Mastering *the* World *of* Psychology

Mastering *the* World *of* Psychology

SECOND EDITION

Samuel E. Wood

Ellen Green Wood

Denise Boyd
Houston Community College System

Boston | New York | San Francisco
Mexico City | Montreal | Toronto | London | Madrid | Munich | Paris
Hong Kong | Singapore | Tokyo | Cape Town | Sydney

Executive Editor: *Susan Hartman*
Editorial Assistant: *Therese Felser*
Senior Development Editor: *Sharon Geary*
Associate Editor: *Jennifer Trebby*
Executive Marketing Manager: *Karen Natale*
Managing Editor: *Michael Granger*
Editorial Production Service: *Andrea Cava*
Composition and Prepress Buyer: *Linda Cox*
Manufacturing Buyer: *Megan Cochran*
Cover Administrator: *Linda Knowles*
Interior Design: *Carol Somberg*
Photo Research: *ImageQuest, Sarah Evertson*
Electronic Composition: *Monotype Composition Company, Inc.*

For related titles and support materials, visit our online catalog at
www.ablongman.com

Between the time website information is gathered and then published, it is not unusual for some sites to have closed. Also, the transcription of URLs can result in unintended typographical errors. The publisher would appreciate notification where these errors occur so that they may be corrected in subsequent editions.

Library of Congress Cataloging-in-Publication Data
Wood, Samuel E.
    Mastering the world of psychology / Samuel E. Wood, Ellen Green Wood, Denise
Boyd.—2nd ed.
        p. cm.
    Includes bibliographical references and indexes.
    ISBN 0-205-45795-9
    1. Psychology—Textbooks.   I. Wood, Ellen R. Green.   II. Boyd, Denise Roberts.   III.
Title.

    BF121.W656 2005
    50—dc21
                                                                                    2005047638

Credits begin on page C-1, which should be considered an extension of the copyright page.

Printed in the United States of America

10 9 8 7 6 5 4 3 2 1   VHP   09 08 07 06 05

Sam and Evie dedicate this book
with love to their children:
Julie Kalina, Bart Green, Alan Wood,
Susan Benson, and Liane Kelly

Denise dedicates this book to the hundreds
of introductory psychology students she has
taught over the past 17 years. Their
questions, comments, and concerns were
the driving force behind her contributions to
Mastering the World of Psychology.

Sam and Evie dedicate this book
with love to their children:
Julie Kalina, Bart Green, Alan Wood,
Susan Benson, and Liane Kelly

Denise dedicates this book to the hundreds
of introductory psychology students she has
taught over the past 17 years. Their
questions, comments, and concerns were
the driving force behind her contributions to
Mastering the World of Psychology.

Brief Contents

Contents

chapter **1**

page 1

Introduction to Psychology

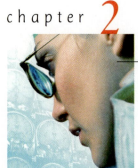

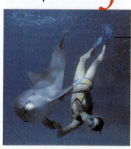

chapter 8

Human Development

page 234

chapter 9

Motivation, Emotion, and Human Sexuality

page 276

chapter 14

Social Psychology

page 424

Preface

A Dedicated Focus on Learning and Application

Today's college students are vastly different from students who filled classrooms just a few years ago. Indeed, students today are more diverse, more mobile, and more technologically astute than ever before.

A good psychology textbook must communicate clearly to this diverse audience. *Mastering the World of Psychology* appeals to students of all educational backgrounds. This book recognizes that different students have different learning preferences and studying and success strategies. It addresses these challenges by offering a wide variety of pedagogical support tools that will help students to master the principles of psychology. No book on the market does more to help students get better grades than *Mastering the World of Psychology*.

Co-Author: Denise Boyd, Ed.D.

Denise Boyd of Houston Community College resumes her co-author role alongside veteran authors Samuel Wood and Ellen Green Wood in bringing extensive experience in teaching thousands of students from varied ages, economic, educational, and cultural backgrounds to the new edition of *Mastering the World of Psychology*. Along with her substantial teaching experience, Dr. Boyd utilizes her background in learning and development to enhance the quality and craftsmanship of the superior student-friendly pedagogical system in the text.

Goals of This Text

We understand that reading about psychology is not enough. We believe that students should be actively involved in psychology. Highly interactive and engaging, *Mastering the World of Psychology* encourages students to think for themselves as they learn about, relate to, and apply the psychological principles that affect their lives. Various tools in this book guide students to success. To accomplish our goals, we set the following objectives:

Maintain a Clear, Understandable Writing Style   First and foremost, a textbook is a teaching instrument. It cannot be a novel; nor should it be an esoteric, academic treatise. A good psychology textbook must communicate clearly to a diverse audience of various ages and levels of academic ability. We seek to achieve this objective by explaining concepts in much the same way as we do in our own psychology classes. This text is filled with everyday examples pertinent to students' lives.

Provide an Accurate, Current, and Thoroughly Researched Textbook Featuring Original Sources   To introduce the world of psychology accurately and clearly, we have gone back to original sources and have read and reread the basic works of the major figures in psychology and the classic studies in the field. This reading has enabled us to write with greater clarity and assurance, rather than having to hedge or write tentatively when discussing what experts in the field have actually said. This book is one of the most carefully researched, up-to-date, accurate, and extensively referenced of all introductory psychology textbooks.

Encourage Students to Become Active Participants in the Learning Process   Reading about psychology is not enough. Students should be able to practice what they have learned, when appropriate. Many of the principles we teach can be demonstrated without elaborate equipment and sometimes as the student reads. Our *Try It* activities personalize psychology, making it simple for students to actively relate psychology to their everyday lives.

Show the Practical Applications of Psychology   One of our goals is to help students apply psychology to their lives. The *Apply It* section near the end of every chapter shows a practical application of psychology and demonstrates the role of psychology in daily life.

Help Students Understand and Appreciate Human Diversity   Diversity is completely integrated throughout *Mastering the World of Psychology*. In addition, every chapter has at least one section that discusses psychological principles as they relate to cultures outside the United States. Highlights of the diversity coverage in the text are as follows:

RACE, ETHNICITY, CULTURE

Chapter 1
Women and minorities in psychology
The sociocultural approach
Chapter 2
Handedness, culture, and genes
Chapter 3
Cultural differences in the perception of illusions
Chapter 4
Culture and altered states of consciousness
Chapter 5
Cultural differences in punishment
Chapter 6
Culturally based schemas
Chapter 7
Learning a second language
Culture-fair testing
Race and IQ
Stereotype threat
Cross-cultural differences in beliefs about intelligence

Chapter 8
Vygostsky's sociological approach
Cultural differences in elders' living arrangements
Chapter 9
Display rules
Cross-cultural differences in intercourse frequency
Chapter 10
Racism and stress
Gender, ethnicity, and health
Chapter 11
Personality and culture
Chapter 12
Suicide and race
Chapter 13
Culturally sensitive therapy
Chapter 14
Prejudice and discrimination
Ethnocentrism
Cross-national differences in domestic abuse

AGING, GENDER, SEXUALITY

Chapter 1
Women and minorities in psychology
Chapter 2
Age and gender differences in the brain
Chapter 4
Age differences in need for sleep
Chapter 6
Estrogen and memory in older women
Chapter 7
Gender differences in cognitive abilities
Chapter 8
Women's career issues including the "glass ceiling"
Successful aging
Stereotypes about later adulthood
The lifespan perspective
Chapter 9
Social attitudes toward gays and lesbians
Determinants of sexual orientation

Gender differences in emotion
Evolutionary versus sociocultural explanations of mating preferences
Gender differences in sexual attitudes and behavior
Sexual behavior among middle-aged and older adults
Chapter 10
Sexually transmitted diseases
Chapter 11
Horney's feminine psychology
Chapter 12
Culture, gender, and depression
Suicide and race, gender, and age
Chapter 13
Culturally sensitive and gender-sensitive therapy
Chapter 14
Aggression: Domestic violence

Our Commitment to Learning

The Second Edition reflects the authors' continued commitment to learning. Based on instructor and student feedback, the authors re-examined and streamlined the pedagogical features and organization of each chapter to provide the best possible opportunities for learning.

The text's commitment to learning begins with the learning method called SQ3R. Made up of five steps—Survey, Question, Read, Recite, and Review—this method serves as the foundation for student success. Introduced in Chapter 1 in both description and in an annotated walkthrough, the SQ3R method is integrated throughout the text to help make the connection between psychology and life, while promoting a more efficient way to approach reading, studying, and test taking.

Among the key learning features in the Second Edition are the following:

Chapter-Opening Vignettes These stories, based on real-life events and people, offer an accessible and interesting introduction to the chapter material.

Margin Learning Questions Margin learning questions form the chapter outlines and appear throughout the chapter to challenge and test comprehension of the chapter coverage and help identify key concepts. These questions have been completely revised to provide an opportunity for students to think more critically about their answers.

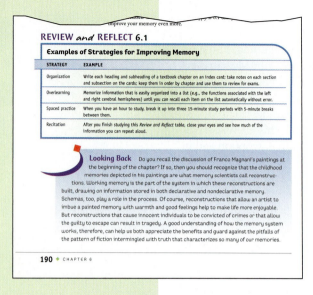

Review and Reflect Tables   These comprehensive summary tables help consolidate major concepts, their components, and their relationships to one another. The tables offer information in a visual form that provides a unique study tool.

Looking Back   End-of-chapter recaps provide a final word on the major concepts of the chapter and make connections within and between chapter topics in the text.

Summary and Key Terms Sections   Organized around the margin learning questions, each summary provides a comprehensive study tool as well as a quick reference to the chapter's key terms, listed alphabetically.

In-text Study Guide   Found at the end of every chapter, each Study Guide contains five sections. Four of the sections are the same in every chapter: Chapter Review, Fill In the Blank, Comprehensive Practice Test, and Critical Thinking. However, the second section in each Study Guide is different, providing an exercise that is tailored to help students review the material in that particular chapter; examples include Identify the Concept, Important Psychologists, and Complete the Diagrams. An answer key for the Study Guides is provided at the end of the book.

Practice Tests Two Practice Tests per chapter can be found at the end of the book. Consisting of 20 multiple-choice questions, 10 true/false questions and a few short-answer questions, each Practice Test gives students the opportunity to learn whether or not they've truly grasped the material in the chapter. Answers can be found in the Solutions Manual, which can be packaged with this book.

Learning through Application

The authors recognize that success lies not only in a strong learning pedagogy but in the ability to relate key psychological principles to life and career choices. The Second Edition provides a variety of opportunities for you to make hands-on use of your studies.

Try It This popular feature provides brief applied experiments, self-assessments, and hands-on activities, which help personalize psychology, making it simple for you to actively relate psychological principles to everyday life. In this edition, the authors have included "Tips" for selected boxes to give students more information on when, where, and how to conduct activities. The following Try Its appear in the text:

1.1 Science or Common Sense? 3
2.1 Hemispheric Interference 53
3.1 A Negative Afterimage 80
4.1 Lucid Dreaming 116
4.2 The Relaxation Response 119
5.1 Using Behavior Modification 155
6.1 A Penny for Your Thoughts 187
7.1 Water Lily Problem 206
8.1 Conservation of Volume 238
8.2 A Moral Dilemma 242
8.3 Estimating Well Being in People Over 65 262
9.1 Recognizing Basic Emotions 290
10.1 Finding a Life Stress Score 310
10.2 Type A or Type B? 320
10.3 AIDS Quiz 328
11.1 Where is Your Locus of Control? 348
12.1 Identifying Anxiety Disorders 374
13.1 A Possible Hierarchy of Fears 403
14.1 Choosing a Mate 430

Apply It At the end of each chapter, an application box combines scientific research with practical advice to show you how to handle difficult or challenging situations that may occur in your personal, academic, or professional life. These boxes cover the following topics:

1.1 More Tips for Effective Studying 28
2.1 Why Consider Genetic Counseling? 64
3.1 Noise and Hearing Loss 98
4.1 Herbal Supplements 129
5.1 How to Win the Battle against Procrastination 160

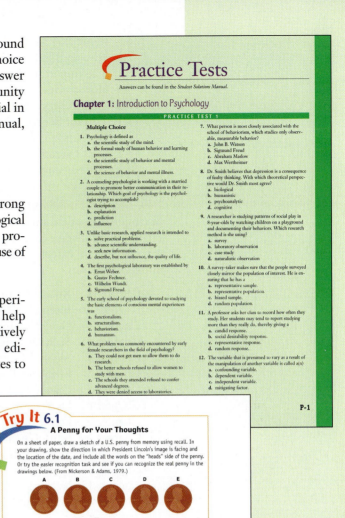

Practice Tests

Answers can be found in the *Student Solutions Manual*.

Chapter 1: Introduction to Psychology

PRACTICE TEST 1

Multiple Choice

1. Psychology is defined as
   a. the scientific study of the mind.
   b. the formal study of human behavior and learning processes.
   c. the scientific study of behavior and mental processes.
   d. the science of behavior and mental illness.

2. A counseling psychologist is working with a married couple to promote better communication in their relationship. Which goal of psychology is the psychologist trying to accomplish?
   a. description
   b. explanation
   c. prediction
   d. influence

3. Unlike basic research, applied research is intended to
   a. solve practical problems.
   b. advance scientific understanding.
   c. seek new information.
   d. describe, but not influence, the quality of life.

4. The first psychological laboratory was established by
   a. Ernst Weber.
   b. Gustav Fechner.
   c. Wilhelm Wundt.
   d. Sigmund Freud.

5. The early school of psychology devoted to studying the basic elements of conscious mental experiences was
   a. structuralism.
   b. functionalism.
   c. behaviorism.
   d. humanism.

6. What problem was commonly encountered by early female researchers in the field of psychology?
   a. They could not get men to allow them to do research.
   b. The better schools refused to allow women to study with men.
   c. The schools they attended refused to confer advanced degrees.
   d. They were denied access to laboratories.

7. What person is most closely associated with the school of behaviorism, which studies only observable, measurable behavior?
   a. John B. Watson
   b. Sigmund Freud
   c. Abraham Maslow
   d. Max Wertheimer

8. Dr. Smith believes that depression is a consequence of faulty thinking. With which theoretical perspective would Dr. Smith most agree?
   a. biological
   b. humanistic
   c. psychoanalytic
   d. cognitive

9. A researcher is studying patterns of social play in 8-year-olds by watching children on a playground and documenting their behaviors. Which research method is she using?
   a. survey
   b. laboratory observation
   c. case study
   d. naturalistic observation

10. A survey-taker makes sure that the people surveyed closely mirror the population of interest. He is ensuring that he has a
    a. representative sample.
    b. representative population.
    c. biased sample.
    d. random population.

11. A professor asks her class to record how often they study. Her students may tend to report studying more than they really do, thereby giving a
    a. candid response.
    b. social desirability response.
    c. representative response.
    d. random response.

12. The variable that is presumed to vary as a result of the manipulation of another variable is called a(n)
    a. confounding variable.
    b. dependent variable.
    c. independent variable.
    d. mitigating factor.

P-1

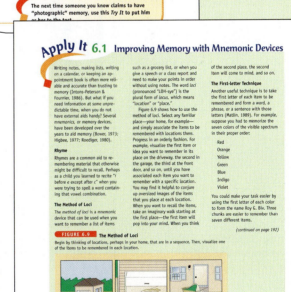

Try It 6.1
A Penny for Your Thoughts

On a sheet of paper, draw a sketch of a U.S. penny from memory using recall. In your drawing, show the direction in which President Lincoln's image is facing and the location of the date, and include all the words on the "heads" side of the penny. Or try the easier recognition task and see if you can recognize the real penny in the drawings below. (From Nickerson & Adams, 1979.)

A   B   C   D   E

Tip

The next time someone you know claims to have "photographic" memory, use this *Try It* to put him or her to the test.

Apply It 6.1   Improving Memory with Mnemonic Devices

Writing notes, making lists, writing on a calendar, or keeping an appointment book is often more reliable and accurate than trusting to memory (Intons-Peterson & Fournier, 1986). But what if you need information at some unpredictable time, when you do not have external aids handy? Several *mnemonics*, or memory devices, have been developed over the years to aid memory (Bower, 1973; Higbee, 1977; Roediger, 1980).

Rhyme

Rhymes are a common aid to remembering material that otherwise might be difficult to recall. Perhaps as a child you learned to recite "*i* before *e* except after *c*" when you were trying to spell a word containing that vowel combination.

The Method of Loci

The *method of loci* is a mnemonic device that can be used when you want to remember a list of items

such as a grocery list, or when you give a speech or a class report and need to make your points in order without using notes. The word *loci* (pronounced "LOH-sye") is the plural form of *locus*, which means "location" or "place."

Figure 6.9 shows how to use the method of loci. Select any familiar place—your home, for example—and simply associate the items to be remembered with locations there. Progress in an orderly fashion. For example, visualize the first item or idea you want to remember in its place on the driveway, the second in the garage, the third at the front door, and so on, until you have associated each item you want to remember with a specific location. You may find it helpful to conjure up oversized images of the items that you place at each location. When you want to recall the items, take an imaginary walk starting at the first place—the first item will pop into your mind. When you think

of the second place, the second item will come to mind, and so on.

The First-letter Technique

Another useful technique is to take the first letter of each item to be remembered and form a word, a phrase, or a sentence with those letters (Matlin, 1989). For example, suppose you had to memorize the seven colors of the visible spectrum in their proper order:

Red
Orange
Yellow
Green
Blue
Indigo
Violet

You could make your task easier by using the first letter of each color to form the name Roy G. Biv. Three chunks are easier to remember than seven different items.

(continued on page 192)

FIGURE 6.9   The Method of Loci

Begin by thinking of locations, perhaps in your home, that are in a sequence. Then, visualize one of the items to be remembered in each location.

MEMORY ◆ 191

How Did You Find Psychology?   This new feature profiles key people in each sub-discipline of the field and explains (in their words) how they came to be a psychologist. Highlighting diverse candidates from all walks of life, this feature will help students still deciding on career paths see that people find their way to psychology from many diffferent avenues.

How Did You Find Psychology?

Elizabeth Loftus

Sometimes sharing an interest with someone whom we love and respect is the basis for a career decision. Eminent memory researcher Elizabeth Loftus, whose name has become virtually synonymous with the repressed-memory controversy, and her father shared the tragedy of losing Loftus's mother just a few years before Loftus began her undergraduate studies at the University of California at Los Angeles. Once her mother was gone, the interest in mathematics Loftus shared with her father became the common ground upon which they maintained their relationship. Thus, it seemed quite natural to Loftus that she should major in mathematics when she entered college. Along the way, however, she took a course in introductory psychology and became fascinated with the subject. She devoted all of the elective hours in her degree plan to psychology courses, ultimately accumulating enough hours to graduate with a double major in math and psychology. Naturally, when she went on to graduate school at Stanford University, Loftus specialized in mathematical psychology, a branch of cognitive science devoted to the development of computational models that can be used to describe psychological processes.

In graduate school, Loftus discovered that she had a gift for experimental design and statistical analysis. Shortly after receiving her Ph.D., she decided that she wanted to apply those talents to issues that could make a real difference in people's lives. Motivated by her lifelong concern for the falsely accused, Loftus applied for a grant to study how eyewitnesses' memories of traffic accidents can become distorted. Once her work was published, her name became known among defense attorneys, and she began to be sought out as an expert witness on the topic of eyewitness memory. These experiences became the catalyst for her controversial work dealing with false memories of abuse—work that has earned her both high praise and harsh criticism.

Her critics argue that Loftus's research obscures the fact that some individuals really do suffer from repressed traumatic memories. However, Loftus is able to empathize with the very real emotional ups and downs of those who believe they have repressed traumatic memories. As mentioned earlier, Loftus's mother died when Loftus was a teenager. For most of her life, she believed that an aunt had discovered her mother's body in the family swimming pool. At a family gathering in the mid-1990s, Loftus's uncle informed her that she had actually been the one who found her mother. Loftus searched her memory and found what she thought was a repressed memory of her discovery of her mother's body. The vivid imagery associated with this memory was particularly striking. As she replayed the memory in her mind, Loftus experienced what she believed to be replays of the emotions that accompanied finding her mother's body. Thus, she was surprised when her uncle telephoned her a few days after the gathering to say that he had been mistaken. For Loftus, this personal experience added further weight to the large body of evidence she and her colleagues have compiled regarding the human memory's vulnerability to external influences.

Loftus's career path demonstrates the importance that your values play in choosing a career. With her gifts for experimental design and statistical analysis, she could easily have spent her entire career in a computer lab cranking out mathematical models of cognitive functions. Instead, Loftus's values led her to choose a career path that hasn't always been easy but that has helped her achieve her goal of making a difference in people's lives.

are accessible to them later in life. The relative inability of older children and adults to recall events from the first few years of life is referred to as **infantile amnesia**.

In light of these developmental limitations, is it possible that some individuals cannot recall incidents of childhood sexual abuse? Widom and Morris (1997) found that 64% of a group of women who had been sexually abused as children reported no memory of the abuse in a 2-hour interview 20 years later. Following up on women who had documented histories of sexual victimization, Williams (1994) found that 38% of them did not report remembering the sexual abuse some 17 years later. Memories of abuse were better when the victimization took place between the ages of 7 and 17 than when it occurred in the first 6 years of life. Keep in mind, however, that it is possible that some of these women may have remembered the abuse but, for whatever reason, chose not

◆ **infantile amnesia**
The relative inability of older children and adults to recall events from the first few years of life.

Instructor Supplements

New! *Mastering the World of Psychology* Instructor's Classroom Kit, Volumes I and II
Our unparalleled Classroom Kit includes every instructional aid an introductory psychology professor needs to manage the classroom. We have made our resources even easier to use by placing all of our print supplements in two convenient volumes. Organized by chapter, each volume contains an instructor's manual, test bank, and slides from the Wood/Wood/Boyd PowerPoint presentation. Each volume also contains our new Classroom Kit CD-ROM with access to all ICK resources, as well as other course materials.

New! *Mastering the World of Psychology* Instructor's Classroom Kit CD-ROM   This exciting new supplement for instructors brings together electronic copies of the Instructor's Manual, the Test Bank, the PowerPoint presentation, images from the text, and video clips for easy instructor access. Highly practical, the CD is organized by chapter and searchable by key terms. The CD-ROMs are available in two volumes as part of the Instructor's Classroom Kit.

Instructor's Manual   Written by text author Denise Boyd, this wonderful tool can be used by first-time or experienced teachers and includes numerous handouts, a sample syllabus, lecture material, chapter outlines, suggested reading and video sources, teaching objectives, and classroom demonstrations.

Test Bank   Written by Paulina Multhaupt of Macomb Community College and featuring more than 100 questions per chapter, the Test Bank includes multiple choice, true/false, short answer, and essay questions, each coded with a difficulty rating, page references, and answer justifications. The Test Bank is also available in a TestGen 5.5 computerized version, for use in personalizing tests.

PowerPoint™ Presentation CD-ROM   An exciting interactive tool created by Stephen Tracy of the Community College of Southern Nevada, the PowerPoint Presentation for *Mastering the World of Psychology* includes images from and key topics covered in the textbook, a link to the companion website for corresponding activities, and the electronic Instructor's Manual files for use in the classroom.

New! Interactive Lecture Questions for Clickers   These lecture questions will jump-start exciting classroom discussions.

Transparencies   The Transparency Kit includes approximately 230 full-color acetates to enhance classroom lecture and discussion, including images from all of Allyn and Bacon's *Introduction to Psychology* texts.

Insights into Psychology Video or DVD, Vol. I-IV   These video programs include two or three short clips per topic, covering such topics as animal research, parapsychology, health and stress, Alzheimer's, bilingual education, genetics and IQ, and much more. A Video Guide containing critical thinking questions accompanies each video. It is also available on DVD.

The Blockbuster Approach: A Guide to Teaching Introductory Psychology with Video
Created by Dena Matzenbacher of McNeese State University, the Blockbuster Guide is a unique print resource for instructors who enjoy enhancing their classroom presentations with film. With heavy coverage of general, abnormal, social, and developmental psychology, this guide suggests a wide range of films to use in class and provides activities, questions for reflection, and other pedagogical tools to make the use of film more effective in the classroom.

Allyn and Bacon Digital Media Archive for Psychology, 4.0 This comprehensive source includes still images, audio clips, web links, and animation and video clips. Highlights include classic psychology experimental footage from Stanley Milgrim's *Invitation to Social Psychology*, biology animations, and more, covering such topics as eating disorders, aggression, therapy, intelligence, and sensation and perception.

Course Management Use these preloaded, customizable content and assessment items to teach your online courses. Available in CourseCompass, Blackboard, and WebCT formats.

MyPsychLab

This interactive and instructive multimedia resource can be used to supplement a traditional lecture course or to administer a course entirely online. It is an all-inclusive tool, a text-specific e-book plus multimedia tutorials, audio, video, simulations, animations, and controlled assessments to completely engage students and reinforce learning. Fully customizable and easy to use, MyPsychLab meets the individual teaching and learning needs of every instructor and every student. Visit the site at www.mypsychlab.com.

Student Supplements

Practice Tests   For additional test preparation, two practice tests per chapter can be found at the end of the text.

Built-In Study Guide FREE with the book   A study guide is included at the end of each chapter to help students reinforce key concepts. Answers to the study guide are included at the end of the book.

Student Solutions Manual   Prepared by David Wasieleski of Valdosta State University, this easy-to-reference manual allows students to check their answers to the practice tests and indicates where further study is needed.

Tutor Center One-on-One Tutoring! (www.ablongman.com/tutorcenter/psych)
Here is a support service that's available when you're not! Every copy of *Mastering the World of Psychology*, Second Edition, is packaged with access to the Tutor Center, providing free, high-quality, one-on-one tutoring to students. Qualified tutors will answer questions students have about material in the text. The Tutor Center is open during peak study hours—in the late afternoon and evenings, 5–12 p.m. (EST), Sunday through Thursday during the academic calendar.

Research Navigator™ (www.ablongman.com/researchnavigator)   The easiest way for students to start a research assignment or research paper, Research Navigator™ helps students quickly and efficiently make the most of their research time and write better papers. The program provides extensive help with the research process and includes three exclusive databases of credible and reliable source material: EBSCO's ContentSelect Academic Journal Database, The New York Times Search by Subject Archive, and our own "Best of the Web" Link Library. The accompanying Research Navigator Guide (with access code) helps point students in the right direction as they explore the tremendous array of information on psychology available on the Internet.

Companion Website (www.ablongman.com/woodmastering2e)   This website is a unique resource for connecting the textbook to the Internet. Each chapter includes learning objectives, chapter summaries, updated and annotated web links for additional sources of information, flash card glossary terms, Introduction to Psychology timeline, online practice tests, and Psychology activities.

Mind Matters II CD-ROM   This resource makes psychology more engaging, interactive, informative, and fun! Mind Matters II covers the concepts of psychology through a combination of text, graphics, simulations, video clips of historic experiments, and activities. Assessments test comprehension at both the topic and unit levels. New to Mind Matters II are innovative modules on personality, developmental psychology, and social psychology.

MyPsychLab

This interactive and instructive multimedia resource can be used to supplement a traditional lecture course or to administer a course entirely online. It is an all-inclusive tool, a text-specific e-book plus multimedia tutorials, audio, video, simulations, animations, and controlled assessments to completely engage students and reinforce learning. Fully customizable and easy to use, MyPsychLab meets the individual teaching and learning needs of every instructor and every student. Visit the site at www.mypsychlab.com.

Acknowledgments

We would like to acknowledge the contributions of the many people who participated in the development of the Second Edition of *Mastering the World of Psychology*.

To begin, we extend our heartfelt thanks to the outstanding psychologists who agreed to participate in our "How Did You Find Psychology?" feature. We would like to personally thank each one of them for answering our questions about their backgrounds and providing us with photos, and for their willingness to serve as role models for undergraduates who may be considering a career in psychology.

Albert Bandura
David Starr Jordan Professor
Department of Psychology
Stanford University

Deanna Barch
Associate Professor
Director of Graduate Studies
Department of Psychology
Co-Director, Cognitive Control and
    Psychopathology Laboratory
Washington University in St. Louis

David Buss
Professor
Head, Individual Differences and
    Evolutionary Psychology Area
Department of Psychology
University of Texas-Austin

Edith Chen
Assistant Professor
Department of Psychology
Co-Director
Psychobiological Determinants of
    Health Laboratory
University of British Columbia

Sean P. A. Drummond
Assistant Professor in Residence
Department of Psychiatry
VA San Diego Health Care System
University of California-San Diego

Robert Guthrie
Emeritus Professor of Psychology
University of Southern Illinois at
    Carbondale

Joseph LeDoux
Henry and Lucy Moses Professor of
    Science
Professor of Neural Science and
    Psychology
Center for Neural Science
New York University

Elizabeth Loftus
Distinguished Professor
Department of Psychology and Social
    Behavior
University of California-Irvine

Darcia Narvaez
Associate Professor of Psychology
Notre Dame University

Miki Paul, Ph.D.
Private Practice
Tucson, Arizona

Nancy Petry
Professor of Psychiatry
Department of Psychiatry and
    Neuropsychiatric Institute
University of Connecticut Health
    Center

Daniel J. Simons
Associate Professor
Head of Laboratory
Department of Psychology
Division of Visual Cognition & Human
    Performance
University of Illinois at Urbana-
    Champaign

Claude M. Steele
Lucie Stern Professor in the Social
  Sciences
Department of Psychology
Stanford University

Sherry Turkle
Abby Rockefeller Mauzé Professor of
  the Social Studies of Science and
  Technology
Director, MIT Initiative on Technology
  and Self
Program in Science, Technology, and
  Society
Massachusetts Institute of Technology

A remarkable team of publishing professionals at Allyn and Bacon deserves a great deal of credit for making this text possible. To our editor, Susan Hartman, we extend our appreciation for everything she has contributed to this revision. Sharon Geary, our development editor, deserves recognition for the long hours, including many nights and weekends, that she spent improving our work and keeping us on schedule. Our supplements editor, Jennifer Trebby, is also to be congratulated for assembling an outstanding set of ancillaries to accompany the text.

Special thanks, too, go to Michael Granger, Allyn and Bacon's managing editor, for keeping the production process on track. We must also thank our project editor, Andrea Cava, for alerting us to needed changes and making our text clearer to its readers.

We are also especially grateful to the superb marketing and sales team at Allyn and Bacon, especially Tim Stookesbury, Pamela Laskey, and Karen Natale, for everything they have done to promote *Mastering the World of Psychology*. They have also helped us and our editors better understand the needs and concerns of the psychology professors who use our books.

To Our Reviewers Numerous reviewers were invaluable to the development of this text. Their help provided a solid foundation for the creation of *Mastering the World of Psychology*, Second Edition:

David W. Alfano, Community College of
  Rhode Island
John Brennecke, Mount San Antonio
  College
Robin Campbell, Brevard Community
  College
Wayne Dixon, Southeastern Oklahoma
  State University
Joseph Feldman, Phoenix College

Julie Hanauer, Suffolk Community
  College
Leslee Koritzke, Los Angeles Trade
  Technical College
Debra Parish, North Harris
  Montgomery Community College
Amy Shapiro, University of
  Massachusetts, Amherst

We would also like to thank reviewers of the first edition of *Mastering the World of Psychology* for their encouragement and insights:

Kenneth Benson, Hinds Community
  College
Cari Cannon, Santiago Canyon
  College
Dennis Cogan, Texas Tech University
Jim Dorman, St. Charles Community
  College
Laura Duvall, Heartland Community
  College
Colleen L. Gift, Highland Community
  College
Paula Goolkasian, UNC Charlotte

Brett Heintz, Delgado Community
  College
Alan Hughes, Nazareth College (NY)
Norman E. Kinney, SE Missouri State U
Leslie Minor-Evans, Central Oregon
  Community College
Michelle Pilati, Rio Hondo College
Vicki Ritts, St. Louis Community
  College, Meramec
Robert Stickgold, Harvard University
Lisa Valentino, Seminole Community
  College

And, last, to all the instructors and students who have taken time out of their busy lives to send along feedback about their experiences teaching and studying from *Mastering the World of Psychology*, we are grateful to you. Please write drdeniseboyd @sbcglobal.net with your comments about the text.

About the Authors

Samuel E. Wood received his doctorate from the University of Florida. He has taught at West Virginia University and the University of Missouri–St. Louis and was a member of the doctoral faculty at both universities. From 1984 to 1996, he served as president of the Higher Education Center, a consortium of 14 colleges and universities in the St. Louis area. He was a co-founder of the Higher Education Cable TV channel (HEC-TV) in St. Louis and served as its president and CEO from its founding in 1987 until 1996.

Ellen Green Wood received her doctorate in educational psychology from St. Louis University and was an adjunct professor of psychology at St. Louis Community College at Meramec. She has also taught in the clinical experiences program in education at Washington University and at the University of Missouri–St. Louis. In addition to her teaching, Dr. Wood has developed and taught seminars on critical thinking. She received the Telecourse Pioneer Award from 1982 through 1988 for her contributions to the field of distance learning.

Denise Boyd received her Ed.D. in educational psychology from the University of Houston and has been a psychology instructor in the Houston Community College system since 1988. She teaches courses in introductory psychology and human development each semester and occasionally teaches statistics and social psychology as well. From 1995 until 1998, she chaired the psychology, sociology, and anthropology department at Houston Community College–Central. Her other texts include, with Samuel Wood and Ellen Green Wood, *The World of Psychology* (Fifth Edition), *Lifespan Development* (Fourth Edition, with Helen Bee), *The Developing Child* (Tenth Edition, with Helen Bee), and *Current Readings in Lifespan Development* (with Genevieve Stevens). A licensed psychologist, she has presented a number of papers at professional meetings, reporting research in child, adolescent, and adult development. She has also presented workshops for teachers whose students range from preschool to college.

Together, Sam, Evie, and Denise have more than 45 years of experience teaching introductory psychology to thousands of students of all ages, backgrounds, and abilities. *Mastering the World of Psychology* is the direct result of their teaching experience.

Mastering *the* World *of* Psychology

Introduction to Psychology

chapter 1

The **SQ3R** method will help you maximize your learning in 5 steps: **SURVEY, QUESTION, READ, RECITE,** and **REVIEW.** This chapter is annotated to show you where each step in the method occurs to help you visualize, practice, and master this learning system.

Psychology: An Introduction
◆ What process do scientists use to answer questions about behavior and mental processes?
◆ What are the goals of psychology?

Exploring Psychology's Roots
◆ What role did Wundt play in the founding of psychology?
◆ What did Titchener contribute to psychology?
◆ Why is functionalism important in the history of psychology?

◆ In what ways have women and minorities shaped the field of psychology, both in the past and today?

Schools of Thought in Psychology
◆ How do behaviorists explain behavior and mental processes?
◆ What do psychoanalytic psychologists believe about the role of the unconscious?
◆ According to Maslow and Rogers, what motivates human behavior and mental processes?
◆ What is the focus of cognitive psychology?

Descriptive Research Methods
◆ How do psychological researchers use naturalistic and laboratory observation?
◆ What are the advantages and disadvantages of the case study?
◆ How do researchers ensure that survey results are useful?

The Experimental Method
◆ Why do researchers use experiments to test hypotheses about cause-effect relationships?

◆ How do independent and dependent variables differ?
◆ Why are experimental and control groups necessary?
◆ What kinds of factors introduce bias into experimental studies?
◆ What are the limitations of the experimental method?

The Correlational Method
◆ What is a correlation coefficient, and what does it mean?
◆ What are the strengths and weaknesses of the correlational method?

Participants in Psychological Research
◆ In what ways can participants bias research results?
◆ What ethical rules must researchers follow when humans are involved in studies?
◆ Why are animals used in research?

Thinking about Theories and Research
◆ How do psychologists compare theories?

1

- How can critical thinking be used to interpret media reports of psychological research?

Current Trends in Psychology
- What is the main idea behind evolutionary psychology?
- How is biological psychology changing the field of psychology?
- What kinds of variables interest psychologists who take a sociocultural approach?
- What are psychological perspectives, and how are they related to an eclectic position?

Psychologists at Work
- Who are some of the specialists working within psychology?
- What kinds of employment opportunities are available for psychology majors?

Have you ever found yourself in this situation? It's the night before an exam, and you have three chapters to read. Of course, you should have read them when they were first assigned, but, between your job and other obligations, you just couldn't find the time. You could have read the chapters last weekend, but how could you pass up the opportunity to take a road trip with your friends or to watch that big game on television? Or perhaps you were caring for a sick child or resolving a relationship issue. The point is that, unless you have an effective plan for studying, you will quickly fall behind. As a result, you now find yourself coping with a tension headache or acid indigestion (or both!) as you try to stay awake all night cramming for the test.

The first step toward avoiding an eleventh-hour, preexam time crunch is to break up the task of reading textbook chapters into manageable and meaningful chunks. The study aids incorporated in *Mastering the World of Psychology* help you do just that. These aids will help you learn to use a series of five learning strategies developed and tested by a psychologist: *Survey, Question, Read, Recite,* and *Review.* Together, these steps are known as the **SQ3R method.** You will learn and remember more if, instead of simply reading each chapter, you follow these steps. Here's how they work.

- *Survey.* First, scan the chapter. The chapter outline helps you preview the content and its organization. Read the section headings and the learning objective questions, which are designed to focus your attention on key information. Glance at the illustrations and tables, including the *Review and Reflect* tables, which organize, review, and summarize key concepts. Then read the *Summary,* located at the end of each chapter. This survey process gives you an overview of the chapter.

- *Question.* Approach each chapter by tackling one major section at a time. Before you actually read a section, reread its learning objective questions. But don't stop there; add a few questions of your own as you glance over the section's subheadings and key terms. For example, the first major section in this chapter is "Psychology: An Introduction." The first subheading is "The Scientific Method," and the associated question is "What process do scientists use to answer questions about behavior and mental processes?" As you look over the section, you might add this question: "What is the difference between common sense and science?" Asking such questions helps focus your reading.

- *Read.* Keeping the learning objective question in mind, read the section and note the examples provided to help you understand major concepts. Once you have grasped the text's examples, try

SURVEY: Begin with a scan of the chapter elements including chapter outline, headings, learning objective questions, illustrations, photos, tables, and end of chapter summary and study guide. This process gives you an overview of the chapter's main points. When approaching each section of the chapter, use the survey method for previewing that section's major coverage and features.

to generate some of your own. If the section includes a *Try It* exercise, complete it and relate the lessons learned to the relevant text. Read each figure or table to which the authors direct your attention. If you don't understand a figure or table, reread the relevant text and look at the figure or table again. Look at the photos and read the captions as well.

- *Recite.* Write a short summary of the material. Your summary should answer the learning objective question. Compare your summary to the answers for the learning objective questions that are provided in the *Summary*. If necessary, reread the section.
- *Review.* If the section includes a *Review and Reflect* table, use it to check your memory and understanding of the section. At the end of each chapter in *Mastering the World of Psychology*, you will find a study guide. The first section of the study guide is a chapter review that includes questions that correspond to each major section of the chapter. As you finish each section, turn to the chapter review

and try to answer the questions that pertain to it. If you cannot, review those parts of the section that you found the most difficult to recall or understand and then answer the questions again. Check your answers against the key provided at the back of the book. When you have finished the entire chapter, go over the *Summary* and the key terms. If you don't know the meaning of a term, turn to the page where that term is defined in the margin. The marginal definitions provide a ready reference for the important terms that appear in **boldface** print in the text. All of these terms and definitions also appear in the end-of-text *Glossary*. Finally, complete the remaining sections of the study guide.

As you work your way through this chapter, you will see that the SQ3R features have been highlighted for you upon first appearance. At the end of the chapter, you can assess how much the SQ3R features helped you. We'll begin our study of psychology by finding out what is (and is *not*) true about psychology.

Psychology: An Introduction

Psychology is defined as the scientific study of behavior and mental processes. Answer true or false for each statement in *Try It 1.1* to see how much you already know about some of the topics we will explore in *Mastering the World of Psychology*. (You'll find the answers in the text below.)

Can we make a valid claim that psychology is a science, or is it just common sense? In the *Try It*, common sense might have led you astray. All of the odd-numbered items are false, and all of the even-numbered items are true. As you see, common sense alone will not get you very far in your study of psychology.

> **QUESTION:** As you begin each chapter section, look over its preview questions in the chapter outline and in the chapter margins to get a sense of the topics being covered. In addition, add any initial questions you may have about the content and key terms for this section. Keep these questions in mind to help focus your reading of each section.

Try It 1.1
Science or Common Sense?

Indicate whether each statement is true (T) or false (F).

1. Once damaged, brain cells never work again.
2. All people dream during a night of normal sleep.
3. As the number of bystanders at an emergency increases, the time it takes for the victim to get help decreases.
4. Humans do not have a maternal instinct.
5. It's impossible for human beings to hear a watch ticking 20 feet away.
6. Eyewitness testimony is often unreliable.
7. Chimpanzees have been taught to speak.
8. Creativity and high intelligence do not necessarily go together.
9. When it comes to close personal relationships, opposites attract.
10. The majority of teenagers have good relationships with their parents.

The Scientific Method

◆ *What process do scientists use to answer questions about behavior and mental processes?*

READ: As you read each chapter section, try to answer the learning objective questions and your own questions that come to mind. If you find particular areas of the section very long or complex, try breaking the section into smaller sections of reading.

The **scientific method** consists of the orderly, systematic procedures that researchers follow as they identify a research problem, design a study to investigate the problem, collect and analyze data, draw conclusions, and communicate their findings. The scientific method is the most objective method known for acquiring knowledge (Christensen, 2001). The knowledge gained is dependable because of the method used to obtain it.

Suppose, for example, a researcher finds that men consistently score higher than women on a test of map reading. If the researcher claims that the gender difference in map-reading scores is attributable to the effects of male and female hormones on the brain, she has moved beyond the domain of facts and into the realm of theory. A **theory** is a general principle or set of principles proposed to explain how a number of separate facts are related. Other researchers may not agree with the explanation. Still, any alternative theory proposed to explain this researcher's findings must be able to account for the fact that men outscore women on tests of map reading. Other psychologists might propose that the difference exists because society encourages men to learn to read maps but discourages women from doing so. They can't simply say that there is no such thing as a gender difference in map reading, especially if the researcher's results have been *replicated* by other scientists. (**Replication** is the process of repeating a study with different participants and preferably a different investigator to verify research findings.)

You might be thinking: Why bother with theories? Why not just report the facts and let people draw their own conclusions? Well, theories enable scientists to fit many separate pieces of data into meaningful frameworks. For example, in the hormone theory of gender differences in map reading, two facts are connected: (1) Men and women have different hormones, and (2) men and women score differently on map-reading tests. Connecting these two facts results in a theory of gender differences from which researchers can make predictions that can be tested.

Theories also stimulate debates that lead to advances in knowledge. The psychologist who thinks gender differences in map reading are due to learning may do a study in which male and female participants are trained in map reading. If the women read maps as well as the men do after training, then the researcher has support for her theory and has added a new fact to the knowledge base. Once the advocates of the hormone view modify their theory to include the new fact, they are likely to carry out new studies to test it. As a result of this back-and-forth process, knowledge about gender differences in map reading increases.

The Goals of Psychology

◆ *What are the goals of psychology?*

What goals do psychological researchers pursue when they plan and conduct their studies? Briefly put, the goals of psychology are to describe, explain, predict, and influence behavior and mental processes. The first goal, *description*, is met when researchers describe the behavior or mental process of interest as accurately and completely as possible. The second and third goals, *explanation* and *prediction*, go hand in hand. After describing a particular behavior or mental process, researchers often devise a tentative explanation for it, one from which they can derive **hypotheses**—or testable predictions about the conditions under which particular behaviors or mental processes may occur. After testing one or more such hypotheses, researchers often find patterns in the results of their studies that help them build more comprehensive explanations, or theories, to explain their original observations. These theories lead to more hypotheses, and tests of these hypotheses help researchers refine their theories. The final goal, *influence*, is attained when the complementary processes of hypothesis testing (prediction) and theory building (explanation) provide researchers

◆ **SQ3R method**

A study method involving the following five steps: (1) survey, (2) question, (3) read, (4) recite, and (5) review.

◆ **psychology**

The scientific study of behavior and mental processes.

◆ **scientific method**

The orderly, systematic procedures that researchers follow as they identify a research problem, design a study to investigate the problem, collect and analyze data, draw conclusions, and communicate their findings.

◆ **theory**

A general principle or set of principles proposed to explain how a number of separate facts are related.

◆ **replication**

The process of repeating a study to verify research findings.

◆ **hypothesis**

A testable prediction about the conditions under which a particular behavior or mental process may occur.

with information they can use to apply a principle or change a condition to prevent unwanted occurrences or to bring about desired outcomes.

Think back to the discussion of gender differences in map-reading skills. When a psychologist carries out a study in which male participants score higher than female participants on a map-reading test, she fulfills the description goal. Psychologists who hypothesize that the difference is due to the influences of male and female hormones and devise a strategy for testing their hypothesis are working toward the explanation and prediction goals. Finally, researchers who devise and test training programs that help women learn to be better map readers are attempting to meet the goal of influence.

Two types of research help psychologists accomplish the four goals just described: basic research and applied research. The purpose of **basic research** is to seek new knowledge and to explore and advance general scientific understanding. Basic research explores such topics as the nature of memory, brain function, motivation, and emotional expression. **Applied research** is conducted specifically for the purpose of solving practical problems and improving the quality of life. Applied research focuses on finding methods to improve memory or increase motivation, therapies to treat psychological disorders, ways to decrease stress, and so on. This type of research is primarily concerned with the fourth goal of psychology—influence—because it specifies ways and means of changing behavior.

The scientific method has enabled psychologists to accumulate a vast knowledge base about behavior and mental processes. However, information alone doesn't necessarily advance our understanding of psychological phenomena. As we noted earlier, using knowledge acquired through the scientific method to develop cohesive theories can help us in the quest for understanding. With that point in mind, we'll turn our attention to some early attempts at psychological theory building and the schools of thought that arose from the debate stimulated by them.

◆ **basic research**
Research conducted to seek new knowledge and to explore and advance general scientific understanding.

◆ **applied research**
Research conducted specifically to solve practical problems and improve the quality of life.

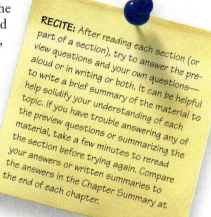

RECITE: After reading each section (or part of a section), try to answer the preview questions and your own questions—aloud or in writing or both. It can be helpful to write a brief summary of the material to help solidify your understanding of each topic. If you have trouble answering any of the preview questions or summarizing the material, take a few minutes to reread the section before trying again. Compare your answers or written summaries to the answers in the Chapter Summary at the end of each chapter.

Exploring Psychology's Roots

If you were to trace the development of psychology from the beginning, you would need to start before the earliest pages of recorded history, beyond even the early Greek philosophers, such as Aristotle and Plato. However, it was not until the scientific method was applied to the study of psychological processes that psychology became recognized as a formal academic discipline.

The Founding of Psychology

Who were the "founders" of psychology? Historians acknowledge that three German scientists—Ernst Weber, Gustav Fechner, and Hermann von Helmholtz—were the first to systematically study behavior and mental processes. But it is Wilhelm Wundt (1832–1920) who is generally thought of as the "father" of psychology. Wundt's vision for the new discipline included studies of social and cultural influences on human thought (Benjafield, 1996).

Wundt established a psychological laboratory at the University of Leipzig in Germany in 1879, an event considered to mark the birth of psychology as a formal academic discipline. Using a method called *introspection*, Wundt and his associates studied the perception of a variety of visual, tactile, and auditory stimuli, including the rhythm patterns produced by metronomes set at different speeds. Introspection as a research method involves looking inward to examine one's own conscious experience and then reporting that experience.

◆ *What role did Wundt play in the founding of psychology?*

Structuralism

◆ What did Titchener contribute to psychology?

Wundt's most famous student, Englishman Edward Bradford Titchener (1867–1927), took the new field to the United States, where he set up a psychological laboratory at Cornell University. He gave the name **structuralism** to this first formal school of thought in psychology, which aimed at analyzing the basic elements, or the structure, of conscious mental experience. Like Wundt before him, Titchener thought that consciousness could be reduced to its basic elements, just as water (H_2O) can be broken down into its constituent elements—hydrogen (H) and oxygen (O). For Wundt, pure sensations—such as sweetness, coldness, or redness—were the basic elements of consciousness. And these pure sensations, he believed, combined to form perceptions.

Even though these children experience the same sensations (sweetness and coldness) as they enjoy eating their ice cream, their reported introspections of the experience would probably differ.

The work of both Wundt and Titchener was criticized for its primary method, introspection. Introspection is not objective, even though it involves observation, measurement, and experimentation. When different introspectionists were exposed to the same stimulus, such as the click of a metronome, they frequently reported different experiences. Therefore, structuralism was not in favor for long. Later schools of thought in psychology were established, partly in a reaction against structuralism, which did not survive after the death of its most ardent spokesperson, Titchener. Nevertheless, the structuralists were responsible for establishing psychology as a science through their insistence that psychological processes could be measured and studied using methods similar to those employed by scientists in other fields.

Functionalism

◆ Why is functionalism important in the history of psychology?

Even as structuralism began losing its influence in the United States in the early 20th century, a new school of psychology called functionalism was taking shape. **Functionalism** was concerned not with the structure of consciousness, but with how mental processes function—that is, how humans and animals use mental processes in adapting to their environment. The influential work of Charles Darwin (1809–1882), especially his ideas about evolution and the continuity of species, was largely responsible for an increasing use of animals in psychological experiments. Even though Darwin, who was British, contributed important seeds of thought that helped give birth to the new school of psychology, functionalism was primarily American in character and spirit.

The famous American psychologist William James (1842–1910) was an advocate of functionalism, even though he did much of his writing before this school of psychology emerged. James's best-known work is his highly regarded and frequently quoted textbook *Principles of Psychology*, published more than a century ago (1890). James taught that mental processes are fluid and have continuity, rather than the rigid, or fixed, structure that the structuralists suggested. James spoke of the "stream of consciousness," which, he said, functions to help humans adapt to their environment.

How did functionalism change psychology? Functionalism broadened the scope of psychology to include the study of behavior as well as mental processes. It also allowed the study of children, animals, and the mentally impaired, groups that could not be studied by the structuralists because they could not be trained to use introspection. Functionalism also focused on an applied, more practical use of psychology by encouraging the study of educational practices, individual differences, and adaptation in the workplace (industrial psychology).

◆ **structuralism**

The first formal school of thought in psychology, aimed at analyzing the basic elements, or structure, of conscious mental experience.

◆ **functionalism**

An early school of psychology that was concerned with how humans and animals use mental processes in adapting to their environment.

Women and Minorities in Psychology

For centuries, conventional thought had held that higher education was exclusively for White males, that women should rear children and be homemakers, and that minorities were best suited for manual labor. However, beginning in the late 19th century, women and minorities overcame these prejudices to make notable achievements in and contributions to the study of psychology.

◆ In what ways have women and minorities shaped the field of psychology, both in the past and today?

Christine Ladd-Franklin (1847–1930) completed the requirements for a Ph.D. at Johns Hopkins University in the mid-1880s but had to wait more than 40 years before receiving her degree in 1926, when the university first agreed to grant it to women. Ladd-Franklin formulated a well-regarded, evolutionary theory of color vision.

In 1895, Mary Whiton Calkins (1863–1930) completed the requirements for a doctorate at Harvard. And even though William James described her as one of his most capable students, Harvard refused to grant the degree to a woman (Dewsbury, 2000). Undeterred, Calkins established a psychology laboratory at Wellesley College and developed the paired-associates test, an important research technique for the study of memory. She became the first female president of the American Psychological Association in 1905.

Margaret Floy Washburn (1871–1939) received her Ph.D. in psychology from Cornell University and later taught at Vassar College (Dewsbury, 2000). She wrote several books, among them *The Animal Mind* (1908), an influential book on animal behavior, and *Movement and Mental Imagery* (1916).

Francis Cecil Sumner (1895–1954) was a self-taught scholar. In 1920, without benefit of a formal high school education, he became the first African American to earn a Ph.D. in psychology, from Clark University (Guthrie, 2004). Sumner translated more than 3,000 articles from German, French, and Spanish. He chaired the psychology department at Howard University and is known as the "father" of African American psychology.

Albert Sidney Beckham (1897–1964), another African American psychologist, conducted some impressive early studies on intelligence and showed how it is related to success in numerous occupational fields. Beckham also established the first psychological laboratory at a Black institution of higher learning—Howard University.

More recently, African American psychologist Kenneth Clark achieved national recognition for his writings on the harmful effects of racial segregation. His work affected the Supreme Court ruling that declared racial segregation in U.S. schools to be unconstitutional (Benjamin & Crouse, 2002). His wife, Mamie Phipps Clark, also achieved recognition when the couple published their works on racial identification and self-esteem, writings that have become classics in the field (Lal, 2002).

Hispanic American Jorge Sanchez conducted studies on bias in intelligence testing during the 1930s. He pointed out that both cultural differences and language differences work against Hispanic students when they take IQ tests.

Native American and Asian American psychologists have made important contributions to psychological research as well. Moreover, they are the fastest-growing minority groups in the field of psychology. The percentage of doctorates awarded to individuals in both groups more than doubled from the mid-1970s to the mid-1990s (National Science Foundation, 2000). One contemporary Native American psychologist, Marigold Linton, is known for her research examining autobiographical memory. In 1999, Richard Suinn, an eminent researcher in behavioral psychology, became the first Asian American president of the American Psychological Association.

Today, more women than men obtain degrees in psychology, and minority group representation is growing. However, there continues to be a gap between the proportion of minorities in the U.S. population and their representation among professional psychologists. Indeed, although the proportion of minorities in the U.S. population is about 28%, only 16% of students pursuing graduate degrees in psychology are of minority ethnicity (APA, 2000). Consequently, the APA and other organizations have established programs to encourage minority enrollment in graduate programs in psychology.

How Did You Find **Psychology?**

Robert Guthrie

As a boy growing up in the rural South during the days of the Great Depression, Robert Guthrie learned that teaching was virtually the only profession open to African Americans. His first encounter with psychology came in an introductory course that was part of the teacher preparation curriculum at Florida A&M University. As Guthrie puts it, "I remember vividly the comments in my introductory psychology class when the textbook read that Black people were 'one standard deviation below the mean on IQ tests.' After that statement I had no reason to accept the 'science' of human behavior" (R. Guthrie, personal communication, November 24, 2004). Nevertheless, he found the subject to be interesting, and because he greatly admired the professor, he kept taking psychology courses. At the same time, Guthrie considered a career in psychology to be impractical as few jobs in the field were open to African Americans.

A tour of duty in the newly integrated U.S. military during the Korean War ultimately changed Guthrie's mind. He felt comfortable working with his White colleagues and began to see that society was changing. When court rulings brought an official end to racial segregation in educational institutions, Guthrie became the first African American graduate student in the psychology department at the University of Kentucky in 1955

(O'Connor, 2001). He found the emotional climate of the campus to be somewhat hostile, however, and committed himself to earning his master's degree as rapidly as possible. Guthrie was also surprised to learn that neither his classmates nor his professors knew anything about minority psychologists such as Francis Cecil Sumner. When he mentioned such individuals to professors, he often heard responses such as "If they were important, I would know about them." While these experiences could have embittered him, they instead instilled in him a desire to educate his White colleagues about the contributions of early African American psychologists.

In the years following his graduation from the University of Kentucky, Guthrie earned a Ph.D. in psychology and achieved success as a psychologist in the military, in private practice, as a government agency researcher, and as a psychology professor. In the 1970s, he turned his attention to the task of educating his colleagues about the African American psychologists whose lives and accomplishments he had found to be so inspiring. He told their stories in a book called *Even the Rat Was White*, first published in 1976. Thanks to Guthrie's determination to gain recognition and respect for those who inspired him, psychology professors can now provide their students with a much fuller understanding of the early years of their discipline. And, like Guthrie, you may find that your introductory psychology course acquaints you with individuals you may want to emulate and exposes you to career options you never knew existed.

Schools of Thought in Psychology

Why don't we hear about structuralism and functionalism today? In the early 20th century, the debate between the two points of view sparked a veritable explosion of theoretical discussion and research examining psychological processes. The foundations of the major schools of thought in the field were established during that period and continue to be influential today.

Behaviorism

◆ *How do behaviorists explain behavior and mental processes?*

◆ **behaviorism**

The school of psychology that views observable, measurable behavior as the appropriate subject matter for psychology and emphasizes the key role of environment as a determinant of behavior.

Psychologist John B. Watson (1878–1958) looked at the study of psychology as defined by the structuralists and functionalists and disliked virtually everything he saw. In his article "Psychology as the Behaviorist Views It" (1913), Watson proposed a radically new approach to psychology, one that rejected the subjectivity of both structuralism and functionalism. This new school redefined psychology as the "science of behavior." Termed **behaviorism** by Watson, this school of psychology confines itself to the study of behavior because behavior is observable and measurable and, therefore, objective and scientific. Behaviorism also emphasizes that behavior is determined primarily by factors in the environment.

Behaviorism was the most influential school of thought in American psychology until the 1960s. It remains a major force in modern psychology, in large part because of the profound influence of B. F. Skinner (1904–1990). Skinner agreed with Watson that concepts such as mind, consciousness, and feelings are neither objective nor measurable and, therefore, not appropriate subject matter for psychology. Furthermore, Skinner argued that these concepts are not needed to explain behavior. One can explain behavior, he claimed, by analyzing the conditions that are present before a behavior occurs and by analyzing the consequences that follow the behavior.

Skinner's research on operant conditioning emphasized the importance of reinforcement in learning and in shaping and maintaining behavior. He maintained that any behavior that is reinforced (followed by pleasant or rewarding consequences) is more likely to be performed again. Skinner's work has had a powerful influence on modern psychology. You will read more about operant conditioning in Chapter 5.

Psychoanalysis

◆ **psychoanalysis**

(SY-ko-ah-NAL-ih-sis) The term Freud used for both his theory of personality and his therapy for the treatment of psychological disorders; the unconscious is the primary focus of psychoanalytic theory.

Sigmund Freud (1856–1939), whose work you will study in Chapter 11, developed a theory of human behavior based largely on case studies of his patients. Freud's theory, **psychoanalysis,** maintains that human mental life is like an iceberg. The smallest, visible part of the iceberg represents the conscious mental experience of the individual. But underwater, hidden from view, floats a vast store of unconscious impulses, wishes, and desires. Freud insisted that individuals do not consciously control their thoughts, feelings, and behavior; these are instead determined by unconscious forces.

◆ *What do psychoanalytic psychologists believe about the role of the unconscious?*

The overriding importance that Freud placed on sexual and aggressive impulses caused much controversy both inside and outside the field of psychology. The most notable of Freud's famous students—Carl Jung, Alfred Adler, and Karen Horney—broke away from their mentor and developed their own theories of personality. These three and their followers are often collectively referred to as *neo-Freudians*. Thus, the psychoanalytic approach continues to be influential, albeit in a form that has been modified considerably over the past several decades by the neo-Freudians.

◆ **humanistic psychology**

The school of psychology that focuses on the uniqueness of human beings and their capacity for choice, growth, and psychological health.

Humanistic Psychology

Humanistic psychologists reject with equal vigor (1) the behaviorist view that behavior is determined by factors in the environment and (2) the view of the psychoanalytic approach stating that human behavior is determined primarily by unconscious forces. **Humanistic psychology** focuses on the uniqueness of human beings and their capacity for choice, growth, and psychological health.

◆ *According to Maslow and Rogers, what motivates human behavior and mental processes?*

Abraham Maslow and other early humanists, such as Carl Rogers (1902–1987), pointed out that Freud based his theory primarily on data from his disturbed patients. By contrast, the humanists emphasize a much more positive view of human nature. They maintain that people are innately good and that they possess free will. The humanists believe that people are capable of making conscious, rational choices, which can lead to personal growth and psychological health. As you will learn in Chapter 9, Maslow proposed a theory of motivation that consists of a hierarchy of needs. He considered the need for self-actualization (developing to one's fullest potential) to be the highest need on the hierarchy. Rogers developed what he called *client-centered therapy*, an approach in which the client, or patient, directs a discussion focused on his or her own view of a problem rather than on the therapist's analysis. Rogers and other humanists also popularized group therapy. Thus, the humanistic perspective continues to be important in research examining human motivation and in the practice of psychotherapy.

◆ **cognitive psychology**

The school of psychology that sees humans as active participants in their environment; studies mental processes such as memory, problem solving, reasoning, decision making, perception, language, and other forms of cognition.

Cognitive Psychology

Cognitive psychology grew and developed partly in response to strict behaviorism, especially in the United States (Robins et al., 1999). **Cognitive psychology** sees humans not as passive recipients who are pushed and pulled by environmental forces, but as active participants who seek out experiences, who

◆ *What is the focus of cognitive psychology?*

◆ **Gestalt psychology**

The school of psychology that emphasizes that individuals perceive objects and patterns as whole units and that the perceived whole is more than the sum of its parts.

alter and shape those experiences, and who use mental processes to transform information in the course of their own cognitive development. It studies mental processes such as memory, problem solving, reasoning, decision making, perception, language, and other forms of cognition. Historically, modern cognitive psychology is derived from two streams of thought: one that began with a small group of German scientists studying human perception in the early twentieth century, and another that grew up alongside the emerging field of computer science in the second half of the century.

Gestalt psychology made its appearance in Germany in 1912. The Gestalt psychologists, notably Max Wertheimer, Kurt Koffka, and Wolfgang Köhler, emphasized that individuals perceive objects and patterns as whole units and that the perceived whole is more than the sum of its parts. The German word Gestalt roughly means "whole, form, or pattern."

To support the Gestalt theory, Wertheimer, the leader of the Gestalt psychologists, performed his famous experiment demonstrating the *phi phenomenon*. In this experiment, two light bulbs are placed a short distance apart in a dark room. The first light is flashed on and then turned off just as the second light is flashed on. As this pattern of flashing the lights on and off continues, an observer sees what appears to be a single light moving back and forth from one position to another. Here, said the Gestaltists, is proof that people perceive wholes or patterns, rather than collections of separate sensations.

When the Nazis came to power in Germany in the 1930s, the Gestalt school disbanded, and its most prominent members emigrated to the United States. Today, the fundamental concept underlying Gestalt psychology—that the mind *interprets* experiences in predictable ways rather than simply reacts to them—is central to cognitive psychologists' ideas about learning, memory, problem solving, and even psychotherapy.

◆ **information-processing theory**

An approach to the study of mental structures and processes that uses the computer as a model for human thinking.

The advent of the computer provided cognitive psychologists with a new way to conceptualize mental structures and processes, known as **information-processing theory.** According to this view, the brain processes information in sequential steps, in much the same way as a computer does serial processing—that is, one step at a time. But as modern technology has changed computers and computer programs, cognitive psychologists have changed their models. "Increasingly, parallel processing models [models in which several tasks are performed at once] are developed in addition to stage models of processing" (Haberlandt, 1997, p. 22).

A central idea of information-processing theory, one that it shares with Gestalt psychology, is that the brain interprets information rather than just responding to it.

For example, consider this statement: *The old woman was sweeping the steps.* If information-processing researchers ask people who have read the sentence to recall whether it includes the word *broom*, a majority will say that it does. According to information-processing theorists, rules for handling information lead us to find associations between new input, such as the statement about a woman sweeping, and previously acquired knowledge, such as our understanding that brooms are used for sweeping. As a result, most of us construct a memory of the sentence that leads us to incorrectly recall that it includes the word *broom*.

Designing computer programs that can process human language in the same way as the human brain is one of the goals of research on *artificial intelligence*. Today, such research represents one of the most important applications of information-processing theory.

Over the past 100 years or so, cognitive psychologists have carried out studies that have greatly increased our knowledge of the human memory system and the mental processes involved in problem solving. Moreover, the principles discovered in these experiments have been used to explain and study all kinds of psychological variables—from gender role development to individual differences in intelligence. As a result, cognitive psychology

Is this person having a bad day? The perceptual processes described by the Gestalt psychologists are observable in everyday life. We often put frustrating events—such as getting up late and then having a flat tire—together to form a "whole" concept, such as "I'm having a bad day."

is currently thought by many psychologists to be the most prominent school of psychological thought (Robins et al., 1999).

If psychologists hold such diverse views about the nature of the phenomena that they study, then what binds them together into a single discipline? The answer is twofold. First, all psychologists pursue the same goals with regard to the study of behavior and mental processes—description, explanation, prediction, and influence. Second, all psychological researchers use a common set of research methods to pursue these goals.

Descriptive Research Methods

The goals of psychological research are often accomplished in stages. In the early stages of research, **descriptive research methods** are usually the most appropriate. Descriptive research methods yield descriptions of behavior and include naturalistic and laboratory observation, the case study, and the survey.

Naturalistic and Laboratory Observation

Have you ever sat in an airport or shopping mall and simply watched what people were doing? Such an activity is quite similar to **naturalistic observation,** a descriptive research method in which researchers observe and record behavior in its natural setting, without attempting to influence or control it. The major advantage of naturalistic observation is the opportunity to study behavior in normal settings, where it occurs more naturally and spontaneously than it does under artificial and contrived laboratory conditions. Sometimes, naturalistic observation is the only feasible way to study behavior—for example, there is no other way to study how people typically react during disasters such as earthquakes and fires.

Naturalistic observation has its limitations, however. Researchers must wait for events to occur; they cannot speed up or slow down the process. And because they have no control over the situation, researchers cannot reach conclusions about cause-effect relationships. Another potential problem with naturalistic observation is *observer bias*, which is a distortion in researchers' observations. Observer bias can result when researchers' expectations about a situation cause them to see what they expect to see or to make incorrect inferences about what they observe. Suppose, for example, that you're a psychologist studying aggression in preschool classrooms. You have decided to count every time a child hits or pushes another child as an aggressive act. Your decision to label this type of physical contact between children as "aggressive" may cause you to notice more such acts, and label them as "aggressive," than you would if you were casually watching a group of children play. The effects of observer bias can be reduced substantially when two or more observers view the same behavior. If you and another observer independently count, say, 23 aggressive acts in an hour of free play, the findings are considered unbiased. If you see 30 such acts and the other observer records only 15, some kind of bias is at work. In such situations, observers usually clarify the criteria for classifying behavior and repeat the observations. Using videotapes can also help eliminate observer bias because behavior can be reviewed several times prior to making classification decisions.

Another method of studying behavior involves observation that takes place not in its natural setting, but in a laboratory. Researchers using **laboratory observation** can exert more control and use more precise equipment to measure responses. Much of what is known about sleep or the human sexual response, for example, has been learned through laboratory observation. However, like other research methods, laboratory observation has limitations. For one, laboratory behavior may not accurately reflect real-world behavior. For example, in sleep studies, some of the behavior people display while asleep in the laboratory may not occur in their homes. As a result, conclusions based on laboratory findings may not generalize beyond the walls of the laboratory itself. Another disadvantage is that building, staffing, equipping, and maintaining research laboratories can be expensive.

◆ **descriptive research methods**
Research methods that yield descriptions of behavior.

◆ **naturalistic observation**
A descriptive research method in which researchers observe and record behavior in its natural setting, without attempting to influence or control it.

◆ *How do psychological researchers use naturalistic and laboratory observation?*

A kind of naturalistic observation occurs on a large scale in England; about a million closed-circuit TV cameras like this one monitor activity in streets and shopping centers.

◆ **laboratory observation**
A descriptive research method in which behavior is studied in a laboratory setting.

The Case Study

◆ *What are the advantages and disadvantages of the case study?*

The **case study**, or case history, is another descriptive research method used by psychologists. In a case study, a single individual or a small number of persons are studied in great depth, usually over an extended period of time. A case study involves the use of observations, interviews, and sometimes psychological testing. Exploratory in nature, the case study's purpose is to provide a detailed description of some behavior or disorder. This method is particularly appropriate for studying people who have uncommon psychological or physiological disorders or brain injuries. Many case studies are written about patients being treated for such problems. In some instances, the results of detailed case studies have provided the foundation for psychological theories. In particular, the theory of Sigmund Freud was based primarily on case studies of his patients.

◆ **case study**

A descriptive research method in which a single individual or a small number of persons are studied in great depth.

◆ **survey**

A descriptive research method in which researchers use interviews and/or questionnaires to gather information about the attitudes, beliefs, experiences, or behaviors of a group of people.

Although the case study has proven useful in advancing knowledge in several areas of psychology, it has certain limitations. Researchers cannot establish the cause of behavior observed in a case study, and observer bias is a potential problem. Moreover, because so few individuals are studied, researchers do not know how applicable, or generalizable, their findings may be to larger groups or to different cultures.

Survey Research

◆ *How do researchers ensure that survey results are useful?*

Have you ever been questioned about your voting behavior or about the kind of toothpaste you prefer? If you have, chances are that you were a participant in another kind of research study. The **survey** is a descriptive research method in which researchers use interviews and/or questionnaires to gather information about the attitudes, beliefs, experiences, or behaviors of a group of people. The results of carefully conducted surveys have provided valuable information about drug use, sexual behavior, and the incidence of various mental disorders.

◆ **population**

The entire group of interest to researchers, to which they wish to generalize their findings; the group from which a sample is selected.

◆ **sample**

A part of a population that is studied to reach conclusions about the entire population.

Researchers in psychology rarely conduct studies using all members of a group. For example, researchers interested in studying the sexual behavior of American women do not survey every woman in the United States. (Imagine trying to interview about 140 million people!) Instead of studying the whole **population** (the entire group of interest to researchers, to which they wish to apply their findings), researchers select a sample for study. A **sample** is a part of a population that is studied to reach conclusions about the entire population.

◆ **representative sample**

A sample that mirrors the population of interest; it includes important subgroups in the same proportions as they are found in that population.

Perhaps you have seen a carton of ice cream that contains three separate flavors—chocolate, strawberry, and vanilla—packed side by side. To properly sample the carton, you would need a small amount of ice cream containing all three flavors in the same proportions as in the whole carton—a representative sample. A **representative sample** mirrors the population of interest—that is, it includes important subgroups in the same proportions as they are found in that population. A *biased sample*, on the other hand, does not adequately reflect the larger population.

The best method for obtaining a representative sample is to select a *random sample* from a list of all members of the population of interest. Individuals are selected in such a way that every member of the larger population has an equal chance of being included in the sample. Using random samples, polling organizations can accurately represent the views of the American public with responses from as few as 1,000 people (O'Brien, 1996).

It might seem that simply interviewing people with a standard set of questions would be the best way to gather survey data. In reality, the truthfulness of participants' responses can be affected by characteristics of the interviewers, such as their gender, age, race, ethnicity, religion, and social class. Thus, to use interviews effectively, survey researchers must select interviewers who have personal characteristics that are appropriate for the intended respondents.

Is the Osbourne family *representative* of the general population of families in the United States? Why or why not?

Questionnaires can be completed more quickly and less expensively than interviews, especially when respondents can fill them out in their homes or online. The Internet offers psychologists a fast and inexpensive way of soliciting participants and collecting questionnaire data, and Internet surveys often generate large numbers of responses (Azar, 2000). For example, an Internet survey posted by researchers who wanted to collect data about suicidal feelings attracted more than 38,000 respondents from all over the world (Mathy, 2002). However, researchers who use Web-based surveys must be cautious about generalizing the results of their studies because respondents represent only the population of Internet users who choose to participate, not the general population or even the entire population of Internet users. Moreover, they must take steps to ensure that a respondent can participate in the study only once (Gosling et al., 2004).

Internet surveys allow psychologists to gather lots of data from large numbers of respondents in a very short period of time. But how representative of the general population are people who respond to Internet surveys? How representative are they of Internet users in general? Questions such as these remain to be answered.

If conducted properly, surveys can provide highly accurate information. They can also track changes in attitudes or behavior over time. For example, Johnston and others (2001) have tracked drug use among high school students since 1975. However, large-scale surveys can be costly and time-consuming. Another important limitation of survey research is that respondents may provide inaccurate information. False information can result from a faulty memory or a desire to please the interviewer. Respondents may try to present themselves in a good light (a phenomenon called the *social desirability response*), or they may even deliberately mislead the interviewer. Finally, when respondents answer questions about sensitive subjects, such as sexual behavior, they are often less candid in face-to-face interviews than in self-administered or computerized questionnaires (Tourangeau et al., 1997).

The Experimental Method

What comes to mind when you hear the word *experiment?* Many people use the word to refer to any kind of study. Among scientists, though, the term *experiment* refers only to one kind of study, the kind in which researchers seek to determine the causes of behavior.

Experiments and Hypothesis Testing

The **experimental method**, or the experiment, is the *only* research method that can be used to identify cause-effect relationships. An experiment is designed to test a hypothesis about a cause-effect relationship between two or more variables. A **variable** is any condition or factor that can be manipulated, controlled, or measured. One variable of interest to you is the grade you will receive in this psychology course. Another variable that probably interests you is the amount of time you will spend studying for this course. Do you suppose that a cause-effect relationship exists between the amount of time students spend studying and the grades they receive? Consider two other variables: alcohol consumption and aggression. Alcohol consumption and aggressive behavior are often observed occurring at the same time. But can we assume that alcohol consumption causes aggressive behavior?

Alan Lang and his colleagues (1975) conducted a classic experiment to determine whether alcohol consumption itself increases aggression or whether the beliefs or expectations about the effects of alcohol cause the aggressive behavior. The participants in the experiment were 96 male college students. Half of the students were given plain tonic to drink; the other half were given a vodka-and-tonic drink in amounts sufficient to raise their blood alcohol level to .10, which is higher than the .08 level that is the legal limit for intoxication in most states. Participants were assigned to four groups:

Group 1: Expected alcohol, received only tonic
Group 2: Expected alcohol, received alcohol mixed with tonic

◆ *Why do researchers use experiments to test hypotheses about cause-effect relationships?*

◆ **experimental method**
The only research method that can be used to identify cause-effect relationships between two or more conditions or variables.

◆ **variable**
Any condition or factor that can be manipulated, controlled, or measured.

Group 3: Expected tonic, received alcohol mixed with tonic
Group 4: Expected tonic, received only tonic

After the students had consumed the designated amount, the researchers had an accomplice, who posed as a participant, purposely provoke half the students by belittling their performance on a difficult task. All the students then participated in a learning experiment, in which the same accomplice posed as the learner. The subjects were told to administer an electric shock to the accomplice each time he made a mistake on a decoding task. Each participant was allowed to determine the intensity and duration of the "shock." (Although the students thought they were shocking the accomplice, no shocks were actually delivered.) The researchers measured the aggressiveness of the students in terms of the duration and the intensity of the shocks they chose to deliver.

What were the results of the experiment? As you might imagine, the students who had been provoked gave the accomplice stronger shocks than those who had not been provoked. But the students who drank the alcohol were not necessarily the most aggressive. Regardless of the actual content of their drinks, the participants who thought they were drinking alcohol gave significantly stronger shocks, whether provoked or not, than those who assumed they were drinking only tonic (see Figure 1.1). The researchers concluded that it was the *expectation* of drinking alcohol, not the alcohol itself, that caused the students to be more aggressive.

Independent and Dependent Variables

◆ *How do independent and dependent variables differ?*

Recall that experiments test hypotheses about cause and effect. Examples of such hypotheses include "Studying causes good grades" and "Taking aspirin causes headaches to go away." Note that each hypothesis involves two variables: One is thought to be the cause (studying, taking aspirin), and the other is thought to be affected by the cause. These two kinds of variables are found in all experiments. An experiment has at least one **independent variable**—a variable that the researcher believes causes a change in some other variable. The researcher deliberately manipulates the independent variable (hypothesized cause) to determine whether it causes any change in another behavior or condition. Sometimes the independent variable is referred to as the *treatment*. The Lang experiment had two independent variables: the alcoholic content of the drink and the expectation of drinking alcohol.

◆ **independent variable**

In an experiment, a factor or condition that is deliberately manipulated to determine whether it causes any change in another behavior or condition.

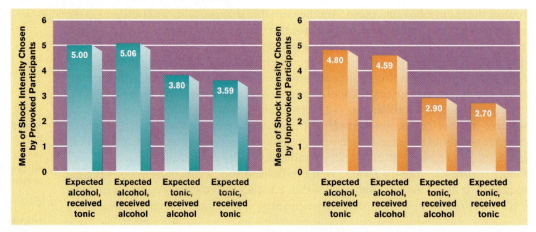

FIGURE 1.1   The Mean Shock Intensity Chosen by Provoked and Unprovoked Participants

In the Lang experiment, participants who thought they were drinking alcohol chose to give significantly stronger shocks, whether provoked or not, than those who believed they were drinking only tonic.   *Source:* Data from Lang et al. (1975).

The second type of variable found in all experiments, the one that the hypothesis states is affected by the independent variable, is the **dependent variable**. It is measured at the end of the experiment and is presumed to vary (increase or decrease) as a result of the manipulations of the independent variable(s). Researchers must provide operational definitions of all variables in an experiment—that is, they must specify precisely how the variables will be observed and measured. In the Lang study, the dependent variable—aggression—was operationally defined as the intensity and duration of the "shocks" the participants chose to deliver to the accomplice.

◆ **dependent variable**
The factor or condition that is measured at the end of an experiment and is presumed to vary as a result of the manipulations of the independent variable(s).

Experimental and Control Groups

Most experiments are conducted using two or more groups of participants. There must always be at least one **experimental group**—a group of participants who are exposed to the independent variable, or the treatment. The Lang experiment used three experimental groups:

◆ *Why are experimental and control groups necessary?*

> *Group 1:* Expected alcohol, received only tonic
> *Group 2:* Expected alcohol, received alcohol mixed with tonic
> *Group 3:* Expected tonic, received alcohol mixed with tonic

Most experiments also have a **control group**—a group that is similar to the experimental group and is also measured on the dependent variable at the end of the experiment, for purposes of comparison. The control group is exposed to the same experimental environment as the experimental group but is not given the treatment. The fourth group in the Lang study was exposed to neither of the two independent variables; that is, this group did not expect alcohol and did not receive alcohol. Because this group was similar to the experimental groups and was exposed to the same experimental environment, it served as a control group.

◆ **experimental group**
In an experiment, the group that is exposed to an independent variable.

◆ **control group**
In an experiment, a group similar to the experimental group that is exposed to the same experimental environment but is not given the treatment; used for purposes of comparison.

You may be wondering why a control group is necessary. Couldn't an experimenter just expose one group to the independent variable and see if a change occurs? While this approach is sometimes used, it is usually preferable to have a control group because people and their behaviors often change without intervention. Having a control group reveals what kinds of changes happen "naturally" and provides a way of separating the effect of the independent variable from such changes. Suppose you want to find out if a certain medication relieves headaches. You could just find some people with headaches, give them the medication, and then count how many still have headaches an hour later. But some headaches go away without treatment. So if the medication appears to work, it may only be because a number of headaches went away on their own. Having a control group allows you to know whether the medicine relieves headaches in addition to those that disappear without treatment.

◆ **confounding variables**
Factors or conditions other than the independent variable(s) that are not equivalent across groups and could cause differences among the groups with respect to the dependent variable.

Sources of Bias in Experimental Research

Can the researcher always assume that the independent variable is the cause of some change in the dependent variable? Not necessarily. Sometimes an experiment is affected by **confounding variables**—factors or conditions other than the independent variable that are not equivalent across groups and that could cause differences among the groups with respect to the dependent variable. By conducting their experiment in a laboratory, Lang and his colleagues were able to control environmental conditions such as extreme noise or heat, which could have acted as confounding variables by increasing aggressive responses. Three additional sources of confounding variables that must be controlled in all experiments are selection bias, the placebo effect, and experimenter bias.

◆ *What kinds of factors introduce bias into experimental studies?*

Why can't researchers allow participants to choose to be in either the experimental group or the control group? Such a procedure would introduce *selection bias* into a study. **Selection bias** occurs when participants are assigned to experimental or control groups in such a way that systematic differences among the groups are present at the beginning

◆ **selection bias**
The assignment of participants to experimental or control groups in such a way that systematic differences among the groups are present at the beginning of the experiment.

of the experiment. If selection bias occurs, then differences at the end of the experiment may not reflect the change in the independent variable but may be due to preexisting differences in the groups. To control for selection bias, researchers must use **random assignment.** This process consists of selecting participants by using a chance procedure (such as drawing the names of participants out of a hat) to guarantee that each participant has an equal probability of being assigned to any of the groups. Random assignment maximizes the likelihood that the groups will be as similar as possible at the beginning of the experiment. If there were preexisting differences in students' levels of aggressiveness in the Lang experiment, random assignment would have spread those differences across all the groups.

Can participants' expectations influence an experiment's results? Yes. The **placebo effect** occurs when a participant's response to a treatment is due to his or her expectations about the treatment rather than to the treatment itself. Suppose a drug is prescribed for a patient and the patient reports improvement. The improvement could be a direct result of the drug, or it could be a result of the patient's expectation that the drug will work. Studies have shown that sometimes patients' remarkable improvement can be attributed solely to the power of suggestion—the placebo effect.

In drug experiments, the control group is usually given a **placebo**—an inert or harmless substance such as a sugar pill or an injection of saline solution. To control for the placebo effect, researchers do not let participants know whether they are in the experimental group (receiving the treatment) or in the control group (receiving the placebo). If participants getting the real drug or treatment show a significantly greater improvement than those receiving the placebo, then the improvement can be attributed to the drug rather than to the participants' expectations about the drug's effects. In the Lang experiment, some students who expected alcohol mixed with tonic were given only tonic. The tonic without alcohol functioned as a placebo, allowing researchers to measure the effect of the expectations alone in producing aggression.

What about the experimenter's expectations? **Experimenter bias** occurs when researchers' preconceived notions or expectations become a self-fulfilling prophecy and cause the researchers to find what they expect to find. A researcher's expectations can be communicated to participants, perhaps unintentionally, through tone of voice, gestures, or facial expressions. These communications can influence the participants' behavior. Expectations can also influence a researcher's interpretation of the experimental results, even if no influence occurred during the experiment. To control for experimenter bias, researchers must not know which participants are assigned to the experimental and control groups until after the research data are collected and recorded. (Obviously, someone assisting the researcher does know.) When neither the participants nor the researchers know which participants are getting the treatment and which are in the control group, the experiment is using the **double-blind technique.**

Limitations of the Experimental Method

◆ *What are the limitations of the experimental method?*

You now know that experiments provide information about cause-effect relationships. But what are their limitations? For one thing, researchers who use the experimental method are able to exercise strict control over the setting, but the more control they exercise, the more unnatural and contrived the research setting becomes. And the more unnatural the setting becomes, the less generalizable findings may be to the real world. Another important limitation of the experimental method is that its use is either unethical or impossible for research in many areas of interest to psychologists. Some treatments cannot be given to human participants because their physical or psychological health would be endangered, or their constitutional rights violated.

What happens when we apply our knowledge about the problems associated with the experimental method to the results of Lang's study? Can we conclude that people in general tend to be more aggressive when they believe they are under the influence of alcohol? Before reaching such a conclusion, we must consider several factors: (1) All participants in this experiment were male college students. We cannot be sure that the same results would have occurred if females or males of other ages had been included. (2) The participants in this experiment were classified as heavy social drinkers. Would the same results have occurred if nondrinkers, moderate social drinkers, or alcoholics had been included? To apply this experiment's findings to other groups, researchers would have to replicate, or repeat, the experiment using different populations of subjects. (3) The amount of alcohol given to the students was just enough to bring their blood alcohol level to .10. We cannot be sure that the same results would have occurred if they had consumed more or less alcohol.

 # The Correlational Method

Can you imagine a principal notifying parents that their son or daughter had been chosen to smoke marijuana for 2 years in an effort to further scientific knowledge? It is often illegal and always unethical to assign people randomly to experimental conditions that could be harmful. For example, to find out if smoking marijuana causes a decline in academic achievement, no researcher would randomly assign high school students to an experimental study that would require participants in the experimental group to smoke marijuana. When an experimental study cannot be performed to determine cause-effect relationships, the **correlational method** is usually used. This research method establishes the *correlation*, or degree of relationship, between two characteristics, events, or behaviors. A group is selected for study, and the variables of interest are measured for each participant. For example, the variables might be the amount of marijuana previously used and grade-point average.

◆ **correlational method**
A research method used to establish the degree of relationship (correlation) between two characteristics, events, or behaviors.

The Correlation Coefficient

What is the relationship between the price of a new car and the social status you gain from owning it? Isn't it true that as price goes up, status goes up as well? And isn't status one of the variables that many people take into account when buying a new car? As this example illustrates, correlations are part of our everyday lives, and we often use them in decision making.

◆ *What is a correlation coefficient, and what does it mean?*

When scientists study correlations, they apply a statistical formula to data representing two or more variables to obtain a *correlation coefficient*. A **correlation coefficient** is a numerical value that indicates the strength and direction of the relationship between two variables. A correlation coefficient ranges from +1.00 (a perfect positive correlation) to .00 (no relationship) to −1.00 (a perfect negative correlation). The number in a correlation coefficient indicates the relative strength of the relationship between two variables—the higher the number, the stronger the relationship. Therefore, a correlation of −.85 is stronger than a correlation of +.64.

The sign of a correlation coefficient (+ or −) indicates whether the two variables vary in the same or opposite directions. A positive correlation indicates that two variables vary in the same direction, like the price of a car and its associated social status.

A negative correlation means that an increase in the value of one variable is associated with a decrease in the value of the other variable. For example, as mileage accumulates on a car's odometer, the less reliable it becomes. Likewise, there is a negative correlation between the number of cigarettes people smoke and the number of years they can expect to live.

◆ **correlation coefficient**
A numerical value that indicates the strength and direction of the relationship between two variables; ranges from +1.00 (a perfect positive correlation) to −1.00 (a perfect negative correlation).

◆ *What are the strengths and weaknesses of the correlational method?*

Strengths and Weaknesses of Correlational Studies

Does the fact that there is a correlation between two variables indicate that one variable causes the other? Remember, only the experimental method can lead to

FIGURE 1.2 — Correlation Does Not Prove Causation

A correlation between two variables does not prove that a cause-effect relationship exists between them. There is a correlation between stress and illness, but that does not mean that stress necessarily causes illness. Both stress and illness may result from another factor, such as poverty or poor general health.

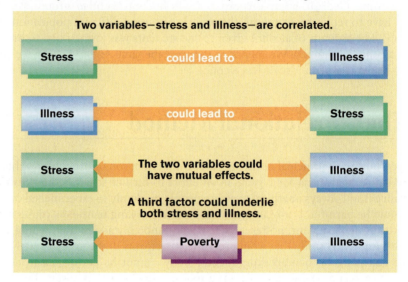

Two variables—stress and illness—are correlated.

Stress → could lead to → Illness

Illness → could lead to → Stress

Stress ← The two variables could have mutual effects. → Illness

A third factor could underlie both stress and illness.

Stress ← Poverty → Illness

conclusions about cause and effect. So, when two variables such as stress and illness are correlated, we cannot conclude that stress makes people sick. It might be that illness causes stress, or that a third factor such as poverty or poor general health causes people to be more susceptible to both illness and stress, as shown in Figure 1.2. For more information on the correlation coefficient, see the discussion of statistical methods in Appendix A, which follows Chapter 14.

At this point, you might be thinking, if a researcher can't draw cause-effect conclusions, why do correlational studies? One reason is that it is sometimes impossible, for ethical reasons, to manipulate variables of interest. Scientists can't ethically ask pregnant women to drink alcohol just so they can find out whether it causes birth defects. The only option available in such cases is the correlational method. Researchers have to ask mothers about their drinking habits and note any association with birth defects in their babies. Knowing the correlation between prenatal alcohol consumption and the incidence of birth defects helps scientists make predictions about what may happen when pregnant women consume alcohol.

In addition, correlational studies can be done more quickly and cheaply than experiments. So, researchers sometimes choose to carry out correlational research even when an experiment would be ethically permissible and the variables could be experimentally controlled.

Temperature is correlated with snow-cone sales. As temperature increases, so does the number of snow cones sold. Is this a positive or a negative correlation? What about the corresponding correlation between temperature and coffee sales? Is it positive or negative?

Participants in Psychological Research

Participant-Related Bias in Psychological Research

Do you remember reading earlier about the importance of representative samples in survey research? With other methods, representativeness becomes an issue when psychologists want to generalize the findings of studies to individuals other than the studies' participants. For example, projections by the U.S. Bureau of the Census (2000) indicate that the percentage of non-Hispanic Whites in the U.S. population is expected to decrease from 71.5% in the year 2000 to 53% in 2050. Yet, Whites are often overrepresented in psychological studies because many researchers draw samples from the college student population, which has a lower proportion of minorities than in the population in general. Moreover, college students, even those of minority ethnicity, are a relatively select group in terms of age, socioeconomic class, and educational level. Thus, they are not representative of the general population. This lack of representativeness in a research sample is a type of *participant-related bias*.

Gender bias is another type of participant-related bias. For example, Ader and Johnson (1994) found that, when conducting research in which all of the participants are of one sex, researchers typically specify the gender of the sample clearly when it is female, but not when the sample is exclusively male. Such a practice, according to Ader and Johnson, reveals a "tendency to consider male participants 'normative,' and results obtained from them generally applicable, whereas female participants are somehow 'different,' and results obtained from them are specific to female participants" (pp. 217–218). On a positive note, these researchers report that over the decades, gender bias in the sampling and selection of research subjects has been decreasing.

In what ways can participants bias research results?

Protecting Research Participants' Rights

Researchers are ethically obligated to protect the rights of all study participants. In 2002, the American Psychological Association (APA) adopted a new set of ethical standards governing research with human participants so as to safeguard their rights while supporting the goals of scientific inquiry. Following are some of the main provisions of the code:

What ethical rules must researchers follow when humans are involved in studies?

- *Legality.* All research must conform to applicable federal, state, and local laws and regulations.
- *Institutional approval.* Researchers must obtain approval from all institutions involved in a study. For example, a researcher cannot conduct a study in a school without the school's approval.
- *Informed consent.* Participants must be informed of the purpose of the study and its potential for harming them.
- *Deception.* Deception of participants is ethical when it is necessary. However, the code of ethics cautions researchers against using deception if another means can be found to test the study's hypothesis.
- *Debriefing.* Whenever a researcher deceives participants, including through the use of placebo treatments, he or she must tell participants about the deception as soon as the study is complete.
- *Clients, patients, students, and subordinates.* When participants are under another's authority (for example, a therapist's client, a patient in a hospital, a student in a psychology class, or an employee), researchers must take steps to ensure that participation in a study, and the information obtained during participation, will not damage the participants in any way. Professors, for example, cannot reduce students' grades if the students refuse to participate in a research study.

- *Payment for participation.* Participants can be paid, but the code of ethics requires that they be fully informed about what is expected in return for payment.
- *Publication.* Psychological researchers must report their findings in an appropriate forum, such as a scientific journal, and they must make their data available to others who want to verify their findings.

The Use of Animals in Research

◆ *Why are animals used in research?*

The APA code of ethics also includes guidelines for using animals in psychological research. Here are a few of the important guidelines:

- *Legality.* Like research with human participants, animal research must follow all relevant federal, state, and local laws.
- *Supervision by experienced personnel.* The use of animals must be supervised by people who are trained in their care. These experienced personnel must teach all subordinates, such as research assistants, how to properly handle and feed the animals and to recognize signs of illness or distress.
- *Minimization of discomfort.* Researchers are ethically bound to minimize any discomfort to research animals. For example, it is unethical to perform surgery on research animals without appropriate anesthesia. And when researchers must terminate the lives of research animals, they must do so in a humane manner.

Even with these safeguards in place, the use of animals in research is controversial. Many animal rights advocates want all animal research stopped immediately.

In a survey of almost 4,000 randomly selected members of the APA, "80% of respondents expressed general support for psychological research on animals" (Plous, 1996, p. 1177). Among the general public, support for animal research is higher when the research is tied to human health and highest when the animals involved in such research are rats and mice rather than dogs, cats, or primates (Plous, 1996). Most agree that there are at least six reasons for using animals in research: (1) They provide a simpler model for studying processes that operate similarly in humans; (2) researchers can exercise far more control over animal subjects and thus be more certain of their conclusions; (3) a wider range of medical and other manipulations can be used with animals; (4) it is easier to study the entire lifespan and even multiple generations in some animal species; (5) animals are more economical to use as research subjects and are available at the researchers' convenience; and (6) some researchers simply want to learn more about the animals themselves.

Thinking about Theories and Research

Students often want to know which of the many psychological theories are "true" and which are "false." However, psychologists don't think about theories in this way. Instead, they evaluate theories in terms of their usefulness.

Likewise, students often wonder whether learning about research methods is of any practical value to people who do not intend to become professional researchers. As you'll see, knowledge about research methods can prove extremely useful in everyday life.

Evaluating Theories

◆ *How do psychologists compare theories?*

As you learned earlier in this chapter, useful theories help psychologists achieve the prediction goal by generating testable hypotheses. When assessed against this criterion, the theories of behaviorists and cognitive psychologists appear more useful than those of psychoanalysts and humanists. B. F. Skinner's prediction that reinforcement increases behavior, for example, is far more testable than Maslow's claim that self-actualization is the highest of all human needs.

Useful theories also lead to the development of solutions to real-world problems. For instance, research based on the information-processing model has resulted in the development of practical strategies for improving memory. Similarly, even though psychoanalytic and humanistic theories have been criticized for lacking testability, they have produced a number of beneficial psychotherapies.

Hypotheses and practical applications are important, but a theory that possesses *heuristic value* is useful even if it falls short in these two areas. A theory that has heuristic value stimulates debate among psychologists and motivates both proponents and opponents of the theory to pursue research related to it. In other words, a theory that possesses heuristic value makes people think and spurs their curiosity and creativity.

All of the theories discussed so far earn high marks for their heuristic value. In fact, even if a theory has limited empirical support, professors who teach introductory psychology are justified in including it in the course if it has been of heuristic importance in the field. This is why we still teach about the structuralists and functionalists, and why we continue to rate Freud's theory as one of the most important in the field. Moreover, such theories usually affect students in the same way that they affect psychologists—that is, learning about them stimulates students' thinking about behavior and mental processes. Thus, introducing these theories helps professors achieve one of their most important instructional goals, that of motivating students to think critically.

Evaluating Research

Another important goal of most professors who teach introductory psychology is to equip students with the intellectual tools needed to evaluate claims based on psychological research. Living in the Information Age, we are bombarded with statistics and claims of all types every day. For instance, not long ago the news media carried a number of reports warning parents of young children that watching too much television in the early years of life might lead to attention deficit/hyperactivity disorder (ADHD) later in childhood (Clayton, 2004). These warnings were based, reporters said, on a scientific study that was published in the prestigious journal *Pediatrics*. How can a person who is not an expert on the subject in question evaluate claims such as these?

◆ *How can critical thinking be used to interpret media reports of psychological research?*

The thinking strategies used by psychologists and other scientists can help us sift through this kind of information. **Critical thinking**, the foundation of the scientific method, is the process of objectively evaluating claims, propositions, and conclusions to determine whether they follow logically from the evidence presented. When we engage in critical thinking, we exhibit these characteristics:

- *Independent thinking.* When thinking critically, we do not automatically accept and believe what we read or hear.
- *Suspension of judgment.* Critical thinking requires gathering relevant and up-to-date information on all sides of an issue before taking a position.
- *Willingness to modify or abandon prior judgments.* Critical thinking involves evaluating new evidence, even when it contradicts preexisting beliefs.

Applying the first of these three characteristics to the television-ADHD study requires recognizing that the validity of any study is not determined by the authority of its source. Prestigious journals—or psychology textbooks for that matter—shouldn't be regarded as sources of fixed, immutable truths. In fact, learning to question accepted "truths" is important to the scientific method itself. For example, as you will learn in Chapter 2, for many years scientists believed that the brain did not develop any new nerve cells after birth. However, once the technology became available to directly study neuronal development, researchers who were willing to challenge the status quo found that the brain produces new nerve cells throughout the lifespan (Gould et al., 1999).

The second and third characteristics of critical thinking, suspension of judgment and willingness to change, may require abandoning some old habits. If you are like most

◆ **critical thinking**
The process of objectively evaluating claims, propositions, and conclusions to determine whether they follow logically from the evidence presented.

people, you respond to media reports about research on the basis of your own personal experiences, a type of evidence scientists call *anecdotal evidence*. For instance, in response to the media report about television and ADHD, a person might say, "I agree with that study because my cousin has such severe ADHD that he had to drop out of high school, and he was always glued to the television when he was little." Another might counter, "I don't agree with that study because I watched a lot of television when I was a kid, and I don't have ADHD."

Suspension of judgment requires that you postpone either accepting or rejecting the study's findings until you have accumulated more evidence. It might involve determining what, if any, findings have been reported by other researchers regarding a possible link between television viewing and ADHD. Analysis of other relevant studies can help to create a comprehensive picture of what the entire body of research says about the issue. Ultimately, when enough evidence has been gathered, a critical thinker must be willing to abandon preconceived notions and prior beliefs that conflict with it.

The quality of the evidence is just as important as the quantity. Thus, a critical thinker would evaluate the findings of the television-ADHD study by considering the methods used to obtain them. Did the researchers randomly assign young children to experimental and control groups who watched different amounts of television and then assess whether experimental and control children differed in ADHD symptoms several years later? If so, then the study was an experiment, and media claims that television viewing in early childhood leads to ADHD might be justified. Conversely, if the researchers simply measured television viewing in early childhood and then correlated this variable with a measure of ADHD later on, then claims of a causal relationship between the two variables would not be justified. Instead, the appropriate response would be to look for underlying variables, such as parental involvement, that might explain the connection. In fact, the research cited in these reports was correlational in nature, so the strong causal claims implied by many media accounts of the study (Christakis et al., 2004) were inappropriate.

Now that you are familiar with how psychologists think about theories and research, let's look at some of the current trends in the field.

 ## Current Trends in Psychology

Psychology is an evolving science in which new theories are being tested and more precise research is being conducted every day. Its ongoing advances will continue to illuminate our thinking and influence our behaviors. So, where is psychology headed today? In addition to the continuing influence of psychodynamic theory, behaviorism, humanistic psychology, and cognitive psychology, several other important trends in psychology have emerged in recent years.

Evolutionary Psychology

◆ *What is the main idea behind evolutionary psychology?*

◆ **evolutionary psychology**
The school of psychology that studies how humans have adapted the behaviors required for survival in the face of environmental pressures over the long course of evolution.

Why do you think most men prefer mates who are younger than they are? This is the kind of question that interests *evolutionary psychologists*. **Evolutionary psychology** focuses on how the human behaviors required for survival have adapted in the face of environmental pressures over the long course of evolution (Archer, 1996). Two widely recognized proponents of evolutionary psychology, Leda Cosmides and John Tooby, hold that this perspective combines the forces of evolutionary biology, anthropology, cognitive psychology, and neuroscience. They explain that an evolutionary perspective can be applied to any topic within the field of psychology (Cosmides & Tooby, 2000). One of the most influential evolutionary psychologists, David Buss, and his colleagues have conducted a number of fascinating studies examining men's and women's patterns of behavior in romantic relationships (2000a, 2000b, 2004; Buss et al., 2001).

One of Buss's consistent findings is that men seem to experience more jealousy when faced with a partner's sexual infidelity than with her emotional infidelity (Buss, 2004; Buss et al., 1992; Shackelford et al., 2002). (Emotional infidelity is the creation of a bond with someone other than one's intimate partner that involves feelings, especially romantic love, that are assumed to have been promised only to that partner.) By contrast, the women in Buss's research appear to be more concerned about emotional rather than sexual unfaithfulness in a partner. Evolutionary psychologists claim that men's jealousy focuses on sexual infidelity because, in the evolutionary past, a man's certainty of his paternity was jeopardized if he learned that his mate had been sexually unfaithful. But the best chance a woman had to pass her genes on to future generations was to be able to rely on material resources, protection, and support from a mate who would help her offspring survive and reach sexual maturity. The man's emotional commitment to her, then, was of paramount importance. Thus, the presumably biological sex difference in reactions to infidelity favors the survival of offspring: Men's insistence on sexual fidelity ensures knowledge of paternity and, therefore, their willingness to commit to an investment in their children's upbringing. Women's insistence on emotional commitment promotes family harmony and continuity, which, in turn, provide a stable environment in which to bring up children.

It's important to note that Buss and his colleagues have gone beyond just asking men and women about jealousy. They have tested participants of both sexes in the laboratory and asked them to imagine the two types of infidelity while connected to instruments for measuring heart or pulse rate, electrodermal response (sweating), and tensing of the brow muscles (frowning). The men showed high physiological distress at the thought of sexual infidelity, but far less distress when considering emotional infidelity. The women tended to exhibit high physiological distress when imagining emotional infidelity by their partner, but much less distress when confronting sexual infidelity. As far as can be determined, these and similar findings appear to be universal. Results of a cross-cultural study in the United States, Germany, the Netherlands, and South Korea are shown in Figure 1.3. As you might suspect, Buss's conclusions are controversial. Other psychologists (e.g., Eagly & Wood, 1999) explain his research results in terms of social and cultural variables.

◆ **biological psychology**
The school of psychology that looks for links between specific behaviors and equally specific biological processes that often help explain individual differences.

Biological (Physiological) Psychology

Sometimes students are confused about the difference between evolutionary psychology and **biological psychology** (also referred to as *physiological psychology*). After all, many think, isn't evolution "biological" in nature? Yes, it is, but evolutionary psychology provides explanations of how certain biologically based behaviors came to be common in an entire species. Consequently, it focuses on *universals*, traits that exist in every member of a species. For instance, language is a human universal.

◆ *How is biological psychology changing the field of psychology?*

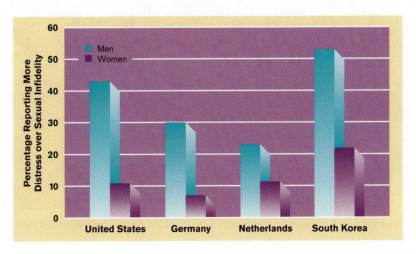

FIGURE 1.3

Gender Differences in Jealousy across Cultures

Across all cultures, men experience greater distress in response to sexual infidelity than women do, while women experience greater distress in response to emotional infidelity than men do.
Source: From Buunk et al. (1996).

◆ **neuroscience**

An interdisciplinary field that combines the work of psychologists, biologists, biochemists, medical researchers, and others in the study of the structure and function of the nervous system.

◆ **sociocultural approach**

The view that social and cultural factors may be just as powerful as evolutionary and physiological factors in affecting behavior and mental processing and that these factors must be understood when interpreting the behavior of others.

By contrast, biological psychologists more often look for links between specific behaviors and particular biological factors that often help explain *individual differences*. They study the structures of the brain and central nervous system, the functioning of neurons, the delicate balance of neurotransmitters and hormones, and the effects of heredity to look for links between these biological factors and behavior. For example, the number of ear infections children have in the first year of life (a *biological* individual difference) is correlated with learning disabilities in the elementary school years (a *behavioral* individual difference) (Spreen et al., 1995). (Remember, this finding doesn't mean that ear infections *cause* learning disabilities; most likely, some other factor links the two.)

Many biological psychologists work under the umbrella of an interdisciplinary field known as **neuroscience.** Neuroscience combines the work of psychologists, biologists, biochemists, medical researchers, and others in the study of the structure and function of the nervous system. Important findings in psychology have resulted from this work. You will read about many such findings in later chapters.

The Sociocultural Approach

◆ *What kinds of variables interest psychologists who take a sociocultural approach?*

How do your background and cultural experiences affect your behavior and mental processing? Just as important as the current trend toward biological explanations is the growing realization among psychologists that social and cultural forces may be as powerful as evolutionary and physiological factors. The **sociocultural approach** emphasizes social and cultural influences on human behavior and stresses the importance of understanding those influences when interpreting the behavior of others. For example, several psychologists (e.g., Tweed & Lehman, 2002) have researched philosophical differences between Asian and Western cultures that may help explain cross-national achievement differences. You will learn about some of these studies in Chapter 7.

◆ **psychological perspectives**

General points of view used for explaining people's behavior and thinking, whether normal or abnormal.

Psychological Perspectives and Eclecticism

◆ *What are psychological perspectives, and how are they related to an eclectic position?*

The views of modern psychologists are frequently difficult to categorize into traditional schools of thought. Thus, rather than discussing schools of thought, it is often more useful to refer to **psychological perspectives**—general points of view used for explaining people's behavior and thinking, whether normal or abnormal. For example, a psychologist may adopt a behavioral perspective without necessarily agreeing with all of Watson's or Skinner's ideas. What is important is that the psychologist taking such a view will explain behavior in terms of environmental forces.

A sociocultural approach helps psychologists explain cross-cultural differences in behavior.

The major perspectives in psychology today and the kinds of variables each emphasizes in explaining behavior are as follows:

- *Behavioral perspective*—environmental factors
- *Psychoanalytic perspective*—emotions, unconscious motivations, early childhood experiences
- *Humanistic perspective*—subjective experiences, intrinsic motivation to achieve self-actualization
- *Cognitive perspective*—mental processes
- *Evolutionary perspective*—inherited traits that enhance adaptability
- *Biological perspective*—biological structures, processes, heredity
- *Sociocultural perspective*—social and cultural variables

Review and Reflect 1.1 lists these perspectives along with an illustration of how each might explain older adults' poor performance on researchers' memory tasks as compared to that of younger adults.

Psychologists need not limit themselves to just one perspective or approach. Many take an *eclectic position*, choosing a combination of approaches to explain a particular behavior. For example, a psychologist may explain a behavior in terms of both environmental factors and mental processes. A child's unruly behavior in school may be seen as maintained by teacher attention (a behavioral explanation) but as initially caused by an emotional reaction to a family event such as divorce (a psychoanalytic explanation). By

REVIEW *and* REFLECT 1.1

Major Perspectives in Psychology

PERSPECTIVE	EMPHASIS	EXPLANATION OF OLDER ADULTS' POOR PERFORMANCE ON RESEARCHERS' MEMORY TASKS
Behavioral	The role of environment in shaping and controlling behavior	Older adults spend little or no time in environments such as school, where they would be reinforced for using their memories.
Psychoanalytic	The role of unconscious motivation and early childhood experiences in determining behavior and thought	Older adults' unconscious fear of impending death interferes with memory processes.
Humanistic	The importance of an individual's subjective experience as a key to understanding his or her behavior	Older adults are more concerned about finding meaning in their lives than about performing well on experimenters' memory tasks.
Cognitive	The role of mental processes—perception, thinking, and memory—that underlie behavior	Older adults fail to use effective memory strategies.
Evolutionary	The roles of inherited tendencies that have proven adaptive in humans	Declines in cognitive and biological functions are programmed into our genes so that younger, and presumably reproductively healthier, people will be more attractive as potential mates.
Biological	The role of biological processes and structures, as well as heredity, in explaining behavior	As the brain ages, connections between neurons break down, causing a decline in intellectual functions such as memory.
Sociocultural	The roles of social and cultural influences on behavior	Older people have internalized the ageist expectations of society and, as a result, expect themselves to perform poorly on memory tasks.

adopting multiple perspectives, psychologists are able to devise more complex theories and research studies, resulting in improved treatment strategies. In this way, their theories and studies can more closely mirror the behavior of real people in real situations.

Psychologists at Work

Specialties in Psychology

◆ *Who are some of the specialists working within psychology?*

Wherever you find human activity, you are very likely to encounter psychologists. These professionals work in a number of specialties, most of which require a master's or a doctoral degree.

Clinical psychologists specialize in the diagnosis and treatment of mental and behavioral disorders, such as anxiety, phobias, and schizophrenia. Some also conduct research in these areas. Most clinical psychologists work in clinics, hospitals, or private practices, but many hold professorships at colleges and universities.

Counseling psychologists help people who have adjustment problems (marital, social, or behavioral) that are generally less severe than those handled by clinical psychologists. Counseling psychologists may also provide academic or vocational counseling. Counselors usually work in a nonmedical setting such as a school or university, or they may have a private practice. Approximately 55% of all psychologists in the United States may be classified as either clinical or counseling psychologists (APA, 1995).

Physiological psychologists, also called *biological psychologists* or *neuropsychologists*, study the relationship between physiological processes and behavior. They study the structure and function of the brain and central nervous system, the role of neurotransmitters and hormones, and other aspects of body chemistry to determine how physical and chemical processes affect behavior in both people and animals.

Experimental psychologists specialize in the use of experimental research methods. They conduct experiments in most areas of psychology—learning, memory, sensation, perception, motivation, emotion, and others. Some experimental psychologists study the brain and nervous system and how they affect behavior; their work overlaps with that of physiological psychologists. Experimental psychologists usually work in a laboratory, where they can exert precise control over the humans or animals being studied. Many experimental psychologists teach and conduct their research as faculty members at colleges or universities. In most of their psychology laboratories, however, the fixtures of the past, such as specimen jars, "have been replaced largely by a single instrument, the computer" (Benjamin, 2000, p. 321).

Developmental psychologists study how people grow, develop, and change throughout the lifespan. Some developmental psychologists specialize in a particular age group, such as infants, children (child psychologists), adolescents, or the elderly (gerontologists). Others may concentrate on a specific aspect of human development, such as physical, language, cognitive, or moral development.

Educational psychologists specialize in the study of teaching and learning. They may help train teachers and other educational professionals or conduct research in teaching and classroom behavior. Some help prepare school curricula, develop achievement tests, or conduct evaluations of teaching and learning.

While most other psychologists are concerned with what makes the individual function, *social psychologists* investigate how the individual feels, thinks, and behaves in a social setting—in the presence of others.

Industry and business have found that expertise in psychology pays off in the workplace. *Industrial/organizational (I/O) psychologists* study the relationships between people and their work environments.

◆ *What kinds of employment opportunities are available for psychology majors?*

Majoring in Psychology

Have you considered majoring in psychology? Many students do. In fact, the number of undergraduate degrees awarded in psychology is second only to the number awarded in business administration (APA, 1995; Horn & Zahn, 2001). There are many jobs open to those with a bachelor's degree in psychology. Many men and women who intend to go on to postgraduate work in other fields—law, for example—major in psychology. You can learn more about careers for psychology majors from the American Psychological Association (www.apa.org) and from the *Occupational Outlook Handbook* published by the U.S. Bureau of Labor Statistics (http://stats.bls.gov).

If you hope to become a professional psychologist, you must have a doctoral degree. The American Psychological Association reports that it takes about 5 years of study beyond the bachelor's degree to obtain a doctoral degree in psychology (APA, 2000). About one-fourth of psychologists who provide psychotherapeutic services to clients are self-employed as either psychotherapists or as consultants (U.S. Bureau of Labor Statistics, 2004). For these psychologists, management and marketing skills are often just as important to their daily work as their background in psychology because a private practice must be managed like any other business. Some psychologists work as salaried employees in health care facilities, government agencies, and private businesses. Others are employed by colleges and universities as professors, counseling center psychologists, and administrators.

Looking Back In this chapter, you have learned a great deal about psychologists, the methods they use, and a tried-and-true approach to studying textbook chapters, the SQ3R method. To be most effective, a general study method such as SQ3R must be adapted to each individual's learning preferences and study skill level. To implement this goal, think about how personally helpful each of the SQ3R strategies was as you worked your way through Chapter 1. Use the following table to rate each feature according to this scale: 2 = very useful, 1 = somewhat useful, and 0 = not useful.

This brief exercise has helped you create a personal SQ3R profile that you can use in future chapters. As you read each chapter, make a conscious effort to follow the SQ3R steps, devoting the most emphasis to those features to which you gave a rating of 1 or 2. Such an approach will enable you to use your study time efficiently and effectively and, we hope, avoid those pre-exam "all-nighters."

Personalizing Your Study Strategy

SQ3R STRATEGIES	TEXT FEATURES	USEFULNESS
Survey	Chapter outline	——
	Review and Reflect	——
	Summary	——
Question	Learning objective questions	——
Read	Examples	——
	Figures	——
	Tables	——
	Photos/captions	——
Recite	Learning objective questions	——
	Summary	——
Review	Review and Reflect	——
	Chapter Review section of Study Guide	——
	Summary	——
	Key terms in margins	——
	Remaining Study Guide sections	——

Apply It 1.1   More Tips for Effective Studying

Decades of research on learning and memory have uncovered a number of strategies that you can use, in addition to the SQ3R method, to make your study time more efficient and effective.

- Establish a quiet place, free of distractions, where you do nothing else but study. You can condition yourself to associate this environment with studying, so that entering the room or area will be your cue to begin work.

- Schedule your study time. Research on memory has proven that spaced learning is more effective than massed practice (cramming). Instead of studying for 5 hours straight, try five study sessions of 1 hour each.

- To be prepared for each class meeting, set specific goals for yourself each week and for individual study sessions. Your goals should be challenging but not overwhelming. If the task for an individual study session is manageable, it will be easier to sit down and face it. Completing the task you have set for yourself will give you a sense of accomplishment.

- The more active a role you play in the learning process, the more you will remember. Spend some of your study time reciting rather than rereading the material. One effective method is to use index cards as flash cards. Write a key term or study question on the front of each card. On the back, list pertinent information from the text and class lectures. Use these cards to help you prepare for tests.

- *Overlearning* means studying beyond the point at which you can just barely recite the information you are trying to memorize. Review the information again and again until it is firmly locked in memory. If you are subject to test anxiety, overlearning will help.

- Forgetting takes place most rapidly within the first 24 hours after you study. No matter how much you have studied for a test, always review shortly before you take it. Refreshing your memory will raise your grade.

- Sleeping immediately after you study will help you retain more of what you have learned. If you can't study before you go to sleep, at least review what you studied earlier in the day. This is also a good time to go through your index cards.

Once you've mastered these study strategies, use them to improve your comprehension and success in all of your courses.

Chapter 1 Summary

◆ Psychology: An Introduction p. 3

◆ What process do scientists use to answer questions about behavior and mental processes? p. 4

The scientific method consists of the orderly, systematic procedures researchers follow.

◆ What are the goals of psychology? p. 4

The four goals of psychology are the description, explanation, prediction, and influence of behavior and mental processes.

◆ Exploring Psychology's Roots p. 5

◆ What role did Wundt play in the founding of psychology? p. 5

Wundt established the first psychological laboratory in 1879.

◆ What did Titchener contribute to psychology? p. 6

Titchener founded the school of thought called structuralism, an approach aimed at analyzing the basic elements of conscious mental experience through introspection.

REVIEW: After you have read each section of the chapter and followed the previous steps—First, review the Summary section at the end of each chapter. Review the questions and try to answer them in your own words. As you review the list of key terms, turn back to the page where the term is defined and review that section if you find you cannot recite the term's meaning. Next, work through the Study Guide at the end of each chapter to test your understanding of the chapter content. Finally, before moving on to the next chapter, take the two sample Practice Tests at the end of the text. If you have trouble with any of the testing, take a few minutes to go back and review that section of the text before moving ahead.

in the study. Participants must give informed consent, may not be deceived unless necessary, and, if deceived, must be debriefed. Subordinates' participation in a study may not negatively affect them in any way. Participants may be paid after being informed about what is expected in return for payment. Researchers must report their findings in an appropriate forum.

◆ Why are animals used in research? p. 20

Animals provide a simpler model for studying similar processes in humans; researchers can exercise more control over animals and use a wider range of medical and other manipulations.

◆ Thinking about Theories and Research p. 20

◆ How do psychologists compare theories? p. 20

Theories are compared in terms of their usefulness. Useful theories generate testable hypotheses and practical solutions to problems. Theories possessing heuristic value are useful for stimulating debate and research.

◆ How can critical thinking be used to interpret media reports of psychological research? p. 21

Critical thinkers are independent, able to suspend judgment, and willing to change prior beliefs. They also use knowledge of research methods to evaluate research findings reported in the news media.

◆ Current Trends in Psychology p. 22

◆ What is the main idea behind evolutionary psychology? p. 22

Evolutionary psychology focuses on how human behaviors necessary for survival have adapted in the face of environmental pressures over the course of evolution.

◆ How is biological psychology changing the field of psychology? p. 23

Biological psychologists look for connections between specific behaviors (such as aggression) and particular biological factors (such as hormone levels) to help explain individual differences. Using modern technology, they have discovered relationships between biological and behavioral variables that have resulted in more effective medications for certain disorders and new insight into the genetic base of many mental illnesses.

◆ What kinds of variables interest psychologists who take a sociocultural approach? p. 24

The sociocultural approach focuses on how factors such as cultural values affect people's behavior.

◆ What are psychological perspectives, and how are they related to an eclectic position? p. 24

Psychological perspectives are general points of view used for explaining people's behavior and thinking. In taking an eclectic position, psychologists use a combination of two or more perspectives to explain a particular behavior.

◆ Psychologists at Work p. 26

◆ Who are some of the specialists working within psychology? p. 26

There are clinical and counseling psychologists, physiological psychologists, experimental psychologists, developmental psychologists, educational psychologists, social psychologists, and industrial/organizational (I/O) psychologists.

◆ What kinds of employment opportunities are available for psychology majors? p. 26

Individuals with bachelor's degrees in psychology are employed in many different settings. Individuals who want to become professional psychologists must do graduate work.

◆ KEY TERMS

Study Guide 1

Answers to all the Study Guide questions are provided at the end of the book.

◆ **SECTION ONE: Chapter Review**

Psychology: An Introduction (pp. 3–5)

1. The orderly, systematic procedures scientists follow in acquiring a body of knowledge is the _____.

2. The four goals of psychology are _____, _____, _____, and _____.

3. The purpose of basic research is to gain knowledge for its own sake. (true/false)

Exploring Psychology's Roots (pp. 5–8)

4. Classify each of the following people and concepts as being associated with (a) Wundt, (b) structuralism, or (c) functionalism. (*Hint:* Some items are associated with more than one.)
   ____ **(1)** James
   ____ **(2)** based on Darwin's theory of evolution
   ____ **(3)** stream of consciousness
   ____ **(4)** elements of experience
   ____ **(5)** Titchener
   ____ **(6)** introspection
   ____ **(7)** became known in the 19th century

5. Match each of the following individuals with his or her contribution to psychology:
   ____ **(1)** Francis Cecil Sumner
   ____ **(2)** Mary Whiton Calkins
   ____ **(3)** Kenneth Clark
   ____ **(4)** Christine Ladd-Franklin
   ____ **(5)** Jorge Sanchez
   a. first female president of APA
   b. published studies on cultural bias in intelligence testing
   c. first African American to receive a Ph.D. in psychology
   d. studied African American children's self-esteem
   e. had to wait 40 years to receive a Ph.D. in psychology after completing the degree requirements

Schools of Thought in Psychology (pp. 8–11)

6. Match the major figure with the appropriate school of psychology. Answer(s) may be used more than once.
   ____ **(1)** Freud
   ____ **(2)** Skinner
   ____ **(3)** Maslow
   ____ **(4)** Wertheimer
   ____ **(5)** Watson
   ____ **(6)** Rogers
   a. Gestalt psychology
   b. humanistic psychology
   c. behavorism
   d. psychoanalysis

7. Match the school of psychology with its major emphasis:
   ____ **(1)** the scientific study of behavior
   ____ **(2)** the perception of whole units or patterns
   ____ **(3)** the unconscious
   ____ **(4)** the computer as a model for human cognition
   ____ **(5)** the uniqueness of human beings and their capacity for growth
   ____ **(6)** the study of mental processes
   a. Gestalt psychology
   b. humanistic psychology
   c. cognitive psychology
   d. behaviorism
   e. information-processing theory
   f. psychoanalysis

Descriptive Research Methods (pp. 11–13)

8. Which descriptive research method would be best for studying each topic?
   ____ **(1)** attitudes toward exercise
   ____ **(2)** gender differences in how people position themselves and their belongings in a library
   ____ **(3)** physiological changes that occur during sleep
   ____ **(4)** the physical and emotional effects of a rare brain injury
   a. naturalistic observation
   b. laboratory observation
   c. case study
   d. survey

9. One problem with _____ _____ is that they often do not generalize to cases other than the one that is the subject of the study.

10. When conducting a survey, a researcher can compensate for a sample that is not representative by using a sample that is very large. (true/false)

The Experimental Method (pp. 13–17)

11. The experimental method is the *only* research method that can be used to identify cause-effect relationships between variables. (true/false)

12. In an experiment, the _____ _____ is manipulated by the researcher, and its effects on the _____ _____ are measured at the end of the study.

13. A researcher investigates the effectiveness of a new antidepressant drug. She randomly assigns depressed patients to two groups. Group 1 is given the drug, and Group 2 is given a placebo. At the end of the experiment, the level of depression of all participants is measured as a score on a test called a depression inventory. Match the elements of this experiment with the appropriate term.
    _____ (1) score on depression inventory
    _____ (2) the antidepressant drug
    _____ (3) Group 1
    _____ (4) Group 2
    a. experimental group   c. independent variable
    b. control group   d. dependent variable

14. Random assignment is used to control for
    a. experimenter bias.   c. selection bias.
    b. the placebo effect.   d. participant bias.

15. The placebo effect occurs when a participant responds according to
    a. the hypothesis.
    b. the actual treatment.
    c. how other participants behave.
    d. his or her expectations.

The Correlational Method (pp. 17–18)

16. The correlational method is used to demonstrate cause-effect relationships. (true/false)

17. The _____ _____ is a number describing the strength and direction of a relationship between two variables.

18. Which of the following correlation coefficients indicates the strongest relationship?
    a. +.65   c. .00
    b. −.78   d. +.25

19. There is a (positive/negative) correlation between the amount of fat people eat and their body weight.

20. A (positive/negative) correlation exists between the temperature and the number of layers of clothing people wear.

21. The main strength of the correlational method is that it can be used to establish cause-effect relationships. (true/false)

Participants in Psychological Research (pp. 19–20)

22. Which of the following groups has *not* been overrepresented as participants in psychological research?
    a. Whites   c. females
    b. males   d. college students

23. Psychologists are required to debrief participants thoroughly after a research study when the study
    a. violates participants' rights to privacy.
    b. deceives participants about the true purpose of the research.
    c. exposes participants to unreasonable risk or harm.
    d. wastes taxpayers' money on trivial questions.

24. Investigators use animals in psychological research to learn more about humans. (true/false)

Thinking about Theories and Research (pp. 20–22)

25. Useful theories
    a. lead to practical solutions to problems.
    b. provide researchers with many testable hypotheses.
    c. Stimulate debate and research.
    d. All of the above.

26. The three characteristics of critical thinkers are _____, _____, and _____.

27. A television reporter claimed that people should stop eating cabbage because scientists have found that it causes cancer. The first response of a critical thinker to this report would be to
    a. find out if the research was published in a prestigious journal.
    b. determine whether the research was correlational or experimental in nature.
    c. find out how many people participated in the study.
    d. stop eating cabbage.

Current Trends in Psychology (pp. 22–26)

28. Match each of the following variables with the psychological approach that is most likely to be interested in it: (a) evolutionary psychology, (b) biological psychology, or (c) sociocultural psychology.
    _____ (1) the effects of drugs and alcohol on reaction time
    _____ (2) the relationship between minority status and self-esteem
    _____ (3) universal behaviors such as infants' attachment to caregivers
    _____ (4) links between hormones and aggression
    _____ (5) gender role beliefs that are consistent across cultures
    _____ (6) gender role beliefs that vary across cultures

29. Match the psychological perspective with its major emphasis.
    ____ **(1)** the role of biological processes and heredity
    ____ **(2)** the role of environmental factors
    ____ **(3)** the role of mental processes
    ____ **(4)** the role of the unconscious and early childhood experience
    ____ **(5)** the importance of the individual's own subjective experience
    ____ **(6)** the role of social and cultural influences
    ____ **(7)** the role of inherited tendencies that have proved adaptive in humans

    a. psychoanalytic   **e.** humanistic
    b. biological   **f.** evolutionary
    c. behavioral   **g.** sociocultural
    d. cognitive

30. Write "Yes" by the statements below that represent electicism in psychology.
    ____ **(1)** Individual differences in aggression are genetic, but parents and teachers can teach highly aggressive children to be less so.

____ **(2)** Children who are highly aggressive have not received enough punishment for their inappropriate behavior.
____ **(3)** Aggressive children are probably using aggression to release pent-up feelings of frustration.
____ **(4)** Going through a trauma like parental divorce may lead to increased aggression in children because they are experiencing strong emotions, and their parents are likely to be too distracted by their own problems to discipline children effectively.

Psychologists at Work (pp. 26–27)

31. The largest proportion of psychologists belong to the _____ subgroup.

32. There are _____ job opportunities for college graduates who major in psychology.

◆ **SECTION TWO: Who Said This?**

Read each statement below and then, in the blank that follows, identify the person mentioned in Chapter 1 who would be most likely to make the statement.

1. I thought that behavior could be explained by analyzing the conditions that were present before it occurs and the consequences it produces. _____

2. I established the first psychological laboratory in Leipzig, Germany. _____

3. I wrote *Principles of Psychology* and advocated functionalism. _____

4. I introduced the term *behaviorism*. _____

5. I proposed a theory of motivation that consists of a hierarchy of needs. _____

6. I was the first African American to earn a Ph.D. in psychology. _____

7. I became the first female president of the American Psychological Association. _____

8. I invented a popular form of psychotherapy called *client-centered therapy*. _____

9. I demonstrated the phi phenomenon.

◆ **SECTION THREE: Fill In the Blank**

1. A _____ is a general principle or set of principles proposed to explain how a number of separate facts are related.

2. Dr. Smith is interested in using _____ to study cooperative versus competitive play in children in nursery school. To accomplish this, she is going to observe and record children's play behaviors at nursery school without attempting to influence or control their behaviors.

3. Dr. Jones is interested in learning about college students in the United States who begin their education after the age of 30. He knows that there are many such students and that he will not be able to study them all, so he decides to carefully define this _____ _____ (the group to which he

hopes to generalize his findings) and then study a _____ _____ of these students. He hopes this approach will allow him to make accurate generalizations.

4. A psychologist believes there is an important relationship between test anxiety and test performance. Her _____ predicts that higher levels of anxiety will interfere with test performance.

5. To test her prediction, the psychologist in question 4 randomly assigns psychology students to two different groups. One group is told that the test they are about to take will determine over half of their semester grade. The other group is told that the test will have no bearing on their grade but will help the psychologist prepare better lectures. The psychologist

believes the two groups will have different levels of anxiety and that the first group will perform less well than the second group on a standardized psychology test. In this experiment, the _____ variable is the pretest instructions, and the _____ variable is the test scores.

6. Psychologists who use the _____ approach are interested in how social and cultural variables influence individual behavior.

7. Correlations can be useful in allowing you to make _____ but should not be used to draw conclusions about _____ and _____.

8. The first formal school of psychology was known as _____, and members of this school were interested in analyzing the basic elements, or structure, of conscious mental experience.

9. Another early school of psychology was _____. Psychologists who used this approach were interested in how mental processes help humans and animals adapt to their environments.

10. The school of psychology that emphasizes the role of unconscious mental forces and conflicts in determining behavior is known as _____.

11. The _____ perspective in psychology studies the role of mental processes—perception, thinking, and memory—in behavior.

12. Sigmund Freud is associated with the _____ perspective in psychology.

13. According to the text, _____ psychologists make up the largest percentage of members of the American Psychological Association.

◆ SECTION FOUR: Comprehensive Practice Test

1. Which of the following psychological perspectives likened human mental life to an iceberg?
   a. behaviorism   c. humanistic psychology
   b. psychoanalysis   d. structuralism

2. _____ is the approach to psychology that arose from the belief that the study of the mind and consciousness was not scientific.
   a. Structuralism   c. Humanistic psychology
   b. Behaviorism   d. Psychoanalysis

3. The _____ perspective in psychology would explain behavior by referring to the operation of the brain and the central nervous system.
   a. evolutionary   c. behavioral
   b. structuralist   d. biological

4. A _____ psychologist specializes in the diagnosis and treatment of mental and behavioral disorders.
   a. social   c. clinical
   b. developmental   d. cognitive

5. "The whole is perceived as greater than the sum of its parts" is a statement you would be most likely to hear from a _____ psychologist.
   a. behavioral   c. Gestalt
   b. cognitive   d. developmental

6. Description, explanation, prediction, and influence of behavior and mental processes are the _____ of psychology.
   a. reasons   c. perspectives
   b. goals   d. methods

7. In an experiment, a researcher would use the double-blind approach to control for _____.
   a. experimenter bias   c. selection bias
   b. placebo bias   d. random bias

8. The disadvantages of survey research include
   a. Respondents may provide inaccurate information.
   b. They can be costly and time-consuming.
   c. The "social desirability effect" may cause respondents to give misleading answers.
   d. All of the above.

9. If a researcher wants to establish evidence for a cause-effect relationship between variables, he should use _____.
   a. naturalistic observation
   b. correlation
   c. the experimental method
   d. the survey method

10. Which of the following psychologists is associated with the humanistic perspective?
    a. Maslow   c. Watson
    b. Darwin   d. Freud

11. Researchers who are interested in the adaptive significance of behavior are known as _____ psychologists.
    a. cognitive   c. evolutionary
    b. humanistic   d. psychoanalytic

12. A social psychologist would be most interested in how individuals behave in isolated settings, such as when they are alone at home. (true/false)

13. Basic research is aimed at solving practical problems and improving the quality of life. (true/false)

14. Watson would suggest that Freud's psychological approach is invalid because of Freud's emphasis on unconscious motivation and other mental events. (true/false)

15. In an experiment, the experimental group is exposed to all aspects of the treatment except the independent variable. (true/false)

16. Structuralism used introspection to study the basic elements of conscious mental experience. (true/false)

17. Most psychologists believe that animal research is of little value in the study of human mental processes and behavior. (true/false)

18. The best way to establish a cause-effect relationship between variables is to use the case study method because that method gives a researcher an in-depth knowledge of the subject matter from spending so much time with just a few participants. (true/false)

19. A researcher is studying the relationship between styles of computer keyboards and typing accuracy. In this case, the dependent variable is the different types of computer keyboards included in the study. (true/false)

20. You would probably expect to find a negative correlation between the number of alcoholic drinks consumed and the number of accidents a participant has while being tested on an experimental driving simulator. (true/false)

21. The proportion of minorities in the field of psychology is lower than that in the overall U.S. population. (true/false)

◆ SECTION FIVE: Critical Thinking

1. Consider three of the major forces in psychology: behaviorism, psychoanalysis, and humanistic psychology. Which appeals to you most and which least, and why?

2. Suppose you hear on the news that a researcher claims to have "proven" that day care is harmful to infants. How could you use what you've learned in this chapter about research methods to evaluate this statement?

3. If you became a psychologist, in which area (developmental, educational, clinical, counseling, social, etc.) would you specialize? Why?

Biology and Behavior

chapter **2**

On September 13, 1848, Phineas Gage, a 25-year-old foreman on a Vermont railroad construction crew, was using dynamite to blast away rock and dirt. Suddenly, an unplanned explosion almost took Gage's head off, sending a 3½-foot-long, 13-pound metal rod under his left cheekbone and out through the top of his skull.

Much of the brain tissue in Gage's frontal lobe was torn away, along with flesh, pieces of his skull, and other bone fragments. This should have been the end of Phineas Gage, but it wasn't. He regained consciousness within a few minutes and was loaded onto a cart and wheeled to his hotel nearly a mile away. He got out of the cart with a little help, walked up the stairs, entered his room, and walked to his bed. He was still conscious when the doctor arrived nearly 2 hours later.

Although Gage recovered in about 5 weeks, he was not the same man. Before the accident, he was described as a hard worker who was polite,

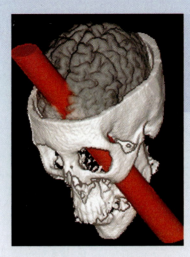

This computer-generated image shows the likely path of the bar that tore through Phineas Gage's skull.

dependable, and well liked. But the new Phineas Gage, without part of his frontal lobe, was loud-mouthed and profane, rude and impulsive, and contemptuous of others. He no longer planned realistically for the future and was no longer motivated and industrious, as he once had been. As a result, Gage lost his job as foreman and ended up joining P. T. Barnum's circus as a sideshow exhibit at carnivals and county fairs (adapted from Harlow, 1848).

Despite the negative impact of the accident on his life, it's remarkable that Gage was able to sustain such a serious head injury and continue to function at all. As his case illustrates, adaptability is the hallmark of the relationship between biology and behavior. This chapter introduces several important contributors to this relationship—the specialized cells and structures of the nervous system and the techniques scientists use to study them, the developmental processes that shape the brain, the hormones that work hand-in-hand with the nervous system, and the patterns of inheritance through which genes contribute to behavior.

◆ **neuron**

(NEW-ron) A specialized cell that conducts impulses through the nervous system and contains three major parts—a cell body, dendrites, and an axon.

 ## The Neurons and the Neurotransmitters

The Neurons

All of our thoughts, feelings, and behavior can ultimately be traced to the activity of **neurons**—the specialized cells that conduct impulses through the nervous system. Neurons perform several important tasks: (1) Afferent (sensory) neurons relay messages from the sense organs and receptors—eyes, ears, nose, mouth, and skin—to the brain or spinal cord; (2) efferent (motor) neurons convey signals from the central nervous system to the glands and the muscles, enabling the body to move; and (3) interneurons, thousands of times more numerous than motor or sensory neurons, carry information between neurons in the brain and between neurons in the spinal cord.

◆ *How are messages transmitted through the nervous system?*

Although no two neurons are exactly alike, nearly all are made up of three important parts: the cell body, the dendrites, and the axon. The **cell body,** or *soma*, contains the nucleus and carries out the metabolic, or life-sustaining, functions of a neuron. Branching out from the cell body are the **dendrites,** which look much like the leafless branches of a tree (*dendrite* comes from the Greek word for "tree"). The dendrites are the primary receivers of signals from other neurons, but the cell body can also receive signals directly. Dendrites also do more than just receive signals from other neurons and relay them to the cell body.

The **axon** is the slender, tail-like extension of the neuron that sprouts into many branches, each ending in a bulbous axon terminal. Signals move from the axon terminals to the dendrites or cell bodies of other neurons and to muscles, glands, and other parts of the body. In humans, some axons are short—only thousandths of an inch long. Others can be as long as a meter (39.37 inches)—long enough to reach from the brain to the tip of the spinal cord, or from the spinal cord to remote parts of the body. Figure 2.1 shows a neuron's structure.

Glial cells are specialized cells in the brain and spinal cord that support the neurons. They are smaller than neurons and make up more than one-half the volume of the human brain. Glial cells remove waste products, such as dead neurons, from the brain by engulfing and digesting them, and they handle other manufacturing, nourishing, and cleanup tasks.

Remarkably, the billions of neurons that send and receive signals are not physically connected. The axon terminals are separated from the receiving neurons by tiny, fluid-filled gaps called *synaptic clefts*. The **synapse** is the junction where the axon terminal of a sending (presynaptic) neuron communicates with a receiving (postsynaptic) neuron across the synaptic cleft. There may be as many as 100 trillion synapses in the human nervous system (Swanson, 1995). A single neuron may also synapse with thousands of other neurons (Kelner, 1997). A technique that has recently been developed to monitor the action at the synapses may soon enable researchers to visualize the activity of all the synapses of a single neuron. If neurons aren't connected, how do they communicate with one another?

A small but measurable electrical impulse is present everytime you move or have a thought. Even though the impulse that travels down the axon is electrical, the axon does not transmit it the way a wire conducts an electrical current. What actually changes is the **permeability** of the cell membrane (its capability of being penetrated or passed through). In other words, the membrane changes in a way that makes it easier for molecules to move through it and into the cell. This process allows ions (electrically charged atoms or molecules) to move into and out of the axon through ion channels in the membrane.

Body fluids contain ions, some with positive electrical charges and others with negative charges. Inside the axon, there are normally more negative than positive ions. When at rest (not firing), the axon membrane carries a negative electrical potential of about –70 millivolts (–70 thousandths of a volt) relative to the fluid outside the cell. This slight negative charge is referred to as the neuron's **resting potential.**

When the excitatory effects on a neuron reach a certain threshold, ion channels begin to open in the cell membrane of the axon at the point closest to the cell body, allowing positive ions to flow into the axon. This inflow of positive ions causes the membrane potential to change abruptly, to a positive value of about +50 millivolts (Pinel, 2000). This sudden reversal of the resting potential, which lasts for about 1 millisecond (1 thousandth of a second), is the **action potential.** Then, the ion channels admitting positive ions close, and other ion channels open, forcing some positive ions out of the axon. As a result, the original negative charge, or resting potential, is restored. The opening and closing of ion channels continues, segment by segment, down the length of the axon, causing the action potential to move along the axon (Cardoso et al., 2000). The action potential operates according to the "all or none" law—a neuron either fires completely or does not fire at all. Immediately after a neuron fires, it enters a *refractory period*, during which it cannot fire again for 1 to 2 milliseconds. But, even with these short resting periods, neurons can fire hundreds of times per second.

◆ **cell body**

The part of a neuron that contains the nucleus and carries out the metabolic functions of the neuron.

◆ **dendrites**

(DEN-drytes) In a neuron, the branchlike extensions of the cell body that receive signals from other neurons.

◆ **axon**

(AK-sahn) The slender, tail-like extension of the neuron that transmits signals to the dendrites or cell body of other neurons and to muscles, glands, and other parts of the body.

◆ **glial cells**

(GLEE-ul) Specialized cells in the brain and spinal cord that support neurons, remove waste products such as dead neurons, and perform other manufacturing, nourishing, and cleanup tasks.

◆ **synapse**

(SIN-aps) The junction where the axon terminal of a sending neuron communicates with a receiving neuron across the synaptic cleft.

◆ **permeability**

(perm-ee-uh-BIL-uh-tee) The capability of being penetrated or passed through.

◆ **resting potential**

The slight negative electrical potential of the axon membrane of a neuron at rest, about –70 millivolts.

◆ **action potential**

The sudden reversal of the resting potential, which initiates the firing of a neuron.

FIGURE 2.1 Structure of a Typical Neuron

A typical neuron has three important parts: (1) a cell body, which carries out the metabolic functions of the neuron; (2) branched fibers called dendrites, which are the primary receivers of the impulses from other neurons; and (3) a slender, tail-like extension called an axon, the transmitting end of the neuron, which sprouts into many branches, each ending in an axon terminal. The photograph shows human neurons greatly magnified.

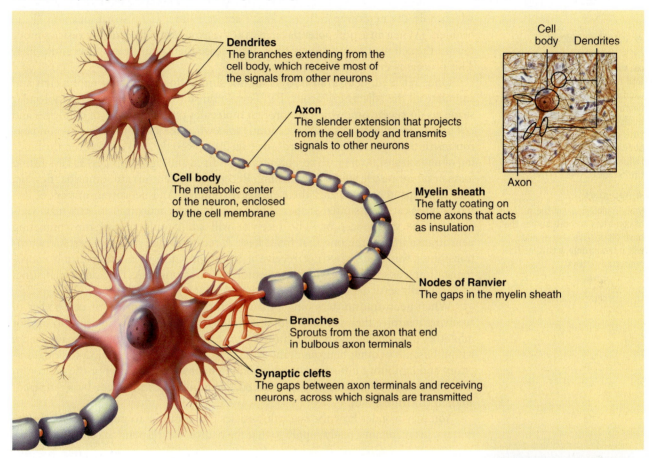

Dendrites
The branches extending from the cell body, which receive most of the signals from other neurons

Axon
The slender extension that projects from the cell body and transmits signals to other neurons

Cell body
The metabolic center of the neuron, enclosed by the cell membrane

Myelin sheath
The fatty coating on some axons that acts as insulation

Nodes of Ranvier
The gaps in the myelin sheath

Branches
Sprouts from the axon that end in bulbous axon terminals

Synaptic clefts
The gaps between axon terminals and receiving neurons, across which signals are transmitted

Cell body   Dendrites

Axon

If a neuron only fires or does not fire, how can we tell the difference between a very strong and a very weak stimulus? In other words, what is the neurological distinction between feeling anxious about being disciplined by your boss for being late to work and running for your life to avoid being the victim of a criminal attacker? The answer lies in the number of neurons firing at the same time and their rate of firing. A weak stimulus may cause relatively few neurons to fire, while a strong stimulus may trigger thousands of neurons to fire at the same time. Also, a weak stimulus may be signaled by neurons firing very slowly; a stronger stimulus may incite neurons to fire hundreds of times per second.

Impulses travel at speeds from about 1 meter per second to approximately 100 meters per second (about 224 miles per hour). The most important factor in speeding the impulse on its way is the **myelin sheath**—a white, fatty coating wrapped around some axons that acts as insulation. If you look again at Figure 2.1, you will see that the coating has numerous gaps, called *nodes of Ranvier*. The electrical impulse is retriggered or regenerated at each node (or naked gap) on the axon. This regeneration makes the impulse up to 100 times faster than impulses in axons without myelin sheaths. Damage to the myelin sheath causes interruptions in the transmission of neural messages. In fact, the disease multiple sclerosis (MS) involves deterioration of the myelin sheath, resulting in loss of coordination, jerky movements, muscular weakness, and disturbances in speech.

This scanning electron micrograph shows numerous axon terminals (the orange, button-shaped structures) that could synapse with the cell body of the neuron (shown in green).

◆ **myelin sheath**
(MY-uh-lin) The white, fatty coating wrapped around some axons that acts as insulation and enables impulses to travel much faster.

Neurotransmitters

◆ *What are neurotransmitters, and what do they contribute to nervous system functioning?*

◆ **neurotransmitter**

(NEW-ro-TRANS-mit-er) A chemical substance that is released into the synaptic cleft from the axon terminal of a sending neuron, crosses a synapse, and binds to appropriate receptor sites on the dendrites or cell body of a receiving neuron, influencing the cell either to fire or not to fire.

◆ **receptors**

Protein molecules on the surfaces of dendrites and cell bodies that have distinctive shapes and will interact only with specific neurotransmitters.

Once a neuron fires, how does it get its message across the synaptic cleft and on to another neuron? Messages are transmitted between neurons by one or more of a large group of chemical substances known as **neurotransmitters**. Where are the neurotransmitters located? Inside the axon terminal are many small, sphere-shaped containers with thin membranes called *synaptic vesicles*, which hold the neurotransmitters. (*Vesicle* comes from a Latin word meaning "little bladder.") When an action potential arrives at the axon terminal, synaptic vesicles move toward the cell membrane, fuse with it, and release their neurotransmitter molecules. This process is shown in Figure 2.2.

Once released, neurotransmitters do not simply flow into the synaptic cleft and stimulate all the adjacent neurons. Each neurotransmitter has a distinctive molecular shape, as do **receptors,** which are protein molecules on the surfaces of dendrites and cell bodies. In other words, each receptor is somewhat like a lock that only certain neurotransmitter keys can unlock (Cardoso et al., 2000; Restak, 1993). However, the binding of neurotransmitters with receptors is not as fixed and rigid a process as keys fitting locks or jigsaw puzzle pieces interlocking. Receptors on neurons are somewhat flexible; they can expand and contract their enclosed volumes. And neurotransmitters of different types can have similar shapes. Thus, two different neurotransmitters may compete for the same receptor. The receptor will admit only one of the competing neurotransmitters—the one that fits it best. A receptor may receive a certain neurotransmitter sometimes, but not receive it in the presence of a better-fitting neurotransmitter whose "affinity with the receptor is even stronger. As in dating and mating, what is finally settled for is always a function of what is available" (Restak, 1993, p. 28).

When neurotransmitters bind with receptors on the dendrites or cell bodies of receiving neurons, their action is either excitatory (influencing the neurons to fire) or inhibitory (influencing them not to fire). Because a single receiving neuron may synapse with thousands of other neurons at the same time, it will always be subject to both excitatory and inhibitory influences from incoming neurotransmitters. For the neuron to fire, the excitatory influences must exceed the inhibitory influences by a sufficient amount (the threshold).

You may wonder how the synaptic vesicles can continue to pour out neurotransmitters, yet maintain a ready supply so that the neuron can respond to continuing stim-

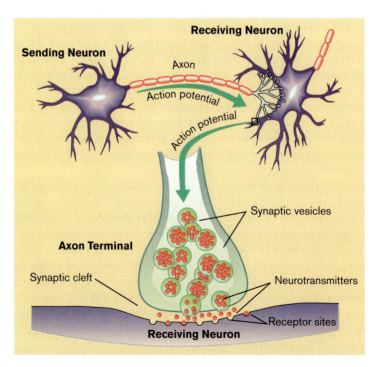

FIGURE 2.2   **Synaptic Transmission**

When a neuron fires, the action potential arrives at the axon terminal and triggers the release of neurotransmitters from the synaptic vesicles. Neurotransmitters flow into the synaptic cleft, and move toward the receiving neuron, which has numerous receptors. The receptors will bind only with neurotransmitters whose molecular shapes match their enclosed volumes. Neurotransmitters influence the receiving neuron to fire or not to fire.

ulation. First, the cell body of the neuron is always working to manufacture more of the neurotransmitter. Second, unused neurotransmitters in the synaptic cleft may be broken down into components and reclaimed by the axon terminal to be recycled and used again. Third, by an important process called **reuptake,** the neurotransmitter is taken back into the axon terminal, intact and ready for immediate use. This terminates the neurotransmitter's excitatory or inhibitory effect on the receiving neuron.

◆ **reuptake**

The process by which neurotransmitters are taken from the synaptic cleft back into the axon terminal for later use, thus terminating their excitatory or inhibitory effect on the receiving neuron.

The Variety of Neurotransmitters

Researchers have identified 75 or more chemical substances that are manufactured in the brain, spinal cord, glands, and other parts of the body and may act as neurotransmitters (Greden, 1994).

◆ *What are the functions of some of the major neurotransmitters?*

One of the most important is **acetylcholine** (Ach). This neurotransmitter exerts excitatory effects on the skeletal muscle fibers, causing them to contract so that the body can move. But it has an inhibitory effect on the muscle fibers in the heart, which keeps the heart from beating too rapidly. Thus, when you run to make it to class on time, acetylcholine helps your leg muscles contract quickly, while simultaneously preventing your heart muscle from pumping so rapidly that you pass out. The differing natures of the receptors on the receiving neurons in the two kinds of muscles cause these opposite effects. Acetylcholine also plays an excitatory role in stimulating the neurons involved in learning new information. So, as you are reading this text, acetylcholine is helping you understand and store the information in your memory.

Dopamine (DA), one of four neurotransmitters called *monoamines*, produces both excitatory and inhibitory effects and is involved in several functions, including learning, attention, movement, and reinforcement. The other three monoamines also serve important functions. **Norepinephrine** (NE) has an effect on eating habits (it stimulates the intake of carbohydrates) and plays a major role in alertness and wakefulness. **Epinephrine** complements norepinephrine by affecting the metabolism of glucose and causing the nutrient energy stored in muscles to be released during strenuous exercise. **Serotonin** plays an important role in regulating mood, sleep, impulsivity, aggression, and appetite. It has also been linked to depression and anxiety disorders (Burghardt et al., 2004).

Two amino acids that serve as neurotransmitters are more common than any other transmitter substances in the central nervous system. **Glutamate** is the primary excitatory neurotransmitter in the brain (Riedel, 1996). It may be released by about 40% of neurons and is active in areas of the brain involved in learning, thought, and emotions (Coyle & Draper, 1996). **GABA** (short for "gamma-*a*mino*b*utyric *a*cid") is the main inhibitory neurotransmitter in the brain (Miles, 1999). It is thought to facilitate the control of anxiety in humans (Mombereau et al., 2004). Tranquilizers, barbiturates, and alcohol appear to have a calming and relaxing effect because they bind with and stimulate one type of GABA receptor, thereby increasing GABA's anxiety-controlling effect. An abnormality in the neurons that secrete GABA is believed to be one of the causes of epilepsy, a serious neurological disorder in which neural activity can become so heightened that seizures result.

◆ **acetylcholine**

(ah-SEET-ul-KOH-leen) A neurotransmitter that plays a role in learning new information, causes the skeletal muscle fibers to contract, and keeps the heart from beating too rapidly.

◆ **dopamine**

(DOE-pah-meen) A neurotransmitter that plays a role in learning, attention, movement, and reinforcement.

◆ **norepinephrine**

(nor-EP-ih-NEF-rin) A neurotransmitter affecting eating, alertness, and sleep.

◆ **epinephrine**

(EP-ih-NEF-rin) A neurotransmitter that affects the metabolism of glucose and nutrient energy stored in muscles to be released during strenuous exercise.

◆ **serotonin**

(ser-oh-TOE-nin) A neurotransmitter that plays an important role in regulating mood, sleep, impulsivity, aggression, and appetite.

◆ **glutamate**

(GLOO-tah-mate) Primary excitatory neurotransmitter in the brain.

◆ **GABA**

Primary inhibitory neurotransmitter in the brain.

◆ **endorphins**

(en-DOR-fins) Chemicals produced naturally by the brain that reduce pain and the stress of vigorous exercise and positively affect mood.

The neurotransmitter acetylcholine helps you process new information by facilitating neural transmissions involved in learning.

Finally, the class of neurotransmitters known as the **endorphins** provide relief from pain or the stress of vigorous exercise and produce feelings of pleasure and well-being. "Runner's high," for example, is attributed to endorphins. Moreover, opiate drugs such as morphine and heroin mimic the endorphins and bind to their receptor sites. You will learn more about how drugs affect the brain's neurotransmitter system in Chapter 4.

Review and Reflect 2.1 (on page 42) summarizes the major neurotransmitters and their functions.

REVIEW and REFLECT 2.1

Major Neurotransmitters and Their Functions

NEUROTRANSMITTER	FUNCTIONS
Acetylcholine (Ach)	Affects movement, learning, memory, REM sleep
Dopamine (DA)	Affects movement, attention, learning, reinforcement
Norepinephrine (NE)	Affects eating, alertness, wakefulness
Epinephrine	Affects metabolism of glucose, energy release during exercise
Serotonin	Affects mood, sleep, appetite, impulsivity, aggression
Glutamate	Active in areas of the brain involved in learning, thought, and emotion
GABA	Facilitates neural inhibition in the central nervous system
Endorphins	Provide relief from pain; feelings of pleasure and well-being

 The Central Nervous System

◆ **central nervous system (CNS)**

The part of the nervous system comprising the brain and the spinal cord.

Human functioning involves much more than the action of individual neurons. Collections of neurons, brain structures, and organ systems also play essential roles in the body. The nervous system is divided into two parts: (1) the **central nervous system (CNS),** which is composed of the brain and the spinal cord, and (2) the peripheral nervous system, which connects the central nervous system to all other parts of the body (see Figure 2.3).

FIGURE 2.3 **Divisions of the Human Nervous System**

The human nervous system is divided into two parts: (1) the central nervous system, consisting of the brain and the spinal cord, and (2) the peripheral nervous system.

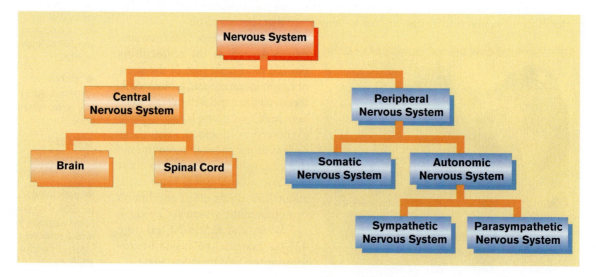

The Spinal Cord

The **spinal cord** can best be thought of as an extension of the brain. A cylinder of neural tissue about the diameter of your little finger, the spinal cord reaches from the base of the brain, through the neck, and down the hollow center of the spinal column. It is protected by bone and also by spinal fluid, which serves as a shock absorber. The spinal cord literally links the body with the brain. It transmits messages between the brain and nerves in other parts of the body. Thus, sensory information can reach the brain, and messages from the brain can be sent to the muscles, the glands, and other parts of the body.

Although the spinal cord and the brain usually function together, the spinal cord can act without help from the brain to protect the body from injury. A simple withdrawal reflex triggered by a painful stimulus—touching a hot stove burner, for example—involves three types of neurons. Sensory neurons in your fingers detect the painful stimulus and relay this information to interneurons in the spinal cord. These interneurons activate motor neurons that control the muscles in your arm and cause you to jerk your hand away. All this happens within a fraction of a second, without any involvement of your brain. However, the brain quickly becomes aware and involved when the pain signal reaches it. At that point, you might plunge your hand into cold water to relieve the pain.

The Brainstem

Brain structures are often grouped into the *hindbrain*, the *midbrain*, and the *forebrain*, as shown in Figure 2.4. The part of the hindbrain known as the **brainstem** begins at the site where the spinal cord enlarges as it enters the skull. The brainstem handles functions that are so critical to physical survival that damage to it is life-threatening. The **medulla** is the part of the brainstem that controls heartbeat, breathing, blood pressure, coughing, and swallowing. Fortunately, the medulla handles these functions automatically, so you do not have to decide consciously to breathe or remember to keep your heart beating.

◆ *Why is an intact spinal cord important to normal functioning?*

◆ **spinal cord**
An extension of the brain, from the base of the brain through the neck and spinal column, that transmits messages between the brain and the peripheral nervous system.

◆ *What are the vital functions handled by the brainstem?*

◆ **brainstem**
The structure that begins at the point where the spinal cord enlarges as it enters the brain and handles functions critical to physical survival. It includes the medulla, the pons, and the reticular formation.

◆ **medulla**
(muh-DUL-uh) The part of the brainstem that controls heartbeat, blood pressure, breathing, coughing, and swallowing.

Corpus callosum

Cerebral cortex

Limbic System
Group of structures involved in emotional expression, memory, and motivation

Thalamus
Relay station between cerebral cortex and lower brain centers

Hypothalamus
Controls functions such as hunger, thirst, body temperature; helps control endocrine system; involved in emotion

Cerebellum
Coordinates skilled movement; regulates muscle tone and posture; plays a role in motor learning and probably cognition

Substantia nigra
Controls unconscious motor actions

Reticular formation
Arousal system; activates cerebral cortex

Pons
Plays role in relaying motor messages between cerebellum and motor cortex; exerts influence on sleep and dreaming

Medulla
Control center for heartbeat, breathing, blood pressure, swallowing, and coughing

Spinal cord
Extension of the brain; controls simple reflexes; connects brain to peripheral nervous system

■ Forebrain
■ Midbrain
■ Hindbrain

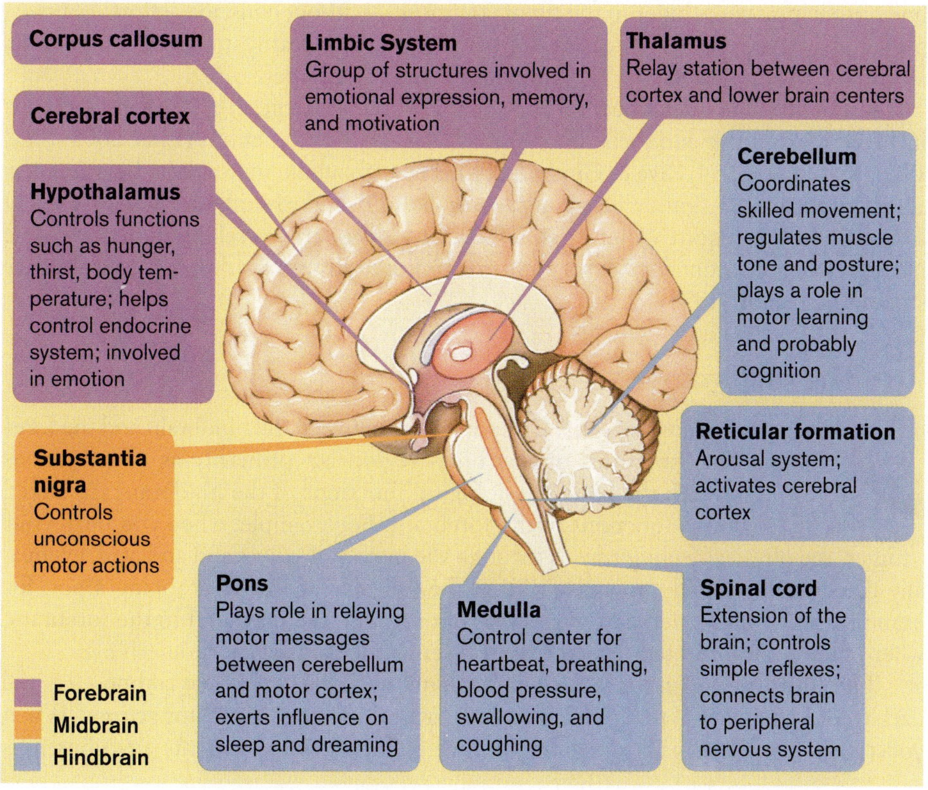

FIGURE 2.4

Major Structures of the Human Brain

This drawing shows some of the major structures of the brain with a brief description of the function of each. The brainstem contains the medulla, the reticular formation, and the pons.

◆ **reticular formation**

A structure in the brainstem that plays a crucial role in arousal and attention and that screens sensory messages entering the brain.

Extending through the central core of the brainstem into the pons is another important structure, the **reticular formation,** sometimes called the *reticular activating system* (RAS) (refer to Figure 2.4). The reticular formation plays a crucial role in arousal and attention (Gadea et al., 2004; Kinomura et al., 1996; Steriade, 1996). Every day, our sense organs are bombarded with stimuli, but we cannot possibly pay attention to everything we see or hear. The reticular formation blocks some messages and sends others on to structures in the midbrain and forebrain for processing. For example, a driver may be listening intently to a radio program when, suddenly, a car cuts in front of him. In response, the reticular formation blocks the sensory information coming from the radio and fixes the driver's attention on the potential danger posed by the other driver's action. Once the traffic pattern returns to normal, the reticular formation allows him to attend to the radio again, while continuing to monitor the traffic situation.

The reticular formation also determines how alert we are. When it slows down, we doze off or go to sleep. But, thanks to the reticular formation, important messages get through even when we are asleep. This is why parents may be able to sleep through a thunderstorm but will awaken to the slightest cry of their baby.

Above the medulla and at the top of the brainstem is a bridgelike structure called the *pons* that extends across the top front of the brainstem and connects to both halves of the cerebellum. The pons plays a role in body movement and even exerts an influence on sleep and dreaming.

The Cerebellum

◆ *What are the primary functions of the cerebellum?*

The **cerebellum** makes up about 10% of the brain's volume and, with its two hemispheres, resembles the larger cerebrum that lies above it (Swanson, 1995). (Refer to Figure 2.4.) The cerebellum is critically important to the body's ability to execute smooth, skilled movements (Spencer et al., 2003). It also regulates muscle tone and posture. Furthermore, it has been found to play a role in motor learning and in retaining memories of motor activities (Lalonde & Botez, 1990). The cerebellum guides the graceful movements of the ballet dancer and the split-second timing of the skilled race car driver. More typically, it coordinates the series of movements necessary to perform many simple activities—such as walking in a straight line or touching your finger to the tip of your nose—without conscious effort. For people who have damage to their cerebellum or who are temporarily impaired by too much alcohol, such simple acts may be difficult or impossible to perform.

◆ **cerebellum**

(sehr-uh-BELL-um) The brain structure that helps the body execute smooth, skilled movements and regulates muscle tone and posture.

Although some researchers remain skeptical, studies suggest that the cerebellum is involved in cognitive and social functions as well as motor functions (Ellis, 2001; Fiez, 1996; Kim et al., 1994; Riva & Giorgi, 2000). The cerebellum may help to heighten our ability to focus attention on incoming sensory stimuli and to shift attention efficiently when conditions require (Allen et al., 1997). In addition, the cerebellum may increase our efficiency in acquiring sensory information and discriminating between sensory stimuli (Gao et al., 1996).

The Midbrain

◆ *What important structure is located in the midbrain?*

As shown in Figure 2.4, the midbrain lies between the hindbrain and the forebrain. The structures of this brain region act primarily as relay stations through which the basic physiological functions of the hindbrain are linked to the cognitive functions of the forebrain. For example, when you burn your finger, the physical feeling travels through the nerves of your hand and arm, eventually reaching the spinal cord, resulting in the reflexive action of dropping a pot, for example. From there, nerve impulses are sent through the midbrain to the forebrain, where they are interpreted ("Next time, I'll remember to use a potholder!").

◆ **substantia nigra**

(sub-STAN-sha NI-gra) The structure in the midbrain that controls unconscious motor movements.

The **substantia nigra** is located in the midbrain. This structure is composed of the darkly colored nuclei of nerve cells that control our unconscious motor actions. When you ride a bicycle or walk up stairs without giving your movements any conscious thought, the nuclei of the cells that allow you to do so are found in the substantia nigra. Recent research indicates that the death of these cells, and the diminished sensitivity of the substantia nigra to various neurotransmitters that results from their death, may explain the inability of people with Parkinson's disease to control their physical movements (Trevitt et al., 2002).

The Thalamus and Hypothalamus

Above the brainstem lie two extremely important structures (refer again to Figure 2.4). The **thalamus,** which has two egg-shaped parts, serves as the relay station for virtually all the information that flows into and out of the forebrain, including sensory information from all the senses except smell. (You'll learn more about the sense of smell in Chapter 3.)

The thalamus, or at least one small part of it, affects our ability to learn new verbal information and plays a role in the production of language (Metter, 1991). Another function of the thalamus is the regulation of sleep cycles, which is thought to be accomplished in cooperation with the pons and the reticular formation (Krosigk, 1993). The majority of people who have had acute brain injury and remain in an unresponsive "vegetative" state have suffered significant damage to the thalamus, to the neural tissue connecting it to parts of the forebrain, or to both (Adams et al., 2000).

The **hypothalamus** lies directly below the thalamus and weighs only about 2 ounces. It regulates hunger, thirst, sexual behavior, and a wide variety of emotional behaviors. The hypothalamus also regulates internal body temperature, starting the process that causes you to perspire when you are too hot and to shiver to conserve body heat when you are too cold. It also houses the biological clock—the mechanism responsible for the timing of the sleep/wakefulness cycle and the daily fluctuation in more than 100 body functions (Ginty et al., 1993). Because of the biological clock, once your body gets used to waking up at a certain time, you tend to awaken at that time every day—even if you forget to set your alarm. The physiological changes in the body that accompany strong emotion—sweaty palms, a pounding heart, a hollow feeling in the pit of your stomach—are also initiated by neurons concentrated primarily in the hypothalamus.

The Limbic System

The **limbic system,** shown in Figure 2.5 (on page 46), is a group of structures in the brain, including the amygdala and the hippocampus, that are collectively involved in emotional expression, memory, and motivation. The **amygdala** plays an important role in emotion, particularly in response to unpleasant or punishing stimuli (LeDoux, 1994, 2000). Heavily involved in the learning of fear responses, the amygdala helps form vivid memories of emotional events, which enable humans and other animals to avoid dangerous situations (Cahill et al., 1995; LeDoux, 1995). The mere sight of frightened faces causes neurons in the amygdala to fire (Morris et al., 1996). Damage to the amygdala can impair a person's ability to recognize facial expressions and tones of voice that are associated with fear and anger (LeDoux, 2000; Scott et al., 1997).

The **hippocampus** is an important brain structure of the limbic system located in the interior temporal lobes (see Figure 2.5). If your hippocampal region—the hippocampus and the underlying cortical areas—were destroyed, you would not be able to store any new personal or cognitive information, such as that day's baseball score or the phone number of the person you met at dinner (Eichenbaum, 1997; Gluck & Myers, 1997; Varga-Khadem et al., 1997). Yet, memories already stored before the hippocampal region was destroyed would remain intact. You will learn more about the central role of the hippocampal region in the formation of memories in Chapter 6.

The hippocampus also plays a role in the brain's internal representation of space in the form of neural "maps" that help us learn our way about in new environments and remember where we have been (Wilson & McNaughton, 1993). An interesting study of taxi drivers in London revealed that their posterior (rear) hippocampus was significantly

◆ *What are the functions of the thalamus and the hypothalamus?*

◆ **thalamus**
(THAL-uh-mus) The structure, located above the brainstem, that acts as a relay station for information flowing into or out of the forebrain.

◆ **hypothalamus**
(HY-po-THAL-uh-mus) A small but influential brain structure that regulates hunger, thirst, sexual behavior, internal body temperature, other body functions, and a wide variety of emotional behaviors.

◆ **limbic system**
A group of structures in the brain, including the amygdala and hippocampus, that are collectively involved in emotional expression, memory, and motivation.

◆ *Which mental processes and behaviors are influenced by the limbic system?*

◆ **amygdala**
(ah-MIG-da-la) A structure in the limbic system that plays an important role in emotion, particularly in response to unpleasant or punishing stimuli.

◆ **hippocampus**
(hip-po-CAM-pus) A structure in the limbic system that plays a central role in the storing of new memories, the response to new or unexpected stimuli, and navigational ability.

FIGURE 2.5

The Principal Structures in the Limbic System

The amygdala plays an important role in emotion; the hippocampus is essential in the formation of new memories.

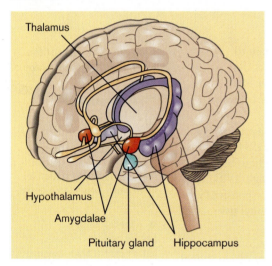

Thalamus

Hypothalamus

Amygdalae

Pituitary gland   Hippocampus

larger than that of participants in a control group who did not have extensive experience navigating the city's streets (Maguire et al., 2000). In fact, the more experience a taxi driver had, the larger that part of the hippocampus was. This study shows that the posterior hippocampus is important for navigational ability. More broadly, the study reveals that an important structure in the adult human brain has *plasticity*, the ability to respond to environmental demands (Maguire et al., 2000).

The Cerebrum

What functions come to mind when you think of the brain? Like most people, you probably identify this organ with logic, problem solving, language comprehension and production, and other "higher" cognitive functions. Though other parts of the brain play important supporting roles in these functions, their primary site is the cerebrum. Indeed, the most essentially human part of our magnificent 3-pound brain is the cerebrum and its cortex.

◆ *What are the components of the cerebrum?*

Components of the Cerebrum

If you could peer into your skull and look down on your brain, what you would see would resemble the inside of a huge walnut. Like a walnut, which has two matched halves connected to each other, the **cerebrum** is composed of two **cerebral hemispheres**—a left and a right hemisphere resting side by side (see Figure 2.6). The two hemispheres are physically connected at the bottom by a thick band of nerve fibers called the **corpus callosum.** This connection makes possible the transfer of information and the coordination of activity between the hemispheres. In general, the right cerebral hemisphere controls movement and feeling on the left side of the body; the left hemisphere controls the right side of the body.

The cerebral hemispheres have a thin outer covering about $1/8$ inch thick called the **cerebral cortex,** which is primarily responsible for the higher mental processes of language, memory, and thinking. The presence of the cell bodies of billions of neurons in the cerebral cortex gives it a grayish appearance. Thus, the cortex is often referred to as *gray matter*. Immediately beneath the cortex are the white myelinated axons (referred to as *white matter*) that connect the neurons of the cortex with those of other brain regions. Research by Andreasen and others (1993) indicated that the amount of gray matter is positively correlated with intelligence in humans.

In humans, the cerebral cortex is very large—if it were spread out flat, it would measure about 2 feet by 3 feet. Because the cortex is roughly three times the size of the cerebrum itself, it does not fit smoothly around the cerebrum. Rather, it is arranged in numerous folds or wrinkles, called *convolutions*. About two-thirds of the cortex is hidden from view in these folds. The cortex of less intelligent animals is much smaller in proportion to total brain size and, therefore, is much less convoluted. The cerebral cortex contains three types of areas: (1) sensory input areas, where vision, hearing, touch, pressure, and temperature register; (2) motor areas, which control voluntary movement; and (3) **association areas,** which house memories and are involved in thought, perception, and language. In each cerebral hemisphere, there are four lobes—the frontal lobe, the parietal lobe, the occipital lobe, and the temporal lobe (see Figure 2.7).

◆ **cerebrum**

(seh-REE-brum) The largest structure of the human brain, consisting of the two cerebral hemispheres connected by the corpus callosum and covered by the cerebral cortex.

◆ **cerebral hemispheres**

(seh-REE-brul) The right and left halves of the cerebrum, covered by the cerebral cortex and connected by the corpus callosum; they control movement and feeling on the opposing sides of the body.

◆ **corpus callosum**

(KOR-pus kah-LO-sum) The thick band of nerve fibers that connects the two cerebral hemispheres and makes possible the transfer of information and the synchronization of activity between the hemispheres.

◆ **cerebral cortex**

(seh-REE-brul KOR-tex) The gray, convoluted covering of the cerebral hemispheres that is responsible for the higher mental processes of language, memory, and thinking.

FIGURE 2.6 **Two Views of the Cerebral Hemispheres**

(a) The two hemispheres rest side by side like two matched halves, physically connected by the corpus callosum. (b) An inside view of the right hemisphere.

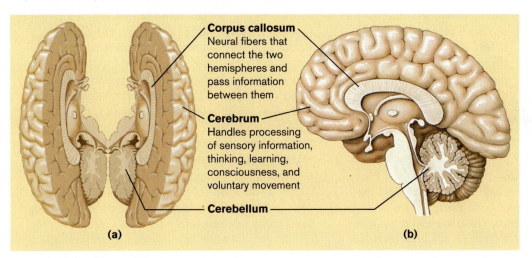

Corpus callosum
Neural fibers that connect the two hemispheres and pass information between them

Cerebrum
Handles processing of sensory information, thinking, learning, consciousness, and voluntary movement

Cerebellum

(a)   (b)

The Frontal Lobes

The largest of the brain's lobes, the **frontal lobes,** begin at the front of the brain and extend to the top center of the skull. They contain the motor cortex, Broca's area, and the frontal association areas.

The **motor cortex** is the area that controls voluntary body movement (refer to Figure 2.7). The right motor cortex controls movement on the left side of the body, and the left motor cortex controls movement on the right side of the body. In 1937, Canadian neurosurgeon Wilder Penfield applied electrical stimulation to the motor cortex of conscious human patients undergoing neurosurgery. He then mapped the primary motor cortex in humans. The parts of the body that are capable of the most finely coordinated movements, such as the fingers, lips, and tongue, have a larger share of the motor cortex. Movements in the lower parts of the body are controlled primarily by neurons at the top of the motor cortex, whereas movements in the upper body parts (face, lips, and tongue) are controlled mainly by neurons near the bottom of the motor cortex. For example, when you wiggle your right big toe, the movement is produced mainly by the firing of a cluster of brain cells at the top of the left motor cortex.

◆ *Which psychological functions are associated with the frontal lobes?*

◆ **association areas**
Areas of the cerebral cortex that house memories and are involved in thought, perception, and language.

◆ **frontal lobes**
The largest of the brain's lobes, which contain the motor cortex, Broca's area, and the frontal association areas.

◆ **motor cortex**
The strip of tissue at the rear of the frontal lobes that controls voluntary body movement and participates in learning and cognitive events.

Motor cortex   Somatosensory cortex

Broca's area

Parietal lobe

Frontal lobe

Occipital lobe

Primary visual cortex

Primary auditory cortex

Temporal lobe

Wernicke's area

Cerebellum

FIGURE 2.7

The Cerebral Cortex of the Left Hemisphere

This illustration of the left cerebral hemisphere shows the four lobes: (1) the frontal lobe, including the motor cortex and Broca's area; (2) the parietal lobe, with the somatosensory cortex; (3) the occipital lobe, with the primary visual cortex; and (4) the temporal lobe, with the primary auditory cortex and Wernicke's area.

How Did You Find Psychology?

Joseph LeDoux

When you were reading about the research linking the amygdala to fear, you may have noticed the name of Joseph LeDoux in the research citations. LeDoux is the director of one of the world's top neuroscience laboratories, located at New York University. You might think that a well-planned career strategy was responsible for his success. However, in describing his own academic and career path, LeDoux noted, "Not everyone knows what they want to do at an early age, and I certainly didn't have a clue" (LeDoux, 2004, p. 141).

As a boy, LeDoux spent Saturday mornings working in his family's butcher shop in a small town in Louisiana. One of his jobs was to extract bullets from the brains of slaughtered cows, an experience that left him intimately acquainted with the physical characteristics of the brain. He marveled at the toughness of the membrane that protects the brain and the mushiness of the brain tissue itself. The intricacies of the brain's convolutions impressed him, too. LeDoux's curiosity about the link between the brain and consciousness was aroused as well, and he couldn't stop wondering what the cow might have thought or felt as the fatal bullet passed through its brain.

Despite his curiosity, pursuing a career in brain research did not occur to the young LeDoux. For the most part, his thoughts about his future were shaped by his desire to avoid the paths the adults in his life wanted to lay out for him. The nuns at the Catholic schools he attended, for instance, went to great lengths to convince him that he was well suited to a career in the priesthood. LeDoux reports that puberty rendered this career option impossible. At the same time, his father made it clear that he expected his son to follow in his footsteps, both in business and in leisure pursuits. In addition to being a butcher, the elder LeDoux was a part-time rodeo cowboy, a hobby in which the younger LeDoux had absolutely no interest.

When high school graduation arrived, LeDoux's primary goal was to escape. He had a good idea about what he wanted to avoid (the priesthood, the meat business, rodeos, and a dull life in a small town) but little insight into what he wanted to pursue. Consequently, LeDoux focused his energies on talking his parents into letting him go away to school—specifically, to the main campus of Louisiana State University in Baton Rouge. Ultimately, LeDoux managed to obtain his parents' blessing to attend LSU on the condition that he would major in business and return to his hometown to work in the local bank.

True to his word, LeDoux studied business at LSU. The topic that most interested him was consumer psychology, so he took a few additional psychology courses and ended up with a minor in psychology. He entered LSU's graduate program in marketing as soon as he completed his bachelor's degree. Still not particularly enthralled by business, LeDoux continued to take psychology courses. One of his professors, a biological psychologist named Robert Thompson, recruited LeDoux to work in his laboratory. Thompson's research sought to identify memory circuits in the brains of rats. The professor was so impressed with LeDoux's work that he encouraged him to apply to Ph.D. programs in biological psychology. Taking his advice, LeDoux obtained his doctorate degree in biological psychology from the State University of New York at Stony Brook. Through several postdoctoral positions, he acquired the academic background and skills needed to work in the interdisciplinary field of neuroscience.

As Joseph LeDoux's story demonstrates, remaining open to new experiences and being willing to change one's goals as new opportunities arise are sometimes more important to career success than having a set goal early in life. If you aren't quite sure what you want to do, bear in mind that your future may hold opportunities to use the knowledge and skills you are acquiring now in ways that you can't yet imagine. After all, it's doubtful that the boy who spent his Saturdays picking bullets out of cows' brains had the slightest inkling that he would someday find himself at the forefront of research aimed at unlocking the mysteries of the human brain.

How accurately and completely does Penfield's map account for the control of body movement? Although it may be useful in a broad sense, more recent research has shown that there is not a precise one-to-one correspondence between specific points on the motor cortex and movement of particular body parts. Motor neurons that control the fingers, for example, play a role in the movement of more than a single finger. In fact, the control of movement of any single finger is handled by a network of neurons that are widely distributed over the entire hand area of the motor cortex (Sanes & Donoghue, 2000; Sanes et al., 1995; Schieber & Hibbard, 1993).

The **plasticity**—the brain's capacity to adapt to changes such as brain damage—of the motor cortex is maintained throughout life. This plasticity allows synapses to

◆ **plasticity**
The capacity of the brain to adapt to changes such as brain damage.

strengthen and reorganize their interconnections when stimulated by experience and practice. Even mental rehearsal, or imaging, can produce changes in the motor cortex (Sanes & Donoghue, 2000), but such changes are not as powerful as those generated by real rehearsal or performance. Thus, athletes often spend time before a game visualizing their upcoming performance on the field or court—but this mental practice never replaces actual, physical practice. Moreover, the motor cortex in humans is responsive to both short-term and long-term experience (Liepert et al., 1999). Simply repeating a sequence of movements rapidly for as little as 5 to 10 minutes can alter the motor cortex (Classen et al., 1998).

In 1861, physician Paul Broca performed autopsies on two patients—one who had been totally without speech, and another who could say only four words (Jenkins et al., 1975). Broca found that both individuals had damage in the left hemisphere, slightly in front of the part of the motor cortex that controls movements of the jaw, lips, and tongue. He concluded that the site of left hemisphere damage he identified through the autopsies was the part of the brain responsible for speech production, now called **Broca's area** (refer to Figure 2.7). Broca's area is involved in directing the pattern of muscle movement required to produce speech sounds.

If Broca's area is damaged as a result of head injury or stroke, **Broca's aphasia** may result. **Aphasia** is a general term for a loss or impairment of the ability to use or understand language, resulting from damage to the brain (Goodglass, 1993). Characteristically, patients with Broca's aphasia know what they want to say but can speak very little or not at all. If they are able to speak, their words are produced very slowly, with great effort, and are poorly articulated.

Much of the frontal lobes consist of association areas involved in thinking, motivation, planning for the future, impulse control, and emotional responses (Stuss et al., 1992). Damage to the frontal association areas produces deficiencies in the ability to plan and anticipate the consequences of actions. Sometimes, pronounced changes in emotional responses occur when the frontal lobes are damaged. Phineas Gage, discussed at the opening of this chapter, represents one case in which damage to the frontal lobes drastically altered impulse control and emotional responses.

The Parietal Lobes

The **parietal lobes** lie directly behind the frontal lobes, in the top middle portion of the brain (refer back to Figure 2.7). The parietal lobes are involved in the reception and processing of touch stimuli. The front strip of brain tissue in the parietal lobes is the **somatosensory cortex,** the site where touch, pressure, temperature, and pain register in the cerebral cortex (Stea & Apkarian, 1992). The somatosensory cortex also makes you aware of movement in your body and the positions of your body parts at any given moment.

The two halves of the somatosensory cortex, in the left and right parietal lobes, are wired to opposite sides of the body. Also, cells at the top of the somatosensory cortex govern feeling in the lower extremities of the body. Drop a brick on your right foot, and the topmost brain cells of the left somatosensory cortex will fire and register the pain sensation. (*Note:* This is *not* a *Try It!*) The large somatosensory areas are connected to sensitive body parts such as the tongue, lips, face, and hand, particularly the thumb and index finger.

Other parts of the parietal lobes are responsible for spatial orientation and sense of direction—for example, helping you to retrace your path when you take a wrong turn. The hippocampus cooperates with these parts of the parietal lobes in performing such functions, as the study of London taxi drivers discussed on pages 45–46 indicates (Maguire et al., 2000).

◆ **Broca's area**
(BRO-kuz) The area in the frontal lobe, usually in the left hemisphere, that controls the production of speech sounds.

◆ **Broca's aphasia**
(BRO-kuz uh-FAY-zyah) An impairment in the physical ability to produce speech sounds or, in extreme cases, an inability to speak at all; caused by damage to Broca's area.

◆ **aphasia**
(uh-FAY-zyah) A loss or impairment of the ability to use or understand language, resulting from damage to the brain.

◆ **parietal lobes**
(puh-RY-uh-tul) The lobes that contain the somatosensory cortex (where touch, pressure, temperature, and pain register) and other areas that are responsible for body awareness and spatial orientation.

◆ **somatosensory cortex**
(so-MAT-oh-SENS-or-ee) The strip of tissue at the front of the parietal lobes where touch, pressure, temperature, and pain register in the cerebral cortex.

◆ *What is the somatosensory cortex, and what does it do?*

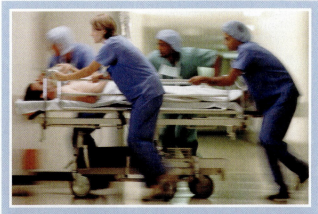

Treatment of brain damage has come a long way since the days of Phineas Gage. Today, more than a million people are treated for head injuries in U.S. hospitals each year. Rapid treatment of head injury patients has contributed to an improved survival rate.

Have you ever fumbled for your keys in a coat pocket, purse, or backpack? How did you distinguish between your keys and other objects without looking? There are association areas in the parietal lobes that house memories of how objects feel against the human skin, a fact that explains why we can identify objects by touch. People with damage to these areas could hold a computer mouse, a CD, or a baseball in their hand but not be able to identify the object by touch alone.

The Occipital Lobes

Behind the parietal lobes at the rear of the brain lie the **occipital lobes,** which are involved in the reception and interpretation of visual information (refer to Figure 2.7). At the very back of the occipital lobes is the **primary visual cortex,** the site where vision registers in the cortex.

Each eye is connected to the primary visual cortex in both the right and the left occipital lobes. Look straight ahead and draw an imaginary line down the middle of what you see. Everything to the left of the line is referred to as the left visual field and registers in the right visual cortex. Everything to the right of the line is the right visual field and registers in the left visual cortex. A person who sustains damage to one half of the primary visual cortex will still have partial vision in both eyes because each eye sends information to both the right and the left occipital lobes.

The association areas in the occipital lobes are involved in the interpretation of visual stimuli. They hold memories of past visual experiences and enable us to recognize what is familiar among the things we see. That's why the face of a friend stands out in a crowd of unfamiliar people. When these areas are damaged, people can lose the ability to identify objects visually, although they will still be able to identify the same objects by touch or through some other sense.

The Temporal Lobes

The **temporal lobes,** located slightly above the ears, are involved in the reception and interpretation of auditory stimuli. The site in the cortex where hearing registers is known as the primary auditory cortex. The **primary auditory cortex** in each temporal lobe receives sound inputs from both ears.

Injury to one of these areas results in reduced hearing in both ears, and the destruction of both areas causes total deafness.

Adjacent to the primary auditory cortex in the left temporal lobe is **Wernicke's area,** which is the language area involved in comprehending the spoken word and in formulating coherent written and spoken language (refer to Figure 2.7). When you listen to someone speak, the sound registers first in the primary auditory cortex. The sound is then sent to Wernicke's area, where the speech sounds are unscrambled into meaningful patterns of words.

Wernicke's aphasia is a type of aphasia resulting from damage to Wernicke's area. Although speech is fluent and words are clearly articulated, the actual message does not make sense to listeners (Maratsos & Matheney, 1994). The content may be vague or bizarre

Because the left hand of a professional string player must rapidly and accurately execute fine movements and slight pressure variations, it is not surprising that these musicians have an unusually large area of the somatosensory cortex dedicated to the fingers of that hand.

◆ *Why are the occipital lobes critical to vision?*

◆ **occipital lobes**

(ahk-SIP-uh-tul) The lobes that are involved in the reception and interpretation of visual information; they contain the primary visual cortex.

◆ **primary visual cortex**

The area at the rear of the occipital lobes where vision registers in the cerebral cortex.

◆ *What are the major areas within the temporal lobes, and what are their functions?*

◆ **temporal lobes**

The lobes that are involved in the reception and interpretation of auditory information; they contain the primary auditory cortex, Wernicke's area, and the temporal association areas.

◆ **primary auditory cortex**

The part of each temporal lobe where hearing registers in the cerebral cortex.

◆ **Wernicke's area**

(VUR-nih-keys) The language area in the left temporal lobe involved in comprehending the spoken word and in formulating coherent speech and written language.

◆ **Wernicke's aphasia**

Aphasia that results from damage to Wernicke's area and in which the person's speech is fluent and clearly articulated but does not make sense to listeners.

and may contain inappropriate words, parts of words, or a gibberish of nonexistent words. One Wernicke's patient, when asked how he was feeling, replied, "I think that there's an awful lot of mung, but I think I've a lot of net and tunged in a little wheat duhvayden" (Buckingham & Kertesz, 1974). People with Wernicke's aphasia are not aware that anything is wrong with their speech. Thus, this disorder is difficult to treat.

The remainder of the temporal lobes consists of the association areas that house memories and are involved in the interpretation of auditory stimuli. For example, the association area where your memories of various sounds are stored enables you to recognize the sounds of your favorite band, a computer booting up, your roommate snoring, and so on. There is also a special association area where familiar melodies are stored.

The Cerebral Hemispheres

You've probably heard about differences between "right-brained" and "left-brained" people. For instance, "right-brained" people are sometimes described as creative, while their "left-brained" counterparts are characterized as logical. Such a notion has no scientific basis, yet it has served to heighten public interest in hemispheric specialization and neuroscience in general (Hellige, 1993). Despite their specialized functions, the right and left hemispheres are always in contact, thanks to the corpus callosum (shown in Figure 2.4). In fact, intellectual ability may be linked to interhemispheric communication; scores on tests of mathematical aptitude are correlated with measures of communication between the left and right hemispheres (Singh & O'Boyle, 2004). But research has shown that some **lateralization** of the hemispheres exists; that is, each hemisphere is specialized to handle certain functions. Let's look at the specific functions associated with the left and right hemispheres.

◆ **lateralization**
The specialization of one of the cerebral hemispheres to handle a particular function.

The Left Hemisphere

The **left hemisphere** handles most of the language functions, including speaking, writing, reading, speech comprehension, and comprehension of written information (Hellige, 1990; Long & Baynes, 2002). Many of these functions have specific regions of the left hemisphere devoted to them. For instance, the sounds and meanings associated with spoken language are processed in different areas of the left hemisphere (Poldrack & Wagner, 2004). The left hemisphere is specialized for mathematics and logic as well (Corballis, 1989). Moreover, researchers have learned that information about the self, including one's sense of well-being, is processed in the left hemisphere (Heatherton et al., 2004; Urry et al., 2004).

The left hemisphere coordinates complex movements by directly controlling the right side of the body and by indirectly controlling the movements of the left side of the body. It accomplishes this by sending orders across the corpus callosum to the right hemisphere so that the proper movements will be coordinated and executed smoothly. (Remember that the cerebellum also plays an important role in helping coordinate complex movements.)

◆ *What are the specialized functions of the left hemisphere?*

◆ **left hemisphere**
The hemisphere that controls the right side of the body, coordinates complex movements, and, in most people, handles most of the language functions.

◆ **right hemisphere**
The hemisphere that controls the left side of the body and, in most people, is specialized for visual-spatial perception.

The Right Hemisphere

The **right hemisphere** is generally considered to be the hemisphere more adept at visual-spatial relations. And the auditory cortex in the right hemisphere appears to be far better able to process music than the left (Zatorre et al., 2002). When you arrange your bedroom furniture or notice that your favorite song is being played on the radio, you are relying primarily on your right hemisphere.

The right hemisphere also augments the left hemisphere's language-processing activities. For example, it produces the unusual verbal associations characteristic of creative thought and problem solving (Seger et al., 2000). As Van Lancker (1987) pointed out, "although the left hemisphere knows best what is being said, the right hemisphere

◆ *What are the specialized functions of the right hemisphere?*

figures out how it is meant and who is saying it" (p. 13). It is the right hemisphere that is able to understand familiar idiomatic expressions, such as "She let the cat out of the bag."

To experience an effect of the specialization of the cerebral hemispheres, try your hand at *Try It 2.1*.

Patients with right hemisphere damage may have difficulty understanding metaphors or orienting spatially, as in finding their way around, even in familiar surroundings. They may have attentional deficits and be unaware of objects in the left visual field, a condition called *unilateral neglect* (Deovell et al., 2000; Halligan & Marshall, 1994). Patients with this condition may eat only the food on the right side of a plate, read only the words on the right half of a page, groom only the right half of the body, or even deny that the arm on the side opposite the brain damage belongs to them (Bisiach, 1996; Chen-Sea, 2000; Posner, 1996; Tham et al., 2000). Researchers have found that a treatment combining visual training with forced movement of limbs on the neglected side helps some patients (Brunila et al., 2002).

As you read earlier, the left hemisphere processes the linguistic aspects of speech. However, researchers have found that the processing of natural language involves an interaction between the two halves of the brain in which the right hemisphere carries out a number of critical functions (Berckmoes & Vingerhoets, 2004). One such function is the comprehension of causal links between statements such as "I fell off my bicycle yesterday. My knee is killing me." (Mason & Just, 2004). The right hemisphere also responds to the emotional message conveyed by another's tone of voice (LeDoux, 2000). Reading and interpreting nonverbal behavior, such as gestures and facial expressions, is another right hemisphere task (Hauser, 1993; Kucharska-Pietura & Klimkowski, 2002). For example, the subtle clues that tell us someone is lying (such as excessive blinking or lack of eye contact) are processed in the right hemisphere (Etcoff et al., 2000).

Evidence also continues to accumulate that brain mechanisms responsible for negative emotions are located in the right hemisphere, while those responsible for positive emotions are in the left hemisphere (Hellige, 1993; Salo et al., 2002). Research shows that patients suffering from major depression experience decreased activity in the left prefrontal cortex, where positive emotions are produced (Drevets et al., 1997). Figure 2.8 summarizes the functions associated with the left and right hemispheres.

The Split Brain

◆ *What do researchers mean by the term "split brain"?*

A great deal of knowledge about lateralization has been gained from studies involving individuals in whom the corpus callosum is absent or has been surgically modified. Many such individuals have had their corpus callosum severed in a drastic surgical procedure called the **split-brain operation.** Neurosurgeons Joseph Bogen and Philip Vogel (1963) found that patients with severe epilepsy, suffering frequent and uncontrollable grand mal seizures, could be helped by surgery that severed their corpus callosum, rendering communication between the two hemispheres impossible. The operation decreases the frequency of seizures in two-thirds of patients and causes minimal loss of cognitive functioning or change in personality (Washington University School of Medicine, 2003).

Research with split-brain patients by Roger Sperry (1964) and colleagues Michael Gazzaniga (1970, 1989) and Jerre

◆ **split-brain operation**

A surgical procedure, performed to treat severe cases of epilepsy, in which the corpus callosum is cut, separating the cerebral hemispheres.

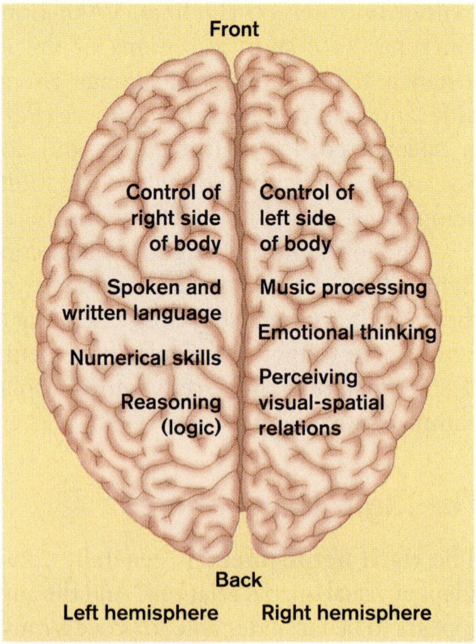

FIGURE 2.8

Lateralized Functions of the Brain

Assigning functions to one hemisphere or the other allows the brain to function more efficiently.

Get a meter stick or yardstick. Try balancing it vertically on the end of your left index finger, as shown in the drawing. Then try balancing it on your right index finger. Most people are better with their dominant hand—the right hand for right-handers, for example. Is this true for you?

Now try this: Begin reciting the ABCs out loud as fast as you can while balancing the stick with your left hand. Do you have less trouble this time? Why should that be? The right hemisphere controls the act of balancing with the left hand. However, your left hemisphere, though poor at controlling the left hand, still tries to coordinate your balancing efforts. When you distract the left hemisphere with a steady stream of talk, the right hemisphere can orchestrate more efficient balancing with your left hand without interference.

Levy (1985) expanded knowledge of the unique capabilities of the individual hemispheres. Sperry (1968) found that when the brain was surgically separated, each hemisphere continued to have individual and private experiences, sensations, thoughts, and perceptions. However, most sensory experiences are shared almost simultaneously because each ear and eye has direct sensory connections to both hemispheres.

Sperry's research, for which he won a Nobel Prize in medicine in 1981, revealed some fascinating findings. In Figure 2.9 (on page 54), a split-brain patient sits in front of a screen that separates the right and left fields of vision. If an orange is flashed to the right field of vision, it will register in the left (verbal) hemisphere. If asked what he saw, the patient will readily reply, "I saw an orange." Suppose that, instead, an apple is flashed to the left visual field and is relayed to the right (nonverbal) hemisphere. The patient will reply, "I saw nothing."

Why could the patient report that he saw the orange but not the apple? Sperry (1964, 1968) maintains that in split-brain patients, only the verbal left hemisphere can report what it sees. In these experiments, the left hemisphere does not see what is flashed to the right hemisphere, and the right hemisphere is unable to report verbally what it has viewed. But did the right hemisphere actually see the apple that was flashed in the left visual field? Yes, because with his left hand (which is controlled by the right hemisphere), the patient can pick out from behind a screen the apple or any other object shown to the right hemisphere. The right hemisphere knows and remembers what it sees just as well as the left, but unlike the left hemisphere, the right cannot name what it has seen. (In these experiments, images must be flashed for no more than $1/10$ or $2/10$ of a second so that the subjects do not have time to refixate their eyes and send the information to the opposite hemisphere.)

Handedness, Culture, and Genes

Since we've been discussing right and left hemispheres, you might be wondering whether right- and left-handedness have anything to do with hemispheric specialization. Investigators have identified differences in the brains of left- and right-handers that suggest that the process of hemispheric specialization and the development of handedness may be related. On average, the corpus callosum of left-handers is 11% larger and contains up to 2.5 million more nerve fibers than that of right-handers (Witelson, 1985). In general, the two sides of the brain are less specialized in left-handers (Hellige et al., 1994). There is also evidence that new learning is more easily transferred from one side of the brain to the other in left-handers (Schmidt et al., 2000).

◆ *How are handedness and brain function related?*

FIGURE 2.9

Testing a Split-Brain Person

Using special equipment, researchers are able to study the independent functioning of the hemispheres in split-brain patients. In this experiment, when a visual image (an orange) is flashed on the right side of the screen, it is transmitted to the left (talking) hemisphere. When asked what he sees, the split-brain patient replies, "I see an orange." When an image (an apple) is flashed on the left side of the screen, it is transmitted only to the right (nonverbal) hemisphere. Because the split-brain patient's left (language) hemisphere did not receive the image, he replies, "I see nothing." But he can pick out the apple by touch if he uses his left hand, proving that the right hemisphere "saw" the apple. *Source:* Based on Gazzaniga (1983).

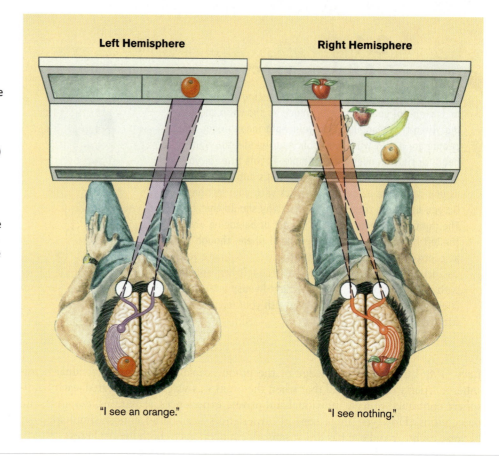

Left Hemisphere   Right Hemisphere

"I see an orange."   "I see nothing."

In addition, left-handers tend to experience less language loss following an injury to either hemisphere. They are also more likely to recover, because the undamaged hemisphere can more easily take over the speech functions. Left-handers are more numerous among artists, musicians, and political leaders (Wilson, 1998). On the other hand, left-handers tend to have higher rates of learning disabilities and mental disorders than right-handers, perhaps because of differences in brain organization (Grouios et al., 1999; Hernandez et al., 1997; Tanner, 1990).

Historical evidence generally supports a genetic explanation for the predominance of right-handedness among humans (Hopkins & Cantalupo, 2004). Archeological studies of ancient populations show that the proportions of left- and right-handers in the human population has been about the same for several thousand years (83% right-handed, 14% left-handed, and 3% ambidexterous; Steele & Mays, 1995). Anthropological studies of ancient artwork and tools from locations all over the world have shown that right-handedness has been dominant for thousands of years (Wilson, 1998). There is even evidence that prehuman species, such as *Homo erectus*, were predominantly right-handed.

Animal studies provide further support for the genetic hypothesis. Studies indicate that right-handedness is almost as prevalent among chimpanzees as among humans (Hopkins et al., 2004). By contrast, studies involving other primate species, which are less genetically similar to humans than chimpanzees are, find a majority of individuals to be left-handed (Westergaard & Lussier, 1999).

 electroencephalogram (EEG)

(ee-lek-tro-en-SEFF-uh-lo-gram) A record of brain-wave activity made by a machine called the electroencephalograph.

◆ **beta wave**

(BAY-tuh) The brain-wave pattern associated with mental or physical activity.

◆ **alpha wave**

The brain-wave pattern associated with deep relaxation.

Discovering the Brain's Mysteries

Modern researchers do not have to perform autopsies or wait for injuries to occur to learn more about the brain. Today, researchers are unlocking the mysteries of the human brain using a variety of techniques.

The EEG and the Microelectrode

In 1924, Austrian psychiatrist Hans Berger invented the electroencephalograph, a machine that records the electrical activity occurring in the brain. This electrical activity, detected by electrodes placed at various points on the scalp and amplified greatly, provides the power to drive a pen across paper, producing a record of brain-wave activity called an **electroencephalogram (EEG).** The **beta wave** is the brain-wave pattern associated with mental or physical activity. The **alpha wave** is associated with deep relaxation, and the **delta wave** with slow-wave (deep) sleep. (You will learn more about these brain-wave patterns in Chapter 4.)

A computerized EEG imaging technique shows the different levels of electrical activity occurring every millisecond on the surface of the brain (Gevins et al., 1995). It can show an epileptic seizure in progress and can be used to study neural activity in people with learning disabilities, schizophrenia, Alzheimer's disease, sleep disorders, and other neurological problems.

Although the EEG is able to detect electrical activity in different areas of the brain, it cannot reveal what is happening in individual neurons. However, the **microelectrode** can. A microelectrode is a wire so small that it can be inserted near or into a single neuron without damaging it. Microelectrodes can be used to monitor the electrical activity of a single neuron or to stimulate activity within it. Researchers have used microelectrodes to discover the exact functions of single cells within the primary visual cortex and the primary auditory cortex.

The CT Scan and Magnetic Resonance Imaging

Since the early 1970s, a number of techniques that provide scientists and physicians with images of the brain's structures have become available. For example, a patient undergoing a **CT scan (computerized axial tomography)** of the brain is placed inside a large, doughnut-shaped structure where an X-ray tube encircles the entire head. The tube rotates in a complete circle, shooting X-rays through the brain as it does so. A series of computerized, cross-sectional images reveal the structures within the brain as well as abnormalities and injuries, including tumors and evidence of old or more recent strokes.

MRI (magnetic resonance imaging), which also became widely available in the 1980s, produces clearer and more detailed images without exposing patients to potentially dangerous X-rays (Potts et al., 1993). MRI can be used to find abnormalities in the central nervous system and in other systems of the body. Although the CT scan and MRI do a remarkable job of showing what the brain looks like both inside and out, they cannot reveal what the brain is doing. But other technological marvels can.

The PET Scan, fMRI, and Other Imaging Techniques

As helpful as they are, CT and MRI images show only structures. By contrast, several techniques capture images of both brain structures and their functions. The oldest of these techniques, the **PET scan (positron-emission tomography)** has been used since the mid-1970s to identify malfunctions that cause physical and psychological disorders. It has also been used to study normal brain activity. A PET scan maps the patterns of blood flow, oxygen use, and glucose consumption (glucose is the food of the brain). It can also show the action of drugs and other biochemical substances in the brain and other bodily organs (Farde, 1996).

A technique that became available in the 1990s, **functional MRI (fMRI),** has several important advantages over PET: (1) It can provide images of both brain structure and brain activity; (2) it requires no injections (of radioactive or other material); (3) it can identify locations of activity more precisely than PET can; and (4) it can detect changes that take place in less than a second, compared with about a minute for PET ("Brain Imaging," 1997).

◆ *What does the electroencephalogram (EEG) reveal about the brain?*

◆ **delta wave**
The brain-wave pattern associated with slow-wave (deep) sleep.

◆ **microelectrode**
A small wire used to monitor the electrical activity of or stimulate activity within a single neuron.

◆ **CT scan (computerized axial tomography)**
A brain-scanning technique that uses a rotating, computerized X-ray tube to produce cross-sectional images of the structures of the brain.

◆ *How are the CT scan and MRI helpful in the study of brain structure?*

◆ **MRI (magnetic resonance imagery)**
A diagnostic scanning technique that produces high-resolution images of the structures of the brain.

◆ *How are the PET scan and newer imaging techniques used to study the brain?*

◆ **PET scan (positron-emission tomography)**
A brain-imaging technique that reveals activity in various parts of the brain, based on patterns of blood flow, oxygen use, and glucose consumption.

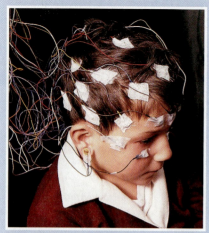

The electroencephalograph, or EEG, uses electrodes placed on the scalp to amplify and record electrical activity in the brain.

Still other imaging devices are now available. SQUID (superconducting quantum interference device) shows brain activity by measuring the magnetic changes produced by the electric current that neurons discharge when they fire. Another imaging marvel, MEG (magnetoencephalography), also measures such magnetic changes and shows neural activity within the brain as rapidly as it occurs, much faster than PET or fMRI. A new kind of MRI, diffusion tensor imaging (DTI), enables researchers to examine individual neuron bundles.

Brain-imaging techniques have helped neuroscientists develop an impressive store of knowledge about normal brain functions such as memory (Zhang et al., 2003). These imaging techniques have also been used to show abnormal brain patterns peculiar to certain psychiatric disorders and to reveal where and how various drugs affect the brain (Juengling et al., 2003; Nestor et al., 2004; Tamminga & Conley, 1997). Furthermore, brain-imaging techniques may someday replace the polygraph (lie dectector) test because imaging studies have shown that lying and truth-telling activate different areas of the brain (Kozel et al., 2004).

◆ **functional MRI (fMRI)**
A brain-imaging technique that reveals both brain structure and brain activity more precisely and rapidly than PET.

Age and Gender Differences in the Brain

The principles of neurological functioning you've learned about—how action potentials occur and so on—work pretty much the same no matter what an individual's age or gender. Still, there are some important age and gender variations in brain structure and function.

The Developing Brain

◆ *What are the major processes at work in the developing brain?*

When do you think the brain reaches full maturity? The answer to this question might surprise you. In fact, the brain grows in spurts from conception until well into adulthood (Fischer & Rose, 1994). In childhood and adolescence, many of these spurts are correlated with major advances in physical and intellectual skills, such as the acquisition of fluency in language that happens around age 4 for most children. Each growth spurt also seems to involve a different brain area. For example, the spurt that begins around age 17 and continues into the early 20s mainly affects the frontal lobes, where the abilities to plan and to control one's emotions are located. Differences between teens and adults in these abilities may be due to this growth spurt. Changes in brain function are influenced by several development processes.

Synapses develop as a result of the growth of both dendrites and axons. This process, known as *synaptogenesis*, occurs in spurts throughout the lifespan. Each spurt is followed by a period of **pruning**, the process through which the developing brain eliminates unnecessary or redundant synapses. The activity of neurotransmitters within the synapses also varies with age. For example, acetylcholine is less plentiful in the brains of children than in the brains of teens and adults. This difference may help explain age differences in memory and other functions influenced by this excitatory neurotransmitter.

The process of *myelination*, or the development of myelin sheaths around axons, begins prior to birth but continues well into adulthood. For example, the brain's association areas are not fully myelinated until age 12 or so (Tanner, 1990). And the reticular formation, which regulates attention, isn't fully myelinated until the mid-20s (Spreen et al., 1995). Thus, differences in myelination may account for differences between children and adults in processing speed, memory, and other functions.

◆ **pruning**
The process through which the developing brain eliminates unnecessary or redundant synapses.

Some degree of hemispheric specialization is present very early in life. Language processing, for example, occurs primarily in the left hemisphere of the fetal and infant brain, just as it does in the adult brain (Chilosi et al., 2001; de Lacoste et al., 1991). Other functions, such as spatial perception, aren't lateralized until age 8 or so. Consequently, children younger than age 8 exhibit much poorer spatial skills than do older children (Roberts & Bell, 2000). For instance, children younger than 8 have difficulty using maps and distinguishing between statements such as *It's on your left* and *It's on my left*.

As you learned earlier, the ability of the brain to reorganize, to reshape itself in response to input from both internal (within the brain) and external (environmental) sources (Clifford, 2000), and to compensate for damage, is termed *plasticity*. Plasticity is greatest in young children within whom the hemispheres are not yet completely lateralized. In fact, the lateralization process itself depends on both maturational and environmental factors. For example, the development of the auditory cortex in infants depends on the presence of patterned auditory input, such as human language, in the environment (Chang & Merzenich, 2003). Moreover, with its superior plasticity, the young brain is remarkably adaptable to serious brain damage. In one case study, researchers found that a prenatal hemorrhage that prevented the development of the left side of the cerebellum in one child was evidenced only by a slight tremor at age 3 (Mancini et al., 2001). As you might suspect, an adult who lost the left side of his or her cerebellum would probably experience much more functional impairment.

However, it is probably also true that the brain retains some degree of plasticity throughout life. For example, researchers have found that the correction of hearing defects in late-middle-aged adults results in changes in all the areas of the brain that are involved in sound perception (Giraud et al., 2001). Moreover, the brains of these individuals appear to develop responses to sounds in areas in which the brains of people with normal hearing do not.

Gender Differences in the Adult Brain

◆ *How do the brains of males and females differ?*

Throughout development, the brains of males and females differ to some degree. However, these differences and their possible links to behavior have been most thoroughly researched among adults. One such difference is that the brains of men have a higher proportion of white matter than do the brains of women (Gur et al., 1999). Moreover, men have a lower proportion of white matter in the left brain than in the right brain. In contrast, in women's brains, the proportions of gray matter and white matter in the two hemispheres are equivalent. Such findings have led some neuropsychologists to speculate that gender differences in the distribution of gray and white matter across the two hemispheres may explain men's superior performance on right-hemisphere tasks such as mental rotation of geometric figures. Likewise, women's superior abilities in the domain of emotional perception (more on this in Chapter 9) may be attributable to the fact that they have more gray matter than men do in the area of the brain that controls emotions (Gur et al., 2002).

Other research has revealed that some tasks stimulate different parts of the brain in men and women. For example, imaging studies have shown that men process navigational information, such as that needed to find the way out of a maze, in the left hippocampus. By contrast, women who are engaged in the same task use the right parietal cortex and the right frontal cortex (Gron et al., 2000). Similarly, studies show that men and women use different areas of the brain when searching for the location of a sound (Lewald, 2004).

What is the meaning of these gender differences in the brain? The short answer is that scientists won't know for certain until a great deal more research is done. Moreover, studies that look for links between these brain differences and actual behavior are needed before any conclusions can be drawn regarding the possible neurological bases for gender differences in behavior.

Aging and Other Influences on the Brain

◆ *How do aging and stroke-related damage affect the brain?*

The brains of males and females alike are subject to the effects of aging. The brain both gains and loses synapses throughout life. At some point in adulthood, however, losses begin to exceed gains (Huttenlocher, 1994). Brain weight begins to decline around age 30. Age-related deficits due to the loss of brain weight are common. For example, elderly people tend to experience problems with balance, they become less steady on their feet, and their gait is affected.

As illustrated by Phineas Gage's story, brain damage can lead to significant changes in brain function. But injuries such as the one Gage suffered aren't the most common source of damage. In the United States, strokes are the most common cause of damage to the adult brain and the third most common cause of death. A **stroke** occurs when a blood clot or plug of fat blocks an artery and cuts off the blood supply to a particular area of the brain or when a blood vessel bursts, often as a result of high blood pressure. High doses of stimulants such as amphetamines and cocaine also increase the risk of stroke.

◆ **stroke**

The most common cause of damage to adult brains, arising when blockage of an artery cuts off the blood supply to a particular area of the brain or when a blood vessel bursts.

Stroke patients, many of whom are older adults, may be left with impaired intellect, loss of coordination or sensation, and/or paralysis. A high percentage of stroke survivors suffer from depression (Angeleri et al., 1997) and about 25% have aphasia. But patients who receive TPA (a blood-clot-dissolving drug used successfully in treating heart attacks) within 3 hours of the onset of a stroke are 30% more likely to have minimal or no disability (Gorman, 1996; National Institute of Neurological Disorders, 1995).

Furthermore, physical therapy can help stroke patients of all ages recover at least partial motor functions, providing yet another example of the brain's plasticity. Indeed, though it was long believed that, once damaged, neurons in the brain were incapable of regeneration, research has shown that this may not be true. Researchers working with monkeys at Princeton Unversity have produced the first solid evidence that new neurons are generated in the lining of the ventricles deep in the center of the adult brain and then migrate to the cerebral cortex (Gould et al., 1999). Thus, the brain should be thought of as dynamic, or constantly changing, throughout the human lifespan.

The Peripheral Nervous System

◆ *What is the difference between the sympathetic and parasympathetic nervous systems?*

What makes your heart pound and palms sweat when you watch a scary movie? Such reactions are the result of signals from the brain's limbic system and other structures that regulate emotions to the peripheral nervous system. The **peripheral nervous system (PNS)** is made up of all the nerves that connect the central nervous system to the rest of the body. It has two subdivisions: the somatic nervous system and the autonomic nervous system. Figure 2.10 shows the subdivisions within the peripheral nervous system.

The *somatic nervous system* consists of (1) all the sensory nerves, which transmit information from the sense receptors—eyes, ears, nose, tongue, and skin—to the central nervous system, and (2) all the motor nerves, which relay messages from the central nervous system to all the skeletal muscles of the body. In short, the nerves of the somatic nervous system make it possible for you to sense your environment and to move, and they are primarily under conscious control.

The *autonomic nervous system* operates without any conscious control or awareness on your part. It transmits messages between the central nervous system and the glands, the cardiac (heart) muscle, and the smooth muscles (such as those in the large arteries and the gastrointestinal system), which are not normally under voluntary control. This system is further divided into two parts—the sympathetic and the parasympathetic nervous systems.

Any time you are under stress or faced with an emergency, the **sympathetic nervous system** automatically mobilizes the body's resources, preparing you for action. This physiological arousal produced by the sympathetic nervous system was named the *fight-or-flight response* by Walter Cannon (1929, 1935). If an ominous-looking stranger

◆ **peripheral nervous system (PNS)**

(peh-RIF-er-ul) The nerves connecting the central nervous system to the rest of the body.

◆ **sympathetic nervous system**

The division of the autonomic nervous system that mobilizes the body's resources during stress and emergencies, preparing the body for action.

FIGURE 2.10 **The Human Nervous System**

The nervous system is divided into two parts: the central nervous system and the peripheral nervous system. The diagram shows the relationships among the parts of the nervous system and provides a brief description of the functions of those parts.

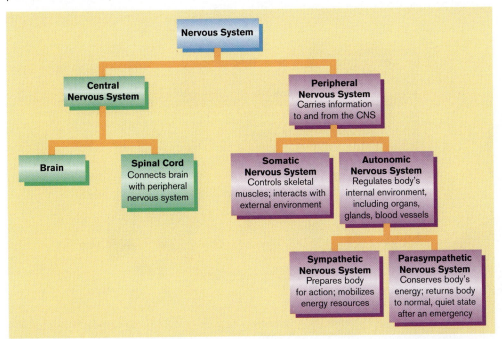

started following you down a dark, deserted street, your sympathetic nervous system would automatically go to work. Your heart would begin to pound, your pulse rate would increase rapidly, your breathing would quicken, and your digestive system would nearly shut down. The blood flow to your skeletal muscles would be enhanced, and all of your bodily resources would be made ready to handle the emergency.

Once the emergency is over, the **parasympathetic nervous system** brings these heightened bodily functions back to normal. As a result of its action, your heart stops pounding and slows to normal, your pulse rate and breathing slow down, and your digestive system resumes its normal functioning. As shown in Figure 2.11 (on page 60), the sympathetic and parasympathetic branches act as opposing but complementary forces in the autonomic nervous system. Their balanced functioning is essential for health and survival.

The Endocrine System

Most people think of the reproductive system when they hear the word *hormones*. Or they may associate hormones with particular physical changes, such as those of puberty, pregnancy, or menopause. However, these substances regulate many other physical and psychological functions, and their influence reaches far beyond the reproductive system.

The **endocrine system** is a series of ductless glands, located in various parts of the body, that manufacture and secrete the chemical substances known as **hormones,** which are manufactured and released in one part of the body but have an effect on other parts of the body. Hormones are released into the bloodstream and travel throughout the circulatory system, but each hormone performs its assigned job only when it connects with the body cells that have receptors for it. Some of the same chemical substances that are neurotransmitters act as hormones as well—norepinephrine and vasopressin, to name two. Figure 2.12 (on page 61) shows the glands in the endocrine system and their locations in the body.

◆ **parasympathetic nervous system**

The division of the autonomic nervous system that brings the heightened bodily responses back to normal following an emergency.

◆ **endocrine system**

(EN-duh-krin) A system of ductless glands in various parts of the body that manufacture hormones and secrete them into the bloodstream, thus affecting cells in other parts of the body.

◆ *What functions are associated with the various glands of the endocrine system?*

◆ **hormone**

A chemical substance that is manufactured and released in one part of the body and affects other parts of the body.

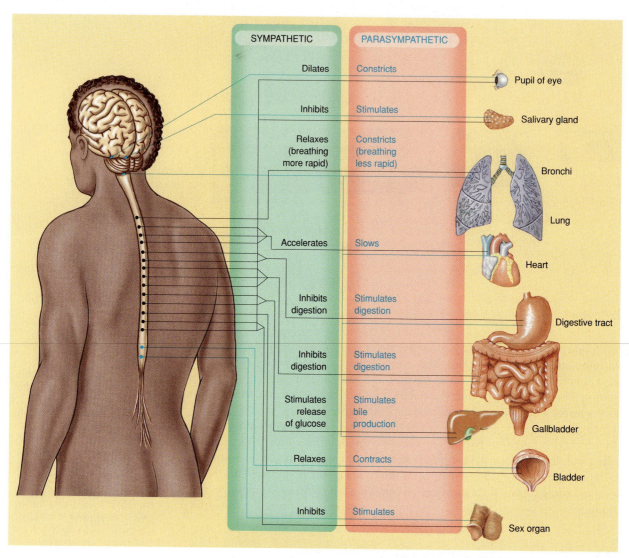

FIGURE 2.11 **The Autonomic Nervous System**

The autonomic nervous system consists of (1) the sympathetic nervous system, which mobilizes the body's resources during emergencies or stress, and (2) the parasympathetic nervous system, which brings the heightened bodily responses back to normal afterward. This diagram shows the opposite effects of the sympathetic and parasympathetic nervous systems on various parts of the body.

SYMPATHETIC	PARASYMPATHETIC	
Dilates	Constricts	Pupil of eye
Inhibits	Stimulates	Salivary gland
Relaxes (breathing more rapid)	Constricts (breathing less rapid)	Bronchi
		Lung
Accelerates	Slows	Heart
Inhibits digestion	Stimulates digestion	Digestive tract
Inhibits digestion	Stimulates digestion	
Stimulates release of glucose	Stimulates bile production	Gallbladder
Relaxes	Contracts	Bladder
Inhibits	Stimulates	Sex organ

◆ **pituitary gland**

The endocrine gland located in the brain that releases hormones that activate other endocrine glands as well as growth hormone; often called the "master gland."

◆ **pineal gland**

The endocrine gland that secretes the hormone that controls the sleep/wakefulness cycle.

◆ **parathyroid glands**

The endocrine glands that produce PTH, a hormone that helps the body absorb minerals from the diet.

The **pituitary gland** rests in the brain just below the hypothalamus and is controlled by it (see Figure 2.12). The pituitary is considered to be the "master gland" of the body because it releases the hormones that activate, or turn on, the other glands in the endocrine system—a big job for a tiny structure about the size of a pea. The pituitary also produces the hormone that is responsible for body growth (Howard et al., 1996). Too little of this powerful substance will make a person a dwarf; too much will produce a giant.

The **pineal gland** lies deep within the brain. Its function is to produce and regulate the hormone *melatonin*. As you will learn in Chapter 4, this hormone regulates sleep and wakefulness. Deficiencies are associated with jet lag and other disturbances of the sleep/wakefulness cycle.

The *thyroid gland* rests in the front, lower part of the neck just below the voice box (larynx). The thyroid produces the important hormone thyroxine, which regulates the rate at which food is metabolized, or transformed into energy. The **parathyroid glands** are attached to the left and right lobes of the thyroid. Parathyroid hormone (PTH) is involved in the absorption of calcium and magnesium from the diet and regulates the levels of these minerals in the bloodstream.

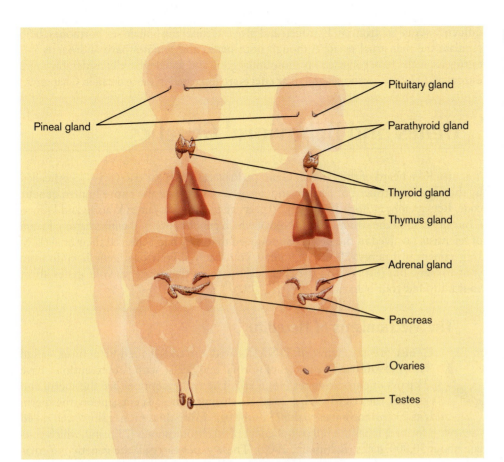

FIGURE 2.12

The Endocrine System

The endocrine system is a series of glands that manufacture and secrete hormones. The hormones travel through the circulatory system and have important effects on many bodily functions.

Pineal gland

Pituitary gland

Parathyroid gland

Thyroid gland

Thymus gland

Adrenal gland

Pancreas

Ovaries

Testes

The **thymus gland,** as you will learn in Chapter 10, produces hormones that are needed for the production of specialized white blood cells that circulate throughout the body and destroy microorganisms that can cause diseases. When the body is threatened by one of these invaders, the thymus gland signals the body to produce more of these cells. The **pancreas** regulates the body's blood sugar levels by releasing the hormones insulin and glucagon into the bloodstream. In people with diabetes, too little insulin is produced. Without insulin to break down the sugars in food, blood-sugar levels can get dangerously high.

The two **adrenal glands,** which rest just above the kidneys (as shown in Figure 2.12), produce epinephrine and norepinephrine. By activating the sympathetic nervous system, these two hormones play an important role in the fight-or-flight syndrome. A group of adrenal hormones called the corticoids are also involved in the fight-or-flight syndrome. Animal research suggests that these hormones contribute to both the emotion of rage and aggressive behavior by signaling the brain to maintain the fight-or-flight response long after the threat that initiated the response has passed (Kruk et al., 2004). Researchers speculate that the flood of corticoid hormones experienced by the brain while in the rage state and/or in the act of behaving aggressively is somehow pleasurable or reinforcing, so the brain allows the adrenals to keep pumping out corticoids even when they are no longer necessary. This property of the corticoids may potentially help explain why, for example, physical aggressors sometimes continue to beat their victims even after the victims have lost consciousness. Ultimately, the adrenals become exhausted under such conditions and are no longer capable of mobilizing the body's defensive systems (as discussed in Chapter 10).

The adrenals also produce small amounts of sex hormones. However, the **gonads** —the ovaries in females and the testes in males—have the primary responsibility for these hormones (refer to Figure 2.12). Activated by the pituitary gland, the gonads release the sex hormones that make reproduction possible and that are responsible for the secondary sex characteristics—pubic and underarm hair in both sexes, breasts in females, and facial hair and a deepened voice in males. Androgens, the male sex hormones,

◆ **thymus gland**

The endocrine gland that produces hormones that are essential to immune system functioning.

◆ **pancreas**

The endocrine gland responsible for regulating the amount of sugar in the bloodstream.

◆ **adrenal glands**

(ah-DREE-nal) A pair of endocrine glands that release hormones that prepare the body for emergencies and stressful situations and also release corticoids and small amounts of the sex hormones.

◆ **gonads**

The ovaries in females and the testes in males; endocrine glands that produce sex hormones.

influence sexual motivation. Estrogen and progesterone, the female sex hormones, help regulate the menstrual cycle. Although both males and females have androgens and estrogens, males have considerably more androgens, and females have considerably more estrogens. (The sex hormones and their effects are discussed in more detail in Chapter 9.)

Genes and Behavioral Genetics

You may have heard of the Human Genome Project, a 13-year enterprise spearheaded by the U.S. Department of Energy and devoted to mapping the entire human genetic code. Remarkably, in April 2003, only 50 years after scientists James Watson and Francis Crick discovered the structure of DNA (of which genes consist), the international team of scientists involved in the project announced that they had achieved their goal (U.S. Department of Energy, 2003). Of course, you received your own genetic code from your parents. But just how do the chemical messages that make up your genes affect your body and your behavior?

The Mechanisms of Heredity

◆ *What patterns of inheritance are evident in the transmission of genetic traits?*

Genes are segments of DNA located on rod-shaped structures called **chromosomes.** The nuclei of normal body cells, with two exceptions, have 23 pairs of chromosomes (46 in all). The two exceptions are the sperm and egg cells, each of which has 23 single chromosomes. At conception, the sperm adds its 23 chromosomes to the 23 of the egg. From this union, a single cell called a *zygote* is formed; it has the full complement of 46 chromosomes (23 pairs), which contain about 30,000 genes (Baltimore, 2000). These genes carry all the genetic information needed to make a human being. The Human Genome Project is aimed at identifying the functions of all the genes and their locations on the chromosomes.

Twenty-two of the 23 pairs of chromosomes are matching pairs, called *autosomes*, and each member of these pairs carries genes for particular physical and mental traits. The chromosomes in the 23rd pair are called *sex chromosomes* because they carry the genes that determine a person's sex. The sex chromosomes of females consist of two X chromosomes (XX); males have an X chromosome and a Y chromosome (XY). The egg cell always contains an X chromosome. Half of a man's sperm cells carry an X chromosome, and half carry a Y. Thus, the sex of an individual depends on which type of chromosome is carried by the sperm that fertilizes the egg. A single gene found only on the Y chromosome causes a fetus to become a male. This gene, which has been labeled Sry, orchestrates the development of the male sex organs (Capel, 2000).

Many traits are influenced by complementary gene pairs, one from the sperm and the other from the egg. In most cases, these gene pairs follow a set of inheritance rules known as the **dominant-recessive pattern.** The gene for curly hair, for example, is dominant over the gene for straight hair. Thus, a person having one gene for curly hair and one for straight hair will have curly hair, and people with straight hair have two recessive genes.

Several neurological and psychological disorders are associated with dominant or recessive genes. For example, *Huntington's chorea*, a degenerative disease of the nervous system is transmitted by a dominant gene, and some kinds of schizophrenia are linked to recessive genes. However, most of the traits of interest to psychologists follow more complex inheritance patterns.

In *polygenic inheritance*, many genes influence a particular characteristic. For example, skin color is determined by several genes. When one parent has dark skin and the other is fair-skinned, the child will have skin that is somewhere between the two. Many polygenic characteristics are subject to **multifactorial inheritance;** that is, they are influenced by both genes and environmental factors. For instance, a man's genes may allow him to reach a height of 6 feet, but if he suffers from malnutrition while still growing, his height may not reach its genetic potential. As you'll learn in later chapters, both intelligence (Chapter 7) and personality (Chapter 11) are believed to be polygenic and

◆ **genes**

The segments of DNA that are located on the chromosomes and are the basic units for the transmission of all hereditary traits.

◆ **chromosomes**

Rod-shaped structures in the nuclei of body cells, which contain all the genes and carry all the genetic information necessary to make a human being.

◆ **dominant-recessive pattern**

A set of inheritance rules in which the presence of a single dominant gene causes a trait to be expressed but two genes must be present for the expression of a recessive trait.

◆ **multifactorial inheritance**

A pattern of inheritance in which a trait is influenced by both genes and environmental factors.

multifactorial in nature. In addition, many neurological disorders, including Alzheimer's disease, are multifactorial (Bird, 2001).

Sex-linked inheritance involves the genes on the X and Y chromosomes. In females, the two X chromosomes function pretty much like the autosomes: If one carries a harmful gene, the other usually has a gene that offsets its effects. In males, however, if the single X chromosome carries a harmful gene, there is no offsetting gene on the Y chromosome because it is very small and carries only the genes needed to create the male body type. Consequently, disorders caused by genes on the X chromosome occur far more often in males than in females. For example, one fairly common sex-linked disorder you will read about in Chapter 3 is *red-green color blindness*. About 5% of men have the disorder, but less than 1% of women suffer from it (Neitz et al., 1996). About 1 in every 1,500 males and 1 in every 2,500 females have a far more serious sex-linked disorder called fragile-X syndrome, which can cause mental retardation (Adesman, 1996).

Behavioral Genetics

Behavioral genetics is a field of research that investigates the relative effects of heredity and environment—nature and nurture—on behavior (Plomin et al., 1997; Bouchard, 2004). In twin studies, behavioral geneticists study identical twins (monozygotic twins) and fraternal twins (dizygotic twins) to determine how much they resemble each other on a variety of characteristics. Identical twins have exactly the same genes because a single sperm of the father fertilizes a single egg of the mother, forming a cell that then splits and forms two human beings—"carbon copies." In the case of fraternal twins, two separate sperm cells fertilize two separate eggs that happen to be released at the same time during ovulation. Fraternal twins are no more alike genetically than any two siblings born to the same parents.

Twins who are raised together, whether identical or fraternal, have similar environments. If identical twins raised together are found to be more alike on a certain trait than fraternal twins raised together, then that trait is assumed to be more influenced by heredity. But if the identical and fraternal twin pairs do not differ on the trait, then that trait is assumed to be influenced more by environment.

In adoption studies, behavioral geneticists study children adopted shortly after birth. Researchers compare the children's abilities and personality traits to those of their adoptive parents and those of their biological parents. This strategy allows researchers to disentangle the effects of heredity and environment (Plomin et al., 1988).

Because heredity and environment work together to influence so many of the variables of interest to psychologists, you'll be reading a great deal more in later chapters about the debate concerning their relative influence.

◆ *What kinds of studies are done by behavioral geneticists?*

◆ **behavioral genetics**
A field of research that uses twin studies and adoption studies to investigate the relative effects of heredity and environment on behavior.

Looking Back We began this chapter by stating that adaptability is the hallmark of the relationship between mind and body. For instance, as the case of Phineas Gage illustrates, many areas of the adult brain are irrevocably committed to certain functions, leaving us with a more vulnerable but more efficient brain than we had as children. Nevertheless, even in the face of devastating injury, the brain may continue to function. The complementary functions of excitatory and inhibitory neurotransmitters enable our brains to respond appropriately to different kinds of situations. Individuals who have split-brain surgery function quite well in everyday life; only in certain kinds of tasks do they show any effects from the loss of interhemispheric communication. When we need to react to an emergency, our endocrine and peripheral nervous systems collaborate to produce the temporary burst of energy we need. Finally, although a few characteristics and diseases are fully determined by our genes, most of our psychological traits are shaped by both heredity and environment, a theme that will be emphasized repeatedly in the coming chapters.

Apply It 2.1 Why Consider Genetic Counseling?

Do you have relatives who suffer from genetic disorders? Surveys suggest that most relatives of individuals who suffer from such disorders or who have diseases, such as breast cancer, that may have a genetic basis are eager to know their own personal risk (Kinney et al., 2001). If you consult a genetic counselor, he or she will carry out a case study involving a detailed family history as well as genetic tests. The purpose of the study will be to estimate your risk of suffering from the same disorders and diseases as your relatives. The counselor will also estimate the likelihood that you will pass genetic defects on to your children.

The goal of genetic counseling is to help people make informed decisions about their own lives and those of their children. This goal is important because most people, especially those whose relatives have genetic disorders, greatly overestimate their own chances of having a genetic defect (Quaid et al., 2001). Generally, genetic counseling leads to more realistic perceptions and feelings of relief (Tercyak et al., 2001). Moreover, parents of children who suffer from genetic diseases report that they feel less guilt about transmitting the disease to their children after receiving genetic counseling (Collins et al., 2001).

However, genetic counseling also has a downside. Once an individual's disease risk is known, especially for life-threatening illnesses such as breast cancer, it may be difficult for him or her to get health insurance (Geer et al., 2001). Although there is no evidence that insurance companies deny coverage based on the results of genetic testing, 28 states have enacted laws to prevent them from doing so in the future (Steinberg, 2000). Geneticists and genetic counselors believe that such legislation is needed because genetic testing is rapidly making prediction of future illness more accurate.

Moreover, a growing number of people are seeking such testing. Experts point out that results from genetic testing do not differ much from the information on the family history that health insurers already use to accept or reject applicants (Steinberg, 2000). Thus, without legal protection in place, genetic testing could become a routine part of the application approval process for health insurance.

Another problem with genetic counseling is that many recipients report feeling overwhelmed by the amount of information provided by counselors and the sometimes difficult task of understanding the complex probability statements that often result from the case studies (Collins et al., 2001). Still, most people who seek genetic counseling say that, on balance, they are better off knowing the facts about potential genetic risks for themselves and their children (Collins et al., 2001).

Chapter 2 Summary

◆ The Neurons and Neurotransmitters p. 37

◆ How are messages transmitted through the nervous system? p. 37

The action potential is the sudden reversal (from a negative value to a positive value) of the resting potential on the cell membrane of a neuron; this reversal initiates the firing of a neuron.

◆ What are neurotransmitters, and what do they contribute to nervous system functioning? p. 40

Neurotransmitters are chemicals released into the synaptic cleft from the axon terminal of the sending neuron. Neurotransmitters regulate the flow of impulses from one neuron to the next.

◆ What are the functions of some of the major neurotransmitters? p. 41

The major neurotransmitters include acetylcholine, dopamine, norepinephrine, epinephrine, serotonin, glutamate, GABA, and endorphins. Acetylcholine (Ach) affects muscle fibers and is involved in learning. Dopamine affects learning, attention, movement, and reinforcement. Norepinephrine and epinephrine help regulate eating and energy release. Serotonin and GABA are inhibitory neurotransmitters that help us sleep; glutamate, an excitatory neurotransmitter, helps us stay awake. Endorphins are natural painkillers.

◆ The Central Nervous System p. 42

◆ Why is an intact spinal cord important to normal functioning? p. 43

The spinal cord must be intact so that sensory information can reach the brain and messages from the brain can reach muscles, glands, and other parts of the body.

◆ What are the vital functions handled by the brainstem? p. 43

The brainstem contains both the medulla, which controls heartbeat, breathing, blood pressure, coughing, and swallowing, and the reticular

formation, which plays a crucial role in arousal and attention.

◆ **What are the primary functions of the cerebellum?** p. 44

The cerebellum allows the body to execute smooth, skilled movements and regulates muscle tone and posture.

◆ **What important structure is located in the midbrain?** p. 44

The substantia nigra, located in the midbrain, controls unconscious motor actions, such as riding a bicycle.

◆ **What are the functions of the thalamus and the hypothalamus?** p. 45

The thalamus acts as a relay station for the information flowing into and out of the forebrain. The hypothalamus regulates hunger, thirst, sexual behavior, and internal body temperature.

◆ **Which mental processes and behaviors are influenced by the limbic system?** p. 45

The limbic system is a group of structures in the brain, including the amygdala and the hippocampus, that are collectively involved in emotional expression, memory, and motivation.

The Cerebrum p. 46

◆ **What are the components of the cerebrum?** p. 46

The cerebral hemispheres are the two halves of the cerebrum, connected by the corpus callosum and covered by the cerebral cortex, which is primarily responsible for higher mental processes.

◆ **Which psychological functions are associated with the frontal lobes?** p. 47

The frontal lobes contain (1) the motor cortex, which controls voluntary motor activity; (2) Broca's area, which functions in speech production; and (3) the frontal association areas, which are involved in thinking, motivation, planning for the future, impulse control, and emotional responses.

◆ **What is the somatosensory cortex, and what does it do?** p. 49

The somatosensory cortex is the front portion of the parietal lobes. It is the site where touch, pressure, temperature, and pain register in the cerebral cortex.

◆ **Why are the occipital lobes critical to vision?** p. 50

The occipital lobes contain the primary visual cortex, where vision registers in the cerebral cortex.

◆ **What are the major areas within the temporal lobes, and what are their functions?** p. 50

The temporal lobes contain (1) the primary auditory cortex; (2) Wernicke's area, which is involved in comprehending the spoken word and in formulating coherent speech and written language; and (3) the temporal association areas, where memories are stored and auditory stimuli are interpreted.

The Cerebral Hemispheres p. 51

◆ **What are the specialized functions of the left hemisphere?** p. 51

The left hemisphere controls the right side of the body, coordinates complex movements, and handles most of the language functions.

What are the specialized functions of the right hemisphere? p. 51

The right hemisphere controls the left side of the body. It is specialized for visual-spatial perception, the interpretation of nonverbal behavior, and the recognition and expression of emotion.

◆ **What do researchers mean by the term "split brain"?** p. 52

In the split-brain operation, a surgeon cuts the corpus callosum, preventing the transfer of information between the two cerebral hemispheres.

◆ **How are handedness and brain function related?** p. 53

In left-handers, the two sides of the brain are less specialized and new learning is more easily transferred. Learning disabilities and mental disorders are more common among left-handed individuals.

Discovering the Brain's Mysteries p. 54

◆ **What does the electroencephalogram (EEG) reveal about the brain?** p. 55

The electroencephalogram (EEG) is a record of brain-wave activity.

◆ **How are the CT scan and MRI helpful in the study of brain structure?** p. 55

Both the CT scan and MRI provide detailed images of brain structures. Functional MRI (fMRI) can also provide information about brain function.

◆ **How are the PET scan and newer imaging techniques used to study the brain?** p. 55

The PET scan reveals patterns of blood flow, oxygen use, and glucose metabolism in the brain. It can also show the action of drugs in the brain and other organs. SQUID and MEG measure magnetic changes to reveal neural activity within the brain as it occurs. DTI shows individual neuron bundles.

Age and Gender Differences in the Brain p. 56

◆ **What are the major processes at work in the developing brain?** p. 56

Growth spurts, synaptogenesis, myelination, and hemispheric specialization are the major processes that contribute to development.

◆ **How do the brains of males and females differ?** p. 57

Men's brains have a higher proportion of white matter in the left brain, while women's brains have equal proportions of gray and white matter in both hemispheres. Some tasks tap different areas in men's brains than in those of women.

◆ **How do aging and stroke-related damage affect the brain?** p. 58

Aging eventually leads to a reduction in the number of synapses. Stroke is the most common cause of damage to the adult brain.

The Peripheral Nervous System p. 58

◆ **What is the difference between the sympathetic and para-sympathetic nervous systems?** p. 58

The sympathetic nervous system mobilizes the body's resources during emergencies or during stress. The parasympathetic nervous system brings the heightened bodily responses back to normal after an emergency.

The Endocrine System p. 59

◆ What functions are associated with the various glands of the endocrine system? p. 59

The pituitary gland releases hormones that control other glands in the endocrine system and also releases a growth hormone. The thyroid gland produces thyroxine, which regulates metabolism. The pancreas produces insulin and glucagon and regulates blood-sugar levels. The adrenal glands release epinephrine and norepinephrine, which prepare the body for emergencies and stressful situations; these glands also release corticoids and small amounts of the sex hormones. The gonads are the sex glands, which produce the sex hormones and make reproduction possible.

Genes and Behavioral Genetics p. 62

◆ What patterns of inheritance are evident in the transmission of genetic traits? p. 62

Some genetic traits follow the dominant-recessive pattern, while others are polygenic and multifactorial.

◆ What kinds of studies are done by behavioral geneticists? p. 63

Behavioral genetics is the study of the relative effects of heredity and environment on behavior. Researchers in this field use twin studies and adoption studies.

◆ SECTION ONE: Chapter Review

The Neurons and Neurotransmitters (pp. 37–42)

1. The branchlike extensions of neurons that act as receivers of signals from other neurons are the
   a. dendrites.
   c. neurotransmitters.
   b. axons.
   d. cell bodies.

2. _____ support neurons, supplying them with nutrients and carrying away their waste products.

3. The junction where the axon of a sending neuron communicates with a receiving neuron is called the
   a. reuptake site.
   c. synapse.
   b. receptor site.
   d. axon terminal.

4. When a neuron fires, neurotransmitters are released from the synaptic vesicles in the _____ terminal into the synaptic cleft.
   a. dendrite
   c. receptor
   b. cell body's
   d. axon

5. The (resting, action) potential is the firing of a neuron that results when the charge within the neuron becomes more positive than the charge outside the cell membrane.

6. Receptor sites on the receiving neuron
   a. receive any available neurotransmitter molecules.
   b. receive only neurotransmitter molecules of specific shapes.
   c. can only be influenced by neurotransmitters from a single neuron.
   d. are located only on the dendrites.

7. The neurotransmitter called *acetylcholine* is involved in
   a. memory.
   b. motor function.
   c. rapid eye movement during sleep.
   d. all of the above.

8. _____ affects eating habits by stimulating the intake of carbohydrates.

9. _____ are neurotransmitters that act as natural painkillers.

10. Both _____ and _____ have been associated with psychological disorders.

The Central Nervous System (pp. 42–46)

11. Match the brain structure with its description.
    ___ (1) connects the brain with the peripheral nervous system
    ___ (2) controls heart rate, breathing, and blood pressure
    ___ (3) consists of the medulla, the pons, and the reticular formation
    ___ (4) influences attention and arousal
    ___ (5) coordinates complex body movements
    ___ (6) serves as a relay station for sensory information flowing into the brain
    ___ (7) controls unconscious movements
    a. medulla
    b. spinal cord
    c. reticular formation
    d. thalamus
    e. cerebellum
    f. brainstem
    g. substantia nigra

12. The hypothalmus regulates all the following except
    a. internal body temperature.
    b. coordinated movement.
    c. hunger and thirst.
    d. sexual behavior.

13. The part of the limbic system primarily involved in the formation of memories is the (amygdala, hippocampus).

14. The _____ is associated with emotions, and the _____ is involved in memory.

The Cerebrum (pp. 46–51)

15. What is the thick band of fibers connecting the two cerebral hemispheres?
    a. cortex
    c. cerebrum
    b. corpus callosum
    d. motor cortex

16. The outer covering of the cerebrum is the
    a. cerebral cortex.
    c. myelin sheath.
    b. cortex callosum.
    d. white matter.

17. Match the lobes with the brain areas they contain.
    _____ **(1)** primary auditory cortex
    _____ **(2)** primary visual cortex
    _____ **(3)** motor cortex
    _____ **(4)** somatosensory cortex
    a. frontal lobes
    b. parietal lobes
    c. occipital lobes
    d. temporal lobes

18. Match the specialized area with the appropriate description of function.
    _____ **(1)** hearing registers
    _____ **(2)** vision registers
    _____ **(3)** touch, pressure, and temperature register
    _____ **(4)** voluntary movement
    _____ **(5)** thinking, motivation, impulse control
    a. primary visual cortex
    b. motor cortex
    c. association areas
    d. auditory cortex
    e. somatosensory cortex

The Cerebral Hemispheres (pp. 51–54)

19. Match the hemisphere with the specialized abilities usually associated with it.
    _____ **(1)** visual-spatial skills
    _____ **(2)** speech
    _____ **(3)** recognition and expression of emotion
    _____ **(4)** singing
    _____ **(5)** mathematics
    a. right hemisphere
    b. left hemisphere

20. Which of these statements is *not* true of the split-brain operation?
    a. It is used on people with severe epilepsy.
    b. It provides a means of studying the functions of the individual hemispheres.
    c. It causes major changes in intelligence, personality, and behavior.
    d. It makes transfer of information between hemispheres impossible.

21. Research suggests that the prevalance of right-handedness in the human population is caused by (genetic, cultural) factors.

Discovering the Brain's Mysteries (pp. 54–56)

22. Match the brain-wave pattern with the state associated with it.
    _____ **(1)** slow-wave (deep) sleep
    _____ **(2)** deep relaxation while awake
    _____ **(3)** physical or mental activity
    a. beta wave   **c.** alpha wave
    b. delta wave

23. The CT scan and MRI are used to
    a. show the amount of activity in various parts of the brain.
    b. produce images of the brain's structures.
    c. measure electrical activity in the brain.
    d. observe neural communication at synapses.

24. Which of the following reveals the electrical activity of the brain by producing a record of brain waves?
    a. electroencephalogram   **c.** PET scan
    b. CT scan   **d.** MRI

25. Which of the following reveals brain activity and function, rather than the structure of the brain?
    a. CT scan   **c.** PET scan
    b. EEG   **d.** MRI

26. Which of the following reveals both brain structure and brain activity?
    a. MRI   **c.** fMRI
    b. PET scan   **d.** CT scan

Age and Gender Differences in the Brain (pp. 56–58)

27. Synaptic development involves growth of
    a. dendrites.
    b. axons.
    c. both dendrites and axons.

28. Two developmental processes that contribute to behavioral differences between children and adults are _____ and _____.

29. Men have a lower proportion of _____ in the right hemisphere than women do.

30. Tasks that require _____ and _____ stimulate different areas of the brain in men and women.

31. As adults get older, brain weight (increases, decreases).

32. _____ is the most common cause of injury to the adult brain.

The Peripheral Nervous System (pp. 58–59)

33. The _____ nervous system connects the brain and spinal cord to the rest of the body.
    a. central   **c.** somatic
    b. peripheral   **d.** autonomic

34. The _____ nervous system mobilizes the body's resources during times of stress; the _____ nervous system brings the heightened bodily responses back to normal when the emergency is over.
    a. somatic; autonomic
    b. autonomic; somatic
    c. sympathetic; parasympathetic
    d. parasympathetic; sympathetic

The Endocrine System (pp. 59–62)

35. Match the endocrine gland with the appropriate description.
    ____ **(1)** keeps body's metabolism in balance
    ____ **(2)** acts as a master gland that activates the other glands
    ____ **(3)** regulates the blood sugar
    ____ **(4)** makes reproduction possible
    ____ **(5)** releases hormones that prepare the body for emergencies
    ____ **(6)** regulates sleep
    a. pituitary gland   **d.** thyroid gland
    b. adrenal glands   **e.** pancreas
    c. gonads   **f.** pineal gland

Genes and Behavioral Genetics (pp. 62–63)

36. A _____ gene will not be expressed unless an individual carries two copies of it.

37. Characteristics that are affected by both genes and environment are said to be
    a. polygenic.
    b. dominant.
    c. recessive.
    d. multifactorial.

38. Researchers use _____ and _____ to examine the effects of heredity and environment.

◆ SECTION TWO: Label the Brain

Identify each of the numbered parts in the brain diagram.

1. _____
2. _____
3. _____
4. _____
5. _____
6. _____
7. _____
8. _____
9. _____

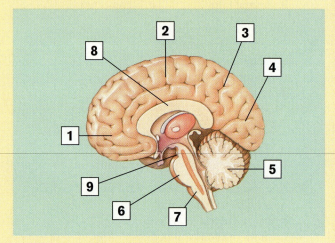

◆ SECTION THREE: Fill In the Blank

1. The _____ is the part of the neuron that receives chemical messages from other neurons.

2. Dopamine, serotonin, and acetylcholine are all examples of _____.

3. The amygdala and the hippocampus are structures in the _____ system.

4. The _____ _____ _____ is at the back of the occipital lobe.

5. The somatosensory cortex is located in the _____ lobe.

6. Phineas Gage suffered damage to his _____ lobe.

7. Broca's area and Wernicke's area are important for language and are located in the _____ hemisphere.

8. The longest part of a neuron is called the _____.

9. The central nervous system is composed of the _____ and the _____.

10. The fight-or-flight response is related to the activity of the _____ nervous system.

11. The _____ monitors and regulates internal body temperature.

12. The _____ _____ occurs when the neuron ion channels open and allow a sudden influx of positive ions into the axon.

13. _____ aphasia is an impairment in the ability to produce speech sounds or, in extreme cases, an inability to speak at all.

14. The limbic system structure thought to play a central role in the formation of memories is the _____.

15. The primary auditory cortex is located in the _____ lobes.

16. You can write notes in class or execute other smooth, skilled body movements because of the action of the _____.

17. The somatic and the autonomic nervous systems are the two primary divisions of the _____ nervous system.

18. People who have Parkinson's disease may have damage to neurons whose nuclei are in the _____.

19. In carrying out navigational tasks, men rely more on the _____ than women do.

20. _____ is a sex-linked disorder that causes mental retardation.

21. _____ is lateralized to the left hemisphere in the fetal brain, just as it is in children and adults.

◆ **SECTION FOUR: Comprehensive Practice Test**

1. Phineas Gage changed from a polite, dependable, well-liked railroad foreman to a rude and impulsive person who could no longer plan realistically for the future after he suffered serious damage to his
   a. occipital lobe.   c. medulla.
   b. frontal lobe.   d. cerebellum.

2. Afferent is to efferent as
   a. sensory is to sensation.
   b. sensation is to perception.
   c. motor is to sensory.
   d. sensory is to motor.

3. _____ plays an important role in regulating mood, sleep, impulsivity, aggression, and appetite.
   a. Dopamine   c. Acetylcholine
   b. Norepinephrine   d. Serotonin

4. Neurons can conduct messages faster if they have
   a. an axon with a myelin sheath.
   b. a positive resting potential.
   c. more than one cell body.
   d. fewer dendrites.

5. The electrical charge inside a neuron is about −70 millivolts and is known as the _____ potential.
   a. action   c. resting
   b. refractory   d. impulse

6. The main divisions of the nervous system are the _____ and the _____ systems.
   a. somatic; autonomic
   b. central; peripheral
   c. brain; spinal cord
   d. sympathetic; parasympathetic

7. The structure that is located above the brainstem and serves as a relay station for information to and from the higher brain centers is the
   a. pituitary gland.   c. thalamus.
   b. hypothalamus.   d. hippocampus.

8. The structure that is located in the brainstem and is important for basic life functions such as heartbeat and breathing is the
   a. pons.   c. hypothalamus.
   b. medulla.   d. amygdala.

9. The _____ is sometimes referred to as the body's thermostat because it controls temperature, hunger, thirst, and emotional behaviors.
   a. corpus callosum   c. cerebellum
   b. pituitary gland   d. hypothalamus

10. The lobe that contains the primary visual cortex is the
    a. parietal lobe.   c. temporal lobe.
    b. occipital lobe.   d. frontal lobe.

11. The primary motor cortex is located in the _____ lobe.
    a. frontal   c. temporal
    b. occipital   d. occulovisual

12. The pituitary gland, known as the master gland, is part of the _____ system.
    a. somatic   c. endocrine
    b. peripheral nervous d. central nervous

13. A researcher interested in getting information about the brain's activity based on the amount of oxygen and glucose consumed should use a(n)
    a. MRI.   c. PET scan.
    b. EEG.   d. CT scan.

14. The _____ nervous system controls skeletal muscles and allows the body to interact with the external environment.
    a. autonomic   c. sympathetic
    b. parasympathetic   d. somatic

15. Damage to Broca's area will result in a type of aphasia in which patients cannot speak. (true/false)

16. Functional MRI (fMRI) reveals both brain structure and brain activity. (true/false)

17. _____ isn't lateralized to the right hemisphere until age 8 or so.

18. Women are more likely than men to process navigational tasks in the _____ lobe of the brain.

19. Red-green color blindness is caused by a defective gene on the _____.

1. Much of the brain research you have read about in this chapter was carried out using animals. In many studies, it is necessary to euthanize animals to study their brain tissues directly. Many people object to this practice, but others say it is justified because it advances knowledge about the brain. Prepare arguments to support both of the following positions:

   a. The use of animals in brain research projects is ethical and justifiable because of the possible benefits to humankind.

   b. The use of animals in brain research projects is not ethical or justifiable on the grounds of possible benefits to humankind.

2. How would your life change if you had a massive stroke affecting your left hemisphere? How would it change if the stroke damaged your right hemisphere? Which stroke would be more tragic for you, and why?

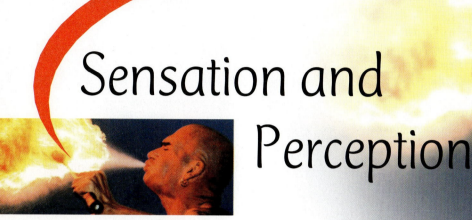

Sensation and Perception

chapter 3

The Process of Sensation
◆ How is sensory information transmitted to the brain?

Vision
◆ How does each part of the eye function in vision?
◆ What path does visual information take from the retina to the primary visual cortex?
◆ How do we detect the difference between one color and another?
◆ What two major theories attempt to explain color vision?

Hearing
◆ What determines the pitch and loudness of a sound, and how is each quality measured?
◆ How do the outer ear, middle ear, and inner ear function in hearing?
◆ What two major theories attempt to explain hearing?

Smell and Taste
◆ What path does a smell message take from the nose to the brain?
◆ What are the primary taste sensations, and how are they detected?

The Skin Senses
◆ How does the skin provide sensory information?
◆ What is the function of pain, and how is pain influenced by psychological factors, culture, and endorphins?

The Spatial Orientation Senses
◆ What kinds of information do the kinesthetic and vestibular senses provide?

Influences on Perception
◆ What is gained and what is lost in the process of attention?

◆ How does prior knowledge influence perception?
◆ How does information from multiple sources aid perception?

Principles of Perception
◆ What are the principles that govern perceptual organization?
◆ What are some of the binocular and monocular depth cues?
◆ How does the brain perceive motion?
◆ What are three types of puzzling perceptions?

Unusual Perceptual Experiences
◆ In what ways does subliminal perception influence behavior?
◆ What have studies of ESP shown?

What would it be like to hear a color or see a song? If you have the condition known as *synesthesia,* the capacity for experiencing unusual sensations along with ordinary ones, you may know. For instance, Sean Day sees the color blue simultaneously with the taste of beef, and an orange blob appears in his field of vision when he consumes foods that have been seasoned with ginger (Carpenter, 2001). Day's unusual sensations do not take the place of those that are experienced by most people in response to these stimuli. Instead, the atypical sensory experiences of synesthetes such as Day supplement the more typical responses.

In the past, many psychologists regarded synesthesia as the result of an overactive imagination or some kind of learned association. In 1993, however, neurologist Richard Cytowic published a popular book called *The Man Who Tasted Shapes,* which sparked interest in the use of modern brain-imaging techniques to study the phenomenon. In the years that followed, many such studies were carried out. The majority suggested that synesthesia has a neurological basis (Cytowic, 2002). In other words, when Sean Day bites into a juicy piece of pot roast, his brain quite literally "sees" blue, just as it would if a blue object were placed in front of his eyes.

Research also indicates that the most common type of synesthesia is one in which individuals sense colors in response to spoken words, known as "colored hearing" (Carpenter, 2001). Neuroimaging studies suggest that colored hearing is not the result of learned associations. Rather, different brain areas are active in synethetes who associate words with colors than in research participants who have been trained to consciously engage in such associations (Nunn et al., 2002).

A number of hypotheses have been proposed to explain synesthesia. Some psychologists speculate that all newborn brains are synesthetic and that the capacity for synesthesia is lost in most people as the various brain areas become more specialized over the years of childhood and adolescence (Mondloch & Maurer, 2004). However, some drugs produce temporary synesthesia, leading a few scientists to hypothesize that the neural connections that underlie synesthetic experiences are present in the brains of both synesthetes and nonsynesthetes alike (Grossenbacher & Lovelace, 2001). Nevertheless, the jury is still out with regard to both the origin and the neurological basis of synesthesia (Carpenter, 2001). A great deal more research needs to be done on this phenomenon.

Studies of synesthesia illustrate the fact that sensing and perceiving stimuli are separate processes. **Sensation** is the process through which the senses pick up visual, auditory, and other sensory stimuli and transmit them to the brain. **Perception** is the process by which the brain actively organizes and interprets sensory information. Sensation furnishes the raw material of sensory experience, whereas perception provides the finished product. Synesthesia is of interest to neuroscientists because it is one of several phenomena that involve perception without sensation. We will return to the topic of unusual sensory and perceptual experiences at the end of the chapter. First, however, we will examine how sensation and perception work in most people most of the time.

The Process of Sensation

◆ *How is sensory information transmitted to the brain?*

◆ **sensation**

The process through which the senses pick up visual, auditory, and other sensory stimuli and transmit them to the brain.

◆ **perception**

The process by which the brain actively organizes and interprets sensory information.

◆ **absolute threshold**

The minimum amount of sensory stimulation that can be detected 50% of the time.

◆ **difference threshold**

A measure of the smallest increase or decrease in a physical stimulus that is required to produce a difference in sensation that is noticeable 50% of the time.

◆ **just noticeable difference (JND)**

The smallest change in sensation that a person is able to detect 50% of the time.

What is the softest sound you can hear, the dimmest light you can see, the most diluted substance you can taste? Researchers in sensory psychology have performed many experiments over the years to answer these questions. Their research has established measures for the senses known as absolute thresholds. Just as the threshold of a doorway is the dividing point between being outside a room and inside, the **absolute threshold** of a sense marks the difference between not being able to perceive a stimulus and being just barely able to perceive it. Psychologists have arbitrarily defined this absolute threshold as the minimum amount of sensory stimulation that can be detected 50% of the time. The absolute thresholds for vision, hearing, taste, smell, and touch are illustrated in Figure 3.1.

If you are listening to music, the very fact that you can hear it means that the absolute threshold has been crossed. But how much must the volume be turned up or down for you to notice a difference? Or, if you are carrying some bags of groceries, how much weight must be added or taken away for you to be able to sense that your load is heavier or lighter? The **difference threshold** is a measure of the smallest increase or decrease in a physical stimulus that is required to produce the **just noticeable difference (JND)**. The JND is the smallest change in sensation that a person is able to detect 50% of the time. If you were holding a 5-pound weight and 1 pound was added, you could easily notice the difference. But if you were holding 100 pounds and 1 additional pound was added, you could not sense the difference. Why not?

More than 150 years ago, researcher Ernst Weber (1795–1878) observed that the JND for all the senses depends on a proportion or percentage of change in a stimulus rather than on a fixed amount of change. This observation became known as **Weber's law.** A weight you are holding must increase or decrease by 1/50, or 2%, for you to notice the difference; thus, adding 1 pound to 100 pounds should not be noticed because the additional weight does not add the required 2% change. In contrast, if you were listening to music, you would notice a difference if a tone became slightly higher or lower in pitch by about only 0.33%. According to Weber's law, the greater the original stimulus, the more it must be increased or decreased for the difference to be noticeable.

FIGURE 3.1   **Absolute Thresholds**

Absolute thresholds have been established for humans for vision, hearing, taste, smell, and touch.

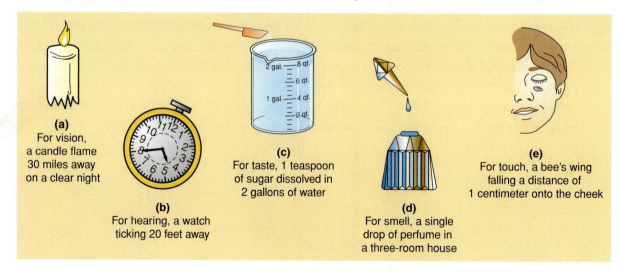

(a)
For vision, a candle flame 30 miles away on a clear night

(b), a watch ticking 20 feet away

(c)
For taste, 1 teaspoon of sugar dissolved in 2 gallons of water

(d)
For smell, a single drop of perfume in a three-room house

(e)
For touch, a bee's wing falling a distance of 1 centimeter onto the cheek

Weber's law best applies to people with average sensitivities and to sensory stimuli that are neither very strong (loud thunder) nor very weak (a faint whisper). For instance, expert wine tasters would know if a particular vintage was a little too sweet, even if its sweetness varied by only a fraction of the 20% necessary for changes in taste. Furthermore, people who have lost one sensory ability often gain greater sensitivity in others. For example, one study found that children with early-onset blindness were more capable of correctly labeling 25 common odors than were sighted children, while another found that congenitally deaf students possessed motion-perception abilities superior to those of hearing students (Bavelier et al., 2000; Rosenbluth et al., 2000).

The sense organs provide only the beginning of sensation, which must be completed by the brain. The body's sense organs are equipped with highly specialized cells called **sensory receptors,** which detect and respond to one type of sensory stimuli—light, sound waves, odors, and so on. The form of each type of sensory receptor is unique.

What is the dimmest light this lifeguard could perceive in the darkness? Researchers in sensory psychology have performed many experiments over the years to answer such questions. Their research has established measures known as absolute thresholds. Just as the threshold of a doorway is the dividing point between being outside a room and being inside it, the absolute threshold of a sense marks the difference between not being able to perceive a stimulus and being just barely able to perceive it.

Through a process known as **transduction,** the sensory receptors convert the sensory stimulation into neural impulses, the electrochemical language of the brain. The neural impulses are then transmitted to precise locations in the brain, such as the primary visual cortex for vision or the primary auditory cortex for hearing. We experience a sensation only when the appropriate part of the brain is stimulated. The sense receptors provide the essential link between the physical sensory world and the brain.

After a time, the sensory receptors grow accustomed to constant, unchanging levels of stimuli—sights, sounds, or smells—so we notice them less and less, or not at all. For example, smokers become accustomed to the smell of cigarette smoke in their homes and on their clothing. This process is known as **sensory adaptation.** Even though it reduces our sensory awareness, sensory adaptation enables us to shift our attention to what is most important at any given moment. However, sensory adaptation is not likely to occur in the presence of a very strong stimulus, such as the smell of ammonia, an ear-splitting sound, or the taste of rancid food.

 ## Vision

Vision is the most studied of all the senses. One thing vision researchers have known for a long time is that there is a great deal more information in the sensory environment than our eyes can take in. Our eyes can respond only to visible light waves, which form a small subgroup of *electromagnetic waves,* a band called the **visible spectrum** (see Figure 3.2, on page 76). These waves are measured in **wavelengths,** the distance from the peak of one wave to the peak of the next. The shortest light waves we can see appear violet, while the longest visible waves appear red. But sight is much more than just response to light.

◆ **Weber's law**

The law stating that the just noticeable difference (JND) for all the senses depends on a proportion or percentage of change in a stimulus rather than on a fixed amount of change.

◆ **sensory receptors**

Highly specialized cells in the sense organs that detect and respond to one type of sensory stimuli—light, sound, or odor, for example—and transduce (convert) the stimuli into neural impulses.

◆ **transduction**

The process through which sensory receptors convert the sensory stimulation into neural impulses.

◆ **sensory adaptation**

The process in which sensory receptors grow accustomed to constant, unchanging levels of stimuli over time.

◆ **visible spectrum**

The narrow band of electromagnetic waves that are visible to the human eye.

◆ **wavelength**

A measure of the distance from the peak of a light wave to the peak of the next.

FIGURE 3.2

The Electromagnetic Spectrum

Human eyes can perceive only a very thin band of electromagnetic waves, known as the visible spectrum.

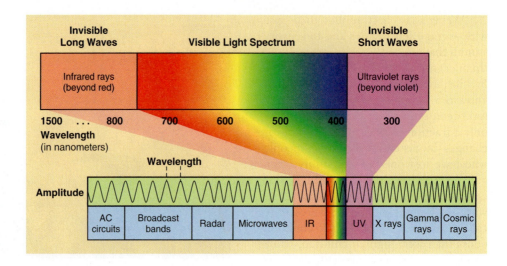

The Eye

The globe-shaped human eyeball, shown in Figure 3.3, measures about 1 inch in diameter. Curving outward from the eye's surface is the **cornea**—the tough, transparent, protective layer covering the front of the eye. The cornea performs the first step in vision by bending the light rays inward. It directs the light rays through the *pupil*, the small, dark opening in the center of the *iris*, or colored part of the eye. The iris dilates and contracts the pupil to regulate the amount of light entering the eye.

Suspended just behind the iris and the pupil, the **lens** is composed of many thin layers and looks like a transparent disk. The lens performs the task of focusing on viewed objects. It flattens as it focuses on objects at a distance and becomes more spherical, bulging in the center, as it focuses on close objects. This flattening and bulging action of the lens is known as **accommodation**. With age, the lens loses the ability to change its shape to accommodate for near vision, a condition called *presbyopia* ("old eyes"). This is why many people over age 40 must hold a book or newspaper at arm's length or use reading glasses to magnify the print.

The lens focuses the incoming image onto the **retina**—a layer of tissue about the size of a small postage stamp and as thin as onion skin, located on the inner surface of the eyeball and containing the sensory receptors for vision. The image that is projected onto the retina is upside down and reversed from left to right, as illustrated in Figure 3.4 (on page 78.)

In some people, the distance through the eyeball (from the lens to the retina) is either too short or too long for proper focusing. Nearsightedness (*myopia*) occurs when the lens focuses images of distant objects in front of, rather than on, the retina. A person with this condition will be able to see near objects clearly, but distant images will be blurred. Farsightedness (*hyperopia*) occurs when the lens focuses images of close objects behind, rather than on, the retina. The individual is able to see far objects clearly, but close objects are blurred. Both conditions are correctable with eyeglasses or contact lenses or by surgical procedures.

At the back of the retina is a layer of light-sensitive receptor cells—the **rods** and the **cones.** Named for their shapes, the rods look like slender cylinders, and the cones appear shorter and more rounded. There are about 120 million rods and 6 million cones in each retina. The cones are the receptor cells that enable us to see color and fine detail in adequate light, but they do not function in very dim light. By contrast, the rods in the human eye are extremely sensitive, allowing the eye to respond to as few as five photons of light (Hecht et al., 1942).

A substance called *rhodopsin* present in the rods enables us to adapt to variations in light. Rhodopsin has two components: *opsin* and *retinal* (a chemical similar to Vitamin A). In bright light, opsin and retinal break apart, as the process of *light adaptation* takes place. During *dark adaptation*, opsin and retinal bond to one another, re-forming

◆ cornea

(KOR-nee-uh) The tough, transparent, protective layer that covers the front of the eye and bends light rays inward through the pupil.

◆ lens

The transparent disk-shaped structure behind the iris and the pupil that changes shape as it focuses on objects at varying distances.

◆ accommodation

The flattening and bulging action of the lens as it focuses images of objects on the retina.

◆ retina

The layer of tissue that is located on the inner surface of the eyeball and contains the sensory receptors for vision.

◆ rods

The light-sensitive receptor cells in the retina that look like slender cylinders and allow the eye to respond to as few as five photons of light.

◆ cones

The light-sensitive receptor cells in the retina that enable humans to see color and fine detail in adequate light but do not function in very dim light.

FIGURE 3.3   **The Major Parts of the Human Eye**

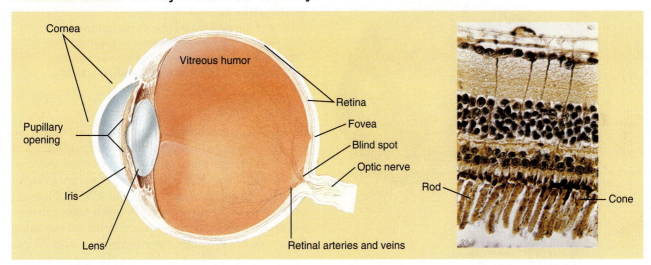

rhodopsin. As you've no doubt experienced, when you move from bright light to total darkness, as when you enter a darkened movie theater, you are momentarily blind until the opsin and retinal recombine. Similarly, when you leave the theater again, you become temporarily blind until the two substances break apart once again.

At the center of the retina is the **fovea,** a small area about the size of the period at the end of this sentence. When you look directly at an object, the image of the object is focused on the center of your fovea. The fovea contains no rods but has about 30,000 cones tightly packed together, providing the clearest and sharpest area of vision in the whole retina. The cones are most densely packed at the center of the fovea; their density decreases sharply just a few degrees beyond the fovea's center and then levels off more gradually to the periphery of the retina.

◆ **fovea**
(FO-vee-uh) A small area at the center of the retina that provides the clearest and sharpest vision because it has the largest concentration of cones.

Vision and the Brain

As you can see in Figure 3.4, the brain is responsible for converting the upside-down retinal images into meaningful visual information. But the first stages of neural processing actually take place in the retina itself. The rods and cones transduce, or change, light waves into neural impulses that are fed to the bipolar cells, which, in turn, pass the impulses along to the ganglion cells. The approximately 1 million axonlike extensions of the ganglion cells are bundled together in a pencil-sized cable that extends through the wall of the retina, leaving the eye and leading to the brain. There are no rods or cones where the cable runs through the retinal wall, so this point is a **blind spot** in each eye.

Beyond the retinal wall of each eye, the cable becomes the **optic nerve** (refer to Figure 3.3). The two optic nerves come together at the *optic chiasm,* a point where some of their nerve fibers cross to the opposite side of the brain. The nerve fibers from the right half of each retina go to the right hemisphere, and those from the left half of each retina go to the left hemisphere. This crossing over is important because it allows visual information from a single eye to be represented in the primary visual cortex of both hemispheres of the brain. Moreover, it plays an important part in depth perception.

From the optic chiasm, the optic nerve fibers extend to the thalamus, where they form synapses with neurons that transmit the impulses to the **primary visual cortex,** the part of the brain that is devoted to visual processing. Thanks to researchers David Hubel and Torsten Wiesel (1959, 1979; Hubel, 1963, 1995), who won a Nobel Prize for their work in 1981, we know a great deal about how specialized the neurons of the primary visual cortex are. By inserting tiny microelectrodes into single cells in the visual cortexes of cats, Hubel and Wiesel (1959) were able to determine what was happening in individual cells when the cats were exposed to different kinds of visual stimuli. They

◆ *What path does visual information take from the retina to the primary visual cortex?*

◆ **blind spot**
The point in each retina where there are no rods or cones because the cable of ganglion cells is extending through the retinal wall.

◆ **optic nerve**
The nerve that carries visual information from each retina to both sides of the brain.

◆ **primary visual cortex**
The part of the brain in which visual information is processed.

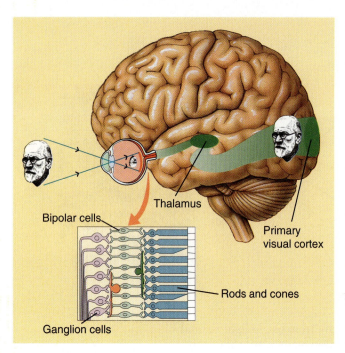

FIGURE 3.4 From Retinal Image to Meaningful Information
Because of the way the lens alters light rays to produce a clear image, images are upside down on the retina. The brain's visual processing system takes the upside-down retinal image and flips it so it is properly orientated.

Thalamus

Bipolar cells

Primary visual cortex

Rods and cones

Ganglion cells

discovered that each neuron responded only to specific patterns. Some neurons responded only to lines and angles, while others fired only when the cat saw a vertical or horizontal line. Still others were responsive to nothing but right angles or lines of specific lengths. Neurons of this type are known as **feature detectors**, and they are already coded at birth to make their unique responses. Yet we see whole images, not collections of isolated features, because visual perceptions are complete only when the primary visual cortex transmits the millions of pieces of visual information it receives to other areas in the brain, where they are combined and assembled into whole visual images (Perry & Zeki, 2000).

The major structures of the visual system are summarized in *Review and Reflect 3.1.*

Color Vision

◆ *How do we detect the difference between one color and another?*

Why does the skin of an apple appear to be red, while its flesh is perceived as an off-white color? Remember, what we actually see is reflected light. Some light waves striking an object are absorbed by it; others are reflected from it. So, why does an apple's skin look red? If you hold a red apple in bright light, light waves of all the different wavelengths strike the apple, but more of the longer red wavelengths of light are reflected from the apple's skin. The shorter wavelengths are absorbed, so you see only the reflected red. Bite into the apple, and it looks off-white. Why? You see the near-white color because, rather than being absorbed, almost all of the wavelengths of the visible spectrum are reflected from the inside part of the apple. The presence of all visible wavelengths gives the sensation of a near-white color. If an object does indeed reflect 100% of visible wavelengths, it appears to be pure white.

Our everyday visual experience goes far beyond the colors in the rainbow. We can detect thousands of subtle color shadings. What produces these fine color distinctions? Researchers have identified three dimensions of light that combine to provide the rich world of color we experience: The chief dimension is **hue**, which refers to the specific color perceived—red, blue, or yellow, for example. **Saturation** refers to the purity of a color; a color becomes less saturated, or less pure, as other wavelengths of light are mixed with it. **Brightness** refers to the intensity of the light energy that is perceived as a color and corresponds to the amplitude (height) of the color's light wave.

◆ **feature detectors**

Neurons in the brain that respond only to specific visual patterns (for example, to lines or angles).

◆ **hue**

The dimension of light that refers to the specific color perceived.

◆ **saturation**

The purity of a color, or the degree to which the light waves producing it are of the same wavelength.

Theories of Color Vision

◆ *What two major theories attempt to explain color vision?*

Scientists know that the cones are responsible for color vision, but exactly how do they work to produce color sensations? Two major theories have been offered to explain color vision, and both were formulated before the development of laboratory technology capable of testing them. The **trichromatic theory**, first proposed by Thomas Young in 1802, was modified by Hermann von Helmholtz about 50 years later. This theory states that there are three kinds of cones in the retina and that each kind makes a maximal chemical response to one of three colors—blue, green, or red. Research conducted in the 1950s and the 1960s

REVIEW and REFLECT 3.1

Major Structures of the Visual System

STRUCTURE	FUNCTION
Cornea	Translucent covering on the front of the eyeball that bends light rays entering the eye inward through the pupil
Iris	Colored part of the eye that adjusts to maintain a constant amount of light entering the eye through the pupil
Pupil	Opening in the center of the iris through which light rays enter the eye
Lens	Transparent disk-shaped structure behind the pupil that adjusts its shape to allow focusing on objects at varying distances
Retina	Layer of tissue on the inner surface of the eye that contains sensory receptors for vision
Rods	Specialized receptor cells in the retina that are sensitive to light changes
Cones	Specialized receptor cells in the retina that enable humans to see fine detail and color in adequate light
Fovea	Small area at the center of the retina, packed with cones, on which objects viewed directly are clearly and sharply focused
Optic nerve	Nerve that carries visual information from the retina to the brain
Blind spot	Area in each eye where the optic nerve joins the retinal wall and no vision is possible

by Nobel Prize winner George Wald (1964; Wald et al., 1954) supports the trichromatic theory. Wald discovered that even though all cones have basically the same structure, the retina does indeed contain three kinds of cones. Subsequent research demonstrated that each kind of cone is particularly sensitive to one of three colors—blue, green, or red (Roorda & Williams, 1999).

The other major attempt to explain color vision is the **opponent-process theory**, which was first proposed by physiologist Ewald Hering in 1878 and revised in 1957 by researchers Leon Hurvich and Dorthea Jamison. According to the opponent-process theory, three kinds of cells respond by increasing or decreasing their rate of firing when different colors are present. The red/green cells increase their firing rate when red is present and decrease it when green is present. The yellow/blue cells have an increased response to yellow and a decreased response to blue. A third kind of cells increase their response rate for white light and decrease it in the absence of light.

If you look long enough at one color in the opponent-process pair and then look at a white surface, your brain will give you the sensation of the opposite color—a negative **afterimage**, a visual sensation that remains after the stimulus is withdrawn. After you have stared at one color in an opponent-process pair (red/green, yellow/blue, white/black), the cell responding to that color tires and the opponent cell begins to fire, producing the afterimage. Demonstrate this for yourself in *Try It 3.1* (on page 80).

But which theory of color vision is correct? It turns out that each theory explains a different phase of color processing. It is now generally accepted that the cones perform color processing in a way that is best explained by the trichromatic theory. The cones pass on information about wavelengths of light to the ganglion cells, the site of opponent processes. And color perception appears to involve more than just these two phases. Researchers think that color processing starts at the level of the retina, continues through the bipolar and ganglion cells, and is completed in the color detectors in the visual cortex (Masland, 1996; Sokolov, 2000).

◆ **brightness**

The dimension of visual sensation that is dependent on the intensity of light reflected from a surface and that corresponds to the amplitude (height) of the light wave.

◆ **trichromatic theory**

The theory of color vision suggesting that three types of cones in the retina each make a maximal chemical response to one of three colors—blue, green, or red.

◆ **opponent-process theory**

The theory of color vision suggesting that three kinds of cells respond by increasing or decreasing their rate of firing when different colors are present.

◆ **afterimage**

A visual sensation that remains after a stimulus is withdrawn.

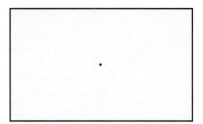

Try It 3.1

A Negative Afterimage

Stare at the dot in the green, black, and yellow flag for approximately 1 minute. Then shift your gaze to the dot in the blank rectangle. You will see the American flag in its true colors—red, white, and blue, which are the opponent-process opposites of green, black, and yellow.

You may have wondered what it means if someone is "color blind." Does that person see the world in black and white? No—the term **color blindness** refers to an inability to distinguish certain colors from one another. About 7% of males experience some kind of difficulty in distinguishing colors, most commonly red from green (Montgomery, 2003). By contrast, fewer than 1% of females suffer from color blindness. (Recall from Chapter 2 that this sex difference is explained by the fact that genes for color vision are carried on the X chromosome.)

Research has shown that color blindness can have degrees; it isn't simply a matter of either-you-have-it-or-you-don't. Why are some of us better able to make fine distinctions between colors, as we must do when sorting black and navy blue socks, for instance? These differences appear to be related to the number of color vision genes individuals have. Researchers have found that, in people with normal color vision, the X chromosome may contain as few as two or as many as nine genes for color perception (Neitz & Neitz, 1995). Those who have more of such genes appear to be better able to make very fine distinctions between colors.

◆ **color blindness**
The inability to distinguish certain colors from one another.

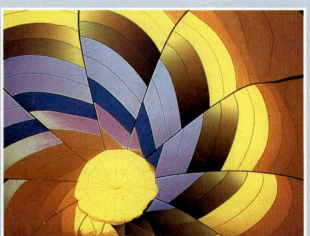

On the left a hot air balloon is shown as it would appear to a person with normal color vision; on the right is the same balloon as it would appear to a person with red-green color blindness.

Hearing

"In space, no one can hear you scream!" Years ago, the frightening science fiction movie *Alien* was advertised this way. Although the movie was fiction, the statement is true. Light can travel through the vast nothingness of space, a vacuum, but sound cannot.

Sound

Sound requires a medium, such as air, water, or a solid object, through which to move. This fact was first demonstrated by Robert Boyle in 1660 when he suspended a ringing pocket watch by a thread inside a specially designed jar. When Boyle pumped all the air out of the jar, he could no longer hear the watch ring. But when he pumped the air back into the jar, he could again hear the watch ringing.

Frequency is determined by the number of cycles completed by a sound wave in one second. The unit used to measure a wave's frequency, or cycles per second, is known as the hertz (Hz). The *pitch*—how high or low the sound is—is chiefly determined by frequency—the higher the frequency (the more cycles per second), the higher the sound. The human ear can hear sound frequencies from low bass tones of around 20 Hz up to high-pitched sounds of about 20,000 Hz. The lowest tone on a piano sounds at a frequency of about 28 Hz, and the highest tone at about 4,214 Hz. Many mammals, such as dogs, cats, bats, and rats, can hear tones much higher in frequency than 20,000 Hz. Amazingly, dolphins can respond to frequencies up to 100,000 Hz.

The loudness of a sound is determined by a measure called **amplitude**. The force or pressure with which air molecules move chiefly determines loudness, which is measured using a unit called the *bel*, named for Alexander Graham Bell. Because the bel is a rather large unit, sound levels are expressed in tenths of a bel, or **decibels (dB).** The threshold of human hearing is set at 0 dB, which does not mean the absence of sound but rather the softest sound that can be heard in a very quiet setting. Each increase of 10 decibels makes a sound 10 times louder. Figure 3.5 shows comparative decibel levels for a variety of sounds.

Another characteristic of sound is **timbre**, the distinctive quality of a sound that distinguishes it from other sounds of the same pitch and loudness. Have you ever thought about why a given musical note sounds different when played on a piano, a guitar, and a violin, even though all three instruments use vibrating strings to produce sounds? The characteristics of the strings, the technique used to initiate the vibrations, and the way the body of the instrument amplifies the vibrations work together to produce a unique "voice," or timbre, for each instrument. Human voices vary in timbre as well, providing us with a way of recognizing individuals when we can't see their faces. Timbres vary from one instrument to another, and from one voice to another, because most sounds consist of several different frequencies rather than a single pitch. The range of those frequencies gives each musical instrument, and each human voice, its unique sound.

◆ *What determines the pitch and loudness of a sound, and how is each quality measured?*

◆ **frequency**
The number of cycles completed by a sound wave in one second, determining the pitch of the sound; expressed in the unit called the hertz.

◆ **amplitude**
The measure of the loudness of a sound; expressed in the unit called the decibel.

◆ **decibel (dB)**
(DES-ih-bel) A unit of measurement for the loudness of sounds.

◆ **timbre**
(TAM-burr) The distinctive quality of a sound that distinguishes it from other sounds of the same pitch and loudness.

FIGURE 3.5

Decibel Levels of Various Sounds

The loudness of a sound (its amplitude) is measured in decibels. Each increase of 10 decibels makes a sound 10 times louder. A normal conversation at 3 feet measures about 60 decibels, which is 10,000 times louder than a soft whisper of 20 decibels. Any exposure to sounds of 130 decibels or higher puts a person at immediate risk for hearing damage.

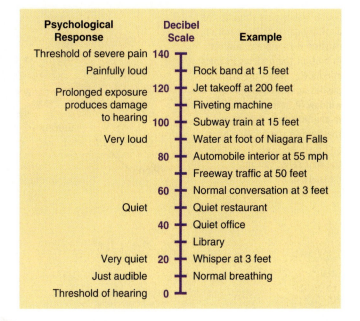

Psychological Response	Decibel Scale	Example
Threshold of severe pain	140	
Painfully loud		Rock band at 15 feet
Prolonged exposure produces damage to hearing	120	Jet takeoff at 200 feet
		Riveting machine
	100	Subway train at 15 feet
Very loud		Water at foot of Niagara Falls
	80	Automobile interior at 55 mph
		Freeway traffic at 50 feet
	60	Normal conversation at 3 feet
Quiet		Quiet restaurant
	40	Quiet office
		Library
Very quiet	20	Whisper at 3 feet
Just audible		Normal breathing
Threshold of hearing	0	

The Ear

Audition is the sensation and process of hearing. The oddly shaped, curved flap of cartilage and skin called the *pinna* is the visible part of the **outer ear** (see Figure 3.6). Inside the ear, the *auditory canal* is about 1 inch long, and its entrance is lined with hairs. At the end of the auditory canal is the *eardrum* (or *tympanic membrane*), a thin, flexible membrane about $1/3$ inch in diameter. The eardrum moves in response to the sound waves that travel through the auditory canal and strike it.

The **middle ear** is no larger than an aspirin tablet. Inside its chamber are the *ossicles*, the three smallest bones in the human body. Named for their shapes, the ossicles—the hammer, the anvil, and the stirrup—are connected in that order, linking the eardrum to the oval window (see Figure 3.6). The ossicles amplify sound waves some 22 times (Békésy, 1957). The **inner ear** begins at the inner side of the oval window, at the **cochlea**—a fluid-filled, snail-shaped, bony chamber. When the stirrup pushes against the oval window, it sets up vibrations that move the fluid in the cochlea back and forth in waves. Inside the cochlea, attached to its thin basilar membrane are about 15,000 sensory receptors called **hair cells,** each with a bundle of tiny hairs protruding from it. The tiny hair bundles are pushed and pulled by the motion of the fluid inside the cochlea. If the tip of a hair bundle is moved only as much as the width of an atom, an electrical impulse is generated, which is transmitted to the brain by way of the auditory nerve.

We can hear some sounds through *bone conduction*, the vibrations of the bones in the face and skull. When you click your teeth or eat crunchy food, you hear these sounds mainly through bone conduction. And, if you have heard a recording of your voice, you may have thought it sounded odd. This is because recordings do not reproduce the sounds you hear through bone conduction when you speak, so you are hearing your voice as it sounds to others.

Having two ears, one on each side of the head, enables you to determine the direction from which sounds are coming (Konishi, 1993). Unless a sound is directly above, below, in front of, or behind you, it reaches one ear very shortly before it reaches the other (Spitzer & Semple, 1991). The brain can detect differences as small as 0.0001 second and interpret them, revealing the direction of the sound (Rosenzweig, 1961). The source of a sound may also be determined by the difference in the intensity of the sound reaching each ear, as well as the position of the head when the sound is detected (Kopinska & Harris, 2003; Middlebrooks & Green, 1991).

◆ *How do the outer ear, middle ear, and inner ear function in hearing?*

◆ **audition**
The sensation and process of hearing.

◆ **outer ear**
The visible part of the ear, consisting of the pinna and the auditory canal.

◆ **middle ear**
The portion of the ear containing the ossicles, which connect the eardrum to the oval window and amplify sound waves.

◆ **inner ear**
The innermost portion of the ear, containing the cochlea, the vestibular sacs, and the semicircular canals.

◆ **cochlea**
(KOK-lee-uh) The fluid-filled, snail-shaped, bony chamber in the inner ear that contains the basilar membrane and its hair cells (the sound receptors).

◆ **hair cells**
Sensory receptors for hearing that are attached to the basilar membrane in the cochlea.

FIGURE 3.6

The Anatomy of the Human Ear

Sound waves pass through the auditory canal to the eardrum, causing it to vibrate and set in motion the ossicles in the middle ear. When the stirrup pushes against the oval window, it sets up vibrations in the inner ear. This moves the fluid in the cochlea back and forth and sets in motion the hair cells, causing a message to be sent to the brain via the auditory nerve.

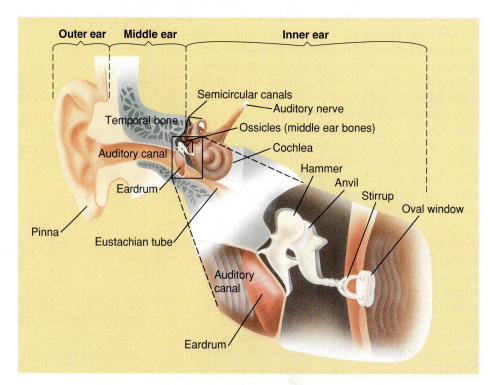

Theories of Hearing

How do the parts of the ear work together to produce auditory sensations? Scientists have proposed two theories to explain hearing.

In the 1860s, Hermann von Helmholtz helped develop **place theory**. This theory of hearing holds that each individual pitch a person hears is determined by the particular spot or place along the basilar membrane that vibrates the most. Observing the living basilar membrane, researchers verified that different locations do, indeed, vibrate in response to differently pitched sounds (Ruggero, 1992). Even so, place theory seems to apply only to frequencies higher than 150 Hz.

Another attempt to explain hearing is **frequency theory**. According to this theory, the hair cells vibrate the same number of times per second as the sounds that reach them. Thus, a tone of 500 Hz would stimulate the hair cells to vibrate 500 times per second. However, frequency theory cannot account for frequencies higher than 1,000 Hz because individual neurons linked to the hair cells cannot fire more than about 1,000 times per second. So, even if a receptor vibrated as rapidly as the sound wave associated with a higher tone, the information necessary to perceive the pitch wouldn't be faithfully transmitted to the brain. Consequently, frequency theory seems to be a good explanation of how we hear low-frequency tones (lower than 500 Hz), but place theory better describes the way in which tones with frequencies higher than 1,000 Hz are heard (Matlin & Foley, 1997). Both frequency and location are involved when we hear sounds whose frequencies are between 500 and 1,000 Hz.

Smell and Taste

Clearly, our sensory experiences would be extremely limited without vision and hearing, but what about the chemical senses—smell and taste?

Smell

If you suddenly lost your capacity for **olfaction** (sense of smell), you might think, "This isn't so bad. I can't smell flowers or food, but, on the other hand, I no longer have to endure the foul odors of life." But your *olfactory system*—the technical name for the organs and brain structures involved in the sense of smell—aids your survival. You smell smoke and can escape before the flames of a fire envelop you. Your nose broadcasts an odor alarm to the brain when certain poisonous gases or noxious fumes are present. Smell, aided by taste, provides your line of defense against putting spoiled food or drink into your body. And, believe it or not, every single individual gives off a unique scent, which is genetically determined (Axel, 1995).

You cannot smell a substance unless some of its molecules vaporize—pass from a solid or liquid into a gaseous state. Heat speeds up the vaporization of molecules, which is why food that is cooking has a stronger and more distinct odor than uncooked food. When odor molecules vaporize, they become airborne and make their way up each nostril to the **olfactory epithelium.** The olfactory epithelium consists of two 1-square-inch patches of tissue, one at the top of each nasal cavity; together these patches contain about 10 million olfactory neurons, which are the receptor cells for smell. Each of these neurons contains only one of the 1,000 different types of odor receptors (Bargmann, 1996). Because humans are able to detect some 10,000 odors, each of the 1,000 types of odor receptors must be able to respond to more than one kind of odor molecule. Moreover, some odor molecules trigger more than one type of odor receptor (Axel, 1995). The intensity of a smell stimulus—how strong or weak it is—is apparently determined by the number of olfactory neurons firing at the same time (Freeman, 1991). Figure 3.7 (on page 84) shows a diagram of the human olfactory system.

Have you ever wondered why dogs have a keener sense of smell than humans? Not only do many dogs have a long snout, but, in some breeds, the olfactory epithelium can

---

◆ *What two major theories attempt to explain hearing?*

◆ **place theory**
The theory of hearing that holds that each individual pitch a person hears is determined by the particular location along the basilar membrane of the cochlea that vibrates the most.

◆ **frequency theory**
The theory of hearing that holds that hair cell receptors vibrate the same number of times per second as the sounds that reach them.

◆ *What path does a smell message take from the nose to the brain?*

◆ **olfaction**
(ol-FAK-shun) The sense of smell.

◆ **olfactory epithelium**
Two 1-square-inch patches of tissue, one at the top of each nasal cavity, which together contain about 10 million olfactory neurons, the receptors for smell.

FIGURE 3.7   The Olfactory System

Odor molecules travel up the nostrils to the olfactory epithelium, which contains the receptor cells for smell. Olfactory receptors are special neurons whose axons form the olfactory nerve. The olfactory nerve relays smell messages to the olfactory bulbs, which pass them on to the thalamus, the orbitofrontal cortex, and other parts of the brain.

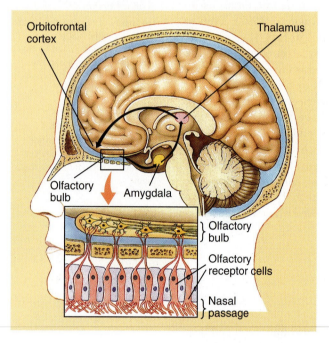

be as large as the area of a handkerchief and can contain 20 times as many olfactory neurons as in humans (Engen, 1982). It is well known that dogs use scent to recognize not only other members of their species, but also the humans with whom they live. Humans have this ability, too. The mothers of newborns can recognize their own babies by smell within hours after birth. But can humans recognize the scents of other species—their own pets, for example? Yes, to a remarkable degree. When presented with blankets permeated with the scents of dogs, some 89% of the dog owners easily identified their own dog by smell (Wells & Hepper, 2000).

Olfactory neurons are different from all other sensory receptors: They both come into direct contact with sensory stimuli and reach directly into the brain. These neurons have a short lifespan; after functioning for only about 60 days, they die and are replaced by new cells (Buck, 1996).

The axons of the olfactory neurons relay a smell message directly to the **olfactory bulbs**—two brain structures the size of matchsticks that rest above the nasal cavities (refer to Figure 3.7). From the olfactory bulbs, the message is relayed to the thalamus and the orbitofrontal cortex, which distinguish the odor and relay that information to other parts of the brain.

The process of sensing odors is the same in every individual, but there are large differences in sensitivity to smells. For example, perfumers and whiskey blenders can distinguish subtle variations in odors that are indistinguishable to the average person. Young people are more sensitive to odors than older people, and nonsmokers are more sensitive than smokers (Matlin & Foley, 1997).

Taste

◆ *What are the primary taste sensations, and how are they detected?*

You might be surprised to learn that much of the pleasure you attribute to the sense of taste actually arises from smells, when odor molecules are forced up the nasal cavity by the action of the tongue, cheeks, and throat when you chew and swallow. Even without a sense of taste, your sense of smell would provide you with some taste sensations. Still, life without the ability to fully experience the tastes of the foods we love would, no doubt, be less enjoyable.

Psychology textbooks have long maintained that **gustation**, the sense of taste, produces four distinct kinds of taste sensations: sweet, sour, salty, and bitter. This is true. But recent research suggests that there is a fifth taste sensation in humans (Herness, 2000). This fifth taste sensation, called *umami*, is triggered by the substance glutamate, which, in the form of monosodium glutamate (MSG), is widely used as a flavoring in Asian foods (Matsunami et al., 2000). Many protein-rich foods, such as meat, milk, aged cheese, and seafood, also contain glutamate.

All five taste sensations can be detected on all locations of the tongue. Indeed, even a person with no tongue could still taste to some extent, thanks to the taste receptors found in the palate, in the mucus lining of the cheeks and lips, and in parts of the throat, including the tonsils. When tastes are mixed, the specialized receptors for each type of flavor are activated and send separate messages to the brain (Frank et al., 2003). In other words, your brain perceives the two distinctive flavors present in sweet and sour sauce quite separately. This analytical quality of the sense of taste prevents your being fooled into eating spoiled or poisoned food when the characteristic taste of either is combined with some kind of pleasant flavor.

◆ **olfactory bulbs**

Two matchstick-sized structures above the nasal cavities, where smell sensations first register in the brain.

◆ **gustation**

The sense of taste.

FIGURE 3.8   The Tongue's Papillae and Taste Buds

(a) A photomicrograph of the surface of the tongue shows several papillae. (b) This vertical cross-section through a papilla reveals the location of the taste buds and taste receptors.

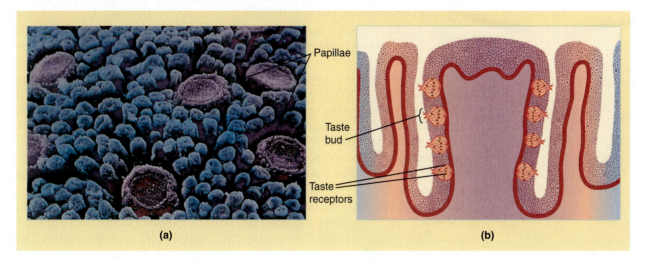

Papillae

Taste bud

Taste receptors

(a)   (b)

If you look at your tongue in a mirror, you will see many small bumps called *papillae*. **Taste buds** lie alongside some of these papillae (see Figure 3.8). Each taste bud is composed of 60 to 100 receptor cells. The lifespan of the taste receptors is very short—only about 10 days—and they are continually being replaced.

Research indicates that individuals vary widely in their capacity for experiencing taste sensations (Yackinous & Guinard, 2002). Nontasters are unable to taste certain sweet and bitter compounds, but they do taste most other substances, albeit with less sensitivity. Supertasters taste these sweet and bitter compounds with far stronger intensity than other people. Researchers are currently investigating links between taste sensitivity, eating behaviors, and health status variables, such as obesity. For example, supertasters who are particularly sensitive to the chemical that gives fruits and vegetables a bitter taste eat less salad than medium tasters and nontasters (Yackinous & Guinard, 2002). Still, supertasters appear no more likely to be overweight than medium tasters or nontasters. In fact, among individuals who report that they never deliberately restrict their diets to try to lose weight, supertasters of the bitter chemical have less body fat than medium tasters or nontasters (Tepper & Ullrich, 2002). So, researchers know that taste sensitivity is linked to food preferences, but not how these preferences may be connected to nutritional status.

◆ **taste buds**
Structures in many of the tongue's papillae that are composed of 60 to 100 receptor cells for taste.

The Skin Senses

How important is the sense of touch? Classic research in the mid-1980s demonstrated that premature infants who were massaged for 15 minutes three times a day gained weight 47% faster than other premature infants who received only regular intensive care treatment (Field et al., 1986). The massaged infants were more responsive and were able to leave the hospital about 6 days earlier on average than those who were not massaged. Thus, the sense of touch is not only one of the more pleasant aspects of life, but is also critical to our survival. And it may be just as important to adult as to infant survival. For instance, you may feel a poisonous spider crawling up your arm and flick it away before it can inflict a deadly bite. The other skin sense—pain—is also vital because it serves as an early warning system for many potentially deadly conditions, as you'll learn in this section.

Touch

◆ How does the skin provide sensory information?

Your natural clothing, the skin, is the largest organ of your body. It performs many important biological functions, while also providing much of what is known as sensual pleasure. **Tactile** information is conveyed to the brain when an object touches and depresses the skin, stimulating one or more of the several distinct types of receptors found in the nerve endings. These sensitive nerve endings in the skin send the touch message through nerve connections to the spinal cord. The message travels up the spinal cord and through the brainstem and the midbrain, finally reaching the somatosensory cortex. (Recall from Chapter 2 that the somatosensory cortex is the strip of tissue at the front of the parietal lobes where touch, pressure, temperature, and pain register.) Once the somatosensory cortex has been activated, you become aware of where and how hard you have been touched. In the 1890s, one of the most prominent researchers of the tactile sense, Max von Frey, discovered the *two-point threshold*—the measure of how far apart two touch points on the skin must be before they are felt as two separate touches.

If you could examine the skin from the outermost to the deepest layer, you would find a variety of nerve endings that differ markedly in appearance. Most or all of these nerve endings appear to respond in some degree to all types of tactile stimulation. The more densely packed with these sensory receptors a part of the body's surface is, the more sensitive it is to tactile stimulation.

Pain

◆ What is the function of pain, and how is pain influenced by psychological factors, culture, and endorphins?

Although the tactile sense delivers a great deal of pleasure, it brings us pain as well. Scientists are not certain how pain works, but one major theory that attempts to answer this question is the *gate-control theory* of Ronald Melzack and Patrick Wall (1965, 1983). These researchers contend that an area in the spinal cord can act like a "gate" and either block pain messages or transmit them to the brain. Only so many messages can go through the gate at any one time. You feel pain when pain messages carried by small, slow-conducting nerve fibers reach the gate and cause it to open. Large, fast-conducting nerve fibers carry other sensory messages from the body; these can effectively tie up traffic at the gate so that it will close and keep many of the pain messages from getting through. What is the first thing you do when you stub your toe or pound your finger with a hammer? If you rub or apply gentle pressure to the injury, you are stimulating the large, fast-conducting nerve fibers, which get their message to the spinal gate first and block some of the pain messages from the slower-conducting nerve fibers. Applying ice, heat, or electrical stimulation to the painful area also stimulates the large nerve fibers and closes the spinal gate.

The gate-control theory also accounts for the fact that psychological factors, both cognitive and emotional, can influence the perception of pain. Melzack and Wall (1965, 1983) contend that messages from the brain to the spinal cord can inhibit the transmission of pain messages at the spinal gate, thereby affecting the perception of pain. This phenomenon explains why soldiers injured in battle or athletes injured during games can be so distracted that they do not experience pain until some time after the injury.

As you learned in Chapter 2, the body produces its own natural painkillers, the **endorphins**, which block pain and produce a feeling of well-being. Endorphins are released when you are injured, when you experience stress or extreme pain, and when you laugh, cry, or exercise. Some people release endorphins even when they merely *think* they are receiving pain medication but are being given, instead, a placebo in the form of a sugar pill or an injection of saline solution. Asthma, high blood pressure, and even heart disease can respond to placebo "treatment" (Brown, 1998). Why? Apparently, when patients believe that they have received a drug for pain, that belief stimulates the release of their own natural pain relievers, the endorphins.

Finally, the proportion of people who suffer from chronic pain, or pain that lasts for three months or longer, varies across cultures. Why? Researchers don't have a definitive answer. However, they do know that the experience of pain has both physical and

◆ **tactile**
Pertaining to the sense of touch.

◆ **endorphins**
(en-DOR-fins) The body's own natural painkillers, which block pain and produce a feeling of well-being.

emotional components, both of which vary from person to person. Pain experts distinguish between pain and suffering—suffering being the affective, or emotional, response to pain. Sullivan and others (1995) found that people suffered most from pain when they harbored negative thoughts about it, feared its potential threat to their well-being, and expressed feelings of helplessness. Thus, cross-cultural variations in chronic pain may be linked to differences in people's emotional states.

The Spatial Orientation Senses

◆ *What kinds of information do the kinesthetic and vestibular senses provide?*

The senses you've learned about so far provide you with valuable information about your environment. But how would you keep from falling if you couldn't sense whether you were standing up straight or leaning to one side? Fortunately, the kinesthetic and vestibular senses keep you apprised of exactly where all parts of your body are and how the location of your body is related to your physical environment.

The **kinesthetic sense** provides information about (1) the position of body parts in relation to each other and (2) the movement of the entire body or its parts. This information is detected by receptors in the joints, ligaments, and muscles. The other senses, especially vision, provide additional information about body position and movement, but the kinesthetic sense works well on its own. Thanks to the kinesthetic sense, we are able to perform smooth and skilled body movements without visual feedback or a studied, conscious effort. (But why do we perceive ourselves as stationary in a moving car? More on this later in the chapter.)

The **vestibular sense** detects movement and provides information about the body's orientation in space. The vestibular sense organs are located in the semicircular canals and the *vestibular sacs* in the inner ear. The **semicircular canals** sense the rotation of your head, such as when you are turning your head from side to side or when you are spinning around (see Figure 3.9). Because the canals are filled with fluid, rotating movements of the head in any direction send the fluid coursing through the tubelike semicircular canals. In the canals, the moving fluid bends the hair cells, which act as receptors and send neural impulses to the brain. Because there are three canals, each positioned on a different plane, rotation in a given direction will cause the hair cells in one canal to bend more than the hair cells in the other canals.

The semicircular canals and the vestibular sacs signal only changes in motion or orientation. If you were blindfolded and had no visual or other external cues, you would not be able to sense motion once your speed reached a constant rate. For example, in an airplane, you would feel the takeoff and the landing, as well as any sudden changes in speed. But once the plane leveled off and maintained a fairly constant cruising speed, your vestibular organs would not signal the brain that you are moving, even if you were traveling at a rate of hundreds of miles per hour.

◆ **kinesthetic sense**
The sense providing information about the position of body parts in relation to each other and the movement of the entire body or its parts.

◆ **vestibular sense**
(ves-TIB-yu-ler) The sense that detects movement and provides information about the body's orientation in space.

◆ **semicircular canals**
Three fluid-filled tubular canals in the inner ear that sense the rotation of the head.

FIGURE 3.9

Sensing Balance and Movement

You sense the rotation of your head in any direction because the movement sends fluid coursing through the tubelike semicircular canals in the inner ear. The moving fluid bends the hair cell receptors, which, in turn, send neural impulses to the brain.

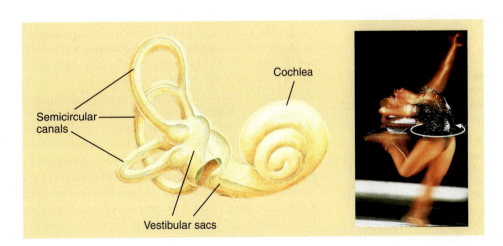

Influences on Perception

So far, you have been reading about *sensation*, the process of taking in information from the outside world through the senses. We've discussed vision, hearing, smell, taste, touch, and the spatial orientation senses. However, we have yet to discuss *perception*, the process through which the brain assigns meaning to sensations. For instance, your senses provide you with information about the color, taste, and smell of an apple, as well as the sound that happens when you bite into one. Sensation even provides you with the kinesthetic sense needed to toss an apple to your roommate. By contrast, perception enables you to link these sensations to the knowledge that apples are food, that you either like or dislike them, and that they have a variety of symbolic associations (e.g., "an apple for the teacher").

Perception is influenced by a number of factors. Before we discuss some of the principles that govern perception in all human beings, we will consider three factors that contribute to perceptual processes: attention, prior knowledge, and cross-modal perception.

Attention

What is gained and what is lost in the process of attention?

In some cases, linking sensations to meanings—the essence of the process of perception—requires very little mental effort. For instance, when reading familiar words, the sensation of seeing the word and the perception of its meaning occur almost simultaneously (Heil et al., 2004). Likewise, while we are driving, perceiving that the other objects on the road with us are cars takes very little mental effort because we are so familiar with them. In other words, connecting the sensation of seeing a car with the perception that the object is a car is an *automatic* (non-effortful) mental process. However, more mental effort is required to determine which cars we should watch most closely. When we engage in this kind of mental effort, the process of *attention* is at work. **Attention** is defined as the process of sorting through sensations and selecting some of them for further processing. Without attention, perception of all but the most familiar sensations would be impossible.

Of course, we cannot pay attention to everything at once. Thus, in a complex perceptual task, such as the everyday experience of driving in traffic, it's important to realize that attention carries certain perceptual costs. Research examining the phenomenon of **inattentional blindness** has helped to illustrate these costs (Mack, 2003; Mack & Rock, 1998; Most et al., 2001). Inattentional blindness occurs when we shift our attention from one object to another and, in the process, fail to notice changes in objects to which we are not directly paying attention (Woodman & Luck, 2003). In many studies of inattentional blindness, experimenters have presented participants with a scene and ask them to attend to a particular element in it. For example, Daniel Simons and colleagues (e.g., Simons & Chabris, 1999) showed participants a videotape of a basketball game in which one team wore white uniforms and the other team wore black uniforms. Participants were instructed to count how many times the ball was passed from one player to another, either on the white team or on the black team. Under such conditions, about one-third of participants typically failed to later recall the appearance on the screen of even extremely incongruent stimuli (for example, a man dressed in a gorilla costume). The inattentional blindness happens even when the incongruous stimulus is present on the screen for a long period of time. Simons's research helps us understand why we sometimes exclaim, "Where did that car come from?" when a car we had been ignoring suddenly swerves into our path.

Similar costs arise when we attend to auditory sensations. Suppose you are standing in a crowded room in which a large number of conversations are going on simultaneously. What would happen if someone mentioned your name? Research shows that you would zero in on the conversation that included your name and ignore others. This *cocktail party phenomenon* was documented in classic research by E. C. Cherry (1953). Remember, perception is the process of attaching meaning to sensations—and what is more meaningful to a person than his or her own name? Thus, when you hear your

◆ **attention**

The process of sorting through sensations and selecting some of them for further processing.

◆ **inattentional blindness**

The phenomenon in which we shift our focus from one object to another and, in the process, fail to notice changes in objects to which we are not directly paying attention.

Daniel J. Simons

Have you had trouble settling on a major? So did psychologist Daniel J. Simons, one of the leading researchers in the study of attention. In fact, Simons considered English, French, physics, and computer science as majors when he was an undergraduate. However, when he took an introductory psychology course, Simons was "hooked" and finally settled on psychology as his field of study. A summer spent doing research with graduate students at the University of Minnesota convinced him that he wanted a career in teaching and research, and he moved on to graduate school as soon as he finished his bachelor's degree.

At the beginning of his graduate career, Simons reports, he was interested in learning how infants acquire concepts (D. Simons, personal communication, November 23, 2004). This interest inspired him to examine perceptual processes in infants more closely. Along the way, he discovered that his greatest interest was in researching the basic processes of perception and attention in adults. When Simons determined that his interests would be better served by transferring to Cornell University, he didn't hesitate to make the change.

The theme that ties together Simons's eclectic academic background and his current research is the joy of discovery. He points out that researchers, although they may have hypotheses in mind, never really know what new kinds of questions may arise out of a study. It is this element of the unexpected, he says, that continues to motivate him. Now, as a professor, he enjoys watching students develop the same kind of passion for discovery that motivates him.

One lesson that you might learn from Simons's experience is that academic and career paths that may appear to outsiders to be somewhat disorganized can reflect some very positive personal characteristics. In other words, his love of the unexpected may be what shaped the paths Simons followed as an undergraduate and graduate student and ultimately guided him to the career that was right for him. Moreover, the same trait has been the impetus for his highly creative research on attention, research that has earned Simons numerous awards. Thus, if you are still stammering and equivocating when people ask "What's your major?", an answer of "I haven't decided" may portend great things for your future.

name, you assume that whatever is to follow will be personally meaningful to you. The process of attending to the conversation that included your name, however, would prevent you from adequately perceiving other conversations. Thus, you might fail to pick up on other conversations that might have more meaning for you but are free from obvious attentional cues such as your name.

Attentional demands involving more than one sense can also lead to attention failures. Research by David Strayer and his colleagues (2003) showed that drivers (using a simulator, not actually driving a car) often failed to perceive vehicles braking directly in front of them while they were engaged in hands-free cellphone conversations. Moreover, participants engaged in cellphone conversations were less able than control participants to recognize other visual stimuli, such as billboards. Consequently, experts advise that you pull off the road when you want to talk on the phone. Furthermore, many communities are banning cellphone use by drivers for these reasons.

Although attending to a stimulus is clearly associated with deficits in the ability to attend to other stimuli, attention is clearly not an all-or-nothing process. We can, and often do, process more than one stimulus at a time. Indeed, research shows that we are capable of accurately perceiving some sensations to which we do not pay direct attention. For example, in the same series of classic studies that led to the discovery of the cocktail party phenomenon, E. C. Cherry (1953) discovered that listeners who were presented with different verbal messages in either ear could remember the content of only the message to which the experimenter directed their attention (e.g., "Pay attention to the message in your left ear"). Nevertheless, they were able to remember many things about the unattended message, such as whether it had been delivered by a male or a female.

Prior Knowledge

◆ *How does prior knowledge influence perception?*

Think back to the example of attending to cars on the road while driving. How do we make judgments about which cars require most of our attention? To a great extent, our past driving experiences, or prior knowledge, help us make such decisions. Prior knowledge is helpful when interpreting the meanings of sensations, but it can lead to perceptual errors as well.

Suppose you were presented with the coded message XBDID FXI XIL. How would you go about deciphering the words? You might conclude that each word uses X to represent a letter, so X must stand for one of the more common letters in English, such as R. You might then insert R in the position of X to see if you could come up with something that makes sense. Such a strategy would involve **bottom-up processing**. This approach begins with the individual components of a stimulus that are detected by the sensory receptors. The bits of information are then transmitted to areas in the brain where they are combined and assembled into patterns. The brain then uses stored information to make inferences about these patterns. For instance, what is the next number in the sequence 2, 7, 12, 17? Your brain infers the pattern $y = x + 5$ (where x is the number that immediately precedes y) from the sequence and proposes that the next number is 22.

What if you noticed that the second and third words in XBDID FXI XIL have two letters in common and are both three letters long and then compared them to real three-letter words in English that share two letters? You would then be using **top-down processing**. In top-down processing, previous experience and conceptual knowledge are applied to recognize the nature of a "whole" and then logically deduce the simpler components of that whole. Of course, we use both bottom-up and top-down processing to form perceptions. Either approach, or a combination of the two, eventually leads to the conclusion that the words in the coded message are ROSES ARE RED.

Prior knowledge also contributes to perception by leading us to expect certain perceptions. For example, if you ordered raspberry sherbet and it was colored green, would it still taste like raspberry, or might it taste more like lime? The **perceptual set**—what we expect to perceive—determines, to a large extent, what we actually see, hear, feel, taste, and smell. Such expectations are, of course, based on prior knowledge (that lime sherbert is usually green). Such expectations do seem to influence perception. So, green raspberry sherbert might, indeed, taste a bit like lime.

In a classic study of perceptual set, psychologist David Rosenhan (1973) and some of his colleagues were admitted as patients to various mental hospitals with "diagnoses" of schizophrenia. Once admitted, they acted normal in every way. The purpose? They wondered how long it would take the doctors and the hospital staff to realize that they were not mentally ill. But the doctors and the staff members saw what they expected to see and not what actually occurred. They perceived everything the pseudo-patients said and did, such as note taking, to be symptoms of their illness. But the real patients were not fooled; they were the first to realize that the psychologists were not really mentally ill.

Cross-Modal Perception

◆ *How does information from multiple sources aid perception?*

Many complex perceptual tasks require the brain to integrate information from more than one sense, a process called **cross-modal perception**. Experiments in which participants are exposed to conflicting visual and auditory information have shown that cross-modal perception is strongly dependent on the availability of accurate sensory information.

You have participated in a cross-modal perception "experiment" if you have ever seen a movie in which the actors' lip movements didn't match their spoken language. Research shows that it is very difficult to understand speech under such conditions (Thomas & Jordan, 2004). In effect, we must block out the visual information to understand what the speakers are saying. The opposite happens when facial expressions and vocal characteristics seem to be conveying different emotional messages. When a person looks angry but speaks in a happy voice, the visual information is typically judged to be more reliable than the auditory input (Vroomen et al., 2001).

◆ **bottom-up processing**

Information processing in which individual components or bits of data are combined until a complete perception is formed.

◆ **top-down processing**

Information processing in which previous experience and conceptual knowledge are applied to recognize the whole of a perception and thus easily identify the simpler elements of that whole.

◆ **perceptual set**

An expectation of what will be perceived, which can affect what actually is perceived.

◆ **cross-modal perception**

A process whereby the brain integrates information from more than one sense.

Principles of Perception

Some influences on perception—particularly the application of prior knowledge to perceptual tasks—can lead to wide variations in how a stimulus is perceived. However, researchers have found a few principles that appear to govern perceptions in all human beings.

Perceptual Organization and Constancy

The Gestalt psychologists maintained that people cannot understand the perceptual world by breaking down experiences into tiny parts and analyzing them separately. When sensory elements are brought together, something new is formed. That is, the whole is more than just the sum of its parts. The German word **Gestalt** has no exact English equivalent, but it roughly refers to the whole form, pattern, or configuration that a person perceives. The Gestalt psychologists claimed that sensory experience is organized according to certain basic principles of perceptual organization:

◆ *What are the principles that govern perceptual organization?*

◆ **Gestalt**
(geh-SHTALT) A German word that roughly refers to the whole form, pattern, or configuration that a person perceives.

- *Figure-ground.* As we view the world, some object (the figure) often seems to stand out from the background (the ground) (see Figure 3.10).
- *Similarity.* Objects that have similar characteristics are perceived as a unit. In Figure 3.11(a), dots of a similar color are perceived as belonging together to form horizontal rows on the left and vertical columns on the right.
- *Proximity.* Objects that are close together in space or time are usually perceived as belonging together. Because of their spacing, the lines in Figure 3.11(b) are perceived as four pairs of lines rather than as eight separate lines.
- *Continuity.* We tend to perceive figures or objects as belonging together if they appear to form a continuous pattern, as in Figure 3.11(c).
- *Closure.* We perceive figures with gaps in them to be complete. Even though parts of the figure in Figure 3.11(d) are missing, we use closure and perceive it as a triangle.

When you say good-bye to friends and watch them walk away, the image they cast on your retina grows smaller and smaller until they finally disappear in the distance.

FIGURE 3.10 **Reversing Figure and Ground**
In this illustration, you can see a white vase as a figure against a black background, or two black faces in profile on a white background. Exactly the same visual stimulus produces two opposite figure-ground perceptions.

FIGURE 3.11 **Gestalt Principles of Grouping**
Gestalt psychologists proposed several principles of perceptual grouping, including similarity, proximity, continuity, and closure.

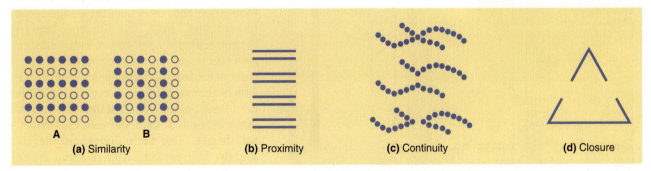

A   B
(a) Similarity   **(b)** Proximity   **(c)** Continuity   **(d)** Closure

So how does your brain know that they are still the same size? Scientists call this phenomenon **perceptual constancy.** Thanks to perceptual constancy, when you watch someone walk away, the information that the retina sends to the brain (the sensation that that person is shrinking in size) does not fool the perceptual system. As objects or people move farther away, you continue to perceive them as being about the same size. This perceptual phenomenon is known as *size constancy.* You do not make a literal interpretation about the size of an object from its retinal image—the image of the object projected onto the retina. If you did, you would believe that objects become larger as they approach and smaller as they move away.

The shape or image of an object projected onto the retina changes according to the angle from which it is viewed. But your perceptual ability includes *shape constancy*—the tendency to perceive objects as having a stable or unchanging shape, regardless of changes in the retinal image resulting from differences in viewing angle. In other words, you perceive a door as rectangular and a plate as round from whatever angle you view them (see Figure 3.12).

We normally see objects as maintaining a constant level of brightness, regardless of differences in lighting conditions—a perceptual phenomenon known as *brightness constancy.* Nearly all objects reflect some part of the light that falls on them, and white objects reflect more light than black objects. However, a black asphalt driveway at noon in bright sunlight actually reflects more light than a white shirt does indoors at night in dim lighting. Nevertheless, the driveway still looks black, and the shirt still looks white. Why? We learn to infer the brightness of objects by comparing it with the brightness of all other objects viewed at the same time.

Depth Perception

◆ *What are some of the binocular and monocular depth cues?*

Depth perception is the ability to perceive the visual world in three dimensions and to judge distances accurately. We judge how far away objects and other people are. We climb and descend stairs without stumbling and perform numerous other actions requiring depth perception. Depth perception is three-dimensional. Yet each eye is able to provide only a two-dimensional view. The images cast on the retina do not contain depth; they are flat, just like a photograph. How, then, do we perceive depth so vividly?

Some cues to depth perception depend on both eyes working together. These **binocular depth cues** include convergence and binocular disparity. *Convergence* occurs when the eyes turn inward to focus on nearby objects—the closer the object, the more the two objects appear to come together. Hold the tip of your finger about 12 inches in front of your nose, and focus on it. Now, slowly begin moving your finger toward your nose. Your eyes will turn inward so much that they virtually cross when the tip of your finger meets the tip of your nose. Many psychologists believe that the tension of the eye muscles as they converge conveys to the brain information that serves as a cue for depth perception. Fortunately, the eyes are just far enough apart, about $2^{1}/_{2}$ inches or so, to give each eye a slightly different view of the objects being focused on and, consequently, a slightly different retinal image. The difference between the two retinal images, known as *binocular disparity* (or *retinal disparity*), provides an important cue for depth perception (see Figure 3.13). The farther away from the eyes (up to 20 feet or so) the objects being viewed, the less the disparity, or difference, between the two retinal images. The brain integrates the two slightly different retinal images and creates the perception of three dimensions.

FIGURE 3.12

Shape Constancy

The door projects very different images on the retina when viewed from different angles. But because of shape constancy, you continue to perceive the door as rectangular.

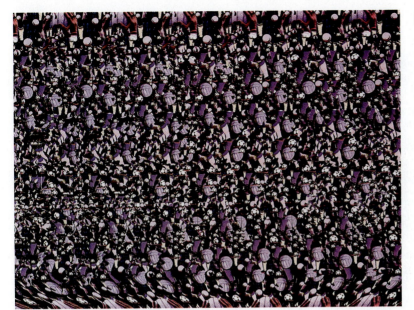

Close one eye, and you will see that you can still perceive depth. The visual depth cues perceived with one eye alone are called **monocular depth cues.** The following is a description of seven monocular depth cues, many of which have been used by artists in Western cultures to give the illusion of depth to their paintings.

◆ **monocular depth cues**
(mah-NOK-yu-ler) Depth cues that can be perceived by one eye alone.

- *Interposition.* When one object partly blocks your view of another, you perceive the partially blocked object as being farther away.
- *Linear perspective.* Parallel lines that are known to be the same distance apart appear to grow closer together, or converge, as they recede into the distance.
- *Relative size.* Larger objects are perceived as being closer to the viewer, and smaller objects as being farther away.
- *Texture gradient.* Objects close to you appear to have sharply defined features, and similar objects that are farther away appear progressively less well defined or fuzzier in texture.
- *Atmospheric perspective* (sometimes called *aerial perspective*). Objects in the distance have a bluish tint and appear more blurred than objects close at hand.
- *Shadow or shading.* When light falls on objects, they cast shadows, which add to the perception of depth.
- *Motion parallax.* When you ride in a moving vehicle and look out the side window, the objects you see outside appear to be moving in the opposite direction and at different speeds; those closest to you appear to be moving faster than those in the distance. Objects very far away, such as the moon and the sun, appear to move in the same direction as the viewer. Photos illustrating each of these cues are shown in Figure 3.14 (on page 94).

Perception of Motion

◆ *How does the brain perceive motion?*

Imagine you're sitting in a bus looking through the window at another bus parked parallel to the one in which you are sitting. Suddenly, you sense your bus moving; then, you realize that it is not your bus that moved but the one next to it. In other words, your ability to perceive the motion of objects has been fooled in some way. This example illustrates the complexity of motion perception.

One of the most important contributors to our understanding of motion perception is psychologist James Gibson. Gibson points out that our perceptions of motion appear to be based on fundamental, but frequently changing, assumptions about stability (Gibson, 1994). Our brains seem to search for some stimulus in the environment to serve as the assumed reference point for stability. Once the stable reference point is

FIGURE 3.14 **Monocular Depth Cues**

Interposition

When one object partially blocks your view of another, you perceive the partially blocked object as being farther away.

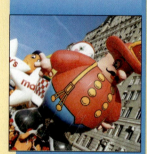

Linear Perspective

Parallel lines are the same distance apart but appear to grow closer together, or converge, as they recede into the distance.

Relative Size

Larger objects are perceived as being closer to the viewer, and smaller objects as being farther away.

Texture Gradient

Objects close to you appear to have sharply defined features, and similar objects farther away appear progressively less well defined, or fuzzier in texture.

Atmospheric Perspective

Objects in the distance have a bluish tint and appear more blurred than objects close at hand (sometimes called *aerial perspective*).

Shadow or Shading

When light falls on objects, they cast shadows, which add to the perception of depth.

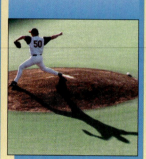

Motion Parallax

When you ride in a moving train and look out the window, the objects you see outside appear to be moving in the opposite direction and at different speeds; those closest to you appear to be moving faster than those in the distance.

chosen, all objects that move relative to that reference point are judged to be in motion. For example, in the bus situation, your brain assumes that the other bus is stable, and when the motion sensors linked to your retina detect movement, it concludes that your bus is moving. And when you're driving a car, you sense the car to be in motion relative to the outside environment. But your brain uses the inside of the car as the stable point of reference for your own movements. Only your movements in relation to the seat, steering wheel, and so on are sensed as motion by your brain.

The fact that the eyes are never really completely still also contributes to perceptions of motion. For instance, if you stare at a single unmoving light in a dark room for a few seconds, the light will appear to begin moving, a phenomenon called the *autokinetic illusion*. If you look away from the light and then return to watching it, it will again appear to be stable. (Could this phenomenon account for some sightings of "unidentified flying objects"?) Two lights placed close to each other will appear to move together, as if they are linked by an invisible string. What is really happening is that your eyes, not the lights, are moving. Because of the darkness of the room, the brain has no stable visual reference point to use in deciding whether the lights are actually moving (Gibson, 1994). But when the room is lit up, the brain immediately "fixes" the error because it has a stable visible background for the lights.

In one kind of study of false-motion perceptions, several stationary lights in a dark room are flashed on and off in sequence, causing participants to perceive a single light moving from one spot to the next. This type of illusion, called the *phi phenomenon* (sometimes called *stroboscopic motion*), was first discussed by Max Wertheimer (1912), one of the founders of Gestalt psychology. You encounter one of the most common examples of the phi phenomenon whenever you go to the movies. As you probably know, movies are simply a series of still photographs shown in rapid succession.

Puzzling Perceptions

Not only can we perceive motion that doesn't exist, but we can also perceive objects that aren't present in a stimulus and misinterpret those that are.

◆ *What are three types of puzzling perceptions?*

When you are faced for the first time with an *ambiguous figure*, you have no experience to call on. Your perceptual system is puzzled and tries to resolve the uncertainty by seeing the ambiguous figure first one way and then another, but not both ways at once. You never get a lasting impression of ambiguous figures because they seem to jump back and forth beyond your control. In some ambiguous figures, two different objects or figures are seen alternately. The best known of these, "Old Woman/Young Woman," by E. G. Boring, is shown in Figure 3.15(a) (on page 96). If you direct your gaze to the left of the drawing, you are likely to see an attractive young woman, her face turned away. But the young woman disappears when you suddenly perceive the image of the old woman. Such examples of object ambiguity offer striking evidence that perceptions are more than the mere sum of sensory parts. It is hard to believe that the same drawing (the same sum of sensory parts) can convey such dramatically different perceptions.

At first glance, many impossible figures do not seem particularly unusual—at least not until you examine them more closely. Would you invest your money in a company that manufactured the three-pronged device shown in Figure 3.15(b)? Such an object could not be made as pictured because the middle prong appears to be in two different places at the same time. However, this type of impossible figure is more likely to confuse people from Western cultures. Classic research in the 1970s showed that people in some African cultures do not represent three-dimensional visual space in their art, and they do not perceive depth in drawings that contain pictorial depth cues. These people see no ambiguity in drawings similar to the three-pronged trident, and they can draw the figure accurately from memory much more easily than people from Western cultures can (Bloomer, 1976).

An **illusion** is a false perception or a misperception of an actual stimulus in the environment. We can misperceive size, shape, or the relationship of one element to another. We need not pay to see illusions performed by magicians. Illusions occur naturally, and we see them all the time. An oar in the water appears to be bent where it meets the water. The moon looks much larger at the horizon than it does overhead. Why? One explanation of the *moon illusion* involves relative size. This idea suggests that the moon looks very large on the horizon because it is viewed in comparison to trees, buildings, and other objects. When viewed overhead, the moon cannot be directly compared with other objects, and it appears smaller.

In Figure 3.15(c), the two lines are the same length, but the diagonals extending outward from both ends of the upper line make it look longer than the lower line, which has diagonals pointing inward, a phenomenon known as the *Müller-Lyer illusion*. The *Ponzo illusion* also plays an interesting trick on our estimation of size. Look at Figure 3.15(d) Contrary to your perceptions, bars A and B are the same length. Again, perceptions of size and distance, which we trust and which are normally accurate in informing us about the real world, can be wrong. If you saw two obstructions like the ones in the illusion on real railroad tracks, the one that looks larger would indeed be larger. So the Ponzo illusion is not a natural illusion but a contrived one. In fact, all these illusions are really misapplications of principles that nearly always work properly in normal everyday experience.

◆ **illusion**
A false perception or a misperception of an actual stimulus in the environment.

FIGURE 3.15 **Some Puzzling Perceptions**

(a) Do you see an old woman or a young woman? (b) Why couldn't you build a replica of this three-pronged device? (c) Which horizontal line appears to be longer? (d) Which bar, A or B, is longer? *Source:* "Old Woman/Young Woman" by E. G. Boring.

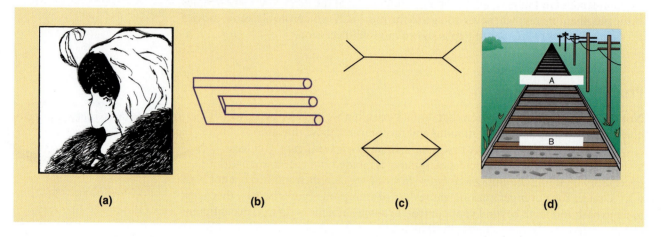

(a)   (b)   (c)   (d)

Because responses to a number of illusions are universal, many psychologists believe they are inborn. However, British psychologist R. L. Gregory believed that susceptibility to the Müller-Lyer and other such illusions is not innate. Rather, the culture in which people live is responsible to some extent for the illusions they perceive. To test whether susceptibility to the Müller-Lyer and similar illusions is due to experience, Segall and others (1966) tested 1,848 adults and children from 15 different cultures in Africa, the Philippines, and the United States. Included were a group of Zulus from South Africa and a group of Illinois residents. The study revealed that "there were marked differences in illusion susceptibility across the cultural groups included in this study" (Segall, 1994, p. 137). People from all the cultures showed some tendency to perceive the Müller-Lyer illusion, indicating a biological component, but experience was clearly a factor. Zulus, who have round houses and see few corners of any kind, are not fooled by this illusion. Illinois residents saw the illusion readily, while the Zulu tribespeople tended not to see it.

In another classic cross-cultural study of illusions, Pedersen and Wheeler (1983) studied perceptions of the Müller-Lyer illusion among two groups of Navajos. The group who lived in rectangular houses and had experienced corners, angles, and edges tended to see the illusion. The members of the other group, like the Zulus, tended not to see it because their cultural experience consisted of round houses.

Some visual illusions seem to be culture-dependent. For example, Zulus and people from other cultures in which the houses lack straight sides and corners do not perceive the Müller-Lyer illusion.

Unusual Perceptual Experiences

At the beginning of the chapter, you read about **synesthesia,** the capacity for responding to stimuli with both unusual perceptions and typical ones. As noted earlier, brain-imaging studies have demonstrated that synesthesia is a very real phenomenon, but what about other kinds of unusual perceptual experiences?

◆ **synesthesia**

The capacity for responding to stimuli simultaneously with normal and unusual perceptions.

Subliminal Perception

Recall that synesthesia involves perception without sensation. For decades, psychologists have studied a similar phenomenon known as **subliminal perception,** the capacity to perceive and respond to stimuli that are presented below the threshold of awareness. Neuroimaging studies show that the brain does, indeed, respond physiologically to subliminally presented stimuli (Brown, 2004; Bernat et al., 2001). Moreover, subliminal information can influence behavior to some degree. For example, when people are subliminally exposed to a picture of one person hitting another, they are more likely to judge a consciously perceived neutral scene, such as two people talking in a restaurant, as involving some kind of aggression (Todorov & Bargh, 2002).

But how strongly does subliminal perception affect behavior? You might remember the infamous "rats" commercial that the Republican party ran during the 2000 presidential campaign, in which the word *bureaucrats* was reduced to *rats* for about $^1/_{30}$ of a second. Democrats accused Republicans of attempting to subliminally influence voters against Albert Gore, the Democratic party candidate. The use of messages presented below the threshold of awareness in advertising, often called *subliminal persuasion,* has been around for decades. However, most research on subliminal perception suggests that, although the phenomenon does exist, it probably cannot produce the kinds of behavior changes claimed by the proponents of its use for advertising purposes (Greenwald, 1992).

Similarly, people who want to lose weight may purchase audiotapes containing subliminal messages such as "I will eat less" embedded in recordings of music or ocean waves in the hopes that listening to the tapes will help them control their appetite. Recordings of this kind are also marketed to people who want to quit smoking. However, experimental, placebo-controlled studies have found that such subliminal messages have no effect on behavior (Greenwald, 1992; Greenwald et al., 1991; Russell et al., 1991).

◆ *In what ways does subliminal perception influence behavior?*

◆ **subliminal perception**

The capacity to perceive and respond to stimuli that are presented below the threshold of awareness.

Extrasensory Perception

Extrasensory perception (ESP) is defined as gaining information about objects, events, or another person's thoughts through some means other than the known sensory channels. Several different kinds of ESP have been proposed to exist. *Telepathy* means gaining awareness of the thoughts, feelings, or activities of another person without the use of the senses—in other words, reading a person's mind. *Clairvoyance* means gaining information about objects or events without use of the senses, such as knowing the contents of a letter before opening it. *Precognition* refers to an awareness of an event before it occurs. Most of the reported cases of precognition in everyday life have occurred while people were dreaming.

Many studies of ESP employ the *Ganzfeld procedure,* a study design in which two individuals, a "sender" and a "receiver," are placed in separate rooms. The rooms are specially designed to minimize distractions and to facilitate deep concentration. Experimenters provide senders with messages that they are supposed to attempt to transmit to receivers. Some studies using the Ganzfeld technique have suggested that ESP exists and that some people are more capable of sending and receiving extrasensory messages than others (Bem & Honorton, 1994). However, in almost all cases, attempts at replication of these studies have failed (Milton & Wiseman, 2001). Thus, most psychologists remain skeptical about the existence of ESP.

◆ *What have studies of ESP shown?*

◆ **extrasensory perception (ESP)**

Gaining information about objects, events, or another person's thoughts through some means other than the known sensory channels.

We began and ended this chapter with an examination of some unusual kinds of perceptual experiences. In synesthesia, one kind of perception (e.g., visual) occurs in response to stimuli that normally elicit another kind of perception (e.g., auditory). Subliminal perception occurs in response to stimuli that we are unaware of having sensed. ESP, if it exists, involves perception in the absence of any sensory stimulus. While such phenomena are intriguing, navigating through our everyday sensory environments would be much more difficult without reliable connections among sensory stimuli, the process of sensation, and the process of perception that mark our more typical sensory and perceptual experiences.

Apply It 3.1 Noise and Hearing Loss

Did you know that every individual has a fairly high risk of suffering from some kind of hearing loss? About one in every 1,000 infants in the United States is born with a hearing loss caused by birth injury or genetic defects (CDC, 2003). In addition, diseases and injuries can cause hearing loss in individuals of any age. *Conduction deafness* occurs when the eardrum or the bones of the middle ear are affected. Most such defects can be repaired medically or surgically. Likewise, there are effective treatments for *sensorineural hearing loss* in which the cochlea suffers damage (i.e., cochlear implant surgery). Congenital hearing losses and those that are caused by disease or injury are preventable only to the extent that the underlying causes are preventable. By contrast, hearing loss due to excessive noise is clearly preventable.

According to experts more than 75% of the cases of hearing loss in older adults are caused by exposure to loud noises (Kalb, 1997). Moreover, cross-cultural research comparing elders in noisy and non-noisy cultural environments supports this conclusion. In one such study, 80-year-old individuals from a rural tribe in the Sudan in Africa scored as well on a hearing test as 20-year-old individuals from industrialized countries (Bennett, 1990).

How much noise does it take to damage hearing? According to the Environmental Protection Agency, just 3 minutes of exposure to sounds above 100 decibels can cause permanent hearing loss (Noise Pollution Council, 2003). Moreover, there are many sources of excessive noise in our everyday environments.

Members of some Sudanese tribes play stringed instruments rather quietly during celebrations. Perhaps because they are not exposed to much noise, these people generally have very sharp hearing.

Noisy Toys

Experts warn that children who play with toy weapons may be at risk for temporary or permanent hearing loss. In an eye-opening classic study, researchers Axelsson and Jerson (1985) tested seven squeaking toys that, at a distance of 10 centimeters, emitted sound levels loud enough to put toddlers at risk for hearing loss at only 2 minutes of daily exposure. These researchers' tests of various toy weapons also found that all exceeded the 130-decibel peak level that is considered the upper limit for exposure to brief explosive sounds if hearing loss is to be avoided.

Fireworks

Firecrackers and other popular fireworks items pose a significant hearing hazard if they explode close enough to the ear. In one study, a number of firecrackers were tested at 3 meters, and sound levels were found to range from 130 decibels to a highly dangerous 190 decibels (Gupta & Vishwakarma, 1989).

Amplified Music

Individuals who routinely crank up the volume on their CD players to full blast expose themselves to potentially damaging sounds every day, often with little or no awareness of the threat posed to hearing. Moreover, this blast of high-decibel sound is often delivered to the inner ear at very close range through headphones or "earbuds." And the decibel levels common at rock concerts can damage hearing very rapidly. For example, rock musician Kathy Peck lost 40% of her hearing in a single evening after her band opened a stadium concert. In 1986, the rock group The Who entered the *Guiness Book of World Records* as the loudest rock band on record, blasting out deafening sound intensities that measured 120 decibels at a distance of 164 feet from the speakers. Unless their ears were protected, audience members within that 164-foot radius probably suffered some irreversible hearing loss. And the band mem-

bers? Pete Townsend of The Who has severely damaged hearing and, in addition, is plagued by *tinnitus,* an annoying condition that causes him to experience continuous ringing in the ears.

Power Tools

Many types of power tools emit sufficient noise to damage hearing. Experts claim that exposure to a lawn mower, for example (a noise level of about 90 decibels), for more than 8 hours in a 24-hour period can damage hearing. For every increase of 5 decibels, maximum exposure time to the tool should be cut in half: 4 hours for 95 decibels, 2 hours for 100 decibels, and 1 hour for 105 decibels.

Protect Yourself from Hearing Loss

How can you protect yourself from the effects of noise?

- If you must be exposed to loud noise, use earplugs (not the kind used for swimming) or earmuffs to reduce noise, or put your fingers in your ears. Leave the scene as soon as possible.

- If you must engage in an extremely noisy activity, such as cutting wood with a chain saw, limit periods of exposure so that stunned hair cells can recover.

- Keep the volume down on your portable radio or CD player. If the volume control is numbered 1 to 10, a volume above 4 probably exceeds the federal standards for noise. If you have ringing or a tickling sensation in your ears after you remove your headset, or if sounds seem muffled, you could have sustained some hearing loss.

Chapter 3 Summary

◆ The Process of Sensation p. 74

◆ How is sensory information transmitted to the brain? p. 74

Stimuli that cross the sensory thresholds are picked up by sensory receptors in the sense organs. Through the process of transduction, these receptors change sensory stimuli into neural impulses.

◆ Vision p. 75

◆ How does each part of the eye function in vision? p. 76

The cornea bends light rays inward through the pupil—the small, dark opening in the eye. The iris dilates and contracts the pupil to regulate the amount of light entering the eye. The

lens changes its shape as it focuses images of objects at varying distances on the retina, a thin layer of tissue that contains the sensory receptors for vision. The cones detect color and fine detail; they function best in adequate light. The rods are extremely sensitive and enable vision in dim light.

◆ What path does visual information take from the retina to the primary visual cortex? p. 77

The rods and the cones transduce light waves into neural impulses that pass from the bipolar cells to the ganglion cells, whose axons form the optic nerve beyond the retinal wall of each eye. At the optic chiasm, the two optic nerves come together, and some of the nerve fibers from each eye cross to the opposite side of the brain. They synapse

with neurons in the thalamus, which transmit the neural impulses to the primary visual cortex.

◆ How do we detect the difference between one color and another? p. 78

The perception of color results from the reflection of particular wavelengths of the visual spectrum from the surfaces of objects.

◆ What two major theories attempt to explain color vision? p. 78

Two major theories that attempt to explain color vision are the trichromatic theory and the opponent-process theory.

◆ Hearing p. 81

◆ What determines the pitch and loudness of a sound, and how is each quality measured? p. 81

The pitch of a sound is determined by the frequency of the sound waves. The loudness of a sound is determined largely by the amplitude of the sound waves.

◆ How do the outer ear, middle ear, and inner ear function in hearing? p. 82

Sound waves enter the pinna and travel to the end of the auditory canal, causing the eardrum to vibrate. This sets in motion the ossicles in the middle ear, which amplify the sound waves. The vibration of the oval window causes activity in the inner ear, setting in motion the fluid in the cochlea. The moving fluid pushes and pulls the hair cells attached to the thin basilar membrane, which transduce the vibrations into neural impulses. The auditory nerve then carries the neural impulses to the brain.

◆ What two major theories attempt to explain hearing? p. 83

Two major theories that attempt to explain hearing are place theory and frequency theory.

◆ Smell and Taste p. 83

◆ What path does a smell message take from the nose to the brain? p. 83

The act of smelling begins when odor molecules reach the smell receptors in the olfactory epithelium, at the top of the nasal cavity. The axons of these receptors relay the smell message to the olfactory bulbs. From there, the smell message travels to the thalamus and the orbitofrontal cortex, which distinguish the odor and relay that information to other parts of the brain.

◆ What are the primary taste sensations, and how are they detected? p. 84

The primary taste sensations are sweet, salty, sour, and bitter, along with a newly discovered one for glutamate, called umami. The receptor cells for taste are found in the taste buds on the tongue and in other parts of the mouth and throat.

◆ The Skin Senses p. 85

◆ How does the skin provide sensory information? p. 86

Sensitive nerve endings in the skin convey tactile information to the brain when an object touches and depresses the skin. The neural impulses for touch sensations ultimately register in the brain's somatosensory cortex.

◆ What is the function of pain, and how is pain influenced by psychological factors, culture, and endorphins? p. 86

Pain can be a valuable warning and a protective mechanism, motivating people to tend to an injury, to restrict activity, and to seek medical help. Negative thinking can influence the perception of pain. Some cultures encourage individuals to suppress (or exaggerate) emotional reactions to pain. Endorphins are natural painkillers produced by the body, which block pain and produce a feeling of well-being.

◆ The Spatial Orientation Senses p. 87

◆ What kinds of information do the kinesthetic and vestibular senses provide? p. 87

The kinesthetic sense provides information about the position of body parts in relation to one another and movement of the entire body or its parts. This information is detected by sensory receptors in the joints, ligaments, and muscles. The vestibular sense detects movement and provides information about the body's orientation in space. Sensory receptors in the semicircular canals and the vestibular sacs sense changes in motion and the orientation of the head.

◆ Influences on Perception p. 88

◆ What is gained and what is lost in the process of attention? p. 88

Attention enables the brain to focus on some sensations while screening others out. Unattended stimuli may be missed altogether or incorrectly perceived.

◆ How does prior knowledge influence perception? p. 90

Individuals use bottom-up and top-down processing to apply prior knowledge to perceptual processes. Expectations based on prior knowledge may predispose people to perceive sensations in a particular way.

◆ How does information from multiple sources aid perception? p. 90

The brain integrates information from different senses to process complex stimuli such as speech and the movement of objects.

◆ Principles of Perception p. 91

◆ What are the principles that govern perceptual organization? p. 91

The Gestalt principles of perceptual organization include figure-ground, similarity, proximity, continuity, and closure. Perceptual constancy is the tendency to perceive objects as maintaining the same size, shape, and brightness, despite changes in lighting conditions or changes in the retinal image that result when an object is viewed from different angles and distances.

◆ What are some of the binocular and monocular depth cues? p. 92

Binocular depth cues include convergence and binocular disparity, which depend on both eyes working together for depth perception. Monocular depth cues, those that can be perceived by one eye, include interposition, linear perspective, relative size, texture gradient, atmospheric perspective, shadow or shading, and motion parallax.

◆ How does the brain perceive motion? p. 93

The brain perceives real motion by comparing the movement of images across the retina to information derived from the spatial orientation senses and to reference points it assumes to be stable.

◆ What are three types of puzzling perceptions? p. 95

Three types of puzzling perceptions are ambiguous figures, impossible figures, and illusions.

◆ Unusual Perceptual Experiences p. 97

◆ In what ways does subliminal perception influence behavior? p. 97

Subliminal perception has subtle influences on behavior but appears to be ineffective at persuading people to buy products or to vote in certain ways.

◆ What have studies of ESP shown? p. 97

Some studies of ESP have suggested that this type of perception exists, but researchers have not been able to replicate their results.

◆ KEY TERMS

absolute threshold, p. 74
accommodation, p. 76
afterimage, p. 79
amplitude, p. 81
attention, p. 88
audition, p. 82
binocular depth cues, p. 92
blind spot, p. 77
bottom-up processing, p. 90
brightness, p. 78
cochlea, p. 82
color blindness, p. 80
cones, p. 76
cornea, p. 76
cross-modal perception, 90
decibel (dB), p. 81
depth perception, p. 92
difference threshold, p. 74
endorphins, p. 86
extrasensory perception, 97
feature detectors, p. 78
fovea, p. 77
frequency, p. 81

frequency theory, p. 83
Gestalt, p. 91
gustation, p. 84
hair cells, p. 82
hue, p. 78
illusion, p. 95
inattentional blindness, p. 88
inner ear, p. 82
just noticeable difference (JND), p. 74
kinesthetic sense, p. 87
lens, p. 76
middle ear, p. 82
monocular depth cues, p. 93
olfaction, p. 83
olfactory bulbs, p. 84
olfactory epithelium, p. 83
opponent-process theory, p. 79
optic nerve, p. 77
outer ear, p. 82
perception, p. 73
perceptual constancy, p. 92

perceptual set, p. 90
place theory, p. 83
primary visual cortex, p. 77
retina, p. 76
rods, p. 76
saturation, p. 78
semicircular canals, p. 87
sensation, p. 73
sensory adaptation, p. 75
sensory receptors, p. 75
subliminal perception, p. 97
synesthesia, p. 97
tactile, p. 86
taste buds, p. 85
timbre, p. 81
top-down processing, p. 90
transduction, p. 75
trichromatic theory, p. 78
vestibular sense, p. 87
visible spectrum, p. 75
wavelength, p. 75
Weber's law, p. 74

◆ **SECTION ONE: Chapter Review**

The Process of Sensation (pp. 74–75)

1. The process through which the senses detect sensory information and transmit it to the brain is called (sensation, perception).

2. The point at which you can barely sense a stimulus 50% of the time is called the (absolute, difference) threshold.

3. The difference threshold is the same for all individuals. (true/false)

4. Which of the following is not true of sensory receptors?
   a. They are specialized to detect certain sensory stimuli.
   b. They transduce sensory stimuli into neural impulses.
   c. They are located in the brain.
   d. They provide the link between the physical sensory world and the brain.

5. The process by which a sensory stimulus is converted into a neural impulse is called _____.

6. Each morning when Jackie goes to work at a dry cleaner, she smells a strong odor of cleaning fluid. After she is there for a few minutes, she is no longer aware of it. What accounts for this?
   a. signal detection theory
   b. sensory adaptation
   c. transduction
   d. the just noticeable difference

Vision (pp. 75–80)

7. Match each part of the eye with its description.
   ___ (1) the colored part of the eye
   ___ (2) the opening in the iris that dilates and constricts
   ___ (3) the transparent covering of the iris
   ___ (4) the transparent structure that focuses an inverted image on the retina
   ___ (5) the thin, photosensitive membrane at the back of the eye on which the lens focuses an inverted image
   a. retina   c. pupil   e. lens
   b. cornea   d. iris

8. The receptor cells in the retina that enable you to see in dim light are the (cones, rods); the cells that enable you to see color and sharp images are (cones, rods).

9. Neural impulses are carried from the retina to the thalamus by the _____ and then relayed to their final destination, the _____.
   a. optic chiasm; primary visual cortex
   b. rods and cones; optic nerve
   c. optic nerve; primary visual cortex
   d. optic nerve; optic chiasm

Hearing (pp. 81–83)

10. Pitch is chiefly determined by _____; loudness is chiefly determined by _____.
    a. amplitude; frequency
    b. wavelength; frequency
    c. intensity; amplitude
    d. frequency; amplitude

11. Pitch is measured in (decibels, hertz); loudness is measured in (decibels, hertz).

12. Match the part of the ear with the structures it contains.
    ___ (1) ossicles   a. outer ear
    ___ (2) pinna, auditory canal   b. middle ear
    ___ (3) cochlea, hair cells   c. inner ear

13. The receptors for hearing are found in the
    a. ossicles.   c. auditory membrane.
    b. auditory canal.   d. cochlea.

14. The two major theories that attempt to explain hearing are
    a. conduction theory and place theory.
    b. hair cell theory and frequency theory.
    c. place theory and frequency theory.
    d. conduction theory and hair cell theory.

Smell and Taste (pp. 83–85)

15. The technical name for the process or sensation of smell is (gustation, olfaction).

16. The olfactory, or smell, receptors are located in the
    a. olfactory tract.   c. olfactory epithelium.
    b. olfactory nerve.   d. olfactory bulbs.

17. The five taste sensations are _____, _____, _____, _____, and _____.

18. Each (papilla, taste bud) contains from 60 to 100 receptor cells.

The Skin Senses (pp. 85–87)

19. Each skin receptor responds only to touch, pressure, warmth, or cold. (true/false)

20. The (kinesthetic, vestibular) sense provides information about the position of body parts in relation to each other and about movement in those body parts.

The Spatial Orientation Senses (p. 87)

21. The receptors for the (kinesthetic, vestibular) sense are located in the semicircular canals and vestibular sacs in the (middle ear, inner ear).

Influences on Perception (pp. 88–90)

22. When people try to keep track of several moving objects at once, they often exhibit _____.

23. When people look for a perceptual pattern in individual bits of sensory information, they are using _____.

24. When a speaker's lips don't match what she is saying, it is difficult to understand what she is saying because speech perception requires _____.

Principles of Perception (pp. 91–96)

25. Match each Gestalt principle with its example:
    ____ (1) **** **** **** perceived as three groups of four
    ____ (2) - - - - -> perceived as an arrow
    ____ (3) ***&&&###@@@ perceived as four groups of three
    a. closure
    b. similarity
    c. proximity

26. Retinal disparity and convergence are two (monocular, binocular) depth cues.

27. Match the appropriate monocular depth cue with each example.
    ____ (1) one building partly blocking another
    ____ (2) railroad tracks converging in the distance
    ____ (3) closer objects appearing to move faster than objects farther away
    ____ (4) objects farther away looking smaller than near objects
    a. motion parallax   c. interposition
    b. linear perspective   d. relative size

28. Rob had been staring at a point of light in the night sky when it suddenly appeared to start moving. Rob's experience is an example of the phi phenomenon. (true/false)

29. An illusion is
    a. an imaginary sensation.
    b. an impossible figure.
    c. a misperception of a real stimulus.
    d. a figure-ground reversal.

30. In situations where you have some prior knowledge and experience, you are likely to rely more on (bottom-up, top-down) processing.

31. Perceptual set is most directly related to a person's
    a. needs.   c. expectations.
    b. interests.   d. emotions.

Unusual Perceptual Experiences (p. 97)

32. Images that are presented below the level of conscious awareness have no effect on subsequent behavior. (true/false)

33. ESP is often studied using the _____.

◆ SECTION TWO: Multiple Choice

1. Perception is the process we use to
   a. organize and interpret stimuli.
   b. detect stimuli.
   c. gather information from the environment.
   d. retrieve information from memory.

2. Which part of the nose serves the same function as the retina in the eye and the basilar membrane in the ear?
   a. olfactory bulbs   c. olfactory neurons
   b. olfactory lining   d. olfactory epithelium

3. The vestibular system is most closely related to
   a. audition.   c. gustation.
   b. olfaction.   d. kinesthetics.

4. As you look down a sandy beach, the sand seems to become more fine as it goes into the distance. This depth cue is called
   a. elevation.   c. texture gradient.
   b. convergence.   d. linear perspective.

5. The minimum amount of physical stimulation necessary for a person to experience a sensation 50% of
the time is called the
   a. figure-to-ground ratio.   c. difference threshold.
   b. blind spot.   d. absolute threshold.

6. Which of the following is the correct sequence of
structures encountered by light moving toward the
retina?
   a. lens, cornea, pupil   c. pupil, cornea, lens
   b. pupil, lens, cornea   d. cornea, pupil, lens

7. Which theory suggests that color vision can be
explained by the existence of three types of cones,
which are maximally sensitive to blue, green, or red?
   a. opponent-process theory
   b. trichromatic theory
   c. signal detection theory
   d. gate-control theory

8. Ms. Scarpaci complains that the street noise in her
apartment is much louder than the noise in her
upstairs neighbor's apartment. To test her claim, you
use a sound meter to check the noise in each apartment. Your meter registers 50 dB in Ms. Scarpaci's
apartment and only 30 dB in her neighbor's. From
these readings, how much louder is Ms. Scarpaci's
apartment than her neighbor's?
   a. 20% louder
   b. 10 times louder
   c. 100 times louder
   d. not enough to be noticeable

9. When you hear a tone of 400 Hz, some of the hair
cells in your ear are stimulated, but most others are
not. This is the basic idea behind the
   a. place theory of hearing.
   b. volley principle of hearing.
   c. frequency theory of hearing.
   d. bone conduction theory of hearing.

10. The receptors for odors are located in the
   a. olfactory epithelium.
   b. projecting septum.
   c. turbinate mucosa.
   d. vestibular membrane.

11. Nerve endings in the skin send signals to the
somatosensory cortex for processing. This area of
the brain is found in the
   a. frontal lobe.   c. parietal lobe.
   b. temporal lobe.   d. occipital lobe.

12. Which of the following sensations would best be
explained by the gate-control theory?
   a. the pain of a pin prick
   b. the smell of dinner cooking
   c. the taste of your favorite cookie
   d. the sound of paper rustling

13. The receptors for the kinesthetic sense are located in
the
   a. middle ear.
   b. inner ear.
   c. joints, ligaments, and muscles.
   d. cortex.

14. The depth cue that occurs when your eyes "cross" to
see an object that is very near your face is called
   a. convergence.   c. aerial perspective.
   b. elevation.   d. binocular disparity.

15. Weber's law applies to
   a. difference thresholds.
   b. absolute thresholds.
   c. transduction thresholds.
   d. retinal thresholds.

16. Gustation is also known as the sense of
   a. taste.   c. smell.
   b. hearing.   d. vision.

17. In the Ponzo illusion, two bars of equal length
are superimposed over a picture of railroad tracks
that recede into the distance and eventually converge
at a single point. One reason the bars appear to be of
unequal lengths is because the illusion takes advantage of
   a. binocular disparity cues.
   b. linear perspective cues.
   c. apparent motion cues.
   d. depth disparity cues.

18. Perceptual set reflects
   a. bottom-up processing.
   b. top-down processing.
   c. subliminal processing.
   d. extrasensory processing.

19. The process through which the senses detect sensory
stimuli and transmit them to the brain is called
   a. consciousness.   c. sensation.
   b. perception.   d. reception.

20. If you were listening to music and your friend wanted to know how far he could turn the volume down
without your noticing, he would need to know your
   a. sensory threshold for sound.
   b. absolute threshold for sound.
   c. transduction threshold for sound.
   d. difference threshold for sound.

21. Margaret is reaching middle age and is having trouble reading fine print. She did not have this problem
when she was younger. Her optometrist has concluded that she has presbyopia, or "old eyes." Given
this diagnosis, you know that Margaret's difficulty is
due to the aging of her
   a. corneas.   c. retinas.
   b. lenses.   d. rods and cones.

22. The trichromatic theory of color is based on the idea that the retina contains three types of
    a. rods.
    b. cones.
    c. bipolar cells.
    d. ganglion cells.

23. Megan watches from the car as her parents drive away from her grandfather's house. Because of _____, Megan knows her grandfather's house remains the same size, even though the image gets smaller as they drive farther away.
    a. the law of good continuation
    b. the law of proximity
    c. size constancy
    d. the Müller-Lyer illusion

24. If you are sitting in a restaurant and hear someone at a nearby table mention your name, research examining the _____ suggests that you are likely to focus your attention on the table where that conversation is occurring.
    a. autokinetic illusion
    b. principle of closure
    c. cocktail party phenomenon
    d. Ponzo illusion

25. _____ is a type of ESP in which people know what is going to happen in the future.
    a. telepathy   b. clairvoyance   c. precognition

SECTION THREE: Fill In the Blank

1. Sensation is to _____ as perception is to _____.

2. The _____ threshold is a measure of the smallest change in a physical stimulus required to produce a noticeable difference in sensation 50% of the time.

3. Researchers in _____ psychology study phenomena related to sensation, such as the least amount of a stimulus required for detection.

4. _____ refers to the process by which a sensory stimulus is changed by the sensory receptors into neural impulses.

5. As part of his training in personnel relations, Ted had to spend a whole day in a very noisy factory. Although the sound seemed almost painful at first, he noticed by the end of the day that it didn't seem so loud anymore. This is an example of _____ _____.

6. One of the major parts of the eye, the _____, performs the first step in vision by bending the light rays inward through the pupil.

7. According to the _____ theory of color vision, certain cells in the visual system increase their rate of firing to signal one color and decrease their firing rate to signal the opposing color.

8. An important characteristic of sound, _____ is determined by the number of cycles completed by a sound wave in 1 second.

9. The taste sensation called _____ results from such protein-rich foods as meat, milk, cheese, and seafood.

10. _____ psychologists studied perception and were guided by the principle that "the whole is more than the sum of its parts."

11. That humans seem to perceive the environment in terms of an object standing out against a background is known as the _____ _____ principle.

12. Ted, an artist, creates pictures that force viewers to fill in gaps in the lines, thereby forming a whole pattern. Ted's art takes advantage of the principle of _____.

13. One important contribution to three-dimensional perception is _____ _____, which results when each eye receives a slightly different view of the objects being viewed.

14. When a person's facial expression and tone of voice don't match, we usually rely on her _____ _____ to make a determination about her actual emotional state.

15. Studies examining _____ _____ show that the brain responds to stimuli that are presented below the threshold of awareness.

SECTION FOUR: Comprehensive Practice Test

1. The process by which humans detect visual, auditory, and other stimuli is known as
    a. perception.
    b. transduction.
    c. sensation.
    d. threshold.

2. The process of organizing and interpreting the information gathered through vision, hearing, and the other senses is known as
    a. perception.
    b. the absolute threshold.
    c. transduction.
    d. sensory induction.

3. The _____ _____ is the minimum amount of stimulus that can be detected 50% of the time.
   a. difference reaction
   b. absolute reaction
   c. difference threshold
   d. absolute threshold

4. The _____ _____ is a measure of the smallest change in a stimulus required for a person to detect a change in the stimulus 50% of the time.
   a. difference reaction
   b. absolute difference
   c. difference threshold
   d. sensory threshold

5. Sense organs have specialized cells called _____ that detect and respond to particular stimuli.
   a. sensory detectors
   b. sensory receptors
   c. perceptual responders
   d. perceptual receptors

6. When you see, hear, taste, smell, or feel a sensory stimulus, the physical energy that caused the stimulus is changed to neural impulses that are processed in your brain. This process is known as
   a. sensory adaptation.
   b. the absolute threshold.
   c. perceptual organization.
   d. transduction.

7. Joe installed an in-ground pool last spring, although his wife thought he was crazy to do so when it was still cool outside. The first day it seemed a little warm Joe jumped in the new pool, but soon he realized just how cold the water really was. As he continued to "enjoy" the water, it seemed to become less cold and even comfortable. This was probably due to a process called
   a. sensory adaptation.
   b. difference threshold.
   c. sensory threshold.
   d. perceptual adaptation.

8. If someone tells you she loves the color of your eyes, she is actually talking about your
   a. pupils.
   b. corneas.
   c. irises.
   d. retinas.

9. Rods are to cones as _____ is to _____.
   a. dim light; color
   b. color; dim light
   c. bright light; color
   d. color; bright light

10. The blind spot in the back of the eye is where
    a. the rods and cones come together.
    b. the retina converges on the fovea.
    c. the optic nerve leaves the eye.
    d. the blood supply enters the eye.

11. When you read a book, the lenses in your eyes are probably a little more spherical, and when you gaze up at the stars at night, your lenses become flatter. These differences are due to a process known as
    a. retinal disparity.
    b. lens reactivity.
    c. accommodation.
    d. adaptation.

12. LaShonda tells her roommate that we see color because three kinds of cones react to one of three colors—blue, green, or red. LaShonda has been reading about the _____ theory of color vision.
    a. opponent-process
    b. trichromatic
    c. relative disparity
    d. complementary color

13. The number of cycles completed by a sound wave in 1 second is the wave's
    a. decibel level.
    b. timbre.
    c. amplitude.
    d. frequency.

14. The job of the _____, also known as the hammer, the anvil, and the stirrup, is to amplify sound as it moves from the eardrum to the oval window.
    a. ossicles
    b. cochlear bones
    c. hair cells
    d. timbre bones

15. Tomas says that we hear different pitches depending on which spot along the basilar membrane vibrates the most. He is talking about the _____ theory of hearing.
    a. frequency
    b. position
    c. cochlea
    d. place

16. Olfaction refers to
    a. the sense of taste.
    b. the sense of smell.
    c. the ability to detect skin temperature.
    d. the ability to differentiate sounds.

17. All parts of the tongue can detect sweet, sour, salty, and bitter. (true/false)

18. Tactile is used in reference to the sense of
    a. smell.
    b. balance.
    c. taste.
    d. touch.

19. The gate-control theory of pain suggests that slow-conducting nerve fibers carry pain messages and that these messages can be blocked by messages from fast-conducting nerve fibers. (true/false)

20. An athlete's ability to move gracefully on the parallel bars is due to the _____ sense.
    a. tactile
    b. olfactory
    c. kinesthetic
    d. eustachian

21. The vestibular sense provides information that allows you to know that a red door is still red even in a dark room. (true/false)

22. The half-time show at a football game involved a hundred people marching on the field—all in different colored uniforms. Then they took on a formation and suddenly all the red uniforms spelled out the initials of the home team. Gestalt psychologists would suggest that the principle of _____ explains why fans could read the initials.
  a. similarity
  b. continuity
  c. closure
  d. constancy

23. Which of the following is not a Gestalt principle of grouping?
  a. closure
  b. similarity
  c. constancy
  d. proximity

24. If you move your finger closer and closer to your nose and focus on perceiving only one image of the finger even when it is almost touching the nose, your eyes begin to turn inward. This eye movement is known as
  a. disparity.
  b. monocular adjustment.
  c. congruity.
  d. convergence.

25. Cues such as interposition, linear perspective, and relative size are known as _____ depth cues.
  a. binocular
  b. divergent
  c. monocular
  d. bimodal

26. Lines of the same length with diagonals at their ends pointing in or out appear to be of different lengths because of the _____ illusion.
  a. Ponzo
  b. Müller-Lyer
  c. trident
  d. ambiguous

27. Bottom-up processing is to _____ stimuli as top-down processing is to _____ stimuli.
  a. unfamiliar; familiar
  b. visual; auditory
  c. familiar; unfamiliar
  d. perceptual; subliminal

28. In the game "Name That Tune," players try to guess the name of a song after hearing only its first few notes. Succeeding at this game requires
  a. top-down processing.
  b. bottom-up processing.
  c. cross-modal perception.

29. Most psychologists think that
  a. subliminal advertising is very effective.
  b. some people have a special talent for ESP.
  c. synesthesia is the result of an overactive imagination.
  d. the brain is capable of perceiving stimuli presented below the threshold of awareness.

◆ **SECTION FIVE: Critical Thinking**

1. Vision and hearing are generally believed to be the two most highly prized senses. How would your life change if you lost your sight? How would your life change if you lost your hearing? Which sense would you find more traumatic to lose? Why?

2. Using what you have learned about how noise contributes to hearing loss, prepare a statement indicating what you think should be done to control noise pollution, even to the extent of banning certain noise hazards. Consider the workplace, the home, automobiles and other vehicles, toys, machinery, rock concerts, and so on.

States of Consciousness

chapter 4

Circadian Rhythms

◆ *In what ways do circadian rhythms affect physiological and psychological functions?*

◆ *How do disruptions in circadian rhythms affect the body and the mind?*

Sleep

◆ *How do NREM and REM sleep differ?*

◆ *What is the progression of NREM stages and REM sleep in a typical night of sleep?*

◆ *How does age influence sleep patterns?*

◆ *What is the difference between the restorative and circadian theories of sleep?*

◆ *How does sleep deprivation affect behavior and neurological functioning?*

◆ *What have researchers learned about dreams, their content, their biological basis, and their controllability?*

◆ *How do the views of contemporary psychologists concerning the nature of dreams differ from those of Freud?*

◆ *What are the various disorders that can trouble sleepers?*

Meditation and Hypnosis

◆ *What are the benefits of meditation?*

◆ *What are the effects of hypnosis, and how do theorists explain them?*

◆ *What is the connection between altered states of consciousness and culture?*

Psychoactive Drugs

◆ *How do drugs affect the brain's neurotransmitter system?*

◆ *What factors influence progression from substance use to substance abuse?*

◆ *What is the difference between physical and psychological drug dependence?*

◆ *What are the effects of stimulants, depressants, and hallucinogens on behavior?*

In 1952, Army Staff Sergeant Raymond Shaw was brought to Washington, D.C., to receive his country's highest military honor. His men spoke glowingly of his courage as they described how their small patrol had been ambushed by Communist North Korean forces. When their situation was at its most desperate, Shaw had single-handedly captured the enemy machine-gun nest that was firing on them, saving the lives of all but two of his men and leading the troops back to safety.

But Shaw's former commanding officer, the man who had brought his heroism to public attention, soon began to be troubled by nightmares that caused him to question what had actually happened. Major Bennett Marco repeatedly dreamed that he watched helplessly as Shaw murdered one of the two soldiers in the platoon who had supposedly died in the ambush. Unable to dismiss these disturbing dreams, he began to investigate Shaw. What he discovered was that the entire story was a lie. The patrol had been captured, but there had been no heroism. Instead, the soldiers had been taken to an enemy base where they were subjected to hypnotic "brainwashing" techniques that erased all memory of their captivity and convinced them that Shaw had saved their lives. In addition, Shaw was trained to carry out cold-blooded killings in response to signals from the hypnotists. Before Shaw left the enemy camp, his controllers tested his obedience by ordering him to murder one of his men in the presence of the entire patrol. Because all of the men were hypnotized when the killings happened, none of them objected or consciously remembered the episode. However, the memory had haunted Marco's dreams.

As Marco continued his investigation, it became clear to him that Shaw had been targeted for brainwashing because his stepfather was a U.S. senator. The plan called for Shaw to return to the United States, where he would be acclaimed as a hero whose loyalty to his country wouldn't be questioned. His family connections and hero status would give him close access to political leaders, putting him in an ideal position to assassinate them when enemy agents signaled him in ways that his controllers had trained him to respond to. What Marco didn't realize was that Shaw's own mother was an enemy spy, and that the ultimate goal of the plot was to put Shaw's stepfather into the position of President of the United States, thereby placing a Communist agent in the position of First Lady.

Thankfully, this story is fictional. It is the plot of a 1959 novel by Richard Condon called *The Manchurian Candidate*. Condon wrote the story at a time when there was a very real concern about the degree to which prisoners of war (POWs) might be brainwashed by their captors. After the Korean War ended in the early 1950s, the public learned that a large percentage of POWs had been subjected to intensive indoctrination designed to induce them—through a combination of psychological pressure, humiliation, repetition, and sometimes torture—to cooperate with their captors. In a small percentage of cases, soldiers had recanted their allegiance to the United States and denounced their country's "war crimes." Some even refused to return to the United States after the war ended. This phenomenon prompted serious questions about what modern scientists could do to erase people's most cherished beliefs and replace them with ideas of their own choosing.

What do scientists say about hypnosis? Could there ever be a real-life Raymond Shaw? The possibilities and limitations of mental states such as those associated with hypnosis and the more mundane ways in which we experience changes in our level of awareness are the subject of this chapter. Such a discussion should always start with clear definitions. **Consciousness** is defined as everything of which we are aware at any given time—our thoughts, feelings, sensations, and perceptions of the external environment. **Altered states of consciousness** are changes in awareness produced by sleep, meditation, hypnosis, and drugs. Before we look more closely at altered states of consciousness, such as meditation and hypnosis, let's first consider our body's physiological rhythms and the important role sleeping and dreaming play in our lives.

Circadian Rhythms

Do you notice changes in the way you feel throughout the day—fluctuations in your energy level, moods, or efficiency? More than 100 bodily functions and behaviors follow **circadian rhythms**—that is, they fluctuate regularly from a high to a low point over a 24-hour period (Dement, 1974).

The Influence of Circadian Rhythms

◆ *In what ways do circadian rhythms affect physiological and psychological functions?*

Physiological functions such as blood pressure, heart rate, appetite, secretion of hormones and digestive enzymes, sensory acuity, elimination, and even the body's response to medication all follow circadian rhythms (Hrushesky, 1994; Morofushi et al., 2001). Many psychological functions—including learning efficiency, the ability to perform a wide range of tasks, and even moods—ebb and flow according to these daily rhythms (Boivin et al., 1997; Johnson et al., 1992; Manly et al., 2002). Indeed, the circadian timing system is involved in the 24-hour variation of virtually every physiological and psychological variable researchers have studied (Kunz & Herrmann, 2000).

◆ **altered state of consciousness**

Changes in awareness produced by sleep, meditation, hypnosis, and drugs

◆ **circadian rhythm**

(sur-KAY-dee-un) Within each 24-hour period, the regular fluctuation from high to low points of certain bodily functions and behaviors.

The biological clock that controls circadian rhythms is the **suprachiasmatic nucleus (SCN),** located in the brain's hypothalamus (Ginty et al., 1993; Ralph, 1989; Ruby et al., 2002). However, the ebb and flow of circadian rhythms is not strictly biological. Environmental cues also play a part. The most significant environmental cue is bright light, particularly sunlight. Specialized cells (photoreceptors) in the retina at the back of each eye respond to the amount of light reaching the eye and relay this information via the optic nerve to the SCN. From dusk until just before dawn, the message from the retina to the SCN is relayed to the pineal gland, causing it to secrete the hormone *melatonin*. During the daylight hours, the pineal gland does not produce melatonin. Researchers have learned that melatonin induces sleep, whereas its absence helps maintain wakefulness (Baringa, 1997).

◆ **suprachiasmatic nucleus (SCN)**

A pair of tiny structures in the brain's hypothalamus that control the timing of circadian rhythms; the biological clock.

Two circadian rhythms of particular importance are the sleep/wakefulness cycle and the daily fluctuation in body temperature. Normal human body temperature ranges from a low of about 97–97.5°F between 3:00 and 4:00 a.m. to a high of about 98.6°F between 6:00 and 8:00 p.m. People sleep best when their body temperature is at its lowest, and they are most alert when their body temperature is at its daily high point. Alertness also follows a circadian rhythm, one that is quite separate from the sleep/wakefulness cycle (Monk, 1989). For most people, alertness decreases between 2:00 and 5:00 p.m. and between 2:00 and 7:00 a.m. (Webb, 1995).

Disruptions in Circadian Rhythms

◆ *How do disruptions in circadian rhythms affect the body and the mind?*

Suppose you fly from Chicago to London, and the plane lands at 12:00 a.m. Chicago time, about the time you usually go to sleep. At the same time that it is midnight in Chicago, it is 6:00 a.m. in London, almost time to get up. The clocks, the sun, and everything else in London tell you it is early morning, but you still feel like it is midnight. You are experiencing jet lag.

Chronic jet lag, such as that experienced by many airline pilots and flight attendants, produces memory deficits that may be permanent (Cho, 2001; Cho et al., 2000). You might think that airline employees who regularly fly across time zones would adjust to their schedules. However, research indicates that experienced airline workers are just as likely to suffer from jet lag as passengers on their first intercontinental flight (Criglington, 1998). Melatonin supplements have been found to be helpful for alleviating jet lag in some long-distance travelers. For others, exposure to bright sunlight during the early morning hours and avoidance of bright lights during the evening may be more effective than melatonin for restoring circadian rhythms (Edwards et al., 2000; Zisapel, 2001).

◆ **subjective night**

The time during a 24-hour period when the biological clock is telling a person to go to sleep.

Similarily, alertness and performance deteriorate if people work during **subjective night,** when their biological clock is telling them to go to sleep (Åkerstedt, 1990; Folkard, 1990). During subjective night, energy and efficiency are at their lowest points, reaction time is slowest, productivity is diminished, and industrial accidents are significantly higher. In one study, more than 17% of a group of commercial long-haul truck drivers admitted to having experienced "near misses" while dozing off behind the wheel (Häkkänen & Summala, 1999). Even the slight circadian disruption due to the 1-hour sleep loss when people put their clocks forward in spring for daylight saving time is associated with an increase in traffic accidents and a short-term but significant 6.5% increase in accidental deaths (Coren, 1996a, 1996b).

Moving work schedules forward from days to evenings to nights makes adjustment easier because people find it easier to go to bed later and wake up later than the reverse. And rotating shifts every three weeks instead of every week lessens the effect on sleep even more (Pilcher et al., 2000). Some researchers are investigating the use of a new wakefulness drug called *modafinil* that helps people remain alert without the side effects of stimulants such as caffeine (Wesensten et al., 2002). Others have used a device called a "light mask"

Research indicates that frequent flyers, such as this airline employee, are just as likely to suffer from jet lag when crossing several time zones as travelers who are on their first intercontinental journey.

to reset shift workers' biological clocks. This mask allows researchers to control the amount of light to which the closed eyelids of research participants are exposed. The findings of light mask studies suggest that exposing participants to bright light during the last 4 hours of sleep is an effective treatment for the kinds of sleep-phase delays experienced by shift workers (Cole et al., 2002). Thus, this device may become important in the treatment of sleep disorders associated with shift work.

Sleep

As noted earlier, the sleep/wakefulness cycle is a circadian rhythm. But what actually happens during our periods of sleep? Before the 1950s, there was little understanding of what goes on during the state of consciousness known as sleep. Then, in the 1950s, several universities set up sleep laboratories where people's brain waves, eye movements, chin-muscle tension, heart rate, and respiration rate were monitored through a night of sleep. From analyses of sleep recordings, known as *polysomnograms*, researchers discovered the characteristics of two major types of sleep.

NREM and REM Sleep

The two major types of sleep are NREM (non–rapid eye movement) sleep and REM (rapid eye movement) sleep. **NREM** (pronounced "NON-rem") **sleep** is sleep in which there are no rapid eye movements. Heart rate and respiration are slow and regular, there is little body movement, and blood pressure and brain activity are at their lowest points of the 24-hour period. There are four stages of NREM sleep— Stages 1, 2, 3, and 4—with Stage 1 being the lightest sleep and Stage 4 being the deepest.

REM sleep, sometimes called "active sleep," constitutes 20–25% of a normal night's sleep in adults. During the REM state, there is intense brain activity. In fact, within 1 to 2 minutes after REM sleep begins, brain metabolism increases, and brain temperature rises rapidly (Krueger & Takahashi, 1997). Epinephrine is released into the system, causing blood pressure to rise and heart rate and respiration to become faster and less regular. In contrast to this storm of internal activity, there is an external calm during REM sleep. The large muscles of the body—arms, legs, trunk—become paralyzed (Chase & Morales, 1990).

Observe a sleeper during the REM state, and you will see her or his eyes darting around under the eyelids. Eugene Azerinsky first discovered these bursts of rapid eye

◆ **NREM sleep**

Non–rapid eye movement sleep, which consists of four sleep stages and is characterized by slow, regular respiration and heart rate, little body movement, an absence of rapid eye movements, and blood pressure and brain activity that are at their 24-hour low points.

◆ *How do NREM and REM sleep differ?*

◆ **REM sleep**

A type of sleep characterized by rapid eye movements, paralysis of large muscles, fast and irregular heart and respiration rates, increased brain-wave activity, and vivid dreams.

movements in 1952, and William Dement and Nathaniel Kleitman (1957) made the connection between rapid eye movements and dreaming. It is during REM sleep that the most vivid dreams occur. When awakened from REM sleep, 80% of people report that they had been dreaming (Carskadon & Dement, 1989). And, if you awaken during REM sleep and remain awake for several minutes, you may not go back into REM sleep for at least 30 minutes. This is why most people have had the disappointing experience of waking in the middle of a wonderful dream and trying to get back to sleep quickly and into the dream again, but failing to do so.

You may have already found out through personal experience that studying all night before a big exam can cause you to yawn frequently and nod off when you take the actual test. But did you know that you can also short-circuit the learning process by engaging in this popular, though ineffective, method of exam preparation? Researchers have found that REM sleep may be critical to the consolidation of memories after learning. Several experiments have shown that participants' performance on previously acquired motor and verbal tasks improves after a period of normal sleep (Fenn et al., 2003; Nader, 2003; Walker et al., 2003). Other studies have suggested that the brain carries out the important function of memory consolidation during REM sleep. Karni and others (1994) found that research participants who were learning a new perceptual skill showed an improvement in performance, with no additional practice, 8 to 10 hours later if they had a normal night's sleep or if the researchers disturbed only their NREM sleep. Performance did not improve, however, in those who were deprived of REM sleep.

There is no doubt that REM sleep serves an important function. When people are deprived of REM sleep as a result of general sleep loss or illness, they will make up for the deprivation by getting an increased amount of REM sleep afterward, a phenomenon called **REM rebound** . Because the intensity of REM sleep is increased during a REM rebound, nightmares often occur. Alcohol, amphetamines, cocaine, and LSD suppress REM sleep, and withdrawal from these drugs results in a REM rebound (Porte & Hobson, 1996).

◆ **REM rebound**

The increased amount of REM sleep that occurs after REM deprivation; often associated with unpleasant dreams or nightmares.

◆ **sleep cycle**

A period of sleep lasting about 90 minutes and including one or more stages of NREM sleep, followed by REM sleep.

Sleep Cycles

◆ *What is the progression of NREM stages and REM sleep in a typical night of sleep?*

We all sleep in cycles. During each **sleep cycle,** which lasts about 90 minutes, a person has one or more stages of NREM sleep, followed by a period of REM sleep. Each of the NREM stages and the periods of REM sleep that occur in each cycle is associated with a distinctive brain wave pattern, as shown in Figure 4.1. Let's look closely at a typical night of sleep for a young adult.

The first sleep cycle begins with a few minutes in Stage 1 sleep, sometimes called "light sleep." Stage 1 is actually a transition stage between waking and sleeping. Irreg-

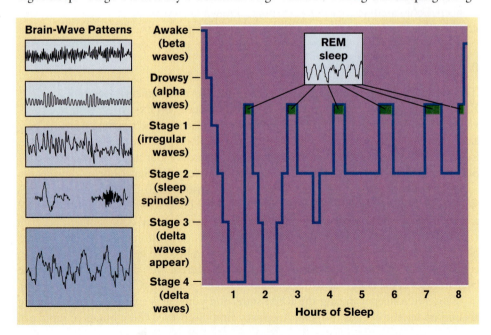

FIGURE 4.1

Brain-Wave Patterns Associated with Different Stages of Sleep

By monitoring brain-wave activity on an EEG throughout a night's sleep, researchers have identified the brain-wave patterns associated with different stages of sleep. As sleepers progress through the four NREM stages, the brain-wave pattern changes from faster, smaller waves in Stages 1 and 2 to the slower, larger delta waves in Stages 3 and 4.

ular waves, some of which are alpha waves, are characteristic of Stage 1. **Sleep spindles,** which are brain waves characterized by alternating short periods of calm and flashes of intense activity, appear in Stage 2. The appearance of sleep spindles in the electroencephalogram (EEG) usually means that the individual is in transition from the light sleep Stage 1 to a state of much deeper sleep. Consequently, sleepers are much more difficult to awaken in Stage 2 than in Stage 1. As sleep gradually becomes deeper, brain activity slows, and more **delta waves** (slow waves) appear in the EEG. When the EEG registers 20% delta waves, sleepers enter Stage 3 sleep, the beginning of **slow-wave sleep** (or deep sleep). Delta waves continue to increase. When they reach more than 50%, people enter **Stage 4 sleep**—the deepest sleep, from which they are hardest to awaken (Carskadon & Rechtschaffen, 1989; Cooper, 1994). Perhaps you have taken an afternoon nap and woke up confused, not knowing whether it was morning or night, a weekday or a weekend. If so, you probably awakened during Stage 4 sleep.

In Stage 4 sleep, delta waves may reach nearly 100% on the EEG, but after about 40 minutes in this stage, brain activity increases and the delta waves begin to disappear. Sleepers ascend back through Stage 3 and Stage 2 sleep, then enter their first REM period, which lasts 10 or 15 minutes. At the end of this REM period, the first sleep cycle is complete, and the second sleep cycle begins. Unless people awaken after the first sleep cycle, they go directly from REM into Stage 2 sleep. They then follow the same progression as in the first sleep cycle, through Stages 3 and 4 and back again into REM sleep.

After the first two sleep cycles of about 90 minutes each (3 hours total), the sleep pattern changes, and sleepers usually get no more Stage 4 sleep. From this point on, during each 90-minute sleep cycle, people alternate mainly between Stage 2 and REM sleep for the remainder of the night. With each sleep cycle, the REM period (and therefore dreaming time) get progressively longer. The last REM period of the night may last 30 to 40 minutes. Most people have about five sleep cycles (7 to 8 hours) and average 1 to 2 hours of slow-wave sleep and 1 to 2 hours of REM sleep. Figure 4.1 shows the progression through NREM and REM sleep during a typical night.

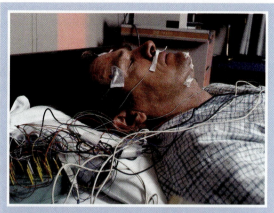

In a sleep laboratory or sleep clinic, researchers attach electrodes to a person's head to monitor brain-wave activity, eye movements, and muscle tension.

◆ **sleep spindles**

Sleep Stage 2 brain waves that feature short periods of calm interrupted by brief flashes of intense activity.

◆ **delta wave**

The slowest brain-wave pattern; associated with Stage 3 and Stage 4 NREM sleep.

◆ **slow-wave sleep**

Deep sleep; associated with Stage 3 and Stage 4 sleep.

◆ **Stage 4 sleep**

The deepest stage of NREM sleep, characterized by an EEG pattern of more than 50% delta waves.

Variations in Sleep

Have you ever compared notes with a friend about how much sleep it takes to make you feel alert and rested the next day? If so, you have probably noticed that the amount of sleep people get varies a lot from one person to another. But how much sleep do we need? Many of us have heard that 8 hours of sleep are required for optimal health. Research suggests that this is not true.

◆ *How does age influence sleep patterns?*

Infants and young children have the longest sleep time and the highest percentages of REM and slow-wave sleep. However, infants and children also have more erratic sleep patterns than individuals in other age groups. By contrast, children from age 6 to puberty are the most consistent sleepers and wakers. They fall asleep easily, sleep soundly for 8 to 9 hours at night, and feel awake and alert during the day. Moreover, they tend to fall asleep and wake up at about the same time every day. By contrast, adolescents' sleep patterns are strongly influenced by their schedules. Factors such as part-time employment and early school start times cause many teenagers to sleep little more than 7 hours on a typical week night (Carskadon et al., 1998). When adolescents are free from

How much sleep does the average person need? The need for sleep varies across individuals, but these people are obviously not getting enough!

such scheduling pressures, however, they tend to sleep even longer than elementary-aged children. Thus, some sleep researchers think that insufficient sleep may be at least partly responsible for discipline and learning problems in secondary schools.

As people age, the quality and quantity of their sleep usually decrease (Reyner & Horne, 1995). In one large study of 9,000 participants aged 65 and older, only 12% reported no sleep problems (Foley et al., 1995). Older adults have more difficulty falling asleep than younger people do and typically sleep more lightly. Moreover, they spend more time in bed but less time asleep, averaging about 6 hours of sleep per night (Prinz et al., 1990). However, while slow-wave sleep decreases substantially from age 30 to age 50 (Mourtazaev et al., 1995; Van Cauter, 2000), the percentage of REM sleep stays about the same (Moran & Stoudemire, 1992).

Explaining the Function of Sleep

♦ What is the difference between the restorative and circadian theories of sleep?

♦ **restorative theory of sleep**

The theory that the function of sleep is to restore body and mind.

♦ **circadian theory of sleep**

The theory that sleep evolved to keep humans out of harm's way during the night; also known as the evolutionary theory.

Are you one of those people who regards sleep as a waste of time—especially when you have a term paper due the next day? (Of course, you wouldn't be facing a sleepless night if you hadn't procrastinated about the paper in the first place!) In fact, consistent sleep habits are probably important to getting good grades. Why?

Two complementary theories have been advanced to explain why we need to sleep. Taken together, they provide us with a useful explanation. One, the **restorative theory of sleep**, holds that being awake produces wear and tear on the body and the brain, while sleep serves the function of restoring body and mind (Gökcebay et al., 1994). There is now convincing evidence for this theory: The functions of sleep do include the restoration of energy and the consolidation of memory (Kunz & Herrmann, 2000). The second explanation, the **circadian theory of sleep**, sometimes called the *evolutionary theory*, is based on the premise that sleep evolved to keep humans out of harm's way during the dark of night, possibly from becoming prey for some nocturnal predator.

Alexander Borbely (1984; Borbely et al., 1989) explains how a synthesis of the circadian and restorative theories can be used to explain the function of sleep. That people feel sleepy at certain times of day is consistent with the circadian theory. And that sleepiness increases the longer a person is awake is consistent with the restorative theory. In other words, the urge to sleep is partly a function of how long a person has been awake and partly a function of the time of day (Webb, 1995).

Sleep Deprivation

♦ How does sleep deprivation affect behavior and neurological functioning?

What is the longest you have ever stayed awake—about 48 hours? According to the *Guinness Book of World Records*, Robert McDonald stayed awake 453 hours and 40 minutes (almost 19 days) in a 1986 rocking-chair marathon. Unlike McDonald, most people have missed no more than a few consecutive nights of sleep, perhaps studying for final exams. If you have ever missed two or three nights of sleep, you may remember having had difficulty concentrating, lapses in attention, and general irritability. Research indicates that even the rather small amount of sleep deprivation associated with delaying your bedtime on weekends leads to decreases in cognitive performance and increases in negative mood on Monday morning (Yang & Spielman, 2001). Thus, the familiar phenomenon of the "Monday morning blues" may be the result of staying up late on Friday and Saturday nights. Moreover, sleep loss is known to impair learning in both children and adults (Drummond et al., 2004; Harrison & Horne, 2000; Raz et al., 2001; Sadeh et al., 2003).

How does a lack of sleep affect the brain? The effects of sleep deprivation go beyond simply feeling tired. In fact, research has shown that failing to get enough sleep affects your ability to learn. So, if you stay up all night to study for a test, you may actually be engaging in a somewhat self-defeating behavior. Drummond and others (2000) used brain-imaging techniques to map the patterns of brain activity during a verbal learning task in two groups of participants: those in an experimental group who were deprived of sleep for about 35 hours, and those in a control group who slept normally. In the control group, the prefrontal cortex was highly active, as were the temporal lobes.

Sean Drummond

Some people have childhood experiences that are so compelling they home in on a particular career path very early in life. That is precisely what happened to Sean Drummond, whose sleep deprivation research you have read about in this chapter. When he was in elementary school, a family member was hospitalized for what he was told was a "nervous breakdown." The young Drummond's curiosity led him to wonder just how a person could be so "nervous" that he or she would have to go to the hospital. In addition, the remarkable improvement he observed in his relative's condition after treatment made him want to become a therapist when he grew up. By the time Drummond entered college, he was firmly committed to majoring in psychology and to continuing on to graduate school. Studying about the mental disorders in his first psychology class, he says, helped him understand that mental health is as complicated and as important as physical health and affirmed his commitment to a career as a therapist.

Drummond's career path took an unexpected turn when he worked as an undergraduate volunteer in the sleep research lab at the University of Arizona. As he puts it, students should take advantage of such opportunities because "you get exposed to science and ideas you never knew existed. In my case, that changed the course of my professional life" (Drummond, personal communication, December 16, 2004). In graduate school, Drummond worked closely with his mentors to develop the sleep research agenda that he continues to pursue today as a clinical psychologist and assistant professor at the University of California at San Diego and the VA San Diego Healthcare System.

What lessons can you learn from Drummond's experiences? First, think back to your childhood. Did you experience anything that you found particularly intriguing? Childhood curiosity can be a powerful motivator even after you reach adulthood. Second, if you are interested in psychology, or any other science for that matter, seek out opportunities to work with experienced researchers. Like Drummond, you may discover ideas that, right now, you don't even know exist.

As expected, on average, these rested participants scored significantly higher on the learning task than did their sleep-deprived counterparts. Surprisingly, however, areas of the prefrontal cortex were even more active in the sleep-deprived participants than in those who slept normally. Moreover, the temporal lobes that were so active in the rested group were almost totally inactive in the sleep-deprived group. The parietal lobes of the latter group became highly active, however, as if to compensate for their sleep-deprived condition. And, the more active the parietal lobes, the higher a sleep-deprived participant scored on the learning task.

This study, the first to use brain-imaging techniques to examine the effects of sleep deprivation on verbal learning, indicates that the cognitive functions used in such learning are significantly impaired by sleep deprivation. It also shows that there are compensatory mechanisms in the parietal lobes that can reduce this impairment to some degree (Drummond et al., 2000; Drummond et al., 2004).

Dreams

What does a young woman mean when she says, "I met the guy of my dreams last night?" Or how about a telemarketer who promises you a "dream vacation" in exchange for listening to a sales pitch? Most of the time, we think of dreaming as a pleasant, imaginative experience. But when a fellow student exclaims, "That exam was a nightmare!" he or she means, of course, that the exam was somewhat less than pleasant, like a frightening dream. Good or bad, just exactly what is a dream?

The vivid dreams people remember and talk about are usually **REM dreams,** the type that occur almost continuously during each REM period. But people also have **NREM dreams,** which occur during NREM sleep, although these are typically less frequent and less memorable than REM dreams (Foulkes, 1996). REM dreams have a

◆ **REM dream**

A type of dream occurring almost continuously during each REM period and having a story-like quality; typically more vivid, visual, and emotional than NREM dreams.

◆ *What have researchers learned about dreams, their biological basis, and their controllability?*

◆ **NREM dream**

A type of dream occurring during NREM sleep that is typically less frequent and memorable than REM dreams are.

storylike or dreamlike quality and are more visual, vivid, and emotional than NREM dreams (Hobson, 1989). Blind people who lose their sight before age 5 usually do not have visual dreams, although they do have vivid dreams involving the other senses.

Brain-imaging studies suggest that the general perception that events in REM dreams are stranger and more emotion-provoking than waking experiences is probably true. The areas of the brain responsible for emotions, as well as the primary visual cortex, are active during REM dreams (Braun et al., 1998). Similarly, vivid REM dreams are associated with distributions of activity in the forebrain that are very similar to those exhibited by individuals with delusional disorders while they are awake (Schwartz & Maquet, 2002). By contrast, the prefrontal cortex, the more rational part of the brain, is suppressed during REM sleep, suggesting that the bizarre events that happen in REM dreams result from the inability of the brain to structure perceptions logically during that type of sleep. Areas associated with memory are also suppressed during REM sleep, which may explain why REM dreams are difficult to remember.

What is it about REM sleep that predisposes people to bizarre dreams? One hypothesis is based on the finding that different neurotransmitters are dominant in the cortex during wakefulness and during REM sleep (Gottesmann, 2000). When we are awake, powerful inhibiting influences exert control over the functioning of the cortex, keeping us anchored to reality, less subject to impulsive thoughts and acts, and more or less "sane." These inhibiting influences are maintained principally by cortical neurons that are responding to serotonin and norepinephrine. These neurotransmitters are far less plentiful during REM dreaming, when a higher level of dopamine causes other cortical neurons to show intense activity. This uninhibited, dopamine-stimulated activity of the dreaming brain has been likened to a psychotic mental state (Gottesmann, 2000).

Finally, do you agree with most people that dreams can't be controlled (Woolley & Boerger, 2002)? If so, you might be surprised to learn that some people have been taught to use **lucid dreams** to control the dreaming process. This technique has been advocated as a means of stopping unpleasant recurring dreams and as an intervention for depression (Newell & Cartright, 2000). *Try It 4.1* introduces a technique for lucid dreaming. Be careful, though. Research shows that intentionally trying *not* to dream about a person or issue will actually cause you to dream about the individual or the issue even more than you would if you hadn't attempted to control your dreams (Wagner et al., 2004).

Interpreting Dreams

◆ *How do the views of contemporary psychologists concerning the nature of dreams differ from those of Freud?*

You may have wondered whether dreams, especially those that frighten us or that recur, have hidden meanings. Sigmund Freud believed that dreams function to satisfy unconscious sexual and aggressive desires. Because such wishes

Try It 4.1

Lucid Dreaming

Next time you wake up during a dream, try the following steps to see if you can engage in lucid dreaming.

1. Relax.
2. Close your eyes and focus on an imaginary spot in your field of vision.
3. Focus on your intention to have a lucid dream.
4. Tell yourself that you're going to dream about whatever you want.
5. Imagine yourself in a dream of the type you want to have.
6. Repeat the steps until you fall asleep.

are unacceptable to the dreamer, they have to be disguised and therefore appear in dreams in symbolic forms. Freud (1900/1953a) claimed that objects such as sticks, umbrellas, tree trunks, and guns symbolize the male sex organ; objects such as chests, cupboards, and boxes represent the female sex organ. Freud differentiated between the **manifest content** of a dream—the content of the dream as recalled by the dreamer—and the **latent content**—or the underlying meaning of the dream—which he considered more significant.

In recent years, there has been a major shift away from the Freudian interpretation of dreams. Now there is a greater focus on the manifest content—the actual dream itself—which is seen as an expression of a broad range of the dreamer's concerns rather than as an expression of sexual impulses (Webb, 1975). And, from an evolutionary viewpoint, dreams are viewed as a mechanism for simulating threatening and dangerous events so that the dreamer can "rehearse" and thus enhance her or his chances for survival (Revensuo, 2000).

Well-known sleep researcher J. Allan Hobson (1988) rejects the notion that nature would equip humans with the capability of having dreams that would require a specialist to interpret. Hobson and McCarley (1977) advanced the **activation-synthesis hypothesis of dreaming**. This hypothesis suggests that dreams are simply the brain's attempt to make sense of the random firing of brain cells during REM sleep. Just as people try to make sense of input from the environment during their waking hours, they try to find meaning in the conglomeration of sensations and memories that are generated internally by this random firing of brain cells. Hobson (1989) believes that dreams also have psychological significance, because the meaning a person imposes on the random mental activity reflects that person's experiences, remote memories, associations, drives, and fears.

Sleep Disorders

So far, our discussion has centered on a typical night for a typical sleeper. But what about the significant number of people who report sleep problems (Rosekind, 1992)?

Do you walk or talk in your sleep? If you do, you suffer from one of the **parasomnias,** sleep disturbances in which behaviors and physiological states that normally occur only in the waking state take place during sleep (Schenck & Mahowald, 2000). Sleepwalking, or *somnambulism*, occurs during a partial arousal from Stage 4 sleep in which the sleeper does not come to full consciousness. *Somniloquy*, the technical term for sleeptalking, can occur in any stage. Typically, sleeptalkers mumble nonsensical words and phrases.

Frightening dreams are also parasomnias. *Sleep terrors* happen during Stage 4 sleep and often begin with a piercing scream. The sleeper springs up in a state of panic—eyes open, heart pounding, perspiring, breathing rapidly, and so on. Typically, such sleep terrors resolve quickly and the individual falls back to sleep. *Nightmares* are more frightening than sleep terrors because they occur during REM sleep and, as a result, are far more vivid. Moreover, sleepers often awaken to full consciousness during a nightmare and remember it in detail. Whereas sleep terrors occur early in the night, nightmares more often occur in the early-morning hours, when REM periods are the longest.

Some sleep disorders can be so debilitating that they affect a person's entire life. For instance, **narcolepsy** is an incurable sleep disorder characterized by excessive daytime sleepiness and uncontrollable attacks of REM sleep, usually lasting 10 to 20 minutes (American Psychiatric Association, 1994). People with narcolepsy, who

◆ **manifest content**
Freud's term for the content of a dream as recalled by the dreamer.

◆ **latent content**
Freud's term for the underlying meaning of a dream.

◆ **activation-synthesis hypothesis of dreaming**
The hypothesis that dreams are the brain's attempt to make sense of the random firing of brain cells during REM sleep.

◆ **parasomnias**
Sleep disturbances in which behaviors and physiological states that normally take place only in the waking state occur while a person is sleeping.

◆ **narcolepsy**
An incurable sleep disorder characterized by excessive daytime sleepiness and uncontrollable attacks of REM sleep.

◆ *What are the various disorders that can trouble sleepers?*

If you dream you are trapped in a virtual reality matrix, does your dream mean that you have problems in your relationship with your parents, or perhaps an unconscious fear of video games?

Sleep researcher William Dement holds a dog that is experiencing a narcoleptic sleep attack. Much has been learned about narcolepsy through research with dogs.

◆ **sleep apnea**

A sleep disorder characterized by periods during sleep when breathing stops and the individual must awaken briefly in order to breathe.

◆ **insomnia**

A sleep disorder characterized by difficulty falling or staying asleep, by waking too early, or by sleep that is light, restless, or of poor quality.

◆ **meditation (concentrative)**

A group of techniques that involve focusing attention on an object, a word, one's breathing, or one's body movements in an effort to block out all distractions, to enhance well-being, and to achieve an altered state of consciousness.

◆ *What are the benefits of meditation?*

number from 250,000 to 350,000 in the United States alone, tend to be involved in accidents virtually everywhere—while driving, at work, and at home (Broughton & Broughton, 1994). Narcolepsy is caused by an abnormality in the part of the brain that regulates sleep, and it appears to have a strong genetic component (Billiard et al., 1994; Partinen et al., 1994). Some dogs are subject to narcolepsy, and much has been learned about the genetics of this disorder from research on canine subjects (Lamberg, 1996). Although there is no cure for narcolepsy, stimulant medications improve daytime alertness in most patients (Guilleminault, 1993; Mitler et al., 1994). Experts also recommend scheduled naps to relieve sleepiness (Garma & Marchand, 1994).

More than 1 million Americans—mostly obese men—suffer from another sleep disorder, **sleep apnea.** Sleep apnea consists of periods during sleep when breathing stops, and the individual must awaken briefly to breathe (White, 1989). The major symptoms of sleep apnea are excessive daytime sleepiness and extremely loud snoring, often accompanied by snorts, gasps, and choking noises. A person with sleep apnea will drop off to sleep, stop breathing altogether, and then awaken struggling for breath. After gasping several breaths in a semi-awakened state, the person falls back to sleep and stops breathing again. People with severe sleep apnea may partially awaken as many as 800 times a night to gasp for air. Alcohol and sedatives aggravate the condition (Langevin et al., 1992).

Severe sleep apnea can lead to chronic high blood pressure, heart problems, and even death (Lavie et al., 1995). Neuroscientists have also found that sleep apnea may cause mild brain damage (Macey et al., 2002). Physicians sometimes treat sleep apnea by surgically modifying the upper airway (Sher et al., 1996). When the surgery is effective, sleep apnea sufferers not only sleep better, but also exhibit higher levels of performance on tests of verbal learning and memory (Dahloef et al., 2002). These findings suggest that the interrupted sleep experienced by individuals with this disorder affects cognitive as well as physiological functioning.

Approximately one-third of adults in the United States suffer from **insomnia,** a sleep disorder characterized by difficulty falling or staying asleep, by waking too early, or by sleep that is light, restless, or of poor quality. Any of these symptoms can lead to distress and impairment in daytime functioning (Costa E Silva et al., 1996; Roth, 1996; Sateia et al., 2000). Transient (temporary) insomnia, lasting 3 weeks or less, can result from jet lag, emotional highs (as when preparing for an upcoming wedding) or lows (losing a loved one or a job), or a brief illness or injury that interferes with sleep (Reite et al., 1995). Much more serious is chronic insomnia, which lasts for months or even years and plagues about 10% of the adult population (Roth, 1996). The percentages are even higher for women, the elderly, and people suffering from psychiatric and medical disorders (Costa E Silva et al., 1996). Chronic insomnia may begin as a reaction to a psychological or medical problem but persist long after the problem is resolved. Individuals with chronic insomnia experience "higher psychological distress [and] greater impairments of daytime functioning, are involved in more fatigue-related accidents, take more sick leave, and utilize health care resources more often than good sleepers" (Morin & Wooten, 1996, p. 522).

Meditation and Hypnosis

We all have to sleep. Even if you fight it, your body will eventually force you to sleep. But there are other forms of altered consciousness that we may experience only if we choose to do so. Meditation and hypnosis are two of these.

Meditation

Do you know that a mental and physical relaxation technique can actually induce an altered state of consciousness? **Meditation** (the concentrative form) is a group of techniques that involve focusing attention on an object, a word, one's breathing, or one's body movements in an effort to block out all distractions, to enhance well-being, and to achieve an altered state of consciousness. Some forms of concentrative meditation, such as yoga, Zen, and transcendental meditation (TM), have their roots in Eastern religions and are practiced by followers of those religions to attain a higher spiritual state. In the United States, these approaches are often used to increase relaxation, reduce arousal, or expand consciousness (Wolsko et al., 2004.) Brain-imaging studies support the conclusion that meditation, in addition to being relaxing, induces an altered state of consciousness (Newberg et al., 2001). Moreover, prayer induces physiological and psychological states very much like those associated with meditation (Bernardi et al., 2001).

Studies suggest that meditation can be helpful for a variety of physical and psychological problems. Researchers have found that regular meditation helps individuals, even those who are severely depressed, learn to control their emotions (Segal et al., 2001). In addition, meditation may prove helpful in lowering blood pressure, cholesterol levels, and other measures of cardiovascular health (Fields et al., 2002; Seeman et al., 2003). Keep in mind, though, that meditation is not a "quick fix" for either mental or physical health problems. Deriving benefits from meditation requires self-discipline and commitment (Murray, 2002). Use the steps in *Try It 4.2* to learn how to induce a relaxation state that is very similar to that experienced by those who meditate; practice the technique until you become proficient in it. You will then be ready to incorporate it into your daily routine.

◆ **hypnosis**

A procedure through which one person, the hypnotist, uses the power of suggestion to induce changes in thoughts, feelings, sensations, perceptions, or behavior in another person, the subject.

Hypnosis

At the beginning of the chapter, you read a fictional story in which hypnosis was used to induce a prisoner of war to become an assassin whose behavior could be controlled by secret signals of which he was not consciously aware. Now, let's consider the scientific basis of this phenomenon. **Hypnosis** may be formally defined as a procedure through which one person, the hypnotist, uses the power of suggestion to induce changes in thoughts, feelings, sensations, perceptions, or behavior in another person, the subject. Under hypnosis, people suspend their usual rational and logical ways of thinking and perceiving and allow themselves to experience distortions in perceptions, memories, and thinking. They may experience positive hallucinations, in which they see, hear, touch, smell, or taste things that are not present in the environment. Or they may have negative hallucinations, in which they fail to perceive things that are actually present.

◆ *What are the effects of hypnosis, and how do theorists explain them?*

Try It 4.2

The Relaxation Response

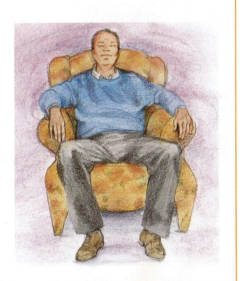

Find a quiet place and sit in a comfortable position.

1. Close your eyes.

2. Relax all your muscles deeply. Beginning with your feet and moving slowly upward, relax the muscles in your legs, buttocks, abdomen, chest, shoulders, neck, and finally your face. Allow your whole body to remain in this deeply relaxed state.

3. Now concentrate on your breathing, and breathe in and out through your nose. Each time you breathe out, silently say the word *one* to yourself.

4. Repeat this process for 20 minutes. (You can open your eyes to look at your watch periodically but don't use an alarm.) When you are finished, remain seated for a few minutes—first with your eyes closed, then with them open.

About 80–95% of people are hypnotizable to some degree, but only 5% can reach the deepest levels of the hypnotic state (Nash & Baker, 1984). The ability to become completely absorbed in imaginative activities is characteristic of highly hypnotizable people (Nadon et al., 1991). Silva and Kirsch (1992) found that individuals' fantasy-proneness and their expectation of responding to hypnotic suggestions are predictors of their hypnotizability.

There are many misconceptions about hypnosis, some of which probably stem from its long association with stage entertainers. Have you ever believed one of these myths?

- *Hypnotized people are under the complete control of the hypnotist and will violate their moral values if told to do so.* Hypnosis is not something that is done to people. Subjects retain the ability to refuse to comply with the hypnotist's suggestions, and they will not do anything that is contrary to their true moral beliefs.
- *People can demonstrate superhuman strength and perform amazing feats under hypnosis.* Subjects are not stronger or more powerful under hypnosis (Druckman & Bjork, 1994).
- *Memory is more accurate under hypnosis.* Although it is true that hypnotized subjects supply more information and are more confident of their recollections, the information is often inaccurate (Dywan & Bowers, 1983; Kihlstrom & Barnhardt, 1993; Nogrady et al., 1985; Weekes et al., 1992). And in the process of trying to help people recall certain events, hypnotists may instead create in them false memories, or *pseudomemories* (Lynn & Nash, 1994; Yapko, 1994).
- *People under hypnosis will reveal embarrassing secrets.* Hypnosis is not like a truth serum. Subjects can keep secrets or lie under hypnosis.
- *People under hypnosis can relive an event that occurred when they were children and can function mentally as if they were that age.* Careful reviews of studies on hypnotic age regression have found no evidence to support this claim. "Although hypnotically regressed subjects may undergo dramatic changes in demeanor and subjective experience, their performance is not accurately childlike" (Nash, 1987, p. 50).

Hypnosis has come a long way from the days when it was used mainly by entertainers. It is now recognized as a viable technique to be used in medicine, dentistry, and psychotherapy (Lynn et al., 2000). Hypnosis is accepted by the American Medical Association, the American Psychological Association, and the American Psychiatric Association. Hypnosis has been particularly helpful in the control of pain (Hilgard, 1975; Kihlstrom, 1985; Montgomery et al., 2000; Patterson, 2004; Tal, 2004). Experimental studies have shown that patients who are hypnotized and exposed to suggestions designed to induce relaxation prior to surgery experience less postsurgery pain than do nonhypnotized patients (Montgomery et al., 2002).

According to the **sociocognitive theory of hypnosis**, the behavior of a hypnotized person is a function of that person's expectations about how subjects behave under hypnosis. People are motivated to be good subjects, to follow the suggestions of the hypnotist, and to fulfill the social role of the hypnotized person as they perceive it (Spanos, 1986, 1991, 1994). Does this mean that hypnotized people are merely acting or faking it? No, "most hypnotized persons are neither faking nor merely complying with suggestions" (Kirsch & Lynn, 1995, p. 847). In fact, using the single most effective and reliable indicator of deception in the laboratory—skin conductance, which indicates emotional response by measuring perspiration—Kinnunen and others (1994) found that 89% of supposedly hypnotized people had been truly hypnotized.

Ernest Hilgard (1986, 1992) has proposed a theory to explain why hypnotized individuals can accomplish very difficult acts, even undergoing surgery without anesthesia. According to his **neodissociation theory of hypnosis,**

◆ **sociocognitive theory of hypnosis**

A theory suggesting that the behavior of a hypnotized person is a function of that person's expectations about how subjects behave under hypnosis.

◆ **neodissociation theory of hypnosis**

A theory proposing that hypnosis induces a split, or dissociation, between two aspects of the control of consciousness: the planning function and the monitoring function.

A hypnotized person is in a state of heightened suggestibility. This hypnotherapist may therefore be able to help the woman control chronic or postsurgery pain.

hypnosis induces a split, or dissociation, between two aspects of the control of consciousness: the planning function and the monitoring function. During hypnosis, it is the planning function that carries out the suggestions of the hypnotist and remains a part of the subject's conscious awareness. The monitoring function monitors or observes everything that happens to the subject, but without his or her conscious awareness. Hilgard called the monitoring function, when separated from conscious awareness, "the hidden observer."

Bowers and his colleagues (Bowers, 1992; Woody & Bowers, 1994) have proposed a view of hypnosis as an authentic altered state of consciousness. Their **theory of dissociated control** maintains that hypnosis does not induce a splitting of different aspects of consciousness, as Hilgard's model suggests. Rather, they believe that hypnosis weakens the control of the executive function over other parts (subsystems) of consciousness, allowing the hypnotist's suggestions to contact and influence those subsystems directly. Bowers further believes that the hypnotized person's responses are automatic and involuntary, like reflexes, and are not controlled by normal cognitive functions (Kirsch & Lynn, 1995). Indeed, some research supports this viewpoint (Bowers & Woody, 1996; Hargadon et al., 1995).

Although the majority of hypnosis researchers seem to support the sociocognitive theory, most clinicians, and some influential researchers in the field, apparently believe that hypnosis is a unique altered state of consciousness (Kirsch & Lynn, 1995; Nash, 1991; Woody & Bowers, 1994). Kihlstrom (1986) has suggested that a more complete picture of hypnosis could emerge from some combination of the sociocognitive and neodissociation theories. But even though researchers still have theoretical differences, hypnosis is being increasingly used in clinical practice and in selected areas of medicine and dentistry.

◆ **theory of dissociated control**

The theory that hypnosis is an authentic altered state of consciousness in which the control the executive function exerts over other subsystems of consciousness is weakened.

Culture and Altered States of Consciousness

In every culture around the world, and throughout recorded history, human beings have found ways to induce altered states of consciousness. Some means of inducing altered states that are used in other cultures may seem strange and exotic to most Westerners. Entering ritual trances and experiencing spirit possession are seen in many cultures in religious rites and tribal ceremonies. Typically, people induce ritual trances by flooding the senses with repetitive chanting, clapping, or singing; by whirling in circles until they achieve a dizzying speed; or by burning strong, pungent incense.

◆ *What is the connection between altered states of consciousness and culture?*

The fact that so many different means of altering consciousness are practiced by members of so many cultures around the world has led some experts to wonder whether "there may be a universal human need to produce and maintain varieties of conscious experiences" (Ward, 1994, p. 60). This may be why some people use drugs to deliberately induce altered states of consciousness.

◆ Psychoactive Drugs

The last time you took a pain reliever or an antibiotic, you probably didn't think of yourself as engaging in a mind-altering experience. However, all chemical substances, even the aspirin you take for a headache, affect the brain because they alter the functioning of neurotransmitters (Munzar et al., 2002). As you can probably guess, most such substances have no noticeable effect on your state of consciousness. Some drugs, however, have especially powerful effects on the brain and induce dramatically altered states of consciousness.

The ritualized spinning dance of the whirling dervishes produces an altered state of consciousness that is recognized as part of their religious practice.

◆ **psychoactive drug**

Any substance that alters mood, perception, or thought; called a controlled substance if approved for medical use.

A **psychoactive drug** is any substance that alters mood, perception, or thought. When psychoactive drugs, such as antidepressants, are approved for medical use, they are called *controlled substances*. The term *illicit* denotes psychoactive drugs that are illegal. Many *over-the-counter drugs*, such as antihistamines and decongestants, as well as many herbal preparations, are psychoactive. Certain foods, such as chocolate, may also alter our moods (Dallard et al., 2001). Note to restaurant servers: Giving customers a piece of chocolate along with their checks increases tips (Strohmetz et al., 2002).

How Drugs Affect the Brain

◆ *How do drugs affect the brain's neurotransmitter system?*

Did you know that all kinds of physical pleasure have the same neurological basis? Whether derived from sex, a psychoactive chemical, or any other source, a subjective sense of physical pleasure is brought about by an increase in the availability of the neurotransmitter dopamine in a part of the brain's limbic system known as the *nucleus accumbens* (Gerrits et al., 2002; Robinson et al., 2001). Thus, it isn't surprising that researchers have found that a surge of dopamine is involved in the rewarding and motivational effects produced by most psychoactive drugs (Carlson, 1998), including marijuana, heroin (Tanda et al., 1997), and nicotine (Pich et al., 1997; Pontieri et al., 1996). Why, then, does the altered state associated with alcohol feel different from that associated with nicotine or marijuana? Because the effect drugs have on the dopamine system is just the beginning of a cascade of effects that involve the brain's entire neurotransmitter system. Each drug influences the whole system differently and is associated with a distinctive altered state of consciousness. Consider a few examples of how different drugs act on neurotransmitters and the associated beneficial effects:

- Opiates such as morphine and heroin mimic the effects of the brain's own endorphins, chemicals that have pain-relieving properties and produce a feeling of well-being. For this reason, opiates are useful in pain management.
- Depressants such as alcohol, barbiturates, and benzodiazepines (Valium and Librium, for example) act on GABA receptors to produce a calming, sedating effect (Harris et al., 1992). Thus, depressants can play a role in reducing a patient's nervousness prior to undergoing a medical procedure.
- Stimulants such as amphetamines and cocaine mimic the effects of epinephrine, the neurotransmitter that triggers the sympathetic nervous system. The effects of the sympathetic nervous system include suppressed hunger and digestion; this is why "diet pills" typically contain some kind of stimulant, such as caffeine.

As we all know, drugs don't always have solely beneficial effects. Why? Because too much of a good thing, or the wrong combination of good things, can lead to disaster. For example, opiates, when taken regularly, will eventually completely suppress the production of endorphins. As a result, natural pain management systems break down, and the brain becomes dependent on the presence of opiates to function normally. Similarly, if ingestion of too much alcohol, or of a combination of alcohol and other depressants, floods the brain with GABA, consciousness will be lost and death may follow. Excessive amounts of a stimulant can send heart rates and blood pressure levels zooming; death can even result from the ingestion of a single, large dose.

◆ **substance abuse**

Continued use of a substance after several episodes in which use of the substance has negatively affected an individual's work, education, and social relationships.

Substance Abuse

◆ *What factors influence progression from substance use to substance abuse?*

When people intentionally use drugs to induce an altered state of consciousness, they risk developing a *substance abuse* problem. Psychologists usually define **substance abuse** as continued use of a substance after several episodes in which use of the substance has negatively affected an individual's work, education, and social relationships (DSM-IV, 1994). For example, a person who has missed work several times because of alcohol intoxication, but who continues to drink, has a substance abuse problem.

What causes people to progress from substance use to substance abuse? The physical pleasure associated with drug-induced altered states of consciousness is one reason. Genetically based differences in the way people respond physiologically to drugs also contribute to substance abuse. For example, some people feel intoxicated after drinking very small amounts of alcohol; others require a much larger "dose" to feel the same effects. People who have to drink more to experience intoxication are more likely to become alcoholics. Genetic researchers are currently searching for the gene or genes that contribute to low response to alcohol (Schuckit et al., 2001). Of course, personality and social factors contribute to substance abuse as well. Impulsivity, for instance, is associated with experimentation with drugs (Simons & Carey, 2002). Stress-related variables, such as a history of having been a victim of child abuse or domestic violence, are associated with substance abuse as well (Goeders, 2004; Gordon, 2002; Sussman & Dent, 2000).

Social and cultural factors play important roles in the development of substance abuse problems, too. For instance, associating with peers who use drugs may influence teenagers to begin doing so or may help to maintain substance abuse behavior once it begins (Curran et al., 1997). However, families can help counteract the effects of peer influence. In one study of 400 California teenagers, researchers found that adolescents from Chinese and Asian/Pacific Island backgrounds were far more likely to abstain from alcohol than their peers in other groups (Faryna & Morales, 2000). (See Figure 4.2.) Researchers attribute these findings to healthy social influences, such as an environment that promotes abstinence and a greater likelihood of having an intact family among Americans of Chinese and Asian/Pacific Islander descent. Also, young Asian Americans spend more time with their families and less time with friends and other peers, thereby minimizing potentially bad influences and peer group pressures (Au & Donaldson, 2000).

Drug Dependence

Some people progress from substance abuse to full-blown substance dependence, commonly called *addiction*. **Physical drug dependence** results from the body's natural ability to protect itself against harmful substances by developing a **drug tolerance**. That is, the user becomes progressively less affected by

◆ **physical drug dependence**
A compulsive pattern of drug use in which the user develops a drug tolerance coupled with unpleasant withdrawal symptoms when the drug use is discontinued.

◆ **drug tolerance**
A condition in which the user becomes progressively less affected by the drug and must take increasingly larger doses to maintain the same effect or high.

◆ *What is the difference between physical and psychological drug dependence?*

FIGURE 4.2   **Alcohol Use among Adolescents of Diverse Ethnicities**

In this study involving more than 400 California high school students, researchers found that differences in cultural values and family structure help to account for these differences in alcohol use. Chinese American and Asian American/Pacific Islander teens were more likely to come from homes in which both parents were present. European American, Latin American, and African American teens spent more time with peers than with their families, but the reverse was true for the Chinese American and Asian American/Pacific Islander high school students.

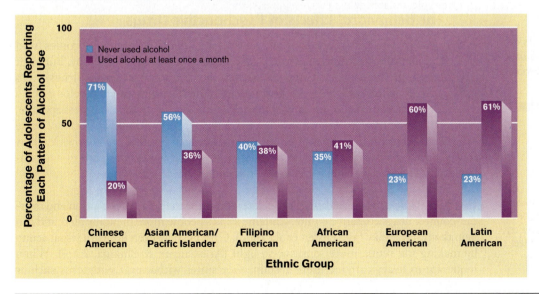

The physical and psychological symptoms (usually the exact opposite of the effects produced by the drug) that occur when a regularly used drug is discontinued and that terminate when the drug is taken again.

◆ **psychological drug dependence**

A craving or irresistible urge for a drug's pleasurable effects.

the drug and must take increasingly larger doses to achieve the same effect or high (Ramsay & Woods, 1997). Tolerance occurs because the brain adapts to the presence of the drug by responding less intensely to it. In addition, the liver produces more enzymes to break down the drug. The various bodily processes adjust so that they can continue to function with the drug in the system.

Once drug tolerance is established, a person cannot function normally without the drug. If the drug is taken away, the user begins to suffer withdrawal symptoms. These **withdrawal symptoms,** which are both physical and psychological, are usually the exact opposite of the effects produced by the drug. For example, withdrawal from stimulants leaves a person exhausted and depressed; withdrawal from tranquilizers leaves a person nervous and agitated. Because taking the drug is the only way to escape these unpleasant symptoms, withdrawal supports continued addiction. Moreover, the lasting behavioral and cognitive effects of abused substances on the brain often interfere with attempts to stop using them. Among other effects, researchers have learned that addiction is associated with attention and memory deficits, loss of the ability to accurately sense the passage of time, and declines in the capacity to plan and control behavior (Bates et al., 2002; Buhusi & Meck, 2002; Lyvers, 2000). Abusers need all of these skills to overcome addiction and rebuild their lives, but regaining them once drug abuse is stopped—if they can be recovered at all—takes time.

Psychological drug dependence is a craving or irresistible urge for the drug's pleasurable effects; it is even more difficult to combat than physical dependence (O'Brien, 1996). Continued use of drugs to which an individual is physically addicted is influenced by the psychological component of the habit. Some drugs that are probably not physically addictive (e.g., marijuana) may nevertheless create psychological dependence.

Learning processes are important in the development and maintenance of psychological dependence. For example, because of classical conditioning, drug-taking cues—the people, places, and things associated with using the drug—can produce a strong craving for the substance of abuse (Hillebrand, 2000). In fact, some researchers have found that people who are addicted to opiates selectively pay attention to drug-related cues, ignoring virtually all non–drug-related cues whenever the drug-taking cues are present (Lubman et al., 2000). In truth, "selective attention" probably isn't the most descriptive term for what is happening in a drug addict's brain. PET scans of cocaine addicts' brains indicate that such cues arouse a cue-specific neural network, which may explain why it is difficult for addicts to divert their attention from them (Bonson et al., 2002). Furthermore, research with animals indicates that drug-related cues elicit the same responses in the brain as the drugs themselves (Kiyatkin & Wise, 2002). These findings underscore the need for further research aimed at revealing the relationships among the physiological effects of drugs and the social contexts in which drug use occurs (Crombag & Robinson, 2004).

The Behavioral Effects of Psychoactive Drugs

◆ *What are the effects of stimulants, depressants, and hallucinogens on behavior?*

Have you ever advised a friend to "switch to decaf"? This advice comes from a bit of drug knowledge we all share: Caffeine can make us jumpy. But what are the specific behavioral effects associated with other kinds of drugs? Let's begin with a look at the stimulants, the group to which caffeine belongs.

Stimulants speed up activity in the central nervous system, suppress appetite, and can make a person feel more awake, alert, and energetic. Stimulants increase pulse rate, blood pressure, and respiration rate, and they reduce cerebral blood flow (Mathew & Wilson, 1991). In higher doses, stimulants make people feel nervous, jittery, and restless, and they can cause shaking or trembling and interfere with sleep.

◆ **stimulants**

A category of drugs that speed up activity in the central nervous system, suppress appetite, and can cause a person to feel more awake, alert, and energetic; also called "uppers."

Caffeine Coffee, tea, cola drinks, chocolate, and more than 100 prescription and over-the-counter drugs contain caffeine. Caffeine makes people more mentally alert and can help them stay awake (Wesensten et al., 2002). Caffeine may even improve visual acuity by making the retina more sensitive to light (Arushanyan & Shikina, 2004). When moderate to heavy caffeine users abstain, they suffer withdrawal symptoms such as nervousness, instability, headaches, drowsiness, and decreased alertness. Using EEGs and sonograms, researchers looked at the effects of caffeine withdrawal symptoms on the brain and were able to correlate the symptoms with significant increases in blood pressure and in the velocity of blood flow in all four of the cerebral arteries. The EEGs also showed an increase in slower brain waves, which correlates with decreased alertness and drowsiness (Jones et al., 2000).

Nicotine Like caffeine, nicotine increases alertness, but few people who have tried to quit smoking doubt its addictive power. (The many serious health problems associated with smoking are discussed in Chapter 10.) Many treatment methods advertised as being helpful to smokers who are trying to quit appear to have limited value. For example, Green and Lynn (2000) reviewed the results of 59 studies of hypnosis and smoking and concluded that hypnosis cannot be considered effective in helping smokers break the habit. However, experiments have shown that over-the-counter nicotine patches help about 1 in 5 smokers quit and enable many others to cut down on the number of cigarettes they smoke (Jolicoeur et al., 2003).

Amphetamines Amphetamines increase arousal, relieve fatigue, improve alertness, suppress the appetite, and give a rush of energy. Animal research suggests that amphetamines stimulate the release of dopamine in the frontal cortex as well as in the nucleus accumbens, which may account for some of their desirable cognitive effects such as increases in attention span and concentration (Frantz et al., 2002). Moreover, these drugs may actually stimulate the growth of neurons in children who suffer from attention problems (Heitjtz et al., 2003). In high doses (100 milligrams or more), however, amphetamines can cause confused and disorganized behavior, extreme fear and suspiciousness, delusions and hallucinations, aggressiveness and antisocial behavior, even manic behavior and paranoia. The powerful amphetamine methamphetamine (known as "crank" or "speed") comes in a smokable form ("ice"), which is highly addictive and can be fatal.

Withdrawal from amphetamines leaves a person physically exhausted; he or she will sleep for 10 to 15 hours or more, only to awaken in a stupor, extremely depressed and intensely hungry. Stimulants constrict the tiny capillaries and the small arteries. Over time, high doses can stop blood flow, causing hemorrhaging and leaving parts of the brain deprived of oxygen. In fact, victims of fatal overdoses of stimulants usually have multiple hemorrhages in the brain.

Cocaine Cocaine, a stimulant derived from coca leaves, can be sniffed as a white powder, injected intravenously, or smoked in the form of crack. The effects of snorting cocaine are felt within 2 to 3 minutes, and the high lasts 30 to 45 minutes. The euphoria from cocaine is followed by an equally intense crash, marked by depression, anxiety, agitation, and a powerful craving for more of the drug.

Cocaine stimulates the reward, or "pleasure," pathways in the brain, which use the neurotransmitter dopamine (Landry, 1997). With continued use, these reward systems fail to function normally, and the user becomes incapable of feeling any pleasure except from the drug. The main withdrawal symptoms are psychological—the inability to feel pleasure and the craving for more cocaine.

Cocaine constricts the blood vessels, raises blood pressure, speeds up the heart, quickens respiration, and can even cause epileptic seizures in people who have no history of epilepsy (Pascual-Leone et al., 1990). Over time, or even quickly in high doses, cocaine can cause heart palpitations, an irregular heartbeat, and heart attacks, and high doses can cause strokes in healthy young individuals. Chronic cocaine use can also result in holes in the nasal septum (the ridge of cartilage running down the middle of the nose) and in the palate (the roof of the mouth) (Armstrong & Shikani, 1996; Sastry et al., 1997).

Animals become addicted more readily to cocaine than to any other drug, and those who are addicted to multiple substances prefer cocaine when offered a choice of drugs (Manzardo et al., 2002). Given unlimited access to cocaine, animals will lose interest in

Amphetamines affect the parts of the brain that control attention and concentration, as well as the nucleus accumbens. This helps explain why these stimulants are useful in the treatment of attention problems in schoolchildren.

◆ **depressants**

A category of drugs that decrease activity in the central nervous system, slow down bodily functions, and reduce sensitivity to outside stimulation; also called "downers."

everything else, including food, water, and sex, and will rapidly and continually self-administer cocaine. They tend to die within 14 days, usually from cardiopulmonary collapse (Gawin, 1991). Cocaine-addicted monkeys will press a lever as many as 12,800 times to get one cocaine injection (Yanagita, 1973).

Crack, or "rock," the most dangerous form of cocaine, can produce a powerful dependency in several weeks. Users who begin with cocaine in powder form are likely to progress to crack, while users who start on crack are more likely to continue using it exclusively. When both powder and crack are used interchangeably, a mutual reinforcement seems to occur, and the user develops a dependence on both forms of cocaine (Shaw et al., 1999).

Another class of drugs, the **depressants,** decrease activity in the central nervous system, slow down bodily functions, and reduce sensitivity to outside stimulation. Within this category are the sedative-hypnotics (alcohol, barbiturates, and minor tranquilizers) and the narcotics (opiates). When different depressants are taken together, their sedative effects are additive and, thus, potentially dangerous.

Alcohol   The more alcohol a person consumes, the more the central nervous system is depressed. As drinking increases, the symptoms of drunkenness mount—slurred speech, poor coordination, staggering. Impaired depth perception—one good reason to avoid driving after you have been drinking—is another feature of alcohol intoxication (Nawrot et al., 2004). Men tend to become more aggressive (Pihl et al., 1997) and more sexually aroused (Roehrich & Kinder, 1991) but less able to perform sexually (Crowe & George, 1989). (We will discuss the health consequences of alcohol abuse in detail in Chapter 10.) Alcohol also decreases the ability to form new memories (Kirchner & Sayette, 2003). That's why an episode of heavy drinking is often followed by a "morning after," during which the drinker is unable to remember the events that occurred while he or she was under the influence of alcohol. Interestingly, alcohol placebos have similar effects on memory function, so a drinker's expectations contribute to alcohol's effects to some extent (Assefi & Garry, 2003).

Barbiturates   Barbiturates depress the central nervous system. Depending on the dose, a barbiturate can act as a sedative or a sleeping pill. People who abuse barbiturates become drowsy and confused, their thinking and judgment suffer, and their coordination and reflexes are affected (Henningfield & Ator, 1986). Barbiturates can kill if taken in overdose, and a lethal dose can be as little as three times the prescribed dose. Alcohol and barbiturates, when taken together, are a potentially fatal combination.

Minor Tranquilizers   The popular minor tranquilizers, the *benzodiazepines*, came on the scene in the early 1960s and are sold under the brand names Valium, Librium, Dalmane, and, more recently, Xanax (also used as an antidepressant). About 90 million prescriptions for minor tranquilizers are filled each year. Benzodiazepines are prescribed for several medical and psychological disorders. Abuse of these drugs is associated with both temporary and permanent impairment of memory and other cognitive functions (Paraherakis et al., 2001). (A more detailed discussion of tranquilizers can be found in Chapter 13.)

Narcotics   **Narcotics** are derived from the opium poppy and produce both pain-relieving and calming effects. Opium affects mainly the brain, but it also paralyzes the intestinal muscles, which is why it is used medically to treat diarrhea. If you have ever taken paregoric, you have had a tincture (extract) of opium. Because opium suppresses the cough center, it is used in some cough medicines. Morphine and codeine, natural constituents of opium, may be found in some drugs prescribed for pain relief. Such drugs, including Oxycontin and Vicodin, are addictive and are sold illegally to millions of people in the United States every year (Drug Enforcement Administration, 2003).

A highly addictive narcotic derived from morphine is heroin. Heroin addicts describe a sudden "rush" of euphoria, followed by drowsiness, inactivity, and impaired concentration. Withdrawal symptoms begin about 6 to 24 hours after use, and the addict becomes physically sick. Nausea, diarrhea, depression, stomach cramps, insomnia, and pain grow worse and worse until they become intolerable—unless the person gets another "fix."

◆ **narcotics**

A class of depressant drugs derived from the opium poppy that produce both pain-relieving and calming effects.

The **hallucinogens,** or *psychedelics*, are drugs that can alter and distort perceptions of time and space, alter mood, and produce feelings of unreality. As the name implies, hallucinogens also cause hallucinations, sensations that have no basis in external reality (Andreasen & Black, 1991; Miller & Gold, 1994). Hallucinogens have been used in religious rituals and ceremonies and recreationally in diverse cultures since ancient times (Millman & Beeder, 1994). Rather than producing a relatively predictable effect like most other drugs, hallucinogens usually magnify the mood of the user at the time the drug is taken. Contrary to the belief of some, hallucinogens hamper rather than enhance creative thinking (Bourassa & Vaugeois, 2001).

Marijuana *THC* (tetrahydrocannabinol), the ingredient in marijuana that produces the high, remains in the body "for days or even weeks" (Julien, 1995). Marijuana impairs attention and coordination and slows reaction time, and these effects make operating complex machinery such as an automobile dangerous, even after the feeling of intoxication has passed. Marijuana can interfere with concentration, logical thinking, and the ability to form new memories (Verdejo-García et al., 2005). It can produce fragmentation in thought and confusion in remembering recent occurrences (Herkenham, 1992). A 17-year longitudinal study of Costa Rican men supports the claim that long-term use of marijuana has a negative impact on short-term memory and the ability to focus sustained attention (Fletcher et al., 1996). Many of the receptors for THC are in the hippocampus, which explains why the drug affects memory (Matsuda et al., 1990).

Chronic use of marijuana has been associated with loss of motivation, general apathy, and decline in school performance, referred to as *amotivational syndrome* (Andreasen & Black, 1991). Studies comparing marijuana users who began taking the drug before age 17 with those who started later show that early marijuana use is associated with a somewhat smaller brain volume and a lower percentage of the all-important gray matter in the brain's cortex. Marijuana users who started younger were also shorter and weighed less than users who started when older (Wilson et al., 2000). Further, marijuana smoke contains many of the same carcinogenic chemicals as cigarette smoke.

However, an advisory panel of the National Institute on Drug Abuse, after reviewing the scientific evidence, concluded that marijuana shows promise as a treatment for certain medical conditions. It has been found effective for treating the eye disease glaucoma, for controlling nausea and vomiting in cancer patients receiving chemotherapy, and for improving appetite and curtailing weight loss in some AIDS patients (Fackelmann, 1997). It may also be helpful in the treatment of spinal cord injuries and other kinds of nerve damage (Wade et al., 2003). However, because pills containing the active ingredients in marijuana are already legally available by prescription, many experts contend that it is not necessary to legalize the use of marijuana cigarettes for medical purposes.

LSD (Llysergic Acid Diethylamide) LSD is lysergic acid diethylamide, sometimes referred to simply as "acid." The average LSD "trip" lasts for 10 to 12 hours and usually produces extreme perceptual and emotional changes, including visual hallucinations and feelings of panic (Miller & Gold, 1994). On occasion, bad LSD trips have ended tragically in accidents, death, or suicide. Former LSD users sometimes experience *flashbacks*, brief recurrences of previous trips that occur suddenly and without warning. Some develop a syndrome called *hallucinogen persisting perception disorder (HPPD)*, in which the visual cortex becomes highly stimulated whenever the individuals shut their eyes, causing them to experience chronic visual hallucinations whenever they try to sleep (Abraham & Duffy, 2001).

Designer Drugs Designer drugs are so called because they are specially formulated to mimic the pleasurable effects of other drugs without, supposedly, their negative side effects. STP (for Serenity, Tranquility, and Peace) and Ecstasy are two common designer drugs. All designer drugs are derived from amphetamines but have hallucinogenic as well as stimulant effects. One reason for their popularity is that most are metabolized by the body differently than are the drugs they imitate (Drug Free Workplace, 2002). As a result, conventional drug tests do not detect the presence of designer drugs in an individual's system. As drug testing has become more common prior to employment and on a random basis in workplaces and some schools, designer drugs have become more popular.

◆ **hallucinogens**
(hal-LU-sin-o-jenz) A category of drugs that can alter and distort perceptions of time and space, alter mood, produce feelings of unreality, and cause hallucinations; also called *psychedelics*.

Rave dances continue to be popular among North American and European teens. When attending raves, many teens use designer drugs such as Ecstasy because they believe these drugs will increase the pleasure they derive from these events.

Users of MDMA (methylene-dioxy-methamphetamine, the chemical for Ecstasy) describe a wonderfully pleasant state of consciousness, in which even the most backward, bashful, self-conscious people shed their inhibitions (U.S. Department of Health and Human Services, 2001; Verdejo-García et al., 2005). However, MDMA is known to impair a variety of cognitive functions, including memory, sustained attention, analytical thinking, and self-control (National Institute on Drug Abuse, 2001). More specifically, the drug is believed to have devastating effects on the critically important neurotransmitter serotonin (Buchert et al., 2004). Serotonin, as you learned in Chapter 2, influences cognitive performance (including memory), as well as moods, sleep cycles, and the ability to control impulses (Reneman et al., 2000; Volkow & Fowler, 2000). Overdoses of MDMA can be fatal (Drug Enforcement Administration, 2003).

Review and Reflect 4.1 provides a summary of the effects and withdrawal symptoms of the major psychoactive drugs.

REVIEW and REFLECT 4.1

The Effects and Withdrawal Symptoms of Some Psychoactive Drugs

PSYCHOACTIVE DRUG	EFFECTS	WITHDRAWAL SYMPTOMS
Stimulants Caffeine	Produces wakefulness and alertness; increases metabolism but slows reaction time	Headache, depression, fatigue
Nicotine (tobacco)	Effects range from alertness to calmness; lowers appetite for carbohydrates; increases pulse rate and other metabolic processes	Irritability, anxiety, restlessness, increased appetite
Amphetamines	Increase metabolism and alertness; elevate mood, cause wakefulness, suppress appetite	Fatigue, increased appetite, depression, long periods of sleep, irritability, anxiety
Cocaine	Brings on euphoric mood, energy boost, feeling of excitement; suppresses appetite	Depression, fatigue, increased appetite, long periods of sleep, irritability
Depressants Alcohol	First few drinks stimulate and enliven while lowering anxiety and inhibitions; higher doses have a sedative effect, slowing reaction time, impairing motor control and perceptual ability	Tremors, nausea, sweating, depression, weakness, irritability, and in some cases hallucinations
Barbiturates	Promote sleep, have calming and sedative effect, decrease muscular tension, impair coordination and reflexes	Sleeplessness, anxiety; sudden withdrawal can cause seizures, cardiovascular collapse, and death
Tranquilizers (e.g., Valium, Xanax)	Lower anxiety, have calming and sedative effect, decrease muscular tension	Restlessness, anxiety, irritability, muscle tension, difficulty sleeping
Narcotics	Relieve pain; produce paralysis of intestines	Nausea, diarrhea, cramps, insomnia

Hallucinogens Marijuana	Generally produces euphoria, relaxation; affects ability to store new memories	Anxiety, difficulty sleeping, decreased appetite, hyperactivity
LSD	Produces excited exhilaration, hallucinations, experiences perceived as insightful and profound	
MDMA (Ecstasy)	Typically produces euphoria and feelings of understanding others and accepting them; lowers inhibitions; often causes overheating, dehydration, nausea; can cause jaw clenching, eye twitching, and dizziness	Depression, fatigue, and in some cases a "crash," during which the person may be sad, scared, or annoyed

Looking Back   This chapter began with a gripping tale of hypnosis-induced brainwashing. But sleep—a far more common altered state of consciousness—was an important part of the story as well. Remember, Major Marco first became aware of what might have happened to him and his fellow soldiers because of nightmares that disturbed his sleep. As you have learned, experts disagree as to whether dreams could hold the key to uncovering memories that have been hidden from consciousness. There is also debate about why people deliberately induce altered states of consciousness through the use of psychoactive drugs, even when those drugs may damage their physical and mental health. As is always the case, more research is needed to help us more fully understand both involuntary and voluntary alterations of consciousness.

Apply It 4.1   Herbal Supplements

Have you ever heard a radio or television commercial touting a "natural" cure for something? Public interest in alternative approaches to health care has grown tremendously in the past few years. One survey of college students found that about half used herbal supplements (Newberry, et al., 2001). Indeed, the use of herbs as medicines is an ancient practice that may be more common in some cultures than the treatments typically employed in Western society.

Do They Work?

Many herbs have the same kinds of effects on the brain as drugs do. However, the kinds of placebo-controlled studies that are common in pharmacological research remain scarce when it comes to investigations of herbal treatments. In the few studies that have been done, researchers have found that many herbal preparations do live up to their claims. Both kava and valerian can make you feel calmer and help you sleep (Mischoulon, 2002; Wheatley, 2001). Kava, in particular, may someday play an important role in the treatment of serious anxiety disorders (Thompson et al., 2004; Watkins et al., 2001), just as St. John's wort may be used to treat depression (Rivas-Vasquez, 2001). Other herbs appear to be effective in treating attention deficit disorder (Lyon et al., 2001). In addition, soy extracts and some other herbs appear to relieve symptoms of premenstrual syndrome and menopause (Chavez & Spitzer, 2002; Huntley & Ernst, 2004).

Are They Safe?

Many people assume that something called "natural" is automatically safe. In reality, research has yet to establish effective and safe dosages for herbal treatments. The dosage issue is an important one, because excessive consumption of herbal supplements has been linked to liver failure, hypertension, allergic reactions, asthma, heightened risk

(continued on page 130)

for sunburn, mania, depression, and potentially dangerous interactions with prescription medications (Escher et al., 2001; Halemaskel et al., 2001; Pyevich & Bogenschultz, 2001; Rivas-Vasquez, 2001). Moreover, people who use herbal therapies to treat illnesses may delay seeking necessary medical care (Brienza et al., 2002). Most experts recommend that, if you take supplements that haven't been tested, you use caution and avoid consuming them in large quantities.

Evaluating Manufacturers' Claims

Claims made by the manufacturers of herbal supplements need to be evaluated using the rules for critical thinking discussed in Chapter 1. To review, when you hear claims that sound as if they are too good to be true ("Cure baldness for only $1 a day!" or "Eat all you want and still lose weight!"), be an independent thinker who doesn't automatically believe everything you hear. If you're really interested in the product, do some research to find out whether any placebo-controlled studies have been performed. If no evidence exists beyond the glowing testimonials from current and former users, then most likely the claims aren't justified. But keep an open mind and be on the lookout for reports of new studies that may come along in the future.

Chapter 4 Summary

◆ Circadian Rhythms p. 110

◆ In what ways do circadian rhythms affect physiological and psychological functions? p. 110

Circadian rhythms regulate all vital life functions. The suprachiasmatic nucleus (SCN) is the body's biological clock. It controls circadian rhythm by signaling the pineal gland to secrete or suppress melatonin, a hormone that acts to induce sleep.

◆ How do disruptions in circadian rhythms affect the body and the mind? p. 110

Jet lag and shift work disrupt circadian rhythms, which can lead to sleep difficulties as well as reduced alertness during periods of wakefulness.

◆ Sleep p. 111

◆ How do NREM and REM sleep differ? p. 111

During NREM sleep, heart rate and respiration are slow and regular, and blood pressure and brain activity are at a 24-hour low point; there is little body movement and no rapid eye movements. During REM sleep, the large muscles of the body are paralyzed, respiration and heart rate are fast and irregular, brain activity increases, and

rapid eye movements and vivid dreams occur. Many psychologists believe that important neurological tasks, such as the consolidation of new learning, take place during REM sleep.

◆ What is the progression of NREM stages and REM sleep in a typical night of sleep? p. 112

During a typical night of sleep, a person goes through about five sleep cycles, each lasting about 90 minutes.

◆ How does age influence sleep patterns? p. 113

Infants and young children have the longest sleep time and largest percentages of REM and slow-wave sleep. Children from age 6 to puberty sleep best. The elderly typically have shorter total sleep time, more awakenings, and substantially less slow-wave sleep.

◆ What is the difference between the restorative and circadian theories of sleep? p. 114

The restorative theory of sleep claims that being awake places stress on the body and the brain; repairs are made during sleep. The circadian (evolutionary) theory maintains that circadian rhythms, which evolved to protect humans from predators during the night, dictate periods of sleep and alertness.

◆ How does sleep deprivation affect behavior and neurological functioning? p. 114

Research examining the effects of sleep deprivation on verbal learning has shown that sleep deprivation may lead to suppression of neurological activity in the temporal lobes. The brain attempts to compensate for this inhibition by increasing activity in the pre-frontal cortex and the parietal lobes.

◆ What have researchers learned about dreams, their biological basis, and their controllability? p. 115

REM dreams have a storylike or dreamlike quality and are more visual, vivid, and emotional than NREM dreams. During REM dreams, areas of the brain responsible for emotions and the primary visual cortex are active. Lucid dreaming is a set of techniques that enable dreamers to exert cognitive control over the content of their dreams.

◆ How do the views of contemporary psychologists concerning the nature of dreams differ from those of Freud? p. 116

Freud believed that dreams carry hidden meanings and function to satisfy unconscious sexual and aggressive desires. Today, some psychologists support the activation-synthesis hypothesis, which claims that dreams are the brain's attempt to make sense of the random firing of brain cells during REM sleep. Others have proposed an evolutionary view of dreams, suggesting that they serve as rehearsals for responses to threatening events.

◆ What are the various disorders that can trouble sleepers? p. 117

Parasomnias such as somnambulism and sleep terrors occur during a partial arousal from Stage 4 sleep. In a sleep terror, the sleeper awakens in a panicked state with a racing heart. Nightmares are frightening dreams that occur during REM sleep. Somniloquy can occur during any sleep stage and is more common in children than adults. The symptoms of narcolepsy include excessive daytime sleepiness and sudden attacks of REM sleep. Sleep apnea is a serious sleep disorder in which a sleeper's breathing stops and the person must awaken briefly to breathe. Insomnia is a sleep disorder characterized by difficulty falling or staying asleep, by waking too early, or by sleep that is light, restless, or of poor quality.

◆ Meditation and Hypnosis p. 118

◆ What are the benefits of meditation? p. 118

Meditation is used to promote relaxation, reduce arousal, or expand consciousness. It may also help prevent and treat cardiovascular disease.

◆ What are the effects of hypnosis, and how do theorists explain them? p. 119

Hypnosis is a procedure through which a hypnotist uses the power of suggestion to induce changes in the thoughts, feelings, sensations, perceptions, or behavior of a subject. It has been used most successfully for the control of pain. The three main theories proposed to explain hypnosis are the sociocognitive theory, the neodissociation theory, and the theory of dissociated control.

◆ What is the connection between altered states of consciousness and culture? p. 121

Practices in many cultures allow individuals to deliberately induce altered states, often as part of tribal ceremonies or religious rituals. For instance, whirling dances and repetitive chanting are capable of producing such states.

◆ Psychoactive Drugs p. 121

◆ How do drugs affect the brain's neurotransmitter system? p. 122

Psychoactive drugs increase the availability of dopamine in the nucleus accumbens. Beyond that, each drug has a unique influence on a specific neurotransmitter or group of neurotransmitters. Consequently, each psychoactive drug is associated with a distinctive altered state of consciousness.

◆ What factors influence progression from subtance use to substance abuse? p. 122

Risk factors for substance abuse include genetics, impulsivity, and association with drug-using peers. Cultural background may have a protective effect.

◆ What is the difference between physical and psychological drug dependence? p. 123

With physical drug dependence, the user develops a drug tolerance, so increasingly larger doses of the drug are needed to achieve the same effect or high. Withdrawal symptoms appear when the drug is discontinued and disappear when the drug is taken again. Psychological drug dependence involves an intense craving for the drug's pleasurable effects.

◆ What are the effects of stimulants, depressants, and hallucinogens on behavior? p. 124

Stimulants (amphetamines, cocaine, caffeine, and nicotine) speed up activity in the central nervous system, suppress appetite, and make a person feel more awake, alert, and energetic. Depressants decrease activity in the central nervous system, slow down bodily functions, and reduce sensitivity to outside stimulation. Depressants include sedative-hypnotics (alcohol, barbiturates, and minor tranquilizers) and narcotics (opiates such as opium, codeine, morphine, and heroin), which have both pain-relieving and calming effects. Hallucinogens—including marijuana, LSD, and MDMA—can alter and distort perceptions of time and space, alter mood, produce feelings of unreality, and cause hallucinations.

◆ KEY TERMS

activation-synthesis hypothesis of dreaming, p. 117
altered state of consciousness, p. 109
circadian rhythm, p. 110
circadian theory of sleep, p. 114
consciousness, p. 109
delta wave, p. 113
depressants, p. 126
drug tolerance, p. 123
hallucinogens, p. 127
hypnosis, p. 119
insomnia, p. 118
latent content, p. 117
lucid dream, p. 116
manifest content, p. 117

meditation (concentrative), p. 118
narcolepsy, p. 117
narcotics, p. 126
neodissociation theory of hypnosis, p. 120
NREM dream, p. 115
NREM sleep, p. 111
parasomnias, p. 117
physical drug dependence, p. 123
psychoactive drug, p. 122
psychological drug dependence, p. 124
REM dream, p. 115
REM rebound, p. 112
REM sleep, p. 111
restorative theory of sleep, p. 114

sleep apnea, p. 118
sleep cycle, p. 112
sleep spindles, p. 113
slow-wave sleep, p. 113
sociocognitive theory of hypnosis, p. 120
Stage 4 sleep, p. 113
stimulants, p. 124
subjective night, p. 110
substance abuse, p. 122
suprachiasmatic nucleus (SCN), p. 110
theory of dissociated control, p. 121
withdrawal symptoms, p. 124

Answers to all the Study Guide questions are provided at the end of the book.

◆ **SECTION ONE: Chapter Review**

1. Which of the following best defines consciousness?
   a. awareness
   b. wakefulness
   c. receptiveness
   d. rationality

Circadian Rhythms (pp. 110–111)

2. The structure that regulates the body's internal clock is the _____.

3. People who are suffering from jet lag or the effects of working rotating shifts or night shifts are experiencing
   a. a deficiency in melatonin production.
   b. an excess of melatonin production.
   c. a defect in their suprachiasmatic nucleus.
   d. a disturbance in their circadian rhythms.

4. The performance of shift workers is enhanced during their subjective night. (true/false)

Sleep (pp. 111–118)

5. State the type of sleep—NREM or REM—that corresponds to each characteristic.
   ____ (1) paralysis of large muscles
   ____ (2) slow, regular respiration and heart rate
   ____ (3) rapid eye movements
   ____ (4) intense brain activity
   ____ (5) vivid dreams
   a. REM
   b. NREM

6. The average length of a sleep cycle in adults is
   a. 30 minutes.
   b. 60 minutes.
   c. 90 minutes.
   d. 120 minutes.

7. After the first two sleep cycles, most people get equal amounts of deep sleep and REM sleep. (true/false)

8. Which type of sleep seems to aid learning and memory?
   a. Stage 1
   b. Stage 2
   c. Stages 3 and 4
   d. REM sleep

9. Following REM deprivation, there is usually
   a. an absence of REM sleep.
   b. an increase in REM sleep.
   c. a decrease in REM sleep.
   d. no change in the amount of REM sleep.

10. Match the age group with the appropriate description of sleep.
    ____ (1) have most difficulty sleeping
    ____ (2) sleep 8 to 9 hours
    ____ (3) have highest percentage of REM and deep sleep
    a. infants
    b. children aged 6 to puberty
    c. elderly adults

11. The two main theories that attempt to explain the function of sleep are the _____ and the _____.

12. Compared to REM dreams, NREM dreams are
    a. more emotional.
    b. more visual.
    c. less storylike.
    d. more vivid.

13. Dreams are difficult to remember because most of them occur during Stage 4 sleep. (true/false)

14. According to researchers,
    a. most dreams are bizarre in nature.
    b. dreams involving bizarre content are more likely to be remembered than other kinds of dreams.
    c. people who have delusional disorders rarely have bizarre dreams.
    d. only children have bizarre dreams.

15. Experts tend to agree on how dreams should be interpreted. (true/false)

16. Sleepwalking and sleep terrors occur during a partial arousal from
    a. Stage 1 sleep.
    b. Stage 2 sleep.
    c. Stage 4 sleep.
    d. REM sleep.

17. Sleep terrors typically occur in Stage 2 sleep. (true/false)

18. Match each sleep problem with the description or associated symptom.
    ____ (1) uncontrollable sleep attacks during the day
    ____ (2) cessation of breathing during sleep
    ____ (3) difficulty falling or staying asleep
    ____ (4) very frightening REM dream
    a. sleep apnea
    b. nightmare
    c. insomnia
    d. narcolepsy

Meditation and Hypnosis (pp. 118–121)

19. Which is not a proposed use of meditation?
    a. to promote relaxation
    b. to substitute for anesthesia during surgery
    c. to bring a person to a higher level of spirituality
    d. to alter consciousness

20. Many people who meditate are motivated by a desire to attain a higher spiritual state of consciousness. (true/false)

21. Meditation can help people control their emotions. (true/false)

22. Which of the following statements is true of people under hypnosis?
    a. They will often violate their moral code.
    b. They are much stronger than they are in the normal waking state.
    c. They can be made to experience distortions in their perceptions.
    d. Their memory is more accurate than it is during the normal waking state.

23. For a fairly hypnotizable person, which use of hypnosis would probably be most successful?
    a. for relief from pain
    b. instead of a general anesthetic during surgery
    c. for treating drug addiction
    d. for improving memory

24. The three main theories proposed to explain hypnosis are the _____, _____, and _____ theories.

Psychoactive Drugs (pp. 121–129)

25. Psychoactive drugs create pleasurable sensations in the brain by stimulating the _____.

26. Which of the following does not necessarily occur with drug tolerance?
    a. The body adjusts to functioning with the drug in the system.
    b. The user needs increasingly larger doses of the drug to achieve the desired effect.
    c. The user becomes progressively less affected by the drug.
    d. The user develops a craving for the pleasurable effects of the drug.

27. During withdrawal from a drug, the user experiences symptoms that are the opposite of the effects produced by the drug. (true/false)

28. Psychological dependence on a drug is more difficult to combat than physical dependence. (true/false)

29. Match the stimulant with the appropriate description.
    ____ (1) used to increase arousal, relieve fatigue, and suppress appetite
    ____ (2) found in coffee
    ____ (3) snorted or injected
    ____ (4) smokable form of cocaine
    a. caffeine
    b. amphetamines
    c. crack
    d. cocaine

30. Decreased activity in the central nervous system is the chief effect of
    a. stimulants.
    b. depressants.
    c. hallucinogens.
    d. narcotics.

31. Which of the following is a narcotic?
    a. cocaine
    b. heroin
    c. LSD
    d. Valium

32. Narcotics have
    a. pain-relieving effects.
    b. stimulating effects.
    c. energizing effects.
    d. perception-altering effects.

33. Which category of drugs alters perception and mood and can cause feelings of unreality?
    a. stimulants
    b. depressants
    c. hallucinogens
    d. narcotics

34. Which of the following is *not* associated with chronic use of marijuana?
    a. decline in school performance
    b. loss of motivation
    c. general apathy
    d. withdrawal symptoms

35. Some addictive drugs increase the effect of the neurotransmitter _____ in the nucleus accumbens.
    a. acetylcholine
    b. GABA
    c. dopamine
    d. serotonin

SECTION TWO: Identify the Drug

Match the description of drug effects with the drug.

___ (1) Produces excited exhilaration and hallucinations

___ (2) Produces wakefulness and alertness with increased metabolism but slowed reaction time

___ (3) Increase metabolism and alertness, elevate mood and wakefulness, and decrease appetite

___ (4) Produce euphoria and relaxation but also affect ability to store new memories

___ (5) Produces an energy boost and feeling of excitement while suppressing appetite

___ (6) Initial doses stimulate and enliven while lowering anxiety, but higher doses have a sedative effect

___ (7) Produces euphoria and feelings of social acceptance; stimulates appetite; leads to depression and fatigue

a. alcohol
b. hallucinogens
c. marijuana
d. caffeine
e. cocaine
f. amphetamines
g. MDMA (Ecstasy)

SECTION THREE: Fill In the Blank

1. The text defined _____ as an awareness of one's own perceptions, thoughts, feelings, sensations, and external environment.

2. The _____ wave is the slowest brain wave and occurs during Stages 3 and 4 sleep.

3. After a person loses REM sleep because of illness or drug use, he or she might experience _____.

4. Luis awoke in the middle of a strange dream in which he flew across a river. This dream probably occurred during _____ sleep.

5. A person who experiences sleepwalking or sleeptalking is suffering from one of a class of sleep disturbances collectively known as _____.

6. Sleep _____ is a condition in which breathing stops during sleep.

7. _____ is characterized by daytime sleepiness and sudden REM sleep.

8. Psychoactive drugs are a group of substances that alter _____, _____, or _____.

9. _____ is a group of techniques designed to block out all distractions so as to achieve an altered state of consciousness.

10. A compulsive pattern of drug use in which the user develops a tolerance coupled with unpleasant withdrawal symptoms when drug use is discontinued is referred to as physical drug _____.

11. The euphoric high from cocaine lasts only a short time and is followed by an equally intense _____, which is marked by depression, anxiety, agitation, and a powerful craving for more cocaine.

12. Cocaine's action in the human brain includes influencing the neurotransmitter _____, thereby leading to the continual excitatory stimulation of the reward pathways in the brain.

13. The most highly addictive drug is _____.

SECTION FOUR: Comprehensive Practice Test

1. The suprachiasmatic nucleus signals the pineal gland to secrete _____ from dusk until dawn.

2. People who work during their _____, when their biological clock is telling them it is time to sleep, can suffer lowered efficiency and productivity.
   a. REM rebound
   b. subjective night
   c. circadian rebound
   d. episodes of narcolepsy

3. REM sleep is the _____ stage of sleep in a typical sleep cycle.
   a. first
   b. second
   c. last
   d. middle

4. Delta waves appear primarily in Stages _____ sleep.
   a. 1 and 2
   b. 2 and 3
   c. 3 and 4
   d. 1 and 4

5. Another name for slow-wave sleep is
   a. light sleep.
   b. deep sleep.
   c. REM sleep.
   d. dream sleep.

6. Researchers have found that REM sleep
   a. is increased in the elderly.
   b. is associated with memory consolidation.
   c. occurs only in some sleep cycles.
   d. is rarely associated with dreaming.

7. As we grow older we sleep more than when we were younger; we also sleep more deeply, with more REM sleep. (true/false)

8. Freud believed dreams functioned to satisfy unconscious _____ and _____ urges.
   a. parental; childhood
   b. sexual; superego
   c. aggressive; violent
   d. sexual; aggressive

9. J. Allan Hobson believes dreams are merely the brain's attempt to make sense of the random firing of brain cells. This view is known as the
   a. Hobson dream hypothesis.
   b. somniloquy hypothesis.
   c. activation-synthesis hypothesis.
   d. physiological activation hypothesis.

10. The technical term for sleepwalking is
    a. somniloquy.   c. narcolepsy.
    b. mobile insomnia.   d. somnambulism.

11. People who talk in their sleep often mumble nonsensical words and phrases. (true/false)

12. Some people suffer from a sleep disorder known as _____, which causes them to stop breathing and then to wake for a brief time so as to start breathing again.
    a. narcolepsy   c. somniloquy
    b. sleep apnea   d. somnambulism

13. The sleep disorder characterized by either difficulty falling asleep or frequently waking is known as
    a. sleep apnea.   c. somnambulism.
    b. insomnia.   d. REM rebound.

14. Jack pleaded not guilty to his public indecency charges. He claimed he would never do such a thing if he were in his right mind and that he was the victim of the effects of hypnosis. A psychologist would probably support this claim. (true/false)

15. Personality has little impact on substance abuse. (true/false)

16. LSD, MDMA, and marijuana are classified as
    a. narcotics.   c. hallucinogens.
    b. stimulants.   d. depressants.

17. Animals addicted to several drugs prefer _____ when offered a choice of drugs.
    a. marijuana
    b. heroin
    c. cocaine
    d. alcohol

18. Caffeine is a depressant. (true/false)

◆ SECTION FIVE: Critical Thinking

1. Suppose you have been hired by a sleep clinic to formulate a questionnaire for evaluating patients' sleep habits. List 10 questions you would include in your questionnaire.

2. Luanne is a full-time student who wants to find a way to keep up her class schedule while working full-time. She decides to work the 11:00 p.m. to 7:00 a.m. shift at a hospital, then attend morning classes. After her classes end at noon, she intends to sleep from 1:00 p.m. until 7:00 p.m., at which time she will get up and study until it is time to leave for work. Based on what you have learned about circadian rhythms in this chapter, what kinds of problems do you think Luanne will encounter in trying to carry out her plan?

3. You have been asked to make a presentation to 7th and 8th graders about the dangers of drugs. What are the most persuasive general arguments you can give to convince them not to start using drugs? What are some convincing, specific arguments against using each of these drugs: alcohol, marijuana, cocaine, and MDMA (Ecstasy)?

Learning

chapter 5

Classical Conditioning

◆ What kind of learning did Pavlov discover and how is it accomplished?

◆ What kinds of changes in stimuli and learning conditions lead to changes in conditioned responses?

◆ How did Watson demonstrate that fear could be classically conditioned?

◆ According to Rescorla, what is the critical element in classical conditioning?

◆ What types of everyday responses can be subject to classical conditioning?

Operant Conditioning

◆ What did Thorndike conclude about learning by watching cats try to escape from his puzzle box?

◆ How do reinforcement and punishment influence behavior?

◆ What is the goal of both positive reinforcement and negative reinforcement, and how is that goal accomplished with each?

◆ What are the four types of schedules of reinforcement, and which type is most effective?

◆ What are the roles of shaping, extinction, generalization, and discriminative stimuli in the operant conditioning process?

◆ How does punishment differ from negative reinforcement?

◆ When is avoidance learning desirable, and when is it maladaptive?

◆ What are some applications of operant conditioning?

Cognitive Learning

◆ What is insight, and how does it affect learning?

◆ What did Tolman discover about the necessity of reinforcement?

◆ How do we learn by observing others?

Training a dolphin to leap high in the air might seem to be fairly simple. After all, wild dolphins jump out of the water at times. Of course, they jump when they feel like it, not when another being signals them to do it. To perform the leaping trick, and to learn to do it at the right time, a dolphin has to acquire several skills.

The process begins with relationship building: The dolphin learns to associate the trainer with things it enjoys, such as food, stroking, and fetching games. These interactions also help the trainer to learn each individual dolphin's personality characteristics: Some enjoy being touched more than playing, some prefer to play "fetch" rather than get stroked, and so on. The pleasant stimuli associated with the trainers serve as potential rewards for desirable behavior. Likewise, trainers can discourage undesirable behaviors by withholding such rewards.

Once the dolphin is responsive to some kind of reward, a long pole with a float on the end is used to teach it to follow directions. Trainers touch the dolphin with the float and then reward it. Next, the float is placed a few feet from the dolphin. When it swims over and touches the float, a reward is administered. The float is moved farther and farther away from the dolphin until the dolphin has been led to the particular location in the tank where the trainer wants it to begin performing the trick.

The pole-and-float device is then used to teach the dolphin to jump. Remember, it has been rewarded for touching the float. To get the dolphin to jump, the trainer raises the float above the water level. The dolphin jumps up to touch the float and receives its reward. The float is raised a little higher each time, until the animal must jump completely out of the water to receive the reward. The process continues until the dolphin has learned to jump to the desired height.

This process might seem to be very time-consuming, but there is one important shortcut in training dolphins: observational learning. Trainers have found that it is much easier to teach an untrained dolphin to perform desired behaviors when a more experienced dolphin participates in the training. In fact, park-bred babies are usually allowed to accompany their mothers during shows so that they learn all of the show behaviors through observation. Some aspects of training must still be accomplished individually, but, like humans, dolphins appear to have a very great capacity for learning complex behaviors by observing others of their species.

Dolphin training takes advantage of all the principles of learning covered in this chapter. Psychologists define **learning** as a relatively permanent change in behavior, knowledge, capability, or attitude that is acquired through experience and cannot be attributed to illness, injury, or maturation. Several parts of this definition warrant further explanation. First, defining learning as a "relatively permanent change" excludes temporary changes that could result from illness, fatigue, or fluctuations in mood. Second, limiting learning to changes that are "acquired through experience" excludes some readily observable changes in behavior that occur as a result of brain injuries or certain diseases. Also, certain observable changes that occur as individuals grow and mature have nothing to do with learning. For example, technically speaking, infants do not *learn* to crawl or walk. Basic motor skills and the maturational plan that governs their development are a part of the genetically programmed behavioral repertoire of every species. The first kind of learning we'll consider is classical conditioning.

◆ **learning**
A relatively permanent change in behavior, knowledge, capability, or attitude that is acquired through experience and cannot be attributed to illness, injury, or maturation.

Classical Conditioning

◆ **classical conditioning**

A type of learning through which an organism learns to associate one stimulus with another.

◆ **stimulus**

(STIM-yu-lus) Any event or object in the environment to which an organism responds; plural is *stimuli*.

Why do sodas that contain artificial sweeteners (so-called diet drinks) make some people hungry? The answer can be found in the principles of **classical conditioning,** a type of learning through which an organism learns to associate one stimulus with another. This kind of learning is sometimes referred to as *Pavlovian conditioning* or *respondent conditioning.* A **stimulus** (the plural is *stimuli*) is any event or object in the environment to which an organism responds. Be patient; at the end of this section, we'll explain why drinking diet sodas might actually cause you to gain weight. As you read about classical conditioning, see if you can figure it out on your own.

Pavlov and the Process of Classical Conditioning

◆ *What kind of learning did Pavlov discover and how is it accomplished?*

Ivan Pavlov (1849–1936) organized and directed research in physiology at the Institute of Experimental Medicine in St. Petersburg, Russia, from 1891 until his death 45 years later. There, he conducted his classic experiments on the physiology of digestion, which won him a Nobel Prize in 1904—the first time a Russian received this honor.

Pavlov's contribution to psychology came about quite by accident. To conduct his study of the salivary response in dogs, Pavlov made a small incision in the side of each dog's mouth. Then he attached a tube so that the flow of saliva could be diverted from inside the animal's mouth, through the tube, and into a container, where the saliva was collected and measured (Figure 5.1). Pavlov's purpose was to collect the saliva that the dogs would secrete naturally in response to food placed inside the mouth. But he noticed that, in many cases, the dogs would begin to salivate even before the food was presented. Pavlov observed drops of saliva collecting in the containers when the dogs heard the footsteps of the laboratory assistants coming to feed them. He observed saliva collecting when the dogs heard their food dishes rattling, saw the attendant who fed them, or spotted their food. How could an involuntary response such as salivation come to be associated with the sights and sounds involved in feeding? Pavlov spent the rest of his life studying this question. The type of learning he studied is known today as classical conditioning.

Pavlov (1927/1960) used tones, bells, buzzers, lights, geometric shapes, electric shocks, and metronomes in his conditioning experiments. In a typical experiment, food

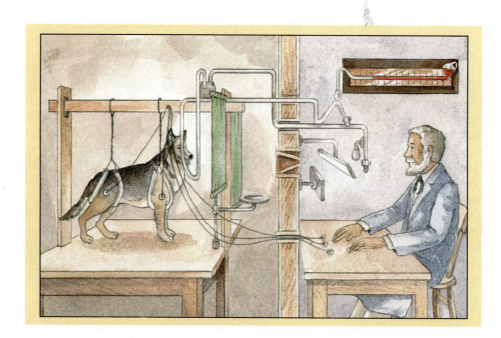

FIGURE 5.1

The Experimental Apparatus Used in Pavlov's Classical Conditioning Studies

In Pavlov's classical conditioning studies, the dog was restrained in a harness in the cubicle and isolated from all distractions. An experimenter observed the dog through a one-way mirror and, by remote control, presented the dog with food and other conditioning stimuli. A tube carried the saliva from the dog's mouth to a container where it was measured.

powder was placed in the dog's mouth, causing salivation. Because dogs do not need to be conditioned to salivate to food, salivation to food is an unlearned response, or **unconditioned response (UR).** Any stimulus, such as food, that without prior learning will automatically elicit, or bring forth, an unconditioned response is called an **unconditioned stimulus (US).**

Following is a list of some common unconditioned reflexes, showing their two components: the unconditioned stimulus and the unconditioned response.

UNCONDITIONED REFLEXES

Unconditioned Stimulus (US)	Unconditioned Response (UR)
food	salivation
loud noise	startle
light in eye	contraction of pupil
puff of air in eye	eyeblink response

Pavlov demonstrated that dogs could be conditioned to salivate to a variety of stimuli never before associated with food, as shown in Figure 5.2. During the conditioning process, the researcher would present a neutral stimulus such as a musical tone shortly before placing food powder in the dog's mouth. The food powder would cause the dog to salivate. Pavlov found that after the tone and the food were paired many times, usually 20 or more, the tone alone would elicit salivation (Pavlov, 1927/1960, p. 385). Pavlov called the tone the learned stimulus, or **conditioned stimulus (CS),** and salivation to the tone the learned response, or **conditioned response (CR).**

♦ **unconditioned response (UR)**

A response that is elicited by an unconditioned stimulus without prior learning.

♦ **unconditioned stimulus (US)**

A stimulus that elicits a specific unconditioned response without prior learning.

♦ **conditioned stimulus (CS)**

A neutral stimulus that, after repeated pairing with an unconditioned stimulus, becomes associated with it and elicits a conditioned response.

♦ **conditioned response (CR)**

The learned response that comes to be elicited by a conditioned stimulus as a result of its repeated pairing with an unconditioned stimulus.

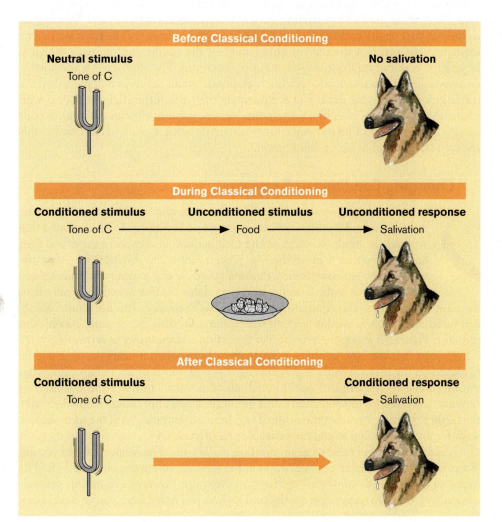

FIGURE 5.2

Classically Conditioning a Salivation Response

A neutral stimulus (a tone) elicits no salivation until it is repeatedly paired with the unconditioned stimulus (food). After many pairings, the neutral stimulus (now called the conditioned stimulus) alone produces salivation. Classical conditioning has occurred.

Before Classical Conditioning

Neutral stimulus
Tone of C

No salivation

During Classical Conditioning

Conditioned stimulus
Tone of C

Unconditioned stimulus
Food

Unconditioned response
Salivation

After Classical Conditioning

Conditioned stimulus
Tone of C

Conditioned response
Salivation

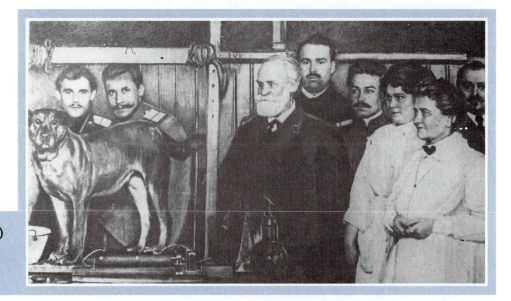

Ivan Pavlov (1849–1936) earned fame by studying the conditioned reflex in dogs.

◆ **higher-order conditioning**

Conditioning that occurs when conditioned stimuli are linked together to form a series of signals.

◆ **extinction**

In classical conditioning, the weakening and eventual disappearance of the conditioned response as a result of repeated presentation of the conditioned stimulus without the unconditioned stimulus.

◆ *What kinds of changes in stimuli and learning conditions lead to changes in conditioned responses?*

◆ **spontaneous recovery**

The reappearance of an extinguished response (in a weaker form) when an organism is exposed to the original conditioned stimulus following a rest period.

◆ **generalization**

In classical conditioning, the tendency to make a conditioned response to a stimulus that is similar to the original conditioned stimulus.

Pavlov also discovered that a neutral stimulus could become a conditioned stimulus simply by pairing it with a previously acquired conditioned stimulus, a process called **higher-order conditioning**. Higher-order conditioning is quite common. Think about what happens when you must have some kind of blood test. Typically, you sit in a chair next to a table on which are arranged materials such as needles, syringes, and such. Next, some kind of constricting device is tied around your arm, and the nurse or technician pats on the surface of your skin until a vein becomes visible. Each step in the sequence tells you that the unavoidable "stick" of the needle and the pain, which is largely the result of reflexive muscle tension, is coming. The stick itself is the unconditioned stimulus, to which you reflexively respond. But all the steps that precede it are conditioned stimuli that cause you to anticipate the pain of the stick itself. And with each successive step, a conditioned response occurs, as your muscles respond to your anxiety by contracting a bit more in anticipation of the stick. Chains of cues such as this are the result of higher-order conditioning.

Changing Conditioned Responses

After conditioning an animal to salivate to a tone, what would happen if you continued to sound the tone but no longer paired it with food? Pavlov found that without the food, salivation to the tone became weaker and weaker and then finally disappeared altogether—a process known as **extinction**. After the response had been extinguished, Pavlov allowed the dog to rest for 20 minutes and then brought it back to the laboratory. He found that the dog would again salivate to the tone. Pavlov called this recurrence **spontaneous recovery**. But the spontaneously recovered response was weaker and shorter in duration than the original conditioned response. Figure 5.3 shows the processes of extinction and spontaneous recovery.

Assume that you have conditioned a dog to salivate when it hears the tone middle C played on the piano. Would it also salivate if you played B or D? Pavlov found that a tone similar to the original conditioned stimulus would produce the conditioned response (salivation), a phenomenon called **generalization**. But the salivation decreased the farther the tone was from the original conditioned stimulus, until the tone became so different that the dog would not salivate at all (Figure 5.4).

It is easy to see the value of generalization in daily life. For instance, when you get in a car, you probably hear a chime or a bell that reminds you to put on a seat belt. The sound of this device is somewhat different in every car, however. Thanks to generalization, you don't have to relearn what to do when you enter a car you've never been

FIGURE 5.3 **Extinction of a Classically Conditioned Response**

When a classically conditioned stimulus (a tone) was presented in a series of trials without the unconditioned stimulus (food), Pavlov's dogs salivated less and less until there was virtually no salivation. But after a 20-minute rest, one sound of the tone caused the conditioned response to reappear in a weakened form (producing only a small amount of salivation), a phenomenon Pavlov called *spontaneous recovery*.   *Source:* Data from Pavlov (1927/1960), p. 58.

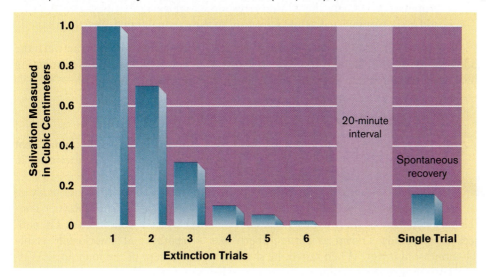

in before. Instead, you can generalize from one car to another even though the sound may be a bit different.

Let's return to the example of a dog being conditioned to a musical tone to trace the process of **discrimination,** the learned ability to distinguish between similar stimuli so that the conditioned response occurs only to the original conditioned stimuli but not to similar stimuli.

◆ **discrimination**

The learned ability to distinguish between similar stimuli so that the conditioned response occurs only to the original conditioned stimulus but not to similar stimuli.

FIGURE 5.4 **Generalization of a Conditioned Response**

Pavlov attached small vibrators to different parts of a dog's body. After conditioning salivation to stimulation of the dog's thigh, he stimulated other parts of the dog's body. Due to generalization, the salivation also occurred when other body parts were stimulated. But the farther away from the thigh the stimulus was applied, the weaker the salivation response.   *Source:* From Pavlov (1927/1960).

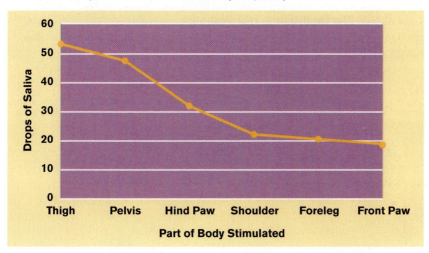

Step 1. The dog is conditioned to salivate in response to the tone C.

Step 2. Generalization occurs, and the dog salivates to a range of musical tones above and below C. The dog salivates less and less as the tone moves farther away from C.

Step 3. The original tone C is repeatedly paired with food. Neighboring tones are also sounded, but they are not followed by food. The dog is being conditioned to discriminate. Gradually, the salivation response to the neighboring tones (A, B, D, and E) is extinguished, while salivation to the original tone C is strengthened.

Like generalization, discrimination has survival value. Discriminating between the odors of fresh and spoiled milk will spare you an upset stomach. Discriminating between a rattlesnake and a garter snake could save your life.

John Watson and Emotional Conditioning

◆ *How did Watson demonstrate that fear could be classically conditioned?*

You may recall from Chapter 1 that John B. Watson (1878–1958) claimed that the influence of environmental factors could explain nearly all variations in human behavior. Recall, too, that Watson coined the term *behaviorism* to refer to the school of thought that proposed limiting psychology to the study of overtly observable behavior. In 1919, Watson and his assistant, Rosalie Rayner, conducted a now-famous study to prove that fear could be classically conditioned. The subject of the study, known as Little Albert, was a healthy and emotionally stable 11-month-old infant. When tested, he showed no fear except of the loud noise Watson made by striking a hammer against a steel bar near his head.

In the laboratory, Rayner presented Little Albert with a white rat. As Albert reached for the rat, Watson struck the steel bar with a hammer just behind Albert's head. This procedure was repeated, and Albert "jumped violently, fell forward and began to whimper" (Watson & Rayner, 1920, p. 4). A week later, Watson continued the experiment, pairing the rat with the loud noise five more times. Then, at the sight of the white rat alone, Albert began to cry.

When Albert returned to the laboratory 5 days later, the fear had generalized to a rabbit and, somewhat less, to a dog, a seal coat, Watson's hair, and a Santa Claus mask (see Figure 5.5). After 30 days, Albert made his final visit to the laboratory. His fears were still evident, although they were somewhat less intense. Watson concluded that conditioned fears "persist and modify personality throughout life" (Watson & Rayner, 1920, p. 12).

Although Watson had formulated techniques for removing conditioned fears, Albert moved out of the city before they could be tried on him. Since Watson apparently knew that Albert would be moving away before these fear-removal techniques could be applied, he clearly showed a disregard for the child's welfare. The American Psycho-

FIGURE 5.5 **The Conditioned Fear Response**

Little Albert's fear of a white rat was a conditioned response that was generalized to other stimuli, including a rabbit and, to a lesser extent, a Santa Claus mask.

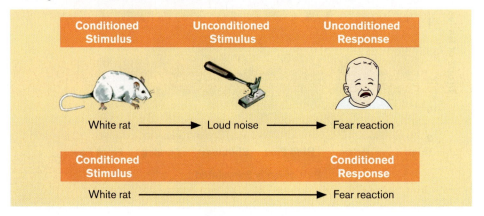

logical Association now has strict ethical standards for the use of human and animal participants in research experiments and would not sanction an experiment such as Watson's.

Some of Watson's ideas for removing fears laid the groundwork for certain behavior therapies used today. Three years after his experiment with Little Albert, Watson and a colleague, Mary Cover Jones (1924), worked with 3-year-old Peter, who was afraid of white rabbits. Peter was brought into the laboratory, seated in a high chair, and given candy to eat. A white rabbit in a wire cage was brought into the room but kept far enough away from Peter that it would not upset him. Over the course of 38 therapy sessions, the rabbit was brought closer and closer to Peter, who continued to enjoy his candy. Occasionally, some of Peter's friends were brought in to play with the rabbit at a safe distance from Peter so that he could see firsthand that the rabbit did no harm. Toward the end of Peter's therapy, the rabbit was taken out of the cage and eventually put in Peter's lap. By the final session, Peter had grown fond of the rabbit.

The Cognitive Perspective

Which aspect of the classical conditioning process is most important? Both Pavlov and Watson believed that the critical element in classical conditioning was the repeated pairing of the conditioned stimulus and the unconditioned stimulus, with only a brief interval between the two. Beginning in the late 1960s, though, researchers began to discover exceptions to some of the general principles Pavlov had identified.

◆ *According to Rescorla, what is the critical element in classical conditioning?*

Robert Rescorla (1967, 1968, 1988; Rescorla & Wagner, 1972) is largely responsible for changing how psychologists view classical conditioning. Rescorla was able to demonstrate that the critical element in classical conditioning is not the repeated pairing of the conditioned stimulus and the unconditioned stimulus. Rather, the important factor is whether the conditioned stimulus provides information that enables the organism to reliably *predict* the occurrence of the unconditioned stimulus. How was Rescorla able to prove that prediction is the critical element?

Using rats as his subjects, Rescorla used a tone as the conditioned stimulus and a shock as the unconditioned stimulus. For one group of rats, the tone and shock were paired 20 times—the shock always occurred during the tone. The other group of rats also received a shock 20 times while the tone was sounding, but this group also received 20 shocks that were not paired with the tone. If the only critical element in classical conditioning were the number of pairings of the conditioned stimulus and the unconditioned stimulus, both groups of rats should have developed a conditioned fear response to the tone, because both groups experienced exactly the same number of pairings of tone and shock. But this was not the case. Only the first group, for which the tone was a reliable predictor of the shock, developed the conditioned fear response to the tone. The second group showed little evidence of conditioning, because the shock was just as likely to occur without the tone as with it. In other words, for this group, the tone provided no additional information about the shock.

Classical Conditioning in Everyday Life

Whether Pavlov's view or that of cognitive psychologists such as Rescorla is the best explanation for classical conditioning, it is clear that this kind of learning is quite common in everyday life. For instance, do you suddenly experience hunger pangs when you smell fresh-baked chocolate chip cookies? Do you cringe in response to the sound of a dental drill? In either case, classical conditioning is the most likely explanation for your behavior.

◆ *What types of everyday responses can be subject to classical conditioning?*

Your stomach rumbles when you smell fresh-baked cookies because smell and taste are so closely linked that food odors, functioning as conditioned stimuli, can actually make you think you are hungry even if you have just finished a large meal. Recall that we began our discussion of classical conditioning by saying that its principles can explain why diet sodas make some people hungry. This can happen because the distinctive flavors of foods can become conditioned stimuli for the digestive processes that typically follow them.

Classical conditioning has proved to be a highly effective tool for advertisers. Here, a neutral product (milk) is paired with an image of an attractive celebrity. Can you identify the UCS, UCR, CS, and CR at work here?

♦ **taste aversion**

The intense dislike and/or avoidance of a particular food that has been associated with nausea or discomfort.

Smell and taste are closely associated because the smell of a particular food is a signal for its taste and the physical sensations associated with eating it. When you look at this photo, can you imagine how the peach smells? When you imagine the smell, do you recall the food's taste and texture? Are you starting to get hungry?

For instance, researchers have found that the pancreas quickly adapts to food cues through the process of classical conditioning (e.g., Stockhorst et al., 1999). Most of the time, the presence of a sweet taste on the tongue (a CS) is a reliable cue indicating that a rise in blood sugar (a UR) will soon occur. As a result, the pancreas "learns" to pump out insulin, the hormone that lowers blood sugar levels, whenever you eat or drink something sweet. A likely consequence of this adaptation is that the pancreas will respond to an artificial sweetener in the same way. Without the presence of real sugar to bring up the blood sugar level, however, the insulin will cause the blood sugar level to drop below normal. Whenever the blood sugar level drops below normal, the body signals the brain to motivate you to eat; in other words, you begin to feel hungry (more on this mechanism in Chapter 10). Over time, of course, the pancreas will probably learn to discriminate between the taste of artificially sweetened beverages and drinks that contain real sugar. The insulin response to artificial sweeteners will then become extinguished, while the link between the taste of sugared beverages and the insulin response will be maintained.

Classical conditioning is also at work when you avoid foods that have made you sick in the past. Have you ever vomited after eating something with a distinctive taste, such as chili or spaghetti? If so, you know that for a few days or weeks afterward, the sight or smell of the offending food can be enough to make you feel nauseous. You certainly don't want to eat any of it. What you are experiencing is a **taste aversion,** an intense dislike and/or avoidance of particular foods that have been associated with nausea. Although classical conditioning usually requires multiple trials, taste aversions can develop after only a single pairing of a food with nausea and/or vomiting. Eventually, the association becomes extinguished and your eating habits return to normal.

For most people, taste aversions are nothing more than a temporary nuisance. For some, however, they can be life-threatening. Helping cancer patients avoid taste aversions, for instance, can be a vital part of their treatment regimen. Bernstein and others (1982; Bernstein, 1985) devised a technique to help cancer patients avoid developing aversions to desirable foods. A group of cancer patients were given a novel-tasting, maple-flavored ice cream before chemotherapy. The nausea caused by the treatment resulted in a taste aversion to the ice cream. The researchers found that when an unusual or unfamiliar food becomes the "scapegoat," or target for a taste aversion, other foods in the patient's diet may be protected, and the patient will continue to eat them regularly. For this reason, cancer patients should refrain from eating preferred or nutritious foods prior to chemotherapy. Instead, they should be given an unusual-tasting food shortly before the treatment. They will then be less likely to develop an aversion to foods they normally eat and, in turn, will be more likely to maintain their body weight during treatment.

Like eating behavior, our fears are influenced by classical conditioning, as was amply demonstrated by Watson's Little Albert experiment. Perhaps you are one of the many people who have developed a dental phobia after having painful dental work. These individuals fear the dentist's drill, along with a wide range of stimuli associated with it—the chair, the waiting room, even the building where the dentist's office is located. In the conditioning of fear, a conditioned stimulus (CS), such as the dentist's drill, is associated with an aversive stimulus (US), such as the pain that can happen in the course of a dental procedure, in a new or unfamiliar environment. After just one such pairing, it is possible to develop a long-lasting fear of the CS and of the context.

As Watson's experiments with Peter revealed, however, classical conditioning also holds the key to overcoming such fears. Thus, if you continue to go to the dentist regularly and, for the most part, experience pain-free treatment, you may well overcome your dental phobia.

Through classical conditioning, environmental cues associated with drug use become conditioned stimuli and later produce the conditioned responses of drug craving (Field & Duka, 2002; London et al., 2000; Sun & Rebec 2005). The conditioned stimuli associated with drugs become powerful, often irresistible forces that lead individuals to seek out and use those substances (Porrino & Lyons, 2000). Consequently, drug counselors strongly urge recovering addicts to avoid any cues (people, places, and things) associated with their past drug use.

Chemotherapy treatments can result in a conditioned taste aversion, but providing patients with a "scapegoat" target for the taste aversion can help them maintain a proper diet.

The prevalence of classical conditioning in our everyday lives raises questions about the degree to which laboratory studies may or may not faithfully represent the process of classical conditioning. As noted earlier, laboratory learning typically requires a large number of trial pairings of conditioned and unconditioned stimuli, but many kinds of everyday conditioning (e.g., taste aversion) can happen after just one experience.

This and other differences have led experts in the field to hypothesize that a stimulus that has "ecological relevance" is more likely to function as a conditioned stimulus (Domjan et al., 2004). In other words, to serve as a conditioned stimulus, a neutral stimulus must have some authentic connection to the unconditioned stimulus. For example, real links exist among smells, tastes, and digestive processes. Likewise, a dental drill really can cause pain, and drugs do create altered states of consciousness. Compare these everyday conditioned stimuli to the arbitrary ones that Pavlov used—musical tones, buzzers, and the like. Research indicates that ecologically valid conditioned stimuli are acquired much more quickly than arbitrary stimuli and are also more resistant to extinction (Domjan et al., 2004).

Some evidence also indicates that we are biologically predisposed to learn some CS-US connections. For example, research has shown that humans can be quite easily conditioned to fear snakes (Ohman & Mineka, 2003). The finding that fear of snakes and other potentially threatening animals is just as common in apes and monkeys as in humans lends further weight to the predisposition hypothesis. Of course, such a predisposition does not mean that everyone is doomed to become fearful of snakes. It simply suggests that nature has prepared us to quickly learn to fear things that can actually harm us.

Operant Conditioning

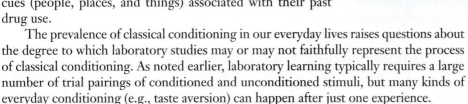

Understanding the principles of classical conditioning can provide a great deal of insight into human behavior. But is there more to human learning than simply responding reflexively to stimuli? Think about a ringing telephone, for example. Do you respond to this stimulus because it has been paired with a natural stimulus of some kind or because of a consequence you anticipate when you hear it? The work of two psychologists, Edward L. Thorndike and B. F. Skinner, helps answer this question.

Thorndike and the Law of Effect

Have you ever watched a dog learn how to turn over a trash can, or a cat learn how to open a door? If so, you probably observed the animal fail several times before finding just the right physical technique for accomplishing the goal. Based on his observations of animal behavior, Edward Thorndike (1874–1949) formulated several laws of learning, the most important being the law of effect (Thorndike, 1911/1970). The **law of effect** states that the consequence, or effect,

◆ **law of effect**
One of Thorndike's laws of learning, which states that the consequence, or effect, of a response will determine whether the tendency to respond in the same way in the future will be strengthened or weakened.

◆ *What did Thorndike conclude about learning by watching cats try to escape from his puzzle box?*

of a response will determine whether the tendency to respond in the same way in the future will be strengthened or weakened. Responses closely followed by satisfying consequences are more likely to be repeated. Thorndike (1898) insisted that it was "unnecessary to invoke reasoning" to explain how the learning took place.

In Thorndike's best-known experiments, a hungry cat was placed in a wooden box with slats, which was called a *puzzle box*. The box was designed so that the animal had to manipulate a simple mechanism—pressing a pedal or pulling down a loop—to escape and claim a food reward that lay just outside the box. The cat would first try to squeeze through the slats; when these attempts failed, it would scratch, bite, and claw the inside of the box. In time, the cat would accidentally trip the mechanism, which would open the door. Each time, after winning freedom and claiming the food reward, the cat was returned to the box. After many trials, the cat learned to open the door almost immediately after being placed in the box.

Thorndike's law of effect was the conceptual starting point for B. F. Skinner's work in operant conditioning.

B. F. Skinner and the Process of Operant Conditioning

Most people in the United States know something about B. F. Skinner because his ideas about learning have strongly influenced American education, parenting practices, and approaches to business management. Like Watson before him, Skinner believed that the causes of behavior lie in the environment and are not rooted in inner mental events such as thoughts, feelings, or perceptions. Instead, Skinner claimed that these inner mental events are themselves behaviors and, like any other behaviors, are shaped and determined by environmental forces.

Skinner conducted much of his research in operant conditioning at the University of Minnesota in the 1930s and wrote *The Behavior of Organisms* (1938), now a classic. Gaining more attention was his first novel, *Walden Two* (1948b), set in a fictional utopian community where reinforcement principles are used to produce happy, productive, and cooperative citizens. In 1948, Skinner returned to Harvard and continued his research and writing. There, he wrote *Science and Human Behavior* (1953), which provides a description of the process of operant conditioning.

In a later and highly controversial book, *Beyond Freedom and Dignity* (1971), Skinner was critical of society's preoccupation with the notion of freedom. He maintained that free will is a myth and that a person's behavior is always shaped and controlled by others—parents, teachers, peers, advertising, television. He argued that rather than leaving the control of human behavior to chance, societies should systematically shape the behavior of their members for the larger good.

Although Skinner's social theories generated controversy, little controversy exists about the significance of his research in **operant conditioning,** the process through which consequences increase or decrease the frequency of a behavior. Skinner's research revealed that the process begins with an **operant,** or voluntary behavior, that accidentally brings about some kind of consequence. A consequence that increases the frequency of an operant is known as a **reinforcer,** while one that decreases an operant's frequency is called a *punisher*. We will examine the process of reinforcement next before taking a closer look at punishment.

Reinforcement

How did you learn the correct sequence of behaviors involved in using an ATM? Simple—a single mistake in the sequence will prevent you from getting your money, so you learn to do it correctly. What about paying bills on time? Doesn't prompt payment allow you to avoid those steep late-payment penalties? In each case, your behavior is reinforced, but in a different way.

Reinforcement is a key concept in operant conditioning and may be defined as any event that follows a response and strengthens or increases the probability of the response being repeated. There are two types of reinforcement, positive and negative.

◆ **operant conditioning**
A type of learning in which the consequences of behavior are manipulated so as to increase or decrease the frequency of an existing response or to shape an entirely new response.

◆ **operant**
A voluntary behavior that accidentally brings about a consequence.

◆ **reinforcer**
Anything that follows a response and strengthens it or increases the probability that it will occur.

◆ **reinforcement**
Any event that follows a response and strengthens or increases the probability that the response will be repeated.

◆ *How do reinforcement and punishment influence behavior?*

◆ *What is the goal of both positive reinforcement and negative reinforcement, and how is that goal accomplished with each?*

Positive reinforcement, which is roughly the same thing as a reward, refers to any pleasant or desirable consequence that follows a response and increases the probability that the response will be repeated. The money you get when you use the correct ATM procedure is a positive reinforcer.

Just as people engage in behaviors to get positive reinforcers, so they also engage in behaviors to avoid or escape aversive, or unpleasant, conditions, such as late-payment penalties. With **negative reinforcement,** a person's or animal's behavior is reinforced by the termination or avoidance of an unpleasant condition. If you find that a response successfully ends an aversive condition, you are likely to repeat it. You will turn on the air conditioner to avoid the heat and will get out of bed to turn off a faucet and end the annoying "drip, drip, drip." Heroin addicts will do almost anything to obtain heroin to terminate their painful withdrawal symptoms. In these instances, negative reinforcement involves putting an end to the heat, the dripping faucet, and the withdrawal symptoms.

Are all reinforcers created equal? Not necessarily. A **primary reinforcer** is one that fulfills a basic physical need for survival and does not depend on learning. Food, water, sleep, and termination of pain are examples of primary reinforcers. And sex is a powerful reinforcer that fulfills a basic physical need for survival of the species. Fortunately, learning does not depend solely on primary reinforcers. If that were the case, people would need to be hungry, thirsty, or sex starved before they would respond at all. Much observed human behavior occurs in response to secondary reinforcers. A **secondary reinforcer** is acquired or learned through association with other reinforcers. Some secondary reinforcers (money, for example) can be exchanged at a later time for other reinforcers. Praise, good grades, awards, applause, attention, and signals of approval, such as a smile or a kind word, are all examples of secondary reinforcers.

For many students, studying with classmates reduces the nervousness they feel about an upcoming exam. They respond to their test anxiety by joining a study group and studying more. Discussing the exam with other students helps alleviate the anxiety as well. Thus, for these students, test anxiety is an important source of negative reinforcement.

◆ **positive reinforcement**
Any pleasant or desirable consequence that follows a response and increases the probability that the response will be repeated.

◆ **negative reinforcement**
The termination of an unpleasant condition after a response, which increases the probability that the response will be repeated.

Schedules of Reinforcement

Think about the difference between an ATM and a slot machine. Under the right conditions, you can get money from either of them. But the ATM gives you a reinforcer every time you use the right procedure, while the slot machine does so only intermittently. These two familiar machines use different **schedules of reinforcement,** or systematic processes for administering reinforcement.

The two basic types of schedules of reinforcement are ratio and interval schedules. Both the ATM and the slot machine use ratio schedules—that is, behavior brings about reinforcement. With interval schedules, a given amount of time must pass before a reinforcer is administered, usually without regard to whether a particular behavior has occurred during that time period. Salaried employees are on an interval schedule. Ratio and variable schedules are further subdivided into fixed and variable categories (see Figure 5.6.). Each kind of schedule has a different effect on behavior.

On a **fixed-ratio schedule,** a reinforcer is given after a fixed number of correct, nonreinforced responses. If the fixed ratio is set at 30 responses (FR-30), a reinforcer is given after 30 correct responses. When wages are paid to factory workers according to the number of units produced and to migrant farm workers for each bushel of fruit they pick, those payments are following a fixed-ratio schedule.

The fixed-ratio schedule is a very effective way to maintain a high response rate, because the number of reinforcers received depends directly on the response rate. The faster people or animals respond, the more reinforcers they earn and the sooner they

◆ *What are the four types of schedules of reinforcement, and which type is most effective?*

◆ **primary reinforcer**
A reinforcer that fulfills a basic physical need for survival and does not depend on learning.

◆ **secondary reinforcer**
A reinforcer that is acquired or learned through association with other reinforcers.

◆ **schedule of reinforcement**
A systematic process for administering reinforcement.

◆ **fixed-ratio schedule**
A schedule in which a reinforcer is given after a fixed number of correct, nonreinforced responses.

FIGURE 5.6 **Four Types of Reinforcement Schedules**

Skinner's research revealed distinctive response patterns for four partial reinforcement schedules (the reinforcers are indicated by the diagonal marks). The ratio schedules, based on the number of responses, yielded a higher response rate than the interval schedules, which are based on the amount of time elapsed between reinforcers.

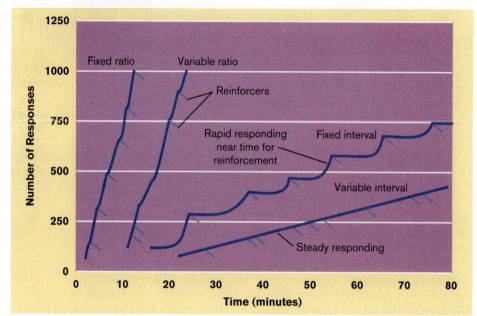

◆ **variable-ratio schedule**

A schedule in which a reinforcer is given after a varying number of nonreinforced responses, based on an average ratio.

◆ **fixed-interval schedule**

A schedule in which a reinforcer is given following the first correct response after a specific period of time has elapsed.

Two examples of variable-ratio schedules of reinforcement: Gamblers can't predict when the payoff (reinforcement) will come, so they are highly motivated to keep playing. Likewise, many computer users find themselves in the predicament of knowing they should stop playing solitaire and get to work, but they just can't seem to tear themselves away from the game. Why?

earn them. When large ratios are used, people and animals tend to pause after each reinforcement but then return to the high rate of responding.

One kind of fixed-ratio schedule, often called *continuous reinforcement*, provides the learner with a reinforcer each time the target behavior occurs (a 1:1 ratio). This kind of reinforcement is provided by an ATM. It is the most effective way to condition a new response. By contrast, when reinforcement occurs intermittently, learning takes longer but is often more resistant to extinction, a phenomenon known as the *partial reinforcement effect*. This reinforcement schedule is employed by slot machines and other kinds of gambling, not to mention a myriad of "addictive" leisure pursuits such as computer solitaire, video games, shooting baskets, and even hunting and fishing.

Intermittent reinforcement is characteristic of a **variable-ratio schedule** in which a reinforcer is provided after a varying number of nonreinforced responses, based on an average ratio. With a variable ratio of 30 responses (VR-30), people might be reinforced one time after 10 responses, another after 50, another after 30 responses, and so on. It would not be possible to predict exactly which responses will be reinforced, but reinforcement would occur 1 in 30 times, on average.

On a **fixed-interval schedule**, a specific period of time must pass before a response is reinforced. For example, on a 60-second fixed-interval schedule (FI-60), a reinforcer is given for the first correct response that occurs 60 seconds after the last reinforced response. People who are on salary, rather than paid an hourly rate, are reinforced on a fixed-interval schedule.

Unlike ratio schedules, reinforcement on interval schedules does not depend on the number of responses made, only on the one correct response made after the time interval has passed. Characteristic of the fixed-interval schedule is a pause or a sharp decline in responding immediately after each reinforcement and a rapid acceleration in responding just before the next reinforcer is due (the "scalloping" effect).

Variable-interval schedules eliminate the pause after reinforcement typical of the fixed-interval schedule. On a **variable-interval schedule,** a reinforcer is given after the first correct response following a varying time of nonreinforced responses, based on an average time. Rather than being given every 60 seconds, for example, a reinforcer might be given after a 30-second interval, with others following after 90-, 45-, and 75-second intervals. But the average time elapsing between reinforcers would be 60 seconds (VI-60). This schedule maintains remarkably stable and uniform rates of responding, but the response rate is typically lower than that for ratio schedules, because reinforcement is not tied directly to the number of responses made. Random drug testing in the workplace is an excellent example of application of the variable-interval schedule that appears to be quite effective.

Review and Reflect 5.1 summarizes the characteristics of the four schedules of reinforcement.

Variations in Operant Conditioning

As the description of dolphin training at the beginning of the chapter illustrates, complex behaviors must be broken down into simpler steps before they can be learned through operant conditioning. Moreover, like learning based on classical conditioning, behaviors acquired through operant conditioning can be altered in a variety of ways.

Skinner demonstrated that **shaping,** an operant conditioning technique in which behaviors are learned in small steps, is particularly effective in training animals to exhibit complex behaviors. With shaping, rather than waiting for the desired response to occur and then reinforcing it, a researcher reinforces any movement in the direction of the desired response, thereby gradually guiding the responses toward the ultimate goal.

◆ **variable-interval schedule**
A schedule in which a reinforcer is given after the first correct response that follows a varying time of nonreinforcement, based on an average time.

◆ **shaping**
An operant conditioning technique that consists of gradually molding a desired behavior (response) by reinforcing any movement in the direction of the desired response, thereby gradually guiding the responses toward the ultimate goal.

◆ *What are the roles of shaping, extinction, generalization, and discriminative stimuli in the operant conditioning process?*

REVIEW *and* REFLECT 5.1

Reinforcement Schedules Compared

SCHEDULE OF REINFORCEMENT	RESPONSE RATE	PATTERN OF RESPONSES	RESISTANCE TO EXTINCTION
Fixed-ratio schedule	Very high	Steady response with low ratio. Brief pause after each reinforcement with very high ratio.	The higher the ratio, the more resistance to extinction.
Variable-ratio schedule	Highest response rate	Constant response pattern, no pauses.	Most resistance to extinction.
Fixed-interval schedule	Lowest response rate	Long pause after reinforcement, followed by gradual acceleration.	The longer the interval, the more resistance to extinction.
Variable-interval schedule	Moderate	Stable, uniform response.	More resistance to extinction than fixed-interval schedule with same average interval.

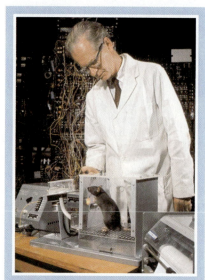

B. F. Skinner shapes a rat's bar-pressing behavior in a Skinner box.

Skinner designed a soundproof apparatus, commonly called a **Skinner box,** with which he conducted his experiments in operant conditioning. One type of box is equipped with a lever, or bar, that a rat presses to gain a reward of food pellets or water from a dispenser. A record of the animal's bar pressing is registered on a device called a *cumulative recorder,* also invented by Skinner. Through the use of shaping, a rat in a Skinner box is conditioned to press a bar for rewards. It may be rewarded first for simply turning toward the bar. The next reward comes only when the rat moves closer to the bar. Each step closer to the bar is rewarded. Next, the rat must touch the bar to receive a reward; finally, it is rewarded only when it presses the bar.

Shaping—rewarding **successive approximations** of the desired response—has been used effectively to condition complex behaviors in people as well as other animals. Parents may use shaping to help their children develop good table manners, praising them each time they show an improvement. Teachers often use shaping with disruptive children, reinforcing them at first for very short periods of good behavior and then gradually expecting them to work productively for longer and longer periods. Through shaping, circus animals have earned to perform a wide range of amazing feats, and pigeons have learned to bowl and play Ping-Pong.

Of course, the motive of the shaper is very different from that of the person or animal whose behavior is being shaped. The shaper seeks to change another's behavior by controlling its consequences. The motive of the person or animal whose behavior is being shaped is to gain rewards or avoid unwanted consequences.

What happens when reinforcement is no longer available? In operant conditioning, **extinction** occurs when reinforcers are withheld. A rat in a Skinner box will eventually stop pressing a bar when it is no longer rewarded with food pellets.

In humans and other animals, the withholding of reinforcement can lead to frustration or even rage. Consider a child having a temper tantrum. If whining and loud demands do not bring the reinforcer, the child may progress to kicking and screaming. If a vending machine takes your coins but fails to deliver candy or soda, you might shake the machine or even kick it before giving up. When we don't get something we expect, it makes us angry.

The process of *spontaneous recovery,* which we discussed in relation to classical conditioning, also occurs in operant conditioning. A rat whose bar pressing has been extinguished may again press the bar a few times when it is returned to the Skinner box after a period of rest.

Skinner conducted many of his experiments with pigeons placed in a specially designed Skinner box. The box contained small illuminated disks that the pigeons could peck to receive bits of grain from a food tray. Skinner found that **generalization** occurs in operant conditioning, just as in classical conditioning. A pigeon reinforced for pecking at a yellow disk is likely to peck at another disk similar in color. The less similar a disk is to the original color, the lower the rate of pecking will be.

Discrimination in operant conditioning involves learning to distinguish between a stimulus that has been reinforced and other stimuli that may be very similar. Discrimination develops when the response to the original stimulus is reinforced but responses to similar stimuli are not reinforced. For example, to encourage discrimination, a researcher would reinforce the pigeon for pecking at the yellow disk but not for pecking at the orange or red disk. Pigeons have even been conditioned to discriminate between a cubist-style Picasso painting and a Monet with 90% accuracy. However, they weren't able to tell a Renoir from a Cezanne ("Psychologists' pigeons . . . ," 1995).

Certain cues come to be associated with reinforcement or punishment. For example, children are more likely to ask their parents for a treat when the parents are smiling than when they are frowning. A stimulus that signals whether a certain response or behavior is likely to be rewarded, ignored, or punished is called a **discriminative stimulus.** If a pigeon's peck at a lighted disk results in a reward but a peck at an unlighted disk does not, the pigeon will soon be pecking exclusively at the lighted disk. The presence or absence

◆ **Skinner box**

A soundproof chamber with a device for delivering food to an animal subject; used in operant conditioning experiments.

◆ **successive approximations**

A series of gradual steps, each of which is more similar to the final desired response.

◆ **extinction**

In operant conditioning, the weakening and eventual disappearance of the conditioned response as a result of the withholding of reinforcement.

◆ **generalization**

In operant conditioning, the tendency to make the learned response to a stimulus similar to that for which the response was originally reinforced.

◆ **discriminative stimulus**

A stimulus that signals whether a certain response or behavior is likely to be rewarded, ignored, or punished.

of the discriminative stimulus—in this case, the lighted disk—will control whether the pecking takes place.

Why do children sometimes misbehave with a grandparent but not with a parent, or make one teacher's life miserable yet be model students for another? The children may have learned that in the presence of some people (the discriminative stimuli), their misbehavior will almost certainly lead to punishment, but in the presence of certain other people, it may even be rewarded.

Punishment

You may be wondering about one of the most common types of consequences, punishment. **Punishment** is the opposite of reinforcement. Punishment usually lowers the probability of a response by following it with an aversive or unpleasant consequence. However, punishment can be accomplished by either adding an unpleasant stimulus or removing a pleasant stimulus. The added unpleasant stimulus might take the form of criticism, a scolding, a disapproving look, a fine, or a prison sentence. The removal of a pleasant stimulus might consist of withholding affection and attention, suspending a driver's license, or taking away a privilege such as watching television.

It is common to confuse punishment and negative reinforcement because both involve an unpleasant condition, but there is a big difference between the two. With punishment, an unpleasant condition may be added; with negative reinforcement, an unpleasant condition is terminated or avoided. Moreover, the two have opposite effects: Unlike punishment, negative reinforcement increases the probability of a desired response by removing an unpleasant stimulus when the correct response is made. "Grounding" can be used as either punishment or negative reinforcement. If a teenager fails to clean her room after many requests to do so, her parents could ground her for the weekend—a punishment. An alternative approach would be to tell her she is grounded until the room is clean—negative reinforcement. Which approach is more likely to be effective?

If punishment can suppress behavior, why do so many people oppose its use? A number of potential problems are associated with the use of punishment:

1. According to Skinner, punishment does not extinguish an undesirable behavior; rather, it suppresses that behavior when the punishing agent is present. But the behavior is apt to continue when the threat of punishment is removed and in settings where punishment is unlikely. If punishment (imprisonment, fines, and so on) reliably extinguished unlawful behavior, there would be fewer repeat offenders in the criminal justice system.
2. Punishment indicates that a behavior is unacceptable but does not help people develop more appropriate behaviors. If punishment is used, it should be administered in conjunction with reinforcement or rewards for appropriate behavior.
3. The person who is severely punished often becomes fearful and feels angry and hostile toward the punisher. These reactions may be accompanied by a desire to retaliate or to avoid or escape from the punisher and the punishing situation. Many runaway teenagers leave home to escape physical abuse. Punishment that involves a loss of privileges is more effective than physical punishment and engenders less fear and hostility (Walters & Grusec, 1977).
4. Punishment frequently leads to aggression. Those who administer physical punishment may become models of aggressive behavior, by demonstrating aggression as a way of solving problems and discharging anger. Children of abusive, punishing parents are at greater risk than other children of becoming aggressive and abusive themselves (Widom, 1989).

If punishment can cause these problems, what can be done to discourage undesirable behavior?

Are there other ways to suppress behavior? Many psychologists believe that removing the rewarding consequences of undesirable behavior is the best way to

◆ **punishment**
The removal of a pleasant stimulus or the application of an unpleasant stimulus, thereby lowering the probability of a response.

◆ *How does punishment differ from negative reinforcement?*

extinguish a problem behavior. According to this view, parents should extinguish a child's temper tantrums not by punishment but by never giving in to the child's demands during a tantrum. A parent might best extinguish problem behavior that is performed merely to get attention by ignoring it and giving attention to more appropriate behavior. Sometimes, simply explaining why a certain behavior is not appropriate is all that is required to extinguish the behavior.

Using positive reinforcement such as praise will make good behavior more rewarding for children. This approach brings with it the attention that children want and need—attention that often comes only when they misbehave.

It is probably unrealistic to believe that punishment will ever become unnecessary. If a young child runs into the street, puts a finger near an electrical outlet, or reaches for a hot pan on the stove, a swift punishment may save the child from a potentially disastrous situation.

When punishment is necessary (e.g., to stop destructive behavior), how can we be sure that it will be effective? Research has revealed several factors that influence the effectiveness of punishment: its timing, its intensity, and the consistency of its application (Parke, 1977).

1. Punishment is most effective when it is applied during the misbehavior or as soon afterward as possible. Interrupting the problem behavior is most effective because doing so abruptly halts its rewarding aspects. The longer the delay between the response and the punishment, the less effective the punishment is in suppressing the response (Camp et al., 1967). When there is a delay, most animals do not make the connection between the misbehavior and the punishment. For example, anyone who has tried to housebreak a puppy knows that it is necessary to catch the animal in the act of soiling the carpet for the punishment to be effective. With humans, however, if the punishment must be delayed, the punisher should remind the perpetrator of the incident and explain why the behavior was inappropriate.

2. Ideally, punishment should be of the minimum severity necessary to suppress the problem behavior. Animal studies reveal that the more intense the punishment, the greater the suppression of the undesirable behavior (Church, 1963). But the intensity of the punishment should match the seriousness of the misdeed. Unnecessarily severe punishment is likely to produce the negative side effects mentioned earlier. The purpose of punishment is not to vent anger, but rather to modify behavior. Punishment meted out in anger is likely to be more intense than necessary to bring about the desired result. Yet, if the punishment is too mild, it will have no effect. Similarly, gradually increasing the intensity of the punishment is not effective because the perpetrator will gradually adapt, and the unwanted behavior will persist (Azrin & Holz, 1966). At a minimum, if a behavior is to be suppressed, the punishment must be more punishing than the misbehavior is rewarding. In human terms, a $200 ticket is more likely to suppress the urge to speed than a $2 ticket.

3. To be effective, punishment must be applied consistently. A parent cannot ignore misbehavior one day and punish the same act the next. And both parents should react to the same misbehavior in the same way. An undesired response will be suppressed more effectively when the probability of punishment is high. Would you be tempted to speed if you saw a police car in your rear-view mirror?

Do you think stoning is an appropriate punishment for adultery? Probably not, unless you come from a culture in which such punishments are acceptable. Punishment is used in every culture to control and suppress people's behavior. It is administered when important values, rules, regulations, and laws are violated. But not all cultures share the same values or have the same laws regulating behavior. U.S. citizens traveling in other countries need to be aware of how different cultures view and administer punishment. For example, selling drugs is a serious crime just about everywhere. In the United States, it carries mandatory prison time; in some other countries, it is a death penalty offense.

More evidence regarding cultural differences in ideas about punishment can be found in the varying national policies and social customs that exist with regard to spanking children. In Sweden, for instance, the law prohibits parents from using corporal punishment (Palmérus & Scarr, 1995). By contrast, in the United States, spanking is both legal and common. Moreover, by the time most children are teenagers, the belief that spanking is an effective and acceptable form of discipline is well established, and youths grow up to be parents who discipline their children in the way they were taught was most effective (Deater-Deckard et al., 2003). However, as noted earlier, punishment of all kinds often has unanticipated effects. Parents would be wise to examine their assumptions about spanking before jumping to the conclusion that it is the most appropriate and effective way of disciplining children.

Cultures differ in their ideas about who can punish whom as well as what kind of punishments are acceptable.

Escape and Avoidance Learning

Remember the earlier example about paying bills on time to avoid late fees? Learning to perform a behavior because it prevents or terminates an aversive event is called *escape learning*, and it reflects the power of negative reinforcement. Running away from a punishing situation and taking aspirin to relieve a pounding headache are examples of escape behavior. In these situations, the aversive event has begun, and an attempt is being made to escape it.

Avoidance learning, in contrast, depends on two types of conditioning. Through classical conditioning, an event or condition comes to signal an aversive state. Drinking and driving may be associated with automobile accidents and death. Because of such associations, people may engage in behaviors to avoid the anticipated aversive consequences. Making it a practice to avoid riding in a car with a driver who has been drinking is sensible avoidance behavior.

Much avoidance learning is maladaptive, however, and occurs in response to phobias. Students who have had a bad experience speaking in front of a class may begin to fear any situation that involves speaking before a group. Such students may avoid taking courses that require class presentations or taking leadership roles that necessitate public speaking. Avoiding such situations prevents them from suffering the perceived dreaded consequences. But the avoidance behavior is negatively reinforced and thus strengthened through operant conditioning. Maladaptive avoidance behaviors are very difficult to extinguish, because people never give themselves a chance to learn that the dreaded consequences probably will not occur, or that they are greatly exaggerated.

There is an important exception to the ability of humans and other animals to learn to escape and avoid aversive situations: **Learned helplessness** is a passive resignation to aversive conditions, learned by repeated exposure to aversive events that are inescapable or unavoidable. The initial experiment on learned helplessness was conducted by Overmeier and Seligman (1967). Dogs in the experimental group were strapped into harnesses from which they could not escape and were exposed to electric shocks. Later, these same dogs were placed in a box with two compartments separated by a low barrier. The dogs then experienced a series of trials in which a warning signal was followed by an electric shock administered through the box's floor. However, the floor was electrified only on one side, and the dogs could have escaped the electric shocks simply by jumping the barrier. Surprisingly, the dogs did not do so. Dogs in the control group had not previously experienced the inescapable shock and behaved in an entirely different manner and quickly learned to jump the barrier when the warning signal sounded and thus escaped the shock. Seligman (1975) later reasoned that humans who have suffered painful experiences they could neither avoid nor escape may also experience learned helplessness. Then, they may simply give up and react to disappointment in life by becoming inactive, withdrawn, and depressed (Seligman, 1991).

◆ *When is avoidance learning desirable, and when is it maladaptive?*

◆ **avoidance learning**
Learning to avoid events or conditions associated with aversive consequences or phobias.

◆ **learned helplessness**
A passive resignation to aversive conditions that is learned through repeated exposure to inescapable or unavoidable aversive events.

Applications of Operant Conditioning

◆ *What are some applications of operant conditioning?*

You have probably realized that operant conditioning is an important learning process that we experience almost every day. Operant conditioning can also be used intentionally by one person to change another person's behavior.

Can you train yourself to control your body's responses to stress? For years, scientists believed that internal responses such as heart rate, brain-wave patterns, and blood flow were not subject to operant conditioning. It is now known that when people are given very precise feedback about these internal processes, they can learn, with practice, to exercise control over them. **Biofeedback** is a way of getting information about internal biological states. Biofeedback devices have sensors that monitor slight changes in these internal responses and then amplify and convert them into visual or auditory signals. Thus, people can see or hear evidence of internal physiological processes, and by trying out various strategies (thoughts, feelings, or images), they can learn which ones routinely increase, decrease, or maintain a particular level of activity.

Biofeedback has been used to regulate heart rate and to control migraine and tension headaches, gastrointestinal disorders, asthma, anxiety tension states, epilepsy, sexual dysfunctions, and neuromuscular disorders such as cerebral palsy, spinal cord injuries, and stroke (Kalish, 1981; L. Miller, 1989; N. E. Miller, 1985).

Can operant conditioning help you get better grades? Perhaps, if you apply its principles to your study behavior. **Behavior modification** is a method of changing behavior through a systematic program based on the learning principles of classical conditioning, operant conditioning, or observational learning (which we will discuss soon). The majority of behavior modification programs use the principles of operant conditioning. *Try It 5.1* challenges you to come up with your own behavior modification plan.

Behavior modification programs have been used to change self-injurious behavior in autistic children and adults. Such programs are highly individualized and are frequently studied in a "one-subject" design, meaning that the study includes only one participant. One such study was designed to address a common problem among adults with autism and their caretakers (Beare et al., 2004). Adults with autism frequently reside in group homes and are employed in modified work settings. However, self-injurious behaviors can disturb these individuals' co-workers and supervisors, interfere with the performance of their duties, and cause them to lose their jobs. In the study, researchers successfully used behavior modification to stop a 41-year-old man with autism from exhibiting such behavior in his workplace, thereby enabling him to keep his job.

Some institutions, such as schools, mental hospitals, and prisons, use a **token economy**—a program that motivates socially desirable behavior by reinforcing it with tokens. The tokens (poker chips or coupons) may later be exchanged for desired items such as candy and privileges such as free time or participation in desired activities. People in the program know in advance exactly what behaviors will be reinforced and how they will be reinforced. Token economies have been used effectively in mental hospitals to encourage patients to attend to grooming, to interact with other patients, and to carry out housekeeping tasks (Ayllon & Azrin, 1965, 1968). Prisons also sometimes use token economies to encourage prosocial behavior among inmates (Seegert, 2004). Even schoolchildren's behavior can be modified with a well-designed token economy that is based on age-appropriate statements of desired behavior (Reitman et al., 2004). Although the positive behaviors generally stop when the tokens are discontinued, this does not mean that the programs are not worthwhile. After all, most people who are employed would probably quit their jobs if they were no longer paid.

Many classroom teachers and parents use *time out*—a behavior modification technique in which a child who is misbehaving is removed for a short time from sources of positive reinforcement. (Remember, according to operant conditioning, a behavior that is no longer reinforced will extinguish.)

Behavior modification is also used successfully in business and industry to increase profits and to modify employee behavior related to health, safety, and job performance (Hickman & Geller, 2003). To keep their premiums low, some companies give annual

◆ biofeedback

The use of sensitive equipment to give people precise feedback about internal physiological processes so that they can learn, with practice, to exercise control over them.

◆ behavior modification

A method of changing behavior through a systematic program based on the learning principles of classical conditioning, operant conditioning, or observational learning.

◆ token economy

A program that motivates socially desirable behavior by reinforcing it with tokens that can be exchanged for desired items or privileges.

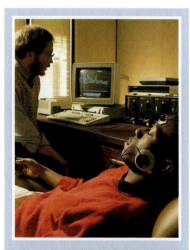

With biofeedback devices, people can see or hear evidence of internal physiological states and learn how to control them through various mental strategies.

Use conditioning to modify your own behavior.

1. *Identify the target behavior.* It must be both observable and measurable. You might choose, for example, to increase the amount of time you spend studying.

2. *Gather and record baseline data.* Keep a daily record of how much time you spend on the target behavior for about a week. Also note where the behavior takes place and what cues (or temptations) in the environment precede any slacking off from the target behavior.

3. *Plan your behavior modification program.* Formulate a plan and set goals to either decrease or increase the target behavior.

4. *Choose your reinforcers.* Any activity you enjoy more can be used to reinforce any activity you enjoy less. For example, you could reward yourself with a movie after a specified period of studying.

5. *Set the reinforcement conditions and begin recording and reinforcing your progress.* Be careful not to set your reinforcement goals so high that it becomes nearly impossible to earn a reward. Keep in mind Skinner's concept of shaping through rewarding small steps toward the desired outcome. Be perfectly honest with yourself and claim a reward only when you meet the goals. Chart your progress as you work toward gaining more control over the target behavior.

rebates to employees who do not use up the deductibles in their health insurance plan. To reduce costs associated with automobile accidents and auto theft, insurance companies offer incentives in the form of reduced premiums for installing airbags and burglar alarm systems. To encourage employees to take company-approved college courses, some companies offer tuition reimbursement to employees who complete such courses with acceptable grades. Many companies promote sales by giving salespeople bonuses, trips, and other prizes for increasing sales. One of the most successful applications of behavior modification has been in the treatment of psychological problems ranging from phobias to addictive behaviors. In this context, behavior modification is called behavior therapy (discussed in Chapter 13).

Cognitive Learning

By now, you are probably convinced of the effectiveness of both classical and operant conditioning. But can either type of conditioning explain how you learned a complex mental function like reading? Behaviorists such as Skinner and Watson believed that any kind of learning could be explained without reference to internal mental processes. Today, however, a growing number of psychologists stress the role of mental processes. They choose to broaden the study of learning to include such **cognitive processes** as thinking, knowing, problem solving, remembering, and forming mental representations. According to cognitive theorists, understanding these processes is critically important to a more complete, more comprehensive view of learning. We will consider the work of three important researchers in the field of cognitive learning: Wolfgang Köhler, Edward Tolman, and Albert Bandura.

◆ **cognitive processes**
(COG-nih-tiv) Mental processes such as thinking, knowing, problem solving, remembering, and forming mental representations.

Learning by Insight

Have you ever been worried about a problem, only to have a crystal clear solution suddenly pop into your mind? If so, you experienced an important kind of cognitive learning first described by Wolfgang Köhler (1887–1967). In his book *The Mentality of Apes* (1925), Köhler described experiments he conducted

◆ *What is insight, and how does it affect learning?*

◆ insight

The sudden realization of the relationship between elements in a problem situation, which makes the solution apparent.

on chimpanzees confined in caged areas. In one experiment, Köhler hung a bunch of bananas inside the caged area but overhead, out of reach of the chimps; boxes and sticks were left around the cage. Köhler observed the chimps' unsuccessful attempts to reach the bananas by jumping up or swinging sticks at them. Eventually, the chimps solved the problem by piling the boxes on top of one another and climbing on the boxes until they could reach the bananas.

Köhler observed that the chimps sometimes appeared to give up in their attempts to get the bananas. However, after an interval, they returned with the solution to the problem, as if it had come to them in a flash of **insight.** They seemed to have suddenly realized the relationship between the sticks or boxes and the bananas. Köhler insisted that insight, rather than trial-and-error learning, accounted for the chimps' successes, because they could easily repeat the solution and transfer this learning to similar problems. In human terms, a solution gained through insight is more easily learned, less likely to be forgotten, and more readily transferred to new problems than a solution learned through rote memorization (Rock & Palmer, 1990).

Latent Learning and Cognitive Maps

◆ *What did Tolman discover about the necessity of reinforcement?*

Like Köhler, Edward Tolman (1886–1959) held views that differed from the prevailing ideas on learning. First, Tolman (1932) believed that learning could take place without reinforcement. Second, he differentiated between learning and performance. He maintained that **latent learning** could occur; that is, learning could occur without apparent reinforcement and not be demonstrated until the organism was motivated to do so. A classic experimental study by Tolman and Honzik (1930) supports this position.

Three groups of rats were placed in a maze daily for 17 days. The first group always received a food reward at the end of the maze. The second group never received a reward, and the third group did not receive a food reward until the 11th day. The first group showed a steady improvement in performance over the 17-day period. The second group showed slight, gradual improvement. The third group, after being rewarded on the 11th day, showed a marked improvement the next day and, from then on, outperformed the rats that had been rewarded daily (see Figure 5.7). The rapid improvement of the third group indicated to Tolman that latent learning had occurred—that the rats had actually learned the maze during the first 11 days but were not motivated to display this learning until they were rewarded for it. Tolman concluded that the rats had learned to form a **cognitive map,** a mental representation or picture, of the maze but had not demonstrated their learning until they were reinforced. In later studies, Tolman showed how rats quickly learn to rearrange their established cognitive maps and readily find their way through increasingly complex mazes.

◆ latent learning

Learning that occurs without apparent reinforcement and is not demonstrated until the organism is motivated to do so.

◆ cognitive map

A mental representation of a spatial arrangement such as a maze.

FIGURE 5.7

Latent Learning

Rats in Group 1 were rewarded every day for running the maze correctly, while rats in Group 2 were never rewarded. Group 3 rats were rewarded only on the 11th day and thereafter outperformed the rats in Group 1. The rats had "learned" the maze but were not motivated to perform until rewarded, demonstrating that latent learning had occurred. *Source:* From Tolman & Honzik (1930).

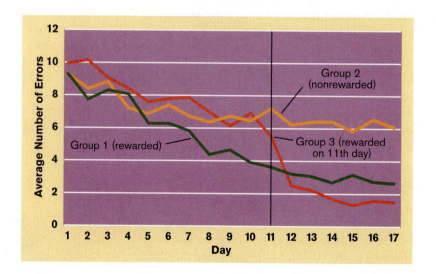

How Did You Find Psychology?

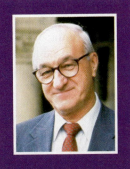

Albert Bandura

Have you ever enrolled in a class simply because it was scheduled at a convenient time? That's how Albert Bandura discovered psychology. Bandura grew up in a tiny town in Alberta, Canada. The town was so small, in fact, that his high school had only two teachers. Bandura's parents were immigrants—his father from Poland and his mother from the Ukraine—who had no formal education. Even so, they pushed their six children to excel in school.

After high school, Bandura worked on a highway repair crew in Alaska before entering the University of British Columbia. The group of students with whom he commuted to campus happened to be enrolled in early morning classes. Bandura had not yet chosen a major, so when he saw an introductory psychology class in the university's early morning schedule, his only thought was that taking the class would fit in well with his transportation arrangements. Once in the class, he became

fascinated with the subject and, in 1949, graduated with a degree in psychology.

Bandura entered graduate school at the University of Iowa as a student of Kenneth Spence, one of the leading researchers in the field of learning at that time. Early on in his graduate studies, Bandura realized that human psychological processes, and the social contexts in which they occur, were far more interesting to him than the animal behavior studies that were common in the field of learning in that era. Thus, he switched his focus to clinical psychology, earning his Ph.D. in that specialty in 1952. When Bandura joined the faculty at Stanford University in 1953, he began a series of collaborations with other psychologists and graduate students that would eventually lead to the development of his theory of observational learning and the famous Bobo Doll experiments you will read about on page 158. Today, Bandura's social-cognitive theory represents one of the leading perspectives in the study of learning. Remember Bandura's experience the next time scheduling priorities influence your enrollment decisions!

Observational Learning

Have you ever wondered why you slow down when you see another driver getting a speeding ticket? In all likelihood, no one has ever reinforced you for slowing down under these conditions, so why do you do it? Psychologist Albert Bandura (1986) contends that many behaviors or responses are acquired through observational learning, or as he calls it, *social-cognitive learning*. **Observational learning**, sometimes called **modeling**, results when people observe the behavior of others and note the consequences of that behavior. Thus, you slow down when you see another driver getting a ticket because you assume that person's consequence will also be your consequence. The same process is involved when we see another person get a free soft drink by hitting the side of a vending machine. We assume that if we hit the machine, we will also get a free drink.

A person who demonstrates a behavior or whose behavior is imitated is called a **model**. Parents, movie stars, and sports personalities are often powerful models for children. The effectiveness of a model is related to his or her status, competence, and power. Other important factors are the age, sex, attractiveness, and ethnicity of the model. Whether learned behavior is actually performed depends largely on whether the observed models are rewarded or punished for their behavior and whether the observer expects to be rewarded for the behavior (Bandura, 1969, 1977a). Recent research has also shown that observational learning is improved when several sessions of observation (watching the behavior) precede attempts to perform the behavior and are then repeated in the early stages of practicing it (Weeks & Anderson, 2000).

But repetition alone isn't enough to cause an observer to learn from a model: An observer must be physically and cognitively capable of performing the behavior in order to learn it. In other words, no matter how much time you devote to watching Serena Williams play tennis or Tiger Woods play golf, you won't be able to acquire skills like

◆ *How do we learn by observing others?*

◆ **observational learning**
Learning by observing the behavior of others and the consequences of that behavior; learning by imitation.

◆ **modeling**
Another name for observational learning.

◆ **model**
The individual who demonstrates a behavior or whose behavior is imitated.

theirs unless you possess physical talents that are equal to theirs. Likewise, it is doubtful that a kindergartener will learn geometry from watching her high-school-aged brother do his homework. Furthermore, the observer must pay attention to the model and store information about the model's behavior in memory. Ultimately, to exhibit a behavior learned through observation, the observer must be motivated to perform the behavior on her or his own.

A model does not have to be a person. For example, when you buy a piece of furniture labeled "assembly required," it usually comes with diagrams and instructions showing how to put it together. Typically, the instructions break down the large task of assembling the piece into a series of smaller steps. Similarly, Chapter 1 opens with an explanation of the SQ3R method that provides step-by-step instructions on how to incorporate the features of this textbook, such as the questions in the chapter outlines, into an organized study method. These instructions serve as a model, or plan, for you to follow in studying each chapter. As is true of learning from human models, you must believe that imitating this kind of verbal model will be beneficial to you. Moreover, you must remember the steps and be capable of applying them as you read each chapter. You will be more likely to keep using the SQ3R method if your experiences motivate you to do so. That is, once you use the model and find that it helps you learn the information in a chapter, you will be more likely to use it for another chapter.

One way people learn from observation is to acquire new responses, a kind of learning called the **modeling effect**. Do you remember learning how to do math problems in school? Most likely, when your teachers introduced a new kind of problems, they demonstrated how to solve them on a chalkboard or overhead projector. Your task was then to follow their procedures, step by step, until you were able to work the new problems independently. For you and your classmates, solving each new kind of problem was a new behavior acquired from a model.

Another kind of observational learning is particularly common in unusual situations. Picture yourself as a guest at an elaborate state dinner at the White House. Your table setting has more pieces of silverware than you have ever seen before. Which fork should be used for what? How should you proceed? You might decide to take your cue from the First Lady. In this case, you wouldn't be learning an entirely new behavior. Instead, you would be using a model to learn how to modify a known behavior (how to use a fork) to fit the needs of an unfamiliar situation. This kind of observational learning is known as the **elicitation effect**.

Sometimes, models influence us to exhibit behaviors that we have previously learned to suppress, a process called the **disinhibitory effect**. For example, we have all learned not to belch in public. However, if we are in a social setting in which others are belching and no one is discouraging them from doing so, we are likely to follow suit. And adolescents may lose whatever resistance they have to drinking, drug use, or sexual activity by seeing or hearing about peers or characters in movies or television shows engaging in these behaviors without experiencing any adverse consequences.

◆ **modeling effect**

Learning a new behavior from a model through the acquisition of new responses.

◆ **elicitation effect**

Exhibiting a behavior similar to that shown by a model in an unfamiliar situation.

◆ **disinhibitory effect**

Displaying a previously suppressed behavior because a model does so without receiving punishment.

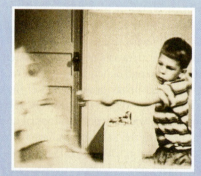

In Bandura's observational learning research, children learned to copy aggression by observing adult models act aggressively toward a Bobo Doll.

However, we may also suppress a behavior upon observing a model receive punishment for exhibiting it (the **inhibitory effect**). This is the kind of observational learning we are displaying when we slow down upon seeing another driver receiving a ticket. When schoolchildren see a classmate punished for talking aloud, the experience has a tendency to suppress that behavior in all of them. Thus, a person does not have to experience the unfortunate consequences of dangerous or socially unacceptable behaviors to avoid them.

◆ **inhibitory effect**

Suppressing a behavior because a model is punished for displaying the behavior.

Fears, too, can be acquired through observational learning. Gerull and Rapee (2002) found that toddlers whose mothers expressed fear at the sight of rubber snakes and spiders displayed significantly higher levels of fear of these objects when tested later than did control group children whose mothers did not express such fears. Conversely, children who see "a parent or peer behaving nonfearfully in a potentially fear-producing situation may be 'immunized'" to feeling fear when confronting a similar frightening situation at a later time (Basic Behavioral Science Task Force, 1996, p. 139).

It's no secret that children see a lot of aggressive behavior on television. Moreover, this behavior isn't confined to programming that features adult characters. Indeed, a recent analysis of nearly 600 commercials in which children were the main characters found that more than one-third of them included aggressive behaviors (Larson, 2003). Recently, psychologist Sarah Coyne has raised concerns about the level of indirect aggression (plotting to ruin a person's reputation) in many television programs, particularly soap operas (Coyne, 2004).

Albert Bandura's pioneering work has greatly influenced current thinking on these issues. In several classic experiments, Bandura demonstrated how children are influenced by exposure to aggressive models. One study involved three groups of preschoolers. Children in one group individually observed an adult model punching, kicking, and hitting a 5-foot, inflated plastic "Bobo Doll" with a mallet, while uttering aggressive phrases (Bandura et al., 1961, p. 576). Children in the second group observed a nonaggressive model who ignored the Bobo Doll and sat quietly assembling Tinker Toys. The children in the control group were placed in the same setting with no adult present. Later, each child was observed through a one-way mirror. Those children exposed to the aggressive model imitated much of the aggression and also engaged in significantly more nonimitative aggression than did children in either of the other groups. The group that observed the nonaggressive model showed less aggressive behavior than the control group.

A further study compared the degree of aggression in children following exposure to (1) an aggressive model in a live situation, (2) a filmed version of the same situation, or (3) a film depicting an aggressive cartoon character using the same aggressive behaviors in a fantasylike setting (Bandura et al., 1963). A control group was not exposed to any of the three situations of aggression. The groups exposed to aggressive models used significantly more aggression than the control group. The researchers concluded that "of the three experimental conditions, exposure to humans on film portraying aggression was the most influential in eliciting and shaping aggressive behavior" (p. 7).

Bandura's research sparked interest in studying the effects of violence and aggression portrayed in other entertainment media. For example, researchers have also shown in a variety of ways—including carefully controlled laboratory experiments with children, adolescents, and young adults—that violent video games increase aggressive behavior (Anderson & Bushman, 2001). Moreover, the effects of media violence are evident whether the violence is presented in music, music videos, or advertising or on the Internet (Villani, 2001). Such research has spawned a confusing array of rating systems that parents may refer to when choos-

Portrayals on television showing violence as an acceptable way to solve problems tend to encourage aggressive behavior in children.

ing media for their children. However, researchers have found that labeling media as "violent" may enhance children's desire to experience it, especially in boys older than the age of 11 years (Bushman & Cantor, 2003).

But, you might argue, if televised violence is followed by appropriate consequences, such as an arrest, it may actually teach children not to engage in aggression. However, experimental research has demonstrated that children do not process information about consequences in the same ways as adults do (Krcmar & Cooke, 2001). Observing consequences for aggressive acts does seem to help preschoolers learn that violence is morally unacceptable. By contrast, school-aged children appear to judge the rightness or wrongness of an act of violence on the basis of provocation; that is, they believe that violence demonstrated in the context of retaliation is morally acceptable even if it is punished by an authority figure.

Remarkably, recently published longitudinal evidence shows that the effects of childhood exposure to violence persist well into the adult years. Psychologist L. Rowell Huesman and his colleagues (2003) found that individuals who had watched the greatest number of violent television programs in childhood were the most likely to have engaged in actual acts of violence as young adults. This study was the first to show that observations of media violence during childhood are linked to real acts of violence in adulthood.

Just as children imitate the aggressive behavior they observe on television, so they also imitate the prosocial, or helping, behavior they see there. Programs such as *Mister Rogers' Neighborhood* and *Sesame Street* have been found to have a positive influence on children. Ideally, the findings of Huesman and his colleagues will also apply to the positive effects of television.

Many avenues of learning are available to humans and other animals. Luckily, people's capacity to learn seems practically unlimited. Certainly, advances in civilization could not have been achieved without the ability to learn.

Looking Back   You may have noticed that most of the principles of learning described in this chapter are employed in training dolphins. Classical conditioning is at work when the dolphins learn to associate their trainers with pleasant stimuli. Operant conditioning techniques—especially shaping—are essential to teaching them to perform tricks. And, as noted in the chapter-opening vignette, dolphins learn through observation. At this point, you may be wondering how the various topics covered in this chapter relate to the mental processes that we commonly associate with academic learning, such as memory and problem solving. The answer is that the principles explained in this chapter represent only a few of the many different kinds of learning that we experience in our daily lives. Other aspects of learning, including memory and problem solving, will be considered in the next two chapters.

Apply It 5.1   How to Win the Battle against Procrastination

Have you often thought that you could get better grades if only you had more time? Do you often find yourself studying for an exam or completing a term paper at the last minute? If so, it makes sense for you to learn how to overcome the greatest time waster of all—procrastination. Research indicates that academic procrastination arises partly out of a lack of confidence in one's ability meet expectations

Apply It 5.1 *(continued)*

(Wolters, 2003). But anyone can overcome procrastination, and gain self-confidence in the process, by using behavior modification techniques. Systematically apply the following suggestions to keep procrastination from interfering with your studying:

- *Identify the environmental cues that habitually interfere with your studying*. Television, computer or video games, and even food can be powerful distractors that consume hours of valuable study time. However, these distractors can be useful positive reinforcers to enjoy after you've finished studying.

- *Schedule your study time and reinforce yourself for adhering to your schedule*. Once you've scheduled it, be just as faithful to your schedule as you would be to a work schedule set by an employer. And be sure to schedule something you enjoy to immediately follow the study time.

- *Get started*. The most difficult part is getting started. Give yourself an extra reward for starting on time and, perhaps, a penalty for starting late.

- *Use visualization*. Much procrastination results from the failure to consider its negative consequences. Visualizing the consequences of not studying, such as trying to get through an exam you haven't adequately prepared for, can be an effective tool for combating procrastination.

- *Beware of jumping to another task when you reach a difficult part of an assignment*. This procrastination tactic gives you the feeling that you are busy and accomplishing something, but it is, nevertheless, an avoidance mechanism.

- *Beware of preparation overkill*. Procrastinators may actually spend hours preparing for a task rather than working on the task itself. For example, they may

gather enough library materials to write a book rather than a five-page term paper. This enables them to postpone writing the paper.

- *Keep a record of the reasons you give yourself for postponing studying or completing important assignments*. If a favorite rationalization is "I'll wait until I'm in the mood to do this," count the number of times in a week you are seized with the desire to study. The mood to study typically arrives after you begin, not before.

Don't procrastinate! Begin now! Apply the steps outlined here to gain more control over your behavior and win the battle against procrastination.

Chapter 5 Summary

◆ Classical Conditioning p. 138

◆ What kind of learning did Pavlov discover and how is it accomplished? p. 138

In classical conditioning, a neutral stimulus (a tone in Pavlov's experiments) is presented shortly before an unconditioned stimulus (food in Pavlov's experiments), which naturally elicits, or brings forth, an unconditioned response (salivation for Pavlov's dogs). After repeated pairings, the conditioned stimulus alone (the tone) comes to elicit the conditioned response.

◆ What kinds of changes in stimuli and learning conditions lead to changes in conditioned responses? p. 140

If the conditioned stimulus (tone) is presented repeatedly without the unconditioned stimulus (food), the conditioned response (salivation) becomes progressively weaker and eventually disappears, a process called extinction. Generalization occurs when an organism makes a conditioned response to a stimulus that is similar to the original conditioned stimulus. Discrimination is the ability to distinguish between similar stimuli, allowing the organism to make the conditioned response only to the original conditioned stimulus.

◆ How did Watson demonstrate that fear could be classically conditioned? p. 142

Watson showed that fear could be classically conditioned by presenting a white rat to Little Albert along with a

loud, frightening noise, thereby conditioning the child to fear the white rat. He also used the principles of classical conditioning to remove the fears of a boy named Peter.

◆ According to Rescorla, what is the critical element in classical conditioning? p. 143

Rescorla found that the critical element in classical conditioning is whether the conditioned stimulus provides information that enables the organism to reliably predict the occurrence of the unconditioned stimulus.

◆ What types of everyday responses can be subject to classical conditioning? p. 143

Types of responses acquired through classical conditioning include positive and negative emotional responses (including likes, dislikes, fears, and phobias), and responses to environmental cues associated with drug use.

◆◆ Operant Conditioning p. 145

◆ What did Thorndike conclude about learning by watching cats try to escape from his puzzle box? p. 145

Thorndike concluded that most learning occurs through trial and error. He claimed that the consequences of a response determine whether the tendency to respond in the same way in the future will be strengthened or weakened (the law of effect).

◆ How do reinforcement and punishment influence behavior? p. 146

Operant conditioning is a method for manipulating the consequences of behavior so as to shape a new response or to increase (reinforcement) or decrease (punishment) the frequency of an existing response. In shaping, a researcher selectively reinforces small steps toward the desired response until that response is achieved. Extinction occurs when reinforcement is withheld.

◆ What is the goal of both positive reinforcement and negative reinforcement, and how is that goal accomplished with each? p. 146

Both positive reinforcement and negative reinforcement are used to strengthen or increase the probability of a response. With positive reinforcement, the desired response is followed by a reward; with negative reinforcement, it is followed by the termination of an aversive stimulus.

◆ What are the four types of schedules of reinforcement, and which type is most effective? p. 147

The four types of schedules of reinforcement are the fixed-ratio, variable-ratio, fixed-interval, and variable-interval schedules. The variable-ratio schedule provides the highest response rate and the most resistance to extinction. The partial-reinforcement effect is the greater resistance to extinction that occurs when responses are maintained under partial reinforcement, rather than under continuous reinforcement.

◆ What are the roles of shaping, extinction, generalization, and discriminative stimuli in the operant conditioning process? p. 149

In shaping, a researcher reinforces small steps toward the desired response. Extinction occurs when reinforcement is withheld. Generalization involves responding to stimuli that are similar to the one with which the behavior was originally learned. Discriminative stimuli are cues that indicate whether a behavior will be reinforced.

◆ How does punishment differ from negative reinforcement? p. 151

Punishment is used to decrease the frequency of a response. Negative reinforcement is used to increase the frequency of a response.

◆ When is avoidance learning desirable, and when is it maladaptive? p. 153

Avoidance learning involves acquisition of behaviors that remove aversive stimuli. Avoidance learning is desirable when it leads to a beneficial response,

such as running away from a potentially deadly snake or buckling a seat belt to stop the annoying sound of a buzzer. It is maladaptive when it occurs in response to fear.

◆ What are some applications of operant conditioning? p. 154

Applications of operant conditioning include using biofeedback to gain control over internal physiological processes and using behavior modification techniques to eliminate undesirable behavior and/or encourage desirable behavior.

◆◆ Cognitive Learning p. 155

◆ What is insight, and how does it affect learning? p. 155

Insight is the sudden realization of the relationship of the elements in a problem situation that makes the solution apparent; this solution is easily learned and transferred to new problems.

◆ What did Tolman discover about the necessity of reinforcement? p. 156

Tolman discovered that rats could learn to run a maze without reinforcement. His hypothesis was that the rats formed a cognitive map of the maze.

◆ How do we learn by observing others? p. 157

Learning by observing the behavior of others (called models) and the consequences of that behavior is known as observational learning. We learn from models when we assume that the consequences they experience will happen to us if we perform their behaviors.

avoidance learning, p. 153
behavior modification, p. 154
biofeedback, p. 154
classical conditioning, p. 138
cognitive map, p. 156
cognitive processes, p. 155
conditioned response (CR), p. 139
conditioned stimulus (CS), p. 139
discrimination, p. 141
discriminative stimulus, p. 150
disinhibitory effect, p. 158
elicitation effect, p. 158
extinction (in classical
  conditioning), p. 140
extinction (in operant
  conditioning), p. 150
fixed-interval schedule, p. 148
fixed-ratio schedule, p. 147

generalization (in classical
  conditioning), p. 140
generalization (in operant
  conditioning), p. 150
higher-order conditioning, p. 140
inhibitory effect, p. 159
insight, p. 156
latent learning, p. 156
law of effect, p. 145
learned helplessness, p. 153
learning, p. 137
model, p. 157
modeling, p. 157
modeling effect, p. 158
negative reinforcement, p. 147
observational learning, p. 157
operant, p. 146
operant conditioning, p. 146

positive reinforcement, p. 147
primary reinforcer, p. 147
punishment, p. 151
reinforcement, p. 146
reinforcer, p. 146
schedule of reinforcement, p. 147
secondary reinforcer, p. 147
shaping, p. 149
Skinner box, p. 150
spontaneous recovery, p. 140
stimulus, p. 138
successive approximations, p. 150
taste aversion, p. 144
token economy, p. 154
unconditioned response (UR), p. 139
unconditioned stimulus (US), p. 139
variable-interval schedule, p. 149
variable-ratio schedule, p. 148

Study Guide 5

Answers to all the Study Guide questions are provided at the end of the book.

◆ **SECTION ONE: Chapter Review**

Classical Conditioning (pp. 138–145)

1. Classical conditioning was originally researched most extensively by _____.

2. A dog's salivation in response to a musical tone is a(n) (conditioned, unconditioned) response.

3. The weakening of a conditioned response that occurs when a conditioned stimulus is presented without the unconditioned stimulus is called _____.

4. For higher-order conditioning to occur, a neutral stimulus is typically paired repeatedly with an (existing conditioned stimulus, unconditioned stimulus).

5. Five-year-old Jesse was bitten by his neighbor's collie. He won't go near that dog but seems to have no fear of other dogs, even other collies. Which learning process accounts for his behavior?
   a. generalization   c. extinction
   b. discrimination   d. spontaneous recovery

6. In Watson's experiment with Little Albert, the white rat was the (conditioned, unconditioned) stimulus, and Albert's crying when the hammer struck the steel bar was the (conditioned, unconditioned) response.

7. Albert's fear of the white rat transferred to a rabbit, a dog, a fur coat, and a mask. What learning process did this demonstrate?
   a. generalization   c. extinction
   b. discrimination   d. spontaneous recovery

8. Rescorla's research suggests that _____ processes play a role in classical conditioning.

9. Taste aversions result from many trials in which a stimulus is paired with nausea. (true/false)

10. Counselors usually advise recovering drug addicts to avoid cues (people, places, and things) that are associated with their past drug use because the environmental cues may serve as conditioned stimuli for drug cravings. (true/false)

Operant Conditioning (pp. 145–155)

11. Who researched trial-and-error learning using cats in puzzle boxes and formulated the law of effect?
    a. Watson   c. Skinner
    b. Thorndike   d. Pavlov

12. Operant conditioning was researched most extensively by
    a. Watson.   c. Skinner.
    b. Thorndike.   d. Pavlov.

13. Which of the following processes occurs in operant conditioning when reinforcers are withheld?
    a. generalization   c. spontaneous recovery
    b. discrimination   d. extinction

14. Many people take aspirin to relieve painful headaches. Taking aspirin is a behavior that is likely to continue because of the effect of (positive, negative) reinforcement.

15. (Partial, Continuous) reinforcement is most effective in conditioning a new response.

16. Jennifer and Ashley are both employed raking leaves. Jennifer is paid $1 for each bag of leaves she rakes; Ashley is paid $4 per hour. Jennifer is paid according to the _____ schedule; Ashley is paid according to the _____ schedule.
    a. fixed-interval; fixed-ratio
    b. variable-ratio; fixed-interval
    c. variable-ratio; variable-interval
    d. fixed-ratio; fixed-interval

17. Which schedule of reinforcement yields the highest response rate and the greatest resistance to extinction?
    a. variable-ratio schedule
    b. fixed-ratio schedule
    c. variable-interval schedule
    d. fixed-interval schedule

18. Danielle's parents have noticed that she has been making her bed every day, and they would like this to continue. Because they understand the partial-reinforcement effect, they will want to reward her every time she makes the bed. (true/false)

19. Punishment is roughly the same as negative reinforcement. (true/false)

20. Depending on the circumstances, avoidance learning can be either adaptive or maladaptive. (true/false)

21. Victims of spousal abuse who have repeatedly failed to escape or avoid the abuse may eventually passively resign themselves to it, a condition known as _____ _____.

22. Using sensitive electronic equipment to monitor physiological processes in order to bring them under conscious control is called _____.

23. Applying learning principles to eliminate undesirable behavior and/or encourage desirable behavior is called _____ _____.

Cognitive Learning (pp. 155–160)

24. The sudden realization of the relationship between the elements in a problem situation that results in the solution to the problem is called (latent learning, insight).

25. Learning that is not demonstrated until one is motivated to perform the behavior is called
    a. learning by insight.
    b. observational learning.
    c. classical conditioning.
    d. latent learning.

26. Hayley has been afraid of snakes for as long as she can remember, and her mother has the same paralyzing fear. Hayley most likely acquired her fear through
    a. learning by insight.
    b. observational learning.
    c. classical conditioning.
    d. latent learning.

27. You are most likely to learn a modeled behavior if you
    a. repeat the behavior many times after watching the model perform it.
    b. are physically capable of performing the behavior.
    c. have never seen the behavior before.
    d. are personally acquainted with the model.

28. Match each of the effects of modeling with its definition:
    ____ (1) modeling
    ____ (2) elicitation
    ____ (3) inhibitory
    ____ (4) disinhibitory
    a. exhibiting a behavior similar to that of a model
    b. exhibiting a previously learned unacceptable behavior after seeing a model do so
    c. learning a new behavior from a model
    d. suppressing a previously learned unacceptable behavior after seeing a model be punished for it

29. Match the researcher with the subject(s) researched.
    ____ (1) Edward Tolman
    ____ (2) Albert Bandura
    ____ (3) Wolfgang Köhler
    a. observational learning
    b. learning by insight
    c. latent learning

SECTION TWO: Identify the Concept

In the blank following each statement below, list the learning principle illustrated by the statement.

1. Ben continues to play a slot machine even though he never knows when it will pay off. _____

2. Alice watched a movie about tornadoes and is now afraid of bad storms. _____

3. Joey is crying and asking for a candy bar. His mother gives in because doing so will make him stop crying for now—but Joey will most likely behave this way again. _____

4. Jan got sick eating lasagna and now never eats food containing tomato sauce. _____

5. Helen washed the dinner dishes, and her mother allowed her to watch television for 30 extra minutes that evening. _____

6. Sarah's parents are advised to stop paying attention to her crying when it is time for bed and instead ignore it. _____

7. Frank is paid for his factory job once every two weeks. _____

8. Marty is scolded for running into the road and never does it again. _____

9. Ellen watches her lab partner mix the chemicals and set up the experiment. She then repeats the same procedure and completes her assignment. _____

10. Through associations with such things as food and shelter, pieces of green paper with pictures of past U.S. presidents on them become very powerful reinforcers. _____

11. Although he studied the problem, Jack did not seem to be able to figure out the correct way to reconnect the pipes under the sink. He took a break before he became too frustrated. Later he returned and immediately saw how to do it. _____

SECTION THREE: Fill In the Blank

1. Classical conditioning is based on the association between _____, and operant conditioning is based on the association between a _____ and its _____.

2. _____ is a relatively permanent change in behavior, knowledge, capability, or attitude that is acquired through experience and cannot be attributed to illness, injury, or maturation.

3. Ed feeds the horses on his ranch every day at the same time. He notices that the horses now run to their feed troughs and whinny as if they know dinner is on its way as soon as they hear his truck coming up the drive. In this example, the conditioned stimulus is _____.

4. In question 3, the unconditioned stimulus is _____.

5. The unconditioned response of Pavlov's dogs was _____.

6. In Pavlov's classic experiment, the bell was originally a(n) _____ stimulus.

7. To get coyotes to stop eating sheep, ranchers poison sheep carcasses in the hope that coyotes that eat the carcasses will get sick enough to avoid eating sheep from that point on. The ranchers hope that the coyotes will avoid all types and sizes of sheep—which is an example of _____ in classical conditioning.

8. The ranchers in question 7 also hope that the coyotes will be able to distinguish between sheep and other more appropriate sources of food. This is an example of _____ in classical conditioning.

9. Eduardo loved eating at a certain fast-food restaurant. After a while even the giant logo sign in front of the restaurant would make him hungry every time he saw it. The restaurant ran a TV ad showing a clown standing by the logo sign. Pretty soon, every time Eduardo saw a clown, he became hungry. Eduardo's responses are examples of _____ conditioning.

10. If Watson had wanted to extinguish Little Albert's conditioned fear of white furry things, he would have presented the _____ stimulus without presenting the _____ stimulus.

11. The law of _____, developed by _____, states that a response that is followed by a satisfying consequence will tend to be repeated, while a response followed by discomfort will tend to be weakened.

12. Since researchers cannot tell rats to press the bar in a Skinner box for food or have them read "The Skinner Box Owner's Manual," they must initiate the bar-pressing response by rewarding _____ _____, an approach known as *shaping*.

13. Reinforcement is any event that follows a response and increases the probability of the response. _____ reinforcement involves the removal of a stimulus and _____ reinforcement involves the presentation of a stimulus.

14. You're driving on an interstate highway and suddenly notice that you've been going 80 miles per hour without realizing it. Immediately after you slow down, you see the flashing light of a state police car, and you know you're about to be pulled over. In this case the flashing light is a _____ stimulus.

15. Food is considered a _____ reinforcer; money is considered a _____ reinforcer.

16. If you were going to train a rat to press a bar for food, you would probably use _____ reinforcement for the initial training period and a _____ -reinforcement schedule to strengthen the learned bar-pressing behavior.

17. Bandura's research demonstrated that children may learn _____ behaviors from watching models perform them on television.

◆ **SECTION FOUR: Comprehensive Practice Test**

1. Pavlov is associated with
   a. classical conditioning.
   b. operant conditioning.
   c. cognitive conditioning.
   d. Watsonian conditioning.

2. This theorist believed that the causes of behavior are in the environment and that inner mental events are themselves shaped by environmental forces.
   a. Bandura   c. Skinner
   b. Pavlov   d. Tolman

3. Which of the following theorists developed the concepts of latent learning and cognitive mapping?
   a. Pavlov   c. Tolman
   b. Köhler   d. Skinner

4. This theorist researched observational learning and the effects of modeling on behavior.
   a. Köhler   c. Skinner
   b. Thorndike   d. Bandura

5. Which of the following theorists is associated with research on reinforcement theory?
   a. Pavlov   c. Tolman
   b. Skinner   d. Bandura

6. The concept that is associated with cognitive learning is
   a. negative reinforcement.
   b. positive reinforcement.
   c. latent learning.
   d. the discriminative stimulus.

7. Jim has been sober since he completed a treatment program for alcoholics. He was told to stay away from his old drinking places. The danger is that he may start drinking again as a result of the conditioned stimuli in those environments. If he did, it would be a practical example of _____ in classical conditioning.
   a. extinction
   b. spontaneous recovery
   c. stimulus generalization
   d. observational response sets

8. The seductive nature of a slot machine in a gambling casino is based on its _____ schedule of reinforcement.
   a. continuous   c. variable-ratio
   b. fixed-interval   d. variable-interval

9. For Little Albert, the conditioned stimulus was
   a. the white rat.
   b. a loud noise.
   c. Watson.
   d. based on negative reinforcement.

10. Positive reinforcement increases behavior; negative reinforcement
    a. decreases behavior.
    b. has no effect on behavior.
    c. removes a behavior.
    d. also increases behavior.

11. A good example of a fixed-interval schedule of reinforcement is
    a. factory piece work.
    b. a child's weekly allowance.
    c. a slot machine.
    d. turning on a light switch.

12. The nice thing about continuous reinforcement is that it creates a behavior that is very resistant to extinction. (true/false)

13. Taste aversion is a real-world example of
    a. operant conditioning.
    b. classical conditioning.
    c. observational learning.
    d. cognitive mapping.

14. In _____ learning, a person or animal learns a response that _____ a negative reinforcer.
    a. escape; prevents the occurrence of
    b. escape; terminates
    c. avoidance; terminates
    d. avoidance; initiates

15. Ms. Doe, a new teacher, is having a difficult time with her misbehaving second graders. When the principal enters the room, the children behave like perfect angels. In this case, the principal may be thought of as a(n)
    a. positive reinforcer.
    b. unconditioned stimulus.
    c. shaping reinforcer.
    d. discriminative stimulus.

16. According to Tolman, _____ is defined as learning that occurs without apparent reinforcement but is not demonstrated until the organism is sufficiently reinforced to do so.
    a. classical conditioning
    b. modeling behavior
    c. latent learning
    d. cognitive mapping

◆ **SECTION FIVE: Critical Thinking**

1. Outline the strengths and limitations of classical conditioning, operant conditioning, and observational learning in explaining how behaviors are acquired and maintained.

2. The use of behavior modification has been a source of controversy among psychologists and others. Prepare arguments supporting each of these positions:
   a. Behavior modification should be used in society to shape the behavior of others.
   b. Behavior modification should not be used in society to shape the behavior of others.

3. Think of a behavior of a friend, family member, or professor that you would like to change. Using what you know about classical conditioning, operant conditioning, and observational learning, formulate a detailed plan for changing the targeted behavior.

Memory

chapter **6**

Remembering

- ◆ *What are the characteristics of each component of memory in the Atkinson-Shiffrin model?*
- ◆ *What are the three methods used by psychologists to measure memory?*

The Nature of Remembering

- ◆ *What is meant by the statement "Memory is reconstructive in nature"?*
- ◆ *What conditions reduce the reliability of eyewitness testimony?*
- ◆ *What is the controversy regarding the therapy used to recover repressed memories of childhood sexual abuse?*

- ◆ *What does research evidence say about flashbulb memories?*
- ◆ *How does culture influence memory?*
- ◆ *What happens when information must be recalled in a particular order?*
- ◆ *How do environmental conditions and emotional states affect memory?*

Biology and Memory

- ◆ *What roles do the hippocampus and the hippocampal region play in memory?*
- ◆ *Why is long-term potentiation important?*
- ◆ *How do hormones influence memory?*

Forgetting

- ◆ *What did Ebbinghaus discover about forgetting?*
- ◆ *What causes forgetting?*

Improving Memory

- ◆ *How can organization, overlearning, spaced practice, and recitation improve memory?*

Franco Magnani was born in 1934 in Pontito, an ancient village in the hills of Tuscany, Italy. His father died when Franco was eight. Soon after that, Nazi troops occupied the village. The Magnani family lived through many years of hardship, at times facing starvation. With the help of the village priest, Franco fulfilled a lifelong dream when he emigrated to the United States in 1958 and settled in San Francisco.

Several years after his arrival in America, Magnani developed a serious illness that required him to stop working for a prolonged period. Troubled and homesick, he decided to take up painting as a hobby. His first effort was a painting of the house in which he had grown up. He had no photograph of the house—only the pictures he carried in his mind. When he had completed the painting, he sent a photograph of it to his mother, who had also left Pontito. Her enthusiasm for the painting and the memories it brought back to her encouraged Magnani to paint more scenes of his hometown. Working entirely from his own memories, Magnani painted a series of pictures of Pontito and the surrounding countryside, scenes that he had not actually seen for decades. Many of Magnani's paintings are extraordinarily accurate when compared with photographs of the originals. For example, look at the pictures below. On the left is a photograph of

the house in which the artist grew up. On the right is his painting of the house. Here Magnani paints not only the house but also a view of his mother inside the house, laying the table for a meal, himself as a boy of about five looking in at her.

As you can see, the painting is a very accurate rendering of the house, but it differs from the photograph in several striking ways. For one, Magnani probably had never actually seen his mother preparing a meal in the way he has shown it in the painting. Instead, the scene he paints represents an inference derived from the connections among the house, his experiences as a young boy, and his mother's cooking that exist in his memory. Likewise, the front steps are much steeper in the painting than in the photograph, suggesting that Magnani remembered the height of each step from the point of view of a small child. Again, the steps and his perspective on them as a boy are interconnected in his memory, perhaps inseparably so. Clearly, too, the painting is imbued with a warmth not evident in the photo. This warmth, no doubt, emanates from the artist's fondness for the places he paints and for a time that is long gone. Thus, the scene Magnani has painted depicts elements that could never have been represented in a photograph. They are the unique product of his memory.

As Magnani's painting suggests, human memory does not function like a tape recorder or a camera in that objective bits of information constitute only one facet of any memory. To these, our memory system adds other pieces of information that are in some way associated with them, as well as emotions and perspectives that are entirely subjective. In this chapter, you will read what psychologists have learned about the fascinating processes that, together, make up human memory.

Photograph

Painting

Remembering

encoding

The process of transforming information into a form that can be stored in memory.

storage

The process of keeping or maintaining information in memory.

consolidation

A physiological change in the brain that allows encoded information to be stored in memory.

What are the characteristics of each component of memory in the Atkinson-Shiffrin model?

retrieval

The process of bringing to mind information that has been stored in memory.

memory

The process of encoding, storage, consolidation, and retrieval of information.

sensory memory

The memory system that holds information from the senses for a period of time ranging from only a fraction of a second to about 2 seconds.

Psychologists think of remembering as involving three processes: encoding, storage, and retrieval (see Figure 6.1). The first process, **encoding,** is the transformation of information into a form that can be stored. For example, if you witness a car crash, you might try to form a mental picture of it to enable yourself to remember it. The second process, **storage**, involves keeping or maintaining information. For encoded information to be stored, some physiological change must take place in the brain—a process called **consolidation**. The final process, **retrieval,** occurs when information is brought to mind. To remember something, you must perform all three processes—encode the information, store it, and then retrieve it. Thus, **memory** is a cognitive process that includes encoding, storage, and retrieval of information.

The Atkinson-Shiffrin Model

How are memories stored? Most current efforts to understand human memory are conducted within a framework known as the *information-processing approach* (Klatzky, 1984). This approach makes use of modern computer science and related fields to provide models that help psychologists understand the processes involved in memory (Kon & Plaskota, 2000; Bishop, 2005).

According to one widely accepted information-processing memory model, the *Atkinson-Shiffrin model*, there are three different, interacting memory systems: sensory memory, short-term memory, and long-term memory (Atkinson & Shiffrin, 1968; Broadbent, 1958). Virtually everything we see, hear, or otherwise sense is held in **sensory memory,** where each piece of information is stored only for the briefest period of time. As shown in Figure 6.2, sensory memory normally holds visual images for a fraction of a second and sounds for about 2 seconds (Crowder, 1992; Klatzky, 1980).

Exactly how long does visual sensory memory last? Glance at the three rows of letters shown below for a fraction of a second, and then close your eyes. How many of the letters can you recall?

```
X  B  D  F
M  P  Z  G
L  C  N  H
```

Most people can correctly recall only four or five of the letters when they are briefly presented. Does this indicate that visual sensory memory can hold only four or five letters at a time? To find out, researcher George Sperling (1960) briefly flashed 12 letters, as shown above, to participants. Immediately upon turning off the display, he sounded a high, medium, or low tone that signaled the participants to report only the top, middle, or bottom row of letters. Before they heard the tone, the participants had no way of knowing which row they would have to report. Yet Sperling found that, when the participants could view the rows of letters for $^{15}/_{1000}$ to $^{1}/_{2}$ second, they could report correctly all the items in any one row nearly 100% of the time. But the items faded from sensory memory so quickly that during the time it took to report three or four of them, the other eight or nine had already disappeared.

FIGURE 6.1

The Processes Required for Remembering

The act of remembering requires successful completion of all three of these processes: encoding, storage, and retrieval.

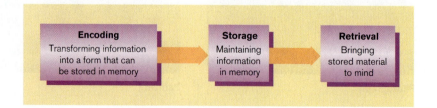

Encoding	Storage	Retrieval
Transforming information into a form that can be stored in memory	Maintaining information in memory	Bringing stored material to mind

FIGURE 6.2 **Characteristics of and Processes Involved in the Three Memory Systems Proposed by Atkinson and Shiffrin**

The three memory systems differ in what and how much they hold and for how long they store it.
Source: Peterson & Peterson (1959).

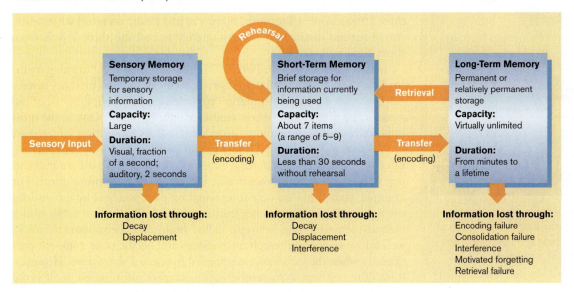

So, you might be thinking, if almost everything flows out of sensory memory, how do we ever remember anything? Fortunately, our ability to attend allows us to grab on to some sensory information and send it to the next stage of processing, **short-term memory (STM).** Short-term memory has a very limited capacity—about seven (plus or minus two) different items or bits of information at one time. This is just enough for phone numbers and ordinary ZIP codes. (Nine-digit ZIP codes strain the capacity of most people's STM.) When short-term memory is filled to capacity, displacement can occur. In **displacement,** each new, incoming item pushes out an existing item, which is then forgotten. Think of what happens when the top of your desk gets too crowded. Things start to "disappear" under other things; some items even fall off the desk. So, you can remember that short-term memory is the limited component of the memory system by associating it with the top of your desk: The desk is limited in size, causing you to lose things when it gets crowded, and the same is true of short-term memory.

One way to overcome the limitation of seven or so bits of information is to use a strategy that George A. Miller (1956), a pioneer in memory research, calls **chunking**—organizing or grouping separate bits of information into larger units, or chunks. A *chunk* is an easily identifiable unit such as a syllable, a word, an acronym, or a number (Cowan, 1988). For example, nine digits, such as 5 2 9 7 3 1 3 2 5, can be divided into three more easily memorized chunks, 529 73 1325. (Notice that this is the form of Social Security numbers in the United States.)

Anytime you chunk information on the basis of knowledge stored in long-term memory—that is, by associating it with some kind of meaning—you increase the effective capacity of short-term memory (Lustig & Hasher, 2002). As a result, chunking is just as useful in remembering large amounts of information as it is in remembering short bits of data such as telephone numbers. For instance, the headings, subheadings, and margin questions in this textbook help you sort information into manageable chunks. Thus, you will remember more of a chapter if you use them as organizers for your notes and as cues to recall information when you are reviewing for an exam.

As you might have guessed, chunking alone won't do the trick. In fact, items in short-term memory are lost in less than 30 seconds unless you repeat them over and over to yourself. This process is known as **rehearsal.** But rehearsal is easily disrupted. It is so fragile, in fact, that an interruption can cause information to be lost in just a few seconds. In a series of early studies, participants were briefly shown three consonants

◆ **short-term memory (STM)**
The memory system that codes information according to sound and holds about seven (from five to nine) items for less than 30 seconds without rehearsal; also called working memory.

◆ **displacement**
The event that occurs when short-term memory is filled to capacity and each new, incoming item pushes out an existing item, which is then forgotten.

◆ **chunking**
A memory strategy that involves grouping or organizing bits of information into larger units, which are easier to remember.

◆ **rehearsal**
The act of purposely repeating information to maintain it in short-term memory.

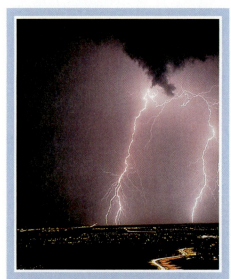

Sensory memory holds a visual image, such as a lightning bolt, for a fraction of a second—just long enough for you to perceive a flow of movement.

(such as H, G, and L) and then asked to count backward by threes from a given number (738, 735, 732, and so on) (Peterson & Peterson, 1959). After intervals lasting from 3 to 18 seconds, participants were instructed to stop counting backward and recall the three letters. Following a delay of 9 seconds, the participants could recall an average of only one of the three letters. After 18 seconds, there was practically no recall whatsoever. An 18-second distraction had completely erased the three letters from short-term memory.

Allan Baddeley (1990, 1992, 1995) has suggested that "working memory" is a more fitting term than short-term memory. This memory system is where you work on information to understand it, remember it, or use it to solve a problem or to communicate with someone. One of the most important working memory processes is the application of *memory strategies*, such as chunking. Using a memory strategy involves manipulating information in ways that make it easier to remember. We use some memory strategies almost automatically, but others require more effort. For example, sometimes we repeat information over and over again until we can recall it easily. (Remember learning those multiplication tables in elementary school?) This strategy, called **maintenance rehearsal**, works well for remembering telephone numbers and license plate numbers, particularly when the information is needed for only a short time. However, it isn't the best way to remember more complex information, such as the kind you find in a textbook. For this kind of information, the best strategy is **elaborative rehearsal**, which involves relating new information to something you already know. For example, suppose you are taking a French class and have to learn the word *éscaliers*, which is equivalent to *stairs* in English. You might remember the meaning of *éscaliers* by associating it with the English word *escalator*.

Maintenance and elaborative rehearsal were first described by memory researchers Fergus Craik and Robert Lockhart (1972) in the context of their *levels-of-processing* model of memory (Baddeley, 1998). This model proposed that maintenance rehearsal involves "shallow" processing (encoding based on superficial features of information, such as the sound of a word), whereas elaborative rehearsal involves "deep" processing (encoding based on the meaning of information). Craik and Lockhart hypothesized that deep processing is more likely to lead to long-term retention than is shallow processing. Their hypothesis was tested in classic research by Craik and Tulving (1975). They had participants answer "yes" or "no" to questions asked about words just before the words were flashed to them for ⅕ of a second. The participants had to process the words in three ways: (1) visually (Is the word in capital letters?); (2) acoustically (Does the word rhyme with another particular word?); and (3) semantically (Does the word make sense when used in a particular sentence?). Thus, this test required shallow processing for the first question, deeper processing for the second question, and still deeper processing for the third question. Later retention tests showed that the deeper the level of processing, the higher the accuracy of memory.

If information is processed effectively in short-term memory, it makes its way to long-term memory. **Long-term memory (LTM)** is a person's vast storehouse of permanent or relatively permanent memories (refer to Figure 6.2).

◆ **maintenance rehearsal**

Repeating information over and over again until it is no longer needed; may eventually lead to storage of information in long-term memory.

◆ **elaborative rehearsal**

A memory strategy that involves relating new information to something that is already known.

◆ **long-term memory (LTM)**

The memory system with a virtually unlimited capacity that contains vast stores of a person's permanent or relatively permanent memories.

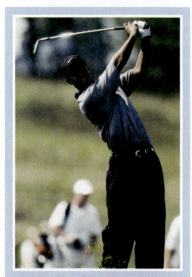

Declarative memories involve facts, information, and personal life events, such as a trip to a foreign country. Nondeclarative memory encompasses motor skills, such as the expert swing of professional golfer Tiger Woods. Once learned, such movements can be carried out with little or no conscious effort.

There are no known limits to the storage capacity of this memory system, and long-term memories can persist for years, some of them for a lifetime. Information in long-term memory is usually stored in semantic form, although visual images, sounds, and odors can be stored there as well.

Some experts believe that there are two main subsystems within long-term memory. The first, **declarative memory** (also called *explicit memory*), stores facts, information, and personal life events that can be brought to mind verbally or in the form of images and then declared or stated. It holds information that we intentionally and consciously recollect. There are two types of declarative memory: episodic memory and semantic memory. **Episodic memory** is the type of declarative memory that records events as they have been subjectively experienced (Wheeler et al., 1997). It is somewhat like a mental diary, a record of the episodes of your life—the people you have known, the places you have seen, and the personal experiences you have had. Using episodic memory, a person might make this statement: "I remember being in Florida on my vacation last spring, lying on the sand, soaking up some rays, and listening to the sound of the waves rushing to the shore." **Semantic memory**, the other type of declarative memory, is memory for general knowledge, or objective facts and information. Semantic memory is involved when a person recalls that Florida is bounded by the Atlantic Ocean on the east and the Gulf of Mexico on the west. It is not necessary to have ever visited Florida to know these facts. Consequently, semantic memory is more like an encyclopedia or a dictionary than a personal diary.

Memory researcher Endel Tulving (1995) points out that the two types of declarative memory do not function independently. For instance, your memory of lying on a beach in Florida (episodic) relies on your understanding of what a beach is (semantic). Likewise, the experience of actually being there (episodic) undoubtedly enhanced your general knowledge of the state (semantic).

The second kind of memory, called **nondeclarative memory** (also called *implicit memory*), is the subsystem within long-term memory that stores motor skills, habits, and simple classically conditioned responses (Squire et al., 1993). Motor skills are acquired through repetitive practice and include such things as eating with a fork, riding a bicycle, or driving a car. Although acquired slowly, once learned, these skills become habit, are quite reliable, and can be carried out with little or no conscious effort. For example, you probably use the keyboard on a computer without consciously being able to name the keys in each row from left to right. Figure 6.3 (on page 174) shows the two subsystems of long-term memory.

Three Kinds of Memory Tasks

How many times have you recognized someone without being able to recall his or her name? This happens to everyone because recognition is an easier memory task than recall. In **recall**, a person must produce required information simply by searching memory. Trying to remember someone's name, the items on a shopping list, or the words of a speech or a poem is a recall task. A recall task may be made a little easier if cues are provided to jog memory. A **retrieval cue** is any stimulus or bit of information that aids in retrieving a particular memory. Think about how you might respond to these two test questions:

What are the four basic memory processes?
The four processes involved in memory are e _____, s _____, c _____, and r _____.

Both questions require you to recall information. However, most students would find the second question easier to answer because it includes four retrieval cues.

Recognition is exactly what the name implies. A person simply recognizes something as familiar—a face, a name, a taste, a melody. Multiple-choice, matching, and true/false questions are examples of test items based on recognition. The main difference between recall and recognition is that a recognition task does not require you to

◆ **declarative memory**
The subsystem within long-term memory that stores facts, information, and personal life events that can be brought to mind verbally or in the form of images and then declared or stated; also called explicit memory.

◆ **episodic memory**
(ep-ih-SOD-ik) The type of declarative memory that records events as they have been subjectively experienced.

◆ **semantic memory**
The type of declarative memory that stores general knowledge, or objective facts and information.

◆ **nondeclarative memory**
The subsystem within long-term memory that stores motor skills, habits, and simple classically conditioned responses; also called implicit memory.

◆ *What are the three methods used by psychologists to measure memory?*

◆ **recall**
A memory task in which a person must produce required information by searching memory.

◆ **retrieval cue**
Any stimulus or bit of information that aids in retrieving particular information from long-term memory.

◆ **recognition**
A memory task in which a person must simply identify material as familiar or as having been encountered before.

FIGURE 6.3 **Subsystems of Long-Term Memory**

Declarative memory can be divided into two subsystems: episodic memory, which stores memories of personally experienced events, and semantic memory, which stores facts and information. Nondeclarative memory consists of motor skills acquired through repetitive practice, habits, and simple classically conditioned responses.

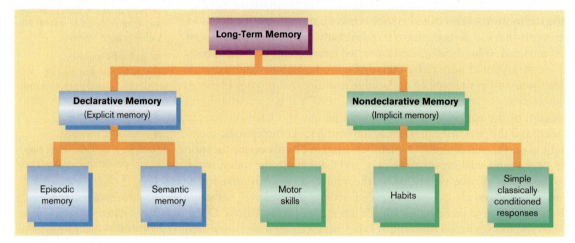

◆ **relearning method**

A measure of memory in which retention is expressed as the percentage of time saved when material is relearned compared with the time required to learn the material originally.

supply the information but only to recognize it when you see it. The correct answer is included along with other items in a recognition question.

There is another, more sensitive way to measure memory. With the **relearning method,** retention is expressed as the percentage of time saved when material is relearned relative to the time required to learn the material originally. Suppose it took you 40 minutes to memorize a list of words, and 1 month later you were tested on those words, using recall or recognition. If you could not recall or recognize a single word, would this mean that you had absolutely no memory of anything on the list? Or could it mean that the recall and recognition tasks were not sensitive enough to measure what little information you may have stored? How could a researcher measure such a remnant of former learning? Using the relearning method, a researcher could time how long it would take you to relearn the list of words. If it took 20 minutes to relearn the list, this would represent a 50% savings over the original learning time of 40 minutes. The percentage of time saved—the *savings score*—reflects how much material remains in long-term memory.

College students demonstrate the relearning method each semester when they study for comprehensive final exams. Relearning material for a final exam takes less time than it took to learn the material originally.

◆ **reconstruction**

An account of an event that has been pieced together from a few highlights, using information that may or may not be accurate.

◆ **schemas**

The integrated frameworks of knowledge and assumptions a person has about people, objects, and events, which affect how the person encodes and recalls information.

The Nature of Remembering

Wilder Penfield (1969), a Canadian neurosurgeon, claimed that experiences leave a "permanent imprint on the brain . . . as though a tape recorder had been receiving it all" (p. 165). Does human memory really function like a tape or video recorder? Probably not.

Memory as a Reconstruction

◆ *What is meant by the statement "Memory is reconstructive in nature"?*

Normally, what a person recalls is not an exact replication of an event. Rather, a memory is a **reconstruction**—an account pieced together from a few highlights, using information that may or may not be accurate (Loftus & Loftus, 1980). A pioneering memory researcher, Sir Frederick Bartlett (1886–1969), suggested that reconstructive memory processes are influenced by **schemas**—frameworks of knowledge and assumptions that we have about people, objects, and events.

In most cases, schemas are helpful to memory because they aid in processing large amounts of material by providing frameworks into which people can incorporate new information. Suppose you read the following headline: "Dog Saves Boy from Drowning." What facts would you expect to be included in the story? You might expect to read about where the incident took place—perhaps it happened at a beach or in a neighborhood swimming pool. By contrast, you would not expect to read about a canine rescue that occurred in a bathtub. Why? Because schemas are based on situational averages. Drownings occur most often in bodies of water in which people swim. Thus, the schema evoked by the headline would cause you to picture the incident taking place in the setting that would be most likely.

Of course, schemas can also lead to inaccurate memories. Bartlett studied this phenomenon by giving participants stories to read and drawings to study; then, after varying time intervals, he had them reproduce the original material. Accurate reports were rare. The participants seemed to reconstruct the material they had learned, rather than actually remember it. They recreated the stories, making them shorter and more consistent with their own individual viewpoints. They adapted puzzling features of the stories to fit their own expectations and often changed details, substituting more familiar objects or events. Errors in memory increased with time, and Bartlett's participants were not aware that they had partly remembered and partly invented. Ironically, the parts his participants had created were often the parts they most adamantly claimed to have remembered (Bartlett, 1932). Bartlett concluded that people systematically distort the facts and the circumstances of experiences.

Are you better at remembering faces than names? Have you ever wondered why? It's because the task involves recognition rather than recall. You must recall the name but merely recognize the face.

Research has shown that autobiographical memories are particularly subject to reconstruction in ways that cause pleasant events to be better remembered than unpleasant ones and that cause memories of unpleasant events to grow more pleasant over time. Researchers call this kind of distortion *positive bias*. Remarkably, research suggests that memories of even the most horrific experiences can be influenced by positive bias. In several studies carried out in the 1980s, Holocaust survivors' recollections of their experiences in Nazi concentration camps were compared to reports they had given to war crimes investigators during and immediately after World War II (1939–1945). In one case, a man reported in the 1940s that he had personally witnessed prisoners being drowned by concentration camp guards. In the 1980s, he claimed that no such incident had occurred and even denied having given the earlier report (Baddeley, 1998). Why are our memories subject to such positive bias? Researchers speculate that positive bias may be important to regulation of current states of emotional well-being (Kennedy et al., 2004). In other words, our current need for emotional well-being is a schema we use to selectively process our memories of past events.

When people recall an event, such as a car accident, they are actually reconstructing it from memory by piecing together bits of information that may or may not be totally accurate.

Eyewitness Testimony

◆ *What conditions reduce the reliability of eyewitness testimony?*

What happens when memory distortions are incorporated into testimony given under oath in legal proceedings? According to Elizabeth Loftus (1993a, 2003), a staggering number of wrongful convictions in the United States each year are based on eyewitness testimony. According to Huff (1995), the number is probably at least 10,000. Yet it was not until October 1999 that the U.S. Department of Justice prepared the first national guidelines for the collection of eyewitness evidence (Wells et al., 2000).

Studies on the accuracy of human memory suggest that eyewitness testimony is highly subject to error, and that it should always be viewed with caution (Loftus, 1979). Nevertheless, it does play a vital role in the U.S. justice system. According to Loftus (1984), "We can't afford to exclude it legally or ignore it as jurors. Sometimes, as in cases of rape, it is the only evidence available, and it is often correct" (p. 24).

Fortunately, eyewitness mistakes can be minimized. Eyewitnesses to crimes typically identify suspects from a lineup. If shown photographs of a suspect before viewing the lineup, eyewitnesses may mistakenly identify that suspect in the lineup because the person looks familiar. Research suggests that it is better to have an eyewitness first describe the perpetrator and then search for photos matching that description than to have the eyewitness start by looking through photos and making judgments as to their similarity to the perpetrator (Pryke et al., 2000).

The composition of the lineup is also important. Other subjects in a lineup must resemble the suspect in age, body build, and certainly race. Even then, if the lineup does not contain the guilty party, eyewitnesses may identify the person who most closely resembles the perpetrator (Gonzalez et al., 1993). Eyewitnesses are less likely to make errors if a sequential lineup is used—that is, if the members of the lineup are viewed one after the other, rather than simultaneously (Loftus, 1993a). Some police officers and researchers prefer a "showup," in which the witness sees only one suspect at a time and indicates whether or not that person is the perpetrator. There are fewer misidentifications with a showup, but also more failures to make a positive identification (Wells, 1993).

Eyewitnesses are more likely to identify the wrong person if the person's race is different from their own. According to Egeth (1993), misidentifications are approximately 15% higher in cross-race than in same-race identifications. Misidentification is also somewhat more likely to occur when a weapon is used in a crime. The witnesses may pay more attention to the weapon than to the physical characteristics of the criminal (Steblay, 1992).

Even the questioning of witnesses after a crime can influence what they later remember. Because leading questions can substantially change a witness's memory of an event, it is critical that the interviewers ask neutral questions (Leichtman & Ceci, 1995). Misleading information supplied after the event can result in erroneous recollections of the actual event, a phenomenon known as the *misinformation effect* (Kroll et al., 1988; Loftus & Hoffman, 1989). Loftus (1997) and her students have conducted "more than 20 experiments involving over 20,000 participants that document how exposure to misinformation induces memory distortion" (p. 71). Furthermore, after eyewitnesses have repeatedly recalled information, whether it is accurate or inaccurate, they become even more confident when they testify in court because the information is so easily retrieved (Shaw, 1996).

Witnessing a crime is highly stressful. How does stress affect eyewitness accuracy? Research suggests that eyewitnesses do tend to remember the central, critical details of the event, even though their arousal is high, but the memory of less important details suffers (Burke et al., 1992; Christianson, 1992).

Furthermore, the confidence eyewitnesses have in their testimony is not necessarily an indication of its accuracy (Loftus, 1993a; Sporer et al., 1995; Loftus & Bernstein, 2005). In fact, eyewitnesses who perceive themselves to be more objective have more confidence in their testimony, regardless of its accuracy, and are more likely to include incorrect information in their verbal descriptions (Geiselman et al., 2000). When witnesses make incorrect identifications with great certainty, they can be highly persuasive to judges and jurors alike. "A false eyewitness identification can create a real-life nightmare for the identified person, friends, and family members. . . . False identifications also mean that the actual culprit remains at large—a double injustice" (Wells, 1993, p. 568).

Recovering Repressed Memories

Memory distortions, as well as "memories" that turn out to be entirely false, have been the subject of debate in regard to the claims made by some therapists about their clients' recoveries of repressed memories of child abuse. In 1988, Ellen Bass and Laura Davis published a best-selling book called *The Courage to Heal*. It became the "bible" for sex abuse victims and the leading "textbook" for some therapists who specialized in treating them. Bass and Davis not only sought to help survivors who remember having suffered sexual abuse, but also reached out to other people who had no memory of any sexual abuse and tried to help them determine whether they might have been abused. They suggested that "if you are unable to remember any specific instances . . . but still have a feeling that something abusive happened to you, it probably did" (p. 21). They offered a definite conclusion: "If you think you were abused and your life shows the symptoms, then you were" (p. 22). And they freed potential victims of sexual abuse from the responsibility of establishing any proof: "You are not responsible for proving that you were abused" (p. 37).

◆ *What is the controversy regarding the therapy used to recover repressed memories of childhood sexual abuse?*

However, many psychologists are skeptical about such "recovered" memories, claiming that they are actually false memories created by the suggestions of therapists. Critics "argue that repression of truly traumatic memories is rare" (Bowers & Farvolden, 1996, p. 355). Moreover, they maintain that "when it comes to a serious trauma, intrusive thoughts and memories of it are the most characteristic reaction" (p. 359). Repressed-memory therapists believe, however, that healing hinges on their patients' being able to recover their repressed memories.

Critics further charge that recovered memories of sexual abuse are suspect because of the techniques therapists usually use to uncover them—namely, hypnosis and guided imagery. As you have learned (in Chapter 4), hypnosis does not improve the accuracy of memory, only the confidence that what one remembers is accurate. And a therapist using guided imagery might tell a patient something similar to what Wendy Maltz (1991) advocates in her book:

> Spend time imagining that you were sexually abused, without worrying about accuracy, proving anything, or having your ideas make sense. . . . Ask yourself . . . these questions: What time of day is it? Where are you? Indoors or outdoors? What kind of things are happening? (p. 50)

Can merely imagining experiences in this way lead people to believe that those experiences had actually happened to them? Yes, according to some studies. Many research participants who are instructed to imagine that a fictitious event happened do, in fact, develop a false memory of that imagined event (Hyman et al., 1995; Hyman & Pentland, 1996; Loftus & Pickrell, 1995; Mazzoni & Memon, 2003; Worthen & Wood, 2001).

False childhood memories can also be experimentally induced. Garry and Loftus (1994) were able to implant a false memory of being lost in a shopping mall at 5 years of age in 25% of participants aged 18 to 53, after verification of the fictitious experience by a relative. Repeated exposure to suggestions of false memories can create those memories (Zaragoza & Mitchell, 1996). Further, researchers have found that adults who claim to have recovered memories of childhood abuse or of abduction by extraterrestrials are more vulnerable to experimentally induced false memories than are adults who do not report such recovered memories (McNally, 2003). So, individual differences in suggestibility may play a role in the recovery of memories.

Critics are especially skeptical of recovered memories of events that occurred in the first few years of life, in part because the hippocampus, vital in the formation of episodic memories, is not fully developed then. And neither are the areas of the cortex where memories are stored (Squire et al., 1993). Furthermore, young children, who are still limited in language ability, do not store semantic memories in categories that

How Did You Find Psychology?

Elizabeth Loftus

Sometimes sharing an interest with someone whom we love and respect is the basis for a career decision. Eminent memory researcher Elizabeth Loftus, whose name has become virtually synonymous with the repressed-memory controversy, and her father shared the tragedy of losing Loftus's mother just a few years before Loftus began her undergraduate studies at the University of California at Los Angelas. Once her mother was gone, the interest in mathematics Loftus shared with her father became the common ground upon which they maintained their relationship. Thus, it seemed quite natural to Loftus that she should major in mathematics when she entered college. Along the way, however, she took a course in introductory psychology and became fascinated with the subject. She devoted all of the elective hours in her degree plan to psychology courses, ultimately accumulating enough hours to graduate with a double major in math and psychology. Naturally, when she went on to graduate school at Stanford University, Loftus specialized in mathematical psychology, a branch of cognitive science devoted to the development of computational models that can be used to describe psychological processes.

In graduate school, Loftus discovered that she had a gift for experimental design and statistical analysis. Shortly after receiving her Ph.D., she decided that she wanted to apply those talents to issues that could make a real difference in people's lives. Motivated by her lifelong concern for the falsely accused, Loftus applied for a grant to study how eyewitnesses' memories of traffic accidents can become distorted. Once her work was published, her name became known among defense attorneys, and she began to be sought out as an expert witness on the topic of eyewitness memory. These experiences became the catalyst for her controversial work dealing with false memories of abuse—work that has earned her both high praise and harsh criticism.

Her critics argue that Loftus's research obscures the fact that some individuals really do suffer from repressed traumatic memories. However, Loftus is able to empathize with the very real emotional ups and downs of those who believe they have repressed traumatic memories. As mentioned earlier, Loftus's mother died when Loftus was a teenager. For most of her life, she believed that an aunt had discovered her mother's body in the family swimming pool. At a family gathering in the mid-1990s, Loftus's uncle informed her that she had actually been the one who found her mother. Loftus searched her memory and found what she thought was a repressed memory of her discovery of her mother's body. The vivid imagery associated with this memory was particularly striking. As she replayed the memory in her mind, Loftus experienced what she believed to be replays of the emotions that accompanied finding her mother's body. Thus, she was surprised when her uncle telephoned her a few days after the gathering to say that he had been mistaken. For Loftus, this personal experience added further weight to the large body of evidence she and her colleagues have compiled regarding the human memory's vulnerability to external influences.

Loftus's career path demonstrates the importance that your values play in choosing a career. With her gifts for experimental design and statistical analysis, she could easily have spent her entire career in a computer lab cranking out mathematical models of cognitive functions. Instead, Loftus's values led her to choose a career path that hasn't always been easy but that has helped her achieve her goal of making a difference in people's lives.

---

are accessible to them later in life. The relative inability of older children and adults to recall events from the first few years of life is referred to as **infantile amnesia.**

In light of these developmental limitations, is it possible that some individuals cannot recall incidents of childhood sexual abuse? Widom and Morris (1997) found that 64% of a group of women who had been sexually abused as children reported no memory of the abuse in a 2-hour interview 20 years later. Following up on women who had documented histories of sexual victimization, Williams (1994) found that 38% of them did not report remembering the sexual abuse some 17 years later. Memories of abuse were better when the victimization took place between the ages of 7 and 17 than when it occurred in the first 6 years of life. Keep in mind, however, that it is possible that some of these women may have remembered the abuse but, for whatever reason, chose not

◆ **infantile amnesia**
The relative inability of older children and adults to recall events from the first few years of life.

to admit it. There is also some indication that individuals who are traumatized develop an attentional style that involves distracting themselves from potentially unpleasant stimuli (DePrince & Freyd, 2004). It is this attentional style, some researchers argue, that prevents such individuals from forming memories of abuse that can be easily recalled.

The American Psychological Association (1994), the American Psychiatric Association (1993a), and the American Medical Association (1994) have issued status reports on memories of childhood abuse. The position of all three groups is that current evidence supports both the possibility that repressed memories exist and the likehood that false memories can be constructed in response to suggestions of abuse. Moreover, individuals who hold false memories are often thoroughly convinced that they are accurate because of the details such memories contain and the strong emotions associated with them (Dodson et al., 2000; Gonsalves et al., 2004; Henkel et al., 2000, 2004; Loftus, 2004; Loftus & Bernstein, 2005; McNally et al., 2004). Neuroimaging studies suggest that engaging in visually vivid mental replays of false memories may serve to strengthen them even further (Lindsay et al., 2004). For these reasons, many experts recommend that recovered memories of abuse should be verified independently before they are accepted as facts.

◆ **flashbulb memory**
An extremely vivid memory of the conditions surrounding one's first hearing the news of a surprising, shocking, or highly emotional event.

Flashbulb Memories

Do you remember where you were and what you were doing when you heard about the tragic events of September 11, 2001? Most people do. Likewise, most people older than age 50 claim to have vivid memories of exactly when and where they received the news of the assassination of President John F. Kennedy. And many of their parents have very clear memories of learning about the attack on Pearl Harbor on December 7, 1941, which marked the entry of the United States into World War II. This type of extremely vivid memory is called a **flashbulb memory** (Bohannon, 1988). Brown and Kulik (1977) suggest that a flashbulb memory is formed when a person learns of an event that is very surprising, shocking, or highly emotional. You might have a flashbulb memory of when you received the news of the death or the serious injury of a close family member or a friend.

◆ *What does research evidence say about flashbulb memories?*

Pillemer (1990) argues that flashbulb memories do not constitute a completely different type of memory. Rather, he suggests, all memories can vary on the dimensions of emotion, consequentiality (the importance of the consequences of the event), and rehearsal (how often people think or talk about the event afterwards). Flashbulb memories rank high in all three dimensions and thus are extremely memorable.

However, several studies suggest that flashbulb memories are not as accurate as people believe them to be. Neisser and Harsch (1992) questioned university freshmen about the televised explosion of the space shuttle *Challenger* the following morning. When the same students were questioned again 3 years later, one-third gave accounts that differed markedly from those given initially, but these individuals were extremely confident about their recollections. Further, flashbulb memories appear to be forgotten at about the same rate and in the same ways as other kinds of memories (Curci et al., 2001).

Eyewitnesses to the aftermath of the terrorist attacks on the Pentagon almost certainly formed flashbulb memories of the horrific events they witnessed. Do you remember where you were and what you were doing when you heard the news on September 11, 2001?

Memory and Culture

◆ How does culture influence memory?

Sir Frederick Bartlett (1932) believed that some impressive memory abilities operate within a social or cultural context and cannot be completely understood as a process. He stated that "both the manner and matter of recall are often predominantly determined by social influences" (p. 244). Studying memory in a cultural context, Bartlett (1932) described the amazing ability of the Swazi people of Africa to remember the slight differences in individual characteristics of their cows. One Swazi herdsman, Bartlett claimed, could remember details of every cow he had tended the year before. Such a feat is less surprising when you consider that the key component of traditional Swazi culture is the herds of cattle the people tend and depend on for their living. Do the Swazi people have super memory powers? Bartlett asked young Swazi men and young European men to recall a message consisting of 25 words. In this case, the Swazi had no better recall ability than the Europeans.

Among many tribal peoples in Africa, the history of the tribe is preserved orally by specialists, who must be able to encode, store, and retrieve huge volumes of historical data (D'Azevedo, 1982). Elders of the Iatmul people of New Guinea are also said to have committed to memory the lines of descent for the various clans of their people, stretching back for many generations (Bateson, 1982). The unerring memory of the elders for the kinship patterns of their people are used to resolve disputed property claims (Mistry & Rogoff, 1994).

Barbara Rogoff, an expert in cultural psychology, maintains that such phenomenal, prodigious memory feats are best explained and understood in their cultural context (Rogoff & Mistry, 1985). The tribal elders perform their impressive memory feats because it is an integral and critically important part of the culture in which they live. Most likely, their ability to remember nonmeaningful information would be no better than your own.

A study examining memory for location among a tribal group in India, the Asur, who do not use artificial lighting of any kind, provides further information about the influence of culture on memory (Mishra & Singh, 1992). Researchers hypothesized that members of this group would perform better on tests of memory for locations than on memory tests involving word pairs, because, without artificial light, they have to remember where things are to be able to move around in the dark without bumping into things. When the tribe members were tested, the results supported this hypothesis: They remembered locations better than word pairs.

In classic research, cognitive psychologists have also found that people more easily remember stories set in their own cultures than those set in others. In one of the first of these studies, researchers told women in the United States and Aboriginal women in Australia a story about a sick child (Steffensen & Calker, 1982). Participants were randomly assigned to groups for whom story outcomes were varied. In one version, the girl got well after being treated by a physician. In the other, a traditional native healer was called in to help the girl. Aboriginal participants better recalled the story with the native healer, while the American women were more accurate in their recall of the story in which a physician treated the girl. Most likely, these results reflect the influence of culturally based schemas. Aboriginal participants' schemas led them to expect a story about a sick child to include a native healer, and the story that fit with these expectations was easier for them to understand and remember. Just the opposite was true for the Western participants.

In many traditional cultures, elders are oral historians, remembering and passing on the details of tribal traditions and myths as well as genealogical data.

Culture also affects autobiographical memory. People in Western cultures, which tend to emphasize the individual more than the society as a whole, typically focus on the emotional aspects of event memories. By contrast, individuals in socially oriented cultures emphasize emotions much less, especially emotions such as anger that can disrupt relationships (Fivush & Nelson, 2004).

The Serial Position Effect

What would happen if you were introduced to a dozen people at a party? You would most likely recall the names of the first few people you met and the last one or two, but forget many of the names in the middle. The reason is the **serial position effect**—the finding that, for information learned in a sequence, recall is better for items at the beginning and the end than for items in the middle of the sequence.

Information at the beginning of a sequence is subject to the **primacy effect**—the tendency to recall the first items in a sequence more readily than the middle items. Such information is likely to be recalled because it already has been placed in long-term memory. Information at the end of a sequence is subject to the **recency effect**—the tendency to recall the last items in a sequence more readily than those in the middle. This information has an even higher probability of being recalled because it is still in short-term memory. The poorer recall of information in the middle of a sequence occurs because that information is no longer in short-term memory and has not yet been placed in long-term memory. The serial position effect lends strong support to the notion of separate systems for short-term and long-term memory (Postman & Phillips, 1965).

Context and Memory

Have you ever stood in your living room and thought of something you needed from your bedroom, only to forget what it was when you got there? Did the item come to mind again when you returned to the living room? Tulving and Thompson (1973) suggest that many elements of the physical setting in which a person learns information are encoded along with the information and become part of the memory. If part or all of the original context is reinstated, it may serve as a retrieval cue. That is why returning to the living room elicits the memory of the object you intended to get from the bedroom. In fact, just visualizing yourself in the living room might do the trick (Smith et al., 1978). (*Hint:* Next time you're taking a test and having difficulty recalling something, try visualizing yourself in the room where you studied.)

Godden and Baddeley (1975) conducted one of the early studies of context and memory with members of a university diving club. Participants memorized a list of words when they were either 10 feet underwater or on land. They were later tested for recall of the words in the same environment or in a different environment. Words learned underwater were best recalled underwater, and words learned on land were best recalled on land. In fact, when the divers learned and recalled the words in the same context, their scores were 47% higher than when the two contexts were different (see Figure 6.4).

In a more recent study of context-dependent memory, participants viewed videotapes and then were tested on their memory of the videos in two separate interviews conducted 2 days apart. The memory context was the same for all the participants, with one exception. Half the participants were questioned by different interviewers, whereas the other half were questioned by the same interviewer in both sessions. As you might expect, participants who were questioned twice by the same interviewer (same context) performed better than the other participants on the memory task (Bjorklund et al., 2000).

Odors can also supply powerful and enduring retrieval cues for memory. In a study by Morgan (1996), participants were placed in isolated cubicles and exposed to a list of

◆ *What happens when information must be recalled in the order in which it was presented?*

◆ **serial position effect**
The finding that, for information learned in a sequence, recall is better for the beginning and ending items than for the middle items in the sequence.

◆ **primacy effect**
The tendency to recall the first items in a sequence more readily than the middle items.

◆ *How do environmental conditions and emotional states affect memory?*

◆ **recency effect**
The tendency to recall the last items in a sequence more readily than those in the middle.

FIGURE 6.4

Context-Dependent Memory

Godden and Baddeley showed the strong influence of environmental context on recall. Divers who memorized a list of words, either on land or underwater, had significantly better recall in the same physical context in which the learning had taken place. *Source:* Data from Godden & Baddeley (1975).

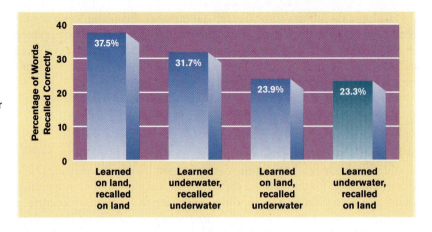

◆ **state-dependent memory effect**

The tendency to recall information better if one is in the same pharmacological or psychological state as when the information was encoded.

40 words. At the same time, they were exposed to different kinds of odors. They were instructed to perform a cognitive task using the words but were not asked to remember them. Then, back in the cubicle 5 days later, participants were unexpectedly tested for recall of the 40 words. Experimental participants who experienced a pleasant odor during learning and again when tested 5 days later had significantly higher recall than did control participants who did not experience the odor during both learning and recall.

People also tend to recall information better if they are in the same emotional state as when the information was encoded. Psychologists call this the **state-dependent memory effect.** For example, when researchers exposed college students to spiders and/or snakes while they were learning lists of words (presumably an anxiety-inducing experience!), the students recalled more words when the creatures were also present during tests of recall (Lang et al., 2001). Adults who are clinically depressed tend to recall more negative life experiences (Clark & Teasdale, 1982) and are likely to recall their parents as unloving and rejecting (Lewinsohn & Rosenbaum, 1987). Moreover, a meta-analysis of 48 studies revealed a significant relationship between depression and memory impairment. And recognition and recall were more impaired in younger depressed patients than in older ones (Burt et al., 1995). But, as depression lifts, the tendency toward negative recall and associated memory impairments reverses itself.

Biology and Memory

Obviously, a person's vast store of memories must exist physically somewhere in the brain. But where?

The Hippocampus and Hippocampal Region

◆ *What roles do the hippocampus and the hippocampal region play in memory?*

Researchers continue to identify specific locations in the brain that house and mediate functions and processes in memory. One important source of information comes from people who have suffered memory loss resulting from damage to specific brain areas. One especially significant case is that of H.M., a man who suffered from such severe epilepsy that, out of desperation, he agreed to a radical surgical procedure. The surgeon removed the part of the brain believed to be causing H.M.'s seizures—the medial portions of both temporal lobes, containing the amygdala and the **hippocampal region**, which includes the hippocampus itself and the underlying cortical areas. It was 1953, and H.M. was 27 years old.

◆ **hippocampal region**

A part of the limbic system, which includes the hippocampus itself and the underlying cortical areas, involved in the formation of semantic memories.

After his surgery, H.M. remained intelligent and psychologically stable, and his seizures were drastically reduced. But unfortunately, the tissue cut from H.M.'s brain housed more than the site of his seizures. It also contained his ability to use working memory to store new information in long-term memory. Though the capacity of his short-term memory remains the same, and he remembers life events that were stored before the operation, H.M. suffers from **anterograde amnesia.** He has not been able to remember a single event that has occurred since the surgery. And though H.M. is in his late seventies, as far as his conscious long-term memory is concerned, it is still 1953 and he is still 27 years old.

Surgery affected only H.M.'s declarative, long-term memory—his ability to store facts, personal experiences, names, faces, telephone numbers, and the like. But researchers were surprised to discover that he could still form nondeclarative memories; that is, he could still acquire skills through repetitive practice, although he could not remember having done so. For example, since the surgery, H.M. has learned to play tennis and improve his game, but he has no memory of ever having played (Milner, 1966, 1970; Milner et al., 1968).

Animal studies support the conclusion that the parts of H.M.'s brain that were removed are critical to working memory function (Ragozzino et al., 2002). Moreover, other patients who have suffered similar brain damage show the same types of memory loss (Squire, 1992).

Most recent research supports the hypothesis that the hippocampus is especially important in forming episodic memories (Eichenbaum, 1997; Eichenbaum & Fortin, 2003; Gluck & Myers, 1997; Spiers et al., 2001). Semantic memory, however, depends not only on the hippocampus, but also on the other parts of the hippocampal region (Vargha-Khadem et al., 1997). Once stored, memories can be retrieved without the involvement of the hippocampus (Gluck & Myers, 1997; McClelland et al., 1995). Consequently, many researchers argue that the neurological underpinnings of episodic and semantic memories are entirely separate (e.g., Tulving, 2002). But the degree to which the brain processes associated with episodic and semantic memories can be clearly distinguished is being questioned by some neuroscientists. Research involving older adults who suffer from semantic dementia due to frontal lobe damage shows that many of them suffer from deficiencies in episodic memory (Nestor et al., 2002). Moreover, other studies show that damage to the temporal and occipital lobes can affect episodic memory (Wheeler & McMillan, 2001).

An interesting recent study (Maguire et al., 2000), which was described briefly in Chapter 2, suggests that the hippocampus may serve special functions in addition to those already known. A part of the hippocampus evidently specializes in navigational skills by helping to create intricate neural spatial maps. Using magnetic resonance imaging (MRI) scans, researchers found that the rear (posterior) region of the hippocampus of London taxi drivers was significantly larger than that of participants in a matched control group whose living did not depend on navigational skills (see Figure 6.5). In addition, the more time spent as a taxi driver, the greater the size of this part of the hippocampus.

◆ **anterograde amnesia**
The inability to form long-term memories of events occurring after a brain injury or brain surgery, although memories formed before the trauma are usually intact and short-term memory is unaffected.

FIGURE 6.5   **MRI Scans Showing the Larger Size of the Posterior Hippocampus in the Brain of an Experienced Taxi Driver**

The posterior (rear) hippocampus of an experienced London taxi driver, shown in red in the MRI scan on the left, is significantly larger than the posterior hippocampus of a research participant who was not a taxi driver, shown in red in the scan on the right.   *Source:* Adapted from Maguire et al. (2000).

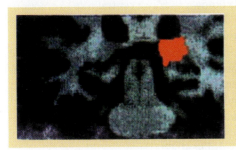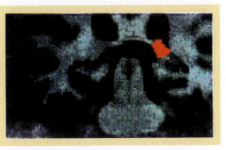

Neuronal Changes and Memory

◆ Why is long-term potentiation important?

Some researchers are exploring memory at deeper levels than the structures of the brain. Some look at the actions of single neurons; others study collections of neurons and their synapses and the neurotransmitters whose chemical action begins the process of recording and storing a memory. The first close look at how memory works in single neurons was provided by Eric Kandel and his colleagues, who traced the effects of learning and memory in the sea snail *Aplysia* (Dale & Kandel, 1990). Using tiny electrodes implanted in several single neurons in this snail, the researchers mapped the neural circuits that are formed and maintained as the animal learns and remembers. They also discovered the different types of protein synthesis that facilitate short-term and long-term memory (Sweatt & Kandel, 1989). Kandel won a Nobel Prize in 2000 for his work.

The studies of learning and memory in *Aplysia* reflect only simple classical conditioning, which is a type of nondeclarative memory. Other researchers studying mammals report that physical changes occur in the neurons and synapses in brain regions involved in declarative memory (Lee & Kesner, 2002).

As far back as the 1940s, Canadian psychologist Donald O. Hebb (1949) argued that learning and memory must involve the enhancement of transmission at the synapses between neurons. The most widely studied model for learning and memory at the level of the neurons meets the requirements of the mechanism Hebb described (Fischbach, 1992). **Long-term potentiation (LTP)** is an increase in the efficiency of neural transmission at the synapses that lasts for hours or longer (Bliss & Lomo, 2000; Martinez & Derrick, 1996; Nguyen et al., 1994). (*Potentiate* means "to make potent, or to strengthen.") Long-term potentiation does not take place unless both the sending neurons and the receiving neurons are activated at the same time by intense stimulation. Also, the receiving neuron must be depolarized (ready to fire) when the stimulation occurs, or LTP will not happen. LTP is common in the hippocampal region, which, as you have learned, is essential in the formation of declarative memories (Eichenbaum & Otto, 1993).

◆ **long-term potentiation (LTP)**

An increase in the efficiency of neural transmission at the synapses that lasts for hours or longer.

If the changes in synapses produced by LTP are the same changes that take place during learning, then blocking or preventing LTP should interfere with learning. And it does. When Davis and others (1992) gave rats a drug that blocks certain receptors in doses large enough to interfere with a maze-running task, they discovered that LTP in the rats' hippocampi was also disrupted. In contrast, Riedel (1996) found that LTP was enhanced and the rats' memory improved when a drug that excites those same receptors was administered shortly after maze training.

Hormones and Memory

◆ How do hormones influence memory?

The strongest and most lasting memories are usually those fueled by emotion. Research by Cahill and McGaugh (1995) suggests that there may be two pathways for forming memories—one for ordinary information and another for memories that are fired by emotion. When a person is emotionally aroused, the adrenal glands release the hormones epinephrine (adrenalin) and norepinephrine (noradrenaline) into the bloodstream. Long known to be involved in the "fight-or-flight response," these hormones enable humans to survive, and they also imprint powerful and enduring memories of the circumstances surrounding threatening situations. Such emotionally laden memories activate the amygdala (known to play a central role in emotion) and other parts of the memory system. This widespread activation in the brain may be the most important factor in explaining the intensity and durability of flashbulb memories.

Other hormones may have important effects on memory. Excessive levels of the stress hormone *cortisol*, for example, have been shown to interfere with memory in patients who suffer from diseases of the adrenal glands, the site of cortisol production (Jelicic & Bonke, 2001). Furthermore, people whose bodies react to experimenter-induced stressors, such as forced public speaking, by releasing higher than average levels of cortisol perform less well on memory tests than those whose bodies release lower than average levels in the same situations (Al'absi et al., 2002).

Estrogen, the female sex hormone, appears to improve working memory efficiency (Dohanich, 2003). This hormone, along with others produced by the ovaries, also plays some role in the development and maintenance of synapses in areas of the brain known to be associated with memory (e.g, the hippocampus). This finding caused researchers to hypothesize that hormone replacement therapy might prevent or reverse the effects of Alzheimer's disease (Dohanich, 2003). However, recent research shows that postmenopausal women who take a combination of synthetic estrogen and progesterone, the two hormones that regulate the menstrual cycle, may actually increase their risk of developing dementia (Rapp et al., 2003; Shumaker et al., 2003). Some researchers have explained these seemingly contradictory findings by claiming that the timing of estrogen replacement is the most critical factor in its effect on memory function (Marriott & Wenk, 2004). They think that women who take estrogen before developing symptoms of Alzheimer's disease may be more likely to benefit from it than those who receive hormone replacement therapy after they have been diagnosed with the disease. Most researchers agree, however, that much more research is needed to ascertain the definitive role of hormone treatment in the prevention and treatment of dementia.

The strongest and most lasting memories are usually fueled by emotion. That's why most people have vivid memories of the events and circumstances that surround the experience of falling in love.

Forgetting

Wouldn't it be depressing if you remembered in exact detail every bad thing that ever happened to you? Most people think of forgetting as a problem to be overcome, but it's actually not always unwelcome. Still, when you need to remember particular information to answer an exam question, forgetting can be very frustrating.

Ebbinghaus and the First Experimental Studies on Forgetting

◆ *What did Ebbinghaus discover about forgetting?*

Hermann Ebbinghaus (1850–1909) conducted the first experimental studies on learning and memory. He performed his studies on memory using 2,300 nonsense syllables as his material and himself as the only participant (1885/1964). He carried out all his experiments at about the same time of day in the same surroundings, eliminating all possible distractions. Ebbinghaus memorized lists of nonsense syllables (strings of letters such as LEJ and XIZ) by repeating them over and over at a constant rate of 2.5 syllables per second, marking time with a metronome or a ticking watch. He repeated a list until he could recall it twice without error, a measure he called *mastery*.

Ebbinghaus recorded the amount of time or the number of trials it took to memorize his lists to mastery. Then, after different periods of time had passed and forgetting had occurred, he recorded the amount of time or number of trials needed to relearn the same list to mastery. Ebbinghaus compared the time or number of trials required for relearning with that for original learning and then computed the percentage of time saved. This savings score represented the percentage of the original learning that remained in memory.

Ebbinghaus learned and relearned more than 1,200 lists of nonsense syllables to discover how rapidly forgetting occurs. Figure 6.6 shows his famous curve of forgetting, which consists of savings scores at various time intervals after the original learning. The curve of forgetting shows that the largest amount of forgetting occurs very quickly, after which forgetting tapers off. Of the information Ebbinghaus retained after a day or two, very little more would be forgotten even a month later. But, remember, this curve of forgetting applies to nonsense syllables. Meaningful material is usually forgotten more slowly, as is material that has been carefully encoded, deeply processed, and frequently rehearsed.

FIGURE 6.6

Ebbinghaus's Curve of Forgetting

After memorizing lists of nonsense syllables similar to those at left, Ebbinghaus measured his retention after varying intervals of time using the relearning method. Forgetting was most rapid at first, as shown by his retention of only 58% after 20 minutes and 44% after 1 hour. Then, the rate of forgetting tapered off, with a retention of 34% after 1 day, 25% after 6 days, and 21% after 31 days. *Source:* Data from Ebbinghaus (1885/1964, 1913).

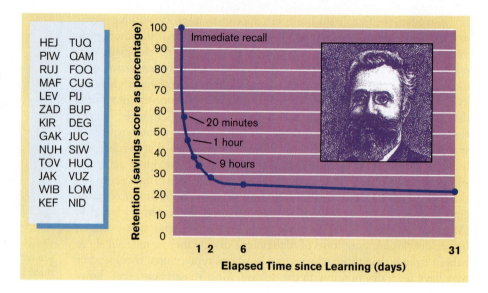

What Ebbinghaus learned about the rate of forgetting is relevant for everyone. Do you, like most students, cram before a big exam? If so, don't assume that everything you memorize on Monday can be held intact until Tuesday. So much forgetting occurs within the first 24 hours that it is wise to spend at least some time reviewing the material on the day of the test. The less meaningful the material is to you, the more you will forget and the more necessary a review is. Recall from Chapter 4 that the quantity and quality of sleep you get between studying and taking the test also influences how much you will remember.

The Causes of Forgetting

◆ *What causes forgetting?*

Why do we fail to remember, even when we put forth a lot of effort aimed at remembering? One possibility is that the item was never stored in memory to begin with. Of course, there is a distinction between forgetting and not being able to remember. *Forgetting* is the inability to recall something that you could recall previously. But often when people say they cannot remember, they have not actually forgotten. The inability to remember is sometimes a result of **encoding failure**—the information was never put into long-term memory in the first place.

Of the many things we encounter every day, it is surprising how little we actually encode. Can you recall accurately, or even recognize, something you have seen thousands of times before? Read *Try It 6.1* to find out.

In your lifetime, you have seen thousands of pennies, but unless you are a coin collector, you probably have not encoded the details of a penny's appearance. If you did poorly on the *Try It*, you have plenty of company. After studying a large group of participants, Nickerson and Adams (1979) reported that few people could reproduce a penny from recall. In fact, only a handful of participants could even recognize an accurate drawing of a penny when it was presented along with incorrect drawings. (The correct penny is the one labeled A in the *Try It*.)

Decay theory, which is probably the oldest theory of forgetting, assumes that memories, if not used, fade with time and ultimately disappear entirely. The word *decay* implies a physiological change in the neurons that recorded the experience. According to this theory, the neuronal record may decay or fade within seconds, days, or even much longer periods of time. While decay, or the fading of memories, is probably a cause of forgetting in sensory and short-term memory, there does not appear to be a gradual, inevitable decay of long-term memories. In one study, Harry Bahrick and others (1975) found that after 35 years, participants could recognize 90% of their high school classmates' names and photographs, the same percentage as for recent graduates.

◆ **encoding failure**

A cause of forgetting that occurs when information was never put into long-term memory.

◆ **decay theory**

The oldest theory of forgetting, which holds that memories, if not used, fade with time and ultimately disappear altogether.

Try It 6.1

A Penny for Your Thoughts

On a sheet of paper, draw a sketch of a U.S. penny from memory using recall. In your drawing, show the direction in which President Lincoln's image is facing and the location of the date, and include all the words on the "heads" side of the penny. Or try the easier recognition task and see if you can recognize the real penny in the drawings below. (From Nickerson & Adams, 1979.)

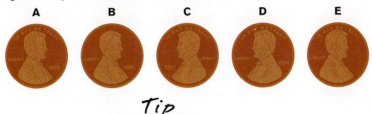

A   B   C   D   E

Tip

The next time someone you know claims to have "photographic" memory, use this *Try It* to put him or her to the test.

A major cause of forgetting that affects people every day is **interference.** Whenever you try to recall any given memory, two types of interference can hinder the effort. Information or associations stored either *before* or *after* a given memory can interfere with the ability to remember it (see Figure 6.7). Interference can reach either forward or backward in time to affect memory—it gets us coming and going. Also, the more similar the interfering associations are to the information a person is trying to recall, the more difficult it is to recall the information (Underwood, 1964).

Proactive interference occurs when information or experiences already stored in long-term memory hinder the ability to remember newer information (Underwood, 1957). For example, Laura's romance with her new boyfriend, Todd, got off to a bad start when she accidentally called him "Dave," her former boyfriend's name. One explanation for proactive interference is the competition between old and new responses (Bower et al., 1994).

Retroactive interference happens when new learning interferes with the ability to remember previously learned information. The more similar the new material is to that learned earlier, the more interference there is. For example, when you take a psychology class, it may interfere with your ability to remember what you learned in your sociology class, especially with regard to theories (e.g., psychoanalysis) that are shared by the two disciplines but applied and interpreted differently. However, research shows that the effects of retroactive interference are often temporary (Lustig et al., 2004). In fact, after some time has passed, the old information may be better remembered than the information that was learned more recently. As a consequence, what a student learned in a previous sociology course may appear to fade when she encounters similar information presented in a somewhat different light in a psychology course. In the long run, however, her sociology knowledge may outlast what she learned in psychology.

Consolidation is the process by which encoded information is stored in memory. When a disruption in this process occurs, a long-term memory usually does not form. **Consolidation failure** can result from anything that causes a person to lose consciousness—a car accident, a blow to the head, a grand mal epileptic seizure, or an electroconvulsive shock treatment given for severe depression. Memory loss of the experiences that occurred shortly before the loss of consciousness is called **retrograde amnesia.**

Researchers Nader and others (2000) demonstrated that conditioned fears in rats can be erased by infusing into the rats' brains a drug that prevents protein synthesis (such synthesis is necessary for memory consolidation). Rats experienced a single pairing of a tone (the conditioned stimulus, CS) and a foot shock (the unconditioned stimulus, US).

◆ **interference**
A cause of forgetting that occurs because information or associations stored either before or after a given memory hinder the ability to remember it.

◆ **consolidation failure**
Any disruption in the consolidation process that prevents a long-term memory from forming.

◆ **retrograde amnesia**
(RET-ro-grade) A loss of memory for experiences that occurred shortly before a loss of consciousness.

FIGURE 6.7 **Retroactive and Proactive Interference**

As shown in Example 1, retroactive interference occurs when new learning hinders the ability to recall information learned previously. As shown in Example 2, proactive interference occurs when prior learning hinders new learning.

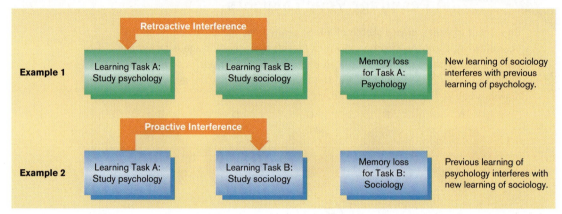

Later, the rats were exposed to the sound of the tone alone (CS) and showed a fear response, "freezing" (becoming totally immobile as if frozen with fright). Clearly, the rats remembered the feared stimulus. Twenty-four hours later, the rats were again exposed to the tone alone, and it elicited fear, causing them to freeze. Immediately, the drug anisomycin, which prevents protein synthesis in the brain, was infused into the rats' amygdalae (the part of the brain that processes fear stimuli). After the drug was infused, the rats were shocked again, but they showed no fear response (freezing). The rats in the study had already consolidated the memory of the fear, but it was completely wiped out after the drug prevented protein synthesis from occurring. This means that fear memories, once activated, must be "reconsolidated," or they may disappear.

We have discussed ways to avoid forgetting, but there are occasions when people may want to avoid remembering—times when they want to forget. Victims of rape or physical abuse, war veterans, and survivors of airplane crashes or earthquakes all have had terrifying experiences that may haunt them for years. These victims are certainly motivated to forget their traumatic experiences, but even people who have not suffered any trauma use **motivated forgetting** to protect themselves from experiences that are painful, frightening, or otherwise unpleasant.

With one form of motivated forgetting, *suppression*, a person makes a conscious, active attempt to put a painful, disturbing, anxiety- or guilt-provoking memory out of mind, but the person is still aware that the painful event occurred. With another type of motivated forgetting, **repression**, unpleasant memories are literally removed from consciousness, and the person is no longer aware that the unpleasant event ever occurred (Freud, 1922). People who have **amnesia** (partial or complete memory loss) that is not due to loss of consciousness or brain damage have repressed the events they no longer remember. Motivated forgetting is probably used by more people than any other method to deal with unpleasant memories. It seems to be a natural human tendency to forget the unpleasant circumstances of life and to remember the pleasant ones (Linton, 1979; Meltzer, 1930). However, as you learned earlier in the chapter, most psychologists believe that unpleasant events are more likely to be remembered than to be repressed.

Prospective forgetting—not remembering to carry out some intended action (e.g., forgetting to go to your dentist appointment)—is another type of motivated forgetting. People are most likely to forget to do the things they view as unimportant, unpleasant, or burdensome. They are less likely to forget things that are pleasurable or important to them (Winograd, 1988). However, as you probably know, prospective forgetting isn't always motivated by a desire to avoid something. Have you ever arrived home and suddenly remembered that you had intended to go to the bank to deposit your paycheck? Or you may have seen a review of a concert in the newspaper and suddenly remembered that you had intended to buy a ticket for it. In such cases, prospective forgetting is more likely to be the result of interference or consolidation failure.

◆ **motivated forgetting**

Forgetting through suppression or repression in an effort to protect oneself from material that is painful, frightening, or otherwise unpleasant.

◆ **repression**

Completely removing unpleasant memories from one's consciousness, so that one is no longer aware that a painful event occurred.

◆ **amnesia**

A partial or complete loss of memory due to loss of consciousness, brain damage, or some psychological cause.

◆ **prospective forgetting**

Not remembering to carry out some intended action.

How many times has this experience happened to you? While taking a test, you can't remember the answer to a question that you are sure you know. Often, people are certain they know something, but are not able to retrieve the information when they need it. This type of forgetting is called **retrieval failure.** A common experience with retrieval failure is known as the *tip-of-the-tongue (TOT) phenomenon* (Brown & McNeil, 1966). You have surely experienced trying to recall a name, a word, or some other bit of information, knowing that you knew it but not able to come up with it. You were on the verge of recalling the word or name, perhaps aware of the number of syllables and the beginning or ending letter. It was on the tip of your tongue, but it just wouldn't quite come out.

Improving Memory

◆ *How can organization, overlearning, spaced practice, and recitation improve memory?*

Have you ever wished there was a magic pill you could take before studying for an exam, one that would make you remember everything in your textbook and lecture notes? Sorry, but there are no magic formulas for improving your memory. Remembering is a skill that, like any other, requires knowledge and practice. How information is organized strongly influences your ability to remember it. For example, almost anyone can name the months of the year in about 10 seconds, but how long would it take to recall them in alphabetical order? These 12 well-known items are much harder to retrieve in alphabetical order, because they are not organized that way in memory. Similarly, you are giving your memory an extremely difficult task if you try to remember large amounts of information in a haphazard fashion. Try to organize items you want to remember in alphabetical order, or according to categories, historical sequence, size, or shape, or in any other way that will make retrieval easier for you.

Do you still remember the words to songs that were popular when you were in high school? You probably can because of **overlearning**, practicing or studying material beyond the point where it can be repeated once without error. Research suggests that people remember material better and longer if they overlearn it (Ebbinghaus, 1885/1964). A pioneering study in overlearning by Krueger (1929) showed very substantial long-term gains for participants who engaged in 50% and 100% overlearning (see Figure 6.8). Furthermore, overlearning makes material more resistant to interference and is perhaps the best insurance against stress-related forgetting. So, the next time you study for a test, don't stop studying as soon as you think you know the material. Spend another hour or so going over it, using features of your textbook such as margin questions and end-of-chapter review questions; you will be surprised at how much more you will remember.

Most students have tried cramming for examinations, but spacing study over several sessions is generally more effective than **massed practice,** learning in one long practice session without rest periods (Glover & Corkill, 1987). You will remember more with less total study time if you engage in **spaced practice**, learning in short practice sessions with rest periods in between. Long periods of memorizing make material particularly subject to interference and often result in fatigue and lowered concentration. When you space your practice, you probably create new memories that may be stored in different places, thus increasing your chances for recall. The spacing effect applies to learning motor skills as well as to learning facts and information. Music students can tell you that it is better to practice for half an hour each day, every day, than to practice many hours in a row once a week.

Do you ever reread a chapter just before a test? Research over many years shows that you will recall more if you increase the amount of recitation in your study. For example, it is better to read a page or a few paragraphs and then recite or practice recalling what you have just read. Then, continue reading, stop and practice reciting again, and so on. When you study for a psychology test and review the assigned chapter, try to answer each of the questions in the *Summary* section at the end of the chapter. Then, read the material that follows each question and check whether you answered the question correctly. This will be your safeguard against encoding failure. Don't simply read each section and assume that you can answer the question. Test yourself before your professor does.

◆ **retrieval failure**
Not remembering something one is certain of knowing.

◆ **overlearning**
Practicing or studying material beyond the point where it can be repeated once without error.

◆ **massed practice**
Learning in one long practice session without rest periods.

◆ **spaced practice**
Learning in short practice sessions with rest periods in between.

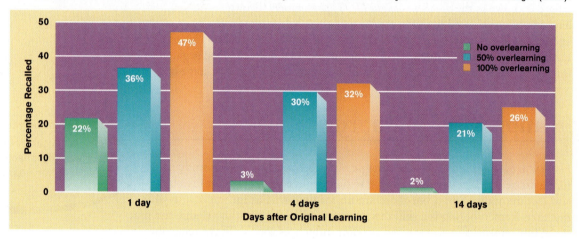

FIGURE 6.8 **Overlearning**

When a person learns material only to the point of one correct repetition, forgetting is very rapid. Just 22% is retained after 1 day, 3% after 4 days, and 2% after 14 days. When participants spend 50% more time going over the material, the retention increases to 36% after 1 day, 30% after 4 days, and 21% after 14 days. *Source:* Data from Krueger (1929).

Review and Reflect 6.1 provides examples for each of the memory improvement techniques discussed in this section, and the *Apply It 6.1* tells you how to use *mnemonics* to improve your memory even more.

REVIEW *and* REFLECT 6.1

Examples of Strategies for Improving Memory

STRATEGY	EXAMPLE
Organization	Write each heading and subheading of a textbook chapter on an index card; take notes on each section and subsection on the cards; keep them in order by chapter and use them to review for exams.
Overlearning	Memorize information that is easily organized into a list (e.g., the functions associated with the left and right cerebral hemispheres) until you can recall each item on the list automatically without error.
Spaced practice	When you have an hour to study, break it up into three 15-minute study periods with 5-minute breaks between them.
Recitation	After you finish studying this *Review and Reflect* table, close your eyes and see how much of the information you can repeat aloud.

Looking Back   Do you recall the discussion of Franco Magnani's paintings at the beginning of the chapter? If so, then you should recognize that the childhood memories depicted in his paintings are what memory scientists call reconstructions. Working memory is the part of the system in which these reconstructions are built, drawing on information stored in both declarative and nondeclarative memory. Schemas, too, play a role in the process. Of course, reconstructions that allow an artist to imbue a painted memory with warmth and good feelings help to make life more enjoyable. But reconstructions that cause innocent individuals to be convicted of crimes or that allow the guilty to escape can result in tragedy. A good understanding of how the memory system works, therefore, can help us both appreciate the benefits and guard against the pitfalls of the pattern of fiction intermingled with truth that characterizes so many of our memories.

Apply It 6.1 Improving Memory with Mnemonic Devices

Writing notes, making lists, writing on a calendar, or keeping an appointment book is often more reliable and accurate than trusting to memory (Intons-Peterson & Fournier, 1986). But what if you need information at some unpredictable time, when you do not have external aids handy? Several *mnemonics,* or memory devices, have been developed over the years to aid memory (Bower, 1973; Higbee, 1977; Roediger, 1980).

Rhyme

Rhymes are a common aid to remembering material that otherwise might be difficult to recall. Perhaps as a child you learned to recite "*i* before *e* except after *c*" when you were trying to spell a word containing that vowel combination.

The Method of Loci

The *method of loci* is a mnemonic device that can be used when you want to remember a list of items such as a grocery list, or when you give a speech or a class report and need to make your points in order without using notes. The word *loci* (pronounced "LOH-sye") is the plural form of *locus,* which means "location" or "place."

Figure 6.9 shows how to use the method of loci. Select any familiar place—your home, for example—and simply associate the items to be remembered with locations there. Progress in an orderly fashion. For example, visualize the first item or idea you want to remember in its place on the driveway, the second in the garage, the third at the front door, and so on, until you have associated each item you want to remember with a specific location. You may find it helpful to conjure up oversized images of the items that you place at each location. When you want to recall the items, take an imaginary walk starting at the first place—the first item will pop into your mind. When you think of the second place, the second item will come to mind, and so on.

The First-letter Technique

Another useful technique is to take the first letter of each item to be remembered and form a word, a phrase, or a sentence with those letters (Matlin, 1989). For example, suppose you had to memorize the seven colors of the visible spectrum in their proper order:

Red

Orange

Yellow

Green

Blue

Indigo

Violet

You could make your task easier by using the first letter of each color to form the name Roy G. Biv. Three chunks are easier to remember than seven different items.

(continued on page 192)

FIGURE 6.9 The Method of Loci

Begin by thinking of locations, perhaps in your home, that are in a sequence. Then, visualize one of the items to be remembered in each location.

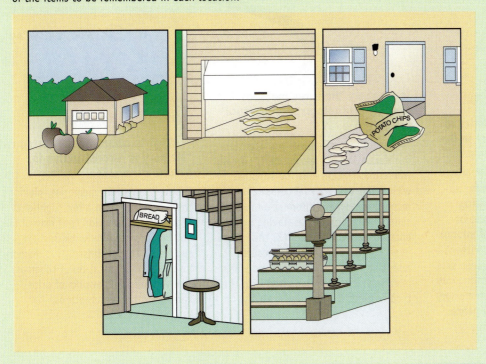

Apply It 6.1 (continued)

The Pegword System

Another mnemonic that has been proven effective is the *pegword system* (Harris & Blaiser, 1997). Developed in England around 1879, it uses rhyming words: *one = bun; two = shoe; three = tree; four = door; five = hive; six = sticks; seven = heaven; eight = gate; nine = wine;* *ten = hen*. The rhyming words are memorized in sequence and then linked through vivid associations with any items you wish to remember in order, as shown in Figure 6.10.

For example, suppose you want to remember to buy five items at the store: milk, bread, grapefruit, laundry detergent, and eggs. Begin by associating the milk with a bun (your first pegword) by picturing milk being poured over a bun. Next, picture a shoe, the second pegword, kicking a loaf of bread. Then, continue by associating each item on your list with a pegword. To recall the items, simply go through your list of pegwords, and the associated word will immediately come to mind.

FIGURE 6.10 The Pegword System

Each item to be recalled is associated with a pegword using a mental image. *Source:* Adapted from Bower (1973).

Item Number	Pegword	Peg Image	Item to Be Recalled	Connecting Image	
1	bun	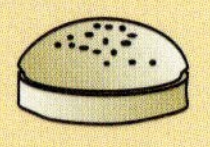	milk		*Milk* pouring onto a soggy hamburger *bun*
2	shoe		bread	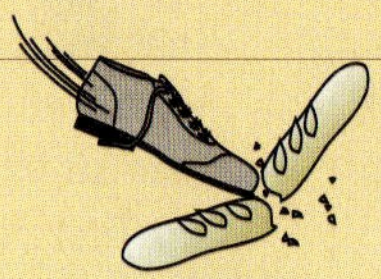	A *shoe* kicking and breaking a brittle loaf of French *bread*

Chapter 6 Summary

◆ Remembering p. 170

◆ What are the characteristics of each component of memory in the Atkinson-Shiffrin model? p. 170

Sensory memory holds information coming in through the senses for up to 2 seconds. Short-term (working) memory holds about seven (plus or minus two) unrelated items of information for less than 30 seconds without rehearsal. Short-term memory also acts as a mental workspace for carrying out any mental activity. Long-term memory is the permanent or relatively permanent memory system with virtually unlimited capacity.

◆ What are the three methods used by psychologists to measure memory? p. 173

Three methods of measuring retention of information in memory are (1) recall, where information must be supplied with few or no retrieval cues; (2) recognition, where information must simply be recognized as having been encountered before; and (3) the relearning method, which measures retention in terms of time saved when relearning material compared with the time required to learn it originally.

◆ The Nature of Remembering p. 174

◆ What is meant by the statement "Memory is reconstructive in nature"? p. 174

People reconstruct memories, piecing them together from a few highlights and using information that may or may not be accurate. Frederick Bartlett suggested that reconstructive memory involves the application of schemas, or integrated frameworks of prior knowledge and assumptions.

◆ **What conditions reduce the reliability of eyewitness testimony?** p. 176

The reliability of eyewitness testimony is reduced when witnesses view a photograph of the suspect before viewing the lineup, when members of a lineup don't sufficiently resemble each other, when members of a lineup are viewed at the same time rather than one by one, when the perpetrator's race is different from that of the eyewitness, when a weapon has been used in the crime, and when leading questions are asked to elicit information from the witness.

◆ **What is the controversy regarding the therapy used to recover repressed memories of childhood sexual abuse?** p. 177

Critics argue that therapists using hypnosis and guided imagery to help their patients recover repressed memories of childhood sexual abuse are actually implanting false memories in those patients. Therapists who use these techniques believe that a number of psychological problems can be treated successfully by helping patients recover repressed memories of sexual abuse.

◆ **What does research evidence say about flashbulb memories?** p. 179

Flashbulb memories, which are formed when a person learns of events that are surprising, shocking, or highly emotional, may not be as accurate as people believe they are.

◆ **How does culture influence memory?** p. 180

The existence of oral historians in some cultures suggests that the ability to remember certain kinds of material may be influenced by culture. In addition, we more easily remember stories set in our own culture.

◆ **What happens when information must be recalled in the order in which it was presented?** p. 181

The serial position effect is the tendency, when recalling a list of items, to remember the items at the beginning of the list (primacy effect) and the items at the end of the list (recency effect) better than items in the middle.

◆ **How do environmental conditions and emotional states influence memory?** p. 181

People tend to recall material more easily if they are in the same physical location during recall as during the original learning. The state-dependent memory effect is the tendency to recall information better if one is in the same emotional state as when the information was learned.

◆ Biology and Memory p. 182

◆ **What roles do the hippocampus and the hippocampal region play in memory?** p. 182

The hippocampus itself is involved primarily in the formation of episodic memories; the rest of the hippocampal region is involved in forming semantic memories.

◆ **Why is long-term potentiation important?** p. 184

Long-term potentiation (LTP) is a long-lasting increase in the efficiency of neural transmission at the synapses. LTP is important because it may be the basis for learning and memory at the level of the neurons.

◆ **How do hormones influence memory?** p. 184

Memories of threatening situations tend to be more powerful and enduring than ordinary memories, perhaps because of the hormones released in such situations. Estrogen may play a role in dementia.

◆ Forgetting p. 185

◆ **What did Ebbinghaus discover about forgetting?** p. 185

Ebbinghaus discovered that the largest amount of forgetting occurs very quickly, then it tapers off.

◆ **What causes forgetting?** p. 186

Encoding failure happens when an item was never stored in memory. Information that has not been retrieved from memory for a long time may fade and ultimately disappear entirely (decay theory). Consolidation failure results from a loss of consciousness as new memories are being encoded. Interference occurs when information or associations stored either before or after a given memory hinder the ability to remember it. Sometimes, we forget because we don't want to remember something, a process called motivated forgetting. At other times, an item is stored in memory, but we are unable to retrieve it (retrieval failure).

◆ Improving Memory p. 189

◆ **How can organization, overlearning, spaced practice, and recitation improve memory?** p. 189

Organization, as in using outlines based on chapter headings, provides retrieval cues for information. Overlearning means practicing or studying material beyond the point where it can be repeated once without error. You remember overlearned material better and longer, and it is more resistant to interference and stress-related forgetting. Short study sessions at different times (spaced practice) allow time for consolidation of new information. Recitation of newly learned material is more effective than simply rereading it.

amnesia, p. 188
anterograde amnesia, p. 183
chunking, p. 171
consolidation, p. 170
consolidation failure, p. 187
decay theory, p. 186
declarative memory, p. 173
displacement, p. 171
elaborative rehearsal, p. 172
encoding, p. 170
encoding failure, p. 186
episodic memory, p. 173
flashbulb memory, p. 179
hippocampal region, p. 182
infantile amnesia, p. 178

interference, p. 187
long-term memory (LTM), p. 172
long-term potentiation (LTP), p. 184
maintenance rehearsal, p. 172
massed practice, p. 189
memory, p. 170
motivated forgetting, p. 188
nondeclarative memory, p. 173
overlearning, p. 189
primacy effect, p. 181
prospective forgetting, p. 188
recall, p. 173
recency effect, p. 181
recognition, p. 173
reconstruction, p. 174

rehearsal, p. 171
relearning method, p. 174
repression, p. 188
retrieval, p. 170
retrieval cue, p. 173
retrieval failure, p. 189
retrograde amnesia, p. 187
schemas, p. 174
semantic memory, p. 173
sensory memory, p. 170
serial position effect, p. 181
short-term memory (STM), p. 171
spaced practice, p. 189
state-dependent memory effect, p. 182
storage, p. 170

Study Guide 6

Answers to all the Study Guide questions are provided at the end of the book.

◆ SECTION ONE: Chapter Review

Remembering (pp. 170–174)

1. Transforming information into a form that can be stored in memory is called _____; bringing to mind the material that has been stored is called

   _____.
   a. encoding; decoding
   b. consolidation; retrieval
   c. consolidation; decoding
   d. encoding; retrieval

2. Match the memory system with the best description of its capacity and the duration of time it holds information.
   ____ (1) sensory memory
   ____ (2) short-term memory
   ____ (3) long-term memory
   a. virtually unlimited capacity; long duration
   b. large capacity; short duration
   c. very limited capacity; short duration

3. Match each example with the appropriate memory system:
   ____ (1) semantic memory
   ____ (2) episodic memory
   ____ (3) nondeclarative memory
   a. movements involved in playing tennis
   b. names of the presidents of the United States
   c. what you did during spring break last year

4. In which subsystem of long-term memory are responses that make up motor skills stored?
   a. episodic memory   c. nondeclarative memory
   b. semantic memory   d. declarative memory

5. Which of the following methods can detect learning when other methods cannot?
   a. recall   c. relearning
   b. recognition   d. retrieval

6. Match the example with the corresponding method of measuring retention:
   ____ (1) identifying a suspect in a lineup
   ____ (2) answering a fill-in-the-blank question on a test
   ____ (3) having to study less for a comprehensive final exam than for all of the previous exams put together
   ____ (4) answering questions in this Study Guide
   ____ (5) reciting one's lines in a play
   a. recognition   b. relearning   c. recall

The Nature of Remembering (pp. 174–182)

7. What early memory researcher proposed the concept of the schema?
   a. Freud   c. Bartlett
   b. Ebbinghaus   d. Skinner

8. Which of the following is *not* true of schemas?
   a. Schemas are the integrated frameworks of knowledge and assumptions a person has about people, objects, and events.
   b. Schemas affect the way a person encodes information.
   c. Schemas affect the way a person retrieves information.
   d. When a person uses schemas, memories are always accurate.

9. There are fewer errors in eyewitness testimony if
   a. eyewitnesses are identifying a person of their own race.
   b. eyewitnesses view suspects' photos prior to a lineup.
   c. a weapon has been used in the crime.
   d. questions are phrased to provide retrieval cues for the eyewitness.

10. As a rule, people's memories are more accurate under hypnosis. (true/false)

11. When you remember where you were and what you were doing when you received a shocking piece of news, you are experiencing
    a. flashbulb memory.   c. semantic imagery.
    b. sensory memory.   d. interference.

12. When children learn the alphabet, they often learn "A, B, C, D" and "W, X, Y, Z" before learning the letters in between. This is due to the
    a. primacy effect.   c. serial position effect.
    b. recency effect.   d. state-dependent memory.

13. Recall is best when it takes place in the same context in which information was learned. (true/false)

14. Scores on recognition tests (either multiple-choice or true/false) will be higher if testing and learning take place in the same physical environment. (true/false)

15. Which best explains why information learned when one is feeling anxious is best recalled when experiencing feelings of anxiety?
    a. consistency effect
    b. state-dependent memory effect
    c. context-dependent effect
    d. consolidation failure

16. Compared to nondepressed people, depressed people tend to have more sad memories. (true/false)

Biology and Memory (pp. 182–185)

17. H.M. retained his ability to add to his nondeclarative memory. (true/false)

18. The hippocampus itself is involved primarily in the formation of _____ memories; the entire hippocampal region is involved primarily in the formation of _____ memories.

19. What is the term for the long-lasting increase in the efficiency of neural transmission at the synapses that may be the basis for learning and memory at the level of the neurons?
    a. long-term potentiation
    b. synaptic facilitation
    c. synaptic potentiation
    d. presynaptic potentiation

20. Memories of circumstances surrounding threatening situations that elicit the "fight-or-flight response" tend to be more powerful and enduring than ordinary memories. (true/false)

Forgetting (pp. 185–189)

21. Who plotted the curve of forgetting?
    a. George Sperling   c. Frederick Bartlett
    b. H. E. Burtt   d. Hermann Ebbinghaus

22. The curve of forgetting shows that memory loss
    a. occurs most rapidly at first and then levels off to a slow decline.
    b. begins to occur about 3 to 4 hours after learning.
    c. occurs at a fairly steady rate over a month's time.
    d. occurs slowly at first and increases steadily over a month's time.

23. Match the example with the appropriate cause of forgetting.
    ____ (1) encoding failure
    ____ (2) consolidation failure
    ____ (3) retrieval failure
    ____ (4) repression
    ____ (5) interference
    a. failing to remember the answer on a test until after you turn in the test
    b. forgetting a humiliating childhood experience
    c. not being able to describe the back of a dollar bill
    d. calling a friend by someone else's name
    e. waking up in the hospital and not remembering you had an automobile accident

24. To minimize interference, it is best to follow learning with
    a. rest.   c. sleep.
    b. recreation.   d. unrelated study.

25. Most psychologists accept decay theory as a good explanation for the loss of information from long-term memory. (true/false)

26. According to the text, the major cause of forgetting is interference. (true/false)

Improving Memory (pp. 189–190)

27. When studying for an exam, it is best to spend
    a. more time reciting than rereading.
    b. more time rereading than reciting.
    c. equal time rereading and reciting.
    d. all of the time reciting rather than rereading.

28. The ability to recite a number of nursery rhymes from childhood is probably due mainly to
    a. spaced practice.
    b. organization.
    c. mnemonics.
    d. overlearning.

◆ SECTION TWO: Complete the Diagrams

Fill in the blanks in each diagram with the missing words.

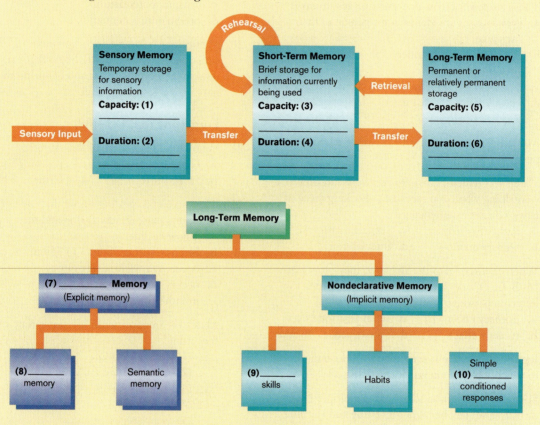

◆ SECTION THREE: Fill In the Blank

1. The first step in the memory process is _____.

2. Short-term memory seems to have a limited life span—less than 30 seconds. If you want to keep a phone number in short-term memory, you will need to use some form of _____, such as repeating the number several times.

3. Another name for short-term memory is _____ memory.

4. When people talk about memory, they are usually talking about _____-term memory.

5. When you take a test in your psychology class, you may be asked to list the names of famous psychologists and their major contributions to psychology. For this task you would use _____ memory.

6. A fill-in-the-blank question requires you to _____ the correct answers.

7. In a list of items, those in the _____ position are the items least easily remembered.

8. The _____ _____ memory effect is the tendency to remember best when in the same physical or psychological state as when the information was encoded.

9. The _____ _____ of the brain appears to be very important in the formation of long-term memory.

10. One theory of memory suggests that neural transmission becomes more efficient at certain synapses along neural paths. This increase in transmission efficiency is known as long-term _____.

11. The capacity of short-term memory can be expanded through the use of _____.
    a. long-term potentiation
    b. working memory
    c. chunking
    d. retrieval consolidation

12. A patient survived delicate brain surgery and displayed no signs of personality change or loss of intelligence. Days after the surgery, the doctor realized that the patient was unable to form long-term memories. He was, however, able to remember everything from before the surgery. The patient was diagnosed as having _____ _____.

13. When Raquel moved to a new town, she had trouble remembering her new ZIP code. Every time she tried to think of her new ZIP code, her old ZIP code seemed to interfere with her recall. This is probably an example of _____ interference.

14. A patient cannot remember the period of his life ranging from age 5 through 7. A doctor can find no physical cause for this amnesia. The patient also has no history of injury or other trauma at any age. This is very likely a case of _____.

15. Serge found himself in trouble during his physics test—he could not remember the formulas from class. He realized that he should have been paying more attention during the lectures. His current memory problem is probably due to _____ failure.

16. Pete started studying for his psychology test six nights ago, spending about 45 minutes per night. Fiona studied for her test all in one night, in a nonstop, 6-hour study session. Pete got a better grade on the test than Fiona. Fiona used a study technique called _____ practice, a strategy that is usually not as effective as spacing sessions.

17. When you study for your next psychology test, you may want to study beyond the point where you think you know the material. If you repeat or rehearse the material over and over, you will probably remember it better. This study technique is known as _____.

◆ SECTION FOUR: Comprehensive Practice Test

1. The first step in the memory process is known as _____, when information is transformed into a form that can be stored in short-term memory.
    a. retrieval   c. encoding
    b. storage   d. rehearsal

2. The process in which information is stored in permanent memory involves a change in the brain's physiology. This change is known as
    a. consolidation.
    b. transformation.
    c. hippocampal transformation.
    d. recalcitration.

3. You are at a party and meet someone you are really interested in. You get that person's phone number but have no way to write it down, so you use the process of _____ to get it into memory.
    a. encoding   c. rehearsal
    b. latent retrieval   d. recalcitration

4. The kind of memory that has a large capacity but a very short duration is _____ memory.
    a. short-term   c. long-term
    b. sensory   d. temporary

5. Alice's ability to remember all the actions required to ride her motorcycle is due to her repetitive practice, to the point where riding it is almost reflexive. Any set of skills acquired this way is part of _____ memory.

6. Implicit memory is to explicit memory as _____ are to _____.
    a. motor skills; facts and information
    b. episodic memories; semantic memories
    c. semantic memories; episodic memories
    d. facts and information; motor skills

7. Cristina and her friends were talking about some great times they had in high school. Recounting those stories as if they had happened yesterday, the friends were relying on _____ memory.
    a. semantic   c. personal
    b. implicit   d. episodic

8. You use _____ memory when you answer questions such as "What is the capital of California?"
    a. episodic   c. geographic
    b. semantic   d. flashbulb

9. An example of good recall is doing well on an essay test. (true/false)

10. An example of good recognition ability is doing well on a fill-in-the-blank test. (true/false)

11. Freud did extensive research on memory. He used nonsense syllables to determine forgetting curves. (true/false)

12. When she was 16 years old, Sarah was severely injured in a car accident and was unconscious for 14 days. She can remember nothing immediately preceding the accident. This is known as _____ amnesia.
   a. trauma
   b. retroactive
   c. proactive
   d. retrograde

13. With retroactive interference, _____ information interferes with _____ information.
   a. new; old
   b. old; new
   c. unpleasant; pleasant
   d. factual; emotional

14. Using _____, a person removes an unpleasant memory from consciousness.
   a. regression
   b. traumatic amnesia
   c. repression
   d. degeneration

15. Penfield's hypothesis that memory functions like a tape recorder has been supported by research. (true/false)

16. Psychologists doubt the validity of people's recovered memories of having been abused in infancy because the hippocampal region of the infant brain is not sufficiently developed to form such memories. (true/false)

17. Experts say that overlearning is basically a waste of time—that is, after you have gone over material once, you will not benefit from further study. (true/false)

18. It appears that the _____ is important in the formation of episodic memory.
   a. hippocampus
   b. cerebellum
   c. amygdala
   d. temporal lobe

19. Pablo's vivid memory of the day Princess Diana was killed is known as a _____ memory.
   a. histrionic
   b. flashbulb
   c. semantic
   d. retroactive

20. Eyewitnesses are more likely to identify the wrong person if the person is of a different race. (true/false)

◆ **SECTION FIVE: Critical Thinking**

1. Some studies cited in this chapter involved only one or a few participants.
   a. Select two of these studies and discuss the possible problems in drawing conclusions based on results from so few participants.
   b. Suggest several possible explanations for the findings other than those proposed by the researchers.

2. Drawing on your knowledge, formulate a plan that you can put into operation to help improve your memory and avoid the pitfalls that cause forgetting.

Cognition, Language, and Intelligence

chapter 7

Cognition

◆ How do images and concepts help us think?

◆ What is the role of heuristics in decision making?

◆ What are some basic approaches to problem solving, and how do they differ?

◆ What are some important applications of artificial intelligence technologies?

Language

◆ What are the necessary components of any language?

◆ What is the evidence concerning the capacity of animals for understanding and producing language?

◆ In what ways does language influence thinking?

◆ What are the advantages and disadvantages of learning a second language at different ages?

Intelligence

◆ How do the views of Spearman, Thurstone, Gardner, and Sternberg differ with regard to the definition of intelligence?

◆ What did Binet, Terman, and Wechsler contribute to the study of intelligence?

◆ Why are reliability, validity, standardization, and cultural bias important in intelligence testing?

◆ How do individuals who are gifted and those with mental retardation differ from others?

◆ What is the evidence supporting the nature and nurture sides of the IQ controversy?

◆ What arguments have been advanced to explain racial differences in IQ scores?

◆ In what ways do the cognitive abilities of males and females differ?

◆ How does creativity differ from other forms of cognition, and how has it been measured?

Who has the highest IQ score ever recorded on an intelligence test? The name of Albert Einstein may quickly come to mind and perhaps a host of other great thinkers of the past—perhaps mostly men. However, the person with the highest IQ score ever recorded happens to be a woman.

Marilyn Mach, born in St. Louis, Missouri, in 1946, scored an amazing 230 on the Stanford-Binet IQ test when she was a 10-year-old elementary school student. How high is a 230 IQ? The average Stanford-Binet IQ score is set at 100, and a score of 116—only about half as high as Mach's lofty score—places a person in the top 16% of the population. Not only does Mach have no peer when it comes to measured intelligence, she does not even have a competitor. Her score is nearly 30 points higher than that of her nearest rival.

Descended from the Austrian philosopher and physicist Ernst Mach, who did pioneering work in the physics of sound (Mach 1, Mach 2), Marilyn Mach added her mother's birth name as an adult and became known as Marilyn Mach vos Savant. She completed about 2 years of college courses but has no college degree. Her primary intellectual interest is creative writing, and she has written 12 books and 3 plays. Her first published work was the Omni IQ Quiz Contest. Mach lives with her husband in New York, where she writes the "Ask Marilyn" column for *Parade* magazine, lectures on intelligence, and pursues various other interests.

Now consider Dr. Robert Jarvik, the world-famous inventor of the Jarvik artificial heart.

Dr. Jarvik combined his medical knowledge and his mechanical genius to produce the world's first functioning artificial heart. But his path wasn't easy. Unlike Marilyn Mach vos Savant, Jarvik was a poor test taker. In fact, he scored too low on intelligence and admissions tests to be admitted to any medical school in the United States. Eventually, despite his low test scores, he was accepted by a medical school in Italy, where he completed his studies and received his M.D. degree. Then, he returned to practice in the United States and made his contribution to medical science—one that kept alive many gravely ill heart patients until a suitable heart transplant could be performed.

How difficult do you think it would be for Dr. Jarvik to improve his IQ test score? Well, he might ask his wife, Marilyn Mach vos Savant-Jarvik, for some help with that.

Like Dr. Jarvik, many highly creative individuals have tested poorly in school. Some of the most prominent are the famous American inventor Thomas A. Edison; Winston Churchill, whose teachers thought he was mentally limited; and even the great Albert Einstein, who was labeled a dunce in math. Consider, too, that when we talk about differences in intelligence we sometimes forget that many aspects of intelligent behavior are common to all human beings and that we share those aspects with other species as well. In this chapter, we will explore some of the universals in human thinking as well as the most important aid to thinking we have—language. Afterward, we will return to the topic of individual differences in intelligence.

Cognition

All of us have an idea of what thinking is. We say, "I think it's going to rain" (a prediction) and "I think this is the right answer" (a decision). But our everyday use of the word *think* obscures the fact that thinking actually involves a number of coordinated subprocesses. Psychologists use the term **cognition** to refer collectively to these processes, which include acquiring, storing, retrieving, and using information (Matlin, 1989). You have already learned about some of them (sensation, perception, and memory) in earlier chapters. Now we turn our attention to some of the other cognitive processes.

Imagery and Concepts

Can you imagine hearing a recording of your favorite song or someone calling your name? In doing such a thing, you take advantage of your own ability to use mental **imagery**—that is, to represent or picture a sensory experience.

According to psychologist Stephen Kosslyn (1988), we mentally construct our images of objects one part at a time. Stored memories of how the parts of an object look are retrieved and assembled in working memory to form a complete image. Such images can be directly analogous to the real world or they can be creative. In the *Apply It* box in Chapter 6, you read about several mnemonic devices that rely on imagery. Such images can be extremely helpful to memory. For example, to remember that the independent variable is the one in an experiment that is manipulated by the experimenter, you might imagine a puppeteer with a large "I" on his forehead manipulating a marionette.

Images can also be helpful in learning or maintaining motor skills. Brain-imaging studies show that, in general, the same brain areas are activated whether a person is performing a given task or mentally rehearsing the same task using imagery (Lotze et al., 1999; Richter et al., 2000; Stephan et al., 1995). Thus, it isn't surprising that professionals whose work involves repetitive physical actions, such as musicians and athletes, use imaging effectively. One remarkable demonstration of the power of imagery may be found in the case of professional pianist Liu Chi Kung, who was imprisoned for 7 years during China's cultural revolution. He mentally rehearsed all the pieces he knew every day and was able to play them all immediately following his release (Garfield, 1986).

The ability to form concepts is another important aid to thinking. A **concept** is a mental category used to represent a class or group of objects, people, organizations, events, situations, or relations that share common characteristics or attributes. *Furniture, tree, student, college,* and *wedding* are all examples of concepts. As fundamental units of thought, concepts are useful tools that help us to order our world and to think and communicate with speed and efficiency.

Thanks to our ability to use concepts, we are not forced to consider and describe everything in great detail before we make an identification. If you see a hairy, brown-and-white, four-legged animal with its mouth open, tongue hanging out, and tail wagging, you recognize it immediately as a representative of the concept *dog. Dog* is a concept that stands for a class of animals that share similar characteristics or attributes, even though they may differ in significant ways. Great Danes, dachshunds, collies, Chihuahuas, and other breeds—you recognize all these varied creatures as fitting into the concept *dog.* Moreover, the concepts we form do not exist in isolation, but rather in hierarchies. For example, dogs represent one subset of the concept animal; at a higher level, animals are a subset of the concept *living things.* Thus, concept formation has a certain logic to it.

Psychologists identify two basic types of concepts: formal (also known as artificial) concepts and natural (also known as fuzzy) concepts. A **formal concept** is one that is clearly defined by a set of rules, a formal definition, or a classification system. Most of the concepts we form and use are **natural concepts,** acquired not from definitions but

◆ cognition
The mental processes that are involved in acquiring, storing, retrieving, and using information and that include sensation, perception, imagery, concept formation, reasoning, decision making, problem solving, and language.

◆ *How do imagery and concepts help us think?*

◆ imagery
The representation in the mind of a sensory experience—visual, auditory, gustatory, motor, olfactory, or tactile.

Many professional athletes use visualization to improve performance.

◆ concept
A mental category used to represent a class or group of objects, people, organizations, events, situations, or relations that share common characteristics or attributes.

◆ formal concept
A concept that is clearly defined by a set of rules, a formal definition, or a classification system; also known as an artificial concept.

◆ natural concept
A concept acquired not from a definition but through everyday perceptions and experiences; also known as a fuzzy concept.

A prototype is an example that embodies the most typical features of a concept. Which of the animals shown here best fits your prototype for the concept *bird*?

through everyday perceptions and experiences. A leading cognition researcher, Eleanor Rosch, and her colleagues studied concept formation in its natural setting and concluded that in real life, natural concepts (such as *fruit*, *vegetable*, and *bird*) are somewhat fuzzy, not clear-cut and systematic (Rosch, 1973, 1978).

Many formal concepts are acquired in school. For example, we learn that an equilateral triangle is one in which all three sides are the same size. We acquire many natural concepts through experiences with examples, or positive instances of the concept. When children are young, parents may point out examples of a car—the family car, the neighbor's car, cars on the street, and pictures of cars in books. But if a child points to some other type of moving vehicle and says "car," the parent will say, "No, that's a truck," or "This is a bus." *Truck* and *bus* are negative instances, or nonexamples, of the concept *car*. After experience with positive and negative instances of the concept, a child begins to grasp some of the properties of a car that distinguish it from other wheeled vehicles.

How do we use concepts in our everyday thinking? One view suggests that, in using natural concepts, we are likely to picture a **prototype** of the concept—an example that embodies its most common and typical features. Your *bird* prototype is more likely to be robin or a sparrow than either a penguin or a turkey: Those birds can fly, while penguins and turkeys can't. Nevertheless, both penguins and turkeys are birds. So not all examples of a natural concept fit it equally well. This is why natural concepts often seem less clear-cut than formal ones. Nevertheless, the prototype most closely fits a given natural concept, and other examples of the concept most often share more attributes with that prototype than with the prototype of any other concept.

A more recent theory of concept formation suggests that concepts are represented by their **exemplars**—individual instances, or examples, of a concept that are stored in memory from personal experience (Estes, 1994). So, if you work with penguins or turkeys every day, your exemplar of *bird* might indeed be a penguin or a turkey. By contrast, most people encounter robins or sparrows far more often than penguins or turkeys (except the roasted variety!). Thus, for the majority of people, robins or sparrows are exemplars of the *bird* concept.

As noted earlier, the concepts we form do not exist in isolation, but rather in hierarchies, or nested categories. Thus, concept formation has a certain orderliness about it, just as the process of *decision making* does—or, at least, sometimes does.

Decision Making

Do you recall the last time you made an important decision? Would you describe the process you used to make the decision as a logical one? Psychologists define **decision making** as the process of considering alternatives and choosing among them. Some psychologists and other scientists with an interest in decision making—particularly economists—maintain that humans make deci-

◆ **prototype**
An example that embodies the most common and typical features of a concept.

◆ **exemplars**
The individual instances, or examples, of a concept that are stored in memory from personal experience.

◆ **decision making**
The process of considering alternatives and choosing among them.

◆ *What is the role of heuristics in decision making?*

sions by systematically examining all possible alternatives and then choosing the one that will be most beneficial to them. You can see a model of this kind of decision making on the website that accompanies this textbook (http://www.ablongman.com/woodmastering2e. Go to Chapter 7 activities). It is a worksheet designed by psychologist Diane Halpern (2000) to help college students make decisions about what they want to do after graduation.

The belief that decision making always proceeds in this fashion was challenged by psychologist Herbert Simon in 1956, when he introduced the notion of *bounded rationality* into the discussion. Bounded rationality simply means that boundaries, or limitations, around the decision-making process prevent it from being entirely logical. One important limitation is the size of working memory. We can think about only so much at any given time. Another limitation is our inability to predict the future. For example, if you are considering marrying someone, how do you know that you will still feel the same way about him or her 20 years from now? Obviously, you can't know, so you have to make an educated guess. For the past several decades, research on decision making has focused on how we form such educated guesses.

In one of the most important early studies of decision making along these lines, psychologist Amos Tversky (1972) suggested that we deal with the limitations on decision making by using a strategy he called **elimination by aspects.** With this approach, the factors on which the alternatives are to be evaluated are ordered from most important to least important. Any alternative that does not satisfy the most important factor is automatically eliminated. The process of elimination continues as each factor is considered in order. The alternative that survives is the one chosen. For example, if the most important factor for your apartment search was that you could afford a maximum rent of $800 per month, then you would automatically eliminate all the apartments that rented for more than that. If the second most important factor was availability of parking, you would then look at the list of apartments that cost $800 or less per month and weed out those without appropriate parking. You would then continue with your third most important factor and so on, until you had trimmed the list down.

Of course, decision making is often less systematic than Tversky's model suggests. For instance, have you ever decided to leave home a bit earlier than necessary so as to allow time for a possible traffic jam? Such decisions are often based on **heuristics**—rules of thumb that are derived from experience. Several kinds of heuristics exist. One that has been studied a great deal is the **availability heuristic,** a rule stating that the probability of an event corresponds to the ease with which the event comes to mind. Thus, a decision to leave home early to avoid a possible traffic jam may result from having been stuck in one recently. Another type of heuristic is the **representativeness heuristic,** a decision strategy based on how closely a new situation resembles a familiar one. For instance, a decision about whether to go out with someone you have just met may be based on how much the person resembles someone else you know.

The **recognition heuristic,** a strategy in which the decision-making process terminates as soon as a factor that moves one toward a decision has been recognized, has also been the subject of much research. Suppose you are voting and the only information you have is the list of names vying for a particular office on the ballot. If you recognize one of the candidates' names as being that of a woman, and you have a predisposition toward seeing more women elected to public office, the recognition heuristic may cause you to decide to vote for the female candidate.

Psychologists have debated the importance of recognition in making decisions. For instance, Gerd Gigerenzer and his colleagues (Gigerenzer et al., 1999; Goldstein & Gigerenzer, 2002) maintain that recognition heuristics enable decision makers to engage in a "fast and frugal" process that leads to rapid decisions that require little cognitive effort. Their research involving computer models of human decision-making processes suggests that the recognition heuristic is just as likely to lead to good decisions as more time-consuming processes. Thus, Gigerenzer argues that the recognition heuristic is our preferred cognitive decision-making tool most of the time because of its efficiency.

Other researchers have challenged Geigerenzer's assertion about the importance of the recognition heuristic (Lee & Cummins, 2004; Newell & Shanks, 2003, 2004). Their studies have shown that research participants use recognition heuristics only when they

◆ **elimination by aspects**

A decision-making approach in which alternatives are evaluated against criteria that have been ranked according to importance.

◆ **heuristic**

(yur-RIS-tik) A rule of thumb that is derived from experience and used in decision making and problem solving, even though there is no guarantee of its accuracy or usefulness.

◆ **availability heuristic**

A cognitive rule of thumb that says that the probability of an event or the importance assigned to it is based on its availability in memory.

◆ **representativeness heuristic**

A thinking strategy based on how closely a new object or situation is judged to resemble or match an existing prototype of that object or situation.

◆ **recognition heuristic**

A strategy in which decision making stops as soon as a factor that moves one toward a decision has been recognized.

How do you choose a fast-food restaurant when you want a quick bite? Chances are you use a representativeness heuristic—a prototype that guides your expectations about how long it will take to get your food and what it will taste like. Restaurant chains use the same ingredients and methods at every location to help establish customers', representativeness heuristics for fast-food buying decisions.

have little or no information about alternative choices and must make a decision in a very limited amount of time. Even under these conditions, all of the participants in a study do not use heuristics. Some individuals, for reasons that are not yet known, prefer to use more time-consuming, logically based strategies even in circumstances in which they have little information or time to make a decision. As a consequence, many psychologists believe that research on decision making needs to address the nature of such individual differences as well as any universals that may exist in the use of heuristics (Lee & Cummins, 2004; Newell, 2005).

Psychologists agree, however, that heuristics can sometimes lead to illogical decisions and, in turn, to tragic outcomes. For example, immediately after the terrorist attacks of September 11, 2001, Gigerenzer hypothesized that the number of deaths due to traffic accidents in the United States would increase dramatically in the ensuing weeks (Gigerenzer, 2004). Why? Gigerenzer believed that memories of the attacks would serve as availability heuristics that would cause people to choose to travel by car rather than by plane, despite the fact that their chances of being the target of a terrorist attack were far less than those associated with getting into an automobile accident. To test his hypothesis, Gigerenzer compared police records of fatal car crashes during September, October, and November of 2001 to the same records for the same months in 1996 through 2000. He found that substantially more such accidents occurred in the months immediately after September 11 than during the same period in the five previous years.

The take-away message from the scholarly debate about the role of heuristics in decision making is that there is little doubt that such strategies help us make rapid decisions with little mental effort, but they can also lead to errors. The challenge we face in everyday decision making is to accurately assess the degree to which a heuristic strategy is appropriate for a given decision. For instance, in the voting booth, we would probably agree that it would be better to base one's decision on information about candidates' positions on issues than to make last-minute decisions on the basis of characteristics such as gender that we may be able to infer from their names.

Likewise, whether we use heuristics or more time-consuming strategies, we should be aware that the manner in which information is presented can affect the decision-making process. For example, **framing** refers to the way information is presented so as to emphasize either a potential gain or a potential loss as the outcome. To study the effects of framing on decision making, Kahneman and Tversky (1984) presented the following options to a group of participants. Which program would you choose?

◆ **framing**
The way information is presented so as to emphasize either a potential gain or a potential loss as the outcome.

The United States is preparing for the outbreak of a dangerous disease, which is expected to kill 600 people. There have been designed two alternative programs to combat the disease. If program A is adopted, 200 people will be saved. If program B is adopted, there is a one-third probability that all 600 will be saved and a two-thirds probability that no people will be saved.

The researchers found that 72% of the participants selected the "sure thing" of program A over the "risky gamble" of program B. Now consider the options as they were reframed:

If program C is adopted, 400 people will die. If program D is adopted, there is a one-third probability that nobody will die and a two-thirds probability that all 600 people will die.

Which program did you choose? Of research participants given this version of the problem, 78% chose program D. A careful reading will reveal that program D has exactly the same consequences as program B in the earlier version. How can this result be explained? The first version of the problem was framed to focus attention on the number of lives that could be saved. And when people are primarily motivated to achieve gains (save lives), they are more likely to choose a safe option over a risky one, as 72% of the participants did. The second version was framed to focus attention on the 400 lives that would be lost. When trying to avoid losses, people appear much more willing to choose a risky option, as 78% of the participants were.

Framing has numerous practical applications to decision making. Customers are more readily motivated to buy products if they are on sale than if they are simply priced lower than similar products to begin with. As a result, customers focus on what they save (a gain) rather than on what they spend (a loss). People seem more willing to purchase an $18,000 car and receive a $1,000 rebate (a gain) than to simply pay $17,000 for the same car. Such reasoning may be the result of our use of **intuition**—rapidly formed judgments based on "gut feelings" or "instincts"— in decision making. Information-processing researchers argue that intuition is based on a mental representation of the gist of a body of information rather than on its factual details (Reyna, 2004). The gist of a car dealer's advertisement for a $1,000 rebate on an $18,000 automobile is "you'll save money if you buy it here," not "$18,000 − $1,000 = $17,000; therefore, it doesn't matter where you buy the car." Furthermore, researchers have found that intuition can lead to errors in reasoning about decisions that carry far greater risks than those associated with buying a car. One study found that intuitive thought processes caused physicians to overestimate the degree to which condoms reduce the risk of sexually transmitted diseases (Reyna & Adam, 2003). Study participants' assessments of the comparative risks of sexual behavior with and without condoms tended to ignore infections that have modes of transmission other than sexual intercourse (e.g., chlamydia).

Problem Solving

The process of decision making shares many features with **problem solving,** the thoughts and actions required to achieve a desired goal. Notably, heuristics are just as important in problem solving as they are in decision making. For instance, the **analogy heuristic** involves comparing a problem to others you have encountered in the past. The idea is that, if strategy A worked with similar problems in the past, it will be effective for solving a new one.

Another heuristic that is effective for solving some problems is **working backward,** sometimes called the *backward search*. This approach starts with the solution, a known condition, and works back through the problem. Once the backward search has revealed the steps to be taken and their order, the problem can be solved. Try working backwards to solve the water lily problem in *Try It 7.1* (on page 206).

Another popular heuristic strategy is **means–end analysis,** in which the current position is compared with a desired goal, and a series of steps are formulated and then taken to close the gap between the two (Sweller & Levine, 1982). Many problems are large and complex and must be broken down into smaller steps or subproblems before a solution can be reached. If your professor assigns a term paper, for example, you probably do not simply sit down and write it. You must first determine how you will approach the topic, research the topic, make an outline, and then write the sections over a period of time. At last, you will be ready to assemble the complete term paper, write several drafts, and put the finished product in final form before handing it in and receiving your A.

◆ **intuition**

Rapidly formed judgments based on "gut feelings" or "instincts."

◆ **problem solving**

Thoughts and actions required to achieve a desired goal that is not readily attainable.

◆ **analogy heuristic**

A rule of thumb that applies a solution that solved a problem in the past to a current problem that shares many features with the past problem.

◆ *What are some basic approaches to problem solving and how do they differ?*

◆ **working backward**

A heuristic strategy in which a person discovers the steps needed to solve a problem by defining the desired goal and working backward to the current condition; also called *backward search*.

◆ **means–end analysis**

A heuristic strategy in which the current position is compared with the desired goal and a series of steps are formulated and taken to close the gap between them.

Try It 7.1
Water Lily Problem

Water lilies double the area they cover every 24 hours. At the beginning of the summer there is one water lily on a pond. It takes 60 days for the pond to become covered with water lilies. On what day is the pond half covered? (From Fixx, 1978.)

Answer: The most important fact is that the lilies double in number every 24 hours. If the pond is to be completely covered on the 60th day, it has to be half covered on the 59th day.

◆ **algorithm**

A systematic, step-by-step procedure, such as a mathematical formula, that guarantees a solution to a problem of a certain type if applied appropriately and executed properly.

◆ **functional fixedness**

The failure to use familiar objects in novel ways to solve problems because of a tendency to view objects only in terms of their customary functions.

◆ **mental set**

The tendency to apply a familiar strategy to the solution of a problem without carefully considering the special requirements of that problem.

When you adopt a heuristic strategy, it may or may not lead to a correct solution. By contrast, an **algorithm** is a problem-solving strategy that always leads to a correct solution if it is applied appropriately. For example, the formula you learned in school for finding the area of a rectangle (width × length) is an algorithm.

Of course, you have to know an algorithm and be able to match it with appropriate problems to use it. Likewise, heuristics must be based on prior knowledge. Thus, one important obstacle to effective problem solving is lack of appropriate knowledge. There are several others.

In some cases, we are hampered in our efforts to solve problems in daily life because of **functional fixedness**—the failure to use familiar objects in novel ways to solve problems. We tend to see objects only in terms of their customary functions. Just think of all the items you use daily—tools, utensils, and other equipment—that help you perform certain functions. Often, the normal functions of such objects become fixed in your thinking so that you do not consider using them in new and creative ways.

Suppose you wanted a cup of coffee, but the glass carafe for your coffeemaker was broken. If you suffered from functional fixedness, you might come to the conclusion that there was nothing you could do to solve your problem at that moment. But, rather than thinking about the object or utensil that you don't have, think about the function that it needs to perform. What you need is something to catch the coffee, not necessarily the specific type of glass carafe that came with the coffeemaker. Could you catch the coffee in a bowl or cooking utensil, or even in coffee mugs?

Another impediment to problem solving, similar to functional fixedness but much broader, is mental set. **Mental set** is a mental rut in one's approach to solving problems, the tendency to continue to use the same old method even though another approach might be better. Perhaps you hit on a way to solve a problem once in the past and continue to use the same technique in similar situations, even though it is not highly effective or efficient. People are much more susceptible to mental set when they fail to consider the special requirements of a problem. Not surprisingly, the same people who are subject to mental set are also more likely to have trouble with functional fixedness when they attempt to solve problems (McKelvie, 1984).

Many of us are hampered in our efforts to solve problems in daily life because of functional fixedness—the failure to use familiar objects in novel ways to solve problems.

Artificial Intelligence

In the previous section you read that mathematical formulas are algorithms, or problem-solving strategies that always lead to a correct solution. Another kind of algorithm tests all possible solutions and then executes the one that works best. In most situations, the limits of human working memory render this kind of algorithm difficult, if not impossible, to employ. By contrast, computers are capable of completing such an algorithm, and doing so in a matter of seconds. This particular feature of computer "thinking" has been well illustrated by **artificial intelligence** programs that have been designed to match the skills of human experts in games such as chess. You may have heard of the series of chess matches that pitted renowned player Garry Kasparov against IBM computers named "Deep Blue" and "Deep Junior." The best Kasparov has been able to do is to play the computers to a draw.

If a computer can beat a human at chess, does it mean that computers process information in exactly the same way as the human brain does? Not necessarily. However, computer scientists hope to design artificial intelligence that accomplishes that goal. Programs designed to mimic human brain functioning are called **artificial neural networks (ANNs).** Such networks have proved very useful in computer programs designed to carry out highly specific functions within a limited domain, known as **expert systems.** One of the first expert systems was MYCIN, a program used by physicians to diagnose blood diseases and meningitis. For the most part, expert systems offer the greatest benefits when acting as assistants to humans. For example, medical diagnosis programs are most often used to confirm doctors' hypotheses or to generate possible diagnoses that have not occurred to them (Brunetti et al., 2002). Remember, too, that any expert system relies on the accumulated knowledge of human experts. Thus, it is impossible for computers to totally replace human professionals.

Moreover, many cognitive tasks that humans find relatively easy to perform are actually quite difficult to teach a computer to do. Many aspects of language processing, for instance, are extremely difficult for computers to manage. For example, what kind of scene comes to mind when you hear the word *majestic*? Perhaps you see a range of snow-capped mountains. Computer scientists are currently working to develop programs that can enable computers to retrieve images on the basis of such vague, abstract cues (Kuroda, 2002). As you will see in the next section, human language, although we use it effortlessly most of the time, is an extremely complex phenomenon.

◆ *What are some important applications of artificial intelligence technologies?*

◆ **artificial intelligence**
The programming of computer systems to simulate human thinking in solving problems and in making judgments and decisions.

◆ **artificial neural networks (ANNs)**
Computer systems that are intended to mimic the human brain.

◆ **expert systems**
Computer programs designed to carry out highly specific functions within a limited domain.

World champion Garry Kasparov contemplates a move against Deep Blue, an IBM computer that exhibited artificial intelligence in the area of top-level chess play.

Language

Language is a means of communicating thoughts and feelings, using a system of socially shared but arbitrary symbols (sounds, signs, or written symbols) arranged according to rules of grammar. Language expands our ability to think because it allows us to consider abstract concepts—such as justice—that are not represented by physical objects. Further, thanks to language, we can share our knowledge and thoughts with one another in an extremely efficient way. Thus, whether spoken, written, or signed, language is our most important cognitive tool. In Chapter 8, we will discuss how language is acquired by infants. Here, we explore the components and the structure of this amazing form of human communication.

◆ **language**
A means of communicating thoughts and feelings, using a system of socially shared but arbitrary symbols (sounds, signs, or written symbols) arranged according to rules of grammar.

The Structure of Language

◆ *What are the necessary components of any language?*

Psycholinguistics is the study of how language is acquired, produced, and used and how the sounds and symbols of language are translated into meaning. Psycholinguists use specific terms for each of the five basic components of language.

The smallest units of sound in a spoken language—such as *b* or *s* in English—are known as **phonemes.** Three phonemes together form the sound of the word *cat: c* (which sounds like *k*), *a*, and *t*. Combinations of letters that form particular sounds are also phonemes, such as the *th* in *the* and the *ch* in *child*. The same phoneme may be represented by different letters in different words; this occurs with the *a* in *stay* and the *ei* in *sleigh*. And the same letter can serve as different phonemes. The letter *a*, for example, is sounded as four different phonemes in *day, cap, watch,* and *law*.

Morphemes are the smallest units of meaning in a language. A few single phonemes serve as morphemes, such as the article *a* and the personal pronoun *I*. The ending *-s* gives a plural meaning to a word and is thus a morpheme in English. Many words in English are single morphemes—*book, word, learn, reason,* and so on. In addition to root words, morphemes may be prefixes (such as *re-* in *relearn*) or suffixes (such as *-ed* to show past tense, as in *learned*). The single morpheme *reason* becomes a dual morpheme in *reasonable*. The morpheme *book* (singular) becomes two morphemes in *books* (plural).

Syntax is the aspect of grammar that specifies the rules for arranging and combining words to form phrases and sentences. The rules of word order, or syntax, differ from one language to another. For example, an important rule of syntax in English is that adjectives usually come before nouns. So English speakers refer to the residence of the U.S. President as "the White House." In Spanish, in contrast, the noun usually comes before the adjective, and Spanish speakers say *"la Casa Blanca,"* or "the House White."

Semantics refers to the meaning derived from morphemes, words, and sentences. The same word can have different meanings depending on how it is used in sentences: "I don't mind." "Mind your manners." "He has lost his mind." Or consider another example: "Loving to read, the young girl read three books last week." Here, the word *read* is pronounced two different ways and, in one case, is the past tense.

Finally, **pragmatics** is the term psycholinguists use to refer to aspects of language such as *intonation*, the rising and falling patterns that are used to express meaning. For example, think about how you would say the single word *cookie* to express each of the following meanings: "Do you want a cookie?" or "What a delicious looking cookie!" or "That's a cookie." The subtle differences reflect your knowledge of the pragmatic rules of English; for example, questions end with a rising intonation, while statements end with a falling intonation. Pragmatic rules also come into play when you speak in one way to your friend and another to your professor. That is, the social rules associated with language use are also included in pragmatics.

◆ **psycholinguistics**

The study of how language is acquired, produced, and used and how the sounds and symbols of language are translated into meaning.

◆ **phonemes**

The smallest units of sound in a spoken language.

◆ **morphemes**

The smallest units of meaning in a language.

◆ **syntax**

The aspect of grammar that specifies the rules for arranging and combining words to form phrases and sentences.

◆ **semantics**

The meaning or the study of meaning derived from morphemes, words, and sentences.

◆ **pragmatics**

The patterns of intonation and social roles associated with a language.

Animal Language

◆ *What is the evidence concerning the capacity of animals for understanding and producing language?*

Ask people what capability most reliably sets humans apart from all other animal species, and most will answer "language." And for good reason. As far as scientists know, humans are the only species to have developed this rich, varied, and complex system of communication. As early as 1933 and 1951, researchers attempted to teach chimpanzees to speak by raising the chimps in their homes. These experiments failed because the vocal tract in chimpanzees and the other apes is not adapted to human speech, so researchers turned to sign language. Psychologists Allen and Beatrix Gardner (1969) took in a 1-year-old chimp named Washoe and taught her sign language. Washoe learned signs for objects and certain commands, such as *flower, give me, come, open,* and *more*. By the end of her fifth year, she had mastered about 160 signs (Fleming, 1974).

Psychologist David Premack (1971) taught another chimp, Sarah, to use an artificial language he developed. Its symbols consisted of magnetized chips of various shapes, sizes, and colors, as shown in Figure 7.1. Premack used operant conditioning

FIGURE 7.1 Sarah's Symbols

A chimpanzee named Sarah learned to communicate using plastic chips of various shapes, sizes, and colors to represent words in an artificial language developed by her trainer, David Premack. *Source:* From Premack (1971).

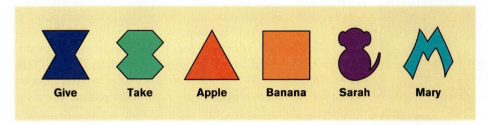

| Give | Take | Apple | Banana | Sarah | Mary |

techniques to teach Sarah to select the magnetic chip representing a fruit and place it on a magnetic language board. The trainer would then reward Sarah with the fruit she had requested. Sarah mastered the concepts of similarities and differences, and eventually she could signal whether two objects were the same or different with nearly perfect accuracy (Premack & Premack, 1983). Even more remarkable, Sarah could view a whole apple and a cut apple and, even though she had not seen the apple being cut, could match the apple with the utensil needed to cut it—a knife.

At the Yerkes Primate Research Center at Emory University, a chimp named Lana participated in a computer-controlled language training program. She learned to press keys imprinted with geometric symbols that represented words in an artificial language called Yerkish. Researcher Sue Savage-Rumbaugh and a colleague (1986; Rumbaugh, 1977) varied the location, color, and brightness of the keys, so Lana had to learn which symbols to use no matter where they were located. One day, her trainer Tim had an orange that she wanted. Lana had available symbols for many fruits—apple, banana, and so on—but none for an orange. Yet there was a symbol for the color orange. So Lana improvised and signaled, "Tim give apple which is orange." Impressive!

But was humanlike language being displayed in these studies with primates? Not according to Herbert Terrace (1979, 1981), who examined the research of others and conducted his own. Terrace and co-workers taught sign language to a chimp they called Nim Chimpsky (after the famed linguist Noam Chomsky) and reported Nim's progress from the age of 2 weeks to 4 years. Nim learned 125 symbols, which is respectable, but does not amount to language, according to Terrace (1985, 1986). Terrace believed that chimps like Nim and Washoe were simply imitating their trainers and making responses to get reinforcers, according to the laws of operant conditioning, not the laws of language. Finally, Terrace suggested that the studies with primates were probably influenced by experimenter bias; trainers might unconsciously tend to interpret the behavior of the chimps as more indicative of progress toward developing language than it really was. However, Terrace had not heard of Kanzi when he expressed his skepticism.

The most impressive performance in language training so far is that of a pygmy chimpanzee, Kanzi, who developed an amazing ability to communicate with his trainers without any formal training. During the mid-1980s, researchers had taught Kanzi's mother to press symbols representing words. Her progress was not remarkable; but her infant son Kanzi, who stood by and observed her during training, was learning rapidly (thanks to observational learning, discussed in Chapter 5). When Kanzi had a chance at the symbol board, his performance quickly surpassed that of his mother and of every other chimp the researchers had tested.

Kanzi demonstrated an advanced understanding (for chimps) of spoken English and could respond correctly even to new commands, such as "Throw your ball to the river," or "Go to the refrigerator and get out a tomato" (Savage-Rumbaugh, 1990; Savage-Rumbaugh et al., 1992). By the time Kanzi was 6 years old, a team of researchers who worked with him had recorded more than 13,000 "utterances" and reported that Kanzi could communicate using some 200 different geometric symbols (Gibbons, 1991). Kanzi could press symbols to ask someone to play chase with him and even ask two others

From their studies of communication among chimps and other animals, researchers have gained useful insights into the nature of language. The pygmy chimp Kanzi became skilled at using a special symbol board to communicate.

to play chase while he watched. And if Kanzi signaled someone to "chase" and "hide," he was insistent that his first command, "chase," be done first (Gibbons, 1991). Kanzi was not merely responding to nearby trainers whose actions or gestures he might have copied. He responded just as well when requests were made over earphones so that no one else in the room could signal to him purposely or inadvertently.

More recent research suggests that chimpanzees may be able to learn numerical as well as linguistic symbols (Beran, 2004; Beran & Rumbaugh, 2001). Researchers trained two chimpanzees to use a joystick to move dots on a computer screen. Then, the chimps were taught to collect specific numbers of dots in association with Arabic numerals. In other words, when *3* was displayed on the screen, the chimp was supposed to use its joystick to move three dots from one location to another. Although the chimps learned the task, they tended to perform poorly with quantities in excess of six or seven. Afterward, the researchers ceased practicing with them because they wanted to find out whether the animals would remember the associations over extended periods of time. When they were retested 6 months later, the chimps were able to perform the task quite well, although they made more errors than when they were first trained. After 3 years, the researchers tested them again and found that they still remembered the symbol–quantity associations.

Most animal species studied by language researchers are limited to motor responses such as sign language, gestures, using magnetic symbols, or pressing keys on symbol boards. But these limitations do not extend to some bird species such as parrots, which are capable of making humanlike speech sounds. One remarkable case is Alex, an African gray parrot that not only mimics human speech but also seems to do so intelligently. Able to recognize and name various colors, objects, and shapes, Alex answers questions about them in English. Asked "Which object is green?" Alex easily names the green object (Pepperberg, 1991, 1994b). And he can count as well. When asked such questions as "How many red blocks?" Alex answers correctly about 80% of the time (Pepperberg, 1994a).

Research with sea mammals such as whales and dolphins has established that they apparently use complicated systems of grunts, whistles, clicks, and other sounds to communicate within their species (Herman, 1981; Savage-Rumbaugh, 1993). Researchers at the University of Hawaii have trained dolphins to respond to fairly complex commands requiring an understanding of directional and relational concepts. Dolphins can learn to pick out an object and put it on the right or left of a basket, for example, and comprehend such commands as "in the basket" and "under the basket" (Chollar, 1989).

Language and Thinking

◆ *In what ways does language influence thinking?*

If language is unique to humans, then does it drive human thinking? Does the fact that you speak English mean that you reason, think, and perceive your world differently than does someone who speaks Spanish, or Chinese, or Swahili? According to one hypothesis presented about 50 years ago, it does. Benjamin Whorf (1956) put forth his **linguistic relativity hypothesis,** suggesting that the language a person speaks largely determines the nature of that person's thoughts. According to this hypothesis, people's worldview is constructed primarily by the words in their language. As proof, Whorf offered his classic example. The languages used by the Eskimo people have a number of different words for snow—"*apikak*, first snow falling; *aniv*, snow spread out; *pukak*, snow for drinking water"—while the English-speaking world has but one word, *snow* (Restak, 1988, p. 222). Whorf claimed that such a rich and varied selection of words for various snow types and conditions enabled Eskimos to think differently about snow than do people whose languages lack such a range of words.

◆ **linguistic relativity hypothesis**

The notion that the language a person speaks largely determines the nature of that person's thoughts.

Eleanor Rosch (1973) tested whether people whose language contains many names for colors would be better at thinking about and discriminating among colors than people whose language has only a few color names. Her participants were English-speaking Americans and the Dani, members of a remote tribe in New Guinea whose language has only two names for colors—*mili* for dark, cool colors and *mola* for bright, warm colors. Rosch showed members of both groups single-color chips of 11 colors—black, white, red, yellow, green, blue, brown, purple, pink, orange, and gray—for 5 seconds each. Then, after 30 seconds, she had the participants select the 11 colors they had viewed from an assortment of 40 color chips. Did the Americans outperform the Dani participants, for whom brown, black, purple, and blue are all *mili*, or dark? No. Rosch found no significant differences between the Dani and the Americans in discriminating, remembering, or thinking about those 11 basic colors. Rosch's study did not support the linguistic relativity hypothesis.

Clearly, however, it would be a mistake to go too far in the opposite direction and assume that language has no influence on how people think. Thought both influences and is influenced by language, and language appears to reflect cultural differences more than it determines them (Pinker, 1994; Rosch, 1987). For example, does it really matter whether we use "he" or "she" to refer to an unspecified person who represents a particular profession? Consider the generic use of the pronoun *he* to refer to any member of a group of people. If your professor says, "I expect each student in this class to do the best he can," does this announcement mean the same to males and females? Studies confirm that the generic use of *he*, *him*, and *his* is interpreted heavily in favor of males (Gastil, 1990; Hamilton, 1988; Henley; 1989; Ng, 1990). If this were not the case, the following sentence would not seem unusual at all: "Like other mammals, man bears his offspring live."

Learning a Second Language

Do you speak more than one language? Most native-born Americans speak only English. But in many other countries around the world, the majority of citizens speak two or even more languages (Snow, 1993). In European countries, most students learn English in addition to the languages of the countries bordering their own. Dutch is the native language of the Netherlands, but all Dutch schoolchildren learn German, French, and English. College-bound German students also typically study three languages (Haag & Stern, 2003). What about the effect of learning two languages on the process of language development itself? (You'll learn more about this process in Chapter 8).

◆ *What are the advantages and disadvantages of learning a second language at various ages?*

Research suggests that there are both advantages and disadvantages to learning two languages early in life. One of the pluses is that, among preschool and school-age children, bilingualism is associated with better *metalinguistic skills*, the capacity to think about language (Bialystok et al., 2000; Mohanty & Perregaux, 1997). On the downside, even in adulthood, bilingualism is sometimes associated with decreased efficiency in memory tasks involving words (Gollan & Silverberg, 2001; McElree et al., 2000). However, bilinguals appear to develop compensatory strategies that allow them to make up these inefficiencies. Consequently, they often perform such tasks as accurately as monolinguals, though they may respond more slowly. Many people would argue, however, that the advantages associated with fluency in two languages are worth giving up a bit of cognitive efficiency.

So, you may ask, what about people who did not have the good fortune to grow up bilingual? Is it still possible to become fluent in a second language after reaching adulthood? Researchers have found that there is no age at which it is impossible to acquire a new lan-

Growing up in a bilingual home provides distinct advantages in adolescence and adulthood. Spanish and English are the languages spoken by the majority of bilinguals in the United States.

FIGURE 7.2 **English Proficiency in Chinese- and Spanish-Speaking Immigrants to the United States**

These research results, based on census data involving more than 2 million individuals, suggest that it is never too late to learn a second language.   *Source:* Hakuta et al. (2003).

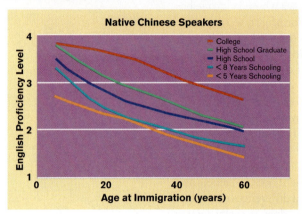

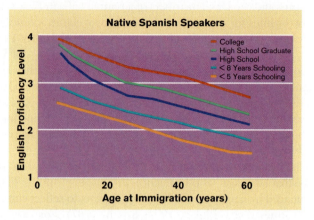

guage. While it is true that those who begin earlier reach higher levels of proficiency, age is not the only determining factor. Kenji Hakuta and his colleagues (2003) used census data to examine relationships among English proficiency, age at entry into the United States, and educational attainment for Chinese- and Spanish-speaking immigrants. The results of their study are shown in Figure 7.2. As you can see, even when immigrants entered the United States in middle and late adulthood, their ability to learn English was predicted by their educational backgrounds. And other studies have shown that the more you know about your first language—its spelling rules, grammatical structure, and vocabulary—the easier it will be for you to learn another language (Meschyan & Hernandez, 2002).

There is one clear advantage to learning two languages earlier in life, however. People who are younger when they learn a new language are far more likely to be able to speak it with an appropriate accent (McDonald, 1997). One reason for this difference between early and late language learners may have to do with slight variations in neural processing in Broca's area, the area of the brain that controls speech production. Research by Kim and others (1997) suggests that bilinguals who learned a second language early (younger than age 10 or 11) rely on the same patch of tissue in Broca's area for both of the languages they speak. In those who learned a second language at an older age, two different sections of Broca's area are active while they are performing language tasks—one section for the first language and another for the second language. Yet, the two sections are very close, only 1/3 inch apart.

 # Intelligence

◆ **intelligence**

An individual's ability to understand complex ideas, to adapt effectively to the environment, to learn from experience, to engage in various forms of reasoning, and to overcome obstacles through mental effort.

Have you ever stopped to think what you really mean when you say someone is "intelligent"? Do you mean that the person learns quickly or that he or she can solve problems that appear to mystify others? Spending a few minutes thinking about intelligence in this way will help you realize that defining intelligence in ways that can be measured is quite a challenge.

The Nature of Intelligence

◆ *How do the views of Spearman, Thurstone, Gardner, and Sternberg differ with regard to the definition of intelligence?*

A task force of experts from the American Psychological Association (APA) defined **intelligence** as possessing several basic facets: an individual's "ability to understand complex ideas, . . . to adapt effectively to the environment, . . . to learn from experience, to engage in various forms of reasoning, and to overcome obstacles by taking thought" (Neisser et al., 1996, p. 77). As you will see, however, there's more to intelligence than this simple definition suggests.

The APA's definition of intelligence includes several factors, such as the ability to understand complex ideas and the capacity for adapting to the environment. But are these manifestations of a single entity or truly separate abilities? This question has fascinated psychologists for more than a century.

English psychologist Charles Spearman (1863–1945) observed that people who are bright in one area are usually bright in other areas as well. In other words, they tend to be generally intelligent. Spearman (1927) came to believe that intelligence is composed of a general ability that underlies all intellectual functions. Spearman concluded that intelligence tests tap this **g factor**, or general intelligence, and a number of *s* factors, or specific intellectual abilities. Spearman's influence can be seen in those intelligence tests, such as the Stanford–Binet, that yield one IQ score to indicate the level of general intelligence.

Another early researcher in testing, Louis L. Thurstone (1938), rejected Spearman's notion of general intellectual ability, or *g* factor. After analyzing the scores of many participants on some 56 separate ability tests, Thurstone identified seven **primary mental abilities:** verbal comprehension, numerical ability, spatial relations, perceptual speed, word fluency, memory, and reasoning. He maintained that all intellectual activities involve one or more of these primary mental abilities. Thurstone and his wife, Thelma G. Thurstone, developed their Primary Mental Abilities Tests to measure these seven abilities. Thurstone believed that a single IQ score obscured more than it revealed. He suggested that a profile showing relative strengths and weaknesses on the seven primary mental abilities would provide a more accurate picture of a person's intelligence.

Harvard psychologist Howard Gardner (Gardner & Hatch, 1989) also denies the existence of a *g* factor. Instead, he proposes eight independent forms of intelligence, or *frames of mind*, as illustrated in Figure 7.3. The eight frames of mind are linguistic, logical-mathematical, spatial, bodily-kinesthetic, musical, interpersonal, intrapersonal, and naturalistic.

Gardner (1983) first developed his theory by studying patients with different types of brain damage that affect some forms of intelligence but leave others intact. He also

◆ **g factor**

Spearman's term for a general intellectual ability that underlies all mental operations to some degree.

◆ **primary mental abilities**

According to Thurstone, seven relatively distinct capabilities that singly or in combination are involved in all intellectual activities.

FIGURE 7.3 **Gardner's Eight Frames of Mind**

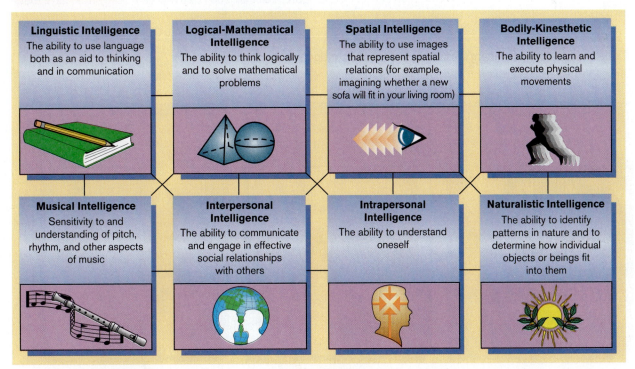

◆ **triarchic theory of intelligence**

Sternberg's theory that there are three types of intelligence: componential (analytical), experiential (creative), and contextual (practical).

studied reports of people with *savant syndrome*, who show a combination of mental retardation and unusual talent or ability. (You'll read more about this phenomenon later in this chapter.) Finally, Gardner considered how various abilities and skills have been valued differently in other cultures and periods of history.

Perhaps the most controversial aspect of Gardner's theory is his view that all forms of intelligence are of equal importance. In fact, different cultures asign varying degrees of importance to the types of intelligence. For example, linguistic and logical mathe-matical intelligences are valued most in the United States and other Western cultures; bodily-kinesthetic intelligence is more highly prized in cultures that depend on hunt-ing for survival.

Psychologist Robert Sternberg (2000) is also critical of heavy reliance on Spear-man's *g* factor for measuring intelligence. But Sternberg is not merely a critic; he has developed his own theory of intelligence. Sternberg (1895a; 1986a) has formulated a **triarchic theory of intelligence**, which proposes that there are three types of intel-ligence (see Figure 7.4). The first type, *componential intelligence*, refers to the mental abil-ities most closely related to success on conventional IQ and achievement tests. He claims that traditional IQ tests measure only componential, or analytical, intelligence.

The second type, *experiential intelligence*, is reflected in creative thinking and prob-lem solving. People with high experiential intelligence are able to solve novel problems and deal with unusual and unexpected challenges. Another aspect of experiential intel-ligence is finding creative ways to perform common daily tasks more efficiently and effectively.

The third type, *contextual intelligence*, or practical intelligence, might be equated with common sense or "street smarts." People with high contextual intelligence are sur-vivors, who capitalize on their strengths and compensate for their weaknesses. They either adapt well to their environment, change the environment so that they can suc-ceed, or, if necessary, find a new environment.

Sternberg and others (1995) argue that IQ-test performance and real-world success are based on two different types of knowledge: *formal academic knowledge*, or the knowl-edge we acquire in school, and *tacit knowledge*. Unlike formal academic knowledge, tacit knowledge is action-oriented and is acquired without direct help from others. Accord-ing to Sternberg, tacit knowledge is more important to successful real-world perfor-mance. Research supports Sternberg's contention that the two forms of knowledge are different (Taub et al., 2001; Grigorenko et al., 2004). However, investigators have found

---

FIGURE 7.4 **Sternberg's Triarchic Theory of Intelligence**

According to Sternberg, there are three types of intelligence: componential, experiential, and contextual.

Componential Intelligence
Mental abilities most closely related to success on traditional IQ and achievement tests

Experiential Intelligence
Creative thinking and problem solving

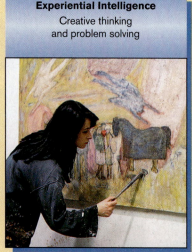

Contextual Intelligence
Practical intelligence or "street smarts"

REVIEW and REFLECT 7.1

Theories of Intelligence

THEORY	DESCRIPTION
Spearman's *g* factor	Intelligence consists of a single factor known as *g*, which represents a general intellectual ability.
Thurstone's primary mental abilities	Intelligence has seven separate components: verbal comprehension, numerical ability, spatial relations, perceptual speed, word fluency, memory, and reasoning.
Gardner's frames of mind	There are eight independent forms of intelligence: linguistic, logical-mathematical, spatial, bodily-kinesthetic, musical, interpersonal, intrapersonal, and naturalistic.
Sternberg's triarchic theory	There are three types of intelligence: componential, experiential, and contextual.

that measures of formal academic knowledge, such as traditional IQ tests, better predict real-world success than do Sternberg's tests of practical intelligence. Sternberg and those who agree with him contend that imperfections in the tests themselves are responsible for such results. Thus, in recent years, Sternberg and his colleagues have focused on developing a reliable and valid intelligence test that measures each of the three hypothesized types of intelligence (Sternberg et al., 2001; Sternberg, 2003a, 2003b).

Sternberg's ideas have become popular among educators. Several studies have shown that teaching methods designed to tap into all three types of intelligence can be effective with students who are low achievers (Grigorenko et al., 2002). In such instruction, teachers emphasize the practical relevance of formal academic knowledge and help students apply it to real-world problems.

Review and Reflect 7.1 summarizes the various theories of intelligence.

Measuring Intelligence

The first successful effort to measure intelligence resulted not from a theoretical approach, but as a practical means of solving a problem. In 1903, the French government formed a special commission to look for a way of assessing the intellectual potential of individual school children. One of the commission members, Alfred Binet (1857–1911), with the help of his colleague, psychiatrist Theodore Simon, developed a variety of tests that eventually became the first intelligence test, the *Binet–Simon Intelligence Scale*, first published in 1905.

◆ *What did Binet, Terman, and Weschler contribute to the study of intelligence?*

The Binet–Simon Scale used a type of score called *mental age*. A child's mental age was based on the number of items she or he got right as compared with the average number right for children of various ages. In other words, if a child's score equaled the average for 8-year-olds, the child was assigned a mental age of 8, regardless of her or his chronological age (age in years). To determine whether children were bright, average, or retarded, Binet compared the children's mental and chronological ages. A child who was mentally 2 years ahead of his or her chronological age was considered bright; one who was 2 years behind was considered retarded. But there was a flaw in Binet's scoring system. A 4-year-old with a mental age of 2 is far more retarded than a 12-year-old with a mental age of 10. How could a similar degree of retardation at different ages be expressed?

German psychologist William Stern (1914) provided an answer. In 1912, he devised a simple formula for calculating an index of intelligence—*the intelligence quotient*. But it was American psychologist Lewis M. Terman, a professor at Stanford University, who perfected this new way of scoring intelligence tests. In 1916, Terman published a

Working with psychiatrist Theodore Simon to develop a test for evaluating children's intelligence, Alfred Binet (shown here) began testing Parisian students in 1904.

thorough revision of the Binet–Simon scale, consisting of items adapted for use with American children. Terman also established new **norms**, or age-based averages, based on the scores of large numbers of children. Within 3 years, 4 million American children had taken Terman's revision, known as the *Stanford–Binet Intelligence Scale*. It was the first test to make use of Stern's concept of the **intelligence quotient (IQ)**. (Terman also introduced the abbreviation *IQ*.) Terman's formula for calculating an IQ score was

$$\frac{\text{Mental age}}{\text{Chronological age}} \times 100 = \text{IQ}$$

For example,

$$\frac{14}{10} \times 100 = 140 \text{ (superior IQ)}$$

The highly regarded Stanford–Binet is an individually administered IQ test for those aged 2 to 23. It contains four subscales: verbal reasoning, quantitative reasoning, abstract visual reasoning, and short-term memory. An overall IQ score is derived from scores on the four subscales, and the test scores correlate well with achievement test scores (Laurent et al., 1992). Intelligence testing became increasingly popular in the United States in the 1920s and 1930s, but it quickly became obvious that the Stanford–Binet was not useful for testing adults. The original IQ formula could not be applied to adults, because at a certain age people achieve maturity in intelligence. According to the original IQ formula, a 40-year-old with the same IQ test score as the average 20-year-old would be considered mentally retarded, with an IQ of only 50. Obviously, something was wrong with the formula when applied to populations of all ages.

In 1939, psychologist David Wechsler developed the first successful individual intelligence test for adults, designed for those aged 16 and older. Scores are based on how much an individual deviates from the average score for adults rather than on mental and chronological ages. The original test has been revised, restandardized, and renamed the *Wechsler Adult Intelligence Scale (WAIS-R)* and is one of the most widely used psychological tests. The test contains both verbal and performance (nonverbal) subtests, which yield separate verbal and performance IQ scores as well as an overall IQ score. This is a key difference from the Stanford–Binet, which yields a single IQ score. Wechsler also published the *Wechsler Intelligence Scale for Children (WISC-R)* and the *Wechsler Preschool and Primary Scale of Intelligence (WPPSI)*, which is normed for children aged 4 to 6½. One advantage of the Wechsler scales is their ability to identify intellectual strengths in nonverbal areas as well as verbal ones. Wechsler also believed that differences in a person's scores on the various verbal and performance subtests could be used for diagnostic purposes.

Individual intelligence tests such as the Stanford–Binet and the Wechsler scales must be given to one person at a time by a psychologist or educational diagnostician. For testing large numbers of people in a short period of time (often necessary due to budget limitations), group intelligence tests are the answer. Group intelligence tests such as the *California Test of Mental Maturity*, the *Cognitive Abilities Test*, and the *Otis–Lennon Mental Ability Test* are widely used.

◆ **norms**
Standards based on the range of test scores of a large group of people who are selected to provide the bases of comparison for those who take the test later.

◆ **intelligence quotient (IQ)**
An index of intelligence, originally derived by dividing mental age by chronological age and then multiplying by 100, but now derived by comparing an individual's score with the scores of others of the same age.

◆ **reliability**
The ability of a test to yield nearly the same score when the same people are tested and then retested on the same test or an alternative form of the test.

◆ *Why are reliability, validity, standardization, and cultural bias important in intelligence testing?*

Requirements of Good Tests

Both individual and group tests of intelligence are judged according to the same criteria. First, they must provide consistent results. What if your watch gains 6 minutes one day and loses 3 or 4 minutes the next day? It would not be reliable. You want a watch you can rely on to give the correct time day after day. Like a watch, an intelligence test must have **reliability**; the test must consistently yield nearly the same score when the same person is tested and then retested on the same test or an alternative form of the test. The higher the correlation between the two scores, the more reliable the test.

Tests can be highly reliable but worthless if they are not valid. **Validity** is the ability or power of a test to measure what it is intended to measure. For example, a thermometer is a valid instrument for measuring temperature; a bathroom scale is valid for measuring weight. But no matter how reliable your bathroom scale is, it will not take your temperature. It is valid only for weighing.

Aptitude tests are designed to predict a person's probable achievement or performance at some future time. Selecting students for admission to college or graduate schools is based partly on the predictive validity of aptitude tests such as the SAT, the American College Testing Program (ACT), and the Graduate Record Examination (GRE). How well do SAT scores predict success in college? The correlation between SAT scores and the grades of first year college students is about .40 (Linn, 1982).

Once a test is proven to be valid and reliable, the next requirement is **standardization.** There must be standard procedures for administering and scoring the test. Exactly the same directions must be given, whether written or oral, and the same amount of time must be allowed for every test taker. But even more important, standardization means establishing norms by which all scores are interpreted. A test is standardized by administering it to a large sample of people who are representative of those who will be taking the test in the future. The group's scores are analyzed, and then the average score, standard deviation, percentile rankings, and other measures are computed. These comparative scores become the norms used as the standard against which all other scores on that test are measured.

One criticism that continues to plague advocates of IQ testing is the suggestion that minority children and those for whom English is a second language are at a disadvantage when they are assessed on conventional tests because their cultural backgrounds differ from that assumed by the tests' authors. In response, attempts have been made to develop **culture-fair intelligence tests** designed to minimize cultural bias. The questions do not penalize individuals whose cultural experience or language differs from that of the mainstream or dominant culture. See Figure 7.5 for an example of the type of test item found on a culture-fair test. Research shows that such tests are moderately correlated with other measures of intellectual ability such as the SAT (Frey & Detterman, 2004). Likewise, high-IQ minority children are more likely to be identified as gifted when culture-fair tests are used than when school officials use conventional IQ tests to screen students for inclusion in programs for the gifted (Shaunessy et al., 2004).

◆ **validity**
The ability of a test to measure what it is intended to measure.

◆ **aptitude test**
A test designed to predict a person's achievement or performance at some future time.

◆ **standardization**
Establishing norms for comparing the scores of people who will take a test in the future; administering tests using a prescribed procedure.

◆ **culture-fair intelligence test**
An intelligence test that uses questions that will not penalize those whose culture differs from the mainstream or dominant culture.

The Range of Intelligence

You may have heard the term *bell curve* and wondered just exactly what it is. When large populations are measured on intelligence or physical characteristics such as height and weight, the frequencies of the various scores or

◆ *How do individuals who are gifted and those with mental retardation differ from others?*

An Example of an Item on a Culture-Fair Test

This culture-fair test item does not penalize test takers whose language or cultural experiences differ from those of the urban middle or upper classes. Test takers select, from the six samples on the right, the patch that completes the pattern. Patch number 3 is the correct answer.
Source: Adapted from the Raven Standard Progressive Matrices Test.

measurements usually conform to a *bell-shaped* distribution known as the *normal curve*—hence the term *bell curve*. The majority of the scores cluster around the mean (average). The more scores deviate from the mean (that is, the farther away from it they fall), either above or below, the fewer there are. And the normal curve is perfectly symmetrical; that is, there are just as many cases above as below the mean. The average IQ test score for all people in the same age group is arbitrarily assigned an IQ score of 100. On the Wechsler intelligence tests, approximately 50% of the scores are in the average range, between 90 and 110. About 68% of the scores fall between 85 and 115, and about 95% fall between 70 and 130. Some 2% of the scores are above 130, which is considered superior, and about 2% fall below 70, in the range of mental retardation (see Figure 7.6).

But what does it mean to have a "superior" IQ? In 1921, to try to answer this question, Lewis Terman (1925) launched a longitudinal study, now a classic, in which 1,528 gifted students were selected and measured at different ages throughout their lives. Tested on the Stanford–Binet, the participants—857 males and 671 females—had unusually high IQs, ranging from 135 to 200, with an average of 151. Terman's early findings put an end to the myth that mentally superior people are more likely to be physically inferior. In fact, Terman's gifted participants excelled in almost all the abilities he studied—intellectual, physical, emotional, moral, and social. Terman also exploded many other myths about the mentally gifted (Terman & Oden, 1947). For example, you may have heard the saying that there is a thin line between genius and madness. Actually, Terman's gifted group enjoyed better mental health than the general population. Terman's participants also earned more academic degrees, achieved higher occupational status and higher salaries, were better adjusted both personally and socially, and were healthier than their less mentally gifted peers. However, most women at that time did not pursue careers outside of the home, so the findings related to occupational success applied primarily to the men. Terman (1925) concluded that "there is no law of compensation whereby the intellectual superiority of the gifted is offset by inferiorities along nonintellectual lines" (p. 16). The Terman study continues today, with the surviving participants in their 80s or 90s. In a report on Terman's study, Shneidman (1989) states its basic findings—that "an unusual mind, a vigorous body, and a relatively well-adjusted personality are not at all incompatible" (p. 687).

At the opposite end of the continuum from Terman's sample are the 2% of the U.S. population whose IQ scores are in the range of mental retardation. There are many causes of mental retardation, including brain injuries, chromosomal abnormalities such

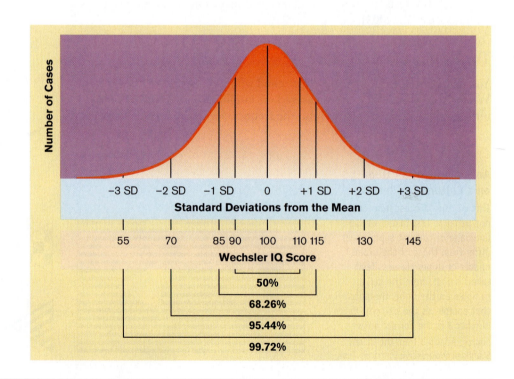

FIGURE 7.6

The Normal Curve

When a large number of test scores are compiled, they are typically distributed in a normal (bell-shaped) curve. On the Wechsler scales, the average, or mean, IQ score is set at 100. As the figure shows, about 68% of the scores fall between 15 IQ points (1 standard deviation) above and below 100 (from 85 to 115), and about 95.5% of the scores fall between 30 points (2 standard deviations) above and below 100 (from 70 to 130).

as Down syndrome, chemical deficiencies, and hazards present during fetal development. And studies continue to document the enduring mental deficits produced by early exposure to lead (Garavan et al., 2000; Morgan et al., 2000). Individuals are not classified as **mentally retarded** unless (1) their IQ score is below 70 and (2) they have a severe deficiency in everyday adaptive functioning—the ability to care for themselves and relate to others (Grossman, 1983). The degrees of retardation range from mild to profound (American Psychiatric Association, 2000). Individuals with IQs ranging from 55 to 70 are considered mildly retarded; from 40 to 54, moderately retarded; from 25 to 39, severely retarded; and below 25, profoundly retarded. Mildly retarded individuals are able to acquire academic skills such as reading up to about a sixth-grade level and may be able to become economically self-supporting. The academic skills of those with moderate retardation are usually limited to the first- or second-grade level; these individuals can learn self-care skills and often function well in sheltered work environments. People with severe levels of retardation typically are unable to acquire academic skills but can communicate verbally and learn habits such as brushing their teeth. At the profound level of retardation, individuals usually learn only rudimentary motor skills and limited self-help skills such as feeding themselves.

Before the late 1960s, mentally retarded children in the United States were educated almost exclusively in special schools. Since then, there has been a movement toward **inclusion**—or educating mentally retarded students in regular schools. Inclusion, also called *mainstreaming*, may involve placing these students in classes with nonhandicapped students for part of the day or in special classrooms in regular schools. Resources spent on training programs for the mentally retarded are proving to be sound investments. Such programs rely heavily on behavior modification techniques and are making it possible for some retarded individuals to become employed workers earning the minimum wage or better. Everyone benefits—the individual, his or her family, and society as a whole.

The IQ Controversy

In many cases, biological factors such as the presence of an extra chromosome are to blame for mental retardation. But what about normal variations in intelligence? To what degree do they result from biological, or genetic, influences? This question arises out of perhaps the most vocal area of disagreement concerning intelligence, the **nature–nurture controversy**, the debate over whether intelligence is primarily the result of heredity or environment. Englishman Sir Francis Galton (1874) initiated this debate, which has raged for more than 100 years, and coined the term. After studying a number of prominent families in England, Galton concluded that intelligence was inherited. Hereditarians agree with Galton, claiming that intelligence is largely inherited—the result of nature. Environmentalists, in contrast, insist that it is influenced primarily by one's environment—the result of nurture. Most psychologists now agree that both nature and nurture contribute to intelligence, but they continue to debate the proportions contributed by each.

As you learned in Chapter 2, *behavioral genetics* is the study of the relative influence of genetics and environment on human behavior and mental processes. Behavioral geneticists sometimes express the results of their studies in terms of **heritability**, an index of the degree to which a characteristic is estimated to be influenced by heredity. Figure 7.7 (on page 220) shows estimates of the proportional contributions of genetic and environmental factors to intelligence. Some research using the adoption study method, comparing children to both their adoptive and biological parents, also supports the assertion that genes strongly influence IQ scores.

Minnesota is the site of the most extensive U.S. study of identical and fraternal twins. The Minnesota Center for Twin and Adoption Research at the University of Minnesota has assembled the *Minnesota Twin Registry*, which in 1998 included more than 10,000 twin pairs (Bouchard, 1998). Since 1979, researchers at the center, headed by Thomas Bouchard, have studied about 60 pairs of fraternal twins and 80 pairs of identical twins who were reared apart. Of all the traits Bouchard and his colleagues studied, the most heritable trait turned out to be intelligence. Bouchard (1997) reports that

◆ **mentally retarded**
Subnormal intelligence reflected by an IQ below 70 and by adaptive functioning severely deficient for one's age.

◆ **inclusion**
Educating mentally retarded students in regular rather than special schools by placing them in regular classes for part of the day or having special classrooms in regular schools; also called *mainstreaming*.

◆ *What is the evidence supporting the nature and nurture sides of the IQ controversy?*

◆ **nature–nurture controversy**
The debate over whether intelligence and other traits are primarily the result of heredity or environment.

◆ **heritability**
An index of the degree to which a characteristic is estimated to be influenced by heredity.

FIGURE 7.7

Correlations between the IQ Scores of Persons with Various Relationships

The more closely related two individuals are, the more similar their IQ scores tend to be. Thus, there is a strong genetic contribution to intelligence. *Source:* Based on data from Bouchard & McGue (1981); Erlenmeyer-Kimling & Jarvik (1963).

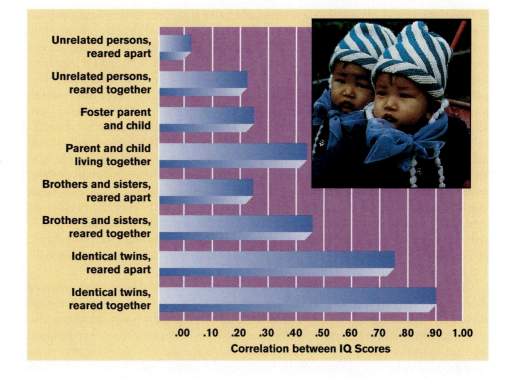

Unrelated persons, reared apart

Unrelated persons, reared together

Foster parent and child

Parent and child living together

Brothers and sisters, reared apart

Brothers and sisters, reared together

Identical twins, reared apart

Identical twins, reared together

.00 .10 .20 .30 .40 .50 .60 .70 .80 .90 1.00

Correlation between IQ Scores

various types of twin studies have consistently yielded heritability estimates of .60 to .70 for intelligence. (The heritability of some personality traits is discussed in Chapter 9.)

Not all researchers agree with Bouchard's heritability estimate for intelligence. Combining data from a number of twin studies, Plomin and others (1994) found the heritability estimate for general intelligence to be .52. Similar findings emerged from analyses of dozens of adoption studies and twin studies involving more than 10,000 pairs of twins. These analyses concluded that the heritability of general cognitive ability is about .50 (McClearn et al., 1997; Plomin et al., 2003). Psychologists who consider environmental factors to be the chief contributors to differences in intelligence also take issue with Bouchard's findings. They claim that most separated identical twins are raised by adoptive parents who have been matched as closely as possible to the biological parents. This fact, the critics say, could account for the similarity in IQ. In response to his critics, Bouchard (1997) has pointed out that children who are not related biologically but are raised in the same home are no more similar in intelligence once they reach adulthood than complete strangers.

Clearly, the high degree of similarity in the intelligence scores of identical twins who have been reared apart makes a strong case for the powerful influence of genes. But even Bouchard and his colleagues (1990) caution against trying to generalize their findings to people raised in disadvantaged environments. Bouchard (1997) states: "A child raised in crushing poverty by illiterate parents is unlikely to score well on IQ tests, no matter what his mental inheritance . . . . Twin studies tend to attract few subjects in such dire straits, so their findings may not always apply to people exposed to extremes of deprivation or privilege" (p. 56).

Several studies indicate that IQ test scores are not fixed but can be modified with an enriched environment. Several decades ago, Sandra Scarr and Richard Weinberg (1976) studied 140 African American and interracial children who had been adopted by highly educated, upper-middle-class White American families; 99 of the children had been adopted in the first year of life. The adoptees were fully exposed to middle-class cultural experiences and vocabulary, the "culture of the tests and the school" (p. 737). How did the children perform on IQ and achievement tests? The average IQ score of the 130 adoptees was 106.3 Their achievement test scores were slightly above the national average, not below. On the average, the earlier the children were adopted, the higher their IQs. The mean IQ score of the 99 early adoptees was 110.4, about 10 IQ

points above the average for White Americans. Similarly, studies in France show that IQ scores and achievement are substantially higher when children from lower-class environments are adopted by middle- and upper-middle-class families (Duyme, 1988; Schiff & Lewontin, 1986).

In addition to these encouraging adoption studies, research examining the effects of early childhood interventions on the IQ scores of children from poor families clearly indicates that early educational experiences can affect IQ scores (Brooks-Gunn, 2003; Schellenberg, 2004). Some of the best known of these interventions have been carried out by developmental psychologist Craig Ramey of the University of North Carolina (Burchinal et al., 1997; Campbell & Ramey, 1994; Campbell et al., 2001; Ramey, 1993; Ramey & Campbell, 1987). And unlike many studies of early interventions, Ramey's research involves true experiments—so it is clear that the outcomes are caused by the interventions.

In one of Ramey's programs (Campbell & Ramey, 1994), 6- to 12-month-old infants of low-IQ, low-income mothers were randomly assigned to either an intensive 40-hour-per-week day-care program that continued throughout the preschool years or a control group that received only medical care and nutritional supplements. When the children reached school age, half in each group (again based on random assignment) were enrolled in a special after-school program that helped their families learn how to support school learning with educational activities at home. Ramey followed the progress of children in all four groups through age 12, giving them IQ tests at various ages. Figure 7.8 shows that those who participated in the infant and preschool program scored higher on IQ tests than peers who received either no intervention or only the school-aged intervention. Perhaps more important, during the elementary school years, about 40% of the control group participants had IQ scores classified as borderline or retarded (scores below 85), compared with only 12.8% of those who were in the infant program. More recent research shows that the cognitive advantage enjoyed by the infant intervention groups has persisted into adulthood (Campbell et al., 2001). Ramey's work clearly shows that the environment has great potential to influence IQ scores.

Historical evidence also suggests that environmental factors have a strong influence on IQ scores. Americans and similarly advantaged populations all over the world have gained about 3 IQ points per decade since 1940. James Flynn (1987, 1999; Dickens & Flynn, 2001) analyzed 73 studies involving some 7,500 participants ranging in age from 12 to 48 and found that "every Binet and Wechsler [standardization group] from 1932 to 1978 has performed better than its predecessor" (Flynn, 1987, p. 225). This consistent improvement in IQ scores over time is known as the *Flynn effect*. The average IQ in Western industrialized nations is currently about 15 points higher than it was 50 years ago.

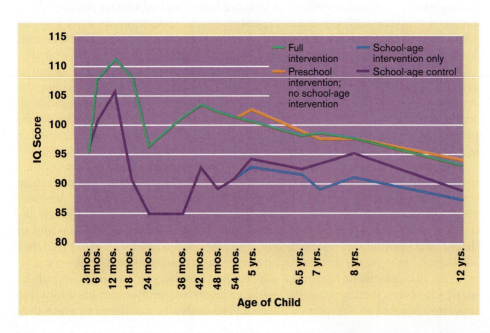

FIGURE 7.8

Ramey's Infant Intervention

In the Ramey study, children were randomly assigned in infancy to an experimental group with special day care (the "full intervention" group) or to a control group. From kindergarten through third grade, half of each group received supplementary family support, and the other half did not. The difference in IQ between the intervention and control groups remained statistically significant even at age 12. *Source:* From Campbell & Ramey (1994).

It should not be surprising that enriched environments alter traits that are highly heritable. Consider the fact that American and British adolescents are 6 inches taller on average than their counterparts a century and a half ago (Tanner, 1990). Height has the same heritability (.90) today as it did in the mid-19th century. So this tremendous average gain in height of 6 inches is entirely attributable to environmental influences: better health, better nutrition, and so on. The highest heritability estimates for intelligence are far lower than those for height. It seems clear, then, that environmental influences have the power to affect intelligence and achievement. For example, poverty affects nutrition, and research clearly shows that malnutrition, especially early in life, can harm intellectual development (Grigorenko, 2003).

Race and IQ

◆ *What arguments have been advanced to explain racial differences in IQ scores?*

The nature–nurture debate has also been important in the discussion of race differences in intelligence test scores. Historically, most studies have shown that Blacks score, on average, about 15 points lower than Whites on standardized IQ tests in the United States (e.g., Loehlin et al., 1975). Other studies have shown similar differences for Blacks and Whites in other nations (e.g., Rushton & Jensen, 2003). But why? Two publications addressing this question stimulated heated debate about the link between race and intelligence in the scientific community and the general public.

In 1969, psychologist Arthur Jensen published an article in which he attributed the IQ gap to genetic differences between the races. Further, he claimed that the genetic influence on intelligence is so strong that the environment cannot make a significant difference. Jensen even went so far as to claim that Blacks and Whites possess qualitatively different kinds of intelligence.

The late psychologist Richard Herrnstein (1930–1994) and political scientist Charles Murray added fresh fuel to the controversy in the mid-1990s with their book *The Bell Curve* (Herrnstein & Murray, 1994). They argued that IQ differences among individuals and between groups explain how those at the top of the ladder in U.S. society got there and why those on the lower rungs remain there. Herrnstein and Murray largely attributed the social ills of modern society—including poverty, welfare dependency, crime, and illegitimacy—to low IQ, which they implied is primarily genetic and largely immune to change by environmental intervention. Yet, their own estimate was that 60% of IQ is genetically inherited, "which, by extension, means that IQ is about 40% a matter of environment" (p. 105). That 40% would seem to leave a lot of room for improvement.

Beliefs such as those expressed by Jensen and Herrnstein and Murray run counter to the results of the studies carried out by Craig Ramey and others that you read about earlier in this chapter. Such studies suggest that racial differences are more likely to result from poverty and lack of access to educational opportunities than from genetics. Moreover, a new testing technique called *dynamic assessment* supports the environmental explanation. In dynamic assessment, examinees are taught the goal and format of each IQ subtest before they are actually tested. The rationale behind the technique is the assumption that children from middle-class backgrounds have more experience with testing procedures and better understand that the goal of testing is to demonstrate competency. Studies of dynamic assessment show that it significantly increases the number of minority children who achieve above-average IQ scores (Lidz & Macrine, 2001).

In recent years, psychologists have begun to investigate another variable called *stereotype threat* that may help explain racial differences in IQ scores. The stereotype threat theory was first proposed by psychologist Claude Steele (Steele & Aronson, 1995). According to Steele, when minority individuals hear discussions of group differences in IQ scores, they may assume that their own intellectual ability is inferior to that of individuals in the majority group. Therefore, when faced with an IQ test, they "disengage," to avoid the threat of being stereotyped as having limited intellectual ability. This disengagement becomes a self-fulfilling prophecy: It causes individuals to obtain low scores, thereby appearing to validate the stereotype. Research has shown that programs designed to help people talk about and overcome the degree to which they

How Did You Find Psychology?

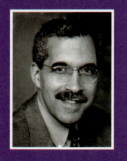

Claude Steele

Can watching television change a person's life? For psychologist Claude Steele, whose work on stereotype threat you read about on page 222, it did ("Claude M. Steele," 2003). At the end of his freshman year at Hiram College in 1964, Steele returned home to Chicago. That summer was marked by riots in Harlem. Steele was intensely interested in the riots because he had been raised by parents who were deeply devoted to the cause of civil rights but who also insisted that the movement never resort to violence to achieve its goals. Consequently, Steele watched all of the television coverage of the riots.

One of the interviews Steele saw featured psychologist Kenneth Clark, whose research you read about in Chapter 1. At that time, Clark was a professor at the Graduate Center of the City University of New York (CUNY). In the interview, he explained his research, which showed that membership in a group that is regarded as inferior by the larger society can affect an individual's self-concept. Up to that point, Steele had been planning to enter a profession such as dentistry and had already taken a required course in introductory psychology. As he listened to Clark, however, he was so impressed with the insight Clark seemed to have into the complexities of human behavior that he decided to take some additional psychology courses. A few years later, Steele graduated from Hiram College with a degree in psychology and applied to graduate school at CUNY, hoping to become one of Clark's students. As a backup plan, Steele also applied to Ohio State University (OSU). As fate would have it, CUNY lost his application, and he ended up going to OSU. At OSU, he was among the first students in what would become one of the top social psychology programs in the United States.

After receiving his Ph.D., Steele went on to establish himself as an eminent researcher in the field over the next few years. While working as a professor at various institutions, Steele served on many graduate school admissions committees. As he sifted through applicants' credentials, he was struck by the lack of qualified minority candidates. Searching for an explanation brought him back to his original interest in Clark's research. Discussions of his line of thinking with his colleagues about the small number of minority individuals who apply to graduate programs in psychology led to Steele's development of the stereotype threat theory.

Steele's experiences show that television can be a positive—even educational—force in people's lives. It can make us aware of people and ideas that we might otherwise never have encountered. And, in some cases, something a person sees on television can change the direction of his or her life in ways that benefit the larger community.

sense stereotype threat when they take cognitive ability tests helps them achieve higher scores (Good et al., 2003). Other psychologists have pointed out that, although studies have shown that stereotype threat does exist, it explains only a fraction of the total average score differences among racial groups (Sackett et al., 2004).

Before leaving the topic of race and IQ, stop and consider why the debates spawned by findings showing that one group has a higher average IQ than another group have stirred so much emotional intensity. One reason might be that in Western societies such as the United States intellectual ability is highly valued. In contrast, studies show that Asians place little value on intellectual ability even though they tend to get higher scores on cognitive ability tests than Whites or other groups (Li, 2003). Instead, Asians emphasize hard work and perseverance as the routes to academic and other kinds of life success (Stevenson, 1992). By contrast, by the time Americans reach the age of 11 or 12, a large majority believe that achievement results more from ability than from effort (Altermatt & Pomerantz, 2003; Heyman et al., 2003). Psychologists suggest that this belief leads American students to fail to appreciate the importance of effort to academic achievement, even for people who are high in ability. It may also help explain research such as that of two researchers who compared the achievement test scores of Australian school children of Asian descent to those of English/Irish ancestry (Dandy & Nettelbeck, 2002). Their findings showed that Asian Australian students scored higher than their English/Irish peers on achievement tests even when they were matched on IQ (Dandy & Nettelbeck, 2002). These results suggest that, on a practical level, teachers and parents should probably be more concerned about helping each student work to achieve his or her full intellectual potential than about the student's IQ score.

Gender Differences in Cognitive Abilities

◆ *In what ways do the cognitive abilities of males and females differ?*

There is some evidence that men and women have different intellectual strengths. For example, Figure 7.9 shows some types of problems on which each gender tends to excel. But you need to keep two important points in mind: First, in general, the differences within each gender are greater than the differences between the genders. Second, even though gender differences in cognitive abilities have been generally small on average, there tends to be more variation in such abilities among males than among females (that is, the range of test scores is typically greater for males).

Girls as young as 18 months of age have been found to have, on average, larger vocabularies than boys of the same age, a difference that persists throughout childhood (Lutchmaya et al., 2002). In one frequently cited large-scale study, Hedges and Nowell (1995) analyzed the results of the National Assessment of Educational Progress (NAEP), which

FIGURE 7.9

Problem-Solving Tasks Favoring Women and Men

(a) A series of problem-solving tasks on which women generally do better than men. (b) Problem-solving tasks on which men do better. *Source:* Kimura (1992).

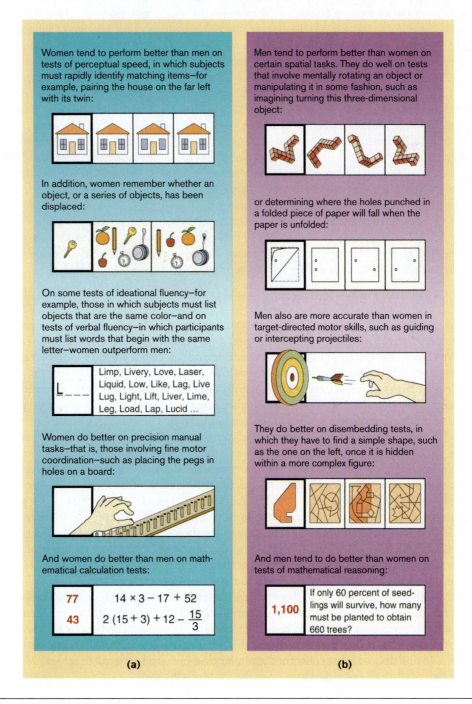

(a)

(b)

has tested a nationally representative sample of 70,000 to 100,000 9-, 13-, and 17-year-olds annually in reading comprehension, writing, math, and science. The researchers compared the achievements of the 17-year-olds from 1971 through 1992 and reported that females outperformed males in reading and writing, while males did better in science and math. Although average gender differences were small, there was one prominent exception: "Females performed substantially better than males in writing every year" (p. 44). Furthermore, Hedges and Nowell reported that more males than females were near the bottom of the distribution, not only in writing, but also in reading comprehension.

As noted above, analyses of NAEP data show that boys display higher levels of achievement in mathematics than girls. Some data indicate that hormonal differences between males and females contribute to the math achievement gender gap (Josephs et al., 2003). However, most researchers agree that social influences are probably more important.

One possible social factor influencing the difference in math achievement is that parents often expect boys to do better than girls in math (Tiedemann, 2000). Could parental expectations become a self-fulfilling prophecy, leading girls to lack confidence in their math ability and to decide not to pursue advanced math courses? Yes, says sex difference researcher Jacqueline Eccles. Eccles's longitudinal research has shown that parents' beliefs about their children's talents at age 6 predict those children's beliefs about their own abilities at age 17 (Fredricks & Eccles, 2002). However, Eccles's research has also revealed that the gender gap in beliefs about math ability is somewhat smaller among today's high school students than it was in the past, suggesting that educators' efforts to increase girls' interest and success in mathematics have been effective.

Another way in which parents influence boys' and girls' ideas about math competence is their tendency to see academically successful girls as "hard workers" and academically successful boys as "talented" (Ratty et al., 2002). Thus, parents' beliefs may help explain why teenage girls who obtain top scores on standardized mathematics tests typically explain their scores as resulting from effort, while their male peers believe that their scores are due to superior natural mathematical talent (Rebs & Park, 2001). Thus, even girls with extraordinary levels of mathematical achievement may see themselves as lacking in ability. Perhaps it isn't surprising that mathematically gifted girls are far less likely than similarly gifted boys to choose math-oriented careers (Webb et al., 2002).

Researchers have found that, in general, males tend to perform somewhat better than females on some, but not all, spatial tasks (Geary, 1996; Kimura, 1992, 2000). Some research has shown that spatial abilities appear to be enhanced by prenatal exposure to high levels of androgens (Berenbaum et al., 1995). Further, high blood levels of testosterone in men are associated with good performance on spatial tasks such as route learning (Choi & Silverman, 2002). However, these findings do not minimize the role of social experiences and expectations in shaping children's abilities and interests. Women also outperform men on some kinds of spatial tasks.

Creativity

Have you ever known a person who was intellectually bright, but lacked creativity? **Creativity** can be thought of as the ability to produce original, appropriate, and valuable ideas and/or solutions to problems. Research indicates that there is only a weak to moderate correlation between creativity and IQ (Lubart, 2003). Remember the mentally gifted individuals studied by Lewis Terman? Not one of them has produced a highly creative work (Terman & Oden, 1959). No Nobel laureates, no Pulitzer prizes. Geniuses, yes; creative geniuses, no. Thus, high intelligence does not necessarily mean high creativity.

Cartoonists often illustrate creative thinking as a flash of insight, a lightbulb that suddenly turns on in the mind. But research studies indicate that useful and genuine creativity rarely appears in the form of sudden flashes (Haberlandt, 1997). For the most part, creative ideas that come to conscious awareness have been incubating for some time. Most experts agree that genuine creativity "is an accomplishment born of intensive study, long reflection, persistence and interest" (Snow, 1993, p. 1033).

◆ How does creativity differ from other forms of cognition, and how has it been measured?

◆ **creativity**
The ability to produce original, appropriate, and valuable ideas and/or solutions to problems.

◆ **divergent thinking**

The ability to produce multiple ideas, answers, or solutions to a problem for which there is no agreed-on solution.

There are basically four stages in the creative problem-solving process (Goleman et al., 1992):

1. *Preparation*—searching for information that may help solve the problem
2. *Incubation*—letting the problem "sit" while the relevant information is digested
3. *Illumination*—being suddenly struck by the right solution
4. *Translation*—transforming the insight into useful action

The incubation stage, perhaps the most important part of the process, takes place below the level of awareness.

What is unique about creative thought? According to psychologist J. P. Guilford (1967), who studied creativity for several decades, creative thinkers are highly proficient at divergent thinking. **Divergent thinking** is the ability to produce multiple ideas, answers, or solutions to a problem for which there is no agreed-on solution (Guilford, 1967). More broadly, divergent thinking is novel, or original, and involves the synthesis of an unusual association of ideas; it is flexible, switching quickly and smoothly from one stream of thought or set of ideas to another; and it requires fluency, or the ability to formulate an abundance of ideas (Csikszentmihalyi, 1996). In contrast to divergent thinking, Guilford defined *convergent thinking* as the type of mental activity measured by IQ and achievement tests; it consists of solving precisely defined, logical problems for which there is a known correct answer.

However, divergent and convergent thinking are not always separate phenomena. Both are required for most cognitive tasks. For example, to be creative, a person must develop divergent thinking, but convergent thinking is required to discriminate between good and bad ideas (Csikszentmihalyi, 1996). Similarly, solving precisely defined problems can involve divergent thinking, as one tries to think of possible solutions.

Researchers are identifying the different brain areas involved in convergent and divergent thinking. In general, convergent thinking is characterized by greater activity in the left frontal cortex, while divergent thinking is marked by higher levels of activity in the right frontal cortex (Razoumnikova, 2000). Other studies show that processes involved in convergent thinking, such as searching for patterns in events, are carried out in the left hemisphere (Wolford et al., 2000). Studies by Carlsson and others (2000) that measured regional cerebral blood flow (rCBF) revealed striking differences in frontal lobe activity between participants who were engaged in highly creative thinking and those who were not. Figure 7.10(a) shows the frontal lobe activity during highly creative thinking. There is activity in both hemispheres but a significantly greater amount in the right frontal cortex. In contrast, Figure 7.10(b) shows that during periods when no creative thinking is occurring, the left frontal lobe is highly active, and there is very little activity in the right hemisphere.

How might individual differences in creativity be measured? Tests designed to measure creativity emphasize original approaches to arriving at solutions for open-ended problems or to producing artistic works (Gregory, 1996). One creativity test, the Unusual Uses Test, asks respondents to name as many uses as possible for an ordinary

FIGURE 7.10

Maps of Regional Cerebral Blood Flow (rCBF)

(a) Highly creative thinking is associated with activity in both hemispheres, but with significantly higher levels in the right hemisphere (red indicates activity). (b) During thinking that is not creative, activity is largely restricted to the left hemisphere. *Source:* Adapted from Carlsson et al. (2000).

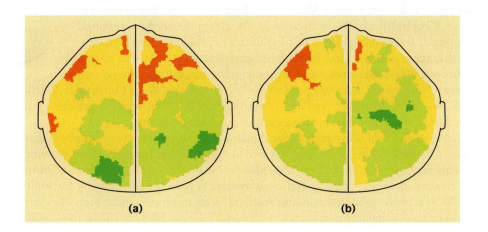

(a)　　　　(b)

object (such as a brick). Another measure of creativity is the Consequences Test, which asks test takers to list as many consequences as they can that would be likely to follow some basic change in the world (such as the force of gravity being reduced by 50%). And researchers Mednick and Mednick (1967), who reasoned that the essence of creativity consists of the creative thinker's ability to fit together ideas that to the noncreative thinker might appear remote or unrelated, created the Remote Associates Test (RAT).

Psychologists studying exceptionally creative individuals (e.g., Bloom et al., 1985) have learned that they share a number of characteristics that distinguish them from less creative individuals. For one, they have a great deal of expertise in a specific area that has been built up over years of disciplined study and practice. Creative individuals are also open to new experiences and ideas, even those that may seem quite odd to others; moreover, they seem to be inherently curious and inquisitive (Sternberg, 1985a). Creative people also tend to be independent thinkers who are less influenced by the opinions of others than their less creative counterparts are. Perhaps because of their independence, creative individuals are more likely to be motivated by the anticipation, excitement, and enjoyment of their work than by a desire to please others. Finally, creative endeavor requires hard work and persistence in the face of failure. For instance, Albert Einstein published 248 papers on his theory of relativity before it was finished, and Mozart, when he died at age 35, had created 609 musical compositions (Haberlandt, 1997).

Looking Back   At the beginning of the chapter, you read about two individuals, Marilyn Mach vos Savant and her husband Robert Jarvik, who are both clearly brilliant but whose records of achievement on intelligence tests are quite different. She attained record-high IQ scores; his performance was mediocre. Clearly, there is much more to intelligence than is captured by IQ test scores. Similarly, although individual differences are important, the remarkable human brain has equipped all of us with the capacity for language and an impressive array of cognitive tools that we could all learn to use more proficiently.

Apply It 7.1   How to Build a Powerful Vocabulary

Of all the cognitive skills humans possess, none is more important for clarity of thinking and academic success than vocabulary. How, then, can you build a more powerful vocabulary? The best way is to realize that almost all words belong to larger networks of meaning and to understand that your mind is already geared toward organizing information in terms of meaning. Thus, with a little effort, you can greatly increase your vocabulary by supporting the kind of learning your brain is already inclined to do. Here are a few techniques for following this advice.

Learn to think analytically about words you already know and relate new words to them.

What do the words *antiseptic* and *septic tank* have in common? You use an *antiseptic* to prevent bacterial infection of a wound; a *septic tank* is used for removing harmful bacteria from water containing human waste. A logical conclusion would be that *septic* has something to do with bacteria. Knowing this, what do you think a doctor means when she says that a patient is suffering from *sepsis*? By linking *sepsis* to *septic tank* and *antiseptic,* you can guess that she is referring to some kind of bacterial infection.

Be aware of word connections that may be hidden by spelling differences.

You may know that both *Caesar* and *Czar* refer to some kind of ruler or leader. But you may not know that they are exactly the same word spoken and spelled somewhat differently

(continued on page 228)

in Ancient Rome (*Caesar*) and in Russia (*Czar*). Now, if you learn in a history class about *Kaiser Wilhelm* who led Germany during World War I, thinking analytically about his title may help you realize that it is exactly the same word as *Caesar* and *Czar*, but with a German spelling. Here's another example: Can you guess something about the location and climate of the nation of *Ecuador* by relating its name to a word that differs only slightly in spelling?

Use your knowledge of word parts to actively seek out new words.

Don't learn new words one at a time. Instead, be on the lookout for "word families"—root words and prefixes and suffixes. Here is one important root word, *spect*. You've seen it in many words. *Spect* means "look," "look at," "watch," "see." And *spect* appears in dozens of different words, such as *inspect*. What do you do when you *inspect* something? You *look* closely at it. Once you are equipped with this knowledge, other *spect* words may start to come to mind along with an entirely new way of thinking about their meanings: *spectacular, spectator, spectacle, spectacles, perspective, prospect, respect, disrespect, retrospect, suspect,* and so on. The word *circumspect*

may be new to you. Look it up in a dictionary, and think about how the literal meaning of the word ("look around") relates to the way this word is frequently used. And, when you read Chapter 1, might it have been easier to understand and remember the meaning of Wundt's research method, *introspection*, if you had thought about the *spect* part of the word? Probably so.

A strong vocabulary based on root words, prefixes, and suffixes will yield the word power that will profit you in many ways.

Chapter 7 Summary

Cognition p. 201

How do images and concepts help us think? p. 201

Imagery aids memory and motor performance. Concepts enable us to use categories to organize our thinking.

What is the role of heuristics in decision making? p. 202

Heuristics help us make decisions quickly with little mental effort.

What are some basic approaches to problem solving, and how do they differ? p. 205

Analogies, working backward, and means–end analysis are problem-solving heuristics that may or may not lead to a correct solution. An algorithm is a strategy that always leads to a correct solution.

What are some important applications of artificial intelligence technologies? p. 207

Artificial neural networks (ANNs) are used to simulate human thinking. They process information like human experts and learn from experience.

Language p. 207

What are the necessary components of any language? p. 208

The components of any language are (1) phonemes, (2) morphemes, (3) syntax, (4) semantics, and (5) pragmatics.

What is the evidence concerning the capacity of animals for understanding and producing language? p. 208

Chimpanzees' communication with humans uses sign language or symbols and consists of constructions strung together rather than actual sentences.

In what ways does language influence thinking? p. 210

In general, thinking has a greater influence on language than language has on thinking. Whorf's linguistic relativity hypothesis has not been supported by research.

What are the advantages and disadvantages of learning a second language at different ages? p. 211

People who learn a second language when they are younger than age 10 or 11 usually speak it without an accent. However, adolescents and adults know more about their own languages, and they can use this knowledge when they are learning a second one.

Intelligence p. 212

How do the views of Spearman, Thurstone, Gardner, and Sternberg differ with regard to the definition of intelligence? p. 212

Spearman believed that intelligence is composed of a general ability factor (*g*) and a number of specific abilities (*s*). Thurstone proposed seven primary mental abilities. Gardner claims that there are eight kinds of intelligence, and Sternberg's triarchic theory proposes that three types exist.

What did Binet, Terman, and Wechsler contribute to the study of intelligence? p. 215

Binet developed the first standardized intelligence test. Terman developed a formula for the intelligence quotient

(IQ) based on chronological age. Wechsler developed a test based on verbal and nonverbal subtests.

◆ Why are reliability, validity, standardization, and cultural bias important in intelligence testing? p. 216

Reliable tests yield consistent results. Tests are valid if they predict appropriate outcome variables. Standardization is necessary so that individuals' scores can be compared. Cultural bias threatens the validity of a test, so test-makers must reduce it as much as possible. Culture-fair tests have been developed in an effort to find a way of measuring intelligence that is independent of culture.

◆ How do individuals who are gifted and those with mental retardation differ from others? p. 217

Terman's longitudinal study demonstrated that gifted individuals enjoy better physical and mental health and are more successful than members of the general population. Mental retardation involves both low IQ and poor adaptive functioning.

◆ What is the evidence supporting the nature and nurture sides of the IQ controversy? p. 219

Twin studies provide evidence that individual differences in intelligence are strongly influenced by genes. Adoption studies and early childhood intervention programs have shown that IQ can also be influenced by environment.

◆ What arguments have been advanced to explain racial differences in IQ scores? p. 222

Some researchers claim that racial differences result from genetics. Others argue that poverty, lack of educational opportunities and familiarity with testing situations, and stereotype threat explain these differences.

◆ In what ways do the cognitive abilities of males and females differ? p. 224

Females outperform males in reading and writing. Males seem to do better in science, math, and some spatial tasks.

◆ How does creativity differ from other forms of cognition, and how has it been measured? p. 225

Guilford suggests that creativity involves divergent thinking. Tests used to measure creativity include the Unusual Uses Test, the Consequences Test, and the Remote Associates Test (RAT).

◆ KEY TERMS

algorithm, p. 206
analogy heuristic, p. 205
aptitude test, p. 217
artificial intelligence, p. 207
artificial neural networks (ANNs) p. 207
availability heuristic, p. 203
cognition, p. 201
concept, p. 201
creativity, p. 225
culture-fair intelligence test, p. 217
decision making, p. 202
divergent thinking, p. 226
elimination by aspects, p. 203
exemplars, p. 202
expert systems, p. 207
formal concept, p. 202
framing, p. 204

functional fixedness, p. 206
g factor, p. 213
heritability, p. 219
heuristic, p. 203
imagery, p. 201
inclusion, p. 219
intelligence, p. 212
intelligence quotient (IQ), p. 216
intuition, p. 205
language, p. 207
linguistic relativity hypothesis, p. 210
means–end analysis, p. 205
mentally retarded, p. 219
mental set, p. 206
morphemes, p. 208
natural concept, p. 202
nature–nurture controversy, p. 219

norms, p. 216
phonemes, p. 208
pragmatics, p. 208
primary mental abilities, p. 213
problem solving, p. 205
prototype, p. 202
psycholinguistics, p. 208
recognition heuristic, p. 203
reliability, p. 216
representativeness heuristic, p. 203
semantics, p. 208
standardization, p. 217
syntax, p. 208
triarchic theory of intelligence, p. 214
validity, p. 217
working backward, p. 205

Answers to all the Study Guide questions are provided at the end of the book.

◆ SECTION ONE: Chapter Review

Cognition (pp. 201–207)

1. The two most common forms of imagery are
   - **a.** visual and motor.
   - **b.** auditory and tactile.
   - **c.** visual and auditory.
   - **d.** visual and gustatory.

2. A mental category that represents a class or group of items that share common characteristics or attributes is called a(n)
   - **a.** image.
   - **b.** concept.
   - **c.** positive instance.
   - **d.** prototype.

3. A prototype is the most _____ example of a concept.
   - **a.** abstract
   - **b.** unusual
   - **c.** recent
   - **d.** typical

4. _____ refers to the way information is presented so as to focus on a potential gain or loss.

5. Which of the following is guaranteed, if properly applied, to result in the correct answer to a problem?
   - **a.** an algorithm
   - **b.** a heuristic
   - **c.** trial and error
   - **d.** applying prior knowledge

6. Working backward and means–end analysis are examples of
   - **a.** algorithms.
   - **b.** heuristics.
   - **c.** mental sets.
   - **d.** functional fixedness.

7. John uses a wastebasket to keep a door from closing. In solving his problem, he was not hindered by
   - **a.** a heuristic.
   - **b.** an algorithm.
   - **c.** functional fixedness.
   - **d.** mental set.

8. One characteristic of good problem solvers is mental set. (true/false)

9. Artificial intelligence systems surpass the problem-solving ability of experts in a number of fields. (true/false)

Language (pp. 207–212)

10. Match the component of language with the appropriate description.
    - _____ (1) the smallest units of meaning
    - _____ (2) the meaning derived from phonemes, morphemes, and sentences
    - _____ (3) grammatical rules for arranging and combining words to form phrases and sentences
    - _____ (4) the smallest units of sound in a spoken language
    - _____ (5) intonation patterns
    - **a.** pragmatics
    - **b.** syntax
    - **c.** morphemes
    - **d.** semantics
    - **e.** phonemes

11. Communication in trained chimpanzees approaches human language in form and complexity. (true/false)

12. The linguistic relativity hypothesis is not supported by research. (true/false)

13. In general, thought influences language more than language influences thought. (true/false)

Intelligence (pp. 212–227)

14. Match the theorist with the theory of intelligence.
    - _____ (1) seven primary abilities
    - _____ (2) multiple intelligences
    - _____ (3) the *g* factor
    - **a.** Spearman
    - **b.** Thurstone
    - **c.** Gardner

15. The first successful effort to measure intelligence was made by
    - **a.** Binet and Simon.
    - **b.** Spearman.
    - **c.** Wechsler.
    - **d.** Terman.

16. According to Terman's formula, what is the IQ of a child with a mental age of 12 and a chronological age of 8?
    - **a.** 75
    - **b.** 150
    - **c.** 125
    - **d.** 100

17. In which range will the scores of the largest percentage of people taking an IQ test fall?
    a. 85 to 115
    b. 85 to 100
    c. 100 to 130
    d. 70 to 85

18. Twin studies suggest that environment is stronger than heredity as a factor in shaping IQ differences. (true/false)

19. In general, differences in cognitive abilities are greater within each gender than between the genders. (true/false)

20. For each cognitive ability, indicate whether males or females, in general, tend to score higher on tests of that ability.
    ____ (1) writing
    ____ (2) science
    ____ (3) spatial ability
    ____ (4) reading comprehension
    ____ (5) mathematics
    a. males
    b. females

21. The ability to produce multiple ideas or answers to a problem is known as
    a. convergent thinking.
    b. practical intelligence.
    c. divergent thinking.
    d. creativity.

22. People with high IQ scores are typically highly creative. (true/false)

23. The stages in the creative problem-solving process occur in the following sequence:
    a. illumination, incubation, preparation, translation
    b. incubation, illumination, preparation, translation
    c. preparation, incubation, illumination, translation
    d. translation, preparation, incubation, illumination

◆ SECTION TWO: Important Concepts and Psychologists

On the line opposite each term, write the name of the theorist or researcher who is most closely associated with it.

1. bounded rationality

2. elimination by aspects

3. linguistic relativity hypothesis

4. *g* factor

5. triarchic theory of intelligence

6. Stanford–Binet Intelligence Scale

7. WAIS-R

8. nature–nurture controversy

9. stereotype threat

10. multiple intelligences

◆ SECTION THREE: Fill In the Blank

1. The mental processes involved in the acquisition, storage, retrieval, and use of knowledge are known as _____.

2. _____ is defined as the representation of sensory experience in the mind.

3. If you are a member of a Western culture, your concept of food probably includes meat. Beef, pork, and chicken most likely are _____ of the concept, but whale blubber probably is not.

4. Jordan must consider many alternatives and factors in making a particular decision. She decides to rank the factors from most important to least important. She then starts to eliminate alternatives as they fail to meet the highest-ranked factors. This is an example of the _____ strategy for decision making.

5. The study of how language is acquired, produced, and used and how sounds and symbols of language are translated into meaning is known as _____.

6. When we speak of the rules of language use, we are talking about _____.

7. Kwoon asserts that the language you use determines the nature of your thoughts. Kwoon is a proponent of the _____ _____ hypothesis.

8. The theory proposing eight kinds of intelligence, including linguistic intelligence and intrapersonal intelligence, was developed by _____.

9. If Taylor scores very low on an IQ test and then is found to be at the top of her class in academic performance, we can assume that the IQ test does not have very good _____.

10. Jack is the kind of person who seems to be able to make the world work for him. He knows how to fit into a situation or change the situation to his needs, and he is very successful in business because of this talent. Sternberg would say that Jack has a high level of _____ intelligence.

11. James takes the same IQ test on two different days. His score on the second day is much higher than his score on the first day. We can assume that the test does not have good _____.

12. The ability to produce original, appropriate, and valuable ideas and/or solutions to problems is known as _____.

◆ **SECTION FOUR: Comprehensive Practice Test**

1. The mental processes involved in acquiring, storing, retrieving, and using knowledge are known collectively as
  a. conceptualization.   **c.** imagery.
  b. cognition.   **d.** thinking.

2. *Dog, car, honesty,* and *trees* are all examples of
  a. images.   **c.** verbal images.
  b. concepts.   **d.** typographs.

3. A gun would be identified by many people as a _____ of the concept *weapon*.

4. Artificial concepts are also known as fuzzy concepts. (true/false)

5. A good example of a formal concept is
  a. the periodic table of the elements.
  b. social display rules.
  c. ethical guidelines.
  d. established table manners.

6. Students who learn systematic, step-by-step procedures to solve their statistics problems are learning
  a. algorithms.   **c.** elimination by aspects.
  b. trial and error.   **d.** means–end analysis.

7. An artificial neural network is a computer system that is designed to mimic
  a. artificial intelligence. **c.** human heuristics.
  b. animal intelligence.   **d.** the human brain.

8. _____ are the smallest units of sound in a spoken language.
  a. phonemes   **c.** morphemes
  b. semantics   **d.** consonants

9. It is obvious that other animals have no real language or communication abilities at all. Any apparent display of such abilities has been shown to be simply a matter of operant conditioning. (true/false)

10. Research suggests that gender-specific pronouns such as "he" influence interpretation of sentences in favor of males. (true/false)

11. Thurstone believed that the single IQ score method of measuring and describing intelligence was the most effective manner of measuring intelligence. (true/false)

12. Sternberg's experiential intelligence includes
  a. the ability to learn from past events.
  b. the ability to manipulate people's opinions.
  c. creative problem solving.
  d. basic academic skills.

13. The WAIS-R intelligence test provides two different subtest scores, in addition to an overall IQ score. The two subtests are
  a. verbal and mathematics.
  b. contextual and componential.
  c. performance and musical.
  d. verbal and performance.

14. Mike has just taken a test that is designed to predict future achievement or performance. Mike took a(n)
    a. aptitude test.
    b. projective test.
    c. intelligence test.
    d. creativity test.

15. About what percentage of IQ test scores fall between −1 and +1 standard deviation from the mean of 100 on a normal curve?
    a. 34%   b. 68%   c. 50%   d. 13%

16. Culture-fair intelligence tests were designed to represent different cultural values equally on the same test. (true/false)

17. Intelligence is not fixed at birth; rather, evidence suggests that improved environmental factors can increase IQ scores. (true/false)

18. Although intelligence may be necessary for creativity, it is not sufficient. (true/false)

◆ SECTION FIVE: Critical Thinking

1. Review the three basic approaches to problem solving discussed in this chapter. Which approach do you think is most practical and efficient for solving everyday problems?

2. Which of the theories of intelligence best fits your notion of intelligence? Why?

3. Prepare an argument supporting each of the following positions:
    a. Intelligence tests should be used in the schools.
    b. Intelligence tests should not be used in the schools.

4. Give several examples of how you might bring more creativity into your educational and personal life.

Human Development

chapter **8**

Do you fear growing old? Many people do because they associate old age with failing health, loneliness, decreased mobility, and impaired mental functioning. Certainly, some very real physical declines inevitably happen as we age. But for some people, even very old age is a time of continuing health and enthusiasm for life. Consider Tom Spear, who, at the advanced age of 102, still plays 18 holes of golf three times a week. And then there's Lily Hearst, age 101, who swims eight laps a day, does yoga, and gives piano lessons. Spear and Hearst are just two of the more than 1,000 centenarians (people who have lived a century or more) whose longevity has been studied by Dr. Thomas Perls and his colleagues at the New England Centenarian Study, located at Boston University Medical School. Perls and his colleagues are gathering data about all aspects of centenarians' lives. So far, they have made the following discoveries:

- Most centenarians have a long history of regular physical activity.
- The majority have remained mentally active by pursuing work or hobbies that they enjoy.
- Ninety percent of centenarians are able to live independently until the age of 90, and 75% do so until the age of 95.
- Many centenarians have experienced long periods of deprivation and hardship. Some were born as slaves; others survived the Holocaust.
- Worldwide, women centenarians outnumber men by a ratio of nine to one.
- Very few centenarians are obese, and most are lean, especially the men.
- A substantial history of smoking is rare.
- Centenarians tend to be optimistic and are able to shrug off worries.
- A good sense of humor seems to be a common trait.
- Most centenarians have one or more parents, siblings, or grandparents who also lived a very long time.
- Centenarians tend to enjoy close family relationships, and many of them live within daily visiting distance of family members.

Perls has developed an online quiz that can help you determine your own chances of living to 100 (www.livingto100.com/quiz.cfm). But the scientific study of old age has ramifications that go far beyond our individual concerns about aging. Centenarians are the fastest-growing segment of the population in developed countries. Approximately 60,000 centenarians now live in the United States, for example; if current trends continue, there will be more than 800,000 by the year 2050. In the rest of the world, the odds of reaching age 100 are considerably lower, but the United Nations predicts that improvements in public health will rapidly increase the proportion of centenarians who live in developing countries. The UN estimates that there will be more than 3 million centenarians in the world by 2050. Social scientists and politicians alike have raised concerns about the costs—both social and economic—of caring for this unprecedented number of extremely elderly individuals. For these reasons, understanding the aging process and those who seem to defy it is vital to our future.

The study of aging has also influenced the way psychologists think about human development. Historically, psychologists considered childhood and adolescence to be periods of change culminating in physical, social, and intellectual maturity. Next, most believed, came several decades of behavioral and psychological stability in adulthood. Finally, the conventional wisdom said, old age ushered in an era of rapid decline that resulted in death. Today, psychologists' approach to all of these periods is strongly influenced by the *lifespan perspective,* the view that change happens throughout the lifespan, literally

Lily Hearst

from "womb to tomb" (Baltes et al., 1980). More-over, most now recognize that, in every era of life, there are both positive and negative changes. Research based in many disciplines—anthropology, sociology, economics, political science, and biology, as well as psychology—is required to fully comprehend human development. In the spirit of this lifespan perspective, we will examine the milestones that occur between the first and final moments of life before returning to our discussion of the challenges associated with the growing number of elderly adults.

◆ developmental psychology

The study of how humans grow, develop, and change throughout the lifespan.

We begin with a discussion of several theories that have strongly influenced the field of **developmental psychology,** the scientific study of how humans grow, develop, and change throughout the lifespan. Then, we will consider the challenges and milestones associated with each of the major phases of development.

Theories of Development

You may not realize it, but you have already learned about several theories of development. The learning theories you studied in Chapter 5, for instance, can explain many age-related changes as resulting from conditioned stimuli, reinforcement, punishment, observational learning, and the like. Learning theories favor the nurture side of the nature–nurture debate you read about in Chapters 2 and 7.

All developmental theories take a position in the nature–nurture debate. Most also address the question of whether development is continuous or occurs in stages. The learning theories assume that development happens in a continuous fashion as the result of environmental influences. Stage theories, by contrast, assert that development occurs in phases—or "leaps" to put it metaphorically—that are distinct from one another. We will begin our discussion of developmental theories with perhaps the most influential of all stage theories, that of Swiss developmentalist Jean Piaget.

Piaget's Theory of Cognitive Development

◆ What did Piaget find regarding stages of cognitive development?

Thanks to the work of Swiss psychologist Jean Piaget (PEE-ah-ZHAY) (1896–1980), psychologists have gained insights into the cognitive processes of children. According to Piaget, cognitive development begins with a few basic **schemes**—cognitive structures or concepts used to identify and interpret objects, events, and other information in the environment. When confronted with new objects, events, experiences, and information, children try to fit them into their existing schemes, a process known as **assimilation.** But not everything can be assimilated into children's existing schemes. If children call a stranger "Daddy" or the neighbor's cat "doggie," assimilation has led them to make an error. When parents or others correct them or when they discover for themselves that something cannot be assimilated into an existing scheme, children will use a process known as **accommodation.** In accommodation, existing schemes are modified or new schemes are created to process new information.

◆ scheme

Piaget's term for a cognitive structure or concept used to identify and interpret information.

◆ assimilation

The process by which new objects, events, experiences, or information is incorporated into existing schemes.

◆ accommodation

The process by which existing schemes are modified and new schemes are created to incorporate new objects, events, experiences, or information.

According to Piaget (1963, 1964; Piaget & Inhelder, 1969), changes in schemes underlie four stages of cognitive development, each of which reflects a qualitatively different way of reasoning and understanding the world. The stages occur in a fixed sequence in which the accomplishments of one stage provide the foundation for the next stage. Although children throughout the world seem to progress through the stages in the same order, they show individual differences in the rate at which they pass through them. And each child's rate is influenced by her or his level of maturation and experiences, such as going to school. The transition from one stage to another is gradual, not abrupt, and children often show aspects of two stages while going through these transitions.

In Piaget's first stage, the *sensorimotor stage* (age birth to 2 years), infants gain an understanding of the world through their senses and their motor activities (actions or body movements). An infant's behavior, which is mostly reflexive at birth, becomes increasingly complex and gradually evolves into intelligent behavior. At this stage, intelligence is about action rather than thought, and it is confined to objects that are present and events that are directly perceived. The child learns to respond to and manipulate objects and to use them in goal-directed activity.

The major achievement of the sensorimotor period is the development of **object permanence**—the realization that objects (including people) continue to exist, even when they are out of sight. This concept develops gradually and is complete when the child is able to represent objects mentally in their absence. The attainment of this ability marks the end of the sensorimotor period.

Children acquire what Piaget called the **symbolic function**—the understanding that one thing can stand for another—during the *preoperational stage* (age 2 to 7 years). Two ways in which children display the symbolic function are through the use of words to represent objects and through *pretend play*, such as imagining that a block is a car or a doll is a real baby. As children practice using symbols, they become increasingly able to represent objects and events mentally with words and images.

During the preoperational stage, children exhibit a tendency Piaget called *egocentrism:* They believe that everyone sees what they see, thinks as they think, and feels as they feel. As a result, their thinking is often illogical. In addition, their thinking about objects is dominated by appearances. For example, a 3-year-old may believe that a cookie is ruined when it breaks. Adults' attempts to convince her otherwise usually fail because adult thinking is based on the assumption that the identity of an object does not change when its appearance changes, a concept that is not yet understood by children in this stage.

In the third stage, the *concrete operations stage* (age 7 to 11 or 12 years), new schemes allow children to understand that a given quantity of matter remains the same despite rearrangement or change in its appearance, as long as nothing is added or taken away—a concept Piaget called **conservation.** Conservation develops because new schemes enable children in this stage to understand the concept of **reversibility**—the understanding that any change in the shape, position, or order of matter can be reversed mentally. As a result, they can think about a broken cookie before and after it broke, realizing that the change in appearance did not change the substance that makes up the cookie. You can see how younger and older children differ in their reasoning about such problems by doing *Try It 8.1* (on page 238).

The concepts of conservation of number, substance (liquid or mass), length, area, weight, and volume are not all acquired at once. They come in a certain sequence and usually at specific ages (see Figure 8.1, on page 239). Moreover, children in the concrete operations stage are unable to apply logic to hypothetical situations. For instance, they find it difficult to think logically about careers they might pursue as adults. They also have difficulty with problems that involve systematically coordinating several variables. For example, they usually cannot solve reasoning problems like these: If Mary is taller than Bill, and Bill is taller than Harry, is Harry shorter than Mary? or How many different two-letter, three-letter, and four-letter combinations of the letters A, B, C, and D are possible? This kind of reasoning isn't possible until children enter the next stage.

The *formal operations stage* (age 11 or 12 years and beyond) is Piaget's fourth and final stage of cognitive development. At this stage, preadolescents and adolescents can apply logical thought to abstract, verbal, and hypothetical situations and to problems in the past, present, or future—a capacity Piaget called **hypothetico-deductive thinking.** Teenagers can comprehend abstract subjects such as philosophy and politics, and they become interested in the world of ideas as they begin to formulate their own theories. However, not all people attain full formal operational thinking (Kuhn, 1984; Neimark, 1981). High school math and science experience seems to facilitate it (Sharp et al., 1979). Failure to achieve formal operational thinking has been associated with below-average scores on intelligence tests (Inhelder, 1966).

Formal operational thinking enables adolescents to think of what might be. Thus, they begin to conceive of "perfect" solutions to the world's and their own problems. For

◆ **object permanence**
The realization that objects continue to exist, even when they can no longer be perceived.

◆ **symbolic function**
The understanding that one thing—an object, a word, a drawing—can stand for another.

◆ **conservation**
The concept that a given quantity of matter remains the same despite being rearranged or changed in appearance, as long as nothing is added or taken away.

◆ **reversibility**
The realization that any change in the shape, position, or order of matter can be reversed mentally.

◆ **hypothetico-deductive thinking**
The ability to base logical reasoning on a hypothetical premise.

Try It 8.1

Conservation of Volume

Show a preschooler two glasses of the same size and then fill them with the same amount of juice. After the child agrees they are the same, pour the juice from one glass into a taller, narrower glass and place that glass beside the other original one. Now ask the child if the two glasses have the same amount of juice, or if one glass has more than the other. Children at this stage will insist that the taller, narrower glass has more juice, although they will quickly agree that you neither added juice nor took any away.

Now, repeat the procedure with a school-aged child. The older child will be able to explain that even though there appears to be more liquid in the taller glass, pouring liquid into a different container doesn't change its quantity.

Tip

Be sure to get permission from the child's parents before you do this *Try It.*

---

example, a teen whose parents are divorced may idealize her noncustodial parent and believe that her life would be wonderful if only she could live with that parent. Piaget used the term **naive idealism** to refer to this kind of thinking.

Psychologist David Elkind (1967, 1974) claims that the early teenage years are marked by another kind of unrealistic thought, *adolescent egocentrism*, which takes two forms: the imaginary audience and the personal fable. The **imaginary audience** consists of admirers and critics that adolescents conjure up and that exist only in their imagination. In their minds, they are always on stage. Teens may spend hours in front of the mirror trying to please this audience. Teenagers also have an exaggerated sense of personal uniqueness and indestructibility that Elkind calls the **personal fable**. Many believe they are somehow indestructible and protected from the misfortunes that befall others, such as unwanted pregnancies or drug overdoses.

Review and Reflect 8.1 (on page 240) provides a summary of Piaget's four stages. Cross-cultural studies have affirmed the universality of the types of reasoning and the sequence of stages formulated by Piaget. But cross-cultural research has also revealed differences in the rates of cognitive development in various domains. Whereas the children Piaget observed began to acquire the concept of conservation between ages 5 and 7, Australian Aboriginal children show this change between the ages of 10 and 13 (Dasen, 1994). Yet the Aboriginal children function at the concrete operations level earlier on spatial tasks than on quantification (counting) tasks, while the reverse is true for Western children. This difference makes sense in light of the high value Aborigines place on spatial skills and the low premium they place on quantification. In the Australian desert, moving from place

◆ **naive idealism**

A type of thought in which adolescents construct ideal solutions for problems.

◆ **imaginary audience**

A belief of adolescents that they are or will be the focus of attention in social situations and that others will be as critical or approving as they are of themselves.

◆ **personal fable**

An exaggerated sense of personal uniqueness and indestructibility, which may be the basis for adolescent risk taking.

FIGURE 8.1
Piaget's Conservation Tasks

Pictured here are several of Piaget's conservation tasks. The ability to answer each task correctly develops at approximately the age indicated. *Source:* Berk, (1994).

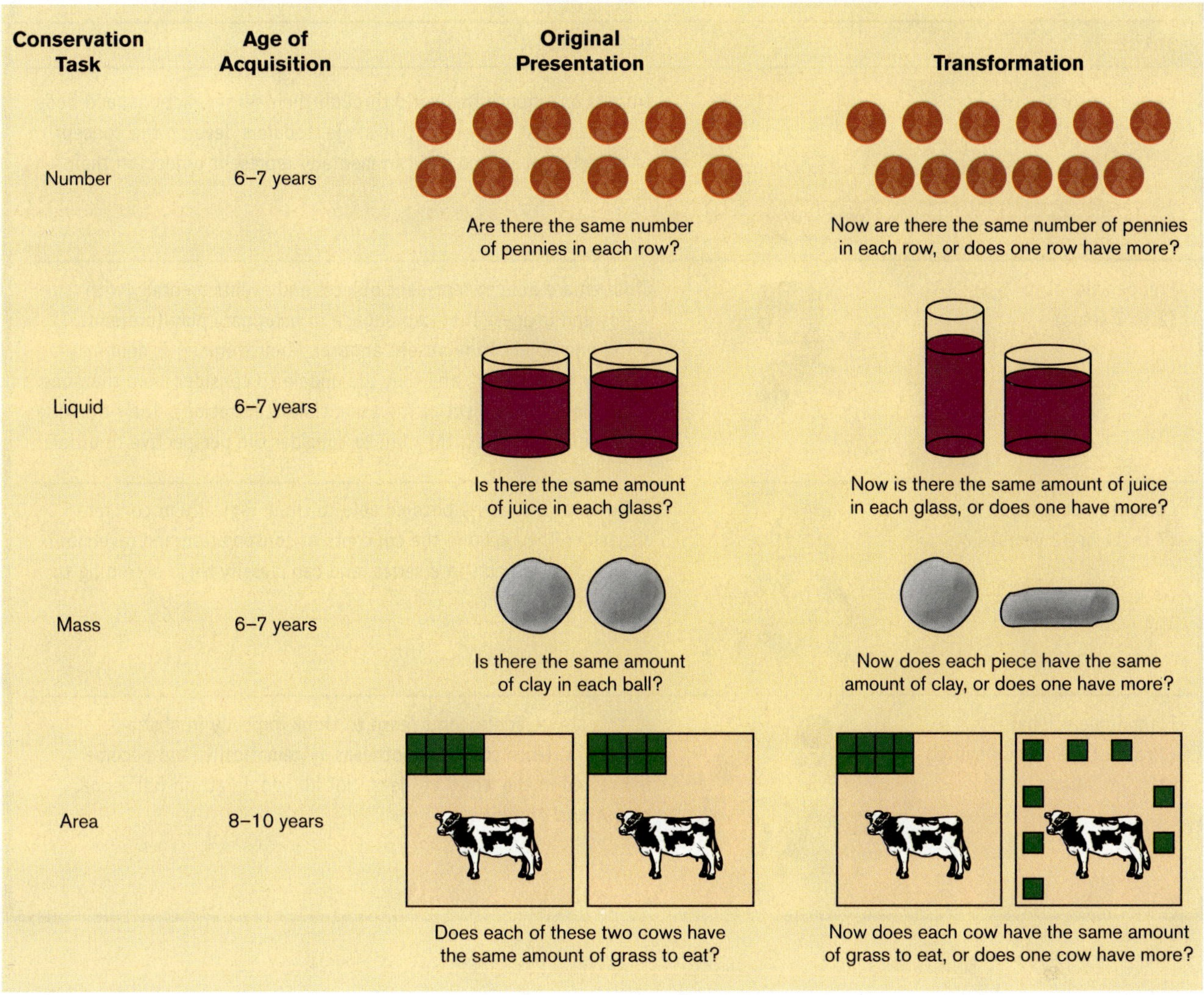

Conservation Task	Age of Acquisition	Original Presentation	Transformation
Number	6–7 years	Are there the same number of pennies in each row?	Now are there the same number of pennies in each row, or does one row have more?
Liquid	6–7 years	Is there the same amount of juice in each glass?	Now is there the same amount of juice in each glass, or does one have more?
Mass	6–7 years	Is there the same amount of clay in each ball?	Now does each piece have the same amount of clay, or does one have more?
Area	8–10 years	Does each of these two cows have the same amount of grass to eat?	Now does each cow have the same amount of grass to eat, or does one cow have more?

to place, hunting, gathering, and searching for water, Aborigines have few possessions and rarely count things. Their language has words for numbers up to five, and their word for "many" applies to anything above five.

Another important cultural variable that contributes to cognitive development is formal education. Developmental psychologists know that children who live in cultures in which they have access to formal education progress more rapidly through Piaget's stages than peers whose societies do not require them to attend school or do not provide them with educational opportunities (Mishra, 1997). Moreover, formal operational thinking is so strongly correlated with formal education that some psychologists have suggested that it may be more a product of specific learning experiences than of a universal developmental process, as Piaget hypothesized.

Although Piaget's genius and his monumental contribution to scientists' knowledge of mental development are rarely disputed, his methods and some of his findings and conclusions have been criticized (Halford, 1989). It now seems clear that children are more advanced cognitively and adults less competent cognitively than Piaget believed (Flavell, 1985, 1992; Mandler, 1990; Siegler, 1991). According to Flavell (1996), "Piaget's greatest contribution was to found the field of cognitive development as we

REVIEW and REFLECT 8.1

Piaget's Stages of Cognitive Development

STAGE		DESCRIPTION
Sensorimotor (0 to 2 years)		Infants experience the world through their senses, actions, and body movements. At the end of this stage, toddlers develop the concept of object permanence and can mentally represent objects in their absence.
Preoperational (2 to 7 years)		Children are able to represent objects and events mentally with words and images. They can engage in imaginary play (pretend), using one object to represent another. Their thinking is dominated by their perceptions, and they are unable to consider more than one dimension of an object at the same time (centration). Their thinking is egocentric; that is, they fail to consider the perspective of others.
Concrete operational (7 to 11 or 12 years)		Children at this stage become able to think logically in concrete situations. They acquire the concepts of conservation and reversibility, can order objects in a series, and can classify them according to multiple dimensions.
Formal operational (11 or 12 years and beyond)		At this stage, adolescents learn to think logically in abstract situations, learn to test hypotheses systematically, and become interested in the world of ideas. Not all people attain full formal operational thinking.

currently know it" (p. 200). Today, few developmental psychologists believe that cognitive development takes place in the general stagelike fashion proposed by Piaget.

Some developmentalists, such as the late Robbie Case (1944–2000), explain age-based differences in performance on the problems Piaget used in his studies as a function of changes in children's use of their working memories (Case, 1992). Research has shown, for instance, that the younger children are, the more slowly they process information (Kail, 2000). Because they process information more slowly, they are more likely to fail to store information in long-term memory before new information comes along and pushes the old information out of working memory. (Recall the interference explanation of forgetting from Chapter 6.) Think about how this might affect children's responses to the conservation of number task shown in Figure 8.1. If Case and his followers are correct, then children younger than age 6 or 7 will likely forget what the original presentation of pennies looked like when they are shown the transformation. As a result, they cannot mentally compare the original and transformed arrays. By contrast, older children, with their faster rates of information processing and more efficient working memories, can keep both presentations in mind as well as the process that was used to make the transformation. As a result, the older children can come up with a correct solution because they are better able to integrate all of the relevant information in working memory.

Vygotsky's Sociocultural Approach

Recall from Chapter 1 that the *sociocultural perspective* explains behavior and mental processes in terms of social and cultural variables. One of the most prominent sociocultural theories resulted from the work of Russian developmentalist Lev Vygotsky (1896–1934). Vygotsky studied Piaget's work and claimed that his theory of cognitive development placed too much emphasis on forces within the child. Vygotsky hypothesized that much of cognitive development results from the child's internalization of information that is acquired socially, primarily through the medium of language.

◆ *How does Vygotsky's theory explain cognitive development?*

For instance, have you ever noticed children talking to themselves as they assemble a puzzle or paint a picture? Vygotsky believed that this and other spontaneous language behaviors exhibited by children are important to the process of cognitive development. Vygotsky maintained that human infants come equipped with basic skills such as perception, the ability to pay attention, and certain capacities of memory not unlike those of many other animal species (Vygotsky, 1934/1986). During the first 2 years of life, these skills grow and develop naturally through direct experiences and interactions with the child's sociocultural world. In due course, children develop the mental ability to represent objects, activities, ideas, people, and relationships in a variety of ways, but primarily through language (speech). With their new ability to represent ideas, activities, and so on through speech, children are often observed "talking to themselves." Vygotsky believed that talking to oneself—*private speech*—is a key component in cognitive development. Through private speech, children can specify the components of a problem and verbalize steps in a process to help them work through a puzzling activity or situation. As young children develop greater competence, private speech fades into barely audible mumbling and muttering, and finally becomes simply thinking.

Vygotsky saw a strong connection among social experience, speech, and cognitive development. He also maintained that a child's readiness to learn resides within a **zone of proximal development** (*proximal* means "potential"). This zone, according to Vygotsky, is a range of cognitive tasks that the child cannot yet perform alone but can learn to perform with the instruction and guidance of a parent, teacher, or more advanced peer. This kind of help, in which a teacher or parent adjusts the quality and degree of instruction and guidance to fit the child's present level of ability or performance, is often referred to as **scaffolding**. In scaffolding, direct instruction is given, at first, for unfamiliar tasks (Maccoby, 1992). But as the child shows increasing competence, the teacher or parent gradually withdraws from direct and active teaching, and the child may continue toward independent mastery of the task. For instance, think about a baby girl who is trying to put a triangular block into a circular hole in a shape-sorting toy. Her father helps her by guiding her hand to the triangular-shaped hole. A few days later, the girl recognizes on her own that the triangular block matches the triangular hole, but she lacks the coordination necessary to get the block all the way through the hole. In response, the father places his hand over hers and gently guides the block through the hole. Comparing the two instances, you can see that the father adjusted the help he provided to fit with what his daughter was able to do on her own. Vygotsky hypothesized that such scaffolding episodes occur frequently within the context of parent–child relationships and are essential to children's cognitive development.

This father teaching his daughter to ride a bike is using Vygotsky's technique called *scaffolding*. A parent or teacher provides direct and continuous instruction at the beginning of the learning process and then gradually withdraws from active teaching as the child becomes more proficient at the new task or skill. How might scaffolding help a child acquire cognitive skills such as reading?

◆ **zone of proximal development**

A range of cognitive tasks that a child cannot yet do but can learn to do through the guidance of an older child or adult.

◆ **scaffolding**

A type of instruction in which an adult adjusts the amount of guidance provided to match a child's present level of ability.

Kohlberg's Theory of Moral Development

Building on a great deal of prior research on cognitive development, Lawrence Kohlberg (1927–1987) proposed a stage theory of moral reasoning that has been extremely influential in the study of moral development. Long before Kohlberg's work began, both Vygotsky and Piaget applied their theories to moral development. Vygotsky (1926/1992) asserted that culture, by means of language and religious instruction, molds individuals to conform to its standards of acceptable behavior. Piaget did not deny the role that culture plays in moral development. However, he hypothesized that children's levels of cognitive development interact with

◆ *What did Kohlberg claim about the development of moral reasoning?*

society's efforts to inculcate moral values in them such that moral reasoning develops in stages that parallel those of cognitive development (Piaget, 1927/1965).

Piaget's ideas about moral reasoning and the methods he used to probe children's reasoning about the physical world were the primary inspiration for Kohlberg's work. Kohlberg (1969) studied moral development by presenting a series of moral dilemmas to male participants from the United States and other countries. Read one of his best-known dilemmas in *Try It 8.2*. Kohlberg was less interested in whether the participants judged Heinz's behavior (as described in the *Try It 8.2*) right or wrong than in the reasons for their responses. He found that moral reasoning could be classified into three levels, with each level having two stages.

At Kohlberg's first level of moral development, the **preconventional level,** moral reasoning is governed by the standards of others rather than one's own internalized standards of right and wrong. An act is judged good or bad based on its physical consequences. In Stage 1, "right" is whatever avoids punishment; in Stage 2, "right" is whatever is rewarded, benefits the individual, or results in a favor being returned. "You scratch my back and I'll scratch yours" is the type of thinking common at this stage. Children usually function at the preconventional level through age 10.

At Kohlberg's second level of moral development, the **conventional level,** the individual has internalized the standards of others and judges right and wrong in terms of those standards. At Stage 3, sometimes called the *good boy–nice girl orientation*, "good behavior is that which pleases or helps others and is approved by them" (Kohlberg, 1968, p. 26). At Stage 4, the orientation is toward "authority, fixed rules, and the maintenance of the social order. Right behavior consists of doing one's duty, showing respect for authority, and maintaining the given social order for its own sake" (p. 26). Kohlberg believed that a person must function at Piaget's concrete operations stage to reason morally at the conventional level.

Kohlberg's highest level of moral development is the **postconventional level,** which requires the ability to think at Piaget's stage of formal operations. Postconventional

◆ **preconventional level**
Kohlberg's lowest level of moral development, in which moral reasoning is based on the physical consequences of an act; "right" is whatever avoids punishment or gains a reward.

◆ **conventional level**
Kohlberg's second level of moral development, in which right and wrong are based on the internalized standards of others; "right" is whatever helps or is approved of by others, or whatever is consistent with the laws of society.

◆ **postconventional level**
Kohlberg's highest level of moral development, in which moral reasoning involves weighing moral alternatives; "right" is whatever furthers basic human rights.

Try It 8.2

A Moral Dilemma

In Europe, a woman was near death from a special kind of cancer. There was one drug the doctors thought might save her. It was a form of radium that a druggist in the same town had recently discovered. The drug was expensive to make, and the druggist was charging ten times what it cost him. He paid $200 for the radium and charged $2,000 for a small dose of the drug. The sick woman's husband, Heinz, went to everyone he knew to borrow the money, but he could only get together $1,000, which was half of what the drug cost. He told the druggist that his wife was dying and asked him to sell it cheaper or let him pay later. But the druggist said, "No, I discovered the drug, and I am going to make money from it." So Heinz got desperate and broke into the man's store to steal the drug for his wife (Colby et al., 1983, p. 77).

What moral judgment would you make about the dilemma? Should Heinz have stolen the drug? Why or why not?

Tip

Compare your responses to the Heinz dilemma to those of classmates from other cultures. Discuss the similarities and differences, and how they might be the result of cultural differences.

reasoning is most often found among middle-class, college-educated people. At this level, people do not simply internalize the standards of others. Instead, they weigh moral alternatives, realizing that the law may sometimes conflict with basic human rights. At Stage 5, the person believes that laws are formulated to protect both society and the individual and should be changed if they fail to do so. At Stage 6, ethical decisions are based on universal ethical principles, which emphasize respect for human life, justice, equality, and dignity for all people. People who reason morally at Stage 6 believe that they must follow their conscience even if it results in a violation of the law.

Review and Reflect 8.2 summarizes Kohlberg's six stages of moral development. Kohlberg claimed that people progress through these stages one at a time in a fixed order, without skipping any stage; if movement occurs, it is to the next higher stage. Postconventional reasoning is not possible, Kohlberg said, until people fully attain Piaget's level of formal operations. They must be able to think abstractly and to apply ethical principles in hypothetical situations (Kohlberg & Gilligan, 1971; Kuhn et al., 1977). As Kohlberg came to realize, discussion of moral dilemmas does not reliably improve moral behavior. He eventually agreed that direct teaching of moral values is necessary and compatible with his theory (Higgins, 1995; Power et al., 1989). Still, as his theory predicts, research shows that general cognitive development strongly influences how children respond to moral teaching. You may remember a story called *The*

REVIEW *and* REFLECT 8.2

Kohlberg's Stages of Moral Development

LEVEL	STAGE
Level I: Preconventional level (Ages 4–10) Moral reasoning is governed by the standards of others; an act is good or bad depending on its physical consequences—whether it is punished or rewarded.	**Stage 1** The stage in which behavior that avoids punishment is right. Children obey out of fear of punishment. **Stage 2** The stage of self-interest. What is right is what benefits the individual or gains a favor in return. "You scratch my back and I'll scratch yours."
Level II: Conventional level (Ages 10–13) The child internalizes the standards of others and judges right and wrong according to those standards.	**Stage 3** The morality of mutual relationships. The "good boy–nice girl" orientation. Child acts to please and help others. **Stage 4** The morality of the social system and conscience. Orientation toward authority. Morality is doing one's duty, respecting authority, and maintaining the social order.
Level III: Postconventional level (After age 13, at young adulthood, or never) Moral conduct is under internal control; this is the highest level and the mark of true morality.	**Stage 5** The morality of contract; respect for individual rights and laws that are democratically agreed on. Rational valuing of the wishes of the majority and the general welfare. Belief that society is best served if citizens obey the law. **Stage 6** The highest stage of the highest social level. The morality of universal ethical principles. The person acts according to internal standards independent of legal restrictions or opinions of others.

How Did You Find **Psychology?**

Darcia Narvaez

A popular poster depicts an array of luxury automobiles with the caption "Justification for Higher Education." Certainly, education and income are related. However, some people are more interested in pursuing knowledge for its own sake than in preparing for a high-paying job. Darcia Narvaez, whose research on children's understanding of moral stories is discussed on this page, is just such a person.

Narvaez grew up in a bilingual home, and her family traveled extensively in Latin America during her childhood. Narvaez reports that the devastating poverty she observed in many Latin American countries is what first sparked her interest in the concept of justice. "I could not understand how the world could be designed so unfairly," she says (Narvaez, personal communication, November 26, 2004).

After receiving her undergraduate degree in Spanish and music, Narvaez first pursued a career in teaching and then became an entrepreneur. Although materially successful, she remained driven by her desire to find a set of ideas that could help her better understand the world. Eventually, she abandoned her successful career to enter a master's degree program in theology at a Lutheran seminary. However, her religious studies didn't provide her with the answers she was seeking. Shortly after graduation, though, the first hints of the career in moral development research that lay ahead for Narvaez became evident.

Narvaez was serving on a church ministry committee that was charged with the responsibility of studying the concept of the common good when she was given the assignment of reading Carol Gilligan's book, *In a Different Voice.* In this classic work, Gilligan claims that Kohlberg's theory of moral development is sex-biased. To better understand Gilligan's criticisms, Narvaez began to read Kohlberg's work as well. When she mentioned her new-found interest in moral development to one of the bishops with whom she worked, he offered to introduce Narvaez to his neighbor, James Rest, who was an educational psychologist at the University of Minnesota. Rest's research, the bishop explained, sought to address many of the unanswered questions in Kohlberg's theory of moral development.

Narvaez met with Rest to discuss his work and, for the first time, embraced the view that the scientific method might be the best way to conduct her search for truth. Ultimately, Narvaez became one of Rest's graduate students and embarked upon a quest to understand how individuals develop divergent views of right and wrong. She continues that quest today in her position as a professor at Notre Dame University. However, she is also concerned with discovering how research findings can improve people's lives. To this end, she studies moral education as well as the basic process of moral development itself.

Sometimes students become so caught up in the idea that the purpose of a college education is to prepare for a career that they overlook a crucial fact: The college environment provides students and faculty alike with opportunities to explore ideas purely for the purpose of personal enlightenment. Narvaez says that it is the privilege of being able to pursue knowledge for its own sake through the medium of psychological research that excites her most about her job. A personal quest like Narvaez's journey may not put you in a position in which you can afford a luxury automobile, but it may lead you to a career in which you can find answers to questions you have been wondering about all of your life.

Little Red Hen in which several lazy animals expect a hard-working hen to share the fruits of her labors with them. The moral message of the story is "If you don't work, you don't eat." Studies carried out by educational psychologist Darcia Narvaez (Narvaez et al., 1999; Narvaez, 2002) show that children younger than about age 10 seldom infer the messages implied in such stories on their own. Further, she has found that young children's ability to infer moral messages is strongly linked to the development of reading comprehension skills. Narvaez's work suggests that parents who use stories like *The Little Red Hen* to teach their children about moral values should provide them with explicit information about the nature of the moral message and how it relates to the characters and events in the story. (Recall Vygotsky's notion of scaffolding.)

Probably because of these links between moral development and general cognitive development, there is a great deal of evidence that Kohlberg's stages of moral reasoning occur in all cultures. In a classic review of 45 studies of Kohlberg's theory conducted in 27 countries, Snarey (1985) found support for the universality of Stages 1 through 4 and for the invariant sequence of these stages in all groups studied. Although extremely rare, Stage 5 was found in almost all samples from urban or middle-class populations and absent in all of the tribal or village folk societies studied. And Snarey's more recent research (1995) supports the conclusions of his earlier work.

One controversy concerning Kohlberg's theory involves the possibility of gender bias. Kohlberg indicated that the majority of women remain at Stage 3, while most men attain Stage 4. Do men typically attain a higher level of moral reasoning than women? Carol Gilligan (1982) asserts that Kohlberg's theory is sex-biased. Not only did Kohlberg fail to include females in his original research, Gilligan points out, but he also limited morality to abstract reasoning about moral dilemmas. And, at his highest level, Stage 6, Kohlberg emphasized justice and equality but not mercy, compassion, love, or concern for others. Gilligan suggests that females, more than males, tend to view moral behavior in terms of compassion, caring, and concern for others. Thus, she agrees that the content of moral reasoning differs between the sexes, but she contends that males and females do not differ in the complexity of their moral reasoning. More recent evidence suggests that females do tend to emphasize care and compassion in resolving moral dilemmas, while males tend to stress justice or at least to give it equal standing with caring (Garmon et al., 1996; Wark & Krebs, 1996). Although Kohlberg's theory does emphasize rights and justice over concern for others, researchers, nevertheless, have found that females score as high as males in moral reasoning (Walker, 1989).

Other critics claim that Kohlberg's theory has a built-in liberal bias and is culture-bound, favoring Western middle-class values (Simpson, 1974; Sullivan, 1977). Yet Snarey (1985), in his review of 45 studies, found that samples from India, kibbutzim in Israel, Taiwan, and Turkey "ranked higher than parallel groups from the United States at one or more points in the life cycle" (p. 228).

Finally, some critics point out that moral reasoning and moral behavior are not one and the same. Kohlberg readily acknowledged that people can be capable of making mature moral judgments yet fail to live morally. But, said Kohlberg (1968), "The man who understands justice is more likely to practice it" (p. 30). Regardless of whether we agree with Kohlberg's theory, most of us would agree that moral reasoning and moral behavior are critically important aspects of human development. Moral individuals make moral societies.

Erikson's Theory of Psychosocial Development

Piaget's, Vygotsky's, and Kohlberg's theories deal with the intellectual aspects of development. Moral reasoning, of course, involves reasoning about the social world, but it doesn't address the process through which individuals come to feel a part of the families, neighborhoods, and cultures in which they live. By contrast, the theories of the psychoanalysts, first mentioned in Chapter 1, focus on precisely this domain of development. We will discuss the developmental theory of the founder of psychoanalysis, Sigmund Freud, in Chapter 11. But the theory of one of Freud's most important revisionists, Erik Erikson (1902–1994), is best discussed in the context of lifespan development, because Erikson (1980) proposed the only major theory of development to include the entire lifespan. According to Erikson, individuals progress through eight **psychosocial stages,** each of which is defined by a conflict involving the individual's relationship with the social environment, which must be resolved satisfactorily for healthy development to occur. The stages are named for a "series of alternative basic attitudes," one of which will result, depending on how the conflict is resolved (Erikson, 1980).

According to Erikson's view, the foundations of adult personality are laid in four childhood stages. During the first stage, *basic trust versus basic mistrust*, infants (birth to 1 year) develop a sense of trust or mistrust depending on the degree and regularity of care, love, and affection they receive from the mother or primary caregiver. Erikson (1980) considered "basic trust as the cornerstone of a healthy personality" (p. 58). During the second stage, *autonomy versus shame and doubt*, children aged 1 to 3 begin to express their independence (often by saying "No!") and develop their physical and mental abilities. In the third stage, *initiative versus guilt*, 3- to 6-year-old children go beyond

♦ How does Erikson's theory describe the process of psychosocial development?

♦ **psychosocial stages**
Erikson's eight developmental stages for the entire lifespan; each is defined by a conflict that must be resolved satisfactorily for healthy personality development to occur.

merely expressing their autonomy and begin to develop initiative. During the fourth stage, *industry versus inferiority*, school-aged children (age 6 years to puberty) begin to enjoy and take pride in making things and doing things.

Erikson's later stages begin with puberty, but they are not as strongly tied to chronological age as those that occur during childhood. Instead, the adolescent and adult stages represent important themes of adult life. These themes occur in a fixed sequence, Erikson claimed, because the resolution of each depends on how well prior stages were resolved.

The first of these stages is *identity versus role confusion*, during which adolescents experience a phenomenon Erikson called the *identity crisis*. During the identity crisis, teens must develop an idea of how they will fit into the adult world. A healthy identity, Erikson claimed, is essential to the next stage, *intimacy versus isolation*, which begins around age 18. During this stage, young adults must find a life partner or come to a healthy acceptance of living in a single state. The next major theme of adult life, *generativity versus stagnation*, is at its peak during the years of middle age. Generativity, according to Erikson, is the desire to guide the next generation, through parenting, teaching, or mentoring. Finally, in later years, adults experience *ego integrity versus despair*. The goal of this stage is an acceptance of one's life in preparation for facing death. *Review and Reflect 8.3* summarizes Erikson's psychosocial stages.

Most research on Erikson's theory has focused on trust in infants, identity formation in adolescents, and generativity in middle-aged adults. Specific predictions derived from Erikson's descriptions of these three stages have received mixed research support. On the positive side, there is a great deal of evidence that a relationship with a trusted caregiver in infancy is critical to later development.

REVIEW *and* REFLECT 8.3

Erikson's Psychosocial Stages of Development

STAGE	AGES	DESCRIPTION
Trust vs. mistrust	Birth to 1 year	Infants learn to trust or mistrust depending on the degree and regularity of care, love, and affection provided by parents or caregivers.
Autonomy vs. shame and doubt	1 to 3 years	Children learn to express their will and independence, to exercise some control, and to make choices. If not, they experience shame and doubt.
Initiative vs. guilt	3 to 6 years	Children begin to initiate activities, to plan and undertake tasks, and to enjoy developing motor and other abilities. If not allowed to initiate or if made to feel stupid and considered a nuisance, they may develop a sense of guilt.
Industry vs. inferiority	6 years to puberty	Children develop industriousness and feel pride in accomplishing tasks, making things, and doing things. If not encouraged or if rebuffed by parents and teachers, they may develop a sense of inferiority.
Identity vs. role confusion	Adolescence	Adolescents must make the transition from childhood to adulthood, establish an identity, develop a sense of self, and consider a future occupational identity. Otherwise, role confusion can result.
Intimacy vs. isolation	Young adulthood	Young adults must develop intimacy—the ability to share with, care for, and commit themselves to another person. Avoiding intimacy brings a sense of isolation and loneliness.
Generativity vs. stagnation	Middle adulthood	Middle-aged people must find some way of contributing to the development of the next generation. Failing this, they may become self-absorbed and emotionally impoverished and reach a point of stagnation.
Ego integrity vs. despair	Late adulthood	Individuals review their lives, and if they are satisfied and feel a sense of accomplishment, they will experience ego integrity. If dissatisfied, they may sink into despair.

In contrast, most research examining the development of identity has shown that the process does begin in adolescence, but it is not complete until well into the early adult years (Waterman, 1985). Many college students, for example, have not yet settled on a major or future career when they begin taking classes, and they use experiences in their first few semesters to make these important decisions. One reason for the apparent delay may be that advances in logical reasoning, such as those associated with Piaget's formal operational stage, are strongly related to identity formation (Klaczynski et al., 1998). Formal operational thinking evolves slowly across the adolescent years. Consequently, people may not have the cognitive ability to engage in the kind of thinking necessary for the development of identity until the early adult years.

With regard to generativity, in one study of young, midlife, and older women, researchers found that generativity did increase in middle age as Erikson's theory predicts (Zucker et al., 2002). However, it did not decline in old age. The oldest group of participants (with an average age of 66) cited generative concerns as important to them just as frequently as the middle-aged group did. So, generativity may be more a characteristic of middle than of early adulthood, as Erikson predicted, but it appears to continue to be important in old age.

Now that you have had an introduction to developmental theories, we will turn our attention to the major milestones of each phase of development. *Prenatal development* refers to the period prior to birth. The first 2 years constitute the period of *infancy*. The period from 2 to 6 years of age is *early childhood*, and *middle childhood* is the period from age 6 to puberty. *Adolescence* begins at puberty and ends when an individual is considered to be an adult in his or her culture. Finally, the adult years are typically divided into phases of *early adulthood* (18 to 40 or 45), *middle adulthood* (40 or 45 to 65), and *late adulthood* (65 and older).

Prenatal Development

> ◆ What happens during each of the three stages of prenatal development?

Many people divide the 9 months of pregnancy into *trimesters*, three periods of 3 months' duration. However, the division of pregnancy into trimesters is arbitrary and has nothing to do with prenatal development. In fact, the third stage of **prenatal development**, or development from conception to birth, begins before the first trimester ends.

Conception, of course, marks the beginning of prenatal development and typically takes place in one of the fallopian tubes. Over the next two weeks, the **zygote**, the cell that results from the union of a sperm and an ovum, travels to the uterus and attaches itself to the uterine wall. This stage is known as the *period of the zygote*. At the end of this stage, the zygote is only the size of the period at the end of this sentence. The second stage is the *period of the embryo*, when the major systems, organs, and structures of the body develop. Lasting from week 3 through week 8, this period ends when the first bone cells form. Only 1 inch long and weighing 1/7 of an ounce, the **embryo** already resembles a human being, with limbs, fingers, toes, and many internal organs that have begun to function. The final stage of prenatal development, called the *period of the fetus*, lasts from the end of the second month until birth. The **fetus** undergoes rapid growth and further development of the structures, organs, and systems of the body. Table 8.1 (on page 248) describes the characteristics of each stage of prenatal development.

During the last several weeks of prenatal development, the fetus is capable of responding to stimuli from the outside world, particularly sounds. Further, newborns remember the stimuli to which they were exposed prior to birth. In a classic study of prenatal learning, DeCasper and Spence (1986) had 16 pregnant women read *The Cat in the Hat* to their developing fetuses twice a day during the final 6 weeks of pregnancy. A few days after birth, the infants could adjust their sucking on specially designed, pressure-sensitive nipples to hear their mother reading either *The Cat in the Hat* or *The King, the Mice, and the Cheese*, a story they had never heard before. By their sucking behavior, the infants showed a definite preference for the familiar story.

◆ **prenatal development**
Development from conception to birth.

◆ **zygote**
Cell that results from the union of a sperm and an ovum.

◆ **embryo**
The developing human organism during the period (week 3 through week 8) when the major systems, organs, and structures of the body develop.

◆ **fetus**
The developing human organism during the period (week 9 until birth) when rapid growth and further development of the structures, organs, and systems of the body occur.

TABLE 8.1 Stages of Prenatal Development

STAGE	TIME AFTER CONCEPTION	MAJOR ACTIVITIES OF THE STAGE
Period of the zygote	1 to 2 weeks	Zygote attaches to the uterine lining. At 2 weeks, zygote is the size of the period at the end of this sentence.
Period of the embryo	3 to 8 weeks	Major systems, organs, and structures of the body develop. Period ends when first bone cells appear. At 8 weeks, embryo is about 1 inch long and weighs $1/7$ of an ounce.
Period of the fetus	9 weeks to birth (38 weeks)	Rapid growth and further development of the body structures, organs, and systems.

As wondrous as the process of prenatal development is, ample evidence indicates that the developing embryo and the fetus are vulnerable to a number of potentially harmful factors. One is lack of prenatal care and another is maternal health. The babies of women who suffer from chronic conditions such as diabetes may experience retardation or acceleration of fetal growth (Levy-Shiff et al., 2002). And when the mother suffers from a viral disease such as *rubella, chicken pox, or HIV,* she may deliver an infant with physical and behavioral abnormalities (Amato, 1998; Kliegman, 1998).

Teratogens are substances that can have a negative impact on prenatal development, causing birth defects and other problems. A teratogen's impact depends on both its intensity and the time during prenatal development when it is present. Teratogens generally have their most devastating consequences during the period of the embryo. During this time, there are **critical periods** when certain body structures develop. If drugs or other harmful substances interfere with development during a critical period, the body structure will not form properly, nor will it develop later (Kopp & Kaler, 1989).

The use of heroin, cocaine, and crack during pregnancy has been linked to miscarriage, prematurity, low birth weight, breathing difficulties, physical defects, and fetal death. Alcohol also crosses the placental barrier, and alcohol levels in the fetus almost match the levels in the mother's blood (Little et al., 1989). Women who drink heavily during pregnancy risk having babies with **fetal alcohol syndrome.** Babies with this syndrome are mentally retarded and have abnormally small heads with wide-set eyes and a short nose. They also have behavioral problems such as hyperactivity (Julien, 1995). Some children prenatally exposed to alcohol have *fetal alcohol effects*—they show some of the characteristics of fetal alcohol syndrome but in less severe form. The Surgeon

◆ **teratogens**
Harmful agents in the prenatal environment, which can have a negative impact on prenatal development or even cause birth defects.

◆ **critical period**
A period so important to development that a harmful environmental influence at that time can keep a bodily structure from developing normally or can impair later intellectual or social development.

◆ **fetal alcohol syndrome**
A condition, caused by maternal alcohol intake during pregnancy, in which the baby is born mentally retarded, with a small head and facial, organ, and behavioral abnormalities.

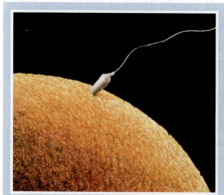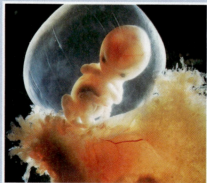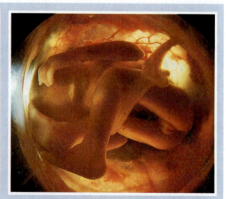

These photos show the fertilization of an egg by a sperm (left), an embryo at 7 weeks (center), and a fetus at 22 weeks (right).

General warns women to abstain from drinking alcohol altogether during pregnancy, but about 20% ignore the warnings (Braun, 1996; Mukherjee & Turk, 2004).

Smoking decreases the amount of oxygen and increases the amount of carbon monoxide crossing the placental barrier. The embryo or fetus is exposed to nicotine and several thousand other chemicals as well. Smoking while pregnant increases the probability that the baby will be premature or of low birth weight (McDonald et al., 1992; Nordentoft et al., 1996). Further, because researchers disagree as to whether heavy caffeine consumption has an adverse effect on the fetus, the wisest course of action is to restrict caffeine consumption to less than 300 milligrams (3 cups) daily.

Most teratogens are associated with an increased risk of delivering either a low-birth-weight or preterm infant. **Low-birth-weight** babies are those weighing less than 5.5 pounds. Infants of this weight born at or before the 37th week are considered **preterm infants.** The smaller and more premature the baby, the greater the risk of problems that range from subtle learning and behavior problems in babies closer to normal birth weight to "severe retardation, blindness, hearing loss, and even death" in the smallest newborns (Apgar & Beck, 1982, p. 69).

Infancy

Neonates (newborn babies) come equipped with an impressive range of **reflexes**—built-in responses to certain stimuli that are needed to ensure survival in their new world. Sucking, swallowing, coughing, and blinking are some necessary behaviors that newborns can perform right away. Newborns will move an arm, a leg, or other body part away from a painful stimulus and will try to remove a blanket or cloth placed over the face. Stroke a baby on the cheek and you will trigger the rooting reflex—the baby opens his or her mouth and actively searches for a nipple. Moreover, all five senses are working at birth, although a number of refinements are still to come.

Perceptual and Motor Development

The newborn already has preferences for certain odors, tastes, sounds, and visual configurations. Hearing is much better developed than vision in the neonate (Busnel et al., 1992). A newborn is able to turn his or her head in the direction of a sound and shows a general preference for female voices. Newborns are able to discriminate among and show preferences for certain odors and tastes (Bartoshuk & Beauchamp, 1994; Leon, 1992). They favor sweet tastes and are able to differentiate between salty, bitter, and sour solutions. Newborns are also sensitive to pain (Porter et al., 1988) and are particularly responsive to touch, reacting positively to stroking and fondling (Field, 2002).

Robert Fantz (1961) made a major breakthrough when he realized that a baby's interest in an object can be gauged by the length of time it fixates on it. Fantz demonstrated that infants prefer the image of a human face to other images such as a black-and-white abstract pattern (see Figure 8.2, on page 250). Fantz's study and others have shown that newborns have clear preferences and powers of discrimination—and even memory recognition and learning ability.

At birth, an infant's vision is about 20/600, and it typically does not reach 20/20 until the child is about 2 years old (Courage & Adams, 1990; Held, 1993). Newborns focus best on objects about 9 inches away, and they can follow a slowly moving object. Infants from 22 to 93 hours old already indicate a preference for their own mother's face over that of an unfamiliar female (Field et al., 1984). Although newborns prefer colored stimuli to gray ones, babies can't distinguish all of the colors adults normally can until they are about 2 months old (Brown, 1990).

One famous experiment was devised to study depth perception in infants and other animals. Gibson and Walk (1960) designed an apparatus called the **visual cliff**, which is "a board laid across a sheet of heavy glass, with a patterned material directly beneath

◆ **low-birth-weight baby**
A baby weighing less than 5.5 pounds.

◆ **preterm infant**
An infant born before the 37th week and weighing less than 5.5 pounds; a premature infant.

◆ *How do infants' perceptual and motor abilities change over the first 18 months of life?*

◆ **neonate**
A newborn infant up to 1 month old.

◆ **reflexes**
Built-in responses to certain stimuli that neonates need to ensure survival in their new world.

◆ **visual cliff**
An apparatus used to test depth perception in infants and young animals.

FIGURE 8.2   Results of Fantz's Study

Using a device called a *viewing box* to observe and record infants' eye movements, Fantz (1961) found that they preferred faces to black-and-white abstract patterns.

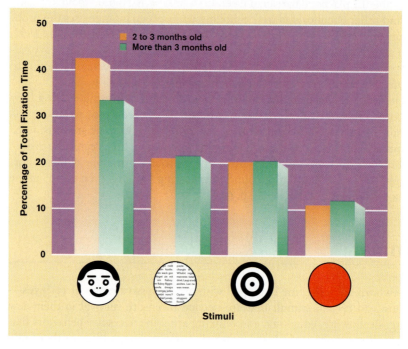

maturation

Changes that occur according to one's genetically determined biological timetable of development.

the glass on one side and several feet below it on the other" (p. 65). This arrangement made it appear that there was a sudden drop-off, or "visual cliff," on one side. Most babies aged 6 to 14 months could be coaxed by their mothers to crawl to the shallow side, but only three would crawl onto the deep side. Gibson and Walk concluded that most babies "can discriminate depth as soon as they can crawl" (p. 64).

Like perceptual skills, an infant's motor skills become increasingly sophisticated over the first 18 months. The rapid changes in motor skills babies undergo arise primarily because of maturation. **Maturation** occurs naturally according to the infant's own genetically determined biological timetable of development. Many motor milestones, such as sitting, standing, and walking (shown in Figure 8.3), depend on the growth and development of the central nervous system.

Still, experience does have some influence on the development of motor skills. For instance, the rate at which milestones are achieved is slowed when an infant is subjected to extremely unfavorable environmental conditions, such as severe malnutrition or maternal or sensory deprivation. Further, cross-cultural research reveals that in some African cultures in Uganda and Kenya, mothers use special motor-training techniques that enable their infants to attain some of the major motor milestones earlier than most infants in the United States (Kilbride & Kilbride, 1975; Super, 1981). But speeding up the attainment of motor skills has no lasting impact on development. Babies will walk, talk, and be toilet-trained according to their own developmental schedules.

When placed on the visual cliff, most infants older than 6 months will not crawl out over the deep side, indicating that they can perceive depth.

Temperament

Is each baby born with an individual behavior style or characteristic way of responding to the environment—a particular **temperament?** The New York Longitudinal Study was undertaken in 1956 to investigate temperament and its effect on development. Thomas, Chess, and Birch (1970) studied 2- to 3-month-old infants and followed them into adolescence and adulthood using observation, interviews with parents and teachers, and psychological tests. They found that "children do show distinct individuality in temperament in the first weeks of life independently of their parents' handling or personality style" (p. 104). Three general types of temperament emerged from the study.

"Easy" children—40% of the group studied—had generally pleasant moods, were adaptable, approached new situations and people positively, and established regular sleeping, eating, and elimination patterns. "Difficult" children—10% of the group—had generally unpleasant moods, reacted negatively to new situations and people, were intense in their emotional reactions, and showed irregularity of bodily functions. "Slow-to-warm-up" children—15% of the group—tended to withdraw, were slow to adapt, and were "somewhat negative in mood." The remaining 35% of the children studied were too inconsistent to categorize.

Thomas and others (1970) believe that personality is molded by the continuous interaction of temperament and environment. Although the environment can intensify, diminish, or modify these inborn behavioral tendencies, "the original characteristics of

◆ *How does temperament shape infants' behavior?*

◆ **temperament**
A person's behavioral style or characteristic way of responding to the environment.

FIGURE 8.3

The Progression of Motor Development

Most infants develop motor skills in the sequence shown in the figure. The ages indicated are only averages, so normal, healthy infants may develop any of these milestones a few months earlier or several months later than the average. *Source:* Frankenburg et al. (1992).

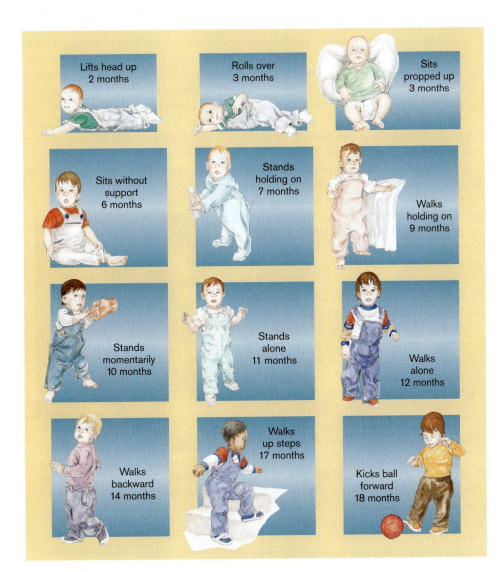

Lifts head up
2 months

Rolls over
3 months

Sits propped up
3 months

Sits without support
6 months

Stands holding on
7 months

Walks holding on
9 months

Stands momentarily
10 months

Stands alone
11 months

Walks alone
12 months

Walks backward
14 months

Walks up steps
17 months

Kicks ball forward
18 months

temperament tend to persist in most children over the years" (p. 104). Adjustment in children seems to rest in part on the fit between individual temperament and the accommodation of family and environment to behavioral style. A difficult child may stimulate hostility and resentment in parents and others, which, in turn, may perpetuate the child's negative behavior. On the other hand, an easy child usually elicits a positive response from parents and others, which reinforces the child's behavior and increases the likelihood that the behavioral style will continue.

Several studies have revealed that children who were undercontrolled or impulsive at a young age tended to become aggressive, danger-seeking, impulsive adolescents (Hart et al., 1997; Hart, Atkins, & Fegley, 2003) with strong negative emotions (Caspi & Silva, 1995). Overcontrolled children were found to be "more prone to social withdrawal" (Hart et al., 1997) and lacking in social potency as adolescents; that is, "they were submissive, not fond of leadership roles, and had little desire to influence others" (Caspi & Silva, 1995, p. 495).

Attachment

◆ *How do the four attachment patterns identified in infants differ?*

Almost all infants form a strong **attachment** to their mothers or primary caregivers. But what precisely is the glue that binds caregiver (usually the mother) and infant?

A series of classic studies conducted by Harry Harlow on attachment in rhesus monkeys was critical to developmentalists' understanding of infant–caregiver attachment. Harlow constructed two surrogate (artificial) monkey "mothers." One was a plain wire-mesh cylinder with a blocky wooden head; the other was a wire-mesh cylinder that was padded, covered with soft terry cloth, and fitted with a somewhat more monkeylike head. A baby bottle could be attached to either surrogate mother for feeding. Newborn monkeys were placed in individual cages where they had equal access to a cloth surrogate and a wire surrogate. The source of their nourishment (cloth or wire surrogate) was unimportant. "The infants developed a strong attachment to the cloth mothers and little or none to the wire mothers" (Harlow & Harlow, 1962, p. 141). Harlow found that it was *contact comfort*—the comfort supplied by bodily contact—rather than nourishment that formed the basis of the infant monkey's attachment to its mother. If the cloth mother was not present when unfamiliar objects were placed in the cage, the monkey would huddle in the corner, clutching its head, rocking, sucking its thumb or toes, and crying in distress. But when the cloth mother was present, it would first cling to her and then explore and play with the unfamiliar objects.

Numerous studies have shown that the attachment process is similar in human infants (Posada et al., 2002). The mother holds, strokes, and talks to the baby and responds to the baby's needs, and the baby gazes at and listens to the mother and even moves in synchrony with her voice (Condon & Sander, 1974; Lester et al., 1985). Once the attachment has formed, infants show **separation anxiety**—fear and distress when the parent leaves them. Occurring from about 8 months to 24 months, separation anxiety peaks between 12 and 18 months of age (Fox & Bell, 1990). At about 6 or 7 months of age, infants develop a fear of strangers called **stranger anxiety**, which increases in intensity until the first birthday and then declines in the second year (Marks, 1987). Stranger anxiety is greater in an unfamiliar setting, when the parent is not close at hand, and when a stranger abruptly approaches or touches the child.

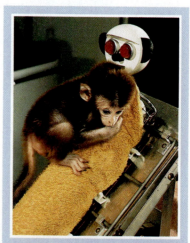

Harlow found that infant monkeys developed a strong attachment to a cloth-covered surrogate mother and little or no attachment to a wire surrogate mother—even when the wire mother provided nourishment.

◆ **attachment**

The strong affectionate bond a child forms with the mother or primary caregiver.

◆ **separation anxiety**

The fear and distress shown by a toddler when the parent leaves, occurring from 8 to 24 months and reaching a peak between 12 and 18 months.

◆ **stranger anxiety**

A fear of strangers common in infants at about 6 months and increasing in intensity until about 12 months, and then declining in the second year.

There are important differences in the quality of attachment. In a classic study of mother–child attachment, Mary Ainsworth (1973, 1979) observed mother–child interactions in the home during the infants' first year and then again at age 12 months in a laboratory. Based on infants' reactions to their mothers after brief periods of separation, Ainsworth and others (1978; Main & Solomon, 1990) identified four patterns of attachment.

The first pattern is *secure attachment* (observed in about 65% of American infants). Although usually distressed when separated from their mother, securely attached infants eagerly seek to reestablish the connection and then show an interest in play. They use the mother as a safe base of operation from which to explore and are typically more responsive, obedient, cooperative, and content than other infants. In addition, secure attachment seems to protect infants from the potentially adverse effects of risk factors such as poverty (Belsky & Fearon, 2002). Further, preschoolers who were securely attached as infants display more advanced social skills, such as the ability to maintain friendships, than peers who were not securely attached to their caregivers (McElwain & Volling, 2004).

Infants with a pattern called *avoidant attachment* (approximately 20% of American infants) are usually not responsive to their mother when she is present and not troubled when she leaves. When the parent returns, the infant may actively avoid contact with her or, at least, not be quick to greet her. In short, these infants do not act much more attached to the parent than to a stranger. Mothers of avoidant infants tend to show little affection and to be generally unresponsive to their infants' needs and cries.

Prior to a period of separation, infants who show *resistant attachment* (10–15% of American infants) seek and prefer close contact with their mother. Yet, in contrast to securely attached infants, they do not tend to branch out and explore. And when the mother returns to the room after a period of separation, the resistant infant displays anger and may push the mother away or hit her. When picked up, the infant is hard to comfort and may continue crying.

The pattern of *disorganized/disoriented attachment* (seen in 5–10% of American infants) is the most puzzling and apparently the least secure pattern. When reunited with the mother, the infant with this pattern of attachment exhibits contradictory and disoriented responses. Rather than looking at the mother while being held, the child may purposely look away or approach the mother with an expressionless or depressed demeanor. Also characteristic are a dazed and vacant facial expression and a peculiar, frozen posture after being calmed by the mother.

Although mother–child, rather than father–child, attachment relationships have been the traditional focus of research, fathers can be as responsive and competent as mothers (Roberts & Moseley, 1996), and their attachments can be just as strong. Indeed, father–child interactions have many enduring positive influences on children. Children who experience regular interaction with their fathers tend to have higher IQs and to do better in social situations and at coping with frustration than children lacking such interaction. They also persist longer in solving problems and are less impulsive and less likely to become violent (Adler, 1997; Bishop & Lane, 2000; Roberts & Moseley, 1996). Positive father–son relationships are also associated with higher-quality parenting behavior by sons when they have children of their own (Shears et al., 2002).

Interactions with fathers may be important for development because mothers and fathers interact differently with infants and children. Fathers engage in more exciting and arousing physical play with children (McCormick & Kennedy, 2000; Paquette, 2004). Mothers are more likely to cushion their children against overstimulation and potential injury. Consequently, some developmentalists believe that fathers are more supportive than mothers of children's confidence and identity development (Moradi, cited in Adler, 1997). For example, fathers allow infants to crawl farther away, up to twice as far as mothers usually allow. And fathers remain farther away as the infant explores novel stimuli and situations. Ideally, of course, children need both kinds of influences.

Fathers tend to engage in more physical play with their children than mothers. However, many fathers today share basic child-care responsibilities, such as feeding and diaper changing, with mothers.

Early and Middle Childhood

Think about how remarkable it is that, at birth, an infant's only means of communication is crying, but by age 11 or so, the average child has a vocabulary of more than 60,000 words (Anglin, 1995). Mastery of language, both spoken and written, is just one of several important developmental processes that happen in early and middle childhood.

Language Development

◆ What are the milestones of language development, and how do various theorists explain them?

During their first few months, infants communicate distress or displeasure through crying. But then they begin rapidly to acquire language.

During the second or third month, infants begin *cooing*—repeatedly uttering vowel sounds such as "ah" and "oo." At about 6 months, infants begin **babbling**. They utter *phonemes*—the basic speech sounds of any language, which form words when combined. During the first part of the babbling stage, infants babble all the basic speech sounds that occur in all the languages of the world. Language up to this point seems to be biologically determined, because all babies throughout the world, even deaf children, vocalize this same range of speech sounds.

At about 8 months, babies begin to focus attention on those speech sounds (phonemes) common to the language spoken around them and on the rhythm and intonation of that language. And by 1 year, the babbling stage gives way to the one-word stage. The first words usually represent objects that move or those that infants can act on or interact with. From 13 to 18 months of age, children markedly increase their vocabulary (Woodward et al., 1994), and 2-year-olds know about 270 words (Brown, 1973).

Initially a child's understanding of words differs from that of an adult. When they lack the correct word, children may act on the basis of shared features and apply a word to a broader range of objects than is appropriate. This is known as **overextension**. For example, any man may be called "dada" and any four-legged animal, "doggie." **Underextension** occurs, too; this is when children fail to apply a word to other members of the class. The family's poodle is a "doggie," but the German shepherd next door is not.

Between 18 and 20 months of age, when their vocabulary is about 50 words, children begin to put nouns, verbs, and adjectives together in two-word phrases and sentences. At this stage, children depend to a great extent on gesture, tone, and context to convey their meaning (Slobin, 1972). Depending on intonation, their sentences may indicate questions, statements, or possession. Children adhere to a rigid word order. You might hear "mama drink," "drink milk," or "mama milk," but not "drink mama," "milk drink," or "milk mama."

Between 2 and 3 years of age, children begin to use short sentences, which may contain three or more words. Labeled **telegraphic speech** by Roger Brown (1973), these short sentences follow a rigid word order and contain only essential content words, leaving out all plurals, possessives, conjunctions, articles, and prepositions. Telegraphic speech reflects the child's understanding of *syntax*—the rules governing how words are ordered in a sentence. When a third word is added to a sentence, it usually fills in the word missing from the two-word sentence (for example, "mama drink milk"). After using telegraphic speech for a time, children gradually begin to add modifiers to make their sentences more precise.

Children pick up grammatical rules intuitively and apply them rigidly. **Overregularization** is the kind of error that results when a grammatical rule is misapplied to a word that has an irregular plural or past tense (Marcus, 1996). Thus, children who have correctly used the words "went," "came," and "did" incorrectly apply the rule for past tenses and begin to say "goed," "comed," and "doed." What the parents see as a regression in speech actually means that the child has acquired a grammatical rule.

Learning theorists have long maintained that language is acquired in the same way as other behaviors—as a result of learning through reinforcement and imitation. B. F. Skinner (1957) asserted that parents selectively criticize incorrect speech and reinforce

◆ **babbling**
Vocalization of the basic speech sounds (phonemes), which begins between 4 and 6 months.

◆ **overextension**
The act of using a word, on the basis of some shared feature, to apply to a broader range of objects than is appropriate.

◆ **underextension**
Restricting the use of a word to only a few, rather than to all, members of a class of objects.

◆ **telegraphic speech**
Short sentences that follow a strict word order and contain only essential content words.

◆ **overregularization**
The act of inappropriately applying the grammatical rules for forming plurals and past tenses to irregular nouns and verbs.

correct speech through praise, approval, and attention. Thus, the child's utterances are progressively shaped in the direction of grammatically correct speech. Others believe that children acquire vocabulary and sentence construction mainly through imitation (Bandura, 1977a). However, imitation cannot account for patterns of speech such as telegraphic speech or for systematic errors such as overregularization. And parents seem to reinforce children more for the content of the utterance than for the correctness of the grammar (Brown et al., 1968).

Noam Chomsky (1957) believes that language ability is largely innate, and he has proposed a very different theory. Chomsky (1968) maintains that the brain contains a *language acquisition device (LAD)*, which enables children to acquire language and discover the rules of grammar easily and naturally. Language develops in stages that occur in a fixed order and appear at about the same times in most normal children. Lenneberg (1967) claims that biological maturation underlies language development in much the same way as it underlies physical and motor development. These claims are known as the *nativist position*.

The nativist position is better able than learning theory to account for the fact that children throughout the world go through the same basic stages in language development. It also accounts for the similar errors all children make when they are first learning to form plurals, past tenses, and negatives—errors not acquired through imitation or reinforcement.

Nevertheless, some environmental factors do contribute to language development. For example, babies whose parents are responsive to their babbling vocalize more than infants whose parents are not responsive to them (Whitehurst et al., 1989). Moreover, parents can facilitate language acquisition by adjusting their speech to their infant's level of development. Parents often use *motherese*—highly simplified speech with shorter phrases and sentences and simpler vocabulary, which is uttered slowly, at a high pitch, and with exaggerated intonation and much repetition (Fernald, 1993; Jones, 2003). Deaf mothers communicate with their infants in a similar way, signing more slowly and with exaggerated hand and arm movements and frequent repetition (Masataka, 1996).

Throughout the industrialized world, children must master written as well as spoken language. As you might expect, many aspects of the development of spoken language are critical to the process of learning to read. *Phonological awareness*, or sensitivity to the sound patterns of a language and how they are represented as letters, is particularly important. Children who can correctly answer questions such as "What would bat be if you took away the [b]?" by the age of 4 or so learn to read more rapidly than their peers who cannot (de Jong & van der Leij, 2002). Moreover, children who have good phonological awareness skills in their first language learn to read more easily even when reading instruction is conducted in a second language (Mumtaz & Humphreys, 2002; Quiroga et al., 2002).

Children seem to learn phonological awareness skills through word play. Among English-speaking children, learning nursery rhymes facilitates the development of these skills (Layton et al., 1996). Japanese parents foster phonological awareness in their children by playing a game with them called *shiritori*, in which one person says a word and another must supply a word that begins with its ending sound (Serpell & Hatano, 1997). Activities in which parents and children work together to read or write a story also foster the development of phonological awareness (Aram & Levitt, 2002).

Deaf mothers use sign language to communicate with their young children, but they do so in "motherese," signing slowly and with frequent repetitions.

◆ **socialization**

The process of learning socially acceptable behaviors, attitudes, and values.

Socialization

The process of learning socially acceptable behaviors, attitudes, and values is called **socialization**. Although parents have the major role in their children's socialization, peers affect the process as well.

A longitudinal study that followed individuals from age 5 to age 41 revealed that "children of warm, affectionate parents were more likely to be socially accomplished

◆ *What outcomes are often associated with the three parenting styles identified by Baumrind?*

adults who, at age 41, were mentally healthy, coping adequately, and psychosocially mature in work, relationships, and generativity" (Franz et al., 1991, p. 593). The methods parents use to control children's behavior contribute to socialization as well. Diane Baumrind (1971, 1980, 1991) studied the continuum of parental control and identified three parenting styles: authoritarian, authoritative, and permissive.

Authoritarian parents make the rules, expect unquestioned obedience from their children, punish misbehavior (often physically), and value obedience to authority. Rather than giving a rationale for a rule, authoritarian parents consider "because I said so" a sufficient reason for obedience. Parents using this parenting style tend to be uncommunicative, unresponsive, and somewhat distant, and Baumrind (1967) found preschool children disciplined in this manner to be withdrawn, anxious, and unhappy. The authoritarian style has been associated with low intellectual performance and lack of social skills, especially in boys (Maccoby & Martin, 1983).

Authoritative parents set high but realistic and reasonable standards, enforce limits, and at the same time encourage open communication and independence. They are willing to discuss rules and supply rationales for them. Knowing why the rules are necessary makes it easier for children to internalize them and to follow them, whether in the presence of their parents or not. Authoritative parents are generally warm, nurturant, supportive, and responsive, and they show respect for their children and their opinions. Their children are more mature, happy, self-reliant, self-controlled, assertive, socially competent, and responsible than their peers. The authoritative parenting style is associated with higher academic performance, independence, higher self-esteem, and internalized moral standards in middle childhood and adolescence (Lamborn et al., 1991; Steinberg et al., 1989).

Although they are rather warm and supportive, **permissive parents** make few rules or demands and usually do not enforce those that are made. They allow children to make their own decisions and control their own behavior. Children raised in this manner are the most immature, impulsive, and dependent, and they seem to be the least self-controlled and self-reliant.

Permissive parents also come in the indifferent, unconcerned, uninvolved variety (Maccoby & Martin, 1983). This parenting style is associated with drinking problems, promiscuous sex, delinquent behavior, and poor academic performance in adolescents.

The positive effects of authoritative parenting have been found across all ethnic groups in the United States (Querido et al., 2002; Steinberg & Dornbusch, 1991). The one exception is among first-generation Asian immigrants, where the authoritarian style is more strongly associated with academic achievement (Chao, 2001). Developmental psychologist Ruth Chao suggests that this finding may be explained by the traditional idea in Asian culture that making a child obey is an act of affection. Moreover, strict parenting tends to be tempered by emotional warmth in Asian families, so children probably get the idea that their parents expect unquestioning obedience because they love them. However, research also shows that the longer first-generation immigrants have lived in the United States, the more the pattern of association between authoritative parenting and social competence resembles that found in other groups (Kim & Chung, 2003).

Friendships begin to develop by the age of 3 or 4, and relationships with peers become increasingly important. These early relationships are usually based on shared activities; two children think of themselves as friends while they are playing together. During the elementary school years, friendships tend to be based on mutual trust (Dunn et al., 2002). By middle childhood, membership in a peer group is central to a child's happiness. Peer groups are usually composed of children of the same race, sex, and social class (Schofield & Francis, 1982). The peer group serves a socializing function by providing models of behavior, dress, and language. Peer groups provide objective measures against which children can evaluate their own traits. They are also a continuing source of both reinforcement for appropriate behavior and punishment for deviant behavior. In fact, peer rejection often results in excessive aggression (Wood et al., 2002).

◆ **authoritarian parents**
Parents who make arbitrary rules, expect unquestioned obedience from their children, punish transgressions, and value obedience to authority.

◆ **authoritative parents**
Parents who set high but realistic standards, reason with the child, enforce limits, and encourage open communication and independence.

◆ **permissive parents**
Parents who make few rules or demands and allow children to make their own decisions and control their own behavior.

Gender Role Development

Traditionally, males have been expected to be independent and competitive; females have been expected to be warm and nurturant. Psychologists use the term **gender roles** to refer to such expectations. Children display play behavior that is consistent with gender roles fairly early in life, by age 2 or so. Psychologists differ in how they explain gender role development.

According to the biological view, genes and prenatal sex hormones have an important influence on gender role development. In a review of studies on the effects of prenatal androgens (male sex hormones), Collaer and Hines (1995) found that these hormones have a reasonably strong influence on children's play behavior. Girls exposed to prenatal androgens are more likely than girls not exposed to these hormones to prefer to play with toys favored by boys, such as trucks, cars, and fire engines (Berenbaum & Snyder, 1995). Prenatal androgens are also known to affect brain development and functioning in humans and many other animal species (Beyenburg et al., 2000).

Of course, biological influences on gender role development don't operate in an environmental vacuum. For example, from infancy on, most of the presents children receive are gender-consistent: Girls are given dolls and tea sets, while boys get trucks and sports equipment. And while a girl may feel complimented if someone calls her a "tomboy," almost every boy considers it an insult to be called a "sissy" (Doyle & Paludi, 1995).

As you might expect, for social learning theorists, environmental influences are considered more important than biological forces in explaining gender role development (Mischel, 1966). These theorists point out that children are usually reinforced for imitating behaviors considered appropriate for their gender. When behaviors are not appropriate (a boy puts on lipstick, or a girl pretends to shave her face), children are quickly informed, often in a reprimanding tone, that boys or girls do not do that. However, there is little evidence that parents reinforce gender role–appropriate behavior in girls and boys often enough to account for the early age at which children begin to show gender-typed behavior (Fagot, 1995). Thus, imitation and reinforcement probably play some part in gender role development, but they do not provide a full explanation of this phenomenon.

Cognitive developmental theory, proposed by Lawrence Kohlberg (1966; Kohlberg & Ullian, 1974), suggests that an understanding of gender is a prerequisite to gender role development. According to Kohlberg, children go through a series of stages in acquiring the concept of gender. Between ages 2 and 3, children acquire *gender identity*—their sense of being a male or a female. Between ages 4 and 5, children acquire the concept of *gender stability*—awareness that boys are boys and girls are girls for a lifetime. Finally, between ages 6 and 8, children understand *gender constancy*—that gender does not change regardless of the activities people engage in or the clothes they wear. Moreover, according to Kohlberg, when children realize their gender is permanent, they are motivated to seek out same-sex models and learn to act in ways considered appropriate for their gender.

Cross-cultural studies reveal that Kohlberg's stages of gender identity, gender stability, and gender constancy occur in the same order in cultures as different as those in Samoa, Kenya, Nepal, and Belize (Munroe et al., 1984). However, this theory fails to explain why many gender-appropriate behaviors and preferences are observed in children as young as age 2 or 3, long before gender constancy is acquired (Bussey & Bandura, 1999; Jacklin, 1989; Martin & Little, 1990).

Gender-schema theory, proposed by Sandra Bem (1981), provides a more complete explanation of gender role development. Like social learning theory, gender-schema theory suggests that young children are motivated to pay attention to and behave in a way consistent with gender-based standards and stereotypes of the culture. Like cognitive developmental theory, gender-schema theory stresses that children begin to use gender as a way to organize and process information (Bussey & Bandura, 1999; Martin & Ruble, 2004). But gender-schema theory holds that this process occurs earlier, when gender identity rather than gender constancy is attained (Bem, 1985). According to Martin and Little (1990), "Once children can accurately label the sexes, they begin to form

◆ **gender roles**
Cultural expectations about the behavior appropriate for each gender.

gender stereotypes and their behavior is influenced by these gender-associated expectations" (p. 1438). They develop strong preferences for sex-appropriate toys and clothing, and they favor same-sex peers over those of the other sex (Powlishta, 1995). To a large extent, children's self-concepts and self-esteem depend on the match between their abilities and behaviors and the cultural definition of what is desirable for their gender. Consequently, the desire to maintain self-esteem, according to gender-schema theory, motivates children to align their behavior with culturally defined gender roles.

Adolescence

The concept of **adolescence**—a period of transition from childhood to adulthood—did not exist until psychologist G. Stanley Hall first wrote about it in his book by that name in 1904. He portrayed this stage in life as one of "storm and stress," the inevitable result of biological changes occurring during the period.

Puberty and Sexual Behavior

◆ How does puberty influence adolescents' self-concepts and behavior?

Adolescence begins with the onset of **puberty**—a period of rapid physical growth and change that culminates in sexual maturity. Although the average onset of puberty is age 10 for girls and age 12 for boys, the normal range extends from age 7 to age 14 for girls and from 9 to 16 for boys (Tanner, 1990).

Puberty begins with a surge in hormone production followed by a marked acceleration in growth known as the *adolescent growth spurt*. On average, the growth spurt occurs from age 10 to 13 in girls and about 2 years later in boys, from age 12 to 15 (Tanner, 1990). Girls attain their full height between ages 16 and 17, and boys, between ages 18 and 20 (Tanner, 1990).

During puberty, the reproductive organs in both sexes mature and **secondary sex characteristics** appear—those physical characteristics not directly involved in reproduction that distinguish the mature male from the mature female. In girls, the breasts develop, and the hips round; in boys, the voice deepens, and facial and chest hair appears; and in both sexes, there is growth of pubic and underarm (axillary) hair. The major landmark of puberty for males is the first ejaculation, which occurs, on average, at age 13 (Jorgensen & Keiding, 1991). For females, it is **menarche**—the onset of menstruation—which occurs at an average age of 12, although from 10 to 15 is considered the normal range (Tanner, 1990).

The timing of puberty can have important psychological consequences, coming as it does at a time when a sense of security is gained from being like other members of the peer group. Many studies show that early-maturing boys, taller and stronger than their classmates, have an advantage in sports and are likely to have a positive body image; to feel confident, secure, independent, and happy; and to be more successful academically (Alsaker, 1995; Blyth et al., 1981; Peterson, 1987). However, early-maturing boys may also be more hostile and aggressive than later-maturing peers (Ge et al., 2002). In addition, among boys from poor families, earlier-than-average puberty is correlated with affiliation with deviant peers (Ge et al., 2002).

Early-maturing girls, who may tower over their peers, feel more self-conscious about their developing bodies and their size. Consequently, they are more likely than late-maturing girls to develop eating disorders (Kaltiala-Heino et al., 2001). In addition to having earlier sexual experiences and more unwanted pregnancies than late-maturing girls, early-maturing girls are more likely to be exposed to alcohol and drug use (Caspi et al., 1993; Cavanaugh, 2004). Late-maturing girls often experience considerable stress when they fail to develop physically along with their peers, but they are likely to be taller and slimmer than their early-maturing age mates.

Puberty brings with it the awakening of sexual desire. As Figure 8.4 indicates, the incidence of sexual activity among teenagers in the United States increases dramatically across grades 9 to 12 (Centers for Disease Control and Prevention [CDC], 2000).

◆ **adolescence**

The developmental stage that begins at puberty and encompasses the period from the end of childhood to the beginning of adulthood.

◆ **puberty**

A period of rapid physical growth and change that culminates in sexual maturity.

◆ **secondary sex characteristics**

Those physical characteristics that are not directly involved in reproduction but distinguish the mature male from the mature female.

◆ **menarche**

(men-AR-kee) The onset of menstruation.

FIGURE 8.4   Incidence of Sexual Activity in U.S. High School Students

This graph, based on a survey of several thousand high school students in 1999, shows that the proportions of sexually active boys and girls increase dramatically from grade 9 to 12.   *Source:* Data from CDC (2000).

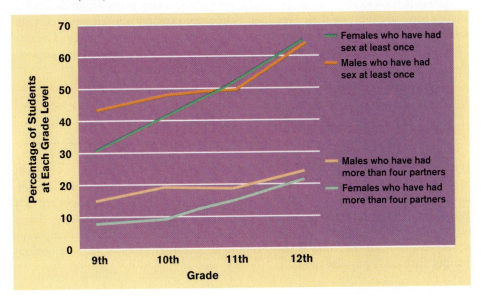

One particularly alarming statistic is the proportion of teens who have had multiple sex partners before leaving high school, because the more partners an individual has (whether teen or adult), the more likely he or she is to contract a sexually transmitted disease.

In addition, the rate of teenage pregnancy is higher in the United States than in any other developed country. For example, there are about 50 births per year for every 1,000 teenage girls in the United States, while the rate is only 4 per 1,000 in Japan (Singh & Darroch, 2000). It's important to keep in mind, though, that most teen pregnancies occur after the age of 16 and that the incidence of teen pregnancy has actually declined in the United States since the 1960s. What has increased is the number of births to *unmarried* adolescent mothers. In the 1960s, about 80% of teen mothers were married, compared with only 20% in the late 1990s (Singh & Darroch, 2000).

Teens who tend to be less experienced sexually attend religious services frequently and live with both biological parents, who are neither too permissive nor too strict in their discipline and rules (Blinn-Pike et al., 2004; Miller et al., 1998; White & DeBlassie, 1992). Early intercourse is also less prevalent among adolescents whose academic achievement is above average and who are involved in sports (Brooks-Gunn & Furstenberg, 1989; Savage & Holcomb, 1999).

Social Relationships

Most adolescents have good relationships with their parents (Steinberg, 1990). In fact, research shows that good relationships with parents are important to the development of self-esteem in adolescents (Wilkinson, 2004). Moreover, of the three parenting styles discussed earlier in the chapter—authoritative, authoritarian, and permissive—the authoritative style is most effective and the permissive least effective for adolescents (Baumrind, 1991; Steinberg et al., 1994). In a study of about 2,300 adolescents, those with permissive parents were more likely to use alcohol and drugs and to have conduct problems and less likely to be interested in academic success than were those with authoritative or authoritarian parents (Lamborn et al., 1991). The authoritarian style was related to more psychological distress and less self-reliance and self-confidence in adolescents.

◆ *In what ways do parents and peers contribute to teens' development?*

Even adolescents who have good relationships with their parents usually feel the need to separate from them to some degree. As a result, friends become a vital source of emotional support and approval for most of them. Adolescents usually choose friends of the same sex and race (Clark & Ayers, 1992), who have similar values, interests, and backgrounds (Duck, 1983; Epstein, 1983). Interactions with peers are critical while young people are forming their identities. Adolescents can try out different roles and observe the reactions of their friends to their behavior and their appearance. The peer group provides teenagers with a standard of comparison for evaluating their personal assets, as well as a vehicle for developing social skills (Berndt, 1992).

Early and Middle Adulthood

As noted earlier, the long period of 50 or more years known as adulthood is generally divided into three parts: young or early adulthood (ages 20 to 40 or 45), middle adulthood (ages 40 or 45 to 65), and late adulthood (after age 65 or 70). These ages are only approximate because there are no biological or psychological events that neatly define the beginning or ending of a period. Obviously, some things change; but, in many ways, adults remain much the same as they were in their earlier years. The most obvious changes are usually physical ones.

Physical Changes

◆ *How does the body change in the early and middle adult years?*

Most people enjoy good general health and vitality in their 20s and 30s, but the first of these decades is the period of top physical condition, when physical strength, reaction time, reproductive capacity, and manual dexterity all peak. After age 30, there is a slight decline in these physical capacities, which is barely perceptible to most people other than professional athletes. Middle-aged people often complain about a loss of physical vigor and endurance. But such losses have to do less with aging than with exercise, diet, and health habits (Boul, 2003). One unavoidable change in the mid- to late 40s, though, is **presbyopia**, a condition in which the lenses of the eyes no longer accommodate adequately for near vision, and reading glasses or bifocals are required for reading.

◆ **presbyopia**
(prez-bee-O-pee-uh) A condition, occurring in the mid- to late 40s, in which the lenses of the eyes no longer accommodate adequately for near vision, and reading glasses or bifocals are required for reading.

◆ **menopause**
The cessation of menstruation, occurring between ages 45 and 55 and signifying the end of reproductive capacity.

The major biological event for women during middle age is **menopause**—the cessation of menstruation, which usually occurs between ages 45 and 55 and signifies the end of reproductive capacity. The most common symptom associated with menopause and the sharp decrease in the level of estrogen is *hot flashes*—sudden feelings of being uncomfortably hot. Some women also experience symptoms such as anxiety, irritability, and/or mood swings, and about 10% become depressed. However, most women do not experience psychological problems in connection with menopause (Busch et al., 1994; Matthews, 1992).

Although men do not have a physical event equivalent to menopause, they do experience a gradual decline in testosterone from age 20 until about age 60. During late middle age, many men also experience a reduction in the functioning of the prostate gland that affects the production of semen. Usually coupled with these reductions in testosterone and semen production is a reduction in the sex drive. However, though women are not able to conceive after menopause, many men can and do father children during late adulthood.

Intellectual Capacity

◆ *In what ways does intellectual capacity improve and decline in adulthood?*

Young adults outperform middle-aged and older adults on tests requiring speed or rote memory. But on tests measuring general information, vocabulary, reasoning ability, and social judgment, older participants usually do better than younger ones because of their greater experience and education (Horn,

1982). Adults actually continue to gain knowledge and skills over the years, particularly when they lead intellectually challenging lives.

Schaie and his colleagues (Schaie, 1994, 1995; Schaie et al., 2004) analyzed data from the Seattle Longitudinal Study, which assessed the intellectual abilities of some 5,000 participants. Many of the participants were tested six times over the course of 35 years. Schaie found that in five areas—verbal meaning, spatial orientation, inductive reasoning, number, and word fluency—participants showed modest gains from young adulthood to the mid-40s. Decline did not occur, on average, until after age 60, and even then the decline was modest until the 80s. Half of the participants, even at age 81, showed no decline compared to their earlier performance. The study also revealed several gender differences: Females performed better on tests of verbal meaning and inductive reasoning; males tended to do better on tests of number and spatial orientation. The only ability found to show a continuous decline from the mid-20s to the 80s was perceptual speed.

Social Development

In days gone by, the primary social tasks of adulthood were marriage and starting a family. While it remains true that the majority of adults marry and have children, there is now a great deal of variability in the ages at which they do so. In 1960, the median age at first marriage was 20 for females and 23 for males; today, the median age is 25 for females and 27 for males (Poponoe & Whitehead, 2000).

◆ What are the milestones of social development in early and middle adulthood?

Likewise, a growing number of couples are delaying parenthood until their 30s. But whenever a person becomes a parent, the adjustment is one of the most challenging— and rewarding—in life. New parents may argue about child-rearing philosophy as well as about who should be responsible for household chores (Reichle & Gefke, 1998). In fact, conflict about the division of labor is believed to be the primary reason for the decline in relationship satisfaction that often follows the birth of a child (Hackel & Ruble, 1992). Thus, it isn't surprising that couples who agree to share household and child-rearing responsibilities have higher levels of satisfaction. Nevertheless, the impact of conflicts about child rearing is evident in surveys that reveal the high levels of relationship satisfaction enjoyed by couples whose children have grown up and left home (Norris & Tindale, 1994).

Child-rearing issues are often central in the lives of working women. In the 1960s, only 18% of mothers with children were employed. Today, 68% of mothers of children younger than age 6 and about 80% of the mothers of school-aged children work outside the home (U.S. Bureau of the Census, 2001). Further, the idea that a career is an important component of a satisfying life is now shared by men and women alike. However, women's work patterns are less likely to be continuous than those of men, often because women take time off to bear and raise children (Drobnic et al., 1999). Studies also show that women are less likely than men to actively seek promotions to upper-level management positions because of potential conflicts between their work and family roles (Sarrio et al., 2002; van Vianen & Fischer, 2002).

Even women who work continuously and actively pursue high-level positions face obstacles such as gender discrimination. Nevertheless, women have steadily increased their representation in upper-level positions in the workforce over the past few decades. For example, in the 1980s, only a handful of corporations were headed by women. Today, about 18% of upper-level managers in U.S. corporations are female, and more women are attaining such positions every year (Adler, 2001). Women have made similar gains in educational institutions and government agencies (Addi-Raccah & Ayalon, 2002; Baker et al., 2002).

Parenthood can cause stress and conflict in a marriage, but it is also immensely satisfying for most couples.

Although career satisfaction is important to most adults, it doesn't necessarily protect them from the negative effects of an increasingly common adult life event—divorce. For women, divorce often means a lower standard of living. And both men and women must usually find a new network of friends after they go through a divorce. Yet, most people who get divorced are not soured on the institution of marriage, because the majority of them eventually remarry.

After negotiating the many challenges associated with establishing relationships (and sometimes ending them) and building careers, it's little wonder that middle-aged people often find themselves in the role of decision maker. This often means that a middle-aged individual occupies the most influential job he or she has ever had. However, it can also be manifested in family roles. For example, many middle-aged women occupy the important family role of *kin-keeper* (Moen, 1996). The kin-keeper maintains lines of communication, solves conflicts among family members, and organizes social events.

In classic research, Bernice Neugarten (1968) found that middle-aged people rarely express a desire to be young again. The social status associated with being middle-aged and the knowledge they have accumulated over the years, most believe, outweigh the physical advantages of early adulthood.

Later Adulthood

In the early years of the 20th century, life expectancy in the United States was only 49 years. By the century's end, the expected lifespan of someone born in the United States was about 76 years. According to the most recent census, people older than age 65 constitute about 15% of the U.S. population; by 2030, that percentage will rise to 20% (FIFARS, 2004; U.S. Bureau of the Census, 2001). As you learned at the beginning of the chapter, a sizable number of these elders are likely to be older than age 100. What are your perceptions of life after 65? The statistics in *Try It 8.3* might surprise you.

Physical Changes

◆ *How does the body change in the later adult years?*

It was long assumed that the number of neurons in the brain declined sharply in later adulthood, but this assumption appears to be false (Gallagher & Rapp, 1997). Research has shown that the shrinking volume of the aging cortex is due

Try It 8.3

Stereotypes about Later Adulthood

Estimate the percentages of people older than age 65 in the United States who exhibit these indicators of well-being:

1. Live alone or with a spouse
2. Have incomes above the poverty level
3. Interact with family at least once every two weeks
4. Need no help with daily activities
5. Need no assistive devices (e.g., cane, wheelchair)
6. Go out to eat at least once every two weeks
7. Attend religious services regularly
8. Are sexually active

Answers: 1. 94% 2. 90% 3. 90% 4. 89% 5. 85% 6. 60% 7. 50% 8. 50%

Sources: FIFARS (2000, 2004); Gingell et al. (2003).

more to breakdown of the myelin that covers the axons in the white matter than to loss of the neurons that make up the gray matter, a process that begins in the early 30s (Peters et al., 1994; Wickelgren, 1996; Bartzokis et al., 2004). As you learned in Chapter 2, the myelin sheath facilitates the rapid conduction of neural impulses. The breakdown of myelin thus explains one of the most predictable characteristics of aging—the slowing of behavior (Birren & Fisher, 1995). With degeneration of the myelin, the brain takes longer to process information, and reaction time is slower.

With advancing age, the elderly typically become more farsighted, have increasingly impaired night vision, and suffer hearing loss in the higher frequencies (Long & Crambert, 1990; Slawinski et al., 1993). Joints become stiffer, and bones lose calcium and become more brittle, increasing the risk of fractures from falls.

About 80% of Americans older than age 65 have one or more chronic conditions. The most common of these ailments is hypertension (high blood pressure), a condition that afflicts 52% of women and 47% of men older than age 65 (FIFARS, 2004). Arthritis, an inflammatory condition that causes stiffness in the joints, is next, with prevalence rates of 39% among females and 31% among males. However, these two conditions can be controlled with medication, and many older adults who have them manage quite well.

Research suggests that physical exercise improves the physical fitness levels of older adults. In one study, 100 frail nursing-home residents, average age 87, exercised their thigh and hip muscles vigorously on exercise machines for 45 minutes three times a week. At the end of 10 weeks, participants had increased their stair-climbing power by 28.4% and their walking speed by 12%, and four of them were able to exchange their walkers for canes (Fiatarone et al., 1994). For many of us, remaining fit and vigorous as we age lies within our power.

Cognitive Changes

Intellectual decline in late adulthood is not inevitable. Older adults who keep mentally and physically active tend to retain their mental skills as long as their health is good (Meer, 1986). They do well on tests of vocabulary, comprehension, and general information, and their ability to solve practical problems is generally higher than that of young adults. And they are just as capable as younger adults at learning new cognitive strategies (Saczynski et al., 2002).

Researchers often distinguish between two types of intelligence (Horn, 1982): **Crystallized intelligence**—one's verbal ability and accumulated knowledge—tends to increase over the lifespan. **Fluid intelligence**—abstract reasoning and mental flexibility—peaks in the early 20s and declines slowly as people age. The rate at which people process information also slows gradually with age (Hertzog, 1991; Lindenberger et al., 1993; Salthouse, 1996, 2004). This explains, in part, why older adults perform more poorly on tests requiring speed.

Is it accurate to equate old age with forgetfulness? In laboratory memory tasks, older people do as well or almost as well as younger people on recognition tasks (Hultsch & Dixon, 1990) and on recall of information in their areas of expertise (Charness, 1989). But on tasks requiring speed of processing in short-term memory or recall of items that hold no particular meaning for them, younger participants do significantly better than older ones (Verhaeghen et al., 1993).

Several factors are positively correlated with good cognitive functioning in the elderly: a higher education level (Anstey et al., 1993; Lyketsos et al., 1999), a complex work environment, a long marriage to an intelligent spouse, and a higher income (Schaie, 1990). And gender is a factor as well. Women not only outlive men, but they also generally show less cognitive decline during old age. But intellectual functioning can be hampered by physical problems (Manton et al., 1986) or by psychological problems such as depression. A study by Shimamura and others (1995) revealed that people who continue to lead intellectually stimulating and mentally active lives are far less likely to suffer mental decline as they age. So, "use it or lose it" is good advice if you want to remain mentally sharp as you age.

◆ *What happens to cognitive ability in later adulthood?*

◆ **crystallized intelligence**
Aspects of intelligence, including verbal ability and accumulated knowledge, that tend to increase over the lifespan.

◆ **fluid intelligence**
Aspects of intelligence involving abstract reasoning and mental flexibility, which peak in the early 20s and decline slowly as people age.

Alzheimer's Disease and Other Types of Dementia

◆ *How does dementia affect older adults' psychological functioning and everyday life?*

Dementia is a state of severe mental deterioration marked by impaired memory and intellect, as well as by altered personality and behavior. It afflicts about 5–8% of those over age 65, 15–20% of those over 75, and 25–50% of those over 85 (American Psychiatric Association, 1997).

Senility is caused by physical deterioration of the brain. It can result from such conditions as cerebral arteriosclerosis (hardening of the arteries in the brain), chronic alcoholism, and irreversible damage by a series of small strokes.

About 50–60% of all cases of senility result from Alzheimer's disease. In **Alzheimer's disease,** there is a progressive deterioration of intellect and personality that results from widespread degeneration of brain cells. Slightly more than 4 million people in the United States suffer from this incurable disorder (National Institute on Aging, 2001). At first, victims show a gradual impairment in memory and reasoning and in efficiency in carrying out everyday tasks. Many have difficulty finding their way around in familiar locations. As the disorder progresses, Alzheimer's patients become confused and irritable, tend to wander away from home, and become increasingly unable to take care of themselves. Eventually, their speech becomes unintelligible, and they become unable to control bladder and bowel functions. If they live long enough, they reach a stage where they do not respond when spoken to and no longer recognize even spouse or children.

Age and a family history of Alzheimer's disease are the two risk factors that have been consistently associated with the disorder (Farrer & Cupples, 1994; Payami et al., 1994; Williams, 2003). Can Alzheimer's disease be delayed? According to Alexander and others (1997), a high IQ coupled with lifelong intellectual activity may delay or lessen the symptoms of Alzheimer's in those who are at risk for the disease. Certain anti-inflammatory drugs (such as ibuprofen) and the antioxidant vitamin E may provide a measure of protection (Nash, 1997; Sano et al., 1997). Other substances and drugs currently being studied for use in the prevention of Alzheimer's include folic acid (Reynolds, 2002), antioxidants such as vitamin C (Brown et al., 2002), and nicotine (Murray & Abeles, 2002).

◆ **dementia**

A state of mental deterioration characterized by impaired memory and intellect and by altered personality and behavior.

◆ **Alzheimer s disease**

(ALZ-hye-merz) An incurable form of dementia characterized by progressive deterioration of intellect and personality, resulting from widespread degeneration of brain cells.

Social Adjustment

◆ *What are some of the adjustment challenges in the social lives of older adults?*

As noted earlier, most elderly adults are both physically and cognitively healthy. Yet old age involves many losses. Adjusting to these losses is one of the challenges of getting older. Fortunately, most older adults are able to cope effectively. For instance, most older adults in the United States (about 88%) are retired (U.S. Census Bureau, 2001). Despite stereotypes, most of them are happy to leave work and do not experience a great deal of stress in adjusting to retirement. Generally, the people who are most reluctant to retire are those who are better educated, hold high-status jobs with a good income, and find fulfillment in their work.

Older adults take more time to learn new skills, but, once learned, they apply new skills as accurately as those who are younger.

Bosse and others (1991) found that only 30% of retirees reported finding retirement stressful, and most of those were likely to be in poor health and to have financial problems.

Another common event that may affect life satisfaction for older adults is the loss of a spouse. For most people, losing a spouse is the most stressful event in a lifetime. Disruption of sleep patterns is among the many physical effects associated with this loss (Steeves, 2002). These physical effects take their toll on the bereaved elderly and lead to tiredness and anxiety. In addition, both widows and widowers are at a greater risk for health problems due to suppressed immune function and have a higher mortality rate, particularly within the first 6 months, than their age-mates who are not bereaved (Martikainen & Valkonen, 1996).

Loss of a spouse often brings with it another challenge for the 44% of women and 14% of older men who experience it (FIFARS, 2004): They must decide whether to alter their living arrangements. In the United States, older Americans of all ethnic groups have a strong preference for remaining independent as long as possible (FIFARS, 2004; Martinez, 2002). As a result, only 5% of elderly women and 9% of older men live with their relatives (FIFARS, 2004). The living arrangements of elders in European countries are similar to those in the United States (Hellstrom & Hallberg, 2004; Osborn et al., 2003). Predictably, maintaining the ability to live alone is an important factor in elders' life satisfaction in these societies (Osborn et al., 2003).

In other countries, the situation is just the opposite. For instance, in Mexico, 90% of elderly widows live with relatives, usually their adult children (Varley & Blasco, 2003). Multigenerational households are commonplace in other Latin American countries as well (De Vos, 1990). Living with relatives is also more common among the elderly in Asian countries than in the United States or Europe (Sung, 1992). Consequently, the psychological effects of living alone are quite different among elders in Latin American and Asian societies than in the United States and Europe. Elders who live alone in societies in which it is considered normative for older adults to live with their adult children express lower levels of life satisfaction than their peers who live with family (Yeh & Lo, 2004).

Successful Aging

As you have learned, for older adults to maintain a sense of life satisfaction, they must be able to adjust to both physical and social changes. Knowing this, you shouldn't be surprised to learn that a majority of older adults rate their health as good (see Figure 8.5), even though 80% of them suffer from some kind of chronic ailment. One reason for this seeming contradiction is that the tendency toward having a generally optimistic outlook on life increases as people get older (Charles et al., 2003). Further, most older adults have learned to think of their lives in relative terms. That is, most believe that others are worse off than they are (Heckhausen & Brim, 1997). In other words, older adults grade their health "on a curve," so to speak.

An optimistic outlook is one of the key components of **successful aging,** the term researchers use to describe maintaining one's physical health, mental abilities, social competence, and overall satisfaction with life as one gets older (Rowe & Kahn, 1997, 1998). Successful aging has been the focus of much aging-related research in recent years. As defined by authors John Rowe and Robert Kahn (1997, 1998), successful aging has three components: good physical health, retention of cognitive abilities, and continuing engagement in social and productive activities.

Much of what happens to us as we age, of course, is somewhat beyond our control. However, successful aging also includes behaviors aimed at warding off age-related declines, such as eating a healthy diet and remaining mentally and socially active, and adaptive responses to the challenges that inevitably accompany aging. For instance, after a stroke, some older adults work diligently to recover lost abilities, while others despair and put little effort into the rehabilitation regimens prescribed for them by doctors and therapists (Ushikubo, 1998). Not surprisingly, individuals who are willing to do the work required for optimal recovery of functioning gain the most from rehabilitation. The kind of attitude that motivates an individual to try to get better after a devastating event such as a stroke represents the spirit of Rowe and Kahn's successful aging concept.

◆ What are the components of successful aging?

◆ **successful aging**
Maintaining one's physical health, mental abilities, social competence, and overall satisfaction with life as one gets older.

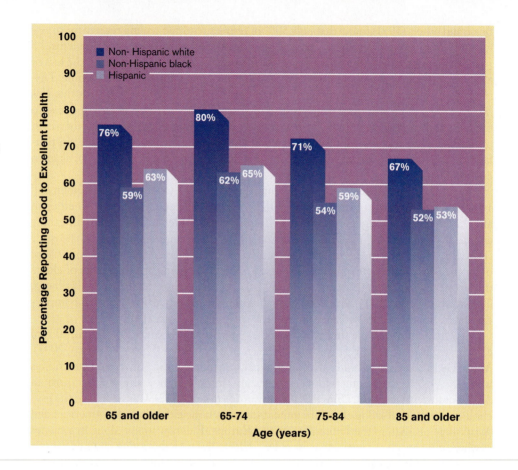

FIGURE 8.5

Percentage of People Age 65 and Older Who Reported Having Good to Excellent Health, by Age Group and Race and Hispanic Origin, 2000—2002 *Source:* FIFARS (2004).

Death and Dying

◆ *How do individuals with terminal illnesses respond to their circumstances?*

One of the developmental tasks for every elderly person is to accept the inevitability of death and to prepare for it. At no time, however, does this task become more critical than when an individual—no matter what age—faces a terminal illness. Elisabeth Kübler-Ross (1969) interviewed some 200 terminally ill people and found they shared common reactions to their impending death. In her book *On Death and Dying*, she identifies five stages people go through in coming to terms with death.

In the first stage, *denial*, most patients react to the diagnosis of their terminal illness with shock and disbelief (surely, the doctors must be wrong). The second stage, *anger*, is marked by feelings of anger, resentment, and envy of those who are young and healthy. In the third stage, *bargaining*, the person attempts to postpone death in return for a promise of "good behavior." An individual may offer God some special service or a promise to live a certain kind of life in exchange for an opportunity to attend a child's wedding or a grandchild's graduation. The fourth stage, *depression*, brings a great sense of loss and may take two forms—depression over past losses and depression over impending losses. Given enough time, patients may reach the final stage, *acceptance*, in which they stop struggling against death and contemplate its coming without fear or despair. Kübler-Ross claims that the family also goes through stages similar to those experienced by the patient.

Critics deny the universality of Kübler-Ross's proposed stages and their invariant sequence (Butler & Lewis, 1982; Kastenbaum, 1992; Wright, 2003). Each person is unique. The reactions of all the terminally ill cannot be expected to conform to some rigid sequence of stages.

Death comes too soon for most people, but not soon enough for others. Some who are terminally ill and subject to intractable pain would welcome an end to their suffering. Should dying patients be left with no choice but to suffer to the end? In answer to this highly controversial question, Dr. Jack Kevorkian has said, "No!" Known as "Dr. Death" to those who oppose his "assisted suicides," Kevorkian has defied both laws and criticism and helped many terminally ill patients end their lives. Although Dr. Kevorkian was convicted of murder in 1999 and remains in prison, he brought to the nation's attention the plight of many hopelessly, terminally ill individuals who wish to end their lives.

A rapidly growing alternative to hospitals and nursing homes is *hospice care*. Hospices are agencies that care for the needs of the dying more humanely and affordably than hospitals can and that use special facilities or, in some cases, the patient's own home. A hospice follows a set of guidelines that make it more attuned to the patient's personal needs and preferences than a hospital or nursing home typically can be.

Finally, many of us have experienced the *grieving process*—the period of bereavement that follows the death of a loved one and sometimes lingers long after the person has gone. Contrary to what many believe, research (Bonanno et al., 1995) has shown that bereaved individuals who suffer the most intense grief initially, who weep inconsolably and feel the deepest pain, do not get through their bereavement more quickly than others. And other research (Folkman et al., 1996) has found that the grieving process for male caregivers whose partners have died of AIDS is very similar to that experienced by spouses.

Death and dying are not pleasant subjects, but remember that life itself is a terminal condition, and each day of life should be treasured like a precious gift.

Looking Back   Our discussion of death and dying has brought us to the end of the human lifespan. As you have seen, gains and losses occur in every phase of development. The accumulated experience available to the elderly is punctuated by losses in physical and psychological speed for most and more serious declines for others. In middle adulthood, many people occupy important social roles at the same time that their reproductive capacity is diminishing. For young adults, the joys of youth are left behind as the responsibilities of adulthood are assumed. In similar fashion, adolescents look back wistfully at the time they spent playing during their childhood years as they use their newly acquired mental and physical abilities to make important decisions about their lives. School-aged children think more logically than when they were younger, but, at the same time, they have forever left behind the pleasures associated with a day spent pretending to be a superhero, for example. The capacity to use one's own behavior as a symbolic representation of something else is the most important ability gained in the preschool years, but it comes with the loss of caregivers' tolerance of dependency. Finally, the infant trades the warm safety of the womb for the opportunity to take in all the sights and sounds of the outside world and to embark on a journey of unknown length but of certain destination. Perhaps it is the ability to balance life's losses against its gains that underlies the remarkable capacity for adjustment exhibited by the centenarians you read about at the beginning of the chapter (Baltes & Baltes, 1990).

Apply It 8.1 Where Are You in the Career Development Process?

Have you ever wondered what type of work you are best suited for? If so, you may want to begin your quest for an answer by looking at two models of career development, the process of choosing and adjusting to a particular career. Recommendations about what you might do to enhance your search for the ideal career can be derived from both. Ultimately, though, the degree to which you are satisfied with your career may depend on how you integrate your work into your life as a whole.

Holland's Personality Types

The work of John Holland has been very influential in shaping psychologists' ideas about personality and career. Holland proposes six basic personality types: realistic, investigative, artistic, social, enterprising, and conventional. His research shows that each of the six types is associated with work preferences. (The types and their associated work preferences are summarized in the table.) As Holland's theory predicts, people whose personality matches their job are also more likely to be satisfied with their work. Thus, a personality assessment may help you make an appropriate occupational choice and give you confidence about the decision (Francis-Smyth & Smith, 1997).

Super's Career Development Stages

Psychologist Donald Super proposed that career development happens in stages that begin in infancy (Super, 1971, 1986). First comes the growth stage (from birth to 14 years), in which you learn about your abilities and interests. Next is the exploratory stage, roughly between the ages of 15 and 24. According to Super, there's a lot of trial and error in this stage, so job changes happen frequently. Next is the establishment stage (also called the stabilization stage), from 25 to 45. This stage begins with learning how things work in your career, the culture of your organization, and progression through the early steps of the career ladder. Sometimes, additional formal training is required during this stage. Setting goals is also important in this stage. You must decide how far you want to go and how you intend to get there. Mentoring by an experienced co-worker often helps you negotiate this stage successfully. Once an individual has become well established in a career, she or he enters the maintenance phase (age 45 through retirement), in which the goal is to protect and maintain the gains made in earlier years. Of course, in today's rapidly changing economy, people are often required to change careers. Thus, an individual may re-enter the exploratory stage at any time. As with most stage theories, the ages associated with Super's stages of career development are less important than the sequence of the stages.

TABLE 8.2 Holland's Personality Types and Work Preferences

TYPE	PERSONALITY TRAITS	WORK PREFERENCES
Realistic	Aggressive, masculine, physically strong, often with low verbal or interpersonal skills	Mechanical activities and tool use; often chooses a job such as mechanic, electrician, or surveyor
Investigative	Oriented toward thinking (particularly abstract thinking), organizing, and planning; low in social skills	Ambiguous, challenging tasks; often a scientist or engineer
Artistic	Asocial	Unstructured, highly individual activity; often an artist
Social	Extraverted; people-oriented, sociable, and needing attention; avoids intellectual activity and dislikes highly ordered activity	Working with people in service jobs like nursing and education
Enterprising	Highly verbal and dominating; enjoys organizing and directing others; persuasive and a strong leader	Often chooses a career in sales
Conventional	Prefers structured activities and subordinate roles; likes clear guidelines; accurate and precise	May choose an occupation such as bookkeeping or filing

Source: Holland (1973, 1992).

Apply It 8.1

Job Satisfaction

The career you choose may suit your personality perfectly, and you may progress through Super's stages with little difficulty. Does this mean that you will be happy in your work? Not necessarily. In fact, the key to job satisfaction probably lies outside of the career development process itself. Research shows, for example, that having a generally optimistic outlook on life predisposes us to be satisfied with our jobs (Diener et al., 2002). So learning to maintain a positive perspective on things may help you more in the long run than trying to find the perfect job.

Additional insight can be gleaned from research linking age and job satisfaction. Younger people tend to be less satisfied in their work (Glenn & Weaver, 1986). Why? Many young people think middle-aged adults are happier in their jobs because they hold higher-status positions and make more money than those who are younger. However, research suggests that the connection between job satisfaction and age exists because as people get older, work becomes less central to their lives (Tamir, 1982). Thus, finding the right balance between work and other pursuits in life may be the key ingredient in job satisfaction.

A Personal Definition of Success

You may be able to avoid the stresses associated with low levels of job satisfaction if you spend some time developing a personal definition of success. Is it wealth? A happy family? Social prestige? How much time do you want to devote to your work? What hobbies would you like to pursue? How important is having a family to you? Whatever your goals, thinking about them now and setting priorities may pay off in reduced stress in the future.

Chapter 8 Summary

◆❖ Theories of Development p. 236

◆ What did Piaget find regarding stages of cognitive development? p. 236

Piaget claimed that cognitive ability develops in four stages, each involving a qualitatively different form of reasoning and understanding. The stages are sensorimotor, preoperational, concrete operational, and formal operational.

◆ How does Vygotsky's theory explain cognitive development? p. 241

Vygotsky hypothesized that cognitive development occurs in a sociocultural context in which parents and teachers provide children with age-appropriate guidance toward the acquisition of cognitive skills. He also claimed that language is required for cognitive development.

◆ What did Kohlberg claim about the development of moral reasoning? p. 241

Kohlberg's research suggests that moral reasoning develops in six stages and is correlated with cognitive development.

◆ How does Erikson's theory describe the process of psychosocial development? p. 245

Erikson proposed eight psychosocial stages that encompass the entire lifespan. Each stage is defined by a conflict with the social environment that must be resolved.

◆❖ Prenatal Development p. 247

◆ What happens during each of the three stages of prenatal development? p. 247

In the period of the zygote, the cell created by the union of a sperm and an ovum moves into the uterus and becomes implanted in the uterine wall. During the period of the embryo, the major organ systems develop. The majority of growth in size occurs during the period of the fetus. The fetus's greatest vulnerability to negative influences occurs during the period of the embryo.

◆❖ Infancy p. 249

◆ How do infants' perceptual and motor abilities change over the first 18 months of life? p. 249

Infants' visual acuity improves dramatically over the first 6 months. They develop depth perception when they begin to crawl. Motor skills develop in a universal sequence that is largely determined by maturation.

◆ How does temperament shape infants' behavior? p. 251

Temperament is an individual infant's characteristic way of responding to the environment. Three temperament categories identified by Thomas and Chess are easy, difficult, and slow-to-warm-up.

◆ How do the four attachment patterns identified in infants differ? p. 252

Securely attached infants protest separation from their caregivers and greet caregivers when they return. Infants with avoidant attachment do not protest being left by caregivers and appear to be indifferent when the caregivers return. Infants with resistant attachment protest separation but display anger when caregivers return. Those with disorganized/disoriented attachment protest separation but display little or no emotion when caregivers return.

Early and Middle Childhood p. 254

What are the milestones of language development, and how do various theorists explain them? p. 254

The stages of language development are cooing, babbling, single words, two-word sentences, and telegraphic speech, followed by the acquisition of grammatical rules. Nativist theories explain language development in terms of an inborn neurological system for acquiring language. Learning theories claim that it is the result of imitation and reinforcement. Cognitive theories emphasize the role of cognitive development.

What outcomes are often associated with the three parenting styles identified by Baumrind? p. 255

Authoritative parenting is most effective and is associated with psychosocial competence in children. Children with authoritarian parents are typically the most anxious and the least socially competent. Permissive parenting is least effective and is often associated with adolescent behavior problems.

How do social learning, cognitive developmental, and gender-schema theorists explain gender role development? p. 257

Social learning claims that gender role development results from modeling and reinforcement. Cognitive developmental theory says that it occurs in a series of stages marked by increasingly sophisticated reasoning about the permanence of gender. Gender-schema theory posits that young children acquire schemas for maleness and femaleness from their cultures and then use them to process information about gender, including their own characteristics and behavior.

Adolescence p. 258

How does puberty influence adolescents' self-concepts and behavior? p. 258

Early maturation provides enhanced self-esteem for boys but has the opposite effect on girls. The reverse is true for late maturation. Puberty brings with it the capacity for sexual behavior. Teens who are involved in school and extracurricular activities and those who believe that premarital sex is morally wrong are less likely to engage in sexual behavior than adolescents who do not have these characteristics.

In what ways do parents and peers contribute to teens' development? p. 259

Parenting styles affect adolescent behavior in ways that are similar to their effects on children's behavior. Peer groups provide them with standards of comparison and a vehicle for developing social skills.

Early and Middle Adulthood p. 260

How does the body change in the early and middle adult years? p. 260

Physical changes associated with increasing age include a need for reading glasses, the end of reproductive capacity in women, and a decline in testosterone level in men.

In what ways does intellectual capacity improve and decline in adulthood? p. 260

Although younger people tend to do better on tests requiring speed or rote memory, the intellectual performance of adults shows modest gains until the mid-40s.

What are the milestones of social development in early and middle adulthood? p. 261

Most adults marry and have children, but today they do so at later ages than in past generations. Adjustment to parenthood often brings conflicts about the division of labor. Careers are important to life satisfaction, and many men and women occupy decision-making roles in middle age.

Later Adulthood p. 262

How does the body change in the later adult years? p. 262

Physical changes associated with later adulthood include a general slowing, a decline in sensory capacity, and the development of chronic conditions such as arthritis, heart disease, and high blood pressure.

What happens to cognitive ability in later adulthood? p. 263

Crystallized intelligence shows no significant age-related decline; fluid intelligence does decline. Both cognitive and physical activity appear to provide some protection against the effects of aging on intellectual functioning.

How does dementia affect older adults' psychological functioning and everyday life? p. 264

Dementia affects older adults' memories and personalities. Patients can become confused and irritable, and they may wander away from their homes. Eventually, those with Alzheimer's disease become unresponsive to those around them.

What are some of the adjustment challenges in the social lives of older adults? p. 264

Older adults typically retire from work. Many lose a spouse and may alter their living arrangements. In Western societies, most elders prefer to live on their own; in other parts of the world, it is more common for older adults to live with family members.

What are the components of successful aging? p. 265

Successful aging includes maintenance of health, active cognitive and engagement, productivity, and life satisfaction.

Death and Dying p. 266

How do individuals with terminal illnesses respond to their circumstances? p. 266

Kübler-Ross suggested five stages of dying: denial, anger, bargaining, depression, and acceptance.

accommodation, p. 236
adolescence, p. 258
Alzheimer's disease, p. 264
assimilation, p. 236
attachment, p. 252
authoritarian parents, p. 256
authoritative parents, p. 256
babbling, p. 254
conservation, p. 237
conventional level, p. 242
critical period, p. 248
crystallized intelligence, p. 263
dementia, p. 264
developmental psychology, p. 236
embryo, p. 247
fetal alcohol syndrome, p. 248
fetus, p. 247
fluid intelligence, p. 263
gender roles, p. 257

hypethetico-deductive thinking,
    p. 237
imaginary audience, p. 238
low-birth-weight baby, p. 249
maturation, p. 250
menarche, p. 258
menopause, p. 260
naive idealism, p. 238
neonate, p. 249
object permanence, p. 237
overextension, p. 254
overregularization, p. 254
permissive parents, p. 256
personal fable, p. 238
postconventional level, p. 242
preconventional level, p. 242
prenatal development, p. 247
presbyopia, p. 260
preterm infant, p. 249

psychosocial stages, p. 245
puberty, p. 258
reflexes, p. 249
reversibility, p. 237
scaffolding, p. 241
scheme, p. 236
secondary sex characteristics, p. 258
separation anxiety, p. 252
socialization, p. 255
stranger anxiety, p. 252
successful aging, p. 265
symbolic function, p. 237
telegraphic speech, p. 254
temperament, p. 251
teratogens, p. 248
underextension, p. 254
visual cliff, p. 249
zone of proximal development, p. 241
zygote, p. 247

Study Guide 8

Answers to all the Study Guide questions are provided at the end of the book.

◆ SECTION ONE: Chapter Review

Theories of Development (pp. 236–247)

1. Which statement reflects Piaget's thinking about the stages of cognitive development?
   a. All people pass through the same stages but not necessarily in the same manner.
   b. All people progress through the stages in the same order but not at the same rate.
   c. All people progress through the stages in the same order and at the same rate.
   d. Very bright children sometimes skip stages.

2. The teenager's personal fable includes all of the following except
   a. a sense of personal uniqueness.
   b. a belief that he or she is indestructible and protected from misfortunes.
   c. a belief that no one has ever felt so deeply before.
   d. a feeling that he or she is always on stage.

3. Match Kohlberg's level of moral reasoning with the rationale for engaging in a behavior.
   ____ (1) to avoid punishment or gain a reward
   ____ (2) to ensure that human rights are protected
   ____ (3) to gain approval or follow the law

   a. conventional
   b. preconventional
   c. postconventional

4. According to Erikson, satisfactory resolution of the conflict associated with each stage of his psychosocial stages is required for healthy development in future stages. (true/false)

Prenatal Development (pp. 247–249)

5. Match the stage of prenatal development with its description.
   ____ (1) first 2 weeks of life
   ____ (2) rapid growth and further development of body structures and systems
   ____ (3) formation of major systems, organs, and structures

   a. period of the fetus
   b. period of the embryo
   c. period of the zygote

Infancy (pp. 249–253)

6. Which of the following statements about infant sensory development is *not* true?
   a. Vision, hearing, taste, and smell are all fully developed at birth.
   b. Vision, hearing, taste, and smell are all functional at birth.
   c. Infants can show preferences in what they want to look at, hear, and smell shortly after birth.
   d. Hearing is better developed at birth than vision.

7. The primary factor influencing the attainment of the major motor milestones is
   a. experience.   c. learning.
   b. maturation.   d. habituation.

8. Which statement best describes Thomas, Chess, and Birch's thinking about temperament?
   a. Temperament develops gradually as a result of parental handling and personality.
   b. Temperament is inborn and is not influenced by the environment.
   c. Temperament is inborn but can be modified by the family and the environment.
   d. Temperament is set at birth and is unchangeable.

9. Ainsworth found that most infants had secure attachment. (true/false)

10. Match the linguistic stage with the example.
    ____ (1) "ba-ba-ba"
    ____ (2) "He eated the cookies"
    ____ (3) "Mama see ball"
    ____ (4) "oo," "ah"
    ____ (5) "kitty," meaning a lion
    a. telegraphic speech
    b. overregularization
    c. babbling
    d. overextension
    e. cooing

Early and Middle Childhood (pp. 254–258)

11. Learning theory is better able than the nativist position to account for how language development can be encouraged. (true/false)

12. Match the parenting style with the approach to discipline.
    ____ (1) expecting unquestioned obedience
    ____ (2) setting high standards, giving rationale for rules
    ____ (3) setting few rules or limits
    a. permissive
    b. authoritative
    c. authoritarian

13. The peer group usually has a negative influence on social development. (true/false)

14. Which theory of gender role development does *not* require that children understand the concept of gender?
    a. Kohlberg's theory
    b. social learning theory
    c. gender-schema theory
    d. none of the above

Adolescence (pp. 258–260)

15. Adolescence is a stormy time for most teenagers. (true/false)

16. The secondary sex characteristics
    a. are directly involved in reproduction.
    b. appear at the same time in all adolescents.
    c. distinguish mature males from mature females.
    d. include the testes and ovaries.

17. Most teenagers have good relationships with their parents. (true/false).

Early and Middle Adulthood (pp. 260–262)

18. During which decade do people reach their peak physically?
    a. teens   b. 30s   c. 20s   d. 40s

Later Adulthood (pp. 262–266)

19. Which of the following statements is true of adults older than age 65?
    a. They are considerably less satisfied with life than young adults are.
    b. Most retirees are happy to be retired.

20. Compared to older adults who are mentally and physically active, younger adults do better on
    a. tests requiring speed.
    b. comprehension tests.
    c. general information tests.
    d. practical problem solving.

Death and Dying (pp. 266–267)

21. According to Kübler-Ross, the first stage experienced by terminally ill patients in coming to terms with death is _____; the last stage is _____ .
    a. anger; depression
    b. denial; depression
    c. bargaining; acceptance
    d. denial; acceptance

On the line opposite each name, list the major concept or theory associated with that name.

Name   **Major Concept or Theory**

1. Piaget   _____

2. Erikson   _____

3. Thomas, Chess, and Birch   _____

4. Ainsworth   _____

5. Chomsky   _____

6. Kohlberg   _____

7. Kübler-Ross   _____

8. Bem   _____

◆ **SECTION THREE: Fill In the Blank**

1. Piaget's term for an individual's cognitive structure or concept that is used to make sense of information is a _____ .

2. According to the concept of the _____ , adolescents may take risks such as driving fast, smoking cigarettes, or having unprotected sex because they believe they are indestructible.

3. Tamara believes that pleasing others defines a good person. She is at the _____ level of moral development.

4. Charles is at a point in his life when he is wrestling with a sense of who he is and where he will go from here. He would be considered to be in Erikson's _____ stage of psychosocial development.

5. The period of the _____ is the first stage of prenatal development.

6. Substances in the prenatal environment that may cause birth defects are called _____ .

7. The pediatrician said that Sandra began to crawl when she did because she had achieved a sufficient degree of _____ in her genetically programmed biological timetable of development.

8. The chapter identified four different patterns of attachment. Ainsworth would say that a child who does not seem to be responsive to his or her mother and does not seem to be troubled when she is gone demonstrates _____ attachment.

9. Watching one of the family dogs sleeping on the couch right next to her, 2-year-old Peg says, "Doggie sleep." This is an example of _____ .

10. One day, her mother asked Peg where the dog was. Peg responded, "Doggie goed outside." This is an example of _____ .

11. According to _____ , children label themselves as boys or girls before they understand that all boys grow up to be men and all girls grow up to be women.

12. _____ intelligence is to verbal ability as _____ intelligence is to abstract reasoning.

13. _____ is the third stage of grieving, according to Kübler-Ross's theory.

◆ **SECTION FOUR: Comprehensive Practice Test**

1. The period of time from conception to birth is called the period of _____ development.
   a. neonatal
   b. prenatal
   c. post-zygotic
   d. post-fertilization

2. The second stage of prenatal development is known as the period of
   a. germination.
   b. the embryo.
   c. the fetus.
   d. the zygote.

3. Researchers have found that resolution of Erikson's stage of intimacy versus isolation typically occurs in adulthood rather than in adolescence. One reason for this finding is that identity development is correlated with
   a. work experience.
   b. cognitive development.
   c. physical maturation.
   d. finding a life partner.

4. A baby is considered preterm if she or he is born
   a. some place other than a hospital.
   b. prior to the parents paying the doctor's bill.
   c. before the 45th week of pregnancy.
   d. before the 37th week of pregnancy.

5. Jorge is just a few days old. He can see, but not as well as he will later. If he is a typical baby, he probably has _____ vision.
   a. 20/40
   b. 20/600
   c. 40/20
   d. 10/40

6. Maturation is
   a. genetically determined biological changes that follow a timetable of development.
   b. behavioral changes based on the child's interaction with the environment.
   c. behavioral changes that take place when the child enters high school.
   d. applicable only to physiology and not to cognition or psychomotor development.

7. Cindy says that her new baby's responses to things that happen in the environment are generally happy and positive. Cindy is talking about her baby's
   a. response system.
   b. temperament.
   c. latent personality.
   d. infant personification.

8. Assimilation is a process used with _____; accommodation is a process used with _____.
   a. new schemas; existing schemas
   b. existing schemas; new schemas
   c. positive responses; negative responses
   d. negative responses; positive responses

9. The nativist position on speech development is that language ability is basically innate. (true/false)

10. Which of the following is *not* an example of a secondary sex characteristic?
    a. development of breasts in females
    b. differentiation of internal reproductive organs
    c. deepening of the voice in males
    d. rounding of the hips in females

11. Piaget's final stage of cognitive development is known as the _____ stage.
    a. concrete operations
    b. cognitive integrity
    c. generativity
    d. formal operations

12. A child in Kohlberg's _____ level of moral reasoning is governed by the standards of others rather than by internalized ideas of right and wrong.
    a. postconventional
    b. conventional
    c. preconventional
    d. preadolescent

13. A person must be at Piaget's stage of formal operations to attain Kohlberg's _____ level of moral reasoning.
    a. conventional
    b. formal conventional
    c. postconventional
    d. ego integrity

14. Evidence suggests that females tend to stress care and compassion in resolving moral dilemmas, whereas males tend to stress _____ (or to give it and caring equal weight).
    a. romance
    b. aggression
    c. justice
    d. morality

15. The children of teenage mothers tend to display academic and/or behavioral difficulties. (true/false)

16. The most obvious changes as an individual gets older are usually
    a. cognitive.
    b. physical.
    c. social.
    d. sexual.

17. One reason for the "in-and-out" career pattern displayed by many women is that
    a. very few women qualify for high-paying jobs.
    b. men demonstrate higher levels of competence on the job and are rewarded accordingly.
    c. women take time off to raise children.
    d. women change careers often.

18. The results of current research seem to indicate that older adults are _____ younger adults.
    a. less happy and satisfied with life than
    b. as satisfied with life as
    c. as dissatisfied with life as
    d. less satisfied but more secure than

19. For the majority of those who stop working, retirement is not as stressful as popularly believed. (true/false)

20. The most stressful event faced by people in their lifetimes is
    a. retirement.
    b. losing a spouse.
    c. children leaving home.
    d. restricted physical ability due to age.

1. Evaluate Erikson's stages of psychosocial development, explaining what aspects of his theory seem most convincing. Support your answer.

2. Using Baumrind's categories, classify the parenting style your mother and/or father used in rearing you.
   a. Cite examples of techniques they used that support your classification.
   b. Do you agree with Baumrind's conclusions about the effects of that parenting style on children? Why or why not?

3. Think back to your junior high school and high school years. To what degree did early or late maturation seem to affect how boys and girls were treated by their peers, their parents, or their teachers? Did early or late maturation affect their adjustment? Explain your answer.

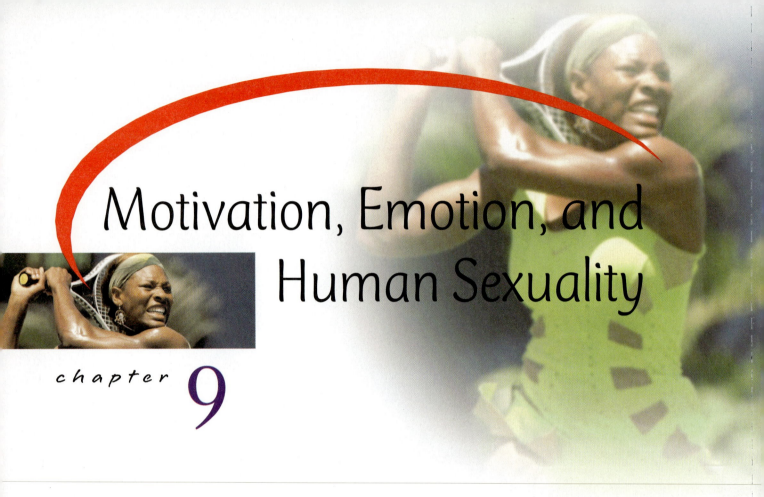

Motivation, Emotion, and Human Sexuality

chapter **9**

Explaining Motivation

◆ What is the difference between intrinsic and extrinsic motivation?

◆ How do drive-reduction and arousal theory explain motivation?

◆ According to Maslow, how do individuals attain self-actualization?

◆ How do need for achievement theory and goal orientation theory explain achievement motivation?

Hunger

◆ How do internal and external cues influence eating behavior?

◆ What are some factors that account for variations in body weight?

◆ What are the proposed causes of eating disorders, and how are these disorders treated?

Emotion

◆ What are the various theories that have been proposed to explain emotion?

◆ What are the neurological processes involved in the fear response?

◆ Which aspects of emotion are universal, and which vary across cultures?

◆ In what ways do males and females differ with regard to emotions?

◆ What are the components of emotional intelligence?

Human Sexuality

◆ How do sexual attitudes and behavior vary across cultures and genders?

◆ What are the four phases of the human sexual response cycle?

◆ What are the various factors that have been suggested as determinants of a gay or lesbian sexual orientation?

How did you find out about sex? Alfred Kinsey and his associates did research in the 1940s that brought the subject of sex out into the open in the United States. They interviewed thousands of men and women about their sexual behaviors and attitudes, publishing the results in a two-volume report—*Sexual Behavior in the Human Male* (1948) and *Sexual Behavior in the Human Female* (1953)—which shocked the public. More than half a century later, Kinsey's work remains controversial.

When first published, Kinsey's report shattered common ideas about sexuality. For instance, despite the fact that sex outside marriage was widely condemned in those days, Kinsey found that 50% of the females and nearly 90% of the males reported having sexual intercourse before marriage. He also reported that about one-fourth of the married women and half of the married men admitted to having had extramarital affairs. Advocates of psychological and cultural approaches to sexuality, such as anthropologist Margaret Mead, criticized Kinsey for taking a strictly biological approach to the subject. Many laypersons were surprised to learn that women and men were equally capable of sexual arousal and orgasm.

Although some people attacked Kinsey's work on moral and theoretical grounds, many others—especially women—found it to be enlightening and empowering.

Another important criticism focused on Kinsey's methods. The survey participants were volunteers, mostly college-educated, and from middle-class backgrounds. Kinsey reported no information on African Americans or other minorities. Moreover, most of those who answered the 300 to 500 survey questions were younger than age 35. Another limitation was that Kinsey's surveys were just that—surveys. Thus, his findings depended largely on the truthfulness of participants.

Despite the limitations of his methods, Alfred Kinsey is credited with having introduced the scientific method into the study of sexuality. Indeed, the publication of his findings served as a catalyst for the thousands of studies of human sexuality that have been done since his name became a household word in the late 1940s. Moreover, the topic of sexuality is discussed more openly now than was true before Kinsey's landmark research findings became known. As these were his primary goals, it is fair to say that he accomplished exactly what he set out to do.

Important though it may be, the desire to express one's sexuality is merely one of many *motives* underlying human behavior. When psychologists use the term **motives,** they are referring to needs or desires that energize and direct behavior toward a goal. The derivative of this term, **motivation,** is a very broad term that encompasses all of the processes that initiate, direct, and sustain behavior.

Psychologists often categorize motives as being either *biological* or *social* in nature. Generally, biological motives are those that are unlearned, whereas social motives are learned. Obviously, sex involves a biological motive, but social motives are also at work in the full expression of human sexuality. We want to experience the physical pleasure associated with sex (biological motive), but we are also usually motivated to do it in a way that fits with our cultural expectations (social motive). Culture, for example, provides guidelines explaining how relationships should begin, be maintained, and end. Clearly, sexuality has an emotional component as well. We call our sexual partners "lovers" and use the term "making love" to refer to sexual activities. Like motives, emotions have both learned and unlearned components. Thinking in this way about sexuality may have helped you see that human motivation, emotion, and sexuality are all fairly complex topics. Before we return to the topic of sexuality, we will take a closer look at both motivation and emotion.

◆ **motives**
Needs or desires that energize and direct behavior toward a goal.

◆ **motivation**
All the processes that initiate, direct, and sustain behavior.

Explaining Motivation

Because of the complexities involved in human motivation, today's motivation researchers typically are not searching for a general theory that explains all types of motivation. Instead, they study particular kinds of motivated behavior (Petri, 1996). Nevertheless, several ideas have been influential across the study of motivation. We begin with a concept that you may recall from the discussion of operant conditioning theory in Chapter 5, the notion that rewards influence behavior.

Intrinsic and Extrinsic Motivation

◆ *What is the difference between intrinsic and extrinsic motivation?*

As noted earlier, motives direct behavior toward a goal. Motives can arise from something inside yourself, such as when you keep studying because you find the subject matter interesting. Such activities are pursued as ends in themselves, simply because they are enjoyable, not because any external reward is attached. This type of motivation is known as **intrinsic motivation.**

Other motives originate from outside, as when some external stimulus, or **incentive,** pulls or entices you to act. When the desire to get a good grade—or to avoid a bad grade—causes you to study, the grade is serving as this kind of external incentive. When we act so as to gain some external reward or to avoid some undesirable consequence, we are pulled by **extrinsic motivation.**

According to B. F. Skinner, a reinforcer is a consequence that increases the frequency of a behavior. Once the link between a behavior and a reinforcer has been established, the expectation of receiving the reinforcer again serves as an incentive to perform the behavior. For example, the prospect of getting a generous tip serves as an incentive for restaurant servers to serve their customers promptly and courteously.

In real life, the motives for many activities are both intrinsic and extrinsic. You may love your job, but you would probably be motivated to leave if your salary, an important extrinsic motivator, were taken away. Although grades are extrinsic motivators, outstanding grades—especially when earned on a particularly difficult assignment or exam—usually bring with them a sense of pride in a job well done (an intrinsic motivator). Table 9.1 gives examples of intrinsic and extrinsic motivation.

◆ **intrinsic motivation**
The desire to behave in a certain way because it is enjoyable or satisfying in and of itself.

◆ **incentive**
An external stimulus that motivates behavior (for example, money or fame).

◆ **extrinsic motivation**
The desire to behave in a certain way in order to gain some external reward or to avoid some undesirable consequence.

TABLE 9.1	Instrinsic and Extrinsic Motivation	
	DESCRIPTION	**EXAMPLES**
Intrinsic motivation	An activity is pursued as an end in itself because it is enjoyable and rewarding.	A person anonymously donates a large sum of money to a university to fund scholarships for deserving students.
		A child reads several books each week because reading is fun.
Extrinsic motivation	An activity is pursued to gain an external reward or to avoid an undesirable consequence.	A person agrees to donate a large sum of money to a university for the construction of a building, provided it will bear the family name.
		A child reads two books each week to avoid losing TV privileges.

Biological Approaches to Motivation

Perhaps you have heard the term *instinct* used to explain why spiders spin webs or birds fly south in the winter. An instinct is a fixed behavior pattern that is characteristic of every member of a species and is assumed to be genetically programmed. Thus, instincts represent one kind of biological motivation. Psychologists generally agree that no true instincts motivate human behavior. However, most also agree that biological forces underlie some human behaviors.

One biological approach to motivation, **drive-reduction theory,** was popularized by Clark Hull (1943). According to Hull, all living organisms have certain biological needs that must be met if they are to survive. A need gives rise to an internal state of tension called a **drive,** and the person or organism is motivated to reduce it. For example, when you are deprived of food or go too long without water, your biological need causes a state of tension—in this case, the hunger or thirst drive. You become motivated to seek food or water to reduce the drive and satisfy your biological need.

Drive-reduction theory is derived largely from the biological concept of **homeostasis**—the tendency of the body to maintain a balanced, internal state to ensure physical survival. Body temperature, blood sugar level, water balance, blood oxygen level—in short, everything required for physical existence—must be maintained in a state of equilibrium, or balance. When such a state is disturbed, a drive is created to restore the balance, as shown in Figure 9.1. But drive-reduction theory cannot fully account for the broad range of human motivation. It cannot explain why some people, often called *sensation seekers* by psychologists, love the thrill they experience when engaging in activities that produce states of tension—like skydiving or bungee-jumping.

Drive-reduction theorists cannot explain sensation seeking because the theory assumes that humans are always motivated to reduce tension. Other theorists argue just the opposite, that humans are sometimes motivated to increase tension. These theorists use the term **arousal** to refer to a person's state of alertness and mental and physical activation. Arousal levels can range from no arousal (when a person is comatose), to moderate arousal (when pursuing normal day-to-day activities), to high arousal (when excited

◆ How do drive-reduction and arousal theory explain motivation?

◆ **drive-reduction theory**

A theory of motivation suggesting that biological needs create internal states of tension or arousal—called drives—which organisms are motivated to reduce.

◆ **drive**

An internal state of tension or arousal that is brought about by an underlying need and that an organism is motivated to reduce.

◆ **homeostasis**

The natural tendency of the body to maintain a balanced internal state in order to ensure physical survival.

◆ **arousal**

A state of alertness and mental and physical activation.

FIGURE 9.1   **Drive-Reduction Theory**

Drive-reduction theory is based on the biological concept of homeostasis—the natural tendency of a living organism to maintain a state of internal balance, or equilibrium. When the equilibrium becomes disturbed (by a biological need such as thirst), a drive (internal state of arousal) emerges. Then the organism is motivated to take action to satisfy the need, thus reducing the drive and restoring equilibrium.

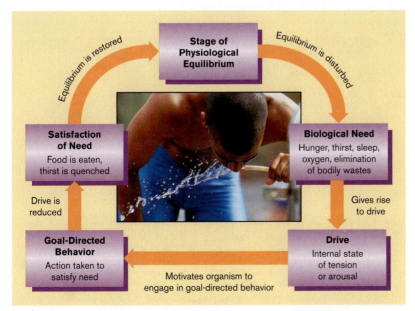

Equilibrium is restored → **Stage of Physiological Equilibrium** → Equilibrium is disturbed

Satisfaction of Need — Food is eaten, thirst is quenched

Biological Need — Hunger, thirst, sleep, oxygen, elimination of bodily wastes

Drive is reduced

Gives rise to drive

Goal-Directed Behavior — Action taken to satisfy need

Motivates organism to engage in goal-directed behavior

Drive — Internal state of tension or arousal

People vary greatly in the amount of arousal they can tolerate. For some people, the heightened level of arousal experienced when hanging off a precipice is enjoyable. Others prefer less arousing activities.

and highly stimulated). **Arousal theory** states that people are motivated to maintain an optimal level of arousal. If arousal is less than the optimal level, we do something to stimulate it; if arousal exceeds the optimal level, we seek to reduce the stimulation.

When arousal is too low, **stimulus motives**—such as curiosity and the motives to explore, to manipulate objects, and to play—cause humans and other animals to increase stimulation. Think about sitting in an airport or at a bus stop, or any other place where people are waiting. How many people do you see playing games on their cellphones or personal digital assistants (PDAs)? Waiting is boring; in other words, it provides no sources of arousal. Thus, people turn to electronic games to raise their level of arousal.

There is often a close link between arousal and performance. According to the **Yerkes-Dodson law,** performance on tasks is best when the person's arousal level is appropriate to the difficulty of the task. Performance on simple tasks is better when arousal is relatively high. Tasks of moderate difficulty are best accomplished when arousal is moderate; complex or difficult tasks, when arousal is lower (see Figure 9.2). But performance suffers when arousal level is either too high or too low for the task. For instance, how often have you heard great athletes who "choke" in critical situations compared to those who "come through" under pressure? Perhaps high-pressure situations push the athletes who choke past the optimal point of arousal but have just the opposite effect on the reliable athletes.

The relationship between arousal and performance is most often explained in terms of attention. Low arousal allows the mind to wander, so performance declines for tasks that require concentration, such as taking a test. By contrast, high arousal interferes with concentration by taking up all the available space in working memory. The ideal level of arousal for test taking, then, is an amount that is sufficient to keep the mind from wandering but not so great as to interfere with the memory demands of

◆ **arousal theory**

A theory of motivation suggesting that people are motivated to maintain an optimal level of alertness and physical and mental activation.

◆ **stimulus motives**

Motives that cause humans and other animals to increase stimulation when the level of arousal is too low (examples are curiosity and the motive to explore).

◆ **Yerkes-Dodson law**

The principle that performance on tasks is best when the arousal level is appropriate to the difficulty of the task: higher arousal for simple tasks, moderate arousal for tasks of moderate difficulty, and lower arousal for complex tasks.

FIGURE 9.2   **The Yerkes-Dodson Law**

The optimal level of arousal varies according to the difficulty of the task. Arousal levels should be relatively high for simple tasks, moderate for moderately difficult tasks, and lower for difficult tasks.

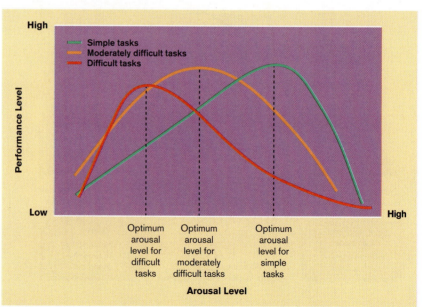

taking the test. Critics of this theory have argued that arousal is merely one of many variables that influence attention (Hanoch & Vitouch, 2004). Moreover, they point out that the Yerkes-Dodson law is based primarily on animal research (Hancock & Ganey, 2003). For these reasons, they caution against generalizing arousal theory to complex human behaviors such as test performance without taking into account other factors that influence how humans allocate attention.

Maslow's Hierarchy of Needs

The motivational theories you've learned about so far emphasize physiological processes such as homeostasis and arousal. Another view of motivation, that associated with the humanistic personality theory of Abraham Maslow, suggests that such motivations are the foundation for so-called higher-level motives (Maslow, 1970). As shown in Figure 9.3, Maslow proposed that our need for self-fulfillment depends on how well our needs for physical well-being, safety, belonging, and esteem have been met. His theory claims that we are motivated by the lowest unmet need. Thus, we don't worry about safety when we are in need of food. Similarly, love and esteem are of little concern when we are in danger.

Maslow studied people he believed were using their talents and abilities to their fullest—in other words, those who exemplified *self-actualization*. He studied some historical figures, such as Abraham Lincoln and Thomas Jefferson, and some individuals who made significant contributions during his own lifetime, including Albert Einstein, Eleanor Roosevelt, and Albert Schweitzer. Maslow found these self-actualizers to be accurate in perceiving reality—able to judge honestly and to spot quickly the fake and the dishonest. Self-actualizers are comfortable with life; they accept themselves and others, and nature as well, with good humor and tolerance. Most of them believe that they have a mission to accomplish or need to devote their life to some larger good. Self-actualizers tend not to depend on external authority or other people but seem to be inner-driven, autonomous, and independent. They feel a strong fellowship with all of humanity, and their relationships with others are characterized by deep and loving

◆ According to Maslow, how do individuals attain self-actualization?

FIGURE 9.3 **Maslow's Hierarchy of Needs**

According to humanistic psychologist Abraham Maslow, "higher" motives, such as the need for love, go unheeded when "lower" motives, such as the need for safety, are not met.

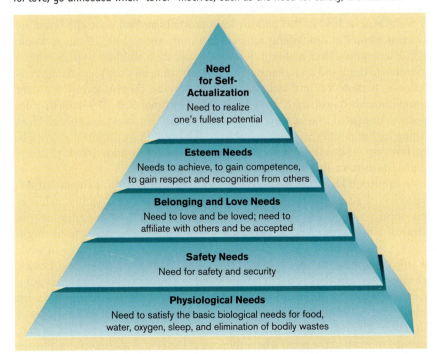

Need for Self-Actualization
Need to realize one's fullest potential

Esteem Needs
Needs to achieve, to gain competence, to gain respect and recognition from others

Belonging and Love Needs
Need to love and be loved; need to affiliate with others and be accepted

Safety Needs
Need for safety and security

Physiological Needs
Need to satisfy the basic biological needs for food, water, oxygen, sleep, and elimination of bodily wastes

bonds. They can laugh at themselves, and their sense of humor—though well developed—never involves hostility or criticism of others. Finally, the hallmark of self-actualizers is frequently occurring *peak experiences*—experiences of deep meaning, insight, and harmony within and with the universe.

Achievement Motivation

◆ How do need for achievement theory and goal orientation theory explain achievement motivation?

Maslow's hierarchy suggests that achievement motivation, one of many esteem needs, will appear somewhat spontaneously as soon as lower needs are met. Other theorists have explained this important dimension of human motivation differently. For instance, in early research, Henry Murray (1938) developed the *Thematic Apperception Test (TAT)*, which consists of a series of pictures of ambiguous situations. The person taking the test is asked to create a story about each picture—to describe what is going on in the picture, what the person or persons pictured are thinking about, what they may be feeling, and what is likely to be the outcome of the situation. The stories are presumed to reveal the test taker's needs and the strength of those needs. One of the motives identified by Murray was the **need for achievement** (abbreviated ***n Ach***), or the motive "to accomplish something difficult. . . . To overcome obstacles and attain a high standard. To excel one's self. To rival and surpass others. To increase self-regard by the successful exercise of talent" (p. 164). The need for achievement, rather than being satisfied with accomplishment, seems to grow as it is fed.

◆ **need for achievement (n Ach)**

The need to accomplish something difficult and to perform at a high standard of excellence.

◆ **goal orientation theory**

The view that achievement motivation depends on which of four goal orientations (mastery-approach, mastery-avoidance, performance-approach, performance-avoidance) an individual adopts.

Researchers David McClelland and John Atkinson have conducted many studies of the need for achievement (McClelland, 1958, 1961, 1985; McClelland et al., 1953). People with a high *n* Ach pursue goals that are challenging, yet attainable through hard work, ability, determination, and persistence. Goals that are too easy, those anyone can reach, offer no challenge and hold no interest because success would not be rewarding (McClelland, 1985). Impossibly high goals and high risks are not pursued because they offer little chance of success and are considered a waste of time. The goals of those with high *n* Ach are self-determined and linked to perceived abilities; thus, these goals tend to be realistic (Conroy et al., 2001).

By contrast, people with low *n* Ach, the researchers claim, are not willing to take chances when it comes to testing their own skills and abilities. They are motivated more by their fear of failure than by their hope and expectation of success. This is why they set either ridiculously low goals, which anyone can attain, or impossibly high goals (Geen, 1984). After all, who can fault a person for failing to reach a goal that is impossible for almost anyone?

Some experts believe that child-rearing practices and values in the home are important factors in developing achievement motivation (McClelland & Pilon, 1983). Parents can foster higher *n* Ach if they give their children responsibilities; teach them to think and act independently from the time they are very young; stress excellence, persistence, and independence; and praise them sincerely for their accomplishments (Ginsberg & Bronstein, 1993; Gottfried et al., 1994). Birth order appears to be related to achievement motivation, with first-born and only children showing higher *n* Ach than younger siblings (Falbo & Polit, 1986). Younger siblings, however, tend to be more sociable and likable than first-born or only children, and this has its rewards, too.

An approach known as **goal orientation theory** provides a somewhat different view of achievement motivation. According to this perspective, achievement motivation varies according to which of four goal orientations an individual adopts (Wolters, 2004). Here's how each of the orienations might affect a college student. Students with a *mastery-approach* orientation will study and engage in other behaviors (e.g., attend class) so as to increase their knowledge and overcome challenges. Those who have a *mastery-avoidance* orientation will exhibit whatever behaviors are necessary to avoid failing to learn (a different outcome than a failing grade, by the way). Students with a *performance-avoidance* orientation will measure their performance against that of other students and are motivated to work to the point where they are at least equal to their peers. Finally,

People with a high need for achievement relish opportunities to take on new challenges. For example, after successful careers in acting and in business, Arnold Schwarezenegger was elected governor of California.

those who have a *performance-approach* orientation try to surpass the performance of their peers in an attempt to enhance their own sense of self-worth. (Stop for a minute and think about which orientation best describes your own.)

Research indicates that college and high school students who adopt either of the mastery orientations are less likely to procrastinate than their peers who adopt either of the performance orientations (Wolters, 2003, 2004). However, a mastery orientation doesn't necessarily mean that a student will get good grades (Harackiewicz et al., 2002). It appears that the performance-approach orientation is more strongly associated with high grades than any of the others (Church et al., 2001).

Hunger

Primary drives are unlearned motives that serve to satisfy biological needs. For instance, thirst is a basic biological drive. The motivation to drink is largely governed by physiological variables, such as the amount of salt in the body's cells. But what about hunger?

Internal and External Cues

Like thirst, hunger is influenced by physiological processes. Researchers have found two areas of the hypothalamus that are of central importance in regulating eating behavior and thus affect the hunger drive (Steffens et al., 1988). As researchers discovered long ago, the **lateral hypothalamus (LH)** acts as a *feeding center* to excite eating. Stimulating the feeding center causes animals to eat even when they are full (Delgado & Anand, 1953). And when the feeding center is destroyed, animals initially refuse to eat (Anand & Brobeck, 1951). The **ventromedial hypothalamus (VMH)** apparently acts as a *satiety* (or *fullness*) *center* that inhibits eating (Hernandez & Hoebel, 1989). If the VMH is surgically removed, animals soon eat their way to gross obesity (Hetherington & Ranson, 1940; Parkinson & Weingarten, 1990). Moreover, some of the substances secreted by the gastrointestinal tract during digestion, such as the hormone cholecystokinin (CCK), act as satiety signals (Bray, 1991; Flood et al., 1990; Woods & Gibbs, 1989).

Changes in blood sugar level and the hormones that regulate it also contribute to sensations of hunger. Blood levels of the sugar called *glucose* are monitored by nutrient detectors in the liver that send this information to the brain (Friedman et al., 1986). Hunger is stimulated when the brain receives the message that blood levels of glucose are low. Similarly, insulin, a hormone produced by the pancreas, chemically converts glucose into energy that is usable by the cells. Elevations in insulin cause an increase in hunger, in food intake, and in a desire for sweets (Rodin et al., 1985). In fact, chronic oversecretion of insulin stimulates hunger and often leads to obesity.

As you may have learned from everyday experience, hunger can also be stimulated by external cues. What happens when you smell a steak sizzling on the grill or chocolate chip cookies baking in the oven? For many, the hands of the clock alone, signaling mealtime, are enough to prompt a quest for food. Table 9.2 (on page 284) summarizes the factors that stimulate and inhibit eating.

Explaining Variations in Body Weight

Health care professionals classify individuals' body weights using a measure of weight relative to height called the **body mass index (BMI).** A BMI that is less than 18.5 is considered underweight, while one in excess of 25 is classified as overweight. To calculate your BMI, use this formula or use the BMI calculator at http://www.cdc.gov/nccdphp/dnpa/bmi/index.htm:

BMI = [Weight in pounds ÷ (height in inches × height in inches)] × 703

◆ **How do internal and external cues influence eating behavior?**

◆ **primary drives**
A state of tension or arousal that arises from a biological need and is unlearned.

◆ **lateral hypothalamus (LH)**
The part of the hypothalamus that acts as a feeding center to incite eating.

◆ **ventromedial hypothalamus (VMH)**
The part of the hypothalamus that acts as a satiety (fullness) center to inhibit eating.

◆ **body mass index (BMI)**
A measure of weight relative to height.

◆ **What are some factors that account for variations in body weight?**

TABLE 9.2 Biological and Environmental Factors That Inhibit and Stimulate Eating

	BIOLOGICAL	ENVIRONMENTAL
Factors that inhibit eating	Activity in ventromedial hypothalamus Raised blood glucose levels Distended (full) stomach CCK (hormone that acts as satiety signal) Sensory-specific satiety	Unappetizing smell, taste, or appearance of food Acquired taste aversions Learned eating habits Desire to be thin Reaction to stress, unpleasant emotional state
Factors that stimulate eating	Activity in lateral hypothalamus Low blood levels of glucose Increase in insulin Stomach contractions Empty stomach	Appetizing smell, taste, or appearance of food Acquired food preferences Being around others who are eating Foods high in fat and sugar Learned eating habits Reaction to boredom, stress, unpleasant emotional state

◆ **obesity**
BMI over 30.

Variations in body weight have emerged as an important public health topic in recent years because of the link between excessive weight and health problems such as heart disease and arthritis (National Center for Health Statistics, 2004). As you can see in Figure 9.4, the prevalence of both overweight (BMI between 25 and 29.9) and **obesity** (BMI over 30) has risen dramatically over the past three decades. Nearly one-third of adults in the United States are obese, and another one-third are overweight.

Why are there such wide variations in human body weight? Heredity is one reason. A review of studies that included more than 100,000 participants found that 74% of identical twin pairs had similar body weights. Only 32% of fraternal twins, however, had comparable body weights. The researchers reported an estimated heritability for body weight between .50 and .90 (Barsh et al., 2000). More than 40 genes appear to be related to body weight regulation (Barsh et al., 2000).

But what exactly do people inherit that affects body weight? Researchers Friedman and colleagues identified the hormone *leptin*, which directly affects the feeding and satiety centers in the brain's hypothalamus and is known to be a key element in the regulation of body weight (Friedman, 1997, 2000; Kochavi et al., 2001). Leptin is produced by the body's fat tissues, and the amount produced is a direct measure of body fat: The

FIGURE 9.4 Age-Adjusted* Prevalence of Overweight and Obesity among U.S. Adults, Age 20–74 Years

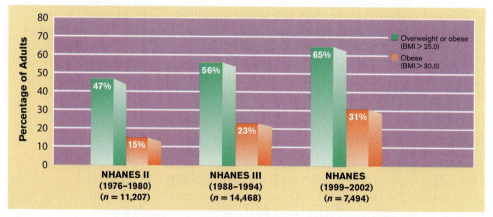

*Age-adjusted by the direct method to the year 2000 U.S. Bureau of the Census estimates using the age groups 20–39, 40–59, and 60–74 years. *Source:* National Center for Health Statistics (2004).

more leptin produced, the higher the level of body fat. Decreases in body fat cause lower levels of leptin in the body, and lower levels of leptin stimulate food intake. When leptin levels increase sufficiently, energy expenditure exceeds food intake, and people lose weight. Obese mice injected with leptin lost 30% of their body weight within 2 weeks (Halaas et al., 1995). In humans, a mutation of the gene that controls leptin receptors can cause obesity as well as pituitary abnormalities (Clément et al., 1998). Changes in the body's leptin levels can affect the immune and reproductive systems as well as the processes involved in bone formation. Thus, leptin plays a key role in linking nutrition to overall human physiology (Friedman, 2000).

The rate at which the body burns calories to produce energy is called the **metabolic rate**, and it is also influenced by genes. Further, *set-point theory* suggests that each person is genetically programmed to carry a certain amount of body weight (Keesey, 1988). **Set point**—the weight the body maintains when one is trying neither to gain nor to lose weight—is affected by the number of fat cells in the body and by metabolic rate, both of which are influenced by the genes (Gurin, 1989).

Researchers think that fat cells send biochemical messages indicating how much energy is stored in them to the hypothalamus (Hallschmid et al., 2004). Presumably, the genes influence what the hypothalamus "believes" to be the appropriate amount of energy to store. One of the most important current lines of research in this area aims to identify these biochemical messages and influence them in ways that will lower the set-points of obese individuals (Hallschmid et al., 2004).

The complexities of the processes involved in appetite regulation and energy metabolism explain why diets often do not work (Campbell & Dhand, 2000). To be effective, any weight-loss program must help people decrease energy intake (eat less), increase energy expenditure (exercise more), or both (Bray & Tartaglia, 2000). Unfortunately, most people who are trying to lose weight focus only on cutting calories. At first, when overweight people begin to diet and cut their calories, they do lose weight. But after a few pounds are shed initially, the dieter's metabolic rate slows down as if to conserve the remaining fat store because fewer calories are being consumed (Hirsch, 1997). Besides making it more difficult to lose weight, this reduction in metabolic rate drains the dieter's energy such that he or she is less able to exercise. This effect appears to be particularly pronounced with today's popular low-carbohydrate diets (Butki, et al., 2003).

Eating Disorders

Eating disorders are a category of mental disorders in which eating and dieting behaviors go far beyond the everyday extremes of overeating and dieting many people experience. Sadly, there has been an increase in the incidence of these disorders in recent years throughout the world (American Psychiatric Association, 2000).

Anorexia nervosa is characterized by an overwhelming, irrational fear of gaining weight or becoming fat, compulsive dieting to the point of self-starvation, and excessive weight loss. Some anorexics lose as much as 20–25% of their original body weight. The disorder typically begins in adolescence, and most of those afflicted are females. About 1–4% of females between ages 12 and 40 suffer from this disorder (American Psychiatric Association, 2000). The greater prevalence of eating disorders among females appears to be a general phenomenon, rather than a culturally specific one. In a large sample of Norwegian adults, for example, women were twice as likely as men to have an eating disorder (Augestad, 2000).

There are important differences between dieting (even obsessive dieting) and anorexia nervosa. For one, anorexics' perception of their body size is grossly distorted. No matter how emaciated they become, they continue to perceive themselves as fat. Researchers have learned that anorexics' unrealistic perceptions of their own bodies may result from a general tendency toward distorted thinking (Tchanturia et al., 2001). Moreover, most individuals with anorexia—as many as 74% in some studies—suffer from another kind of psychiatric disorder along with their eating disorder (Milos, et al.,

◆ **metabolic rate**

(meh-tuh-BALL-ik) The rate at which the body burns calories to produce energy.

◆ **set point**

The weight the body normally maintains when one is trying neither to gain nor to lose weight.

◆ *What are the proposed causes of eating disorders, and how are these disorders treated?*

◆ **anorexia nervosa**

An eating disorder characterized by an overwhelming, irrational fear of gaining weight or becoming fat, compulsive dieting to the point of self-starvation, and excessive weight loss.

Jamie-Lynn Discala, who plays the daughter of James Gandolfini on the hit TV series *The Sopranos,* suffered from anorexia: I would hide from mirrors because I didn't want to see what I had become. She is currently recovering from the disease while pursuing her acting and musical careers.

◆ **bulimia nervosa**

An eating disorder characterized by repeated and uncontrolled (and often secretive) episodes of binge eating.

2004). An unusually high proportion of them, nearly 25%, have been diagnosed with *obsessive-compulsive disorder,* a disorder that involves an excessive need for control (APA, 2000; Milos et al., 2002). These findings suggest that, for some sufferers, anorexia may be only one component of a larger psychiatric problem.

Frequently, anorexics not only starve themselves but also exercise relentlessly in an effort to accelerate the weight loss. Further, anorexics don't necessarily avoid food or the ritual of eating. Indeed, most anorexics are fascinated with food and the process of preparing it (Faunce, 2002). Many become skilled in giving the appearance of eating while not actually swallowing food. To accomplish this, some anorexics habitually chew and spit out their food, often with such dexterity that others with whom they eat don't notice (Kovacs et al., 2002).

Among young female anorexics, progressive and significant weight loss eventually results in amenorrhea (cessation of menstruation). Anorexics may also develop low blood pressure, impaired heart function, dehydration, electrolyte disturbances, and sterility (American Psychiatric Association, 1993b), as well as decreases in the gray matter volume in the brain, which are thought to be irreversible (Lambe et al., 1997). Moreover, prolonged self-starvation induces changes in the lining of the stomach that can make it extremely difficult for anorexics to recover normal functioning of the digestive system even after they have begun eating normally (Ogawa et al., 2004). Unfortunately, as many as 20% of those suffering from anorexia nervosa eventually die of starvation or complications from organ damage (Brotman, 1994).

It is difficult to pinpoint the cause of this disorder. Most anorexic individuals are well behaved and academically successful (Vitousek & Manke, 1994). Psychological risk factors for eating disorders include being overly concerned about physical appearance, worrying about perceived attractiveness, and feeling social pressure in favor of thinness (Whisenhunt et al., 2000). Some investigators believe that young women who refuse to eat are attempting to control a portion of their lives, which they may feel unable to control in other respects.

Anorexia is very difficult to treat. Most anorexics are steadfast in their refusal to eat, while insisting that nothing is wrong with them. The main thrust of treatment, therefore, is to get the anorexic individual to gain weight. The patient may be admitted to a hospital, fed a controlled diet, and given rewards for small weight gains and increases in food intake. The treatment usually includes some type of psychotherapy and/or a self-help group. Some studies show that antidepressant drugs may help in the treatment of anorexia (Barbarich et al., 2004). Others suggest that protein-rich supplements help individuals with anorexia regain their normal appetites (Latner & Wilson, 2004). Multidimensional treatment programs—that is, those that combine medication, nutritional therapy, and psychotherapy—may prove to be the most successful approach (Bean et al., 2004). However, no matter which treatment approach is used, most individuals with anorexia experience relapses (Hogan & McReynolds, 2004).

As many as 50% of anorexics also develop **bulimia nervosa,** a chronic disorder characterized by repeated and uncontrolled (and often secretive) episodes of binge eating (American Psychiatric Association, 1993b). And individuals who are not anorexic can develop bulimia alone. Many bulimics come from families in which family members make frequent negative comments about others' physical appearances (Crowther et al., 2002).

An episode of binge eating has two main features: (1) the consumption of much larger amounts of food than most people would eat during the same period of time, and (2) a feeling that one cannot stop eating or control the amount eaten. Binges—which generally involve foods that are rich in carbohydrates, such as cookies, cake, and candy—are frequently followed by purging. Purging consists of self-induced vomiting and/or the use of large quantities of laxatives and diuretics. Bulimics may also engage in excessive dieting and exercise. Athletes are especially susceptible to this disorder. But many bulimics are of average size and purge after an eating binge simply to maintain their weight.

Bulimia nervosa can cause a number of physical problems. The stomach acid in vomit eats away at the teeth and may cause them to rot, and the delicate balance of body chemistry is destroyed by excessive use of laxatives and diuretics. The bulimic may have a chronic sore throat as well as a variety of other symptoms, including dehydration, swelling of the salivary glands, kidney damage, and hair loss. The disorder also has a strong emotional component; the bulimic person is aware that the eating pattern is abnormal and feels unable to control it. Depression, guilt, and shame accompany both binging and purging. Some evidence suggests that decreased function of the neurotransmitter serotonin appears to contribute to this disorder (Jimerson et al., 1997).

Bulimia nervosa tends to appear in the late teens and affects about 1 in 25 women (Kendler et al., 1991). Like anorexics, bulimics have high rates of obsessive-compulsive disorder (Milos et al., 2002). Further, perhaps as many as one-third of bulimics have engaged in other kinds of self-injurious behavior, such as cutting themselves intentionally (Paul et al., 2002).

About 10–15% of all bulimics are males, and homosexuality or bisexuality seems to increase males' risk for bulimia (Carlat et al., 1997). In addition, researchers are finding more evidence of a cultural component to bulimia. Westernized attitudes in Turkey, for example, are clashing with the country's traditional values and, according to researchers, creating an increase in cases of bulimia (Elal et al., 2000). Apparently, some Turkish citizens are succumbing to Western media pressure to have an ultrathin body.

Bulimia, like anorexia, is difficult to treat. Sometimes treatment is complicated by the fact that a person with an eating disorder is likely to have a personality disorder as well or to be too shy to interact effectively with therapists (Goodwin & Fitzgibbon, 2002; Rosenvinge et al., 2000). Some behavior modification programs have helped extinguish bulimic behavior (Traverso et al., 2000), and cognitive-behavioral therapy has been used successfully to help bulimics modify their eating habits and their abnormal attitudes about body shape and weight (Halmi, 1996; Johnson et al., 1996). Certain antidepressant drugs have been found to reduce the frequency of binge eating and purging and to result in significant attitudinal change (Agras et al., 1994; "Eating disorders," 1997).

Emotion

Much of our motivation to act is fueled by emotional states. In fact, the root of the word **emotion** means "to move," indicating the close relationship between motivation and emotion. But what, precisely, are emotions?

Explaining the Components of Emotions

Typically, psychologists have studied emotions in terms of three components: the physical, the cognitive, and the behavioral (Wilken et al., 2000). The three components appear to be interdependent. For instance, in one study, participants who were better at detecting heartbeat variations (the physical component) rated their subjective experiences of emotion (the cognitive component) as being more intense than did participants who were less able to detect physical changes (Wilken et al., 2000). However, neither the physical nor the cognitive components completely determine how emotion is expressed (the behavioral component). Moreover, there is a long-standing debate among psychologists about which component comes first in the overall experience of emotion.

American psychologist William James (1884) argued that an event causes physiological arousal and a physical response, after which the individual perceives the physical response as an emotion. At about the same time James proposed his theory, a Danish physiologist and psychologist, Carl Lange, independently formulated nearly the same theory. The **James-Lange theory** of emotion (Lange & James, 1922) suggests that different patterns of arousal in the autonomic nervous system produce the different emotions people feel, and that the physiological arousal appears before the emotion is perceived. (See Figure 9.5, on page 288.)

Another early theory of emotion that challenged the James-Lange theory was proposed by Walter Cannon (1927), who did pioneering work on the fight-or-flight

> ◆ *What are the various theories that have been proposed to explain emotion?*

◆ **emotion**
An identifiable feeling state involving physiological arousal, a cognitive appraisal of the situation or stimulus causing that internal body state, and an outward behavior expressing the state.

◆ **James-Lange theory**
The theory that emotional feelings result when an individual becomes aware of a physiological response to an emotion-provoking stimulus (for example, feeling fear because of trembling).

Stimulus situation → Physiological arousal, action → Experience of emotion based on interpretation of arousal and action

Fear

A dog growls at you. → Your heart pounds; you run. → "My heart is racing and I'm running. I must be afraid."

The James Lange Theory of Emotion

The James-Lange theory of emotion is the exact opposite of what subjective experience tells us. If a dog growls at you, the James-Lange interpretation is that the dog growls, your heart begins to pound, and only after perceiving that your heart is pounding do you conclude that you must be afraid.

◆ **Cannon-Bard theory**

The theory that an emotion-provoking stimulus is transmitted simultaneously to the cerebral cortex, providing the conscious mental experience of the emotion, and to the sympathetic nervous system, causing the physiological arousal.

◆ **Schachter-Singer theory**

A two-factor theory stating that for an emotion to occur, there must be (1) physiological arousal and (2) a cognitive interpretation or explanation of the arousal, allowing it to be labeled as a specific emotion.

◆ **Lazarus theory**

The theory that a cognitive appraisal is the first step in an emotional response and all other aspects of an emotion, including physiological arousal, depend on it.

response and the concept of homeostasis. Cannon claimed that the bodily changes caused by the various emotions are not sufficiently distinct to allow people to distinguish one emotion from another. Cannon's original theory was later expanded by physiologist Philip Bard (1934). The **Cannon-Bard theory** suggests that the following chain of events occurs when a person feels an emotion: Emotion-provoking stimuli are received by the senses and are then relayed simultaneously to the cerebral cortex, which provides the conscious mental experience of the emotion, and to the sympathetic nervous system, which produces the physiological state of arousal. In other words, the feeling of an emotion (fear, for example) occurs at about the same time as the experience of physiological arousal (a pounding heart). One does not cause the other.

Stanley Schachter believed that the early theories of emotion left out a critical component—the subjective cognitive interpretation of why a state of arousal has occurred. Schachter and Singer (1962) proposed a two-factor theory. According to the **Schachter-Singer theory,** two things must happen for a person to feel an emotion: (1) The person must first experience physiological arousal; and (2) there must then be a cognitive interpretation, or explanation, of the physiological arousal so that the person can label it as a specific emotion. Thus, Schachter concluded, a true emotion can occur only if a person is physically aroused and can find some reason for it. When people are in a state of physiological arousal but do not know why they are aroused, they tend to label the state as an emotion that is appropriate to their situation at the time. Some attempts to replicate the findings of Schachter and Singer have been unsuccessful (Marshall & Zimbardo, 1979). Also, the notion that arousal is general rather than specific has been questioned by later researchers who have identified some distinctive patterns of arousal for some of the basic emotions (Ekman et al., 1983; Levenson, 1992; Scherer & Wallbott, 1994).

The theory of emotion that most heavily emphasizes the cognitive aspect has been proposed by Richard Lazarus (1991a, 1991b, 1995). According to the **Lazarus theory,** a cognitive appraisal is the first step in an emotional response; all other aspects of an emotion, including physiological arousal, depend on the cognitive appraisal. This theory is most compatible with the subjective experience of an emotion's sequence of events—the sequence that William James reversed long ago. Faced with a stimulus—an event—a person first appraises it. This cognitive appraisal determines whether the person will have an emotional response and, if so, what type of response. The physiological arousal and all other aspects of the emotion flow from the appraisal. In short, Lazarus contends that emotions are provoked when cognitive appraisals of events or circumstances are positive or negative—but not neutral.

Critics of the Lazarus theory point out that some emotional reactions are instantaneous—occurring too rapidly to pass through a cognitive appraisal (Zajonc, 1980, 1984). Lazarus (1984, 1991a) responds that some mental processing occurs without conscious awareness. And there must be some form of cognitive realization, however brief, or else a person would not know what he or she is responding to or what emotion to feel—fear, happiness, embarrassment, and so on. Further, researchers have found that reappraisal, or changing one's thinking about an emotional stimulus, is related to a reduction in physiological response (Gross, 2002).

Review and Reflect 9.1 summarizes the four major theories of emotion: James-Lange, Cannon-Bard, Schachter-Singer, and Lazarus.

REVIEW and REFLECT 9.1

Theories of Emotion

THEORY	VIEW	EXAMPLE
James-Lange theory	An event causes physiological arousal. You experience an emotion only *after* you interpret the physical response.	You are walking home late at night and hear footsteps behind you. Your heart pounds and you begin to tremble. You interpret these physical responses as fear.
Cannon-Bard theory	An event causes a physiological *and* an emotional response simultaneously. One does not cause the other.	You are walking home late at night and hear footsteps behind you. Your heart pounds, you begin to tremble, and you feel afraid.
Schachter-Singer theory	An event causes physiological arousal. You must then be able to identify a reason for the arousal to label the emotion.	You are walking home late at night and hear footsteps behind you. Your heart pounds and you begin to tremble. You know that walking alone at night can be dangerous, so you feel afraid.
Lazarus theory	An event occurs, a cognitive appraisal is made, and then the emotion and physiological arousal follow.	You are walking home late at night and hear footsteps behind you. You think it could be a mugger. So you feel afraid, and your heart starts to pound and you begin to tremble.

Emotion and the Brain

Fear has stimulated more research by neuroscientists than any other emotion (LeDoux, 1996, 2000). And the brain structure most closely associated with fear is the amygdala (see Figure 9.6). Information comes to the amygdala directly from all five of the senses and is acted on immediately, without initial involvement of the primary "thinking" area of the brain, the cortex. But, as with reflex actions, the cortex does become involved as soon as it "catches up" with the amygdala (LeDoux, 2000). Once it does so, the cortex tempers the amygdala's fear response with its interpretation of the fear-provoking situation. The ability of the cortex to control the amygdala's fear response is also vital to our ability to overcome previously learned fears (Sotres-Bayon, et al., 2004). Thus, when people manage to conquer, say, the fear associated with taking an important exam, they can thank their cortex's ability to regulate the amygdala.

When the emotion of fear first materializes, much of the brain's processing is nonconscious. The person becomes conscious of it later, of course, but the amygdala is activated before she or he is aware that a threat is present (Damasio, 1994, 1999). Interestingly, the amygdala becomes more highly activated when a person looks at photos of angry- or fearful-looking faces than it does when the person views photos of happy faces (LeDoux, 2000).

Emotions may also be lateralized. Sad feelings, for example, are associated with greater activity in the left cerebral hemisphere (Papousek & Schoulter, 2002). Perception of others' emotions appears to be lateralized to the right side of the brain. However, this pattern of lateralization may be more pronounced in females than in males. In one study, participants listened to emotional expressions alternately with the left and right ears. (Recall that the left ear feeds the right side of the brain, while the right ear sends information to the left side.) A left-ear advantage for accurate identification of a speaker's emotional state was evident only for women (Voyer & Rodgers, 2002).

◆ *What are the neurological processes involved in the fear response?*

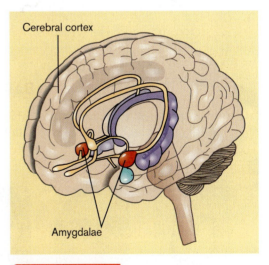

FIGURE 9.6

Emotion and the Amygdala

The amygdala plays an important role in emotion. It is activated by fear before any direct involvement of the cerebral cortex occurs.

The Expression of Emotion

◆ *Which aspects of emotion are universal, and which vary across cultures?*

Expressing emotions comes as naturally to humans as breathing. Two leading researchers on emotion, Paul Ekman (1993) and Carroll Izard (1992), insist that there are a limited number of basic emotions. **Basic emotions** are unlearned and universal; that is, they are found in all cultures, are reflected in the same facial expressions, and emerge in children according to their own biological timetable of development. Fear, anger, disgust, surprise, joy or happiness, and sadness or distress are usually considered basic emotions. Izard (1992, 1993) suggests that there are distinct neural circuits that underlie each of the basic emotions, and Levenson and others (1990) point to specific autonomic nervous system activity associated with the basic emotions.

In studying the range of emotion, Ekman (1993) has suggested considering emotions as comprising families. The anger family would range from annoyed to irritated, angry, livid, and, finally, enraged. Furthermore, the anger family, if it exists, also includes various forms in which the emotion is expressed, according to Ekman (1993). Resentment, for example, is a form of anger "in which there is a sense of grievance" (p. 386). Just as there are many words in the English language to describe the variations in the range of any emotion, Ekman and Friesen claim that subtle distinctions in the facial expression of a single emotion convey its intensity (Ekman, 1993).

Charles Darwin (1872/1965) maintained that most emotions and the facial expressions that convey them are genetically inherited and characteristic of the entire human species. If Darwin was right, then everyone should label the expressions in *Try It! 9.1* the same way. Do your labels agree with those of others?

Strong support for the notion that facial expressions are universal comes from the way in which they develop in infants. Like the motor skills of crawling and walking, facial expressions of emotions develop according to a biological timetable of maturation and are influenced very little by experience. In fact, blind babies develop them in exactly the same sequence and at the same times as infants who can see.

While the facial expressions of the basic emotions are much the same in cultures around the world, each culture can have very different **display rules**—cultural rules that dictate how emotions should generally be expressed and where and when their expression is appropriate (Ekman, 1993; Ekman & Friesen, 1975; Scherer & Wallbott, 1994). Often a society's display rules require people to give evidence of certain emotions

◆ **basic emotions**

Emotions that are unlearned and universal, that are reflected in the same facial expressions across cultures, and that emerge in children according to their biological timetable of development; fear, anger, disgust, surprise, happiness, and sadness are usually considered basic emotions.

◆ **display rules**

Cultural rules that dictate how emotions should generally be expressed and when and where their expression is appropriate.

Try It 9.1
Recognizing Basic Emotions

Look carefully at the six photographs. Which basic emotion is portrayed in each?
Match the number of the photograph with the basic emotion it conveys.

a. happiness　　b. sadness　　c. fear　　d. anger　　e. surprise　　f. disgust

   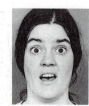  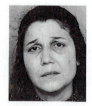

1. _____　　2. _____　　3. _____　　4. _____　　5. _____　　6. _____

Answers: 1. d　2. c　3. f　4. e　5. a　6. b

There are many situations in which people must disguise their emotions to comply with the display rules of their culture, which dictate when and how feelings should be expressed. For example, these soccer players—both winners and losers—are expected to be good sports, even if it means hiding their true feelings.

that they may not actually feel or to disguise their true feelings. For example, Americans are expected to look sad at funerals, to hide disappointment at not winning, and to refrain from making facial expressions of disgust when served food that tastes bad. Display rules in Japanese culture dictate that negative emotions must be disguised when other people are present (Ekman, 1972; Triandis, 1994). In East Africa, young males from traditional Masai society are expected to appear stern and stony-faced and to "produce long, unbroken stares" (Keating, 1994).

There are variations in display rules across groups within the same culture as well. For instance, researchers have found that, in most work settings, supervisors expect the workers they manage to express more positive than negative emotions (Dienfendorff & Richard, 2004). Similarly, researchers have learned that, in the United States, teens conform to unspoken display rules acquired from peers that discourage public displays of emotion. The resulting subdued emotional expressions can cause them to appear to be aloof, uncaring, and even rude to parents and other adults (Salisch, 2001). Psychologists speculate that conformity to these peer-based display rules may be the basis of much miscommunication between teens and their parents and teachers.

Most of us learn display rules very early and abide by them most of the time. Yet you may not be fully aware that such rules dictate where, when, how, and even how long certain emotions should be expressed.

Finally, you may have heard that it is always "healthy" to express one's emotions. However, research has failed to support this idea. Consider what happens when you express feelings such as anger. Does it typically help or hinder you in accomplishing your goals? If you are good at controlling your emotions, you can express them when they are helpful and suppress them when they are not (Salovey & Pizarro, 2003).

Could controlling one's facial expressions be a means of controlling the emotions themselves? The idea that the muscular movements involved in certain facial expressions produce the corresponding emotion is called the **facial-feedback hypothesis** (Izard, 1971, 1977, 1990; Strack et al., 1988). Some evidence supports this notion. In classic research, Ekman and colleagues (1983) demonstrated that physiological measures of emotion such as heart rate and muscle tension changed in response to changes in research participants' facial expressions. More recently, researchers have found that people's facial expressions are more likely to change the intensity of the emotion they

◆ **facial-feedback hypothesis**

The idea that the muscular movements involved in certain facial expressions produce the corresponding emotions (for example, smiling makes one feel happy).

are really feeling than to enable them to change from one state to another (Soussignan, 2002). Thus, if you are angry and you adopt an angry expression, you will feel angrier. However, such findings could be interpreted to mean that neutralizing your facial expression is the first step toward gaining control when your emotions are heading in a direction that you think may be more harmful than helpful.

Gender Differences in Emotion

◆ *In what ways do males and females differ with regard to emotions?*

Do females and males differ significantly in the way they experience their emotions? According to the evolutionary perspective, your answer to the following question is likely to be gender-specific: What emotion would you feel first if you were betrayed or harshly criticized by another person? When asked to respond to this question, male research participants in a classic study were more likely to report that they would feel angry; female participants were more likely to say that they would feel hurt, sad, or disappointed (Brody, 1985). Of course, both males and females express anger, but typically not in the same ways. Women are just as likely as men to express anger in private (at home) but much less likely than men to express it publicly (Cupach & Canary, 1995). The reason that women may fail to show anger in public is that emotion display rules are, at least to some extent, gender-specific. Researchers in the United States have found that, in general, women are expected to suppress negative emotions and express positive ones (Simpson & Stroh, 2004). The pattern of expectations is just the opposite for men.

Researchers have also found sex differences in the intensity of emotional response. Grossman and Wood (1993) tested male and female participants for the intensity of emotional responses on five basic emotions—joy, love, fear, sadness, and anger. They found that "women reported more intense and more frequent emotions than men did, with the exception of anger" (p. 1013). More joy, more sadness, more fear, more love! But these were self-reports. How did Grossman and Wood know that the female participants actually felt four

emotional intelligence
The ability to apply knowledge about emotions to everyday life.

of the five emotions more intensely than the males? The researchers also measured physiological arousal. The participants viewed slides depicting the various emotions while they were hooked up to an electromyograph, which measured tension in the facial muscles. The researchers found that "women not only reported more intense emotional experience than men, but they also generated more extreme physiological reactions" (p. 1020). Other researchers agree that, in general, women respond with greater emotional intensity than men and thus can experience both greater joy and greater sorrow (Fujita et al., 1991).

In another interesting study of gender differences in emotional intensity, researchers measured levels of *cortisol*, a stress hormone that increases with emotional arousal, in husbands and wives after discussions of positive and negative events in their relationships (Kiecolt-Glaser, 2000). The researchers found that women's cortisol levels increased after discussions of negative events, while men's levels remained constant. This finding suggests that women are more physiologically sensitive to negative emotions than men are.

Some studies indicate that females are more attuned than males are to verbal and nonverbal expressions of emotion. Do these findings fit with your experiences?

Emotional Intelligence

◆ *What are the components of emotional intelligence?*

Whether one is male or female, the understanding we possess about our own and others' emotions influences how we think about ourselves and manage our interactions with others. **Emotional intelligence** is the ability to apply knowledge about emotions to everyday life (Salovey & Pizarro, 2003) Two leading researchers in the field, Peter Salovey and David Pizarro, argue that emotional intelligence is just as important to many important outcome variables, including how we fare in our chosen careers, as the kind of intelligence that is measured by IQ tests. Research supports this view, showing that emotional intelligence is unrelated to IQ scores (Lam & Kirby, 2002; van der Zee et al., 2002). At the same time, emotional intelligence is correlated with both academic and social success (Rozell et al., 2002).

Emotional intelligence includes two sets of components. The first, known as the *personal* aspects of emotional intelligence, includes awareness and management of our own emotions. People who are able to monitor their feelings as they arise are less likely to be ruled by them. However, managing emotions does not mean suppressing them; nor does it mean giving free rein to every feeling. Instead, effect management of emotions involves expressing them appropriately. Emotion management also involves engaging in activities that cheer us up, soothe our hurts, or reassure us when we feel anxious.

The *interpersonal* aspects of emotional intelligence make up the second set of components. *Empathy*, or sensitivity to others' feelings, is one such component. One key indicator of empathy is the ability to read others' nonverbal behavior—the gestures, vocal inflections, tones of voice, and facial expressions of others. Another of the interpersonal components is the capacity to manage relationships. However, it is related to both the personal aspects of emotional intelligence and to empathy. In other words, to effectively manage the emotional give-and-take involved in social relationships, we have to be able to manage our own feelings and be sensitive to those of others.

In a recent study, men were found to process emotions, especially positive ones, predominantly in the left hemisphere of the brain, while women were found to use both cerebral hemispheres more equally for processing emotions (Coney & Fitzgerald, 2000). This finding could account for some of the emotional difference between the genders.

Human Sexuality

At the beginning of the chapter, you learned that Alfred Kinsey's research opened the door to the scientific study of human sexuality. Since his work was published, research examining this important part of life has proliferated. We will begin by discussing cultural and gender differences in sexual attitudes and behavior.

Sexual Attitudes and Behavior

You probably won't be surprised to learn that a large majority of adults all over the world are sexually active. As you can see in Figure 9.7 (on page 294), the average frequency of sexual intercourse varies considerably from one culture to another (Durex Global Sex Survey, 2002). Nevertheless, even in the nation with the lowest frequency in the survey on which Figure 9.7 is based, Singapore, the rate of intercourse works out to be about once every three or four days. Of course, individuals vary considerably around the averages identified in Figure 9.7. Some people have sex several times each day; while others never have sex at all.

◆ *How do sexual attitudes and behavior vary across cultures and genders?*

As you learned in Chapter 8, sexual activity continues throughout the lifespan. In one very large survey involving people aged 40 to 80 in 13 different countries, researchers found that 83% of men and 66% of women had engaged in intercourse at least once in the last year (Gingell et al., 2003). One reason why intercourse frequency was lower among women was that many of the elderly women in the study were widows who lacked access to a partner. Nevertheless, men and women of all ages differ with regard to sexual attitudes and behavior, even when both have equal access to a partner.

On average, men are more interested in sex and think about it more often than women do (Peplau, 2003). And they are more likely than women to be interested in purely physical sex and to have more permissive attitudes toward sex (Baldwin & Baldwin, 1997; Dantzker & Eisenman, 2003). A study of first-year college students illustrates this difference quite well (Cohen & Shotland, 1996). These researchers found that the male students expected sexual intercourse to become part of a dating relationship far sooner than the female students did. Nearly all of the men in the study

FIGURE 9.7

Frequency of Sexual Intercourse around the World

Results of an international survey conducted by the Durex Corporation, a manufacturer of condoms, shows that the frequency of intercourse varies from country to country.

Source: Durex Global Sex Survey (2002).

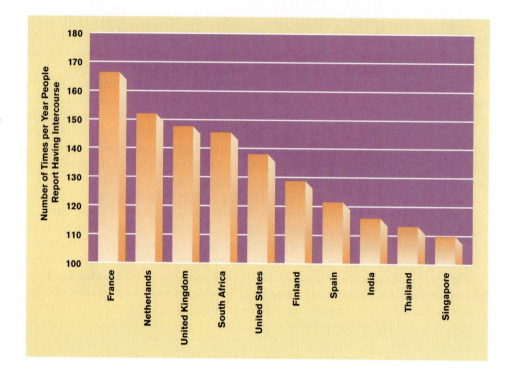

◆ **parental investment**

A term used by evolutionary psychologists to denote the amount of time and effort men or women must devote to parenthood.

expressed a willingness to have sex on a basis of physical attraction only, with no emotional involvement; fewer than two-thirds of the women were willing to do so. Approximately 30% of the men but only 5% of the women admitted to having had sex with someone they were neither attracted to nor emotionally involved with.

Why do these gender differences exist? Evolutionary psychologists often explain these differences as resulting from the influence of evolution on men's and women's mating behaviors. Many use the term **parental investment** to denote the amount of time and effort men or women must devote to parenthood. According to parental investment theory, women and men have adopted mating strategies that correspond to their respective investments in parenting (Buss, 1999, 2000b). Men are assumed to be interested in making only a short-term biological investment in parenting, so they typically seek women who are young, healthy (physical attractiveness is taken as a sign of good health), and well suited for child bearing. Because parenting requires a greater investment from women (9 months of pregnancy and a long period of dependency), they tend to prefer men who are somewhat older, more stable and with sufficient resources, generous, emotionally attached, and strong enough to provide protection for the family (Buss, 1999). These and related gender differences are apparently not culture-specific, since they have been found in 37 different countries (Buss, 1994).

As you learned in Chapter 1, Buss's research also supported evolutionary predictions regarding differential patterns of jealousy in men and women. He found that men were mostly concerned about sexual fidelity, presumably because they wanted to be certain that any children conceived would be their own. Women, by contrast, were most interested in emotional fidelity, or the idea that they should be able to count on a man to be fully committed to a psychological and social partnership with them. Other researchers have replicated these findings in more recent work (Hughes, et al., 2004). Moreover, Buss and his colleagues have replicated them in both elderly (average age = 67) and young adult (average age = 20) samples (Shackelford et al., 2004).

Finally, as evolutionary theory would predict, women appear to have the strongest desire for sex around the time of ovulation when they are most likely to conceive a child (Pillsworth et al., 2004). Similarly, studies conducted by Viennese researcher Karl Grammar (cited in Holden, 1996) indicate that increases in men's testosterone levels are linked to the *pheromones*, odor-producing hormones, that are found in women's vaginal secretions at the time of ovulation. Thus, it is likely that men are the most rapidly aroused in the presence of female partners who are ovulating.

How Did You Find Psychology?

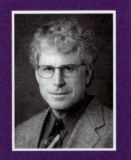

David Buss

"The man always pays" were the words of relationship advice a supervisor offered to David Buss when he was a teenaged high school dropout working the night shift at a New Jersey truck stop (Buss, 2004, p.14). But Buss was skeptical about his middle-aged supervisor's assertion. Liberated men, Buss informed him, unlike their unfortunate forebears, no longer had to be concerned about "paying" for sex either materially or through long-term commitments, thanks to the sexual revolution. Years later, when Buss completed his study of mate preferences in 37 cultures, he realized that his supervisor's words had contained an element of truth (Buss, 2004).

Buss grew up sandwiched between a brother who was "the brilliant one" and a sister who was "the creative one" (Buss, 2004, p. 14). His only distinguishing characteristic, as far as his family could determine, was good vision. By his teenaged years, Buss had lost interest in school. He got into a couple of scrapes with the police, and ended up leaving high school.

Buss's job at the truck stop convinced him that the world had little to offer to individuals who lacked education, so he took night classes and managed to get a high school diploma. Next, he headed for Europe. On a flight bound for Amsterdam, Buss met and fell in love with a female scientist who changed his life. They began living together in Austin, Texas, and Buss applied to the University of Texas. As chance would have it, he won an admissions lottery and enrolled at the university.

For the first time in his life, academic learning captured Buss's interest. When he encountered Darwin's theory of evolution in a geology class, he was fascinated with it. By his junior year, Buss knew that he wanted to pursue a career in psychological research and began to formulate an evolutionary hypothesis to explain mating behavior. He wrote a paper in an advanced psychology class in which he postulated that men were highly motivated to claw their way up the status hierarchy because dominant men have more access to sexual partners than their nondominant peers. Buss was surprised when the professor praised his paper to the entire class and asked Buss to formally present it to them. When he moved on to graduate school at the University of California, Buss continued developing his evolutionary theory of mating behavior. He received his Ph.D. in 1981.

Today, Buss serves as a professor of psychology and head of the Individual Difference and Evolutionary Psychology Area at the University of Texas at Austin, and is a leading figure in the field of evolutionary psychology—a remarkable turnaround for a fellow who earlier in life had decided to drop out of school. Buss's story tells us that we should never give up on people (or on ourselves!) even when they appear to have taken a wrong turn in life.

Other researchers question whether women's reported mate preferences and concerns about emotional fidelity are thoroughly biological in nature. Researchers Eagly and Wood (1999) cite research demonstrating that gender differences in mate preferences are significantly smaller when economic and social conditions for males and females are more equal, as they are becoming in developed countries in the 21st century. In other words, when women are economically dependent on men, the mating "rules" described by evolutionary psychologists may apply; however, gender differences in mate preferences decline as women gain independence. Under conditions of equality, physical attractiveness in a mate would be likely to be just as important to women as to men. And a woman's earning capacity might be more highly valued by men.

Eagly and Wood may be right. Recent research indicates that, in societies with egalitarian attitudes about gender roles, marital status and income are correlated. Longitudinal, prospective research has shown that the higher a woman's economic status, the more likely she is to get married (Ono, 2003). Moreover, the sexual/emotional fidelity distinction appears to be larger among older women than among college students, so younger cohorts of women may be developing beliefs about fidelity that are more similar to those held by men (Shackelford et al., 2004). Today's men may be looking for more in their mates than just good looks and child-bearing potential, and today's women may be more concerned about sexual fidelity than their mothers and grandmothers were.

Sexual Desire and Arousal

◆ What are the four phases of the human sexual response cycle?

Dr. William Masters and Dr. Virginia Johnson conducted the first laboratory investigations of the human sexual response in 1954. They monitored their volunteer participants, who engaged in sex while connected to electronic sensing devices. Masters and Johnson (1966) concluded that both males and females experience a **sexual response cycle** with four phases, as shown in Figure 9.8.

The *excitement phase* is the beginning of the sexual response. Visual cues such as watching a partner undress are more likely to initiate the excitement phase in men than in women. Tender, loving touches coupled with verbal expressions of love arouse women more readily than visual stimulation. And men can become aroused almost instantly, while arousal for women is often a more gradual, building process. For both partners, muscular tension increases, heart rate quickens, and blood pressure rises. As additional blood is pumped into the genitals, the male's penis becomes erect and the female feels a swelling of the clitoris. Vaginal lubrication occurs as the inner two-thirds of the vagina expands and the inner lips of the vagina enlarge. In women especially, the nipples harden and stand erect.

After the excitement phase, the individual enters the *plateau phase*, when excitement continues to mount. Blood pressure and muscle tension increase still more, and breathing becomes heavy and more rapid. The man's testes swell, and drops of liquid, which can contain live sperm cells, may drip from the penis. The outer part of the woman's vagina swells as the increased blood further engorges the area. The clitoris withdraws under the clitoral hood (its skin covering), and the breasts become engorged with blood. Excitement builds steadily during the plateau phase.

The *orgasm*, the shortest of the phases, is the highest point of sexual pleasure, marked by a sudden discharge of accumulated sexual tension. Involuntary muscle contractions may seize the entire body during orgasm, and the genitals contract rhythmically. Orgasm is a two-stage experience for the male. First is his awareness that ejaculation is near and that he can do nothing to stop it; second is the ejaculation itself, when semen is released from the penis in forceful spurts. The experience of orgasm in

◆ **sexual response cycle**

The four phases—excitement, plateau, orgasm, and resolution—that make up the human sexual response in both males and females, according to Masters and Johnson.

FIGURE 9.8 **The Sexual Response Cycle**

Masters and Johnson identified four phases in the sexual response patterns of men and women. However, progression through the phases differs for males and females.

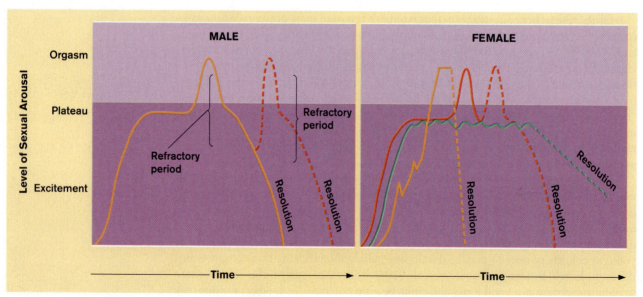

women builds in much the same way as for men. Marked by powerful, rhythmic contractions, the female's orgasm usually lasts longer than that of the male. About 40–50% of women regularly experience orgasm during intercourse (Wilcox & Hager, 1980).

The orgasm gives way to the *resolution phase*, a tapering-off period, when the body returns to its unaroused state. Men experience a *refractory period* in the resolution phase, during which they cannot have another orgasm. The refractory period may last from only a few minutes for some men to as long as several hours for others. Women do not have a refractory period and may, if restimulated, experience another orgasm right away.

The sexual response cycle is strongly influenced by hormones. The sex glands manufacture hormones—*estrogen* and *progesterone* in the ovaries, and androgens in the testes. The adrenal glands in both sexes also produce small amounts of these hormones. Females have considerably more estrogen and progesterone than males do, so these are known as the female sex hormones. Males have considerably more androgens, the male sex hormones.

Psychological factors play an important role in sexual attraction and arousal. Such factors include preferences and attitudes we learn from our culture.

Testosterone, the most important androgen, influences the development and maintenance of male sex characteristics, as well as sexual motivation. Males must have a sufficient level of testosterone to maintain sexual interest and have an erection. Females, too, need small amounts of testosterone in the bloodstream to maintain sexual interest and responsiveness (Andersen & Cyranowski, 1995). Deficiencies in sexual interest and activity can sometimes be reversed in both men and women with the use of testosterone patches or ointments (Meyer, 1997). However, researchers point out that many hormones work in concert with testosterone to regulate the sexual response cycle and warn against the assumption that pharmacological manipulation of testosterone alone is adequate to solve problems with sexual functioning (Halaris, 2003). You will learn more about the topic of sexual dysfunctions in Chapter 12.

Psychological factors play a large role in sexual arousal. Part of the psychological nature of sexual behavior stems from preferences and practices that people learn from their culture. And cultural norms about sexual behavior vary widely, covering everything from the age at which initiation of sexual behavior is proper to the partners, conditions, settings, positions, and specific sexual acts that are considered acceptable. Moreover, what is perceived as sexually attractive in a male and a female may differ dramatically from culture to culture.

Sexual fantasies also influence sexual arousal. Both men and women are likely to fantasize during intercourse. Most sexual fantasies involve conventional imagery about one's current or past partner or an imaginary lover. There are consistent gender differences in fantasies: "Men more than women imagine doing something sexual to their partner, whereas women more than men imagine something sexual being done to them" (Leitenberg & Henning, 1995, p. 491). Men's fantasies generally involve more specific visual imagery, and women's fantasies have more emotional and romantic content. Although 95% of males and females admit to having sexual fantasies, about 25% experience strong guilt about them (Leitenberg & Henning, 1995). But research seems to suggest an association between a higher incidence of sexual fantasies and a more satisfactory sex life and fewer sexual problems.

Sexual Orientation

Now we turn our attention to **sexual orientation**—the direction of an individual's sexual preference, erotic feelings, and sexual activity. In heterosexuals, the human sexual response is oriented toward members of the opposite sex; in

◆ **sexual orientation**
The direction of one's sexual preference—toward members of the opposite sex (heterosexuality), toward one's own sex (homosexuality), or toward both sexes (bisexuality)

◆ *What are the various factors that have been suggested as determinants of a gay or lesbian sexual orientation?*

homosexuals, toward those of the same sex; and in bisexuals, toward members of both sexes. Homosexuality has been reported in all societies throughout recorded history (Carrier, 1980; Ford & Beach, 1951). Kinsey and his associates (1948, 1953) estimated that 4% of the male participants had nothing but homosexual relations throughout life, and 2–3% of the female participants had been in mostly or exclusively lesbian relationships. Gay and lesbian rights groups, however, claim that about 10% of the U.S. population is predominantly homosexual. In what is said to be the most definitive and reliable sex survey to date, Laumann and others (1994) reported that the percentages of Americans who identified themselves as homosexual or bisexual were 2.8% of men and 1.4% of women. But 5.3% of men and 3.5% of women said that they had had a sexual experience with a person of the same sex at least once since puberty. And even larger percentages of those surveyed—10% of males and 8–9% of females—said that they had felt some same-sex desires. More recent surveys of gay men, although they have included much smaller samples, have found similar prevalence rates to those of Laumann and his colleagues (Bagley & Tremblay, 1998). Notably, all estimates suggest that homosexuality is twice as prevalent in males as in females.

Psychologists continue to debate whether sexual orientation is biologically fixed or acquired through learning and experience. Some researchers have suggested that abnormal levels of androgens during prenatal development might influence sexual orientation (Collaer & Hines, 1995; Hershberger & Segal, 2004). Too much or too little androgen at critical periods of brain development might masculinize or feminize the brain of the developing fetus, making a homosexual orientation more likely (Berenbaum & Snyder, 1995). A few studies have revealed an increase in the incidence of lesbianism among females who had been exposed prenatally to synthetic estrogen (Meyer-Bahlburg et al., 1995) or to an excess of androgens (Ehrhardt et al., 1968; Money & Schwartz, 1977).

Neuroscientist Simon LeVay (1991) reported that an area in the hypothalamus governing sexual behavior is about twice as large in heterosexual men as in homosexual men. Critics were quick to point out that all of the gay men included in LeVay's sample died of AIDS. Many researchers questioned whether the brain differences LeVay observed might have resulted from AIDS, rather than being associated with sexual orientation (Byne, 1993). However, recent animal studies have also suggested a link between the hypothalamus and sexual orientation. Among domestic species of sheep, about 10% of males (i.e., rams) exhibit homosexual behavior. Researchers have found that, like LeVay's subjects, male-oriented rams have a smaller hypothalamus than those who prefer exclusively female partners do (Roselli et al., 2004).

Some researchers looking for a genetic contribution to sexual orientation suggest that a number of "feminizing" genes work together to shift male brain development in the female direction (Miller, 2000). These researchers believe that if only a few of these feminizing genes are acting, males who inherit them are more tender-minded and sensitive. But if many such genes are active during development, their effect probably contributes to homosexuality. Moreover, a similar effect may occur with other genes, resulting in lesbianism in females (Miller, 2000). Ample evidence exists to support the hypothesis that some kind of genetic predisposition increases the likelihood of a homosexual orientation in both men and women. Twin studies show that 50–60% of the identical co-twins of gay men are also gay, and slightly less than 50% of the identical co-twins of lesbian women are also lesbians (Bailey & Pillard, 1991; Whitam et al., 1993; Bailey et al., 1993). However, researchers have yet to identify a specific set of genes that accounts for homosexual orientation or the molecular mechanism through which genes may influence sexual orientation (Mustanski et al., 2002).

Some researchers (Byne & Parsons, 1993, 1994) maintain that, in the absence of studies of identical twins reared apart, the influence of environment cannot be ruled out as the cause of a higher incidence of homosexuality in certain families. Furthermore, they suggest that if one or more genes are involved, they may not be genes directly influencing sexual orientation. Rather, they could be genes affecting personality or temperament, which might influence how people react to environmental stimuli (Byne, 1994).

Consequently, many psychologists, such as Charlotte Patterson (1995), suggest that sexual orientation should be studied as a complex interaction of nature and nurture, using theoretical models similar to those used by developmental psychologists to explain other phenomena. For instance, developmentalists often study the ways in which family characteristics contribute to the development of children's traits and behavior. In one early study that examined homosexuality from this perspective, Bell, Weinberg, and Hammersmith (1981) conducted extensive face-to-face interviews with 979 homosexual participants (293 women, 686 men) and 477 heterosexual controls. The researchers found no single condition of family life that in and of itself appeared to be a factor in either homosexual or heterosexual development.

In the United States, social attitudes concerning homosexuality appear to be moving slowly toward acceptance. However, men continue to hold more negative attitudes about homosexuality than women do.

Other researchers have examined whether homosexuality in adulthood is related in some consistent way to childhood behavior. Some researchers (e.g., Zuger, 1990) believe that effeminate behavior in boys is an early stage of homosexuality. Such effeminate behavior might include a boy's cross-dressing, expressing the desire to be a girl or insisting that he is in fact a girl, and/or preferring girls as playmates and girls' games over boys' games and sports.

In another study of recalled childhood experiences and sexual orientation, Phillips and Over (1995) found that lesbian women were more likely than heterosexual peers to recall imagining themselves as males, preferring boy's games, and being called "tomboys." Yet, some heterosexual women recalled childhood experiences similar to those of the majority of lesbians, and some lesbians recalled experiences more like those of the majority of heterosexual women. The link between childhood behaviors such as play preferences and adult sexual orientation is clearly not strong enough to make it possible to predict which children will be homosexual and which will be heterosexual in adulthood.

Looking Back   Sexual researchers such as Kinsey and Masters and Johnson are sometimes accused of reducing the sex act to its clinical, physical components. However, scientific understanding of a phenomenon doesn't rob it of its personal meaning. As Masters and Johnson noted in their book *The Pleasure Bond* (1975), the physical act of sex must not be separated from its emotional and motivational foundations. In Maslow's hierarchy, the need for love and acceptance arises once our needs for physical sustenance and safety have been met. In the context of a committed relationship, sex can be an important ingredient in the achievement of this goal. Recall, too, that fulfillment of our need for love and acceptance is required before we can go on to greater things.

Apply It 9.1 How to Get a Date

You think you have met Mr. or Ms. Right. So, what do you do? How do you go about making a date? Psychologists have learned that we can enhance our social skills, including our date-seeking skills, through the technique of *successive approximations*. That means that we can practice a series of tasks that are graded in difficulty, honing our social skills and gaining self-confidence at each step. We can try out some of our skills on friends, who can role-play the prospective date and give honest feedback about our behavior.

Here is a series of graduated (step-by-step) tasks that may help you sharpen your own date-seeking skills.

Easy Practice Level

- Select a person with whom you are friendly, but whom you have no desire to date. Practice making small talk about the weather, new films, TV shows, concerts, museum shows, political events, and personal hobbies.

- Select a person you might have some interest in dating. Smile when you pass this person at work, school, or elsewhere, and say, "Hi." Engage in this activity with other people of both genders to increase your skills at greeting others.

Medium Practice Level

- Sit down next to the person you want to date, and engage in small talk. If you are in a classroom, talk about a homework assignment, the seating arrangement, or the instructor (be kind). If you are at work, talk about the building or some recent interesting event in the neighborhood. Ask your intended date how he or she feels about the situation.

- Engage in small talk about the weather and local events. Channel the conversation into an exchange of personal information. Give your "name, rank, and serial number"—who you are, your major field or your occupation, where you're from, and why or how you came to the school or company. The other person is likely to reciprocate and provide equivalent information.

- Rehearse asking the person out before your mirror, a family member, or a confidant. You may wish to suggest a cup of coffee or a film. It is somewhat less threatening to ask someone out to a gathering at which "some of us will be getting together." Or you may rehearse asking the person to accompany you to a cultural event, such as an exhibition at a museum or a concert—it's sort of a date, but less anxiety-inducing.

Target Behavior Level

- Ask the person out on a date in a manner that is consistent with your behavior rehearsal. If the person says he or she has a previous engagement or can't make it, you might wish to say something like "That's too bad" or "I'm sorry you can't make it" and add something like "Perhaps another time." You should be able to get a feeling for whether the person you asked out was just seeking an excuse or has a genuine interest in you and could not, in fact, accept the specific invitation.

- Before asking the person out again, pay attention to his or her apparent comfort level when you return to small talk on a couple of occasions. If there is still a chance, the other person should smile and return your eye contact; he or she might also offer you an invitation. In any event, if you are turned down twice, do not ask a third time. And don't make a catastrophe out of the refusal. Look up. Note that the roof hasn't fallen in. The birds are still chirping in the trees. You are still paying taxes. Then give someone else a chance to appreciate your fine qualities.

Source: Rathus et al. (2000).

◆ Explaining Motivation p. 278

◆ What is the difference between intrinsic and extrinsic motivation? p. 278

With intrinsic motivation, an act is performed because it is satisfying or pleasurable in and of itself. With extrinsic motivation, an act is performed to bring a reward or to avert an undesirable consequence.

◆ How do drive-reduction and arousal theory explain motivation? p. 279

Drive-reduction theory suggests that a biological need creates an unpleasant state of emotional arousal that impels the organism to engage in behavior that will reduce the arousal level. Arousal theory suggests that the aim of motivation is to maintain an optimal level of arousal.

◆ According to Maslow, how do individuals attain self-actualization? p. 281

Maslow claimed that individuals must satisfy physiological and safety needs before addressing needs for love, esteem, and self-actualization.

◆ How do need for achievement theory and goal orientation theory explain achievement motivation? p. 281

Murray's need for achievement theory claims that some individuals vary in the need to accomplish something difficult and to perform at a high standard of excellence. Goal orientation theory asserts that individuals vary in their adoption of mastery and performance goals. Mastery goals measure achievement against a desired level of knowledge acquisition. Performance goals measure achievement against that of others.

◆ Hunger p. 283

◆ How do internal and external cues influence eating behavior? p. 283

When the lateral hypothalamus (LH) is activated, it signals the organism to eat. When the ventromedial hypothalamus (VMH) is activated, it signals the organism to stop eating. Signals that activate these two structures include the fullness of the stomach and glucose and insulin levels in the bloodstream. External cues include the smell of food and the time of day.

◆ What are some factors that account for variations in body weight? p. 283

Variations in body weight are influenced by genes, metabolic rate, set point, activity level, and eating habits.

◆ What are the proposed causes of eating disorders, and how are these disorders treated? p. 285

Eating disorders are associated with a distorted view of the body. Cultural images that exalt thinness may also influence their development. An excessive need for control may contribute to eating disorders as well. The most successful treatments combine nutritional intervention, medication, and psychotherapy.

◆ Emotion p. 287

◆ What are the various theories that have been proposed to explain emotion? p. 287

According to the James-Lange theory, environmental stimuli produce a physiological response, and then awareness of the response allows that response to be experienced as an emotion. The Cannon-Bard theory suggests that emotions are experienced physiologically and psychologically at the same time. The Schachter-Singer theory states that emotions involve attributions of meaning to physiological responses to stimuli. The Lazarus theory claims that emotion-provoking stimuli trigger cognitive appraisals.

◆ What are the neurological processes involved in the fear response? p. 289

The physiological component of the fear response is relayed to the amygdala before going to the cortex. When the cortex catches up, it regulates the amygdala's influence on the fight-or-flight response.

◆ Which aspects of emotion are universal, and which vary across cultures? p. 290

Recognition of basic emotional expressions is universal. Cultures vary in their guidelines for how and when emotions should be expressed. Groups within the same culture may also have different rules concerning emotional expressions.

◆ In what ways do males and females differ with regard to emotions? p. 292

Men are more prone to anger when betrayed; women are more likely to feel sad. Men are more likely to express anger publicly. Women's physiological responses to negative emotions may be more intense than those of men's responses.

◆ What are the components of emotional intelligence? p. 292

The personal components of emotional intelligence are an awareness of one's emotions, an ability to manage them, and self-motivation. The interpersonal components are empathy and the ability to handle relationships.

◆ **How do sexual attitudes and behavior vary across cultures and genders?** p. 293

The frequency of sexual activity varies across cultures. Evolutionary psychologists have identified variables that are consistent across cultures, such as men's preference for younger partners. Men are more likely than women to think of sex in purely physical terms and to hold more permissive attitudes toward sex.

◆ **What are the four phases of the human sexual response cycle?** p. 296

The sexual response cycle consists of the excitement phase, the plateau phase, orgasm, and the resolution phase.

◆ **What are the various factors that have been suggested as determinants of a gay or lesbian sexual orientation?** p. 298

Biological factors that may influence sexual orientation include genes, hormones, and brain structures.

◆ KEY TERMS

anorexia nervosa, p. 285
arousal, p. 279
arousal theory, p. 280
basic emotions, p. 290
body mass index (BMI), p. 283
bulimia nervosa, p. 286
Cannon-Bard theory, p. 288
display rules, p. 290
drive, p. 279
drive-reduction theory, p. 279
emotion, p. 287
emotional intelligence, p. 292

extrinsic motivation, p. 278
facial-feedback hypothesis, p. 291
goal orientation theory, p. 282
homeostasis, p. 279
incentive, p. 278
intrinsic motivation, p. 278
James-Lange theory, p. 287
lateral hypothalamus (LH), p. 283
Lazarus theory, p. 288
metabolic rate, p. 285
motivation, p. 277
motives, p. 277

need for achievement (n Ach), p. 282
obesity, p. 284
parental investment, p. 294
primary drives, p. 283
Schachter-Singer theory, p. 288
set point, p. 285
sexual orientation, p. 297
sexual response cycle, p. 296
stimulus motives, p. 280
ventromedial hypothalamus (VMH), p. 283
Yerkes-Dodson law, p. 280

Study Guide 9

Answers to all the Study Guide questions are provided at the end of the book.

◆ SECTION ONE: Chapter Review

Explaining Motivation (pp. 278–283)

1. When you engage in an activity to gain a reward or to avoid an unpleasant consequence, your motivation is (intrinsic, extrinsic).

2. Drive-reduction theory states that people are motivated to
   a. reduce tension created by biological drives.
   b. seek emotional highs such as the feelings you have on a roller coaster.
   c. obey genetically programmed instincts.
   d. maintain appropriate levels of arousal.

3. According to arousal theory, people seek _____ arousal.
   a. minimized
   b. increased
   c. decreased
   d. optimal

4. According to Maslow's hierarchy of needs, which needs must be satisfied before a person will try to satisfy the belonging and love needs?
   a. safety and self-actualization needs
   b. self-actualization needs and esteem needs
   c. physiological and safety needs
   d. physiological and esteem needs

5. Murray used the Thematic Apperception Test (TAT) to study the need for achievement. (true/false)

6. Goals that are too easy are not interesting to people who are high in *n* Ach. (true/false)

7. People who are high in *n* Ach usually attribute success to luck or other factors beyond their control. (true/false)

8. Individuals who have a (mastery/performance) goal orientation are less likely to procrastinate than others.

Hunger (pp. 283–287)

9. The lateral hypothalamus (LH) acts as a (feeding, satiety) center; the ventromedial hypothalamus (VMH) acts as a (feeding, satiety) center.

10. All of the following are hunger signals except
    a. activity of the lateral hypothalamus.
    b. low levels of glucose in the blood.
    c. the hormone CCK.
    d. a high insulin level.

11. The smell of food
    a. has little effect on hunger.
    b. can substitute for food itself when you are dieting.
    c. may make you feel hungry even when you are not.
    d. motivates you to eat only when you are very hungry.

12. Which factor is most responsible for how fast your body burns calories to produce energy?
    a. calories consumed   c. eating habits
    b. fat cells   d. metabolic rate

13. According to set-point theory, the body works to (increase, decrease, maintain) body weight.

14. Which of the following might indicate a tendency for obesity to be inherited?
    a. metabolic rate
    b. set point
    c. hormones
    d. all of the above

15. Adopted children are more likely to be very thin or obese if their (biological, adoptive) parents are very thin or obese.

16. Increased exercise during dieting is important to counteract the body's tendency to
    a. increase the fat in the fat cells.
    b. increase the number of fat cells.
    c. lower its metabolic rate.
    d. raise its metabolic rate.

17. Self-starvation is the defining symptom of _____; binge eating followed by purging is the main symptom of _____.

Emotion (pp. 287–293)

18. According to the text, emotions have all of the following except a _____ component.
    a. physical   c. sensory
    b. cognitive   d. behavioral

19. Which theory of emotion holds that you feel a true emotion only when you become physically aroused and can identify some cause for the arousal?
    a. Schachter-Singer theory
    b. James-Lange theory
    c. Cannon-Bard theory
    d. Lazarus theory

20. Which theory of emotion suggests that you would feel fearful because you were trembling?
    a. Schachter-Singer theory
    b. James-Lange theory
    c. Cannon-Bard theory
    d. Lazarus theory

21. Which theory suggests that the feeling of emotion and the physiological response to an emotional situation occur at about the same time?
    a. Schachter-Singer theory
    b. James-Lange theory
    c. Cannon-Bard theory
    d. Lazarus theory

22. Which theory suggests that the physiological arousal and the emotion flow from a cognitive appraisal of an emotion-provoking event?
    a. Schachter-Singer theory
    b. James-Lange theory
    c. Cannon-Bard theory
    d. Lazarus theory

23. Which of the following is *not* true of the basic emotions?
    a. They are reflected in distinctive facial expressions.
    b. They are found in all cultures.
    c. There are several hundred known to date.
    d. They are unlearned.

24. All of the following are true of display rules *except* that they
    a. are the same in all cultures.
    b. dictate when and where emotions should be expressed.
    c. dictate what emotions should not be expressed.
    d. often cause people to display emotions they do not feel.

25. The idea that making a happy, sad, or angry face can actually trigger the psychological response and feeling associated with the emotion is called the
    a. emotion production theory.
    b. emotion and control theory.
    c. facial-feedback hypothesis.
    d. facial expression theory.

26. Which of the following does *not* demonstrate emotional intelligence?
    a. Feeling depressed and distracted, Kyra takes a break and goes to the movies.
    b. When he fails a test, Alan gets angry at his girlfriend for taking up so much of his study time.
    c. Mike notices that his boss is in a bad mood and stays out of her way for the afternoon.
    d. Gisela knows how to get her team moving to solve a problem.

Human Sexuality (pp. 293–299)

27. Who conducted the first major surveys of sexual attitudes and behaviors of American males and females?
    a. Alfred Kinsey   c. George Gallup
    b. Masters and Johnson   d. Laumann and others

28. Which of the following statements about the human sexual response is false?
    a. It consists of four phases.
    b. It occurs in sexual intercourse and can occur in other types of sexual activity.
    c. It is quite different in males and females.
    d. It was researched by Masters and Johnson.

29. Androgens, estrogen, and progesterone are present in both males and females. (true/false)

30. Testosterone plays a role in maintaining sexual interest in males and females. (true/false)

31. The direction of one's sexual preference—toward members of the opposite sex or members of one's own sex—is termed one's
    a. sexual role.   c. sexual desire.
    b. sexual orientation.   d. sexual motive.

32. Statistics suggest that homosexuality is twice as common in males as in females. (true/false)

33. Which of the following did Bell, Weinberg, and Hammersmith's study reveal about the childhood experiences of their gay and lesbian participants?
    a. Abuse was more common in their families than in those of heterosexuals.
    b. No single characteristic of family life distinguished their families from those of heterosexuals.
    c. Most were raised in single-parent homes.
    d. Most were from middle-class backgrounds.

34. Evolutionary theory suggests that gender differences in sexual behavior are caused by gender differences in
    a. hormones.
    b. parental investment.
    c. cultural roles.
    d. ideas about the importance of physical attractiveness.

◆ **SECTION TWO: Important Psychologists and Concepts**

On the line opposite each name, list the major concept or theory discussed in this chapter.

Name   **Major Concept or Theory**

1. Hull _____

2. Maslow _____

3. Murray _____

4. James and Lange _____

5. Cannon and Bard _____

6. Lazarus _____

7. Salovey and Pizarro _____

◆ **SECTION THREE: Fill In the Blank**

1. _____ are needs or desires that energize and direct behavior toward a goal.

2. Anthony mows his parents' lawn and, in the winter, shovels his own and his elderly neighbor's sidewalk. He does this because he enjoys helping others. Anthony is responding to _____ motivation.

3. Cleo will help around the house only if she receives a financial reward or special privilege. Cleo responds to _____ motivation.

4. Jack always wants to ride the wildest rides at the amusement park. He also seems to get bored very easily and then finds a way to create action in his environment. His behavior would probably best be explained by the _____ theory of motivation.

5. The _____ hypothalamus acts as the feeding center, and the _____ hypothalamus acts as the satiety center.

6. The most important factor in successful long-term weight loss is _____.

7. _____ nervosa involves rigid restriction of calorie intake; _____ nervosa involves a cycle of binging and purging.

8. The _____ theory of emotion says that we experience emotion as a result of becoming aware of our physical response to a situation.

9. The _____ theory of emotion says that our physical response to a stimulus and our emotional response occur at the same time.

10. The _____ theory of emotion says that we experience a physical response to a stimulus and then give it meaning; from this comes our emotional response.

11. Feelings of fear, anger, disgust, surprise, joy, or happiness have been identified as _____ emotions.

12. The _____ phase is the beginning of the human sexual response cycle.

13. Males must have a sufficient level of _____ to maintain sexual interest and have an erection.

14. The tendency of the body to maintain a balanced internal state with regard to oxygen level, body temperature, blood sugar, water balance, and so forth is called _____.

15. Simon LeVay, a neuroscientist, reported that an area in the hypothalamus governing sexual behavior is about twice as large in _____ men as in _____ men.

16. _____ is the ability to use knowledge about emotions in everyday life.

◆ **SECTION FOUR: Comprehensive Practice Test**

1. If James is responding to an incentive, he is responding to an _____ stimulus.
   a. external
   b. internal
   c. explicit
   d. intrinsic

2. Courtney reads books on research and statistics because these subjects fascinate her; she really enjoys learning about new approaches to research and the results of major research projects. Courtney is being driven by _____ motivation.
   a. intrinsic
   b. intellectual
   c. academic
   d. extrinsic

3. Keisha studies chemistry every night because she wants to excel in this field; she believes she will make a great deal of money as a chemist. Keisha is being driven mainly by _____ motivation.
   a. career
   b. intrinsic
   c. extrinsic
   d. academic

4. A _____ is a state of tension or arousal brought about by an underlying need, which motivates one to engage in behavior that will satisfy the need and reduce the tension.
   a. drive
   b. balance stimulus
   c. tension stimulus
   d. homeostatic condition

5. Angel's behavior sometimes scares his friends. He drives his motorcycle fast, he loves bungee jumping, and he can't wait for his first parachute jump. These interests could be explained by the _____ theory of motivation.
   a. instinct
   b. risky shift
   c. arousal
   d. homeostasis

6. According to Maslow, the need for love and affiliation is satisfied _____ basic biological needs and the need for safety.
   a. instead of
   b. before
   c. at the same time as
   d. after

7. Cody realizes that the goals he has set for himself are going to take too much time and effort so he decides to compromise and go for what he considers less difficult but more rational goals. Cody is a good example of a high achiever. (true/false)

8. When you are hungry, you experience the effects of the _____ hypothalamus; when you have eaten and feel full, you experience the effects of the _____ hypothalamus.
   a. proximal; distal
   b. distal; proximal
   c. ventromedial; lateral
   d. lateral; ventromedial

9. Murray developed the Thematic Apperception Test as a way to measure
   a. anger.
   b. personal perceptions of success.
   c. social needs.

10. A person with a _____ n Ach is likely to set either very low goals or impossibly high goals.
    a. high
    b. moderate
    c. low
    d. borderline

11. Which of the following theories asserts that, when presented with an emotion-producing stimulus, we feel the physiological effects and the subjective experience of emotion at about the same time?
    a. James-Lange
    b. Lazarus
    c. Cannon-Bard
    d. Schachter-Singer

12. All researchers who are doing work in the physiology of emotions agree that humans experience both basic emotions and responses such as fear, rage, and joy. (true/false)

13. Trina smiled and thanked her friend for a birthday gift that she really did not like. Trina has learned the _____ of her culture.
    a. social rules   c. display rules
    b. interpersonal rules   d. expressive rules

14. The facial-feedback hypothesis states that the muscular movements that cause facial expressions trigger the corresponding emotions. (true/false)

15. Emotional intelligence is similar to the kind of intelligence that is measured by IQ tests. (true/false)

16. The orgasm is the shortest phase in the sexual response cycle. (true/false)

17. Masters and Johnson concluded that the sexual response cycle is _____ for males and females.
    a. quite similar
    b. different
    c. variable
    d. instinctive

18. Boys who display early effeminate behavior usually are homosexual in adulthood. (true/false)

◆ **SECTION FIVE: Critical Thinking**

1. In your view, which theory or combination of theories best explains motivation: drive-reduction theory, arousal theory, or Maslow's hierarchy of needs? Which theory do you find least convincing? Support your answers.

2. Which level of Maslow's hierarchy provides the strongest motivation for your behavior in general? Give specific examples to support your answer.

3. In your view, which is the better explanation of gender differences in sexual attitudes and behavior: parental investment theory or the social factors proposed by Eagly and Wood?

Health and Stress

chapter **10**

Sources of Stress

◆ What was the Social Readjustment Rating Scale designed to reveal?

◆ What roles do hassles and uplifts play in the stress of life, according to Lazarus?

◆ How do approach-approach, avoidance-avoidance, and approach- avoidance conflicts differ?

◆ How do the unpredictability and lack of control over a stressor affect its impact?

◆ For people to function effectively and find satisfaction on the job, what nine variables should fall within their comfort zone?

◆ How do people typically react to catastrophic events?

◆ How might historical racism affect the health of African Americans?

Responding to Stress

◆ What is the general adaptation syndrome?

◆ What are the roles of primary and secondary appraisals when a person is confronted with a potentially stressful event?

◆ What is the difference between problem-focused and emotion-focused coping?

Health and Illness

◆ How do the biomedical and biopsychosocial models differ in their approaches to health and illness?

◆ What are the Type A and Type B behavior patterns?

◆ How do psychological factors influence cancer patients' quality of life?

◆ What are the effects of stress on the immune system?

◆ What four personal factors are associated with health and resistance to stress?

◆ What are the relationships among gender, ethnicity, and health?

Lifestyle and Health

◆ What is the most dangerous health-threatening behavior?

◆ What are some health risks of alcohol abuse?

◆ What is the difference between bacterial and viral STDs?

◆ What are some benefits of regular aerobic exercise?

◆ What are the benefits and risks associated with alternative medicine?

Lance Armstrong was, in his own words, "born to race bikes." As a teenager, and the child of a divorced working mother in Plano, Texas, he trained and competed hard. On weekends, he rode his bicycle so far that he sometimes had to phone his mother to pick him up. Armstrong's dedication to his training was so single-minded that he neglected his schoolwork and nearly failed his senior year of high school, but managed to squeak by. After high school, his life was a whirlwind of amateur competitions, the 1992 Olympics, and then the professional cycling circuit.

In his first professional race, Armstrong came in dead last, but he won ten titles the following year. By 1996, he was a household name in Europe and was gaining fame in the United States as well—heady stuff for any 25-year-old. It seemed that everything was going his way. But one fall day, Armstrong experienced an excruciating pain. Shockingly, tests revealed that he had advanced testicular cancer that had spread to his lungs and his brain. Doctors recommended surgeries to remove his malignant testicle and the cancer in his brain. Following those procedures, he would undergo an aggressive course of chemotherapy. The physicians told Armstrong that, even with the best treatment, he had less than a 50-50 chance to recover. This young, powerful man who had been on top of the world just days before now faced his own mortality.

The chemotherapy weakened Armstrong severely, and he lost 20 pounds. However, his years of training gave him great reserves of physical strength and, at least as importantly, his will was strong. Armstrong has said cancer caused him to take a hard look at himself. He realized that he had relied on his tremendous natural physical abilities and had not learned the discipline, strategy, and teamwork that would be necessary to become a truly great cyclist. He had never given himself the full opportunity to train. He would start, then stop, then start again just a month before a big race. His natural ability was so great that he still won many races, but not the long-distance ones for which more skill is required. Now that Armstrong could take nothing for granted, he realized how important it was to develop into the best cycler he could be. He had a strong network of family and friends he could count on for emotional support. And, even in the midst of his own treatment, he wanted to do something for others. To this end, he established the Lance Armstrong Foundation to help other cancer victims and raise awareness about the importance of early detection. "Having cancer," he says, "was the best thing that ever happened to me."

Armstrong believes that his dedication to rebuilding his health and turning a tragedy into opportunity helped him to recover rapidly. His oncologist described the cyclist as "the most willful person I have ever met . . . he wasn't *willing* to die." Just 5 months after the diagnosis, he began to train again and vowed to return better than ever. But his sponsors, doubtful that he would ever be able to achieve this goal, dropped him. Armstrong signed a much less lucrative contract with another sponsor and continued to train, but his initial efforts left him exhausted and depressed. Afraid of failing, afraid that his strength would never rebound, afraid of a humiliating loss, afraid that his cancer would return, again and again Armstrong had to fight the desire to quit when things were too tough. One day, riding high in the mountains of North Carolina, he felt his unquenchable spirit return. A few days earlier, his coach had had to coax him to try just one more race. Now he was on top of the world again, spoiling for a competition.

Armstrong won his first post-cancer race in 1998, but his real comeback arrived in 1999, when he won Tour de France, a grueling 21 days of riding totaling 2,110 miles. He became an inspiration and a role model to young people and cancer survivors around the world. In 2001, 5 years after his diagnosis, Armstrong was pronounced cancer free. He undergoes regular testing to ensure that the disease has not recurred. He also continues to work with his foundation. In 2004, Armstrong won his sixth Tour de France race, setting a world record.

Why would someone say, as Armstrong did, that cancer was the best thing that ever happened to him? Such statements represent a deliberate choice to view what anyone would agree is a "stressor" as an opportunity for growth. As you will learn in this chapter, the way that an individual views his or her challenges in life greatly influences whether we succeed in overcoming them. We will begin by considering the various sources of stress in our lives.

Sources of Stress

What do you mean when you say you are "stressed out"? Most psychologists define **stress** as the physiological and psychological response to a condition that threatens or challenges an individual and requires some form of adaptation or adjustment. Stress is associated with the **fight-or-flight response,** in which the body's sympathetic nervous system and the endocrine glands prepare the body to fight or escape from a threat (see Chapter 2). Most of us frequently experience other kinds of **stressors,** stimuli or events that are capable of producing physical or emotional stress.

Holmes and Rahe's Social Readjustment Rating Scale

Researchers Holmes and Rahe (1967) developed the **Social Readjustment Rating Scale (SRRS)** to measure stress by ranking different life events from most to least stressful and assigning a point value to each event. Life events that produce the greatest life changes and require the greatest adaptation are considered the most stressful, regardless of whether the events are positive or negative. The 43 life events on the scale range from death of a spouse (assigned 100 stress points) to minor law violations such as getting a traffic ticket (11 points). Find your life stress score by completing *Try It 10.1* (on page 310).

Holmes and Rahe claim that there is a connection between the degree of life stress and major health problems. People who score 300 or more on the SRRS, the researchers say, run about an 80% risk of suffering a major health problem within the next 2 years. Those who score between 150 and 300 have a 50% chance of becoming ill within a 2-year period (Rahe et al., 1964). More recent research has shown that the weights given to life events by Holmes and Rahe continue to be appropriate for adults in North America and that SRRS scores are correlated with a variety of health indicators (Faisal-Cury et al., 2004; Hobson & Delunas, 2001; Scully et al., 2000).

Some researchers have questioned whether a high score on the SRRS is a reliable predictor of future health problems (Krantz et al., 1985; McCrae, 1984). One of the main shortcomings of the SRRS is that it assigns a point value to each life change without taking into account how an individual copes with that stressor. One study found that SRRS scores did reliably predict disease progression in multiple sclerosis patients (Mohr et al., 2002). But the patients who used more effective coping strategies displayed less disease progression than did those who experienced similar stressors but coped poorly with them.

◆ **stress**
The physiological and psychological response to a condition that threatens or challenges a person and requires some form of adaptation or adjustment.

◆ **fight-or-flight response**
A response to stress in which the sympathetic nervous system and the endocrine glands prepare the body to fight or flee.

◆ **stressor**
Any stimulus or event capable of producing physical or emotional stress.

◆ *What was the Social Readjustment Rating Scale designed to reveal?*

◆ **Social Readjustment Rating Scale (SRRS)**
Holmes and Rahe's measure of stress, which ranks 43 life events from most to least stressful and assigns a point value to each.

Even positive life events, such as getting married, can cause stress.

Try It 10.1

Finding a Life Stress Score

To assess your level of life changes, check all of the events that have happened to you in the past year. Add up the points to derive your life stress score. (Based on Holmes & Masuda, 1974.)

Rank	Life Event	Life Change Unit Value	Your Points
1	Death of spouse	100	____
2	Divorce	73	____
3	Marital separation	65	____
4	Jail term	63	____
5	Death of close family member	63	____
6	Personal injury or illness	53	____
7	Marriage	50	____
8	Getting fired at work	47	____
9	Marital reconciliation	45	____
10	Retirement	45	____
11	Change in health of family member	44	____
12	Pregnancy	40	____
13	Sex difficulties	39	____
14	Gain of new family member	39	____
15	Business readjustment	39	____
16	Change in financial state	38	____
17	Death of close friend	37	____
18	Change to different line of work	36	____
19	Change in number of arguments with spouse	35	____
20	Taking out loan for major purchase (e.g., home)	31	____
21	Foreclosure of mortgage or loan	30	____
22	Change in responsibilities at work	29	____
23	Son or daughter leaving home	29	____
24	Trouble with in-laws	29	____
25	Outstanding personal achievement	28	____
26	Spouse beginning or stopping work	26	____
27	Beginning or ending school	26	____
28	Change in living conditions	25	____
29	Revision of personal habits	24	____
30	Trouble with boss	23	____
31	Change in work hours or conditions	20	____
32	Change in residence	20	____
33	Change in schools	20	____
34	Change in recreation	19	____
35	Change in church activities	19	____
36	Change in social activities	18	____
37	Taking out loan for lesser purchase (e.g., car or TV)	17	____
38	Change in sleeping habits	16	____
39	Change in number of family get-togethers	15	____
40	Change in eating habits	15	____
41	Vacation	13	____
42	Christmas	12	____
43	Minor violation of the law	11	____

Life stress score: ____

Daily Hassles and Uplifts

Which is more stressful—major life events or those little problems and frustrations that seem to crop up every day? Richard Lazarus believes that the little stressors, which he calls **hassles,** cause more stress than major life events do. Daily hassles are the "irritating, frustrating, distressing demands and troubled relationships that plague us day in and day out" (Lazarus & DeLongis, 1983, p. 247). Kanner and others (1981) developed the Hassles Scale to assess various categories of hassles. Unlike the Holmes and Rahe scale, the Hassles Scale takes into account the facts that items may or may not represent stressors to individuals and that the amount of stress produced by an item varies from person to person. People completing the scale indicate the items that have been a hassle for them and rate those items for severity on a 3-point scale. Table 10.1 shows the ten hassles most frequently reported by college students.

DeLongis and others (1988) studied 75 American couples over a 6-month period and found that daily stress (as measured on the Hassles Scale) related significantly to present and future "health problems such as flu, sore throat, headaches, and backaches" (p. 486). Research also indicates that minor hassles that accompany stressful major life events, such as those measured by the SRRS, are better predictors of a person's level of psychological distress than the major events themselves (Pillow et al., 1996).

According to Lazarus, **uplifts,** or positive experiences in life, may neutralize the effects of many hassles. Lazarus and his colleagues also constructed an Uplifts Scale. As with the Hassles Scale, people completing this scale make a cognitive appraisal of what they consider to be an uplift. Research has demonstrated links among hassles, uplifts, and a personal sense of well-being. It appears that a hectic daily schedule increases hassles, decreases uplifts, and diminishes their subjective sense of how well they feel (Erlandsson & Eklund, 2003). However, items viewed as uplifts by some people may actually be stressors for others. For middle-aged people, uplifts are often health- or family-related, whereas for college students uplifts often take the form of having a good time (Kanner et al., 1981).

◆ *What roles do hassles and uplifts play in the stress of life, according to Lazarus?*

◆ **hassles**
Little stressors, including the irritating demands that can occur daily, that may cause more stress than major life changes do.

◆ **uplifts**
The positive experiences in life, which may neutralize the effects of many hassles.

TABLE 10.1	**The Ten Most Common Hassles for College Students**	
HASSLE		**PERCENTAGE OF TIMES CHECKED**
1. Troubling thoughts about future		76.6
2. Not getting enough sleep		72.5
3. Wasting time		71.1
4. Inconsiderate smokers		70.7
5. Physical appearance		69.9
6. Too many things to do		69.2
7. Misplacing or losing things		67.0
8. Not enough time to do the things you need to do		66.3
9. Concerns about meeting high standards		64.0
10. Being lonely		60.8

Source: Kanner et al. (1981).

Making Choices

◆ *How do approach-approach, avoidance-avoidance, and approach-avoidance conflicts differ?*

What happens when you have to decide which movie to see or which new restaurant to try? Simply making a choice, even among equally desirable alternatives (an **approach-approach conflict**), can be stressful. Some approach-approach conflicts are minor, such as deciding which movie to see. Others can have major consequences, such as the conflict between building a promising career or interrupting that career to raise a child. In an **avoidance-avoidance conflict**, a person must choose between two undesirable alternatives. For example, you may want to avoid studying for an exam, but at the same time you want to avoid failing the test. An **approach-avoidance conflict** involves a single choice that has both desirable and undesirable features. The person facing this type of conflict is simultaneously drawn to and repelled by a choice—for example, wanting to take a wonderful vacation but having to empty a savings account to do so.

Unpredictability and Lack of Control

◆ *How do the unpredictability and lack of control over a stressor affect its impact?*

"Good morning, class. Today, we are going to have a pop quiz," your professor says. Do these words cause a fight-or-flight response in your body? Such reactions are common, because unpredictable stressors are more difficult to cope with than predictable stressors. Laboratory tests have shown that rats receiving electric shocks without warning develop more ulcers than rats given shocks just as often but only after receiving a warning (Weiss, 1972). Likewise, humans who are warned of a stressor before it occurs and have a chance to prepare themselves for it experience less stress than those who must cope with an unexpected stressor.

Our physical and psychological well-being is profoundly influenced by the degree to which we feel a sense of control over our lives (Rodin & Salovey, 1989). Langer and Rodin (1976) studied the effects of control on nursing-home residents. Residents in one group were given some measure of control over their lives, such as choices in arranging their rooms and in the times they could see movies. They showed improved health and well-being and had a lower death rate than another group who were not given such control. Within 18 months, 30% of the residents given no choices had died, compared with only 15% of those who had been given some control over their lives. Control is important for cancer patients, too. Some researchers suggest that a sense of control over their daily physical symptoms and emotional reactions may be even more important for cancer patients than control over the course of the disease itself (Thompson et al., 1993).

Several studies suggest that we are less subject to stress when we have the power to do something about it, whether we exercise that power or not (John, 2004). Glass and Singer (1972) subjected two groups of participants to the same loud noise. Participants in one group were told that they could, if necessary, terminate the noise by pressing a switch. These participants suffered less stress, even though they never did exercise the control they were given. Friedland and others (1992) suggest that when people experience a loss of control because of a stressor, they are motivated to try to reestablish control in the stressful situation. Failing this, they often attempt to increase their sense of control in other areas of their lives.

◆ **approach-approach conflict**

A conflict arising from having to choose between equally desirable alternatives.

◆ **avoidance-avoidance conflict**

A conflict arising from having to choose between undesirable alternatives.

◆ **approach-avoidance conflict**

A conflict arising when the same choice has both desirable and undesirable features.

Stress in the Workplace

◆ *For people to function effectively and find satisfaction on the job, what nine variables should fall within their comfort zone?*

Perhaps there is no more troublesome source of stress than the workplace. Everyone who works is subject to some job-related stress, but the amount and sources of the stress differ, depending on the type of job and the kind of organization. Albrecht (1979) suggests that if people are to function effectively and find satisfaction on the job, the following nine variables must fall within their comfort zone (see also Figure 10.1):

FIGURE 10.1   **Variables in Work Stress**

For a person to function effectively and find satisfaction on the job, these nine variables should fall within the person's comfort zone.   *Source:* Albrecht (1979).

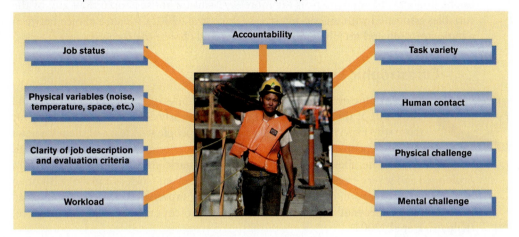

- *Workload.* Too much or too little to do can cause people to feel anxious, frustrated, and unrewarded.
- *Clarity of job description and evaluation criteria.* Anxiety arises from confusion about job responsibilities and performance criteria or from a job description that is too rigidly defined to leave room for individual initiative.
- *Physical variables.* Temperature, noise, humidity, pollution, amount of workspace, and the physical positions (standing or sitting) required to carry out job duties should fall within a person's comfort zone.
- *Job status.* People with very low-paying, low-status jobs may feel psychological discomfort; those with celebrity status often cannot handle the stress that fame brings.
- *Accountability.* Accountability overload occurs when people have responsibility for the physical or psychological well-being of others but only a limited degree of control (air-traffic controllers, emergency room nurses and doctors); accountability underload occurs when workers perceive their jobs as meaningless.
- *Task variety.* To function well, people need a comfortable amount of variety and stimulation.
- *Human contact.* Some workers have virtually no human contact on the job (forest-fire lookouts); others have almost continuous contact with others (welfare and employment office workers). People vary greatly in how much interaction they enjoy or even tolerate.
- *Physical challenge.* Jobs range from being physically demanding (construction work, professional sports) to requiring little to no physical activity. Some jobs (firefighting, police work) involve physical risk.
- *Mental challenge.* Jobs that tax people beyond their mental capability, as well as those that require too little mental challenge, can be frustrating.

Workplace stress can be especially problematic for women because of sex-specific stressors, including sex discrimination and sexual harassment in the workplace and difficulties in combining work and family roles. These added stressors have been shown to increase the negative effects of occupational stress on the health and well-being of working women (Swanson, 2000).

Air-traffic controllers have an extremely high-stress job. The on-the-job stress they experience increases the risk of coronary disease and stroke.

Job stress can have a variety of consequences. Perhaps the most frequently cited is reduced effectiveness on the job. But job stress can also lead to absenteeism, tardiness, accidents, substance abuse, and lower morale (Wilhelm et al., 2004). However, as you might predict, unemployment is far more stressful for most people than any of the variables associated with on-the-job stress (Price et al., 2002). Given a choice between a high-stress job and no job at all, most of us would choose the former.

Catastrophic Events

◆ *How do people typically react to catastrophic events?*

Catastrophic events such as the terrorist attacks of September 11, 2001, and the crash of the space shuttle Columbia in early 2003 are stressful both for those who experience them directly and for people who learn of them via news media. Most people are able to manage the stress associated with such catastrophes. However, for some, these events lead to **posttraumatic stress disorder (PTSD),** a prolonged and severe stress reaction to a catastrophic event (such as a plane crash or an earthquake) or to severe, chronic stress (such as that experienced by soldiers engaged in combat or residents of neighborhoods in which violent crime is a daily occurrence) (Kilpatrick et al., 2003).

The potential impact of catastrophic events on the incidence of PTSD is illustrated by surveys conducted before and after September 11, 2001. Prior to the terrorist attacks, most surveys found that between 1% and 2% of Americans met the diagnostic criteria for PTSD (Foa & Meadows, 1997). Two months after the attacks, about 17% of Americans surveyed by researchers at the University of California–Irvine reported symptoms of PTSD. When the researchers conducted follow-up interviews with survey participants 6 months after the attacks, 6% of them were still experiencing distress. Other researchers have found additional lingering effects associated with September 11 (see Figure 10.2). As you might predict, however, individuals with a personal connection to the events of September 11 were more likely to experience long-term symptoms of PTSD. For example, a survey of flight attendants conducted in summer 2002 found that 17% of them continued to suffer from PTSD symptoms (Lating et al., 2004).

People with PTSD often have flashbacks, nightmares, or intrusive memories that make them feel as though they are actually reexperiencing the traumatic event. They suffer increased anxiety and startle easily, particularly in response to anything that reminds them of the trauma (Green et al., 1985). Many survivors of war or catastrophic events experience *survivor guilt* because they lived while others died; some feel that

◆ **posttraumatic stress disorder (PTSD)**

A prolonged and severe stress reaction to a catastrophic event or to severe, chronic stress.

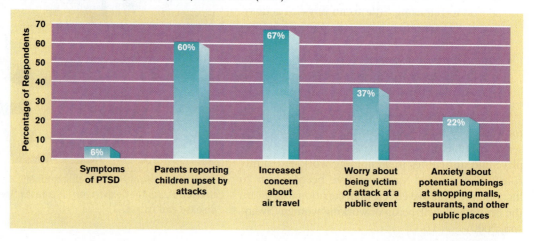

FIGURE 10.2 Americans' Stress Levels after September 11, 2001

Researchers have found that Americans continued to experience increased levels of stress and anxiety several months after the terrorist attacks of September 11, 2001. *Sources:* Clay (2002), Clay et al. (2002), Schlenger et al. (2002), Silver et al. (2002).

perhaps they could have done more to save others. Extreme combat-related guilt in Vietnam veterans is a risk factor for suicide or preoccupation with suicide (Hendin & Haas, 1991). One study of women with PTSD revealed that they were twice as likely as women without PTSD to experience first-onset depression and three times as likely to develop alcohol problems (Breslau et al., 1997). PTSD sufferers also experience cognitive difficulties, such as poor concentration (Vasterling et al., 2002).

Racism and Stress

A significant source of chronic stress is being a member of a minority group in a majority culture. A study of White and African American participants' responses to a questionnaire about ways of managing stress revealed that a person may experience racial stress from simply being one of the few or only members of a particular race in any of a variety of settings, such as a classroom, the workplace, or a social situation (Plummer & Slane, 1996). The feelings of stress experienced in such situations can be intense, even in the absence of racist attitudes, discrimination, or any other overt evidence of racism.

◆ How might historical racism affect the health of African Americans?

Some theorists have proposed that a phenomenon called *historical racism*—experienced by members of groups that have a history of repression—can also be a source of stress (Troxel et al., 2003). Researchers interested in the effects of historical racism have focused primarily on African Americans. Many of these researchers claim that the higher incidence of high blood pressure among African Americans is attributable to stress associated with historical racism. Surveys have shown that African Americans experience more race-related stress than members of other minority groups do (Utsey et al., 2002). Those African Americans who express the highest levels of concern about racism display higher levels of cardiovascular reactivity to experimentally induced stressors, such as sudden loud noises, than do peers who express less concern (Bowen-Reid & Harrell, 2002). At least one study has demonstrated a correlation between African Americans' perceptions of racism and hypertension (Din-Dzietham et al., 2004). Researchers found that African Americans who reported the highest levels of race-related stressors in their workplaces were more likely to have high blood pressure than workers who reported fewer such stressors.

African Americans are also more likely than members of other minority groups to have a strong sense of ethnic identity, a factor that helps moderate the effects of racial stress (Utsey et al., 2002). But some studies show that personal characteristics, such as hostility, may increase the effects of racial stress (Fang & Myers, 2001; Raeikkoenen et al., 2003). So, the relationship between historical racism and cardiovascular health is probably fairly complex and varies considerably across individuals. Moreover, some researchers believe that the association must be studied more thoroughly in other historically oppressed groups, such as Native Americans, before firm conclusions can be drawn (Belcourt-Dittloff & Stewart, 2000).

A strong sense of ethnic identity helps African Americans cope with the stress that may arise from living with racism.

Responding to Stress

◆ **general adaptation syndrome (GAS)**

The predictable sequence of reactions (alarm, resistance, and exhaustion stages) that organisms show in response to stressors.

How do you respond to stress? Psychologists have different views of the ways in which people respond to stressful experiences. Each approach can help us gain insight into our own experiences and, perhaps, deal more effectively with stress.

Selye and the General Adaptation Syndrome

◆ *What is the general adaptation syndrome?*

Hans Selye (1907–1982), the researcher most prominently associated with the effects of stress on health, established the field of stress research. At the heart of Selye's concept of stress is the **general adaptation syndrome (GAS),** the predictable sequence of reactions that organisms show in response to stressors. It consists of three stages: the alarm stage, the resistance stage, and the exhaustion stage (Selye, 1956). (See Figure 10.3.)

The first stage of the body's response to a stressor is the **alarm stage,** in which the adrenal cortex releases hormones called *glucocorticoids* that increase heart rate, blood pressure, and blood-sugar levels, supplying a burst of energy that helps the person deal with the stressful situation (Pennisi, 1997). Next, the organism enters the **resistance stage,** during which the adrenal cortex continues to release glucocorticoids to help the body resist stressors. The length of the resistance stage depends both on the intensity of the stressor and on the body's power to adapt. If the organism finally fails in its efforts to resist, it reaches the **exhaustion stage,** at which point all the stores of deep energy are depleted, and disintegration and death follow.

Selye found that the most harmful effects of stress are due to the prolonged secretion of glucocorticoids, which can lead to permanent increases in blood pressure, suppression of the immune system, weakening of muscles, and even damage to the hippocampus (Stein-Behrens et al., 1994). Thanks to Selye, the connection between extreme, prolonged stress and certain diseases is now widely accepted by medical experts.

◆ **alarm stage**

The first stage of the general adaptation syndrome, in which the person experiences a burst of energy that aids in dealing with the stressful situation.

◆ **resistance stage**

The second stage of the general adaptation syndrome, when there are intense physiological efforts to either resist or adapt to the stressor.

◆ **exhaustion stage**

The third stage of the general adaptation syndrome, which occurs if the organism fails in its efforts to resist the stressor.

Lazarus's Cognitive Theory of Stress

◆ *What are the roles of primary and secondary appraisals when a person is confronted with a potentially stressful event?*

Is it the stressor itself that upsets us, or the way we think about it? Richard Lazarus (1966; Lazarus & Folkman, 1984) contends that it is not the stressor that causes stress, but rather a person's perception of it. According to Lazarus, when people are confronted with a potentially stressful event, they engage in a cognitive process that involves a primary and a secondary appraisal. A **primary appraisal** is an evaluation of the meaning and significance of the situation—whether its effect on one's well-being is positive, irrelevant, or negative. An

◆ **primary appraisal**

A cognitive evaluation of a potentially stressful event to determine whether its effect is positive, irrelevant, or negative.

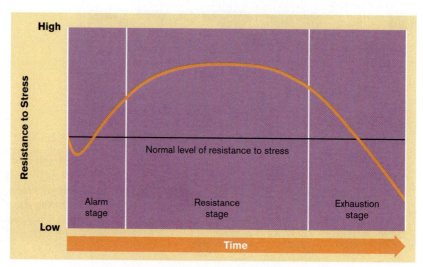

FIGURE 10.3

The General Adaptation Syndrome

The three stages in Selye's general adaptation syndrome are (1) the alarm stage, during which there is emotional arousal and the defensive forces of the body are mobilized for fight or flight; (2) the resistance stage, in which intense physiological efforts are exerted to resist or adapt to the stressor; and (3) the exhaustion stage, when the organism fails in its efforts to resist the stressor. *Source:* Selye (1956).

event appraised as stressful could involve (1) harm or loss—that is, damage that has already occurred; (2) threat, or the potential for harm or loss; or (3) challenge—that is, the opportunity to grow or to gain. An appraisal of threat, harm, or loss can occur in relation to anything important to you—a friendship, a part of your body, your property, your finances, your self-esteem. When people appraise a situation as involving threat, harm, or loss, they experience negative emotions such as anxiety, fear, anger, and resentment (Folkman, 1984). An appraisal that sees a challenge, on the other hand, is usually accompanied by positive emotions such as excitement, hopefulness, and eagerness.

During **secondary appraisal**, if people judge the situation to be within their control, they make an evaluation of available resources—physical (health, energy, stamina), social (support network), psychological (skills, morale, self-esteem), material (money, tools, equipment), and time. Then, they consider the options and decide how to deal with the stressor. The level of stress they feel is largely a function of whether their resources are adequate to cope with the threat, and how severely those resources will be taxed in the process. Figure 10.4 summarizes the Lazarus and Folkman psychological model of stress. Research supports their claim that the physiological, emotional, and behavioral reactions to stressors depend partly on whether the stressors are appraised as challenging or threatening.

◆ **secondary appraisal**
A cognitive evaluation of available resources and options prior to deciding how to deal with a stressor.

Coping Strategies

If you're like most people, the stresses you have experienced have helped you develop some coping strategies. **Coping** refers to a person's efforts through action and thought to deal with demands perceived as taxing or overwhelming. **Problem-focused coping** is direct; it consists of reducing, modifying, or eliminating the source of stress itself. If you are getting a poor grade in history and appraise this as a threat, you may study harder, talk over your problem with your professor, form a study group with other class members, get a tutor, or drop the course.

Emotion-focused coping involves reappraising a stressor an effort to reduce its emotional impact. Research has shown that emotion-focused coping can be a very effective way of managing stress (Austenfeld & Stanton, 2004). If you lose your job, you may decide that it isn't a major tragedy and instead view it as a challenge, an opportunity to

◆ *What is the difference between problem-focused and emotion-focused coping?*

◆ **coping**
Efforts through action and thought to deal with demands that are perceived as taxing or overwhelming.

◆ **problem-focused coping**
A direct response aimed at reducing, modifying, or eliminating a source of stress.

◆ **emotion-focused coping**
A response involving reappraisal of a stressor to reduce its emotional impact.

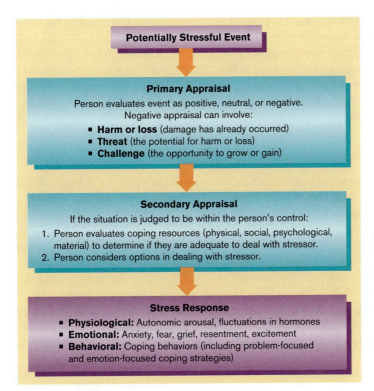

FIGURE 10.4

Lazarus and Folkman's Psychological Model of Stress

Lazarus and Folkman emphasize the importance of a person's perceptions and appraisal of stressors. The stress response depends on the outcome of the primary and secondary appraisals, whether the person's coping resources are adequate to cope with the threat, and how severely the resources are taxed in the process. *Source:* Folkman (1984).

REVIEW and REFLECT 10.1

Theories of Stress Responses

THEORY	DESCRIPTION
Selye's general adaptation syndrome (GAS)	Three stages: alarm, resistance, and exhaustion
Lazarus's cognitive theory	Primary appraisal (evaluation of stressor), followed by secondary appraisal (evaluation of resources and options)
Coping strategies	Problem-focused coping, directed toward stressor; emotion-focused coping, directed toward the emotional response to the stressor

find a better job with a higher salary. Despite what you may have heard, ignoring a stressor—one form of emotion-focused coping—can be an effective way of managing stress. Researchers studied 116 people who had experienced heart attacks (Ginzburg et al., 2002). All of the participants reported being worried about suffering another attack. However, those who tried to ignore their worries were less likely to exhibit anxiety-related symptoms such as nightmares and flashbacks. Other emotion-focused strategies, though, such as keeping a journal in which you write about your worries and track how they change over time, may be even more effective (Pennebaker & Seagal, 1999; Solano et al., 2003).

A combination of problem-focused and emotion-focused coping is probably the best stress-management strategy (Folkman & Lazarus, 1980). For example, a heart patient may ignore her anxiety (emotion-focused coping) while conscientiously adopting recommended lifestyle changes such as increasing exercise (problem-focused coping).

Review and Reflect 10.1 summarizes the key aspects of the various theories concerning humans' response to stress.

Health and Illness

Have you heard the term *wellness* and wondered exactly what was meant by it? This word is associated with a new approach to thinking about health, used by both professionals and laypersons. This approach encompasses a growing emphasis on lifestyle, preventive care, and the need to maintain wellness rather than thinking of health matters only when the body is sick. Health psychologists are discovering how stress, through its influence on the immune system, may affect people's health. They are also examining how personal and demographic factors are related to both illness and wellness.

Two Approaches to Health and Illness

◆ **biomedical model**
A perspective that explains illness solely in terms of biological factors.

◆ **biopsychosocial model**
A perspective that focuses on health as well as illness and holds that both are determined by a combination of biological, psychological, and social factors.

◆ *How do the biomedical and biopsychosocial models differ in their approaches to health and illness?*

◆ **health psychology**
The subfield within psychology that is concerned with the psychological factors that contribute to health, illness, and recovery.

For many decades, the predominant view in medicine was the **biomedical model,** which explains illness in terms of biological factors. Today, physicians and psychologists alike recognize that the **biopsychosocial model** provides a fuller explanation of both health and illness (see Figure 10.5) (Engel, 1977, 1980; Schwartz, 1982). This model considers health and illness to be determined by a combination of biological, psychological, and social factors.

Growing acceptance of the biopsychosocial approach has given rise to a new subfield, **health psychology,** which is "the field within psychology devoted to understanding psychological influences on how people stay healthy, why they become ill, and how they respond when they do get ill" (Taylor, 1991, p. 6). Health psychology is particularly important today because several prevalent diseases, including heart disease and cancer, are related to unhealthy lifestyles and stress (Taylor & Repetti, 1997).

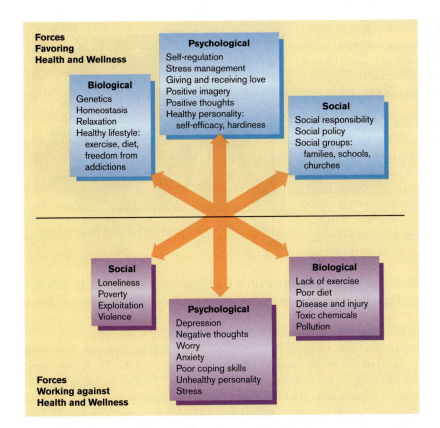

FIGURE 10.5

The Biopsychosocial Model of Health and Illness

The biopsychosocial model focuses on health as well as on illness and holds that both are determined by a combination of biological, psychological, and social factors. Most health psychologists endorse the biopsychosocial model. *Source:* Green & Shellenberger (1990).

Coronary Heart Disease

To survive, the heart muscle requires a steady, sufficient supply of oxygen and nutrients carried by the blood. Coronary heart disease is caused by the narrowing or the blockage of the coronary arteries, the arteries that supply blood to the heart muscle. Although coronary heart disease remains the leading cause of death in the United States, responsible for 28% of all deaths, deaths due to this cause have declined 50% during the past 30 years (National Center for Health Statistics, 2004).

A health problem of modern times, coronary heart disease is largely attributable to lifestyle and is therefore an important field of study for health psychologists. A *sedentary lifestyle*—one that includes a job at which one spends most of the time sitting and less than 20 minutes of exercise three times per week—is the primary modifiable risk factor contributing to death from coronary heart disease (Gallo et al., 2003). Other modifiable risk factors are high serum cholesterol level, cigarette smoking, and obesity.

Though not modifiable, another important risk factor is family history. The association between family history and coronary heart disease is both genetic and behavioral. For instance, individuals whose parents have high blood pressure, but who have not yet developed the disorder themselves, exhibit the same kinds of emotional reactivity and poor coping strategies as their parents (Frazer et al., 2002).

High levels of stress and job strain have also been associated with increased risk for coronary heart disease and stroke (Rosengren et al., 1991; Siegrist et al., 1990). Apparently, the effects of stress enter the bloodstream almost as if they were injected intravenously. Malkoff and others (1993) report that after an experimental group of participants had experienced laboratory-induced stress, their blood platelets (special clotting cells) released large amounts of a substance that promotes the buildup of plaque in blood vessels and may lead to heart attack and stroke. No changes were found in the blood platelets of unstressed control-group participants.

Personality type is also associated with an individual's risk of heart disease. After extensive research, cardiologists Meyer Friedman and Ray Rosenman (1974) concluded that there are two types of personality: Type A, associated with a high rate of coronary

◆ *What are the Type A and Type B behavior patterns?*

heart disease, and Type B, commonly found in persons unlikely to develop heart disease. Do you have characteristics similar to those of a Type A or a Type B person? Before reading further, complete *Try It 10.2* and find out.

People with the **Type A behavior pattern** have a strong sense of time urgency and are impatient, excessively competitive, hostile, and easily angered. They are "involved in a chronic, incessant struggle to achieve more and more in less and less time" (Friedman & Rosenman, 1974, p. 84).

Hostility is a key component of the Type A behavior pattern.

Type A's would answer "true" to most or all of the questions in the *Try It*. In contrast, people with the **Type B behavior pattern** are relaxed and easygoing and are not driven by a sense of time urgency. They are not impatient or hostile and are able to relax without guilt. They play for fun and relaxation rather than to exhibit superiority over others. Yet, a Type B individual may be as bright and ambitious as a Type A person, and more successful as well. Type B's would answer "false" to most or all of the *Try It* questions.

Using meta-analysis, Miller and others (1991) found that 70% of middle-aged men with coronary heart disease exhibited the Type A behavior pattern, compared to 46% of healthy middle-aged men. Research indicates that the lethal core of the Type A personality is not time urgency but anger and hostility, which fuel an aggressive, reactive

Try It 10.2

Type A or Type B?

Answer true (T) or false (F) for each of the statements below. (Adapted from Friedman & Rosenman, 1974.)

_____ 1. I forcefully emphasize key words in my everyday speech.

_____ 2. I usually walk and eat quickly.

_____ 3. I get irritated and restless around slow workers.

_____ 4. When talking to others, I get impatient and try to hurry them along.

_____ 5. I get very irritated, even hostile, when the car in front of me drives too slowly.

_____ 6. When others are talking, I often think about my own concerns.

_____ 7. I usually think of or do at least two things at the same time.

_____ 8. I get very impatient when I have to wait.

_____ 9. I usually take command and move the conversation to topics that interest me.

_____ 10. I usually feel guilty when I relax and do nothing.

_____ 11. I am usually too absorbed in my work to notice my surroundings.

_____ 12. I keep trying to do more and more in less time.

_____ 13. I sometimes punctuate my conversation with forceful gestures such as clenching my fists or pounding the table.

_____ 14. My accomplishments are due largely to my ability to work faster than others.

_____ 15. I don't play games just for fun. I play to win.

_____ 16. I am more concerned with acquiring things than with becoming a better person.

_____ 17. I usually use numbers to evaluate my own activities and the activities of others.

temperament (Miller et al., 1996; Räikkönen, et al., 2004; Smith & Ruiz, 2002; Williams, 1993). Hostility is not only highly predictive of coronary heart disease but is also associated with ill health in general (Miller et al., 1996).

Cancer

◆ How do psychological factors influence cancer patients' quality of life?

Cancer is the second leading cause of death in the United States, accounting for 22% of all deaths (National Center for Health Statistics, 2004). Cancer strikes frequently in the adult population, and about 30% of Americans—more than 75 million people—will develop cancer at some time in their lives. The young are not spared the scourge of cancer, for it takes the lives of more children aged 3 to 14 than any other disease.

Cancer, a collection of diseases rather than a single illness, can invade cells in any part of a living organism—humans, other animals, and even plants. Normal cells in all parts of the body divide, but fortunately they have built-in instructions about when to stop dividing. Unlike normal cells, cancer cells do not stop dividing. And, unless caught in time and destroyed, they continue to grow and spread, eventually killing the organism. Health psychologists point out that an unhealthy diet, smoking, excessive alcohol consumption, promiscuous sexual behavior, or becoming sexually active in the early teens (especially for females) are all behaviors that increase the risk of cancer.

The more than 1 million people in the United States who are diagnosed with cancer each year have the difficult task of adjusting to a potentially life-threatening disease and the chronic stressors associated with it. Thus, researchers claim that cancer patients need more than medical treatment. Their therapy should include help with psychological and behavioral factors that can influence their quality of life. Carver and others (1993) found that 3 months and 6 months after surgery, breast cancer patients who maintained an optimistic outlook, accepted the reality of their situation, and maintained a sense of humor experienced less distress. Patients who engaged in denial—refusal to accept the reality of their situation—and had thoughts of giving up experienced much higher levels of distress. Dunkel-Schetter and others (1992) found that the most effective elements of a strategy for coping with cancer were social support (such as through self-help groups), a focus on the positive, and distraction. Avoidant coping strategies such as fantasizing, denial, and social withdrawal were associated with more emotional distress.

This group of cancer patients is involved in art therapy, which is believed to lower the stress level associated with having a serious illness.

The Immune System and Stress

◆ *What are the effects of stress on the immune system?*

Composed of an army of highly specialized cells and organs, the immune system works to identify and search out and destroy bacteria, viruses, fungi, parasites, and any other foreign matter that may enter the body. The key components of the immune system are white blood cells known as **lymphocytes,** which include B cells and T cells. *B cells* are so named because they are produced in the bone marrow. *T cells* derive their name from the thymus gland where they are produced. All cells foreign to the body, such as bacteria, viruses, and so on, are known as *antigens*. B cells produce proteins called *antibodies*, which are highly effective in destroying antigens that live in the bloodstream and in the fluid surrounding body tissues (Paul, 1993). For defeating harmful foreign invaders that have taken up residence inside the body's cells, however, T cells are critically important.

Psychoneuroimmunology is a field of study in which psychologists, biologists, and medical researchers combine their expertise to learn the effects of psychological factors—emotions, thinking, and behavior—on the immune system (Fleshner & Laudenslager, 2004). Researchers now know that the immune system is not just a means for fighting off foreign invaders. Rather, it is an incredibly complex, interconnected defense system working with the brain to keep the body healthy (Ader, 2000).

Psychological factors, emotions, and stress are all related to immune system functioning (Kiecolt-Glaser et al., 2002). The immune system exchanges information with the brain, and what goes on in the brain can apparently enhance or suppress the immune system. In one study, researchers gave volunteers nasal drops containing a cold virus. Within the next few days, symptoms of the viral infection rose sharply in some of the 151 women and 125 men who participated in the study, but less so or not at all in others. Participants with a rich social life in the form of frequent interactions with others—spouses, children, parents, co-workers, friends, and volunteer and religious groups—seemed to enjoy a powerful shield of protection against the virus infection. This pattern of protection held across age and racial groups, for both sexes, at all educational levels, and at every season of the year (Ader, 2000; Cohen et al., 1997).

Close social ties—to family, friends, and others—apparently have good effects on the immune system. Ill effects often come from stress. Periods of high stress are correlated with increased symptoms of many infectious diseases, including oral and genital herpes, mononucleosis, colds, and flu. Stress may also decrease the effectiveness of certain kinds of vaccines (Miller et al., 2004; Moynihan et al., 2004) and decrease levels of the immune system's B and T cells. Kiecolt-Glaser and others (1996) found that elderly men and women experiencing chronic stress as a result of years of caring for a spouse with Alzheimer's disease showed an impaired immune response to flu shots. Physicians have long observed that stress and anxiety can worsen autoimmune diseases. And "if fear can produce relapses [in autoimmune diseases], then even the fear of a relapse may become a self-fulfilling prophecy" (Steinman, 1993, p. 112). Stress is also associated with an increase in illness behaviors—reporting physical symptoms and seeking medical care (Cohen & Herbert, 1996; Cohen & Williamson, 1991).

Stress has the power to suppress the immune system long after the stressful experience is over. An experimental group of medical students who were enduring the stress of major exams was compared with a control group of medical students who were on vacation from classes and exams. When tested for the presence of disease-fighting antibodies, participants in the exam group, but not those in the control group, had a significant reduction in their antibody count because of the stress. The lowered antibody count was still present 14 days after the exams were over. At that point, the students were not even aware that they were still stressed and reported feeling no stress (Deinzer et al., 2000).

In addition to academic pressures, poor marital relationships and sleep deprivation have been linked to lowered immune response (Kiecolt-Glaser et al., 1987; Maier & Laudenslager, 1985). Several researchers have reported that severe, incapacitating depression is also related to lowered immune system activity (Herbert & Cohen, 1993). For several months after the death of a spouse, the widow or widower suffers weakened immune system function and is at a higher risk of mortality. Severe bereavement weakens

---

◆ **lymphocytes**

The white blood cells—including B cells and T cells—that are the key components of the immune system.

◆ **psychoneuroimmunology**

(sye-ko-NEW-ro-IM-you-NOLL-oh-gee) A field in which psychologists, biologists, and medical researchers combine their expertise to study the effects of psychological factors on the immune system.

the immune system, increasing a person's chance of suffering from a long list of physical and mental ailments for as long as 2 years following a partner's death (Prigerson et al., 1997).

Personal Factors Reducing the Impact of Stress and Illness

There are several personal factors that seem to offer protection against the effects of stress and illness. People who are generally optimistic tend to cope more effectively with stress, which, in turn may reduce their risk of illness (Seligman, 1990). An important characteristic shared by optimists is that they generally expect good outcomes. Such positive expectations help make them more stress-resistant than pessimists, who tend to expect bad outcomes. Similarly, individuals who are optimistic seem to be able to find positives even in the darkest of circumstances (Rini et al., 2004). An especially lethal form of pessimism is hopelessness. A longitudinal study of a large number of Finnish men revealed that participants who reported feeling moderate to high hopelessness died from all causes at two to three times the rates of those reporting low or no hopelessness (Everson et al., 1996).

In addition, studying male executives with high levels of stress, psychologist Suzanne Kobasa (1979; Kobasa et al., 1982) found three psychological characteristics that distinguished those who remained healthy from those who had a high incidence of illness. The three qualities, which she referred to collectively as **hardiness**, are *commitment*, *control*, and *challenge*. Hardy individuals feel a strong sense of commitment to both their work and their personal life. They see themselves not as victims of whatever life brings, but as people who have control over consequences and outcomes. They act to solve their own problems, and they welcome challenges in life, viewing them not as threats but as opportunities for growth and improvement. Other researchers have found that the dimensions of hardiness are related to the subjective sense of well-being among the elderly (Smith et al., 2004).

Another personal factor that contributes to resistance to stress and illness is religious faith (Dedert et al., 2004; Miller & Thoresen, 2003). A meta-analysis of 42 separate studies combined data on some 126,000 individuals and revealed that religious involvement is positively associated with measures of physical health and lower rates of cancer, heart disease, and stroke (McCullough et al., 2000). Why is religious involvement linked to health? Researchers are currently examining a number of hypotheses (Powell et al., 2003). One proposal is that individuals who frequent religious services experience proportionately more positive emotions than those who do not attend.

Religious involvement may also provide people with a stronger form of social support than is available to those who are not religious (Seeman et al., 2003). **Social support** is support provided, usually in time of need, by a spouse, other family members, friends, neighbors, colleagues, support groups, or others. It can involve tangible aid, information, and advice, as well as emotional support. It can also be viewed as the feeling of being loved, valued, and cared for by those toward whom we feel a similar obligation.

Social support appears to have positive effects on the body's immune system as well as on the cardiovascular and endocrine systems (Moynihan et al., 2004; Holt-Lunstad et al., 2003; Miller et al., 2002; Uchino et al., 1996). Social support may help encourage health-promoting behaviors and reduce the impact of stress so that people are less likely to resort to unhealthy methods of coping, such as smoking or drinking. Further, social support has been shown to reduce depression and enhance self-esteem in individuals who suffer from chronic illnesses such as kidney disease (Symister & Friend, 2003). A large study of soldiers who had enlisted in the U.S. Army showed that a high level of social support from peers

◆ *What four personal factors are associated with health and resistance to stress?*

◆ **hardiness**
A combination of three psychological qualities—commitment, control, and challenge—shared by people who can handle high levels of stress and remain healthy.

◆ **social support**
Tangible and/or emotional support provided in time of need by family members, friends, and others; the feeling of being loved, valued, and cared for by those toward whom we feel a similar obligation.

A strong social support network can help a person recover faster from an illness.

was an essential ingredient in reducing stress (Bliese & Castro, 2000). People with social support recover more quickly from illnesses and lower their risk of death from specific diseases. Social support may even increase the probability of surviving a heart attack because it buffers the impact of stress on cardiovascular function (Steptoe, 2000).

Gender, Ethnicity, and Health

◆ What are the relationships among gender, ethnicity, and health?

The degree of wellness and the leading health risk factors are not the same for all Americans (CDC, 2003a). For example, researchers have found that women are more likely than men to seek medical care (Addis & Mahalik, 2003). Nevertheless, most medical research in the past, much of it funded by the U.S. government, rejected women as participants in favor of men (Matthews et al., 1997). One area where the failure to study women's health care needs has been particularly evident is in research examining mortality risk following open-heart surgery. Women are more likely to die after such surgery than are men. To date, studies have shown that the gender gap in surgical survival narrows with age, but researchers are still investigating why women's postsurgical mortality rate is higher than men's (Vaccarino et al., 2002). Women are also slighted in general health care and treatment (Rodin & Ickovics, 1990). Physicians are more likely to see women's health complaints as "emotional" in nature rather than due to physical causes (Council on Ethical and Judicial Affairs, American Medical Association [AMA], 1991).

There are health disparities across ethnic groups as well. For example, African American infants are at twice the risk of death within their first year of life as White American infants (CDC, 2005). Compared to White Americans, African Americans have higher rates of diabetes, arthritis, and, as you learned earlier in this chapter, high blood pressure (National Center for Health Statistics, 2004). African Americans are 40% more likely than White Americans to die of heart disease and 30% more likely to die of cancer. Even when African and White Americans of the same age suffer from similar illnesses, the mortality rate of African Americans is higher (CDC, 2003a). And the rate of AIDS is more than three times higher among African Americans than among White Americans.

Hispanic Americans account for more than 20% of new tuberculosis cases in the United States (CDC, 2003a). Hypertension and diabetes are also more prevalent among Hispanic Americans than among non-Hispanic White Americans, but heart problems are less prevalent (CDC, 2005). Rates of diabetes are also dramatically higher among Native Americans than for other groups (CDC, 2005). In addition, the infant mortality rate among Native Americans is two times higher than among Whites (CDC, 2005).

Asian Americans, who make up 3.6% of the U.S. population, are comparatively very healthy. However, there are wide disparities among subgroups. For example, Vietnamese women are five times more likely to suffer from cervical cancer than White women are (CDC, 2005). Similarly, the overall age-adjusted death rate for Asian American males is 40% lower than that for White American males, but their death rate from stroke is 8% higher. Of all U.S. ethnic groups, infant mortality is lowest for Chinese Americans, at 3 deaths per 1,000 births, compared with 7 per 1,000 for the overall population (National Center for Health Statistics, 2000).

Some of the variations in health across ethnic groups can be explained by socioeconomic status (Franks, et al., 2003). African Americans, Hispanic Americans, and Native Americans are more likely to be poor than their White counterparts. Health psychologist Edith Chen points out that poverty predisposes individuals—and particularly children—to poor health for a number of reasons (Chen, 2004). One important reason is lack of access to health care. Another is stress—individuals who live in poverty are exposed to more physical and psychological stress than others. Nevertheless, changes in health-related behaviors such as dietary choices and exercise benefit individuals who are poor just as much as they do more affluent people, so taking steps to ensure that individuals across all racial groups are aware of these behaviors are likely to bring about improvements in health for all concerned (Beets & Pitetti, 2004; CDC, 2005).

How Did You Find **Psychology?**

Edith Chen

Where would you expect to find a gifted 14-year-old with a keen interest in science? You might be surprised to learn that adolescents with these characteristics, such health psychology researcher Edith Chen, are often accepted as volunteeer research assistants in university labs.

That route is precisely how Chen got her start in research. While still in high school, she worked at the University of Miami doing research on the effects of neurotransmitters on muscle fiber contraction. The professor she assisted even let Chen present a paper at a scientific conference, as she puts it, "before [I] was old enough to appreciate (and be intimidated by) the reputation of established leaders in the field" ("Edith Chen," 2004, p. 707).

Ever the ambitious student, Chen began her undergraduate work at Harvard University intending to pursue a double major in chemistry and philosophy. However, when she found out that she would have to do a senior thesis integrating the two fields, she looked elsewhere for a major. She inadvertently discovered the interdisciplinary major known as history of science and was intrigued by the opportunity it offered to take a combination of science and liberal arts courses. When she took an abnormal psychology course in her junior year, the professor invited her to work on a research project examining memory bias and anxiety. The project sparked her interest in applying to graduate programs in clinical psy-

chology. Because Chen had taken only one psychology course, she thought she wouldn't be able to get in. Her professor encouraged her to take introductory psychology and a statistics class prior to applying to graduate school. With his help, she was admitted to the program at the University of California–Los Angeles.

At UCLA, Chen initially continued the work on memory bias and anxiety that had first interested her at Harvard. Eventually, UCLA's health psychology program caught her attention. She worked with faculty in the program to apply her interests in anxiety to issues related to pain management. Her dissertation dealt with helping children with cancer learn to reflect on their memories of treatment in ways that helped to minimize their anxiety responses to future treatments.

After receiving her Ph.D., Chen worked as a postdoctoral fellow at the University of Pittsburgh. While there, she began the research program examining correlations between immune system functioning and socioeconomic status that she continues to pursue today. Currently, Chen is investigating these correlations in children who suffer from asthma.

Chen's story is similar to that of many young researchers in that her career path has been strongly shaped by mentors. If her first psychology professor hadn't been willing to help her get into graduate school, Chen might have dismissed her interest in graduate work in psychology as beyond her reach as a nonpsychology major. If you have an interest in a particular field, seek out an experienced person who can advise you about the best strategy for pursuing a career in that area.

 ## Lifestyle and Health

Think about your own health for a moment. What do you think is the greatest threat to your personal well-being and longevity? For most Americans, health enemy number one is their own habits—lack of exercise, too little sleep, alcohol or drug abuse, an unhealthy diet, and overeating. What can make someone change an unhealthy lifestyle? Perhaps vanity is the key. Researchers have found that people are more likely to adopt healthy behaviors if they believe behavioral change will make them look better or appear more youthful than if they simply receive information about the health benefits of the suggested change (Mahler et al., 2003). Still, there are some health-threatening behaviors that carry such grave risks that everyone ought to take them seriously. The most dangerous unhealthy behavior of all is smoking.

Smoking and Health

Smoking remains the foremost cause of preventable diseases and deaths in the United States (U.S. Department of Health and Human Services, 2000). That message appears to be taking root because the prevalence of smoking among American adults has been decreasing and is currently less than 25% (National

◆ *What is the most dangerous health-threatening behavior?*

Center for Health Statistics, 2004). Moreover, smoking is more likely to be viewed as a socially unacceptable behavior now than in the past (Chassin et al., 2003). But there are wide variations in smoking habits according to gender and ethnic group. The highest rates of smoking are found among Native American men (41%) and women (29%), while the lowest rates are reported for Asian American men (18%) and women (11%) (U.S. Department of Health and Human Services, 2000).

Even though the prevalence of smoking is decreasing, every year more than 1 million young Americans become regular smokers, and more than 400,000 American adults die from diseases related to tobacco use (U.S. Department of Health and Human Services, 2000). Smoking increases the risk for heart disease, lung cancer, other smoking-related cancers, and emphysema. It is now known that smoking suppresses the action of T cells in the lungs, increasing susceptibility to respiratory tract infections and tumors (McCue et al., 2000).

Other negative consequences from smoking include the widespread incidence of chronic bronchitis and other respiratory problems; the deaths and injuries from fires caused by smoking; and the low birth weight and retarded fetal development in babies born to smoking mothers. Furthermore, mothers who smoke during pregnancy tend to have babies who are at greater risk for anxiety and depression and are five times more likely to become smokers themselves (Cornelius et al., 2000). And millions of non-smokers engage in *passive smoking* by breathing smoke-filled air—with proven ill effects. Research indicates that nonsmokers who are regularly exposed to *second-hand smoke* have twice the risk of heart attack of those who are not exposed (Kawachi et al., 1997)

Because smoking is so addictive, smokers have great difficulty breaking the habit. Even so, 90% of ex-smokers quit smoking on their own (Novello, 1990). The average smoker makes five or six attempts to quit before finally succeeding (Sherman, 1994). Some aids, such as nicotine gum and the nicotine patch, help many people kick the habit. A meta-analysis involving 17 studies and more than 5,000 participants revealed that 22% of people who used the nicotine patch stopped smoking compared with only 9% of those who received a placebo. And 27% of those receiving the nicotine patch plus antismoking counseling or support remained smoke-free (Fiore, cited in Sherman, 1994). But even with the patch, quitting is difficult, because the patch only lessens withdrawal symptoms, which typically last 2 to 4 weeks (Hughes, 1992). Half of all relapses occur within the first 2 weeks after people quit, and relapses are most likely when people are experiencing stressful negative emotions or are using alcohol. It takes just one cigarette, sometimes only one puff, to cause a relapse.

Alcohol Abuse

◆ *What are some health risks of alcohol abuse?*

Do you use alcohol regularly? Many Americans do. Recall from Chapter 4 that *substance abuse* is defined as continued use of a substance that interferes with a person's major life roles at home, in school, at work, or elsewhere and contributes to legal difficulties or any psychological problems (American Psychiatric Association, 1994). Alcohol is perhaps the most frequently abused substance of all, and the health costs of alcohol abuse are staggering—in fatalities, medical bills, lost work, and family problems.

Approximately 10 million Americans are alcoholics (Neimark et al., 1994). Alcohol abuse is three times more prevalent in males than in females (American Psychiatric Association, 2000). And people who begin drinking before age 15 are four times more likely than those who begin later to become alcoholics (Grant & Dawson, 1998). For many, alcohol provides a method of coping with life stresses they feel otherwise powerless to control (Seeman & Seeman, 1992). As many as 80% of men and women who are alcoholics complain of episodes of depression. The presence of depression or other psychiatric problems decreases the likelihood that an alcoholic who enters treatment will recover (Green et al., 2004). A large study of almost 3,000 alcoholics concluded that some depressive episodes are independent of alcohol, whereas others are substance-induced (Schuckit et al., 1997).

Alcohol can damage virtually every organ in the body, but it is especially harmful to the liver and is the major cause of cirrhosis, which kills 26,000 people each year (Neimark et al., 1994). Other causes of death are more common in alcoholics than in nonalcoholics as well. One Norwegian longitudinal study involving more than 40,000 male participants found that the rate of death prior to age 60 was significantly higher among alcoholics than nonalcoholics (Rossow & Amundsen, 1997). Alcoholics are about three times as likely to die in automobile accidents or of heart disease as non-alcoholics, and they have twice the rate of deaths from cancer.

Shrinkage in the cerebral cortex of alcoholics has been found by researchers using MRI scans (Jernigan et al., 1991). CT scans also show brain shrinkage in a high percentage of alcoholics, even in those who are young and in those who show normal cognitive functioning (Lishman, 1990). Moreover, heavy drinking can cause cognitive impairment that continues for several months after the drinking stops (Sullivan et al., 2002). The only good news in recent studies is that some of the effects of alcohol on the brain seem to be partially reversible with prolonged abstinence.

Since the late 1950s, the American Medical Association has maintained that alcoholism is a disease, and once an alcoholic, always an alcoholic. According to this view, even a small amount of alcohol can cause an irresistible craving for more, leading alcoholics to lose control of their drinking (Jellinek, 1960). Thus, total abstinence is seen as the only acceptable and effective method of treatment. Alcoholics Anonymous (AA) also endorses both the disease concept and the total abstinence approach to treatment. And there is a drug that may make abstinence somewhat easier. German researchers report that the drug acamprosate helps prevent relapse in recovering alcoholics (Sass et al., 1996).

Some studies suggest a genetic influence on alcoholism and lend support to the disease model. For example, neuroscientist Henri Begleiter and his colleagues have accumulated a large body of evidence suggesting that the brains of alcoholics respond differently to visual and auditory stimuli than those of nonalcoholics (Hada et al., 2000, 2001; Prabhu et al., 2001). Further, many relatives of alcoholics, even children and adults who have never consumed any alcohol in their lives, display the same types of response patterns (Zhang et al., 2001). The relatives of alcoholics who do display these patterns are more likely to become alcoholics themselves or to suffer from other types of addictions (Anokhin et al., 2000; Beirut et al., 1998). Consequently, Begleiter has suggested that the brain-imaging techniques he uses in his research may someday be used to determine which relatives of alcoholics are genetically predisposed to addiction (Porjesz et al., 1998).

Sexually Transmitted Diseases

What is the most common infectious disease in the United States? You might be surprised to learn that it is *chlamydia*, a sexually transmitted disease (CDC, 2003b). **Sexually transmitted diseases (STDs)** are infections spread primarily through sexual contact. Each year, approximately 15 million Americans contract an STD. The incidence of many STDs has increased dramatically over the past 30 years or so. This trend can be partly explained by more permissive attitudes toward sex and increased sexual activity among young people, some of whom have had several sexual partners by the time they graduate from high school (look back at Figure 8.4 on page 259). Another factor is the greater use of nonbarrier methods of contraception, such as the birth control pill, which do not prevent the spread of STDs. Barrier methods, such as condoms and vaginal spermicide, provide some protection against STDs.

Chlamydia is one of many **bacterial STDs,** diseases that can be cured by antibiotics. It can be transmitted through many kinds of physical contact involving the genitals as well as actual intercourse (CDC, 2003b). Women are about three times as likely as men to suffer from chlamydia. The prevalence of another bacterial STD, *gonorrhea*, has declined considerably in recent years, but the strains that exist today are far more resistant to antibiotics than those that existed decades ago (CDC, 2003b). One of the long-term effects of both chlamydia and gonorrhea is *pelvic inflammatory disease*, an infection of the female reproductive tract that can cause infertility.

◆ *What is the difference between bacterial and viral STD's?*

◆ **sexually transmitted diseases**
Infections that are spread primarily through intimate sexual contact.

◆ **bacterial STDs**
Sexually transmitted diseases that are caused by bacteria and can be treated with antibiotics.

Another bacterial STD is *syphilis*, which can lead to serious mental disorders and death if it is not treated in the early stages of infection. At one time, syphilis had been almost completely eradicated. However, in 2002, about 7,000 cases were reported to the Centers for Disease Control and Prevention (CDC, 2003b). Most of these cases involved homosexual males who live in urban areas (CDC, 2003b). Educating such men about the dangers of syphilis and measures that may be taken to prevent its transmission has become a major focus of public health officials in recent years.

Unlike STDs caused by bacteria, **viral STDs** cannot be treated with antibiotics and are considered to be incurable. One such disease is *genital herpes*, a disease that can be acquired through either intercourse or oral sex. The Centers for Disease Control and Prevention reports that 20% of the adult population in the United States is infected with herpes (CDC, 2001a). Outbreaks of the disease, which include the development of painful blisters on the genitals, occur periodically in most people who carry the virus.

A more serious viral STD is *genital warts* caused by infection with *human papillomavirus (HPV)*. The primary symptom of the disease, the presence of growths on the genitals, is not its most serious effect, however. HPV is strongly associated with cervical cancer (CDC, 2003b). Studies indicate that, in the United States, 25% of women in their twenties, and 10% of women older than the age 30 are infected with HPV (Stone et al., 2002).

The most feared STD is **acquired immune deficiency syndrome (AIDS),** caused by infection with the **human immunodeficiency virus (HIV).** The virus attacks the T cells, gradually but relentlessly weakening the immune system until it is essentially nonfunctional. Although the first case was diagnosed in this country in 1981, there is still no cure for AIDS. However, efforts to develop a way to immunize people against HIV have yielded several potential vaccines, at least one of which is currently being tested on humans (Beyrer, 2003). By the end of 2001, 816,249 cases of AIDS and 467,910 deaths from AIDS had been reported to the Centers for Disease Control and Prevention (2002). Worldwide, in 2001, 3 million people died from AIDS and 40 million people were living with HIV infection (CDC, 2002). Concerns about the HIV-AIDS crisis has been heightened by the recent discovery of a strain of the virus that leads to full-blown AIDS in as short a period as a few months (Lombardi, 2005). Test your knowledge about AIDS in *Try It 10.3*.

Try It 10.3

AIDS Quiz

Answer true or false for each statement.

1. AIDS is a single disease. (true/false)

2. AIDS symptoms vary widely from country to country, and even from risk group to risk group. (true/false)

3. Those at greatest risk for getting AIDS are people who have sex without using condoms, drug users who share needles, and infants born to AIDS-infected mothers. (true/false)

4. AIDS is one of the most highly contagious diseases. (true/false)

5. One way to avoid contracting AIDS is to use an oil-based lubricant with a condom. (true/false)

Answers:

1. **False:** AIDS is not a single disease. Rather, a severely impaired immune system leaves a person with AIDS highly susceptible to a whole host of infections and diseases.

2. **True:** In the United States and Europe, AIDS sufferers may develop Kaposi's sarcoma (a rare form of skin cancer), pneumonia, and tuberculosis. In Africa, people with AIDS usually waste away with fever, diarrhea, and symptoms caused by tuberculosis.

3. **True:** Those groups are at greatest risk. Screening of blood donors and testing of donated blood have greatly reduced the risk of contracting AIDS through blood transfusions. Today, women make up the fastest-growing group of infected people worldwide, as AIDS spreads among heterosexuals, especially in Africa.

4. **False:** AIDS is not among the most highly infectious diseases. You cannot get AIDS from kissing, shaking hands, or using objects handled by people who have AIDS.

5. **False:** Do not use oil-based lubricants, which can eat through condoms. Latex condoms with an effective spermicide are safer. Learn the sexual history of any potential partner, including HIV test results. Don't have sex with prostitutes.

HIV attacks the immune system, leaving it severely impaired and virtually unable to function. The diagnosis of AIDS is made when the immune system is so damaged that victims develop rare forms of cancer or pneumonia or other so-called opportunistic infections. The average time from infection with HIV to advanced AIDS is about 10 years, but the time may range from 2 years to as long as 15 years or more (Nowak & McMichael, 1995). The disease progresses faster in smokers, in the very young, in people older than 50, and, apparently, in women. AIDS also progresses faster in those who are repeatedly exposed to the virus and in those who were infected by someone in an advanced stage of the disease.

Researchers believe that HIV is transmitted primarily through the exchange of blood, semen, or vaginal secretions during sexual contact or when IV (intravenous) drug users share contaminated needles or syringes. Figure 10.6 illustrates the proportion of AIDS cases attributable to each means of transmitting the disease. The rate of AIDS among gay men is higher than in other groups because gay men are likely to have anal intercourse. Anal intercourse is more dangerous than coitus because rectal tissue often tears during penetration, allowing HIV ready entry into the bloodstream.

It is a mistake to view AIDS as a disease confined to gay men, however. About 25% of the AIDS cases reported in the United States in 2001 were females, 40% of whom contracted it through heterosexual contact and 20% through IV drug abuse (CDC, 2002). In Africa, where AIDS is currently epidemic and is believed to have originated, it strikes men and women about equally, and heterosexual activity is believed to be the primary means of transmission (Quinn, 2002). AIDS is transmitted 12 times more easily from infected men to women than vice versa (Padian et al., 1991). AIDS may also be transmitted from mother to child during pregnancy or breast-feeding (Prince, 1998).

What are the psychological effects on people who struggle to cope with this fearsome disease? The reaction to the news that one is HIV-positive is frequently shock, bewilderment, confusion, or disbelief. Stress reactions to the news are typically so common and so acute that experts strongly recommend pretest counseling so that those who do test positive may know in advance what to expect (Maj, 1990). Another common reaction is anger—at past or present sexual partners, family members, health care professionals, or society in general. Often, a person's response includes guilt, a sense that one is being punished for homosexuality or drug abuse. Other people exhibit denial, ignoring medical advice and continuing to act as if nothing has changed in their lives. Then, of course, there is fear—of death; of mental and physical deterioration; of rejection by friends, family, and co-workers; of sexual rejection; of abandonment. Experiencing emotional swings ranging from shock to anger to guilt to fear can lead to serious clinical depression and apathy (Tate et al., 2003). Once apathy sets in, HIV-positive patients may become less likely to comply with treatment (Dorz et al., 2003).

There are only two foolproof ways to protect oneself from becoming infected with an STD through intimate sexual contact. The first is obvious: Abstain from sexual contact. The second is to have a mutually faithful (monogamous) relationship with a partner who is free of infection. Any other course of action will place a person at risk. Much has been written in recent decades about the joy of sex. It is true that the pleasures sex brings to life are many, but fear of STDs may interfere with those pleasures. Thus, safe sex practices are essential—not only for health, but also for the enjoyment of sex.

The producers of *Sesame Street* introduced an HIV-positive Muppet to the show's cast to help educate young viewers about the plight of children living with the infection.

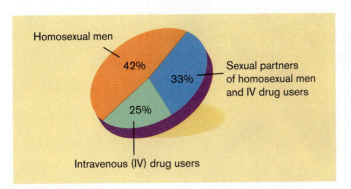

FIGURE 10.6

How HIV Has Been Transmitted in AIDS Cases in the United States
Source: CDC (2001b).

Homosexual men — 42%

Sexual partners of homosexual men and IV drug users — 33%

Intravenous (IV) drug users — 25%

Discharges, blisters, sores, rashes, warts, odors, or any other unusual symptoms are warning signs of STDs. Yet, many people who have no visible symptoms carry STDs. What you don't know can hurt you. People who choose to practice risky sex cannot be safe but can reduce the risks by using a latex condom along with a spermicide such as an intravaginal contraceptive foam, jelly, or cream.

The potential for risky sexual behavior is increased when people are under the influence of alcohol and other drugs (Leigh & Stall, 1993). People put themselves at risk for AIDS when they have multiple sex partners or have sex with prostitutes, IV drug users, or anyone carrying HIV (Bellis et al., 2002). Anyone who fears that he or she might have been exposed to an STD should go to a doctor or clinic to be tested. Many STDs are easily treated, and serious complications can be avoided if the treatment is prompt. Initiating a discussion of sexual history with a potential partner can be stressful but will enable you to make informed decisions about your behavior. And, anyone who has an STD should discuss it with his or her partner so that the partner can be checked and treated.

Exercise

◆ *What are some benefits of regular aerobic exercise?*

How much exercise do you get? Many studies show that regular exercise pays rich dividends in the form of physical and mental fitness. However, many people still express reluctance to exercise. More than 30% of Americans get no exercise at all (National Center for Health Statistics, 2004). Some simply prefer not to be physically active; others blame such factors as the cost of joining a health club or even the unpredictability of the weather for their lack of physical activity (Salmon et al., 2003). Such individuals are missing out on one of the simplest and most effective ways of enhancing one's health.

◆ **aerobic exercise**
(ah-RO-bik) Exercise that uses the large muscle groups in continuous, repetitive action and increases oxygen intake and breathing and heart rates.

Aerobic exercise (such as running, swimming, brisk walking, bicycling, rowing, and jumping rope) is exercise that uses the large muscle groups in continuous, repetitive action and increases oxygen intake and breathing and heart rates. To improve cardiovascular fitness and endurance and to lessen the risk of heart attack, an individual should perform aerobic exercise regularly—three or four times a week for 20–30 minutes, with additional 5–10-minute warm-up and cool-down periods (Alpert et al., 1990; Shepard, 1986). Less than 20 minutes of aerobic exercise three times a week has "no measurable effect on the heart," and more than 3 hours per week "is not known to reduce cardiovascular risk any further" (Simon, 1988, p. 3). However, individuals who engage in more than 3 hours of aerobic activity each week are more successful at losing excess weight and keeping it off than are those who exercise less (Votruba et al., 2000).

In case you are not yet convinced, consider the following benefits of exercise (Fiatarone et al., 1988):

- Increases the efficiency of the heart, enabling it to pump more blood with each beat, and reduces the resting pulse rate and improves circulation

Regular aerobic exercise improves cardiovascular fitness in people of all ages.

- Raises levels of HDL (the good blood cholesterol), which (1) helps rid the body of LDL (the bad blood cholesterol) and (2) removes plaque buildup on artery walls
- Burns up extra calories, enabling you to lose weight or maintain your weight
- Makes bones denser and stronger, helping to prevent osteoporosis in women
- Moderates the effects of stress
- Gives you more energy and increases your resistance to fatigue
- Benefits the immune system by increasing natural killer cell activity

Alternative Medicine

Do you take vitamins or herbal supplements in hopes of positively influencing your health? According to surveys, Americans spend billions of dollars each year on unconventional treatments—herbs, massage, self-help groups, megavitamins, folk remedies, and homeopathy—for a variety of illnesses and conditions. In one such survey, the National Science Foundation (NSF, 2002) found that 88% of Americans believe that there are valid ways of preventing and curing illnesses that are not recognized by the medical profession. Moreover, a growing number of people are turning to alternative health care providers for treatment of their mental health problems (Simon et al., 2004). And college-educated Americans are more likely to use unconventional treatments than those who have less education.

◆ *What are the benefits and risks associated with alternative medicine?*

The National Science Foundation (2002) defines **alternative medicine** as any treatment or therapy that has not been scientifically demonstrated to be effective. Even a simple practice such as taking vitamins sometimes falls into this category. For instance, *scurvy* (a condition whose symptoms include bleeding gums and easy bruising) has been scientifically determined to be caused by Vitamin C deficiency. So, taking Vitamin C to prevent or cure scurvy is not considered an alternative therapy. However, if you take Vitamin C to protect yourself against the common cold, you are using alternative medicine because Vitamin C has not been scientifically proven to prevent colds.

If alternative treatments lack scientific support, why do so many people believe in them? One possibility is that it is easier to take a vitamin than to make a lifestyle change. But it is also true that people who do their own research about alternative therapies may happen upon effective treatments of which their physicians are unaware. However, most patients who use alternative treatments do not inform their physicians about them. Health professionals cite this tendency toward secrecy as a major risk factor in the use of alternative medicine (Yale-New Haven Hospital, 2003). They point out that many therapies, especially those that involve food supplements, have pharmacological effects that can interfere with treatments prescribed by physicians. Consequently, individuals who use alternative treatments should tell their physicians about them. While doctors may be skeptical about the utility of the alternative treatments, they need to have this information about their patients to practice conventional medicine effectively. Moreover, faith in an alternative treatment may cause an individual to delay seeking necessary conventional medical treatment.

Although it is true that some alternative therapies may be helpful in both preventing and treating illness, most health professionals agree that lifestyle changes bring greater health benefits than do any methods of alternative medicine. Unfortunately, many people resist making lifestyle changes because they see them as taking too long to be effective or being too difficult to carry out. A smoker may think, "I've been smoking so long, quitting now won't make a difference." An obese person may be so overwhelmed by the amount of weight loss necessary to attain an ideal weight that she or he gives up. However, Table 10.2 (on page 332) shows that the benefits of various lifestyle changes, some of which are fairly easy to achieve, can be well worth the effort. And remember, to be healthier, you don't have to make *all* of the changes. You might consider starting with just one. Even if you never make another change, you are likely to live longer and be healthier than you would have otherwise.

◆ **alternative medicine**
Any treatment or therapy that has not been scientifically demonstrated to be effective.

TABLE 10.2 **Benefits of Lifestyle Changes**

LIFESTYLE CHANGE	BENEFITS
If overweight, lose just 10 pounds.	34% reduction in triglyceride levels; 16% decrease in total cholesterol; 18% increase in HDL ("good" cholesterol); significant reduction in blood pressure; decreased risk of diabetes, sleep apnea, and osteoarthritis (Still, 2001).
Add 20 to 30 grams of fiber to your diet each day.	Improved bowel function; reduced risk of colon cancer and other digestive system diseases; decrease in total cholesterol; reduced blood pressure; improved insulin function in both diabetics and nondiabetics (HCF, 2003).
Engage in moderate physical activity every day (e.g., walk up and down stairs for 15 minutes; spend 30 minutes washing a car).	Reduced feelings of anxiety and sadness; increased bone density; reduced risk of diabetes, heart disease, high blood pressure, and many other life-shortening diseases (CDC, 1999).
Stop smoking at any age, after any number of years of smoking.	*Immediate:* improved circulation; reduced blood level of carbon monoxide; stabilization of pulse rate and blood pressure; improved sense of smell and taste; improved lung function and endurance; reduced risk of lung infections such as pneumonia and bronchitis.
	Long-term: reduced risk of lung cancer (declines substantially with each year of abstinence); decreased risk of other smoking-related illnesses such as emphysema and heart disease; decreased risk of cancer recurrence in those who have been treated for some form of cancer (National Cancer Institute, 2000).

Looking Back At the beginning of the chapter, you read about the remarkable recovery of Lance Armstrong. What were the keys to his success? To put it succinctly, Armstrong took control of those things that he realistically could control, such as what he ate and how much exercise he got, and sought the best medical treatment available. At the same time, he approached the challenges he faced with an optimistic outlook. In doing so, he provided others in his circumstances with a superb role model.

Apply It 10.1 Interpreting Health Information on the Internet

An increasing number of people are turning to the Internet for information about their health. One study of 188 women with breast cancer found that about half of them used the Internet to find out more about the disease (Fogel et al., 2002). Surveys of older adults and HIV-positive individuals have shown that using the Internet helps them gain a sense of control over their health care decisions (Benotsch et al., 2004; Kalichman et al., 2003; McMellon &

Schiffman, 2002). Chat rooms devoted to specific diseases may represent an important source of social support for patients, especially those suffering from rare disorders (Kummervold et al., 2002). And using e-mail to coach and encourage patients in the management of chronic diseases such as diabetes has proven to be effective both for patients' health and for health care professionals' time management (McKay et al., 2002).

But how reliable is the information available on the Internet? In a large-scale study of health-related websites sponsored by the American Medical Association, researchers found that the quality of information varied widely from one site to another (Eysenbach et al., 2002). A study of Internet-based advice for managing children's fever sponsored by the British Medical Association found that most websites contained erroneous information. Moreover, in a follow-up

Apply It 10.1

study done 4 years later, the researchers found that about half of the sites were no longer available; those that remained showed little improvement in the quality of information.

Despite these difficulties, physicians' organizations acknowledge the potential value of the Internet in helping patients learn about and manage their own health. And because so many older adults are using the Internet to learn about health issues, the American Association of Retired Persons (2002) has published a list of points to keep in mind when surfing the Web for health information and advice:

- *Remember that there are no rules governing what is published on the Internet*. Unlike scientific journal articles, which are usually written and reviewed by experts in the field, Internet articles can be posted by anyone, without review of any kind. Without expert knowledge, it is extremely difficult to tell whether the information and advice these articles contain are valid.

- *Consider the source*. Generally, websites sponsored by medical schools, government agencies, and public health organizations are reliable. Others, especially those promoting a health-related product, should be considered suspect.

- *Get a second opinion*. Ask your health care provider about Internet-based information, or read what's available from several different sources on the topic.

- *Examine references*. Sites that refer to credible sources (e.g., books, other websites) that you can find on the Internet or in a library or bookstore are probably more reliable than sites that offer no references to support their advice.

- *How current is the information?* Health-related information changes frequently. Be certain that you are reading the most current findings and recommendations.

- *Is it too good to be true?* As in all areas of life, if something sounds too good to be true (e.g., a vitamin that cures cancer), it probably is. Try to find experimental, placebo-controlled studies that support any claims.

Using these guidelines, you can become a better consumer of Internet-based health information.

Chapter 10 Summary

Sources of Stress p. 309

◆ What was the Social Readjustment Rating Scale designed to reveal? p. 309

The SRRS assesses stress in terms of life events, positive or negative, that necessitate change and adaptation. Holmes and Rahe found a relationship between degree of life stress (as measured on the scale) and major health problems.

◆ What roles do hassles and uplifts play in the stress of life, according to Lazarus? p. 311

According to Lazarus, daily hassles typically cause more stress than major life changes. Positive experiences in life—or uplifts—can neutralize the effects of many of the hassles, however.

◆ How do approach-approach, avoidance-avoidance, and approach-avoidance conflicts differ? p. 312

In an approach-approach conflict, a person must decide between equally desirable alternatives. In an avoidance-avoidance conflict, the choice is between two undesirable alternatives. In an approach-avoidance conflict, a person is both drawn to and repelled by a single choice.

◆ How do the unpredictability and lack of control over a stressor affect its impact? p. 312

Stressors that are unpredictable and uncontrollable have greater impact than those that are predictable and controllable.

◆ For people to function effectively and find satisfaction on the job, what nine variables should fall within their comfort zone? p. 312

The nine variables that should fall within a worker's comfort zone are workload, clarity of job description and evaluation criteria, physical variables, job status, accountability, task variety, human contact, physical challenge, and mental challenge.

◆ How do people typically react to catastrophic events? p. 314

Most people cope quite well with catastrophic events. However, some people develop posttraumatic stress disorder (PTSD), a prolonged, severe stress reaction, often characterized by flashbacks, nightmares, or intrusive memories of the traumatic event.

◆ How might historical racism affect the health of African Americans? p. 315

Some researchers believe that African Americans have higher levels of high blood pressure than members of other groups because of stress due to historical racism. African Americans who express high levels of concern about racism display larger cardiovascular responses to experimentally induced stressors than do their peers who express lower levels of concern.

◆ Responding to Stress p. 316

◆ What is the general adaptation syndrome? p. 316

The general adaptation syndrome (GAS) proposed by Selye is the predictable sequence of reactions that organisms show in response to stressors. It consists of the alarm stage, the resistance stage, and the exhaustion stage.

◆ What are the roles of primary and secondary appraisals when a person is confronted with a potentially stressful event? p. 316

Lazarus maintains that, when confronted with a potentially stressful event, a person engages in a cognitive appraisal process consisting of (1) a primary appraisal, to evaluate the relevance of the situation to one's well-being (whether it will be positive, irrelevant, or negative), and (2) a secondary appraisal, to evaluate one's resources and determine how to cope with the stressor.

◆ What is the difference between problem-focused and emotion-focused coping? p. 317

Problem-focused coping is a direct response, aimed at reducing, modifying, or eliminating the source of stress; emotion-focused coping involves reappraising a stressor in an effort to reduce its emotional impact.

◆ Health and Illness p. 318

◆ How do the biomedical and biopsychosocial models differ in their approaches to health and illness? p. 318

The biomedical model focuses on illness rather than on health and explains illness in terms of biological factors. The biopsychosocial model focuses on health as well as on illness and holds that both are determined by a combination of biological, psychological, and social factors.

◆ What are the Type A and Type B behavior patterns? p. 319

The Type A behavior pattern, often cited as a risk factor for coronary heart disease, is characterized by a sense of time urgency, impatience, excessive competitive drive, hostility, and easily aroused anger. The Type B behavior pattern is characterized by a relaxed, easy-going approach to life, without the time urgency, impatience, and hostility of the Type A pattern.

◆ How do psychological factors influence cancer patients' quality of life? p. 321

Cancer patients can improve their quality of life by maintaining an optimistic outlook, accepting the reality of their situation, and maintaining a sense of humor. Social support and psychotherapy can help them do so.

◆ What are the effects of stress on the immune system? p. 322

Stress has been associated with lowered immune response and with increased symptoms of many infectious diseases.

◆ What four personal factors are associated with health and resistance to stress? p. 323

Personal factors related to health and resistance to stress are optimism, hardiness, religious involvement, and social support.

◆ What are the relationships among gender, ethnicity, and health? p. 324

Women are more likely than men to seek medical care, but women's needs have often been ignored by medical researchers and health care providers. African Americans, Hispanic Americans, and Native Americans have higher rates of many diseases than do White Americans. Asian Americans are comparatively very healthy.

◆ Lifestyle and Health p. 325

◆ What is the most dangerous health-threatening behavior? p. 325

Smoking is considered the most dangerous health-related behavior because it is directly related to more than 400,000 deaths each year, including deaths from heart disease, lung cancer, respiratory diseases, and stroke.

◆ What are some health risks of alcohol abuse? p. 326

Alcohol abuse damages virtually every organ in the body, including the liver, stomach, skeletal muscles, heart, and brain. Alcoholics are three times as likely to die in motor vehicle accidents as nonalcoholics.

◆ What is the difference between bacterial and viral STDs? p. 327

Bacterial STDs can be treated and, in most cases, cured with antiobiotics. Viral STDs are considered to be incurable.

◆ What are some benefits of regular aerobic exercise? p. 330

Regular aerobic exercise reduces the risk of cardiovascular disease, increases muscular strength, moderates the effects of stress, makes bones denser and stronger, and helps one maintain a desirable weight.

◆ What are the benefits and risks associated with alternative medicine? p. 331

Alternative medicine, or the use of any treatment that has not been proven scientifically to be effective, can benefit individuals who find alternative treatments that are effective. However, many patients increase their risk of poor outcomes by not telling their physicians about their use of alternative treatments. And some people delay seeking necessary conventional medical treatment because they believe that alternative approaches will work.

acquired immune deficiency
 syndrome (AIDS), p. 328
aerobic exercise, p. 330
alarm stage, p. 316
alternative medicine, p. 331
approach-approach conflict, p. 312
approach-avoidance conflict, p. 312
avoidance-avoidance conflict, p. 312
bacterial STDs, p. 327
biomedical model, p. 318
biopsychosocial model, p. 318
coping, p. 317
emotion-focused coping, p. 317
exhaustion stage, p. 316

fight-or-flight response, p. 309
general adaptation syndrome (GAS),
 p. 316
hardiness, p. 323
hassles, p. 311
health psychology, p. 318
human immunodeficiency virus
 (HIV), p. 328
lymphocytes, p. 322
posttraumatic stress disorder (PTSD)
 p. 314
primary appraisal, p. 316
problem-focused coping, p. 317
psychoneuroimmunology, p. 322

resistance stage, p. 316
secondary appraisal, p. 317
sexually transmitted diseases
 (STDs), p. 327
Social Readjustment Rating Scale
 (SRRS), p. 309
social support, p. 323
stress, p. 309
stressor, p. 309
Type A behavior pattern, p. 320
Type B behavior pattern, p. 320
uplifts, p. 311
viral STDs, p. 328

Study Guide 10

Answers to all the Study Guide questions are provided at the end of the book.

◆ SECTION ONE: Chapter Review

Sources of Stress (pp. 309–315)

1. On the Social Readjustment Rating Scale, only negative life changes are considered stressful. (true/false)

2. The Social Readjustment Rating Scale takes account of the individual's perceptions of the stressfulness of the life change in assigning stress points. (true/false)

3. According to Lazarus, hassles typically account for more life stress than major life changes. (true/false)

4. Lazarus's approach to measuring hassles and uplifts considers individual perceptions of stressful events. (true/false)

5. Travis cannot decide whether to go out or stay home and study for his test. What kind of conflict does he have?
   a. approach-approach
   b. avoidance-avoidance
   c. approach-avoidance
   d. ambivalence-ambivalence

6. What factor or factors increase stress, according to research on the topic?
   a. predictability of the stressor
   b. unpredictability of the stressor
   c. predictability of and control over the stressor
   d. unpredictability of and lack of control over the stressor

7. Sources of workplace stress for women include
   a. sexual harassment.
   b. discrimination.
   c. balancing family and work demands.
   d. all of the above.

8. Victims of catastrophic events usually panic. (true/false)

9. Posttraumatic stress disorder is a prolonged and severe stress reaction that results when a number of common sources of stress occur simultaneously. (true/false)

10. The group that has received the most attention from researchers interested in the association between stress and racism is
   a. Native Americans.
   b. Hispanic Americans.
   c. Asian Americans.
   d. African Americans.

Responding to Stress (pp. 316–318)

11. The stage of the general adaptation syndrome marked by intense physiological efforts to adapt to the stressor is the (alarm, resistance) stage.

12. Susceptibility to illness increases during the (alarm, exhaustion) stage of the general adaptation syndrome.

13. Selye focused on the (psychological, physiological) aspects of stress; Lazarus focused on the (psychological, physiological) aspects of stress.

14. During secondary appraisal, a person
    a. evaluates his or her coping resources and considers options for dealing with the stressor.
    b. determines whether an event is positive, neutral, or negative.
    c. determines whether an event involves loss, threat, or challenge.
    d. determines whether an event causes physiological or psychological stress.

15. Coping aimed at reducing, modifying, or eliminating a source of stress is called (emotion-focused, problem-focused) coping; that aimed at reducing an emotional reaction to stress is called (emotion-focused, problem-focused) coping.

16. People typically use a combination of problem-focused and emotion-focused coping when dealing with a stressful situation. (true/false)

Health and Illness (pp. 318–325)

17. The biomedical model focuses on _____; the biopsychosocial model focuses on _____.
    a. illness; illness
    b. health and illness; illness
    c. illness; health and illness
    d. health and illness; health and illness

18. Most research has pursued the connection between the Type A behavior pattern and
    a. cancer.   c. stroke.
    b. coronary heart disease.   d. ulcers.

19. Recent research suggests that the most toxic component of the Type A behavior pattern is
    a. hostility.   c. a sense of time urgency.
    b. impatience.   d. perfectionism.

20. Viral STDs are those that can be effectively treated with antibiotics. (true/false)

21. HIV eventually causes a breakdown in the _____ system.
    a. circulatory   c. immune
    b. vascular   d. respiratory

22. The incidence of AIDS in the United States is highest among
    a. homosexuals and IV drug users.
    b. homosexuals and hemophiliacs.
    c. homosexuals and bisexuals.
    d. heterosexuals, IV drug users, and hemophiliacs.

23. Lowered immune response has been associated with
    a. stress.   c. stress and depression.
    b. depression.   d. neither stress nor depression.

24. Some research suggests that optimists are more stress-resistant than pessimists. (true/false)

25. Which of the following is not a dimension of psychological hardiness?
    a. a feeling that adverse circumstances can be controlled and changed
    b. a sense of commitment and deep involvement in personal goals
    c. a tendency to look on change as a challenge rather than a threat
    d. close, supportive relationships with family and friends

26. Social support tends to reduce stress but is unrelated to health outcomes. (true/false)

Lifestyle and Health (pp. 325–332)

27. Which is the most important factor leading to disease and death?
    a. unhealthy lifestyle
    b. a poor health care system
    c. environmental hazards
    d. genetic disorders

28. Which health-compromising behavior is responsible for the most deaths?
    a. overeating   c. lack of exercise
    b. smoking   d. excessive alcohol use

29. (Alcohol, Smoking) damages virtually every organ in the body.

30. To improve cardiovascular fitness, aerobic exercise should be done
    a. 15 minutes daily.
    b. 1 hour daily.
    c. 20 to 30 minutes daily.
    d. 20 to 30 minutes three or four times a week.

31. Alternative health treatments have proven to be just as effective as traditional approaches to illness. (true/false)

List at least two forces for each of the following:

1. Biological forces favoring health and wellness   _____

2. Biological forces working against health and wellness   _____

3. Psychological forces favoring health and wellness   _____

4. Psychological forces working against health and wellness _____

5. Social forces favoring health and wellness   _____

6. Social forces working against health and wellness   _____

SECTION THREE: Fill In the Blank

1. Medicine has been dominated by the _____ model, which focuses on illness rather than on health, whereas the _____ model asserts that both health and illness are determined by a combination of biological, psychological, and social factors.

2. The field of psychology that is concerned with the psychological factors that contribute to health, illness, and recovery is known as _____ _____.

3. The fight-or-flight response is controlled by the _____ and the endocrine glands.

4. The first stage of the general adaptation syndrome is the _____ stage.

5. The stage of the general adaptation syndrome during which the adrenal glands release hormones to help the body resist stressors is called the _____ stage.

6. Lazarus's theory is considered a _____ theory of stress and coping.

7. Noelle knew that her upcoming job interview would be difficult, so she tried to anticipate the kinds of questions she would be asked and practiced the best possible responses. Noelle was practicing _____ coping.

8. The most feared disease related to the immune system is _____.

9. The primary means of transmission of HIV is through sexual contact between _____.

10. Daily _____ are the "irritating, frustrating, distressing demands and troubled relationships that plague us day in and day out."

11. Tiffany is a psychologist who works with biologists and medical researchers to determine the effects of psychological factors on the immune system. Tiffany works in the field of _____.

12. People with the Type _____ behavior pattern have a strong sense of time urgency and are impatient, excessively competitive, hostile, and easily angered.

13. The effects of alcohol on _____ may continue for several months after an alcoholic stops drinking.

14. _____ appraisal is an evaluation of the significance of a potentially stressful event according to how it will affect one's well-being—whether it is perceived as irrelevant or as involving harm, loss, threat, or challenge.

15. African Americans may have a greater incidence of _____ _____ _____ than White Americans because of the stress associated with historical racism.

16. A _____ is any event capable of producing physical or emotional stress.

17. Cole wants to get a flu shot, but he is also very afraid of needles. He is faced with an _____-_____ conflict.

SECTION FOUR: Comprehensive Practice Test

1. Stress consists of the threats and problems we encounter in life. (true/false)

2. Hans Selye developed the
   a. diathesis stress model.
   b. general adaptation syndrome model.
   c. cognitive stress model.
   d. conversion reaction model.

3. The fight-or-flight response is seen in the _____ stage of the general adaptation syndrome.
   a. alarm
   c. resistance
   b. exhaustion
   d. arousal

4. Lack of exercise, poor diet, and disease and injury are considered to be _____ forces that work against health and wellness.
   a. environmental
   c. biological
   b. psychological
   d. social

5. Charlotte has been looking for new bedroom furniture and has found two styles that she really likes. She is trying to decide which one she will purchase. Charlotte is experiencing an _____ conflict.
   a. approach-approach
   b. approach-avoidance
   c. avoidance-avoidance
   d. avoidance-approach

6. People's sense of control over a situation can have an important beneficial influence on how a stressor affects them even if they do not exercise that control. (true/false)

7. Posttraumatic stress disorder leaves some people more vulnerable to future mental health problems. (true/false)

8. Which of the following is not a variable in work stress?
   a. workload
   b. clarity of job description
   c. perceived equity of pay for work
   d. task variety

9. Research indicates that African Americans who are highly concerned about _____ are more sensitive to stressors than their peers who are less concerned.

10. Religious faith helps people cope with negative life events. (true/false)

11. Lazarus's term for the positive experiences that can serve to cancel out the effects of day-to-day hassles is
    a. stress assets.
    c. uplifts.
    b. coping mechanisms.
    d. appraisals.

12. Type B behavior patterns seem to be more correlated with heart disease than do Type A behavior patterns. (true/false)

13. B cells produce antibodies that are effective in destroying antigens that live _____ the body cells; T cells are important in the destruction of antigens that live _____ the body cells.
    a. outside; inside
    b. inside; outside

14. AIDS is caused by HIV, often called the AIDS virus. (true/false)

15. HIV weakens the immune system by attacking T cells. (true/false)

◆ SECTION FIVE: Critical Thinking

1. In your view, which is more effective for evaluating stress: the Social Readjustment Rating Scale or the Hassle Scale? Explain the advantages and disadvantages of each.

2. Prepare two arguments: one supporting the position that alcoholism is a genetically inherited disease, and the other supporting the position that alcoholism is not a medical disease but results from learning.

3. Choose several stress-producing incidents from your life and explain what problem-focused and emotion-focused coping strategies you used. From the knowledge you have gained in this chapter, list other coping strategies that might have been more effective.

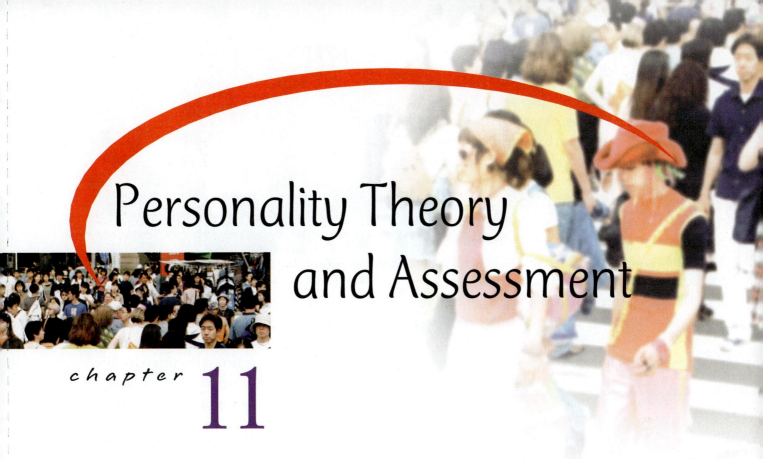

Personality Theory and Assessment

chapter **11**

In 1924, two young Chicago men, 18-year-old Nathan Leopold and 19-year-old Richard Loeb, brutally killed a 13-year-old boy in an effort to prove their intellectual superiority. They believed that their superior cognitive abilities exempted them from society's rules. Moreover, they thought that their intelligence would enable them to murder at will, without risk of detection by the presumably intellectually inferior authorities. However, the police were able to trace a pair of glasses Leopold carelessly left at the murder scene and arrested the two a few days after the crime.

Leopold and Loeb confessed, and their wealthy families hired well-known attorney Clarence Darrow to try to save them from the death penalty. Arguing from several books and articles by Sigmund Freud, Darrow tried to convince the judge who would pass sentence that Leopold and Loeb's parents were at least partially responsible for the crime because they had deprived the young men of emotional warmth when they were children (Higdon, 1975). Darrow hired psychologists to testify that the two murderers were emotionally equivalent to young children and should not be put to death for their crime. At the end of the trial, the judge sided with Darrow and sentenced the two young men to life in prison.

Publicity surrounding the Leopold and Loeb trial was how Freud's theory first became widely known among the general public in the United States (Torrey, 1992). The claim that two murderers' parents might be morally responsible

Richard Loeb (left) and Nathan Leopold (right) in prison, 1924, for the murder of Robert Franks.

for their heinous crime caused many people to see Freud's theory as repugnant. But it was Darrow, not Freud, who turned the theory into a "blame your parents" legal defense. Indeed, Freud's assertion that early childhood experiences contribute to adult behavior is accepted by both psychologists and nonpsychologists and may be his most enduring contribution. But can early childhood experiences alone account for variations among adults?

Even though most people agree that variations in early childhood experiences contribute to differences among adults, most also realize that many other factors must be taken into account to explain the full range of behaviors collectively referred to as "personality"—all the ways in which one person differs from another. **Personality** is formally defined as an individual's characteristic patterns of behaving, thinking, and feeling (Carver & Scheier, 1996). In this chapter, we explore some of the theories, including Freud's, that have been proposed to explain personality.

◆ **personality**

A person's characteristic patterns of behaving, thinking, and feeling.

◆ **psychoanalysis**

(SY-co-ah-NAL-ih-sis) Freud's term for his theory of personality and his therapy for treating psychological disorders.

Sigmund Freud and Psychoanalysis

When you hear the term **psychoanalysis,** do you picture a psychiatrist treating a troubled patient on a couch? Many people do, but the term refers not only to a therapy for treating psychological disorders devised by Sigmund Freud, but also to the influential personality theory he proposed. The central idea of psychoanalytic theory is that unconscious forces shape human thought and behavior.

The Conscious, the Preconscious, and the Unconscious

Freud believed that there are three levels of awareness in consciousness: the conscious, the preconscious, and the unconscious. The **conscious** consists of whatever we are aware of at any given moment—thoughts, feelings, sensations, or memories. The **preconscious** is somewhat like long-term memory: It contains all the memories, feelings, experiences, and perceptions that we are not consciously thinking about at the moment, but that may be easily brought to consciousness.

The most important of the three levels is the **unconscious**, which Freud believed to be the primary motivating force of human behavior. The unconscious holds memories that once were conscious but were so unpleasant or anxiety-provoking that they were repressed (involuntarily removed from consciousness). The unconscious also contains all of the instincts (sexual and aggressive), wishes, and desires that have never been allowed into consciousness. Freud traced the roots of psychological disorders to these impulses and repressed memories.

◆ *What are the three levels of awareness in consciousness?*

◆ **conscious**
(KON-shus) The thoughts, feelings, sensations, or memories of which a person is aware at any given moment.

◆ **preconscious**
The thoughts, feelings, and memories that a person is not consciously aware of at the moment but that may be easily brought to consciousness.

The Id, the Ego, and the Superego

Freud also proposed three systems of personality. Figure 11.1 shows these three systems and how they relate to his conscious, preconscious, and unconscious levels of awareness. These systems do not exist physically; they are only concepts, or ways of looking at personality.

The **id** is the only part of the personality that is present at birth. It is inherited, primitive, inaccessible, and completely unconscious. The id contains (1) the life instincts, which are the sexual instincts and the biological urges such as hunger and thirst, and (2) the death instinct, which accounts for aggressive and destructive impulses (Freud, 1933/1965). Operating according to the *pleasure principle*, the id tries to seek pleasure, avoid pain, and gain immediate gratification of its wishes. The id is the source of the *libido*, the psychic energy that fuels the entire personality; yet, the id can only wish, image, fantasize and demand.

The **ego** is the logical, rational, realistic part of the personality. The ego evolves from the id and draws its energy from the id. One of the ego's functions is to satisfy the id's urges. But the ego, which is mostly conscious, acts according to the *reality principle*. It considers the constraints of the real world in determining appropriate times, places, and objects for gratification of the id's wishes. The art of the possible is its guide, and sometimes compromises must be made—such as settling for a fast-food hamburger instead of steak or lobster.

When a child is age 5 or 6, the **superego**, the moral component of the personality, is formed. The superego has two parts: (1) The *conscience* consists of all the behaviors for which the child has been punished and about which he or she feels guilty; and (2) the *ego ideal* comprises the behaviors for which the child has been praised and rewarded and

◆ *What are the roles of the id, the ego, and the superego?*

Sigmund Freud (1856–1939), with his daughter Anna.

◆ **unconscious**
(un-KON-shus) For Freud, the primary motivating force of human behavior, containing repressed memories as well as instincts, wishes, and desires that have never been conscious.

◆ **id**
(ID) The unconscious system of the personality, which contains the life and death instincts and operates on the pleasure principle; source of the libido.

◆ **ego**
(EE-go) In Freud's theory, the logical, rational, largely conscious system of personality, which operates according to the reality principle.

FIGURE 11.1 **Freud's Conception of Personality**

According to Freud, personality, which may be conceptualized as a giant iceberg, is composed of three structures: the id, the ego, and the superego. The id, completely unconscious, is wholly submerged, floating beneath the surface. The ego is largely conscious and visible, but partly unconscious. The superego also operates at both the conscious and unconscious levels.

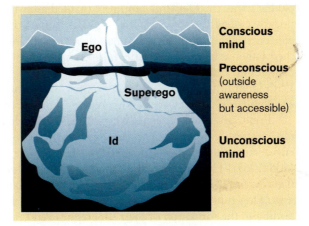

Ego

Superego

Id

Conscious mind

Preconscious (outside awareness but accessible)

Unconscious mind

◆ **superego**

(sue-per-EE-go) The moral system of the personality, which consists of the conscience and the ego ideal.

about which he or she feels pride and satisfaction. At first, the superego reflects only the parents' expectations of what is good and right, but it expands over time to incorporate teachings from the broader social world. In its quest for moral perfection, the superego sets guidelines that define and limit the ego's flexibility. A harsher judge than any external authority, including one's parents, the superego judges not only behavior, but also thoughts, feelings, and wishes.

Defense Mechanisms

◆ *What is the purpose of defense mechanisms?*

All would be well if the id, the ego, and the superego had compatible aims. But the id's demands for pleasure are often in direct conflict with the superego's desire for moral perfection. At times the ego needs some way to defend itself against the anxiety created by the excessive demands of the id and the harsh judgments of the superego. When it cannot solve problems directly, the ego may use a **defense mechanism**, a technique used to defend against anxiety and to maintain self-esteem. All people use defense mechanisms to some degree, but research supports Freud's view that the overuse of defense mechanisms can adversely affect mental health (Watson, 2002).

◆ **defense mechanism**

A means used by the ego to defend against anxiety and to maintain self-esteem.

According to Freud, *repression* is the most frequently used defense mechanism. It involves removing painful or threatening memories, thoughts, or perceptions from consciousness and keeping them in the unconscious. It may also prevent unconscious sexual and aggressive impulses from breaking into consciousness. Several studies have shown that people do, indeed, try to repress unpleasant thoughts (Koehler et al., 2002). Freud believed that repressed thoughts lurk in the unconscious and can cause psychological disorders in adults. He thought that the way to cure such disorders was to bring the repressed material back to consciousness, and this was the basis for his system of therapy—psychoanalysis.

The Psychosexual Stages of Development

◆ *What are the psychosexual stages, and why did Freud consider them important in personality development?*

The sex instinct, Freud said, is the most important factor influencing personality. It is present at birth and then develops through a series of **psychosexual stages.** Each stage centers on a particular part of the body that provides pleasurable sensations (an *erogenous zone*) and around which a conflict arises (Freud, 1905/1953b, 1920/1963b). If the conflict is not readily resolved, the child may develop a **fixation.** This means that a portion of the libido (psychic energy) remains invested at that particular stage, leaving less energy to meet the challenges of future stages. Overindulgence at any stage may leave a person psychologically unwilling to move on to the next stage, whereas too little gratification may leave the person trying to make up for unmet needs. Freud believed that certain personality characteristics develop as a result of difficulty at one or another of the stages. *Review and Reflect 11.1* (on page 343) summarizes Freud's psychosexual stages.

◆ **psychosexual stages**

A series of stages through which the sexual instinct develops; each stage is defined by an erogenous zone around which conflict arises.

◆ **fixation**

Arrested development at a psychosexual stage occurring because of excessive gratification or frustration at that stage.

◆ **Oedipus complex**

(ED-uh-pus) Occurring in the phallic stage, a conflict in which the child is sexually attracted to the opposite-sex parent and feels hostility toward the same-sex parent.

One of the most controversial features of Freud's theory is the central theme of the phallic stage, the **Oedipus complex** (named after the central character in the Greek tragedy *Oedipus Rex*, by Sophocles). Freud claimed that, during the phallic stage, "boys concentrate their sexual wishes upon their mother and develop hostile impulses against their father as being a rival" (1925/1963a, p. 61). The boy usually resolves the Oedipus complex by identifying with his father and repressing his sexual feelings for his mother. With identification, the child takes on his father's behaviors, mannerisms, and superego standards; in this way, the superego develops (Freud, 1930/1962).

Freud proposed an equally controversial developmental process for girls in the phallic stage. When they discover they have no penis, girls in this stage develop "penis envy," and they turn to their father because he has the desired organ (Freud, 1933/1965). They feel sexual desires for him and develop jealousy and rivalry toward their mother. But eventually girls, too, experience anxiety as a result of their hostile feelings. They repress their sexual feelings toward the father and identify with the mother, leading to the formation of their superego (Freud, 1930/1962).

REVIEW and REFLECT 11.1

Freud's Psychosexual Stages of Development

STAGE	PART OF THE BODY	CONFLICTS/ EXPERIENCES	ADULT TRAITS ASSOCIATED WITH PROBLEMS AT THIS STAGE
Oral (birth to 1 year)	Mouth	Weaning Oral gratification from sucking, eating, biting	Optimism, gullibility, dependency, pessimism, passivity, hostility, sarcasm, aggression
Anal (1 to 3 years)	Anus	Toilet training Gratification from expelling and withholding feces	Excessive cleanliness, orderliness, stinginess, messiness, rebelliousness, destructiveness
Phallic (3 to 5 or 6 years)	Genitals	Oedipal conflict Sexual curiosity Masturbation	Flirtatiousness, vanity, promiscuity, pride, chastity
Latency (5 or 6 years to puberty)	None	Period of sexual calm Interest in school, hobbies, same-sex friends	
Genital (from puberty on)	Genitals	Revival of sexual interests Establishment of mature sexual relationships	

According to Freud, failure to resolve these conflicts can have serious consequences for both boys and girls: Tremendous guilt and anxiety may be carried over into adulthood and cause sexual problems, great difficulty relating to members of the opposite sex, or homosexuality.

Evaluating Freud's Contribution

◆ How are Freud's ideas evaluated by modern psychologists?

Some of Freud's ideas may seem odd or even bizarre to you, but psychology is indebted to Freud for introducing the idea that unconscious forces may motivate behavior and for emphasizing the influence of early childhood experiences on later development. Some psychologists also say that Freud's theory may better explain the emotional aspects of psychological experience than today's popular learning and cognitive theories (Turkle, 2004b). Moreover, as Freud's theory predicts, many children who are rejected by their parents have behavioral and psychological difficulties later in life (Akse et al., 2004). Therapists point out that psychoanalysis is still a useful therapeutic technique (Bartlett, 2002). And Freud's concept of defense mechanisms provides a useful way of categorizing the cognitive strategies that people use to manage stress (Fauerbach et al., 2002; Tori & Bilmes, 2002).

Freud believed that a fixation at the anal stage, resulting from harsh parental pressure, could lead to an anal retentive personality—characterized by excessive stubbornness, rigidity, and neatness.

However, critics charge that much of Freud's theory defies scientific testing. Too much of the time, any act of behavior or even no act of behavior at all can be interpreted to support Freud's theory. How, for instance, can we ever test the idea that little boys are in love with their mothers and want to get rid of their fathers? How can we verify or falsify the idea that one component of personality is motivated entirely by the pursuit of pleasure? Chiefly because of the difficulty involved in finding scientific answers to such questions, there are very few strict Freudians among today's psychologists.

The Neo-Freudians

◆ How do the views of the neo-Freudians differ from those of Freud?

Is it possible to construct a theory of personality that builds on the strengths of Freud's approach and avoids its weaknesses? Several personality theorists, referred to as *neo-Freudians*, have attempted to do so. Most started their careers as followers of Freud but began to disagree on certain basic principles of psychoanalytic theory.

One of the most important neo-Freudians, Carl Jung (1875–1961), did not consider the sexual instinct to be the main factor in personality, nor did he believe that the personality is almost completely formed in early childhood. For Jung (1933), middle age was an even more important period for personality development. Jung conceived of the personality as consisting of three parts: the ego, the personal unconscious, and the collective unconscious, as shown in Figure 11.2. He saw the ego as the conscious component of personality, which carries out normal daily activities. Like Freud, he believed the ego to be secondary in importance to the unconscious.

The **personal unconscious** develops as a result of one's own experience and is therefore unique to each person. It contains all the experiences, thoughts, and perceptions accessible to the conscious, as well as repressed memories, wishes, and impulses. The **collective unconscious**, the most inaccessible layer of the unconscious, contains the universal experiences of humankind throughout evolution. This is how Jung accounted for the similarity of certain myths, dreams, symbols, and religious beliefs in

◆ **personal unconscious**

In Jung's theory, the layer of the unconscious that contains all of the thoughts, perceptions, and experiences accessible to the conscious, as well as repressed memories, wishes, and impulses.

◆ **collective unconscious**

In Jung's theory, the most inaccessible layer of the unconscious, which contains the universal experiences of humankind throughout evolution.

Carl Gustav Jung
(1875–1961)

FIGURE 11.2   Jung's Conception of Personality

Like Freud, Jung saw three components in personality. The ego and the personal unconscious are unique to each individual. The collective unconscious accounts for the similarity of myths and beliefs in diverse cultures.

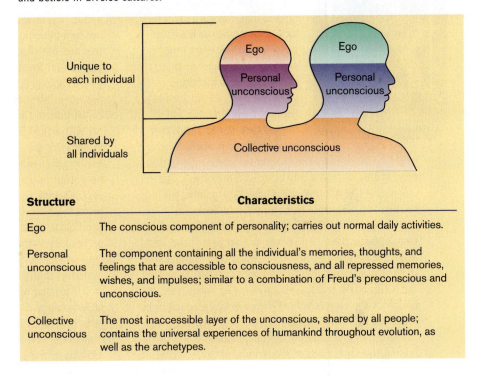

Structure	Characteristics
Ego	The conscious component of personality; carries out normal daily activities.
Personal unconscious	The component containing all the individual's memories, thoughts, and feelings that are accessible to consciousness, and all repressed memories, wishes, and impulses; similar to a combination of Freud's preconscious and unconscious.
Collective unconscious	The most inaccessible layer of the unconscious, shared by all people; contains the universal experiences of humankind throughout evolution, as well as the archetypes.

cultures widely separated by distance and time. Moreover, the collective unconscious contains what he called **archetypes,** inherited tendencies to respond to universal human situations in particular ways. Jung would say that the tendencies of people to believe in a god, a devil, evil spirits, and heroes all result from inherited archetypes that reflect the shared experience of humankind.

Another neo-Freudian, Alfred Adler (1870–1937), emphasized the unity of the personality rather than the separate warring components of id, ego, and superego. Adler (1927, 1956) also maintained that the drive to overcome feelings of inferiority acquired in childhood motivates most of our behavior. He claimed that people develop a "style of life" at an early age—a unique way in which the child and later the adult will go about the struggle to achieve superiority (Adler, 1956). Sometimes inferiority feelings are so strong that they prevent personal development, a condition Adler called the *inferiority complex* (Dreikurs, 1953). Because Adler's theory stresses the uniqueness of each individual's struggle to achieve superiority and refers to the "creative self," a conscious, self-aware component of an individual's personality, it is known as *individual psychology.*

The work of neo-Freudian Karen Horney (1885–1952) centered on two main themes: the neurotic personality (Horney, 1937, 1945, 1950) and feminine psychology (Horney, 1967). Horney did not accept Freud's division of personality into id, ego, and superego, and she flatly rejected his psychosexual stages and the concepts of the Oedipus complex and penis envy. Furthermore, Horney thought Freud overemphasized the role of the sexual instinct and neglected cultural and environmental influences on personality. While she did stress the importance of early childhood experiences, Horney (1939) believed that personality could continue to develop and change throughout life.

Horney argued forcefully against Freud's notion that a woman's desire to have a child and to have a man is nothing more than a conversion of the unfulfilled wish for a penis. Horney (1945) believed that many of women's psychological difficulties arise from failure to live up to an idealized version of themselves. To be psychologically

◆ **archetype**

(AR-ka-type) Existing in the collective unconscious, an inherited tendency to respond to universal human situations in particular ways.

How Did You Find **Psychology?**

Sherry Turkle

Psychologist Sherry Turkle reports that, "despite my total lack of musicality or dramatic gifts, for several years [my mother] was convinced that I would become a nightclub singer" (Turkle, 2004a, p. 145). For her tenth birthday, Turkle's mother took her to a Brooklyn supper club, hoping that she would be inspired by the chanteuse. Turkle reports that even at ten she had a way to resist her mother's campaign. She had another role model, Nancy Drew, the heroine in a series of children's mystery books.

Money was tight in Turkle's home, so books were precious commodities. Neither she nor her best friend could believe their great good fortune when they found a stack of 19 Nancy Drew books in a neighbor's trash. They read the books again and again, marveling at Nancy's ability to unlock the secrets behind the objects she found in her detective work. To develop her own detective skills, Turkle began investigating her neighbors in hopes of finding the same kinds of mysterious lost objects and suspicious life patterns that Nancy Drew always seemed to uncover, a practice ultimately discovered and forbidden by her parents. Thankfully, though, she had another outlet. At her grandparents' home, Turkle was allowed to explore the "memory closet," a cupboard in which items from her family's past were stored. There she found old letters, photographs, school notebooks, and the like, and she wondered about the context in which each object had entered her family members' lives. She pondered questions such as why people keep some photographs

but not others and a central question about her own past and its mysteries: why had she not been allowed to know her own biological father? Out of such materials, intellectual and personal, Turkle envisioned herself in an occupation that involved solving such mysteries.

Psychology entered Turkle's awareness via one of the few books her family owned, a career guidance book called *How to Choose the Right Job.* The book provided her with valuable insight into the individual differences in behavior she observed in her relatives and friends. And it provided her with an idea that would be central to her future work on the psychology of technology: For people's work to be fulfilling, they need to love the objects, the material of that work. A future psychoanalytic psychologist was born, perhaps, when the ideas about personality in the book helped Turkle realize that people—as well as objects—can be the bearers of mysteries.

Today, Sherry Turkle is a professor of the social studies of science and technology at the Massachusetts Institute of Technology. She studies the ways in which people's objects represent extensions of themselves, particularly their computers, personal digital assistants (PDAs), and other artifacts of the Information Age. Like the secret doors, rusty keys, and old clocks that beckoned Nancy Drew into new mysteries, some aspects of human behavior, says Turkle, are best thought of as clues that require insightful decoding. Turkle believes (February 5, 2005, personal communication) that she found a way to follow the essence of her mother's dream: to find a way to find personal self-expression in her work. If your dreams for yourself conflict with those of your parents, take from Turkle's story the idea that there may be a way to find the essence of what they wish for you and make it your own.

healthy, she claimed, women—and men, for that matter—must learn to overcome irrational beliefs about the need for perfection. Her influence may be seen in modern cognitive-behavioral therapies, which we will explore in Chapter 13.

Learning Theories and Personality

What are the components of Bandura's concept of reciprocal determinism and Rotter's locus of control?

Do you recall the importance of reinforcement in B. F. Skinner's principles of operant conditioning? As you might expect, learning theorists view personality as just one more result of learning. Thus, according to Skinner, we consistently exhibit certain behaviors, called "personality" by most, because we have been reinforced for doing so. And, of course, behaviors and reinforcements are far more easily observed than are internal factors such as Freud's id, ego, and superego. For this reason, many psychologists regard explanations of personality that are based on learning theories as more scientific than Freud's psychoanalysis. However, learning theories are often criticized for paying too little attention to emotions and other internal processes.

One learning theory that does take internal factors into account is the *social-cognitive approach* of Albert Bandura (1977a, 1986). He maintains that cognitive factors (such as an individual's stage of cognitive development), individual behaviors, and the external environment are all influenced by each other (Bandura, 1989). This mutual relationship Bandura calls **reciprocal determinism** (see Figure 11.3).

One of the cognitive factors that Bandura (1997a, 1997b) considers especially important is **self-efficacy**, the perception people have of their ability to perform competently whatever they attempt. Cross-cultural researchers examining self-efficacy in 25 countries found it to be an important individual difference in all of them (Scholz et al., 2002). According to Bandura, people high in self-efficacy approach new situations confidently, set high goals, and persist in their efforts because they believe success is likely. People low in self-efficacy, on the other hand, expect failure; consequently, they avoid challenges and typically give up on tasks they find difficult. Bandura's research has shown that people with high self-efficacy are less likely to experience depression than those with low self-efficacy (Bandura, 1997b).

Julian Rotter proposes a similar cognitive factor, **locus of control**. Some people see themselves as primarily in control of their behavior and its consequences. This perception Rotter (1966, 1971, 1990) defines as an *internal locus of control*. Other people perceive that whatever happens to them is in the hands of fate, luck, or chance. These individuals exhibit an *external locus of control* and may claim that it does not matter what they do because "whatever will be, will be." Rotter contends that people with an external locus of control are less likely to change their behavior as a result of reinforcement, because they do not see reinforcers as being tied to their own actions. Students who have an external locus of control tend to be procrastinators and, thus, are less likely to be academically successful than those with an internal locus of control (Janssen & Carton, 1999). Similarly, construction workers who have an internal locus of control are more likely than their external-locus co-workers to take the time to implement safety procedures before beginning a dangerous project (Kuo & Tsaur, 2004). External locus of control is also associated with lower levels of life satisfaction (Kirkcaldy et al., 2002). Where is your locus of control? To find out, complete *Try It 11.1* (on page 348).

Individuals who are high in self-efficacy pursue challenging goals and persist in their efforts until they reach them.

◆ **reciprocal determinism**

Bandura's concept of a mutual influential relationship among behavior, cognitive factors, and environment.

◆ **self-efficacy**

The perception a person has of his or her ability to perform competently whatever is attempted.

◆ **locus of control**

Rotter's concept of a cognitive factor that explains how people account for what happens in their lives—either seeing themselves as primarily in control of their behavior and its consequences (internal locus of control) or perceiving what happens to them to be in the hands of fate, luck, or chance (external locus of control).

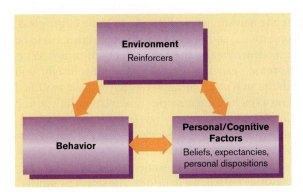

FIGURE 11.3

Bandura's Reciprocal Determinism

Bandura takes a social-cognitive view of personality. He suggests that three components—the external environment, individual behaviors, and cognitive factors, such as beliefs, expectancies, and personal dispositions—are all influenced by each other and play reciprocal roles in determining personality.

Try It 11.1
Where Is Your Locus of Control?

For each statement, indicate whether you agree or disagree.

1. Heredity determines most of a person's personality.
2. Chance has a lot to do with being successful.
3. Whatever plans you make, something will always interfere.
4. Being at the right place at the right time is essential for getting what you want in life.
5. Intelligence is a given, and it cannot be improved.
6. If I successfully accomplish a task, it's because it was an easy one.
7. You cannot change your destiny.
8. School success is mostly a result of one's socioeconomic background.
9. People are lonely because they are not given the chance to meet new people.

10. Setting goals for yourself is of little use because nobody knows what might happen in the future to interfere with them.

Give yourself 1 point for each "agree" and 0 points for each "disagree." How close did you get to a score of 10? The closer your score to 10, the more external your locus of control.

Tip

Try this quiz with your friends and explain the concept of locus of control to them afterward. Ask them how they think their lives might be different if their locus of control was either more external or internal, depending on their individual results.

Humanistic Personality Theories

◆ *What are the contributions of humanistic theorists to the study of personality?*

In *humanistic psychology*, people are assumed to have a natural tendency toward growth and the realization of their fullest potential. Thus, humanistic personality theories are more optimistic than Freud's psychoanalytic theory and more sensitive to emotional experiences than the learning theories. However, like Freud's theory, these perspectives are often criticized as being difficult to test scientifically.

For humanistic psychologist Abraham Maslow (1908–1970), motivational factors are at the root of personality. You may remember from Chapter 9 that Maslow constructed a hierarchy of needs, ranging from physiological needs at the bottom upward to safety needs, belonging and love needs, esteem needs, and finally to the highest need—self-actualization (see Figure 9.3 on page 281). **Self-actualization** means developing to one's fullest potential. A healthy person is continually striving to become all that he or she can be.

In his research, Maslow found self-actualizers to be accurate in perceiving reality—able to judge honestly and to spot quickly the fake and the dishonest. Most of them believe they have a mission to accomplish or the need to devote their life to some larger good. Self-actualizers tend not to depend on external authority or other people but seem to be inner-driven, autonomous, and independent. Finally, the hallmark of self-actualizers is having frequently occurring *peak experiences*—experiences of deep meaning, insight, and harmony within themselves and with the universe. Current researchers have modified Maslow's definition of self-actualization to include effective personal relationships as well as peak experiences (Hanley & Abell, 2002).

According to another humanistic psychologist, Carl Rogers (1902–1987), our parents set up **conditions of worth,** or conditions on which their positive regard hinges. Conditions of worth force us to live and act according to someone else's values rather than our own. In our efforts to gain positive regard, we deny our true selves by inhibit-

◆ **self-actualization**
Developing to one's fullest potential.

◆ **conditions of worth**
Conditions on which the positive regard of others rests.

ing some of our behavior, denying or distorting some of our perceptions, and closing off parts of our experience. In so doing, we experience stress and anxiety, and our whole self-structure may be threatened.

For Rogers, a major goal of psychotherapy is to enable people to open themselves up to experiences and begin to live according to their own values rather than living by the values of others in an attempt to gain positive regard. He called his therapy *person-centered therapy*, preferring not to use the term *patient* (Rogers's therapy will be discussed further in Chapter 13). Rogers believed that the therapist must give the client **unconditional positive regard**—that is, unqualified caring and nonjudgmental acceptance, no matter what the client says, does, has done, or is thinking of doing. Unconditional positive regard is designed to reduce threat, eliminate conditions of worth, and bring the person back in tune with his or her true self. If successful, the therapy helps the client become what Rogers called a *fully functioning person*, one who is functioning at an optimal level and living fully and spontaneously according to his or her own inner value system.

Abraham Maslow (1908–1970)

◆ **unconditional positive regard**
Unqualified caring and nonjudgmental acceptance of another.

Although humanists have been criticized for being unscientific and for seeing, hearing, and finding no evil within the human psyche, they have inspired the study of positive personality qualities, including altruism, cooperation, love, acceptance of others, and especially self-esteem. One source of variations in self-esteem arises from comparisons of actual to desired traits. For example, a tone-deaf person who desires to be an accomplished musician might suffer from low self-esteem. However, most of us do not form a global idea about our own self-worth on the basis of a single area of competence. Instead, we view ourselves in terms of strengths and weaknesses. When our strengths lie in areas that we value and believe to be important, we have high self-esteem. Conversely, even outstanding achievements in areas we consider to be of little value may not affect our self-esteem. So, a person who is a great plumber, but who believes that being a good plumber isn't very important, is likely to have low self-esteem. At the same time, a person who feels incompetent because he has to pay a plumber a handsome sum to fix a leaking faucet might be in awe of the plumber's skill.

Trait Theories

Traits are personal qualities or characteristics that make it possible for us to face a wide variety of situational demands and deal with unforeseen circumstances (De Raad & Kokkonen, 2000). *Trait theories* are attempts to explain personality and differences among people in terms of personal characteristics that are stable across situations.

◆ **trait**
A personal characteristic that is stable across situations and is used to describe or explain personality.

Early Trait Theories

One of the early trait theorists, Gordon Allport (1897–1967), claimed that each person inherits a unique set of raw materials for given traits, which are then shaped by experiences (Allport & Odbert, 1936). A *cardinal trait* is "so pervasive and so outstanding in a life that . . . almost every act seems traceable to its influence" (Allport, 1961, p. 365). It is so strong a part of a person's personality that he or she may become identified with or known for that trait. For example, what comes to mind when you hear the name *Einstein?* Most likely, you associate this name with intellectual genius; in fact, it is sometimes used as a synonym for genius. Thus, for Albert Einstein, genius is a cardinal trait. *Central traits* are those, said Allport (1961), that we would "mention in writing a careful letter of recommendation" (p. 365).

Raymond Cattell (1950) referred to observable qualities of personality as *surface traits*. Using observations and questionnaires, Cattell studied thousands of people and found certain clusters of surface traits that appeared together time after time. He

◆ *What were some of the ideas proposed by early trait theorists?*

thought these were evidence of deeper, more general, underlying personality factors, which he called *source traits*. People differ in the degree to which they possess each source trait. For example, Cattell claimed that intelligence is a source trait: Everyone has it, but the amount possessed varies from person to person.

Cattell found 23 source traits in normal individuals, 16 of which he studied in great detail. Cattell's Sixteen Personality Factor Questionnaire, commonly called the *16PF*, yields a personality profile (Cattell, 1950; Cattell et al., 1977). This test continues to be widely used in research (e.g., Aluja & Blanch, 2004; Brody et al., 2000) and for personality assessment in career counseling, schools, and employment settings. Results from the 16PF are usually plotted on a graph such as that shown in Figure 11.4.

Factor Models of Personality

◆ *What do factor theorists consider to be the most important dimensions of personality?*

The early trait theories represented the beginning of a movement that continues to be important in personality research. Cattell's notion of personality factors has been especially influential. One factor model that has shaped a great deal of personality research is that of British psychologist Hans Eysenck (1990), who places particular emphasis on two dimensions: Extroversion (extroversion versus introversion) and Neuroticism (emotional stability versus instability). Extroverts are sociable, outgoing, and active, whereas introverts are withdrawn, quiet, and introspective. Emotionally stable people are calm, even-tempered, and often easygoing, while emotionally unstable people are anxious, excitable, and easily distressed.

Extroversion and Neuroticism are also important dimensions in the most talked-about personality theory today—the **five-factor theory**, also known as the *Big Five* (Wiggins, 1996). We will consider the Big Five personality dimensions and the traits associated with them using the names assigned by Robert McCrae and Paul Costa (1987; McCrae, 1996), the most influential proponents of the five-factor theory.

◆ **five-factor theory**

A trait theory that attempts to explain personality using five broad dimensions, each of which is composed of a constellation of personality traits.

1. *Extroversion.* This dimension contrasts such traits as sociable, outgoing, talkative, assertive, persuasive, decisive, and active with more introverted traits such as withdrawn, quiet, passive, retiring, and reserved.
2. *Neuroticism.* People high on Neuroticism are prone to emotional instability. They tend to experience negative emotions and to be moody, irritable, nervous, and

FIGURE 11.4 **The 16PF Personality Profile**

Results from Cattell's 16PF can be plotted on a chart like this one. The profile is represented by a line connecting an individual's score points on each dimension (e.g., reserved–warm). How would you draw your own profile? Circle the point along each of the dimensions, and connect them with a line to find out.

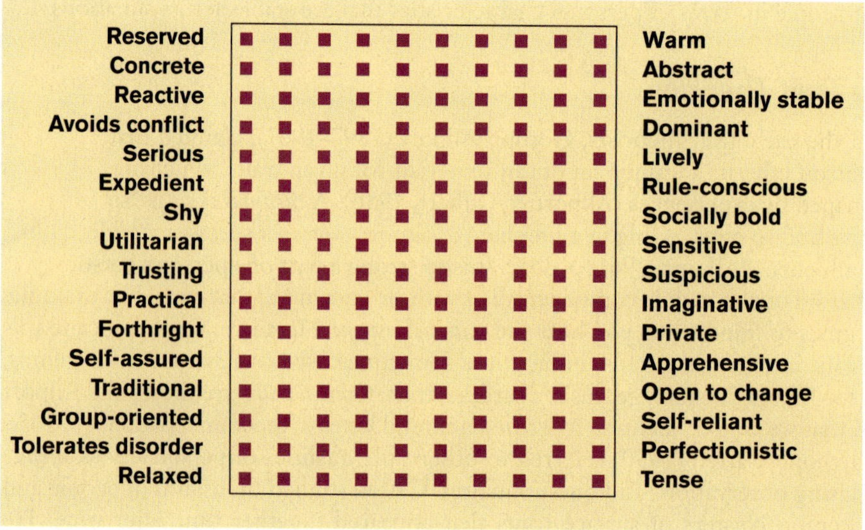

		Warm
Reserved		Warm
Concrete		Abstract
Reactive		Emotionally stable
Avoids conflict		Dominant
Serious		Lively
Expedient		Rule-conscious
Shy		Socially bold
Utilitarian		Sensitive
Trusting		Suspicious
Practical		Imaginative
Forthright		Private
Self-assured		Apprehensive
Traditional		Open to change
Group-oriented		Self-reliant
Tolerates disorder		Perfectionistic
Relaxed		Tense

inclined to worry. This dimension differentiates people who are anxious, excitable, and easily distressed from those who are emotionally stable and thus calm, even-tempered, easygoing, and relaxed.

3. *Conscientiousness.* This dimension differentiates individuals who are dependable, organized, reliable, responsible, thorough, hard-working, and persevering from those who are undependable, disorganized, impulsive, unreliable, irresponsible, careless, negligent, and lazy.

4. *Agreeableness.* This dimension is composed of a collection of traits that range from compassion to antagonism toward others. A person high on Agreeableness would be a pleasant person, who is good-natured, warm, sympathetic, and cooperative; one low on Agreeableness would tend to be unfriendly, unpleasant, aggressive, argumentative, cold, even hostile and vindictive.

5. *Openness to Experience.* This dimension contrasts individuals who seek out varied experiences and who are imaginative, intellectually curious, and broad-minded with those who are concrete-minded and practical and whose interests are narrow. Researchers have found that being high on Openness to Experience is a requirement for creative accomplishment (King et al., 1996).

To measure the Big Five dimensions of personality, Costa and McCrae (1985, 1992, 1997) developed the NEO Personality Inventory (NEO-PI) and, more recently, the Revised NEO Personality Inventory (NEO-PI-R). The NEO and other measures of the Big Five are currently being used in a wide variety of personality research studies. For example, psychologists in the Australian army have used the test to measure personality differences between effective and ineffective leaders (McCormack & Mellor, 2002). And all five factors have been found in cross-cultural studies involving participants from Canada, Finland, Poland, Germany, Russia, Hong Kong, Croatia, Italy, South Korea, the Czech Republic, and Portugal (McCrae et al., 2000, 2004; Paunonen et al., 1996).

But how important are the Big Five in our everyday experiences? One line of research addressing this question focuses on connections among personality, physical health, and mental health. For instance, researchers have learned that high scores on the dimension of Neuroticism are associated with peptic ulcer disease (Goodwin & Stein, 2003). Individuals with such high scores are also more likely to suffer from attention problems (Szymura & Wodniecka, 2003). Understanding the connection between personality traits and problems such as these may help prevent these problems in the future or may help health professionals more effectively treat individuals who suffer from them.

Researchers have also found connections between the Big Five and other domains of behavior such as entertainment preferences (Schutte & Malouff, 2004). For instance, the higher an individual's score on the dimension of Openness to Experience, the more likely she is to prefer classical, jazz, or rock music to country or rap (Rentfrow & Gosling, 2003). Moreover, scores on the Big Five are related to the physical characteristics of an individual's home (Gosling et al., 2002). For instance, those who score high on Extroversion are likely to arrange their living spaces in ways that are cheerful, colorful, and stylish, but a bit cluttered and unconventional. People who score high on Conscientiousness create efficient furniture arrangements and organize their possessions so that they can be easily located. Thus, it appears that the different ways in which people respond to questions on personality inventories are, indeed, meaningfully linked to everyday behavior.

The Situation versus Trait Debate

How well do trait theories explain behavior? This question has been addressed by one of the severest critics of trait theories, Walter Mischel (1968, 2004). Mischel initiated the *situation–trait debate*, an ongoing discussion among psychologists about the relative importance of factors within the situation and factors within the person in accounting for behavior (Rowe, 1987). For instance, you probably wouldn't steal money from a store, but what if you see a stranger unknowingly drop a $5

◆ *What is the situation–trait debate about?*

Research on personality suggests that some traits, such as agreeableness, actually increase as we get older.

bill? Mischel and those who agree with him say that characteristics of the two situations dictate your behavior, not a trait such as honesty. Stealing from a store might require devising and carrying out a complicated plan, and it would carry a heavy penalty if you were caught, so you opt for honesty. Picking up a $5 bill is easy and may only result in embarrassment if you get caught, so you may do it. Mischel (1973, 1977) later modified his original position and admitted that behavior is influenced by both the person and the situation. Mischel views a trait as a conditional probability that a particular action will occur in response to a particular situation (Wright & Mischel, 1987).

Advocates of the trait side of the situation–trait debate point out that support for trait theories has come from many longitudinal studies (McCrae, 2002; Pesonen et al., 2003). McCrae and Costa (1990) studied personality traits of subjects over time and found them to be stable for periods of 3 to 30 years. Typically, personality changes very little with age. As McCrae (1993) puts it, "Stable individual differences in basic dimensions are a universal feature of adult personality" (p. 577). Indeed, a large meta-analysis demonstrated that consistency of personality traits actually increases over the adult years (Roberts & DelVecchio, 2000).

The weight of evidence supports the view that there are internal traits that strongly influence behavior across situations (Carson, 1989; McAdams, 1992). Still, situational variables do affect personality traits. In one study of elderly women, researchers found that life changes such as decreases in social support and increases in physical disability resulted in increases in Neuroticism (Maiden et al., 2003). Similarly, the organizational demands of adult life appear to lead to increases in Conscientiousness throughout adulthood that are most marked between the ages of 20 and 30 (Srivastava et al., 2003). (There's hope for even the most disorganized among us!) And, researchers say, the stereotype of "grumpy old men" is a myth; agreeableness actually increases as we get older (Srivastava et al., 2003). Thus, characteristic traits determine how we behave most of the time, not all of the time.

Nature, Nurture, and Personality

So, you might be wondering, how do we acquire our personality traits? This question leads us back to the great debate we have encountered before—the nature–nurture controversy. Recall from Chapter 2 that *behavioral genetics* is the field of study that uses twin studies and adoption studies to investigate the relative effects of heredity and environment on behavior. Personality traits have been studied extensively by researchers in this field.

Twin and Adoption Studies

◆ What have twin and adoption studies revealed about the influence of genes on personality?

As you learned in Chapter 7, one of the best-known studies in psychology, the Minnesota twin study, revealed that the IQ scores of identical twins are strongly correlated, regardless of whether the twins are raised in the same or different environments (Bouchard, 1997). Using data from the same participants, Tellegen and others (1988) found that identical twins are also quite similar on several personality factors, again regardless of whether they are raised together or apart.

In another classic twin study, Rushton and colleagues (1986) found that nurturance, empathy, and assertiveness are substantially influenced by heredity. Even altruism and aggressiveness, traits we might expect to be strongly influenced by parental upbringing, are actually more heavily influenced by heredity. A meta-analysis by Miles and Carey (1997) revealed that the heritability of aggressiveness may be as high as .50 (or 50%). Moreover, a number of longitudinal studies indicate that heredity makes substantial contributions to individual differences in the Big Five personality dimensions, as shown in Figure 11.5 (Bouchard, 1994; Caspi, 2000; Loehlin, 1992). These studies suggest that genes exert more influence on Extroversion and Neuroticism than on the other dimensions of the Big Five (Krueger & Johnson, 2004). Thus, genetically based similarities in personality, rather than modeling, may be responsible for the ways in which our adult lives relate to those of our parents.

Adoption studies have also shown that heredity strongly influences personality. Loehlin and others (1987) assessed the personalities of 17-year-olds who had been adopted at birth. When the adopted children were compared to other children in the family, the researchers found that the shared family environment had virtually no influence on their personalities. In another study, Loehlin and colleagues (1990) measured change in personality of adoptees over a 10-year period and found that children tended "to change on the average in the direction of their genetic parents' personalities" (p. 221). The prevailing thinking among behavioral geneticists, then, is that the shared environment plays a negligible role in the formation of personality (Loehlin et al., 1988), although there has been some opposition to this view (Rose et al., 1988).

Clearly, heredity influences personality. However, it is equally clear that personality is not determined by genes in the same way as physical traits such as eye color and blood type are. Instead, according to many psychologists, genes *constrain* the ways in which environments affect personality traits (Kagan, 2003). For example, a child who has a genetic tendency toward shyness may be encouraged by parents to be more sociable. As a result, he will be more outgoing than he would have been without such encouragement but will still be less sociable than a child who is genetically predisposed to be extroverted.

FIGURE 11.5 **Estimated Influence of Heredity and Environment on the Big Five Personality Dimensions**

The Minnesota study of twins reared apart yielded an average heritability estimate of .41 (41%) for the Big Five personality factors; the Loehlin twin studies, a heritability estimate of .42 (42%). Both studies found the influence of the shared environment to be only about .07 (7%). The remaining percentage represents a combination of nonshared environmental influences and measurement error. *Source:* Adapted from Bouchard (1994).

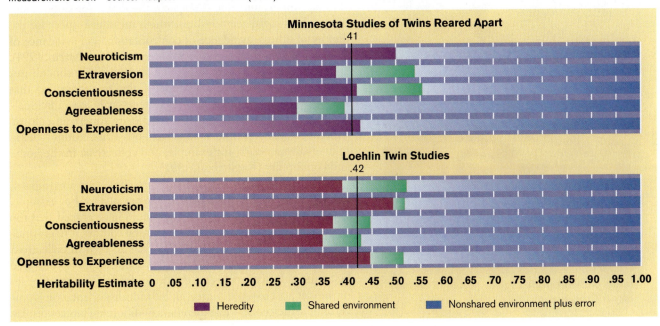

Personality and Culture

◆ How does personality differ across cultures?

◆ **individualism/ collectivism dimension**

A measure of a culture's emphasis on either individual achievement or social relationships.

Important environmental influences on personality also arise from the diverse cultures in which humans live and work. In classic research, Hofstede (1980, 1983) analyzed questionnaire responses measuring the work-related values of more than 100,000 IBM employees in 53 countries around the world. Factor analysis revealed four separate dimensions related to culture and personality, of which one, the **individualism/collectivism dimension,** is of particular interest here. In individualist cultures, more emphasis is placed on individual achievement than on group achievement. High-achieving individuals are accorded honor and prestige in individualist cultures. People in collectivist cultures, on the other hand, tend to be more interdependent and define themselves and their personal interests in terms of their group membership. Asians, for example, have highly collectivist cultures, and collectivism is compatible with Confucianism, the predominant religion of these Eastern cultures. In fact, according to the Confucian values, the individual finds his or her identity in interrelatedness, as a part of the larger group. Moreover, this interrelatedness is an important ingredient of happiness for Asians (Kitayama & Markus, 2000).

Hofstede rank-ordered the 53 countries from the IBM study on each of the four dimensions. The United States ranked as the most individualist culture in the sample, followed by Australia, Great Britain, Canada, and the Netherlands. At the other end of the continuum were the most collectivist cultures: Guatemala, Ecuador, Panama, Venezuela, and Colombia, all Latin American countries.

Although, according to Hofstede, the United States ranks first in individualism, there are many distinct minority cultural groups in the United States, which may be decidedly less individualist. Native Americans number close to 2 million, but even within this relatively small cultural group, there are more than 200 different tribes, and no single language, religion, or culture (Bennett, 1994). Yet, Native Americans have many shared (collectivist) values, such as the importance of family, community, cooperation, and generosity. Native Americans value a generous nature as evidenced by gift giving and helpfulness. Such behaviors bring more honor and prestige than accumulating property and building individual wealth.

For these native Alaskans, participating in the traditional blanket toss ceremony is one manifestation of their culture's values related to community and cooperation.

Hispanic Americans, who represent about 13% of the U.S. population (U.S. Census Bureau, 2001) also tend to be more collectivist than individualist. Despite significant cultural differences among various Hispanic American groups, there are striking similarities as well. The clearest shared cultural value is a strong identification with and attachment to the extended family. Another important value is *simpatía*, the desire for smooth and harmonious social relationships, which includes respect for the dignity of others, avoidance of confrontation, and avoidance of words or actions that might hurt another's feelings (Marín, 1994).

Although the Native American and Hispanic subcultures are more collectivist than individualist, that does not mean that any one member of these cultures is necessarily less individualist than any given member of the majority American culture. Moreover, many people may value both orientations—being individualist at work, for example, and collectivist in the home and community (Kagitcibasi, 1992).

It is important to note that some psychologists warn against overemphasizing cultural differences in personality. For example, Constantine Sedikides and her colleagues have argued that the goal of all individuals, regardless of cultural context, is to enhance self-esteem (Sedikides et al., 2003). That is, even in collectivist cultures, the process of conforming to one's culture is motivated by an individualistic concern, the desire for self-esteem. Consequently, at least to some degree, an individualist orientation is universal. Furthermore, while members of different cultures display varying commitments to an individualistic philosophy, autonomy—a sense of personal control over one's life—predicts well-being in all cultures (Ryan et al., 2003).

Personality Assessment

Have you ever taken a personality test? You may have as part of a job application and screening process. Personality assessment is commonly used in business and industry to aid in hiring decisions. Various ways of measuring personality are used by clinical psychologists, psychiatrists, and counselors in the diagnosis of patients and in the assessment of progress in therapy.

Observation, Interviews, and Rating Scales

Psychologists use observation in personality assessment in a variety of settings—hospitals, clinics, schools, and workplaces. Behaviorists, in particular, prefer observation to other methods of personality assessment. Using an observational technique known as *behavioral assessment*, psychologists can count and record the frequency of particular behaviors. This method is often used in behavior modification programs in settings such as psychiatric hospitals, where psychologists may chart patients' progress toward reducing aggressive acts or other undesirable or abnormal behaviors. However, behavioral assessment is time-consuming, and behavior may be misinterpreted. Probably the most serious limitation is that the very presence of the observer can alter the behavior being observed.

◆ *How do psychologists use observations, interviews, and rating scales?*

Clinical psychologists and psychiatrists use interviews to help in the diagnosis and treatment of patients. Counselors use interviews to screen applicants for admission to college or other special programs, and employers use them to evaluate job applicants and employees for job promotions. Interviewers consider not only a person's answers to questions but the person's tone of voice, speech, mannerisms, gestures, and general appearance also. Interviewers often use a *structured interview*, in which the content of the questions and even the manner in which they are asked are carefully planned ahead of time. The interviewer tries not to deviate in any way from the structured format so that more reliable comparisons can be made between different subjects.

Examiners sometimes use *rating scales* to record data from interviews or observations. Such scales are useful because they provide a standardized format, including a list of traits or behaviors to evaluate. A rating scale helps to focus the rater's attention on all the relevant traits to be considered so that none is overlooked or weighed too heavily. The major limitation of these scales is that the ratings are often subjective. A related problem is the *halo effect*—the tendency of raters to be excessively influenced in their overall evaluation of a person by one or a few favorable or unfavorable traits. Often, traits or attributes that are not even on the rating scale, such as physical attractiveness or similarity to the rater, heavily influence a rater's perception of an individual. To overcome these limitations, it is often necessary to have individuals rated by more than one interviewer.

◆ **inventory**
A paper-and-pencil test with questions about a person's thoughts, feelings, and behaviors, which measures several dimensions of personality and can be scored according to a standard procedure.

◆ **Minnesota Multiphasic Personality Inventory (MMPI)**
The most extensively researched and widely used personality test, which is used to screen for and diagnose psychiatric problems and disorders; revised as MMPI-2.

Personality Inventories

As useful as observations, interviews, and rating scales are, another method of measuring personality offers greater objectivity. This method is the **inventory**, a paper-and-pencil test with questions about an individual's thoughts, feelings, and behaviors, which measures several dimensions of personality and can be scored according to a standard procedure. Psychologists favoring the trait approach prefer the inventory because it reveals where people fall on various dimensions of personality, and it yields a personality profile.

The most widely used personality inventory is the **Minnesota Multiphasic Personality Inventory (MMPI)** or its revision, the MMPI-2. The MMPI is the most heavily researched personality test for diagnosing psychiatric problems and disorders

◆ *What is an inventory, and what are the MMPI-2 and the CPI designed to reveal?*

(Butcher & Rouse, 1996). There have been more than 115 recognized translations of the MMPI, and it is used in more than 65 countries (Butcher & Graham, 1989).

Developed in the late 1930s and early 1940s by researchers J. Charnley McKinley and Starke Hathaway, the MMPI was originally intended to identify tendencies toward various types of psychiatric disorders. The researchers administered more than 1,000 questions about attitudes, feelings, and specific symptoms to groups of psychiatric patients at the University of Minnesota hospital who had been clearly diagnosed with various specific disorders and to a control group of individuals who had no diagnosed disorders. They retained the 550 items that differentiated the specific groups of psychiatric patients from the group of participants considered to be normal.

Because the original MMPI had become outdated, the MMPI-2 was published in 1989 (Butcher et al., 1989). Most of the original test items were retained, but new items were added to more adequately cover areas such as alcoholism, drug abuse, suicidal tendencies, eating disorders, and the Type A behavior pattern. The MMPI had often been unreliable for African Americans, women, and adolescents (Levitt & Duckworth, 1984). Thus, new norms were established to reflect national census data and achieve a better geographical, racial, and cultural balance (Ben-Porath & Butcher, 1989).

Table 11.1 shows the 10 clinical scales of the MMPI-2. Following are examples of items on the test, which are to be answered "true," "false," or "cannot say."

I wish I were not bothered by thoughts about sex.
When I get bored, I like to stir up some excitement.
In walking I am very careful to step over sidewalk cracks.
If people had not had it in for me, I would have been much more successful.

A high score on any of the scales does not necessarily mean that a person has a problem or a psychiatric symptom. Rather, the psychologist looks at the individual's

TABLE 11.1   The Clinical Scales of the MMPI-2

SCALE NAME	INTERPRETATION
1. Hypochondriasis (Hs)	High scorers exhibit an exaggerated concern about their physical health.
2. Depression (D)	High scorers are usually depressed, despondent, and distressed.
3. Hysteria (Hy)	High scorers complain often about physical symptoms that have no apparent organic cause.
4. Psychopathic deviate (Pd)	High scorers show a disregard for social and moral standards.
5. Masculinity/femininity (Mf)	High scorers show "traditional" masculine or feminine attitudes and values.
6. Paranoia (Pa)	High scorers demonstrate extreme suspiciousness and feelings of persecution.
7. Psychasthenia (Pt)	High scorers tend to be highly anxious, rigid, tense, and worrying.
8. Schizophrenia (Sc)	High scorers tend to be socially withdrawn and to engage in bizarre and unusual thinking.
9. Hypomania (Ma)	High scorers are usually emotional, excitable, energetic, and impulsive.
10. Social introversion (S)	High scorers tend to be modest, self-effacing, and shy.

MMPI profile—the pattern of scores on all the scales—and then compares it to the profiles of normal individuals and those with various psychiatric disorders.

But what if someone lies on the test to appear mentally healthy? Embedded in the test to provide a check against lying are questions such as these:

Once in a while, I put off until tomorrow what I ought to do today.
I gossip a little at times.
Once in a while, I laugh at a dirty joke.

Most people would almost certainly have to answer "true" in response to such items—unless, of course, they were lying. Another scale controls for people who are faking psychiatric illness, as in the case of someone hoping to be judged not guilty of a crime by reason of insanity. Research seems to indicate that the validity scales in the MMPI-2 are effective in detecting test takers who were instructed to fake a psychological disturbance or to lie to make themselves appear more psychologically healthy (Bagby et al., 1994; Butcher et al., 1995). Even when given specific information about various psychological disorders, test takers could not produce profiles similar to those of people who actually suffered from the disorder (Wetter et al., 1993).

The MMPI-2 is reliable, easy to administer and score, and inexpensive to use. It is useful in the screening, diagnosis, and clinical description of abnormal behavior, but it does not reveal normal personality differences very well. A special form of the test, the MMPI-A, was developed for adolescents in 1992. The MMPI-A includes some items that are especially relevant to adolescents, such as those referring to eating disorders, substance abuse, and problems with school and family. The MMPI-2 has been translated for use in Belgium, Chile, China, France, Hong Kong, Israel, Korea, Italy, Japan, Norway, Russia, Spain, and Thailand (Butcher, 1992). Lucio and others (1994) administered the Mexican (Spanish) version of MMPI-2 to more than 2,100 Mexican college students. They found the profiles of these students "remarkably similar" to profiles of U.S. college students.

An important limitation of the MMPI-2, though, is that it was designed specifically to assess abnormality. By contrast, the **California Personality Inventory (CPI)** is a highly regarded personality test developed especially for normal individuals aged 13 and older. Similar to the MMPI, the CPI even has many of the same questions, but it does not include any questions designed to reveal psychiatric illness (Gough, 1987). The CPI is valuable for predicting behavior, and it has been "praised for its technical competency, careful development, cross-validation and follow-up, use of sizable samples and separate sex norms" (Domino, 1984, p. 156). The CPI was revised in 1987, to make it provide "a picture of the subject's life-style and the degree to which his or her potential is being realized" (McReynolds, 1989, p. 101). The CPI is particularly useful in predicting school achievement in high school and beyond, leadership and executive success, and the effectiveness of police, military personnel, and student teachers (Gregory, 1996).

The **Myers-Briggs Type Indicator (MBTI)** is another personality inventory that is useful for measuring normal individual differences. This test is based on Jung's personality theory. The MBTI scored on four separate bipolar dimensions:

Extraversion (E) ←——→ Introversion (I)
Sensing (S) ←——→ Intuition (N)
Thinking (T) ←——→ Feeling (F)
Judging (J) ←——→ Perceptive (P)

A person can score anywhere along a continuum for each of the four bipolar dimensions, and these individual scores are usually summarized according to a system of personality types. Sixteen types of personality profiles can be derived from the possible combinations of the four bipolar dimensions. For example, a person whose scores were more toward the Extraversion, Intuition, Feeling, and Perceptive ends of the four dimensions would be labeled an ENFP personality type, which is described as follows:

Relates more readily to the outer world of people and things than to the inner world of ideas (E); prefers to search for new possibilities over working with known facts and conventional ways of doing things (N); makes decisions and solves problems on the basis of personal values and feelings rather than relying on logical thinking and analy-

◆ **California Personality Inventory (CPI)**

A highly regarded personality test developed especially for normal individuals aged 13 and older.

◆ **Myers-Briggs Type Indicator (MBTI)**

A personality inventory useful for measuring normal individual differences; based on Jung's theory of personality.

sis (F); and prefers a flexible, spontaneous life to a planned and orderly existence (P). (Gregory, 1996)

The MBTI is growing in popularity, especially in business and educational settings (Sample, 2004). Critics point to the absence of rigorous, controlled validity studies of the inventory (Pittenger, 1993). And it has also been criticized for being interpreted too often by unskilled examiners, who have been accused of making overly simplistic interpretations (Gregory, 1996). However, sufficiently sophisticated methods for interpreting the MBTI do exist, as revealed by almost 500 research studies to date (Allen, 1997). Many of these studies have shown that the MBTI personality types are associated with career choices and job satisfaction. For example, physicians who choose different specialties (e.g., pediatrics, surgery) tend to have different MBTI types (Stilwell et al., 2000). Consequently, the MBTI continues to enjoy popularity among career counselors.

Projective Tests

How do projective tests provide insight into personality, and what are some of the most commonly used projective tests?

Responses on interviews and questionnaires are conscious responses and, for this reason, are less useful to therapists who wish to probe the unconscious. Such therapists may choose a completely different technique called a projective test. A **projective test** is a personality test consisting of inkblots, drawings of ambiguous human situations, or incomplete sentences for which there are no correct or incorrect responses. People respond by projecting their inner thoughts, feelings, fears, or conflicts onto the test materials.

One of the oldest and most popular projective tests is the **Rorschach Inkblot Method** developed by Swiss psychiatrist Hermann Rorschach (ROR-shok) in 1921. It consists of 10 inkblots, which the test taker is asked to describe (see Figure 11.6). To develop his test, Rorschach put ink on paper and then folded the paper so that symmetrical patterns would result. Earlier, psychologists had used standardized series of inkblots to study imagination and other variables, but Rorschach was the first to use inkblots to investigate personality. He experimented with thousands of inkblots on different groups of people and found that 10 of the inkblots could be used to discriminate among different diagnostic groups, such as manic depressives, paranoid schizophrenics, and so on. These 10 inkblots—5 black and white, and 5 with color—were standardized and are still widely used.

The Rorschach can be used to describe personality, make differential diagnoses, plan and evaluate treatment, and predict behavior (Ganellen, 1996; Weiner, 1997, 2004). For the last 20 years, it has been second in popularity to the MMPI for use in research and clinical assessment (Butcher & Rouse, 1996). The test taker is shown the 10 inkblots and asked to tell everything that he or she thinks about what each inkblot looks like or resembles. The examiner writes down the test taker's responses and then goes through the cards again, asking questions to clarify what the test taker has reported. In scoring the Rorschach, the examiner considers whether the test taker has used the whole inkblot in the description or only parts of it. The test taker is asked whether the shape of the inkblot, its color, or something else prompted the response. The examiner also considers whether the test taker sees movement, human figures or parts, animal figures or parts, or other objects in the inkblots.

Until the 1990s, the main problem with the Rorschach was that the results were too dependent on the interpretation and judgment of the examiner. In response to such criticisms, Exner (1993) developed

◆ **projective test**

A personality test in which people respond to inkblots, drawings of ambiguous human situations, or incomplete sentences by projecting their inner thoughts, feelings, fears, or conflicts onto the test materials.

◆ **Rorschach Inkblot Method**

(ROR-shok) A projective test composed of 10 inkblots that the test taker is asked to describe; used to assess personality, make differential diagnoses, plan and evaluate treatment, and predict behavior.

FIGURE 11.6

An Inkblot Similar to One Used for the Rorschach Inkblot Method

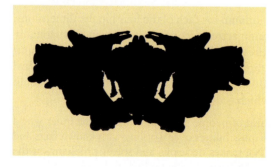

the Comprehensive System, a more reliable procedure for scoring the Rorschach. It provides some normative data so that the responses of a person taking the test can be compared to those of others with known personality characteristics. Using this system, some researchers have found high agreement among different raters interpreting the same responses (interrater agreement) (McDowell & Acklin, 1996). Others believe that more research is necessary before it can be concluded that the Comprehensive System yields reliable and valid results (Wood et al., 1996). However, a number of meta-analyses indicate that the Rorschach Inkblot Method has "psychometric soundness and practical utility" (Weiner, 1996).

Another projective test is the **Thematic Apperception Test (TAT)** developed by Henry Murray and his colleagues in 1935 (Morgan & Murray, 1935; Murray, 1938). You may remember from Chapter 9 that researchers have used the TAT to study the need for achievement, but it is also useful for assessing other aspects of personality. The TAT consists of 1 blank card and 19 other cards showing vague or ambiguous black-and-white drawings of human figures in various situations. If you were taking the TAT, this is what you would be told:

> This is a test of your creative imagination. I shall show you a picture, and I want you to make up a plot or story for which it might be used as an illustration. What is the relation of the individuals in the picture? What has happened to them? What are their present thoughts and feelings? What will be the outcome? (Morgan & Murray, 1962, p. 532)

What does the story you write have to do with your personality or your problems or motives? Murray (1965) stresses the importance of "an element or theme that recurs three or more times in the series of stories" (p. 432). For example, if a person uses many story themes about illness, sex, fear of failure, aggression, power, or interpersonal conflict, such a recurring theme is thought to reveal a problem in the person's life. Murray (1965) also claims that the strength of the TAT is "its capacity to reveal things that the patient is unwilling to tell or is unable to tell because he [or she] is unconscious of them" (p. 427).

The TAT is time-consuming and difficult to administer and score. Although it has been used extensively in research, it suffers from the same weaknesses as other projective techniques: (1) It relies heavily on the interpretation skills of the examiner, and (2) it may reflect too strongly a person's temporary motivational and emotional states and not indicate more permanent aspects of personality.

◆ **Thematic Apperception Test (TAT)**

A projective test consisting of drawings of ambiguous human situations, which the test taker describes; thought to reveal inner feelings, conflicts, and motives, which are projected onto the test materials.

Looking Back   At the beginning of the chapter, we posed a question about the sufficiency of childhood experiences to explain personality differences among adults. At this point, you should realize that, although they are important, childhood experiences are but one source of variation that helps explain these differences. Other views of personality are needed to explain why similar childhood experiences have different effects on individuals. The experience of parental divorce, for example, is traumatic to all children. But, for some, it helps to forge a resolve to establish lasting relationships in adulthood. For others, it leads to difficulty in trusting others enough to form relationships. Humanistic, learning, and trait theories may help us understand why individuals respond differently to these experiences. Thus, like so many other issues in psychology, personality is best approached from a variety of perspectives, rather than from a single theory that we assume to be the "right" one.

Apply It 11.1 Put Your Best Foot Forward

As you learned in the chapter, interviews are an important assessment tool used by psychologists. But did you ever think of a job interview as an assessment? You should, because that's precisely what it is. The interviewer isn't measuring your personality, of course, as a psychologist would. Instead, he or she is assessing whether you fit the organization's needs and whether you can fit in with the others who work there. Here are a few tips for successful interviewing.

Impression Management

Think of the interview as an opportunity to make a particular impression on a potential employer. Psychologists use the term impression management to refer to the process of deliberately controlling your behavior in ways that will create the impression you desire. For instance, dressing appropriately and using polite language are components of impression management. Researchers have found that interviewees who display these kinds of impression management behaviors are viewed more positively by interviewers (Bolino & Turnley, 2003). However, you should refrain from using strategies such as exaggerating your qualifications or experience. Experienced interviewers are skilled at recognizing such exaggerations and tend to look unfavorably upon interviewees who use them (Paulhus et al., 2003).

Educate Yourself

One of the most often overlooked keys to successful interviewing is learning about the job you're applying for. You should learn as much as you can about the business or industry you want to work in and about the particular firm to which you are applying. Many major corporations and organizations host websites that provide extensive information on their history, mission statement, products, employees, and job listings. These sites can be a great place to start researching potential employers. Study the job qualifications, both required and preferred, if they're available, and get a good idea of how your qualifications match up.

Prepare an Effective Resume

Even if the job you're applying for doesn't require a resume, it's a good idea to prepare one and take it—along with some extra copies—with you to the interview. For one thing, preparing a resume will provide an opportunity for you to rehearse your knowledge about your work history, job skills, and other qualifications. As a result, you'll be able to retrieve the information from your memory more rapidly when the interviewer questions you. A good resume is a quick source of information for the interviewer, who needs to know about your entire work history to create questions based on it. This preparation will leave more time for you to discuss more substantive issues with the interviewer. Most colleges and universities have career centers that provide advice on resume preparation and related services.

Practice

Practice answering interview questions with a friend. Many college career centers have lists of frequently asked interview questions, and you should always create your own list of questions that you think the interviewer might ask. Try to avoid saying negative things about yourself. Remember, too, that consistent eye contact will show the interviewer that you have confidence.

Dress Professionally

When you are interviewing for a job, your clothing, visible adornments on your body (e.g., tattoos, jewelry), how well groomed you are, and even the way you smell can be forms of communication. Thus, details are important. Male interviewees should consider the research finding that both male and female interviewers respond more positively to clean-shaven applicants (de Souza et al., 2003).

Ideally, your appearance should communicate to the interviewer that you understand the environment in which you hope to be working. For example, if you are interviewing for a position as a construction worker, jeans and a T-shirt, along with a pair of sturdy shoes, are appropriate. When interviewing for an office job, a suit and dress shoes would be better choices. Keep in mind, too, that your appearance influences your own self-confidence. Researchers have found that the more formal interviewees' clothing is, the more positive are the remarks they make about themselves during the interview (Hannover & Kuehnen, 2002).

Be Punctual

Do you feel frustrated when others keep you waiting? Interviewers respond emotionally to tardiness, just as you do. Consequently, it's best to arrive early. And if you are unavoidably delayed, call and reschedule.

Greet the Interviewer Appropriately

Your greeting plays an important role in the interview process as well. In the United States, it's best to look your interviewer directly in the eyes, shake hands firmly, pronounce her or his name correctly, and have good posture.

Follow Up

After the interview, it's a good idea to send a thank-you note. If you met with more than one interviewer, send a note to each of them, mentioning some specific aspect of the discussion that you found interesting. This will indicate that you were fully engaged in the conversation, listening intently, and interested in the interviewer's knowledge about the open position and the organization. The note should also express your appreciation for the interviewer's time and your interest in the position.

Sigmund Freud and Psychoanalysis p. 340

◆ What are the three levels of awareness in consciousness? p. 341

The three levels of awareness in consciousness are the conscious, the preconscious, and the unconscious. The conscious mind includes everything we are thinking about at any given moment. The preconscious includes thoughts and feelings we can easily bring to mind. The unconscious contains thoughts and feelings that are difficult to call up because they have been repressed.

◆ What are the roles of the id, the ego, and the superego? p. 341

The id is the primitive, unconscious part of the personality, which contains the instincts and operates on the pleasure principle. The ego is the rational, largely conscious system, which operates according to the reality principle. The superego is the moral system of the personality, consisting of the conscience and the ego ideal.

◆ What is the purpose of defense mechanisms? p. 342

A defense mechanism is a means used by the ego to defend against anxiety and to maintain self-esteem. For example, through repression, painful memories, thoughts, ideas, or perceptions are involuntarily removed from consciousness.

◆ What are the psychosexual stages, and why did Freud consider them important in personality development? p. 342

Freud believed that the sexual instinct is present at birth and develops through a series of psychosexual stages, providing the driving force for all feelings and behaviors. The stages are the oral stage, anal stage, phallic stage (followed by the latency period), and genital stage.

◆ How are Freud's ideas evaluated by modern psychologists? p. 344

Freud is credited with calling attention to the unconscious, the importance of early childhood experiences, and the role of defense mechanisms. However, his theory is often criticized because it is difficult to test scientifically.

The Neo-Freudians p. 344

◆ How do the views of the neo-Freudians differ from those of Freud? p. 344

Jung conceived of the personality as having three parts: the ego, the personal unconscious, and the collective unconscious. Adler claimed that the predominant force of the personality is not sexual in nature but rather the drive to overcome and compensate for feelings of weakness and inferiority and to strive for superiority or significance. Horney took issue with Freud's sexist view of women and added the feminine dimension to the world of psychology.

Learning Theories and Personality p. 346

◆ What are the components of Bandura's concept of reciprocal determinism and Rotter's locus of control? p. 346

The external environment, behavior, and cognitive factors are the three components of reciprocal determinism, each influencing and being influenced by the others. According to Rotter, people with an internal locus of control see themselves as primarily in control of their behavior and its consequences; those with an external locus of control believe their destiny is in the hands of fate, luck, or chance.

Humanistic Personality Theories p. 348

◆ What are the contributions of humanistic theorists to the study of personality? p. 348

According to Maslow, the goal of personality development is to reach a level where most behavior is motivated by self-actualization, the drive to attain one's fullest potential. According to Rogers, individuals often do not become fully functioning persons because in childhood they did not receive unconditional positive regard from their parents. To gain positive regard, they had to meet their parents' conditions of worth.

Trait Theories p. 349

◆ What were some of the ideas proposed by early trait theorists? p. 349

Allport defined a cardinal trait as a personal quality that pervades a person's personality to the point where he or she may become identified with that trait. A central trait is the type you might mention when writing a letter of recommendation. Cattell used the term *surface traits* to refer to observable qualities of personality. Source traits, which underlie the surface traits, are possessed in varying amounts by people.

◆ What do factor theorists consider to be the most important dimensions of personality? p. 350

Eysenck considers the two most important dimensions of personality to be Extroversion (extroversion versus introversion) and Neuroticism (emotional stability versus instability). According to McCrae and Costa, personality is influenced by five dimensions. The Big Five are Neuroticism, Extroversion, Conscientiousness, Agreeableness, and Openness to Experience.

◆ **What is the situation–trait debate about?** p. 351

The situation–trait debate mainly concerns the degree to which situations influence the manifestation of personality traits. The trait side says that behavior is strongly influenced by traits in all situations. The situation side says that situations are more strongly related to behavior.

Nature, Nurture, and Personality p. 352

◆ **What have twin and adoption studies revealed about the influence of genes on personality?** p. 352

Both twin and adoption studies have shown that heredity strongly influences personality.

◆ **How does personality differ across cultures?** p. 354

The cultural dimension known as individualism/collectivism is associated with personality. Individualist cultures encourage people to view themselves as separate from others and to value independence and assertiveness. Collectivist cultures emphasize social connectedness among people and encourage individuals to define themselves in terms of their social relationships.

Personality Assessment p. 355

◆ **How do psychologists use observations, interviews, and rating scales?** p. 355

During observations, psychologists count behaviors that may be representative of an individual's personality. They use structured interviews to compare the responses of one interviewee to those of others given under similar circumstances. Rating scales are used to quantify behaviors that occur during observations or interviews.

◆ **What is an inventory, and what are the MMPI-2 and the CPI designed to reveal?** p. 355

An inventory is a test with questions about a person's thoughts, feelings, and behaviors. The MMPI-2 is designed to screen and diagnose psychiatric problems, and the CPI is designed to assess the normal personality.

◆ **How do projective tests provide insight into personality, and what are some of the most commonly used projective tests?** p. 358

In a projective test, people respond to inkblots or drawings of ambiguous human situations by projecting their inner thoughts, feelings, fears, or conflicts onto the test materials.

◆ **KEY TERMS**

Study Guide 11

Answers to all the Study Guide questions are provided at the end of the book.

◆ **SECTION ONE: Chapter Review**

Sigmund Freud and Psychoanalysis (pp. 340–344)

1. Psychoanalysis is both a theory of personality and a therapy for the treatment of psychological disorders. (true/false)

2. Freud considered the (conscious, unconscious) to be the primary motivating force of human behavior.

3. The part of the personality that would make you want to eat, drink, and be merry is your
   a. id.   c. superego.
   b. ego.

4. You just found a gold watch in a darkened movie theater. Which part of your personality would urge you to turn it in to the lost and found?
   a. id   c. superego
   b. ego

5. The part of the personality that determines appropriate ways to satisfy biological urges is the
   a. id.   c. superego.
   b. ego.

6. Defense mechanisms are used only by psychologically unhealthy individuals. (true/false)

7. Repression is used to avoid unpleasant thoughts. (true/false)

8. According to Freud, the sex instinct arises at (birth, puberty).

9. Which of the following lists presents Freud's stages in the order in which they occur?
   a. anal, oral, genital, phallic
   b. genital, anal, oral, phallic
   c. oral, phallic, anal, genital
   d. oral, anal, phallic, genital

10. Rich's excessive concern with cleanliness and order could indicate a fixation at the _____ stage.
   a. oral   b. anal   c. phallic   d. genital

11. When a young boy develops sexual feelings toward his mother and hostility toward his father, he is said to have a conflict called the _____
   _____.

12. According to Freud, which of the following represents a primary source of influence on personality?
   a. heredity
   b. life experiences after beginning school
   c. the relative strengths of the id, ego, and superego
   d. the problems experienced during adolescence

The Neo-Freudians (pp. 344–346)

13. In Jung's theory, the inherited part of the personality that stores the experiences of humankind is the (collective, personal) unconscious.

14. Which personality theorist believed that the basic human drive is to overcome and compensate for inferiority and strive for superiority and significance?
   a. Sigmund Freud   c. Alfred Adler
   b. Carl Jung   d. Karen Horney

15. On which of the following did Horney focus?
   a. psychoanalysis
   b. trait theory
   c. feminine psychology
   d. humanistic psychology

Learning Theories and Personality (pp. 346–348)

16. Bandura's concept of reciprocal determinism refers to the mutual effects of
   a. a person's behavior, personality, and thinking.
   b. a person's feelings, attitudes, and thoughts.
   c. a person's behavior, personal/cognitive factors, and the environment.
   d. classical and operant conditioning and observational learning.

17. Which statement is *not* true of people low in self-efficacy?
   a. They persist in their efforts.
   b. They lack confidence.
   c. They expect failure.
   d. They avoid challenge.

18. Who proposed the concept of locus of control?
   a. B. F. Skinner   c. Hans Eysenck
   b. Albert Bandura   d. Julian Rotter

Humanistic Personality Theories (pp. 348–349)

19. Humanistic psychologists would *not* say that
    a. human nature is innately good.
    b. human beings have a natural tendency toward self-actualization.
    c. human beings have free will.
    d. researchers should focus primarily on observable behavior.

20. Which psychologist identified characteristics that he believed self-actualized persons share?
    a. Carl Rogers   c. Abraham Maslow
    b. Gordon Allport   d. Hans Eysenck

21. Which psychologist believed that individuals often do not become fully functioning persons because, in childhood, they fail to receive unconditional positive regard from their parents?
    a. Carl Rogers   c. Abraham Maslow
    b. Gordon Allport   d. Hans Eysenck

Trait Theories (pp. 349–352)

22. According to Allport, the kind of trait that is a defining characteristic of one's personality is a _____ trait.
    a. common   c. secondary
    b. source   d. cardinal

23. According to Cattell, the differences between people are explained by the number of source traits they possess. (true/false)

24. Who claimed that psychologists can best understand personality by assessing people on two major dimensions, Extroversion and Neuroticism?
    a. Hans Eysenck
    b. Gordon Allport
    c. Raymond Cattell
    d. Carl Jung

25. This chapter suggests that, according to a growing consensus among trait theorists, there are _____ major dimensions of personality.
    a. 3   c. 7
    b. 5   d. 16

Nature, Nurture, and Personality (pp. 352–355)

26. Behavioral geneticists have found that the shared family environment has a (strong, negligible) effect on personality development.

27. Children adopted at birth are more similar in personality to their adoptive parents than to their biological parents. (true/false)

Personality Assessment (pp. 355–359)

28. Match each personality test with its description.
    ____ (1) MMPI-2
    ____ (2) Rorschach
    ____ (3) TAT
    ____ (4) CPI
    ____ (5) MBTI
    a. inventory used to diagnose psychopathology
    b. inventory used to assess normal personality
    c. projective test using inkblots
    d. projective test using drawings of ambiguous human situations
    e. inventory used to assess personality types

29. Clay has an unconscious resentment toward his father. Which test might best detect this?
    a. MMPI-2   c. MBTI
    b. CPI   d. TAT

30. Which of the following items might appear on the MMPI-2?
    a. What is happening in the picture?
    b. Hand is to glove as foot is to _____.
    c. My mother was a good person.
    d. What is your favorite food?

◆ SECTION TWO: Complete the Table

Approach	Key Theorist(s)	Major Assumption about Behavior
1. Psychoanalytic	_____	_____
2. Social-cognitive	_____	_____
3. Humanistic	_____	_____
4. Trait	_____	_____

1. According to Freud, the _____ is the personality structure that is completely unconscious and operates on the pleasure principle.

2. According to Freud, the _____ is the logical and rational part of the personality.

3. Freud's _____ is very much like long-term memory.

4. The stages of psychosexual development, in the proper order, are _____, _____, _____, _____, and _____.

5. Mother Teresa would be said to have possessed the _____ trait of altruism.

6. According to Cattell, _____ traits are the observable qualities of personality.

7. Bandura asserted that personal/cognitive factors, one's behavior, and the external environment all influence each other and are influenced by each other. He called this relationship _____.

8. According to Jung, the _____ _____ accounts for the similarity of certain myths, dreams, symbols, and religious beliefs in different cultures.

9. According to Eysenck, _____ are more important in determining personality than is the _____.

10. Psychologists who adopt a behavioral perspective on personality usually prefer the _____ method to other methods of personality assessment.

11. The Myers-Briggs Type Indicator is a personality inventory that is based on _____ theory of personality.

12. The Rorschach Inkblot Method is an example of a _____ test.

13. The _____ is the most widely used of the many different personality inventories.

14. _____ refers to a person's belief that he or she can perform competently in what is attempted.

15. Cattell defined _____ traits as those traits that make up the most basic personality structure and cause behavior.

16. In Jung's view, an _____ exists in the collective unconscious and is an inherited tendency to respond in particular ways to universal human situations.

17. Cultures that encourage people to define themselves in terms of social relationships represent the _____ side of the _____/_____ dimension.

◆ **SECTION FOUR: Comprehensive Practice Test**

1. A person's unique pattern of behaving, thinking, and feeling is his or her
   a. motivation.
   c. personality.
   b. emotion.
   d. cognition.

2. Freud's theory of personality and his therapy for the treatment of psychological disorders are both known as
   a. behaviorism.
   c. psychoanalysis.
   b. psychosocialism.
   d. humanism.

3. Of Freud's three conceptual systems of personality, the _____ is mainly in the conscious, the _____ is split between the conscious and the unconscious, and the _____ is completely unconscious.
   a. id; ego; superego
   c. superego; ego; id
   b. ego; superego; id
   d. ego; id; superego

4. The libido is Freud's name for the psychic or sexual energy that comes from the superego and provides the energy for the entire personality. (true/false)

5. Ava is 13 months old, and whatever she can pick up is likely to go into her mouth. Ava is in Freud's _____ stage of psychosexual development.
   a. anal
   c. phallic
   b. oral
   d. genital

6. Clint is 5 years old, and he thinks his mother is as beautiful as a princess; he would rather spend time with her than with his father. Clint is in Freud's _____ stage of psychosexual development.
   a. anal
   c. phallic
   b. oral
   d. genital

7. A central theme in Adler's theory is the individual's quest for feelings of
   a. superiority.
   c. adequacy.
   b. the collective unconscious.
   d. ego integrity.

8. According to Horney, maladjustment is often caused by
   a. guilt related to failing to live up to an ideal self.
   b. observation of maladjusted role models.
   c. inherited traits.
   d. repressed memories.

9. Allport and Cattell were proponents of the _____ theory of personality.
   a. stage
   b. trait
   c. biological
   d. humanistic

10. Which of the following Big Five personality factors has been found to be a requirement for creative accomplishment?
   a. Extroversion
   b. Conscientiousness
   c. Neuroticism
   d. Openness to Experience

11. Bandura's theory includes the concept of _____, the belief a person has regarding his or her ability to perform competently whatever is attempted.
   a. reciprocal determinism
   b. self-efficacy
   c. extroversion
   d. conditions of worth

12. Trey believes that what happens to him is based on fate, luck, or chance, and his philosophy of life is "whatever will be, will be." Rotter would say that Trey has a(n) _____ locus of control.
   a. internal
   b. explicit
   c. external
   d. regressed

13. Rogers's theory included the concept of conditions of worth—the idea that our parents teach us important values in life and that we as individuals will be motivated to seek out those values. (true/false)

14. The MMPI-2 is a good example of a projective personality test. (true/false)

15. The California Psychological Inventory was developed to evaluate the personalities of
   a. the mentally ill.
   b. males.
   c. normal people.
   d. females.

16. You are shown a black-and-white scene and asked to tell a story about it. You are probably responding to
   a. the Rorschach Inkblot Method.
   b. the CPI.
   c. the Myers-Briggs Type Indicator.
   d. the TAT.

◆ **SECTION FIVE: Critical Thinking**

1. In your opinion, which of the major personality theories discussed in this chapter is the most accurate, reasonable, and realistic? Which is the least accurate, reasonable, and realistic? Give reasons to support your answers.

2. Most social scientists say that American culture is individualist. What aspects of culture in the United States exemplify individualism? Are there some features of American culture that are collectivist in nature? If so, what are they?

3. How do you think the Big Five dimensions of personality affect your behavior?

Psychological Disorders

chapter **12**

What Is Abnormal?

◆ What criteria can be used to determine whether behavior is abnormal?

◆ How prevalent are psychological disorders?

◆ What are the theoretical approaches that attempt to explain the causes of psychological disorders?

Anxiety Disorders

◆ How is generalized anxiety disorder manifested?

◆ How does panic disorder affect the lives of those who suffer from it?

◆ What are the characteristics of the three categories of phobias?

◆ What thought and behavior patterns are associated with obsessive-compulsive disorder?

Mood Disorders

◆ What are the symptoms of major depressive disorder?

◆ How are culture, gender, and depression related?

◆ What are the extremes of mood suffered by those with bipolar disorder?

◆ What are some suggested causes of mood disorders?

◆ What are some of the risk factors for suicide?

Schizophrenia

◆ What are the major positive symptoms of schizophrenia?

◆ What normal functions are reduced or absent in schizophrenics?

◆ What does research indicate about the neurological functioning of schizophrenics?

◆ What are the four types of schizophrenia?

◆ What factors increase the risk of developing schizophrenia?

Other Psychological Disorders

◆ What are two somatoform disorders, and what symptoms do they share?

◆ How do the various dissociative disorders affect behavior?

◆ What are the main characteristics of the various sexual disorders?

◆ What behaviors are associated with personality disorders in Clusters A, B, and C?

Sarah, a student in an Introduction to Psychology class, was fascinated by her professor's lecture on obsessive-compulsive disorder (OCD). As she listened, however, she noticed that many of the symptoms the professor described sounded familiar. Just that morning, Sarah had been driving out of her driveway to go to class when she was seized with the worry that she had left the iron on. Afraid it might cause a fire, she had gone inside to check it, only to find the iron perfectly cold. Sarah remembered other times when she had felt the need to go back and confirm that she had locked her front door, even at the risk of being late for class. And she was a very organized person. She never went to bed at night without first cleaning the kitchen and carefully laying out her clothes and school materials for the next day. Sometimes friends teased her about being a "control freak."

Concerned, Sarah went to the library to read more about OCD. By the time she finished, she was alarmed, having found several other resemblances between her behavior and the symptoms described in books: She often counted steps when she went up or down stairs. She remembered, as a child, having disturbing thoughts about her beloved pet dog being lost or stolen. She felt slightly uncomfortable all day if she forgot to wear her good-luck bracelet, so she tried to remember to put it on every morning. Sarah left the library wondering whether she needed medication, therapy, or both. That night, she made an appointment to see a psychologist at the campus counseling center. She went to bed feeling frightened at the thought that she might have a mental disorder.

At the appointment the next day, the psychologist asked Sarah a number of questions about her behavior. First, he asked, were Sarah's symptoms causing her significant distress? No, she replied, she had never really thought about them until she heard the lecture on OCD. "Do they take up more than an hour each day?" the psychologist asked. "No, probably more like 15 minutes," said Sarah. He went on to ask whether the symptoms hindered Sarah's functioning at school, on the job, or in social relationships. "Not really," Sarah answered. Finally, the psychologist asked, did Sarah think that her symptoms were unreasonable or excessive? "Well," said Sarah, "I didn't think so before, but now I'm not so sure." The psychologist smiled and told Sarah that she could stop worrying and that what she was experiencing was very common. "It is so common," the psychologist said, "that it has a name: *intern's syndrome*," the tendency of students to believe they have the disorders they are learning about in class. The psychologist showed Sarah the description of OCD in *Diagnostic and Statistical Manual of Mental Disorders,* the book that mental health professionals use to diagnose mental disorders. While it was true that Sarah did some of the same kinds of things that people with OCD do, it was clear that she was far from meeting the diagnostic criteria for the disorder.

In this chapter, you'll read about the concept of abnormality, theoretical perspectives on the causes of abnormality, and psychological disorders. The symptoms of psychological disorders range from mild to severe, and you will probably notice that you or people close to you have some of the symptoms described. Beware of developing intern's syndrome!

What Is Abnormal?

◆ **psychological disorders**
Mental processes and/or behavior patterns that cause emotional distress and/or substantial impairment in functioning.

Psychological disorders are mental processes and/or behavior patterns that cause emotional distress and/or substantial impairment in functioning. We begin our examination of them with a basic question: What is abnormal?

Defining Mental Disorders

Human behavior lies along a continuum, from well adjusted to maladaptive. But where along the continuum does behavior become abnormal? Several questions can help determine when behavior is abnormal:

◆ *What criteria can be used to determine whether behavior is abnormal?*

- *Is the behavior considered strange within the person's own culture?* What is considered normal and abnormal in one culture is not necessarily considered so in another. In some cultures, it is normal for women to appear in public bare-breasted, but it would be abnormal for a female executive in an industrialized culture to go to work that way.
- *Does the behavior cause personal distress?* When people experience considerable emotional distress without any life experience that warrants it, they may be diagnosed as having a psychological or mental disorder. Some people may be sad and depressed, and some anxious; others may be agitated or excited; and still others may be frightened, or even terrified, by delusions and hallucinations.
- *Is the behavior maladaptive?* Some experts believe that the best way to differentiate between normal and abnormal behavior is to consider whether it leads to healthy or impaired functioning. Washing your hands before you eat is adaptive; washing them 100 times a day is maladaptive.
- *Is the person a danger to self or others?* Another consideration is whether people pose any danger to themselves or others. To be committed to a mental hospital, a person must be judged both mentally ill and a danger to self or others.
- *Is the person legally responsible for his or her acts?* Often, the term *insanity* is used to label those who behave abnormally, but mental health professionals do not use this term. It is a legal term used by the courts to declare people not legally responsible for their acts. Mass murderer Jeffrey Dahmer was ruled legally responsible for his acts, yet his behavior was clearly abnormal.

Abnormal behavior is defined by each culture. For example, homelessness is considered abnormal in some cultures and completely normal in others.

FIGURE 12.1 **Annual Prevalence Rates of Selected Mental Disorders among Adults in the United States** *Source:* NIMH (2001).

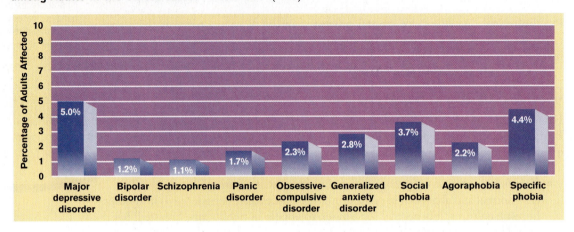

Prevalence of Psychological Disorders

◆ *How prevalent are psychological disorders?*

Would you be surprised to learn that psychological disorders are more common than many physical ailments? For instance, each year in the United States, less than 1% of adults, about 1.3 million people, are diagnosed with cancer (American Cancer Society, 2002). By contrast, 22%, or more than 44 million adults, are diagnosed with a mental disorder of some kind (NIMH, 2001). Figure 12.1 shows the annual prevalence rates of a few of the more common mental disorders.

Another way of thinking about the frequency of a disorder is to examine how likely an individual is to be diagnosed with it in his or her lifetime. The lifetime prevalence rate of cancer in the United States is about 30%; in other words, about 30% of Americans will be diagnosed with cancer sometime in their lives (NCHS, 2000). Again, mental disorders are more common, with a lifetime prevalence rate of nearly 50% (Kessler et al., 1994). Lifetime rates of a few disorders are shown in Figure 12.2. Clearly, mental disorders represent a significant source of personal misery for individuals and of lost productivity for society. Thus, research aimed at identifying their causes and treatments is just as important as research examining the causes and treatments of physical diseases.

FIGURE 12.2 **Lifetime Prevalence of Psychological Disorders**

The percentages of males and females in the United States who suffer from various psychological disorders during their lifetime are based on the findings of the National Comorbidity Survey. Males and females had about the same rate for experiencing some type of disorder. Males had higher rates for substance abuse and antisocial personality disorder. Females had higher rates for anxiety disorders and mood disorders. *Source:* Data from Kessler et al. (1994).

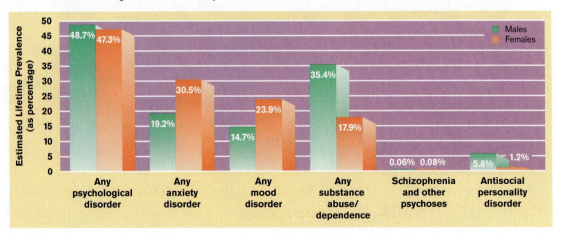

Explaining Psychological Disorders

What causes psychological disorders, and how can they be treated? This is the question addressed by the various theoretical approaches summarized in *Review and Reflect 12.1*. Each perspective has its place in the description, analysis, and treatment of psychological disorders.

◆ *What are the theoretical approaches that attempt to explain the causes of psychological disorders?*

The *biological perspective* views abnormal behavior as arising from a physical cause, such as genetic inheritance, biochemical abnormalities or imbalances, structural abnormalities within the brain, and/or infection. Thus, its adherents favor biological treatments such as drug therapy.

The *biopsychosocial perspective* agrees that physical (biological) causes are of central importance but also recognizes the influence of psychological and social factors in the study, identification, and treatment of psychological disorders. Consequently, biopsychosocial psychologists often advocate treatment strategies that include both drugs and psychotherapy.

Originally proposed by Freud, the *psychodynamic perspective* maintains that psychological disorders stem from early childhood experiences and unresolved, unconscious conflicts, usually of a sexual or aggressive nature. The cause assumed by the psychodynamic approach also suggests the cure—psychoanalysis, which Freud developed to uncover and resolve such unconscious conflicts.

According to the *learning perspective*, psychological disorders are thought to be learned and sustained in the same way as any other behavior. According to this view, people who exhibit abnormal behavior either are victims of faulty learning or have failed to learn appropriate patterns of thinking and acting. Behavior therapists use the learning principles of classical and operant conditioning to eliminate distressing behavior and to establish new, more appropriate behavior in its place.

REVIEW *and* REFLECT 12.1

Perspectives on Psychological Disorders

PERSPECTIVE	CAUSES OF PSYCHOLOGICAL DISORDERS	TREATMENT
Biological perspective	A psychological disorder is a symptom of an underlying physical disorder caused by a structural or biochemical abnormality in the brain, by genetic inheritance, or by infection.	Diagnose and treat like any other physical disorder Drugs, electroconvulsive therapy, or psychosurgery
Biopsychosocial perspective	Psychological disorders result from a combination of biological, psychological, and social causes.	An eclectic approach employing treatments that include both drugs and psychotherapy
Psychodynamic perspective	Psychological disorders stem from early childhood experiences and unresolved, unconscious sexual or aggressive conflicts.	Bring disturbing repressed material to consciousness and help patient work through unconscious conflicts Psychoanalysis
Learning perspective	Abnormal thoughts, feelings, and behaviors are learned and sustained like any other behaviors, or there is a failure to learn appropriate behaviors.	Use classical and operant conditioning and modeling to extinguish abnormal behavior and to increase adaptive behavior Behavior therapy Behavior modification
Cognitive perspective	Faulty thinking or distorted perceptions can cause psychological disorders.	Change faulty, irrational, and/or negative thinking Beck's cognitive therapy Rational-emotive therapy

◆ **DSM-IV**

Diagnostic and Statistical Manual of Mental Disorders, 4th edition, a manual published by the American Psychiatric Association, which describes the criteria used to classify and diagnose mental disorders.

The *cognitive perspective* suggests that faulty thinking or distorted perceptions can contribute to some types of psychological disorders. Treatment based on this perspective is aimed at changing thinking, which presumably will lead to a change in behavior. Moreover, the cognitive perspective offers advice that may prevent psychological disorders. For example, one step toward healthy thinking is to recognize and avoid five cognitive traps: (1) setting unrealistic standards for yourself; (2) negative "what if" thinking (such as "What if I lose my job?"); (3) turning a single negative event, such as a poor grade, into a catastrophe ("I'll never pass this course"); (4) judging anything short of perfection to be a failure; and (5) demanding perfection in yourself and others. If your happiness depends on any of these conditions, you are setting the stage for disappointment, or even depression.

Regardless of their theoretical perspective, all clinicians and researchers use the same set of criteria to classify and diagnose psychological disorders. These criteria can be found in a manual published by the American Psychiatric Association. The most recent edition, *Diagnostic and Statistical Manual of Mental Disorders,* 4th edition, commonly known as **DSM-IV**, appeared in 1994. An updated version, DSM-IV-TR (Text Revision), was published in 2000. The major categories used in DSM-IV-TR to classify psychological disorders are listed in Table 12.1.

TABLE 12.1 **Major DSM-IV Categories of Mental Disorders**

DISORDER	SYMPTOMS	EXAMPLES
Schizophrenia and other psychotic disorders	Disorders characterized by the presence of psychotic symptoms, including hallucinations, delusions, disorganized speech, bizarre behavior, and loss of contact with reality	Schizophrenia, paranoid type Schizophrenia, disorganized type Schizophrenia, catatonic type Delusional disorder, jealous type
Mood disorders	Disorders characterized by periods of extreme or prolonged depression or mania or both	Major depressive disorder Bipolar disorder
Anxiety disorders	Disorders characterized by anxiety and avoidance behavior	Panic disorder Social phobia Obsessive-compulsive disorder Posttraumatic stress disorder
Somatoform disorders	Disorders in which physical symptoms are present that are psychological in origin rather than due to a medical condition	Hypochondriasis Conversion disorder
Dissociative disorders	Disorders in which one handles stress or conflict by forgetting important personal information or one's whole identity, or by compartmentalizing the trauma or conflict into a split-off alter personality	Dissociative amnesia Dissociative fugue Dissociative identity disorder
Personality disorders	Disorders characterized by long-standing, inflexible, maladaptive patterns of behavior beginning early in life and causing personal distress or problems in social and occupational functioning	Antisocial personality disorder Histrionic personality disorder Narcissistic personality disorder Borderline personality disorder
Substance-related disorders	Disorders in which undesirable behavioral changes result from substance abuse, dependence, or intoxication	Alcohol abuse Cocaine abuse Cannabis dependence
Disorders usually first diagnosed in infancy, childhood, or adolescence	Disorders that include mental retardation, learning disorders, communication disorders, pervasive developmental disorders, attention-deficit and disruptive behavior disorders, tic disorders, and elimination disorders	Conduct disorder Autistic disorder Tourette's syndrome Stuttering
Eating disorders	Disorders characterized by severe disturbances in eating behavior	Anorexia nervosa Bulimia nervosa

Source: Based on DSM-IV (American Psychiatric Association, 1994).

Anxiety Disorders

According to chronically anxious comic strip hero Charlie Brown, the secret to life is to "replace one worry with another." Everyone worries to some degree. But, as Charlie Brown suggests, for some people, worrying is a way of life. And when vague, fearful thoughts about what might happen in the future (a state of mind referred to as *anxiety* by psychologists) become so frequent that they interfere with a person's social and occupational functioning, worrying can develop into a serious psychological disorder. In fact, **anxiety disorders** are the most common category of mental disorders and account for more than 4 million visits to doctors' offices each year in the United States (NCHS, 2002b). Figure 12.3 shows the percentages of males and females in the United States who have suffered from various anxiety disorders during their lifetimes. Take a minute now to complete the anxiety disorder checklist in *Try It 12.1* (on page 374).

◆ **anxiety disorders**
Psychological disorders characterized by frequent fearful thoughts about what might happen in the future.

◆ **generalized anxiety disorder**
An anxiety disorder in which people experience chronic, excessive worry for 6 months or more.

Generalized Anxiety Disorder

Generalized anxiety disorder (GAD) is the diagnosis given to people who are plagued by chronic, excessive worry for 6 months or more. These people expect the worst; their worrying is either unfounded or greatly exaggerated and, thus, difficult to control. They may be unduly worried about their finances, their own health or that of family members, their performance at work, or their ability to function socially. Their excessive anxiety may cause them to feel tense, tired, and irritable, and to have difficulty concentrating and sleeping. Other symptoms may include trembling, palpitations, sweating, dizziness, nausea, diarrhea, or frequent urination. This disorder affects twice as many women as men and leads to considerable distress and impairment (Brawman-Mintzer & Lydiard, 1996, 1997; Kranzler, 1996). Antidepressant drugs may be helpful in the treatment of GAD (Mogg et al., 2004). As troubling as this disorder is, however, it is less severe than panic disorder.

◆ *How is generalized anxiety disorder manifested?*

◆ **panic attack**
An episode of overwhelming anxiety, fear, or terror.

Panic Disorder

For some anxiety disorder sufferers, feelings of fear and dread happen in spurts rather than continuously. During **panic attacks**—episodes of overwhelming anxiety, fear, or terror—people commonly report a pounding heart, uncontrollable trembling or shaking, and sensations of choking or smothering. Some say they believe they are going to die or are "going crazy." Recent studies

◆ *How does panic disorder affect the lives of those who suffer from it?*

FIGURE 12.3 Lifetime Prevalence of Anxiety Disorders

The percentages of males and females in the United States who have suffered from various anxiety disorders during their lifetime are based on the findings of the National Comorbidity Survey. *Source:* Data from Kessler et al. (1994).

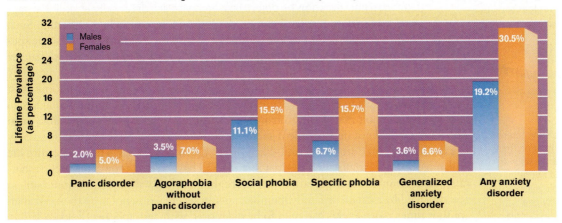

◆ **panic disorder**

An anxiety disorder in which a person experiences recurring, unpredictable episodes of overwhelming anxiety, fear, or terror.

◆ **phobia**

(FO-bee-ah) A persistent, irrational fear of some specific object, situation, or activity that poses little or no real danger.

have revealed that the more catastrophic such beliefs are, the more intense the panic attack is likely to be (Hedley et al., 2000). People who suffer from recurring panic attacks may be diagnosed with **panic disorder.** Panic disorder sufferers must cope both with repeated attacks and with anxiety about the occurrence and consequences of further attacks. This anxiety can lead people to avoid situations that have been associated with previous panic attacks. About 2% of men and 5% of women in the United States suffer from panic disorder (Kessler et al., 1994).

Panic disorder can have significant social and health consequences (Sherbourne et al., 1996). Panic disorder sufferers visit doctors' offices and emergency rooms quite frequently (Katon, 1996) and are at increased risk for abuse of alcohol and other drugs (Marshall, 1997). However, effective treatments for this disorder are available. Most individuals with panic disorder respond to a combination of medication and psychotherapy (Biondi & Picardi, 2003).

Phobias

◆ *What are the characteristics of the three categories of phobias?*

Is there some situation or object of which you are dreadfully afraid? Perhaps you fear snakes, insects, heights, or closed-in spaces such as elevators. Such fears are quite common. A **phobia** is a persistent, irrational fear of some specific object, situation, or activity that poses no real danger (or whose danger is blown out of proportion). Phobics realize their fears are irrational, but they nevertheless feel compelled to avoid the feared situations or objects. The phobia most likely to drive people to seek professional help is **agoraphobia.** An agoraphobic has an intense fear of being in a situation from which immediate escape is not possible or in which help would not be available if she or he should become overwhelmed by anxiety or experience a panic attack or panic-like symptoms. In some cases, a person's entire life is planned around avoiding feared situations such as busy streets, crowded stores, restaurants, and/or public transportation. An agoraphobic often will not leave home unless accompanied by a friend or family member, and, in severe cases, not even then. Women are four times more likely than men to be diagnosed with agoraphobia (Bekker, 1996).

◆ **agoraphobia**

(AG-or-uh-FO-bee-ah) An intense fear of being in a situation from which escape is not possible or in which help would not be available if one experienced overwhelming anxiety or a panic attack.

Although agoraphobia can occur without panic attacks, it typically begins during the early adult years with repeated panic attacks (Horwath et al., 1993). The intense fear of having another attack causes the person to avoid any place or situation where previous attacks have occurred. Panic disorder with agoraphobia (PDA) is one of the most debilitating of psychological disorders, and it is more common in women than in men. It can affect most areas of life—physical, psychological, social, occupational, interpersonal, and economic.

People who suffer from **social phobia** are intensely afraid of any social or performance situation in which they might embarrass or humiliate themselves in front of others—by shaking, blushing, sweating, or in some other way appearing clumsy, foolish, or incompetent. Social phobia is the most common type of anxiety disorder (Tillfors, 2004), and may take the form of *performance anxiety*. Surprisingly, many professional entertainers experience this kind of specific social phobia; Barbra Streisand's extreme performance anxiety kept her from appearing live in concert for many years. About one-third of social phobics only fear speaking in public (Kessler et al., 1998). And in a survey of 449 individuals who had not been formally diagnosed with social phobia, one-third said they would experience excessive anxiety if they had to speak in front of a large audience (Stein et al., 1996). If you are one of the millions who are afraid of public speaking, see *Apply It 12.1* at the end of this chapter for advice on overcoming your fear.

Although less debilitating than agoraphobia, social phobia can be a disabling disorder (Stein & Kean, 2000). In its extreme form, it can seriously affect people's performance at work, preventing them from advancing in their careers or pursuing an education and severely restricting their social lives (Bruch et al., 2003; Greist, 1995; Stein & Kean, 2000). Often, those with social phobia turn to alcohol and tranquilizers to lessen their anxiety in social situations. Baseball legend Mickey Mantle, for example, used alcohol to calm himself when making public appearances (Jefferson, 1996).

A **specific phobia** is a marked fear of a specific object or situation. This general label is applied to any phobia other than agoraphobia and social phobia. Faced with the object or situation they fear, people afflicted with a specific phobia experience intense anxiety, even to the point of shaking or screaming. They will go to great lengths to avoid the feared object or situation. The categories of specific phobias, in order of frequency of occurrence, are (1) situational phobias (fear of elevators, airplanes, enclosed places, heights, tunnels, or bridges); (2) fear of the natural environment (fear of storms or water); (3) animal phobias (fear of dogs, snakes, insects, or mice); and (4) blood-injection-injury phobia (fear of seeing blood or an injury, or of receiving an injection) (Fredrikson et al., 1996). Two types of situational phobias—*claustrophobia* (fear of closed spaces) and *acrophobia* (fear of heights)—are the specific phobias treated most often by therapists.

The causes of phobias vary, depending on the type of phobia. However, heredity is an important factor in the development of phobias (Rapee & Spence, 2004). Beyond genetics, frightening experiences appear to set the stage for the acquisition of phobias. Many specific and social phobias are acquired in childhood or adolescence through direct conditioning, modeling, or the transmission of information (Rachman, 1997). For instance, a person may be able to trace the beginning of a specific phobia to a traumatic childhood experience with the feared object or situation (Hirschfeld, 1995; Jefferson, 1996; Stemberger et al., 1995). Phobias may be acquired also through observational learning. For example, children who hear their parents talk about a frightening encounter with a dog may develop a fear of dogs.

Principles of learning are often used to treat phobias. A therapist may use classical conditioning principles to teach patients to associate pleasant emotions with feared objects or situations. For example, a child who fears dogs might be given ice cream while in a room where a dog is present. Behavior modification, in which patients are reinforced for exposing themselves to fearful stimuli, may also be useful. Observation of models who do not exhibit fear in response to the object or situation of which a phobic is afraid has also been an effective treatment technique. Finally, antidepressant drugs have been shown to help agoraphobics overcome their fears (Kampman et al., 2002; Marshall, 1997).

◆ **social phobia**
An irrational fear and avoidance of any social or performance situation in which one might embarrass or humiliate oneself in front of others by appearing clumsy, foolish, or incompetent.

◆ **specific phobia**
A marked fear of a specific object or situation; a general label for any phobia other than agoraphobia and social phobia.

Obsessive-Compulsive Disorder

◆ *What thought and behavior patterns are associated with obsessive-compulsive disorder?*

What would your life be like if every time you left your home you were so fearful of having left your door unlocked that you had to go back and check it again and again? **Obsessive-compulsive disorder (OCD)** is an anxiety disorder in which a person suffers from recurrent obsessions or compulsions, or both. **Obsessions** are persistent, involuntary thoughts, images, or impulses that invade consciousness and cause a person great distress. People with obsessions might worry about contamination by germs or about whether they performed a certain act, such as turning off the stove or locking the door (Insel, 1990). Other types of obsessions center on aggression, religion, or sex. One minister reported obsessive thoughts of running naked down the church aisle and shouting obscenities at his congregation.

A person with a **compulsion** feels a persistent, irresistible, irrational urge to perform an act or ritual repeatedly. The individual knows such acts are senseless but cannot resist performing them without experiencing an intolerable buildup of anxiety—which can be relieved only by yielding to the compulsion. Many of us have engaged in compulsive behavior like stepping over cracks on the sidewalk, counting stairsteps, or performing little rituals from time to time. The behavior becomes a psychological problem only if the person cannot resist performing it, if it is very time-consuming, and if it interferes with the person's normal activities and relationships with others.

Compulsions exhibited by people with obsessive-compulsive disorder often involve cleaning and washing behaviors, counting, checking, touching objects, hoarding, and excessive organizing. These cleaning and checking compulsions affect 75% of OCD patients receiving treatment (Ball et al., 1996). Sometimes, compulsive acts or rituals seem to reflect superstitious thinking in that they must be performed faithfully to ward off some danger. People with OCD do not enjoy the endless counting, checking, or cleaning. They realize that their behavior is not normal, but they simply cannot help themselves, as shown in the following example.

> Mike, a 32-year-old patient, performed checking rituals that were preceded by a fear of harming other people. When driving, he had to stop the car often and return to check whether he had run over people, particularly babies. Before flushing the toilet, he had to check to be sure that a live insect had not fallen into the toilet, because he did not want to be responsible for killing a living thing. At home he repeatedly checked to see that the doors, stoves, lights, and windows were shut or turned off. . . . Mike performed these and many other checking rituals for an average of 4 hours a day. (Kozak et al., 1988, p. 88)

Mike's checking compulsion is quite extreme, but it has been estimated that perhaps 2–3% of the U.S. population will suffer from OCD at some time in life. Fairly similar rates have been reported in studies in Canada, Puerto Rico, Germany, Korea, and New Zealand (Weissman et al., 1994).

Studies have shown that early auto-immune system diseases, early strep infections, and changes in the brain caused by infection may predispose a person to develop OCD (Giedd et al., 2000; Hamilton & Swedo, 2001; Swedo & Grant, 2004). Several twin and family studies suggest that a genetic factor is involved in the development of OCD as well (Nestadt et al., 2000; Rasmussen & Eisen, 1990). Genes affecting serotonin functioning are suspected of causing OCD in some people, many of whom are helped by antidepressant drugs that increase serotonin levels in the brain (Pigott, 1996).

◆ obsessive-compulsive disorder (OCD)

An anxiety disorder in which a person suffers from recurrent obsessions and/or compulsions.

◆ obsession

A persistent, involuntary thought, image, or impulse that invades consciousness and causes great distress.

◆ compulsion

A persistent, irresistible, and irrational urge to perform an act or ritual repeatedly.

Like this woman, many people with obsessive-compulsive disorder take great pains to avoid contamination from germs and dirt.

Mood Disorders

Like anxiety disorders, mood disorders are fairly common. **Mood disorders** are characterized by extreme and unwarranted disturbances in emotion. Of course, everyone experiences ups and downs, but true mood disorders involve changes in mood that are characterized by the criteria for abnormality you read about at the beginning of the chapter. In other words, people with these disorders have symptoms that are severe enough to interfer with their normal functioning.

◆ **mood disorders**
Disorders characterized by extreme and unwarranted disturbances in emotion or mood.

Major Depressive Disorder

People with **major depressive disorder** feel an overwhelming sadness, despair, and hopelessness, and they usually lose their ability to experience pleasure. They may have changes in appetite, weight, or sleep patterns; loss of energy; and difficulty in thinking or concentrating. Key symptoms of major depressive disorder are psychomotor disturbances (Sobin & Sackeim, 1997). For example, body movements, reaction time, and speech may be so slowed that some depressed people seem to be doing everything in slow motion. Others experience the opposite extreme and are constantly moving and fidgeting, wringing their hands, and pacing. Depression can be so severe that its victims suffer from delusions or hallucinations, which are symptoms of *psychotic depression*. The more deeply a person descends into depression over an extended period, the more she or he withdraws from social activities (Judd et al., 2000).

◆ *What are the symptoms of major depressive disorder?*

◆ **major depressive disorder**
A mood disorder marked by feelings of great sadness, despair, and hopelessness as well as the loss of the ability to experience pleasure.

According to the American Psychiatric Association (1994), 1 year after their initial diagnosis of major depressive disorder, 40% of patients are without symptoms; 40% are still suffering from the disorder; and 20% are depressed, but not enough to warrant a diagnosis of major depression. Slightly less than one-half of those hospitalized for major depressive disorder are fully recovered after 1 year (Keitner et al., 1992). For many, recovery is aided by antidepressant drugs. However, some studies show that psychotherapy can be just as effective (Hollon et al., 2002). Some people suffer only one major depressive episode, but 50–60% of patients will have a recurrence. Risk of recurrence is greatest for females (Winokur et al., 1993) and for individuals with an onset of depression before age 15 (Brown, 1996). Recurrences may be frequent or infrequent, and for 20–35% of patients, the episodes are chronic, lasting 2 years or longer. Thus, finding a way to prevent recurrences is important in depression research. Most researchers suggest that medication, psychotherapy, social support, and even physical exercise may all play some role in the prevention of recurrent episodes of depression (Sher, 2004).

Culture, Gender, and Depression

How is it possible to study depression—or any mental disorder, for that matter—across cultures, since cultural context must be taken into consideration when defining abnormality? Indeed, it is extremely difficult to construct surveys or other instruments for measuring mental disorders that are valid in a variety of cultures (Girolamo & Bassi, 2003). Nevertheless, a few researchers have managed to produce a limited, but informative, body of data about cross-cultural differences in depression (Girolamo & Bassi, 2003). One large study involving participants from 10 countries revealed that the lifetime risk for developing depression varied greatly around the world (see Figure 12.4, on page 378), with Asian countries (Taiwan and Korea) having significantly lower rates of the disorder (Weissman et al., 1996). Despite these variations, major depressive disorder is the number one cause of disability throughout the world (NIMH, 1999b), especially in women.

◆ *How are culture, gender, and depression related?*

In most countries, the rate of depression for females is about twice that for males (Culbertson, 1997). Before boys reach puberty, they are more likely than girls to be depressed, but a dramatic reversal of the gender-related depression rates takes place in adolescence

FIGURE 12.4 **Lifetime Risk for Developing Depression in 10 Countries**

The lifetime prevalence of depression for 38,000 men and women in 10 different countries reveals that women are more susceptible to depression worldwide. *Source:* Data from Weissman et al. (1996).

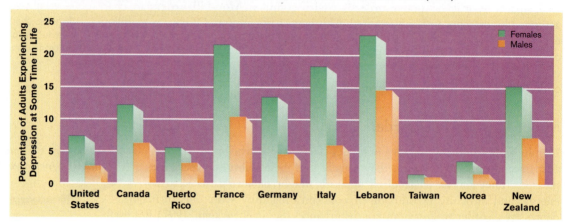

(Cyranowski et al., 2000). Not only are women more likely than men to suffer from depression, but they are also more likely to be affected by negative consequences as a result. Early-onset major depressive disorder adversely affects the educational attainment and earning power of women, but not men (Berndt et al., 2000). The National Task Force on Women and Depression suggests that the higher rate of depression in women is largely due to social and cultural factors. In fulfilling her many roles—mother, wife, lover, friend, daughter, neighbor—a woman is likely to put the needs of others ahead of her own.

Bipolar Disorder

◆ *What are the extremes of mood suffered by those with bipolar disorder?*

Have you ever heard about the bizarre episode in which painter Vincent van Gogh cut off his own ear? Based on analyses of his artistic productivity and personal writings, mental health professionals believe that van Gogh suffered from **bipolar disorder** (Blumer, 2002). Individuals with bipolar disorder exhibit two radically different moods—the extreme highs of manic episodes (or *mania*) and the extreme lows of major depression—usually with relatively normal periods in between.

Van Gogh's ear-cutting episode occurred in the aftermath of a violent argument with another artist, Paul Gauguin, most likely in the context of a **manic episode.** Such episodes are marked by excessive euphoria, inflated self-esteem, wild optimism, and hyperactivity. People in a manic state have temporarily lost touch with reality and frequently have delusions of grandeur along with their euphoric highs. They may waste large sums of money on get-rich-quick schemes. If family members or friends try to stop them, they are likely to become irritable, hostile, enraged, or even dangerous; they may even harm themselves as van Gogh did. Quite often, patients must be hospitalized during manic episodes to protect them and others from the disastrous consequences of their poor judgment.

Van Gogh was hospitalized shortly after severing his ear. After his release from the hospital, and consistent with the modern-day diagnosis of bipolar disorder, his career was marked by intense bursts of creativity. In one 2-month period in 1889, he produced 60 paintings, some of which are regarded as his best works (Thomas & Bracken, 2001). Between these frantic periods of almost nonstop work, van Gogh experienced phases of deep despair, in which he could do no work at all. Tragically, he committed suicide at age 37.

Bipolar disorder is much less common than major depressive disorder, affecting about 1.2% of the U.S. population in any given year, and the lifetime prevalence rates are about the same for males and females (NIMH, 2001). Bipolar disorder tends to appear in late adolescence or early adulthood. About 90% of those with the disorder have recurrences, and about 50% experience another episode within a year of recovering from

◆ **bipolar disorder**

A mood disorder in which manic episodes alternate with periods of depression, usually with relatively normal periods in between.

◆ **manic episode**

(MAN-ik) A period of excessive euphoria, inflated self-esteem, wild optimism, and hyperactivity, often accompanied by delusions of grandeur and by hostility if activity is blocked.

a previous one. The good news is that 70–80% of the patients return to a state of emotional stability (American Psychiatric Association, 2000), even though mild cognitive deficits, such as difficulty with planning, persist in many patients following a manic episode (Chowdhury et al., 2003). Still, in many cases, individuals with bipolar disorder can manage their symptoms, and thereby live a normal life, with the help of drugs such as lithium and divalproex. Moreover, psychotherapy can help them cope with the stress of facing life with a potentially disabling mental illness (Hollon et al., 2002).

Causes of Mood Disorders

Biological factors such as heredity and abnormal brain chemistry play a major role in bipolar disorder and major depressive disorder. PET scans have revealed abnormal patterns of brain activity in patients with both disorders (George et al., 1993). Drevets and others (1997) located a brain area that may trigger both the sadness of major depression and the mania of bipolar disorder. A small, thimble-size patch of brain tissue in the lower prefrontal cortex (about 2–3 inches behind the bridge of the nose) is a striking 40–50% smaller in people with major depression. Earlier research established that this area of the brain plays a key role in the control of emotions. Moreover, the personality trait called *Neuroticism* is associated with both depression and abnormalities in the brain's serotonin levels (Fanous et al., 2002; Lesch, 2003). Research has shown that abnormal levels of serotonin are strongly linked to depression and to suicidal thoughts (Oquendo et al., 2003). Thus, individuals who are at the neurotic end of the Big Five personality dimension of Neuroticism may be predisposed to develop depression and to have suicidal thoughts.

◆ *What are some suggested causes of mood disorders?*

Researchers have also found that the production, transport, and reuptake patterns for dopamine, GABA, and norepinephrine in people suffering from mood disorders differ from those in normal individuals (Kalidini & McGuffin, 2003). Neurotransmitter abnormalities may reflect genetic variations, thus helping to explain the significant heritability rates for mood disorders. Based on a study of 1,721 identical and fraternal female twins, Kendler, Neale, Kessler, and others (1993) estimated the heritability of major depressive disorder to be 70% and the contribution of environment to be 30%.

Evidence for a genetic basis for bipolar disorder is also strong. In one twin study, researchers found that 50% of the identical twins of bipolar sufferers had also been diagnosed with a mood disorder, compared to only 7% of fraternal twins (Kalidini & McGuffin, 2003). Mounting evidence indicates that the genetic and neurological bases of bipolar disorder are more like those of schizophrenia than those of major depressive disorder (Molnar et al., 2003). These findings may explain why biological relatives of bipolar disorder sufferers are at increased risk of developing a number of mental disorders, while those of major depressive disorder sufferers display an increased risk only for that disorder (Kalidini & McGuffin, 2003).

Of course, genetics isn't the whole story, especially with regard to depression. Cognitive factors are important as well. For example, depressed individuals tend to view themselves, their world, and their future all in negative ways (Beck, 1967, 1991). They see their interactions with the world as a series of burdens and obstacles that usually end in failure. Depressed persons believe they are deficient, unworthy, and inadequate, and they attribute their perceived failures to their own physical, mental, or moral inadequacies. Depressed patients may think: "Everything always turns out wrong." "I never win." "Things will never get better." "It's no use."

Life stresses are also associated with depression. The vast majority of first episodes of depression strike after major life stress (Brown et al., 1994; Frank et al., 1994; Tennant, 2002). A longitudinal study of Harvard graduates that continued for over 40 years found that negative life events as well as family history played significant roles in the development of mood disorders (Cui & Vaillant, 1996). This seems particularly true of women, who are more likely to have experienced a severe negative life event just prior to the onset of depression (Spangler et al., 1996). Yet, recurrences of depression, at least in people who are biologically predisposed, often occur without significant life stress (Brown et al., 1994).

Suicide and Race, Gender, and Age

◆ *What are some of the risk factors for suicide?*

Some depressed people commit the ultimate act of desperation—suicide. Mood disorders and schizophrenia, along with substance abuse, are major risk factors for suicide in all age groups (Mościcki, 1995; Pinikahana et al., 2003; Shaffer et al., 1996). Suicide risk also increases when people are exposed to particularly troubling life stressors, such as the violent death of a child (Murphy et al., 2003). There is also evidence that suicidal behavior runs in families (Brent et al., 1996; 2002). Even among people who have severe mood disturbances, such as bipolar disorder, those with a family history of suicide attempts are far more likely to kill themselves than are those without such history (Tsai et al., 2002).

Between 30,000 and 31,000 suicides are reported annually in the United States. Figure 12.5 shows the differences in U.S. suicide rates according to race, gender, and age (NCHS, 2001a, 2002a). As you can see, White Americans are more likely than African Americans to commit suicide. Native American suicide rates are similar to those of White Americans; rates for Hispanic Americans are similar to those of African Americans (NCHS, 2001b). Asian Americans have the lowest suicide rates of all ethnic groups in the United States (NCHS, 2002a).

You will also note in the Figure 12.5 that suicide rates are far lower for both White and African American women than for men. However, studies show that women are four times more likely than men to attempt suicide (Anderson, 2002). The higher rate of completed suicides in males is due to the methods men and women use. Emergency room records show that the rate of firearms use by suicide attempters and completers is 10 times higher in males than in females, while the rates of poisoning and drug overdose are higher in females (CDC, 2002). Consequently, a higher proportion of male suicide attempters succeed in killing themselves.

Although suicide rates among teens and young adults have increased in the past few decades, older Americans are at far greater risk for suicide than younger people. White males aged 85 and older have the highest recorded suicide rate, with more than 75 suicides for every 100,000 people in that age group, about five times the average national suicide rate of 15.2 per 100,000 (U.S. Census Bureau, 1999). Poor general health, serious illness, loneliness (often due to the death of a spouse), and decline in social and economic status are conditions that may push many older Americans, especially those aged 75 and older, to commit suicide.

Evidence suggests that suicidal behavior tends to run in families. Les Franklin founded the Shaka Franklin Foundation for Youth, a suicide prevention organization, in memory of his son Shaka, who had killed himself. Ten years later, Franklin's other son, Jamon, also committed suicide.

About 90% of individuals who commit suicide leave clues (Shneidman, 1994). They may communicate verbally: "You won't be seeing me again." They may provide behavioral clues, such as giving away their most valued possessions; withdrawing from friends, family, and associates; taking unnecessary risks; showing personality changes; acting and looking depressed; and losing interest in favorite activities. These warning signs should always be taken seriously. If you suspect you are dealing with a suicidal person, the best thing you can do is to encourage the person to get professional help. There are 24-hour suicide hotlines all over the country. A call might save a life.

In every age group, the suicide rate is highest for White American males and second-highest for African American males. The general conclusion is that males are more likely to commit suicide than females, and that White Americans are more likely to do so than are African Americans. Suicide rates indicated by asterisks (*) are too low to be statistically reliable. *Source:* Data from NCHS (2001a, 2002a).

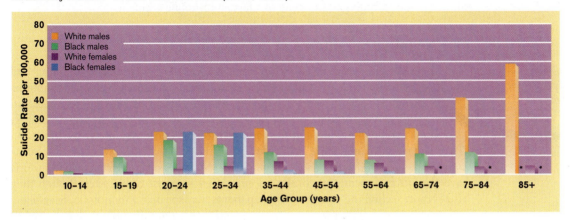

Schizophrenia

Schizophrenia is a serious psychological disorder characterized by loss of contact with reality (a condition often referred to as **psychosis**), hallucinations, delusions, inappropriate or flat affect, some disturbance in thinking, social withdrawal, and/or other bizarre behavior.

Positive Symptoms of Schizophrenia

The *positive symptoms* of schizophrenia are the abnormal behaviors that are present in people with the disorder. (By the way, *positive* means "added" not "good.") One of the clearest positive symptoms of schizophrenia is the presence of **hallucinations,** or imaginary sensations. Schizophrenic patients may see, hear, feel, taste, or smell strange things in the absence of any stimulus in the environment, but hearing voices is the most common type of hallucination. Most often, the voices accuse or curse the patients or engage in a running commentary on their behavior. Visual hallucinations, less common than auditory hallucinations, are usually in black and white and commonly take the form of friends, relatives, God, Jesus, or the devil. Schizophrenics also may experience exceedingly frightening and painful bodily sensations and feel that they are being beaten, burned, or sexually violated.

Having **delusions,** or false beliefs not generally shared by others in the culture, is another positive symptom of schizophrenia. Schizophrenics with **delusions of grandeur** may believe they are a famous person (the president or Moses, for example) or a powerful or important person who possesses some great knowledge, ability, or authority. Those with **delusions of persecution** have the false notion that some person or agency is trying to harass, cheat, spy on, conspire against, injure, kill, or in some other way harm them.

Another positive symptom is the loosening of associations, or *derailment,* that is evident when a schizophrenic does not follow one line of thought to completion but, on the basis of vague connections, shifts from one subject to another in conversation or writing. A schizophrenic's *grossly disorganized behavior,* another positive symptom, can include such things as childlike silliness, inappropriate sexual behavior (masturbating in public), disheveled appearance, and peculiar dress. There may also be unpredictable

◆ **schizophrenia**
(SKIT-soh-FREE-nee-ah) A severe psychological disorder characterized by loss of contact with reality, hallucinations, delusions, inappropriate or flat affect, some disturbance in thinking, social withdrawal, and/or other bizarre behavior.

◆ *What are the major positive symptoms of schizophrenia?*

◆ **psychosis**
(sy-CO-sis) A condition characterized by loss of contact with reality.

◆ **hallucination**
An imaginary sensation.

◆ **delusion**
A false belief, not generally shared by others in the culture.

◆ **delusion of grandeur**
A false belief that one is a famous person or a powerful or important person who has some great knowledge, ability, or authority.

◆ **delusion of persecution**
A false belief that some person or agency is trying in some way to harm one.

agitation, including shouting and swearing, and unusual or inappropriate motor behavior, including strange gestures, facial expressions, or postures. Schizophrenics may also display *inappropriate affect*; that is, their facial expressions, tone of voice, and gestures may not reflect the emotion that would be expected under the circumstances. A person might cry when watching a TV comedy and laugh when watching a news story showing bloody bodies at the scene of a fatal automobile accident.

Negative Symptoms of Schizophrenia

◆ What normal functions are reduced or absent in schizophrenics?

A *negative symptom* of schizophrenia is a loss of or deficiency in thoughts and behaviors that are characteristic of normal functioning. Negative symptoms include social withdrawal, apathy, loss of motivation, lack of goal-directed activity, very limited speech, slowed movements, poor hygiene and grooming, poor problem-solving abilities, and a distorted sense of time (Davalos et al., 2002; Hatashita-Wong et al., 2002; Skrabalo, 2000). Many also have difficulty forming new memories (Matthews & Barch, 2004). Some who suffer from schizophrenia have *flat affect*, showing practically no emotional response at all, even though they often report feeling the emotion. These patients may speak in a monotone, have blank and emotionless facial expressions, and act and move more like robots than humans.

Not all schizophrenics have negative symptoms. Those who do seem to have the poorest outcomes (Fenton & McGlashan, 1994). Negative symptoms are predictors of impaired overall social and vocational functioning. Schizophrenics tend to withdraw from normal social contacts and retreat into their own world. They have difficulty relating to people, and often their functioning is too impaired for them to hold a job or even to care for themselves.

Brain Abnormalities in Schizophrenics

◆ What does research indicate about the neurological functioning of schizophrenics?

Several abnormalities in brain structure and function have been found in schizophrenic patients, such as low levels of neural activity in the frontal lobes (Glantz & Lewis, 2000; Kim et al., 2000). Many schizophrenics have defects in the neural circuitry of the cerebral cortex and the limbic system (Benes, 2000; MacDonald et al., 2003; McGlashan & Hoffman, 2000). There is also evidence of reduced volume in the hippocampus, amygdala, thalamus, and frontal lobes (Gur et al., 2000; Sanfilippo et al., 2000; Staal et al., 2000). Further, schizophrenics display abnormal lateralization of brain functions and slow communication between left and right hemispheres (Florio et al., 2002).

Abnormal dopamine activity in the brain is observed in many schizophrenics. Such altered dopamine activity sometimes results from cocaine abuse, which can pose an increased risk for schizophrenia (Benes, 2000; Tzschentke, 2001). Much of the brain's dopamine activity occurs in the limbic system, which is involved in human emotions. Drugs that are effective in reducing the symptoms of schizophrenia block dopamine action, although about one-third of the patients who take these drugs do not show improvement.

Types of Schizophrenia

◆ What are the four types of schizophrenia?

Even though various symptoms are commonly shared by schizophrenics, certain features distinguish one type of schizophrenia from another. For example, people with **paranoid schizophrenia** usually suffer from delusions of grandeur or persecution. They may be convinced that they have an identity other than their own—that they are the president, the Virgin Mary, or God—or that they possess great ability or talent. They may feel that they are in charge of the hospital or on a secret assignment for the government. Paranoid schizophrenics often show exaggerated anger and suspiciousness. If they have delusions of persecution and feel that they are being harassed or threatened, they may become violent in an attempt to defend themselves against their imagined persecutors. Usually, the behavior of a patient with

◆ **paranoid schizophrenia**
(PAIR-uh-noid) A type of schizophrenia characterized by delusions of grandeur or persecution.

How Did You Find **Psychology?**

Deanna Barch

You may have heard it said that learning about something in school is very different from encountering it in the real world. Real-world problems were what first attracted Deanna Barch to a career in psychology ("Deanna M. Barch," 2002). By the time she reached high school, Barch knew that she wanted to be a psychologist and planned to work with school children who had learning and behavioral problems. With this goal in mind, she majored in psychology at Northwestern University.

Until Barch took a course in abnormal psychology, the thought of focusing her career on research, rather than on the professional practice of psychology, had not occurred to her. When the professor asked Barch to join her research group, Barch agreed. The experience of working collaboratively with other students and faculty led her to seriously consider a research career. Her interest in people's real-world problems, however, prompted Barch to take a position as a case manager working with people who had serious psychological disorders after graduation rather than going straight to graduate school.

During her year as a case manager working primarily with individuals who suffered from schizophrenia, Barch saw a side of life that she had never encountered previously. She had been an excellent student and possessed a great deal of academic knowledge about schizophrenia. Nevertheless, the personal devastation she observed in

individuals who suffered from the disorder touched her as nothing had before in her life. Barch reports that she met one particular young man, close to her own age, who had been planning a life very much like the one she was living before the disease struck him. His case and others like it convinced her that her research both in graduate school and afterward would focus on schizophrenia.

Graduate studies at the University of Illinois helped Barch hone her research skills and determine the aspects of schizophrenia that most interested her. With the help of her advisor, she began to do research on language production in schizophrenics. As an intern at the Western Psychiatric Institute and Clinic at the University of Pittsburgh, Barch acquired the knowledge and skills required to add a neurobiological component to her research. Today, she conducts research aimed at identifying preschizophrenic behaviors with the goal of preventing full-blown expression of the disorder. She also continues to research both the psychological and the neurobiological aspects of schizophrenics' language production problems.

If you think you might want to pursue a career that involves working with individuals who have psychological disorders, you would do well to follow Barch's example and gain some real-world experience. Your professors and your textbooks can undoubtedly teach you a great deal about psychological disorders. But no one can explain what it is like to have one's life turned upside-down by a disorder like schizophrenia in the same way as an individual who lives with it every day.

---

paranoid schizophrenia is not so obviously disturbed as that of one with the catatonic or disorganized type, and the chance for recovery is better.

Disorganized schizophrenia, the most serious type, tends to occur at an earlier age than the other types and is marked by extreme social withdrawal, hallucinations, delusions, silliness, inappropriate laughter, grimaces, grotesque mannerisms, and other bizarre behavior. These patients show flat or inappropriate affect and are frequently incoherent. They often exhibit obscene behavior, may masturbate openly, and may swallow almost any kind of object or material. Disorganized schizophrenia results in the most severe disintegration of the personality, and its victims have the poorest chance of recovery (Fenton & McGlashan, 1991).

Persons with **catatonic schizophrenia** may display complete stillness and stupor or great excitement and agitation. Frequently, they alternate rapidly between the two. They may become frozen in a strange posture or position and remain there for hours without moving. **Undifferentiated schizophrenia** is the general term used when schizophrenic symptoms either do not conform to the criteria of any one type of schizophrenia or conform to more than one type.

◆ **disorganized schizophrenia**
The most serious type of schizophrenia, marked by extreme social withdrawal, hallucinations, delusions, silliness, inappropriate laughter, grotesque mannerisms, and other bizarre behavior.

◆ **catatonic schizophrenia**
(KAT-uh-TAHN-ik) A type of schizophrenia characterized by complete stillness or stupor or great excitement and agitation; patients may assume an unusual posture and remain in it for long periods of time.

◆ **undifferentiated schizophrenia**
A catchall term used when schizophrenic symptoms either do not conform to the criteria of any one type of schizophrenia or conform to more than one type.

Risk Factors in Schizophrenia

◆ *What factors increase the risk of developing schizophrenia?*

Genetic factors appear to play a major role in the development of schizophrenia (Cannon et al., 1998; Gottesman, 1991; Kendler & Diehl, 1993; Owen & O'Donovan, 2003). Figure 12.6 shows how the chance of developing schizophrenia varies with the degree of relationship to a schizophrenic person. However, genes are not destiny; schizophrenia develops when there is both a genetic predisposition toward the disorder and more stress than a person can handle. Any environmental factor—birth trauma, a virus, malnutrition, head injury, and so on—that can interfere with normal brain development brings an increased risk for schizophrenia (McDonald & Murray, 2000; McNeil et al., 2000).

Schizophrenia is more likely to strike men than women. Men also tend to develop the disorder at an earlier age (Takahashi et al., 2000), they do not respond as well to treatment, they spend more time in mental hospitals, and they are more likely to relapse. The earlier age of onset of the disorder among males appears to be independent of culture and socioeconomic variables. Studies of male and female schizophrenics conducted in Japan more than 40 years apart (in the 1950s and the 1990s) revealed that the Japanese males had an earlier onset of the disorder than the Japanese females did and that the average age of onset did not change over the 40-year period. Thus, the age of onset was not influenced by the dramatic cultural and socioeconomic changes in Japan during the postwar period (Takahashi et al., 2000).

Other Psychological Disorders

So far, you have learned about anxiety disorders, mood disorders, and schizophrenia—three major categories of psychological disorders. Several others exist as well, and we will consider four of them in this section. Perhaps you know or have heard about someone who exhibits signs of one of them. But remember Sarah's story at the beginning of the chapter, and beware of intern's syndrome.

Somatoform Disorders

◆ *What are two somatoform disorders, and what symptoms do they share?*

Have you heard the word *psychosomatic* applied to a symptom or illness? Laypersons usually use this term to refer to physical disorders of psychological origin. The DSM-IV-TR uses the term *somatoform disorder* to refer to such conditions. The **somatoform disorders** involve physical symptoms that are due to psychological causes rather than any known medical condition. Although their symptoms are psychological in origin, patients are sincerely convinced that they spring from real physical disorders. People with somatoform disorders are not consciously faking illness to avoid work or other activities.

◆ **somatoform disorders**
(so-MAT-uh-form) Disorders in which physical symptoms are present that are due to psychological causes rather than any known medical condition.

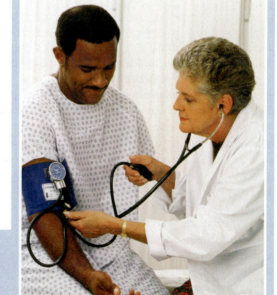

A person with catatonic schizophrenia may become frozen in an unusual position, like a statue, for hours at a time.

A person who continually complains of various symptoms and seeks medical treatment for them, even though doctors can discover nothing wrong, may be suffering from a somatoform disorder.

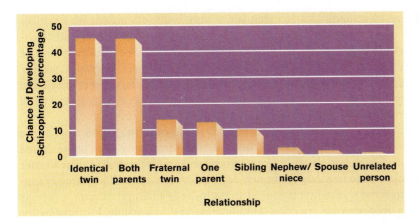

FIGURE 12.6

Genetic Similarity and Probability of Developing Schizophrenia

Research strongly indicates a genetic factor associated with schizophrenia. Identical twins have identical genes, and if one twin develops schizophrenia, the other twin has a 46% chance of also developing it. In fraternal twins, the chance is only 14%. A person with one schizophrenic parent has a 13% chance of developing schizophrenia, but a 46% chance if both parents are schizophrenic. *Source:* Data from Nicol & Gottesman (1983).

People with **hypochondriasis** are overly concerned about their health and fear that their bodily symptoms are a sign of some serious disease. A person with this somatoform disorder "might notice a mole and think of skin cancer or read about Lyme disease and decide it might be the cause of that tired feeling" (Barsky, 1993, p. 8). Yet, the symptoms are not usually consistent with known physical disorders, and even when a medical examination reveals no physical problem, people with hypochondriasis are not convinced. They may "doctor shop," going from one physician to another, seeking confirmation of their worst fears. Unfortunately, hypochondriasis is not easily treated, and there is usually a poor chance for recovery.

A person is diagnosed with a **conversion disorder** when there is a loss of motor or sensory functioning in some part of the body, which is not due to a physical cause but which solves a psychological problem. A person may become blind, deaf, or unable to speak or may develop a paralysis in some part of the body. Many of Freud's patients suffered from conversion disorder, and he believed that they unconsciously developed a physical disability to help resolve an unconscious sexual or aggressive conflict.

Dissociative Disorders

Imagine how disconcerting it would be if you were unable to recognize your own leg. In his book *A Leg to Stand On*, neurologist Oliver Sacks (1984) described the case of a hospitalized man who could not feel or even recognize his own leg. This patient insisted that the leg wasn't even connected to his body, and his attempts to throw the leg out of his bed resulted in numerous falls. This unfortunate man was suffering from a profound disintegration of his physical and psychological self. Mental health professionals refer to this process as *dissociation*—the loss of one's ability to integrate all the components of self into a coherent representation of one's identity. In this case, the patient's dissociation was the result of an underlying physical illness. In many other instances, dissociation has a psychological rather than a physical cause.

In response to unbearable stress, some people develop a **dissociative disorder,** in which they lose the ability to consciously integrate their identities. Their consciousness becomes dissociated from their identity or their memories of important personal events, or both. For example, **dissociative amnesia** is a complete or partial loss of the ability to recall personal information or identify past experiences that cannot be attributed to ordinary forgetfulness or substance use. It is often caused by a traumatic experience—a psychological blow, so to speak—or a situation that creates unbearable anxiety causing the person to escape by "forgetting."

Several people previously thought to have been killed in the terrorist attacks on the World Trade Center on September 11, 2001, were discovered in mental hospitals many months later with diagnoses of dissociative amnesia (*Daily Hampshire Gazette*, 2002). They had been brought to hospitals on the day of the tragedy but were carrying no identification and were unable to remember their names or other identifying information. Extensive investigative work, including DNA testing in some cases, was required

◆ **hypochondriasis**

(HI-poh-kahn-DRY-uh-sis) A somatoform disorder in which persons are preoccupied with their health and fear that their physical symptoms are a sign of some serious disease, despite reassurance from doctors to the contrary.

◆ **conversion disorder**

A somatoform disorder in which a person suffers a loss of motor or sensory functioning in some part of the body; the loss has no physical cause but solves some psychological problem.

◆ *How do the various dissociative disorders affect behavior?*

◆ **dissociative disorders**

Disorders in which, under unbearable stress, consciousness becomes dissociated from a person's identity or her or his memories of important personal events, or both.

◆ **dissociative amnesia**

A dissociative disorder in which there is a complete or partial loss of the ability to recall personal information or identify past experiences.

◆ **dissociative fugue**

(FEWG) A dissociative disorder in which one has a complete loss of memory of one's entire identity, travels away from home, and may assume a new identity.

◆ **dissociative identity disorder (DID)**

A dissociative disorder in which two or more distinct, unique personalities occur in the same person, and there is severe memory disruption concerning personal information about the other personalities.

before they were identified. The fact that some were homeless people with schizophrenia who lived on the streets or in the subway stations near the World Trade Center made the task of identifying them all the more difficult. Such cases illustrate a puzzle concerning dissociative amnesia: Sufferers forget items of personal reference, such as their name, age, and address, and may fail to recognize their parents, other relatives, and friends, but they do not forget how to carry out routine tasks or how to read and write or solve problems, and their basic personality structure remains intact.

Even more puzzling than dissociative amnesia is **dissociative fugue.** In a fugue state, people not only forget their identity, but they also travel away from home. Some take on a new identity that is usually more outgoing and uninhibited than their former identity. The fugue state may last for hours, days, or even months. The fugue is usually a reaction to some severe psychological stress, such as a natural disaster, a serious family quarrel, a deep personal rejection, or military service in wartime. Fortunately for most people, recovery from dissociative fugue is rapid, although they may have no memory of the initial stressor that brought on the fugue state. When people recover from the fugue, they often have no memory of events that occurred during the episode.

In **dissociative identity disorder (DID),** two or more distinct, unique personalities exist in the same individual, and there is severe memory disruption concerning personal information about the other personalities. In 50% of the cases, there are more than 10 different personalities. The change from one personality to another often occurs suddenly and usually during stress. The personality in control of the body the largest percentage of time is known as the *host personality* (Kluft, 1984). The alternate personalities, or *alter personalities*, may differ radically in intelligence, speech, accent, vocabulary, posture, body language, hairstyle, taste in clothes, manners, and even handwriting and sexual orientation. In 80% of the cases of dissociative identity disorder, the host personality does not know of the alter personalities, but the alters have varying levels of awareness of each other (Putnam, 1989). The host and alter personalities commonly show amnesia for certain periods of time or for important life events such as a graduation or wedding. A common complaint is of "lost time"—periods for which a given personality has no memory because he or she was not in control of the body.

Dissociative identity disorder usually begins in early childhood but is rarely diagnosed before adolescence (Vincent & Pickering, 1988). About 90% of the treated cases have been women (Ross et al., 1989), and more than 95% of the patients reveal early histories of severe physical and/or sexual abuse (Coons, 1994; Putnam, 1992). The splitting off of separate personalities is apparently a way of coping with intolerable abuse. Researchers have found evidence to confirm the severe trauma and abuse suffered by many patients with DID (Gleaves, 1996). Dissociative identity disorder can be treated, often by psychotherapy, and some evidence indicates that DID patients respond well to treatment (Ellason & Ross, 1997).

Sexual Disorders

◆ *What are the main characteristics of the various sexual disorders?*

Most psychologists define **sexual disorders** as behavior patterns that are related to sexuality or sexual functioning and are destructive, guilt- or anxiety-producing, compulsive, or a cause of discomfort or harm to one or both parties involved.

Perhaps the most common of all of the sexual disorders are the *sexual dysfunctions*—persistent, recurrent, and distressing problems involving sexual desire, sexual arousal, or the pleasure associated with sex or orgasm (see Chapter 9). Drug treatments for sexual dysfunctions have been successful for both men and women. For men, the drug *sildenafil citrate (Viagra)* has been proven effective in restoring erectile function. And orgasmic disorders and other sexual dysfunctions in women are increasingly being treated with hormones such as *dehydroepiandrosterone (DHEA)* (Munarriz et al., 2002). However, experts in sexual dysfunction point out that while biochemical treatments may restore or enhance physiological functions, other interventions, including individual and couples therapy, are required to improve sufferers' intimate relationships (Besharat, 2001; Heiman, 2002; Lieblum, 2002).

◆ **sexual disorders**

Disorders with a sexual basis that are destructive, guilt- or anxiety-producing, compulsive, or a cause of discomfort or harm to one or both parties involved.

Another important aspect of treatment concerns the link between depression and sexual dysfunction in both men and women (Seidman, 2002). Depression is both a cause and an effect of sexual dysfunctions. Consequently, researchers advise health professionals to question patients who complain of sexual difficulties about factors that may indicate the presence of depression. However, antidepressant drugs often increase the incidence of sexual difficulties (Coleman et al., 2001). Thus, experts advocate combined biochemical and psychological interventions that address both mood and sexual functioning for depressed patients (Montejo et al., 2001).

Paraphilias are disorders in which a person experiences recurrent sexual urges, fantasies, or behaviors involving children, other nonconsenting persons, nonhuman objects, or the suffering or humiliation of the individual or his or her partner. To be diagnosed as having a paraphilia, the person must experience considerable psychological distress or an impairment in functioning in an important area of his or her life.

Gender identity disorder is characterized by a problem accepting one's identity as male or female; children either express a desire to be or insist that they are the other gender. They show a strong preference for the clothes, games, pastimes, and playmates of the opposite sex. Twin studies suggest that genes strongly influence the development of gender identity disorder (Coolidge et al., 2002). The cross-sex preferences of individuals with this disorder go far beyond the cross-gender play behaviors of other children. In fact, these children often express the desire to *be* the other sex, not just engage in the activities associated with it. In adulthood, an individual may feel so strongly that she or he is psychologically of the other gender that *sex-reassignment surgery* is undergone.

Personality Disorders

Do you know someone who is impossible to get along with and who always blames others for his or her problems? Such a person may have a **personality disorder**—a long-standing, inflexible, maladaptive pattern of behaving and relating to others, which usually begins early in childhood or adolescence. Personality disorders are among the most common of mental disorders; the DSM-IV-TR indicates that 10–15% of North Americans have one or more personality disorders. People who suffer from other disorders, especially mood disorders, are often diagnosed with personality disorders as well (Brieger et al., 2003; Joyce et al., 2003). In most cases, the causes of personality disorders have yet to be identified.

People with personality disorders are extremely difficult to get along with. As a result, most have unstable work and social histories. Some sufferers know that their behavior causes problems, yet they seem unable to change. But more commonly, they blame other people or situations for their problems. Thus, because medications have not proved to be very useful in the treatment of personality disorders, treatment options are few. After all, to seek and benefit from therapy, a person must realize that he or she has a problem and be somewhat cooperative with the therapist. Most individuals with personality disorders seek treatment only when forced to by legal authorities or family members and, once in therapy, seldom engage in the kind of self-reflection that is essential to successful psychotherapy.

Several types of personality disorders exist, and the criteria used to differentiate among them overlap considerably. For this reason, the DSM-IV-TR groups personality disorders into *clusters*, as shown in Table 12.2 (on page 388). The individual disorders within each cluster share certain similarities. For example, all of the disorders in Cluster A are characterized by odd behavior such as extreme suspiciousness.

Cluster B disorders involve erratic, overly dramatic behavior. A person with a Cluster B disorder might complain loudly in a store when he feels slighted by a clerk. These disorders carry a higher risk of suicide than other personality disorders (Lambert, 2003). Individuals with borderline personality disorder are especially prone to suicidal thoughts and to self-mutilation. Many have histories of childhood abuse and experience intense fears of abandonment in adult relationships (Trull et al., 2003).

Another Cluster B disorder, antisocial personality disorder, is believed to afflict 20% or more of the men and women who are serving prison sentences in the United States

◆ **paraphilias**
Sexual disorders in which recurrent sexual urges, fantasies, or behavior involve nonhuman objects, children, other nonconsenting persons, or the suffering or humiliation of the individual or his or her partner.

◆ **gender identity disorder**
Sexual disorder characterized by a problem accepting one's identity as male or female.

◆ *What behaviors are associated with personality disorders in Clusters A, B, and C?*

◆ **personality disorder**
A long-standing, inflexible, maladaptive pattern of behaving and relating to others, which usually begins in early childhood or adolescence.

(DSM-IV-TR, 2000). In most of these individuals, a pattern of behavior characterized by lying, cheating, and cruelty to others became established in childhood (Arehart-Treichel, 2002). People with Cluster B disorders typically lack empathy, and many experts believe that this feature of their thinking predisposes them to antisocial behavior (Habel et al., 2002).

Cluster C disorders are characterized by intense feelings of anxiety. Individuals with obsessive-compulsive disorder, for example, may become severely distressed if their normal routines are disrupted. The anxieties of those with either avoidant or dependent personality disorder center on social relationships.

Because the characteristics involved in personality disorders closely resemble normal variations in personality, it is especially important when thinking about them to remember the criteria for abnormality discussed at the beginning of this chapter. So, if a friend suspects a neighbor of poisoning his cat, and you think this is an unreasonable suspicion, don't jump to the conclusion that your friend has paranoid personality disorder. This tendency toward suspiciousness is likely to be simply a personality trait of your friend.

TABLE 12.2 Types of Personality Disorders

PERSONALITY DISORDER	SYMPTOMS
Cluster A: Odd behavior	
Paranoid	Individual is highly suspicious, untrusting, guarded, hypersensitive, easily slighted, lacking in emotion; holds grudges.
Schizoid	Individual isolates self from others; appears unable to form emotional attachments; behavior may resemble that of autistic children.
Schizotypal	Individual dresses in extremely unusual ways; lacks social skills; may have odd ideas resembling the delusions of schizophrenia.
Cluster B: Erratic, overly dramatic behavior	
Narcissistic	Individual has exaggerated sense of self-importance and entitlement; is self-centered, arrogant, demanding, exploitive, envious; craves admiration and attention; lacks empathy.
Histrionic	Individual seeks attention and approval; is overly dramatic, self-centered, shallow, demanding, manipulative, easily bored, suggestible; craves excitement; often, is attractive and sexually seductive.
Borderline	Individual is unstable in mood, behavior, self-image, and social relationships; has intense fear of abandonment; exhibits impulsive and reckless behavior and inappropriate anger; makes suicidal gestures and performs self-mutilating acts.
Antisocial	Individual disregards rights and feelings of others; is manipulative, impulsive, selfish, aggressive, irresponsible, reckless, and willing to break the law, lie, cheat, and exploit others for personal gain, without remorse; fails to hold jobs.
Cluster C: Anxious, fearful behavior	
Obsessive-compulsive	Individual is concerned with doing things the "right" way and is generally a perfectionist; relationships are emotionally shallow.
Avoidant	Individual fears criticism and rejection; avoids social situations in order to prevent being judged by others.
Dependent	Person overly dependent on others for advice and approval; may cling to lovers and friends, fearing abandonment.

As Sarah observed when the psychologist shared the diagnostic criteria for obsessive-compulsive disorder with her, in some cases the difference between "normal" and "abnormal" is one of degree. Think about depression. Everyone feels sad from time to time, but most of us manage these feelings without experiencing the severe disturbances in functioning that are characteristic of individuals with major depressive disorder. It is also true, however, that some disorders have little in common with the ordinary experiences of most people. The delusions of schizophrenia, for example, are qualitatively different from everyday experiences, with the possible exception of the vivid REM dreams you read about in Chapter 4. Of course, we know that these dreams aren't real, while schizophrenics may find themselves living in a world in which they have little or no certainty about what is and is not real. Although you might not think so, intern's syndrome can actually be helpful to your efforts to understand mental illness. As the psychologist said to Sarah, "It's a good thing that people who study mental disorders can see some aspects of those disorders in themselves, because it helps us to understand and empathize with people who have more serious problems. It makes it more difficult for us to indulge in the wish to distance the 'normal us' from the 'abnormal them.'"

Apply It 12.1 Overcoming the Fear of Public Speaking

Do you break out in a cold sweat and start trembling when you have to speak in public? If so, cheer up; you're in good company: Fear of public speaking is the number one fear reported by American adults in surveys. More people fear public speaking than flying, sickness, or even death (*CBS News,* July 31, 2002)!

What Causes It?

Fear of public speaking is a form of performance anxiety, a common type of social phobia. Much of the fear of public speaking stems from fear of being embarrassed or of being judged negatively by others. Some people cope with this fear by trying to avoid situations in which they may be required to speak in public. A more practical approach is to examine the incorrect beliefs that can cause the fear of public speaking and then take specific steps to overcome it. Here are some incorrect beliefs associated with public speaking (Orman, 1996):

- To succeed, a speaker has to perform perfectly. (Not true; no audience expects perfection.)

- A good speaker presents as many facts and details about the subject as possible. (Not true; all you need is two or three main points.)

- If some members of the audience aren't paying attention, the speaker needs to do something about it. (Not true; you can't please everyone, and it's a waste of time to try to do so.)

What Can You Do?

Some of the steps you can take to manage fear of public speaking deal with how you present yourself to your audience; others focus on what's going on inside you. Here are some of the many suggestions offered by experts at Toastmasters International (2003), an organization devoted to helping people improve their public speaking skills:

- *Know your material well.* Practice aloud, and revise your speech, if necessary.

- *Visualize your speech.* Imagine yourself giving your speech in a confident, clear manner.

- *Relax.* Reduce your tension by doing deep breathing or relaxation exercises.

- *Be familiar with the place where you will speak.* Arrive early, and practice using the microphone and any other equipment you plan to use.

- *Connect with the audience.* Greet some members of the audience as they arrive; then, when you give your speech, speak to the audience as though they were a group of your friends.

- *Project confidence through your posture.* Stand or sit in a self-assured manner, smile, and make eye contact with the audience.

- *Focus on your message, not on yourself.* Turn your attention away from your nervousness and focus on the purpose of your speech, which is to transmit information to your audience.

- *Remember that the audience doesn't expect you to be perfect.* Don't apologize for any problems you think you have with your speech. Just be yourself.

By applying these few simple tips, you can overcome nervousness and speak confidently on any topic—even on the spur of the moment.

◆ What Is Abnormal? p. 369

◆ What criteria can be used to determine whether behavior is abnormal? p. 369

Behavior might be considered abnormal if it differs radically from what is considered normal in the person's own culture, if it leads to personal distress or impaired functioning, or if it results in the person's being a danger to self and/or others.

◆ How prevalent are psychological disorders? p. 370

Psychological disorders are more common than many physical diseases. About 22% of Americans are diagnosed with a psychological disorder each year. The lifetime risk of developing such a disorder is 50% in the United States.

◆ What are the theoretical approaches that attempt to explain the causes of psychological disorders? p. 371

Five theoretical perspectives on the causes of psychological disorders are the biological perspective, the biopsychosocial perspective, the psychodynamic perspective, the learning perspective, and the cognitive perspective.

◆ Anxiety Disorders p. 373

◆ How is generalized anxiety disorder manifested? p. 373

Generalized anxiety disorder is characterized by chronic, excessive worry that is so severe that it interferes with daily functioning.

◆ How does panic disorder affect the lives of those who suffer from it? p. 373

Panic disorder is marked by recurrent, unpredictable panic attacks—episodes of overwhelming anxiety, fear, or terror, during which people experience a pounding heart, uncontrollable trembling or shaking, choking or smothering sensations, and the feeling that they are going to die or lose their sanity.

◆ What are the characteristics of the three categories of phobias? p. 374

The three categories of phobias are (1) agoraphobia, an intense fear of being in situations where immediate escape is impossible or help is not available in case of incapacitating anxiety; (2) social phobia, an intense fear of social or performance situations where one might be embarrassed or humiliated by appearing clumsy, foolish, or incompetent; and (3) specific phobia, a marked fear of a specific object or situation (any phobia other than agoraphobia or social phobia).

◆ What thought and behavior patterns are associated with obsessive-compulsive disorder? p. 376

Obsessive-compulsive disorder is characterized by recurrent obsessions (persistent, involuntary thoughts, images, or impulses that cause great distress) and/or compulsions (persistent, irresistible, irrational urges to perform an act or ritual repeatedly).

◆ Mood Disorders p. 377

◆ What are the symptoms of major depressive disorder? p. 377

Major depressive disorder is characterized by feelings of great sadness, despair, and hopelessness, as well as a loss of the ability to feel pleasure.

◆ How are culture, gender, and depression related? p. 377

Lifetime rates of depression vary widely from one culture to another. However, worldwide, women are more likely to suffer from depression than men.

◆ What are the extremes of mood suffered by those with bipolar disorder? p. 378

Bipolar disorder is a mood disorder in which a person suffers from manic episodes (periods of wild optimism, inflated self-esteem, excessive euphoria, and hyperactivity) that alternate with periods of major depression.

◆ What are some suggested causes of mood disorders? p. 379

Some of the proposed causes of mood disorders are (1) a genetic predisposition; (2) disturbances in the brain's serotonin levels; (3) abnormal patterns in the neurotransmitters dopamine, GABA, and norepinephrine; (4) distorted and negative views of oneself, the world, and the future; and (5) major life stress.

◆ What are some of the risk factors for suicide? p. 380

Depression, mood disorders, schizophrenia, and substance abuse are major risk factors for suicide. Elderly, White males commit suicide more often than members of other race or age groups. Women are more likely to attempt suicide, but men are more likely to be successful.

◆ Schizophrenia p. 381

◆ What are the major positive symptoms of schizophrenia? p. 381

The positive symptoms of schizophrenia are abnormal behaviors and characteristics, including hallucinations, delusions, derailment, grossly disorganized behavior, and inappropriate affect.

◆ What normal functions are reduced or absent in schizophrenics? p. 382

The negative symptoms of schizophrenia represent loss of or deficiencies in thoughts and behavior that are characteristic of normal functioning. They include social withdrawal, apathy, loss of motivation, lack of goal-directed activity, very limited speech, slowed movements, flat affect, poor problem-solving abilities, a distorted sense of time, and poor hygiene and grooming.

◆ What does research indicate about the neurological functioning of schizophrenics? p. 382

Schizophrenics exhibit low levels of neural activity in the frontal lobes. Many also have defects in the neural circuitry of the cerebral cortex and limbic system, as well as abnormalities in the hippocampus, amygdala, thalamus, and frontal lobes. They display abnormal lateralization of brain functions and slow communication between left and right hemispheres. Dopamine activity is also abnormal in many schizophrenics.

◆ What are the four types of schizophrenia? p. 382

The four types of schizophrenia are paranoid, disorganized, catatonic, and undifferentiated schizophrenia.

◆ What factors increase the risk of developing schizophrenia? p. 384

Some risk factors for schizophrenia are a genetic predisposition, more stress than a particular individual can handle, any environmental factor that can interfere with normal brain development, and excessive dopamine activity in the brain. Men are more likely than women to develop schizophrenia.

◆ Other Psychological Disorders p. 384

◆ What are two somatoform disorders, and what symptoms do they share? p. 384

Hypochondriasis involves a persistent fear that bodily symptoms are the sign of some serious disease. Conversion disorder involves a loss of motor or sensory functioning in some part of the body, which has no physical cause but does solve a psychological problem.

◆ How do the various dissociative disorders affect behavior? p. 385

People with dissociative amnesia have a complete or partial loss of memory of important personal events and/or their entire personal identity. In dissociative fugue, people forget their entire identity, travel away from home, and may assume a new identity somewhere else. In dissociative identity disorder, two or more distinct, unique personalities exist in the same person.

◆ What are the main characteristics of the various sexual disorders? p. 385

A sexual dysfunction is a problem with sexual desire, sexual arousal, or the pleasure associated with sex or orgasm.

Paraphilias are disorders in which sufferers have recurrent sexual urges, fantasies, and behaviors that involve children, other nonconsenting persons, nonhuman objects, or the suffering and humiliation of the individual or his or her partner. People who feel that their psychological gender identity is different from that typically associated with their biological sex may suffer from gender identity disorder.

◆ What behaviors are associated with personality disorders in Clusters A, B, and C? p. 387

People with personality disorders have long-standing, inflexible, maladaptive patterns of behavior that cause problems in their social relationships and at work and often cause personal distress. Cluster A disorders are characterized by odd behavior. The disorders in Cluster B involve erratic, overly dramatic behavior. Cluster C includes disorders that are associated with fearful and anxious behaviors.

◆ KEY TERMS

agoraphobia, p. 374
anxiety disorders, p. 373
bipolar disorder, p. 378
catatonic schizophrenia, p. 383
compulsion, p. 376
conversion disorder, p. 385
delusion, p. 381
delusion of grandeur, p. 381
delusion of persecution, p. 381
disorganized schizophrenia, p. 383
dissociative amnesia, p. 385
dissociative disorders, p. 385
dissociative fugue, p. 386
dissociative identity disorder (DID), p. 386

DSM-IV, p. 372
gender identity disorder, p. 387
generalized anxiety disorder, p. 373
hallucination, p. 381
hypochondriasis, p. 384
major depressive disorder, p. 377
manic episode, p. 378
mood disorders, p. 377
obsession, p. 376
obsessive-compulsive disorder (OCD), p. 376
panic attack, p. 373
panic disorder, p. 374
paranoid schizophrenia, p. 382
paraphilias, p. 387

personality disorder, p. 387
phobia, p. 374
psychological disorders, p. 369
psychosis, p. 381
schizophrenia, p. 381
sexual disorders, p. 386
social phobia, p. 375
somatoform disorders, p. 384
specific phobia, p. 375
undifferentiated schizophrenia, p. 383

Study Guide 12

Answers to all the Study Guide questions are provided at the end of the book.

◆ SECTION ONE: Chapter Review

What is Abnormal? (pp. 369–372)

1. It is relatively easy to differentiate normal behavior from abnormal behavior. (true/false)

2. The DSM-IV is a manual that is published by the American Psychiatric Association and is used to
   a. diagnose psychological disorders.
   b. explain the causes of psychological disorders.
   c. outline the treatments for various psychological disorders.
   d. assess the effectiveness of treatment programs.

3. Match the perspective with its suggested cause of abnormal behavior.
   ____ (1) faulty learning
   ____ (2) unconscious, unresolved conflicts
   ____ (3) genetic inheritance or biochemical or structural abnormalities in the brain
   ____ (4) faulty thinking
   a. psychodynamic
   b. biological
   c. learning
   d. cognitive

Anxiety Disorders (pp. 373–376)

4. Anxiety disorders are the least common of all psychological disorders. (true/false)

5. Phobias may result from frightening experiences and observational learning. (true/false)

6. Obsessive-compulsive disorder appears to be caused primarily by psychological rather than biological factors. (true/false)

7. Match the anxiety disorder with the example.
   ____ (1) Lana refuses to eat in front of others for fear her hand will shake.
   ____ (2) Ronin is excessively anxious about his health and his job, even though there is no concrete reason to be.
   ____ (3) Kyla has been housebound for 4 years.
   ____ (4) Jackson gets hysterical when a dog approaches him.
   ____ (5) Lauren has incapacitating attacks of anxiety that come on her suddenly.
   ____ (6) Michael repeatedly checks his doors, windows, and appliances before he goes to bed.

a. panic disorder
b. agoraphobia
c. specific phobia
d. generalized anxiety disorder
e. social phobia
f. obsessive-compulsive disorder

Mood Disorders (pp. 377–381)

8. Monteil has periods in which he is so depressed that he becomes suicidal. At other times he is wildly euphoric. He would probably receive the diagnosis of
   a. antisocial personality disorder.
   b. dissociative fugue.
   c. bipolar disorder.
   d. major depressive disorder.

9. Match the type of factor with the proposed cause of depression:
   ____ (1) negative thoughts about oneself, the world, and one's future
   ____ (2) hereditary predisposition or biochemical imbalance
   ____ (3) negative life events
   a. stress
   b. cognitive factor
   c. biological factor

10. Drugs are seldom used in the treatment of mood disorders. (true/false)

11. The suicide rate is lower for
    a. males than for females.
    b. African American males than for White males.
    c. the elderly than for teenagers.
    d. people who suffer psychological disorders than for those who do not.

Schizophrenia (pp. 381–384)

12. Match the symptom of schizophrenia with the example.
    ____ (1) Brendon believes he is Moses.
    ____ (2) Dina thinks her family is spreading rumors about her.
    ____ (3) Avi hears voices cursing him.
    ____ (4) Dean laughs at tragedies and cries when he hears a joke.
    a. delusions of grandeur   c. inappropriate affect
    b. hallucinations   d. delusions of persecution

392 ◆ CHAPTER 12

13. There is substantial research evidence that all of the following have roles as causes of schizophrenia *except*
    a. genetic factors.
    b. stress in people predisposed to the disorder.
    c. abnormal dopamine activity.
    d. unhealthy family interaction patterns.

14. Match the subtype of schizophrenia with the example.
    ____ (1) Amy stands for hours in the same strange position.
    ____ (2) Trevin believes the CIA is plotting to kill him.
    ____ (3) Matt makes silly faces, laughs a lot, and masturbates openly.
    ____ (4) Francesca has the symptoms of schizophrenia but does not fit any one type.
    a. paranoid schizophrenia
    b. disorganized schizophrenia
    c. catatonic schizophrenia
    d. undifferentiated schizophrenia

Other Psychological Disorders (pp. 384–388)

15. Somatoform disorders have physiological rather than psychological causes. (true/false)

16. Dissociative disorders are often associated with trauma. (true/false)

17. Match the psychological disorder with the example.
    ____ (1) Jan is convinced he has some serious disease, although his doctors can find nothing physically wrong.
    ____ (2) Lonnie is found far away from his home town, calling himself by another name and having no memory of his past.
    ____ (3) Natalia suddenly loses her sight, but doctors can find no physical reason for the problem.
    ____ (4) Colane has no memory of being in the boat with other family members the day her older brother drowned.
    ____ (5) Cassandra has no memory for blocks of time in her life and often finds clothing in her closet that she cannot remember buying.
    a. dissociative identity disorder
    b. dissociative fugue
    c. dissociative amnesia
    d. hypochondriasis
    e. conversion disorder

18. (Sexual dysfunctions, Paraphilias) are disorders in which sexual urges, fantasies, and behaviors involve children, other nonconsenting partners, or objects.

19. Which statement is true of personality disorders?
    a. Personality disorders usually begin in adulthood.
    b. Persons with these disorders usually realize that they have a problem.
    c. Personality disorders typically cause problems in social relationships and at work.
    d. Persons with these disorders typically seek professional help.

20. Bruce lies, cheats, and exploits others without feeling guilty. His behavior best fits the diagnosis of _____ personality disorder.
    a. avoidant
    b. histrionic
    c. antisocial
    d. narcissistic

◆ SECTION TWO: Identifying the Disorder

Name the disorder characterized by each set of symptoms.

Symptoms   **Disorder**

1. Markedly diminished interest or pleasure in all or most activities, combined with psychomotor disturbances, fatigue, insomnia, feelings of worthlessness, and recurrent thoughts of death

    _____

2. Grossly disorganized behavior combined with inappropriate affect, disturbed speech and loose associations, and delusions of grandeur—for example, a belief that one is working for a secret government agency and is being followed by foreign spies

    _____

3. Intense mood swings, ranging from euphoric and hyperactive highs marked by delusions of grandeur to extreme depression

    _____

4. Intense fear of being in a situation from which immediate escape is not possible or help is not available in the case of panic

    _____

5. Complete loss of the ability to recall personal information or past experiences, with no physical explanation for the problem

   _____

6. A pattern of unstable and intense interpersonal relationships combined with impulsivity, inappropriate and intense anger, a poor self-image, and recurrent thoughts of suicide

   _____

7. Problems involving sexual desire, sexual arousal, or the pleasure associated with sex or orgasm

   _____

8. Spending excessive amounts of time engaged in daily rituals such as counting and cleaning, accompanied by obsessions

   _____

◆ **SECTION THREE: Fill In the Blank**

1. The _____ perspective views abnormal behavior as a symptom of an underlying physical disorder.

2. Hallucinations, delusions, and disorganized speech are considered to be _____ symptoms of schizophrenia.

3. Ricardo believes that there are three men who follow him around and whisper messages in his ear, telling him to do bad things. Ricardo's false belief is called a _____.

4. Symptoms such as social withdrawal, apathy, slowed movements, and limited speech are examples of the _____ symptoms of schizophrenia.

5. Alice has been unable to make herself go to work for several weeks. She lies in bed for hours wishing for death. Alice may be suffering from _____ _____ _____.

6. Yolanda called her best friend one night at 2 a.m., extremely excited about her great idea: She was going to have U2 perform in her backyard for her birthday. She planned to call the band members as soon as she got off the phone with her friend. Yolanda was probably having a _____ episode.

7. Hypochondriasis is an example of a _____ disorder.

8. Taryn experiences sudden and unexplained waves of fear that seem to come out of nowhere. She is suffering from _____ disorder.

9. An obsession is characterized by _____ _____ _____; a compulsion involves a _____ _____ _____.

10. There seems to be no physical reason for Jason's paralysis. It is likely that he is suffering from a _____ disorder.

11. The disorder in which an individual has two or more distinct personalities is called _____ _____ disorder.

12. Histrionic, borderline, antisocial, and narcissistic disorders are collectively known as _____ disorders.

13. Kim has never felt comfortable with her gender and believes she should have been a male. According to the DSM-IV she has _____ _____ disorder.

14. _____ are sensory perceptions in the absence of any external stimulation—for example, seeing things that are not really there.

15. A _____ is a persistent, irrational fear of an object, situation, or activity that a person feels compelled to avoid.

16. The _____ personality disorder is marked by a lack of feeling for others, selfishness, aggressive and irresponsible behavior, and a willingness to break the law or exploit others for personal gain.

◆ **SECTION FOUR: Comprehensive Practice Test**

1. Which perspective sees abnormal behavior as a symptom of an underlying physical disorder?
   a. cognitive
   b. psychoanalytic
   c. biological
   d. behavioral

2. Which perspective sees abnormal behavior as the result of faulty and negative thinking?
   a. psychoanalytic
   b. cognitive
   c. behavioral
   d. biological

3. Which perspective sees abnormal behavior as the result of early childhood experiences and unconscious sexual and aggressive conflicts?
   a. cognitive
   b. biological
   c. humanistic
   d. psychoanalytic

4. Which perspective sees psychological disorders as resulting from both physical and psychological causes?
   a. cognitive
   b. biopsychosocial
   c. biological
   d. behavioral

5. Psychosis is a loss of contact with reality. (true/false)

6. Panic disorder, phobia, and obsessive-compulsive disorder are all examples of _____ disorders.
   a. neurotic
   b. anxiety
   c. personality
   d. somatoform

7. Dawn is convinced that she has a disease and goes from one doctor to another searching for a diagnosis; however, every doctor she consults says there is nothing physically wrong with her. Dawn is suffering from
   a. hypochondriasis.
   b. dissociative identity disorder.
   c. a conversion disorder.
   d. body dysmorphic disorder.

8. Dissociative amnesia, characterized by loss of memory of one's identity, is generally brought on by physical trauma. (true/false)

9. A common early experience of patients with dissociative identity disorder is
   a. drug use by their mother while pregnant.
   b. measles or mumps when young.
   c. parental divorce.
   d. early physical and/or sexual abuse.

10. Hallucinations, delusions, and disorganized thinking and speech are _____ symptoms of schizophrenia.
    a. negative
    b. positive
    c. dissociative
    d. obsessive

11. Thao's belief that he is a secret agent for the devil is a good example of a delusion. (true/false)

12. A patient who sits completely still for hours as if he were in a stupor and sometimes experiences periods of great agitation and excitement is suffering from _____ schizophrenia.
    a. disorganized
    b. undifferentiated
    c. paranoid
    d. catatonic

13. Major depression and bipolar disorder are examples of _____ disorders.
    a. personality
    b. psychotic
    c. mood
    d. emotional

14. Depression is diagnosed more often in women than in men. (true/false)

15. _____ is characterized by periods of inflated self-esteem, wild optimism, and hyperactivity known as manic episodes.
    a. Schizophrenia
    b. Major depression
    c. Borderline personality disorder
    d. Bipolar disorder

16. The risk of suicide is especially high in patients who suffer from
    a. catatonic schizophrenia.
    b. paraphilias.
    c. depression.
    d. simple phobia.

17. The psychoanalytic perspective asserts that depression stems from faulty thinking and distorted perceptions. (true/false)

18. Depression seems to be the result of
    a. biological factors only.
    b. both biological and environmental factors.
    c. environmental factors only.
    d. poor parenting in early childhood.

◆ SECTION FIVE: Critical Thinking

1. Formulate a specific plan that will help you recognize and avoid the five cognitive traps that contribute to unhealthy thinking. You might enlist the help of a friend to monitor your negative statements.

2. Some psychological disorders are more common in women (depression, agoraphobia, and simple phobia), and some are more common in men (antisocial personality disorder and substance abuse). Give some possible reasons for such gender differences in the prevalence of these disorders. Support your answer.

3. There is continuing controversy over whether specific psychological disorders are chiefly biological in origin (nature) or result primarily from learning and experience (nurture). Select any two disorders from this chapter, and prepare arguments for both the nature and nurture positions for both disorders.

Therapies

chapter 13

Insight Therapies

◆ *What are the basic techniques of psychoanalysis, and how are they used to help patients?*

◆ *What are the role and the goal of the therapist in person-centered therapy?*

◆ *What is the major emphasis of Gestalt therapy?*

Relationship Therapies

◆ *What problems commonly associated with major depression does interpersonal therapy focus on?*

◆ *What is the goal of family therapy?*

◆ *What are some advantages of group therapy?*

Behavior Therapies

◆ *How do behavior therapists modify clients' problematic behavior?*

◆ *What behavior therapies are based on classical conditioning?*

◆ *How does participant modeling help people overcome their fears?*

Cognitive Therapies

◆ *What is the aim of rational-emotive therapy?*

◆ *How does Beck's cognitive therapy help people overcome depression and panic disorder?*

Biological Therapies

◆ *What are the advantages and disadvantages of using drugs to treat psychological disorders?*

◆ *What is electroconvulsive therapy (ECT) used for?*

◆ *What is psychosurgery, and for what problems is it used?*

Evaluating the Therapies

◆ *What therapy, if any, is most effective in treating psychological disorders?*

Culturally Sensitive and Gender-Sensitive Therapy

◆ *What characterizes culturally sensitive and gender-sensitive therapy?*

396

Jane is an intelligent and attractive young woman who works part-time at a local sporting goods store and attends college. She is studying to be a computer programmer. For as long as she can remember, Jane has worried about things that might go wrong, even when there are no signs of trouble. She worries about her grades, although she always does well in her classes. She worries that she will lose her job and have to drop out of school, although her performance reviews are always positive. She worries about home safety issues—radon gas, carbon monoxide, and black mold—and has spent hundreds of dollars on home inspections to make sure that the air in her home is safe. All of the inspectors have given Jane's home a clean bill of health, but she still can't stop worrying. She worries that Sam, her boyfriend, doesn't care about her as much as she cares about him, although he is quick to reassure her whenever she voices her fears.

Along with these large worries, Jane worries about small, everyday things, such as being late, not wearing the appropriate clothes, getting a traffic ticket, or hurting other people's feelings. Her body is always tense. She frequently experiences aches and pains that trouble her but that her physician can't trace to any physical illness or injury. She tires easily, has difficulty concentrating, and doesn't sleep well.

Many days, Jane feels depressed by her inability to stop worrying about things, and she feels that her anxiety takes a toll on those closest to her. She frequently asks for reassurance, but it brings only temporary relief. Sometimes her boyfriend is hurt that she doesn't seem to trust his feelings for her. Jane worries that her need for reassurance and her inability to believe it when it is given will eventually drive Sam away. She says, "I'm always waiting for the other shoe to drop, and it's not a good way to live, but I can't seem to stop thinking about what bad thing will happen next."

As you may recognize from what you learned in Chapter 12, Jane suffers from generalized anxiety disorder. If you were a psychotherapist, how would you treat someone who is experiencing these distressing symptoms? In this chapter, you will discover the many kinds of therapy available to help people suffering from psychological disorders. As you read, keep Jane in mind, and ask yourself how each kind of therapist would try to help her with her anxiety.

Psychotherapy uses psychological rather than biological means to treat psychological disorders. The practice of psychotherapy has grown and changed enormously since its beginnings more than 100 years ago, when Freud and his colleagues began using it.

Insight Therapies

Do you recall a form of learning called insight that you read about in Chapter 5? Such learning is the foundation of several approaches to psychotherapy. These approaches, fittingly enough, are collectively referred to as **insight therapies** because their assumption is that psychological well-being depends on self-understanding—understanding of one's own thoughts, emotions, motives, behavior, and coping mechanisms.

◆ **psychotherapy**
Any type of approach that uses psychological rather than biological means to treat psychological disorders.

◆ **insight therapies**
Approaches to psychotherapy based on the notion that psychological well-being depends on self-understanding.

Psychodynamic Therapies

◆ *What are the basic techniques of psychoanalysis, and how are they used to help patients?*

Psychodynamic therapies attempt to uncover repressed childhood experiences that are thought to explain a patient's current difficulties. The techniques associated with the first such therapy—Freud's **psychoanalysis**—are still used by psychodynamic therapists today (Epstein et al., 2001). One such technique is **free association,** in which the patient is asked to reveal whatever thoughts, feelings, or images come to mind, no matter how trivial, embarrassing, or terrible they might seem. The analyst then pieces together the free-flowing associations, explains their meanings, and helps patients gain insight into the thoughts and behaviors that are troubling them. But some patients avoid revealing certain painful or embarrassing thoughts while engaging in free association, a phenomenon Freud called *resistance.* Resistance may take the form of halting speech during free association, "forgetting" appointments with the analyst, or arriving late.

Dream analysis is another technique used by psychoanalysts. Freud believed that areas of emotional concern repressed in waking life are sometimes expressed in symbolic form in dreams. He claimed that patient behavior may have a symbolic quality as well. At some point during psychoanalysis, Freud said, the patient reacts to the analyst with the same feelings that were present in another significant relationship—usually with the mother or father. This reaction of the patient is called **transference.** Freud believed that encouraging patients to achieve transference was a essential part of psychotherapy. He claimed that transference allows the patient to relive troubling experiences from the past with the analyst as a parent substitute, thereby resolving any hidden conflicts.

Many therapists today practice brief psychodynamic therapy, in which the therapist and patient decide on the issues to explore at the outset rather than waiting for them to emerge in the course of treatment. The therapist assumes a more active role and places more emphasis on the present than in traditional psychoanalysis. Brief psychodynamic therapy may require only one or two visits per week for as few as 12 to 20 weeks. In a meta-analysis of 11 well-controlled studies, Crits-Christoph (1992) found brief psychodynamic therapy to be as effective as other psychotherapies. More recent research has also shown brief psychodynamic therapy to be comparable to other forms of psychotherapy in terms of successful outcomes (Hager et al., 2000). Brief psychotherapy appears to be most effective with patients who do not have multiple psychological disorders, who lack significant social relationship problems, and who believe that the therapy will be effective (Crits-Christoph et al., 2004).

◆ **psychodynamic therapies**

Psychotherapies that attempt to uncover repressed childhood experiences that are thought to explain a patient's current difficulties.

◆ **psychoanalysis**

(SY-ko-uh-NAL-ul-sis) The first psychodynamic therapy, which was developed by Freud and uses free association, dream analysis, and transference.

◆ **free association**

A psychoanalytic technique used to explore the unconscious by having patients reveal whatever thoughts, feelings, or images come to mind.

◆ **transference**

An emotional reaction that occurs during psychoanalysis, in which the patient displays feelings and attitudes toward the analyst that were present in another significant relationship.

Freud's famous couch was used by his patients during psychoanalysis.

Humanistic Therapies

Humanistic therapies assume that people have the ability and freedom to lead rational lives and make rational choices. **Person-centered therapy**, developed by Carl Rogers (1951), is one of the most frequently used humanistic therapies. According to this view, people are innately good and, if allowed to develop naturally, will grow toward *self-actualization*—the realization of their inner potential. The humanistic perspective suggests that psychological disorders result when a person's natural tendency toward self-actualization is blocked either by oneself or by others. In the 1940s and 1950s, person-centered therapy enjoyed a strong following among psychologists.

The person-centered therapist attempts to create an accepting climate, based on *unconditional positive regard* (explained in Chapter 12) for the client. The therapist also empathizes with the client's concerns and emotions. When the client speaks, the therapist responds by restating or reflecting back her or his ideas and feelings. Using these techniques, the therapist allows the client to control the direction of the therapy sessions. Rogers rejected all forms of therapy that cast the therapist in the role of expert and clients in the role of patients who expect the therapist to prescribe something that "cures" their problem. Thus, person-centered therapy is called a **nondirective therapy**.

Gestalt Therapy

Gestalt therapy, developed by Fritz Perls (1969), emphasizes the importance of clients' fully experiencing, in the present moment, their feelings, thoughts, and actions and then taking responsibility for them. The goal of Gestalt therapy is to help clients achieve a more integrated self and become more authentic and self-accepting. In addition, they learn to assume personal responsibility for their behavior rather than blaming society, past experiences, parents, or others.

Gestalt therapy is a **directive therapy**, one in which the therapist takes an active role in determining the course of therapy sessions and provides answers and suggestions to the client. The well-known phrase "getting in touch with your feelings" is a major objective of Gestalt therapy. Perls suggested that those of us who are in need of therapy carry around a heavy load of unfinished business, which may be in the form of resentment toward or conflicts with parents, siblings, lovers, employers, or others. If not resolved, these conflicts are carried forward into our present relationships. One method for dealing with unfinished business is the "empty chair" technique (Paivio & Greenberg, 1995). The client sits facing an empty chair and imagines, for example, that a wife, husband, father, or mother sits there. The client proceeds to tell the chair what he or she truly feels about that person. Then, the client moves to the empty chair and role-plays what the imagined person's response would be to what was said.

Carl Rogers (at upper right) facilitates discussion in a therapy group.

> ◆ *What are the role and the goal of the therapist in person-centered therapy?*

◆ **humanistic therapies**
Psychotherapies that assume that people have the ability and freedom to lead rational lives and make rational choices.

◆ **person-centered therapy**
A nondirective, humanistic therapy developed by Carl Rogers, in which the therapist creates an accepting climate and shows empathy, freeing clients to be themselves and releasing their natural tendency toward self-actualization.

> ◆ *What is the major emphasis of Gestalt therapy?*

◆ **nondirective therapy**
Any type of psychotherapy in which the therapist allows the direction of the therapy sessions to be controlled by the client; an example is person-centered therapy.

◆ **Gestalt therapy**
A therapy that was originated by Fritz Perls and that emphasizes the importance of clients' fully experiencing, in the present moment, their feelings, thoughts, and actions and then taking responsibility for them.

◆ **directive therapy**
Any type of psychotherapy in which the therapist takes an active role in determining the course of therapy sessions and provides answers and suggestions to the patient; an example is Gestalt therapy.

Relationship Therapies

◆ **relationship therapies**
Therapies that attempt to improve patients' interpersonal relationships or create new relationships to support patients' efforts to address psychological problems.

Insight therapies focus on the self, which is not always the most appropriate approach to a psychological problem. **Relationship therapies** look not only at the individual's internal struggles but also at his or her interpersonal relationships. Some deliberately create new relationships for people that can support them in their efforts to address their problems.

Interpersonal Therapy

◆ *What problems commonly associated with major depression does interpersonal therapy focus on?*

Interpersonal therapy (IPT) is a brief psychotherapy that has proven very effective in the treatment of depression (Elkin et al., 1989, 1995; Klerman et al., 1984). It can be carried out with individual clients or with groups (Mufson et al., 2004). IPT is designed specifically to help patients understand and cope with four types of interpersonal problems commonly associated with major depression:

1. *Unusual or severe responses to the death of a loved one.* The therapist and patient discuss the patient's relationship with the deceased person and feelings (such as guilt) that may be associated with the death.
2. *Interpersonal role disputes.* The therapist helps the patient to understand others' points of view and to explore options for bringing about change.
3. *Difficulty in adjusting to role transitions, such as divorce, career change, and retirement.* Patients are helped to see the change not as a threat but as a challenge that they can master and an opportunity for growth.
4. *Deficits in interpersonal skills.* Through role-playing and analysis of the patient's communication style, the therapist tries to help the patient develop the interpersonal skills necessary to initiate and sustain relationships.

◆ **interpersonal therapy (IPT)**
A brief psychotherapy designed to help depressed people better understand and cope with problems relating to their interpersonal relationships.

Interpersonal therapy is relatively brief, consisting of 12 to 16 weekly sessions. A large study conducted by the National Institute of Mental Health found IPT to be an effective treatment even for severe depression and to have a low dropout rate (Elkin et al., 1989, 1995). Research also indicates that patients who recover from major depression can enjoy a longer period without relapse when they continue with monthly sessions of IPT (Frank et al., 1991).

Family Therapy and Couples Therapy

◆ *What is the goal of family therapy?*

Some therapists work with couples to help them resolve their difficulties. Others specialize in treating troubled families. In **family therapy,** parents and children enter therapy as a group. The therapist pays attention to the dynamics of the family unit—how family members communicate, how they act toward one another, and how they view one another. The goal of the therapist is to help family members reach agreement on certain changes that will help heal the wounds of the family unit, improve communication patterns, and create more understanding and harmony within the group (Hawley & Weisz, 2003).

Couples therapy and family therapy appear to have positive effects in treating a number of disorders and clinical problems (Lebow & Gurman, 1995; Walitzer & Demen, 2004). Couples therapy can be helpful in the treatment of sexual dysfunctions (Gehring, 2003). And, when it accompanies medication, family therapy can be beneficial in the treatment of schizophrenia and can reduce relapse rates (Carpenter, 1996). Schizophrenic patients are more likely to relapse if their family members express emotions, attitudes, and behaviors that involve criticism, hostility, or emotional overinvolvement (Linszen et al., 1997); this pattern is labeled *high in expressed emotion,* or *high EE* (Falloon, 1988; Jenkins & Karno, 1992). Family therapy can help other family members modify their behavior toward the patient. It also seems to be the most favorable setting for treating adolescent drug abuse (Lebow & Gurman, 1995).

◆ **family therapy**
Therapy involving an entire family, with the goal of helping family members reach agreement on changes that will help heal the family unit, improve communication problems, and create more understanding and harmony within the group.

Therapists working with couples pay attention to the dynamics between the two people—how they communicate, act toward each other, and view each other.

Group Therapy

Group therapy is a form of therapy in which several clients (usually 7 to 10) meet regularly with one or more therapists to resolve personal problems. Besides being less expensive than individual therapy, group therapy gives the individual a sense of belonging and opportunities to express feelings, to get feedback from other members, and to give and receive help and emotional support. Learning that others also share their problems helps people feel less alone and ashamed. A meta-analysis of studies comparing prisoners who participated in group therapy to those who did not found that group participation was helpful for a variety of problems, including anxiety, depression, and low self-esteem (Morgan & Flora, 2002).

A variant of group therapy is the *self-help group*. Approximately 12 million people in the United States participate in roughly 500,000 self-help groups, most of which focus on a single problem such as substance abuse or depression. Self-help groups usually are not led by professional therapists. They are simply groups of people who share a common problem and meet to give and receive support.

One of the oldest and best-known self-help groups is Alcoholics Anonymous, which claims 1.5 million members worldwide. Other self-help groups patterned after Alcoholics Anonymous have been formed to help individuals overcome many other addictive behaviors, from overeating (Overeaters Anonymous) to gambling (Gamblers Anonymous). One study indicated that people suffering from anxiety-based problems were helped by participating in groups that used a multimedia self-help program called Attacking Anxiety. Of the 176 individuals who participated in the study, 62 were reported to have achieved significant improvement, and another 40 reported some improvement (Finch et al., 2000).

> ◆ *What are some advantages of group therapy?*

> ◆ **group therapy**
> A form of therapy in which several clients (usually 7 to 10) meet regularly with one or more therapists to resolve personal problems.

Group therapy can give individuals a sense of belonging and an opportunity to give and receive emotional support.

Behavior Therapies

◆ **behavior therapy**

A treatment approach that is based on the idea that abnormal behavior is learned and that applies the principles of operant conditioning, classical conditioning, and/or observational learning to eliminate inappropriate or maladaptive behaviors and replace them with more adaptive responses.

◆ **behavior modification**

An approach to therapy that uses learning principles to eliminate inappropriate or maladaptive behaviors and replace them with more adaptive responses.

◆ *How do behavior therapists modify clients' problematic behavior?*

◆ **token economy**

A behavior modification technique that rewards appropriate behavior with tokens that can be exchanged later for desired goods and/or privileges.

◆ **time out**

A behavior modification technique used to eliminate undesirable behavior, especially in children and adolescents, by withdrawing all reinforcers for a period of time.

A time out is effective because it prevents a child from receiving reinforcers for undesirable behaviors. The child learns that once the behavior is under control, he or she will again have access to reinforcers. Similar behavioral techniques, such as token economies, are useful with adults in mental hospitals and other institutions.

Sometimes, individuals seek help from a mental health professional because they want to rid themselves of a troublesome habit, or they want to develop a better way to respond to specific situations in their lives. In such cases, psychotherapists may employ a behavioral approach.

A **behavior therapy** is a treatment approach consistent with the learning perspective on psychological disorders—that abnormal behavior is learned. Instead of viewing maladaptive behavior as a symptom of some underlying disorder, the behavior therapist sees the behavior itself as the disorder. If a person comes to a therapist with a fear of flying, that fear of flying is seen as the problem. Behavior therapies use learning principles to eliminate inappropriate or maladaptive behaviors and replace them with more adaptive responses—an approach referred to as **behavior modification.** The goal is to change the troublesome behavior, not to change the individual's personality structure or to search for the origin of the problem behavior.

Behavior Modification Techniques Based on Operant Conditioning

Behavior modification techniques based on operant conditioning seek to control the consequences of behavior. Extinction of an undesirable behavior is accomplished by terminating, or withholding, the reinforcement that is maintaining that behavior (Lerman & Iwata, 1996). Behavior therapists also seek to reinforce desirable behavior to increase its frequency. Institutional settings such as hospitals, prisons, and school classrooms are well suited to behavior modification techniques, because they provide a restricted environment where the consequences of behavior can be strictly controlled.

Some institutions use **token economies** that reward appropriate behavior with tokens such as poker chips, play money, gold stars, or the like. These tokens can later be exchanged for desired goods (candy, gum, cigarettes) and/or privileges (weekend passes, free time, participation in desirable activities). Sometimes, individuals are fined a certain number of tokens for undesirable behavior. Mental hospitals have successfully used token economies with chronic schizophrenics for decades to improve their self-care skills and social interactions (Ayllon & Azrin, 1965, 1968). Similar interventions have been helpful in motivating clients at substance abuse clinics to remain abstinent (Petry et al., 2004).

Other behavior therapies based on operant conditioning have been effective in modifying some behaviors of seriously disturbed people. Although these techniques do not cure schizophrenia, autism, or mental retardation, they can increase the frequency of desirable behaviors and decrease the frequency of undesirable behaviors. For example, a large proportion of people who suffer from schizophrenia smoke cigarettes. Among this group, monetary reinforcement has been found to be as effective as nicotine patches for the reduction of smoking (Tidey et al., 2002). Sometimes, modifying such behaviors enables the family members of people with schizophrenia to accept and care for them more easily.

Another effective method used to eliminate undesirable behavior, especially in children and adolescents, is **time out** (Kazdin & Benjet, 2003). Children are told in advance that if they engage in certain undesirable behaviors, they will be removed from the situation and will have to pass a period of time (usually no more than 15 minutes) in a place containing no reinforcers (no television, books, toys, friends, and so on). Theoretically, the undesirable behavior will stop if it is no longer followed by attention or any other positive reinforcers.

Behavior modification techniques can also be used by people who want to break bad habits such as smoking and overeating or to develop good habits such as a regular exercise regime. If you want to modify any of your behaviors, devise a reward system for desirable behaviors, and remember the principles of shaping. Reward gradual changes in the direction of your ultimate goal. If you are trying to develop better eating habits, don't try to change a lifetime of bad habits all at once. Begin with a small step, such as substituting frozen yogurt for ice cream. Set realistic weekly goals that you are likely to be able to achieve.

Behavior Therapies Based on Classical Conditioning

Behavior therapies based on classical conditioning can be used to rid people of fears and other undesirable behaviors. These therapies include systematic desensitization, flooding, exposure and response prevention, and aversion therapy.

One of the pioneers in the application of classical conditioning techniques to therapy, psychiatrist Joseph Wolpe (1958, 1973), reasoned that if he could get people to relax and stay relaxed while they thought about a feared object, person, place, or situation, they could conquer their fear. In Wolpe's therapy, known as **systematic desensitization**, clients are trained in deep muscle relaxation. Then, they confront a hierarchy of fears—a graduated series of anxiety-producing situations—either *in vivo* (in real life) or in their imagination, until they can remain relaxed even in the presence of the most feared situation. The technique can be used for everything from fear of animals to claustrophobia, social phobia, and other situational fears. Try creating such a hierarchy in *Try It 13.1*.

◆ *What behavior therapies are based on classical conditioning?*

◆ **systematic desensitization**

A behavior therapy that is based on classical conditioning and used to treat fears by training clients in deep muscle relaxation and then having them confront a graduated series of anxiety-producing situations (real or imagined) until they can remain relaxed while confronting even the most feared situation.

Try It 13.1
A Possible Hierarchy of Fears

Use what you have learned about systematic desensitization to create a step-by-step approach to help someone overcome a fear of taking tests. The person's hierarchy of fears begins with reading in the syllabus that a test will be given and culminates in actually taking the test. Fill in successive steps, according to a possible hierarchy of fears, that will lead to the final step. One set of possible steps is given below.

Suggested Answers: (1) Preparing for each class session by reading the assigned material and/or completing any homework assignments. (2) Attending each class session and taking notes on the material the test will cover. (3) Reviewing the new notes after each class period. (4) Reviewing all class materials beginning one week before the test. (5) Reciting key information from memory the day before the test. (6) Arriving early to take the test, having gotten a good night's sleep.

Taking the test in class

6. _____

5. _____

4. _____

3. _____

2. _____

1. _____

Reading in the syllabus that a test will be given on a certain day

Flooding can be a useful treatment for phobias, such as fear of dogs.

Many experiments, demonstrations, and case reports confirm that systematic desensitization is a highly successful treatment for eliminating fears and phobias in a relatively short time (Kalish, 1981; Rachman & Wilson, 1980). It has proved effective for specific problems such as test anxiety, stage fright, and anxiety related to sexual disorders.

Flooding is a behavior therapy used in the treatment of phobias. It involves exposing clients to the feared object or event (or asking them to imagine it vividly) for an extended period, until their anxiety decreases. The person is exposed to the fear all at once, not gradually as in systematic desensitization. An individual with a fear of heights, for example, might have to go onto the roof of a tall building and remain there until the fear subsided.

Flooding sessions typically last from 30 minutes to 2 hours and should not be terminated until patients are markedly less afraid than they were at the beginning of the session. Additional sessions are required until the fear response is extinguished or reduced to an acceptable level. It is rare for a patient to need more than six treatment sessions (Marshall & Segal, 1988). *In vivo* flooding, the real-life experience, works faster and is more effective than simply imagining the feared object (Chambless & Goldstein, 1979; Marks, 1972). Thus, a person who fears flying would benefit more from taking an actual plane trip than from just thinking about one.

Exposure and response prevention has been successful in treating obsessive-compulsive disorder (Baer, 1996; Foa, 1995; Rhéaume & Ladouceur, 2000). The first component of this technique involves *exposure*—exposing patients to objects or situations they have been avoiding because they trigger obsessions and compulsive rituals. The second component is *response prevention*, in which patients agree to resist performing their compulsive rituals for progressively longer periods of time.

Initially, the therapist identifies the thoughts, objects, or situations that trigger the compulsive ritual. For example, touching a doorknob, a piece of unwashed fruit, or a garbage bin might send people with a fear of contamination to the nearest bathroom to wash their hands. Patients are gradually exposed to stimuli that they find more and more distasteful and anxiety-provoking. They must agree not to perform the normal ritual (hand washing, bathing, or the like) for a specified period of time after each exposure. A typical treatment course—about 10 sessions over a period of 3 to 7 weeks—can bring about considerable improvement in 60–70% of patients (Jenike, 1990). And patients treated with exposure and response prevention are less likely to relapse after treatment than those treated with drugs alone (Greist, 1992). Exposure and response prevention has also proved useful in the treatment of posttraumatic stress disorder (Cloitre et al., 2002).

Aversion therapy is used to stop a harmful or socially undesirable behavior by pairing it with a painful, sickening, or otherwise aversive stimulus. Electric shock, emetics (which cause nausea and vomiting), or other unpleasant stimuli are paired with the undesirable behavior time after time until a strong negative association is formed and the person comes to avoid that behavior. Treatment continues until the bad behavior loses its appeal and becomes associated with pain or discomfort.

Alcoholics are sometimes given a nausea-producing substance such as Antabuse, which reacts violently with alcohol and causes a person to retch and vomit until the stomach is empty (Grossman & Ruiz, 2004). But for most problems, aversion therapy need not be so intense as to make a person physically ill. A controlled comparison of treatments for chronic nail biting revealed that mild aversion therapy—painting a bitter-tasting substance on the fingernails—yielded significant improvement (Allen, 1996).

◆ **flooding**

A behavior therapy based on classical conditioning and used to treat phobias by exposing clients to the feared object or event (or asking them to imagine it vividly) for an extended period, until their anxiety decreases.

◆ **exposure and response prevention**

A behavior therapy that exposes patients with obsessive-compulsive disorder to stimuli that trigger obsessions and compulsive rituals, while patients resist performing the compulsive rituals for progressively longer periods of time.

◆ **aversion therapy**

A behavior therapy in which an aversive stimulus is paired with a harmful or socially undesirable behavior until the behavior becomes associated with pain or discomfort.

Participant Modeling

Therapies derived from Albert Bandura's work on observational learning are based on the belief that people can overcome fears and acquire social skills through modeling. The most effective type of therapy based on observational learning theory is called **participant modeling** (Bandura, 1977a; Bandura et al., 1975, 1977). In this therapy, not only does the model demonstrate the appropriate response in graduated steps, but the client also attempts to imitate the model step by step, while the therapist gives encouragement and support. Most specific phobias can be extinguished in only 3 or 4 hours of client participation in modeling therapy. For instance, participant modeling could be used to help someone overcome a fear of dogs. A session would begin with the client watching others petting and playing with a dog. As the client becomes more comfortable, he or she would be encouraged to join in. Alternatively, a client would be shown a video of people playing with a dog and then would be encouraged to play with a live dog.

◆ *How does participant modeling help people overcome their fears?*

◆ **participant modeling**
A behavior therapy in which an appropriate response to a feared stimulus is modeled in graduated steps and the client attempts to imitate the model step by step, encouraged and supported by the therapist.

How Did You Find **Psychology?**

Nancy Petry

Do you think that a distinguished career in research could begin as a fascination with a psychology textbook? If not, then you need to consider the example of Nancy Petry, whose research on behavioral treatments for compulsive gamblers and substance abusers has been widely acclaimed ("Nancy M. Petry," 2003). Petry reports that, when she was 8 years old, her mother was pursuing a degree in nursing and was enrolled in a psychology class. The bright third-grader picked up her mother's textbook and became fascinated with the subject matter. A few days later, her teacher asked members of Petry's class to write about what kind of job they wanted to have when they grew up. The first thing that popped into Petry's mind was the textbook. She wanted to write that she was hoping to become a psychologist, but she couldn't remember the correct spelling of the word,—so she wrote about being a flight attendant instead.

After high school, Petry studied in Japan and in England. While in England, she worked as a waitress in a pub and happened to meet a group of physiological psychologists. She mentioned her interest in psychology to them and ended up working in their behavioral pharmacology lab. Petry later returned to the United States and, after earning her degree from Randolph-Macon Women's College, began her graduate studies at Harvard University. With her Ph.D. in hand, Petry turned her attention to applied research focusing on treatments for drug addiction. As a researcher at the substance abuse clinic located at the University of Vermont at Burlington, Petry experimented with adding behavioral treatments such as token economies to conventional pharmacological therapies.

After Petry moved on to the University of Connecticut Health Center's substance abuse clinic, she faced an administrative problem. The center had established a program in which addicts received vouchers for prizes every time they visited the center and passed a drug test, but the program was becoming increasingly expensive. To save money, Petry changed the rules so that a drug-free urine sample earned patients the right to draw a voucher from a bowl. The vouchers represented prizes of different values and, as in a lottery, the probabilities associated with drawing vouchers for the various prizes were negatively related to the value of the prizes. In other words, there were a lot of vouchers for inexpensive prizes and a few vouchers for expensive prizes.

Critics of the new voucher system argued that it might cause patients to develop gambling problems, so Petry added this variable to her research agenda. Remarkably, in preparing a proposal explaining her research, she discovered that there had never been any systematic studies of pathological gambling treatment. Petry then obtained funding from several sources to initiate the first such study. As mentioned on page 406, she found that cognitive-behavioral therapy was an effective treatment for gambling addiction.

Petry's experience with her mother's psychology textbook provides a good illustration of the different ways children and adults view the world. To Petry's mother, reading the book probably represented a chore that had to be completed to obtain her nursing degree. To the young Petry, the book was a treasure trove of intriguing information—one that shaped her views of what kind of career she wanted to have in a far distant future. Perhaps it would be helpful to you to look at your textbooks through the eyes of a curious child who is thirsty for information about the world. Try it. You might find yourself irresistibly attracted to the knowledge they contain.

Cognitive Therapies

Recall from earlier chapters that behavioral theories have often been criticized for ignoring internal variables such as thinking and emotion. As you might predict, behavior therapies are often criticized for the same reason. Cognitive psychologists argue that behaviors cannot be changed in isolation from the thoughts that produce them. Accordingly, they have developed cognitively based therapeutic approaches.

Cognitive therapies, which are based on the cognitive perspective, assume that maladaptive behavior can result from irrational thoughts, beliefs, and ideas, which the therapist tries to change. Cognitive therapies are also often referred to as *cognitive-behavioral approaches* because they combine the insights into behavior provided by cognitive psychology with the methodological approaches of behaviorism (Carson et al., 2000). That is, cognitive therapists seek to change the way clients think (cognitive), and they determine the effectiveness of their interventions by assessing changes in clients' behavior (behavioral). Cognitive-behavioral therapy has been shown to be effective in treating a wide variety of problems, including anxiety disorders (Kellett et al., 2004), hypochondriasis (Martinez & Belloch, 2004), psychological drug dependence (Babor, 2004), and pathological gambling (Petry, 2002).

◆ **cognitive therapies**

Therapies that assume maladaptive behavior can result from irrational thoughts, beliefs, and ideas.

◆ **rational-emotive therapy**

A directive form of psychotherapy, developed by Albert Ellis and designed to challenge clients' irrational beliefs about themselves and others.

Rational-Emotive Therapy

◆ *What is the aim of rational-emotive therapy?*

Clinical psychologist Albert Ellis (1961, 1977, 1993) developed **rational-emotive therapy** in the 1950s. Ellis claims to have developed the technique as a way of addressing his own problems with incapacitating anxiety (Ellis, 2004a). This type of therapy is based on Ellis's *ABC theory*. The A refers to the activating event, the B to the person's belief about the event, and the C to the emotional consequence that follows. Ellis claims that it is not the event itself that causes the emotional consequence, but rather the person's belief about the event. In other words, A does not cause C; B causes C. If the belief is irrational, then the emotional consequence can be extreme distress, as illustrated in Figure 13.1.

FIGURE 13.1 **The ABCs of Rational-Emotive Therapy**

Rational-emotive therapy teaches clients that it is not the activating event (A) that causes the upsetting consequences (C). Rather, it is the client's beliefs (B) about the activating event. According to Albert Ellis, irrational beliefs cause emotional distress. Rational-emotive therapists help clients identify their irrational beliefs and replace them with rational ones.

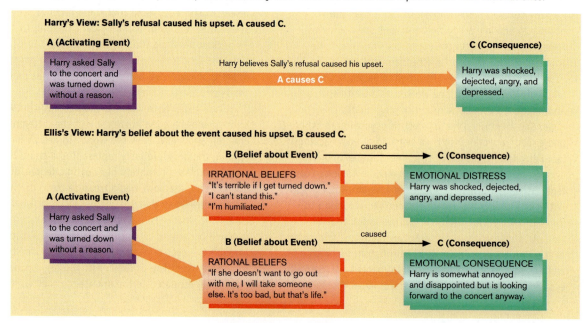

Rational-emotive therapy is a directive form of psychotherapy designed to challenge clients' irrational beliefs about themselves and others. Most clients in rational-emotive therapy see a therapist individually, once a week, for 5 to 50 sessions. In Ellis's view, clients do not benefit from warm, supportive therapeutic approaches that help them feel better but do not address the irrational thoughts that underlie their problems (Ellis, 2004b). Instead, he argues, as clients begin to replace irrational beliefs with rational ones, their emotional reactions become more appropriate, less distressing, and more likely to lead to constructive behavior. For example, a client might tell a therapist that he is feeling anxious and depressed because of his supervisor's unreasonable demands. Using Ellis's rational-emotive therapeutic model, the therapist would help the client distinguish between the supervisor's demands and the client's emotional reactions to them. The goal would be to help the client understand that his reactions to his supervisor's demands are the source of his anxiety and depression, not the demands themselves. Ultimately, the rational-emotive therapist would lead the client to the conclusion that while he may not be able to control his supervisor's demands, he is capable of controlling his emotional reactions to them. Once the client changes his thinking about the problem, the rational-emotive therapist helps him learn behavioral strategies, such as relaxation techniques, that can help him control his emotional reactions.

One meta-analysis of 28 studies showed that individuals receiving rational-emotive therapy did better than those receiving no treatment or a placebo, and about the same as those receiving systematic desensitization (Engels et al., 1993).

Beck's Cognitive Therapy

Psychiatrist Aaron T. Beck (1976) claims that much of the misery endured by a depressed and anxious person can be traced to *automatic thoughts*—unreasonable but unquestioned ideas that rule the person's life ("To be happy, I must be liked by everyone"; "If people disagree with me, it means they don't like me"). Beck (1991) believes that depressed persons hold "a negative view of the present, past, and future experiences" (p. 369). These individuals notice only negative, unpleasant things and jump to upsetting conclusions.

◆ *How does Beck's cognitive therapy help people overcome depression and panic disorder?*

The goal of Beck's **cognitive therapy** is to help clients stop their negative thoughts as they occur and replace them with more objective thoughts. After identifying and challenging the client's irrational thoughts, the therapist sets up a plan and guides the client so that her or his personal experience can provide actual evidence in the real world to refute the false beliefs. Clients are given homework assignments, such as keeping track of automatic thoughts and the feelings evoked by them and then substituting more rational thoughts.

Cognitive therapy is brief, usually lasting only 10 to 20 sessions (Beck, 1976). This therapy has been researched extensively and is reported to be highly successful in the treatment of mild to moderately depressed individuals (Hollon et al., 2002; Thase et al., 1991). There is some evidence that depressed people who have received cognitive therapy are less likely to relapse than those who have been treated with antidepressant drugs (Evans et al., 1992; Scott, 1996).

Cognitive therapy has also been shown to be effective for treating panic disorder (Addis et al., 2004; Barlow, 1997; Power et al., 2000). By teaching clients to change the catastrophic interpretations of their symptoms, cognitive therapy helps prevent the symptoms from escalating into panic. Studies have shown that after 3 months of cognitive therapy, about 90% of individuals with panic disorder are panic-free (Robins & Hayes, 1993). Not only does cognitive therapy have a low dropout rate and a low relapse rate, but clients often continue to improve even after treatment is completed (Öst & Westling, 1995). And cognitive therapy has proved effective for generalized anxiety disorder (Beck, 1993; Wetherell et al., 2003), OCD (Abramowitz, 1997), cocaine addiction (Carroll et al., 1994), insomnia (Quesnel et al., 2003), and bulimia (Agras et al., 2000). Some research even indicates that cognitive therapy is effective in treating both negative and positive symptoms of schizophrenia (Bach & Hayes, 2002; Lecomte & Lecomte, 2002; Sensky et al., 2000).

◆ **cognitive therapy**
A therapy designed by Aaron Beck to help patients stop their negative thoughts as they occur and replace them with more objective thoughts.

Biological Therapies

◆ **biological therapy**

A therapy (drug therapy, electroconvulsive therapy, or psychosurgery) that is based on the assumption that psychological disorders are symptoms of underlying physical problems.

Do you know someone who takes or has taken a drug prescribed by a physician or psychiatrist as a means of overcoming a psychological problem? Chances are good that you do, because millions of people the world over are now taking various medications for just such reasons. Treatment with drugs is a cornerstone of the biological approach to therapy. Predictably, professionals who favor the biological perspective—the view that psychological disorders are symptoms of underlying physical problems—usually favor a **biological therapy**. The three main biological therapies are drug therapy, electroconvulsive therapy (ECT), and psychosurgery.

Drug Therapy

◆ *What are the advantages and disadvantages of using drugs to treat psychological disorders?*

The most frequently used biological treatment is drug therapy. Breakthroughs in drug therapy, coupled with the federal government's effort to reduce involuntary hospitalization of mental patients, lowered the mental hospital patient population in the United States from about 560,000 in 1955, when the drugs were introduced, to about 100,000 by 1990 (see Figure 13.2); this figure continued to drop throughout the 1990s. Furthermore, the average stay of patients who do require hospitalization is now usually a matter of days.

◆ **antipsychotic drugs**

Drugs used to control severe psychotic symptoms, such as delusions, hallucinations, disorganized speech, and disorganized behavior, by inhibiting dopamine activity; also known as neuroleptics.

Antipsychotic drugs known as *neuroleptics* are prescribed primarily for schizophrenia. You may have heard of these drugs by their brand names—Thorazine, Stelazine, Compazine, and Mellaril. Their purpose is to control hallucinations, delusions, disorganized speech, and disorganized behavior (Andreasen et al., 1995). The neuroleptics work primarily by inhibiting the activity of the neurotransmitter dopamine. About 50% of patients have a good response to the standard antipsychotics (Kane, 1996). But many patients, particularly those with an early onset of schizophrenia, are not helped by them (Meltzer et al., 1997), and others show only slight or modest improvement in symptoms. The long-term use of typical antipsychotic drugs carries a high risk of a severe side effect, *tardive dyskinesia*—almost continual twitching and jerking movements of the face and tongue, and squirming movements of the hands and trunk (Glazer et al., 1993).

Newer antipsychotic drugs called *atypical neuroleptics* (clozapine, risperidone, olanzipine) can treat not only the positive symptoms of schizophrenia but also the negative symptoms, leading to marked improvement in patients' quality of life (Worrel et al., 2000). Atypical neuroleptics target both dopamine and serotonin receptors (Kawanishi et al., 2000). About 10% of patients who take clozapine find the results so dramatic that they almost feel as though they have been reborn. Clozapine produces fewer side effects than standard neuroleptics, and patients taking it are less likely to develop tardive dyskinesia (Casey, 1996). It may also be more effective at suicide prevention than

---

FIGURE 13.2

Decrease in Patient Populations in State and County Mental Hospitals (1950–2000)

State and county mental hospital patient populations peaked at approximately 560,000 in 1955, the same year that antipsychotic drugs were introduced. These drugs, coupled with the federal government's efforts to reduce involuntary hospitalization of mental patients, resulted in a dramatic decrease in the patient population to fewer than 100,000 in 2000.
Source: Data from Mandersheid & Henderson (2001).

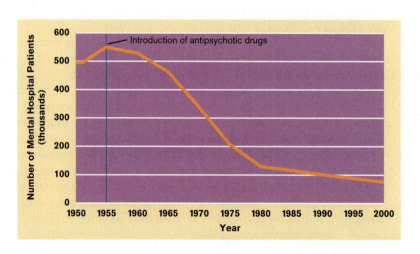

other antipsychotic drugs (Meltzer et al., 2003). However, clozapine is extremely expensive, and without careful monitoring, it can cause a fatal blood defect in 1–2% of patients who take it. For this reason, the levels of various liver enzymes and other substances in patients who take the drug must be monitored regularly (Erdogan et al., 2004). Risperidone appears to be effective and safe and also has fewer side effects than standard neuroleptics (Marder, 1996; Tamminga, 1996). Another advantage of risperidone is that it is much more effective than other neuroleptics in treating the negative symptoms of schizophrenia (Marder, 1996).

Antidepressant drugs act as mood elevators for people who are severely depressed (Elkin et al., 1995) and are also helpful in the treatment of certain anxiety disorders. About 65–75% of patients who take antidepressants find themselves significantly improved, and 40–50% of those are essentially completely recovered (Frazer, 1997). It is important to note, though, that most antidepressant research involves severely depressed patients—those who are most likely to show a significant change after treatment (Zimmerman et al., 2002). Thus, these studies may not apply to mildly depressed individuals. Moreover, research has shown that participants respond almost as frequently to placebo treatments as to real drugs (Walsh et al., 2002). In fact, EEG studies of patients who receive placebos have documented neurological changes that, while different from those in patients receiving real drugs, are associated with improvements in mood (Leuchter et al., 2002). Recall from Chapter 1 that placebo effects in patients are attributable to the belief that a given treatment will help. Consequently, many researchers think that depressed patients' responses to antidepressant drugs result from a combination of the physiological effects of these medications on the brain and patients' confidence in the effectiveness of drug treatment.

The first-generation antidepressants are known as the *tricyclics* (amitriptyline, imipramine) (Nutt, 2000). The tricyclics work against depression by blocking the reuptake of norepinephrine and serotonin into the axon terminals, thus enhancing the action of these neurotransmitters in the synapses. But tricyclics can have some unpleasant side effects, including sedation, dizziness, nervousness, fatigue, dry mouth, forgetfulness, and weight gain (Frazer, 1997). Progressive weight gain (an average of more than 20 pounds) is the main reason people stop taking tricyclics, in spite of the relief these drugs provide from distressing psychological symptoms.

The second-generation antidepressants, the *selective serotonin reuptake inhibitors (SSRIs)*, block the reuptake of the neurotransmitter serotonin, increasing its availability at the synapses in the brain (Nutt, 2000; Vetulani & Nalepa, 2000). SSRIs (fluoxetine, clomipramine) have fewer side effects (Nelson, 1997) and are safer than tricyclics if an overdose occurs (Thase & Kupfer, 1996). SSRIs have been found to be promising in treating obsessive-compulsive disorder (Goodwin, 1996), social phobia (Jefferson, 1995), panic disorder (Coplan et al., 1997; Jefferson, 1997), genaralized anxiety disorder (Mogg et al., 2004), and binge eating (Hudson et al., 1996). However, SSRIs can cause sexual dysfunction, although normal sexual functioning returns when the drug is discontinued. Reports indicating that SSRIs, especially fluoxetine (Prozac), increase the risk of suicide have not been substantiated (Ham, 2003; Warshaw & Keller, 1996). However, concerns about a link between antidepressant treatment and suicidal thinking and nonfatal suicidal behaviors in children and adolescents have led officials in the United States and other countries to recommend that patients younger than 18 be closely monitored during the first few weeks of treatment (U.S. Food and Drug Administration, 2004).

Another line of treatment for depression is the use of *monoamine oxidase (MAO) inhibitors* (sold under the names Marplan, Nardil, and Parnate). By blocking the action of an enzyme that breaks down norepinephrine and serotonin in the synapses, MAO inhibitors increase the availability of these neurotransmitters. MAO inhibitors are usually prescribed for depressed patients who do not respond to other antidepressants (Thase et al., 1992). They are also effective in treating panic disorder (Sheehan & Raj, 1988) and social phobia (Marshall et al., 1994). But MAO inhibitors have many of the same unpleasant side effects as tricyclic antidepressants, and patients taking MAO inhibitors must avoid certain foods or run the risk of stroke.

◆ **antidepressant drugs**
Drugs that act as mood elevators for severely depressed people and are also prescribed to treat some anxiety disorders.

◆ **lithium**

A drug used to treat bipolar disorder, which at proper maintenance dosage reduces both manic and depressive episodes.

Lithium, a naturally occurring salt, is considered a wonder drug for 40–50% of patients suffering from bipolar disorder (Thase & Kupfer, 1996). It is said to begin to quiet the manic state within 5 to 10 days. This is an amazing accomplishment, because the average episode, if untreated, lasts about 3 to 4 months. A proper maintenance dose of lithium reduces depressive episodes as well as manic ones. Published reports over a period of three decades show that the clinical effectiveness of lithium for treating depression and bipolar disorder is unmatched (Ross et al., 2000). But 40–60% of those who take a maintenance dose will experience a recurrence (Thase & Kupfer, 1996). Also, monitoring of the level of lithium in the patient's blood every 2 to 6 months is necessary to guard against lithium poisoning and permanent damage to the nervous system (Schou, 1997).

Recent research suggests that *anticonvulsant drugs,* such as Depakote (divalproex), may be just as effective for managing bipolar symptoms as lithium, with fewer side effects (Kowatch et al., 2000). Moreover, many bipolar patients, especially those whose manic states include symptoms of psychosis, benefit from taking antipsychotic drugs along with the anticonvulsants (Bowden et al., 2000, 2004; Sachs et al., 2002; Vieta, 2003).

The family of minor tranquilizers called *benzodiazepines* includes, among others, the well-known drugs sold as Valium and Librium and the newer high-potency drug Xanax (pronounced "ZAN-ax"). Used primarily to treat anxiety, benzodiazepines are prescribed more often than any other class of psychoactive drugs (Medina et al., 1993). They have been found to be effective in treating panic disorder (Davidson, 1997; Noyes et al., 1996) and generalized anxiety disorder (Lydiard et al., 1996).

Xanax, the largest-selling psychiatric drug (Famighetti, 1997), appears to be particularly effective in relieving anxiety and depression. When used to treat panic disorder (Noyes et al., 1996), Xanax works faster and has fewer side effects than antidepressants (Ballenger et al., 1993; Jonas & Cohon, 1993). However, if patients discontinue treatment, relapse is likely (Rickels et al., 1993). There is a downside to Xanax. Many patients, once they no longer experience panic attacks, find themselves unable to discontinue the drug because they experience moderate to intense withdrawal symptoms, including intense anxiety (Otto et al., 1993). Valium seems to be just as effective as Xanax for treating panic disorder, and withdrawal is easier. Although withdrawal is a problem with benzodiazepines, the abuse and addiction potential of these drugs is fairly low (Romach et al., 1995).

Beyond the drugs' unpleasant or dangerous side effects, another disadvantage in using drug therapy is the difficulty in establishing the proper dosages. Also, it's important to note that drugs do not cure psychological disorders, so patients usually experience a relapse if they stop taking the drugs when their symptoms lift. Maintenance doses of antidepressants following a major depressive episode reduce the probability of recurrence (Prien & Kocsis, 1995). Maintenance doses are usually required with anxiety disorders as well, or symptoms are likely to return (Rasmussen et al., 1993). Further, some studies suggest that the trend away from involuntary hospitalization brought about by the availability of antipsychotic and other psychiatric drugs has led to an increase in homelessness among people who suffer from chronic mental illnesses such as schizophrenia (Carson et al., 2000). Unfortunately, after being discharged from mental hospitals because they have shown favorable responses to antipsychotic drugs, many schizophrenic patients do not get adequate follow-up care. As a result, some stop taking their medications, relapse into psychotic states, and are unable to support themselves.

◆ **electroconvulsive therapy (ECT)**

A biological therapy in which an electric current is passed through the right hemisphere of the brain; usually reserved for severely depressed patients who are suicidal.

Electroconvulsive Therapy

◆ *What is electroconvulsive therapy (ECT) used for?*

Antidepressant drugs are relatively slow-acting. A severely depressed patient needs at least 2 to 6 weeks to obtain relief, and 30% of these patients don't respond at all. This situation can be too risky for suicidal patients. **Electroconvulsive therapy (ECT)** is sometimes used with such patients. ECT has a bad reputation because it was misused and overused in the 1940s and 1950s. Nevertheless, when used appropriately, ECT is a highly effective treatment for major depression (Folkerts, 2000; Little et al., 2002; McCall et al., 2004). And depressed patients who are 75 and older tolerate the procedure as well as younger patients do and reap comparable therapeutic benefits (Tew et al., 1999).

For many years, ECT was performed by passing an electric current through both cerebral hemispheres, a procedure known as *bilateral ECT*. Today, electric current is administered to the right hemisphere only, and the procedure is called *unilateral ECT*. Research suggests that unilateral ECT is as effective as the more intense bilateral form while producing milder cognitive effects (Sackeim et al., 2000). Also, a patient undergoing ECT today is given anesthesia, controlled oxygenation, and a muscle relaxant.

Experts think that ECT changes the biochemical balance in the brain, resulting in a lifting of depression. When ECT is effective, cerebral blood flow in the prefrontal cortex is reduced, and delta waves (usually associated with slow-wave sleep) appear (Sackeim et al., 1996). Some psychiatrists and neurologists have spoken out against the use of ECT, claiming that it causes pervasive brain damage and memory loss. But advocates of ECT say that claims of brain damage are based on animal studies in which dosages of ECT were much higher than those now used in human patients. No structural brain damage from ECT has been revealed by studies comparing MRI or CT scans before and after a series of treatments (Devanand et al., 1994).

Toward the end of the 20th century, a new brain-stimulation therapy known as *rapid transcranial magnetic stimulation (rTMS)* was developed. This magnetic therapy is not invasive in any way. Performed on patients who are not sedated, it causes no seizures, leads to no memory loss, and has no known side effects. Its therapeutic value is similar to that of ECT, and it is much more acceptable to the public (Vetulani & Nalepa, 2000). This therapy has been used effectively in conjunction with SSRIs in treating depressed patients (Conca et al., 2000).

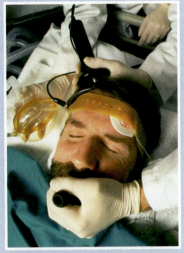

In electroconvulsive therapy, a mild electric current is passed through the right hemisphere of the brain for 1 to 2 seconds, causing a brief seizure.

Psychosurgery

An even more drastic procedure than ECT is **psychosurgery**—brain surgery performed to alleviate serious psychological disorders, such as severe depression, severe anxiety, or obsessions, or to provide relief from unbearable chronic pain. The first experimental brain surgery for human patients, the *lobotomy*, was developed by Portuguese neurologist Egas Moniz in 1935 to treat severe phobias, anxiety, and obsessions. Surgeons performing a lobotomy would sever the neural connections between the frontal lobes and the deeper brain centers involved in emotion. But no brain tissue was removed. At first, the procedure was considered a tremendous contribution, and Moniz won for the Nobel Prize in medicine in 1949. Eventually, however, it became apparent that this treatment left patients in a severely deteriorated condition.

Modern psychosurgery procedures result in less intellectual impairment because, rather than using conventional surgery, surgeons deliver electric currents through electrodes to destroy a much smaller, more localized area of brain tissue. In one procedure, called a *cingulotomy*, electrodes are used to destroy the *cingulum*, a small bundle of nerves connecting the cortex to the emotional centers of the brain. Several procedures, including cingulotomy, have been helpful for some extreme cases of obsessive-compulsive disorder (Baer et al., 1995; Trivedi, 1996). But the results of psychosurgery are still not predictable, and the consequences—whether positive or negative—are irreversible. For these reasons, the treatment is considered experimental and absolutely a last resort (Balon, 2004).

◆ *What is psychosurgery, and for what problems is it used?*

◆ **psychosurgery**
Brain surgery performed to alleviate serious psychological disorders or unbearable chronic pain.

Evaluating the Therapies

If you look over the summaries of the various therapeutic approaches in *Review and Reflect 13.1*, you will notice that they share many similarities. For example, several therapies help clients reflect on their own thoughts and/or emotions. Analyses of therapy sessions representing different perspectives suggest that therapists use a core set of techniques no matter which perspective they adopt; at the same time, each

◆ *What therapy, if any, is most effective in treating psychological disorders?*

REVIEW and REFLECT 13.1

Summary and Comparison of the Therapies

TYPE OF THERAPY	PERCEIVED CAUSE OF DISORDER	GOALS OF THERAPY	METHODS USED	PRIMARY DISORDERS OR SYMPTOMS TREATED
Psycho-analysis	Unconscious sexual and aggressive urges or conflicts; fixations; weak ego	Help patient bring disturbing, repressed material to consciousness and work through unconscious conflicts; strengthen ego functions	Psychoanalyst analyzes and interprets dreams, free associations, resistance, and transference.	General feelings of unhappiness; unresolved problems from childhood
Person-centered therapy	Blocking of normal tendency toward self-actualization; incongruence between real and desired self; overdependence on positive regard of others	Increase self-acceptance and self-understanding; help patient become more inner-directed; increase congruence between real and desired self; enhance personal growth	Therapist shows empathy, unconditional positive regard, and genuineness, and reflects client's expressed feelings back to client.	General feelings of unhappiness; interpersonal problems
Inter-personal therapy	Difficulty with relationships and/or life transitions, as well as possible biological causes	Adjust to bereavement; overcome interpersonal role disputes; improve interpersonal skills; adjust to role transitions such as divorce, career change, and retirement	Therapist helps patient (1) release the past, (2) understand others' points of view and explore options for change, (3) view change as a challenge rather than a threat, and/or (4) improve interpersonal skills, using techniques such as role-playing.	Depression
Family therapy and couples therapy	Problems caused by faulty communication patterns, unreasonable role expectations, drug and/or alcohol abuse, and so on	Create more understanding and harmony within the relationships; improve communication patterns; heal wounds of family unit	Therapist sees clients individually or several family members at a time and explores such things as communication patterns, power struggles, and unreasonable demands and expectations.	Family problems such as marriage or relationship problems, troubled or troublesome teenagers, abusive relationships, drug or alcohol problems, schizophrenic family member
Behavior therapy	Learning of maladaptive behaviors or failure to learn appropriate behaviors	Extinguish maladaptive behaviors and replace with more adaptive ones; help patient acquire needed social skills	Therapist uses methods based on classical and operant conditioning and modeling, which include systematic desensitization, flooding, exposure and response prevention, and aversion therapy.	Fears, phobias, panic disorder, obsessive-compulsive disorder, bad habits
Cognitive therapy	Irrational and negative assumptions and ideas about self and others	Change faulty, irrational, and/or negative thinking	Therapist helps client identify irrational and negative thinking and substitute rational thinking.	Depression, anxiety, panic disorder, general feelings of unhappiness
Biological therapies	Underlying physical disorder caused by structural or biochemical abnormality in the brain; genetic inheritance	Eliminate or control biological cause of abnormal behavior; restore balance of neurotransmitters	Physician prescribes drugs such as antipsychotics, antidepressants, lithium, or tranquilizers; uses ECT or psychosurgery.	Schizophrenia, depression, bipolar disorder, anxiety disorders

therapeutic approach has elements that distinguish it from others (Gazzola & Stalikas, 2004; Trijsburg, et al., 2004; Waldron & Helm, 2004). But to what degree do the various therapies differ in effectiveness? In a classic study of therapeutic effectiveness, Smith and his colleagues (1980) analyzed the results of 475 studies, which involved 25,000 patients. Their findings revealed that psychotherapy was better than no treatment, but that no one type of psychotherapy was more effective than another. A subsequent reanalysis of the same data by Hans Eysenck (1994), however, showed a slight advantage for behavior therapies over other types. A study by Hollon and others (2002) found that cognitive and interpersonal therapies had an advantage over psychodynamic approaches for depressed patients.

But how do the patients themselves rate the therapies? To answer this question, *Consumer Reports* (1995) conducted the largest survey to date on patient attitudes toward psychotherapy. Martin Seligman (1995, 1996), a consultant for the study, summarized its findings:

- Overall, patients believed that they benefited substantially from psychotherapy.
- Patients seemed equally satisfied with their therapy, whether it was provided by a psychologist, a psychiatrist, or a social worker.

- Patients who were in therapy for more than 6 months did considerably better than the rest; generally, the longer patients stayed in therapy, the more they improved.
- Patients who took a drug such as Prozac or Xanax believed it helped them, but overall, psychotherapy alone seemed to work about as well as psychotherapy plus drugs.

Choosing a therapist with the type of training best suited to your problem can be crucial to how helpful the therapy turns out to be. Table 13.1 lists the various types of

TABLE 13.1 Mental Health Professionals

PROFESSIONAL TITLE	TRAINING	SERVICES PROVIDED
Psychiatrist	Medical degree (M.D. or O.D.); residency in psychiatry	Psychotherapy; drug therapy; hospitalization for serious psychological disorders
Psychoanalyst	M.D., Ph.D., or Psy.D.; additional training in psychoanalysis	Psychodynamic therapy
Clinical psychologist	Ph.D. or Psy.D.; internship in clinical psychology	Diagnosis and treatment of psychological disorders; can prescribe drugs in some settings after additional training; psychological testing
Counseling psychologist	Ph.D. or Ed.D.; internship in counseling psychology	Assessment and therapy for normal problems of life (e.g., divorce); psychological testing
School psychologist	Ph.D., Ed.D., or master's degree; internship in school psychology	Assessment and treatment of school problems in children and adolescents; psychological testing
Clinical or psychiatric social worker (M.S.W.)	Master's degree; internship in psychiatric social work	Diagnosis and treatment of psychological disorders; identification of supportive community services
Licensed professional counselor (L.P.C.)	Master's degree; internship in counseling	Assessment and therapy for normal problems of life; some psychological testing
Licensed marriage and family therapist (L.M.F.T.)	Master's degree; internship in couples therapy and family therapy	Assessment and therapy for relationship problems
Licensed chemical dependency counselor (L.C.D.C.)	Educational requirements vary from one state to another; often former addicts themselves	Treatment and education for substance abuse problems

mental health professionals. One important difference among professionals, about which many people are confused, is that a **psychologist** has an advanced degree, usually at the doctoral level, in psychology, while a **psychiatrist** is a medical doctor. Historically, drug therapy has been available only from psychiatrists. At present, however, there is a movement that is gaining momentum in the United States to allow psychologists with special training in psychopharmacology to prescribe drugs. Only the U.S. military and a few states have authorized prescribing privileges for psychologists so far.

Regardless of their training or theoretical orientation, all therapists are bound by ethical standards established by professional organizations and, in most cases, codified in state laws. Each profession (e.g., psychologists, social workers) has its own ethical standards, but certain features are common to all of them and are exemplified by the ethics code of the American Psychological Association (2002). One important standard is the requirement for *informed consent*. Therapists must inform clients of the cost and expected duration of therapy prior to beginning any intervention. Moreover, clients must be informed of the legal limits of confidentiality. For example, if a client reveals that she or he has committed a crime, in most cases the therapist is obligated to report the confession to the appropriate authorities. In addition, some insurance companies require that therapists' notes be available for review without regard to clients' confidentiality.

The nature of the therapeutic relationship is also governed by ethical standards. Therapists are forbidden to engage in any kind of intimate relationship with a client or with anyone close to the client. They are also prohibited from providing therapeutic services to former intimate partners. When ending a therapeutic relationship, a therapist must counsel a client about the reason for terminating therapy and provide him or her with alternatives.

With regard to testing, therapists are ethically obligated to use tests that are reliable and valid. Moreover, they must have appropriate training for administering, scoring, and evaluating each test they use. They are also required to explain the purpose of testing to clients and to provide them with test results in a timely and confidential manner.

Culturally Sensitive and Gender-Sensitive Therapy

◆ *What characterizes culturally sensitive and gender-sensitive therapy?*

Think for a moment about the role played by culture and gender in our social relationships. Do you think it's possible that these variables could affect relationships between therapists and their clients?

Among most psychotherapists, there is a growing awareness of the need to consider cultural variables in diagnosing and treating psychological disorders (Bernal & Castro, 1994). In fact, the American Psychological Association recently published guidelines to help psychologists be more sensitive to cultural issues (APA, 2003). Similarly, many psychologists have expressed concern about the need for awareness of gender differences when practicing psychotherapy (Addis & Mahalik, 2003; Gehart & Lyle, 2001).

According to Kleinman and Cohen (1997), people experience and suffer from psychological disorders within a cultural context that may dramatically affect the meaning of symptoms, outcomes, and responses to therapy. And cultural differences between therapist and client may undermine the *therapeutic alliance*, the bond between therapist and client that is known to be a factor in the effectiveness of psychotherapy (Blatt et al., 1996). Thus, many experts advocate an approach called **culturally sensitive psychotherapy** in which knowledge of clients' cultural backgrounds guides the choice of therapeutic interventions (Kumpfer et al., 2002).

Culturally sensitive therapists recognize that language differences between therapists and patients can pose problems (Santiago-Rivera & Altarriba, 2002). For example, a patient who speaks both Spanish and English but is more fluent in Spanish may

When therapist and client have the same racial or ethnic background, they are more likely to share cultural values and communication styles, which can facilitate the therapeutic process.

exhibit hesitations, back-tracking, and delayed responses to questions when being interviewed in English. As a result, the therapist may erroneously conclude that this patient is suffering from the kind of disordered thinking that is often displayed by people with schizophrenia (Martinez, 1986). Such language differences may also affect patients' results on standardized tests used by clinicians. In one frequently cited study, researchers found that when a group of Puerto Rican patients took the Thematic Apperception Test (TAT) in English, their pauses and their choices of words were incorrectly interpreted as indications of psychological problems (Suarez, 1983). Thus, culturally sensitive therapists become familiar with patients' general fluency in the language in which they will be assessed prior to interviewing and testing them.

When working with recent immigrants to the United States, culturally sensitive therapists take into account the impact of the immigration experience on patients' thoughts and emotions (Lijtmaer, 2001; Smolar, 1999; Sluzki, 2004). Some researchers who have studied the responses of recent Asian immigrants to psychotherapy recommend that, prior to initiating diagnosis and treatment, therapists encourage patients who are immigrants to talk about the feelings of sadness they have experienced as a result of leaving their native culture, as well as their anxieties about adapting to life in a new society. Using this strategy, therapists may be able to separate depression and anxiety related to the immigration experience from true psychopathology.

Some advocates of culturally sensitive therapy point out that sometimes cultural practices can be used as models for therapeutic interventions. Traditional Native American *healing circles*, for example, are being used by many mental health practitioners who serve Native Americans (Garrett et al., 2001). Members of a healing circle are committed to promoting the physical, mental, emotional, and spiritual well-being of one another. Healing circle participants typically engage in member-led activities such as discussion, meditation, and prayer. However, some more structured healing circles include a recognized Native American healer who leads the group in traditional healing ceremonies.

Culturally sensitive therapists also attempt to address group differences that can affect the results of therapy. For example, many studies have found that African Americans with mental disorders are less likely than White Americans with the same diagnoses to follow their doctor's or therapist's instruction about taking medications. (Fleck et al., 2002; Hazlett-Stevens et al., 2002). A culturally sensitive approach to this problem might be based on a therapist's understanding of the importance of kinship networks and community relationships in African American culture. A therapist might increase an African American patient's compliance level by having the patient participate in a support group with other African Americans suffering from the same illness and taking the same medications (Muller, 2002). In addition, researchers and experienced therapists recommend that non–African American therapists and African American patients openly discuss their differing racial perspectives prior to beginning therapy (Bean et al., 2002).

gender-sensitive therapy

An approach to therapy that takes into account the effects of gender on both the therapist's and the client's behavior.

Many psychotherapists also note the need for **gender-sensitive therapy,** a therapeutic approach that takes into the account the effects of gender on both the therapist's and the client's behavior (Gehart & Lyle, 2001). To implement gender-sensitive therapy, therapists must examine their own gender-based prejudices. They may assume men to be more analytical and women to be more emotional, for example. These stereotypical beliefs may be based on a therapist's socialization background or knowledge of research findings on gender differences.

Advocates of gender-sensitive therapy point out that knowledge of real differences between the sexes is important to the practice of gender-sensitive therapy. For instance, because of men's gender role socialization, interventions focused on emotional expression may be less effective for them than for women. Moreover, men may view seeking therapy as a sign of weakness or as a threat to their sense of masculinity (Addis & Mahalik, 2003). As a result, researchers advise therapists to try to avoid creating defensiveness in their male clients. Nevertheless, therapists must guard against using research findings as a basis for stereotyping either male or female clients. They have to keep in mind that there is more variation within each gender than across genders, and thus each man or women must be considered as an individual.

Some therapists who are motivated by a sincere desire to be sensitive to gender issues may place too much emphasis on gender issues and misinterpret clients' problems (Addis & Mahalik, 2003). For example, in one study, researchers found that therapists expect people who are working in nontraditional fields—female engineers and male nurses, for instance—to have more psychological problems (Rubinstein, 2001). As a result, therapists may assume that such clients' difficulties arise from gender role conflicts, when, in reality, their problems have completely different origins.

Looking Back   At the beginning of the chapter, you read about Jane, a college student who suffers from generalized anxiety disorder. Did you think about how each type of therapy might be applied to her case? If so, these suggestions may be similar to your own inferences. An insight therapist would almost certainly ask Jane to reflect on her problems and how they might have developed. A therapist whose focus is on relationships might have suggested couples therapy for Jane and Sam. Another therapist might have encouraged Jane to participate in group sessions with other students who have anxiety problems. Behavior therapists would have helped Jane identify ways of modifying her anxious responses to different kinds of stimuli. Those who focus on modeling might have suggested that Jane read books about others who have overcome anxiety disorders. Cognitive therapists would provide Jane with homework assignments that would help her change her thinking about the issues that make her anxious. Jane might also have been advised to try anxiety-reducing medications. Which method would work best? Most likely, the therapy in which Jane has the most confidence will be the one that works best for her. Jane's own determination to overcome her anxiety disorder and willingness to make necessary changes would likely be important to her response to therapy as well.

Apply It 13.1 Is E-therapy Right for You?

If you were trying to overcome a substance abuse problem or needed help getting through a period of bereavement, would you turn to an online support group? Many people do. For example, researchers Taylor and Luce (2003) reported that when Senator Edward Kennedy mentioned a website for a particular support group on a nationally televised program, the site received more than 400,000 e-mail inquiries over the next few days. But what about psychotherapy? Can online sessions with a trained therapist be just as effective as face-to-face therapy?

Some studies suggest that therapy delivered via the Internet can be highly effective (Kenwright & Marks, 2004). But people aren't waiting for scientific studies that demonstrate the effectiveness of these innovative treatments. Thousands have already turned to *e-therapy*—ongoing online interaction with a trained therapist (Alleman, 2002; Taylor & Luce, 2003). This form of therapy typically involves the exchange of e-mail messages over a period of hours or days but can also include video-conferencing and telephone sessions (Day & Schneider, 2002).

Advantages of E-therapy

E-therapy enables clients to be much less inhibited than they might be in a face-to-face situation. It is also less expensive than traditional therapy (Roan, 2000). Another advantage is that the therapist and the client do not have to be in the same place at the same time. The client can write to the therapist whenever he or she feels like it and can keep records of "sessions" (e-mail correspondence) to refer to later (Ainsworth, 2000; Stubbs, 2000). A therapist can also keep accurate records of communications with clients and can answer their questions at times of day when telephone calls are inconvenient, thus

making his or her therapy practice more efficient (Andrews & Erskine, 2003). Ainsworth (2000) and Walker (2000) have found that e-therapy can be an especially helpful alternative to psychotherapy for people with any of several characteristics:

- They are often away from home or have full schedules.
- They cannot afford traditional therapy.
- They live in rural areas and do not have access to mental health care.
- They have disabilities.
- They are too timid or embarrassed to make an appointment with a therapist.
- They are good at expressing their thoughts and feelings in writing.

Disadvantages of E-therapy

Because of the anonymity of Internet interactions, it is easy for imposters to pose as therapists. So far, there is no system for regulating or licensing e-therapists. In addition, e-therapy poses some potential ethical problems, such as the possibility of breaches of confidentiality. But like all reputable therapists, the best e-therapists do everything they can to protect clients' privacy and confidentiality—except when it is necessary to protect them or someone else from immediate harm (Ainsworth, 2000). Perhaps the most serious drawback

of e-therapy is the fact that the therapist cannot see the client and therefore cannot use visual and auditory cues to determine when the person is becoming anxious or upset. This reduces the effectiveness of treatment (Roan, 2000; Walker, 2000).

Another important limitation of e-therapy is that it is not appropriate for diagnosing and treating serious psychological disorders, such as schizophrenia or bipolar disorder (Manhal-Baugus, 2001). In addition, e-therapy is not appropriate for someone who is in the midst of a serious crisis. There are better ways to get immediate help, such as suicide hotlines.

Finding an E-therapist

If you wish to locate an e-therapist, the best place to start is http://www.metanoia.org. This site lists online therapists whose credentials have been checked by Mental Health Net. It provides information about the location of the therapist, the services offered, the payment method, and so forth (Roan, 2000).

When choosing a therapist, be sure to do the following (Ainsworth, 2000):

- Make sure the person's credentials have been verified by a third party.
- Get real-world contact information.
- Verify that you'll receive a personal reply to your messages.
- Find out in advance how much the therapist charges.

If you decide to contact an e-therapist, bear this in mind: While e-therapy may be a good way to get started, if you have persistent problems, it would be wise in the long run to obtain traditional psychotherapy (Roan, 2000).

◆ Insight Therapies p. 397

◆ What are the basic techniques of psychoanalysis, and how are they used to help patients? p. 398

The techniques associated with psychoanalysis are free association, dream analysis, and transference. They are used to uncover the repressed memories, impulses, and conflicts presumed to be the cause of the patient's problems.

◆ What are the role and the goal of the therapist in person-centered therapy? p. 399

Person-centered therapy is a nondirective therapy in which the therapist provides empathy and a climate of unconditional positive regard. The goal is to allow the client to determine the direction of the therapy sessions and to move toward self-actualization.

◆ What is the major emphasis of Gestalt therapy? p. 399

Gestalt therapy emphasizes the importance of clients' fully experiencing, in the present moment, their feelings, thoughts, and actions and taking personal responsibility for their behavior.

◆ Relationship Therapies p. 400

◆ What problems commonly associated with major depression does interpersonal therapy focus on? p. 400

Interpersonal therapy (IPT) is designed to help depressed patients cope with unusual or severe responses to the death of a loved one, interpersonal role disputes, difficulty in adjusting to role transitions, and deficits in interpersonal skills.

◆ What is the goal of family therapy? p. 400

The goal of family therapy is to help family members heal their wounds, improve communication patterns, and create more interpersonal understanding and harmony.

◆ What are some advantages of group therapy? p. 401

Group therapy is less expensive than individual therapy, and it gives people opportunities to express their feelings, to get feedback from other group members, and to give and receive help and emotional support.

◆ Behavior Therapies p. 402

◆ How do behavior therapists modify clients' problematic behavior? p. 402

Behavior therapists use operant conditioning techniques such as the use of reinforcement to shape or increase the frequency of desirable behaviors (token economies) and the withholding of reinforcement to eliminate undesirable behaviors (time out).

◆ What behavior therapies are based on classical conditioning? p. 403

Behavior therapies based on classical conditioning are systematic desensitization, flooding, exposure and response prevention, and aversion therapy.

◆ How does participant modeling help people overcome their fears? p. 405

In participant modeling, an appropriate response to a feared stimulus is modeled in graduated steps, and the client is asked to imitate each step with the encouragement and support of the therapist. This process extinguishes the client's fear response.

◆ Cognitive Therapies p. 406

◆ What is the aim of rational-emotive therapy? p. 406

Rational-emotive therapy is a directive form of therapy whose aim is to challenge and modify a client's irrational beliefs, which are believed to be the cause of personal distress.

◆ How does Beck's cognitive therapy help people overcome depression and panic disorder? p. 407

Beck's cognitive therapy helps people overcome depression and panic disorder by pointing out the irrational thoughts causing them misery and by helping them learn other, more realistic ways of looking at themselves and their experiences.

◆ Biological Therapies p. 408

◆ What are the advantages and disadvantages of using drugs to treat psychological disorders? p. 408

The use of drug therapy has reduced the number of patients in mental hospitals. Antipsychotic drugs control the major symptoms of schizophrenia by inhibiting the activity of dopamine. Antidepressants are helpful in the treatment of severe depression and certain anxiety disorders. Lithium and anticonvulsant drugs can control symptoms of manic episodes and can even out the mood swings in bipolar disorder. Some problems with the use of drugs are unpleasant or dangerous side effects, the difficulty in establishing the proper dosages, and the fact that relapse is likely if the drug therapy is discontinued. Also, the movement away from hospitalization has led to an increase in the number of homeless people with mental disorders.

◆ What is electroconvulsive therapy (ECT) used for? p. 410

The unilateral form of ECT is used to treat people with severe depression, especially those who are in imminent danger of committing suicide.

◆ What is psychosurgery, and for what problems is it used? p. 411

Psychosurgery is brain surgery performed to relieve some severe, persistent, and debilitating psychological disorders or unbearable chronic pain. A highly controversial technique, psychosurgery is considered experimental and a last resort.

◆ Evaluating the Therapies p. 411

◆ What therapy, if any, is most effective in treating psychological disorders? p. 411

Although no one therapeutic approach has proved generally superior overall, specific therapies have proven to be most effective for treating particular disorders. For example, cognitive and interpersonal therapies are preferred for depressed patients.

◆ Culturally Sensitive and Gender-Sensitive Therapy p. 414

◆ What characterizes culturally sensitive and gender-sensitive therapy? p. 414

These approaches to therapy help mental health professionals be more aware of cultural variables and gender differences that may influence patients' responses to the therapy and the therapist as well as therapists' responses to patients. Patients' cultural backgrounds and practices may be useful in guiding the choice of therapeutic interventions.

◆ KEY TERMS

antidepressant drugs, p. 409
antipsychotic drugs, p. 408
aversion therapy, p. 404
behavior modification, p. 402
behavior therapy, p. 402
biological therapy, p. 408
cognitive therapies, p. 406
cognitive therapy, p. 407
culturally sensitive therapy, p. 414
directive therapy, p. 399
electroconvulsive therapy (ECT), p. 410
exposure and response prevention, p. 404

family therapy, p. 400
flooding, p. 404
free association, p. 398
gender-sensitive therapy, p. 416
Gestalt therapy, p. 399
group therapy, p. 401
humanistic therapies, p. 399
insight therapies, p. 397
interpersonal therapy (IPT), p. 400
lithium, p. 410
nondirective therapy, p. 399
participant modeling, p. 405
person-centered therapy, p. 399

psychiatrist, p. 414
psychoanalysis, p. 398
psychodynamic therapies, p. 398
psychologist, p. 414
psychosurgery, p. 411
psychotherapy, p. 397
rational-emotive therapy, p. 406
relationship therapies, p. 400
systematic desensitization, p. 403
time out, p. 402
token economy, p. 402
transference, p. 398

Study Guide **13**

Answers to all the Study Guide questions are provided at the end of the book.

◆ SECTION ONE: Chapter Review

Insight Therapies (pp. 397–399)

1. In psychoanalysis, the technique whereby a patient reveals every thought, idea, or image that comes to mind is called _____; the patient's attempt to avoid revealing certain thoughts is called _____.
   a. transference; resistance
   b. free association; transference
   c. revelation; transference
   d. free association; resistance

2. (Person-centered, Gestalt) therapy is the directive therapy that emphasizes the importance of the client's fully experiencing, in the present moment, his or her thoughts, feelings, and actions.

3. (Person-centered, Gestalt) therapy is the nondirective therapy developed by Carl Rogers in which the therapist creates a warm, accepting climate so that the client's natural tendency toward positive change can be released.

4. (Psychodynamic, Humanistic) therapy presumes that the cause of the patient's problems are repressed childhood experiences.

Relationship Therapies (pp. 400–401)

5. Which depressed person would be *least* likely to be helped by interpersonal therapy (IPT)?
   a. Tyrone, who is unable to accept the death of his wife
   b. Beth, who has been depressed since she was forced to retire
   c. Jen, who was sexually abused by her father
   d. Tony, who feels isolated and alone because he has difficulty making friends

6. Which of the following is *not* true of group therapy?
   a. It allows people to get feedback from other members.
   b. It allows individuals to receive help and support from other members.
   c. It is conducted by untrained therapists.
   d. It is less expensive than individual therapy.

7. Self-help groups are generally ineffective because they are not led by professionals. (true/false)

Behavior Therapies (pp. 402–405)

8. Techniques based on (classical, operant) conditioning are used to change behavior by reinforcing desirable behavior and removing reinforcers for undesirable behavior.

9. Behavior therapies based on classical conditioning are used mainly to
   a. shape new, more appropriate behaviors.
   b. rid people of fears and undesirable behaviors or habits.
   c. promote development of social skills.
   d. demonstrate appropriate behaviors.

10. Exposure and response prevention is a treatment for people with
    a. panic disorder.
    b. phobias.
    c. generalized anxiety disorder.
    d. obsessive-compulsive disorder.

11. Match the description with the therapy.
    ___ (1) flooding
    ___ (2) aversion therapy
    ___ (3) systematic desensitization
    ___ (4) participant modeling
    a. practicing deep muscle relaxation during gradual exposure to feared object
    b. pairing painful or sickening stimuli with undesirable behavior
    c. being exposed directly to a feared object without relaxation
    d. imitating a model responding appropriately in a feared situation

Cognitive Therapies (pp. 406–407)

12. Cognitive therapists believe that, for the most part, emotional disorders
    a. have physical causes.
    b. result from unconscious conflict and motives.
    c. result from faulty and irrational thinking.
    d. result from environmental stimuli.

13. Rational-emotive therapy is a nondirective therapy that requires a warm, accepting therapist. (true/false)

14. The goal of cognitive therapy is best described as helping people
    a. develop effective coping strategies.
    b. replace automatic thoughts with more objective thoughts.
    c. develop an external locus of control.
    d. develop realistic goals and aspirations.

15. Cognitive therapy has proved very successful in the treatment of
    a. depression and mania.
    b. schizophrenia.
    c. fears and phobias.
    d. anxiety disorders and depression.

Biological Therapies (pp. 408–411)

16. For the most part, advocates of biological therapies assume that psychological disorders have a physical cause. (true/false)

17. Match the disorder with the drug most often used for its treatment.
    ___ (1) panic disorder
    ___ (2) schizophrenia
    ___ (3) bipolar disorder
    ___ (4) depression
    ___ (5) obsessive-compulsive disorder
    a. lithium
    b. antipsychotics
    c. antidepressants

18. Medication that relieves the symptoms of schizophrenia is thought to work by blocking the action of
    a. serotonin.   c. norepinephrine.
    b. dopamine.   d. epinephrine.

19. Which of the following is *not* true of drug therapy for psychological disorders?
    a. Some patients must take more than one psychiatric drug to relieve their symptoms.
    b. Drugs sometimes have unpleasant side effects.
    c. Patients often relapse if they stop taking the drugs.
    d. Drugs are usually not very effective.

20. For which disorder is ECT typically used?
   a. severe depression   **c.** anxiety disorders
   b. schizophrenia   **d.** panic disorder

21. The major side effect of ECT is tardive dyskinesia. (true/false)

22. Psychosurgery techniques are now so precise that the exact effects of the surgery can be predicted in advance. (true/false)

Evaluating the Therapies (pp. 411–414)

23. What is true regarding the effectiveness of therapies?
   a. All are equally effective for any disorder.
   b. Specific therapies have proved effective in treating particular disorders.
   c. Insight therapies are consistently best.
   d. Therapy is no more effective than no treatment for emotional and behavioral disorders.

24. Match the problem with the most appropriate therapy.
   _____ **(1)** fears, bad habits
   _____ **(2)** schizophrenia
   _____ **(3)** general unhappiness, interpersonal problems
   _____ **(4)** severe depression
   a. behavior therapy
   b. insight therapy
   c. drug therapy

25. One must have a medical degree to become a
   a. clinical psychologist.
   b. sociologist.
   c. psychiatrist.
   d. clinical psychologist, psychiatrist, or psychoanalyst.

Culturally Sensitive and Gender-Sensitive Therapy (pp. 414–416)

26. The responses and outcomes of patients in therapy (are, are not) influenced by cultural factors.

◆ SECTION TWO: Identify the Therapy

Indicate which type of therapy each sentence is describing: (a) psychoanalytic, (b) behavioral, (c) humanistic, (d) cognitive, (e) Gestalt, (f) interpersonal, or (g) biological.

_____ **1.** This directive therapy has as an important objective "getting in touch with your feelings"; clients are encouraged to fully experience the present moment.

_____ **2.** This approach emphasizes early childhood experience and the conflicts one encounters in different stages of development; important concepts include free association and transference.

_____ **3.** Practitioners of this approach believe that faulty and irrational thinking results in emotional distress; a popular application of this approach is rational-emotive therapy.

_____ **4.** This therapy is considered a brief psychotherapy and is used in cases of depression due to problems such as the death of a loved one or deficits in interpersonal skills.

_____ **5.** This approach is based on the principles of learning theory and includes treatment strategies that use operant conditioning, classical conditioning, and observational learning.

_____ **6.** This approach sees psychological problems as symptoms of underlying physical disorders and uses medical treatments such as drug therapy and electroconvulsive therapy.

_____ **7.** This approach views people as having free choice; clients are encouraged to seek personal growth and fulfill their potential.

◆ SECTION THREE: Fill In the Blank

1. Psychotherapy uses _____ rather than _____ means to treat emotional and behavioral disorders.

2. Helene begins to behave toward her therapist the same way she behaved toward a significant person in her past. Helene is experiencing _____.

3. A therapy approach in which the therapist takes an active role in determining the course of therapy sessions and provides answers and suggestions to the client is known as _____ therapy.

4. One approach to treating depression is _____ therapy, which has been shown to be especially helpful for people dealing with problems such as severe bereavement and difficulty in adjusting to role transitions.

5. An approach that has been shown to be helpful for problems such as troubled or troublesome teenagers, alcoholic parents, and abusive family situations is _____ therapy.

6. Alcoholics Anonymous is the prototypical example of a _____ _____ _____ .

7. The techniques of token economy and time out are based on _____ conditioning.

8. Marco acts out in class by throwing spitballs, making funny noises, and passing notes to classmates. The teacher decides to ignore Marco when he behaves this way, in the hope that withholding attention will reduce the behavior. The teacher is using a _____ _____ technique.

9. Rational-emotive therapy is a type of _____ therapy.

10. The class of drugs known as neuroleptics is mainly used to treat _____ .

11. SSRIs and MAO inhibitors are drugs that are used mainly to treat _____ .

12. Lithium is used to treat _____ _____ .

13. Electroconvulsive therapy, although an extremely controversial method of therapy, may be the treatment of choice for patients suffering from _____ _____ .

14. A _____ psychologist specializes in the assessment, treatment, and/or researching of psychological problems and behavioral disturbances.

15. The psychoanalytic technique that involves having patients reveal whatever thoughts or images come to mind is known as _____ _____ .

16. Emily sends her son to his room for 20 minutes each time he misbehaves. Emily is using the behavior modification technique known as _____ _____ .

17. A surgical technique known as _____ involves severing the nerve fibers connecting the frontal lobes and the deeper brain.

18. Gender-sensitive therapists must examine their own _____ _____ and how they may affect their interactions with both male and female clients.

◆ **SECTION FOUR: Comprehensive Practice Test**

1. Your therapist asks you to reveal whatever thoughts, feelings, or images come to mind, no matter how trivial, embarrassing, or terrible they might seem. Your therapist is using a technique known as
   b. analysis of resistance.   c. free association.
   b. psychodrama.   d. stimulus satiation.

2. Which of the following is *not* considered an insight therapy?
   a. psychoanalysis   c. rational-emotive therapy
   b. Gestalt therapy   d. person-centered therapy

3. Which of the following is important in humanistic therapy?
   a. challenging irrational beliefs
   b. dream analysis
   c. empathy
   d. behavior modification

4. Person-centered therapy is most effective when the therapist proposes valuable solutions and offers solid advice while directing the therapeutic process. (true/false)

5. In this directive form of therapy, the therapist helps clients to experience their feelings as deeply and genuinely as possible, and then to admit responsibility for them.
   a. behavioral modification
   b. psychodynamic therapy
   c. rational-emotive therapy
   d. Gestalt therapy

6. Which type of therapy seems to offer the most effective setting for treating adolescent drug abuse?
   a. family therapy   c. person-centered therapy
   b. Gestalt therapy   d. behavioral therapy

7. This therapy involves the application of principles of classical and operant conditioning.
   b. Gestalt therapy   c. psychoanalysis
   b. behavior modification   d. humanistic therapy

8. A therapist treating you for fear of heights takes you to the top floor of a tall building and asks you to look out the window toward the ground until she can see that your fear is significantly diminished. What technique is she using?
   a. flooding   c. systematic desensitization
   b. psychodrama   d. stimulus satiation

9. Which therapy emphasizes acceptance and unconditional positive regard?
   a. person-centered therapy
   b. cognitive therapy
   c. rational-emotive therapy
   d. psychoanalysis

10. A technique based on Albert Bandura's observational learning theory is
    a. flooding.
    b. participant modeling.
    c. systematic desensitization.
    d. implosive therapy.

11. A type of therapy that is used to treat phobias and employs relaxation training techniques is called
    a. cognitive-behavioral therapy.
    b. systematic desensitization.
    c. psychoanalysis.
    d. client-centered therapy.

12. Which insight therapy was developed by Fritz Perls?
    a. Gestalt therapy
    b. rational-emotive therapy
    c. client-centered therapy
    d. psychoanalysis

13. This type of biological therapy helps reduce symptoms of severe depression by producing a seizure in the patient.
    a. psychosurgery   c. electroconvulsive therapy
    b. lobotomy   d. chemotherapy

14. This biological therapy uses an electrical current to destroy a localized section of brain cells.
    a. psychosurgery
    b. prefrontal lobotomy
    c. electroconvulsive therapy
    d. chemotherapy

15. This group of drugs includes tricyclics, MAO inhibitors, and SSRIs.
    a. antimania drugs   c. antianxiety drugs
    b. antidepressant drugs d. antipsychotic drugs

16. This group of drugs is used to treat symptoms including hallucinations and delusions.
    a. antimania drugs
    b. antidepressant drugs
    c. antianxiety drugs
    d. antipsychotic drugs

17. The most severe side effect of typical antipsychotic drugs is
    a. cramps.   c. tardive dyskinesia.
    b. muscle spasms.   d. mania.

18. In a major review of 475 studies, researchers concluded that people who received therapy were better off than those who did not. (true/false)

19. The main problem with interpersonal therapy is the fact that it is so time-consuming. (true/false)

20. The B in Albert Ellis's ABC theory of rational-emotive therapy stands for *behavior*. (true/false)

◆ SECTION FIVE: Critical Thinking

1. What are the major strengths and weaknesses of the following approaches to therapy: psychoanalysis, person-centered therapy, behavior therapy, cognitive therapy, and drug therapy?

2. From what you have learned in this chapter, prepare a strong argument to support each of these positions:
   a. Psychotherapy is generally superior to drug therapy in the treatment of psychological disorders.
   b. Drug therapy is generally superior to psychotherapy in the treatment of psychological disorders.

3. In selecting a therapist for yourself or advising a friend or family member, what are some important questions you would ask a therapist in an effort to determine whether he or she would be a good choice?

Social Psychology

chapter 14

Social Perception

- ◆ Why are first impressions so important?
- ◆ What is the difference between a situational attribution and a dispositional attribution?

Attraction

- ◆ What factors contribute to attraction?
- ◆ How important is physical attractiveness to attraction?
- ◆ How do psychologists explain romantic attraction and mating?

Conformity, Obedience, and Compliance

- ◆ What did Asch find in his famous experiment on conformity?
- ◆ What did researchers find when they varied the circumstances of Milgram's classic study of obedience?
- ◆ What are three techniques used to gain compliance?

Group Influence

- ◆ How does social facilitation affect performance?
- ◆ What is social loafing, and what factors reduce it?
- ◆ How do social roles influence individual behavior?

Attitudes and Attitude Change

- ◆ What are the three components of an attitude?
- ◆ What is cognitive dissonance, and how can it be reduced?
- ◆ What are the elements of persuasion?

Prosocial Behavior

- ◆ What motivates one person to help another?
- ◆ What is the bystander effect, and why does it occur?

Aggression

- ◆ What biological factors are thought to be related to aggression?
- ◆ What other factors contribute to aggression?
- ◆ According to social learning theory, what causes aggressive behavior?

Prejudice and Discrimination

- ◆ What factors contribute to the development of prejudice and discrimination?
- ◆ What evidence suggests that prejudice and discrimination are decreasing?

Are there any circumstances under which you could be persuaded to deliberately harm another person? Many people think they could never be persuaded to do such a thing. But a classic study suggests otherwise.

In the 1960s, an advertisement appeared in newspapers in New Haven, Connecticut, and other communities near Yale University. It read: "Wanted: Volunteers to serve as subjects in a study of memory and learning at Yale University." Many people responded to the ad, and 40 male participants between the ages of 20 and 50 were selected. Yet, instead of a memory experiment, a staged drama was planned. The cast of characters was as follows:

- The Experimenter: A 31-year-old high school biology teacher, dressed in a gray laboratory coat, who assumed a stern and serious manner
- The Learner: A middle-aged man (an actor and accomplice of the experimenter)
- The Teacher: One of the volunteers

The experimenter led the teacher and the learner into one room, where the learner was strapped into an electric-chair apparatus. The teacher was delivered a sample shock of 45 volts, supposedly for the purpose of testing the equipment and showing the teacher what the learner would feel. Next, the script called for the learner to complain of a heart condition and say that he hoped the electric shocks would not be too painful. The experimenter admitted that the stronger shocks would hurt but hastened to add, "Although the shocks can be extremely painful, they cause no permanent tissue damage" (Milgram, 1963, p. 373).

Then, the experimenter took the teacher to an adjoining room and seated him in front of an instrument panel with 30 lever switches arranged horizontally across the front. The first switch on the left, he was told, delivered only 15 volts, but each successive switch was 15 volts stronger than the previous one, up to the last switch, which carried 450 volts. The switches on the instrument panel were labeled with designations ranging from "Slight Shock" to "Danger: Severe Shock." The experimenter instructed the teacher to read a list of word pairs to the learner and then test his memory. When the learner made the right choice, the teacher was supposed to go on to the next pair. If the learner missed a question, the teacher was told to flip a switch and shock him, moving one switch to the right—delivering 15 additional volts—each time the learner missed a question.

The learner performed well at first but then began missing about three out of every four questions. The teacher began flipping the switches. When he hesitated, the experimenter urged him to continue. If he still hesitated, the experimenter said, "The experiment requires that you continue," or more strongly, "You have no other choice, you must go on" (Milgram, 1963, p. 374). At the 20th switch, 300 volts, the script required the learner to pound on the wall and scream, "Let me out of here, let me out, my heart's bothering me, let me out!" (Meyer, 1972, p. 461). From this point on, the learner answered no more questions. If the teacher expressed concern or a desire to discontinue the experiment, the experimenter answered, "Whether the learner likes it or not, you must go on" (Milgram, 1963, p. 374). At the flip of the next switch—315 volts—the teacher heard only groans from the learner. Again, if the teacher expressed reluctance to go on, the experimenter said, "You have no other choice, you must go on" (Milgram, 1963, p. 374). If the teacher insisted on stopping at this point, the experimenter allowed him to do so.

How many of the 40 participants in the Milgram study do you think obeyed the experimenter to the end—450 volts? Not a single participant stopped before the 20th switch, at supposedly 300 volts, when the learner began pounding the wall. Amazingly, 26 participants—65% of the sample—obeyed the experimenter to the bitter end. But this experiment took a terrible toll on the participants. They "were observed to sweat, tremble, stutter, bite their lips, groan, and dig their fingernails into their flesh. These were characteristic rather than exceptional responses to the experiment" (Milgram, 1963, p. 375).

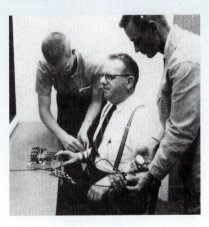

Social psychology

The subfield that attempts to explain how the actual, imagined, or implied presence of others influences the thoughts, feelings, and behavior of individuals.

confederate

A person who poses as a participant in an experiment but is actually assisting the experimenter.

naive subject

A person who has agreed to participate in an experiment but is not aware that deception is being used to conceal its real purpose.

You have just read a description of a classic experiment in **social psychology,** the subfield that attempts to explain how the actual, imagined, or implied presence of others influences the thoughts, feelings, and behavior of individuals. A study like Milgram's could not be performed today because it would violate the American Psychological Association's code of ethics for researchers. Still, deception has traditionally been a part of social psychologists' research. To accomplish this deception, a researcher often must use one or more **confederates**—people who pose as participants in a psychology experiment but who are actually assisting the researcher, like the learner in the Milgram experiment. A **naive subject**—like the teacher in Milgram's study—is a person who has agreed to participate in an experiment but is not aware that deception is being used to conceal its real purpose. You will continue to see why it is often necessary to conceal the purpose of an experiment as you read about other classic studies in social psychology.

Social Perception

What are the strategies we use to assess and make judgments of other people? Our ability to understand others is important because we live in a social world. The process we use to obtain critically important social information about others is known as *social perception* (Allison et al., 2000).

Impression Formation

Why are first impressions so important?

When we meet people for the first time, we begin forming impressions about them right away, and, of course, they are busily forming impressions of us. Naturally, we notice the obvious attributes first—gender, race, age, dress, and how physically attractive or unattractive someone appears (Shaw & Steers, 2001). Such attributes, combined with people's verbal and nonverbal behavior, play a part in establishing first impressions. Research shows that a firm handshake still makes a powerful first impression (Chaplin et al., 2000). It conveys that a person is positive, confident, and outgoing, not shy or weak-willed. Moods also play a part. When we are happy, our impressions of others are usually more positive than when we are unhappy.

A number of studies reveal that an overall impression or judgment of another person is influenced more by the first information that is received about that person than by information that comes later (Luchins, 1957). This phenomenon is called the **primacy effect.** It seems that we attend to initial information more carefully; once an impression is formed, it provides the framework through which we interpret later infor-

primacy effect

The tendency for an overall impression of another to be influenced more by the first information that is received about that person than by information that comes later.

mation (Gawronski et al., 2002). Any information that is consistent with the first impression is likely to be accepted, thus strengthening the impression. Information that does not fit with the earlier information is more likely to be disregarded. Remember, any time you list your personal traits or qualities, always list your most positive qualities first. It pays to put your best foot forward—first.

What is your first impression of the person shown here?

Attribution

Why do people do the things they do? To answer this question, we make **attributions**—that is, we assign or attribute causes to explain the behavior of others or of ourselves. One kind of attribution is called a **situational attribution** (an external attribution), in which we attribute a person's behavior to some external cause or factor operating within the situation. After failing an exam, you might say, "The test was unfair" or "The professor didn't give us enough time." Or you might make a **dispositional attribution** (an internal attribution) and attribute the behavior to some internal cause, such as a personal trait, motive, or attitude. For example, you might attribute a poor grade to lack of ability or to a poor memory. To some degree, attributions are influenced by informal psychological theories we develop through our observations of and interactions with people (Plaks et al., 2005). One such theory might be that children's behavior is primarily a function of parental discipline. Nevertheless, several other factors influence whether we make situational or dispositional attributions.

We tend to use situational attributions to explain our own failures, because we are aware of factors in the situation that influenced us to act as we did (Jones, 1976, 1990; Jones & Nisbett, 1971). When we explain others' failures, we focus more on personal factors than on the factors operating within the situation (Gilbert & Malone, 1995; Leyens et al., 1996; van Boven et al., 2003). The tendency to attribute our own shortcomings primarily to external, or situational, factors and those of others to internal, or dispositional, factors is known as the **actor-observer effect.** Members of both Catholic and Protestant activist groups in Northern Ireland are subject to the actor-observer effect, for example. Each group attributes the violence of the other group to dispositional characteristics (e.g., they are murderers, they have evil intentions), and each group attempts to justify its own violence by attributing it to situational causes (e.g., we were just protecting ourselves, we were only retaliating) (Hunter et al., 2000).

There is one striking inconsistency in the way we view our own behavior: the **self-serving bias.** We use the self-serving bias when we attribute our successes to dispositional causes and blame our failures on situational causes (Baumgardner et al., 1986; Brown & Rogers, 1991; Pansu & Gilibert, 2002). For example, if you interview for a job and get it, you tell yourself it is because you have the right qualifications; if someone else gets the job, it is probably because he or she knew the right people. The self-serving bias allows us to take credit for our successes and shift the blame for our failures to the situation. Research examining the attributions of professional athletes, for example, has shown that they attribute victories to internal traits, such as ability and effort, and losses to situational factors, such as poor officiating and the like (Roesch & Amirkhan, 1997). Interestingly, managers prefer job applicants who make dispositional attributions during interviews, especially when the attributions focus on effort rather than natural ability (Pansu & Gilibert, 2002).

Culture apparently contributes to attributional biases as well. In a series of studies, researchers compared Koreans' and Americans' situational and dispositional attributions for both desirable and undesirable behaviors (Choi et al., 2003). They found that Koreans, on average, made more situational attributions than Americans did, no matter what kind of behavior participants were asked to explain. The reason for the difference, according to the researchers, was that the Koreans took into account more information than the Americans did before making attributions.

◆ What is the difference between a situational attribution and a dispositional attribution?

◆ **attribution**
An assignment of a cause to explain one's own or another's behavior.

◆ **situational attribution**
Attributing a behavior to some external cause or factor operating within the situation; an external attribution.

◆ **dispositional attribution**
Attributing a behavior to some internal cause, such as a personal trait, motive, or attitude; an internal attribution.

◆ **actor-observer effect**
The tendency to attribute one's own behavior primarily to situational factors and the behavior of others primarily to dispositional factors.

◆ **self-serving bias**
The tendency to attribute one's successes to dispositional causes and one's failures to situational causes.

Attraction

Think for a moment about your friends. What makes you like, or even fall in love with, one person and ignore or react negatively to someone else?

Factors Influencing Attraction

◆ *What factors contribute to attraction?*

Several factors influence attraction. One is **proximity,** or physical or geographic closeness. Obviously, it is much easier to make friends with people who are close at hand. One reason proximity matters is the **mere-exposure effect,** the tendency to feel more positively toward a stimulus as a result of repeated exposure to it. People, food, songs, and clothing styles become more acceptable the more we are exposed to them. Advertisers rely on the positive effects of repeated exposure to increase people's liking for products and even for political candidates.

Our own moods and emotions, whether positive or negative, can influence how much we are attracted to people we meet. We may develop positive or negative feelings toward others simply because they are present when very good or very bad things happen to us. Further, we tend to like the people who also like us—or who we *believe* like us—a phenomenon called *reciprocity* or *reciprocal liking.*

Beginning in elementary school and continuing through life, people are also more likely to pick friends of the same age, gender, race, and socioeconomic class. We tend to choose friends and lovers who have similar views on most things that are important to us. Similar interests and attitudes toward leisure-time activities make it more likely that time spent together is rewarding.

◆ **proximity**

Physical or geographic closeness; a major influence on attraction.

◆ **mere-exposure effect**

The tendency to feel more positively toward a stimulus as a result of repeated exposure to it.

Physical Attractiveness

◆ *How important is physical attractiveness to attraction?*

Perhaps no other factor influences attraction more than physical attractiveness. People of all ages have a strong tendency to prefer physically attractive people (Langlois et al., 2000). Even 6-month-old infants, when given the chance to look at a photograph of an attractive or an unattractive woman, man, or infant, will spend more time looking at the attractive face (Ramsey et al., 2004). How people behave, especially the simple act of smiling, influences our perceptions of their attractiveness (Reis et al., 1990). But physical appearance matters as well.

Based on studies using computer-generated faces, researchers Langlois and Roggman (1990) reported that perceptions of attractiveness are based on features that are approximately the mathematical average of the features in a general population. In addition, Perrett and others (1994) found that averaging faces tends to make them more symmetrical. Symmetrical faces and bodies, are seen as more attractive and sexually appealing (Singh, 1995; Thornhill & Gangestad, 1994).

In a review of 11 meta-analyses of cross-cultural studies of attractiveness, Langlois and others (2000) found that males and females across many cultures have similar ideas about the physical attractiveness of members of the opposite sex. When native Asian, Hispanic American, and White American male students rated photographs of Asian, Hispanic, African American, and White females on attractiveness, Cunningham and others (1995) reported a very high mean correlation (.93) among the groups in attractiveness ratings. When African American and White American men rated photos of African American women, their agreement on facial features was also very high—a correlation of .94. Evolutionary psychologists suggest that this cross-cultural similarity is because of a tendency, shaped by natural selection, to look for indicators of health in potential mates (Fink & Penton-Voak, 2002).

Why does physical attractiveness matter? When people have one trait that we either admire or dislike very much, we often assume that they have other positive or negative traits—a phenomenon known as the **halo effect** (Nisbett & Wilson, 1977). Dion and others (1972) found that people generally attribute additional favorable qualities to those who are attractive. Attractive people are seen as more exciting, personable, interesting, and socially desirable than unattractive people. As a result, job interviewers are

◆ **halo effect**

The tendency to assume that a person has generally positive or negative traits as a result of observing one major positive or negative trait.

The halo effect—the attribution of other favorable qualities to those who are attractive—helps explain why physical attractiveness is so important.

more likely to recommend highly attractive people (Dipboye et al., 1975). Similarly, when asked to rate pictures of women with regard to the likelihood of career success, research participants give higher ratings to those who are thin than to those who are overweight or obese (Wade & DiMaria, 2003).

Does this mean that unattractive people don't have a chance? Fortunately not. Eagly and her colleagues (1991) suggest that the impact of physical attractiveness is strongest in the perception of strangers. But once we get to know people, other qualities assume more importance. In fact, as we come to like people, they begin to look more attractive to us, while people with undesirable personal qualities begin to look less attractive.

Romantic Attraction and Mating

You probably have heard that opposites attract, but is this really true? The **matching hypothesis** suggests that we are likely to end up with a partner similar to ourselves in physical attractiveness and other assets (Berscheid et al., 1971; Feingold, 1988; Walster & Walster, 1969). Furthermore, couples mismatched in attractiveness are more likely to end the relationship (Cash & Janda, 1984). It has been suggested that we estimate our social assets and realistically expect to attract someone with approximately equal assets. In terms of physical attractiveness, some people might consider a movie star or supermodel to be the ideal man or woman, but they do not seriously consider their ideal to be a realistic, attainable possibility. Fear of rejection keeps many people from pursuing those who are much more attractive than they are. But instead of marrying an extremely handsome man, a very beautiful woman may opt for money and social status. Extremely handsome men have been known to make similar "sacrifices."

Most research, however, indicates that similarity in needs is mainly what attracts (Buss, 1984; Phillips et al., 1988). Similarities in personality, physical traits, intellectual ability, education, religion, ethnicity, socioeconomic status, and attitudes are also related to partner choice (O'Leary & Smith, 1991; Luo & Klohnen, 2005). And similarities in needs and in personality appear to be related to marital success as well as to marital choice (O'Leary & Smith, 1991). Similarities wear well. If you were to select a marriage partner, what qualities would attract you? Complete *Try It 14.1* (on page 430) to evaluate your own preferences.

Compare your rankings from the *Try It* to those of men and women from 33 countries and 5 major islands around the world. Generally, men and women across those cultures rate these four qualities as most important in mate selection: (1) mutual attraction/love, (2) dependable character, (3) emotional stability and maturity, and (4) pleasing disposition (Buss et al., 1990). Aside from these first four choices, however, women and men differ somewhat in the attributes they prefer. According to the views of evolutionary psychologist David Buss (1994), "Men prefer to mate with beautiful young women, whereas women prefer to mate with men who have resources and social status" (p. 239). These preferences, he claims, have been adaptive in human evolutionary history. To a male, beauty and youth suggest health and fertility—the best opportunity to send his genes into the next generation. To a female, resources and social status provide security for her and her children (Buss, 2000b). As was noted in Chapter 9, social role theorists maintain that gender differences in mate preferences are influenced by economic and social forces as well as evolutionary forces (Eagly & Wood, 1999).

◆ *How do psychologists explain romantic attraction and mating?*

◆ **matching hypothesis**
The notion that people tend to have lovers or spouses who are similar to themselves in physical attractiveness and other assets.

You are more likely to be attracted to someone who is similar to you than to someone who is your opposite.

Try It 14.1

Choosing a Mate

In your choice of a mate, which qualities are most and least important to you? Rank these 18 qualities of a potential mate from most important (1) to least important (18) to you.

_____ Ambition and industriousness

_____ Chastity (no previous sexual intercourse)

_____ Desire for home and children

_____ Education and intelligence

_____ Emotional stability and maturity

_____ Favorable social status or rating

_____ Good cooking and housekeeping skills

_____ Similar political background

_____ Similar religious background

_____ Good health

_____ Good looks

_____ Similar education

_____ Pleasing disposition

_____ Refinement/neatness

_____ Sociability

_____ Good financial prospects

_____ Dependable character

_____ Mutual attraction/love

Tip

You can use this checklist to test Buss's hypothesis that men and women have different priorities in mating. Ask several male and female classmates to complete the list, and then compare their rankings.

Conformity, Obedience, and Compliance

Conformity

◆ *What did Asch find in his famous experiment on conformity?*

Do you like to think of yourself as a nonconformist? Many people do, but research suggests that everyone is subject to social influence in some way. **Conformity** is changing or adopting a behavior or an attitude in an effort to be consistent with the social norms of a group or the expectations of other people. **Social norms** are the standards of behavior and the attitudes that are expected of members of a particular group. Some conformity is necessary if we are to have a society at all. We cannot drive on the other side of the road anytime we please. And we conform to other people's expectations to have their esteem or approval, their friendship or love, or even their company (Christensen et al., 2004). In fact, researchers have found that teenagers who attend schools where the majority of students are opposed to smoking, drinking, and drug use are less likely to use these substances than are peers who attend school where the majority approves of these behaviors (Kumar et al., 2002).

The best-known experiment on conformity was conducted by Solomon Asch (1951, 1955), who designed the simple test shown in Figure 14.1. Eight male participants were seated around a large table and were asked, one by one, to tell the experimenter which of the three lines matched the standard line. But only one of the eight was an actual participant; the others were confederates assisting

◆ **conformity**

Changing or adopting a behavior or an attitude in an effort to be consistent with the social norms of a group or the expectations of other people.

◆ **social norms**

The attitudes and standards of behavior expected of members of a particular group.

In this scene from Asch's experiment on conformity, all but one of the "subjects" were really confederates of the experimenter. They deliberately chose the wrong line to try to influence the naive subject (second from right) to go along with the majority.

the experimenter. There were 18 trials—18 different lines to be matched. During 12 of these trials, the confederates all gave the same wrong answer, which of course puzzled the naive participant. Remarkably, Asch found that 5% of the subjects conformed to the incorrect, unanimous majority all of the time, 70% conformed some of the time, but 25% remained completely independent and were never swayed by the group.

Varying the experiment with groups of various sizes, Asch found that the tendency to go along with the majority opinion remained in full force even when there was a unanimous majority of only 3 confederates. Surprisingly, unanimous majorities of 15 confederates produced no higher conformity rate than did those of 3. Asch also discovered that if just one other person voices a dissenting opinion, the tendency to conform is not as strong. When just one confederate in the group disagreed with the incorrect majority, the naive subjects' errors dropped drastically, from 32% to 10.4%.

Groupthink is the term social psychologist Irving Janis (1982) applied to the kind of conformity often seen in the decision-making processes of tightly knit groups. When a tightly knit group is more concerned with preserving group solidarity and uniformity than with objectively evaluating all possible alternatives in decision making, individual members may hesitate to voice any dissent. The group may also discredit opposing views from outsiders and begin to believe it is incapable of making mistakes. To guard against groupthink, Janis suggests that it is necessary to encourage open discussion of alternative views and the expression of any objections and doubts. He further recommends that outside experts sit in and challenge the views of the group. At least one group member should take the role of devil's advocate whenever a policy alternative is evaluated. Finally, to avoid groupthink in workplace situations, managers should withhold their own opinions when problem-solving and decision-making strategies are being considered (Bazan, 1998).

Other research on conformity and the Big Five personality dimensions reveals that people who are low in Neuroticism but high in Agreeableness and Conscientiousness are more likely to conform than those who score oppositely on those dimensions (DeYoung et al., 2002). But, contrary to conventional wisdom, women are no more likely to conform than men (Eagly & Carli, 1981). And an individual's conformity is greater if the sources of influence are perceived as belonging to that person's own group (Abrams et al., 1990). Even so, those who hold minority opinions on an issue have more influence in changing a majority view if they present a well-organized, clearly stated argument and if they are especially consistent in advocating their views (Wood et al., 1994).

Obedience

Can you imagine a world where each person always did exactly what he or she wanted, without regard for rules or respect for authority? We would stop at red lights only when we felt like it or weren't in a hurry. Someone might decide that he likes your car better than his own and take it. Or worse, someone might kill you because of an interest in your intimate partner.

Clearly, most people must obey most rules and respect those in authority most of the time if society is to survive and function. However, unquestioned obedience can cause humans to commit unbelievably horrible acts. One of the darkest chapters in human history arose from the obedience of officials in Nazi Germany, who carried out Adolph Hitler's orders to exterminate Jews and other "undesirables."

The study you read about at the beginning of this chapter demonstrated how far ordinary citizens would go to obey orders; remember, more than 60% of Milgram's participants delivered the "maximum" voltage, despite the pleading and eventual collapse of the "learner." Another researcher repeated the experiment in a three-room office suite in a run-down building rather than at prestigious Yale University. Even there, 48% of the participants administered the maximum shock (Meyer, 1972).

Milgram (1965) conducted a variation of the original experiment: Each trial involved three teachers, two of whom were confederates and the other, a naive participant. One confederate was instructed to refuse to continue after 150 volts, and the other confederate after 210 volts. In this situation, 36 out of 40 naive participants (90%)

FIGURE 14.1

Asch's Classic Study of Conformity

If you were one of eight participants in the Asch experiment who were asked to pick the line (1, 2, or 3) that matched the standard line shown above them, which line would you choose? If the other participants all chose line 3, would you conform and answer line 3? *Source:* Based on Asch (1955).

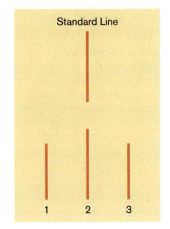

Standard Line

1   2   3

◆ *What did researchers find when they varied the circumstances of Milgram's classic study of obedience?*

◆ **groupthink**

The tendency for members of a tightly knit group to be more concerned with preserving group solidarity and uniformity than with objectively evaluating all alternatives in decision making.

defied the experimenter before the maximum shock could be given, compared with only 14 out of 40 participants in the original experiment (Milgram, 1965). In Milgram's experiment, as in Asch's conformity study, the presence of another person who refused to go along gave many of the participants the courage to defy authority.

Compliance

◆ What are three techniques used to gain compliance?

◆ **compliance**
Acting in accordance with the wishes, suggestions, or direct requests of other people.

◆ **foot-in-the-door technique**
A strategy designed to gain a favorable response to a small request at first, with the intent of making the person more likely to agree later to a larger request.

◆ **door-in-the-face technique**
A strategy in which someone makes a large, unreasonable request with the expectation that the person will refuse but will then be more likely to respond favorably to a smaller request later.

◆ **low-ball technique**
A strategy in which someone makes a very attractive initial offer to get a person to commit to an action and then makes the terms less favorable.

How often do you do what others want you to do? There are many times when people act, not out of conformity or obedience, but in accordance with the wishes, suggestions, or direct requests of others. This type of action is called **compliance.** One strategy people use to gain the compliance of others, the **foot-in-the-door technique,** is designed to gain a favorable response to a small request first. The intent is to make the person more likely to agree later to a larger request (the result desired from the beginning).

In a classic study of the foot-in-the-door technique, a researcher claiming to represent a consumers' group called a number of homes and asked whether the people answering the phone would mind responding to a few questions about the soap products they used. Then, a few days later, the same person called those who had agreed to the first request and asked if he could send five or six of his assistants to conduct an inventory of the products in their home. The researcher told the people that the inventory would take about 2 hours and that the inventory team would have to search all drawers, cabinets, and closets in the house. Nearly 53% of those asked preliminary questions agreed to the larger request, compared to 22% of a control group who were contacted only once with the larger request (Freedman & Fraser, 1966).

With the **door-in-the-face technique,** a large, unreasonable request is made first. The expectation is that the person will refuse but will then be more likely to respond favorably to a smaller request later (the result desired from the beginning). In one of the best-known studies on the door-in-the-face technique, college students were approached on campus. They were asked to agree to serve without pay as counselors to juvenile delinquents for 2 hours each week for a minimum of 2 years. As you would imagine, not a single person agreed (Cialdini et al., 1975). Then, the experimenters presented a much smaller request, asking if the students would agree to take a group of juveniles on a 2-hour trip to the zoo. Half the students agreed, a fairly high compliance rate. The researchers used another group of college students as controls, asking them to respond only to the smaller request, for the zoo trip. Only 17% agreed when the smaller request was presented alone.

Another method used to gain compliance is the **low-ball technique.** A very attractive initial offer is made to get people to commit themselves to an action, and then the terms are made less favorable. In a frequently cited study of this technique, college students were asked to enroll in an experimental course for which they would receive credit. After the students had agreed to participate, they were informed that the class would meet at 7:00 a.m. Control group participants were told about the class meeting time when first asked to enroll. More than 50% of the low-balled group agreed to participate, but only 25% of control participants did so (Cialdini et al., 1978).

Group Influence

Have you ever done something you really didn't want to do just to maintain harmony with a friend or friends? You may have seen a movie in which you really weren't interested or gone to the beach when you would have preferred to stay home. Being part of a group often means giving up a bit of individuality, but the reward is the support and camaraderie of the group. Clearly, we behave differently in a variety of ways when we are part of a group, small or large. What happens when the group of which we are a part is made up of strangers? Do such groups influence our behavior as well?

Social Facilitation

In certain cases, individual performance can be either helped or hindered by the mere physical presence of others. The term **social facilitation** refers to any effect on performance, whether positive or negative, that can be attributed to the presence of others. Research on this phenomenon has focused on two types of effects: (1) **audience effects**, the impact of passive spectators on performance, and (2) **co-action effects**, the impact on performance caused by the presence of other people engaged in the same task.

In one of the first studies in social psychology, Norman Triplett (1898) looked at co-action effects. He had observed in official records that bicycle racers pedaled faster when they were pedaling against other racers than when they were racing against the clock. Was this pattern of performance peculiar to competitive bicycling? Or was it part of a more general phenomenon whereby people would work faster and harder in the presence of others than when performing alone? Triplett set up a study in which he told 40 children to wind fishing reels as quickly as possible under one of two conditions: (1) alone, or (2) in the presence of other children performing the same task. He found that children worked faster when other reel turners were present. But later studies on social facilitation found that, in the presence of others, people's performance improves on easy tasks but suffers on difficult tasks (Michaels et al., 1982). See Figure 14.2.

◆ How does social facilitation affect performance?

◆ **social facilitation**
Any positive or negative effect on performance that can be attributed to the presence of others, either as an audience or as co-actors.

◆ **audience effects**
The impact of passive spectators on performance.

◆ **co-action effects**
The impact on performance of the presence of other people engaged in the same task.

Social Loafing

Have you ever been assigned by a teacher or professor to work in a group and, at the end of the project, felt that you had carried more than your fair share of the workload? Such feelings are not uncommon. Researcher Bibb Latané used the term **social loafing** to refer to people's tendency to put forth less effort when working with others on a common task than they do when they are working alone (Latané et al., 1979). Social loafing occurs in situations where no one person's contribution to the group can be identified and individuals are neither praised for a good performance nor blamed for a poor one (Williams et al., 1981). Social loafing is a problem in many workplaces, especially where employees have unlimited access to the Internet (Lim, 2002).

You may have noticed the phenomenon of social loafing if you have ever had to do a group project for a class. Interestingly, though, achievement motivation influences social loafing (Hart et al., 2004). Researchers tested participants with regard to their levels of achievement motivation and then assigned them to pairs. Each pair was asked to generate as many uses for a knife that they could think of. The amount of effort exhibited by participants who were low in achievement motivation depended on their partner's effort. When paired with partners who worked hard, individuals with low achievement motivation contributed little, that is, they engaged in social loafing. They did the opposite, however, when paired with others who didn't work. By contrast, participants who were high in achievement motivation worked hard at the task no matter what their partner's level of participation was.

◆ What is social loafing, and what factors reduce it?

◆ **social loafing**
The tendency to put forth less effort when working with others on a common task than when working alone.

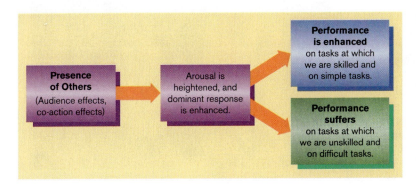

FIGURE 14.2 **Social Facilitation: Performing in the Presence of Others**
The presence of others (either as an audience or as co-actors engaged in the same task) may have opposite effects, either helping or hindering an individual's performance. Why? First, the presence of others heightens arousal. Second, heightened arousal leads to better performance on tasks the individual is good at and worse performance on tasks that are difficult for him or her. *Source:* Based on Zajonc & Sales (1966).

Studying in a group could lead to social loafing through a diffusion of responsibility effect.

Some 80 experimental studies have been conducted on social loafing in diverse cultures, including those of Taiwan, Japan, Thailand, India, China, and the United States. Social loafing on a variety of tasks was evident to some degree in all of the cultures studied. But it appears to be more common in individualistic Western cultures such as the United States (Karau & Williams, 1993).

Social Roles

◆ *How do social roles influence individual behavior?*

◆ **social roles**
Socially defined behaviors considered appropriate for individuals occupying certain positions within a given group.

Social roles are socially defined behaviors that are considered appropriate for individuals occupying certain positions within a given group. These roles can shape our behavior, sometimes quickly and dramatically. Consider a classic experiment (the Stanford Prison Experiment) in which psychologist Philip Zimbardo (1972) simulated a prison experience. College student volunteers were randomly assigned to be either guards or prisoners. The guards, wearing uniforms and carrying small clubs, strictly enforced harsh rules. The prisoners were stripped naked, searched, and deloused. Then, they were given prison uniforms, assigned numbers, and locked away in small, bare cells. The guards quickly adapted to their new role, some even to the point of becoming heartless and sadistic. One guard remembered forcing prisoners to clean toilets with their bare hands. And the prisoners began to act debased and subservient. The role playing became all too real—so much so that the experiment had to be ended in only 6 days.

Of course, social roles have positive effects on behavior as well. In classic research examining adolescents with learning disabilities, Palinscar and Brown (1984) reported that students' learning behaviors were powerfully affected by their being assigned to play either the "teacher" or the "student" role in group study sessions. Participants summarized reading assignments more effectively, and as a result learned more from them, when functioning as a teacher than when functioning as a student.

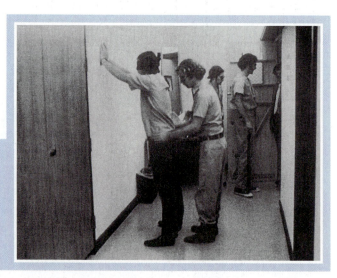

Zimbardo's experiment simulated the prison environment by randomly assigning participants to the social roles of prison guards or inmates. The social roles influenced the participants' behavior: The prisoners began acting like real prisoners, and the prison guards, like real prison guards.

Attitudes and Attitude Change

We use the word *attitude* frequently in everyday speech. We say that someone has a "bad attitude," for instance. But what is an attitude?

Attitudes

Essentially, **attitudes** are relatively stable evaluations of persons, objects, situations, or issues, along a continuum ranging from positive to negative (Petty et al., 1997). Most attitudes have three components: (1) a cognitive component, consisting of thoughts and beliefs about the attitudinal object; (2) an emotional component, made up of feelings toward the attitudinal object; and (3) a behavioral component, composed of predispositions concerning actions toward the object (Breckler, 1984). See Figure 14.3. Attitudes enable us to appraise people, objects, and situations, and provide structure and consistency in the social environment (Fazio, 1989). Attitudes also help us process social information (Pratkanis, 1989), guide our behavior (Sanbonmatsu & Fazio, 1990), and influence our social judgments and decisions (Jamieson & Zanna, 1989).

Some attitudes are acquired through firsthand experiences with people, objects, situations, and issues. Others are acquired when children hear parents, family, friends, and teachers express positive or negative attitudes toward certain issues or people. The mass media, including advertising, influence people's attitudes and reap billions of dollars annually for their efforts. As you might expect, however, the attitudes that people form through their own direct experience are stronger than those they acquire vicariously and are also more resistant to change (Wu & Shaffer, 1987). Once formed, however, attitudes tend to strengthen when we associate with others who share them (Visser & Mirabile, 2004).

Lively discussions of controversial topics, even when those discussions take place only with others who agree with us, may improve our ability to think analytically about our attitudes. Researchers Joseph Lao and Deanna Kuhn (2002) asked college students to engage in a series of six discussions of a controversial topic with another student. Participants were assigned to three experimental conditions. In one arm of the study, all of the discussions involved a partner who agreed with them. In another, all of the partners disagreed. In the third condition, three discussion partners agreed and three disagreed with the participant. Six weeks later, Lao and Kuhn found that participants who had discussed the topic either with those who agreed with them or with an equal number of agreers and disagreers showed the greatest improvement in critical thinking about the topic. They inferred from these findings that discussing a controversial issue with people who disagree

◆ *What are the three components of an attitude?*

◆ **attitude**
A relatively stable evaluation of a person, object, situation, or issue, along a continuum ranging from positive to negative.

FIGURE 14.3 **The Three Components of an Attitude**

An attitude is a relatively stable evaluation of a person, object, situation, or issue. Most of our attitudes have (1) a cognitive component, (2) an emotional component, and (3) a behavioral component.

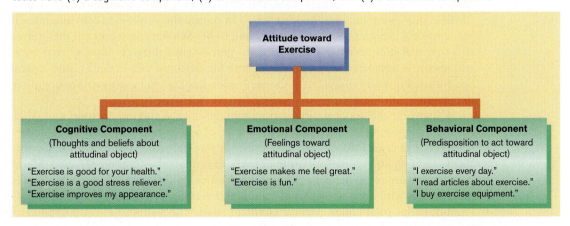

with you is helpful only if it is balanced by discussions with others who share your views. Despite ageist stereotypes, many studies have found that older adults are more likely to change their attitudes than are middle-aged adults (Visser & Krosnick, 1998).

We often hear that attitude change is the key to behavior change. However, a number of studies in the mid-20th century showed that attitudes predict behavior only about 10% of the time (Wicker, 1969). People, for example, may express strong attitudes in favor of protecting the environment and conserving natural resources, yet not take their aluminum cans to a recycling center or join a carpool. However, attitudes are better predictors of behavior if they are strongly held, are readily accessible in memory (Bassili, 1995; Fazio & Williams, 1986; Kraus, 1995), and vitally affect the holder's interests (Sivacek & Crano, 1982).

Cognitive Dissonance

◆ *What is cognitive dissonance, and how can it be reduced?*

◆ **cognitive dissonance**
The unpleasant state that can occur when people become aware of inconsistencies between their attitudes or between their attitudes and their behavior.

What happens when attitudes contradict one another, or when attitudes and behaviors are inconsistent? According to psychologist Leon Festinger (1957), if people discover that some of their attitudes are in conflict or that their attitudes are not consistent with their behavior, they are likely to experience an unpleasant state called **cognitive dissonance**. Psychologists believe that cognitive dissonance results from a desire to maintain self-esteem (Stone, 2003). Moreover, individuals can experience such dissonance when observing conflicts in the attitudes and/or behaviors of others—this is *vicarious cognitive dissonance* (Norton et al., 2003). People usually try to reduce the dissonance by changing the behavior or the attitude or by somehow explaining away the inconsistency or minimizing its importance (Aronson, 1976; Festinger, 1957; Matz & Wood, 2005). By changing the attitude, individuals retain their self-esteem and reduce the discomfort caused by dissonance (Elliot & Devine, 1994).

In classic research, Festinger and Carlsmith (1959) placed research participants alone in a room to play a boring game. Upon completing the game, participants were instructed to tell the next participants that the game was fun. Participants were randomly assigned to two experimental groups. One group was paid $1 for following instructions, while the other was paid $20. Festinger and Carlsmith assumed that the conflict between participants' self-esteem and their lying behavior would cause cognitive dissonance. How could participants resolve this dissonance and get rid of the threat to self-esteem caused by lying? Just as Festinger and Carlsmith had hypothesized, participants who were paid $1 resolved the conflict by convincing themselves that the game really had been fun—a change in attitude. By contrast, participants who were paid $20 resolved the conflict by justifying their actions on the basis of having been paid a fairly large sum of money relative to the amount of effort it had required to lie to the next participant. Consequently, they did not view the lie as a threat to their self-esteem.

Smoking creates a perfect situation for cognitive dissonance. Faced with a mountain of evidence linking smoking to a number of diseases, what are smokers to do? The healthiest, but perhaps not the easiest, way to reduce cognitive dissonance is to change the behavior—quit smoking. Another way is to change the attitude, to convince oneself that smoking is not as dangerous as it is said to be. Smokers may also tell themselves that they will stop smoking long before any permanent damage is done, or that medical science is advancing so rapidly that a cure for cancer or emphysema is just around the corner. Figure 14.4 illustrates the methods a smoker may use to reduce cognitive dissonance.

Expanding the applicability of cognitive dissonance theory, Aronson and Mills (1959) argued that the more people have to sacrifice, give up, or suffer to become a member of an organization—say, a fraternity or sorority—the more positive their attitudes are likely to become toward the group, in order to justify their sacrifice. Members of cults are often required to endure hardships and make great sacrifices, such as severing ties with their families and friends and turning over their property and possessions to the group. Such extreme sacrifice can then be justified only by a strong and radical defense of the cult, its goals, and its leaders.

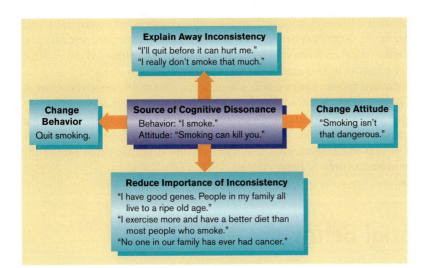

FIGURE 14.4

Methods of Reducing Cognitive Dissonance

Cognitive dissonance can occur when people become aware of inconsistencies in their attitudes or between their attitudes and their behavior. People try to reduce dissonance by (1) changing their behavior, (2) changing their attitude, (3) explaining away the inconsistency, or (4) reducing its importance. Here are examples of how a smoker might use these methods to reduce the cognitive dissonance created by his or her habit.

Persuasion

Have you ever tried to convince another person to agree with your political opinions or to do something you wanted them to do? **Persuasion** is a deliberate attempt to influence the attitudes and/or the behavior of another person. Attempts at persuasion are pervasive parts of work experience, social experience, and even family life. Researchers have identified four elements of persuasion: (1) the source of the communication (who is doing the persuading), (2) the audience (who is being persuaded), (3) the message (what is being said), and (4) the medium (the means by which the message is transmitted).

Some factors that make the source (the communicator) more persuasive are credibility, attractiveness, and likability. A credible communicator is one who has expertise (knowledge of the topic at hand) and trustworthiness (truthfulness and integrity). Other characteristics of the source—including physical attractiveness, celebrity status, and similarity to the audience—also contribute to our responses to the sources of persuasive messages.

Audience characteristics influence responses to persuasion as well. In general, people with low IQs are easier to persuade than those with high IQs (Rhodes & Wood, 1992). Evidence suggests that a one-sided message is usually most persuasive if the audience is not well informed on the issue, is not highly intelligent, or already agrees with the point of view. A two-sided message (where both sides of an issue are mentioned) works best when the audience is well informed on the issue, is fairly intelligent, or is initially opposed to the point of view. A two-sided appeal will usually sway more people than will a one-sided appeal (Hovland et al., 1949; McGuire, 1985). And people tend to scrutinize arguments that are contrary to their existing beliefs more carefully and exert more effort refuting them; they are also more likely to judge such arguments as being weaker than those that support their beliefs (Edwards & Smith, 1996).

A message can be well reasoned, logical, and unemotional ("just the facts"); it can be strictly emotional ("make their hair stand on end"); or it can be a combination of the two. Arousing fear seems to be an effective method for persuading people to quit smoking, get regular chest X rays, wear seat belts, and get flu vaccine shots (Dillard & Anderson, 2004). Appeals based on fear are most effective

◆ *What are the elements of persuasion?*

◆ **persuasion**
A deliberate attempt to influence the attitudes and/or behavior of another person.

Celebrity status can make someone more persuasive than she or he would otherwise be, a key factor in political campaigning.

when the presentation outlines definite actions the audience can take to avoid the feared outcomes (Buller et al., 2000; Stephenson & Witte, 1998). However, nutritional messages are more effective when framed in terms of the benefits of dietary change rather than the harmful effects of a poor diet (van Assema et al., 2002).

Another important factor in persuasion is repetition. The more often a product or a point of view is presented, the more people will be persuaded to buy it or embrace it. Advertisers apparently believe in the mere-exposure effect, because they repeat their messages over and over (Bornstein, 1989). But messages are likely to be less persuasive if they include vivid elements (colorful language, striking examples) that hinder the reception of the content (Frey & Eagly, 1993).

Prosocial Behavior

According to the Association of Fundraising Professionals, Americans contributed nearly $250 billion to various causes in 2002 ("Charity holds its own," 2003). This giving supports our belief in the basic goodness of human beings. But what does it mean when people ignore others in need? In a now-famous case from 1964, New York City resident Kitty Genovese was murdered while her neighbors looked on, apparently indifferent to her plight. More recently, in early 2003, several people were caught on videotape doing nothing as a man who had just been shot lay dying in a gas station driveway (CNN.com, 2003). One person even stared at the victim for a few minutes and then calmly returned to the task of filling a can with kerosene. What causes such extreme variations in helping behavior?

Reasons for Helping

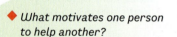

What motivates one person to help another?

There are many kinds of **prosocial behavior**—behavior that benefits others, such as helping, cooperation, and sympathy. Such impulses arise early in life. Researchers agree that young children respond sympathetically to companions in distress, usually before their second birthday (Hay, 1994; Kochanska, 1993). The term **altruism** is usually reserved for behavior that is aimed at helping others, requires some self-sacrifice, and is not performed for personal gain. Batson and colleagues (1989) believe that we help out of *empathy*—the ability to take the perspective of others, to put ourselves in their place.

Commitment is another factor influencing altruism. We are more likely to behave in an altruistic fashion in the context of relationships to which we are deeply committed (Powell & Van Vugt, 2003). The influence of commitment is strongest when the cost of an altruistic act is high. For instance, you would probably be more likely to volunteer to donate a kidney, let's say, to a family member than to a stranger.

The degree to which society values altruism is another variable that can influence individual decisions about altruistic behavior. Cultures vary in their norms for helping others—that is, their *social responsibility norms*. According to Miller and others (1990), people in the United States tend to feel an obligation to help family members, friends, and even strangers in life-threatening circumstances, but only family members in moderately serious situations. In contrast, in India the social responsibility norm extends to strangers whose needs are only moderately serious or even minor.

Whatever the motive for altruism, people who regularly engage in behavior that helps others reap significant benefits (Seenoo & Takagi, 2003). One interesting benefit is that, the more people help, the more altruistic they become. In other words, behaving altruistically generates or enhances an individual's altruistic attitudes. Along with this attitude change comes an increased appreciation for life. Thus, the costs of altruistic behavior are balanced by its benefits, both for those who are helped and for the helpers themselves.

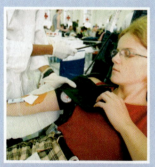

Altruistic acts, such as donating blood, may be motivated by social responsibility norms.

The Bystander Effect

A variety of social circumstances contribute to the decision to help another person. One example is the **bystander effect**: As the number of bystanders at an emergency increases, the probability that the victim will receive help from them decreases, and the help, if given, is likely to be delayed. Psychologists have suggested that the bystander effect explains the failure of Kitty Genovese's neighbors to help her.

◆ *What is the bystander effect, and why does it occur?*

In now-classic research, Darley and Latané (1968a) placed a series of research participants alone in a small room and told them that they would be participating in a discussion group by means of an intercom system. Some participants were told that they would be communicating with only one other participant, some believed that two other participants would be involved, and some were told that five other people would participate. There really were no other participants in the study—only the prerecorded voices of confederates assisting the experimenter. Shortly after the discussion began, the voice of one confederate was heard over the intercom calling for help, indicating that he was having an epileptic seizure. Of the participants who believed that they alone were hearing the victim, 85% went for help before the end of the seizure. When participants believed that one other person

Why do people ignore someone who is unconscious on the sidewalk? Diffusion of responsibility is one possible explanation.

heard the seizure, 62% sought help. But when they believed that four other people were aware of the emergency, only 31% tried to get help before the end of the seizure. Figure 14.5 shows how the number of bystanders affects both the number of people who try to help and the speed of response.

Darley and Latané (1968a) suggest that, when bystanders are present in an emergency, they generally feel that the responsibility for helping is shared by the group, a phenomenon known as **diffusion of responsibility.** Consequently, each person feels less compelled to act than if she or he were alone and felt the total responsibility; each bystander thinks, "Somebody else must be doing something." Another reason for the bystander effect is the influence of other bystanders who appear calm. When others seem calm, we may conclude that nothing is really wrong and that no intervention is necessary (Darley & Latané, 1968b).

Ironically, with regard to catastrophes, such as the events of September 11, 2001, and the tsunami disaster in December 2004, the bystander effect is greatly reduced. In fact, people are likely to put forth extraordinary effort to help others in such situations (Shepperd, 2001).

◆ **bystander effect**

A social factor that affects prosocial behavior: As the number of bystanders at an emergency increases, the probability that the victim will receive help decreases, and the help, if given, is likely to be delayed.

◆ **diffusion of responsibility**

The feeling among bystanders at an emergency that the responsibility for helping is shared by the group, making each person feel less compelled to act than if he or she alone bore the total responsibility.

FIGURE 14.5

The Bystander Effect

In their intercom experiment, Darley and Latané showed that the more people a participant believed were present during an emergency, the longer it took the participant to respond and help a person in distress. *Source:* Data from Darley & Latané (1968a).

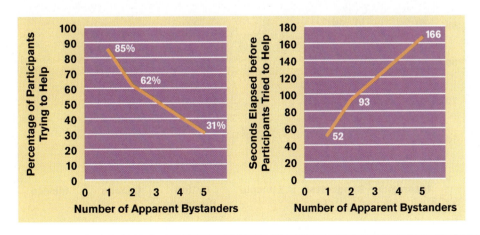

Aggression

One of the enduring themes of research in social psychology for many years has been the study of aggression. **Aggression** is the intentional infliction of physical or psychological harm on others. Aggression has many forms and takes place in a variety of locations—at home, at work, and even among drivers on the road. As Figure 14.6 suggests, being the target of an aggressive act is an all-too-common experience. Of course, domestic violence represents only one of many forms of aggression. But why does one person intentionally harm another?

◆ **aggression**

The intentional infliction of physical or psychological harm on others.

Biological Factors in Aggression

◆ *What biological factors are thought to be related to aggression?*

Sigmund Freud believed that humans have an aggressive instinct that can be turned inward as self-destruction or outward as aggression or violence toward others. While rejecting this view, many psychologists do concede that biological factors are involved. A meta-analysis of 24 twin and adoption studies of several personality measures of aggression revealed a heritability estimate of about .50 for aggression (Miles & Carey, 1997). Twin and adoption studies have also revealed a genetic link for criminal behavior (DiLalla & Gottesman, 1991). Cloninger and others (1982) found that adoptees with a criminal biological parent were four times as likely as members of the general population to commit crimes, while adoptees with a criminal adoptive parent were at twice the risk of committing a crime. But adoptees with both a criminal biological and a criminal adoptive parent were 14 times as likely to commit crimes, indicating the power of the combined influences of nature and nurture. Thus, many researchers believe that genes that predispose individuals to aggressive behavior may cause them to be more sensitive to models of aggressiveness in the environment (Rowe, 2003).

One biological factor that seems very closely related to aggression is a low arousal level of the autonomic nervous system (Raine, 1996). Low arousal level (low heart rate and lower reactivity) has been linked to antisocial and violent behavior (Brennan et al., 1997). People with a low arousal level tend to seek stimulation and excitement and often exhibit fearlessness, even in the face of danger.

FIGURE 14.6 **Rate of Physical Abuse in Various Nations**

These data on physical abuse are based on a World Health Organization international survey of medical records.   *Source:* WHO (2000).

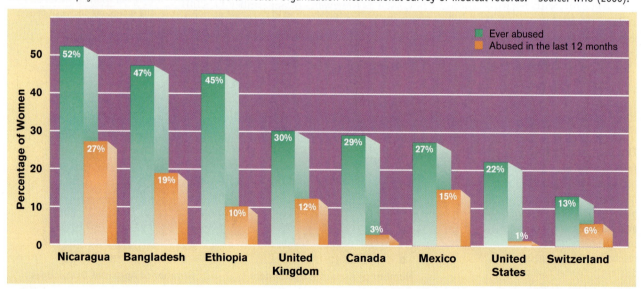

How Did You Find **Psychology?**

Miki Paul

Imagine for a moment that you are a young mother living out your childhood fantasies. Your husband is a successful doctor whose income provides you with many luxuries, and you have two adorable children. In your elegantly decorated home, several places are particularly special to you. Why? Because they are the places where you hide, where you try to become invisible, when you are afraid that your husband is about to beat you again. According to counseling psychologist Miki Paul, this is the secret life of terror that is lived by many victims of domestic violence, especially those who appear to outsiders to be living ideal lives ("Miki Paul," 2004). Paul specializes in counseling such women and is a survivor of domestic violence herself.

Paul's interest in psychology began when she was an undergraduate majoring in English literature at Indiana University. "It was the rich emotional lives and the motivations behind the characters' actions that drove my curiosity and passion for psychology," she says (Paul, personal communication, December 10, 2004). However, her upbringing in a traditional home predisposed her to give marriage and motherhood a higher priority. A few years after she married, Paul realized that she needed the stimulation that comes from being in school and pursuing one's passion, so she began working toward a master's degree in counseling. Her path to an advanced degree was not an easy one, though. Years later, after Paul had become a psychologist, she wrote an article describing the journey from abused wife to successful psychologist that was experienced by a fictitious woman named "Ellen." The character, says Paul, was a composite based on her own experiences and those of many of her clients ("Miki Paul," 2004). Here are some of the highlights of Ellen's story.

Ellen thought she had made the perfect match when she married a handsome, young doctor with whom she was passionately in love. She was stunned when he began beating her shortly after the wedding. Like most battered women, Ellen worked hard at being a perfect wife. The cycle of beatings, followed by apologies and expensive gifts, led her to conclude over and over again that her husband's behavior would change. Even so, the abuse continued, and Ellen wondered why her husband continued beating her when she tried so diligently to please him. This question drove her to begin part-time graduate work in counseling psychology. In the midst of her master's degree program, however, her husband decided to move the family to another state. Once again, domestic concerns took priority over Ellen's personal goals. But she persisted, transferring to another program in the new location.

After a particularly frightening episode of abuse, Ellen mustered all of her courage and turned a deaf ear to the voices of self-doubt in her head that told her that she would never make it on her own. She walked away from her comfortable life into single parenthood and economic deprivation. Her parents offered to take Ellen and her children in, but she was determined to be independent to prove that the voices were wrong. When she graduated, Ellen's degree was more than an academic credential. It was a symbol of the courage that had been required to create a new life for herself.

Like Ellen, Paul earned her master's degree in counseling amidst the economic and emotional struggles involved in divorcing her husband. The success that she experienced as a master's-level counselor gave her the confidence she needed to enter the doctoral program in counseling psychology at Ball State University. With the support of family and friends, Paul managed to successfully juggle the demands of single parenthood with the pressures of being a doctoral student. After earning her Ph.D., Paul obtained a license to practice independently as a psychologist.

Today, Paul is considered an authority on domestic abuse. Interviews with her have appeared in the news media, and she regularly gives talks about abuse to community and professional groups. She has won numerous awards for her professional work and for her service to the community. Clearly, the Miki Paul of today is a far cry from the young woman who wanted nothing more than to become a good wife and mother and, instead, found herself the target of domestic violence. She believes that, given appropriate support, other women who find themselves in abusive situations can do the same.

Men are more physically aggressive than women (Green et al., 1996), and a correlation between high testosterone levels and aggressive behavior has been found in males (Archer, 1991; Dabbs & Morris, 1990). In fact, the primary biological variable related to domestic violence (both verbal and physical abuse) appears to be high testosterone levels, which are highly heritable (Soler et al., 2000). Harris and others (1996) found testosterone levels in male and female college students to be positively correlated with aggression and negatively correlated with prosocial behavior. Furthermore, violent behavior has been associated with low levels of the neurotransmitter serotonin (Gartner & Whitaker-Azimitia, 1996; Mitsis et al., 2000; Toot et al., 2004).

Brain damage, brain tumors, and temporal lobe epilepsy have all been related to aggressive and violent behavior (Mednick et al., 1988; van Elst et al., 2000). A study of 15 death row inmates revealed that all had histories of severe head injuries (Lewis et al., 1986). According to Eronen and others (1996), homicide rates are 8 times higher among men with schizophrenia and 10 times higher among men with antisocial personality disorder. The risk of violence is even greater when individuals with these disorders abuse alcohol (Hodgins et al., 1996; Tiihonen et al., 1997). In children, high levels of lead exposure (Needleman et al., 1996) and low IQ and problems paying attention (Loeber & Hay, 1997) are related to aggressive behavior and delinquency.

Alcohol and aggression are frequent partners. A meta-analysis of 30 experimental studies indicated that alcohol is related to aggression (Bushman & Cooper, 1990). The use of alcohol and other drugs that affect the brain's frontal lobes may lead to aggressive behavior in humans and other animals by disrupting normal executive functions (Lyvers, 2000). Ito and others (1996) found that alcohol intoxication is particularly likely to lead to aggression in response to frustration. People who are intoxicated commit the majority of murders, spouse beatings, stabbings, and instances of physical child abuse.

Review and Reflect 14.1 summarizes the possible biological causes of aggression.

Other Influences on Aggression

◆ *What other factors contribute to aggression?*

Beyond biological factors, what other variables contribute to aggression? The **frustration-aggression hypothesis** suggests that frustration produces aggression (Dollard et al., 1939; Miller, 1941). If a traffic jam caused you to be late for an appointment and you were frustrated, would you lean on your horn, shout obscenities out of your window, or just sit patiently and wait? Frustration doesn't always cause aggression, but it is especially likely to do so if it is intense and seems to be unjustified (Doob & Sears, 1939; Pastore, 1950). Berkowitz (1988) points out that even if frustration is justified and not aimed specifically at an individual, it can cause aggression if it arouses negative emotions.

Aggression in response to frustration is not always focused on the actual cause of the frustration. If the preferred target is too threatening or not available, the aggression may be displaced. For example, children who are angry with their parents may take out their frustration on a younger sibling. Sometimes, members of minority groups or other innocent targets who are not responsible for a frustrating situation become targets of displaced aggression, a practice known as **scapegoating** (Koltz, 1983).

People often become aggressive when they are in pain (Berkowitz, 1983) or are exposed to loud noise or foul odors (Rotton et al., 1979). Extreme heat has also been linked to aggression in several studies (Anderson & Anderson, 1996; Rotton & Cohn, 2000). These and other studies lend support to the *cognitive-neoassociationistic model* proposed by Berkowitz (1990). He has suggested that anger and aggression result from aversive events and from unpleasant emotional states, such as sadness, grief, and depression. The cognitive component of Berkowitz's model occurs when the angered person appraises the aversive situation and makes attributions about the motives of the people involved. As a result of the cognitive appraisal, the initial reaction of anger can be intensified, reduced, or suppressed. This process makes the person either more or less likely to act on his or her aggressive tendency.

Personal space is an area surrounding each individual, much like an invisible bubble, that the person considers part of himself or herself and uses to regulate the close-

◆ **frustration-aggression hypothesis**

The hypothesis that frustration produces aggression.

◆ **scapegoating**

Displacing aggression onto members of minority groups or other innocent targets not responsible for the frustrating situation.

◆ **personal space**

An area surrounding each person, much like an invisible bubble, that the person considers part of himself or herself and uses to regulate the level of intimacy with others.

REVIEW and REFLECT 14.1

Possible Biological Causes of Aggression

CAUSE	EVIDENCE
Heredity	If one identical twin is aggressive, there is a 50% chance that the other twin is aggressive as well. Adopted children's aggressive tendencies are more like those of their biological parents than their adopted parents.
Low arousal level	People with low levels of arousal seek stimulation and excitement to increase arousal.
High testosterone level	High levels of testosterone have been found to be correlated with some forms of aggression, such as intimate partner abuse, in both men and women.
Neurological disorders	Brain tumors and other neurological diseases have been linked to aggressive behavior.
Alcohol abuse	People who are intoxicated commit the majority of murders and most other violent crimes.

ness of interactions with others. Personal space serves to protect privacy and to regulate the level of intimacy with others. The size of personal space varies according to the person or persons with whom an individual is interacting and the nature of the interaction. When personal space is reduced, aggression can result.

Crowding—the subjective judgment that there are too many people in a confined space—often leads to higher physiological arousal, and males typically experience its effects more negatively than females do. The effects of crowding also vary across cultures and situations. Researchers have studied its effects on such diverse populations as male heads of households in India and middle-class male and female college students in the United States (Evans & Lepore, 1993). In both of these studies, psychological distress was linked to household crowding. Furthermore, studies in prisons have shown that the more inmates per cell, the greater the number of violent incidents (Paulus et al., 1988). However, keep in mind that a prison is an atypical environment with a population whose members have been confined precisely because they tend to be aggressive.

◆ **crowding**
The subjective judgment that there are too many people in a confined space.

Finally, researchers Roy and Judy Eidelson have identified several beliefs that may lead members of a group of people to act aggressively toward outsiders (Eidelson & Eidelson, 2003). One such belief is a group's conviction that its members are superior to others, together with a sense of "chosenness" for a particular task. The view that one's own group has a legitimate grievance against outsiders can also spark aggression. Group members who believe themselves to be vulnerable may justify aggression as a form of defense. Similarly, those who are convinced that promises made by outsiders to respect the rights of group members cannot be trusted may act aggressively. Finally, group members who believe that aggression is the only strategy available to them for addressing grievances or protecting themselves may resort to violence. Group leaders play an important role in either encouraging or discouraging these beliefs among group members. For example, positive leadership may be able to prevent intergroup aggression.

The Social Learning Theory of Aggression

The *social learning theory of aggression* holds that people learn to behave aggressively by observing aggressive models and by having their aggressive responses reinforced (Bandura, 1973). It is well known that aggression levels are higher in groups and subcultures that condone violent behavior and accord high status to aggressive members. A leading advocate of the social learning theory of aggression, Albert Bandura (1976), claims that aggressive models in the subculture, the family, and the media all play a part in increasing the level of aggression in society.

◆ *According to social learning theory, what causes aggressive behavior?*

There is some truth to this belief. Abused children certainly experience aggression and see it modeled day after day. On the basis of original research and an analysis of 60 other studies, Oliver (1993) concludes that one-third of people who are abused go on to become abusers, one-third do not, and the final one-third may become abusers if their lives are highly stressful. Further, individuals who were sexually abused as children are more likely than others to become child sexual abusers as adults (Burton, 2003).

Most abusive parents, however, were not abused as children (Widom, 1989). Although abused and neglected children are at higher risk of becoming delinquent, criminal, or violent, the majority do not become abusive themselves (Widom & Maxfield, 1996). Several researchers suggest that the higher risk for aggression may not be due solely to an abusive family environment but may be partly influenced by the genes (DiLalla & Gottesman, 1991). Some abused children become withdrawn and isolated rather than aggressive and abusive (Dodge et al., 1990).

The research evidence overwhelmingly supports a relationship between TV violence and viewer aggression (Coyne et al., 2004; Huesmann & Moise, 1996; Singer et al., 1999). And the negative effects of TV violence are even worse for individuals who are, by nature, highly aggressive (Bushman, 1995). According to Eron (1987, p. 438), "One of the best predictors of how aggressive a young man would be at age 19 was the violence of the TV programs he preferred when he was 8 years old." A longitudinal study conducted in Finland also found that the viewing of TV violence was related to criminality in young adulthood (Viemerö, 1996). Moreover, a review of 28 studies of the effects of media violence on children and adolescents revealed that "media violence enhances children's and adolescents' aggression in interactions with strangers, classmates, and friends" (Wood et al., 1991, p. 380). It may stimulate physiological arousal, lower inhibitions, cause unpleasant feelings, and decrease sensitivity to violence and make it more acceptable to people.

Researchers have also found a correlation between playing violent video games and aggression (Anderson & Dill, 2000; Carnagey & Anderson, 2004). Moreover, aggressiveness increases as more time is spent playing such games (Colwell & Payne, 2000). However, researchers in the Netherlands found that boys who choose aggressive video games tend to be more aggressive, less intelligent, and less prosocial in their behavior (Weigman & van Schie, 1998). So, the link between aggression and video games may be due to the tendency of aggressive individuals to prefer entertainment media that feature aggression.

◆ **prejudice**

Attitudes (usually negative) toward others based on their gender, religion, race, or membership in a particular group.

◆ **discrimination**

Behavior (usually negative) directed toward others based on their gender, religion, race, or membership in a particular group.

◆ **realistic conflict theory**

The view that as competition increases among social groups for scarce resources, so do prejudice, discrimination, and hatred.

◆ *What factors contribute to the development of prejudice and discrimination?*

Prejudice and Discrimination

Do you know the difference between *prejudice* and *discrimination*? **Prejudice** consists of attitudes (usually negative) toward others based on their gender, religion, race, or membership in a particular group. Prejudice involves beliefs and emotions (not actions) that can escalate into hatred. **Discrimination** consists of behavior—actions (usually negative) toward others based on their gender, religion, race, or membership in a particular group. Many Americans have experienced prejudice and discrimination—minority racial groups (racism), women (sexism), the elderly (ageism), the handicapped, homosexuals, religious groups, and others. What are the roots of prejudice and discrimination?

The Roots of Prejudice and Discrimination

Social psychologists have proposed several theories to explain the psychological bases for prejudice and discrimination. Moreover, a number of studies have provided insight into their origins.

One of the oldest explanations as to how prejudice arose cites competition among various social groups that must struggle against each other for scarce resources—good jobs, homes, schools, and so on. Commonly called the **realistic conflict theory,** this view suggests that as competition increases, so do prejudice, discrimina-

tion, and hatred among the competing groups. Some historical evidence supports the realistic conflict theory. Prejudice and hatred were high between the American settlers and the Native Americans, who struggled over land during the westward expansion. The multitudes of Irish and German immigrants who came to the United States in the 1830s and 1840s felt the sting of prejudice and hatred from other Americans who were facing economic scarcity. But prejudice and discrimination are attitudes and actions too complex to be explained solely by economic conflict and competition.

Prejudice can also spring from the distinct social categories into which people divide the world, employing an "us-versus-them" mentality (Turner et al., 1987). An **in-group** is a social group with a strong sense of togetherness, from which others are excluded. Members of college fraternities and sororities often exhibit strong in-group feelings. The **out-group** consists of individuals specifically identified by the in-group as not belonging. Us-versus-them thinking can lead to excessive competition, hostility, prejudice, discrimination, and even war. Prejudiced individuals are reluctant to admit outsiders to their racial in-group if there is the slightest doubt about the outsiders' racial purity (Blascovich et al., 1997).

A famous study by Sherif and Sherif (1967) shows how in-group/out-group conflict can escalate into prejudice and hostility rather quickly, even between groups that are very much alike. The researchers set up their experiment at the Robber's Cave summer camp. Their subjects were 22 bright, well-adjusted, 11- and 12-year-old White middle-class boys from Oklahoma City. Divided into two groups and housed in separate cabins, the boys were kept apart for all their daily activities and games. During the first week, in-group solidarity, friendship, and cooperation developed within each of the groups. One group called itself the "Rattlers"; the other group took the name "Eagles."

During the second week of the study, competitive events were purposely scheduled so that the goals of one group could be achieved "only at the expense of the other group" (Sherif, 1958, p. 353). The groups were happy to battle each other, and intergroup conflict quickly emerged. Name-calling began, fights broke out, and accusations were hurled back and forth. During the third week of the experiment, the researchers tried to put an end to the hostility and to turn rivalry into cooperation. They simply brought the groups together for pleasant activities, such as eating meals and watching movies. "But far from reducing conflict, these situations only served as opportunities for the rival groups to berate and attack each other. . . . They threw paper, food and vile names at each other at the tables" (Sherif, 1956, pp. 57–58).

Finally, experimenters manufactured a series of crises that could be resolved only if all the boys combined their efforts and resources and cooperated. The water supply, sabotaged by the experimenters, could be restored only if all the boys worked together. After a week of several activities requiring cooperation, cut-throat competition gave way to cooperative exchanges. Friendships developed between groups, and before the end of the experiment, peace was declared. Working together toward shared goals had turned hostility into friendship.

According to *social-cognitive theory*, people learn attitudes of prejudice and hatred the same way they learn other attitudes. If children hear their parents, teachers, peers, and others openly express prejudices toward different racial, ethnic, or cultural groups, they may be quick to learn such attitudes. And if parents, peers, and others reward children with smiles and approval for parroting their own prejudices (operant conditioning), children may learn these prejudices even more quickly. Phillips and Ziller (1997) suggest that people learn to be nonprejudiced in the same way.

Social cognition refers to the ways in which people typically process social information—the mental processes used to notice, interpret, and remember information about the social world. The very processes we use to simplify, categorize, and order the social world are the same processes that distort our views of it. So, prejudice may arise not only from heated negative emotions and hatred toward other social groups, but also from cooler cognitive processes that govern how we think and process social information (Kunda & Oleson, 1995).

One way people simplify, categorize, and order the world is by using stereotypes. **Stereotypes** are widely shared beliefs about the characteristic traits, attitudes, and

◆ **in-group**
A social group with a strong sense of togetherness, from which others are excluded.

◆ **out-group**
A social group made up of individuals specifically identified by the in-group as not belonging.

◆ **social cognition**
The mental processes that people use to notice, interpret, and remember information about the social world.

◆ **stereotypes**
Widely shared beliefs about the characteristic traits, attitudes, and behaviors of members of various social groups (racial, ethnic, or religious), including the assumption that the members of such groups are usually all alike.

Can you perceive differences among the young girls shown here? Research shows that people typically perceive more variability among members of groups to which they belong and more similarity among members of groups with which they are unfamiliar.

behaviors of members of various social groups (racial, ethnic, or religious), including the assumption that "they" are usually all alike. Once a stereotype is in place, people tend to pay more attention to information that confirms their beliefs than to information that challenges them (Wigboldus et al., 2003).

Some research has revealed that people tend to perceive more diversity or more variability within the groups to which they belong (in-groups), but they see more similarity among members of other groups (out-groups) (Ostrom et al., 1993). For example, White Americans see more diversity among themselves but more sameness within groups of African Americans or Asian Americans. This tendency in thinking can also be based on gender, age, or any other characteristic. One study showed that a group of 100 young college students believed there was much more variability or diversity in their group than in a group of 100 elderly Americans, whom the students perceived to be much the same (Linville et al., 1989). And a study involving elderly adults showed that they perceived more variability within their own age group than among college students. Age stereotypes can be even more pronounced and negative than gender stereotypes (Kite et al., 1991).

The tendency to be less sensitive to variations among members of other groups may arise from a general tendency to look at people and situations from the perspective of one's own racial or cultural group. This tendency is often called **ethnocentrism.** In work settings, ethnocentrism may prevent us from realizing that co-workers from different backgrounds sometimes perceive the same incidents quite differently. For example, researchers have found that African Americans are more likely than Whites to perceive negative encounters between supervisors and subordinates of different races as being racial in nature (Johnson et al., 2003). To complicate matters further, members of each group believe that such opinions are either right or wrong. Because of ethnocentrism, Whites will insist that their view is the correct one; African Americans will take the same position about their view. To address this problem, many organizations provide workers with training geared toward helping them understand that such differences do not involve one view that is right and another that is wrong. Instead, each perspective is deserving of respect by the other.

◆ **ethnocentrism**

The tendency to look at situations from one's own racial or cultural perspective.

Is Prejudice Decreasing?

◆ *What evidence suggests that prejudice and discrimination are decreasing?*

Few people will readily admit to being prejudiced. Gordon Allport (1954), a pioneer in research on prejudice, said, "Defeated intellectually, prejudice lingers emotionally" (p. 328). Even those who are sincerely intellectually opposed to prejudice may still harbor some prejudiced feelings (Devine, 1989). However, most people feel guilty when they catch themselves having prejudiced thoughts or engaging in discriminatory behavior (Volis et al., 2002).

Is there any evidence that prejudice is decreasing in U.S. society? Gallup polls have revealed that White Americans became more racially tolerant over the final decades of the 20th century (Gallup & Hugick, 1990). When White Americans were asked in 1990 whether they would move if African Americans were to move next door to them, 93% said no, compared with 65% in 1965. Even if African Americans were to move into their neighborhood in great numbers, 68% of White Americans still said they would not move. Moreover, both White and African Americans overwhelmingly agree that conditions have improved for minorities in the United States over the past several decades (Public Agenda Online, 2002). However, there are still marked differences of opinion among ethnic groups as to whether racism continues to be a problem in the United States, as you can see in Figure 14.7. Moreover, studies show that people continue to cite fear of rejection as the reason why they don't engage in more social contact with others of different races (Shelton & Richeson, 2005).

FIGURE 14.7   **Perceptions of Racism in the United States**

African Americans and Hispanic Americans are more likely than White Americans to say that racism is a major problem in various areas of life.   *Source:* Data from Princeton Survey Research/Kaiser Family Foundation (1999).

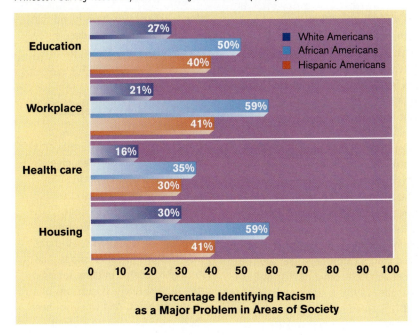

Percentage Identifying Racism as a Major Problem in Areas of Society

Recall, too, that attitudes do not always predict behavior. In a recent study, researchers asked participants to judge whether a fictitious woman was qualified to be the president of a parent-teacher organization (Lott & Saxon, 2002). Participants were provided with information about the woman's occupation and education. In addition, they were told, based on random assignment, that the woman was Hispanic, Anglo-Saxon, or Jewish in ethnic origin. The experimenters found that participants who believed the woman to be Hispanic were more likely to say that she was not qualified for the position than those who thought her to be Anglo-Saxon or Jewish. Moreover, researchers have learned that teachers are more likely to attribute White children's behavior problems to situational factors and those of minority children to dispositional factors (Jackson, 2002).

Such studies suggest that racial stereotyping is still evident in the United States. But there are many things we can do to combat prejudice and discrimination, as you will learn from reading the *Apply It* (on page 448).

Looking Back   At the beginning of the chapter, you learned about the disturbing findings from studies conducted by one of the pioneers of social psychology, Stanley Milgram. As you have seen, his research demonstrated only one of the many ways that social forces can influence individual behavior. You may have also noticed that many of the theories and studies in social psychology arose out of a desire to answer important questions about life. Milgram's brilliant experiment began as an effort to comprehend what appeared to be an incomprehensible event, the Holocaust. His work and that of other social psychologists demonstrate that psychology is a field with a great deal of relevance to the real world, whether that world consists of momentous historical events or the more ordinary happenings of everyday life.

Apply It 14.1 "Unlearning" Prejudice

Today's college population is more diverse than ever before. In the United States, members of minority groups are attending college in higher numbers. And people from cultures all over the world come to the United States to further their educations. Consequently, for many young people, campus life represents a unique opportunity to interact with others of different racial, ethnic, or cultural groups. How can students make the most of this opportunity to "unlearn" the prejudices they may bring with them to college?

Intergroup Contact

As you learned from the Robber's Cave experiment (Sherif & Sherif, 1967), intergroup contact can sometimes lead to increased stereotyping. Under the right conditions, though, intergroup contact can reduce prejudice. College can provide a context in which students from diverse backgrounds study together, endure the same trials (midterms and finals), develop a shared sense of school spirit, join clubs in which members from different backgrounds share common goals, and so on.

The Jigsaw Technique

Methods such as the *jigsaw technique,* a strategy that works well in college classrooms and as a game in less formal interactions, represent a more direct approach. Each participant in a jigsaw group is given a small amount of information and asked to teach it to other participants. The group must use all the individual pieces of information to solve a problem. This approach increases interaction among participants and helps them develop empathy for members of other ethnic and racial groups (Aronson, 1988; Aronson et al., 1978; Singh, 1991; Walker & Crogan, 1998). A side benefit is that it is an effective way of learning a new solution to a problem.

Diversity Education

Many colleges offer students and faculty opportunities to participate in seminars and workshops designed to combat racism. In such settings, participants learn about racial and cultural perspectives that may differ from their own. They also learn to identify behaviors that may be construed as racist by others, even when that may not be what they intend. Researchers have found that such programs help to reduce automatic stereotyping among participants (Hill & Augoustinos, 2001; Rudman et al., 2001).

Open Discussions of Prejudice and Discrimination

Perhaps the greatest potential of the college campus for reducing prejudice and discrimination lies in the nature of its intellectual climate. Traditionally, college classes, as well as club meetings, gatherings at restaurants, all-night study sessions in coffee shops, and late-night debates in dorm rooms, often feature lively discussions of a variety of topics. And when we hear others speak passionately about racism, sexism, and other types of injustice, we are likely to adopt more tolerant attitudes ourselves.

So, the next time you hear someone make a statement you feel is racist or sexist or prejudiced in any way, speak up! You never know how influential your voice might be.

Chapter 14 Summary

◆ Social Perception p. 426

◆ Why are first impressions so important? p. 426

First impressions are important because (1) people attend more carefully to the first information they receive about another person, and (2) once formed, an impression acts as a framework through which later information is interpreted.

◆ What is the difference between a situational attribution and a dispositional attribution? p. 427

In making a situational attribution, people attribute the cause of the behavior to some factor operating within the situation. With a dispositional attribution, the inferred cause is internal, such as some personal trait, motive, or attitude.

◆ Attraction p. 428

◆ What factors contribute to attraction? p. 428

Proximity contributes to attraction and increases the likelihood that there will be repeated contacts. There is a tendency to feel more positively toward a stimulus as a result of repeated exposure to it (the mere-exposure effect). Our moods and emotions influence how much we are attracted to those we meet. We also tend to like people who like us (reciprocity). Other factors that contribute to attraction are similarities in age, gender, race, and socioeconomic class and similar views and interests.

◆ **How important is physical attractiveness to attraction?**   p. 428

Physical attractiveness is a major factor in attraction for people of all ages. People attribute positive qualities to those who are physically attractive, a phenomenon called the halo effect.

◆ **How do psychologists explain romantic attraction and mating?** p. 429

Psychologists have proposed the matching hypothesis to explain the finding that people are often attracted to others who are similar to themselves. Evolutionary psychologists argue that men and women are attracted to one another on the basis of what each can contribute to the creation and support of a family.

◆ **Conformity, Obedience, and Compliance** p. 430

◆ **What did Asch find in his famous experiment on conformity?**   p. 430

In Asch's classic study on conformity, 5% of the participants went along with the incorrect, unanimous majority all the time; 70% went along some of the time; and 25% remained completely independent.

◆ **What did researchers find when they varied the circumstances of Milgram's classic study of obedience?**   p. 431

Participants were almost as likely to obey experimenters when the study was repeated at a shabby office building rather than at Yale University. However, when participants were paired with confederates who refused to obey the experimenter, they were less likely to obey.

◆ **What are three techniques used to gain compliance?**   p. 432

Three techniques often used to gain compliance are the foot-in-the-door technique, the door-in-the-face technique, and the low-ball technique.

◆ **Group Influence** p. 433

◆ **How does social facilitation affect performance?**   p. 433

When others are present, either as an audience or as co-actors, people's performance on easy tasks is usually improved through social facilitation. However, performance on difficult tasks is usually impaired.

◆ **What is social loafing, and what factors reduce it?**   p. 433

Social loafing is people's tendency to put forth less effort when they are working with others on a common task than when working alone. It is less likely to occur when individual output can be monitored or when people have a personal stake in the outcome.

◆ **How do social roles influence individual behavior?**   p. 434

Individual behavior can be guided by the expectations associated with certain social roles. The effects of such roles can be either negative or positive.

◆ **Attitudes and Attitude Change** p. 435

◆ **What are the three components of an attitude?**   p. 435

An attitude usually has a cognitive, an emotional, and a behavioral component.

◆ **What is cognitive dissonance, and how can it be reduced?**   p. 436

Cognitive dissonance is an unpleasant state that can occur when people become aware of inconsistencies among their attitudes or between their attitudes and their behavior. People can reduce cognitive dissonance by changing the behavior or the attitude or by explaining away the inconsistency or minimizing its importance.

◆ **What are the elements of persuasion?**   p. 437

The four elements of persuasion are the source of the communication, the audience, the message, and the medium.

◆ **Prosocial Behavior** p. 438

◆ **What motivates one person to help another?**   p. 438

Some prosocial behavior is motivated by altruism. In other cases, cultural norms influence helping behavior. We are more likely to help those in need if we are in a committed relationship with them or we perceive them to be similar to us.

◆ **What is the bystander effect, and why does it occur?**   p. 439

The bystander effect is a social factor that affects prosocial behavior: As the number of bystanders at an emergency increases, the probability that the victim will receive help decreases, and the help, if given, is likely to be delayed. The bystander effect may be due in part to diffusion of responsibility or the influence of other bystanders who seem calm.

◆ **Aggression** p. 440

◆ **What biological factors are thought to be related to aggression?** p. 440

Biological factors thought to be related to aggression are a genetic link in criminal behavior, low arousal levels, high testosterone levels, low levels of serotonin, and brain damage or certain brain disorders.

◆ **What other factors contribute to aggression?**   p. 442

The frustration-aggression hypothesis holds that frustration produces aggression and that this aggression may be directed at the person causing the frustration or displaced onto another target, as in scapegoating. Aggression has been associated with aversive conditions such as pain, heat, loud noise, and foul odors and with unpleasant emotional states such as sadness, grief, and depression. Invasions of privacy and crowding may also contribute to aggression. Finally, belief in the superiority of one's own group may lead to aggression toward outsiders.

◆ **According to social learning theory, what causes aggressive behavior?**   p. 443

According to social learning theory, people acquire aggressive responses by observing aggressive models, in the family, the subculture, and the media, and by having aggressive responses reinforced.

◆ Prejudice and Discrimination p. 444

◆ What factors contribute to the development of prejudice and discrimination? p. 444

Prejudice consists of attitudes (usually negative) toward others based on their gender, religion, race, or membership in a particular group. Discrimination consists of actions (usually negative) against others based on the same factors. Prejudice can arise out of competition for scarce resources or from people's tendency to divide the world into distinct social categories—in-groups and out-groups. According to social-cognitive theory, prejudice is learned in the same way that other attitudes are—through modeling and reinforcement.

◆ What evidence suggests that prejudice and discrimination are decreasing? p. 446

White Americans are less likely to object to living in racially mixed neighborhoods than in the past. But ethnic groups still have varying views of the degree to which prejudice and discrimination continue to be problematic in the United States.

Study Guide 14

Answers to all the Study Guide questions are provided at the end of the book.

◆ SECTION ONE: Chapter Review

Social Perception (pp. 426–427)

1. Which of the following statements about first impressions is *false?*
   a. People usually pay closer attention to early information they receive about a person than to later information.
   b. Early information forms a framework through which later information is interpreted.
   c. First impressions often serve as self-fulfilling prophecies.
   d. The importance of first impressions is greatly overrated.

2. People tend to make _____ attributions to explain their own behavior and _____ attributions to explain the behavior of others.
   a. situational; situational
   b. situational; dispositional
   c. dispositional; situational
   d. dispositional; dispositional

3. Attributing Mike's poor grade to his lack of ability is a dispositional attribution. (true/false)

Attraction (pp. 427–430)

4. Match each term with a description.
   ____ (1) Brian sees Kelly at the library often and begins to like her.
   ____ (2) Lori assumes that because Michael is handsome, he must be popular and sociable.
   ____ (3) Kate and Kurt are going together and are both very attractive.
   a. matching hypothesis
   b. halo effect
   c. mere-exposure effect

5. Physical attractiveness is a very important factor in initial attraction. (true/false)

6. People are usually drawn to those who are more opposite than similar to themselves. (true/false)

Conformity, Obedience, and Compliance (pp. 430–432)

7. Match the technique for gaining compliance with the appropriate example.
   ____ (1) Meghan agrees to sign a letter supporting an increase in taxes for road construction. Later she agrees to make 100 phone calls urging people to vote for the measure.
   ____ (2) Jude refuses a phone request for a $24 donation to send four needy children to the circus but does agree to give $6.
   ____ (3) Lexie agrees to babysit for her next-door neighbors' two girls and then is informed that their three nephews will be there, too.
   a. door-in-the-face technique
   b. low-ball technique
   c. foot-in-the-door technique

8. What percentage of subjects in the Asch study never conformed to the majority's unanimous incorrect response?
   a. 70%   c. 25%
   b. 33%   d. 5%

9. What percentage of the subjects in Milgram's original obedience experiment administered what they thought was the maximum 450-volt shock?
   a. 85%   c. 45%
   b. 65%   d. 25%

Group Influence (pp. 432–434)

10. Which of the following statements regarding the effects of social facilitation (the presence of other people) is true?
    a. Performance improves on all tasks.
    b. Performance worsens on all tasks.
    c. Performance improves on easy tasks and worsens on difficult tasks.
    d. Performance improves on difficult tasks and worsens on easy tasks.

11. Social loafing is most likely to occur when
    a. individual output is monitored.
    b. individual output is evaluated.
    c. a task is challenging.
    d. individual output cannot be identified.

12. What occurs when members of a very cohesive group are more concerned with preserving group solidarity than with evaluating all possible alternatives in making a decision?
    a. groupthink   c. social facilitation
    b. group polarization d. social loafing

Attitudes and Attitude Change (pp. 435–438)

13. Which of the following is *not* one of the three components of an attitude?
    a. cognitive component
    b. emotional component
    c. physiological component
    d. behavioral component

14. All of the following are ways to reduce cognitive dissonance *except*
    a. changing an attitude.
    b. changing a behavior.
    c. explaining away the inconsistency.
    d. strengthening the attitude and behavior.

15. People who have made a great sacrifice to join a group usually decrease their liking for the group. (true/false)

16. Credibility relates most directly to the communicator's
    a. attractiveness.
    b. expertise and trustworthiness.
    c. likability.
    d. personality.

17. With a well-informed audience, two-sided messages are more persuasive than one-sided messages. (true/false)

18. High-fear appeals are more effective than low-fear appeals if they provide definite actions that people can take to avoid dreaded outcomes. (true/false)

Prosocial Behavior (pp. 438–439)

19. The bystander effect is influenced by all of the following *except*
    a. the number of bystanders.
    b. the personalities of bystanders.
    c. whether the bystanders appear calm.
    d. whether the situation is ambiguous.

20. Altruism is one form of prosocial behavior. (true/false)

21. As the number of bystanders at an emergency increases, the probability that the victim will receive help decreases. (true/false)

22. In an ambiguous situation, a good way to determine if an emergency exists is to look at the reactions of other bystanders. (true/false)

Aggression (pp. 440–444)

23. Social psychologists generally believe that aggression stems from an aggressive instinct. (true/false)

24. Pain, extreme heat, loud noise, and foul odors have all been associated with an increase in aggressive responses. (true/false)

25. According to the frustration-aggression hypothesis, frustration _____ leads to aggression.
   a. always   **b.** often   **c.** rarely   **d.** never

26. Which of the following statements is *not* true of personal space?
   a. It functions to protect privacy and regulate intimacy.
   b. How much personal space a person requires is affected by culture, race, gender, and personality.
   c. The size of a person's personal space is fixed.
   d. Invasions of personal space are usually perceived as unpleasant.

27. The social learning theory of aggression emphasizes all of the following *except* that
   a. aggressive responses are learned from the family, the subculture, and the media.
   b. aggressive acts are learned through modeling.
   c. most aggression results from frustration.
   d. when aggression responses are reinforced, they are more likely to continue.

28. Research tends to support the notion that a person can drain off aggressive energy by watching others behave aggressively in sports or on television. (true/false)

29. Research suggests that media violence is probably related to increased aggression. (true/false)

Prejudice and Discrimination (pp. 444–447)

30. Match the example with the term.
   _____ **(1)** Carlotta hired a woman to be her assistant because she doesn't like working with men.
   _____ **(2)** Darlene thinks that all Asian students are good at math.
   _____ **(3)** Bill canceled a blind date with Ellen when he heard that she was overweight.
   a. stereotypic thinking
   b. discrimination
   c. prejudice

31. Social learning theory asserts that prejudice develops and is maintained through
   a. competition.
   b. us-versus-them thinking.
   c. modeling and reinforcement.
   d. genetic inheritance.

32. African Americans no longer believe that racism is a major problem in U.S. society. (true/false)

33. Ethnocentrism is the tendency to look at others from their own group's point of view. (true/false)

◆ **SECTION TWO: Match Terms with Definitions**

_____ **(1)** effect of one major positive or negative trait

_____ **(2)** as more viewers gather at the scene of an emergency, a victim's chances of help are reduced

_____ **(3)** geographic closeness

_____ **(4)** the blocking of an impulse

_____ **(5)** attitudes and standards of a group

_____ **(6)** relatively stable evaluation of a person, object, situation, or issue

_____ **(7)** impact of passive spectators on performance

_____ **(8)** the tendency of individuals to go along with the group even if they disagree

_____ **(9)** widely shared beliefs about traits of members of certain groups

_____ **(10)** the fact that one's overall impression is influenced by a first impression

_____ **(11)** displacing aggression onto innocent people

_____ **(12)** making a large request in the hope of gaining compliance with a subsequent small request

_____ **(13)** the intentional infliction of harm on another

a. frustration

b. proximity

c. aggression

d. scapegoating

e. bystander effect

f. halo effect

g. door-in-the-face technique

h. social norms

i. attitude

j. groupthink

k. stereotypes

l. audience effect

m. primacy effect

1. A(n) _____ is a relatively stable evaluation of a person, object, situation, or issue.

2. Research reveals that our overall impression of another person is more influenced by the first information we have about the individual than by later information about the person. This tendency is called the _____ _____.

3. Jaime explained his poor grade on his math test by saying that he is a right-brained person and, therefore, more the artistic type than the analytical type. He is making a _____ attribution.

4. We tend to use _____ factors to explain our own behavior and _____ factors to explain the behavior of others.

5. Sal tends to attribute his successes to internal factors and his failure to situational factors. This tendency is known as the _____ _____ _____.

6. People tend to infer generally positive or negative traits in a person as a result of observing one major positive or negative trait. This tendency is known as the _____ effect.

7. A classic study in social psychology is Milgram's research on _____. His experiment revealed that most participants were willing to follow orders and deliver the strongest possible shock to a confederate for giving wrong answers in a memory test.

8. Individual performance may be affected by the mere physical presence of others. This effect is known as _____ _____.

9. Group polarization refers to the tendency of group members, following a discussion, to take a more _____ position on the issue at hand.

10. A(n) _____ is a widely shared belief about the characteristics of members of various social groups and includes the assumption that all members of a social group are alike.

11. As the number of bystanders at an emergency increases, the probability that anyone will help a victim decreases. This phenomenon is known as the _____ effect.

12. Theo suffered serious injury while attempting to save a child from being run over by a car. Theo's action is an example of _____.

13. The _____ hypothesis suggests that frustration can result in aggression.

14. _____ occurs when a person is the undeserving victim of someone else's displaced aggression, which is due to that person's frustration.

15. A(n) _____ is an inference about the cause of our own or another's behavior.

16. _____ is changing or adopting an attitude or behavior to be consistent with the norms of a group or the expectations of others.

◆ **SECTION FOUR: Comprehensive Practice Test**

1. Dispositional attribution is to _____ as situational attribution is to _____.
   a. external factors; internal factors
   b. others; self
   c. self; others
   d. internal factors; external factors

2. Crystal attributed Asher's poor oral presentation to his basic lack of motivation to be a good student and to be prepared for class. Assuming Crystal was wrong and Asher's poor performance was due to some other, external factor, Crystal was making an error called the self-serving bias. (true/false)

3. Crystal's own oral presentation was also poor. She explained that the students in the front row were goofing off and distracting her. Crystal was excusing her performance with the
   a. primary attribution error.
   b. fundamental self-bias error.
   c. self-serving bias.
   d. error of external factors.

4. The concept of proximity relates to
   a. attribution.   c. aggression.
   b. attraction.   d. prejudice.

5. In the past few decades people have become less influenced by physical attractiveness and more influenced by internal factors such as personality. (true/false)

6. Jesse's mother reminded him to check his tie and comb his hair prior to meeting the interviewer at his college admissions interview. Jesse's mother was probably concerned about the _____ effect.
   a. attenuation   c. Harvard
   b. Soloman   d. halo

7. The old adage "Birds of a feather flock together" summarizes the concept of _____, one of the factors that influence attraction.
   a. attribution
   b. social influence
   c. similarity
   d. proximity

8. Research reveals that low autonomic nervous system arousal levels seem to be related to aggressive behavior. (true/false)

9. Messsages about smoking are most effective if framed _____, while those about dietary change are best if framed _____.
   a. positively, negatively
   b. negatively, positively

10. The terms *stereotype* and *prejudice* are actually different words for the same thing. (true/false)

11. A negative attitude toward a person based on gender, religion, race, or membership in a certain group is known as
   a. discrimination.
   b. prejudice.
   c. a stereotype.
   d. social dissonance.

12. Strategies such as changing a behavior, changing an attitude, explaining away an inconsistency, or minimizing the importance of an inconsistency are all used to reduce
   a. cognitive distortion bias.
   b. relative attribution frustration.
   c. cognitive dissonance.
   d. inconsistency anxiety.

13. _____ are the attitudes and standards of behavior expected of members of a particular group.
   a. Values
   b. Social rules
   c. Social norms
   d. Social postures

14. Those who hold a minority opinion have more influence on a majority group if
   a. the opinion is stated vaguely so its departure from the majority opinion is disguised.
   b. the opinion is clearly stated and well organized.

c. the opinion is stated as a question.
d. the opinion is stated with qualifications that complement the majority opinion.

15. One strategy to induce compliance to a request is known as the _____ technique. In this strategy, the person making the request secures a favorable response to a small request with the aim of making the person more likely to agree to a larger request later.
   a. door-in-the-face
   b. low-ball
   c. foot-in-the-door
   d. risky shift

16. A good example of the door-in-the-face technique is to ask $10,000 for your used car, hoping that the buyer, who is likely to refuse to pay that much, will then be willing to agree to pay $8,000, the price you wanted in the first place. (true/false)

17. Social loafing refers to
   a. the tendency to avoid social contact and interpersonal relationships.
   b. the tendency to exert less effort when working with others on a common task.
   c. the tendency to be less productive when working alone than with others.
   d. the tendency to see others' work as more externally motivated than one's own.

18. A common finding on audience effects is that when we are being watched, we tend to do better on easy tasks and on more difficult tasks at which we are more proficient. (true/false)

19. Which of the following is *not* listed as a component of an attitude?
   a. social component
   b. behavioral component
   c. cognitive component
   d. emotional component

◆ **SECTION FIVE: Critical Thinking**

1. Prepare a convincing argument supporting each of these positions:
   a. The Milgram study should have been conducted because it provided vitally important information about the troubling human tendency to inflict pain and suffering on others in obedience to authority figures.
   b. Despite the value of the knowledge the Milgram study provided, it should never have been conducted because it subjected research participants to tremendous stress.

2. Prepare a convincing argument supporting each of these positions:
   a. Aggression results largely from biological factors (nature).
   b. Aggression is primarily learned (nurture).

3. Review the factors influencing impression formation and attraction discussed in this chapter. Prepare a dual list of behaviors indicating what you should and should not do if you wish to make a better impression on other people and to increase their liking for you.

Appendix

Statistical Methods

Statistics, a branch of mathematics, enables psychologists and other scientists to organize, describe, and draw conclusions about the quantitative results of their studies. We will explore the two basic types of statistics that psychologists use—descriptive statistics and inferential statistics.

Descriptive Statistics

Descriptive statistics are statistics used to organize, summarize, and describe data. Descriptive statistics include measures of central tendency, variability, and relationship.

Measures of Central Tendency

A **measure of central tendency** is a measure or score that describes the center, or middle, of a distribution of scores. The most widely used and most familiar measure of central tendency is the **mean,** the arithmetic average of a group of scores. The mean is computed by adding all the single scores and dividing the sum by the number of scores.

Carl sometimes studies and does well in his classes, but he occasionally procrastinates and fails a test. Table A.1 shows how Carl performed on the seven tests in his psychology class last semester. Carl computes his mean score by adding up all his test scores and dividing the sum by the number of tests. Carl's mean, or average, score is 80.

The mean is an important and widely used statistical measure of central tendency, but it can be misleading when a group of scores contains one or several extreme scores. Table A.2 (on page AP-2) lists the annual incomes of ten people in rank order. When an income of $1 million is averaged with several more modest incomes, the mean does not provide a true picture of the group. Therefore, when one or a few individuals score far above or below the middle range of a group, a different measure of central tendency should be used. The **median** is the middle score or value when a group of scores are arranged from highest to lowest. When there are an odd number of scores, the score in the middle is the median. When there are an even number of scores, the median is the average of the two middle scores. For the ten incomes arranged from highest to lowest in Table A.2, the median is $27,000, which is the average of the middle incomes, $28,000 and $26,000. The $27,000 median income is a truer reflection of the comparative income of the group than is the $124,700 mean.

Another measure of central tendency is the **mode.** The mode is easy to find because it is the score that occurs most frequently in a group of scores. The mode of the annual-income group in Table A.2 is $22,000.

Describing Data with Tables and Graphs

A researcher tested 100 students for recall of 20 new vocabulary words 24 hours after they had memorized the list. The researcher organized the scores in a **frequency distribution**—an arrangement showing the numbers of scores that fall

---

◆ **descriptive statistics**

Statistics used to organize, summarize, and describe data.

◆ **measure of central tendency**

A measure or score that describes the center, or middle, of a distribution of scores (example: mean, median, or mode).

◆ **mean**

The arithmetic average of a group of scores; calculated by adding all the single scores and dividing the sum by the number of scores.

◆ **median**

The middle score or value when a group of scores are arranged from highest to lowest.

◆ **mode**

The score that occurs most frequently in a group of scores.

◆ **frequency distribution**

An arrangement showing the numbers of scores that fall within equal-sized class intervals.

TABLE A.1 Carl's Psychology Test Scores	
Test 1	98
Test 2	74
Test 3	86
Test 4	92
Test 5	56
Test 6	68
Test 7	86
Sum:	560
Mean: 560 ÷ 7 = 80	

TABLE A.2 — Annual Income for Ten People

SUBJECT	ANNUAL INCOME
1	$1,000,000
2	$50,000
3	$43,000
4	$30,000
5	$28,000
6	$26,000
7	$22,000
8	$22,000
9	$16,000
10	$10,000
Sum:	$1,247,000

$27,000 = Median

Mode

Mean: $1,247,000 ÷ 10 = $124,700
Median: $27,000
Mode: $22,000

within equal-sized class intervals. To organize the 100 test scores, the researcher decided to use intervals of 2 points each. Next, the researcher tallied the frequency (number of scores) within each 2-point interval. Table A.3 presents the resulting frequency distribution.

The researcher then made a **histogram**, a bar graph that depicts the number of scores within each class interval in the frequency distribution. The intervals are plotted along the horizontal axis, and the frequency of scores in each interval is plotted along the vertical axis. Figure A.1 shows the histogram for the 100 test scores.

◆ **histogram**

A bar graph that depicts the number of scores within each class interval in a frequency distribution.

TABLE A.3 — Frequency Distribution of 100 Vocabulary Test Scores

CLASS INTERVAL	TALLY OF SCORES IN EACH CLASS INTERVAL	NUMBER OF SCORES IN EACH CLASS INTERVAL (FREQUENCY)
1–2	|	1
3–4	||	2
5–6	JHT |	6
7–8	JHT JHT JHT |||	18
9–10	JHT JHT JHT JHT |||	23
11–12	JHT JHT JHT JHT |||	23
13–14	JHT JHT JHT ||	17
15–16	JHT |||	8
17–18	|	1
19–20	|	1

FIGURE A.1 A Frequency Histogram

Vocabulary test scores from the frequency distribution in Table A.3 are plotted here in the form of a histogram. Class intervals of 2 points each appear on the horizontal axis. Frequencies of the scores in each class interval are plotted on the vertical axis.

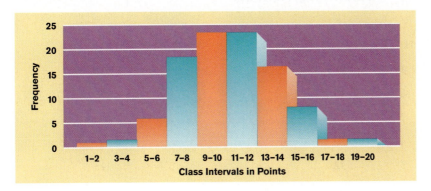

Another common method of representing frequency data is the **frequency polygon**. As in a histogram, the class intervals are plotted along the horizontal axis and the frequencies are plotted along the vertical axis. However, in a frequency polygon, each class interval is represented by a graph point that is placed at the middle (midpoint) of the class interval so that its vertical distance above the horizontal axis shows the frequency of that interval. Lines are drawn to connect the points, as shown in Figure A.2. The histogram and the frequency polygon are simply two different ways of presenting data.

Measures of Variability

In addition to a measure of central tendency, researchers need a measure of the **variability** of a set of scores—how much the scores spread out, away from the mean. Both groups in Table A.4 (on page AP-4) have a mean and a median of 80. However, the scores in Group II cluster tightly around the mean, while the scores in Group I vary widely from the mean.

The simplest measure of variability is the **range**—the difference between the highest and lowest scores in a distribution of scores. Table A.4 reveals that Group I has a range of 47, indicating high variability, while Group II has a range of only 7, showing low variability. Unfortunately, the range reveals only the difference between the lowest score and the highest score; it tells nothing about the scores in between.

The **standard deviation** is a descriptive statistic reflecting the average amount that scores in a distribution deviate, or vary, from their mean. The larger the standard deviation, the greater the variability in a distribution of scores. Refer to Table A.4 and note the standard deviations for the two distributions of test scores. In Group I, the relatively large standard deviation of 18.1 reflects the wide variability in that distribution. By contrast, the small standard deviation of 2.14 in Group II indicates that the variability is low, and you can see that the scores cluster tightly around the mean.

The Normal Curve

Psychologists and other scientists often use descriptive statistics in connection with an important type of frequency distribution known

◆ **frequency polygon**
A line graph that depicts the frequency, or number, of scores within each class interval in a frequency distribution.

◆ **variability**
How much the scores in a distribution spread out, away from the mean.

◆ **range**
The difference between the highest score and the lowest score in a distribution of scores.

◆ **standard deviation**
A descriptive statistic reflecting the average amount that scores in a distribution deviate, or vary, from their mean.

FIGURE A.2 A Frequency Polygon

Vocabulary test scores from the frequency distribution in Table A.3 are plotted here in the form of a frequency polygon. Class intervals of 2 points each appear on the horizontal axis. Frequencies of the scores in each class interval are plotted on the vertical axis.

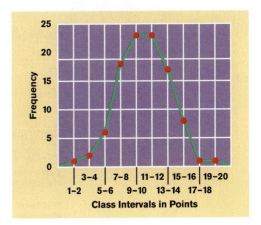

| TABLE A.4 | Comparison of Range and Standard Deviation for Two Small Groups of Scores Having Identical Means and Medians |

GROUP I			GROUP II		
TEST	SCORE		TEST	SCORE	
1	99		1	83	
2	99		2	82	
3	98		3	81	
4	80	Median	4	80	Median
5	72		5	79	
6	60		6	79	
7	52		7	76	
Sum:	560		Sum:	560	

Mean: 560 ÷ 7 = 80
Median: 80
Range: 99 − 52 = 47
Standard deviation: 18.1

Mean: 560 ÷ 7 = 80
Median: 80
Range: 83 − 76 = 7
Standard deviation: 2.14

◆ **normal curve**

A symmetrical, bell-shaped frequency distribution that represents how scores are normally distributed in a population; most scores fall near the mean, and fewer and fewer scores occur in the extremes either above or below the mean.

as the **normal curve,** pictured in Figure A.3. If a large number of people are measured on any of a wide variety of traits (such as height or IQ score), the great majority of values will cluster in the middle, with fewer and fewer individuals measuring extremely low or high on these variables. Note that slightly more than 68% of the scores in a normal distribution fall within 1 standard deviation of the mean (34.13% within 1 standard deviation above the mean, and 34.13% within 1 standard deviation below the mean). Almost 95.5% of the scores in a normal distribution lie between 2 standard deviations

FIGURE A.3 The Normal Curve

The normal curve is a symmetrical, bell-shaped curve that represents how scores are normally distributed in a population. Slightly more than 68% of the scores in a normal distribution fall within 1 standard deviation above and below the mean. Almost 95.5% of the scores lie between 2 standard deviations above and below the mean, and about 99.75% fall between 3 standard deviations above and below the mean.

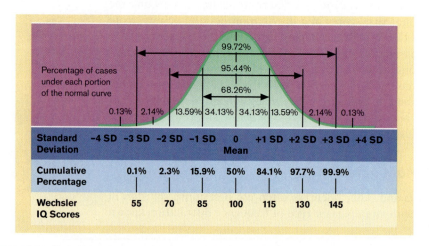

above and below the mean. The vast majority of scores in a normal distribution—99.72%—fall between 3 standard deviations above and below the mean.

Using the properties of the normal curve and knowing the mean and the standard deviation of a normal distribution, we can find where any score stands (how high or low) in relation to all the other scores in the distribution. For example, on the Wechsler intelligence scales, the mean IQ is 100 and the standard deviation is 15. Thus, 99.72% of the population has an IQ score within 3 standard deviations above and below the mean, ranging from an IQ of 55 to an IQ of 145.

The Correlation Coefficient

A **correlation coefficient** is a number that indicates the degree and direction of relationship between two variables. Correlation coefficients can range from +1.00 (a perfect positive correlation) to .00 (no correlation) to −1.00 (a perfect negative correlation), as illustrated in Figure A.4. A **positive correlation** indicates that two variables vary in the same direction. An increase in one variable is associated with an increase in the other variable, or a decrease in one variable is associated with a decrease in the other. There is a positive correlation between the number of hours college students spend studying and their grades. The more hours they study, the higher their grades are likely to be. A **negative correlation** means that an increase in one variable is associated with a decrease in the other variable. There may be a negative correlation between the number of hours students spend watching television and studying. The more hours they spend watching TV, the fewer hours they may spend studying, and vice versa.

The sign (+ or −) in a correlation coefficient merely tells whether the two variables vary in the same or opposite directions. (If no sign appears, the correlation is assumed to be positive.) The number in a correlation coefficient indicates the relative strength of the relationship between the two variables—the higher the number, the stronger the relationship. For example, a correlation of −.70 is higher than a correlation of +.56; a correlation of −.85 is just as strong as one of +.85. A correlation of .00

◆ **correlation coefficient**
A numerical value indicating the strength and direction of relationship between two variables, which ranges from +1.00 (a perfect positive correlation) to −1.00 (a perfect negative correlation).

◆ **positive correlation**
A relationship between two variables in which both vary in the same direction.

◆ **negative correlation**
A relationship between two variables in which an increase in one variable is associated with a decrease in the other variable.

FIGURE A.4 **Understanding Correlation Coefficients**

Correlation coefficients can range from −1.00 (a perfect negative correlation) through .00 (no correlation) to +1.00 (a perfect positive correlation). As the arrows indicate, a negative correlation exists when an increase in one variable is associated with a decrease in the other variable, and vice versa. A positive correlation exists when both variables tend to either increase or decrease together.

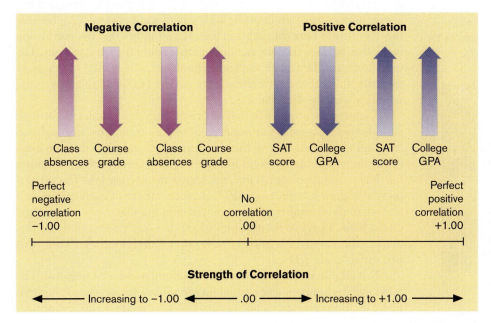

TABLE A.5	High School and College GPAs for 11 Students	
STUDENT	HIGH SCHOOL GPA (VARIABLE X)	COLLEGE GPA (VARIABLE Y)
1	2.0	1.8
2	2.2	2.5
3	2.3	2.5
4	2.5	3.1
5	2.8	3.2
6	3.0	2.2
7	3.0	2.8
8	3.2	3.3
9	3.3	2.9
10	3.5	3.2
11	3.8	3.5

indicates that no relationship exists between the variables. IQ and shoe size are examples of two variables that are not correlated.

Table A.5 shows the measurements of two variables—high school GPA and college GPA for 11 college students. Looking at the data, we can see that 6 of the 11 students had a higher GPA in high school, while 5 of the students had a higher GPA in college. A clearer picture of the actual relationship is shown by the *scatterplot* in Figure A.5. High school GPA (variable X) is plotted on the horizontal axis, and college GPA (variable Y) is plotted on the vertical axis.

One dot is plotted for each of the 11 students at the point where high school GPA, variable X, and college GPA, variable Y, intersect. For example, the first student is represented by a dot at the point where her high school GPA of 2.0 on the horizontal (x) axis and college GPA of 1.8 on the vertical (y) axis intersect. The scatterplot in Figure A.5 reveals a relatively high correlation between high school and college GPAs, because the dots cluster near the diagonal line. It also shows that the correlation is positive, because the dots run diagonally upward from left to right. The correlation coefficient for the high school and college GPAs of these 11 students is .71. If the correlation were perfect (1.00), all the dots would fall exactly on the diagonal line.

A scatterplot shows whether a correlation is low, moderate, or high and whether it is positive or negative. Scatterplots that run diagonally up from left to right reveal positive correlations. Scatterplots that run diagonally down from left to right indicate negative correlations. The closer the dots are to the diagonal line, the higher the correlation. The scatterplots in Figure A.6 (on page AP-7) depict a variety of correlations. It is important to remember that correlation does not demonstrate cause and effect. Even a perfect correlation (+1.00 or −1.00) does not mean that one variable causes or is caused by the other. Correlation shows only that two variables are related.

Not all relationships between variables are positive or negative. The relationships between some variables are said to be *curvilinear*. A curvilinear relationship exists when two variables correlate positively (or neg-

FIGURE A.5   **A Scatterplot**

A scatterplot reveals a relatively high positive correlation between the high school and college GPAs of the 11 students listed in Table A.5. One dot is plotted for each of the 11 students at the point where high school GPA (plotted on the horizontal axis) and college GPA (plotted on the vertical axis) intersect.

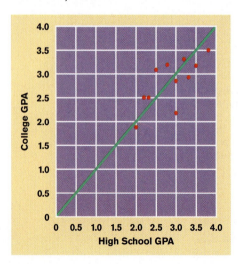

A scatterplot moving diagonally up from left to right, as in (a), indicates a positive correlation. A scatterplot moving diagonally down from left to right, as in (c), indicates a negative correlation. The more closely the dots cluster around a diagonal line, the higher the correlation. Scatterplot (b) indicates no correlation. Scatterplot (d) shows a curvilinear relationship that is positive up to a point and then becomes negative. Age and strength of handgrip have a curvilinear relationship: Handgrip increases in strength up to about age 40 and then decreases with continued aging.

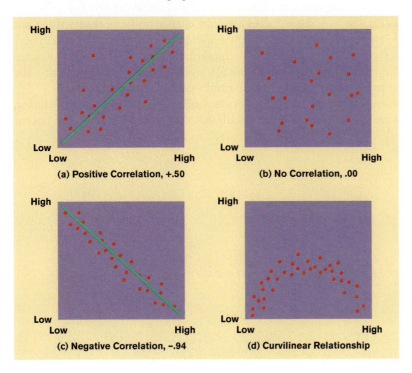

(a) Positive Correlation, +.50

(b) No Correlation, .00

(c) Negative Correlation, −.94

(d) Curvilinear Relationship

atively) up to a certain point and then change direction. For example, there is a positive correlation between physical strength and age up to about 40 or 45 years of age. As age increases from childhood to middle age, so does the strength of handgrip pressure. But beyond middle adulthood, the relationship becomes negative, and increasing age is associated with decreasing handgrip strength. Figure A.6(d) shows a scatterplot of this curvilinear relationship.

Inferential Statistics

Inferential statistics allow researchers (1) to make inferences about the characteristics of the larger population from their observations and measurements of a sample and (2) to derive estimates of how much faith or confidence can be placed in those inferences. In statistical theory, a **population** is the entire group that is of interest to researchers—the group to which they wish to apply their findings. For example, a population could be all the registered voters in the United States. Usually, researchers cannot directly measure and study the entire population of interest. Consequently, they make inferences about a population from a relatively small **sample** selected from that population. For researchers to draw conclusions about the larger population, the sample must be representative—that is, its characteristics must mirror those of the larger population. (See Chapter 1 for more information about representative samples.)

◆ **inferential statistics**
Statistical procedures that allow researchers to make inferences about the characteristics of the larger population from observations and measurements of a sample and to derive estimates of how much confidence can be placed in those inferences.

◆ **population**
The entire group of interest to researchers and to which they wish to generalize their findings; the group from which a sample is selected.

◆ **sample**
The portion of any population that is selected for study and from which generalizations are made about the entire population.

Statistical Significance

Suppose 200 students are randomly assigned either to an experimental group that will be taught psychology with innovative materials or to a control group that will receive traditional instruction. At the end of the semester, researchers find that the mean test scores of the experimental group are considerably higher than those of the control group. To conclude that the instructional methods caused the difference, the researchers must use **tests of statistical significance** to estimate how often the experimental results could have occurred by chance alone. The estimates derived from tests of statistical significance are stated as probabilities. A probability of .05 means that the experimental results would be expected to occur by chance no more than 5 times out of 100. The .05 level of significance is usually required as a minimum for researchers to conclude that their findings are statistically significant. Often the level of significance reached is even more impressive, such as the .01 level. The .01 level means that the probability is no more than 1 in 100 that the results occurred by chance.

The inferences researchers make are not absolute. They are based on probability, and there is always a possibility, however small, that experimental results could occur by chance. For this reason, replication of research studies is recommended.

◆ **tests of statistical significance**
Statistical tests that estimate the probability that a particular research result could have occurred by chance.

Answers to Study Guide Questions

Chapter 1

Section One: Chapter Review   1. scientific method
2. describe, explain, predict, influence   3. false   4. (1) c, (2) c,
(3) c, (4) a, (5) b, (6) a, (7) a, b, c 5. (1) c, (2) a, (3) d, (4) e, (5) b
6. (1) d, (2) c, (3) b, (4) a, (5) c, (6) b   7. (1) d, (2) a, (3) f, (4) e,
(5) b, (6) c   8. (1) d, (2) a, (3) b, (4) c   9. case study   10. false
11. true   12. independent variable, dependent variable   13. (1) d,
(2) c, (3) a, (4) b   14. c   15. d   16. false   17. correlation
coefficient   18. b   19. positive   20. negative   21. false   22. c
23. b   24. true   25. d   26. independent thinking, suspension of
judgment, willingness to modify or abandon prior judgements
27. b   28. (1) b, (2) c, (3) a, (4) b, (5) a, (6) c   29. (1) b, (2) c,
(3) d, (4) a, (5) e, (6) g, (7) f   30. (1) Yes, (2) No, (3) No, (4) No
31. clinical or counseling   32. many

Section Two: Who Said This?   1. Skinner   2. Wundt
3. James   4. Watson   5. Maslow   6. Sumner   7. Calkins
8. Rogers   9. Wertheimer

Section Three: Fill In the Blank   1. theory   2. naturalistic
observation   3. population, representative sample   4. hypothesis   5. independent, dependent   6. sociocultural   7. prediction,
cause, effect   8. structuralism   9. functionalism   10. psychoanalysis   11. cognitive   12. psychoanalytic   13. clinical and
counseling

Section Four: Comprehensive Practice Test   1. b   2. b
3. d   4. c   5. c   6. b   7. a   8. d   9. c   10. a   11. c   12. false
13. false   14. true   15. false   16. true   17. false   18. false
19. false   20. false   21. true

Chapter 2

Section One: Chapter Review   1. a   2. glial cells   3. c   4. d
5. action   6. b   7. b   8. Norepinephrine   9. Endorphins
10. GABA, serotonin   11. (1) b, (2) a, (3) f, (4) c, (5) e, (6) d,
(7) g   12. b   13. hippocampus   14. amygdala, hippocampus
15. b   16. a   17. (1) d, (2) c, (3) a, (4) b   18. (1) d, (2) a, (3) e,
(4) b, (5) c   19. (1) a, (2) b, (3) a, (4) b, (5) a   20. c   21. genetic
22. (1) b, (2) c, (3) a   23. b   24. a   25. c   26. c   27. c
28. synaptogenesis, myelination   29. white matter
30. processing navigation information, locating sounds
31. decreases   32. Stroke   33. b   34. c   35. (1) d, (2) a, (3) e,
(4) c, (5) b, (6) f   36. recessive   37. d   38. twin studies,
adoption studies

Section Two: Label the Brain   1. frontal lobe   2. motor
cortex   3. parietal lobe   4. occipital lobe   5. cerebellum
6. pons   7. medulla   8. corpus callosum   9. pituitary gland

Section Three: Fill In the Blank   1. dendrites   2. neurotransmitters   3. limbic   4. primary visual cortex   5. parietal
6. frontal   7. left   8. axon   9. brain, spinal cord   10. sympathetic   11. hypothalamus   12. action potential   13. Broca's
14. hippocampus   15. temporal   16. cerebellum   17. peripheral   18. cerebellum   19. left hippocampus   20. Fragile X
syndrome   21. Language processing

Section Four: Comprehensive Practice Test   1. b   2. d
3. d   4. a   5. c   6. b   7. c   8. b   9. d   10. b   11. a   12. c
13. c   14. d   15. true   16. true   17. Spatial perception
18. parietal   19. X chromosome

Chapter 3

Section One: Chapter Review   1. sensation   2. absolute
3. false   4. c   5. transduction   6. b   7. (1) d, (2) c, (3) b, (4) e,
(5) a   8. rods, cones   9. c   10. d   11. hertz, decibels   12. (1)
b, (2) a, (3) c   13. d   14. c   15. olfaction   16. c   17. sweet,
sour, salty, bitter, umami   18. taste bud   19. false   20. kinesthetic
21. vestibular, inner ear   22. inattention blindness   23. attention   24. cross-modal perception   25. (1) c, (2) a, (3) b
26. binocular   27. (1) c, (2) b, (3) a (4) d   28. false   29. c
30. top-down   31. c   32. false   33. Ganzfeld procedure

Section Two: Multiple Choice   1. a   2. d   3. d   4. c   5. c
6. d   7. b   8. c   9. a   10. a   11. c   12. a   13. c   14. a   15. a
16. a   17. b   18. b   19. c   20. d   21. b   22. b   23. c   24. c
25. c

Section Three: Fill In the Blank   1. seeing, hearing, etc.;
interpreting what is seen and heard, etc.   2. difference
3. sensory   4. Transduction   5. sensory adaptation   6. cornea
7. opponent-process theory   8. frequency   9. umami
10. Gestalt   11. figure ground   12. closure   13. binocular
disparity   14. cross-modal perception   15. subliminal perception

Section Four: Comprehensive Practice Test   1. c   2. a
3. d   4. c   5. b   6. d   7. a   8. c   9. a   10. c   11. c   12. b
13. d   14. a   15. d   16. b   17. true   18. d   19. true   20. c
21. false   22. a   23. c   24. d   25. c   26. b   27. a
28. b   29. d

Chapter 4

Section One: Chapter Review   1. a   2. suprachiasmatic
nucleus (SCN)   3. d   4. false   5. (1) a, (2) b, (3) a, (4) a, (5) a
6. c   7. false   8. d   9. b   10. (1) c, (2) b, (3) a   11. restorative
theory of sleep, circadian theory of sleep   12. c   13. false   14.
b   15. false   16. c   17. false   18. (1) d, (2) a, (3) c, (4) b   19. b
20. true   21. true   22. c   23. a   24. theory of dissociated control, neodissociation theory of hypnosis, sociocognitive theory
of hypnosis   25. nucleus accumbens   26. d   27. true   28. true
29. (1) b, (2) a, (3) d, (4) c   30. b   31. b   32. a   33. c   34. d   35. c

Section Two: Identify the Drug   (1) b, (2) d, (3) f, (4) c,
(5) e, (6) a, (7) g

Section Three: Fill In the Blank   1. consciousness   2. delta
3. REM rebound   4. REM   5. parasomnias   6. apnea
7. narcolepsy   8. mood, perception, thought   9. Meditation
10. dependence   11. crash   12. dopamine   13. cocaine

Section Four: Comprehensive Practice Test   1. melatonin
2. b   3. c   4. c   5. b   6. b   7. false   8. d   9. c   10. d   11. true
12. b   13. b   14. false   15. true   16. c   17. c   18. false

Chapter 5

Section One: Chapter Review 1. Pavlov 2. conditioned 3. extinction 4. existing conditioned stimulus 5. b 6. conditioned, unconditioned 7. a 8. cognitive 9. false 10. true 11. b 12. c 13. d 14. negative 15. Continuous 16. d 17. a 18. false 19. false 20. true 21. learned helplessness 22. biofeedback 23. behavior modification 24. insight 25. d 26. b 27. b 28. (1) c, (2) a, (3) d, (4) b 29. (1) b, (2) a, (3) c

Section Two: Identify the Concept 1. variable-ratio reinforcement 2. classical conditioning of emotions 3. negative reinforcement 4. generalization 5. positive reinforcement 6. extinction in operant conditioning 7. fixed-interval reinforcement 8. punishment 9. observational learning 10. secondary reinforcement 11. insight

Section Three: Fill In the Blank 1. stimuli, response, consequences 2. Learning 3. the sound of the truck 4. the food 5. salivation 6. neutral 7. generalization 8. discrimination 9. higher-order 10. conditioned, unconditioned 11. effect, Edward Thorndike 12. successive approximations 13. negative, positive 14. discriminative 15. primary, secondary 16. continuous, partial 17. aggressive

Section Four: Comprehensive Practice Test 1. a 2. c 3. c 4. d 5. b 6. c 7. b 8. c 9. a 10. d 11. b 12. false 13. b 14. b 15. d 16. c

Chapter 6

Section One: Chapter Review 1. d 2. (1) b, (2) c, (3) a 3. (1) b, (2) c, (3) a 4. c 5. c 6. (1) a, (2) c, (3) b, (4) a, (5) c 7. c 8. d 9. a 10. false 11. a 12. c 13. true 14. false 15. b 16. true 17. true 18. episodic, semantic 19. a 20. true 21. d 22. a 23. (1) c, (2) e, (3) a, (4) b, (5) d 24. c 25. false 26. true 27. a 28. d

Section Two: Complete the Diagram 1. large 2. visual, fraction of a second; auditory, 2 seconds 3. about 7 items 4. less than 30 seconds 5. unlimited 6. from minutes to a lifetime 7. declarative 8. episodic 9. motor 10. classically

Section Three: Fill In the Blank 1. encoding 2. rehearsal 3. working 4. long 5. semantic 6. recall 7. middle 8. state dependent 9. hippocampal region 10. potentiation 11. c 12. anterograde amnesia 13. proactive 14. encoding 15. massed 16. overlearning

Section Four: Comprehensive Practice Test 1. c 2. a 3. c 4. b 5. nondeclarative 6. a 7. d 8. b 9. false 10. true 11. false 12. d 13. a 14. c 15. false 16. true 17. false 18. a 19. b 20. true

Chapter 7

Section One: Chapter Review 1. c 2. b 3. d 4. Framing 5. a 6. b 7. c 8. false 9. false 10. (1) c, (2) d, (3) b, (4) e, (5) a 11. false 12. true 13. true 14. (1) b, (2) c, (3) a 15. a 16. b 17. a 18. false 19. true 20. (1) b, (2) a, (3) a, (4) b, (5) a 21. c 22. false 23. c

Section Two: Important Concepts and Psychologists 1. Simon 2. Tversky 3. Newell and Simon 4. Spearman 5. Sternberg 6. Terman 7. Wechsler 8. Galton 9. Steele 10. Gardner

Section Three: Fill In the Blank 1. cognition 2. Imagery 3. exemplar 4. elimination by aspects 5. psycholinguistics

6. syntax 7. linguistic relativity 8. Howard Gardner 9. validity 10. contextual 11. reliability 12. creativity

Section Four: Comprehensive Practice Test 1. b 2. b 3. prototype 4. false 5. a 6. a 7. d 8. a 9. false 10. true 11. false 12. c 13. d 14. a 15. b 16. false 17. true 18. true

Chapter 8

Section One: Chapter Review 1. b 2. d 3. (1) b, (2) c, (3) a 4. true 5. (1) c, (2) a, (3) b 6. a 7. b 8. c 9. true 10. (1) c, (2) b, (3) a, (4) e, (5) d 11. true 12. (1) c, (2) b, (3) a 13. false 14. b 15. false 16. c 17. true 18. c 19. b 20. a 21. d

Section Two: Important Concepts and Psychologists 1. cognitive development 2. psychosocial development 3. temperament 4. attachment 5. nativist view of language development 6. moral reasonings 7. death and dying 8. gender schema theory

Section Three: Fill In the Blank 1. schema 2. personal fable 3. third 4. identity versus role confusion 5. zygote 6. teratogens 7. maturation 8. avoidant 9. telegraphic speech 10. overregularization 11. Kohlberg 12. Crystallized, fluid 13. Bargaining

Section Four: Comprehensive Practice Test 1. b 2. b 3. d 4. d 5. b 6. a 7. b 8. b 9. true 10. b 11. d 12. c 13. c 14. c 15. true 16. b 17. c 18. b 19. true 20. b

Chapter 9

Section One: Chapter Review 1. extrinsic 2. a 3. d |4. c 5. true 6. true 7. false 8. mastery 9. feeding, satiety 10. d 11. c 12. d 13. maintain 14. d 15. biological 16. c 17. anorexia nervosa, bulimia nervosa 18. c 19. b 20. c 21. d 22. c 23. c 24. a 25. a 26. b 27. a 28. c 29. true 30. true 31. b 32. true 33. b 34. b

Section Two: Important Psychologists and Concepts 1. drive-reduction theory 2. hierarchy of needs 3. need for achievement 4. event creates physical arousal, which is identified as an emotion 5. event creates physical arousal plus emotion 6. cognitive appraisal of a stimulus results in emotion 7. facial-feedback hypothesis

Section Three: Fill In the Blank 1. motives 2. intrinsic 3. extrinsic 4. arousal 5. lateral; ventromedial 6. exercise 7. anorexia; bulimia 8. James-Lange 9. Cannon-Bard 10. Schachter-Singer 11. basic 12. excitement 13. testosterone 14. homeostasis 15. heterosexual; homosexual 16. emotional intelligence

Section Four: Comprehensive Practice Test 1. a 2. a 3. c 4. a 5. c 6. d 7. true 8. d 9. true 10. c 11. c 12. a 13. false 14. c 15. false 16. c 17. true 18. false

Chapter 10

Section One: Chapter Review 1. false 2. false 3. true 4. true 5. c 6. d 7. d 8. false 9. false 10. d 11. resistance 12. exhaustion 13. physiological, psychological 14. a 15. problem-focused, emotion-focused 16. true 17. c 18. b 19. a 20. false 21. c 22. a 23. c 24. true 25. d 26. false 27. a 28. b 29. Alcohol 30. d 31. false

Section Two: The Biopsychosocial Model of Health and Illness   1. genetics, relaxation, healthy lifestyle   2. lack of exercise, poor diet, disease and injury, toxic chemicals, pollution   3. stress management skills, giving and receiving love, optimism   4. depression, pessimism, worry, anxiety, poor coping skills, stress   5. social responsibility, social policy, social groups   6. loneliness, poverty, exploitation, violence

Section Three: Fill In the Blank   1. biomedical; biopsychosocial   2. health psychology   3. sympathetic nervous system   4. alarm   5. resistance   6. cognitive   7. proactive   8. AIDS   9. homosexual and bisexual males   10. hassles   11. psychoneuroimmunology   12. A   13. cognition   14. Primary   15. high blood pressure   16. stressor   17. approach-avoidance

Section Four: Comprehensive Practice Test   1. false   2. b   3. a   4. c   5. a   6. true   7. true   8. c   9. racism   10. true   11. c   12. false   13. a   14. true   15. true

Chapter 11

Section One: Chapter Review   1. true   2. unconscious   3. a   4. c   5. b   6. false   7. true   8. birth   9. d   10. b   11. Oedipus complex   12. c   13. collective   14. c   15. c   16. c   17. a   18. d   19. d   20. c   21. a   22. d   23. false   24. a   25. b   26. negligible   27. false   28. (1) a, (2) c, (3) d, (4) b, (5) e   29. d   30. c

Section Two: Complete the Table   1. Freud; Behavior arises mostly from unconscious conflict between pleasure-seeking id and moral-perfectionistic superego, with ego as mediator.   2. Bandura, Rotter; Behavior results from an interaction between internal cognitive factors and environmental factors.   3. Maslow, Rogers; Behavior springs from the person's motivation to become self-actualized or fully functioning and reflects the person's unique perception of reality and conscious choices.   4. Allport, Cattell, Eysenck; Behavior springs from personality traits that may be influenced by both heredity and environment.

Section Three: Fill In the Blank   1. id   2. ego   3. preconscious   4. oral, anal, phallic, genital   5. cardinal   6. surface; source   7. reciprocal determinism   8. collective unconscious   9. genes; environment   10. observation   11. Jung's   12. projective   13. Minnesota Multiphasic Personality Inventory   14. self-efficacy   15. source   16. archetype   17. collectivist; individualistic/collectivist

Section Four: Comprehensive Practice Test   1. c   2. c   3. b   4. false   5. b   6. c   7. a   8. a   9. b   10. d   11. b   12. c   13. false   14. false   15. c   16. d

Chapter 12

Section One: Chapter Review   1. false   2. a   3. (1) c, (2) a, (3) b, (4) d   4. false   5. true   6. false   7. (1) e, (2) d, (3) b, (4) c, (5) a, (6) f   8. c   9. (1) b, (2) c, (3) a   10. false   11. b   12. (1) a, (2) d, (3) b, (4) c   13. d   14. (1) c, (2) a, (3) b, (4) d   15. false   16. true   17. (1) d, (2) b, (3) e, (4) c, (5) a   18. paraphilias   19. c   20. c

Section Two: Identifying the Disorder   1. major depression   2. paranoid schizophrenia   3. bipolar disorder   4. agoraphobia   5. dissociative amnesia   6. borderline personality disorder   7. sexual dysfunction   8. obsessive-compulsive disorder

Section Three: Fill In the Blank   1. biological   2. positive   3. delusion   4. negative   5. major depressive disorder   6. manic   7. somatoform   8. panic   9. persistent involuntary thoughts, persistent irrational urge   10. conversion   11. dissociative identity disorder   12. personality   13. gender identity   14. Hallucinations   15. phobia   16. antisocial

Section Four: Comprehensive Practice Test   1. c   2. b   3. d   4. b   5. true   6. b   7. a   8. false   9. d   10. b   11. true   12. d   13. c   14. true   15. d   16. c   17. false   18. b

Chapter 13

Section One: Chapter Review   1. d   2. Gestalt   3. Person-centered   4. Psychodynamic   5. c   6. c   7. false   8. operant   9. b   10. d   11. (1) c, (2) b, (3) a, (4) d   12. c   13. false   14. b   15. d   16. true   17. (1) c, (2) b, (3) a, (4) c, (5) c   18. b   19. d   20. a   21. false   22. false   23. b   24. (1) a, (2) c, (3) b, (4) c   25. c   26. are

Section Two: Identify the Therapy   1. e   2. a   3. d   4. f   5. b   6. g   7. c

Section Three: Fill In the Blank   1. psychological; biological   2. transference   3. directive   4. interpersonal   5. family   6. self-help group   7. operant   8. behavior modification   9. cognitive   10. schizophrenia   11. depression   12. bipolar disorder   13. suicidal depression   14. clinical   15. free association   16. time out   17. lobotomy   18. psychoanalyst

Section Four: Comprehensive Practice Test   1. c   2. c   3. b   4. false   5. d   6. a   7. b   8. a   9. a   10. b   11. b   12. a   13. c   14. a   15. b   16. d   17. c   18. true   19. false   20. false

Chapter 14

Section One: Chapter Review   1. d   2. b   3. true   4. (1) c, (2) b, (3) a   5. true   6. false   7. (1) c, (2) a, (3) b   8. c   9. b   10. c   11. d   12. a   13. c   14. d   15. false   16. b   17. true   18. true   19. b   20. true   21. true   22. false   23. false   24. true   25. b   26. c   27. c   28. false   29. true   30. (1) a, (2) b, (3) c   31. c   32. false   33. true

Section Two: Match Terms with Definitions   1. f   2. e   3. b   4. a   5. h   6. i   7. l   8. j   9. k   10. m   11. d   12. g   13. c

Section Three: Fill In the Blank   1. attitude   2. primacy effect   3. dispositional   4. situational; personality   5. self-serving bias   6. halo   7. obedience   8. social facilitation   9. extreme   10. stereotype   11. bystander   12. altruism   13. frustration-aggression   14. scapegoating   15. attribution   16. conformity

Section Four: Comprehensive Practice Test   1. d   2. false   3. c   4. b   5. false   6. d   7. c   8. true   9. b   10. false   11. b   12. c   13. c   14. b   15. c   16. true   17. b   18. true   19. a

References

Note: Bracketed numbers following references indicate chapter(s) in which they are cited.

Abraham, H., & Duffy, F. (2001). EEG coherence in post-LSD visual hallucinations. *Psychiatry Research: Neuroimaging, 107,* 151–163. [4]

Abramowitz, J. S. (1997). Effectiveness of psychological and pharmacological treatments for obsessive-compulsive disorder: A quantitative review. *Journal of Consulting and Clinical Psychology, 65,* 44–52. [13]

Abrams, D., Wetherell, M., Cochrane, S., Hogg, M. A., & Turner, J. C. (1990). Knowing what to think by knowing who you are: Self-categorization and the nature of norm formation, conformity and group polarization. *British Journal of Social Psychology, 29*(Pt. 2), 97–119. [14]

Adams, J. H., Graham, D. I., & Jennett, B. (2000). The neuropathology of the vegetative state after an acute brain insult. *Brain, 123,* 1327–1338. [2]

Addi-Raccah, Q., & Ayalon, H. (2002). Gender inequality in leadership positions of teachers. *British Journal of Sociology of Education, 23,* 157–177. [8]

Addis, M., Hatgis, C., Krasnow, A., Jacob, K., Bourne, L., & Mansfield, A. (2004). Effectiveness of cognitive-behavioral treatment for panic disorder versus treatment as usual in a managed care setting. *Journal of Consulting & Clinical Psychology, 72,* 625–635. [13]

Addis, M., & Mahalik, J. (2003). Men, masculinity, and the contexts of help seeking. *American Psychologist, 58,* 5–14. [10, 13]

Ader, D. N., & Johnson, S. B. (1994). Sample description, reporting, and analysis of sex in psychological research: A look at APA and APA division journals in 1990. *American Psychologist, 49,* 216–218. [1]

Ader, R. (2000). On the development of psychoneuroimmunology. *European Journal of Pharmacology, 405,* 167–176. [10]

Adesman, A. (1996). Fragile X syndrome. In A. Capute & P. Accardo (Eds.). *Developmental disabilities in infancy and childhood* (2nd ed., Vol. 2, pp. 255–269). Baltimore: Brookes. [2]

Adler, A. (1927). *Understanding human nature.* New York: Greenberg. [11]

Adler, A. (1956). In H. L. Ansbacher & R. R. Ansbacher (Eds.), *The individual psychology of Alfred Adler: A systematic presentation in selections from his writings.* New York: Harper & Row. [11]

Adler, J. (1997, Spring/Summer). It's a wise father who knows. . . . *Newsweek* [Special Edition], p. 73. [8]

Adler, R. (2001). *Glass ceiling basics.* Malibu, CA: Glass Ceiling Research Institute. Retrieved January 22, 2003, from http://www.glass-ceiling.com/ArticlesFolder/GlassCeilingBasicsPage1.html [8]

Agras, W. S., Rossiter, E. M., Arnow, B., Telch, C. F., Raeburn, S. D., Bruce, B., & Koran, L. M. (1994). One-year follow-up of psychosocial and pharmacologic treatments for bulimia nervosa. *Journal of Clinical Psychiatry, 55,* 179–183. [9]

Agras, W. S., Walsh, T., Fairburn, C. G., Wilson, T., & Kraemer, H. C. (2000). A multicenter comparison of cognitive-behavioral therapy and interpersonal psychotherapy for bulimia nervosa. *Archives of General Psychiatry, 57,* 459–466. [13]

Ainsworth, M. (2000). ABCs of "internet therapy." *Metanoia* [Electronic version]. Retrieved from www.metanoia.org [13]

Ainsworth, M. D. S. (1973). The development of infant-mother attachment. In B. Caldwell & H. Ricciuti (Eds.), *Review of child development research* (Vol. 3). Chicago: University of Chicago Press. [8]

Ainsworth, M. D. S. (1979). Infant-mother attachment. *American Psychologist, 34,* 932–937. [8]

Ainsworth, M. D. S., Blehar, M. C., Walters, E., & Wall, S. (1978). *Patterns of attachment.* Hillsdale, NJ: Erlbaum. [8]

Åkerstedt, T. (1990). Psychological and psychophysiological effects of shift work. *Scandinavian Journal of Work and Environmental Health, 16,* 67–73. [4]

Akse, J., Hale, W., Engels, R., Raaijmakers, Q., & Meeus, W. (2004). Personality, perceived parental rejection and problem behavior in adolescence. *Social Psychiatry & Psychiatric Epidemiology, 39,* 980–988. [11]

Al'absi, M., Hugdahl, K., & Lovallo, W. (2002). Adrenocortical stress responses and altered working memory performance. *Psychophysiology, 39,* 95–99. [6]

Albrecht, K. (1979). *Stress and the manager: Making it work for you.* Englewood Cliffs, NJ: Prentice-Hall. [10]

Alexander, G. E., Furey, M. L., Grady, C. L., Pietrini, P., Brady, D. R., Mentis, M. J., & Schapiro, M. B. (1997). Association of premorbid intellectual function with cerebral metabolism in Alzheimer's disease: Implications for the cognitive reserve hypotheses. *American Journal of Psychiatry, 154,* 165–172. [8]

Alleman, J. (2002). Online counseling: The Internet and mental health treatment. *Psychotherapy: Theory, Research, Practice, Training, 39,* 199–209. [13]

Allen, B. P. (1997). *Personality theories: Development, growth, and diversity* (2nd ed.). Boston: Allyn & Bacon. [11]

Allen, G., Buxton, R. B., Wong, E. C., & Courchesne, E. (1997). Attentional activation of the cerebellum independent of motor involvement. *Science, 275,* 1940–1943. [2]

Allen, K. W. (1996). Chronic nailbiting: A controlled comparison of competing response and mild aversion treatments. *Behaviour Research and Therapy, 34,* 269–272. [13]

Allison, T., Puce, A., & McCarthy, G. (2000). Social perception from visual cues: Role of the STS region. *Trends in Cognitive Sciences, 4,* 267–278. [14]

Allport, G. W. (1954). *The nature of prejudice.* Reading, MA: Addison-Wesley. [14]

Allport, G. W. (1961). *Pattern and growth in personality.* New York: Holt, Rinehart & Winston. [11]

Allport, G. W., & Odbert, J. S. (1936). Trait names: A psycholexical study. *Psychological Monographs, 47*(1, Whole No. 211), 1–171. [11]

Alpert, B., Field, T., Goldstein, S., & Perry, S. (1990). Aerobics enhances cardiovascular fitness and agility in preschoolers. *Health Psychology, 9,* 48–56. [10]

Alsaker, F. D. (1995). Timing of puberty and reactions to pubertal changes. In M. Rutter (Ed.), *Psychosocial disturbances in young people* (pp. 37–82). New York: Cambridge University Press. [8]

Altermatt, E., & Pomerantz, E. (2003). The development of competence-related and motivational beliefs: An investigation of similarity and influence among friends. *Journal of Educational Psychology, 95,* 111–123. [7]

Aluja, A., & Blanch, A. (2004). Replicability of first-order 16PF-5 factors: An analysis of three parcelling methods. *Personality & Individual Differences, 37,* 667–677. [11]

Amato, S. (1998). Human genetics and dysmorphy. In R. Behrman & R. Kliegman (Eds.), *Nelson essentials of pediatrics* (3rd ed., pp. 167–225). Philadelphia: W. B. Saunders. [8]

American Association of Retired Persons. (2002). *Evaluating health information on the Internet: How good are your sources?* Retrieved November 1, 2002, from http://www.aarp.org/confacts/health/wwwhealth.html [10]

American Cancer Society. (2002). *Cancer facts & figures/2002.* Retrieved November 10, 2002, from http://www.cancer.org/downloads/STT/CancerFacts&Figures2002TM [12]

American Medical Association. (1994). *Report of the Council on Scientific Affairs: Memories of childhood abuse.* CSA Report 5-A-94. [6]

American Psychiatric Association. (1993a). *Statement approved by the Board of Trustees, December 12, 1993.* Washington, DC: Author. [6]

American Psychiatric Association. (1993b). Practice guideline for eating disorders. *American Journal of Psychiatry, 150,* 212–228. [9]

American Psychiatric Association. (1994). *Diagnostic and statistical manual of mental disorders* (4th ed.). Washington DC: Author. [4, 10, 12]

American Psychiatric Association. (1997). Practice guideline for the treatment of patients with Alzheimer's disease and other dementias of late life. *American Journal of Psychiatry, 154,* 1–39. [8]

American Psychiatric Association. (2000). *The diagnostic and statistical manual of mental disorders* (4th ed., Text Revision). Washington, DC: Author. [10, 12]

American Psychiatric Association (APA). (2000). *Practice guidelines for eating disorders.* Retrieved January 31, 2005, from http://www.psych.org [9]

American Psychological Association. (1994). *Interim report of the APA Working Group on Investigation of Memories of Childhood Abuse.* Washington, DC: Author. [6]

American Psychological Association. (1995). Psychology: Scientific problem-solvers—Careers for the 21st century. Retrieved March 7, 2002, from http://www.apa.org/students/brochure/outlook.html#bachelors [1]

American Psychological Association. (2000). Psychologists in the red [Online factsheet]. Retrieved March 7, 2002, from http://www.apa.org/ppo/issues/ebsinthered.html [1]

American Psychological Association (APA). (2002). Ethical principles of psychologists and code of conduct. *American Psychologist, 57,* 1060–1073. [13]

American Psychological Association (APA). (2003). Guidelines on multicultural education, training, research, practice, and organizational change for psychologists. *American Psychologist, 58,* 377–402. [13]

Anand, B. K., & Brobeck, J. R. (1951). Hypothalamic control of food intake in rats and cats. *Yale Journal of Biological Medicine, 24,* 123–140. [9]

Andersen, B. L., & Cyranowski, J. M. (1995). Women's sexuality: Behaviors, responses, and individual differences. *Journal of Consulting and Clinical Psychology, 63,* 891–906. [9]

Anderson, C., & Bushman, B. (2001). Effects of violent video games on aggressive behavior, aggressive cognition, aggressive affect, physiological arousal, and prosocial behavior: A meta-analytic review of the scientific literature. *Psychological Science, 12,* 353–359. [5]

Anderson, C. A., & Anderson, K. B. (1996). Violent crime rate studies in philosophical context: A destructive testing approach to heat and southern culture of violence effects. *Journal of Personality and Social Psychology, 70,* 740–756. [14]

Anderson, C. A., & Dill, K. E. (2000). Video games and aggressive thoughts, feelings, and behavior in the laboratory and in life. *Journal of Personality & Social Psychology, 78,* 772–790. [14]

Anderson, R. (2002). Deaths: Leading causes for 2000. *National Vital Statistics Reports, 50* (16), 1–86. [12]

Andreasen, N. C., Arndt, S., Alliger, R., Miller, D., & Flaum, M. (1995). Symptoms of schizophrenia: Methods, meanings, and mechanisms. *Archives of General Psychiatry, 52,* 341–351. [13]

Andreasen, N. C., & Black, D. W. (1991). *Introductory textbook of psychiatry.* Washington, DC: American Psychiatric Press. [4]

Andreasen, N. C., Flaum, M., Swayze, V., O'Leary, D. S., Alliger, R., Cohen, G., Ehrhardt, J., & Yuh, W. T. C. (1993). Intelligence and brain structure in normal individuals. *American Journal of Psychiatry, 150,* 130–134. [2]

Andrews, G., & Erskine, A. (2003). Reducing the burden of anxiety and depressive disorders: The role of computerized clinician assistance. *Current Opinion in Psychiatry, 16,* 41–44. [13]

Angeleri, F., Angeleri, V. A., Foschi, N., Giaquinto, S., Nolfe, G., Saginario, A., & Signorino, M. (1997). Depression after stroke: An investigation through catamnesis. *Journal of Clinical Psychiatry, 58,* 261–265. [2]

Anglin, J. (1995, March). *Word learning and the growth of potentially knowable vocabulary.* Paper presented at the biennial meetings of the Society for Research in Child Development, Indianapolis, IN. [8]

Anokhin, A., Vedeniapin, A., Sitevaag, E., Bauer, L., O'Connor, S., Kuperman, S., Porjesz, B., Reich, T., Begleiter, H., Polich, J., & Rohrbaugh, J. (2000). The P300 brain potential is reduced in smokers. *Psychopharmacology, 149,* 409–413. [10]

Anstey, K., Stankov, L., & Lord, S. (1993). Primary aging, secondary aging, and intelligence. *Psychology and Aging, 8,* 562–570. [8]

Apgar, V., & Beck, J. (1982). A perfect baby. In H. E. Fitzgerald & T. H. Carr (Eds.), *Human Development 82/83* (pp. 66–70). Guilford, CT: Dushkin. [8]

Aram, D., & Levitt, I. (2002). Mother-child joint writing and storybook reading: Relations with literacy among low SES kindergarteners. *Merrill-Palmer Quarterly, 48,* 202–224. [8]

Archer, J. (1991). The influence of testosterone on human aggression. *British Journal of Social Psychology, 82*(Pt. 1), 1–28. [14]

Archer, J. (1996). Sex differences in social behavior: Are the social role and evolutionary explanations compatible? *American Psychologist, 51,* 909–917. [1]

Arehart-Treichel, J. (2002). Researchers explore link between animal cruelty, personality disorders. *Psychiatric News, 37,* 22. [12]

Armstrong, M., & Shikani, A. (1996). Nasal septal necrosis mimicking Wegener's granulomatosis in a cocaine abuser. *Ear Nose Throat Journal, 75,* 623–626. [4]

Aronson, E. (1976). Dissonance theory: Progress and problems. In E. P. Hollander & R. C. Hunt (Eds.), *Current perspectives in social psychology* (4th ed., pp. 316–328). New York: Oxford University Press. [14]

Aronson, E. (1988). *The social animal* (3rd ed.). San Francisco: W. H. Freeman. [18]

Aronson, E., & Mills, J. (1959). The effect of severity of initiation on liking for a group. *Journal of Abnormal and Social Psychology, 59,* 177–181. [14]

Aronson, E., Stephan, W., Sikes, J., Blaney, N., & Snapp, M. (1978). *Cooperation in the classroom.* Beverly Hills, CA: Sage. [14]

Arushanyan, E., & Shikina, I. (2004). Effect of caffeine on light and color sensitivity of the retina in healthy subjects depending on psychophysiological features and time of day. *Human Physiology, 30,* 56–61. [4]

Asch, S. E. (1951). Effects of group pressure upon the modification and distortion of judgments. In H. Guetzkow (Ed.), *Groups, leadership, and men.* Pittsburgh, PA: Carnegie Press. [14]

Asch, S. E. (1955). Opinions and social pressure. *Scientific American, 193,* 31–35. [14]

Assefi, S., & Garry, M. (2003). Absolut memory distortions: Alcohol placebos influence the misinformation effect. *Psychological Science, 14,* 77–80. [4]

Atkinson, R. C., & Shiffrin, R. M. (1968). Human memory: A proposed system and its controlled processes. In K. W. Spence & J. T. Spence (Eds.), *The psychology of learning and motivation* (Vol. 2, pp. 89–195). New York: Academic. [6]

Au, J. G., & Donaldson, S. I. (2000). Social influences as explanations for substance use differences among Asian-American and European-American adolescents. *Journal of Psychoactive Drugs, 32,* 15–23. [4]

Augestad, L. B. (2000). Prevalence and gender differences in eating attitudes and physical activity among Norwegians. *Eating and Weight Disorders: Studies on Anorexia, Bulimia, and Obesity, 5,* 62–72. [9]

Austenfeld, J., & Stanton, A. (2004). Coping through emotional approach: A new look at emotion, coping, and health-related outcomes. *Journal of Personality, 72,* 1335–1363. [10]

Axel, R. (1995, October). The molecular logic of smell. *Scientific American, 273,* 154–159. [3]

Axelsson, A., & Jerson, T. (1985). Noisy toys: A possible source of sensorineural hearing loss. *Pediatrics, 76,* 574–578. [3]

Ayllon, T., & Azrin, N. (1965). The measurement and reinforcement of behavior of psychotics. *Journal of the Experimental Analysis of Behavior, 8,* 357–383. [5, 13]

Ayllon, T., & Azrin, N. (1968). *The token economy: A motivational system for therapy and rehabilitation.* New York: Appleton-Century-Crofts. [5, 13]

Azar, B. (2000). A web of research. *Monitor on Psychology, 31* [Online version]. Retrieved March 13, 2002, from http://www.apa.org/monitor/ [1]

Azrin, N. H., & Holz, W. C. (1966). Punishment. In W. K. Honig (Ed.), *Operant behavior: Areas of research and application.* New York: Appleton-Century-Crofts. [5]

Babor, T. (2004). Brief treatments for cannabis dependence: Findings from a randomized multisite trial. *Journal of Consulting & Clinical Psychology, 72,* 455–466. [13]

Bach, P., & Hayes, S. (2002). The use of acceptance and commitment therapy to prevent the rehospitalization of psychotic patients: A randomized controlled trial. *Journal of Consulting and Clinical Psychology, 70,* 1129–1139. [13]

Baddeley, A. D. (1990). *Human memory.* Boston, MA: Allyn & Bacon. [6]

Baddeley, A. D. (1992). Working memory. *Science, 255,* 556–559. [6]

Baddeley, A. D. (1995) Working memory. In M. S. Gazzaniga (Ed.), *The cognitive neurosciences.* Cambridge, MA: MIT Press. [6]

Baer, J. (1996). The effects of task-specific divergent-thinking training. *Journal of Creative Behavior, 30,* 183–187. [8]

Baer, L. (1996). Behavior theory: Endogenous serotonin therapy? *Journal of Clinical Psychiatry, 57*(6, Suppl.), 33–35. [13]

Baer, L., Rauch, S. L., Ballantine, T., Jr., Martuza, R., Cosgrove, R., Cassem, E., Giriunas, I., Manzo, P. A., Dimino, C., & Jenike, M. A. (1995). Cingulotomy for intractable obsessive-compulsive disorder. *Archives of General Psychiatry, 52,* 384–392. [13]

Bagby, R. M., Rogers, R., & Buis, T. (1994). Detecting malingered and defensive responding on the MMPI-2 in a forensic inpatient sample. *Journal of Personality Assessment, 62,* 191–203. [11]

Bagley, C., & Tremblay, P. (1998). On the prevalence of homosexuality and bisexuality in a random community survey of 750 men aged 18 to 27. *Journal of Homosexuality, 36,* 1–18. [9]

Bahrick, H. P., Bahrick, P. O., & Wittlinger, R. P. (1975). Fifty years of memory for names and faces: A cross-sectional approach. *Journal of Experimental Psychology: General, 104,* 54–75. [6]

Bailey, J. M., & Pillard, R. C. (1991). A genetic study of male sexual orientation. *Archives of General Psychiatry, 48,* 1089–1096. [9]

Bailey, J. M., Pillard, R. C., Neale, M. C., & Agyei, Y. (1993). Heritable factors influence sexual orientation in women. *Archives of General Psychiatry, 50,* 217–223. [9]

Baker, B., Wendt, A., & Slonaker, W. (2002). An analysis of gender equity in the federal labor relations career field. *Public Personnel Management, 31,* 559–567. [8]

Baldwin, J. D., & Baldwin, J. I. (1997). Gender differences in sexual interest. *Archives of Sexual Behavior, 26,* 181–210. [9]

Ball, S. G., Baer, L., & Otto, M. W. (1996). Symptom subtypes of obsessive-compulsive disorder in behavioral treatment studies: A quantitative review. *Behaviour Research and Therapy, 34,* 47–51. [12]

Ballenger, J. C., Pecknold, J., Rickels, K., & Sellers, E. M. (1993). Medication discontinuation in panic disorder. *Journal of Clinical Psychiatry, 54*(10, Suppl.), 15–21. [13]

Balon, R. (2004). Developments in treatment of anxiety disorders; Psychotherapy, pharmacotherapy, and psychosurgery. *Depression & Anxiety, 19,* 63–76. [13]

Baltes, P., & Baltes, M. (1990). Psychological perspectives on successful aging: The model of selective optimization with compensation. In P. Baltes & M. Baltes (Eds.), *Successful aging* (pp. 1–34). Cambridge, England: Cambridge University Press. [8]

Baltes, P. B., Reese, H. W., & Lipsitt, L. P. (1980). Life-span developmental psychology. *Annual Review of Psychology, 31,* 65–110. [8]

Baltimore, D. (2000). Our genome unveiled. *Nature, 409,* 814–816. [2, 8]

Bandura, A. (1969). *Principles of behavior modification.* New York: Holt, Rinehart & Winston. [5]

Bandura, A. (1973). *Aggression: A social learning analysis.* Englewood Cliffs, NJ: Prentice-Hall. [14]

Bandura, A. (1976). On social learning and aggression. In E. P. Hollander & R. C. Hunt (Eds.), *Current perspectives in social psychology* (4th ed., pp. 116–128). New York: Oxford University Press. [14]

Bandura, A. (1977a). *Social learning theory.* Englewood Cliffs, NJ: Prentice-Hall. [5, 8, 10, 13]

Bandura, A. (1986). *Social functions of thought and action: A social-cognitive theory.* Englewood Cliffs, NJ: Prentice-Hall. [5, 11]

Bandura, A. (1989). Social cognitive theory. *Annals of Child Development, 6,* 1–60. [11]

Bandura, A. (1997a, March). Self-efficacy. *Harvard Mental Health Letter, 13*(9), 4–6. [11]

Bandura, A. (1997b). *Self-efficacy: The exercise of control.* New York: Freeman. [11]

Bandura, A., Adams, N. E., & Beyer, J. (1977). Cognitive processes mediating behavioral change. *Journal of Personality and Social Psychology, 35,* 125–139. [13]

Bandura, A., Jeffery, R. W., & Gajdos, E. (1975). Generalizing change through participant modeling with self-directed mastery. *Behaviour Research and Therapy, 13,* 141–152. [13]

Bandura, A., Ross, D., & Ross, S. A. (1961). Transmission of aggression through imitation of aggressive models. *Journal of Abnormal and Social Psychology, 63,* 575–582. [5]

Bandura, A., Ross, D., & Ross, S. A. (1963). Imitation of film-mediated aggressive models. *Journal of Abnormal and Social Psychology, 66,* 3–11. [5]

Barbarich, N., McConaha, C., Gaskill, J., La Via, M., Frank, G., Achenbach, S., Plotnicov, K., & Kaye, W. (2004). An open trial of olanzapine in anorexia nervosa. *Journal of Clinical Psychiatry, 65,* 1480–1482. [9]

Barch, Deanna M. Award for distinguished scientific early career contributions to psychology. (2002). *American Psychologist, 57,* 852–854.

Bard, P. (1934). The neurohumoral basis of emotional reactions. In C. A. Murchison (Ed.), *Handbook of general experimental psychology.* Worcester, MA: Clark University Press. [9]

Bargmann, C. (1996). From the nose to the brain. *Nature, 384,* 512–513. [3]

Barinaga, M. (1997). How jet-lag hormone does double duty in the brain. *Science, 277,* 480. [4]

Barlow, D. H. (1997). Cognitive-behavioral therapy for panic disorder: Current status. *Journal of Clinical Psychiatry, 58*(6, Suppl.), 32–36. [13]

Barsh, G. S., Farooqi, I. S., & O'Rahilly, S. (2000). Genetics of body-weight regulation. *Nature, 404,* 644–651. [9]

Barsky, A. J. (1993, August). How does hypochondriasis differ from normal concerns about health? *Harvard Mental Health Letter, 10*(3), 8. [12]

Bartlett, A. (2002). Current perspectives on the goals of psychoanalysis. *Journal of the American Psychoanalytic Association, 50,* 629–638. [11]

Bartlett, F. C. (1932). *Remembering: A study in experimental and social psychology.* London: Cambridge University Press. [6]

Bartoshuk, L. M., & Beauchamp, G. K. (1994). Chemical senses. *Annual Review of Psychology, 45,* 419–449. [8]

Bartzokis, G., Sultzer, D., Lu, P., Huechterlein, K., Mintz, J., & Cummings, J. (2004). Heterogeneous age-related breakdown of white matter structural integrity: Implications for cortical "disconnection" in aging and Alzheimer's disease. *Neurobiology of Aging, 25,* 843–851. [8]

Basic Behavioral Science Task Force of the National Advisory Mental Health Council. (1996). Basic behavioral science research for mental health: Perception, attention, learning, and memory. *American Psychologist, 51,* 133–142. [5]

Bass, E., & Davis, L. (1988). *The courage to heal.* New York: Harper & Row. [6]

Bassili, J. N. (1995). Response latency and the accessibility of voting intentions: What contributes to accessibility and how it affects vote choice. *Personality and Social Psychology Bulletin, 21,* 686–695. [14]

Bates, M., Labouvie, D., & Voelbel, G. (2002). Individual differences in latent neuropsychological abilities at addictions treatment entry. *Psychology of Addictive Behaviors, 16,* 35–46. [4]

Bateson, G. (1982). Totemic knowledge in New Guinea. In U. Neisser (Ed.), *Memory observed: Remembering in natural contexts.* San Francisco: W. H. Freeman. [6]

Batson, C. D., Batson, J. G., Griffitt, C. A., Barrientos, S., Brandt, J. R., Sprengelmeyer, P., & Bayly, M. J. (1989). Negative-state relief and the empathy-altruism hypothesis. *Journal of Personality and Social Psychology, 56,* 922–933. [14]

Baumgardner, A. H., Heppner, P. P., & Arkin, R. M. (1986). Role of causal attribution in personal problem solving. *Journal of Personality and Social Psychology, 50,* 636–643. [14]

Baumrind, D. (1967). Child care practices anteceding three patterns of preschool behavior. *Genetic Psychology Monographs, 75,* 43–88. [8]

Baumrind, D. (1971). Current patterns of parental authority. *Developmental Psychology Monographs, 4*(1, Pt. 2). [8]

Baumrind, D. (1980). New directions in socialization research. *American Psychologist, 35,* 639–652. [8]

Baumrind, D. (1991). The influence of parenting style on adolescent competence and substance use. *Journal of Early Adolescence, 11,* 56–95. [8]

Bavelier, D., Tomann, A., Hutton, C., Mitchell, T., Corina, D., Liu, G., & Neville, H. (2000). Visual attention to the periphery is enhanced in congenitally deaf individuals. *Journal of Neuroscience, 20,* 1–6. [3]

Bazan, S. (1998). Enhancing decision-making effectiveness in problem-solving teams. *Clinical Laboratory Management Review, 12,* 272–276. [14]

Bean, P., Loomis, C., Timmel, P., Hallinan, P., Moore, S., Mammel, J., & Weltzin, T. (2004). Outcome variables for anorexic males and females one year after discharge from residential treatment. *Journal of Addictive Diseases, 23,* 83–94. [9]

Bean, R., Perry, B., & Bedell, T. (2002). Developing culturally competent marriage and family therapists: Treatment guidelines for non-African American therapists working with African American families. *Journal of Marital & Family Therapy, 28,* 153–164. [13]

Beare, P., Severson, S., & Brandt, P. (2004). The use of a positive procedure to increase engagement on-task and decrease challenging behavior. *Behavior Modification, 28,* 28–44. [5]

Beck, A. T. (1967). *Depression: Causes and treatment.* Philadelphia: University of Pennsylvania Press. [12]

Beck, A. T. (1976). *Cognitive therapy and the emotional disorders.* New York: New American Library. [13]

Beck, A. T. (1991). Cognitive therapy: A 30-year retrospective. *American Psychologist, 46,* 368–375. [12, 13]

Beck, A. T. (1993). Cognitive therapy: Past, present, and future. *Journal of Consulting and Clinical Psychology, 61,* 194–198. [13]

Beets, M., & Pitetti, K. (2004). One-mile run/walk and body mass index of an ethnically diverse sample of youth. *Medicine & Science in Sports & Exercise, 36,* 1796–1803. [10]

Beirut, L., Dinwiddie, S., Begleiter, H., Crowe, R., Hesselbrock, V., Nurnberger, J., Porjesz, B., Schuckit, M., & Reich, T. (1998). Familial transmission of substance dependence: Alcohol, marijuana, cocaine, and habitual smoking: A report from the collaborative study on the genetics of alcoholism. *Archives of General Psychiatry, 55,* 982–988. [10]

Békésy, G. von. (1957). The ear. *Scientific American, 197,* 66–78. [3]

Bekker, M. H. J. (1996). Agoraphobia and gender: A review. *Clinical Psychology Review, 16,* 129–146. [12]

Belcourt-Dittloff, A., & Stewart, J. (2000). Historical racism: Implications for Native Americans. *American Psychologist, 55,* 1164–1165. [10]

Bell, A. P., Weinberg, M. S., & Hammersmith, S. K. (1981). *Sexual preference: Its development in men and women.* Bloomington: Indiana University Press. [9]

Bellis, M., Cook, P., Clark, P., Syed, Q., & Hoskins, A. (2002). Re-emerging syphilis in gay men: A case-control study of behavioural risk factors and HIV status. *Journal of Epidemiology & Community Health, 56,* 235–236. [10]

Belsky, J., & Fearon, R. (2002). Infant-mother attachment security, contextual risk, and early development: A moderational analysis. *Development & Psychopathology, 14,* 293–310. [8]

Bem, D., & Honorton, C. (1994). Does psi exist? Replicable evidence for an anomalous process of information transfer. *Psychological Bulletin, 115,* 4–18. [3]

Bem, S. L. (1981). Gender schema theory: A cognitive account of sex typing. *Psychological Review, 88,* 354–364. [8]

Bem, S. L. (1985). Androgyny and gender schema theory: A conceptual and empirical integration. In T. B. Sonderegger (Ed.), *Nebraska symposium on motivation: Psychology of gender* (Vol. 32, pp. 179–226). Lincoln: University of Nebraska Press. [8]

Benes, F. M. (2000). Emerging principles of altered neural circuitry in schizophrenia. *Brain Research Reviews, 31,* 251–269. [12]

Benjafield, J. G. (1996). *A history of psychology.* Boston: Allyn & Bacon. [1]

Benjamin, L., & Crouse, E. (2002). The American Psychological Association's response to *Brown v. Board of Education*: The case of Kenneth B. Clark. *American Psychologist, 57,* 38–50. [1]

Benjamin, L. T. (2000). The psychology laboratory at the turn of the 20th century. *American Psychologist, 55,* 318–321. [1]

Bennett, S. K. (1994). The American Indian: A psychological overview. In W. J. Lonner & R. Malpass (Eds.), *Psychology and culture* (pp. 35–39). Boston: Allyn & Bacon. [11]

Bennett, W. I. (1990, November). Boom and doom. *Harvard Health Letter, 16,* 1–4. [3]

Benotsch, E., Kalichman, S., & Weinhardt, L. (2004). HIV-AIDS patients' evaluation of health information on the Internet: The digital divide and vulnerability to fraudulent claims. *Journal of Consulting & Clinical Psychology, 72,* 1004–1011. [10]

Butcher, J. N., & Graham, J. R. (1989). *Topics in MMPI-2 interpretation*. Minneapolis: Department of Psychology, University of Minnesota. [11]

Butcher, J. N., Graham, J. R., & Ben-Porath, Y. S. (1995). Methodological problems and issues in MMPI, MMPI-2, and MMPI-A research. *Psychological Assessment, 7*, 320–329. [11]

Butcher, J. N., & Rouse, S. V. (1996). Personality: Individual differences and clinical assessment. *Annual Review of Psychology, 47*, 89–111. [11]

Butki, B., Baumstark, J., & Driver, S. (2003). Effects of a carbohydrate-restricted diet on affective responses to acute exercise among physically active participants. *Perceptual & Motor Skills, 96*, 607–615. [9]

Butler, R., & Lewis, M. (1982). *Aging and mental health* (3rd ed.). St. Louis: Mosby. [8]

Buunk, B. P., Angleitner, A., Oubaid, V., & Buss, D. M. (1996). Sex differences in jealousy in evolutionary and cultural perspective: Tests from the Netherlands, Germany and the United States. *Psychological Science, 7*, 359–363. [1]

Byne, W. (1994). The biological evidence challenged. *Scientific American, 270*, 50–55. [9]

Byne, W., & Parsons, B. (1993). Human sexual orientation: The biologic theories reappraised. *Archives of General Psychiatry, 50*, 228–239. [9]

Byne, W., & Parsons, B. (1994). Biology and human sexual orientation. *Harvard Mental Health Letter, 10*(8), 5–7. [9]

Cahill, L., Babinsky, R., Markowitsch, H. J., & McGaugh, J. L. (1995). The amygdala and emotional memory. *Nature, 377*, 295–296. [2, 6]

Cahill, L., & McGaugh, J. (1995). A novel demonstration of enhanced memory associated with emotional arousal. *Consciousness & Cognition, 4*, 410–421. [6]

Camp, D. S., Raymond, G. A., & Church, R. M. (1967). Temporal relationship between response and punishment. *Journal of Experimental Psychology, 74*, 114–123. [5]

Campbell, F., Pungello, E., Miller-Johnson, S., Burchinal, M., & Ramey, C. (2001). The development of cognitive and academic abilities: Growth curves from an early childhood educational experiment. *Developmental Psychology, 37*, 231–242. [7]

Campbell, F., & Ramey, C. (1994). Effects of early intervention on intellectual and academic achievement: A follow-up study of children from low-income families. *Child Development, 65*, 684–698. [7]

Campbell, P., & Dhand, R. (2000). Obesity. *Nature, 404*, 631. [9]

Cannon, T. D., Kaprio, J., Lönnqvist, J., Huttunen, M., & Koskenvuo, M. (1998). The genetic epidemiology of schizophrenia in a Finnish twin cohort: A population-based modeling study. *Archives of General Psychiatry, 55*, 67–74. [12]

Cannon, W. B. (1927). The James-Lange theory of emotions: A critical examination as an alternative theory. *American Journal of Psychology, 39*, 106–112. [9]

Cannon, W. B. (1929). *Bodily changes in pain, hunger, fear and rage* (2nd ed.). New York: Appleton. [2]

Cannon, W. B. (1935). Stresses and strains of homeostasis. *American Journal of Public Health, 189*, 1–14. [2]

Capel, B. (2000). The battle of the sexes. *Mechanisms of Development, 92*, 89–103. [2]

Cardoso, S. H., de Mello, L. C., & Sabbatini, R. M. E. (2000). How nerve cells work. Retrieved from http://www.epub.org.br/cm/n09/fundamentos/transmissao/voo_i.htm [2]

Carlat, D. J., Camargo, C. A., Jr., & Herzog, D. B. (1997). Eating disorders in males: A report on 135 patients. *American Journal of Psychiatry, 154*, 1127–1132. [9]

Carlsson, I., Wendt, P. E., & Risberg, J. (2000). On the neurobiology of creativity. Differences in frontal activity between high and low creative subjects. *Neuropsychologia, 38*, 873–885. [7]

Carnagey, N., & Anderson, C. (2004). Violent video game exposure and aggression: A literature review. *Minerva Psichiatrica, 45*, 1–18. [14]

Carpenter, S. (2001, March). Everyday fantasia: The world of synesthesia. *APA Monitor on Psychology* [Online version], *32*. [3]

Carpenter, S. (2001). Sights unseen. *Monitor on Psychology, 32* [Electronic version]. Retrieved May 13, 2003, from http://www.apa.org/monitor/apr01/blindness.html [3]

Carpenter, W. T., Jr. (1996). Maintenance therapy of persons with schizophrenia. *Journal of Clinical Psychiatry, 57*(9, Suppl.), 10–18. [13]

Carrier, J. (1980). Homosexual behavior in cross-cultural perspective. In J. Marmor (Ed.), *Homosexual behavior* (pp. 100–122). New York: Basic Books. [9]

Carroll, K. M., Rounsaville, B. J., Nich, C., Gordon, L. T., Wirtz, P. W., & Gawin, F. (1994). One-year follow-up of psychotherapy and pharmacotherapy for cocaine dependence: Delayed emergence of psychotherapy effects. *Archives of General Psychiatry, 51*, 989–997. [13]

Carskadon, M. A., & Dement, W. C. (1989). Normal human sleep: An overview. In M. H. Kryger, T. Roth, & W. C. Dement (Eds.), *Principles and practice of sleep medicine* (pp. 3–13). Philadelphia: W. B. Saunders. [4]

Carskadon, M. A., & Rechtschaffen, A. (1989). Monitoring and staging human sleep. In M. H. Kryger, T. Roth, & W. C. Dement (Eds.), *Principles and practice of sleep medicine* (pp. 665–683). Philadelphia: W. B. Saunders. [4]

Carson, R., Butcher, J., & Mineka, S. (2000). *Abnormal psychology and modern life* (11th ed.). Boston: Allyn & Bacon. [13]

Carson, R. C. (1989). Personality. *Annual Review of Psychology, 40*, 227–248. [11]

Carver, C. S., Pozo, C., Harris, S. D., Noriega, V., Scheier, M. F., Robinson, D. S., Ketcham, A. S., Moffat, F. L., Jr., & Clark, K. C. (1993). How coping mediates the effect of optimism on distress: A study of women with early stage breast cancer. *Journal of Personality and Social Psychology, 65*, 375–390. [10]

Carver, C. S., & Scheier, M. F. (1996). *Perspectives on personality* (3rd ed.). Boston: Allyn & Bacon. [11]

Case, R. (Ed.). (1992). *The mind's staircase: Exploring the conceptual underpinnings of children's thought and knowledge*. Hillsdale, NJ: Erlbaum. [8]

Casey, D. E. (1996). Side effect profiles of new antipsychotic agents. *Journal of Clinical Psychiatry, 57*(11, Suppl.), 40–45. [13]

Cash, T. F., & Janda, L. H. (1984, December). The eye of the beholder. *Psychology Today*, 46–52. [14]

Caspi, A. (2000). The child is father of the man: Personality continuities from childhood to adulthood. *Journal of Personality & Social Psychology, 78*, 158–172. [11]

Caspi, A., Lynam, D., Moffitt, T. E., & Silva, P. A. (1993). Unraveling girls' delinquency: Biological, dispositional, and contextual contributions to adolescent misbehavior. *Developmental Psychology, 29*, 19–30. [8]

Caspi, A., & Silva, P. A. (1995). Temperamental qualities at age three predict personality traits in young adulthood: Longitudinal evidence from a birth cohort. *Child Development, 66*, 486–498. [8]

Cattell, R. B. (1950). *Personality: A systematic, theoretical, and factual study*. New York: McGraw-Hill. [11]

Cattell, R. B., Eber, H. W., & Tatsuoka, M. M. (1977). *Handbook for the 16 personality factor questionnaire*. Champaign, IL: Institute of Personality and Ability Testing. [11]

Cavanaugh, S. (2004). The sexual debut of girls in early adolescence: The intersection of race, pubertal timing, and friendship group. *Journal of Research on Adolescence, 14*, 285–312. [8]

Brooks-Gunn, J., & Furstenberg, F. F. (1989). Adolescent sexual behavior. *American Psychologist, 44*, 249–257. [8]

Brotman, A. W. (1994). What works in the treatment of anorexia nervosa? *Harvard Mental Health Letter, 10*(7), 8. [9]

Broughton, W. A., & Broughton, R. J. (1994). Psychosocial impact of narcolepsy. *Sleep, 17*, S45–S49. [4]

Brown, A. (1996, Winter). Mood disorders in children and adolescents. *NARSAD Research Newsletter*, pp. 11–14. [12]

Brown, A. (2004). The déjà vu illusion. *Current Directions in Psychological Science, 13*, 256–259. [3]

Brown, A. M. (1990). Development of visual sensitivity to light and color vision in human infants: A critical review. *Vision Research, 30*, 1159–1188. [8]

Brown, G. W., Harris, T. O., & Hepworth, C. (1994). Life events and endogenous depression: A puzzle reexamined. *Archives of General Psychiatry, 51*, 525–534. [12]

Brown, J. D., & Rogers, R. J. (1991). Self-serving attributions: The role of physiological arousal. *Personality and Social Psychology Bulletin, 17*, 501–506. [14]

Brown, R. (1973). *A first language: The early stages.* Cambridge, MA: Harvard University Press. [8]

Brown, R., Cazden, C., & Bellugi, U. (1968). The child's grammar from I to III. In J. P. Hill (Ed.), *Minnesota symposium on child psychology* (Vol. 2, pp. 28–73). Minneapolis: University of Minnesota Press. [8]

Brown, R., & Kulik, J. (1977). Flashbulb memories. *Cognition, 5*, 73–99. [6]

Brown, R., & McNeil, D. (1966). The "tip of the tongue" phenomenon. *Journal of Verbal Learning and Verbal Behavior, 5*, 325–337. [6]

Brown, W., O'Connell, A., & Fillit, H. (2002). New developments in pharmacotherapy for Alzheimer disease. *Drug Benefit Trends, 14*, 34–44. [8]

Brown, W. A. (1998, January). The placebo effect. *Scientific American, 278*, 90–95. [3]

Brownlee, S., & Schrof, J. M. (1997, March 17). The quality of mercy. *U.S. News & World Report*, pp. 54–67. [3]

Bruch, M., Fallon, M., & Heimberg, R. (2003). Social phobia and difficulties in occupational adjustment. *Journal of Counseling Psychology, 50*, 109–117. [12]

Brunetti, A., Carta, P., Cossu, G., Ganadu, M., Golosio, B., Mura, G., & Pirastru, M. (2002). A real-time classification system of thalassemic pathologies based on artificial neural networks. *Medical Decision Making, 22*, 18–26. [7]

Brunila, T., Lincoln, N., Lindell, A., Tenovuo, O., & Haemelaeinen, H. (2002). Experiences of combined visual training and arm activation in the rehabilitation of unilateral visual neglect: A clinical study. *Neuropsychological Rehabilitation, 12*, 27–40. [2]

Buchert, R., Thomasius, R., Wilke, F., Petersen, K., Nebeling, B., Obrocki, J., Schulze, O., Schmidt, U., & Clausen, M. (2004). A voxel-based PET investigation of the long-term effects of "ecstasy" consumption on brain serotonin transporters. *American Journal of Psychiatry, 161*, 1181–1189. [4]

Buck, L. B. (1996). Information coding in the vertebrate olfactory system. *Annual Review of Neuroscience, 19*, 517–544. [3]

Buckingham, H. W., Jr., & Kertesz, A. (1974). A linguistic analysis of fluent aphasics. *Brain and Language, 1*, 29–42. [2]

Buhusi, C., & Meck, W. (2002). Differential effects of methamphetamine and haloperidol on the control of an internal clock. *Behavioral Neuroscience, 116*, 291–297. [4]

Buller, D. B., Burgoon, M., Hall, J. R., Levine, N., Taylor, A. M., Beach, B. H., Melcher, C., Buller, M. K., Bowen, S. L., Hunsaker, F. G., & Bergen, A. (2000). Using language intensity to increase the success of a family intervention to protect children from ultraviolet radiation: Predictions from language expectancy theory. *Preventive Medicine, 30*, 103–113. [14]

Burchinal, M., Campbell, F., Bryant, D., Wasik, B., & Ramey, C. (1997). Early intervention and mediating processes in cognitive performance of children of low-income African American families. *Child Development, 68*, 935–954. [7]

Burghardt, N., Sullivan, G., McEwen, B., Gorman, J., & LeDoux, J. (2004). The selective serotonin reuptake inhibitor citalopram increases fear after acute treatment but reduces fear with chronic treatment: A comparison with tianeptine. *Biological Psychiatry, 55*, 1171–1178. [2]

Burke, A., Heuer, F., & Reisberg, D. (1992). Remembering emotional events. *Memory and Cognition, 20*, 277–290. [6]

Burt, D. B., Zembar, M. J., & Niederehe, G. (1995). Depression and memory impairment: A meta-analysis of the association, its pattern, and specificity. *Psychological Bulletin, 117*, 285–305. [6]

Burton, D. (2003). Male adolescents: Sexual victimization and subsequent sexual abuse. *Child & Adolescent Social Work Journal, 20*, 277–296. [14]

Busch, C. M., Zonderman, A. B., & Costa, P. T. (1994). Menopausal transition and psychological distress in a nationally representative sample: Is menopause associated with psychological distress? *Journal of Aging and Health, 6*, 209–228. [8]

Bushman, B., & Cantor, J. (2003). Media ratings for violence and sex: Implications for policymakers and parents. *American Psychologist, 58*, 130–141. [5]

Bushman, B. J. (1995). Moderating role of trait aggressiveness in the effects of violent media on aggression. *Journal of Personality and Social Psychology, 69*, 950–960. [14]

Bushman, B. J., & Cooper, H. M. (1990). Effects of alcohol on human aggression: An integrative research review. *Psychological Bulletin, 107*, 341–354. [14]

Busnel, M. C., Granier-Deferre, C., & Lecanuet, J. P. (1992). Fetal audition. *Annals of the New York Academy of Sciences, 662*, 118–134. [8]

Buss, D. (2004a). *Evolutionary psychology* (2nd ed.). Boston, MA: Allyn & Bacon. [1, 9]

Buss, D. (2004b). The bumbling apprentice. In J. Brockman (Ed.), *Curious minds: How a child becomes a scientist* (pp. 13–18). New York: Pantheon Books. [9]

Buss, D. M. (1984). Marital assortment for personality dispositions: Assessment with three different data sources. *Behavioral Genetics, 14*, 111–123. [14]

Buss, D. M. (1994). The strategies of human mating. *American Scientist, 82*, 238–249. [9, 14]

Buss, D. M. (1999). *Evolutionary psychology: The new science of the mind.* Boston: Allyn & Bacon. [9]

Buss, D. M. (2000a). *The dangerous passion: Why jealousy is as necessary as sex and love.* New York: Free Press. [1, 5]

Buss, D. M. (2000b). Desires in human mating. *Annals of the New York Academy of Sciences, 907*, 39–49. [1, 9, 14]

Buss, D. M., Abbott, M., Angleitner, A., Asherian, A., Biaggio, A., Blanco-Villasenor, A., Bruchon-Schweitzer, M., et al. (1990). International preferences in selecting mates: A study of 37 cultures. *Journal of Cross-Cultural Psychology, 21*, 5–47. [14]

Buss, D. M., Larson, R., Westen, D., & Semmelroth, J. (1992). Sex differences in jealousy: Evolution, physiology, and psychology. *Psychological Science, 3*, 251–255. [1]

Buss, D., Shackelford, T., Kirkpatrick, L., & Larsen, R. (2001). A half century of mate preferences: The cultural evolution of values. *Journal of Marriage and the Family, 63*, 491–503. [1]

Bussey, K., & Bandura, A. (1999). Social cognitive theory of gender development and differentiation. *Psychological Review, 106*, 676–713. [8]

Butcher, J. N. (1992, October). International developments with the MMPI-2. *MMPI-2 News & Profiles, 3*, 4. [11]

Butcher, J. N., Dahlstrom, W. G., Graham, J. R., Tellegen, A., & Kaemmer, B. (1989). *Manual for the restandardized Minnesota Multiphasic Personality Inventory: MMPI-2. An administrative and interpretive guide.* Minneapolis: University of Minnesota Press. [11]

CBS News. (July 31, 2002). Fear of public speaking. Retrieved February 14, 2003, from http://www.cbsnews.com/stories/2002/07/30 [12]

Centers for Disease Control and Prevention (CDC). (1999). Physical activity and health. Retrieved January 29, 2003, from http://www.cdc.gov/needphp/sgr/ataglan.htm [10]

Centers for Disease Control and Prevention (CDC). (2000). Youth risk behavior surveillance—United States, 1999. *Morbidity and Mortality Weekly Report, 49,* 1–96. [8]

Centers for Disease Control and Prevention (CDC). (2001a). Genital herpes. Retrieved January 27, 2003, from http://www.cdc.gov/nchstp/dst/Fact_Sheets_facts_Gnital_Herpes_htm [10]

Centers for Disease Control and Prevention (CDC). (2001b). HIV/AIDS update: A glance at the HIV epidemic. Retrieved January 24, 2003, from http://www.cdc.gov/nchstp/od/news/At-a-Glance.pdf [10]

Centers for Disease Control and Prevention. (2002). *HIV/AIDS Surveillance Report: Year-end Edition, 13,* 1–44. [10]

Centers for Disease Control and Prevention. (2002). Nonfatal self-inflicted injuries treated in hospital emergency departments—United States, 2000. *Morbidity & Mortality Weekly Report, 51,* 436–438. [12]

Centers for Disease Control and Prevention (CDC). (2003a). About minority health. Retrieved August 8, 2003, from http://www.cdc.gov/omh/AMH/AMH.htm [10]

Centers for Disease Control and Prevention (CDC). (2003b). Sexually transmitted disease surveillance, 2002. Retrieved August 18, 2004, from http://www.cdc.gov/std/stats/natoverview.htm [10]

Centers for Disease Control and Prevention (CDC). (2003). *Hearing Loss* [Online factsheet]. Retrieved May 13, 2003, from http://www.cdc.gov/ncbddd/dd/ddhi.htm [3]

Centers for Disease Control and Prevention (CDC). (2005). About minority health. Retrieved February 2, 2005, from http://www.cdc.govomh/AMH/AMH.htm [10]

Chambless, D. L., & Goldstein, A. J. (1979). Behavioral psychotherapy. In R. J. Corsini (Ed.), *Current psychotherapies* (2nd ed., pp. 230–272). Itasca, IL: F. E. Peacock. [13]

Chang, E., & Merzenich, M. (2003). Environmental noise retards auditory cortical development. *Science, 300,* 498–502. [2]

Chao, R. (2001). Extending research on the consequences of parenting style for Chinese Americans and European Americans. *Child Development, 72,* 1832–1843. [8]

Chaplin, W. F., Philips, J. B., Brown, J. D., Clanton, N. R., & Stein, J. L. (2000). Handshaking, gender, personality, and first impressions. *Journal of Personality and Social Psychology, 19,* 110–117. [14]

"Charity holds its own in tough times." (2003). Press release. Retrieved November 25, 2003, from http://www.aafrc.org/press_releases/trustreleases/charityholds.html [14]

Charles, S., Mather, M., & Carstensen, L. (2003). Aging and emotional memory: The forgettable nature of negative images for older adults. *Journal of Experimental Psychology, 132,* 310–324. [8]

Charness, N. (1989). Age and expertise: Responding to Talland's challenge. In L. W. Poon, D. C. Rubin, & B. A. Wilson (Eds.), *Everyday cognition in adulthood and old age.* New York: Cambridge University Press. [8]

Chase, M. H., & Morales, F. R. (1990). The atonia and myoclonia of active (REM) sleep. *Annual Review of Psychology, 41,* 557–584. [4]

Chassin, L., Presson, C., Sherman, S., & Kim, K. (2003). Historical changes in cigarette smoking and smoking-related beliefs after 2 decades in a midwestern community. *Health Psychology, 22,* 347–353. [10]

Chavez, M., & Spitzer, M. (2002). Herbals and other dietary supplements for premenstrual syndrome and menopause. *Psychiatric Annals, 32,* 61–71. [4]

Chen, E. (2004). Why socioeconomic status affects the health of children: A psychosocial perspective. *Current Directions in Psychological Science, 13,* 112–115. [10]

Chen-Sea, M.-J. (2000). Validating the Draw-A-Man Test as a personal neglect test. *American Journal of Occupational Therapy, 54,* 391–397. [2]

Cherry, E. (1953). Some experiments on the recognition of speech with one and two ears. *Journal of the Acoustical Society of America, 25,* 975–979. [3]

Chickering, A., & Reisser, L. (1993). *Education and identity* (2nd ed.). San Francisco: Jossey-Bass. [10]

Chilosi, A., Cipriani, P., Bertuccelli, B., Pfanner, L., & Cioni, G. (2001). Early cognitive and communication development in children with focal brain lesions. *Journal of Child Neurology, 16,* 309–316. [2]

Cho, K. (2001). Chronic "jet lag" produces temporal lobe atrophy and spatial cognitive deficits. *Nature Neuroscience, 4,* 567–568. [4]

Cho, K., Ennaceur, A., Cole, J., & Kook Suh, C. (2000). Chronic jet lag produces cognitive deficits. *Journal of Neuroscience, 20,* RC66. [4]

Choi, I., Dalal, R., Kim-Prieto, C., & Park, H. (2003). Culture and judgment of causal relevance. *Journal of Personality & Social Psychology, 84,* 46–59. [14]

Choi, J., & Silverman, I. (2002). The relationship between testosterone and route-learning strategies in humans. *Brain & Cognition, 50,* 116–120. [7]

Chollar, S. (1989). Conversation with the dolphins. *Psychology Today, 23,* 52–57. [7]

Chomsky, N. (1957). *Syntactic structures.* The Hague: Mouton. [8]

Chomsky, N. (1968). *Language and mind.* New York: Harcourt, Brace & World. [8]

Chowdhury, R., Ferrier, I., & Thompson, J. (2003). Cognitive dysfunction in bipolar disorder. *Current Opinion in Psychiatry, 16,* 7–12. [12]

Christakis D., Zimmerman, F., Giuseppe, D., & McCarty, C. (2004). Early television exposure and subsequent attentional problems in children. *Pediatrics, 113,* 708–713. [1]

Christensen, L. B. (2001). *Experimental methodology* (8th ed.). Boston: Allyn & Bacon. [1]

Christensen P., Rothgerber, H., Wood, W., & Matz, D. (2004). Social norms and identity relevance: A motivational approach to normative behavior. *Journal of Personality & Social Psychology Bulletin, 30,* 1295–1309. [14]

Christianson, S-Å. (1992). Emotional stress and eyewitness memory: A critical review. *Psychological Bulletin, 112,* 284–309. [6]

Church, M., Elliot, A., & Gable, S. (2001). Perceptions of classroom environment, achievement goals, and achievement outcomes. *Journal of Educational Psychology, 93,* 43–54. [9]

Church R. M. (1963). The varied effects of punishment on behavior. *Psychological Review, 70,* 369–402. [5]

Cialdini, R. B., Cacioppo, J. T., Basset, R., & Miller, J. A. (1978). Low-ball procedure for producing compliance: Commitment then cost. *Journal of Personality and Social Psychology, 36,* 463–476. [14]

Cialdini, R. B., Vincent, J. E., Lewis, S. K., Catalan, J., Wheeler, D., & Darby, B. L. (1975). Reciprocal concessions procedure for inducing compliance: The door-in-the-fact technique. *Journal of Personality and Social Psychology, 31,* 206–215. [14]

Clark, D. M., & Teasdale, J. D. (1982). Diurnal variation in clinical depression and accessibility of memories of positive and negative experiences. *Journal of Abnormal Psychology, 91,* 87–95. [6]

Clark, M. L., & Ayers, M. (1992). Friendship similarity during early adolescence: Gender and racial patterns. *Journal of Psychology, 126*, 393–405. [8]

Classen, J., Liepert, J., Wise, S., Hallett, M., & Cohen, L. (1998). Rapid plasticity of human cortical movement representation induced by practice. *Journal of Neurophysiology, 79*, 1117–1123. [2]

Claude M. Steele: Award for distinguished senior career contributions to the public interest. (2003). *American Psychologist, 58*, 909–911. [7]

Clay, R. (2002). Research on 9/11: What psychologists have learned so far. *APA Monitor on Psychology, 33*, 28–30. [10]

Clay, R., Daw, J., & Dittman, M. (2002). More research on America's response. *APA Monitor on Psychology, 33*, 31. [10]

Clayton, V. (2004, September 8). *What's to blame for the rise in ADHD?* Retrieved November 22, 2004, from http:www/msnbc.msn.com/id/5933775/ [1]

Clément, K., Vaisse, C., Lahlou, N., Cabrol, S., Pelloux, V., Cassuto, D., Gourmelen, M., Dina, C., Chambaz, J., Lacorte, J-M., Basdevant, A., Bougnères, P., Lubouc, Y., Froguel, P., & Guy-Grand, B. (1998). A mutation in the human leptin receptor gene causes obesity and pituitary dysfunction. *Nature, 392*, 398–401. [9]

Clifford, E. (2000). Neural plasticity: Merzenich, Taub, and Greenough. *Harvard Brain* [Special Issue], *6*, 16–20. [2]

Cloitre, M., Koenen, K., Cohen, L., & Han, H. (2002). Skills training in affective and interpersonal regulation followed by exposure: A phase-based treatment for PTSD related to childhood abuse. *Journal of Consulting and Clinical Psychology, 70*, 1067–1074. [13]

Cloninger, C. R., Sigvardsson, S., Bohman, M., & von Knorring, A. L. (1982). Predispositions to petty criminality in Swedish adoptees, II. Cross-fostering analysis of gene-environment interaction. *Archives of General Psychiatry, 39*, 1242–1249. [14]

CNN.com. (February 16, 2003). Fatal shooting caught on tape. Retrieved February 17, 2003, from http://www.cnn.com/2003/US/South/02/16/gas.shooting.ap/index.html [14]

Cohen, L. L., & Shotland, R. L. (1996). Timing of first sexual intercourse in a relationship: Expectations, experiences, and perceptions of others. *Journal of Sex Research, 33*, 291–299. [9]

Cohen, S., Doyle, W. J., Skoner, D. P., Rabin, B. S., & Gwaltney, J. M., Jr. (1997). Social ties and susceptibility to the common cold. *Journal of the American Medical Association, 277*, 1940–1944. [10]

Cohen, S., & Herbert, T. B. (1996). Health psychology: Psychological factors and physical disease from the perspective of human psychoneuroimmunology. *Annual Review of Psychology, 47*, 113–142. [10]

Cohen, S., & Williamson, G. M. (1991). Stress and infectious disease in humans. *Psychological Bulletin, 109*, 5–54. [10]

Colby, A., Kohlberg, L., Gibbs, J., & Lieberman, M. (1983). A longitudinal study of moral judgment. *Monographs of the Society for Research in Child Development, 48*(1–2, Serial No. 200). [8]

Cole, R., Smith, J., Alcala, Y., Elliott, J., & Kripke, D. (2002). Bright-light mask treatment of delayed sleep phase syndrome. *Journal of Biological Rhythms, 17*, 89–101. [4]

Coleman, C., King, B., Bolden-Watson, C., Book, M., Segraves, R., Richard, N., Ascher, J., Batey, S., Jamerson, B., & Metz, A. (2001). A placebo-controlled comparison of the effects on sexual functioning of bupropion sustained release and fluoxetine. *Clinical Therapeutics: The International Peer-Reviewed Journal of Drug Therapy, 23*, 1040–1058. [12]

Collaer, M. L., & Hines, M. (1995). Human behavioral sex differences: A role for gonadal hormones during early development. *Psychological Bulletin, 118*, 55–107. [8, 9]

Collins, V., Halliday, J., Kahler, S., & Williamson, R. (2001). Parents' experiences with genetic counseling after the birth of a baby with a genetic disorder: An exploratory study. *Journal of Genetic Counseling, 10*, 53–72. [2]

Colwell, J., & Payne, J. (2000). Negative correlates of computer game play in adolescents. *British Journal of Psychology, 91* (Pt. 3), 295–310. [14]

Conca, A., Swoboda, E., König, P., Koppi, S., Beraus, W., Künz, A., et al. (2000). Clinical impacts of single transcranial magnetic stimulation (sTMS) as an add-on therapy in severely depressed patients under SSRI treatment. *Human Psychopharmacology: Clinical and Experimental, 15*, 429–438. [13]

Condon, W. S., & Sander, L. W. (1974). Neonatal movement is synchronized with adult speech: Interactional participation and language acquisition. *Science, 183*, 99–101. [8]

Coney, J., & Fitzgerald, J. (2000). Gender differences in the recognition of laterally presented affective nouns. *Cognition and Emotion, 14*, 325–339. [9]

Conroy, D., Poczwardowski, A., & Henschen, K. (2001). Evaluative criteria and consequences associated with failure and success for elite athletes and performing artists. *Journal of Applied Sport Psychology, 13*, 300–322. [9]

Consumer Reports. (1995, November) Mental health: Does therapy help?, 734–739. [13]

Coolidge, F., Thede, L., & Young, S. (2002). The heritability of gender identity disorder in a child and adolescent twin sample. *Behavior Genetics, 32*, 251–257. [12]

Coons, P. M. (1994). Confirmation of childhood abuse in child and adolescent cases of multiple personality disorder and dissociative disorder not otherwise specified. *Journal of Nervous and Mental Disease, 182*, 461–464. [12]

Cooper, R. (1994). Normal sleep. In R. Cooper (Ed.), *Sleep.* New York: Chapman & Hall. [4]

Coplan, J. D., Papp, L. A., Pine, D., Marinez, J., Cooper, T., Rosenblum, L. A., Klein, D. F., & Gorman, J. M. (1997). Clinical improvement with fluoxetine therapy and noradrenergic function in patients with panic disorder. *Archives of General Psychiatry, 54*, 643–648. [13]

Corballis, M. C. (1989). Laterality and human evolution. *Psychological Review, 96*, 492–509. [2]

Coren, S. (1996a). Accidental death and the shift to daylight savings time. *Perceptual and Motor Skills, 83*, 921–922. [4]

Coren, S. (1996b). Daylight savings time and traffic accidents. *New England Journal of Medicine, 334*, 924. [4]

Cornelius, M. D., Leech, S. L., Goldschmidt, L., & Day, N. L. (2000). Prenatal tobacco exposure: Is it a risk factor for early tobacco experimentation? *Nicotine & Tobacco Research, 2*, 45–52. [10]

Cosmides, L., & Tooby, J. (2000). Evolutionary psychology and the emotions. In M. Lewis, Jr., & J. M. Haviland-Jones (Eds.), *Handbook of emotions* (2nd ed.). New York: Guilford. [1]

Costa, P. T., Jr., & McCrae, R. R. (1985). *The NEO Personality Inventory.* Odessa, FL: Psychological Assessment Resources. [11]

Costa, P. T., Jr., & McCrae, R. R. (1992). *NEO-PI-R: Revised NEO Personality Inventory (NEO-PI-R).* Odessa, FL: Psychological Assessment Resources. [11]

Costa, P. T., Jr., & McCrae, R. R. (1997). Stability and change in personality assessment: The Revised NEO Personality Inventory in the year 2000. *Journal of Personality Assessment, 68*, 8694. [11]

Costa E Silva, J. A., Chase, M., Sartorius, N., & Roth, T. (1996). Special report from a symposium held by the World Health Organization and the World Federation of Sleep Research Societies: An overview of insomnias and related disorders—recognition, epidemiology, and rational management. *Sleep, 19*, 412–416. [4]

Council on Ethical and Judicial Affairs, American Medical Association. (1991). Gender disparities in clinical decision making. *Journal of the American Medical Association, 266*, 559–562. [10]

Courage, M. L., & Adams, R. J. (1990). Visual acuity assessment from birth to three years using the acuity card procedures: Cross-sectional and longitudinal samples. *Optometry and Vision Science, 67*, 713–718. [8]

Cowan, N. (1988). Evolving conceptions of memory storage, selective attention, and their mutual constraints within the human information-processing system. *Psychological Bulletin, 104*, 163–191. [6]

Coyle, J., & Draper, E. S. (1996). What is the significance of glutamate for mental health? *Harvard Mental Health Letter, 13*(6), 8. [2]

Coyne, S. (2004). Indirect aggression on screen: A hidden problem? *The Psychologist, 17*, 688–690. [5]

Coyne, S., Archer, J., & Eslea, M. (2004). Cruel intentions on television and in real life: Can viewing indirect aggression increase viewers' subsequent indirect aggression? *Journal of Experimental Child Psychology, 88*, 234–253. [14]

Craik, F. I. M., & Lockhart, R. S. (1972). Levels of processing: A framework for memory research. *Journal of Verbal Learning and Verbal Behavior, 11*, 671–684. [6]

Craik, F. I. M., & Tulving, E. (1975). Depth of processing and the retention of words in episodic memory. *Journal of Experimental Psychology: General, 104*, 268–294. [6]

Criglington, A. (1998). Do professionals get jet lag? A commentary on jet lag. *Aviation, Space, & Environmental Medicine, 69*, 810. [4]

Crits-Christoph, P. (1992). The efficacy of brief dynamic psychotherapy: A meta-analysis. *American Journal of Psychiatry, 149*, 151–158. [13]

Crits-Christoph, P., Gibbons, M., Losardo, D., Narducci, J., Schamberger, M., & Gallop, R. (2004). Who benefits from brief psychodynamic therapy for generalized anxiety disorder? *Canadian Journal of Psychoanalysis, 12*, 301–324. [13]

Crombag, H., & Robinson, T. (2004). Drugs, environment, brain, and behavior. *Current Directions in Psychological Science, 13*, 107–111. [4]

Crowder, R. G. (1992) Sensory memory. In L. R. Squire (Ed.), *Encyclopedia of learning and memory.* New York: Macmillan. [6]

Crowe, L. C., & George, W. H. (1989). Alcohol and human sexuality: Review and integration. *Psychological Bulletin, 105*, 374–386. [4]

Crowther, J., Kichler, J., Shewood, N., & Kuhnert, M. (2002). The role of familial factors in bulimia nervosa. *Eating Disorders: The Journal of Treatment & Prevention, 10*, 141–151. [9]

Csikszentmihalyi, M. (1996, July/August). The creative personality. *Psychology Today, 29*, 36–40. [7]

Cui, X-J., & Vaillant, G. E. (1996). Antecedents and consequences of negative life events in adulthood: A longitudinal study. *American Journal of Psychiatry, 153*, 21–26. [12]

Culbertson, F. M. (1997). Depression and gender: An international review. *American Psychologist, 52*, 25–31. [12]

Cunningham, M. R., Roberts, A. R., Barbee, A. P., Druen, P. B., & Wu, C-H. (1995). "Their ideas of beauty are, on the whole, the same as ours": Consistency and variability in the cross-cultural perception of female physical attractiveness. *Journal of Personality and Social Psychology, 68*, 261–279. [14]

Cupach, W. R., & Canary, D. J. (1995). Managing conflict and anger: Investigating the sex stereotype hypothesis. In P. J. Kalbfleisch & M. J. Cody (Eds.), *Gender, power, and communication in human relationships.* Hillsdale, NJ: Erlbaum. [9]

Curci, A., Luminet, O., Finkenauer, C., & Gisler, L. (2001). Flashbulb memories in social groups: A comparative test-retest study of the memory of French president Mitterrand's death in a French and a Belgian group. *Memory, 9*, 81–101. [6]

Curran, P. J., Stice, E., & Chassin, L. (1997). The relation between adolescent alcohol use and peer alcohol use: A longitudinal random coefficients model. *Journal of Consulting and Clinical Psychology, 65*, 130–140. [4]

Cyranowski, J. M., Frand, E., Young, E., & Shear, M. K. (2000). Adolescent onset of the gender difference in lifetime rates of major depression. *Archives of General Psychiatry, 57*, 21–27. [12]

Cytowic, R. (1993). *The man who tasted shapes.* Cambridge, MA: MIT Press. [3]

Cytowic, R. (2002). *Synesthesia: A union of the senses* (2nd ed.). Cambridge, MA: MIT Press. [3]

Dabbs, J. M., Jr., & Morris, R. (1990). Testosterone, social class, and antisocial behavior in a sample of 4,462 men. *Psychological Science, 1*, 209–211. [14]

Dahloef, P., Norlin-Bagge, E., Hedner, J., Ejnell, H., Hetta, J., & Haellstroem, T. (2002). Improvement in neuropsychological performance following surgical treatment for obstructive sleep apnea syndrome. *Acta Oto-Laryngologica, 122*, 86–91. [4]

Daily Hampshire Gazette [Electronic version]. (September 7, 2002). Two missing after 9/11 found. Retrieved November 8, 2002, from http://www.gazettenet.com [12]

Dale, N., & Kandel, E. R. (1990). Facilitatory and inhibitory transmitters modulate spontaneous transmitter release at cultured Aplysia sensorimotor synapses. *Journal of Physiology, 421*, 203–222. [6]

Dallard, I., Cathebras, P., & Sauron, C. (2001). Is cocoa a psychotropic drug? Psychopathological study of self-labeled "chocolate addicts." *Encephale, 27*, 181–186. [4]

Damasio, A. R. (1994). *Descartes' error: Emotion, reason, and the human brain.* New York: Lyons Press. [9]

Damasio, A. R. (1999). *The feeling of what happens: Body and emotion in the making of consciousness.* New York: Harcourt. [9]

Dandy, J., & Nettelbeck, T. (2002). The relationship between IQ, homework, aspirations and academic achievement for Chinese, Vietnamese and Anglo-Celtic Australian school children. *Educational Psychology, 22*, 267–276. [7]

Dantzker, M., & Eisenman, R. (2003). Sexual attitudes among Hispanic college students: Differences between males and females. *International Journal of Adolescence & Youth, 11*, 79–89. [9]

Darley, J. M., & Latané, B. (1968a). Bystander intervention in emergencies: Diffusion of responsibility. *Journal of Personality and Social Psychology, 8*, 377–383. [14]

Darley, J. M., & Latané, B. (1968b, December). When will people help in a crisis? *Psychology Today,* 54–57, 70–71. [14]

Darwin, C. (1872/1965). *The expression of emotion in man and animals.* Chicago: University of Chicago Press. (Original work published 1872). [9]

Dasen, P. R. (1994). Culture and cognitive development from a Piagetian perspective. In W. J. Lonner & R. Malpass (Eds.), *Psychology and culture* (pp. 145–149). Boston: Allyn & Bacon. [8]

Davalos, D., Kisley, M., & Ross, R. (2002). Deficits in auditory and visual temporal perception in schizophrenia. *Cognitive Neuropsychiatry, 7*, 273–282. [12]

Davidson, J. R. T. (1997). Use of benzodiazepines in panic disorder. *Journal of Clinical Psychiatry, 58*(2, Suppl.), 26–28. [13]

Davis, S., Butcher, S. P., & Morris, R. G. M. (1992). The NMDA receptor antagonist D-2-amino-5-phosphonopentanoate (D-AP5) impairs spatial learning and LTP in vivo at intracerebral concentrations comparable to those that block LTP in vitro. *Journal of Neuroscience, 12*, 21–34. [6]

Day, S., & Schneider, P. (2002). Psychotherapy using distance technology: A comparison of face-to-face, video, and audio treatment. *Journal of Counseling Psychology, 49*, 499–503. [13]

D'Azevedo, W. A. (1982). Tribal history in Liberia. In U. Neisser (Ed.), *Memory observed: Remembering in natural contexts.* San Francisco: W. H. Freeman. [6]

de Jong, P., & vander Leij, A. (2002). Effects of phonological abilities and linguistic comprehension on the development of reading. *Scientific Studies of Reading, 6,* 51–77. [8]

de Lacoste, M., Horvath, D., & Woodward, J. (1991). Possible sex differences in the developing human fetal brain. *Journal of Clinical and Experimental Neuropsychology, 13,* 831. [2]

De Souza, A., Baiao, V., & Otta, E. (2003). Perception of men's personal qualities and prospect of employment as a function of facial hair. *Psychological Reports, 92,* 201–208. [11]

De Vos, S. (1990). Extended family living among older people in six Latin American countries. *Journal of Gerontology: Social Sciences, 45,* S87–S94. [8]

Deater-Deckard, K., Lansford, J., Dodge, K., Pettit, G., & Bates, J. (2003). The development of attitudes about physical punishment: An 8-year longitudinal study. *Journal of Family Psychology, 17,* 351–360. [5]

DeCasper, A. J., & Spence, M. J. (1986). Prenatal maternal speech influences newborns' perception of speech sounds. *Infant Behavior and Development, 9,* 133–150. [8]

Dedert, E., Studts, J., Weissbecker, I., Salmon, P., Banis, P., & Sephton, S. (2004). Religiosity may help preserve the cortisol rhythm in women with stress-related illness. *International Journal of Psychiatry in Medicine, 34,* 61–77. [10]

Deinzer, R., Kleineidam, C., Stiller-Winkler, R., Idel, H., & Bachg, D. (2000). Prolonged reduction of salivary immunoglobulin (sIgA) after a major academic exam. *International Journal of Psychophysiology, 37,* 219–232. [10]

Delgado, J. M. R., & Anand, B. K. (1953). Increased food intake induced by electrical stimulation of the lateral hypothalamus. *American Journal of Physiology, 172,* 162–168. [9]

DeLongis, A., Folkman, S., & Lazarus, R. S. (1988). The impact of daily stress on health and mood: Psychological and social resources as mediators. *Journal of Personality and Social Psychology, 54,* 486–495. [10]

Dement, W. C. (1974). *Some must watch while some must sleep.* San Francisco: W. H. Freeman. [4]

Dement, W., & Kleitman, N. (1957). The relation of eye movements during sleep to dream activity: An objective method for the study of dreaming. *Journal of Experimental Psychology, 53,* 339–346. [4]

Deovell, L. Y., Bentin, S., & Soroker, N. (2000). Electrophysiological evidence for an early (pre-attentive) information processing deficit in patients with right hemisphere damage and unilateral neglect. *Brain, 123,* 353–365. [2]

DePrince, A., & Freyd, J. (2004). Forgetting trauma stimuli. *Psychological Science, 15,* 488–492. [6]

Devanand, D. P., Dwork, A. J., Hutchinson, M. S. E., Bolwig, T. G., & Sackeim, H. A. (1994). Does ECT alter brain structure? *American Journal of Psychiatry, 151,* 957–970. [13]

Devine, P. G. (1989). Stereotypes and prejudice: Their automatic and controlled components. *Journal of Personality and Social Psychology, 56,* 5–18. [14]

Dewsbury, D. A. (2000). Introduction: Snapshots of psychology circa 1900. *American Psychologist, 55,* 255–259. [1]

DeYoung, C., Peterson, J., & Higgins, D. (2002). Higher-order factors of the Big Five predict conformity: Are there neuroses of health? *Personality & Individual Differences, 33,* 533–552. [14]

Dickens, W., & Flynn, R. (2001). Heritability estimates versus large environmental effects: The IQ paradox resolved. *Psychological Review, 108,* 346–369. [7]

Diefendorff, J., & Richard, E. (2003). Antecedents and consequences of emotional display rule perceptions. *Journal of Applied Psychology, 88i,* 284–294. [9]

Diener, E., Nickerson, C., Lucas, R., & Sandvik, E. (2002). Dispositional affect and job outcomes. *Social Indicators Research, 59,* 229–259. [8]

DiLalla, L. F., & Gottesman, I. I. (1991). Biological and genetic contributors to violence—Widom's untold tale. *Psychological Bulletin, 109,* 125–129. [14]

Dillard, J., & Anderson, J. (2004). The role of fear in persuasion. *Psychology & Marketing, 21,* 909–926. [14]

Din-Dzietham, R., Nembhard, W., Collins, R., & Davis, S. (2004). Perceived stress following race-based discrimination at work is associated with hypertension in African-Americans. *Social Science & Medicine, 58,* 449–461. [10]

Dion, K., Berscheid, E., & Walster, E. (1972). What is beautiful is good. *Journal of Personality and Social Psychology, 24,* 285–290. [14]

Dipboye, R. L., Fromkin, H. L., & Wilback, K. (1975). Relative importance of applicant sex, attractiveness, and scholastic standing in evaluation of job applicant resumes. *Journal of Applied Psychology, 60,* 39–43. [14]

Dodge, K. A., Bates, J. E., & Pettit, G. S. (1990). Mechanisms in the cycle of violence. *Science, 250,* 1678–1683. [14]

Dodson, C. S., Koutstaal, W., & Schacter, D. L. (2000). Escape from illusion: Reducing false memories. *Trends in Cognitive Sciences, 4,* 391–397. [6]

Dohanich, G. (2003). Ovarian steroids and cognitive function. *Current Directions in Psychological Science, 12,* 57–61. [6]

Dollard, J., Doob, L. W., Miller, N., Mowrer, O. H., & Sears, R. R. (1939). *Frustration and aggression.* New Haven: Yale University Press. [14]

Domino, G. (1984). California Psychological Inventory. In D. J. Keyser & R. C. Sweetland (Eds.), *Test Critiques* (Vol. 1, pp. 146–157). Kansas City: Test Corporation of America. [11]

Domjan, M., Cusato, B., & Krause, M. (2004). Learning with arbitrary versus ecological conditioned stimuli: Evidence from sexual conditioning. *Psychonomic Bulletin & Review, 11,* 232–246. [5]

Doob, L. W., & Sears, R. R. (1939). Factors determining substitute behavior and the overt expression of aggression. *Journal of Abnormal and Social Psychology, 34,* 293–313. [14]

Dorz, S., Lazzarini, L., Cattelan, A., Meneghetti, F., Novara, C., Concia, E., Sica, C., & Sanavio, E. (2003). Evaluation of adherence to antiretroviral therapy in Italian HIV patients. *AIDS Patient Care & STDs, 17,* 33–41. [10]

Doyle, J. A., & Paludi, M. A. (1995). *Sex and gender* (3rd ed.). Madison, WI: Brown & Benchmark. [8]

Dreikurs, R. (1953). *Fundamentals of Adlerian psychology.* Chicago: Alfred Adler Institute. [11]

Drevets, W. C., Price, J. L., Simpson, J. R., Jr., Todd, R. D., Reich, T., Vannier, M., & Raichle, M. E. (1997). Subgenual prefrontal cortex abnormalities in mood disorders. *Nature, 386,* 824–827. [2, 12]

Drobnic, S., Blossfeld, H., & Rohwer, G. (1999). Dynamics of women's employment patterns over the family life course: A comparison of the United States and Germany. *Journal of Marriage & the Family, 61,* 133–146. [8]

Druckman, D., & Bjork, R. A. (Eds.) (1994). *Learning, remembering, believing: Enhancing human performance.* Washington, DC: National Academy Press. [4]

Drug Enforcement Administration. National Drug Intelligence Center. (2003). *National Drug Threat Assessment/2003* [Online report]. Retrieved October 22, 2003, from http://www.usdoj.gov/ndic/pubs3/3300/pharm.htm [4]

Drug Free Workplace. (2002, September). Designer Drugs. *National Medical Report* [Electronic version]. Retrieved May 25, 2003, from http://www.drugfreeworkplace.com/drugsofabuse/designer.htm [4]

Drummond, S., Brown, G., Salamat, J., & Gillin, J. (2004). Increasing task difficulty facilitates the cerebral compensatory response to total sleep deprivation. *Sleep: Journal of Sleep & Sleep Disorders Research, 27,* 445–451. [4]

Drummond, S. P. A., Brown, G. G., Gillin, J. C., Stricker, J. L., Wong, E. C., & Buxton, R. B. (2000). Altered brain response to verbal learning following sleep deprivation. *Nature, 403,* 655–657. [4]

Duck, S. (1983). *Friends for life: The psychology of close relationships.* New York: St. Martin's Press. [8]

Dunkel-Schetter, C., Feinstein, L. G., Taylor, S. E., & Falke, R. L. (1992). Patterns of coping with cancer. *Health Psychology, 11,* 79–87. [10]

Dunn, J., Cutting, A., & Fisher, N. (2002). Old friends, new friends: Predictors of children's perspective on their friends at school. *Child Development, 73,* 621–635. [8]

Durex Global Sex Survey. (2002). Retrieved January 20, 2003, from http://www.durex.com/uk/sexsurvey/globalsexsurvey2002/global_sex2002_freqb.htm [9]

Duyme, M. (1988). School success and social class: An adoption study. *Developmental Psychology, 24,* 203–209. [7]

Dywan, J., & Bowers, K. (1983). The use of hypnosis to enhance recall. *Science, 222,* 184–185. [4, 6]

Eagly, A. H., Ashmore, R. D., Makhijani, M. G., & Longo, L. C. (1991). What is beautiful is good . . . : A meta-analytic review of research on the physical attractiveness stereotype. *Psychological Bulletin, 110,* 109–128. [14]

Eagly, A. H., & Carli, L. (1981). Sex of researchers and sex-typed communications as determinants of sex differences in influence-ability: A meta-analysis of social influence studies. *Psychological Bulletin, 90,* 1–20. [14]

Eagly, A. H., & Wood, W. (1999). The origins of sex differences in human behavior: Evolved dispositions versus social roles. *American Psychologist, 54,* 408–423. [1, 9, 14]

Earlandsson, L., & Eklund, M. (2003). The relationships among hassles and uplifts to experience of health in working women. *Women & Health, 38,* 19–37. [10]

Eating disorders—part II. (1997, November). *Harvard Mental Health Letter, 14*(5), 1–5. [9]

Ebbinghaus, H. (1913). *Memory* (H. Ruyer & C. E. Bussenius, Trans.). New York: Teacher's College Press. (Original work published 1885) [6]

Ebbinghaus, H. E. (1885/1964). *Memory: A contribution to experimental psychology* (H. A. Ruger & C. E. Bussenius, Trans.). New York: Dover. (Original work published 1885). [6]

Edith Chen: Award for distinguished scientific early career contributions to psychology. (2004). *American Psychologist, 59,* 707–709. [10]

Edwards, B., Atkinson, G., Waterhouse, J., Reilly, T., Godfrey, R., & Budgett, R. (2000). Use of melatonin in recovery from jet-lag following an eastward flight across 10 time-zones. *Ergonomics, 43,* 1501–1513. [4]

Edwards, K., & Smith, E. E. (1996). A disconfirmation bias in the evaluation of arguments. *Journal of Personality and Social Psychology, 71,* 5–24. [14]

Egeth, H. E. (1993). What do we not know about eyewitness identification? *American Psychologist, 48,* 577–580. [6]

Ehrhardt, A. A., Evers, K., & Money, J. (1968). Influence of androgen and some aspects of sexual dimorphic behavior in women with the late-treated adrenogenital syndrome. *Johns Hopkins Medical Journal, 123,* 115–122. [9]

Eichenbaum, H. (1997). Declarative memory: Insights from cognitive neurobiology. *Annual Review of Psychology, 48,* 547–572. [2, 6]

Eichenbaum, H., & Fortin, N. (2003). Episodic memory and the hippocampus: It's about time. *Current Directions in Psychological Science, 12,* 53–57. [6]

Eichenbaum, H., & Otto, T. (1993). LTP and memory: Can we enhance the connection? *Trends in Neurosciences, 16,* 163. [6]

Eidelson, R., & Eidelson, J. (2003). Dangerous ideas. *American Psychologist, 58,* 182–192. [14]

Ekman, P. (1972). Universals and cultural differences in facial expression of emotion. In J. Cole (Ed.), *Nebraska symposium on motivation* (Vol. 19). Lincoln: University of Nebraska Press. [9]

Ekman, P. (1993). Facial expression and emotion. *American Psychologist, 48,* 384–392. [9]

Ekman, P., & Friesen, W. V. (1975). *Unmasking the face: A guide to recognizing emotions from facial clues.* Englewood Cliffs, NJ: Prentice-Hall. [9]

Ekman, P., Levenson, R. W., & Friesen, W. V. (1983). Autonomic nervous system activity distinguishes among emotions. *Science, 221,* 1208–1210. [9]

Elal, G., Altug, A., Slade, P., & Tekcan, A. (2000). Factor structure of the Eating Attitudes Test (EAT) in a Turkish university sample. *Eating and Weight Disorders: Studies on Anorexia, Bulimia, and Obesity, 5,* 46–50. [9]

Elkin, I., Gibbons, R. D., Shea, M. T., Sotsky, S. M., Watkins, J. T., Pikonis, P. A., & Hedeker, D. (1995). Initial severity and differential treatment outcome in the National Institute of Mental Health Treatment of Depression Collaborative Research Program. *Journal of Consulting and Clinical Psychology, 63,* 841–847. [13]

Elkin, I., Shea, M. T., Watkins, J. T., et al. (1989). National Institute of Mental Health Treatment of Depression Collaborative Research Program: General effectiveness of treatments. *Archives of General Psychology, 46,* 971–982. [13]

Elkind, D. (1967). Egocentrism in adolescence. *Child Development, 38,* 1025–1034. [8]

Elkind, D. (1974). *Children and adolescents: Interpretive essays on Jean Piaget* (2nd ed.). New York: Oxford University Press. [8]

Ellason, J. W., & Ross, C. A. (1997). Two-year follow-up of inpatients with dissociative identity disorder. *American Journal of Psychiatry, 154,* 832–839. [12]

Elliot, A. J., & Devine, P. G. (1994). On the motivational nature of cognitive dissonance: Dissonance as psychological discomfort. *Journal of Personality and Social Psychology, 67,* 382–394. [14]

Ellis, A. (1961). *A guide to rational living.* Englewood Cliffs, NJ: Prentice-Hall. [13]

Ellis, A. (1977). The basic clinical theory of rational-emotive therapy. In A. Ellis & R. Grieger (Eds.), *Handbook of rational-emotive therapy* (pp. 3–33). New York: Springer. [13]

Ellis, A. (1993). Reflections on rational-emotive therapy. *Journal of Consulting and Clinical Psychology, 61,* 199–201. [13]

Ellis, A. (2004a). Why I (really) became a therapist. *Journal of Rational-Emotive & Cognitive Behavior Therapy, 22,* 73–77. [13]

Ellis, A. (2004b). Why rational-emotive behavior therapy is the most comprehensive and effective form of behavior therapy. *Journal of Rational-Emotive & Cognitive Behavior Therapy, 22,* 85–92. [13]

Ellis, R. (2001). A theoretical model of the role of the cerebellum in cognition, attention and consciousness. *Consciousness & Emotion, 2,* 300–309. [2]

Engel, G. L. (1977). The need for a new medical model: A challenge for biomedicine. *Science, 196,* 126–129. [10]

Engel, G. L. (1980). The clinical application of the biopsychosocial model. *American Journal of Psychiatry, 137,* 535–544. [10]

Engen, T. (1982). *The perception of odors.* New York: Academic Press. [3]

Epstein, J. (1983). Examining theories of adolescent friendships. In J. Epstein & N. Karweit (Eds.), *Friends in school.* New York: Academic Press. [8]

Epstein, J., Stern, E., & Silbersweig, D. (2001). Neuropsychiatry at the millennium: The potential for mind/brain integration through emerging interdisciplinary research strategies. *Clinical Neuroscience Research, 1,* 10–18. [13]

Erdogan, A., Kocabasoglu, N., Yalug, I., Ozbay, G., & Senturk, H. (2004). Management of marked liver enzyme increase during clozapine treatment: A case report and review of the literature. *International Journal of Psychiatry in Medicine, 34,* 83–89. [13]

Erikson, E. H. (1980). *Identity and the life cycle.* New York: Norton. [8]

Erlenmeyer-Kimling, L., & Jarvik, L. F. (1963). Genetics and intelligence: A review. *Science, 142,* 1477–1479. [7]

Eron, L. D. (1987). The development of aggressive behavior from the perspective of a developing behaviorism. *American Psychologist, 42,* 435–442. [14]

Eronen, M., Hakola, P., & Tiihonen, J. (1996). Mental disorders and homicidal behavior in Finland. *Journal of Personality and Social Psychology, 53,* 497–501. [14]

Escher, M., Desmeules, J., Giostra, E., & Mentha, G. (2001). Hepatitis associated with kava, a herbal remedy for anxiety. *BMJ: British Medical Journal, 322,* 139. [4]

Estes, W. K. (1994). *Classification and cognition.* New York: Oxford University Press. [7]

Etcoff, N., Ekman, P., Magee, J., & Frank, M. (2000). Lie detection and language comprehension. *Nature, 405,* 139. [2]

Evans, G. W., & Lepore, S. J. (1993). Household crowding and social support: A quasiexperimental analysis. *Journal of Personality and Social Psychology, 65,* 308–316. [14]

Evans, M. D., Hollon, S. D., DeRubeis, R. J., Piasecki, J. M., Grove, W. M., Garvey, M. J., & Tuason, V. B. (1992). Differential relapse following cognitive therapy and pharmacotherapy for depression. *Archives of General Psychiatry, 49,* 802–808. [13]

Everson, S. A., Goldberg, D. E., Kaplan, G. A., Cohen, R. D., Pukkala, E., Tuomilehto, J., & Salonen, J. T. (1996). Hopelessness and risk of mortality and incidence of myocardial infarction and cancer. *Psychosomatic Medicine, 58,* 113–121. [10]

Exner, J. E. (1993). *The Rorschach: A comprehensive system: Vol. 1. Basic foundations* (3rd ed.). New York: Wiley. [11]

Eysenbach, G., Powell, J., Kuss, O., & Sa, E. (2002). Empirical studies of health information for consumers on the World Wide Web: A systematic review. *JAMA: Journal of the American Medical Association, 287,* 2691–2700. [10]

Eysenck, H. J. (1990). Genetic and environmental contributions to individual differences: The three major dimensions of personality. *Journal of Personality, 58,* 245–261. [11]

Eysenck, H. J. (1994). The outcome problem in psychotherapy: What have we learned? *Behaviour Research and Therapy, 32,* 477–495. [13]

Fackelmann, K. (1997). Marijuana on trial: Is marijuana a dangerous drug or a valuable medicine? *Science News, 151,* 178–179, 183. [4]

Fagot, B. (1995). Observations of parent reactions to sex-stereotyped behavior: Age and sex effects. *Child Development, 62,* 617–628. [8]

Faisal-Cury, A., Tedesco, J., Kahhale, S., Menezes, P., & Zugaib, M. (2004). Postpartum depression: In relation to life events and patterns of coping. *Archives of Women's Mental Health, 7,* 123–131. [10]

Falbo, T., & Polit, D. F. (1986). Quantitative review of the only child literature: Research evidence and theory development. *Psychological Bulletin, 100,* 176–189. [9]

Falloon, I. R. H. (1988). Expressed emotion: Current status. *Psychological Medicine, 18,* 269–274. [13]

Famighetti, R. (Ed.). (1997). *The world almanac and book of facts 1998.* Mahwah, NJ: World Almanac Books. [13]

Fang, C., & Myers, H. (2001). The effects of racial stressors and hostility on cardiovascular reactivity in African American and Caucasian men. *Health Psychology, 20,* 64–70. [10]

Fanous, A., Gardner, C., Prescott, C., Cancro, R., & Kendler, K. (2002). Neuroticism, major depression and gender: A population-based twin study. *Psychological Medicine, 32,* 719–728. [12]

Fantz, R. L. (1961). The origin of form perception. *Scientific American, 204,* 66–72. [8]

Farde, L. (1996). The advantage of using positron emission tomography in drug research. *Trends in Neurosciences, 19,* 211–214. [2]

Farrer, L. A., & Cupples, A. (1994). Estimating the probability for major gene Alzheimer disease. *American Journal of Human Genetics, 54,* 374–383. [8]

Faryna, E., & Morales, E. (2000). Self-efficacy and HIV-related risk behaviors among multiethnic adolescents. *Cultural Diversity and Ethnic Minority Psychology, 6,* 42–56. [4]

Fauerbach, J., Lawrence, J., Haythornthwaite, J., & Richter, L. (2002). Coping with the stress of a painful medical procedure. *Behaviour Research & Therapy, 40,* 1003–1015. [11]

Faunce, G. (2002). Eating disorders and attentional bias: A review. *Eating Disorders: The Journal of Treatment & Prevention, 10,* 125–139. [9]

Fazio, R. H., & Williams, C. J. (1986). Attitude accessibility as a moderator of the attitude perception and attitude-behavior relations: An investigation of the 1984 presidential election. *Journal of Personality and Social Psychology, 51,* 505–514. [14]

Federal Interagency Forum on Aging-Related Statistics (FIFARS). (2000). Older Americans 2000: Key indicators of well-being. Retrieved January 27, 2005, from http://www.agingstats.gov/chartbook2004/default.htm [8]

Federal Interagency Forum on Aging-Related Statistics (FIFARS). (2004). Older Americans 2004: Key indicators of well-being. Retrieved January 27, 2005, from http://www.agingstats.gov/chartbook2004/default.htm [8]

Feingold, A. (1988). Matching for attractiveness in romantic partners and same-sex friends: A meta-analysis and theoretical critique. *Psychological Bulletin, 104,* 226–235. [14]

Fenn, K., Nusbaum, H., & Margoliash, D. (2003). Consolidation during sleep of perceptual learning of spoken language. *Nature, 425,* 614–616. [4]

Fenton, W. S., & McGlashan, T. H. (1991). Natural history of schizophrenia subtypes: I. Longitudinal study of paranoid, hebephrenic, and undifferentiated schizophrenia. *Archives of General Psychiatry, 48,* 969–977. [12]

Fenton, W. S., & McGlashan, T. H. (1994). Antecedents, symptom progression, and long-term outcome of the deficit syndrome in schizophrenia. *American Journal of Psychiatry, 151,* 351–356. [12]

Fernald, A. (1993). Approval and disapproval: Infant responsiveness to vocal affect in familiar and unfamiliar languages. *Child Development, 64,* 637–656. [8]

Fernandez, M. (1997). Domestic violence by extended family members in India. *Journal of Interpersonal Violence, 12,* 433–455. [5]

Festinger, L. (1957). *A theory of cognitive dissonance.* Evanston, IL: Row, Peterson. [14]

Festinger, L., & Carlsmith, J. M. (1959). Cognitive consequences of forced compliance. *Journal of Abnormal and Social Psychology, 58,* 203–210. [14]

Fiatarone, M. A., Morley, J. E., Bloom, E. T., Benton, D., Makinodan, T., & Solomon, G. F. (1988). Endogenous opioids and the exercise-induced augmentation of natural killer cell activity. *Journal of Laboratory and Clinical Medicine, 112,* 544–552. [10]

Fiatarone, M. A., O'Neill, E. F., Ryan, N. D., Clements, K. M., Solares, G. R., Nelson, M. E., Roberts, S. B., Kehayias, J. J., Lipsitz, L. A., & Evans, W. J. (1994). Exercise training and nutritional supplementation for physical frailty in very elderly people. *New England Journal of Medicine, 330,* 1769–1775. [8]

Field, M., & Duka, T. (2002). Cues paired with a low dose of alcohol acquire conditioned incentive properties in social drinkers. *Psychopharmacology, 159,* 325–334. [5]

Field, T. (2002). Infants' need for touch. *Human Development, 45,* 100–103. [8]

Field, T., Schanberg, S. M., Scfidi, F., Bauer, C. R., Vega-Lahr, N., Garcia, R., Nystrom, J., & Kuhn, C. (1986, May). Tactile/kinesthetic stimulation effects on preterm neonates. *Pediatrics, 77,* 654–658. [3]

Field, T. M., Cohen, D., Garcia, R., & Greenberg, R. (1984). Mother-stranger face discrimination by the newborn. *Infant Behavior and Development, 7,* 19–25. [8]

Fields, J., Walton, K., & Schneider, R. (2002). Effect of a multi-modality natural medicine program on carotid atherosclerosis in older subjects: A pilot trial of Maharishi Verdic Medicine. *American Journal of Cardiology, 89,* 952–958. [4]

Fiez, J. A. (1996). Cerebellar contributions to cognition. *Neuron, 16,* 13–15. [2]

Finch, A. E., Lambert, M. J., & Brown, G. (2000). Attacking anxiety: A naturalistic study of a multimedia self-help program. *Journal of Clinical Psychology, 56,* 11–21. [13]

Fink, B., & Penton-Voak, I. (2002). Evolutionary psychology of facial attractiveness. *Current Directions in Psychological Science, 11,* 154–158. [14]

Fischbach, G. D. (1992). Mind and brain. *Scientific American, 267,* 48–56. [6]

Fischer, K., & Rose, S. (1994). Dynamic development of coordination of components in brain and behavior: A framework for theory and research. In K. Fischer & G. Dawson (Eds.), *Human Behavior and the Developing Brain* (pp. 3–66). New York: Guilford Press. [2]

Fivush, R., & Nelson, K. (2004). Culture and language in the emergence of autobiographical memory. *Psychological Science, 15,* 573–577. [6]

Fixx, J. F. (1978). *Solve It! A perplexing profusion of puzzles.* New York: Doubleday. [7]

Flavell, J. H. (1985). *Cognitive development.* Englewood, NJ: Prentice-Hall. [8]

Flavell, J. H. (1992). Cognitive development: Past, present, and future. *Developmental Psychology, 28,* 998–1005. [8]

Flavell, J. H. (1996). Piaget's legacy. *Psychological Science, 7,* 200–203. [8]

Fleck, D., Hendricks, W., DelBellow, M., & Strakowski, S. (2002). Differential prescription of maintenance antipsychotics to African American and White patients with new-onset bipolar disorder. *Journal of Clinical Psychiatry, 63,* 658–664. [13]

Fleming, J. D. (1974, July). Field report: The state of the apes. *Psychology Today,* 31–46. [7]

Fleshner, M., & Laudenslager, M. (2004). Psychoneuroimmunology: Then and now. *Behavioral & Cognitive Neuroscience Reviews, 3,* 114–130. [10]

Fletcher, J. M., Page, B., Francis, D. J., Copeland, K., Naus, M. J., Davis, C. M., Morris, R., Krauskopf, D., & Satz, P. (1996). Cognitive correlates of long-term cannabis use in Costa Rican men. *Archives of General Psychiatry, 53,* 1051–1057. [4]

Flood, J. F., Silver, A. J., & Morley, J. E. (1990). Do peptide-induced changes in feeding occur because of changes in motivation to eat? *Peptides, 11,* 265–270. [9]

Florio, V., Fossella, S., Maravita, A., Miniussi, C., & Marzi, C. (2002). Interhemispheric transfer and laterality effects in simple visual reaction time in schizophrenics. *Cognitive Neuropsychiatry, 7,* 97–111. [12]

Flynn, J. (1999). Searching for justice: The discovery of IQ gains over time. *American Psychologist, 54,* 5–20. [7]

Flynn, J. R. (1987). Race and IQ: Jensen's case refuted. In S. Modgil, & C. Modgil (Eds.), *Arthur Jensen: Consensus and controversy.* New York: Palmer Press. [7]

Foa, E. B. (1995). How do treatments for obsessive-compulsive disorder compare? *Harvard Mental Health Letter, 12*(1), 8. [13]

Foa, E. B., & Meadows, E. A. (1997). Psychosocial treatments for posttraumatic stress disorder: A critical review. *Annual Review of Psychology, 48,* 449–480. [10]

Fogel, J., Albert, S., Schnabel, F., Ditkoff, B., & Neugut, A. (2002). Internet use and social support in women with breast cancer. *Health Psychology, 21,* 398–404. [10]

Foley, D. J., Monjan, A. A., Brown, S. L., Simonsick, E. M., Wallace, R. B., & Blazer, D. G. (1995). Sleep complaints among elderly persons: An epidemiologic study of three communities. *Sleep, 18,* 425–432. [4]

Folkard, S. (1990). Circadian performance rhythms: Some practical and theoretical implications. *Philosophical Transactions of the Royal Society of London. Series B: Biological Sciences, 327,* 543–553. [4]

Folkerts, H. (2000). Electroconvulsive therapy of depressive disorders. *Ther. Umsch, 57,* 290–294. [13]

Folkman, S. (1984). Personal control and stress and coping processes: A theoretical analysis. *Journal of Personality and Social Psychology, 46,* 839–852. [10]

Folkman, S., Chesney, M., Collette, L., Boccellari, A., & Cooke, M. (1996). Postbereavement depressive mood and its prebereavement predictors in HIV+ and HIV- gay men. *Journal of Personality and Social Psychology, 70,* 336–348. [8]

Folkman, S., & Lazarus, R. S. (1980). An analysis of coping in a middle-aged community sample. *Journal of Health and Social Behavior, 21,* 219–239. [10]

Ford, C. S., & Beach, F. A. (1951). *Patterns of sexual behavior.* New York: Harper & Row. [9]

Foulkes, D. (1996). Sleep and dreams: Dream research: 1953–1993. *Sleep, 19,* 609–624. [4]

Fox, N. A., & Bell, M. A. (1990). Electrophysiological indices of frontal lobe development: Relations to cognitive and affective behavior in human infants over the first year of life. *Annals of the New York Academy of Sciences, 608,* 677–698. [8]

Frank, E., Anderson, B., Reynolds, C. F., III, Ritenour, A., & Kupfer, D. J. (1994). Life events and the research diagnostic criteria endogenous subtype. *Archives of General Psychiatry, 51,* 519–524. [12]

Frank, E., Kupfer, D. J., Wagner, E. F., McEachran, A. B., & Cornes, C. (1991). Efficacy of interpersonal psychotherapy as a maintenance treatment of recurrent depression: Contributing factors. *Archives of General Psychiatry, 48,* 1053–1059. [13]

Frank, M., Formaker, B., & Hettinger, T. (2003). Taste response to mixtures: Analytic processing of quality. *Behavioral Neuroscience, 117,* 228–235. [3]

Frankenburg, W. K., Dodds, J. B., Archer, P., et al. (1992). *Denver II training manual.* Denver: Denver Developmental Materials. [8]

Franks, P., Gold, M., & Fiscella, K. (2003). Sociodemographics, self-rated health, and mortality in the U.S. *Social Science & Medicine, 56,* 2505–2514. [10]

Frantz, K., Hansson, K., Stouffer, D., & Parsons, L. (2002). 5-HT-sub-6 receptor antagonism potentiates the behavioral and neurochemical effects of amphetamine but not cocaine. *Neuropharmacology, 42,* 170–180. [4]

Franz, C. E., McClelland, D. C., & Weinberger, J. (1991). Childhood antecedents of conventional social accomplishment in midlife adults: A 36-year prospective study. *Journal of Personality and Social Psychology, 60,* 586–595. [8]

Frazer, A. (1997). Antidepressants. *Journal of Clinical Psychiatry, 58*(6, Suppl.), 9–25. [13]

Frazer, N., Larkin, K., & Goodie, J. (2002). Do behavioral responses mediate or moderate the relation between cardiovascular reactivity to stress and parental history of hypertension? *Health Psychology, 21,* 244–253. [10]

Fredricks, J., & Eccles, J. (2002). Children's competence and value beliefs from childhood through adolescence growth trajectories in two male-sex-typed domains. *Developmental Psychology, 38,* 519–533. [7]

Fredrikson, M., Annas, P., Fischer, H., & Wik, G. (1996). Gender and age differences in the prevalence of specific fears and phobias. *Behaviour Research and Therapy, 34,* 33–39. [12]

Freedman, J. L., & Fraser, S. C. (1966). Compliance without pressure: The foot-in-the-door technique. *Journal of Personality and Social Psychology, 4,* 195–202. [14]

Freeman, W. J. (1991). The physiology of perception. *Scientific American, 264,* 78–85. [3]

Freud, S. (1900/1953a). The interpretation of dreams. In J. Strachey (Ed. and Trans.), *The standard edition of the complete psychological works of Sigmund Freud* (Vols. 4 and 5). London: Hogarth Press. (Original work published 1900). [4]

Freud, S. (1905/1953b). Three essays on the theory of sexuality. In J. Strachey (Ed. and Trans.), *The standard edition of the complete psychological works of Sigmund Freud* (Vol. 7). London: Hogarth Press. (Original work published 1905). [11]

Freud, S. (1920/1963b). *A general introduction to psycho-analysis* (J. Riviere, Trans.). New York: Simon & Schuster. (Original work published 1920). [11]

Freud, S. (1922). *Beyond the pleasure principle.* London: International Psychoanalytic Press. [6]

Freud, S. (1925/1963a). *An autobiographical study* (J. Strachey, Trans.). New York: W.W. Norton. (Original work published 1925). [11]

Freud, S. (1930/1962). *Civilization and its discontents* (J. Strachey, Trans.). New York: W. W. Norton. (Original work published 1930). [11]

Freud, S. (1933/1965). *New introductory lectures on psychoanalysis* (J. Strachey, Trans.). New York: W. W. Norton. (Original work published 1933). [11]

Frey, K. P., & Eagly, A. H. (1993). Vividness can undermine the persuasiveness of messages. *Journal of Personality and Social Psychology, 65,* 32–44. [14]

Frey, M., & Detterman, D. (2004). Scholastic assessment or *g?* The relationship between the scholastic assessment test and general cognitive ability. *Psychological Science, 15,* 373–378. [7]

Friedland, N., Keinan, G., & Regev, Y. (1992). Controlling the uncontrollable: Effects of stress on illusory perceptions of controllability. *Journal of Personality and Social Psychology, 63,* 923–931. [10]

Friedman, J. M. (1997). The alphabet of weight control. *Nature, 385,* 119–120. [9]

Friedman, J. M. (2000). Obesity in the new millennium. *Nature, 404,* 632–634. [9]

Friedman, M., & Rosenman, R. H. (1974). *Type A behavior and your heart.* New York: Fawcett. [10]

Friedman, M. I., Tordoff, M. G., & Ramirez, I. (1986). Integrated metabolic control of food intake. *Brain Research Bulletin, 17,* 855–859. [9]

Fujita, F., Diener, E., & Sandvik, E. (1991). Gender differences in negative affect and well-being: The case for emotional intensity. *Journal of Personality and Social Psychology, 61,* 427–434. [9]

Gadea, M., Martinez-Bisbal, M., Marti-Bonmati, Espert, R., Casanova, B., Coret, F., & Celda, B. (2004). Spectroscopic axonal damage of the right locus coeruleus relates to selective attention impairment in early stage relapsing-remitting multiple sclerosis. *Brain, 127,* 89–98. [2]

Gallagher, M., & Rapp, P. R. (1997). The use of animal models to study the effects of aging on cognition. *Annual Review of Psychology, 48,* 339–370. [8]

Gallo, L., Troxel, W., Matthews, K., Jansen-McWilliams, L., Kuller, L., & Suton-Tyrrell, K. (2003). Occupation and subclinical carotid artery disease: Are clerical workers at greater risk? *Health Psychology, 22,* 19–29. [10]

Gallup, G., Jr., & Hugick, L. (1990). Racial tolerance grows, progress on racial equality less evident. *Gallup Poll Monthly,* No. 297, 23–32. [14]

Galton, F. (1874). *English men of science: Their nature and nurture.* London: Macmillan. [7]

Ganellen, R. J. (1996). Comparing the diagnostic efficiency of the MMPI, MCMI-II, and Rorschach: A review. *Journal of Personality Assessment, 67,* 219–243. [11]

Gao, J-H., Parsons, L. M., Bower, J. M., Xiong, J., Li, J., & Fox, P. T. (1996). Cerebellum implicated in sensory acquisition and discrimination rather than motor control. *Science, 272,* 545–547. [2]

Garavan, H., Morgan, R. E., Levitsky, D. A., Hermer-Vasquez, L., & Strupp, B. J. (2000). Enduring effects of early lead exposure: Evidence for a specific deficit in associative ability. *Neurotoxicology and Teratology, 22,* 151–164. [7]

Gardner, H. (1983). *Frames of mind: The theory of multiple intelligences.* New York: Basic Books. [7]

Gardner, H., & Hatch, T. (1989). Multiple intelligences go to school: Educational implication of the theory of multiple intelligences. *Educational Researcher, 18*(8), 6. [7]

Gardner, R. A., & Gardner, B. T. (1969). Teaching sign language to a chimpanzee. *Science, 165,* 664–672. [7]

Garfield, C. (1986). *Peak performers: The new heroes of American business.* New York: Morrow. [7]

Garma, L., & Marchand, F. (1994). Non-pharmacological approaches to the treatment of narcolepsy. *Sleep, 17,* S97–S102. [4]

Garmon, L. C., Basinger, K. S., Gregg, V. R., & Gibbs, J. C. (1996). Gender differences in stage and expression of moral judgment. *Merrill-Palmer Quarterly, 42,* 418–437. [8]

Garrett, M., Garrett, J., & Brotherton, D. (2001). Inner circle/outer circle: A group technique based on Native American healing circles. *Journal for Specialists in Group Work, 26,* 17–30. [13]

Garry, M., & Loftus, E. F. (1994). Pseudomemories without hypnosis. *International Journal of Clinical and Experimental Hypnosis, 42,* 363–373. [6]

Gartner, J., & Whitaker-Azimitia, P. M. (1996). Developmental factors influencing aggression: Animal models and clinical correlates. *Annals of the New York Academy of Sciences, 794,* 113–120. [14]

Gastil, J. (1990). Generic pronouns and sexist language: The oxymoronic character of masculine generics. *Sex Roles, 23,* 629–643. [7]

Gawin, F. H. (1991). Cocaine addiction: Psychology and neurophysiology. *Science, 251,* 1580–1586. [4]

Gawronski, B., Alshut, E., Grafe, J., Nespethal, J., Ruhmland, A., & Schulz, L. (2002). Processes of judging known and unknown persons. *Zeitschrift fuer Sozialpsychologie, 33,* 25–34. [14]

Gazzaniga, M. (1970). *The bisected brain.* New York: Appleton-Century-Crofts. [2]

Gazzaniga, M. (1989). Organization of the human brain. *Science, 245,* 947–952. [2]

Gazzaniga, M. S. (1983). Right hemisphere language following brain bisection: A 20-year perspective. *American Psychologist, 38,* 525–537. [2]

Gazzola, N., & Stalikas, A. (2004). Therapist interpretations and client processes in three therapeutic modalities: Implications for psychotherapy integration. *Journal of Psychotherapy Integration, 14,* 397–418. [13]

Ge, X., Brody, G., Conger, R., Simons, R., & Murry, V. (2002). Contextual amplification of pubertal transition effects on deviant peer affiliation and externalizing behavior among African American children. *Developmental Psychology, 38,* 42–54. [8]

Geary, D. C. (1996). Sexual selection and sex differences in mathematical abilities. *Behavioral and Brain Sciences, 19*, 229–284. [7]

Geen, R. G. (1984). Human motivation: New perspectives on old problems. In A. M. Rogers & C. J. Scheier (Eds.), *The G. Stanley Hall lecture series* (Vol. 4). Washington, DC: American Psychological Association. [8]

Geer, K., Ropka, M., Cohn, W., Jones, S., & Miesfeldt, S. (2001). Factors influencing patients' decisions to decline cancer genetic counseling services. *Journal of Genetic Counseling, 10*, 25–40. [2]

Gehart, D., & Lyle, R. (2001). Client experience of gender in therapeutic relationships: An interpretive ethnography. *Family Process, 40*, 443–458. [13]

Gehring, D. (2003). Couple therapy for low sexual desire: A systematic approach. *Journal of Sex & Marital Therapy, 29*, 25–38. [13]

Geiselman, R. E., Schroppel, T., Tubridy, A., Konishi, T., & Rodriguez, V. (2000). Objectivity bias in eye witness performance. *Applied Cognitive Psychology, 14*, 323–332. [6]

George, M. S., Ketter, T. A., & Post, R. M. (1993). SPECT and PET imaging in mood disorders. *Journal of Clinical Psychiatry, 54*(11, Suppl.), 6–13. [12]

Gergen, K. J., Gulerce, A., Lock, A., & Misra, G. (1996). Psychological science in cultural context. *American Psychologist, 51*, 496–503. [1]

Gerull, F., & Rapee, R. (2002). Mother knows best: The effects of maternal modelling on the acquisition of fear and avoidance behaviour in toddlers. *Behaviour Research & Therapy, 40*, 279–287. [5]

Gevins, A., Leong, H., Smith, M. E., Le, J., & Du, R. (1995). Mapping cognitive brain function with modern high-resolution electroencephalography. *Trends in Neurosciences, 18*, 429–436. [2]

Gibbons, A. (1991). Déjà vu all over again: Chimp-language wars. *Science, 251*, 1561–1562. [7]

Gibson, E., & Walk, R. D. (1960). The "visual cliff." *Scientific American, 202*, 64–71. [8]

Gibson, J. (1994). The visual perception of objective motion and subjective motion. *Psychological Review, 101*, 318–323. [3]

Giedd, J. N., Rapoport, J. L., Garvey, M. A., Perlmutter, S., & Swedo, S. E. (2000). MRI assessment of children with obsessive-compulsive disorder or tics associated with streptococcal infection. *American Journal of Psychiatry, 157*, 2281–2283. [12]

Gigerenzer, G. (2004). Dread risk, September 11, and fatal traffic accidents. *Psychological Science, 15*, 286–287. [7]

Gigerenzer, G., & Todd, P., for the ABC Research Group (1999). *Simple heuristics that make us smart.* Oxford, England: Oxford University Press. [7]

Gilbert, D. T., & Malone, P. S. (1995). The correspondence bias. *Psychological Bulletin, 117*, 21–38. [14]

Gilligan, C. (1982). *In a different voice: Psychological theory and women's development.* Cambridge, MA: Harvard University Press. [8]

Gingell, C., Nicolosi, A., Buvat, J., Glasser, D., Simsek, F., Hartmann, U., & Laumann, E. (2003, March). *Sexual activity and dysfunction among men and women aged 40 to 80 years.* Poster presented at the XVIIIth Congress of the European Association of Urology, Madrid. [8, 9]

Ginsberg, G., & Bronstein, P. (1993). Family factors related to children's intrinsic/extrinsic motivational orientation and academic performance. *Child Development, 64*, 1461–1474. [9]

Ginty, D. D., Kornhauser, J. M., Thompson, M. A., Bading, H., Mayo, K. E., Takahashi, J. S., & Greenberg, M. E. (1993). Regulation of CREB phosphorylation in the suprachiasmatic nucleus by light and a circadian clock. *Science, 260*, 238–241. [2, 4]

Ginzburg, K., Solomon, Z., & Bleich, A. (2002). Repressive coping style, acute stress disorder, and post-traumatic stress disorder after myocardial infarction. *Journal of the American Psychosomatic Society, 64*, 748–757. [10]

Giraud, A., Price, C., Graham, J., & Frackowisk, R. (2001). *Neuropsychopharmacology, 124*, 1307–1316. [2]

Girolamo, G., & Bassi, M. (2003). Community surveys of mental disorders: Recent achievements and works in progress. *Current Opinion in Psychiatry, 16*, 403–411. [12]

Glantz, L. A., & Lewis, D. A. (2000). Decreased dendritic spine density on prefrontal cortical pyramidal neurons in schizophrenia. *Archives of General Psychiatry, 57*, 65–73. [12]

Glass, D. C., & Singer, J. E. (1972). *Urban stress: Experiments in noise and social stressors.* New York: Academic Press. [10]

Glazer, W. M., Morgenstern, H., & Doucette, J. T. (1993). Predicting the long-term risk of tardive dyskinesia in outpatients maintained on neuroleptic medications. *Journal of Clinical Psychiatry, 54*, 133–139. [13]

Gleaves, D. J. (1996). The sociocognitive model of dissociative identity disorder: A reexamination of the evidence. *Psychological Bulletin, 120*, 42–59. [12]

Glenn, N., & Weaver, C. (1985). Age, cohort, and reported job satisfaction in the United States. In A. Blau (Ed.), *Current perspectives on aging and the life cycle. A research annual, Vol. 1. Work, retirement, and social policy* (pp. 89–110). Greenwich, CT: JAI Press. [8]

Glover, J. A., & Corkill, A. J. (1987). Influence of paraphrased repetitions on the spacing effect. *Journal of Educational Psychology, 79*, 198–199. [6]

Gluck, M. A., & Myers, C. E. (1997). Psychobiological models of hippocampal function in learning and memory. *Annual Review of Psychology, 48*, 481–514. [2, 6]

Godden, D. R., & Baddeley, A. D. (1975). Context-dependent memory in two natural environments: On land and underwater. *British Journal of Psychology, 66*, 325–331. [6]

Goeders, N. (2004). Stress, motivation, and drug addiction. *Current Directions in Psychological Science, 13*, 33–35. [4]

Gökcebay, N., Cooper, R., Williams, R. L., Hirshkowitz, M., & Moore, C. A. (1994). Function of sleep. In R. Cooper (Ed.), *Sleep.* New York: Chapman & Hall. [4]

Goldstein, D., & Gigerenzer, G. (2002). Models of ecological rationality: The recognition heuristic. *Psychological Review, 109*, 75–90. [7]

Goleman, D., Kaufman, P., & Ray, M. (1992). *The creative spirit.* New York: Dutton. [7]

Gollan, T., & Silverberg, N. (2001). Tip-of-the-tongue states in Hebrew-English bilinguals. *Bilingualism: Language and Cognition, 4*, 63–83. [7]

Gonsalves, B., Reber, P., Gitelman, D., Parrish, T., Mesulam, M., & Paller, K. (2004). Neural evidence that vivid imagining can lead to false remembering. *Psychological Science, 15*, 655–660. [6]

Gonzalez, R., Ellsworth, P. C., & Pembroke, M. (1993). Response biases in lineups and showups. *Journal of Personality and Social Psychology, 64*, 525–537. [6]

Good, C., Aronson, J., & Inzlicht, M. (2003). Improving adolescents' standardized test performance: An intervention to reduce the effects of stereotype threat. *Applied Developmental Psychology, 24*, 645–662. [7]

Goodglass, H. (1993). *Understanding aphasia.* San Diego, CA: Academic Press. [2]

Goodwin, G. M. (1996). How do antidepressants affect serotonin receptors? The role of serotonin receptors in the therapeutic and side effect profile of the SSRIs. *Journal of Clinical Psychiatry, 57*(4, Suppl.), 9–13. [13]

Goodwin, R., & Fitzgibbon, M. (2002). Social anxiety as a barrier to treatment for eating disorders. *International Journal of Eating Disorders, 32*, 103–106. [9]

Goodwin, R., & Stein, M. (2003). Peptic ulcer disease and neuroticism in the United States adult population. *Psychotherapy & Psychosomatics, 72,* 10–15. [11]

Gordon, H. (2002). Early environmental stress and biological vulnerability to drug abuse. *Psychoneuroendocrinology, 27,* 115–126. [4]

Gorman, C. (1996, Fall). Damage control. *Time* [Special Issue], 31–35. [2]

Gosling, S., Ko, S., Mannarelli, T., & Morris, M. (2002). A room with a cue: Personality judgments based on offices and bedrooms. *Journal of Personality & Social Psychology, 82,* 379–398. [11]

Gosling, S., Vazire, S., Srivastava, S., & John, O. (2004). Should we trust Web-based studies? A comparative analysis of six preconceptions about Internet questionnaires. *American Psychologist, 59,* 93–104. [1]

Gottesman, I. I. (1991). *Schizophrenia genesis: The origins of madness.* New York: W. H. Freeman. [12]

Gottesmann, C. (2000). Hypothesis for the neurophysiology of dreaming. *Sleep Research Online, 3,* 1–4. [4]

Gottfried, A. E., Fleming, J. S., & Gottfried, A. W. (1994). Role of parental motivational practices in children's academic intrinsic motivation and achievement. *Journal of Educational Psychology, 86,* 104–113. [9]

Gough, H. (1987). *California Psychological Inventory: Administrator's Guide.* Palo Alto: Consulting Psychologists Press. [11]

Gould, E. R., Reeves, A. J., Graziano, M. S. A., & Gross, C. (1999). Neurogenesis in the neocortex of adult primates. *Science, 286,* 548. [1, 2]

Grant, B. F., & Dawson, D. A. (1998). Age at onset of alcohol use and its association with *DSM-IV* alcohol abuse and dependence: Results from the National Longitudinal Alcohol Epidemiologic Survey. *Journal of Substance Abuse, 9,* 103–110. [10]

Greden, J. F. (1994). Introduction Part III. New agents for the treatment of depression. *Journal of Clinical Psychiatry, 55*(2, Suppl.), 32–33. [2]

Green, B. L., Lindy, J. D., & Grace, M. C. (1985). Post-traumatic stress disorder: Toward DSM-IV. *Journal of Nervous and Mental Disorders, 173,* 406–411. [10]

Green, C., Polen, M., Lynch, F., Dickinson, D., & Bennett, M. (2004). Gender differences in outcomes in an HMO-based substance abuse treatment program. *Journal of Addictive Diseases, 23,* 47–70. [10]

Green, J., & Shellenberger, R. (1990). *The dynamics of health and wellness: A biopsychosocial approach.* Fort Worth: Holt, Rinehart & Winston. [10]

Green, J. P., & Lynn, S. J. (2000). Hypnosis and suggestion-based approaches to smoking cessation: An examination of the evidence. *International Journal of Clinical Experimental Hypnosis, 48,* 195–224. [4]

Green, L. R., Richardson, D. R., & Lago, T. (1996). How do friendship, indirect, and direct aggression relate? *Aggressive Behavior, 22,* 81–86. [14]

Greenwald, A. (1992). New look 3: Unconscious cognition reclaimed *American Psychologist, 47,* 766–779. [3]

Greenwald, A., Spangenberg, E., Pratkanis, A., & Eskenazi, J. (1991). Double-blind tests of subliminal self-help audiotapes. *Psychological Science, 2,* 119–122. [3]

Gregory, R. J. (1996). *Psychological testing: History, principles, and applications* (2nd ed.). Boston: Allyn & Bacon. [7, 11]

Greist, J. H. (1992). An integrated approach to treatment of obsessive compulsive disorder. *Journal of Clinical Psychiatry, 53*(4, Suppl.), 38–41. [13]

Greist, J. H. (1995). The diagnosis of social phobia. *Journal of Clinical Psychiatry, 56*(5, Suppl.), 5–12. [12]

Grigorenko, E. (2003). Epistasis and the genetics of complex traits. In R. Plomin, J. DeFries, I. Craig, & P. McGuffin (Eds.), *Behavioral genetics in the postgenomic era.* (pp. 247–266). Washington, DC: American Psychological Association. [7]

Grigorenko, E., Jarvin, L., & Sternberg, R. (2002). School-based tests of the triarchic theory of intelligence: Three settings, three samples, three syllabi. *Contemporary Educational Psychology, 27,* 167–208. [7]

Grigorenko, E., Meier, E., Lipka, J., Mohatt, G., Yanez, E., & Sternberg, R. (2004). Academic and practical intelligence: A case study of the Yup'ik in Alaska. *Learning & Individual Differences, 14,* 183–207. [7]

Gron, G., Wunderlich, A. P., Spitzer, M., Tomczrak, R., & Riepe, M. W. (2000). Brain activation during human navigation: Gender-different neural networks as substrate of performance. *Nature Neuroscience, 3,* 404–408. [2]

Gross, J. (2002). Emotion regulation: Affective, cognitive, and social consequences. *Psychophysiology, 39,* 281–291. [9]

Grossenbacher, P., & Lovelace, C. (2001). Mechanisms of synesthesia: Cognitive and physiological constraints. *Trends in Cognitive Sciences, 5,* 36–41. [3]

Grossman, H. J. (Ed.). (1983). *Manual on terminology and classification in mental retardation.* Washington, DC: American Association on Mental Deficiency. [7]

Grossman, J., & Ruiz, P. (2004). Shall we make a leap-of-faith to disulfiram (Antabuse)? *Addictive Disorders & Their Treatment, 3,* 129–132. [13]

Grossman, M., & Wood, W. (1993). Sex differences in intensity of emotional experience: A social role interpretation. *Journal of Personality and Social Psychology, 65,* 1010–1022. [9]

Grouios, G., Sakadami, N., Poderi, A., & Alevriadou, A. (1999). Excess of non-right handedness among individuals with intellectual disability: Experimental evidence and possible explanations. *Journal of Intellectual Disability Research, 43,* 306–313. [2]

Guilford, J. P. (1967). *The nature of human intelligence.* New York: McGraw-Hill. [7]

Guilleminault, C. (1993). 1. Amphetamines and narcolepsy: Use of the Stanford database. *Sleep, 16,* 199–201. [4]

Gupta, D., & Vishwakarma, M. S. (1989). Toy weapons and firecrackers: A source of hearing loss. *Laryngoscope, 99,* 330–334. [3]

Gur, R., Gunning-Dixon, F., Bilker, W., & Gur, R. (2002). Sex differences in temporo-limbic and frontal brain volumes of healthy adults. *Cerebral Cortex, 12,* 998–1003. [2]

Gur, R. C., Turetsky, B., Mastsui, M., Yan, M., Bilker, W., Hughett, P., & Gur, R. E. (1999). Sex differences in brain gray and white matter in healthy young adults: Correlations with cognitive performance. *Journal of Neuroscience, 19,* 4067–4072. [2]

Gur, R. E., Cowell, P. E., Latshaw, A., Turetsky, B. I., Grossman, R. I., Amold, S. E., Bilker, W. B., & Gur, R. C. (2000). Reduced dorsal and orbital prefrontal gray matter volumes in schizophrenia. *Archives of General Psychiatry, 57,* 761–768. [12]

Gurin, J. (1989, June). Leaner, not lighter. *Psychology Today,* 32–36. [9]

Guthrie, R. (2004). *Even the rat was white* (classic ed.). Boston, MA: Allyn & Bacon. [1]

Haag, L., & Stern E. (2003). In search of the benefits of learning Latin. *Journal of Educational Psychology, 95,* 174–178. [7]

Habel, U., Kuehn, E., Salloum, J., Devos, H., & Schneider, F. (2002). Emotional processing in psychopathic personality. *Aggressive Behavior, 28,* 394–400. [12]

Haberlandt, D. (1997). *Cognitive psychology* (2nd ed.). Boston: Allyn & Bacon. [1, 7]

Hackel, L. S., & Ruble, D. N. (1992). Changes in the marital relationship after the first baby is born: Predicting the impact of expectancy disconfirmation. *Journal of Personality and Social Psychology, 62,* 944–957. [8]

Hada, M., Porjesz, B., Begleiter, H., & Polich, J. (2000). Auditory P3a assessment of male alcoholics. *Biological Psychiatry, 48,* 276–286. [10]

Hada, M., Porjesz, B., Chorlian, D., Begleiter, H., & Polich, J. (2001). Auditory P3a deficits in male subjects at high risk for alcoholism. *Biological Psychiatry, 49,* 726–738. [10]

Hager, W., Leichsenring, F., & Schiffler, A. (2000). When does a study of different therapies allow comparisons of their relative efficacy? *Psychother. Psychosom. Med. Psychol., 50,* 251–262. [13]

Haj-Yahia, M. (2002). Beliefs of Jordanian women about wife-beating. *Psychology of Women Quarterly, 26,* 282–291. [5]

Häkkänen, H., & Summala, H. (1999). Sleepiness at work among commercial truck drivers. *Sleep, 23,* 49–57. [4]

Hakuta, K., Bialystok, E., & Wiley, E. (2003). Critical evidence: A test of the critical-period hypothesis for second-language acquisition. *Psychological Science, 14,* 31–38. [7]

Halaas, J. L., Gajiwala, K. S., Maffei, M., Cohen, S. L., Chait, B. T., Rabinowitz, D., Lallone, R. L., Burley, S. K., & Friedman, J. M. (1995). Weight-reducing effects of the plasma protein encoded by the obese gene. *Science, 269,* 543–546. [9]

Halaris, A. (2003). Neurochemical aspects of the sexual response cycle. *CNS Spectrums, 8,* 211–216. [9]

Halemaskel, B., Dutta, A., & Wutoh, A. (2001). Adverse reactions and interactions among herbal users. *Issues in Interdisciplinary Care, 3,* 297–300. [4]

Halford, G. S. (1989). Reflections on 25 years of Piagetian cognitive developmental psychology, 1963–1988. *Human Development, 32,* 325–327. [8]

Halligan, P. W., & Marshall, J. C. (1994). Toward a principled explanation of unilateral neglect. *Cognitive Neuropsychology, 11,* 167–206. [2]

Hallschmid, M., Benedict, C., Born, J., Fehm, H., & Kern, W. (2004). Manipulating central nervous mechanisms of food intake and body weight regulation by intranasal administration of neuropeptides in man. *Physiology & Behavior, 83,* 55–64. [9]

Halmi, K. A. (1996). Eating disorder research in the past decade. *Annals of the New York Academy of Sciences, 789,* 67–77. [9]

Halpern, D. (2000). Making sound decisions: The worksheet method. Retrieved January 20, 2005, from http://wps.ablongman.com/ab_wood_worldofpsy_5/0,9166,1378162-,00.html [7]

Ham, P. (2003). Suicide risk not increased with SSRI antidepressants. *Journal of Family Practice, 52,* 537–588.

Hamilton, C. S., & Swedo, S. E. (2001). Autoimmune-mediated, childhood onset obsessive-compulsive disorder and tics: A review. *Clinical Neuroscience Research, 1,* 61–68. [12]

Hamilton, M. C. (1988). Using masculine generics: Does generic "he" increase male bias in the user's imagery? *Sex Roles, 19,* 785–789. [7]

Hancock, P., & Ganey, H. (2003). From the inverted-u to the extended-u: The evolution of a law of psychology. *Journal of Human Performance in Extreme Environments, 7,* 5–14. [9]

Hanley, S., & Abell, S. (2002). Maslow and relatedness: Creating an interpersonal model of self-actualization. *Journal of Humanistic Psychology, 42,* 37–56. [11]

Hannover, B., & Kuehnen, U. (2002). "The clothing makes the self" via knowledge activation. *Journal of Applied Social Psychology, 32,* 2513–2525. [11]

Hanoch, Y., & Vitouch, O. (2004). When less is more: Information, emotional arousal and the ecological reframing of the Yerkes-Dodson law. *Theory & Psychology, 14,* 427–452. [9]

Harackiewicz, A., Barron, A., Pintrich, A., Elliot, A., & Thrash, A. (2002). Revision of achievement goal theory: Necessary and illuminating. *Journal of Educational Psychology, 94,* 638–645. [9]

Hargadon, R., Bowers, K. S., & Woody, E. Z. (1995). Does counterpain imagery mediate hypnotic analgesia? *Journal of Abnormal Psychology, 104,* 508–516. [4]

Harlow, H. F., & Harlow, M. K. (1962). Social deprivation in monkeys. *Scientific American, 207,* 137–146. [8]

Harlow, J. M. (1848). Passage of an iron rod through the head. *Boston Medical and Surgical Journal, 39,* 389–393. [2]

Harris, J. A., Rushton, J. P., Hampson, E., & Jackson, D. N. (1996). Salivary testosterone and self-report aggressive and pro-social personality characteristics in men and women. *Aggressive Behavior, 22,* 321–331. [14]

Harris, L. J., & Blaiser, M. J. (1997). Effects of a mnemonic peg system on the recall of daily tasks. *Perceptual and Motor Skills, 84,* 721–722. [6]

Harris, R. A., Brodie, M. S., & Dunwiddie, T. V. (1992). Possible substrates of ethanol reinforcement: GABA and dopamine. *Annals of the New York Academy of Sciences, 654,* 61–69. [4]

Harrison, Y., & Horne, J. A. (2000). Sleep loss and temporal memory. *Journal of Experimental Psychology, 53,* 271–279. [4]

Hart, D., Atkins, R., & Fegley, S. (2003). Personality and development in childhood: A person-centered approach. *Monographs of the Society for Research in Child Development, 68*(1). [8]

Hart, D., Hofmann, V., Edelstein, W., & Keller, M. (1997). The relation of childhood personality types to adolescent behavior and development: A longitudinal study of Icelandic children. *Developmental Psychology, 33,* 195–205. [8]

Hart, J., Karau, S., Stasson, M., & Kerr, N. (2004). Achievement motivation, expected coworker performance, and collective task motivation: Working hard or hardly working? *Journal of Applied Social Psychology, 34,* 984–1000. [14]

Hatashita-Wong, M., Smith, T., Silverstein, S., Hull, J., & Willson, D. (2002). Cognitive functioning and social problem-solving skills in schizophrenia. *Cognitive Neuropsychiatry, 7,* 81–95. [12]

Hauser, M. D. (1993). Right hemisphere dominance for the production of facial expression in monkeys. *Science, 261,* 475–477. [2]

Hawley, K., & Weisz, J. (2003). Child, parent and therapist (dis)agreement on target problems in outpatient therapy: The therapist's dilemma and its implications. *Journal of Consulting & Clinical Psychology, 71,* 62–70. [13]

Hay, D. F. (1994). Prosocial development. *Journal of Child Psychology and Psychiatry, 35,* 29–71. [14]

Hazlett-Stevens, H., Craske, M., Roy-Byrne, P., Sherbourne, C., Stein, M., & Bystritsky, A. (2002). Predictors of willingness to consider medication and psychosocial treatment for panic disorder in primary care patients. *General Hospital Psychology, 24,* 316–321. [13]

HCF Nutrition Foundation. (2003). *The benefits of fiber.* Retrieved January 29, 2003 from http://www.hcf-nutrition.org/fiber/fiberben_article.html [10]

Heatherton, T., Macrae, N., & Kelley, W. (2004). What the social brain sciences can tell us about the self. *Current Directions in Psychological Science, 13,* 190–193. [2]

Hebb, D. O. (1949). *The organization of behavior.* New York: John Wiley & Sons. [6]

Hecht, S., Shlaer, S., & Pirenne, M. H. (1942). *Journal of General Physiology, 25,* 819. [3]

Heckhausen, J., & Brian, O. (1997). Perceived problems for self and others: Self-protection by social downgrading throughout adulthood. *Psychology & Aging, 12,* 610–619. [8]

Hedges, L. B., & Nowell, A. (1995). Sex differences in mental test scores, variability, and numbers of high-scoring individuals. *Science, 269,* 41–45. [7]

Hedley, L. M., Hoffart, A., Dammen, T., Ekeberg, O., & Friis, S. (2000). The relationship between cognitions and panic attack intensity. *Acta Psychiatrica Scandinavica, 102,* 300–302. [12]

Heil, M., Rolke, B., & Pecchinenda, A. (2004). Automatic semantic activation is no myth. *Psychological Science, 15,* 852–857. [3]

Heiman, J. (2002). Psychologic treatments for female sexual dysfunction: Are they effective and do we need them? *Archives of Sexual Behavior, 31,* 445–450. [12]

Heitjtz, R., Kolb, B., & Forssberg, H. (2003). Can a therapeutic dose of amphetamine during pre-adolescence modify the pattern of synaptic organization in the brain? *European Journal of Neuroscience, 18,* 3394–3399. [4]

Held, R. (1993). What can rates of development tell us about underlying mechanisms? In C. E. Granrud (Ed.), *Visual perception and cognition in infancy* (pp. 75–89). Hillsdale, NJ: Erlbaum. [8]

Hellige, J. B. (1990). Hemispheric asymmetry. *Annual Review of Psychology, 41,* 55–80. [2]

Hellige, J. B. (1993). *Hemispheric asymmetry: What's right and what's left.* Cambridge, MA: Harvard University Press. [2]

Hellige, J. B., Bloch, M. I., Cowin, E. L., Eng, T. L., Eviatar, Z., & Sergent, V. (1994). Individual variation in hemispheric asymmetry: Multitask study of effects related to handedness and sex. *Journal of Experimental Psychology: General, 123,* 235–256. [2]

Hellstrom, Y., & Hallberg, I. (2004). Determinants and characteristics of help provision for eldery people living at home and in relation to quality of life. *Scandinavian Journal of Caring Sciences, 18,* 387–395. [8]

Hendin, H., & Haas, A. P. (1991). Suicide and guilt as manifestations of PTSD in Vietnam combat veterans. *American Journal of Psychiatry, 148,* 586–591. [10]

Henkel, L. A., Franklin, N., & Johnson, M. K. (2000). Cross-modal source monitoring confusions between perceived and imagined events. *Journal of Experimental Psychology: Learning, Memory, and Cognition, 26,* 321–335. [6]

Henley, N. M. (1989). Molehill or mountain? What we know and don't know about sex bias in language. In M. Crawford & M. Gentry (Eds.), *Gender and thought: Psychological perspectives.* New York: Springer-Verlag. [7]

Henningfield, J. E., & Ator, N. A. (1986). *Barbiturates: Sleeping potion or intoxicant?* New York: Chelsea House. [4]

Herbert, T. B., & Cohen, S. (1993). Depression and immunity: A meta-analytic review. *Psychological Bulletin, 113,* 472–486. [10]

Herkenham, M. (1992). Cannabinoid receptor localization in brain: Relationship to motor and reward systems. *Annals of the New York Academy of Sciences, 654,* 19–32. [4]

Herman, L. (1981). Cognitive characteristics of dolphins. In L. Herman (Ed.), *Cetacean behavior.* New York: Wiley. [7]

Hernandez, L., & Hoebel, B. G. (1989). Food intake and lateral hypothalamic self-stimulation covary after medial hypothalamic lesions or ventral midbrain 6-hydroxydopamine injections that cause obesity. *Behavioral Neuroscience, 103,* 412–422. [9]

Hernandez, S., Camacho-Rosales, J., Nieto, A., & Barroso, J. (1997). Cerebral asymmetry and reading performance: Effect of language lateralization and hand preference. *Child Neuropsychology, 3,* 206–225. [2]

Herness, S. (2000). Coding in taste receptor cells: The early years of intracellular recordings. *Physiology and Behavior, 69,* 17–27. [3]

Herrnstein, R. J., & Murray, C. (1994). *The bell curve: Intelligence and class structure in American life.* New York: Free Press. [7]

Hershberger, S., & Segal, N. (2004). The cognitive, behavioral, and personality profiles of a male monozygotic triplet set discordant for sexual orientation. *Archives of Sexual Behavior, 33,* 497–514. [9]

Hertzog, C. (1991). Aging, information processing speed, and intelligence. In K. W. Schaie & M. P. Lawton (Eds.), *Annual Review of Gerontology and Geriatrics* (Vol. 11, pp. 55–79). [8]

Heyman, G., Gee, C., & Giles, J. (2003). Preschool children's reasoning about ability. *Child Development, 74,* 516–534. [7]

Hickman, J., & Geller, E. (2003). A safety self-management intervention for mining operations. *U.S. Journal of Safety Research, 34,* 299–308. [5]

Higbee, K. L. (1977). *Your memory: How it works and how to improve it.* Englewood Cliffs, NJ: Prentice-Hall. [6]

Higdon, H. (1975). *The crime of the century.* New York: G. P. Putnam's Sons. [11]

Higgins, A. (1995). Educating for justice and community: Lawrence Kohlberg's vision of moral education. In W. M. Kurtines & J. L. Gerwirtz (Eds.), *Moral development: An introduction* (pp. 49–81). Boston: Allyn & Bacon. [8]

Hilgard, E. R. (1975). Hypnosis. *Annual Review of Psychology, 26,* 19–44. [4]

Hilgard, E. R. (1986). *Divided consciousness: Multiple controls in human thought and action.* New York: Wiley. [4]

Hilgard, E. R. (1992). Dissociation and theories of hypnosis. In E. Fromm & M. R. Nash (Eds.), *Contemporary hypnosis research.* New York: Guilford. [4]

Hill, M., & Augoustinos, M. (2001). Stereotype change and prejudice reduction: Short- and long-term evaluation of a cross-cultural awareness programme. *Journal of Community & Applied Social Psychology, 11,* 243–262. [14]

Hillebrand, J. (2000). New perspectives on the manipulation of opiate urges and the assessment of cognitive effort associated with opiate urges. *Addictive Behaviors, 25,* 139–143. [4]

Hirsch, J. (1997). Some heat but not enough light. *Nature, 387,* 27–28. [9]

Hirschfeld, M. A. (1995). The impact of health care reform on social phobia. *Journal of Clinical Psychiatry, 56*(5, Suppl.), 13–17. [12]

Hobson, C., & Delunas, L., (2001). National norms and life-event frequencies for the revised Social Readjustment Rating Scale. *International Journal of Stress Management, 8,* 299–314. [10]

Hobson, J. A. (1988). *The dreaming brain.* New York: Basic Books. [4]

Hobson, J. A. (1989). *Sleep.* New York: Scientific American Library. [4]

Hobson, J. A., & McCarley, R. W. (1977). The brain as a dream state generator: An activation-synthesis hypothesis of the dream process. *American Journal of Psychiatry, 134,* 1335–1348. [4]

Hodgins, S., Mednick, S. A., Brennan, P. A., Schulsinger, F., & Engberg, M. (1996). Mental disorder and crime: Evidence from a Danish birth cohort. *Journal of Personality and Social Psychology, 53,* 489–496. [14]

Hofstede, G. (1980). *Culture's consequences: International differences in work-related values.* Beverly Hills, CA: Sage. [11]

Hofstede, G. (1983). Dimensions of national cultures in fifty countries and three regions. In J. Deregowski, S. Dzuirawiec, and R. Annis (Eds.), *Explications in cross-cultural psychology.* Lisse: Swets and Zeitlinger. [11]

Hogan, E., & McReynolds, C. (2004). An overview of anorexia nervosa, bulimia nervosa, and binge eating disorders: Implications for rehabilitation professionals. *Journal of Applied Rehabilitation Counseling, 35,* 26–34. [9]

Hollon, S., Thase, M., & Markowitz, J. (2002). Treatment and prevention of depression. *Psychological Science in the Public Interest, 3,* 39–77. [12, 13]

Holmes, T. H., & Masuda, M. (1974). Life change and illness susceptibility. In B. S. Dohrenwend & B. P. Dohrenwend (Eds.), *Stressful life events: Their nature and effects.* New York: Wiley. [10]

Holmes, T. H., & Rahe, R. H. (1967). The social readjustment rating scale. *Journal of Psychosomatic Research, 11,* 213–218. [10]

Holt-Lunstad, J., Uchino, B., Smith, T., Olson-Cerny, C., & Nealey-Moore, J. (2003). Social relationships and ambulatory blood pressure: Structural and qualitative predictors of cardiovascular function during everyday social interactions. *Health Psychology, 22,* 388–397. [10]

Hopkins, W., & Cantalupo, C. (2004, in press). Handedness in chimpanzees (*Pan troglodytes*) is associated with asymmetries of the primary motor cortex but not with homologous language areas. *Behavioral Neuroscience, 118,* 1176–1183. [2]

Hopkins, W., Wesley, M., Izard, M., Hook, M., & Schapiro, S. (2004). Chimpanzees (*Pan troglodytes*) are predominantly right-handed: Replication in three populations of apes. *Behavioral Neuroscience, 118,* 659–663. [2]

Horn, J. L. (1982). The theory of fluid and crystallized intelligence in relation to concepts of cognitive psychology and aging in adulthood. In F. I. M. Craik & S. Trehub (Eds.), *Aging and cognitive processes* (pp. 201–238). New York: Plenum Press. [8]

Horn, L. J., & Zahn, L. (2001). From bachelor's degree to work: Major field of study and employment outcomes of 1992–93 bachelor's degree recipients who did not enroll in graduate education by 1997 (NCES 2001–165). Retrieved March 7, 2002, from http://nces.ed.gov/pubs2001/quarterly/spring/q5_2.html [1]

Horney, K. (1937). *The neurotic personality of our time.* New York: W. W. Norton. [11]

Horney, K. (1939). *New ways in psychoanalysis.* New York: W. W. Norton. [11]

Horney, K. (1945). *Our inner conflicts.* New York: W. W. Norton. [11]

Horney, K. (1950). *Neurosis and human growth.* New York: W. W. Norton. [11]

Horney, K. (1967). *Feminine psychology.* New York: W. W. Norton. [11]

Horwath, E., Lish, J. D., Johnson, J., Hornig, C. D., & Weissman, M. M. (1993). Agoraphobia without panic: Clinical reappraisal of an epidemiologic finding. *American Journal of Psychiatry, 150,* 1496–1501. [12]

Hovland, C. I., Lumsdaine, A. A., & Sheffield, F. D. (1949). *Experiments on mass communication.* Princeton, NJ: Princeton University Press. [14]

Howard, A. D., Feighner, S. D., Cully, D. F., Arena, J. P., Liberator, P. A., Rosenblum, C. I., et al. (1996). A receptor in pituitary and hypothalamus that functions in growth hormone release. *Science, 273,* 974–977. [2]

Hrushesky, W. J. M. (1994, July/August). Timing is everything. *The Sciences,* 32–37. [4]

Hubel, D. H. (1963). The visual cortex of the brain. *Scientific American, 209,* 54–62. [3]

Hubel, D. H. (1995). *Eye, brain, and vision.* New York: Scientific American Library. [3]

Hubel, D. H., & Wiesel, T. N. (1959). Receptive fields of single neurons in the cat's striate cortex. *Journal of Physiology, 148,* 547–591. [3]

Hubel, D. H., & Wiesel, T. N. (1979). Brain mechanisms of vision. *Scientific American, 241,* 130–144. [3]

Hudson, J. I., Carter, W. P., & Pope, H. G., Jr. (1996). Antidepressant treatment of binge-eating disorder: Research findings and clinical guidelines. *Journal of Clinical Psychiatry, 57*(8, Suppl.), 73–79. [13]

Huesman, L., Moise-Titus, J., Podolski, C., & Eron, L. (2003). Longitudinal relations between children's exposure to television violence and their aggressive and violent behavior in young adulthood. *Developmental Psychology, 39,* 201–221. [5]

Huesmann, L. R., & Moise, J. (1996, June). Media violence: A demonstrated public health threat to children. *Harvard Mental Health Letter, 12*(12), 5–7. [14]

Huff, C. R. (1995). *Convicted but innocent.* Thousand Oaks, CA: Sage. [6]

Hughes, J. R. (1992). Tobacco withdrawal in self-quitters. *Journal of Consulting and Clinical Psychology, 60,* 689–697. [10]

Hughes, S., Harrison, M., & Gallup, G. (2004). Sex differences in mating strategies: Mate guarding, infidelity and multiple concurrent sex partners. *Evolution & Gender, 6,* 3–13. [9]

Hull, C. L. (1943). *Principles of behavior.* New York: Appleton-Century-Crofts. [9]

Hultsch, D. F., & Dixon, R. A. (1990). Learning and memory in aging. In J. E. Birren & K. W. Schaie (Eds.), *Handbook of the psychology of aging* (3rd ed., pp. 359–374). San Diego: Academic Press. [8]

Hunter, J. A., Reid, J. M., Stokell, N. M., & Platow, M. J. (2000). Social attribution, self-esteem, and social identity. *Current Research in Social Psychology, 5,* 97–125. [14]

Huntley, A., & Ernst, E. (2004). Soy for the treatment of perimenopausal symptoms—A systematic review. *Maturitas, 47,* 1–9. [4]

Hurvich, L. M., & Jameson, D. (1957). An opponent-process theory of color vision. *Psychological Review, 64,* 384–404. [3]

Huttenlocher, P. (1994). Synaptogenesis, synapse elimination, and neural plasticity in human cerebral cortex. In C. Nelson (Ed.), *The Minnesota symposia on child psychology* (Vol. 27, pp. 35–54). Hillsdale, NJ: Erlbaum. [2]

Hyman, I. E., Jr., Husband, T. H., & Billings, E. J. (1995). False memories of childhood. *Applied Cognitive Psychology, 9,* 181–197. [6]

Hyman, I. E., Jr., & Pentland, J. (1996). The role of mental imagery in the creation of false childhood memories. *Journal of Memory and Language, 35,* 101–117. [6]

Insel, T. R. (1990). Phenomenology of obsessive compulsive disorder. *Journal of Clinical Psychiatry, 51*(2, Suppl.), 4–8. [12]

Intons-Peterson, M. J., & Fournier, J. (1986). External and internal memory aids: When and how often do we use them? *Journal of Experimental Psychology: General, 115,* 267–280. [6]

Isenberg, D. J. (1986). Group polarization: A critical review and meta-analysis. *Journal of Personality and Social Psychology, 50,* 1141–1151. [14]

Ito, T. A., Miller, N., & Pollock, V. E. (1996). Alcohol and aggression: A meta-analysis on the moderating effects of inhibitory cues, triggering events, and self-focused attention. *Psychological Bulletin, 120,* 60–82. [14]

Izard, C. E. (1971). *The face of emotion.* New York: Appleton-Century-Crofts. [9]

Izard, C. E. (1977). *Human emotions.* New York: Plenum Press. [9]

Izard, C. E. (1990). Facial expressions and the regulation of emotions. *Journal of Personality and Social Psychology, 58,* 487–498. [9]

Izard, C. E. (1992). Basic emotions, relations among emotions, and emotion-cognition relations. *Psychological Review, 99,* 561–565. [9]

Izard, C. E. (1993). Four systems for emotion activation: Cognitive and noncognitive processes. *Psychological Review, 100,* 68–90. [9]

Jacklin, C. N. (1989). Female and male: Issues of gender. *American Psychologist, 44,* 127–133. [8]

Jackson, S. (2002). A study of teachers' perceptions of youth problems. *Journal of Youth Studies, 5,* 313–322. [14]

Jacobs, B. (2004). Depression: The brain finally gets into the act. *Current Directions in Psychological Science, 13,* 103–106. [2]

James, W. (1884). What is an emotion? *Mind, 9,* 188–205. [9]

James, W. (1890). *Principles of psychology.* New York: Holt. [1, 9]

Jamieson, D. W., & Zanna, M. P. (1989). Need for structure in attitude formation and expression. In A. R. Pratkanis, S. J. Breckler, & A. G. Greenwald (Eds.), *Attitude structure and function* (pp. 383–406). Hillsdale, NJ: Erlbaum. [14]

Janis, I. L. (1982). *Groupthink: Psychological studies of policy decisions and fiascoes* (2nd ed.). Boston: Houghton Mifflin. [14]

Janssen, T., & Carton, J. (1999). The effects of locus of control and task difficulty on procrastination. *Journal of Genetic Psychology, 160,* 436–442. [11]

Jefferson, J. W. (1995). Social phobia: A pharmacologic treatment overview. *Journal of Clinical Psychiatry, 56*(5, Suppl.), 18–24. [13]

Jefferson, J. W. (1996). Social phobia: Everyone's disorder? *Journal of Clinical Psychiatry, 57*(6, Suppl.), 28–32. [12]

Jefferson, J. W. (1997). Antidepressants in panic disorder. *Journal of Clinical Psychiatry, 58*(2, Suppl.), 20–24. [13]

Jelicic, M., & Bonke, B. (2001). Memory impairments following chronic stress? A critical review. *European Journal of Psychiatry, 15*, 225–232. [6]

Jellinek, E. M. (1960). *The disease concept of alcoholism.* New Brunswick, NJ: Hillhouse Press. [10]

Jenike, M. A. (1990, April). Obsessive-compulsive disorder. *Harvard Medical School Health Letter, 15*, 4–8. [13]

Jenkins, J. H., & Karno, M. (1992). The meaning of expressed emotion: Theoretical issues raised by cross-cultural research. *American Journal of Psychiatry, 149*, 9–21. [13]

Jenkins, J. J., Jimenez-Pabon, E., Shaw, R. E., & Sefer, J. W. (1975). *Schuell's aphasia in adults: Diagnosis, prognosis, and treatment* (2nd ed.). Hagerstown, MD: Harper & Row. [2]

Jensen, A. (1969). How much can we boost IQ and scholastic achievement? *Harvard Educational Review, 39*, 1–123. [7]

Jernigan, T. L., Butters, N., DiTraglia, G., Schafer, K., Smith, T., Irwin, M., Grant, I., Schuckit, M., & Cermak, L. S. (1991). Reduced cerebral grey matter observed in alcoholics using magnetic resonance imaging. *Alcoholism: Clinical and Experimental Research, 15*, 418–427. [10]

Jimerson, D. C., Wolfe, B. E., Metzger, E. D., Finkelstein, D. M., Cooper, T. B., & Levine, J. M. (1997). Decreased serotonin function in bulimia nervosa. *Archives of General Psychiatry, 54*, 529–534. [9]

John, L. (2004). Subjective well-being in a multicultural urban population: Structural and multivariate analyses of the Ontario Health Survey well-being scale. *Social Indicators Research, 68*, 107–126. [10]

Johnson, J., Simmons, C., Trawalter, S., Ferguson, T., & Reed, W. (2003). Variation in black anti-white bias and target distancing cues: Factors that influence perceptions of "ambiguously racist" behavior. *Personality & Social Psychology Bulletin, 29*, 609–622. [14]

Johnson, M. P., Duffy, J. F., Dijk, D-J., Ronda, J. M., Dyal, C. M., & Czeisler, C. A. (1992). Short-term memory, alertness and performance: A reappraisal of their relationship to body temperature. *Journal of Sleep Research, 1*, 24–29. [4]

Johnson, W. G., Tsoh, J. Y., & Varnado, P. J. (1996). Eating disorders: Efficacy of pharmacological and psychological interventions. *Clinical Psychology Review, 16*, 457–478. [9]

Johnston, L. E., O'Malley, P. M., & Bachman, J. G. (2001). *Monitoring the Future national results on adolescent drug use: Overview of key findings, 2000* (NIH Publication No. 01-4923). Rockville MD: National Institute on Drug Abuse. [1, 4]

Jolicoeur, D., Richter, K., Ahgluwalia, J., Mosier, M., & Resnicow, K. (2003). Smoking cessation, smoking reduction, and delayed quitting among smokers given nicotine patches and a self-help pamphlet. *Substance Abuse, 24*, 101–106. [4]

Jonas, J. M., & Cohon, M. S. (1993). A comparison of the safety and efficacy of alprazolam versus other agents in the treatment of anxiety, panic, and depression: A review of the literature. *Journal of Clinical Psychiatry, 54* (10, Suppl.), 25–45. [13]

Jones, E. E. (1976). How do people perceive the causes of behavior? *American Scientist, 64*, 300–305. [14]

Jones, E. E. (1990). *Interpersonal perception.* New York: Freeman. [14]

Jones, E. E., & Nisbett, R. E. (1971). *The actor and the observer: Divergent perceptions of the causes of behavior.* New York: General Learning. [14]

Jones, H. E., Herning, R. I., Cadet, J. L., & Griffiths, R. R. (2000). Caffeine withdrawal increases cerebral blood flow velocity and alters quantitative electroencephalography (EEG) activity. *Psychopharmacology, 147*, 371–377. [4]

Jones, M. C. (1924). A laboratory study of fear: The case of Peter. *Pedagogical Seminary, 31*, 308–315. [5]

Jones, R. (2003). Listen and learn. *Nature Reviews Neuroscience, 4*, 699. [8]

Jorgensen, M., & Keiding, N. (1991). Estimation of spermarche from longitudinal spermaturia data. *Biometrics, 47*, 177–193. [8]

Josephs, R., Newman, M., Brown, R., & Beer, J. (2003). Status, testosterone, and human intellectual performance. *Psychological Science, 14*, 158–163. [7]

Joyce, P., Mulder, R., Luty, S., McKenzie, J., Sullivan, P., & Cloninger, R. (2003). Borderline personality disorder in major depression: Symptomatology, temperament, character, differential drug response, and 6-month outcome. *Comprehensive Psychiatry, 44*, 35–43. [12]

Judd, L. L., Akiskal, H. S., Zeller, P. J., Paulus, M., Leon, A. C., Maser, J. D., Endicott, J., Coryell, W., Kunovac, J. L., Mueller, T. I., Rice, J. P., & Keller, M. B. (2000). Psychosocial disability during the long-term course of unipolar major depressive disorder. *Archives of General Psychiatry, 57*, 375–380. [12]

Juengling, F., Schmahl, C., Heblinger, B., Ebert, D., Bremner, J., Gostomzyk, J., Bohus, M., & Lieb, K. (2003). Positron emission tomography in female patients with borderline personality disorder. *Journal of Psychiatric Research, 37*, 109–115. [2]

Julien, R. M. (1995). *A primer of drug action* (7th ed.). New York: W.H. Freeman. [4, 8]

Jung, C. G. (1933). *Modern man in search of a soul.* New York: Harcourt Brace Jovanovich. [11]

Kagan, J. (2003). Foreward: A behavioral science perspective. In R. Plomin, J. DeFries, I. Craig, & P. McGuffin (Eds.), *Behavioral genetics in the postgenomic era* (pp. xvii–xxiii). Washington, DC: American Psychological Association. [11]

Kagitcibasi, C. (1992). A critical appraisal of individualism-collectivism: Toward a new formulation. In U. Kim, H. C. Triandis, and G. Yoon (Eds.), *Individualism and collectivism: Theoretical and methodological issues.* Newbury Park, CA: Sage. [11]

Kahneman, D., & Tversky, A. (1984). Choices, values, and frames. *American Psychologist, 39*, 341–350. [7]

Kail, R. (2000). Speed of information processing: Developmental change and links to intelligence. *Journal of School Psychology, 38*, 51–61. [8]

Kaiser Family Foundation. (1999, October). Race, ethnicity, & medical care: A survey of public perceptions and experiences. Retrieved November 26, 2003, from http://www.kff.org/content/1999/19901014a/chartpack.pdf [14]

Kalb, C. (1997, August 25). Our embattled ears: Hearing loss once seemed a normal part of aging, but experts now agree that much of it is preventable. How to protect yourself. *Newsweek, 130*, 75–76. [3]

Kalichman, S., Benotsch, E., Weinhardt, L., Austin, J., Webster, L., & Chauncey, C. (2003). Health-related Interent use, coping, social support, and health indicators in people living with HIV/AIDS: Preliminary results from a community survey. *Health Psychology, 22*, 111–116. [10]

Kalidini, S., & McGuffin, P. (2003). The genetics of affective disorders: Present and future. In R. Plomin, J. Defries, I. Craig, & P. McGuffin (Eds.), *Behavioral genetics in the postgenomic era* (pp. 481–502). Washington, DC: American Psychological Association. [12]

Kalish, H. I. (1981). *From behavioral science to behavior modification.* New York: McGraw-Hill. [5, 13]

Kaltiala-Heino, R., Rimpelae, M., Rissanen, A., & Rantanen, P. (2001). Early puberty and early sexual activity are associated with bulimic-type eating pathology in middle adolescence. *Journal of Adolescent Health, 28*, 346–352. [8]

Kampman, M., Keijsers, G., Hoogduin, C., & Hendriks, G. (2002). A randomized, double-blind, placebo-controlled study of the effects of adjunctive paroxetine in panic disorder patients unsuccessfully treated with cognitive-behavioral therapy alone. *Journal of Clinical Psychiatry, 63*, 772–777. [12]

Kane, J. M. (1996). Treatment-resistant schizophrenic patients. *Journal of Clinical Psychiatry, 57*(9, Suppl.), 35–40. [13]

Kanner, A. D., Coyne, J. C., Schaefer, C., & Lazarus, R. S. (1981). Comparison of two modes of stress measurement: Daily hassles and uplifts versus major life events. *Journal of Behavioral Medicine, 4*, 1–39. [10]

Karau, S. J., & Williams, K. D. (1993). Social loafing; a meta-analytic review and theoretical integration. *Journal of Personality and Social Psychology, 65*, 681–706. [14]

Karni, A., Tanne, D., Rubenstein, B. S., Askenasy, J. J. M., & Sagi, D. (1994). Dependence on REM sleep of overnight improvement of a perceptual skill. *Science, 265*, 679–682. [4]

Kastenbaum, R. (1992). *The psychology of death.* New York: Springer-Verlag. [8]

Katon, W. (1996). Panic disorder: Relationship to high medical utilization, unexplained physical symptoms, and medical costs. *Journal of Clinical Psychiatry, 57*(10, Suppl.), 11–18. [12]

Kawachi, I., Colditz, G. A., Speizer, F. E., Manson, J. E., Stampfer, M. J., Willett, W. C., & Hennekens, C. H. (1997). A prospective study of passive smoking and coronary heart disease. *Circulation, 95*, 2374–2379. [10]

Kawanishi, Y., Tachikawa, H., & Suzuki, T. (2000). Pharmacogenomics and schizophrenia. *European Journal of Pharmacology, 410*, 227–241. [13]

Kazdin, A., & Benjet, C. (2003). Spanking children: Evidence and issues. *Current Directions in Psychological Science, 12*, 99–103. [13]

Keating, C. R. (1994). World without words: Messages from face and body. In W. J. Lonner & R. Malpass (Eds.), *Psychology and culture* (pp. 175–182). Boston: Allyn & Bacon. [9]

Keitner, G. I., Ryan, C. E., Miller, I. W., & Norman, W. H. (1992). Recovery and major depression: Factors associated with twelve-month outcome. *American Journal of Psychiatry, 149*, 93–99. [12]

Kellett, S., Newman, D., Matthews, L., & Swift, A. (2004). Increasing the effectiveness of large group format CBT via the application of practice-based evidence. *Behavioural & Cognitive Psychotherapy, 32*, 231–234. [13]

Kelner, K. L. (1997). Seeing the synapse. *Science, 276*, 547. [2]

Kendler, K. S., & Diehl, S. R. (1993). The genetics of schizophrenia: A current genetic-epidemiologic perspective. *Schizophrenia Bulletin, 19*, 261–285. [12]

Kendler, K. S., MacLean, C., Neale, M., Kessler, R., Heath, A., & Eaves, L. (1991). The genetic epidemiology of bulimia nervosa. *American Journal of Psychiatry, 148*, 1627–1637. [9]

Kendler, K. S., Neale, M. C., Kessler, R. C., Heath, A. C., & Eaves, L. J. (1993). The lifetime history of major depression in women: Reliability of diagnosis and heritability. *Archives of General Psychiatry, 50*, 863–870. [12]

Kennedy, Q., Mather, M., & Carstensen, L. (2004). The role of motivation in the age-related positivity effect in autobiographical memory. *Psychological Science, 15*, 208–214. [6]

Kenwright, M., & Marks, I. (2004). Computer-aided self-help for phobia/panic via Internet at home: A pilot study. *British Journal of Psychiatry, 184*, 448–449. [13]

Kessler, R. C., McGonagle, K. A., Zhao, S., Nelson, C. B., Hughes, M., Eshleman, S., Wittchen, H-U., & Kendler, K. S. (1994). Lifetime and 12-month prevalence of *DSM-III-R* psychiatric disorders in the United States: Results from the National Comorbidity Survey. *American Journal of Psychiatry, 51*, 8–19. [12]

Kessler, R. C., Stein, M. B., & Berglund, P. (1998). Social phobia subtypes in the National Comorbidity Survey. *American Journal of Psychiatry, 155*, 613–619. [12]

Kiecolt-Glaser, J. (2000). *Friends, lovers, relaxation, and immunity: How behavior modifies health. Cortisol and the language of love: Text analysis of newlyweds' relationship stories.* Paper presented at the annual meeting of the American Psychological Association, Washington, DC. [9]

Kiecolt-Glaser, J. K., Fisher, L. D., Ogrocki, P., Stout, J., Speicher, C. E., & Glaser, R. (1987). Marital quality, marital disruption, and immune function. *Psychosomatic Medicine, 49*, 13–34. [10]

Kiecolt-Glaser, J. K., Glaser, R., Gravenstein, S., Malarkey, W. B., & Sheridan, J. (1996). Chronic stress alters the immune response to influenza virus vaccine in older adults. *Proceedings of the National Academy of Science, 93*, 3043–3047. [10]

Kiecolt-Glaser, J., McGuire, L., Robles, T., & Glaser, R. (2002). Psychoneuroimmunology: Psychological influences on immune function and health. *Journal of Consulting and Clinical Psychology, 70* , 537–547. [10]

Kihlstrom, J. F. (1985). Hypnosis. *Annual Review of Psychology, 26*, 557–591. [4]

Kihlstrom, J. F. (1986). Strong inferences about hypnosis. *Behavioral and Brain Sciences, 9*, 474–475. [4]

Kihlstrom, J. F., & Barnhardt, T. M. (1993). The self-regulation of memory: For better and for worse, with and without hypnosis. In D. M. Wegner & J. W. Pennebaker (Eds.), *Handbook of mental control.* Englewood Cliffs, NJ: Prentice Hall. [4]

Kilbride, J. E., & Kilbride, P. L. (1975). Sitting and smiling behavior of Baganda infants. *Journal of Cross-Cultural Psychology, 6*, 88–107. [8]

Kilpatrick, D., Ruggiero, K., Acierno, R., Saunders, B., Resnick, H., & Best, C. (2003). Violence and risk of PTSD, major depression, substance abuse/dependence, and comorbidity: Results from the National Survey of Adolescents. *Journal of Consulting and Clinical Psychology, 71*, 692–700. [10]

Kim, H., & Chung, R. (2003). Relationship of recalled parenting style to self-perception in Korean American college students. *Journal of Genetic Psychology, 164*, 481–492. [8]

Kim, J. J., Mohamed, S., Andreasen, N. C., O'Leary, D. S., Watkins, L., Ponto, L. L. B., & Hichwa, R. D. (2000). Regional neural dysfunctions in chronic schizophrenia studied with positron emission tomography. *American Journal of Psychiatry, 157*, 542–548. [12]

Kim, K. H. S., Relkin, N. R., Lee, K-M., & Hirsch, J. (1997). Distinct cortical areas associated with native and second languages. *Nature, 388*, 171–174. [7]

Kim, S-G., Ugurbil, K., & Strick, P. L. (1994). Activation of a cerebellar output nucleus during cognitive processing. *Science, 265*, 949–951. [2]

Kimura, D. (1992). Sex differences in the brain. *Scientific American, 267*, 118–125. [7]

Kimura, D. (2000). *Sex and cognition.* Cambridge, MA: MIT Press. [7]

King, L. A., Walker, L. M., & Broyles, S. J. (1996). Creativity and the five-factor model. *Journal of Research on Personality, 30*, 189–203. [11]

Kinney, A., Croyle, R., Bailey, C., Pelias, M., & Neuhausen, S. (2001). Knowledge, attitudes, and interest in breast-ovarian cancer gene testing: A survey of a large African American kindred with a BRCA1 mutation. *Journal of Genetic Counseling, 10*, 41–51. [2]

Kinnunen, T., Zamansky, H. S., & Block, M. L. (1994). Is the hypnotized subject lying? *Journal of Abnormal Psychology, 103*, 184–191. [4]

Kinomura, S., Larsson, J., Gulyás, B., & Roland, P. E. (1996). Activation by attention of the human reticular formation and thalamic intralaminar nuclei. *Science, 271*, 512–515. [2]

Kinsey, A. C., Pomeroy, W. B., & Martin, C. E. (1948). *Sexual behavior in the human male.* Philadelphia: W. B. Saunders. [9]

Kinsey, A. C., Pomeroy, W. B., Martin, C. E., & Gebhard, P. H. (1953). *Sexual behavior in the human female.* Philadelphia: W. B. Saunders. [9]

Kirchner, T., & Sayette, M. (2003). Effects of alcohol on controlled and automatic memory processes. *Experimental & Clinical Psychopharmacology, 11*, 167–175. [4]

Kirkcaldy, B., Shephard, R., & Furnham, A. (2002). The influence of Type A behavior and locus of control upon job satisfaction and occupational health. *Personality & Individual Differences, 33*, 1361–1371. [11]

Kirsch, I., & Lynn, S. J. (1995). The altered state of hypnosis: Changes in the theoretical landscape. *American Psychologist, 50*, 846–858. [4]

Kitayama, S., & Markus, H. R. (2000). The pursuit of happiness and the realization of sympathy: Cultural patterns of self, social relations, and well-being. In E. Diener & E. M. Suh (Eds.), *Subjective well-being across cultures.* Cambridge, MA: MIT Press. [11]

Kite, M. E., Deaux, K., & Miele, M. (1991). Stereotypes of young and old: Does age outweigh gender? *Psychology and Aging, 6*, 19–27. [14]

Kiyatkin, E., & Wise, R. (2002). Brain and body hyperthermia associated with heroin self-administration in rats. *Journal of Neuroscience, 22*, 1072–1080. [4]

Klaczynski, P., Fauth, J., & Swanger, A. (1998). Adolescent identity: Rational vs. experiential processing, formal operations, and critical thinking beliefs. *Journal of Youth & Adolescence, 27*, 185–207. [8]

Klatzky, R. L. (1980). *Human memory: Structures and processes* (2nd ed.). New York: W. H. Freeman. [6]

Klatzky, R. L. (1984). *Memory and awareness: An information-processing perspective.* New York: W. H. Freeman. [6]

Kleinman, A., & Cohen, A. (1997, March). Psychiatry's global challenge. *Scientific American, 276*, 86–89. [13]

Klerman, G. L., Weissman, M. N., Rounsaville, B. J., & Chevron, E. S. (1984). *Interpersonal therapy of depression.* New York: Academic Press. [13]

Kliegman, R. (1998). Fetal and neonatal medicine. In R. Behrman & R. Kliegman (Eds.), *Nelson essentials of pediatrics* (3rd ed., pp. 167–225). Philadelphia: W. B. Saunders. [8]

Kluft, R. P. (1984). An introduction to multiple personality disorder. *Psychiatric Annals, 14*, 19–24. [12]

Kobasa, S. (1979). Stressful life events, personality, and health: An inquiry into hardiness. *Journal of Personality and Social Psychology, 37*, 1–11. [10]

Kobasa, S. C., Maddi, S. R., & Kahn, S. (1982). Hardiness and health: A prospective study. *Journal of Personality and Social Psychology, 42*, 168–177. [10]

Kochanska, G. (1993). Toward a synthesis of parental socialization and child temperament in early development of conscience. *Child Development, 64*, 325–347. [14]

Kochavi, D., Davis, J., & Smith, G. (2001). Corticotropin-releasing factor decreases meal size by decreasing cluster number in Koletsky (LA/N) rats with and without a null mutation of the leptin receptor. *Physiology & Behavior, 74*, 645–651. [9]

Koehler, T., Tiede, G., & Thoens, M. (2002). Long and short-term forgetting of word associations: An experimental study of the Freudian concepts of resistance and repression. *Zeitschrift fuer Klinische Psychologie, Psychiatrie und Psychotherapie, 50*, 328–333. [11]

Kohlberg, L. (1966). A cognitive-developmental analysis of children's sex-role concepts and attitudes. In E. E. Maccoby (Ed.), *The development of sex differences* (pp. 82–173). Stanford, CA: Stanford University Press. [8]

Kohlberg, L. (1968, September). The child as a moral philosopher. *Psychology Today,* 24–30. [8]

Kohlberg, L. (1969). *Stages in the development of moral thought and action.* New York: Holt, Rinehart & Winston. [8]

Kohlberg, L., & Gilligan, C. (1971). The adolescent as a philosopher: The discovery of the self in a postconventional world. *Daedalus, 100*, 1051–1086. [8]

Kohlberg, L., & Ullian, D. Z. (1974). In R. C. Friedman, R. M. Richart, & R. L. Vande Wiele (Eds.), *Sex differences in behavior* (pp. 209–222). New York: Wiley. [8]

Köhler, W. (1925). *The mentality of apes* (E. Winter, Trans.). New York: Harcourt Brace Jovanovich. [5]

Koltz, C. (1983, December). Scapegoating. *Psychology Today,* 68–69. [14]

Kon, M. A., & Plaskota, L. (2000). Information complexity of neural networks. *Neural Networks, 13*, 365–375. [6]

Konishi, M. (1993). Listening with two ears. *Scientific American, 268*, 66–73. [3]

Kopinska, A., & Harris, L. (2003). Spatial representation in body coordinates: Evidence from errors in remembering positions of visual and auditory targets after active eye, head, and body movements. *Canadian Journal of Experimental Psychology, 57*, 23–37. [3]

Kopp, C. P., & Kaler, S. R. (1989). Risk in infancy: Origins and implications. *American Psychologist, 44*, 224–230. [8]

Kosslyn, S. M. (1988). Aspects of a cognitive neuroscience of mental imagery. *Science, 240*, 1621–1626. [7]

Kovacs, D., Mahon, J., & Palmer, R. (2002). Chewing and spitting out food among eating-disordered patients. *International Journal of Eating Disorders, 32*, 112–115. [9]

Kowatch, R., Suppes, T., Carmody, T., Bucci, J., Hume, J., Kromelis, M., Emslie, G., Weinberg, W., & Rush, A. (2000). Effect size of lithium, divalproex sodium, and carbamazepine in children and adolescents with bipolar disorder. *Journal of the American Academy of Child & Adolescent Psychiatry, 39*, 713–720. [13]

Kozak, M. J., Foa, E. B., & McCarthy, P. R. (1988). Obsessive-compulsive disorder. In C. G. Last & M. Herson (Eds.), *Handbook of anxiety disorders* (pp. 87–108). New York: Pergamon Press. [12]

Kozel, F., Padgett, T., & George, M. (2004). A replication study of the neural correlates of deception. *Behavioral Neuroscience, 118*, 852–856. [2]

Krantz, D. S., Grunberg, N. E., & Baum, A. (1985). Health psychology. *Annual Review of Psychology, 36*, 349–383. [10]

Kranzler, H. R. (1996). Evaluation and treatment of anxiety symptoms and disorders in alcoholics. *Journal of Clinical Psychiatry, 57*(6, Suppl.). [12]

Kraus, S. J. (1995). Attitudes and the prediction of behavior: A meta-analysis of the empirical literature. *Personality and Social Psychology Bulletin, 21*, 58–75. [14]

Krcmar, M., & Cooke, M. (2001). Children's moral reasoning and their perceptions of television violence. *Journal of Communication, 51*, 300–316. [5]

Kroll, N. E. A., Ogawa, K. H., & Nieters, J. E. (1988). Eyewitness memory and the importance of sequential information. *Bulletin of the Psychonomic Society, 26*, 395–398. [6]

Krosigk, M. von. (1993). Cellular mechanisms of a synchronized oscillation in the thalamus. *Science, 261*, 361–364. [2]

Krueger, J. M., & Takahashi, S. (1997). Thermoregulation and sleep: Closely linked but separable. *Annals of the New York Academy of Sciences, 813*, 281–286. [4]

Krueger, R., & Johnson, W. (2004). Genetic and environmental structure of adjectives describing the domains of the Big Five model of personality: A nationwide U.S. twin study. *Journal of Research in Personality, 38*, 448–472. [11]

Krueger, W. C. F. (1929). The effect of overlearning on retention. *Journal of Experimental Psychology, 12*, 71–81. [6]

Kruk, M., Meelis, W., Halasz, J., & Haller, J. (2004). Fast positive feedback between the adrenocortical stress response and a brain mechanism involved in aggressive behavior. *Behavioral Neuroscience, 118*, 1062–1070. [2]

Kübler-Ross, E. (1969). *On death and dying.* New York: Macmillan. [8]

Kucharska-Pietura, K., & Klimkowski, M. (2002). Perception of facial affect in chronic schizophrenia and right brain damage. *Acta Neurobiologiae Experimentalis, 62*, 33–43. [2]

Kuhn, D. (1984). Cognitive development. In M. H. Bernstein & M. E. Lamb (Eds.), *Developmental psychology.* Hillsdale, NJ: Erlbaum. [8]

Kuhn, D., Kohlberg, L., Langer, J., & Haan, N. (1977). The development of formal operations in logical and moral judgment. *Genetic Psychology Monographs, 95*, 97–188. [8]

Kuhn, D., & Lao, J. (1996). Effects of evidence on attitudes: Is polarization the norm? *Psychological Science, 7*, 115–120. [14]

Kumar, R., O'Malley, P., Johnston, L., Schulenberg, J., & Bachman, J. (2002). Effects of school-level norms on student substance abuse. *Prevention Science, 3*, 105–124. [14]

Kummervold, P., Gammon, D., Bergvik, S., Johnsen, J., Hasvold, T., & Rosenvinge, J. (2002). Social support in a wired world: Use of online mental health forums in Norway. *Nordic Journal of Psychiatry, 56*, 59–65. [10]

Kumpfer, K., Alvarado, R., Smith, P., & Ballamy, N. (2002). Cultural sensitivity and adaptation in family-based prevention interventions. *Prevention Science, 3*, 241–246. [13]

Kunda, Z., & Oleson, K. C. (1995). Maintaining stereotypes in the face of disconfirmation: Construction grounds for subtyping deviants. *Journal of Personality and Social Psychology, 68*, 565–579. [14]

Kunz, D., & Herrmann, W. M. (2000). Sleep-wake cycle, sleep-related disturbances, and sleep disorders: A chronobiological approach. *Comparative Psychology, 41*(2, Suppl. 1), 104–105. [4]

Kuo, C., & Tsaur, C. (2004). Locus of control, supervisory support and unsafe behavior: The case of the construction industry in Taiwan. *Chinese Journal of Psychology, 46*, 392–405. [11]

Kuroda, K. (2002). An image retrieval system by impression words and specific object names-IRIS. *Neurocomputing: An International Journal, 43*, 259–276. [7]

Lal, S. (2002). Giving children security: Mamie Phipps Clark and the racialization of child psychology. *American Psychologist, 57*, 20–28. [1]

Lalonde, R., & Botez, M. I. (1990). The cerebellum and learning processes in animals. *Brain Research Reviews, 15*, 325–332. [2]

Lam, L., & Kirby, S. (2002). Is emotional intelligence an advantage? An exploration of the impact of emotional and general intelligence on individual performance. *Journal of Social Psychology, 142*, 133–143. [9]

Lambe, E. K., Katzman, D. K., Mikulis, D. J., Kennedy, S. H., & Zipursky, R. B. (1997). Cerebral gray matter volume deficits after weight recovery from anorexia nervosa. *Archives of General Psychiatry, 54*, 537–542. [9]

Lamberg, L. (1996). Narcolepsy researchers barking up the right tree. *Journal of the American Medical Association, 276*, 265–266. [4]

Lambert, M. (2003). Suicide risk assessment and management: Focus on personality disorders. *Current Opinion in Psychiatry, 16*, 71–76. [12]

Lamborn, S. D., Mounts, N. S., Steinberg, L., & Dornbusch, S. M. (1991). Patterns of competence and adjustment among adolescents from authoritative, authoritarian, indulgent, and neglectful families. *Child Development, 62*, 1049–1065. [8]

Lamm, H. (1988). A review of our research on group polarization: Eleven experiments on the effects of group discussion on risk acceptance, probability estimation, and negotiation positions. *Psychological Reports, 62*, 807–813. [14]

Lang, A., Craske, M., Brown, M., & Ghaneian, A. (2001). Fear-related state dependent memory. *Cognition & Emotion, 15*, 695–703. [6]

Lang, A. R., Goeckner, D. J., Adesso, V. J., & Marlatt, G. A. (1975). Effects of alcohol on aggression in male social drinkers. *Journal of Abnormal Psychology, 84*, 508–518. [1]

Lange, C. G., & James, W. (1922). *The emotions* (I. A. Haupt, Trans.). Baltimore: Williams and Wilkins. [9]

Langer, E. J., & Rodin, J. (1976). The effects of choice and enhanced personal responsibility for the aged: A field experiment in an institutional setting. *Journal of Personality and Social Psychology, 34*, 191–198. [10]

Langevin, B., Sukkar, F., Léger, P., Guez, A., & Robert, D. (1992). Sleep apnea syndromes (SAS) of specific etiology: Review and incidence from a sleep laboratory. *Sleep, 15*, S25–S32. [4]

Langlois, J. H., Kalakanis, L., Rubenstein, A. J., Larson, A., Hallam, M., & Smoot, M. (2000). Maxims or myths of beauty? A meta-analytic and theoretical review. *Psychological Bulletin, 126*, 390–423. [14]

Langlois, J. H., & Roggman, L. A. (1990). Attractive faces are only average. *Psychological Science, 1*, 115–121. [14]

Lao, J., & Kuhn, D. (2002). Cognitive engagement and attitude development. *Cognitive Development, 17*, 1203–1217. [14]

Larson, M. (2003). Gender, race, and aggression in television commercials that feature children. *Sex Roles, 48*, 67–75. [5]

Latané, B., Williams, K., & Harkins, S. (1979). Many hands make light the work: The causes and consequences of social loafing. *Journal of Personality and Social Psychology, 37*, 822–832. [14]

Lating, J., Sherman, M., Lowry, J., Everly, G., & Peragine, T. (2004). PTSD reactions and coping responses of East Coast and West Coast American Airlines flight attendants after September 11: A possible psychological contagion effect? *Journal of Nervous & Mental Disease, 192*, 876–879. [10]

Latner, J., & Wilson, T. (2004). Binge eating and satiety in bulimia nervosa and binge eating disorder: Effects of macronutrient intake. *International Journal of Eating Disorders, 36*, 402–415. [9]

Laumann, E. O., Gagnon, J. H., Michael, R. T., & Michaels, S. (1994). *The social organization of sexuality.* Chicago: University of Chicago Press. [9]

Laurent, J., Swerdik, M., & Ryburn, M. (1992). Review of validity research on the Stanford-Binet Intelligence Scale: Fourth Edition. *Psychological Assessment, 4*, 102–112. [7]

Lavie, P., Herer, P., Peled, R., Berger, I., Yoffe, N., Zomer, J., & Rubin, A-H. (1995). Mortality in sleep apnea patients: A multivariate analysis of risk factors. *Sleep, 18*, 149–157. [4]

Layton, L., Deeny, K., Tall, G., & Upton, G. (1996). Researching and promoting phonological awareness in the nursery class. *Journal of Research in Reading, 19*, 1–13. [8]

Lazarus, R. S. (1966). *Psychological stress and the coping process.* New York: McGraw-Hill. [10]

Lazarus, R. S. (1984). On the primacy of cognition. *American Psychologist, 39*, 124–129. [9]

Lazarus, R. S. (1991a). Cognition and motivation in emotion. *American Psychologist, 46*, 352–367. [9]

Lazarus, R. S. (1991b). Progress on a cognitive-motivational-relational theory of emotion. *American Psychologist, 46*, 819–834. [9]

Lazarus, R. S. (1995). Vexing research problems inherent in cognitive-mediational theories of emotion—and some solutions. *Psychological Inquiry, 6*, 183–187. [9]

Lazarus, R. S., & DeLongis, A. (1983). Psychological stress and coping in aging. *American Psychologist, 38*, 245–253. [10]

Lazarus, R. S., & Folkman, S. (1984). *Stress, appraisal, and coping.* New York: Springer. [10]

Lebow, J. L., & Gurman, A. S. (1995). Research assessing couple and family therapy. *Annual Review of Psychology, 46*, 27–57. [13]

Lecomte, T., & Lecomte, C. (2002). Toward uncovering robust principles of change inherent to cognitive-behavioral therapy for psychosis. *American Journal of Orthopsychiatry, 72*, 50–57. [13]

LeDoux, J. (2004). Brains through the back door. In J. Brockman (Ed.), *Curious minds: How a child becomes a scientist* (pp. 141–144). New York: Pantheon Books. [2]

LeDoux, J. E. (1994). Emotion, memory, and the brain. *Scientific American, 270*, 50–57. [2]

LeDoux, J. E. (1995). Emotion: clues from the brain. *Annual Review of Psychology, 46*, 209–235. [2]

LeDoux, J. E. (1996). *The emotional brain: The mysterious underpinnings of emotional life.* New York: Simon & Schuster. [9]

LeDoux, J. E. (2000). Emotion circuits in the brain. *Annual Review of Neuroscience, 23*, 155–184. [2, 9]

Lee, I., & Kesner, R. (2002). Differential contribution of NMDA receptors in hippocampal subregions to spatial working memory. *Nature Neuroscience, 5*, 162–168. [6]

Lee, M., & Cummins, T. (2004). Evidence accumulation in decision making: Unifying the "take the best" and the "rational" models. *Psychonomic Bulletin & Review, 11*, 343–352. [7]

Leichtman, M. D., & Ceci, S. J. (1995). The effects of stereotypes and suggestions on preschoolers' reports. *Developmental Psychology, 31*, 568–578. [6]

Leigh, B. C., & Stall, R. (1993). Substance use and risky sexual behavior for exposure to HIV: Issues in methodology, interpretation, and prevention. *American Psychologist, 48*, 1035–1045. [10]

Leitenberg, H., & Henning, K. (1995). Sexual fantasy. *Psychological Bulletin, 117*, 469–496. [9]

Lenneberg, E. (1967). *Biological foundations of language.* New York: Wiley. [8]

Leon, M. (1992). The neurobiology of filial learning. *Annual Review of Psychology, 43*, 337–398. [8]

Lerman, D. C., & Iwata, B. A. (1996). Developing a technology for the use of operant extinction in clinical settings: An examination of basic and applied research. *Journal of Applied Behavior Analysis, 29*, 345–382. [13]

Lesch, K. (2003). Neuroticism and serotonin: A developmental genetic perspective. In R. Plomin, J. DeFries, I. Craig, & P. McGuffin (Eds.), *Behavioral genetics in the postgenomic era* (pp. 389–423). Washington, DC: American Psychological Association. [12]

Lester, B., Hoffman, J., & Brazelton, T. (1985). The rhythmic structure of mother-infant interaction in term and preterm infants. *Child Development, 56*, 15–27. [8]

Leuchter, A., Cook, I., Witte, E., Morgan, M., & Abrams, M. (2002). Changes in brain function of depressed subjects during treatment with placebo. *American Journal of Psychiatry, 159*, 122–129. [13]

LeVay, S. (1991). A difference in hypothalamic structure between heterosexual and homosexual men. *Science, 253*, 1034–1037. [9]

Levenson, R. W. (1992). Autonomic nervous system differences among emotions. *Psychological Science, 3*, 23–27. [9]

Levenson, R. W., Ekman, P., & Friesen, W. (1990). Voluntary facial action generates emotion-specific autonomic nervous system activity. *Psychophysiology, 27*, 363–385. [9]

Levitt, E. E., & Duckworth, J. C. (1984). Minnesota Multiphasic Personality Inventory. In D. J. Keyser & R. C. Sweetland (Eds.), *Test critiques* (Vol. 1, pp. 466–472). Kansas City: Test Corporation of America. [11]

Levy, J. (1985, May). Right brain, left brain: Fact and fiction. *Psychology Today,* pp. 38–44. [2]

Levy-Shiff, R., Lerman, M., Har-Even, D., & Hod, M. (2002). Maternal adjustment and infant outcome in medically defined high-risk pregnancy. *Developmental Psychology, 38*, 93–103. [8]

Lewald, J. (2004). Gender-specific hemispheric asymmetry in auditory space perception. *Cognitive Brain Research, 19*, 92–99. [2]

Lewinsohn, P. M., & Rosenbaum, M. (1987). Recall of parental behavior by acute depressives, remitted depressives, and nondepressives. *Journal of Personality and Social Psychology, 52*, 611–619. [6]

Lewis, D. O., Pincus, J. H., Feldman, M., Jackson, L., & Bard, B. (1986). Psychiatric, neurological, and psychoeducational characteristics of 15 death row inmates in the United States. *American Journal of Psychiatry, 143*, 838–845. [14]

Leyens, J-P., Yzerbyt, V., & Olivier, C. (1996). The role of applicability in the emergence of the overattribution bias. *Journal of Personality and Social Psychology, 70*, 219–229. [14]

Li, J. (2003). U.S. and Chinese cultural beliefs about learning. *Journal of Educational Psychology, 95*, 258–267. [7]

Lidz, C., & Macrine, S. (2001). An alternative approach to the identification of gifted culturally and linguistically diverse learners: The contribution of dynamic assessment. *School Psychology International, 22*, 74–96. [7]

Lieblum, S. (2002). After sildenafil: Bridging the gap between pharmacologic treatment and satisfying sexual relationships. *Journal of Clinical Psychiatry, 63*, 17–22. [12]

Liepert, J., Terborg, C., & Weiller, C. (1999). Motor plasticity induced by synchronized thumb and foot movements. *Experimental Brain Research, 125*, 435–439. [2]

Lijtmaer, R. (2001). Splitting and nostalgia in recent immigrants: Psychodynamic considerations. *Journal of the American Academy of Psychoanalysis, 29*, 427–438. [13]

Lim, V. (2002). The IT way of loafing on the job: Cyberloafing, neutralizing and organizational justice. *Journal of Organizational Behavior, 23*, 675–694. [14]

Lindenberger, U., Mayr, U., & Kliegl, R. (1993). Speed and intelligence in old age. *Psychology and Aging, 8*, 207–220. [8]

Lindsay, D., Hagen, L., Read, J., Wade, K., & Garry, M. (2004). True photographs and false memories. *Psychological Science, 15*, 149–154. [6]

Linn, R. L. (1982). Ability testing: Individual differences, prediction, and differential prediction. In A. K. Wigdor & W. R. Garner (Eds.), *Ability testing: Uses, consequences, and controversies* (Part II). Washington, DC: National Academy Press. [7]

Linszen, D. H., Dingemans, P. M., Nugter, M. A., Van der Does, J. W., Scholte, W. F., & Lenior, M. A. (1997). Patient attributes and expressed emotion as risk factors for psychotic relapse. *Schizophrenia Bulletin, 23*, 119–130. [13]

Linton, M. (1979, July). I remember it well. *Psychology Today,* 80–86. [6]

Linville, P. W., Fischer, G. W., & Salovey, P. (1989). Perceived distributions of the characteristics of in-group and out-group members: Empirical evidence and a computer simulation. *Journal of Personality and Social Psychology, 57*, 165–188. [14]

Lishman, W. A. (1990). Alcohol and the brain. *British Journal of Psychiatry, 156*, 635–644. [10]

Little, J., McFarlane, J., & Ducharme, H. (2002). ECT use delayed in the presence of comorbid mental retardation: A review of clinical and ethical issues. *Journal of ECT, 18*, 218–222. [13]

Little, R. E., Anderson, K. W., Ervin, C. H., Worthington-Roberts, B., & Clarren, S. K. (1989). Maternal alcohol use during breast-feeding and infant mental and motor development at one year. *New England Journal of Medicine, 321*, 425–430. [8]

Loeber, R., & Hay, D. (1997). Key issues in the development of aggression and violence from childhood to early adulthood. *Annual Review of Psychology, 48*, 371–410. [14]

Loehlin, J. C. (1992). *The limits of family influence: Genes, experience, and behavior.* New York: Guilford. [11]

Loehlin, J. C., Horn, J. M., & Willerman, L. (1990). Heredity, environment, and personality change: Evidence from the Texas Adoption Project. *Journal of Personality, 58*, 221–243. [11]

Loehlin, J. C., Lindzey, G., & Spuhler, J. N. (1975). *Race differences in intelligence.* San Francisco: Freeman. [7]

Loehlin, J. C., Willerman, L., & Horn, J. M. (1987). Personality resemblance in adoptive families: A 10-year follow-up. *Journal of Personality and Social Psychology, 53*, 961–969. [11]

Loehlin, J. C., Willerman, L., & Horn, J. M. (1988). Human behavior genetics. *Annual Review of Psychology, 39*, 101–133. [11]

Loftus, E. (2003). Our changeable memories: Legal and practical implications. *Nature Reviews: Neuroscience, 4*, 231–234. [6]

Loftus, E. (2004). Memories of things unseen. *Current Directions in Psychological Science, 13*, 145–147. [6]

Loftus, E., & Bernstein, D. (2005). Rich false memories: The royal road to success. In A. Healy (Ed.), *Experimental cognitive psychology and its applications.* Washington, DC: American Psychological Association. (pp. 101–113). [6]

Loftus, E. F. (1979). *Eyewitness testimony.* Cambridge, MA: Harvard University Press. [6]

Loftus, E. F. (1984, February). Eyewitnesses: Essential but unreliable. *Psychology Today,* 22–27. [6]

Loftus, E. F. (1993). Psychologists in the eyewitness world. *American Psychologist, 48,* 550–552. [6]

Loftus, E. F. (1997). Creating false memories. *Scientific American, 277,* 71–75. [6]

Loftus, E. F., & Hoffman, H. G. (1989). Misinformation and memory: The creation of new memories. *Journal of Experimental Psychology: General, 118,* 100–104. [6]

Loftus, E. F., & Loftus, G. R. (1980). On the permanence of stored information in the human brain. *American Psychologist, 35,* 409–420. [6]

Loftus, E. F., & Pickrell, J. (1995). The formation of false memories. *Psychiatric Annals, 25,* 720–725. [6]

Lombardi, F. (2005, February 11). Vicious new AIDS strain. *New York Daily News* [Online edition]. Retrieved February 21, 2005, from http://www.nydailynews.com/front/story/280163p-240060c.html [10]

London, E. D., Ernst, M., Grant, S., Bonson, K., & Weinstein, A. (2000). Orbitofrontal cortex and human drug abuse: Functional imaging. *Cerebral Cortex, 10,* 334–342. [5]

Long, D., & Baynes, K. (2002). Discourse representation in the two cerebral hemispheres. *Journal of Cognitive Neuroscience, 14,* 228–242. [2]

Long, G. M., & Crambert, R. F. (1990). The nature and basis of age-related changes in dynamic visual acuity. *Psychology and Aging, 5,* 138–143. [8]

Lott, B., & Saxon, S. (2002). The influence of ethnicity, social class and context on judgments about U.S. women. *Journal of Social Psychology, 142,* 481–499. [14]

Lotze, M., Montoya, P., Erb, M., Hulsmann, E., Flor, H., Klose, U., Birbaumer, N., & Grodd, W. (1999). Activation of cortical and cerebellar motor areas during executed and imagined hand movements: An fMRI study. *Journal of Cognitive Neuroscience, 11,* 491–501. [7]

Lubart, T. (2003). In search of creative intelligence. In R. Sternberg, J. Lautrey, & T. Lubart (Eds.), *Models of intelligence: International perspective* (pp. 279–292). Washington, DC: American Psychological Association. [7]

Lubman, D. I., Peters, L. A., Mogg, K., Bradley, B. P., & Deakin, J. F. (2000). Attentional bias for drug cues in opiate dependence. *Psychological Medicine, 30,* 169–175. [4]

Luchins, A. S. (1957). Experimental attempts to minimize the impact of first impressions. In C. I. Hovland (Ed.), *Yale studies in attitude and communication: Vol. 1. The order of presentation in persuasion* (pp. 62–75). New Haven, CT: Yale University Press. [14]

Lucio, E., Reyes-Lagunes, I., & Scott, R. L. (1994). MMPI-2 for Mexico: Translation and adaptation. *Journal of Personality Assessment, 63,* 105–116. [11]

Luo, S., & Klohnen, E. (2005). Assortative mating and marital quality in newlyweds: A couple-centered approach. *Journal of Personality & Social Psychology, 88,* 304–326. [14]

Lustig, C., & Hasher, L. (2002). Working memory span: The effect of prior learning. *American Journal of Psychology, 115,* 89–101. [6]

Lustig, C., Konkel, A., & Jacoby, L. (2004). Which route to recovery? Controlled retrieval and accessibility bias in retroactive interference. *Psychological Science, 15,* 729–735. [6]

Lutchmaya, S., Baron-Cohen, S., & Raggatt, P. (2002). Foetal testosterone and vocabulary size in 18- and 24-month-old infants. *Infant Behavior & Development, 24,* 418–424. [7]

Lydiard, R. B., Brawman-Mintzer, O., & Ballenger, J. C. (1996). Recent developments in the psychopharmacology of anxiety disorders. *Journal of Consulting and Clinical Psychology, 64,* 660–668. [13]

Lyketsos, C. G., Chen, L.-S., & Anthony, J. C. (1999). Cognitive decline in adulthood: An 11.5-year follow-up of the Baltimore Epidemiologic Catchment Area Study. *American Journal of Psychiatry, 156,* 56–58. [8]

Lynn, S. J., Kirsch, I., Barabasz, A., Cardena, E., & Patterson, D. (2000). Hypnosis as an empirically supported clinical intervention: The state of the evidence and a look to the future. *International Journal of Clinical Experimental Hypnosis, 48,* 239–259. [4]

Lynn, S. J., & Nash, M. R. (1994). Truth in memory: Ramifications for psychotherapy and hypnotherapy. *American Journal of Clinical Hypnosis, 36,* 194–208. [4]

Lyon, M., Cline, J., Totosy de Zepetnek, J., Jie Shan, J., Pang, P., & Benishin, C. (2001). Effect of the herbal extract combination *Panax quinquefolium* and *Ginko biloba* on attention-deficit hyperactivity disorder: A pilot study. *Journal of Psychiatry & Neuroscience. 26,* 221–228. [4]

Lyvers, M. (2000). "Loss of control" in alcoholism and drug addiction: A neuroscientific interpretation. *Experimental and Clinical Psychopharmacology, 8,* 225–245. [4]

Lyvers, M. (2000). Cognition, emotion, and the alcohol–aggression relationship: Comment on Giancola. *Experimental Clinical Psychopharmacology, 8,* 612–617. [14]

Maccoby, E. E. (1992). The role of parents in the socialization of children: An historical overview. *Developmental Psychology, 28,* 1006–1017. [8]

Maccoby, E. E., & Martin, J. A. (1983). Socialization in the context of the family: Parent-child interaction. In P. H. Mussen (Ed.), *Handbook of child psychology* (4th ed., Vol. 4). New York: John Wiley. [8]

MacDonald, A., Pogue-Geile, M., Johnson, M., & Carter, C. (2003). A specific deficit in context processing in the unaffected siblings of patients with schizophrenia. *Archives of General Psychiatry, 60,* 57–65. [12]

Macey, P., Henderson, L., Macey, K., Alger, J., Frysinger, R., Woo, M., Harper, R., Yan-Go, F., & Harper, R. (2002). Brain morphology associated with obstructive sleep apnea. *American Journal of Respiratory and Critical Care Medicine, 166,* 1382–1387. [4]

Mack, A. (2003). Inattentional blindness: Looking without seeing. *Current Directions in Psychological Science, 12,* 180–184. [3]

Mack, A., & Rock, I. (1998). *Inattentional blindness.* Cambridge, MA: MIT Press. [3]

Maguire, E. A., Gadian, D. G., Johnsrude, I. S., Good, C. D., Ashburner, J., Frackowiak, R. S. J., & Frith, C. D. (2000). Navigation-related structural change in the hippocampi of taxi drivers. *Proceedings of the National Academy of Science, 97,* 4398–4403. [2, 6]

Mahler, H., Kulik, J., Gibbons, F., Gerrard, M., & Harrell, J. (2003). Effects of appearance-based intervention on sun protection intentions and self-reported behaviors. *Health Psychology, 22,* 199–209. [10]

Maiden, R., Peterson, S., Caya, M., & Hayslip, B. (2003). Personality changes in the old-old: A longitudinal study. *Journal of Adult Development, 10,* 31–39. [11]

Maier, S. F., & Laudenslager, M. (1985, August). Stress and health: Exploring the links. *Psychology Today,* 44–49. [10]

Main, M., & Solomon, J. (1990). Procedures for identifying infants as disorganized/disoriented during the Ainsworth Strange Situation. In M. Greenberg, D. Cicchetti, & M. Cummings (Eds.), *Attachment in the preschool years: Theory, research, and intervention* (pp. 121–160). Chicago: University of Chicago Press. [8]

Maj, M. (1990). Psychiatric aspects of HIV–1 infection and AIDS. *Psychological Medicine, 20,* 547–563. [10]

Malkoff, S. B., Muldoon, M. F., Zeigler, Z. R., & Manuck, S. B. (1993). Blood platelet responsivity to acute mental stress. *Psychosomatic Medicine, 55,* 477–482. [10]

Maltz, W. (1991). *The sexual healing journey: A guide for survivors of sexual abuse.* New York: HarperCollins. [6]

Mancini, J., Lethel, V., Hugonenq, C., & Chabrol, B. (2001). Brain injuries in early foetal life: Consequences for brain development. *Developmental Medicine & Child Neurology, 43,* 52–60. [2]

Manderscheid, R., & Henderson, M. (2001). *Mental health, United States, 2000.* Rockville, MD: Center for Mental Health Services. Retrieved January 14, 2003, from http://www.mental-health.org/publications/allpubs/SMA01-3537/ [13]

Mandler, J. M. (1990). A new perspective on cognitive development in infancy. *American Scientist, 78*(3), 236–243. [8]

Manhal-Baugus, M. (2001). E-therapy: Practical, ethical, and legal issues. *CyberPsychology and Behavior, 4,* 551–563. [13]

Manly, T., Lewis, G., Robertson, I., Watson, P., & Datta, A. (2002). Coffee in the cornflakes: Time-of-day as a modulator of executive response control. *Neuropsychologia, 40,* 1–6. [4]

Manton, K. G., Siegler, I. C., & Woodbury, M. A. (1986). Patterns of intellectual development in later life. *Journal of Gerontology, 41,* 486–499. [8]

Manzardo, A., Stein, L., & Belluzi, J. (2002). Rats prefer cocaine over nicotine in a two-level self-administration choice test. *Brain Research, 924,* 10–19. [4]

Maratsos, M., & Matheny, L. (1994). Language specificity and elasticity: Brain and clinical syndrome studies. *Annual Review of Psychology, 45,* 487–516. [2]

Marcus, G. F. (1996). Why do children say "breaked"? *Current Directions in Psychological Science, 5,* 81–85. [8]

Marder, S. R. (1996). Clinical experience with risperidone. *Journal of Clinical Psychiatry, 57*(9, Suppl.), 57–61. [13]

Marín, G. (1994). The experience of being a Hispanic in the United States. In W. J. Lonner & R. Malpass (Eds.), *Psychology and culture* (pp. 23–27). Boston: Allyn & Bacon. [11]

Marks, I. (1987). The development of normal fear: A review. *Journal of Child Psychology and Psychiatry, 28,* 667–697. [8]

Marks, I. M. (1972). Flooding (implosion) and allied treatments. In W. S. Agras (Ed.), *Behavior modification.* New York: Little, Brown. [13]

Marriott, L., & Wenk, G. (2004). Neurobiological consequences of long-term estrogen therapy. *Current Directions in Psychological Science, 13,* 173–176. [6]

Marshall, G. D., & Zimbardo, P. G. (1979). Affective consequences of inadequately explained physiological arousal. *Journal of Personality and Social Psychology, 37,* 970–988. [9]

Marshall, J. R. (1997). Alcohol and substance abuse in panic disorder. *Journal of Clinical Psychiatry, 58*(2, Suppl.), 46–49. [12]

Marshall, R. D., Schneier, F. R., Fallon, B. A., Feerick, J., & Liebowitz, M. R. (1994). Medication therapy for social phobia. *Journal of Clinical Psychiatry, 56*(6, Suppl.), 33–37. [13]

Marshall, W. L., & Segal, Z. (1988). Behavior therapy. In C. G. Last & M. Hersen (Eds.), *Handbook of anxiety disorders* (pp. 338–361). New York: Pergamon. [13]

Martikainen, P., & Valkonen, R. (1996). Mortality after the death of a spouse: Rates and causes of death in a large Finnish cohort. *American Journal of Public Health, 86,* 1087–1093. [8]

Martin, C., & Ruble, D. (2004). Children's search for gender cues: Cognitive perspectives on gender development. *Current Directions in Psychological Science, 13,* 67–70. [8]

Martin, C. L., & Little, J. K. (1990). The relation of gender understanding to children's sex-typed preferences and gender stereotypes. *Child Development, 61,* 1427–1439. [8]

Martinez, C. (1986). Hispanics: Psychiatric issues. In C. B. Wilkinson (Ed.), *Ethnic psychiatry* (pp. 61–88). New York: Plenum. [13]

Martinez, I. (2002). The elder in the Cuban American family: Making sense of the real and ideal. *Journal of Comparative Family Studies, 33,* 359–375. [8]

Martinez, J. L., Jr., & Derrick, B. E. (1996). Long-term potentiation and learning. *Annual Review of Psychology, 47,* 173–203. [6]

Martinez, M., & Belloch, A. (2004). The effects of a cognitive-behavioural treatment for hypochondriasis on attentional bias. *International Journal of Clinical & Health Psychology, 4,* 299–311. [13]

Masataka, N. (1996). Perception of motherese in a signed language by 6-month-old deaf infants. *Developmental Psychology, 32,* 874–879. [8]

Masland, R. H. (1996). Unscrambling color vision. *Science, 271,* 616–617. [3]

Maslow, A. H. (1970). *Motivation and personality* (2nd ed.). New York: Harper & Row. [9]

Mason, R., & Just, M. (2004). How the brain processes causal inferences in text: A theoretical account of generation and integration component processes utilizing both cerebral hemispheres. *Psychological Science, 15,* 1–7. [2]

Masters, W. H., & Johnson, V. E. (1966). *Human sexual response.* Boston: Little, Brown. [9]

Masters, W. H., & Johnson, V. E. (1975). *The pleasure bond: A new look at sexuality and commitment.* Boston: Little, Brown. [9]

Mathew, R. J., & Wilson, W. H. (1991). Substance abuse and cerebral blood flow. *American Journal of Psychiatry, 148,* 292–305. [4]

Mathews, J., & Barch, D. (2004). Episodic memory for emotional and nonemotional words in schizophrenia. *Cognition & Emotion, 18,* 721–740. [12]

Mathy, R. (2002). Suicidality and sexual orientation in five continents: Asia, Australia, Europe, North America, and South America. *International Journal of Sexuality & Gender Studies, 7,* 215–225. [1]

Matlin, M. W. (1989). *Cognition* (2nd ed.). New York: Holt, Rinehart & Winston. [6, 7]

Matlin, M. W., & Foley, H. J. (1997). *Sensation and perception* (4th ed.). Boston: Allyn & Bacon. [3]

Matsuda, L., Lolait, S. J., Brownstein, M. J., Young, A. C., & Bonner, T. I. (1990). Structure of a cannabinoid receptor and functional expression of the cloned CDNA. *Nature, 346,* 561–564. [4]

Matsunami, H., Montmayeur, J-P., & Buck, L. B. (2000). A family of candidate taste receptors in human and mouse. *Nature, 404,* 601–604. [3]

Matthews, K. A. (1992). Myths and realities of the menopause. *Psychosomatic Medicine, 54,* 1–9. [8]

Matthews, K. A., Shumaker, S. A., Bowen, D. J., Langer, R. D., Hunt, J. R., Kaplan, R. M., Klesges, R. C., & Ritenbaugh, C. (1997). Women's health initiative: Why now? What is it? What's new? *American Psychologist, 52,* 101–116. [10]

Matz, D., & Wood, W. (2005). Cognitive dissonance in groups: The consequences of disagreement. *Journal of Personality & Social Psychology, 88,* 22–37. [14]

Mazzoni, G., & Memon, A. (2003). Imagination can create false autobiographical memories. *Psychological Science, 14,* 186–188. [6]

McAdams, D. P. (1992). The five-factor model in personality: A critical appraisal. *Journal of Personality, 60,* 329–361. [11]

McAnulty, R. D., & Burnette, M. M. (2001). *Exploring human sexuality: Making healthy decisions* (pp. 144–150). Boston: Allyn & Bacon. [8]

McCall, W., Dunn, A., & Rosenquist, P. (2004). Quality of life and function after electroconvulsive therapy. *British Journal of Psychiatry, 185,* 405–409. [13]

McClearn, G. E., Johansson, B., Berg, S., Pedersen, N. L., Ahern, F., Petrill, S. A., & Plomin, R. (1997). Substantial genetic influence on cognitive abilities in twins 80 or more years old. *Science, 276,* 1560–1563. [7]

McClelland, D. C. (1958). Methods of measuring human motivation. In J. W. Atkinson (Ed.), *Motives in fantasy, action and society: A method of assessment and study.* Princeton, NJ: Van Nostrand. [9]

McClelland, D. C. (1961). *The achieving society.* Princeton, NJ: Van Nostrand. [9]

McClelland, D. C. (1985). *Human motivation*. New York: Cambridge University Press. [9]

McClelland, D. C., & Pilon, D. A. (1983). Sources of adult motives in patterns of parent behavior in early childhood. *Journal of Personality and Social Psychology, 44,* 564–574. [9]

McClelland, D. C., Atkinson, J. W., Clark, R. W., & Lowell, E. L. (1953). *The achievement motive*. New York: Appleton-Century-Crofts. [9]

McClelland, J. L., McNaughton, B. L., & O'Reilly, R. C. (1995). Why there are complementary learning systems in the hippocampus and neocortex: Insights from the successes and failures of connectionist models of learning and memory. *Psychological Bulletin, 102,* 419–457. [6]

McCormack, L., & Mellor, D. (2002). The role of personality in leadership: An application of the five-factor model in the Australian military. *Military Psychology, 14,* 179–197. [11]

McCormick, C. B., & Kennedy, J. H. (2000). Father–child separation, retrospective and current views of attachment relationship with father and self-esteem in late adolescence. *Psychological Reports, 86,* 827–834. [8]

McCrae, R. (1984). Situational determinants of coping responses: Loss, threat, and challenge. *Journal of Personality and Social Psychology, 46,* 919–928. [10]

McCrae, R. (2002). The maturation of personality psychology: Adult personality development and psychological well-being. *Journal of Research in Personality, 36,* 307–317. [11]

McCrae, R., Costa, P., Hrebíčková, M., Urbánek, T., Martin, T., Oryol, V., Rukavishnikov, A., & Senin, I. (2004). Age differences in personality traits across cultures: Self-report and observer perspectives. *European Journal of Personality, 18,* 143–157. [11]

McCrae, R. R. (1993). Moderated analyses of longitudinal personality stability. *Journal of Personality and Social Psychology, 65,* 577–583. [11]

McCrae, R. R. (1996). Social consequences of experiential openness. *Psychological Bulletin, 120,* 323–337. [11]

McCrae, R. R., & Costa, P. T., Jr. (1987). Validation of the five-factor model of personality across instruments and observers. *Journal of Personality and Social Psychology, 52,* 81–90. [11]

McCrae, R. R., & Costa, P. T., Jr. (1990). *Personality in adulthood.* New York: Guilford. [11]

McCrae, R. R., Costa, P. T., Jr., Ostendorf, F., Angleitner, A., Hrebickova, M., Avia, S. J., Sanchez-Bernardos, M. L., Kusdil, M. E., Woodfield, R., Saunders, P. R., & Smith, P. B. (2000). Nature over nurture: Temperament, personality, and life span development. *Journal of Personality & Social Psychology, 78,* 173–186. [11]

McCue, J. M., Link, K. L., Eaton, S. S., & Freed, B. M. (2000). Exposure to cigarette tar inhibits ribonucleotide reductase and blocks lymphocyte proliferation. *Journal of Immunology, 165,* 6771–6775. [10]

McCullough, M. E., Hoyt, W. T., Larson, D. B., Koenig, H. G., & Thoresen, C. (2000). Religious involvement and mortality: A meta-analytic review. *Health Psychology, 19,* 211–222. [10]

McDonald, A. D., Armstrong, B. G., & Sloan, M. (1992). Cigarette, alcohol, and coffee consumption and prematurity. *American Journal of Public Health, 82,* 87–90. [8]

McDonald, C., & Murray, R. M. (2000). Early and late environmental risk factors for schizophrenia. *Brain Research Reviews, 31,* 130–137. [12]

McDonald, J. L. (1997). Language acquisition: The acquisition of linguistic structure in normal and special populations. *Annual Review of Psychology, 48,* 215–241. [7]

McDowell, C., & Acklin, M. W. (1996). Standardizing procedures for calculating Rorschach interrater reliability: Conceptual and empirical foundations. *Journal of Personality Assessment, 66,* 308–320. [11]

McElree, B., Jia, G., & Litvak, A. (2000). The time course of conceptual processing in three bilingual populations. *Journal of Memory & Language, 42,* 229–254. [7]

McElwain, N., & Volling, B. (2004). Attachment security and parental sensitivity during infancy: Associations with friendship quality and false-belief understanding at age 4. *Journal of Social & Personal Relationships, 21,* 639–667. [8]

McGlashan, T. H., & Hoffman, R. E. (2000). Schizophrenia as a disorder of developmentally reduced synaptic connectivity. *Archives of General Psychiatry, 57,* 637–648. [12]

McGuire, W. J. (1985). Attitudes and attitude change. In G. Lindzey & E. Aronson (Ed.), *Handbook of social psychology* (Vol. 2, 3rd ed.). New York: Random House. [14]

McKay, H., Glasgow, R., Feil, E., Boles, S., & Barrera, M. (2002). Internet-based diabetes self-management and support: Initial outcomes from the Diabetes Network Project. *Rehabilitation Psychology, 47,* 31–48. [10]

McMellon, C., & Schiffman, L. (2002). Cybersenior empowerment: How some older individuals are taking control of their lives. *Journal of Applied Gerontology, 21,* 157–175. [10]

McNally, R. (2003). Recovering memories of trauma: A view from the laboratory. *Current Directions in Psychological Science, 12,* 32–35. [6]

McNally, R., Lasko, N., Clancy, S., Macklin, M., Pitman, R., & Orr, S. (2004). Psychophysiological responding during script-driven imagery in people reporting abduction by space aliens. *Psychological Science, 15,* 493–497. [6]

McNeil, T. F., Cantor-Graae, E., & Weinberger, D. R. (2000). Relationship of obstetric complications and differences in size of brain structures in monozygotic twin pairs discordant for schizophrenia. *American Journal of Psychiatry, 157,* 203–212. [12]

McReynolds, P. (1989). Diagnosis and clinical assessment: Current status and major issues. *Annual Review of Psychology, 40,* 83–108. [11]

Medina, J. H., Paladini, A. C., & Izquierdo, I. (1993). Naturally occurring benzodiazepines and benzodiazepine-like molecules in brain. *Behavioural Brain Research, 58,* 1–8. [13]

Mednick, S. A., Brennan, P., & Kandel, E. (1988). Predisposition to violence. *Aggressive Behavior, 14,* 25–33. [14]

Mednick, S. A., & Mednick, M. T. (1967). *Examiner's manual, Remote Associates Test.* Boston: Houghton-Mifflin. [7]

Meer, J. (1986, June). The age of reason. *Psychology Today,* 60–64. [8]

Meltzer, H. (1930). Individual differences in forgetting pleasant and unpleasant experiences. *Journal of Educational Psychology, 21,* 399–409. [6]

Meltzer, H., Alphs, L., Green, A., Altamura, A., Anand, R., Bertoldi, A., Bourgeois, M., Chouinard, G., Islam, Z., Kane, J., Krishnan, R., Lindenmayer, J., & Potkin, S. (2003). Clozapine treatment for suicidality in schizophrenia: International suicide prevention trial. *Archives of General Psychiatry, 60,* 82–91. [13]

Meltzer, H. Y., Rabinowitz, J., Lee, M. A., Cola, P. A., Ranjan, R., Findling, R. L., & Thompson, P. A. (1997). Age at onset and gender of schizophrenic patients in relation to neuroleptic resistance. *American Journal of Psychiatry, 154,* 475–482. [13]

Melzack, R., & Wall, P. D. (1965). Pain mechanisms: A new theory. *Science, 150,* 971–979. [3]

Melzack, R., & Wall, P. D. (1983). *The challenge of pain.* New York: Basic Books. [3]

Meschyan, G., & Hernandez, A. (2002). Is native-language decoding skill related to second-language learning? *Journal of Educational Psychology, 94,* 14–22. [7]

Metter, E. J. (1991). Brain-behavior relationships in aphasia studied by positron emission tomography. *Annals of the New York Academy of Sciences, 620,* 153–164. [2]

Meyer, A. (1997, March/April). Patching up testosterone. *Psychology Today, 30,* 54–57, 66–70. [9]

Meyer, P. (1972). If Hitler asked you to electrocute a stranger, would you? In R. Greenbaum & H. A. Tilker (Eds.), *The challenge of psychology* (pp. 456–465). Englewood Cliffs, NJ: Prentice-Hall. [14]

Meyer-Bahlburg, H. F. L., Ehrhardt, A. A., Rosen, L. R., & Gruen, R. S. (1995). Prenatal estrogens and the development of homosexual orientation. *Developmental Psychology, 31,* 12–21. [9]

Michaels, J. W., Bloomel, J. M., Brocato, R. M., Linkous, R. A., & Rowe, J. S. (1982). Social facilitation and inhibition in a natural setting. *Replications in Social Psychology, 2,* 21–24. [14]

Middlebrooks, J. C., & Green, D. M. (1991). Sound localization by human listeners. *Annual Review of Psychology, 42,* 135–159. [3]

Miki Paul: Award for distinguished professional contributions to independent or institutional practice in the private sector. (2004). *American Psychologist, 59,* 807–816. [14]

Miles, D. R., & Carey, G. (1997). Genetic and environmental architecture of human aggression. *Journal of Personality and Social Psychology, 72,* 207–217. [11, 14]

Miles, R. (1999). A homeostatic switch. *Nature, 397,* 215–216. [2]

Milgram, S. (1963). Behavioral study of obedience. *Journal of Abnormal and Social Psychology, 67,* 371–378. [14]

Milgram, S. (1965). Liberating effects of group pressure. *Journal of Personality and Social Psychology, 1,* 127–134. [14]

Miller, B., Norton, M., Curtis, T., Hill, E., Schvaneveldt, P., & Young, M. (1998). The timing of sexual intercourse among adolescents: Family, peer, and other antecedents: Erratum. *Youth & Society, 29,* 390. [8]

Miller, E. M. (2000). Homosexuality, birth order, and evolution: Toward an equilibrium reproductive economics of homosexuality. *Archives of Sexual Behavior, 29,* 11–34. [9]

Miller, G., Cohen, S., Pressman, S., Barkin, A., Rabin B., & Treanor, J. (2004). Psychological stress and antibody response to influenza vaccination: When is the critical period for stress, and how does it get inside the body? *Psychosomatic Medicine, 66,* 215–223. [10]

Miller, G., Cohen, S., & Ritchey, A. (2002). Chronic psychological stress and the regulation of pro-inflammatory cytokines: A glucocorticoid-resistance model. *Health Psychology, 21,* 531–541. [10]

Miller, G. A. (1956). The magical number seven, plus or minus two: Some limits on our capacity for processing information. *Psychological Review, 63,* 81–97. [6]

Miller, J. G., Bersoff, D. M., & Harwood, R. L. (1990). Perceptions of social responsibilities in India and in the United States: Moral imperatives or personal decisions? *Journal of Personality and Social Psychology, 58,* 33–47. [14]

Miller, L. (1989, November). What biofeedback does (and doesn't) do. *Psychology Today,* pp. 22–23. [5]

Miller, N. E. (1941). The frustration-aggression hypothesis. *Psychological Review, 48,* 337–342. [14]

Miller, N. E. (1985, February). Rx: Biofeedback. *Psychology Today,* 54–59. [5]

Miller, N. S., & Gold, M. S. (1994). LSD and Ecstasy: Pharmacology, phenomenology, and treatment. *Psychiatric Annals, 24,* 131–133. [4]

Miller, T. Q., Smith, T. W., Turner, C. W., Guijarro, M. L., & Hallet, A. J. (1996). A meta-analytic review of research on hostility and physical health. *Psychological Bulletin, 119,* 322–348. [10]

Miller, T. Q., Turner, C. W., Tindale, R. S., Posavac, E. J., & Dugoni, B. L. (1991). Reasons for the trend toward null findings in research on Type A behavior. *Psychological Bulletin, 110,* 469–485. [10]

Miller, W., & Thoresen, C. (2003). Spirituality, religion, and health: An emerging research field. *American Psychologist, 58,* 24–35. [10]

Millman, R. B., & Beeder, A. B. (1994). The new psychedelic culture: LSD, Ecstasy, "rave" parties and The Grateful Dead. *Psychiatric Annals, 24,* 148–150. [4]

Milner, B. (1966). Amnesia following operation on the temporal lobes. In C. W. M. Whitty & O. L. Zangwill (Eds.), *Amnesia* (pp. 109–133). London: Butterworth. [6]

Milner, B. (1970). Memory and the medial temporal regions of the brain. In K. H. Pribram & D. E. Broadbent (Eds.), *Biology of memory.* New York: Academic Press. [6]

Milner, B., Corkin, S., & Teuber, H. L. (1968). Further analysis of the hippocampal amnesic syndrome: 14-year follow-up study of H. M. *Neuropsychologia, 6,* 215–234. [6]

Milos, G., Spindler, A., Ruggiero, G., Klaghofer, R., & Schnyder, U. (2002). Comorbidity of obsessive-compulsive disorders and duration of eating disorders. *International Journal of Eating Disorders, 31,* 284–289. [9]

Milos, G., Spindler, A., & Schnyder, U. (2004). Psychiatric comorbidity and Eating Disorder Inventory (EDI) profiles in eating disorder patients. *Canadian Journal of Psychiatry, 49,* 179–184. [9]

Milton, J., & Wiseman, R. (2001). Does psi exist? Reply to Storm and Ertel (2001). *Psychological Bulletin, 127,* 434–438. [3]

Mischel, W. (1966). A social-learning view of sex differences in behavior. In E. E. Maccoby (Ed.), *The development of sex differences* (pp. 56–81). Stanford, CA: Stanford University Press. [8]

Mischel, W. (1968). *Personality and assessment.* New York: Wiley. [11]

Mischel, W. (1973). Toward a cognitive social learning reconceptualization of personality. *Psychological Review, 80,* 252–283. [11]

Mischel, W. (1977). The interaction of person and situation. In D. Magnusson & N. S. Endler (Eds.), *Personality at the crossroads: Current issues in interactional psychology.* Hillsdale, NJ: Lawrence Erlbaum. [11]

Mischel, W. (2004). Toward an integrative science of the person. *Annual Review of Psychology, 55,* 1–22. [11]

Mischoulon, D. (2002). The herbal anxiolytics kava and valerian for anxiety and insomnia. *Psychiatric Annals, 32,* 55–60. [4]

Mishra, R. (1997). Cognition and cognitive development. In J. Berry, P. Dasen, & T. Sarswthi (Eds.), *Handbook of cross-cultural psychology* (Vol. 2). Boston, MA: Allyn & Bacon. [8]

Mishra, R., & Singh, T. (1992). Memories of Asur children for locations and pairs of pictures. *Psychological Studies, 37,* 38–46. [6]

Mistry, J., & Rogoff, B. (1994). Remembering in cultural context. In W. J. Lonner & R. Malpass (Eds.), *Psychology and culture* (pp. 139–144). Boston: Allyn & Bacon. [6]

Mitler, M. M., Aldrich, M. S., Koob, G. F., & Zarcone, V. P. (1994). Narcolepsy and its treatment with stimulants. *Sleep, 17,* 352–371. [4]

Mitsis, E. M., Halperin, J. M., & Newcorn, J. H. (2000). Serotonin and aggression in children. *Current Psychiatry Reports, 2,* 95–101. [14]

Moen, H. (1996). Gender, age, and the life course. In R. H. Binstock & L. K. George (Eds.), *Handbook of aging and the social sciences* (4th ed., pp. 171–187). San Diego, CA: Academic Press. [8]

Mogg, K., Baldwin, D., Brodrick, P., & Bradley, B. (2004). Effect of short-term SSRI treatment on cognitive bias in generalised anxiety disorder. *Psychopharmacology, 176,* 466–470. [12, 13]

Mohanty, A., & Perregaux, C. (1997). Language acquisition and bilingualism. In J. Berry, P. Dasen, & T. Saraswathi (Eds.), *Handbook of cross-cultural psychology* (pp. 217–254). Boston: Allyn & Bacon. [7]

Mohr, D., Goodkin, D., Nelson, S., Cox, D., & Weiner, M. (2002). Moderating effects of coping on the relationship between stress and the development of new brain lesions in multiple sclerosis. *Psychosomatic Medicine, 64,* 803–809. [10]

Molnar, M., Potkin, S., Bunney, W., & Jones, E. (2003). MRNA expression patterns and distribution of white matter neurons in dorsolateral prefrontal cortex of depressed patients differ from those in schizophrenia patients. *Biological Psychiatry, 53*, 39–47. [12]

Mombereau, C., Kaupmann, K., Froestl, W., Sansig, G., van der Putten, H., & Cryan, J. (2004). Genetic and pharmaceutical evidence of a role for GABA-sub(b) receptors in the modulation of anxiety- and antidepressant-like behavior. *Neuropsychopharmacology, 29*, 1050–1062. [1]

Mondloch, C., & Maurer, D. (2004). Do small white balls squeak? Pitch-object correspondences in young children. *Cognitive, Affective, & Behavioral Neuroscience, 4*, 133–136. [3]

Money, J., & Schwartz, M. (1977). Dating, romantic and nonromantic friendships, and sexuality in 17 early-treated adrenogenital females, aged 16–25. In P. A. Lee et al. (Eds.), *Congenital adrenal hyperplasia*. Baltimore: University Park Press. [9]

Monk, T. H. (1989). Circadian rhythms in subjective activation, mood, and performance efficiency. In M. H. Kryger, T. Roth, & W. C. Dement (Eds.), *Principles and practice of sleep medicine* (pp. 163–172). Philadelphia: W. B. Saunders. [4]

Montejo, A., Llorca, G., Izquierdo, J., & Rico-Villademoros, F. (2001). Incidence of sexual dysfunction associated with antidepressant agents: A prospective multicenter study of 1022 outpatients. *Journal of Clinical Psychiatry, 62*, 10–21. [12]

Montgomery, G. (2003). Color blindness: More prevalent among males. *Seeing, Hearing, and Smelling the World*. Retrieved May 13, 2003, from http://www.hhmi.org/senses/b130.html [3]

Montgomery, G., Weltz, C., Seltz, M., & Bovbjerg, D. (2002). Brief presurgery hypnosis reduces distress and pain in excisional breast biopsy patients. *International Journal of Clinical & Experimental Hypnosis, 50*, 17–32. [4]

Montgomery, G. H., DuHamel, K. N., & Redd, W. H. (2000). A meta-analysis of hypnotically induced analgesia: How effective is hypnosis? *International Journal of Clinical Experimental Hypnosis, 48*, 138–153. [4]

Moran, M. G., & Stoudemire, A. (1992). Sleep disorders in the medically ill patient. *Journal of Clinical Psychiatry, 53*(6, Suppl.), 29–36. [4]

Morgan, C. D., & Murray, H. A. (1935). A method for investigating fantasies: The Thematic Apperception Test. *Archives of Neurology and Psychiatry, 34*, 289–306. [11]

Morgan, C. D., & Murray, H. A. (1962). Thematic Apperception Test. In H. A. Murray et al. (Eds.), *Explorations in personality: A clinical and experimental study of fifty men of college age* (pp. 530–545). New York: Science Editions. [11]

Morgan, C. L. (1996). Odors as cues for the recall of words unrelated to odor. *Perceptual and Motor Skills, 83*, 1227–1234. [6]

Morgan, R., & Flora, D. (2002). Group psychotherapy with incarcerated offenders: A research synthesis. *Group Dynamics: Theory, Research, and Practice, 6*, 203–218. [13]

Morgan, R. E., Levitsky, D. A., & Strupp, B. J. (2000). Effects of chronic lead exposure on learning and reaction time in a visual discrimination task. *Neurotoxicology and Teratology, 22*, 337–345. [7]

Morin, C. M., & Wooten, V. (1996). Psychological and pharmacological approaches to treating insomnia: Critical issues in assessing their separate and combined effects. *Clinical Psychology Review, 16*, 521–542. [4]

Morofushi, M., Shinohara, K., & Kimura, F. (2001). Menstrual and circadian variations in time perceptions in healthy women and women with premenstrual syndrome. *Neuroscience Research, 41*, 339–344. [4]

Morris, J. S., Frith, C. D., Perrett, D. I., Rowland, D., Young, A. W., Calder, A. J., & Dolan, R. J. (1996). A differential neural response in the human amygdala to fearful and happy facial expressions. *Nature, 383*, 812–815. [2]

Mościcki, E. K. (1995). Epidemiology of suicidal behavior. *Suicide and Life-Threatening Behavior, 25*, 22–31. [12]

Most, S., Simons, D., Scholl, B., Jimenez, R., Clifford, E., & Chabris, C. (2001). How not to be seen: The contribution of similarity and selective ignoring to sustained inattentional blindness. *Psychological Science, 12*, 9–17. [3]

Moulin, D., Clark, A., Speechley, M., & Morley-Forster, P. (2002). Chronic pain in Canada: Prevalence, treatment, impact and the role of opioid analgesia. *Pain Research & Management, 7*, 179–184. [3]

Mourtazaev, M. S., Kemp, B., Zwinderman, A. H., & Kamphuisen, H. A. C. (1995). Age and gender affect different characteristics of slow waves in the sleep EEG. *Sleep, 18*, 557–564. [4]

Moynihan, J., Larson, M., Treanor, J., Duberstein, P., Power, A., Shre, B., & Ader, R. (2004). Psychosocial factors and the response to influenza vaccination in older adults. *Psychosomatic Medicine, 66*, 950–953. [10]

Mufson, L., Gallagher, T., Dorta, K., & Young, J. (2004). A group adaptation of interpersonal psychotherapy for depressed adolescents. *American Journal of Psychotherapy, 58*, 220–237. [13]

Mukherjee, R., & Turk, J. (2004). Fetal alcohol syndrome. *Lancet, 363*, 1556. [8]

Muller, L. (2002). Group counseling for African American males: When all you have are European American counselors. *Journal for Specialists in Group Work, 27*, 299–313. [13]

Mumtaz, S., & Humphreys, G. (2002). The effect of Urdu vocabulary size on the acquisition of single word reading in English. *Educational Psychology, 22*, 165–190. [8]

Munarriz, R., Talakoub, L., Flaherty, E., Gioia, M., Hoag, L., Kim, N., Traish, A., Goldstein, I., Guay, A., & Spark, R. (2002). Androgen replacement therapy with dehydroepiandrosterone for androgen insufficiency and female sexual dysfunction: Androgen and questionnaire results. *Journal of Sex & Marital Therapy, 28*, 165–173. [12]

Munroe, R. H., Shimmin, H. S., & Munroe, R. L. (1984). Gender role understanding and sex role preference in four cultures. *Developmental Psychology, 20*, 673–682. [8]

Munzar, P., Li, H., Nicholson, K., Wiley, J., & Balster, R. (2002). Enhancement of the discriminative stimulus effects of phencyclidine by the tetracycline antibiotics doxycycline and minocycline in rats. *Psychopharmacology, 160*, 331–336. [4]

Murphy, S., Tapper, V., Johnson, L., & Lohan, J. (2003). Suicide ideation among parents bereaved by the violent deaths of their children. *Issues in Mental Health Nursing, 24*, 5–25. [12]

Murray, B. (2002). Finding the peace within us. *APA Monitor on Psychology, 33*, 56–57. [4]

Murray, H. (1938). *Explorations in personality*. New York: Oxford University Press. [9, 11]

Murray, H. A. (1965). Uses of the Thematic Apperception Test. In B. I. Murstein (Ed.), *Handbook of projective techniques* (pp. 425–432). New York: Basic Books. [11]

Murray, K., & Abeles, N. (2002). Nicotine's effect on neural and cognitive functioning in an aging population. *Aging & Mental Health, 6*, 129–138. [8]

Mustanski, B., Chivers, M., & Bailey, J. (2002). A critical review of recent biological research on human sexual orientation. *Annual Review of Sex Research, 13*, 89–140. [9]

Myers, D. G., & Bishop, G. D. (1970). Discussion effects on racial attitudes. *Science, 169*, 778–779. [14]

Myers, D. G., & Lamm, H. (1975). The polarizing effect of group discussion. *American Scientist, 63*, 297–303. [14]

Nader, K. 2003. Re-recording human memories. *Nature, 425*, 571–572. [4]

Nader, K., Schafe, G. E., & Le Doux, J. E. (2000). Fear memories require protein synthesis in the amygdala for reconsolidation after retrieval. *Nature, 406*, 722–726. [6]

Nadon, R., Hoyt, I. P., Register, P. A., & Kilstrom, J. F. (1991). Absorption and hypnotizability: Context effects reexamined. *Journal of Personality and Social Psychology, 60*, 144–153. [4]

Nancy M. Petry: Award for distinguished scientific early career contributions to psychology. (2003). *American Psychologist, 58,* 878–881. [13]

Narvaez, D. (2002). Does reading moral stories build character? *Educational Psychology Review, 14,* 155–171. [8]

Narvaez, D., Gleason, T., Mitchell, C., & Bentley, J. (1999). Moral theme comprehension in children. *Journal of Educational Psychology, 91,* 477–487. [8]

Nash, J. M. (1997, March 24). Gift of love. *Time,* pp. 80–82. [8]

Nash, M. (1987). What, if anything, is regressed about hypnotic age regression? A review of the empirical literature. *Psychological Bulletin, 102,* 42–52. [4]

Nash, M., & Baker, E. (1984, February). Trance encounters: Susceptibility to hypnosis. *Psychology Today, 18,* 72–73. [4]

Nash, M. R. (1991). Hypnosis as a special case of psychological regression. In S. J. Lynn & J. W. Rhue (Eds.), *Theories of hypnosis: Current models and perspectives* (pp. 171–194). New York: Guilford. [4]

National Cancer Institute. (2000). *Questions and answers about smoking cessation.* Retrieved January 29, 2003, from http://cis.nci.nih.gov/fact/ 8_13.htm [10]

National Center for Health Statistics. (2000). *Health, United States, 2000 with adolescent health chartbook.* Retrieved from http://www.cdc.gov/nchs/products/pubs/pubd/hus/hestatus .htm [10]

National Center for Health Statistics. (2001). Death rates for 358 selected causes, by 10-year age groups, race, and sex: United States, 1999–2000. *National Vital Statistics Report, 49,* (8). [Electronic version]. Retrieved November 10, 2002, from http://www.cdc.gov/nchs/data/dvs/VS00100.WTABLE 12.pdf [12]

National Center for Health Statistics. (2002). Deaths, percent of total deaths, and death rates for the 15 leading causes of death in 5-year age groups, by race and sex: United States, 1999–2000. *National Vital Statistics Report, 50,* (16). [Electronic version]. Retrieved November 10, 2002, from http://www.cdc.gov/nchs/data/dvs/LCWK1_2000.pdf [12]

National Center for Health Statistics (NCHS). (2004). *Health in the U.S. 2004.* Retrieved February 1, 2005, from http://www.cdc.gov/nchs/hus.htm [10]

National Center for Health Statistics (NCHS). (2004). Prevalence of overweight and obesity among adults: United States, 1999–2002. Retrieved February 1, 2005, from http://www.cdc.gov/nchs/products/pubs/pubd/hestats/obese/ obse99.htm [9]

National Institute of Mental Health. (1999a). Does this sound like you? Retrieved from http://www.nimh.nih.gov/soundlikeyou .htm [12]

National Institute of Mental Health. (1999b). The invisible disease—depression Retrieved from http://www.nimh.nih.gov/ publicat/ invisible.cfm [12]

National Institute of Mental Health (NIMH). (2001). *The numbers count: Mental disorders in America* (NIMH Report No. 01–4584). Washington, DC: Author. [12]

National Institute of Neurological Disorders and Stroke rt-PA Stroke Study Group. (1995). Tissue plasminogen activator for acute ischemic stroke. *New England Journal of Medicine, 333,* 1581–1587. [2]

National Institute on Aging. (2001). Progress report on Alzheimer's Disease: Taking the next steps. Silver Spring, MD: Alzheimer's Disease Education and Referral Center (ADEAR) of the National Institute on Aging. [8]

National Institute on Drug Abuse (NIDA). (2001). Ecstasy: What we know and don't know about MDMA: A scientific review [Online report]. Retrieved October 17, 2003, from http:// www.nida.nih.gov/Meetings/MDMA/MDMAExSummary .html [4]

National Science Foundation (NSF). (2000). Women, minorities, and persons with disabilities in science and engineering: Annual report to the U.S. Congress. Washington, DC: Author. [1]

National Science Foundation (NSF). (2002). *Science and engineering: Indicators 2002.* Retrieved January 29, 2003, from http://www.nsf.gov/sbc/srs/seind02/toc.htm [10]

Nawrot, M., Nordenstrom, B., & Olson, A. (2004). Disruption of eye movements by ethanol intoxication affects perception of depth from motion parallax. *Psychological Science, 15,* 858–865. [4]

Needleman, H. L., Riess, J. A., Tobin, M. J., Biesecker, G. E., & Greenhouse, J. B. (1996). Bone lead levels and delinquent behavior. *Journal of the American Medical Association, 275,* 363–369. [14]

Neimark, E. D. (1981). Confounding with cognitive style factors: An artifact explanation for the apparent nonuniversal incidence of formal operations. In I. Sigel, D. Brodzinsky, & R. Golinkoff (Eds.), *New directions in Piagetian research and theory.* Hillsdale, NJ: Erlbaum. [8]

Neimark, J., Conway, C., & Doskoch, P. (1994, September/October). Back from the drink. *Psychology Today,* 46–53. [10]

Neisser, U., Boodoo, G., Bouchard, T. J., Jr., Boykin, A. W., Brody, N., Ceci, S. J., Halpern, D. F., Loehlin, J. C., Perloff, R., Sternberg, R. J., & Urbina, S. (1996). Intelligence: Knowns and unknowns. *American Psychologist, 51,* 77–101. [7]

Neisser, U., & Harsch, N. (1992). Phantom flashbulbs: False recollections of hearing the news about Challenger. In E. Winograd & U. Neisser (Eds.), *Affect and accuracy in recall: Studies of "flashbulb" memories* (pp. 9–31). New York: Cambridge University Press. [6]

Neitz, J., Neitz, M., & Kainz, M. (1996). Visual pigment gene structure and the severity of color vision defects. *Science, 274,* 801–804. [2]

Neitz, M., & Neitz, J. (1995). Numbers and ratios of visual pigment genes for normal red-green color vision. *Science, 267,* 1013–1016. [3]

Nelson, J. C. (1997). Safety and tolerability of the new antidepressants. *Journal of Clinical Psychiatry, 58*(6, Suppl.), 26–31. [13]

Nestadt, G., Samuels, J., Riddle, M., Bienvenu, J., Liang, K., LaBuda, M., Walkup, J., Grados, M., & Hoehn-Saric, R. (2000). A family study of obsessive-compulsive disorder. *Archives of General Psychiatry, 57,* 358–363. [12]

Nestor, P., Graham, K., Bozeat, S., Simons, J., & Hodges, J. (2002). Memory consolidation and the hippocampus: Further evidence from studies of autobiographical memory in semantic dementia and frontal variant frontotemporal dementia. *Neuropsychologia, 40,* 633–654. [6]

Nestor, P., Kubicki, M., Gurrera, R., Niznikiewica, M., Frumin, M., McCarley, R., & Shenton, M. (2004). Neuropsychological correlates of diffusion tensor imaging in schizophrenia. *Neuropsychology, 18,* 629–637. [2]

Newberg, A., Alavi, A. Baime, M., Pourdehnad, M., Santanna, J. d'Aquili, E. (2001). The measurement of cerebral blood flow during the complex cognitive task of meditation: A preliminary SPECT study. *Psychiatry Research: Neuroimaging, 106,* 113–122. [4]

Newberry, H., Duncan, S., McGuire, M., & Hillers, V. (2001). Use of nonvitamin, nonmineral dietary supplements among college students. *Journal of American College Health, 50,* 123–129. [4]

Newell, B. (2005). Re-visions of rationality? *Trends in the Cognitive Sciences, 9,* 11–15. [7]

Newell, B., & Shanks, D. (2003). Take the best or look at the rest? Factors influencing "one-reason" decision making. *Journal of Experimental Psychology: Learning, Memory, and Cognition, 29,* 53–65. [7]

Newell, B., & Shanks, D. (2004). On the role of recognition in decision making. *Journal of Experimental Psychology: Learning, Memory and Cognition, 30*, 923–935. [7]

Newell, P., & Cartwright, R. (2000). Affect and cognition in dreams: A critique of the cognitive role in adaptive dream functioning and support for associative models. *Psychiatry: Interpersonal & Biological Processes, 63*, 34–44. [4]

Ng K., Tsui, S., & Chan, W. (2002). Prevalence of common chronic pain in Hong Kong adults. *Clinical Journal of Pain, 18*, 275–281. [3]

Ng, S. H. (1990). Androcentric coding of *man* and *his* in memory by language users. *Journal of Experimental Social Psychology, 26*, 455–464. [7]

Nguyen, P. V., Abel, T., & Kandel, E. R. (1994). Requirement of a critical period of transcription for induction of a late phase of LTP. *Science, 265*, 1104–1107. [6]

Nickerson, R. S., & Adams, M. J. (1979). Long-term memory for a common object. *Cognitive Psychology, 11*, 287–307. [6]

Nicol, S. E., & Gottesman, I. I. (1983). Clues to the genetics and neurobiology of schizophrenia. *American Scientist, 71*, 398–404. [12]

Nisbett, R. E., & Wilson, T. D. (1977). The halo effect: Evidence for unconscious alteration of judgments. *Journal of Personality and Social Psychology, 35*, 250–256. [14]

Nogrady, H., McConkey, K. M., & Perry, C. (1985). Enhancing visual memory: Trying hypnosis, trying imagination, and trying again. *Journal of Abnormal Psychology, 94*, 195–204. [4]

Noise Pollution Council. (2003). Comparing standards for safe noise exposure. Retrieved May 16, 2003, from http://www.nonoise.org/hearing/exposure/standardschart.htm [3]

Nordentoft, M., Lou, H. C., Hansen, D., Nim, J., Pryds, O., Rubin, P., & Hemmingsen, R. (1996). Intrauterine growth retardation and premature delivery: The influence of maternal smoking and psychosocial factors. *American Journal of Public Health, 86*, 347–354. [8]

Norris, J. E., & Tindale, J. A. (1994). *Among generations: The cycle of adult relationships.* New York: Freeman. [8]

Norton, M., Moniu, B., Cooper, J., & Hogg, M. (2003). Vicarious dissonance: Attitude change from the inconsistency of others. *Journal of Personality & Social Psychology, 85*, 47–62. [14]

Novello, A. C. (1990). The Surgeon General's 1990 report on the health benefits of smoking cessation: Executive summary. *Morbidity and Mortality Weekly Report, 39* (No. RR–12). [10]

Nowak, M. A., & McMichael, A. J. (1995). How HIV defeats the immune system. *Scientific American, 273*, 58–65. [10]

Noyes, R., Jr., Burrows, G. D., Reich, J. H., Judd, F. K., Garvey, M. J., Norman, T. R., Cook, B. L., & Marriott, P. (1996). Diazepam versus alprazolam for the treatment of panic disorder. *Journal of Clinical Psychiatry, 57*, 344–355. [13]

Nunn, J., Gregory, L., Brammer, M., Williams, S., Parslow, D., Morgan, M., Morris, R., Bullmore, E., Baron-Cohen, S., & Gray, J. (2002). Functional magnetic resonance imaging of synesthesia: Activation of V4/V8 by spoken words. *Nature Neuroscience, 5*, 371–375. [3]

Nutt, D. (2000). Treatment of depression and concomitant anxiety. *European Neuropsychopharmacology, 10* (Suppl. 4), S433–S437. [13]

O'Brien, C. P. (1996). Recent developments in the pharmacotherapy of substance abuse. *Journal of Consulting and Clinical Psychology, 64*, 677–686. [1, 4]

O'Connor, E. (2001). An "American psychologist." APA Monitor on Psychology [Online] Retrieved November 26, 2004, from http://www.apa.org/monitor/nov01/american.html [1]

Ogawa, A., Mizuta, I., Fukunaga, T., Takeuchi, N., Honaga, E., Sugita, Y., Mikami, A., Inoue, Y., & Takeda, M. (2004). Electrogastrography abnormality in eating disorders. *Psychiatry & Clinical Neurosciences, 58*, 300–310. [9]

Ohman, A., & Mineka, S. (2003). The malicious serpent: Snakes as a prototypical stimulus for an evolved module of fear. *Current Directions in Psychological Science, 12*, 5–8. [5]

O'Leary, K. D., & Smith, D. A. (1991). Marital interactions. *Annual Review of Psychology, 42*, 191–212. [14]

Oliver, J. E. (1993). Intergenerational transmission of child abuse: Rates, research, and clinical implications. *American Journal of Psychiatry, 150*, 1315–1324. [14]

Ono, H. (2003). Women's economic standing, marriage timing and cross-national contexts of gender. *Journal of Marriage & Family, 65*, 275–286. [9]

Oquendo, M., Placidi, G., Malone, K., Campbell, C., Kelp, J., Brodsky, B., Cagoules, L., Cooper, T., Parsey, R., Van Heertum, R., & Mann, J. (2003). Positron emission tomography of regional brain metabolic responses to a serotonergic challenge and lethality of suicide attempts in major depression. *Archives of General Psychiatry, 60*, 14–22. [12]

Orman, M. (1996). How to conquer public speaking fear. Retrieved February 15, 2003, from http://www.stresscure.com/jobstress/speak.html [12]

Osborn, D., Fletcher, A., Smeeth, L., Sitrling, S., Bulpitt, C., Breeze, E., Ng, E., Nunes, M., Jones, D., & Tulloch, A. (2003). Factors associated with depression in a representative sample of 14,217 people aged 75 and over in the United Kingdom: Results from the MRC trial of assessment and management of older people in the community. *International Journal of Geriatric Psychiatry, 18*, 623–630. [8]

Öst, L-G., & Westling, B. E. (1995). Applied relaxation vs. cognitive behavior therapy in the treatment of panic disorder. *Behavior Research and Therapy, 33*, 145–158. [13]

Ostrom, T. M., Carpenter, S. L., Sedikides, C., & Li, F. (1993). Differential processing of in-group and out-group information. *Journal of Personality and Social Psychology, 64*, 21–34. [14]

Otto, M. W., Pollack, M. H., Sachs, G. S., Reiter, S. R., Meltzer-Brody, S., & Rosenbaum, J. F. (1993). Discontinuation of benzodiazepine treatment: Efficacy of cognitive-behavioral therapy for patients with panic disorder. *American Journal of Psychiatry, 150*, 1485–1490. [13]

Overmeier, J. B., & Seligman, M. E. P. (1967). Effects of inescapable shock upon subsequent escape and avoidance responding. *Journal of Comparative and Physiological Psychology, 67*, 28–33. [5]

Owen, M., & O'Donovan, M. (2003). Schizophrenia and genetics. In R. Plomin, J. Defries, I. Craig, & P. McGuffin (Eds.), *Behavioral genetics in the postgenomic era* (pp. 463–480). Washington, DC: American Psychological Association. [12]

Padian, N. S. et al. (1991). Female-to-male transmission of human immunodeficiency virus. *Journal of the American Medical Association, 266*, 1664–1667. [10]

Paivio, S. C., & Greenberg, L. S. (1995). Resolving "unfinished business": Efficacy of experiential therapy using empty-chair dialogue. *Journal of Consulting and Clinical Psychology, 63*, 419–425. [13]

Palinscar, A. S., & Brown, A. L. (1984). Reciprocal teaching of comprehension-fostering and comprehension-monitoring activities. *Cognition and Instruction, 1*, 117–175. [14]

Palmérus, K., & Scarr, S. (1995, April). *How parents discipline young children: Cultural comparisons and individual differences.* Paper presented at the annual meeting of the Society for Research in Child Development, Indianapolis, IN. [5]

Pansu, P., & Gilibert, D. (2002). Effect of causal explanations on work-related judgments. *Applied Psychology: An International Review, 51*, 505–526. [14]

Papousek, I., & Schulter, G. (2002). Covariations of EEG asymmetries and emotional states indicate that activity at frontopolar locations is particularly affected by state factors. *Psychophysiology, 39*, 350–360. [9]

Paquette, D. (2004). Dichotomizing paternal and maternal functions as a means to better understand their primary contributions. *Human Development, 47,* 237–238. [8]

Paraherakis, A., Charney, D., & Gill, K. (2001). Neuropsychological functioning in substance-dependent patients. *Substance Use & Misuse, 36,* 257–271. [4]

Parke, R. D. (1977). Some effects of punishment on children's behavior–revisited. In E. M. Hetherington, E. M. Ross, & R. D. Parke (Eds.), *Contemporary readings in child psychology.* New York: McGraw-Hill. [5]

Partinen, M., Hublin, C., Kaprio, J., Koskenvuo, M., & Guilleminault, C. (1994). Twin studies in narcolepsy. *Sleep, 17,* S13–S16. [4]

Pascual-Leone, A., Dhuna, A., Altafullah, I., & Anderson, D. C. (1990). Cocaine-induced seizures. *Neurology, 40,* 404–407. [4]

Pastore, N. (1950). The role of arbitrariness in the frustration-aggression hypothesis. *Journal of Abnormal and Social Psychology, 47,* 728–731. [14]

Patterson, C. J. (1995). Sexual orientation and human development: An overview. *Developmental Psychology, 31,* 3–11. [9]

Patterson, D. (2004). Treating pain with hypnosis. *Current Directions in Psychological Science, 13,* 252–255. [4]

Paul, T., Schroeter, K., Dahme, B., & Nutzinger, D. (2002). Self-injurious behavior in women with eating disorders. *American Journal of Psychiatry, 159,* 408–411. [9]

Paul, W. E. (1993). Infectious diseases and the immune system. *Scientific American, 269,* 90–99. [10]

Paulhus, D., Harms, P., Bruce, M., & Lysy, D. (2003). The overclaiming technique: Measuring self-enhancement independent of ability. *Journal of Personality & Social Psychology, 84,* 890–904. [11]

Paulus, P. B., Cox, V. C., & McCain, G. (1988). *Prison crowding: A psychological perspective.* New York: Springer-Verlag. [14]

Paunonen, S. V., Keinonen, M., Trzebinski, J., Forsterling, F., Grishenko-Roze, N., Kouznetsova, L., & Chan, D. W. (1996). The structure of personality in six cultures. *Journal of Cross-Cultural Psychology, 27,* 339–353. [11]

Pavlov, I. P. (1927/1960). *Conditioned reflexes: An investigation of the physiological activity of the cerebral cortex* (G. V. Anrep, Trans.). New York: Dover. (Original translation published 1927). [5]

Payami, H., Montee, K., & Kaye, J. (1994). Evidence for familial factors that protect against dementia and outweigh the effect of increasing age. *American Journal of Human Genetics, 54,* 650–657. [8]

Pedersen, D. M., & Wheeler, J. (1983). The Müller-Lyer illusion among Navajos. *Journal of Social Psychology, 121,* 3–6. [3]

Penfield, W. (1969). Consciousness, memory, and man's conditioned reflexes. In K. Pribram (Ed.), *On the biology of learning* (pp. 129–168). New York: Harcourt Brace Jovanovich. [6]

Pennebaker, J., & Seagal, J. (1999). Forming a story: The health benefits of narrative. *Journal of Clinical Psychology, 55,* 1243–1254. [10]

Pennisi, E. (1997). Tracing molecules that make the brain-body connection. *Science, 275,* 930–931. [10]

Pepperberg, I. M. (1991, Spring). Referential communication with an African grey parrot. *Harvard Graduate Society Newsletter,* 1–4. [7]

Pepperberg, I. M. (1994a). Numerical competence in an African grey parrot (*Psittacus erithacus*). *Journal of Comparative Psychology, 108,* 36–44. [7]

Pepperberg, I. M. (1994b). Vocal learning in grey parrots (*Psittacus erithacus*): Effects of social interaction, reference, and context. *The Auk, 111,* 300–314. [7]

Perls, F. S. (1969). *Gestalt therapy verbatim.* Lafayette, CA: Real People Press. [13]

Perrett, D. I., May, K. A., & Yoshikawa, S. (1994). Facial shape and judgements of female attractiveness. *Nature, 368,* 239–242. [14]

Perry, R. & Zeki, S. (2000). The neurology of saccades and covert shifts in spatial attention: An event-related fMRI study. *Brain, 123,* 2273–2288. [3]

Pesonen, A., Raeikkoenen, K., Keskivaara, P., & Keltikangas-Jaervinen, L. (2003). Difficult temperament in childhood and adulthood: Continuity from maternal perceptions to self-ratings over 17 years. *Personality & Individual Differences, 34,* 19–31. [11]

Peters, A., Leahu, D., Moss, M. B., & McNally, J. (1994). The effects of aging on area 46 of the frontal cortex of the rhesus monkey. *Cerebral Cortex, 6,* 621–635. [8]

Peterson, A. C. (1987, September). Those gangly years. *Psychology Today,* 28–34. [8]

Peterson, L. R., & Peterson, M. J. (1959). Short-term retention of individual verbal items. *Journal of Experimental Psychology, 58,* 193–198. [6]

Petri, H. L. (1996). *Motivation: Theory, research, and applications* (4th ed.). Pacific Grove, CA: Brooks/Cole. [9]

Petry, N. (2002). Psychosocial treatments for pathological gambling: Current status and future directions. *Psychiatric Annals, 32,* 192–196. [13]

Petry, N., Tedford, J., Austin, M., Nich, C., Carroll, K., & Rounsaville, B. (2004). Prize reinforcement contingency management for treating cocaine users: How low can we go, and with whom? *Addiction, 99,* 349–360. [13]

Petty, R. E., Wegener, D. T., & Fabrigar, L. R. (1997). Attitudes and attitude change. *Annual Review of Psychology, 48,* 609–647. [14]

Phillips, G. P., & Over, R. (1995). Differences between heterosexual, bisexual, and lesbian women in recalled childhood experiences. *Archives of Sexual Behavior, 24,* 1–20. [9]

Phillips, K., Fulker, D. W., Carey, G., & Nagoshi, C. T. (1988). Direct marital assortment for cognitive and personality variables. *Behavioral Genetics, 18,* 347–356. [14]

Phillips, S. T., & Ziller, R. C. (1997). Toward a theory and measure of the nature of nonprejudice. *Journal of Personality and Social Psychology, 72,* 420–434. [14]

Piaget, J. (1927/1965). *The moral judgment of the child.* New York: Free Press. [8]

Piaget, J. (1963). *Psychology of intelligence.* Patterson, NJ: Littlefield, Adams. [8]

Piaget, J. (1964). *Judgment and reasoning in the child.* Patterson, NJ: Littlefield, Adams. [8]

Piaget, J., & Inhelder, B. (1969). *The psychology of the child.* New York: Basic Books. [8]

Pigott, T. A. (1996). OCD: Where the serotonin selectivity story begins. *Journal of Clinical Psychiatry, 57*(6, Suppl.), 11–20. [12]

Pihl, R. O., Lau, M. L., & Assaad, J-M. (1997). Aggressive disposition, alcohol, and aggression. *Aggressive Behavior, 23,* 11–18. [4]

Pilcher, J. J., Lambert, B. J., & Huffcutt, A. I. (2000). Differential effects of permanent and rotating shifts on self-report sleep length: A meta-analytic review. *Sleep, 23,* 155–163. [4]

Pillemer, D. B. (1990). Clarifying the flashbulb memory concept: Comment on McCloskey, Wible, and Cohen (1988). *Journal of Experimental Psychology: General, 119,* 92–96. [6]

Pillow, D. R., Zautra, A. J., & Sandler, I. (1996). Major life events and minor stressors: Identifying mediational links in the stress process. *Journal of Personality and Social Psychology, 70,* 381–394. [10]

Pillsworth, E., Haselton, M., & Buss, D. (2004). Ovulatory shifts in female sexual desire. *Journal of Sex Research, 41,* 55–65. [9]

Pinel, J. P. L. (2000). *Biopsychology* (4th ed.). Boston: Allyn & Bacon. [2]

Pinikahana, J., Happell, B., & Keks, N. (2003). Suicide and schizophrenia: A review of literature for the decade (1990–1999) and implications for mental health nursing. *Issues in Mental Health Nursing, 24,* 27–43. [12]

Pinker, S. (1994). *The language instinct: How the mind creates language.* New York: Morrow. [7]

Pittenger, D. J. (1993). The utility of the Myers-Briggs Type Indicator. *Review of Educational Research, 63,* 467–488. [11]

Plaks, J., Grant, H., & Dweck, C. (2005, in press). Violations of implicit theories and the sense of prediction and control: Implications for motivated person perception. *Journal of Personality & Social Psychology, 88.* [14]

Plomin, R., DeFries, J. C., & Fulker, D. W. (1988). *Nature and nurture during infancy and early childhood.* New York: Cambridge University Press. [2]

Plomin, R., DeFries, J. C., McClearn, G. E., & Rutter, M. (1997). *Behavioral genetics* (3rd ed.). New York: Freeman. [2]

Plomin, R., Owen, M. J., & McGuffin, P. (1994). The genetic basis of complex human behaviors. *Science, 264,* 1733–1739. [7]

Plous, S. (1996). Attitudes toward the use of animals in psychological research and education: Results from a national survey of psychologists. *American Psychologist, 51,* 1167–1180. [1]

Plummer, D. L., & Slane S. (1996). Patterns of coping in racially stressful situations. *Journal of Black Psychology, 22,* 302–315. [10]

Poldrack, R., & Wagner, A. (2004). What can neuroimaging tell us about the mind? Insights from prefrontal cortex. *Current Directions in Psychological Science, 13,* 177–181. [2]

Poponoe, D., & Whitehead, B. D. (2000). Sex without strings, relationships without rings: Today's young singles talk about mating and dating. In National Marriage Project, "The State of Our Unions, 2000." Retrieved from http://marriage.rutgers.edu/2000.htm [8]

Porjesz, B., Begleiter, H., Reich, T., Van Eerdewegh, P., Edenberg, H., Foroud, T., Goate, A., Litke, A., Chorlian, D., Stimus, A., Rice, J., Blangero, J., Almasy, L., Sorbell, J., Bauer, L., Kuperman, S., O'Connor, S., & Rohrbaugh, J. (1998). Amplitude of visual P3 event-related potential as a phenotypic marker for a predisposition to alcoholism: Preliminary results from the COGA project. *Alcoholism: Clinical & Experimental Research, 22,* 1317–1323. [10]

Porrino, L. J., & Lyons, D. (2000). Orbital and medial prefrontal cortex and psychostimulant abuse: Studies in animal models. *Cerebral Cortex, 10,* 326–333. [5]

Porte, H. S., & Hobson, J. A. (1996). Physical motion in dreams: One measure of three theories. *Sleep, 105,* 3329–3335. [4]

Porter, F. L., Porges, S. W., & Marshall, R. E. (1988). Newborn pain cries and vagal tone: Parallel changes in response to circumcision. *Child Development, 59,* 495–505. [8]

Posada, G., Jacobs, A., Richmond, M., Carbonell, O., Alzate, G., Bustamante, M., & Quiceno, J. (2002). Maternal caregiving and infant security in two cultures. *Developmental Psychology, 38,* 67–78. [8]

Posner, M. I. (1996, September). Attention and psychopathology. *Harvard Mental Health Letter, 13*(3), 5–6. [2]

Postman, L., & Phillips, L. W. (1965). Short-term temporal changes in free recall. *Quarterly Journal of Experimental Psychology, 17,* 132–138. [6]

Potts, N. L. S., Davidson, J. R. T., & Krishman, K. R. R. (1993). The role of nuclear magnetic resonance imaging in psychiatric research. *Journal of Clinical Psychiatry, 54*(12, Suppl.), 13–18. [2]

Powell, C., & Van Vugt, M. (2003). Genuine giving or selfish sacrifice? The role of commitment and cost level upon willingness to sacrifice. *European Journal of Social Psychology, 33,* 403–412. [14]

Powell, L., Shahabi, L., & Thoresen, C. (2003). Religion and spirituality: Linkages to physical health. *American Psychologist, 58,* 36–52. [10]

Power, F. C., Higgins, A., & Kohlberg, L. (1989). *Lawrence Kohlberg's approach to moral education.* New York: Columbia University Press. [8]

Power, K. G., Sharp, D. M., Swanson, V., & Simpson, R. J. (2000). Therapist contact in cognitive behaviour therapy for panic disorder and agoraphobia in primary care. *Clinical Psychology & Psychotherapy, 7,* 37–46. [13]

Powlishta, K. K. (1995). Intergroup processes in childhood: Social categorization and sex role development. *Developmental Psychology, 31,* 781–788. [8]

Prabhu, V., Porjesz, B., Chorlian, D., Wang, K., Stimus, A., & Begleiter, H. (2001). Visual P3 in female alcoholics. *Alcoholism: Clinical & Experimental Research, 25,* 531–539. [10]

Pratkanis, A. R. (1989). The cognitive representation of attitudes. In A. R. Pratkanis, S. J. Breckler, & A. G. Greenwald (Eds.), *Attitude structure and function* (pp. 71–93). Hillsdale, NJ: Erlbaum. [14]

Premack, D. (1971). Language in chimpanzees. *Science, 172,* 808–822. [7]

Premack, D., & Premack, A. J. (1983). *The mind of an ape.* New York: Norton. [7]

Price, R., Choi, J., & Vinokur, A. (2002). Links in the chain of adversity following job loss: How financial strain and loss of personal control lead to depression, impaired functioning, and poor health. *Journal of Occupational Health Psychology, 7,* 302–312. [10]

Prien, R. F., & Kocsis, J. H. (1995). Long-term treatment of mood disorders. In F. E. Bloom & D. J. Kupfer (Eds.), *Psychopharmacology: The fourth generation of progress* (pp. 1067–1079). New York: Raven. [13]

Prigerson, H. G., Bierhals, A. J., Kasl, S. V., Reynolds, C. F., III, Shear, M. K., Day, N., Beery, L. C., Newsom, J. T., & Jacobs, S. (1997). Traumatic grief as a risk factor for mental and physical mortality. *American Journal of Psychiatry, 154,* 616–623. [10]

Prince, A. (1998). Infectious diseases. In B. Kliegman (Ed.), *Nelson essentials of pediatrics* (pp. 315–418). Philadelphia: W.B. Saunders. [10]

Prinz, P. N., Vitiello, M. V., Raskind, M. A., & Thorpy, M. J. (1990). Geriatrics: Sleep disorders and aging. *New England Journal of Medicine, 323,* 520–526. [4]

Pryke, S., Lindsay, R. C. L., & Pozzulo, J. D. (2000). Sorting mug shots: Methodological issues. *Applied Cognitive Psychology, 14,* 81–96. [6]

Psychologists' pigeons score 90 pct. picking Picasso. (1995, May 7). *St. Louis Post-Dispatch,* p. 2A. [5]

Public Agenda Online. (2002). *The issues: Race.* Retrieved November 13, 2002 from http://www.publicagenda.com/issues/overview.dfm?issue_type=race [14]

Putnam, F. W. (1989). *Diagnosis and treatment of multiple personality disorder.* New York: Guilford Press. [12]

Putnam, F. W. (1992). Altered states: Peeling away the layers of a multiple personality. *The Sciences, 32,* 30–36. [12]

Pyevich, D., & Bogenschultz. M. (2001). Herbal diuretics and lithium toxicity. *American Journal of Psychiatry, 158,* 1329. [4]

Quaid, K., Aschen, S., Smiley, C., Nurnberger, J. (2001). Perceived genetic risks for bipolar disorder in patient population: An exploratory study. *Journal of Genetic Counseling, 10,* 41–51. [2]

Querido, J., Warner, T., & Eyberg, S. (2002). Parenting styles and child behavior in African American families of preschool children. *Journal of Clinical Child & Adolescent Psychology, 31,* 272–277. [8]

Quesnel, C., Savard, J., Simard, S., Ivers, H., & Morin, C. (2003). Efficacy of cognitive-behavioral therapy for insomnia in women treated for nonmetastatic breast cancer. *Journal of Consulting & Clinical Psychology, 71,* 189–200. [13]

Quinn, T. (2002). The global HIV/AIDS pandemic 2002: A status report. *The Hopkins HIV report* [September 2002 online edition]. Retrieved December 28, 2002, from http://hopkins-aids.edu/publications/report/sept02_5.html [10]

Quiroga, T., Lemos-Britton, Z., Mostafapour, E., Abbott, R., & Berninger, V. (2002). Phonological awareness and beginning reading in Spanish-speaking ESL first graders: Research into practice. *Journal of School Psychology, 40,* 85–111. [8]

Rachman, S. (1997). The conditioning theory of fear acquisition: A critical examination. *Behavior Research and Therapy, 15,* 375–387. [12]

Rachman, S. J., & Wilson, G. T. (1980). *The effects of psychological therapy* (2nd ed.). New York: Pergamon. [13]

Raeikkoenen, K., Matthews, K., & Salomon, K. (2003). Hostility predicts metabolic syndrome risk factors in children and adolescents. *Health Psychology, 22,* 279–286. [10]

Ragozzino, M., Detrick, S., & Kesner, R. (2002). The effects of prelimbic and infralimbic lesions on working memory for visual objects in rats. *Neurobiology of Learning & Memory, 77,* 29–43. [6]

Rahe, R. J., Meyer, M., Smith, M., Kjaer, G., & Holmes, T. H. (1964). Social stress and illness onset. *Journal of Psychosomatic Research, 8,* 35–44. [10]

Räikkönen, K., Matthews, K., Sutton-Tyrrell, K., & Kuller, L. (2004). Trait anger and the metabolic syndrome predict progression of carotid atherosclerosis in healthy middle-aged women. *Psychosomatic Medicine, 66,* 903–908. [10]

Raine, A. (1996). Autonomic nervous system factors underlying disinhibited, antisocial, and violent behavior: Biosocial perspectives and treatment implications. *Annals of the New York Academy of Sciences, 794,* 46–59. [14]

Ralph, M. R. (1989, November/December). The rhythm maker: Pinpointing the master clock in mammals. *The Sciences, 29,* 40–45. [4]

Ramey, C. (1993). A rejoinder to Spitz's critique of the Abecedarian experiment. *Intelligence, 17,* 25–30. [7]

Ramey, C., & Campbell, F. (1987). The Carolina Abecedarian project. An educational experiment concerning human malleability. In J. J. Gallagher & C. T. Ramey (Eds.), *The malleability of children,* (pp. 127–140). Baltimore: Brookes. [7]

Ramsay, D. S., & Woods, S. C. (1997). Biological consequences of drug administration: Implications for acute and chronic tolerance. *Psychological Review, 104,* 170–193. [4]

Ramsey, J., Langlois, J., Hoss, R., Rubenstein, A., & Griffin, A. (2004). Origins of a stereotype: Categorization of facial attractiveness by 6-month-old infants. *Developmental Science, 7,* 201–211. [14]

Rapee, R., & Spence, S. (2004). The etiology of social phobia: Empirical evidence and an initial model. *Clinical Psychology Review, 24,* 737–767. [12]

Rapp, S., Espeland, M., Shumaker, S., Henderson, V., Brunner, R., Manson, J., Gass, M., Stefanick, M., Lane, D., Hays, J., Johnson, K., Coker, L., Dailey, M., & Bowen, D. (2003). Effect of estrogen plus progestin on global cognitive function in postmenopausal women: The Women's Health Initiative Memory Study: A randomized controlled trial. *Journal of the American Medical Association (JAMA), 289,* 2663–2672. [6]

Rasmussen, S. A., & Eisen, J. L. (1990). Epidemiology of obsessive compulsive disorder. *Journal of Clinical Psychiatry, 51(2,* Suppl.), 10–13. [12]

Rasmussen, S. A., Eisen, J. L., & Pato, M. T. (1993). Current issues in the pharmacologic management of obsessive compulsive disorder. *Journal of Clinical Psychiatry, 54(6,* Suppl.), 4–9. [13]

Rathus, S. A., Nevid, J. S., & Fichner-Rathus, L. (2000). *Human sexuality in a world of diversity* (4th ed., pp. 216–217). Boston: Allyn & Bacon. [9]

Ratty, H., Vaenskae, J., Kasanen, K., & Kaerkkaeinen, R. (2002). Parents' explanations of their child's performance in mathematics and reading: A replication and extension of Yee and Eccles. *Sex Roles, 46,* 121–128. [7]

Raz, A., Deouell, L., & Bentin, S. (2001). Is pre-attentive processing compromised by prolonged wakefulness? Effects of total sleep deprivation on the mismatch negativity. *Psychophysiology, 38,* 787–795. [4]

Razoumnikova, O. M. (2000). Functional organization of different brain areas during convergent and divergent thinking: An EEG investigation. *Cognitive Brain Research, 10,* 11–18. [7]

Rebs, S., & Park, S. (2001). Gender differences in high-achieving students in math and science. *Journal for the Education of the Gifted, 25,* 52–73. [7]

Reichle, B., & Gefke, M. (1998). Justice of conjugal divisions of labor—you can't always get what you want. *Social Justice Research, 11,* 271–287. [8]

Reis, H. T., Wilson, I. M., Monestere, C., Bernstein, S., Clark, K., Seidl, E., Franco, M., Gioioso, E., Freeman, L., & Radoane, K. (1990). What is smiling is beautiful and good. *European Journal of Social Psychology, 20,* 259–267. [14]

Reite, M., Buysse, D., Reynolds, C., & Mendelson, W. (1995). The use of polysomnography in the evaluation of insomnia. *Sleep, 18,* 58–70. [4]

Reitman, D., Murphy, M., Hupp, S., & O'Callaghan, P. (2004). Behavior change and perceptions of change: Evaluating the effectiveness of a token economy. *Child & Family Behavior Therapy, 26,* 17–36. [5]

Reneman, L., Booij, J., Schmand, B., van den Brink, W., & Gunning, B. (2000). Memory disturbances in "Ecstasy" users are correlated with an altered brain serotonin neurotransmission. *Psychopharmacology, 148,* 322–324. [4]

Rentfrow, P., & Gosling, S. (2003). The do re mi's of everyday life: The structure and personality correlates of music preferences. *Journal of Personality & Social Psychology, 84,* 1236–1256. [11]

Rescorla, R. A. (1967). Pavlovian conditioning and its proper control procedures. *Psychological Review, 74,* 71–80. [5]

Rescorla, R. A. (1968). Probability of shock in the presence and absence of CS in fear conditioning. *Journal of Comparative and Physiological Psychology, 66,* 1–5. [5]

Rescorla, R. A. (1988). Pavlovian conditioning: It's not what you think it is. *American Psychologist, 43,* 151–160. [5]

Rescorla, R. A., & Wagner, A. R. (1972). A theory of Pavlovian conditioning: Variations in the effectiveness of reinforcement and nonreinforcement. In A. Black & W. F. Prokasy (Eds.), *Classical conditioning: II. Current research and theory.* New York: Appleton. [5]

Restak, R. (1988). *The mind.* Toronto: Bantam. [7]

Restak, R. (1993, September/October). Brain by design. *The Sciences,* pp. 27–33. [2]

Revensuo, A. (2000). The reinterpretation of dreams: An evolutionary hypothesis of the function of dreaming. *Behavioral & Brain Science, 23.* [4]

Reyna, V. (2004). How people make decisions that involve risk: A dual-processes approach. *Current Directions in Psychological Science, 13,* 60–66. [7]

Reyna, V., & Adam, M. (2003). Fuzzy-trace theory, risk communication, and product labeling in sexually transmitted diseases. *Risk Analysis, 23,* 325–342. [7]

Reyner, A., & Horne, J. A. (1995). Gender- and age-related differences in sleep determined by home-recorded sleep logs and actimetry from 400 adults. *Sleep, 18,* 127–134. [4]

Reynolds, E. (2002). Benefits and risks of folic acid to the nervous system. *Journal of Neurology, 72,* 567–571. [8]

Rhéaume, J., & Ladouceur, R. (2000). Cognitive and behavioural treatments of checking behaviours: An examination of individual cognitive change. *Clinical Psychology & Psychotherapy, 7,* 118–127. [13]

Rhodes, N., & Wood, W. (1992). Self-esteem and intelligence affect influenceability: The medicating role of message reception. *Psychological Bulletin, 111,* 156–171. [14]

Richter, W., Somorjai, R., Summers, R., Jarmasz, M., Ravi, S., Menon, J. S., et al. (2000). Motor area activity during mental rotation studied by time-resolved single-trial fMRI. *Journal of Cognitive Neuroscience, 12,* 310–320. [7]

Rickels, K., Schweizer, E., Weiss, S., & Zavodnick, S. (1993). Maintenance drug treatment for panic disorder II. Short- and long-term outcome after drug taper. *Archives of General Psychiatry, 50,* 61–68. [13]

Riedel, G. (1996). Function of metabotropic glutamate receptors in learning and memory. *Trends in Neurosciences, 19,* 219–224. [2, 6]

Rini, C., Manne, S., DuHamel, K., Austin, J., Ostroff, J., Boulad, F., Parsons, S., Martini, R., Williams, S., Mee, L., Sexson, S., & Redd, W. (2004). Mothers' perceptions of benefit following pediatric stem cell transplantation: A longitudinal investigation of the roles of optimism, medical risk, and sociodemographic resources. *Annals of Behavioral Medicine, 28,* 132–141. [10]

Riva, D., & Giorgi, C. (2000). The cerebellum contributes to higher functions during development. *Brain, 123,* 1051–1061. [2]

Rivas-Vasquez, R. (2001). St. John's Wort (Hypericum Perforatum): Practical considerations based on the evidence. *Professional Psychology: Research and Practice, 32,* 329–332. [4]

Roan, S. (2000, March 6). Cyber analysis. *L.A. Times.* [13]

Roberts, B. W., & DelVecchio, W. F. (2000). The rank-order consistency of personality traits from childhood to old age: A quantitative review of longitudinal studies. *Psychological Bulletin, 126,* 3–25. [11]

Roberts, P., & Moseley, B. (1996, May/June). Fathers' time. *Psychology Today, 29,* 48–55, 81. [8]

Robins, C. J., & Hayes, A. M. (1993). An appraisal of cognitive therapy. *Journal of Consulting and Clinical Psychology, 61,* 205–214. [13]

Robins, R. W., Gosling, S. D., & Craik, K. H. (1999). An empirical analysis of trends in psychology. *American Psychologist, 54,* 117–128. [1]

Rock, I., & Palmer, S. (1990). The legacy of Gestalt psychology. *Scientific American, 263,* 84–90. [5]

Rodin, J., & Ickovics, J. R. (1990). Women's health: Review and research agenda as we approach the 21st century. *American Psychologist, 45,* 1018–1034. [10]

Rodin, J., & Salovey, P. (1989). Health psychology. *Annual Review of Psychology, 40,* 533–579. [10]

Rodin, J., Wack, J., Ferrannini, E., & DeFronzo, R. A. (1985). Effect of insulin and glucose on feeding behavior. *Metabolism, 34,* 826–831. [9]

Roediger, H. L., III. (1980). The effectiveness of four mnemonics in ordering recall. *Journal of Experimental Psychology: Human Learning and Memory, 6,* 558–567. [6]

Roehrich, L., & Kinder, B. N. (1991). Alcohol expectancies and male sexuality: Review and implications for sex therapy. *Journal of Sex and Marital Therapy, 17,* 45–54. [4]

Roesch, S. C., & Amirkhan, J. H. (1997). Boundary condition for self-serving attributions: Another look at the sports pages. *Journal of Applied Social Psychology, 27,* 245–261. [14]

Rogers, C. R. (1951). *Client-centered therapy: Its current practice, implications, and theory.* Boston: Houghton Mifflin. [13]

Rogoff, B., & Mistry, J. (1985). Memory development in cultural context. In M. Pressley & C. Brainerd (Eds.), *The cognitive side of memory development.* New York: Springer-Verlag. [6]

Romach, M., Busto, U., Somer, G., et al. (1995). Clinical aspects of chronic use of alprazolam and lorazepam. *American Journal of Psychiatry, 152,* 1161–1167. [13]

Roorda, A., & Williams, D. R. (1999). The arrangement of the three cone classes in the living human eye. *Nature, 397,* 520–521. [3]

Rosch, E. (1978). Principles of categorization. In E. Rosch & B. Lloyd (Eds.), *Cognition and categorization.* Hillsdale, NJ: Erlbaum. [7]

Rosch, E. H. (1973). Natural categories. *Cognitive Psychology, 4,* 328–350. [7]

Rosch, E. H. (1987). Linguistic relativity. *Et Cetera, 44,* 254–279. [7]

Rose, R. J., Koskenvuo, M., Kaprio, J., Sarna, S., & Langinvainio, H. (1988). Shared genes, shared experiences, and similarity of personality: Data from 14,288 adult Finnish co-twins. *Journal of Personality and Social Psychology, 54,* 161–171. [11]

Rosekind, M. R. (1992). The epidemiology and occurrence of insomnia. *Journal of Clinical Psychiatry, 53*(6, Suppl.), 4–6. [4]

Roselli, C., Larkin, K., Schrunk, J., & Stormshak, F. (2004). Sexual partner preference, hypothalamic morphology and aromatase in rams. *Physiology & Behavior, 83,* 233–245. [9]

Rosenbluth, R., Grossman, E. S., & Kaitz, M. (2000). Performance of early-blind and sighted children on olfactory tasks. *Perception, 29,* 101–110. [3]

Rosengren, A., Tibblin, G., & Wilhelmsen, L. (1991). Self-perceived psychological stress and incidence of coronary artery disease in middle-aged men. *American Journal of Cardiology, 68,* 1171–1175. [10]

Rosenhan, D. L. (1973). On being sane in insane places. *Science, 179,* 250–258. [3]

Rosenvinge, J. H., Matinussen, M., & Ostensen, E. (2000). The comorbidity of eating disorders and personality disorders: A meta-analytic review of studies published between 1983 and 1998. *Eating and Weight Disorders: Studies on Anorexia, Bulimia, and Obesity, 5,* 52–61. [9]

Rosenzweig, M. R. (1961). Auditory localization. *Scientific American, 205,* 132–142. [3]

Ross, C. A., Norton, G. R., & Wozney, K. (1989). Multiple personality disorder: An analysis of 236 cases. *Canadian Journal of Psychiatry, 34,* 413–418. [12]

Ross, J., Baldessarini, R. J., & Tondo, L. (2000). Does lithium treatment still work? Evidence of stable responses over three decades. *Archives of General Psychiatry, 57,* 187–190. [13]

Rossow, I., & Amundsen, A. (1997). Alcohol abuse and mortality: a 40-year prospective study of Norwegian conscripts. *Social Science & Medicine, 44,* 261–267. [10]

Roth, T. (1996). Social and economic consequences of sleep disorders. *Sleep, 19,* S46–S47. [4]

Rotter, J. B. (1966). Generalized expectancies for internal versus external control of reinforcement. *Psychological Monographs, 80*(1, Whole No. 609). [11]

Rotter, J. B. (1971, June). External control and internal control. *Psychology Today,* pp. 37–42, 58–59. [11]

Rotter, J. B. (1990). Internal versus external control of reinforcement: A case history of a variable. *American Psychologist, 45,* 489–493. [11]

Rotton, J., & Cohn, E. G. (2000). Violence is a curvilinear function of temperature in Dallas: A replication. *Journal of Personality & Social Psychology, 78,* 1074–1082. [14]

Rotton, J., Frey, J., Barry, T., Milligan, M., & Fitzpatrick, M. (1979). The air pollution experience and physical aggression. *Journal of Applied Social Psychology, 9,* 397–412. [14]

Rowe, D. (2003). Assessing genotype-environment interactions and correlations in the postgenomic era. In R. Plomin, J. DeFries, I. Craig, & P. McGuffin (Eds.), *Behavioral genetics in the postgenomic era* (pp. 71–86). Washington, DC: American Psychological Association. [14]

Rowe, D. C. (1987). Resolving the person-situation debate: Invitation to an interdisciplinary dialogue. *American Psychologist, 42,* 218–227. [11]

Rowe, J., & Kahn, R. (1998). *Successful aging.* New York: Pantheon. [8]

Rozell, E., Pettijohn, C., & Parker, R. (2002). An empirical evaluation of emotional intelligence: The impact on management development. *Journal of Management Development, 21,* 272–289. [9]

Rubinstein, G. (2001). Sex-role reversal and clinical judgment of mental health. *Journal of Sex & Marital Therapy, 27,* 9–19. [13]

Ruby, N., Dark, J., Burns, D., Heller, H., & Zucker, I. (2002). The suprachiasmatic nucleus is essential for circadian body temperature rhythms in hibernating ground squirrels. *Journal of Neuroscience, 22,* 357–364. [4]

Rudman, L., Ashmore, R., & Gary, M. (2001). "Unlearning" automatic biases: The malleability of implicit prejudice and stereotypes. *Journal of Personality & Social Psychology, 81,* 856–868. [14]

Ruggero, M. A. (1992). Responses to sound of the basilar membrane of the mammalian cochlea. *Current Opinion in Neurobiology, 2,* 449–456. [3]

Rumbaugh, D. (1977). *Language learning by a chimpanzee: The Lana project.* New York: Academic Press. [7]

Rushton, J. P., Fulker, D. W., Neale, M. C., Nias, D. K. B., & Eysenck, H. J. (1986). Altruism and aggression: The heritability of individual differences. *Journal of Personality and Social Psychology, 50,* 1192–1198. [11]

Rushton, J., & Jensen, A. (2003). African-White IQ differences from Zimbabwe on the Wechsler Intelligence Scale for Children-Revised are mainly on the *g* factor. *Personality & Individual Differences, 34,* 177–183. [7]

Russell, T., Rowe, W., & Smouse, A. (1991). Subliminal self-help tapes and academic achievement: An evaluation. *Journal of Counseling and Development, 69,* 359–362. [3]

Ryan, R., Kim, Y., & Kaplan, U. (2003). Differentiating autonomy from individualism and independence: A self-determination theory perspective on internalization of cultural orientations and well-being. *Journal of Personality and Social Psychology, 84,* 97–110. [11]

Sachs, G., Grossman, F., Ghaemi, S., Okamoto, A., & Bosden, C. (2002). Combination of a mood stabilizer with risperidone or haloperidol for treatment of acute mania: A double-blind, placebo-controlled comparison of efficacy and safety. *American Journal of Psychiatry, 159,* 1146–1154. [13]

Sackeim, H. A., Luber, B., Katzman, G. P., Moeller, J. R., Prudic, J., Devanand, D. P., & Nobler, M. S. (1996). The effects of electroconvulsive therapy on quantitative electroencephalograms. *Archives of General Psychiatry, 53,* 814–824. [13]

Sackeim, H. A., Prudic, J., Devanand, D. P., Nobler, M. S., Lisanby, S. H., Peyser, S., Fitzsimons, L., Moody, B. J., & Clark, J. (2000). A prospective, randomized, double-blind comparison of bilateral and right unilateral electroconvulsive therapy at different stimulus intensities. *Archives of General Psychiatry, 57,* 425–434. [13]

Sackett, P., Hardison, C., & Cullen, M. (2004). On interpreting stereotype threat as accounting for African American–White differences on cognitive tests. *American Psychologist, 59,* 7–13. [7]

Sacks, O. (1984). *A leg to stand on.* New York: Harper & Row. [12]

Saczynski, J., Willis, S., & Schaie, K. W. (2002). Strategy use in reasoning training with older adults. *Aging, Neuropsychology, & Cognition, 9,* 48–60. [8]

Sadeh, A., Gruber, R., & Raviv, A. (2003). The effect of sleep restriction and extension on school-age children: What a difference an hour makes. *Child Development, 74,* 444–455. [4]

Salisch, M. (2001). Children's emotional development: Challenges in their relationships to parents, peers, and friends. *International Journal of Behavioural Development, 25,* 310–319. [9]

Salmon, J., Owen, N., Crawford, D., Bauman, A., & Sallis, J. (2003). Physical activity and sedentary behavior: A population-based study of barriers, enjoyment, and preference. *Health Psychology, 22,* 178–188. [10]

Salo, J., Niemelae, A., Joukamaa, M., & Koivukangas, J. (2002). Effect of brain tumour laterality on patients' perceived quality of life. *Journal of Neurology, Neurosurgery, & Psychiatry, 72,* 373–377. [2]

Salovey, P., & Pizarro, D. (2003). The value of emotional intelligence. In R. Sternberg, J. Lautrey, & T. Lubart (Eds.), *Models of intelligence: International perspective* (pp. 263–278). Washington, DC: American Psychological Association. [9]

Salthouse, T. (2004). What and when of cognitive aging. *Current Directions in Psychological Science, 13,* 140–144. [8]

Salthouse, T. A. (1996). The processing-speed theory of adult age differences in cognition. *Psychological Review, 103,* 403–428. [8]

Sample, J. (2004). The Myers-Briggs type indicator and OD: Implications for practice from research. *Organization Development Journal, 22,* 67–75. [11]

Sanbonmatsu, D. M., & Fazio, R. H. (1990). The role of attitudes in memory-based decision making. *Journal of Personality and Social Psychology, 59,* 614–622. [14]

Sanes, J. N., & Donoghue, J. P. (2000). Plasticity and primary motor cortex. *Annual Review of Neuroscience, 23,* 393–415. [2]

Sanes, J. N., Donoghue, J. P., Thangaraj, V., Edelman, R. R., & Warach, S. (1995). Shared neural substrates controlling hand movements in human motor cortex. *Science, 268,* 1775. [2]

Sanfilippo, M., Lafargue, T., Rusinek, H., Arena, L., Loneragan, C., Lautin, A., Feiner, D., Rotrosen, J., & Wolkin, A. (2000). Volumetric measure of the frontal and temporal lobe regions in schizophrenia. *Archives of General Psychiatry, 57,* 471–480. [12]

Sano, M., Ernesto, C., Thomas, R. G., Kauber, M. R., Schafer, K., Grundman, M., Woodbury, P., Growdon, J., Cotman, C. W., Pfeiffer, E., Schneider, L. S., & Thal, L. J. (1997). A controlled trial of selegiline, alpha-tocopherol, or both as treatment for Alzheimer's disease. *New England Journal of Medicine, 336,* 1216–1222. [8]

Santiago-Rivera, A., & Altarriba, J. (2002). The role of language in therapy with the Spanish-English bilingual client. *Professional Psychology: Research & Practice, 33,* 30–38. [13]

Sarrio, M., Barbera, E., Ramos, A., & Candela, C. (2002). The glass ceiling in the professional promotion of women. *Revista de Psicologia Social, 17,* 167–182. [8]

Sass, H., Soyha, M., Mann, K., & Zieglgänsberger, W. (1996). Relapse prevention by acamprosate: Results from a placebo-controlled study on alcohol dependence. *Archives of General Psychiatry, 53,* 673–680. [10]

Sastry, R., Lee, D., & Har-El, G. (1997). Palate perforation from cocaine abuse. *Otolaryngol Head Neck Surgery, 116,* 565–566. [4]

Sateia, M. J., Doghramji, K., Hauri, P. J., & Morin, C. M. (2000). Evaluation of chronic insomnia. An American Academy of Sleep Medicine review. *Sleep, 23,* 243–308. [4]

Savage, M., & Holcomb, D. (1999). Adolescent female athletes' sexual risk-taking behaviors. *Journal of Youth and Adolescence, 28,* 583–594. [8]

Savage-Rumbaugh, E. S. (1986). *Ape language.* New York: Columbia University Press. [7]

Savage-Rumbaugh, E. S. (1990). Language acquisition in a nonhuman species: Implications for the innateness debate. *Developmental Psychology, 26,* 599–620. [7]

Savage-Rumbaugh, E. S. (1993). Language learnability in man, ape, and dolphin. In H. L. Roitblat, L. M. Herman, & P. E. Nachtigall (Eds.), *Language and communication: Comparative perspectives. Comparative cognition and neuroscience* (pp. 457–484). Hillsdale, NJ: Erlbaum. [7]

Savage-Rumbaugh, E. S., Sevcik, R. A., Brakke, K. E., & Rumbaugh, D. M. (1992). Symbols: Their communicative use, communication, and combination by bonobos (*Pan paniscus*). In L. P. Lipsitt & C. Rovee-Collier (Eds.). *Advances in infancy research* (Vol. 7, pp. 221–278). Norwood, NJ: Ablex. [7]

Scarr, S., & Weinberg, R. (1976). The influence of "family background" on intellectual attainment. *American Sociological Review, 43,* 674–692. [7]

Schachter, S., & Singer, J. E. (1962). Cognitive, social, and physiological determinants of emotional state. *Psychological Review, 69,* 379–399. [9]

Schaie, K. W. (1990). Late life potential and cohort differences in mental abilities. In M. Perlmutter (Ed.), *Late life potential* (pp. 43–61). Washington, DC: Gerontological Society. [8]

Schaie, K. W. (1994). The course of adult intellectual development. *American Psychologist, 49*, 304–313. [8]

Schaie, K. W. (1995). *Intellectual development in adulthood: The Seattle Longitudinal Study.* New York: Cambridge University Press. [8]

Schaie, W., Willis, S., & Caskie, G. (2004). The Seattle longitudinal study: Relationship between personality and cognition. *Aging, Neuropsychology & Cognition, 11*, 304–324. [8]

Schellenberg, E. (2004). Music lessons enhance IQ. *Psychological Science, 15*, 511–514. [7]

Schenck, C. H., & Mahowald, M. W. (2000). Parasomnias. Managing bizarre sleep-related behavior disorders. *Postgraduate Medicine, 107*, 145–156. [4]

Scherer, K. R., & Wallbott, H. G. (1994). Evidence for universality and cultural variation of differential emotion response patterning. *Journal of Personality and Social Psychology, 66*, 310–328. [9]

Schieber, M. H., & Hibbard, L. S. (1993). How somatotopic is the motor cortex hand area? *Science, 261*, 489–492. [2]

Schiff, M., & Lewontin, R. (1986). *Education and class: The irrelevance of IQ genetic studies.* Oxford, England: Clarendon. [7]

Schlenger, W., Caddell, J., Ebert, L., Jordan, B., Rourke, K., Wilson, D., Thalji, L., Dennis, J., Fairbank, J., & Kulka, R. (2002). Psychological reactions to terrorist attacks: Findings from the National Study of Americans' Reactions to September 11. *JAMA: Journal of the American Medical Association, 288*, 581–588. [10]

Schmidt, S., Oliveira, R., Rocha, F., & Abreu-Villaca, Y. (2000). Influence of handedness and gender on the grooved pegboard task. *Brain & Cognition, 44*, 445–454. [2]

Schofield, J. W., & Francis, W. D. (1982). An observational study of peer interaction in racially mixed "accelerated" classrooms. *Journal of Educational Psychology, 74*, 722–732. [8]

Scholz, U., Dona, B., Sud, S., & Schwarzer, R. (2002). Is general self-efficacy a universal construct? Psychometric findings from 25 countries. *European Journal of Psychological Assessment, 18*, 242–251. [11]

Schou, M. (1997). Forty years of lithium treatment. *Archives of General Psychiatry, 54*, 9–13. [13]

Schuckit, M., Edenberg, H., Kalmijn, J., Flury, L., Smith, T., Reich, T., Beirut, L., Goate, A., & Foroud, T. (2001). A genome-wide search for gens that relate to a low level of response to alcohol. *Alcoholism: Clinical & Experimental Research, 25*, 323–329. [4]

Schuckit, M. A., Tipp, J. E., Bergman, M., Reich, W., Hesselbrock, V. M., & Smith, T. L. (1997). Comparison of induced and independent major depressive disorders in 2,945 alcoholics. *American Journal of Psychiatry, 154*, 948–957. [10]

Schutte, N., & Malouff, J. (2004). University student reading preferences in relation to the Big Five personality dimensions. *Reading Psychology, 25*, 273–295. [11]

Schwartz, G. E. (1982). Testing the biopsychosocial model: The ultimate challenge facing behavioral medicine? *Journal of Consulting and Clinical Psychology, 50*, 1040–1052. [10]

Schwartz, S., & Maquet, P. (2002). Sleep imaging and the neuropsychological assessment of dreams. *Trends in Cognitive Sciences, 6*, 23–30. [4]

Scott, J. (1996). Cognitive therapy of affective disorders: A review. *Journal of Affective Disorders, 37*, 1–11. [13]

Scott, S. K., Young, A. W., Calder, A. J., Hellawell, D. J., Aggleton, J. P., & Johnson, M. (1997). Impaired auditory recognition of fear and anger following bilateral amygdala lesions. *Nature, 385*, 254–257. [2]

Scully, J., Tosi, H., & Banning, K. (2000). Life event checklists: Revisiting the Social Readjustment Rating Scale after 30 years. *Educational & Psychological Measurement, 60*, 864–876. [10]

Sedikides, C., Gaertner, L., & Toguchi, Y. (2003). Pancultural self-enhancement. *Journal of Personality & Social Psychology, 84*, 60–79. [11]

Seegert, C. (2004). Token economies and incentive programs: Behavioral improvement in mental health inmates housed in state prisons. *Behavior Therapist, 26*, 210–211. [5]

Seeman, M., & Seeman, A. Z. (1992). Life strains, alienation, and drinking behavior. *Alcoholism: Clinical and Experimental Research, 16*, 199–205. [10]

Seeman, T., Dubin, L., & Seeman, M. (2003). Religiosity/spirituality and health. *American Psychologist, 58*, 53–63. [4, 10]

Seenoo, K., & Takagi, O. (2003). The effect of helping behaviors on helper: A case study of volunteer work for local resident welfare. *Japanese Journal of Social Psychology, 18*, 106–118. [14]

Segal, Z., Williams, M., & Teasdale, J. (2001). *Mindfulness-based cognitive therapy for depression.* New York: Guilford Press. [4]

Segall, M. H. (1994). A cross-cultural research contribution to unraveling the nativist/empiricist controversy. In J. Lonner & R. Malpass (Eds.), *Psychology and culture* (pp. 135–138). Boston: Allyn & Bacon. [3]

Segall, M. H., Campbell, D. T., & Herskovitz, M. J. (1966). *The influence of culture on visual perception.* Indianapolis: Bobbs-Merrill. [3]

Seger, C. A., Desmond, J. E., Glover, G. H., & Gabrieli, J. D. E. (2000). Functional magnetic resonance imaging evidence for right-hemisphere involvement in processing unusual semantic relationships. *Neuropsychology, 14*, 361–369. [2]

Seidman, S. (2002). Exploring the relationship between depression and erectile dysfunction in aging men. *Journal of Clinical Psychiatry, 63*, 5–12. [12]

Seligman, M. E. P. (1975). *Helplessness: On depression, development and death.* San Francisco: Freeman. [5]

Seligman, M. E. P. (1990). *Learned optimism: How to change your mind and your life.* New York: Simon & Schuster. [10]

Seligman, M. E. P. (1991). *Learned optimism.* New York: Knopf. [5]

Seligman, M. E. P. (1995). The effectiveness of psychotherapy: The *Consumer Reports* Study. *American Psychologist, 50*, 965–974. [13]

Seligman, M. E. P. (1996). Science as an ally of practice. *American Psychologist, 51*, 1072–1079. [13]

Selye, H. (1956). *The stress of life.* New York: McGraw-Hill. [10]

Sensky, T., Turkington, D., Kingdon, D., Scott, J. L., Scott, J., Siddle, R., O'Carroll, M., & Barnes, T. R. E. (2000). A randomized controlled trial of cognitive-behavioral therapy for persistent symptoms in schizophrenia resistant to medication. *Archives of General Psychiatry, 57*, 165–172. [13]

Serpell R., & Hatano, G. (1997). Education, schooling, and literacy. In J. Berry, P. Dasen, & T. Sarswthi (Eds.), *Handbook of cross-cultural psychology* (Vol. 2). Boston, MA: Allyn & Bacon. [8]

Shackelford, T., Buss, D., & Bennett, K. (2002). Forgiveness or breakup: Sex differences in responses to a partner's infidelity. *Cognition & Emotion, 16*, 299–307. [1]

Shackelford, T., Voracek, M., Schmitt, D., Buss, D., Weekes-Shackelford, V., & Michalski, R. (2004). Romantic jealousy in early adulthood and in later life. *Human Nature, 15*, 283–300. [9]

Shaffer, D., Gould, M. S., Fisher, P., Trautman, P., Moreau, D., Kleinman, M., & Flory, M. (1996). Psychiatric diagnosis in child and adolescent suicide. *Archives of General Psychiatry, 53*, 339–348. [12]

Sharp, D., Cole, M., & Lave, C. (1979). Education and cognitive development: The evidence from experimental research. *Monographs of the Society for Research in Child Development, 44*(1–2, Serial No. 178). [8]

Shaunessy, E., Karnes, F., & Cobb, Y. (2004). Assessing potentially gifted students from lower socioeconomic status with nonverbal measures of intelligence. *Perceptual & Motor Skills, 98*, 1129–1138. [7]

Shaw, J. I., & Steers, W. N. (2001). Gathering information to form an impression: Attribute categories and information valence. *Current Research in Social Psychology, 6,* 1–21. [14]

Shaw, J. S., III. (1996). Increases in eyewitness confidence resulting from postevent questioning. *Journal of Experimental Psychology: Applied, 2,* 126–146. [6]

Shaw, V. N., Hser, Y.-I., Anglin, M. D., & Boyle, K. (1999). Sequences of powder cocaine and crack use among arrestees in Los Angeles County. *American Journal of Drug and Alcohol Abuse, 25,* 47–66. [4]

Shears, J., Robinson, J., & Emde, R. (2002). Fathering relationships and their associations with juvenile delinquency. *Infant Mental Health Journal, 23,* 79–87. [8]

Sheehan, D. V., & Raj, A. B. (1988). Monoamine oxidase inhibitors. In C. G. Last & M. Hersen (Eds.), *Handbook of anxiety disorders* (pp. 478–506). New York: Pergamon. [13]

Shelton, J., & Richeson, J. (2005). Intergroup contact and pluralistic ignorance. *Journal of Personality & Social Psychology, 88,* 91–107. [14]

Shepard, R. J. (1986). Exercise in coronary heart disease. *Sports Medicine, 3,* 26–49. [10]

Shepperd, J. (2001). The desire to help and behavior in social dilemmas: Exploring responses to catastrophes. *Group Dynamics, 5,* 304–314. [14]

Sher, A. E., Schechtman, K. B., & Piccirillo, J. F. (1996). The efficacy of surgical modifications of the upper airway in adults with obstructive sleep apnea syndrome. *Sleep, 19,* 156–177. [4]

Sher, L. (2004). Hypothalamic-pituitary-adrenal function and preventing major depressive episodes. *Canadian Journal of Psychiatry, 49,* 574–575. [12]

Sherbourne, C. D., Wells, K. B., & Judd, L. L. (1996). Functioning and well-being of patients with panic disorder. *American Journal of Psychiatry, 153,* 213–218. [12]

Sherif, M. (1956). Experiments in group conflict. *Scientific American, 195,* 53–58. [14]

Sherif, M. (1958). Superordinate goals in the reduction of intergroup conflict. *American Journal of Sociology, 63,* 349–358. [14]

Sherif, M., & Sherif, C. W. (1967). The Robbers' Cave study. In J. F. Perez, R. C. Sprinthall, G. S. Grosser, & P. J. Anastasiou, *General psychology: Selected readings* (pp. 411–421). Princeton, NJ: D. Van Nostrand. [14]

Sherman, C. (1994, September/October). Kicking butts. *Psychology Today,* 41–45. [10]

Shimamura, A. P., Berry, J. M., Mangela, J. A., Rusting, C. L., & Jurica, P. J. (1995). Memory and cognitive abilities in university professors: Evidence for successful aging. *Psychological Science, 6,* 271–277. [8]

Shneidman, E. (1989). The Indian summer of life: A preliminary study of septuagenarians. *American Psychologist, 44,* 684–694. [7]

Shneidman, E. S. (1994). Clues to suicide, reconsidered. *Suicide and Life-Threatening Behavior, 24,* 395–397. [12]

Shumaker, S., Legault, C., Rapp, S., Thal, L., Wallace, R., Ockene, J., Hendrix, S., Jones, B., Assaf, A., Jackson, R., Kotchen, J., Wassertheil-Smoller, S., & Wactawski-Wende, J. (2003). Estrogen plus progestin and the incidence of dementia and mild cognitive impairment in postmenopausal women: The Women's Health Initiative Memory Study: A randomized controlled trial. *Journal of the American Medical Association (JAMA), 289,* 2651–2662. [12]

Siegler, R. S. (1991). *Children's thinking* (2nd ed.). Englewood Cliffs, NJ: Prentice-Hall. [8]

Siegrist, J., Peter, R., Junge, A., Cremer, P., & Seidel, D. (1990). Low status control, high effort at work and ischemic heart disease: Prospective evidence from blue-collar men. *Social Science and Medicine, 31,* 1127–1134. [10]

Silva, C. E., & Kirsch, I. (1992). Interpretive sets, expectancy, fantasy proneness, and dissociation as predictors of hypnotic response. *Journal of Personality and Social Psychology, 63,* 847–856. [4]

Silver, R., Holman, E., McIntosh, D., Poulin, M., & Gil-Rivas, V. (2002). Nationwide longitudinal study of psychological responses to September 11. *JAMA: Journal of the American Medical Association, 288,* 1235–1244. [10]

Simon, G., Cherkin, D., Sherman, K., Eisenberg, D., Deyo, R., & Davis, R. (2004). Mental health visits to complementary and alternative medicine providers. *General Hospital Psychiatry, 26,* 171–177. [10]

Simon, H. (1956). Rational choice and the structure of the environment. *Psychological Review, 63,* 129–138. [7]

Simon, H. B. (1988, June). Running and rheumatism. *Harvard Medical School Health Letter, 13,* 2–4. [10]

Simons, D. & Chabris, C. (1999). Gorillas in our midst: Sustained inattentional blindness for dynamic events. *Perception, 28,* 1059–1074. [3]

Simons, J., & Carey, K. (2002). Risk and vulnerability for marijuana use problems. *Psychology of Addictive Behaviors, 16,* 72–75. [4]

Simpson, E. L. (1974). Moral development research. *Human Development, 17,* 81–106. [8]

Simpson, P., & Stroh, L. (2004). Gender differences: Emotional expression and feelings of personal inauthenticity. *Journal of Applied Psychology, 89,* 715–721. [9]

Singer, M. I., Miller, D. B., Guo, S., Flannery, D. J., Frierson, T., & Slovak, K. (1999). Contributors to violent behavior among elementary and middle school children. *Pediatrics, 104*(Pt. 1), 878–884. [14]

Singh, B. (1991). Teaching methods for reducing prejudice and enhancing academic achievement for all children. *Educational Studies, 17,* 157–171. [14]

Singh, D. (1995). Female health, attractiveness, and desirability for relationships: Role of breast asymmetry and waist-hip ratio. *Ethology and Sociobiology, 16,* 445–481. [14]

Singh, H., & O'Boyle, M. (2004). Interhemispheric interaction during global–local processing in mathematically gifted adolescents, average-ability youth, and college students. *Neuropsychology, 18,* 371–377. [2]

Singh, S., & Darroch, J. (2000). Adolescent pregnancy and childbearing: Levels and trends in industrialized countries. *Family Planning Perspectives, 32,* 14–23. [8]

Sivacek, J., & Crano, W. D. (1982). Vested interest as a moderator of attitude-behavior consistency. *Journal of Personality and Social Psychology, 43,* 210–221. [14]

Skinner, B. F. (1938). *The behavior of organisms.* New York: Appleton-Century-Crofts. [5]

Skinner, B. F. (1948). *Walden two.* New York: Macmillan. [5]

Skinner, B. F. (1953). *Science and human behavior.* New York: Macmillan. [5, 14]

Skinner, B. F. (1957). *Verbal behavior.* New York: Appleton Century. [8]

Skinner, B. F. (1971). *Beyond freedom and dignity.* New York: Knopf. [5]

Skrabalo, A. (2000). Negative symptoms in schizophrenia(s): The conceptual basis. *Harvard Brain, 7,* 7–10. [12]

Slawinski, E. B., Hartel, D. M., & Kline, D. W. (1993). Self-reported hearing problems in daily life throughout adulthood. *Psychology and Aging, 8,* 552–561. [8]

Slobin, D. (1972, July). Children and language: They learn the same all around the world. *Psychology Today,* pp. 71–74, 82. [8]

Sluzki, C. (2004). House taken over by ghosts: Culture, migration, and the developmental cycle of a Moroccan family invaded by hallucination. *Families, Systems, & Health, 22,* 321–337. [13]

Smith, B., Elliott, A., Chambers, W., Smith, W., Hannaford, P., & Penny, K. (2001). The impact of chronic pain in the community. *Family Practice, 18,* 292–299. [3]

Smith, M. L., Glass, G. V., & Miller, T. I. (1980). *The benefits of psychotherapy.* Baltimore, MD: Johns Hopkins University Press. [13]

Smith, N., Young, A., & Lee, C. (2004). Optimism, health-related hardiness and well-being among older Australian women. *Journal of Health Psychology, 9*, 741–752. [10]

Smith, S. M., Glenberg, A., & Bjork, R. A. (1978). Environmental context and human memory. *Memory & Cognition, 6*, 342–353. [6]

Smith, T., & Ruiz, J. (2002). Psychosocial influences on the development and course of coronary heart disease: Current status and implications for research and practice. *Journal of Consulting and Clinical Psychology, 70* , 548–568. [10]

Smolar, A. (1999). Bridging the gap: Technical aspects of the analysis of an Asian immigrant. *Journal of Clinical Psychoanalysis, 8*, 567–594. [13]

Snarey, J. R. (1985). Cross-cultural universality of social-moral development: A critical review of Kohlbergian research. *Psychological Bulletin, 97*, 202–232. [8]

Snarey, J. R. (1995). In communitarian voice: The sociological expansion of Kohlbergian theory, research, and practice. In W. M. Kurtines & J. L. Gerwirtz (Eds.), *Moral development: An introduction* (pp. 109–134). Boston: Allyn & Bacon. [8]

Snow, C. E. (1993). Bilingualism and second language acquisition. In J. B. Gleason & N. B. Ratner (Eds.), *Psycholinguistics*. Fort Worth, TX: Harcourt. [7]

Sobin, C., & Sackeim, H. A. (1997). Psychomotor symptoms of depression. *American Journal of Psychiatry, 154*, 4–17. [12]

Sokolov, E. N. (2000). Perception and the conditioning reflex: Vector encoding. *International Journal of Psychophysiology, 35*, 197–217. [3]

Solano, L., Donati, V., Pecci, F., Perischetti, S., & Colaci, A. (2003). Postoperative course after papilloma resection: Effects of written disclosure of the experience in subjects with different alexithymia levels. *Psychosomatic Medicine, 65*, 477–484. [10]

Soler, H., Vinayak, P., & Quadagno, D. (2000). Biosocial aspects of domestic violence. *Psychoneuroendocrinology, 25*, 721–739. [14]

Sotres-Bayon, F., Bush, D., & LeDoux, J. (2004). Emotional perseveration: An update on prefrontal–amygdala interactions in fear extinction. *Learning & Memory, 11*, 525–535. [9]

Soussignan, R. (2002). Duchenne smile, emotional experience, and autonomic reactivity: A test of the facial feedback hypothesis. *Emotion, 2*, 52–74. [9]

Spangler, D. L., Simons, A. D., Monroe, S. M., & Thase, M. E. (1996). Gender differences in cognitive diathesis-stress domain match: Implications for differential pathways to depression. *Journal of Abnormal Psychology, 105*, 653–657. [12]

Spanos, N. P. (1986). Hypnotic behavior: A social-psychological interpretation of amnesia, analgesia, and "trance logic." *Behavioral and Brain Sciences, 9*, 499–502. [4]

Spanos, N. P. (1991). A sociocognitive approach to hypnosis. In S. J. Lynn & J. W. Rhue (Eds.), *Theories of hypnosis: Current models and perspectives* (pp. 324–361). New York: Guilford. [4]

Spanos, N. P. (1994). Multiple identity enactments and multiple personality disorder: A sociocognitive perspective. *Psychological Bulletin, 116*, 143–165. [4]

Spearman, C. (1927). *The abilities of man*. New York: Macmillan. [7]

Spencer, R., Zelaznik, H., Diedrichsen, J., & Ivry, R. (2003). Disrupted timing of discontinuous but not continuous movements by cerebellar lesions. *Science, 300*, 1437–1439. [2]

Sperling, G. (1960). The information available in brief visual presentations. *Psychological Monographs: General and Applied 74* (Whole No. 498), 1–29. [6]

Sperry, R. W. (1964). The great cerebral commissure. *Scientific American, 210*, 42–52. [2]

Sperry, R. W. (1968). Hemisphere deconnection and unity in conscious experience. *American Psychologist, 23*, 723–733. [2]

Spitzer, M. W., & Semple, M. N. (1991). Interaural phase coding in auditory midbrain: Influence of dynamic stimulus features. *Science, 254*, 721–724. [3]

Sporer, S. L., Penrod, S., Read, D., & Cutler, B. (1995). Choosing, confidence, and accuracy: A meta-analysis of the confidence-accuracy relation in eyewitness identification studies. *Psychological Bulletin, 118*, 315–327. [6]

Spreen, O., Risser, A., & Edgell, D. (1995). *Developmental neuropsychology*. New York: Oxford University Press. [1, 2]

Squire, L. R. (1992). Memory and the hippocampus: A synthesis from findings with rats, monkeys, and humans. *Psychological Review, 99*, 195–231. [6]

Squire, L. R., Knowlton, B., & Musen, G. (1993). The structure and organization of memory. *Annual Review of Psychology, 44*, 453–495. [6]

Srivastava, S., John, O., Gosling, S., & Potter, J. (2003). Development of personality in early and middle adulthood: Set like plaster or persistent change? *Journal of Personality & Social Psychology, 84*, 1041–1053. [11]

Staal, W. G., Pol, H. E. H., Schnack, H. G., Hoogendoorn, M. L. C., Jellema, K., & Kahn, R. S. (2000). Structural brain abnormalities in patients with schizophrenia and their healthy siblings. *American Journal of Psychiatry, 157*, 416–421. [12]

Stea, R. A., & Apkarian, A. V. (1992). Pain and somatosensory activation. *Trends in Neurosciences, 15*, 250–251. [2]

Steblay, N. M. (1992). A meta-analytic review of the weapon focus effect. *Law and Human Behavior, 16*, 413–424. [6]

Steele, C., & Aronson, J. (1995). Stereotype threat and the intellectual test performance of African Americans. *Journal of Personality & Social Psychology, 69*, 797–811. [7]

Steele, J., & Mayes, S. (1995). Handedness and directional asymmetry in the long bones of the human upper limb. *International Journal of Osteoarchaeology, 5*, 39–49. [2]

Steeves, R. (2002). The rhythms of bereavement. *Family & Community Health, 25*, 1–10. [8]

Steffens, A. B., Scheurink, A. J., & Luiten, P. G. (1988). Hypothalamic food intake regulating areas are involved in the homeostasis of blood glucose and plasma FFA levels. *Physiology and Behavior, 44*, 581–589. [9]

Steffensen, M., & Calker, L. (1982). Intercultural misunderstandings about health care: Recall of descriptions of illness and treatments. *Social Science and Medicine, 16*, 1949–1954. [6]

Stein, M. B., & Kean, Y. M. (2000). Disability and quality of life in social phobia: Epidemiologic findings. *American Journal of Psychiatry, 157*, 1606–1613. [12]

Stein, M. B., Walker, J. R., & Forde, D. R. (1996). Public-speaking fears in a community sample: Prevalence, impact on functioning, and diagnostic classification. *Archives of General Psychiatry, 53*, 169–174. [12]

Stein-Behrens, B., Mattson, M. P., Chang, I., Yeh, M., & Sapolsky, R. (1994). Stress exacerbates neuron loss and cytoskeletal pathology in the hippocampus. *Journal of Neuroscience, 14*, 5373–5380. [10]

Steinberg, K. (2000). Risks associated with genetic testing: Health insurance discrimination or simply business as usual? *Journal of the American Medical Womens Association, 55*, 241–242. [2]

Steinberg, L. (1990). Autonomy, conflict, and harmony in the family relationship. In S. S. Feldman & R. E. Glen (Eds.). *At the threshold: The developing adolescent*. Cambridge, MA: Harvard University Press. [8]

Steinberg, L., & Dornbusch, S. (1991). Negative correlates of part-time employment during adolescence: Replication and elaboration. *Developmental Psychology, 27*, 304–313. [8]

Steinberg, L., Elman, J. D., & Mounts, N. S. (1989). Authoritative parenting, psychosocial maturity, and academic success among adolescents. *Child Development, 60*, 1424–1436. [8]

Steinberg, L., Lamborn, S. D., Darling, N., Mounts, N. S., & Dornbusch, S. M. (1994). Over-time changes in adjustment and competence among adolescents from authoritative, authoritarian, indulgent, and neglectful families. *Child Development, 65*, 754–770. [8]

Steinman, L. (1993). Autoimmune disease. *Scientific American, 269,* 106–114. [10]

Stemberger, R. T., Turner, S. M., Beidel, D. C., & Calhoun, K. S. (1995). Social phobia: An analysis of possible developmental factors. *Journal of Abnormal Psychology, 104,* 526–531. [12]

Stephan, K. M., Fink, G. R., Passingham, R. E., Silbersweig, D., Ceballos-Baumann, A. O., Frith, C. D., & Frackowiak, R. S. J. (1995). Functional anatomy of the mental representation of upper extremity movements in healthy subjects. *Journal of Neurophysiology, 73,* 373–386. [7]

Stephenson, M. T., & Witte, K. (1998). Fear, threat, and perceptions of efficiency from frightening skin cancer messages. *Public Health Review, 26,* 147–174. [14]

Steptoe, A. (2000). Stress, social support and cardiovascular activity over the working day. *International Journal of Psychophysiology, 37,* 299–308. [10]

Steriade, M. (1996). Arousal: Revisiting the reticular activating system. *Science, 272,* 225–226. [2]

Stern, W. (1914). *The psychological methods of testing intelligence.* Baltimore: Warwick and York. [7]

Sternberg, R. (2003a). Our research program validating the triarchic theory of successful intelligence: Reply to Gottfredson. *Intelligence, 31,* 399–413. [7]

Sternberg, R. (2003b). Issues in the theory and measurement of successful intelligence: A reply to Brody. *Intelligence, 31,* 331–337. [7]

Sternberg, R., Castejon, J., Prieto, M., Hautamacki, J., & Grigorenko, E. (2001). Confirmatory factor analysis of the Sternberg Triarchic Abilities Test in three international samples: An empirical test of the triarchic theory of intelligence. *European Journal of Psychological Assessment, 17,* 1–16. [7]

Sternberg, R. J. (1985a). *Beyond IQ: A triarchic theory of human intelligence.* New York: Cambridge University Press. [7]

Sternberg, R. J. (1985b). Human intelligence: The model is the message. *Science, 230,* 1111–1118. [7]

Sternberg, R. J. (1986). *Intelligence applied: Understanding and increasing your intellectual skills.* San Diego: Harcourt Brace Jovanovich. [7]

Sternberg, R. J. (2000). The holey grail of general intelligence. *Science, 289,* 399–401. [7]

Sternberg, R. J., Wagner, R. K., Williams, W. M., & Horvath, J. A. (1995). Testing common sense. *American Psychologist, 50,* 912–927. [7]

Still, C. (2001). Health benefits of modest weight loss. Retrieved January 29, 2003, from http://abcnews.go.com/sections/living/ Healthology/weightloss_benefits011221.html [10]

Stilwell, N., Wallick, M., Thal, S., & Burleson, J. (2000). Myers-Briggs type and medical specialty choice: A new look at an old question. *Teaching & Learning in Medicine, 12,* 14–20. [11]

Stockhorst, U., Gritzmann, E., Klopp, K., Schottenfeld-Naor, Y., Hübinger, A., Berresheim, H., Stingrüber, H., & Gries, F. (1999). Classical conditioning of insulin effects in healthy humans. *Psychosomatic Medicine, 61,* 424–435. [5]

Stone, J. (2003). Self-consistency for low self-esteem in dissonance processes: The role of self-standards. *Personality & Social Psychology Bulletin, 29,* 846–858. [14]

Stone, K., Karem, K., Sternberg, M., McQuillan, G., Poon, A., Unger, E., & Reeves, W. (2002). Seroprevalence of human papillomavirus type 16 infection in the United States. *Journal of Infectious Diseases, 186,* 1396–1402. [10]

Strack, F., Martin, L. L., & Stepper, S. (1988). Inhibiting and facilitating conditions of facial expressions: A nonobtrusive test of the facial feedback hypothesis. *Journal of Personality and Social Psychology, 54,* 768–777. [9]

Strayer, D., Drews, F., & Johnston, W. (2003). Cell phone-induced failures of visual attention during simulated driving. *Journal of Experimental Psychology: Applied, 9,* 23–32. [3]

Strohmetz, D., Rind, B., Fisher, R., & Lynn, M. (2002). *Journal of Applied Social Psychology, 32,* 300–309. [4]

Stubbs, P. (2000). *Mental health care online.* [13]

Stuss, D. T., Gow, C. A., & Hetherington, C. R. (1992). "No longer Gage": Frontal lobe dysfunction and emotional changes. *Journal of Consulting and Clinical Psychology, 60,* 349–359. [2]

Suarez, M. G. (1983). Implications of Spanish-English bilingualism in the TAT stories. Unpublished doctoral dissertation, University of Connecticut. [13]

Sullivan, E., Fama, R., Rosenbloom, M., & Pfefferbaum, A. (2002). A profile of neuropsychological deficits in alcoholic women. *Neuropsychology, 16,* 74–83. [10]

Sullivan, E. V. (1977). A study of Kohlberg's structural theory of moral development: A critique of liberal social science ideology. *Human Development, 20,* 352–376. [8]

Sullivan, M. J. L., Bishop, S. R., & Pivik, J. (1995). The pain catastrophizing scale: Development and validation. *Psychological Assessment, 7,* 524–532. [3]

Sun, W., & Rebec, G. (2005). The role of prefrontal cortex D1-like and D2-like receptors in cocaine-seeking behavior in rats. *Psychopharmacology, 177,* 315–323. [5]

Sung, K-T. (1992). Motivations for parent care: The case of filial children in Korea. *International Journal of Aging and Human Development, 34,* 109–124. [8]

Super, C. W. (1981). Behavioral development in infancy. In R. H. Munroe, R. L. Munroe, & B. B. Whiting (Eds.), *Handbook of cross-cultural human development* (pp. 181–269). Chicago: Garland. [8]

Super, D. (1971). A theory of vocational development. In H. J. Peters & J. C. Hansen (Eds.), *Vocational guidance and career development* (pp. 111–122). New York: Macmillan. [8]

Super, D. (1986). Life career roles: Self-realization in work and leisure. In D. T. H. & Associates (Eds.), *Career development in organizations* (pp. 95–119). San Francisco: Jossey-Bass. [8]

Sussman, S., & Dent, C. W. (2000). One-year prospective prediction of drug use from stress-related variables. *Substance Use & Misuse, 35,* 717–735. [4]

Swanson, L. W. (1995). Mapping the human brain: past, present, and future. *Trends in Neurosciences, 18,* 471–474. [2]

Swanson, N. G. (2000). Working women and stress. *Journal of the American Medical Womens Association, 55,* 276–279. [10]

Sweatt, J. D., & Kandel, E. R. (1989). Persistent and transcriptionally dependent increase in protein phosphorylation in long-term facilitation of Aplysia sensory neurons. *Nature, 339,* 51–54. [6]

Swedo, S., & Grant, P. (2004). PANDAS: A model for autoimmune neuropsychiatric disorders. *Primary Psychiatry, 11,* 28–33. [12]

Sweller, J., & Levine, M. (1982). Effects of goal specificity on means-end analysis and learning. *Journal of Experimental Psychology: Learning, Memory, and Cognition, 8,* 463–474. [7]

Symister, P., & Friend, R. (2003). The influence of social support and problematic support on optimism and depression in chronic illness: A prospective study evaluating self-esteem as a mediator. *Health Psychology, 22,* 123–129. [10]

Szymura, B., & Wodniecka, Z. (2003). What really bothers neurotics? In search for factors impairing attentional performance. *Personality & Individual Differences, 34,* 109–126. [11]

Takahashi, S., Matsuura, M., Tanabe, E., Yara, K., Nonaka, K., Fukura, Y., Kikuchi, M., & Kojima, T. (2000). Age at onset of schizophrenia: Gender differences and influence of temporal socioeconomic change. *Psychiatry and Clinical Neurosciences, 54,* 153–156. [12]

Tal, M. (2004). Focused analgesia and generalized relaxation produce differential hypnotic analgesia in response to ascending stimulus intensity. *Journal of Psychophysiology, 52,* 187–196. [4]

Tamir, L. (1982). *Men in their forties: The transition to middle age.* New York: Springer. [8]

Tamminga, C. A. (1996, Winter). The new generation of antipsychotic drugs. *NARSAD Research Newsletter,* pp. 4–6. [13]

Tamminga, C. A., & Conley, R. R. (1997). The application of neuroimaging techniques to drug development. *Journal of Clinical Psychiatry, 58*(10, Suppl.), 3–6. [2]

Tanner, J. (1990). *Fetus into man: Physical growth from conception to maturity.* Cambridge, MA: Harvard University Press. [2]

Tanner, J. M. (1990). *Fetus into man* (2nd ed.). Cambridge MA: Harvard University Press. [7, 8]

Tate, D., Paul, R., Flanigan, T., Tashima, K., Nash, J., Adair, C., Boland, R., & Cohen, R. (2003). The impact of apathy and depression on quality of life in patients infected with HIV. *AIDS Patient Care & STDs, 17,* 117–120. [10]

Taub, G., Hayes, B., Cunningham, W., & Sivo, S. (2001). Relative roles of cognitive ability and practical intelligence in the prediction of success. *Psychological Reports, 88,* 931–942. [7]

Taylor, C., & Luce, K. (2003). Computer- and Internet-based psychotherapy interventions. *Current Directions in Psychological Science, 12,* 18–22. [13]

Taylor, S. E. (1991). *Health psychology* (2nd ed.). New York: McGraw-Hill. [10]

Taylor, S. E., & Repetti, R. L. (1997). Health psychology: What is an unhealthy environment and how does it get under the skin? *Annual Review of Psychology, 48,* 411–447. [10]

Tchanturia, K., Serpell, L., Troop, N., & Treasure, J. (2001). Perceptual illusions in eating disorders: Rigid and fluctuating styles. *Journal of Behavior Therapy & Experimental Psychiatry, 32,* 107–115. [9]

Tellegen, A., Lykken, D. T., Bouchard, T. J., Jr., Wilcox, K. J., Segal, N. L., & Rich, S. (1988). Personality similarity in twins reared apart and together. *Journal of Personality and Social Psychology, 54,* 1031–1039. [11]

Tennant, C. (2002). Life events, stress and depression: A review of the findings. *Australian & New Zealand Journal of Psychiatry, 36,* 173–182. [12]

Tepper, B., & Ullrich, N. (2002). Influence of genetic taste sensitivity to 6-n-propylthiouracil (PROP), dietary restraint and disinhibition on body mass index in middle-aged women. *Physiology & Behavior, 75,* 305–312. [3]

Tercyak, K., Johnson, S., Roberts, S., & Cruz, A. (2001). Psychological response to prenatal genetic counseling and amniocentesis. *Patient Education & Counseling, 43,* 73–84. [2]

Terman, L. M. (1925). *Genetic studies of genius, Vol. 1: Mental and physical traits of a thousand gifted children.* Stanford, CA: Stanford University Press. [7]

Terman, L. M., & Oden, M. H. (1947). *Genetic studies of genius, Vol. 4: The gifted child grows up.* Stanford, CA: Stanford University Press. [7]

Terman, L. M., & Oden, M. H. (1959). *Genetic studies of genius, Vol. 5: The gifted group at mid-life.* Stanford, CA: Stanford University Press. [7]

Terrace, H. (1979, November). How Nim Chimpski changed my mind. *Psychology Today,* 65–76. [7]

Terrace, H. S. (1981). A report to an academy. *Annals of the New York Academy of Sciences, 364,* 115–129. [7]

Tew, J. D., Mulsant, B. H., Haskett, R. F., Prudic, J., Thase, M. E., Crowe, R. R., Dolata, D., Begley, A. E., Reynolds, C. F., III, & Sackeim, H. A. (1999). Acute efficacy of ECT in the treatment of major depression in the old-old. *American Journal of Psychiatry, 156,* 1865–1870. [13]

Tham, K., Borell, L., & Gustavsson, A. (2000). The discovery of disability: A phenomenological study of unilateral neglect. *American Journal of Occupational Therapy, 54,* 398–406. [2]

Thase, M. E., Frank, E., Mallinger, A. G., Hammer, T., & Kupfer, D. J. (1992). Treatment of imipramine-resistant recurrent depression, III: Efficacy of monoamine oxidise inhibitors. *Journal of Clinical Psychiatry, 53*(1, Suppl.), 5–11. [13]

Thase, M. E., & Kupfer, D. J. (1996). Recent developments in the pharmacotherapy of mood disorders. *Journal of Consulting and Clinical Psychology, 64,* 646–659. [13]

Thase, M. E., Simons, A. D., Cahalane, J. F., & McGeary, J. (1991). Cognitive behavior therapy of endogenous depression: Part 1: An outpatient clinical replication series. *Behavior Therapy, 22,* 457–467. [13]

Thomas, A., Chess, S., & Birch, H. G. (1970). The origin of personality. *Scientific American, 223,* 102–109. [8]

Thomas, P., & Bracken, P. (2001). Vincent's bandage: The art of selling a drug for bipolar disorder. *British Medical Journal, 323,* 1434. [12]

Thomas, S., & Jordan, T. (2004). Contributions of oral and extraoral facial movement to visual and audiovisual speech perception. *Journal of Experimental Psychology: Human Perception & Performance, 30,* 873–888. [3]

Thompson, R., Ruch, W., & Hasenöhrl, R. (2004). Enhanced cognitive performance and cheerful mood by standardized extracts of *Piper methysticum* (Kava-kava). *Human Psychopharmacology: Clinical & Experimental, 19,* 243–250. [4]

Thompson, S. C., Sobolew-Shubin, A., Galbraith, M. E., Schwankovsky, L., & Cruzen, D. (1993). Maintaining perceptions of control: Finding perceived control in low-control circumstances. *Journal of Personality and Social Psychology, 64,* 293–304. [10]

Thorndike, E. (1898). Some experiments on animal intelligence. *Science, 7*(181), 818–824. [5]

Thorndike, E. L. (1911/1970). *Animal intelligence: Experimental studies.* New York: Macmillan. (Original work published 1911). [5]

Thornhill, R., & Gangestad, G. W. (1994). Human fluctuating asymmetry and sexual behavior. *Psychological Science, 5,* 297–302. [14]

Thurstone, L. L. (1938). *Primary mental abilities.* Chicago: University of Chicago Press. [7]

Tidey, J., O'Neill, S., & Higgins, S. (2002). Contingent monetary reinforcement of smoking reductions, with and without transferal nicotine, in outpatients with schizophrenia. *Experimental and Clinical Psychopharmacology, 10,* 241–247. [13]

Tiedemann, J. (2000). Parents' gender stereotypes and teachers' beliefs as predictors of children's concept of their mathematical ability in elementary school. *Journal of Educational Psychology, 92,* 144–151. [7]

Tiihonen, J., Isohanni, M., Räsänen, P., Koiranen, M., & Moring, J. (1997). Specific major mental disorders and criminality: A 26-year prospective study of the 1966 northern Finland birth cohort. *American Journal of Psychiatry, 154,* 840–845. [14]

Tillfors, M. (2004). Why do some individuals develop social phobia? A review with emphasis on neurobiological influences. *Nordic Journal of Psychiatry, 58,* 267–276. [12]

Toastmasters International. (2003). Ten tips for successful public speaking. Retrieved November 25, 2003, from http://www.toastmasters.org/pdfs/top10.pdf [12]

Todorov, A., & Bargh, J. (2002). Automatic sources of aggression. *Aggression & Violent Behavior, 7,* 53–68. [3]

Tolman, E. C. (1932). *Purposive behavior in animals and men.* New York: Appleton-Century-Crofts. [5]

Tolman, E. C., & Honzik, C. H. (1930). Introduction and removal of reward, and maze performance in rats. *University of California Publications in Psychology, 4,* 257–275. [5]

Toot, J., Dunphy, G., Turner, M., & Ely, D. (2004). The SHR Y-chromosome increases testosterone and aggression, but decreases serotonin as compared to the SKY Y-chromosome in the rat model. *Behavior Genetics, 34,* 515–524. [14]

Tori, C., & Bilmes, M. (2002). Multiculturalism and psychoanalytic psychology: The validation of a defense mechanism's measure in an Asian population. *Psychoanalytic Psychology, 19,* 701–721. [11]

Torrey, E., (1992). *Freudian fraud: The malignant effect of Freud's theory on American thought and culture.* New York: Harper Collins. [11]

Tourangeau, R., Smith, T. W., & Rasinski, K. A. (1997). Motivation to report sensitive behaviors on surveys: Evidence from a bogus pipeline experiment. *Journal of Applied Social Psychology, 27,* 209–222. [1]

Traverso, A., Ravera, G., Lagattolla, V., Testa, S., & Adami, G. F. (2000). Weight loss after dieting with behavioral modification for obesity: The predicting efficiency of some psychometric data. *Eating and Weight Disorders: Studies on Anorexia, Bulimia, and Obesity, 5,* 102–107. [9]

Trevitt, J., Carolson, B., Correa, M., Keene, A., Morales, M., & Salamone, J. (2002). Interactions between dopamine D1 receptors and gamma-aminobutyric acid mechanisms in substantia nigra pars reticulata of the rat: Neurochemical and behavioral studies. *Psychopharmacology, 159,* 229–237. [2]

Triandis, H. C. (1994). *Culture and social behavior.* New York: McGraw-Hill. [9]

Trijsburg, R., Perry, J., & Semeniuk, T. (2004). An empirical study of the differences in interventions between psychodynamic therapy and cognitive-behavioural therapy for recurrent major depression. *Canadian Journal of Psychoanalysis, 12,* 325–345. [13]

Triplett, N. (1898). The dynamogenic factors in pacemaking and competition. *American Journal of Psychology, 9,* 507–533. [14]

Trivedi, M. J. (1996). Functional neuroanatomy of obsessive-compulsive disorder. *Journal of Clinical Psychiatry, 57*(8, Suppl.), 26–36. [13]

Troxel, W., Matthews, K., Bromberger, J., & Sutton-Tyrrell, K. (2003). Chronic stress burden, discrimination, and subclinical carotid artery disease in African American and Caucasian women. *Health Psychology, 22,* 300–309. [10]

Trull, T., Stepp, S., & Durrett, C. (2003). Research on borderline personality disorder: An update. *Current Opinion in Psychiatry, 16,* 77–82. [12]

Tsai, S., Kuo, C., Chen, C., & Lee, H. (2002). Risk factors for completed suicide in bipolar disorder. *Journal of Clinical Psychiatry, 63,* 469–476. [12]

Tulving, E. (1995). Organization of memory: Quo vadis? In M. S. Gazzaniga (Ed.), *The cognitive neurosciences.* Cambridge, MA: MIT Press. [6]

Tulving, E. (2002). Episodic memory: From mind to brain. *Annual Review of Psychology, 53,* 1–25. [6]

Tulving, E., & Thompson, D. M. (1973). Encoding specificity and retrieval processes in episodic memory. *Psychological Review, 80,* 352–373. [6]

Turkle, S. (2004a). The objects of our lives. In P. Brockman (Ed.), *Curious minds: How a child becomes a scientist* (pp. 145–152). New York: Pantheon Books. [11]

Turkle, S. (2004b). Whither psychoanalysis in computer culture? *Psychoanalytic Psychology, 21,* 16–30. [11]

Turner, J. C., Hogg, M. A., Oakes, P. J., Reicher, S. D., & Wetherell, M. S. (1987). *Rediscovering the social group: A self-categorization theory.* Oxford, England: Blackwell. [14]

Tversky, A. (1972). Elimination by aspects: A theory of choice. *Psychological Review, 79,* 281–299. [7]

Tweed, R., & Lehman, D. (2002). Learning considered within a cultural context: Confucian and Socratic approaches. *American Psychologist, 57,* 89–99. [1]

Tzschentke, T. M. (2001). Pharmacology and behavioral pharmacology of mesocortical dopamine system. *Progress in Neurobiology, 63,* 241–320. [12]

Uchino, B. N., Cacioppo, J. T., & Kiecolt-Glaser, J. K. (1996). The relationship between social support and physiological processes: A review with emphasis on underlying mechanisms and implications for health. *Psychological Bulletin, 119,* 488–531. [10]

Underwood, B. J. (1957). Interference and forgetting. *Psychological Review, 64,* 49–60. [6]

Underwood, B. J. (1964). Forgetting. *Scientific American, 210,* 91–99. [6]

Urry, H., Nitschke, J., Dolski, I., Jackson, D., Dalton, K., Mueller, C., Rosenkranz, M., Ryff, C., Singer, B., & Davidson, R. (2004). Making a life worth living: Neural correlates of well-being. *Psychological Science, 15,* 367–372. [2]

U.S. Bureau of the Census. (2001). *Statistical abstract of the United States.* Washington, DC: U.S. Government Printing Office. [8, 11]

U.S. Bureau of Labor Statistics. (2004). Psychologists. *Occupational outlook handbook* (2004–2005 ed.). Retrieved November 23, 2004, from http://stats.bls.gov/oco/ocos056.htm [1]

U.S. Census Bureau. (1999). *Statistical abstracts of the United States 1999* (119th ed.). Washington DC: U.S. Government Printing Office. [12]

U.S. Census Bureau. (2000). Native resident population estimates of the United States by sex, race, and Hispanic origin. Population Estimates Program, Population Division. Retrieved from http://www.census.gov/populationestimates/nation/nativity/nbtab003.txt [1, 10]

U.S. Census Bureau. (2001). *Statistical abstract of the United States.* Washington, DC: Author. [8]

U.S. Department of Energy. (2003). *International consortium completes Human Genome Project.* Retrieved January 16, 2005, from http://www.ornl.gov/sci/techresources/Human_Genome/project/50yr/press4_2003.shtml [2]

U.S. Department of Health and Human Services. (2000). *Reducing tobacco use: A report of the Surgeon General—executive summary.* Atlanta: Department of Health and Human Services, Centers for Disease Control and Prevention, National Center for Chronic Disease Prevention and Health Promotion, Office on Smoking and Health. [10]

U.S. Department of Health and Human Services. (2001). Ecstasy: Teens speak out [Online factsheet]. Retrieved October 22, 2003, from http://www.health.org/govpubs/prevalert/v4/8.aspx [4]

U.S. Food and Drug Administration. (2004, October 15). Suicidality in children and adolescents being treated with antidepressant medication. Retrieved May 12, 2005, from http://www.fda.gov/cder/drug/antidepressants/SSRIPHA200410.htm [13]

Ushikubo, M. (1998). A study of factors facilitating and inhibiting the willingness of the institutionalized disabled elderly for rehabilitation: A United States–Japanese comparison. *Journal of Cross-Cultural Gerontology, 13,* 127–157. [8]

Utsey, S., Chae, M., Brown, C., & Kelly, D. (2002). Effect of ethnic group membership on ethnic identity, race-related stress and quality of life. *Cultural Diversity & Ethnic Minority Psychology, 8,* 367–378. [10]

Vaccarino, V., Abramson, J., Veledar, E., & Weintraub, W. (2002). Sex differences in hospital mortality after coronary artery bypass surgery: Evidence for a higher mortality in younger women. *Circulation, 105,* 1176. [10]

Van Assema, P., Martens, M., Ruiter, A., & Brug, J. (2002). Framing of nutrition education messages in persuading consumers of the advantages of a healthy diet. *Journal of Human Nutrition & Dietetics, 14,* 435–442. [14]

Van Boven, L., White, K., Kamada, A., & Gilovich, T. (2003). Intuitions about situational correction in self and others. *Journal of Personality & Social Psychology, 85,* 249–258. [14]

Van Cauter, E. (2000). Slow-wave sleep and release of growth hormone. *Journal of the American Medical Association, 284,* 2717–2718. [4]

Van der Zee, K., Thijs, M., & Schakel, L. (2002). The relationship of emotional intelligence with academic intelligence and the Big Five. *European Journal of Personality, 16,* 103–125. [9]

van Elst, L. T., Woermann, F. G., Lemieux, L., Thompson, P. J., & Trimble, M. R. (2000). Affective aggression in patients with temporal lobe epilepsy. *Brain, 123,* 234–243. [14]

Van Lancker, D. (1987, November). Old familiar voices. *Psychology Today,* 12–13. [2]

van Vianen, A., & Fischer, A. (2002). Illuminating the glass ceiling: The role of organizational culture preferences. *Journal of Occupational & Organizational Psychology, 75,* 315–337. [8]

Vargha-Khadem, F., Gadian, D. G., Watkins, D. E., Connelly, A., Van Paesschen, W., & Mishkin, M. (1997). Differential effects of early hippocampal pathology on episodic and semantic memory. *Science, 277,* 376–380. [2, 6]

Varley, A., & Blasco, M. (2003). Older women's living arrangements and family relationships in urban Mexico. *Women's Studies International Forum, 26,* 525–539. [8]

Vasterling, J., Duke, L., Brailey, K., Constans, J., Allain, A., & Sutker, P. (2002). Attention, learning, and memory performances and intellectual resources in Vietnam veterans: PTSD and no disorder comparisons. *Neuropsychology, 16,* 5–14. [10]

Verdejo-García, A., López-Torrecillas, F., Aguilar de Arcos, F., & Pérez-García, M. (2005). Differential effects of MDMA, cocaine, and cannabis use severity on distinctive components of the executive functions in polysubstance users: A multiple regression analysis. *Addictive Behaviors, 30,* 89–101. [4]

Verhaeghen, P., Marcoen, A., & Goossens, L. (1993). Facts and fiction about memory aging. A quantitative integration of research findings. *Journal of Gerontology, 48,* 157–171. [8]

Vetulani, J., & Nalepa, I. (2000). Antidepressants: Past, present and future. *European Journal of Pharmacology, 405,* 351–363. [13]

Viemerö, V. (1996). Factors in childhood that predict later criminal behavior. *Aggressive Behavior, 22,* 87–97. [14]

Vieta, E. (2003). Atypical antipsychotics in the treatment of mood disorders. *Current Opinion in Psychiatry, 16,* 23–27. [13]

Villani, S. (2001). Impact of media on children and adolescents: A 10-year review of the research. *Journal of the American Academy of Child & Adolescent Psychiatry, 40,* 392–401. [5]

Vincent, M., & Pickering, M. R. (1988). Multiple personality disorder in childhood. *Canadian Journal of Psychiatry, 33,* 524–529. [12]

Vinokur, A., & Burnstein, E. (1978). Depolarization of attitudes in groups. *Journal of Personality and Social Psychology, 36,* 872–885. [14]

Visser, P., & Mirabile, R. (2004). Attitudes in the social context: The impact of social network composition on individual-level attitude strength. *Journal of Personality & Social Psychology, 87,* 779–795. [14]

Visser, P. S., & Krosnick, J. A. (1998). Development of attitude strength over the life cycle: Surge and decline. *Journal of Personality & Social Psychology, 75,* 1389–1410. [14]

Vitousek, K., & Manke, F. (1994). Personality variables and disorders in anorexia nervosa and bulimia nervosa. *Journal of Abnormal Psychology, 103,* 137–147. [9]

Volis, C., Ashburn-Nardo, L., & Monteith, M. (2002). Evidence of prejudice-related conflict and associated affect beyond the college setting. *Group Processes & Intergroup Relations, 5,* 19–33. [14]

Volkow, N. D., & Fowler, J. S. (2000). Addiction, a disease of compulsion and drive: Involvement of the orbitofrontal cortex. *Cerebral Cortex, 10,* 318–325. [5]

Votruba, S., Horvitz, M., & Schoeller, D. (2000). The role of exercise in the treatment of obesity. *Nutrition, 16,* 179–188. [10]

Voyer, D., & Rodgers, M. (2002). Reliability of laterality effects in a dichotic listening task with nonverbal material. *Brain & Cognition, 48,* 602–606. [9]

Vroomen, J., Driver, J., & deGelder, B. (2001). Is cross-modal integration of emotional expressions independent of attentional resources? *Cognitive, Affective & Behavioral Neuroscience, 1,* 382–387. [3]

Vygotsky, L. (1926/1992). *Educational psychology.* Boca Raton, FL: St. Lucie Press. [8]

Vygotsky, L. S. (1934/1986). *Thought and language* (A. Kozulin, Trans.). Cambridge, MA: MIT Press. (Original work published 1936). [8]

Wade, D., Robson, P., House, H., Makela, P., & Aram, J. (2003). A preliminary controlled study to determine whether whole-plant cannabis extracts can improve intractable neurogenic symptoms. *Clinical Rehabilitation, 17,* 21–29. [4]

Wade, T., & DiMaria, C. (2003). Weight halo effects: Individual differences in perceived life success as a function of women's race and weight. *Sex Roles, 48,* 461–465. [14]

Wagner, D., Wenzlaff, R., & Kozak, M. (2004). Dream rebound: The return of suppressed thoughts in dreams. *Psychological Science, 15,* 232–236. [4]

Wald, G. (1964). The receptors of human color vision. *Science, 145,* 1007–1017. [3]

Wald, G., Brown, P. K., & Smith, P. H. (1954). Iodopsin. *Journal of General Physiology, 38,* 623–681. [3]

Waldron, S., & Helm, F. (2004). Psychodynamic features of two cognitive-behavioural and one psychodynamic treatment compared using the analytic process scales. *Canadian Journal of Psychoanalysis, 12,* 346–368. [13]

Walitzer, K., & Demen, K. (2004). Alcohol-focused spouse involvement and behavioral couples therapy: Evaluation of enhancements to drinking reduction treatment for male problem drinkers. *Journal of Consulting & Clinical Psychology, 72,* 944–955. [13]

Walker, D. (2000). Online therapy? Not yet. *CBS News.* New York: CBS. [13]

Walker, I., & Crogan, M. (1998). Academic performance, prejudice and the jigsaw classroom: New pieces to the puzzle. *Journal of Community & Applied Social Psychology, 8,* 381–393. [14]

Walker, L. (1989). A longitudinal study of moral reasoning. *Child Development, 60,* 157–166. [8]

Walker, M., Brakefield, T., Hobson, J., & Stickgold, R. (2003). Dissociable stages of human memory consolidation and reconsolidation. *Nature, 425,* 616–620. [4]

Walsh, B., Seidman, S., Sysko, R., & Gould, M. (2002). Placebo response in studies of major depression: Variable, substantial, and growing. *JAMA: Journal of the American Medical Association, 287,* 1840–1847. [13]

Walster, E., & Walster, G. W. (1969). The matching hypothesis. *Journal of Personality and Social Psychology, 6,* 248–253. [14]

Walters, C. C., & Grusec, J. E. (1977). *Punishment.* San Francisco: Freeman. [5]

Ward, C. (1994). Culture and altered states of consciousness. In W. J. Lonner & R. Malpass (Eds.), *Psychology and culture* (pp. 59–64). Boston: Allyn & Bacon. [4]

Wark, G. R., & Krebs, D. L. (1996). Gender and dilemma differences in real-life moral judgment. *Developmental Psychology, 32,* 220–230. [8]

Warshaw, M. G., & Keller, M. B. (1996). The relationship between fluoxetine use and suicidal behavior in 654 subjects with anxiety disorders. *Journal of Clinical Psychiatry, 57,* 158–166. [13]

Washington University School of Medicine. (2003). *Epilepsy surgery* [Online factsheet]. Retrieved September 29, 2003, from http://neurosurgery.wustl.edu/clinprog/epilepsysurg.htm [2]

Waterman, A. (1985). Identity in the context of adolescent psychology. *Child Development, 30,* 5–24. [8]

Watkins, L., Connor, K., & Davidson, J. (2001). Effect of kava on vagal cardiac control in generalized anxiety disorder: Preliminary findings. *Journal of Psychopharmacology, 15,* 283–286. [4]

Watson, D. (2002). Predicting psychiatric symptomatology with the Defense Style Questionnaire-40. *International Journal of Stress Management, 9,* 275–287. [11]

Watson, J. B., & Rayner, R. (1920). Conditioned emotional reactions. *Journal of Experimental Psychology, 3*, 1–14. [5]

Webb, R., Lubinski, D., & Benbow, C. (2002). Mathematically facile adolescents with math-science aspirations: New perspectives on their educational and vocational development. *Journal of Educational Psychology, 94*, 785–794. [7]

Webb, W. (1995). The cost of sleep-related accidents: A reanalysis. *Sleep, 18*, 276–280. [4]

Webb, W. B. (1975). *Sleep: The gentle tyrant.* Englewood Cliffs, NJ: Prentice-Hall. [4]

Weekes, J. R., Lynn, S. J., Green, J. P., & Brentar, J. T. (1992). Pseudomemory in hypnotized and task-motivated subjects. *Journal of Abnormal Psychology, 101*, 356–360. [4]

Weeks, D. L., & Anderson, L. P. (2000). The interaction of observational learning with overt practice: Effects on motor skill learning. *Acta Psychologia, 104*, 259–271. [5]

Weigman, O., & van Schie, E. G. (1998). Video game playing and its relations with aggressive and prosocial behaviour. *British Journal of Social Psychology, 37*(Pt. 3), 367–378. [14]

Weiner, I. (2004). Monitoring psychotherapy with performance-based measures of personality functioning. *Journal of Personality Assessment, 83*, 323–331. [11]

Weiner, I. B. (1996). Some observations on the validity of the Rorschach Inkblot Method. *Psychological Assessment, 8*, 206–213. [11]

Weiner, I. B. (1997). Current status of the Rorschach Inkblot Method. *Journal of Personality Assessment, 68*, 5–19. [11]

Weiss, J. M. (1972). Psychological factors in stress and disease. *Scientific American, 226*, 104–113. [10]

Weissman, M. M., Bland, R. C., Canino, G. J., Faravelli, C., Greenwald, S., Hwu, H-G., Joyce, P. R., Karam, E. G., Lee, C-K., Lellouch, J., Lepine, J-P., Newman, S. C., Rubio-Stepic, M., Wells, J. E., Wickramaratne, P. J., Wittchen, H-U., & Yeh, E-K. (1996). Cross-national epidemiology of major depression and bipolar disorder. *Journal of the American Medical Association, 276*, 293–299. [12]

Weissman, M. M., Bland, R. C., Canino, G. J., Greenwald, S., Hwu, H-G., Lee, C. K., Newman, S. C., Oakley-Browne, M. A., Rubio-Stipec, M., Wickramaratne, P. J., Wittchen, H-U., & Yeh, E-K. (1994). The cross national epidemiology of obsessive compulsive disorder. *Journal of Clinical Psychiatry, 55*(3, Suppl.), 5–10. [12]

Wells, D. L., & Hepper, P. G. (2000). The discrimination of dog odours by humans. *Perception, 29*, 111–115. [3]

Wells, G. L. (1993). What do we know about eyewitness identification? *American Psychologist, 48*, 553–571. [6]

Wells, G. L., Malpass, R. S., Lindsay, R. C., Fisher, R. P., Turtle, J. W., & Fulero, S. M. (2000). From the lab to the police station. A successful application of eyewitness research. *American Psychologist, 55*, 6581–6598. [6]

Wertheimer, M. (1912). Experimental studies of the perception of movement. *Zeitschrift fur Psychologie, 61*, 161–265. [3]

Wesensten, N., Balenky, G., Kautz, M., Thorne, D., Reichardt, R., & Balkin, T. (2002). Maintaining alertness and performance during sleep deprivation: Modafinil versus caffeine. *Psychopharmacology, 159*, 238–247. [4]

Westergaard, G., & Lussier, I. (1999). Left-handedness and longevity in primates. *International Journal of Neuroscience, 99*, 79–87. [2]

Wetherell, J., Gatz, M., & Craske, M. (2003). Treatment of generalized anxiety disorder in older adults. *Journal of Consulting & Clinical Psychology, 71*, 31–40. [13]

Wetter, M. W., Baer, R. A., Berry, T. R., Robison, L. H., & Sumpter, J. (1993). MMPI-2 profiles of motivated fakers given specific symptom information: A comparison to matched patients. *Psychological Assessment, 5*, 317–323. [11]

Wheatley, D. (2001). Stress-induced insomnia treated with kava and valerian. Singly and in combination. *Human Psychopharmacology Clinical & Experimental, 16*, 353–356. [4]

Wheeler, M., & McMillan, C. (2001). Focal retrograde amnesia and the episodic-semantic distinction. *Cognitive, Affective & Behavioral Neuroscience, 1*, 22–36. [6]

Wheeler, M. A., Stuss, D. T., & Tulving, E. (1997). Toward a theory of episodic memory: The frontal lobes and autonoetic consciousness. *Psychological Bulletin, 121*, 331–354. [6]

Whisenhunt, B. L., Williamson, D. A., Netemeyer, R. G., & Womble, L. G. (2000). Reliability and validity of the Psychosocial Risk Factors Questionnaire (PRFQ). *Eating and Weight Disorders: Studies on Anorexia, Bulimia, and Obesity, 5*, 1–6. [9]

Whitam, F. L., Diamond, M., & Martin, J. (1993). Homosexual orientation in twins: A report on 61 pairs and three triplet sets. *Archives of Sexual Behavior, 22*, 187–296. [9]

White, D. P. (1989). Central sleep apnea. In M. H. Kryger, T. Roth, & W. C. Dement (Eds.), *Principles and practice of sleep medicine* (pp. 513–524). Philadelphia: W. B. Saunders. [4]

White, S. D., & DeBlassie, R. R. (1992). Adolescent sexual behavior. *Adolescence, 27*, 183–191. [8]

Whitehurst, G. J., Fischel, J. E., Caulfield, M. B., DeBaryshe, B. D., & Valdez-Menchaca, M. C. (1989). Assessment and treatment of early expressive language delay. In P. R. Zelazo & R. Barr (Eds.), *Challenges to developmental paradigms: Implications for assessment and treatment* (pp. 113–135). Hillsdale, NJ: Erlbaum. [8]

Whorf, B. L. (1956). Science and linguistics. In J. B. Carroll (Ed.), *Language, thought, and reality: Selected writings of Benjamin Lee Whorf.* Cambridge, MA: MIT Press. [7]

Wickelgren, I. (1996). For the cortex, neuron loss may be less than thought. *Science, 273*, 48–50. [8]

Wicker, A. W. (1969). Attitudes versus action: The relationship of verbal and overt behavioral responses to attitude objects. *Journal of Social Issues, 25*, 41–78. [14]

Widom, C. S., & Maxfield, M. G. (1996). A prospective examination of risk for violence among abused and neglected children. *Annals of the New York Academy of Sciences, 794*, 224–237. [14]

Widom, C. S., & Morris, S. (1997). Accuracy of adult recollections of childhood victimization: Part 2. Childhood sexual abuse. *Psychological Bulletin, 9*, 34–46. [6]

Wigboldus, D., Dijksterhuis, A., & Van Knippenberg, A. (2003). When stereotypes get in the way: Stereotypes obstruct stereotype-inconsistent trait inferences. *Journal of Personality & Social Psychology, 84*, 470–484. [14]

Wiggins, J. S. (Ed.). (1996). *The five-factor model of personality: Theoretical perspectives.* New York: Guilford. [11]

Wilcox, D., & Hager, R. (1980). Toward realistic expectation for orgasmic response in women. *Journal of Sex Research, 16*, 162–179. [9]

Wilhelm, K., Kovess, V., Rios-Seidel, C., & Finch, A. (2004). Work and mental health. *Social Psychiatry & Psychiatric Epidemiology, 39*, 866–873. [10]

Wilken, J. A., Smith, B. D., Tola, K., & Mann, M. (2000). Trait anxiety and prior exposure to non-stressful stimuli: Effects on psychophysiological arousal and anxiety. *International Journal of Psychophysiology, 37*, 233–242. [9]

Wilkinson, R. (2004). The role of parental and peer attachment in the psychological health and self-esteem of adolescents. *Journal of Youth & Adolescence, 33*, 479–493. [8]

Williams, J. (2003). Dementia and genetics. In R. Plomin, J. de Fries, I. Craig, & P. McGuffin (Eds.), *Behavioral genetics in the postgenomic era* (pp. 503–528). Washington, DC: APA. [8]

Williams, K., Harkins, S. G., & Latané, B. (1981). Identifiability as a deterrent to social loafing: Two cheering experiments. *Journal of Personality and Social Psychology, 40*, 303–311. [14]

Williams, L. M. (1994). Recall of childhood trauma: A prospective study of women's memories of child sexual abuse. *Journal of Consulting and Clinical Psychology, 62*, 1167–1176. [6]

Williams, R. (1993). *Anger kills.* New York: Times Books. [10]

Wilson, F. R. (1998). *The hand: How its use shapes the brain, language, and human culture*. New York: Pantheon. [2]

Wilson, M. A., & McNaughton, B. L. (1993). Dynamics of the hippocampal ensemble code for space. *Science, 261,* 1055–1058. [2]

Wilson, W., Mathew, R., Turkington, T., Hawk, T., Coleman, R. E., & Provenzale, J. (2000). Brain morphological changes and early marijuana use: A magnetic resonance and positron emission tomography study. *Journal of Addictive Diseases, 19,* 1–22. [4]

Winograd, E. (1988). Some observations on prospective remembering. In M. M. Gruneberg, P. E. Morris, & R. N. Sykes (Eds.), *Practical aspects of memory: Current research and issues: Vol. 1* (pp. 348–353). Chichester, England: John Wiley & Sons. [6]

Winokur, G., Coryell, W., Keller, M., Endicott, J., & Akiskal, H. S. (1993). A prospective follow-up of patients with bipolar and primary unipolar affective disorder. *Archives of General Psychiatry, 50,* 457–465. [12]

Witelson, S. F. (1985). The brain connection: The corpus callosum is larger in left-handers. *Science, 229,* 665–668. [2]

Wolford, G., Miller, M. B., & Gazzaniga, M. (2000). The left hemisphere's role in hypothesis formation. *Journal of Neuroscience, 20,* 1–4. [7]

Wolpe, J. (1958). *Psychotherapy by reciprocal inhibition*. Stanford, CA: Stanford University Press. [13]

Wolpe, J. (1973). *The practice of behavior therapy* (2nd ed.). New York: Pergamon. [13]

Wolsko, P., Eisenberg, D., Davis, R., & Phillips, R. (2004). Use of mind-body medical therapies: Results of a national survey. *Journal of General Internal Medicine, 19,* 43–50. [4]

Wolters, C. (2003). Understanding procrastination from a self-regulated learning perspective. *Journal of Educational Psychology, 95,* 179–187. [5, 9]

Wolters, C. (2004). Advancing achievement goal theory using goal structures and goal orientations to predict students' motivation, cognition, and achievement. *Journal of Educational Psychology, 96,* 136–250. [9]

Wood, J., Cowan, P., & Baker, B. (2002). Behavior problems and peer rejection in preschool boys and girls. *Journal of Genetic Psychology, 163,* 72–88. [8]

Wood, J. M., Nezworski, M. T., & Stejskal, W. J. (1996). The Comprehensive System for the Rorschach: A critical examination. *Psychological Science, 7,* 3–10. [11]

Wood, W., Lundgren, S., Ovellette, J. A., Busceme, S., & Blackstone, T. (1994). Minority influence: A meta-analytic review of social influence processes. *Psychological Bulletin, 115,* 323–345. [14]

Wood, W., Wong, F. Y., & Chachere, J. G. (1991). Effects of media violence on viewers' aggression in unconstrained social interaction. *Psychological Bulletin, 109,* 371–383. [14]

Woodman, G., & Luck, S. (2003). Serial deployment of attention during visual search. *Journal of Experimental Psychology: Human Perception and Performance, 29,* 121–138. [3]

Woods, S. C., & Gibbs, J. (1989). The regulation of food intake by peptides. *Annals of the New York Academy of Sciences, 575,* 236–243. [9]

Woodward, A. L., Markman, E. M., & Fitzsimmons, C. M. (1994). Rapid word learning in 13- and 18-month-olds. *Developmental Psychology, 30,* 553–566. [8]

Woody, E. Z., & Bowers, K. S. (1994). A frontal assault on dissociated control. In S. J. Lynn & J. W. Rhue (Eds.), *Dissociation: Clinical, theoretical and research perspectives* (pp. 52–79). New York: Guilford. [4]

Woolley, J., & Boerger, E. (2002). Development of beliefs about the origins and controllability of dreams. *Development Psychology, 38,* 24–41. [4]

World Health Organization. (2000). *Violence against women* [Online report]. Retrieved September 1, 2000, from http://www.who.int [14]

Worrel, J. A., Marken, P. A., Beckman, S. E., & Ruehter, V. L. (2000). Atypical antipsychotic agents: A critical review. *American Journal of Health System Pharmacology, 57,* 238–255. [13]

Worthen, J., & Wood, V. (2001). Memory discrimination for self-performed and imagined acts: Bizarreness effects in false recognition. *Quarterly Journal of Experimental Psychology, 54A,* 49–67. [6]

Wright, J. C., & Mischel, W. (1987). A conditional approach to dispositional constructs: The local predictability of social behavior. *Journal of Personality and Social Psychology, 53,* 1159–1177. [11]

Wu, C., & Shaffer, D. R. (1987). Susceptibility to persuasive appeals as a function of source credibility and prior experience with the attitude object. *Journal of Personality and Social Psychology, 52,* 677–688. [14]

Yackinous, C., & Guinard, J. (2002). Relation between PROP (6-n-propylthiouracil) taster status, taste anatomy and dietary intake measures for young men and women. *Appetite, 38,* 201–209. [3]

Yale-New Haven Hospital. (2003). Making the right choice: Speak up about complementary and alternative therapies. Retrieved August 6, 2003, from http://www.ynhh.org/choice/cam.html [10]

Yanagita, T. (1973). An experimental framework for evaluation of dependence liability in various types of drugs in monkeys. *Bulletin of Narcotics, 25,* 57–64. [4]

Yang, C., & Spielman, A. (2001). The effect of a delayed weekend sleep pattern on sleep and morning functioning. *Psychology & Health, 16,* 715–725. [4]

Yapko, M. D. (1994). Suggestibility and repressed memories of abuse: A survey of psychotherapists' beliefs. *American Journal of Clinical Hypnosis, 36,* 163–171. [4]

Yeh, S., & Lo, S. (2004). Living alone, social support, and feeling lonely among the elderly. *Social Behavior & Personality, 32,* 129–138. [8]

Zajonc, R. B. (1980). Feeling and thinking: Preferences need no inferences. *American Psychologist, 35,* 151–175. [9]

Zajonc, R. B. (1984). On the primacy of affect. *American Psychologist, 39,* 117–123. [9]

Zajonc, R. B., & Sales, S. M. (1966). Social facilitation of dominant and subordinate responses. *Journal of Experimental Social Psychology, 2,* 160–168. [14]

Zaragoza, M. S., & Mitchell, K. J. (1996). Repeated exposure to suggestion and the creation of false memories. *Psychological Science, 7,* 294–300. [6]

Zhang, D., Li, Z., Chen, X., Wang, Z., Zhang, X., Meng, X., He, S., & Hu, X. (2003). Functional comparison of primacy, middle and recency retrieval in human auditory short-term memory: An event-related fMRI study. *Cognitive Brain Research, 16,* 91–98. [2]

Zhang, X., Cohen, H., Porjesz, B., & Begleiter, H. (2001). Mismatch negativity in subjects at high risk for alcoholism. *Alcoholism: Clinical & Experimental Research, 25,* 330–337. [10]

Zimbardo, P. G. (1972). Pathology of imprisonment. *Society, 9,* 4–8. [14]

Zimmerman, M., Posternak, K., & Chelminski, I. (2002). Symptom severity and exclusion from antidepressant efficacy trials. *Journal of Clinical Psychopharmacology, 22,* 610–614. [13]

Zisapel, N. (2001). Circadian rhythm sleep disorders: Pathophysiology and potential approaches to management. *CNS Drugs, 15,* 311–328. [4]

Zucker, A., Ostrove, J., & Stewart A. (2002). College-educated women's personality development in adulthood: Perceptions and age differences. *Psychology & Aging, 17,* 236–244. [8]

Zuger, B. (1990, August). Changing concepts of the etiology of male homosexuality. *Medical Aspects of Human Sexuality, 24,* 73–75. [9]

Glossary

absolute threshold   The minimum amount of sensory stimulation that can be detected 50% of the time.

accommodation   The flattening and bulging action of the lens as it focuses images of objects on the retina.

accommodation   The process by which existing schemes are modified and new schemes are created to incorporate new objects, events, experiences, or information.

acetylcholine   (ah-SEET-ul-KOH-leen) A neurotransmitter that plays a role in learning new information, causes the skeletal muscle fibers to contract, and keeps the heart from beating too rapidly.

acquired immune deficiency syndrome (AIDS)   A devastating and incurable illness that is caused by infection with the human immunodeficiency virus (HIV) and progressively weakens the body's immune system, leaving the person vulnerable to opportunistic infections that usually cause death.

action potential   The sudden reversal of the resting potential, which initiates the firing of a neuron.

activation-synthesis hypothesis of dreaming   The hypothesis that dreams are the brain's attempt to make sense of the random firing of brain cells during REM sleep.

actor-observer effect   The tendency to attribute one's own behavior primarily to situational factors and the behavior of others primarily to dispositional factors.

adolescence   The developmental stage that begins at puberty and encompasses the period from the end of childhood to the beginning of adulthood.

adrenal glands   (ah-DREE-nal) A pair of endocrine glands that release hormones that prepare the body for emergencies and stressful situations and also release corticoids and small amounts of the sex hormones.

aerobic exercise   Exercise that uses the large muscle groups in continuous, repetitive action and increases oxygen intake and breathing and heart rates.

afterimage   A visual sensation that remains after a stimulus is withdrawn.

aggression   The intentional infliction of physical or psychological harm on others.

agoraphobia   (AG-or-uh-FO-bee-ah) An intense fear of being in a situation from which escape is not possible or in which help would not be available if one experienced overwhelming anxiety or a panic attack.

alarm stage   The first stage of the general adaptation syndrome, in which the person experiences a burst of energy that aids in dealing with the stressful situation.

algorithm   A systematic, step-by-step procedure, such as a mathematical formula, that guarantees a solution to a problem of a certain type if applied appropriately and executed properly.

alpha wave   The brain-wave pattern associated with deep relaxation.

altered state of consciousness   Changes in awareness produced by sleep, meditation, hypnosis, and drugs

alternative medicine   Any treatment or therapy that has not been scientifically demonstrated to be effective.

altruism   Behavior that is aimed at helping another, requires some self-sacrifice, and is not performed for personal gain.

Alzheimer's disease   (ALZ-hye-merz) An incurable form of dementia characterized by progressive deterioration of intellect and personality, resulting from widespread degeneration of brain cells.

amnesia   A partial or complete loss of memory due to loss of consciousness, brain damage, or some psychological cause.

amplitude   The measure of the loudness of a sound; expressed in the unit called the decibel.

amygdala   (ah-MIG-da-la) A structure in the limbic system that plays an important role in emotion, particularly in response to unpleasant or punishing stimuli.

analogy heuristic   A rule of thumb that applies a solution that solved a problem in the past to a current problem that shares many features with the past problem.

anorexia nervosa   An eating disorder characterized by an overwhelming, irrational fear of gaining weight or becoming fat, compulsive dieting to the point of self-starvation, and excessive weight loss.

anterograde amnesia   The inability to form long-term memories of events occurring after a brain injury or brain surgery, although memories formed before the trauma are usually intact and short-term memory is unaffected.

antidepressant drugs   Drugs that act as mood elevators for severely depressed people and are also prescribed to treat some anxiety disorders.

antipsychotic drugs   Drugs used to control severe psychotic symptoms, such as delusions, hallucinations, disorganized speech, and disorganized behavior, by inhibiting dopamine activity; also known as neuroleptics.

anxiety disorders   Psychological disorders characterized by frequent fearful thoughts about what might happen in the future.

aphasia   (uh-FAY-zyah) A loss or impairment of the ability to use or understand language, resulting from damage to the brain.

applied research   Research conducted specifically to solve practical problems and improve the quality of life.

approach-approach conflict A conflict arising from having to choose between equally desirable alternatives.

approach-avoidance conflict A conflict arising when the same choice has both desirable and undesirable features.

aptitude test A test designed to predict a person's achievement or performance at some future time.

archetype (AR-ka-type) Existing in the collective unconscious, an inherited tendency to respond to universal human situations in particular ways.

arousal A state of alertness and mental and physical activation.

arousal theory A theory of motivation suggesting that people are motivated to maintain an optimal level of alertness and physical and mental activation.

artificial intelligence The programming of computer systems to simulate human thinking in solving problems and in making judgments and decisions.

artificial neural networks (ANNs) Computer systems that are intended to mimic the human brain.

assimilation The process by which new objects, events, experiences, or information is incorporated into existing schemes.

association areas Areas of the cerebral cortex that house memories and are involved in thought, perception, and language.

attachment The strong affectionate bond a child forms with the mother or primary caregiver.

attention The process of sorting through sensations and selecting some of them for further processing.

attitude A relatively stable evaluation of a person, object, situation, or issue, along a continuum ranging from positive to negative.

attribution An assignment of a cause to explain one's own or another's behavior.

audience effects The impact of passive spectators on performance.

audition The sensation and process of hearing.

authoritarian parents Parents who make arbitrary rules, expect unquestioned obedience from their children, punish transgressions, and value obedience to authority.

authoritative parents Parents who set high but realistic standards, reason with the child, enforce limits, and encourage open communication and independence.

availability heuristic A cognitive rule of thumb that says that the probability of an event or the importance assigned to it is based on its availability in memory.

aversion therapy A behavior therapy in which an aversive stimulus is paired with a harmful or socially undesirable behavior until the behavior becomes associated with pain or discomfort.

avoidance learning Learning to avoid events or conditions associated with aversive consequences or phobias.

avoidance-avoidance conflict A conflict arising from having to choose between undesirable alternatives.

axon (AK-sahn) The slender, tail-like extension of the neuron that transmits signals to the dendrites or cell body of other neurons and to muscles, glands, and other parts of the body.

babbling Vocalization of the basic speech sounds (phonemes), which begins between 4 and 6 months.

bacterial STDs Sexually transmitted diseases that are caused by bacteria and can be treated with antibiotics.

basic emotions Emotions that are unlearned and universal, that are reflected in the same facial expressions across cultures, and that emerge in children according to their biological timetable of development; fear, anger, disgust, surprise, happiness, and sadness are usually considered basic emotions.

basic research Research conducted to seek new knowledge and to explore and advance general scientific understanding.

behavior modification A method of changing behavior through a systematic program based on the learning principles of classical conditioning, operant conditioning, or observational learning. An approach to therapy that uses learning principles to eliminate inappropriate or maladaptive behaviors and replace them with more adaptive responses.

behavior therapy A treatment approach that is based on the idea that abnormal behavior is learned and that applies the principles of operant conditioning, classical conditioning, and/or observational learning to eliminate inappropriate or maladaptive behaviors and replace them with more adaptive responses.

behavioral genetics A field of research that uses twin studies and adoption studies to investigate the relative effects of heredity and environment on behavior.

behaviorism The school of psychology that views observable, measurable behavior as the appropriate subject matter for psychology and emphasizes the key role of environment as a determinant of behavior.

beta wave (BAY-tuh) The brain-wave pattern associated with mental or physical activity.

binocular depth cues Depth cues that depend on both eyes working together.

biofeedback The use of sensitive equipment to give people precise feedback about internal physiological processes so that they can learn, with practice, to exercise control over them.

biological psychology The school of psychology that looks for links between specific behaviors and equally specific biological processes that often help explain individual differences.

biological therapy A therapy (drug therapy, electroconvulsive therapy, or psychosurgery) that is based on the assumption that psychological disorders are symptoms of underlying physical problems.

biomedical model A perspective that explains illness solely in terms of biological factors.

biopsychosocial model A perspective that focuses on health as well as illness and holds that both are determined by a combination of biological, psychological, and social factors.

bipolar disorder A mood disorder in which manic episodes alternate with periods of depression, usually with relatively normal periods in between.

blind spot The point in each retina where there are no rods or cones because the cable of ganglion cells is extending through the retinal wall.

body mass index (BMI) A measure of weight relative to height.

bottom-up processing Information processing in which individual components or bits of data are combined until a complete perception is formed.

brainstem The structure that begins at the point where the spinal cord enlarges as it enters the brain and handles functions critical to physical survival. It includes the medulla, the pons, and the reticular formation.

brightness The dimension of visual sensation that is dependent on the intensity of light reflected from a surface and that corresponds to the amplitude (height) of the light wave.

Broca's aphasia (BRO-kuz uh-FAY-zyah) An impairment in the physical ability to produce speech sounds or, in extreme cases, an inability to speak at all; caused by damage to Broca's area.

Broca's area (BRO-kuz) The area in the frontal lobe, usually in the left hemisphere, that controls the production of speech sounds.

bulimia nervosa An eating disorder characterized by repeated and uncontrolled (and often secretive) episodes of binge eating.

bystander effect A social factor that affects prosocial behavior: As the number of bystanders at an emergency increases, the probability that the victim will receive help decreases, and the help, if given, is likely to be delayed.

California Personality Inventory (CPI) A highly regarded personality test developed especially for normal individuals aged 13 and older.

Cannon-Bard theory The theory that an emotion-provoking stimulus is transmitted simultaneously to the cerebral cortex, providing the conscious mental experience of the emotion, and to the sympathetic nervous system, causing the physiological arousal.

case study A descriptive research method in which a single individual or a small number of persons are studied in great depth.

catatonic schizophrenia (KAT-uh-TAHN-ik) A type of schizophrenia characterized by complete stillness or stupor or great excitement and agitation; patients may assume an unusual posture and remain in it for long periods of time.

cell body The part of a neuron that contains the nucleus and carries out the metabolic functions of the neuron.

central nervous system (CNS) The part of the nervous system comprising the brain and the spinal cord.

cerebellum (sehr-uh-BELL-um) The brain structure that helps the body execute smooth, skilled movements and regulates muscle tone and posture.

cerebral cortex (seh-REE-brul KOR-tex) The gray, convoluted covering of the cerebral hemispheres that is responsible for the higher mental processes of language, memory, and thinking.

cerebral hemispheres (seh-REE-brul) The right and left halves of the cerebrum, covered by the cerebral cortex and connected by the corpus callosum; they control movement and feeling on the opposing sides of the body.

cerebrum (seh-REE-brum) The largest structure of the human brain, consisting of the two cerebral hemispheres connected by the corpus callosum and covered by the cerebral cortex.

chromosomes Rod-shaped structures in the nuclei of body cells, which contain all the genes and carry all the genetic information necessary to make a human being.

chunking A memory strategy that involves grouping or organizing bits of information into larger units, which are easier to remember.

circadian rhythm (sur-KAY-dee-un) Within each 24-hour period, the regular fluctuation from high to low points of certain bodily functions and behaviors.

circadian theory of sleep The theory that sleep evolved to keep humans out of harm's way during the night; also known as the evolutionary theory.

classical conditioning A type of learning through which an organism learns to associate one stimulus with another.

co-action effects The impact on performance of the presence of other people engaged in the same task.

cochlea (KOK-lee-uh) The fluid-filled, snail-shaped, bony chamber in the inner ear that contains the basilar membrane and its hair cells (the sound receptors).

cognition The mental processes that are involved in acquiring, storing, retrieving, and using information and that include sensation, perception, imagery, concept formation, reasoning, decision making, problem solving, and language.

cognitive dissonance The unpleasant state that can occur when people become aware of inconsistencies between their attitudes or between their attitudes and their behavior.

cognitive map A mental representation of a spatial arrangement such as a maze.

cognitive processes (COG-nih-tiv) Mental processes such as thinking, knowing, problem solving, remembering, and forming mental representations.

cognitive psychology The school of psychology that sees humans as active participants in their environment; studies mental processes such as memory, problem solving, reasoning, decision making, perception, language, and other forms of cognition.

cognitive therapies Therapies that assume maladaptive behavior can result from irrational thoughts, beliefs, and ideas.

cognitive therapy A therapy designed by Aaron Beck to help patients stop their negative thoughts as they occur and replace them with more objective thoughts.

collective unconscious In Jung's theory, the most inaccessible layer of the unconscious, which contains the universal experiences of humankind throughout evolution.

color blindness   The inability to distinguish certain colors from one another.

compliance   Acting in accordance with the wishes, suggestions, or direct requests of other people.

compulsion   A persistent, irresistible, and irrational urge to perform an act or ritual repeatedly.

concept   A mental category used to represent a class or group of objects, people, organizations, events, situations, or relations that share common characteristics or attributes.

conditioned response (CR)   The learned response that comes to be elicited by a conditioned stimulus as a result of its repeated pairing with an unconditioned stimulus.

conditioned stimulus (CS)   A neutral stimulus that, after repeated pairing with an unconditioned stimulus, becomes associated with it and elicits a conditioned response.

conditions of worth   Conditions on which the positive regard of others rests.

cones   The light-sensitive receptor cells in the retina that enable humans to see color and fine detail in adequate light but do not function in very dim light.

confederate   A person who poses as a participant in an experiment but is actually assisting the experimenter.

conformity   Changing or adopting a behavior or an attitude in an effort to be consistent with the social norms of a group or the expectations of other people.

confounding variables   Factors or conditions other than the independent variable(s) that are not equivalent across groups and could cause differences among the groups with respect to the dependent variable.

conscious   (KON-shus) The thoughts, feelings, sensations, or memories of which a person is aware at any given moment.

consciousness   Everything of which we are aware at any given time-our thoughts, feelings, sensations, and external environment.

conservation   The concept that a given quantity of matter remains the same despite being rearranged or changed in appearance, as long as nothing is added or taken away.

consolidation   A physiological change in the brain that allows encoded information to be stored in memory.

consolidation failure   Any disruption in the consolidation process that prevents a long-term memory from forming.

control group   In an experiment, a group similar to the experimental group that is exposed to the same experimental environment but is not given the treatment; used for purposes of comparison.

conventional level   Kohlberg's second level of moral development, in which right and wrong are based on the internalized standards of others; "right" is whatever helps or is approved of by others, or whatever is consistent with the laws of society.

conversion disorder   A somatoform disorder in which a person suffers a loss of motor or sensory functioning in some part of the body; the loss has no physical cause but solves some psychological problem.

coping   Efforts through action and thought to deal with demands that are perceived as taxing or overwhelming.

cornea   (KOR-nee-uh) The tough, transparent, protective layer that covers the front of the eye and bends light rays inward through the pupil.

corpus callosum   (KOR-pus kah-LO-sum) The thick band of nerve fibers that connects the two cerebral hemispheres and makes possible the transfer of information and the synchronization of activity between the hemispheres.

correlation coefficient   A numerical value that indicates the strength and direction of the relationship between two variables; ranges from +1.00 (a perfect positive correlation) to −1.00 (a perfect negative correlation).

correlational method   A research method used to establish the degree of relationship (correlation) between two characteristics, events, or behaviors.

creativity   The ability to produce original, appropriate, and valuable ideas and/or solutions to problems.

critical period   A period so important to development that a harmful environmental influence at that time can keep a bodily structure from developing normally or can impair later intellectual or social development.

critical thinking   The process of objectively evaluating claims, propositions, and conclusions to determine whether they follow logically from the evidence presented.

cross-modal perception   A process whereby the brain integrates information from more than one sense.

crowding   The subjective judgment that there are too many people in a confined space.

crystallized intelligence   Aspects of intelligence, including verbal ability and accumulated knowledge, that tend to increase over the lifespan.

CT scan (computerized axial tomography)   A brain-scanning technique that uses a rotating, computerized X-ray tube to produce cross-sectional images of the structures of the brain.

culturally sensitive therapy   An approach to therapy in which knowledge of clients' cultural backgrounds guides the choice of therapeutic interventions.

culture-fair intelligence test   An intelligence test that uses questions that will not penalize those whose culture differs from the mainstream or dominant culture.

decay theory   The oldest theory of forgetting, which holds that memories, if not used, fade with time and ultimately disappear altogether.

decibel (dB)   (DES-ih-bel) A unit of measurement for the loudness of sounds.

decision making   The process of considering alternatives and choosing among them.

declarative memory   The subsystem within long-term memory that stores facts, information, and personal life events that can be brought to mind verbally or in the form of images and then declared or stated; also called explicit memory.

defense mechanism   A means used by the ego to defend against anxiety and to maintain self-esteem.

delta wave   The brain-wave pattern associated with slow-wave (deep) sleep. The slowest brain-wave pattern; associated with Stage 3 and Stage 4 NREM sleep.

delusion   A false belief, not generally shared by others in the culture.

delusion of grandeur   A false belief that one is a famous person or a powerful or important person who has some great knowledge, ability, or authority.

delusion of persecution   A false belief that some person or agency is trying in some way to harm one.

dementia   A state of mental deterioration characterized by impaired memory and intellect and by altered personality and behavior.

dendrites   (DEN-drytes) In a neuron, the branchlike extensions of the cell body that receive signals from other neurons.

dependent variable   The factor or condition that is measured at the end of an experiment and is presumed to vary as a result of the manipulations of the independent variable(s).

depressants   A category of drugs that decrease activity in the central nervous system, slow down bodily functions, and reduce sensitivity to outside stimulation; also called "downers."

depth perception   The ability to perceive the visual world in three dimensions and to judge distances accurately.

descriptive research methods   Research methods that yield descriptions of behavior.

developmental psychology   The study of how humans grow, develop, and change throughout the lifespan.

difference threshold   A measure of the smallest increase or decrease in a physical stimulus that is required to produce a difference in sensation that is noticeable 50% of the time.

diffusion of responsibility   The feeling among bystanders at an emergency that the responsibility for helping is shared by the group, making each person feel less compelled to act than if he or she alone bore the total responsibility.

directive therapy   Any type of psychotherapy in which the therapist takes an active role in determining the course of therapy sessions and provides answers and suggestions to the patient; an example is Gestalt therapy.

discrimination   Behavior (usually negative) directed toward others based on their gender, religion, race, or membership in a particular group. The learned ability to distinguish between similar stimuli so that the conditioned response occurs only to the original conditioned stimulus but not to similar stimuli.

discriminative stimulus   A stimulus that signals whether a certain response or behavior is likely to be rewarded, ignored, or punished.

disinhibitory effect   Displaying a previously suppressed behavior because a model does so without receiving punishment.

disorganized schizophrenia   The most serious type of schizophrenia, marked by extreme social withdrawal, hallucinations, delusions, silliness, inappropriate laughter, grotesque mannerisms, and other bizarre behavior.

displacement   The event that occurs when short-term memory is filled to capacity and each new, incoming item pushes out an existing item, which is then forgotten.

display rules   Cultural rules that dictate how emotions should generally be expressed and when and where their expression is appropriate.

dispositional attribution   Attributing a behavior to some internal cause, such as a personal trait, motive, or attitude; an internal attribution.

dissociative amnesia   A dissociative disorder in which there is a complete or partial loss of the ability to recall personal information or identify past experiences.

dissociative disorders   Disorders in which, under unbearable stress, consciousness becomes dissociated from a person's identity or her or his memories of important personal events, or both.

dissociative fugue   (FEWG) A dissociative disorder in which one has a complete loss of memory of one's entire identity, travels away from home, and may assume a new identity.

dissociative identity disorder (DID)   A dissociative disorder in which two or more distinct, unique personalities occur in the same person, and there is severe memory disruption concerning personal information about the other personalities.

divergent thinking   The ability to produce multiple ideas, answers, or solutions to a problem for which there is no agreed-on solution.

dominant-recessive pattern   A set of inheritance rules in which the presence of a single dominant gene causes a trait to be expressed but two genes must be present for the expression of a recessive trait.

door-in-the-face technique   A strategy in which someone makes a large, unreasonable request with the expectation that the person will refuse but will then be more likely to respond favorably to a smaller request later.

dopamine   (DOE-pah-meen) A neurotransmitter that plays a role in learning, attention, movement, and reinforcement.

double-blind technique   A procedure in which neither the participants nor the experimenter knows who is in the experimental and control groups until after the data have been gathered; a control for experimenter bias.

drive   An internal state of tension or arousal that is brought about by an underlying need and that an organism is motivated to reduce.

drive-reduction theory   A theory of motivation suggesting that biological needs create internal states of tension or arousal—called drives—which organisms are motivated to reduce.

drug tolerance   A condition in which the user becomes progressively less affected by the drug and must take increasingly larger doses to maintain the same effect or high.

DSM-IV   *Diagnostic and Statistical Manual of Mental Disorders*, 4th edition, a manual published by the American Psychiatric Association, which describes the criteria used to classify and diagnose mental disorders.

ego (EE-go) In Freud's theory, the logical, rational, largely conscious system of personality, which operates according to the reality principle.

elaborative rehearsal A memory strategy that involves relating new information to something that is already known.

electroconvulsive therapy (ECT) A biological therapy in which an electric current is passed through the right hemisphere of the brain; usually reserved for severely depressed patients who are suicidal.

electroencephalogram (EEG) (ee-lek-tro-en-SEFF-uh-lo-gram) A record of brain-wave activity made by a machine called the electroencephalograph.

elicitation effect Exhibiting a behavior similar to that shown by a model in an unfamiliar situation.

elimination by aspects A decision-making approach in which alternatives are evaluated against criteria that have been ranked according to importance.

embryo The developing human organism during the period (week 3 through week 8) when the major systems, organs, and structures of the body develop.

emotion An identifiable feeling state involving physiological arousal, a cognitive appraisal of the situation or stimulus causing that internal body state, and an outward behavior expressing the state.

emotional intelligence The ability to apply knowledge about emotions to everyday life.

emotion-focused coping A response involving reappraisal of a stressor to reduce its emotional impact.

encoding The process of transforming information into a form that can be stored in memory.

encoding failure A cause of forgetting that occurs when information was never put into long-term memory.

endocrine system (EN-duh-krin) A system of ductless glands in various parts of the body that manufacture hormones and secrete them into the bloodstream, thus affecting cells in other parts of the body.

endorphins (en-DOR-fins) The body's own natural painkillers, which block pain and produce a feeling of well-being. Chemicals produced naturally by the brain that reduce pain and the stress of vigorous exercise and positively affect mood.

epinephrine (EP-ih-NEF-rin) A neurotransmitter that affects the metabolism of glucose and nutrient energy stored in muscles to be released during strenuous exercise.

episodic memory (ep-ih-SOD-ik) The type of declarative memory that records events as they have been subjectively experienced.

ethnocentrism The tendency to look at situations from one's own racial or cultural perspective.

evolutionary psychology The school of psychology that studies how humans have adapted the behaviors required for survival in the face of environmental pressures over the long course of evolution.

exemplars The individual instances, or examples, of a concept that are stored in memory from personal experience.

exhaustion stage The third stage of the general adaptation syndrome, which occurs if the organism fails in its efforts to resist the stressor.

experimental group In an experiment, the group that is exposed to an independent variable.

experimental method The only research method that can be used to identify cause-effect relationships between two or more conditions or variables.

experimenter bias A phenomenon that occurs when a researcher's preconceived notions or expectations in some way influence participants' behavior and/or the researcher's interpretation of experimental results.

expert systems Computer programs designed to carry out highly specific functions within a limited domain.

exposure and response prevention A behavior therapy that exposes patients with obsessive-compulsive disorder to stimuli that trigger obsessions and compulsive rituals, while patients resist performing the compulsive rituals for progressively longer periods of time.

extinction In classical conditioning, the weakening and eventual disappearance of the conditioned response as a result of repeated presentation of the conditioned stimulus without the unconditioned stimulus. In operant conditioning, the weakening and eventual disappearance of the conditioned response as a result of the withholding of reinforcement.

extrasensory perception (ESP) Gaining information about objects, events, or another person's thoughts through some means other than the known sensory channels.

extrinsic motivation The desire to behave in a certain way to gain some external reward or to avoid some undesirable consequence.

facial-feedback hypothesis The idea that the muscular movements involved in certain facial expressions produce the corresponding emotions (for example, smiling makes one feel happy).

family therapy Therapy involving an entire family, with the goal of helping family members reach agreement on changes that will help heal the family unit, improve communication problems, and create more understanding and harmony within the group.

feature detectors Neurons in the brain that respond only to specific visual patterns (for example, to lines or angles).

fetal alcohol syndrome A condition, caused by maternal alcohol intake during pregnancy, in which the baby is born mentally retarded, with a small head and facial, organ, and behavioral abnormalities.

fetus The developing human organism during the period (week 9 until birth) when rapid growth and further development of the structures, organs, and systems of the body occur.

fight-or-flight response A response to stress in which the sympathetic nervous system and the endocrine glands prepare the body to fight or flee.

five-factor theory A trait theory that attempts to explain personality using five broad dimensions, each of which is composed of a constellation of personality traits.

fixation Arrested development at a psychosexual stage occurring because of excessive gratification or frustration at that stage.

fixed-interval schedule A schedule in which a reinforcer is given following the first correct response after a specific period of time has elapsed.

fixed-ratio schedule A schedule in which a reinforcer is given after a fixed number of correct, nonreinforced responses.

flashbulb memory An extremely vivid memory of the conditions surrounding one's first hearing the news of a surprising, shocking, or highly emotional event.

flooding A behavior therapy based on classical conditioning and used to treat phobias by exposing clients to the feared object or event (or asking them to imagine it vividly) for an extended period, until their anxiety decreases.

fluid intelligence Aspects of intelligence involving abstract reasoning and mental flexibility, which peak in the early 20s and decline slowly as people age.

foot-in-the-door technique A strategy designed to gain a favorable response to a small request at first, with the intent of making the person more likely to agree later to a larger request.

formal concept A concept that is clearly defined by a set of rules, a formal definition, or a classification system; also known as an artificial concept.

fovea (FO-vee-uh) A small area at the center of the retina that provides the clearest and sharpest vision because it has the largest concentration of cones.

framing The way information is presented so as to emphasize either a potential gain or a potential loss as the outcome.

free association A psychoanalytic technique used to explore the unconscious by having patients reveal whatever thoughts, feelings, or images come to mind.

frequency The number of cycles completed by a sound wave in one second, determining the pitch of the sound; expressed in the unit called the hertz.

frequency theory The theory of hearing that holds that hair cell receptors vibrate the same number of times per second as the sounds that reach them.

frontal lobes The largest of the brain's lobes, which contain the motor cortex, Broca's area, and the frontal association areas.

frustration-aggression hypothesis The hypothesis that frustration produces aggression.

functional fixedness The failure to use familiar objects in novel ways to solve problems because of a tendency to view objects only in terms of their customary functions.

functional MRI (fMRI) A brain-imaging technique that reveals both brain structure and brain activity more precisely and rapidly than PET.

functionalism An early school of psychology that was concerned with how humans and animals use mental processes in adapting to their environment.

_g_ factor Spearman's term for a general intellectual ability that underlies all mental operations to some degree.

GABA Primary inhibitory neurotransmitter in the brain.

gender identity disorder Sexual disorder characterized by a problem accepting one's identity as male or female.

gender roles Cultural expectations about the behavior appropriate for each gender.

gender-sensitive therapy An approach to therapy that takes into account the effects of gender on both the therapist's and the client's behavior.

general adaptation syndrome (GAS) The predictable sequence of reactions (alarm, resistance, and exhaustion stages) that organisms show in response to stressors.

generalization In classical conditioning, the tendency to make a conditioned response to a stimulus that is similar to the original conditioned stimulus. In operant conditioning, the tendency to make the learned response to a stimulus similar to that for which the response was originally reinforced.

generalized anxiety disorder An anxiety disorder in which people experience chronic, excessive worry for 6 months or more.

genes The segments of DNA that are located on the chromosomes and are the basic units for the transmission of all hereditary traits.

Gestalt (geh-SHTALT) A German word that roughly refers to the whole form, pattern, or configuration that a person perceives.

Gestalt psychology The school of psychology that emphasizes that individuals perceive objects and patterns as whole units and that the perceived whole is more than the sum of its parts.

Gestalt therapy A therapy that was originated by Fritz Perls and that emphasizes the importance of clients' fully experiencing, in the present moment, their feelings, thoughts, and actions and then taking responsibility for them.

glial cells (GLEE-ul) Specialized cells in the brain and spinal cord that support neurons, remove waste products such as dead neurons, and perform other manufacturing, nourishing, and cleanup tasks.

glutamate (GLOO-tah-mate) Primary excitatory neurotransmitter in the brain.

goal orientation theory The view that achievement motivation depends on which of four goal orientations (mastery-approach, mastery-avoidance, performance-approach, performance-avoidance) an individual adopts.

gonads The ovaries in females and the testes in males; endocrine glands that produce sex hormones.

group therapy A form of therapy in which several clients (usually 7 to 10) meet regularly with one or more therapists to resolve personal problems.

groupthink The tendency for members of a tightly knit group to be more concerned with preserving group solidarity and uniformity than with objectively evaluating all alternatives in decision making.

gustation The sense of taste.

hair cells Sensory receptors for hearing that are attached to the basilar membrane in the cochlea.

hallucination   An imaginary sensation.

hallucinogens   (hal-LU-sin-o-jenz) A category of drugs that can alter and distort perceptions of time and space, alter mood, produce feelings of unreality, and cause hallucinations; also called *psychedelics*.

halo effect   The tendency to assume that a person has generally positive or negative traits as a result of observing one major positive or negative trait.

hardiness   A combination of three psychological qualities—commitment, control, and challenge—shared by people who can handle high levels of stress and remain healthy.

hassles   Little stressors, including the irritating demands that can occur daily, that may cause more stress than major life changes do.

health psychology   The subfield within psychology that is concerned with the psychological factors that contribute to health, illness, and recovery.

heritability   An index of the degree to which a characteristic is estimated to be influenced by heredity.

heuristic   (yur-RIS-tik) A rule of thumb that is derived from experience and used in decision making and problem solving, even though there is no guarantee of its accuracy or usefulness.

higher-order conditioning   Conditioning that occurs when conditioned stimuli are linked together to form a series of signals.

hippocampal region   A part of the limbic system, which includes the hippocampus itself and the underlying cortical areas, involved in the formation of semantic memories.

hippocampus   (hip-po-CAM-pus) A structure in the limbic system that plays a central role in the storing of new memories, the response to new or unexpected stimuli, and navigational ability.

homeostasis   The natural tendency of the body to maintain a balanced internal state in an effort to ensure physical survival.

hormone   A chemical substance that is manufactured and released in one part of the body and affects other parts of the body.

hue   The dimension of light that refers to the specific color perceived.

human immunodeficiency virus (HIV)   The virus that causes AIDS.

humanistic psychology   The school of psychology that focuses on the uniqueness of human beings and their capacity for choice, growth, and psychological health.

humanistic therapies   Psychotherapies that assume that people have the ability and freedom to lead rational lives and make rational choices.

hypnosis   A procedure through which one person, the hypnotist, uses the power of suggestion to induce changes in thoughts, feelings, sensations, perceptions, or behavior in another person, the subject.

hypochondriasis   (HI-poh-kahn-DRY-uh-sis) A somatoform disorder in which persons are preoccupied with their health and fear that their physical symptoms are a sign of some serious disease, despite reassurance from doctors to the contrary.

hypothalamus   (HY-po-THAL-uh-mus) A small but influential brain structure that regulates hunger, thirst, sexual behavior, internal body temperature, other body functions, and a wide variety of emotional behaviors.

hypothesis   A testable prediction about the conditions under which a particular behavior or mental process may occur.

hypothetico-deductive thinking   The ability to base logical reasoning on a hypothetical premise.

id   (ID) The unconscious system of the personality, which contains the life and death instincts and operates on the pleasure principle; source of the libido.

illusion   A false perception or a misperception of an actual stimulus in the environment.

imagery   The representation in the mind of a sensory experience—visual, auditory, gustatory, motor, olfactory, or tactile.

imaginary audience   A belief of adolescents that they are or will be the focus of attention in social situations and that others will be as critical or approving as they are of themselves.

inattentional blindness   The phenomenon in which we shift our focus from one object to another and, in the process, fail to notice changes in objects to which we are not directly paying attention.

incentive   An external stimulus that motivates behavior (for example, money or fame).

inclusion   Educating mentally retarded students in regular rather than special schools by placing them in regular classes for part of the day or having special classrooms in regular schools; also called *mainstreaming*.

independent variable   In an experiment, a factor or condition that is deliberately manipulated to determine whether it causes any change in another behavior or condition.

individualism/ collectivism dimension   A measure of a culture's emphasis on either individual achievement or social relationships.

infantile amnesia   The relative inability of older children and adults to recall events from the first few years of life.

information-processing theory   An approach to the study of mental structures and processes that uses the computer as a model for human thinking.

in-group   A social group with a strong sense of togetherness, from which others are excluded.

inhibitory effect   Suppressing a behavior because a model is punished for displaying the behavior.

inner ear   The innermost portion of the ear, containing the cochlea, the vestibular sacs, and the semicircular canals.

insight   The sudden realization of the relationship between elements in a problem situation, which makes the solution apparent.

insight therapies   Approaches to psychotherapy based on the notion that psychological well-being depends on self-understanding.

insomnia A sleep disorder characterized by difficulty falling or staying asleep, by waking too early, or by sleep that is light, restless, or of poor quality.

intelligence An individual's ability to understand complex ideas, to adapt effectively to the environment, to learn from experience, to engage in various forms of reasoning, and to overcome obstacles through mental effort.

intelligence quotient (IQ) An index of intelligence, originally derived by dividing mental age by chronological age and then multiplying by 100, but now derived by comparing an individual's score with the scores of others of the same age.

interference A cause of forgetting that occurs because information or associations stored either before or after a given memory hinder the ability to remember it.

interpersonal therapy (IPT) A brief psychotherapy designed to help depressed people better understand and cope with problems relating to their interpersonal relationships.

intrinsic motivation The desire to behave in a certain way because it is enjoyable or satisfying in and of itself.

intuition Rapidly formed judgments based on "gut feelings" or "instincts."

inventory A paper-and-pencil test with questions about a person's thoughts, feelings, and behaviors, which measures several dimensions of personality and can be scored according to a standard procedure.

James-Lange theory The theory that emotional feelings result when an individual becomes aware of a physiological response to an emotion-provoking stimulus (for example, feeling fear because of trembling).

just noticeable difference (JND) The smallest change in sensation that a person is able to detect 50% of the time.

kinesthetic sense The sense providing information about the position of body parts in relation to each other and the movement of the entire body or its parts.

laboratory observation A descriptive research method in which behavior is studied in a laboratory setting.

language A means of communicating thoughts and feelings, using a system of socially shared but arbitrary symbols (sounds, signs, or written symbols) arranged according to rules of grammar.

latent content Freud's term for the underlying meaning of a dream.

latent learning Learning that occurs without apparent reinforcement and is not demonstrated until the organism is motivated to do so.

lateral hypothalamus (LH) The part of the hypothalamus that acts as a feeding center to incite eating.

lateralization The specialization of one of the cerebral hemispheres to handle a particular function.

law of effect One of Thorndike's laws of learning, which states that the consequence, or effect, of a response will determine whether the tendency to respond in the same way in the future will be strengthened or weakened.

Lazarus theory The theory that a cognitive appraisal is the first step in an emotional response and all other aspects of an emotion, including physiological arousal, depend on it.

learned helplessness A passive resignation to aversive conditions that is learned through repeated exposure to inescapable or unavoidable aversive events.

learning A relatively permanent change in behavior, knowledge, capability, or attitude that is acquired through experience and cannot be attributed to illness, injury, or maturation.

left hemisphere The hemisphere that controls the right side of the body, coordinates complex movements, and, in most people, handles most of the language functions.

lens The transparent disk-shaped structure behind the iris and the pupil that changes shape as it focuses on objects at varying distances.

limbic system A group of structures in the brain, including the amygdala and hippocampus, that are collectively involved in emotional expression, memory, and motivation.

linguistic relativity hypothesis The notion that the language a person speaks largely determines the nature of that person's thoughts.

lithium A drug used to treat bipolar disorder, which at proper maintenance dosage reduces both manic and depressive episodes.

locus of control Rotter's concept of a cognitive factor that explains how people account for what happens in their lives—either seeing themselves as primarily in control of their behavior and its consequences (internal locus of control) or perceiving what happens to them to be in the hands of fate, luck, or chance (external locus of control).

long-term memory (LTM) The memory system with a virtually unlimited capacity that contains vast stores of a person's permanent or relatively permanent memories.

long-term potentiation (LTP) An increase in the efficiency of neural transmission at the synapses that lasts for hours or longer.

low-ball technique A strategy in which someone makes a very attractive initial offer to get a person to commit to an action and then makes the terms less favorable.

low-birth-weight baby A baby weighing less than 5.5 pounds.

lucid dream A dream that an individual is aware of dreaming and whose content the individual is often able to influence while the dream is in progress.

lymphocytes The white blood cells—including B cells and T cells—that are the key components of the immune system.

maintenance rehearsal Repeating information over and over again until it is no longer needed; may eventually lead to storage of information in long-term memory.

major depressive disorder A mood disorder marked by feelings of great sadness, despair, and hopelessness as well as the loss of the ability to experience pleasure.

manic episode (MAN-ik) A period of excessive euphoria, inflated self-esteem, wild optimism, and hyperactivity, often accompanied by delusions of grandeur and by hostility if activity is blocked.

manifest content Freud's term for the content of a dream as recalled by the dreamer.

massed practice Learning in one long practice session without rest periods.

matching hypothesis The notion that people tend to have lovers or spouses who are similar to themselves in physical attractiveness and other assets.

maturation Changes that occur according to one's genetically determined biological timetable of development.

means–end analysis A heuristic strategy in which the current position is compared with the desired goal and a series of steps are formulated and taken to close the gap between them.

meditation (concentrative) A group of techniques that involve focusing attention on an object, a word, one's breathing, or one's body movements in an effort to block out all distractions, to enhance well-being, and to achieve an altered state of consciousness.

medulla (muh-DUL-uh) The part of the brainstem that controls heartbeat, blood pressure, breathing, coughing, and swallowing.

memory The process of encoding, storage, consolidation, and retrieval of information.

menarche (men-AR-kee) The onset of menstruation.

menopause The cessation of menstruation, occurring between ages 45 and 55 and signifying the end of reproductive capacity.

mental set The tendency to apply a familiar strategy to the solution of a problem without carefully considering the special requirements of that problem.

mentally retarded Subnormal intelligence reflected by an IQ below 70 and by adaptive functioning severely deficient for one's age.

mere-exposure effect The tendency to feel more positively toward a stimulus as a result of repeated exposure to it.

metabolic rate (meh-tuh-BALL-ik) The rate at which the body burns calories to produce energy.

microelectrode A small wire used to monitor the electrical activity of or stimulate activity within a single neuron.

middle ear The portion of the ear containing the ossicles, which connect the eardrum to the oval window and amplify sound waves.

Minnesota Multiphasic Personality Inventory (MMPI) The most extensively researched and widely used personality test, which is used to screen for and diagnose psychiatric problems and disorders; revised as MMPI-2.

model The individual who demonstrates a behavior or whose behavior is imitated.

modeling Another name for observational learning.

modeling effect Learning a new behavior from a model through the acquisition of new responses.

monocular depth cues (mah-NOK-yu-ler) Depth cues that can be perceived by one eye alone.

mood disorders Disorders characterized by extreme and unwarranted disturbances in emotion or mood.

morphemes The smallest units of meaning in a language.

motivated forgetting Forgetting through suppression or repression in an effort to protect oneself from material that is painful, frightening, or otherwise unpleasant.

motivation All the processes that initiate, direct, and sustain behavior.

motives Needs or desires that energize and direct behavior toward a goal.

motor cortex The strip of tissue at the rear of the frontal lobes that controls voluntary body movement and participates in learning and cognitive events.

MRI (magnetic resonance imagery) A diagnostic scanning technique that produces high-resolution images of the structures of the brain.

multifactorial inheritance A pattern of inheritance in which a trait is influenced by both genes and environmental factors.

myelin sheath (MY-uh-lin) The white, fatty coating wrapped around some axons that acts as insulation and enables impulses to travel much faster.

Myers-Briggs Type Indicator (MBTI) A personality inventory useful for measuring normal individual differences; based on Jung's theory of personality.

naive idealism A type of thought in which adolescents construct ideal solutions for problems.

naive subject A person who has agreed to participate in an experiment but is not aware that deception is being used to conceal its real purpose.

narcolepsy An incurable sleep disorder characterized by excessive daytime sleepiness and uncontrollable attacks of REM sleep.

narcotics A class of depressant drugs derived from the opium poppy that produce both pain-relieving and calming effects.

natural concept A concept acquired not from a definition but through everyday perceptions and experiences; also known as a fuzzy concept.

naturalistic observation A descriptive research method in which researchers observe and record behavior in its natural setting, without attempting to influence or control it.

nature–nurture controversy The debate over whether intelligence and other traits are primarily the result of heredity or environment.

need for achievement (*n* Ach) The need to accomplish something difficult and to perform at a high standard of excellence.

negative reinforcement The termination of an unpleasant condition after a response, which increases the probability that the response will be repeated.

neodissociation theory of hypnosis A theory proposing that hypnosis induces a split, or dissociation, between two aspects of the control of consciousness: the planning function and the monitoring function.

neonate A newborn infant up to 1 month old.

neuron (NEW-ron) A specialized cell that conducts impulses through the nervous system and contains three major parts—a cell body, dendrites, and an axon.

neuroscience An interdisciplinary field that combines the work of psychologists, biologists, biochemists, medical researchers, and others in the study of the structure and function of the nervous system.

neurotransmitter (NEW-ro-TRANS-mit-er) A chemical substance that is released into the synaptic cleft from the axon terminal of a sending neuron, crosses a synapse, and binds to appropriate receptor sites on the dendrites or cell body of a receiving neuron, influencing the cell either to fire or not to fire.

nondeclarative memory The subsystem within long-term memory that stores motor skills, habits, and simple classically conditioned responses; also called implicit memory.

nondirective therapy Any type of psychotherapy in which the therapist allows the direction of the therapy sessions to be controlled by the client; an example is person-centered therapy.

norepinephrine (nor-EP-ih-NEF-rin) A neurotransmitter affecting eating, alertness, and sleep.

norms Standards based on the range of test scores of a large group of people who are selected to provide the bases of comparison for those who take the test later.

NREM dream A type of dream occurring during NREM sleep that is typically less frequent and memorable than REM dreams are.

NREM sleep Non–rapid eye movement sleep, which consists of four sleep stages and is characterized by slow, regular respiration and heart rate, little body movement, an absence of rapid eye movements, and blood pressure and brain activity that are at their 24-hour low points.

obesity BMI over 30.

object permanence The realization that objects continue to exist, even when they can no longer be perceived.

observational learning Learning by observing the behavior of others and the consequences of that behavior; learning by imitation.

obsession A persistent, involuntary thought, image, or impulse that invades consciousness and causes great distress.

obsessive-compulsive disorder (OCD) An anxiety disorder in which a person suffers from recurrent obsessions and/or compulsions.

occipital lobes (ahk-SIP-uh-tul) The lobes that are involved in the reception and interpretation of visual information; they contain the primary visual cortex.

Oedipus complex (ED-uh-pus) Occurring in the phallic stage, a conflict in which the child is sexually attracted to the opposite-sex parent and feels hostility toward the same-sex parent.

olfaction (ol-FAK-shun) The sense of smell.

olfactory bulbs Two matchstick-sized structures above the nasal cavities, where smell sensations first register in the brain.

olfactory epithelium Two 1-square-inch patches of tissue, one at the top of each nasal cavity, which together contain about 10 million olfactory neurons, the receptors for smell.

operant A voluntary behavior that accidentally brings about a consequence.

operant conditioning A type of learning in which the consequences of behavior are manipulated so as to increase or decrease the frequency of an existing response or to shape an entirely new response.

opponent-process theory The theory of color vision suggesting that three kinds of cells respond by increasing or decreasing their rate of firing when different colors are present.

optic nerve The nerve that carries visual information from each retina to both sides of the brain.

outer ear The visible part of the ear, consisting of the pinna and the auditory canal.

out-group A social group made up of individuals specifically identified by the in-group as not belonging.

overextension The act of using a word, on the basis of some shared feature, to apply to a broader range of objects than is appropriate.

overlearning Practicing or studying material beyond the point where it can be repeated once without error.

overregularization The act of inappropriately applying the grammatical rules for forming plurals and past tenses to irregular nouns and verbs.

pancreas The endocrine gland responsible for regulating the amount of sugar in the bloodstream.

panic attack An episode of overwhelming anxiety, fear, or terror.

panic disorder An anxiety disorder in which a person experiences recurring, unpredictable episodes of overwhelming anxiety, fear, or terror.

paranoid schizophrenia (PAIR-uh-noid) A type of schizophrenia characterized by delusions of grandeur or persecution.

paraphilias Sexual disorders in which recurrent sexual urges, fantasies, or behavior involve nonhuman objects, children, other nonconsenting persons, or the suffering or humiliation of the individual or his or her partner.

parasomnias Sleep disturbances in which behaviors and physiological states that normally take place only in the waking state occur while a person is sleeping.

parasympathetic nervous system The division of the autonomic nervous system that brings the heightened bodily responses back to normal following an emergency.

parathyroid glands The endocrine glands that produce PTH, a hormone that helps the body absorb minerals from the diet.

parental investment A term used by evolutionary psychologists to denote the amount of time and effort men or women must devote to parenthood.

parietal lobes (puh-RY-uh-tul) The lobes that contain the somatosensory cortex (where touch, pressure, temperature, and pain register) and other areas that are responsible for body awareness and spatial orientation.

participant modeling A behavior therapy in which an appropriate response to a feared stimulus is modeled in graduated steps and the client attempts to imitate the model step by step, encouraged and supported by the therapist.

perception The process by which the brain actively organizes and interprets sensory information.

perceptual constancy The phenomenon that allows us to perceive objects as maintaining stable properties, such as size, shape, and brightness, despite differences in distance, viewing angle, and lighting.

perceptual set An expectation of what will be perceived, which can affect what actually is perceived.

peripheral nervous system (PNS) (peh-RIF-er-ul) The nerves connecting the central nervous system to the rest of the body.

permeability (perm-ee-uh-BIL-uh-tee) The capability of being penetrated or passed through.

permissive parents Parents who make few rules or demands and allow children to make their own decisions and control their own behavior.

personal fable An exaggerated sense of personal uniqueness and indestructibility, which may be the basis for adolescent risk taking.

personal space An area surrounding each person, much like an invisible bubble, that the person considers part of himself or herself and uses to regulate the level of intimacy with others.

personal unconscious In Jung's theory, the layer of the unconscious that contains all of the thoughts, perceptions, and experiences accessible to the conscious, as well as repressed memories, wishes, and impulses.

personality A person's characteristic patterns of behaving, thinking, and feeling.

personality disorder A long-standing, inflexible, maladaptive pattern of behaving and relating to others, which usually begins in early childhood or adolescence.

person-centered therapy A nondirective, humanistic therapy developed by Carl Rogers, in which the therapist creates an accepting climate and shows empathy, freeing clients to be themselves and releasing their natural tendency toward self-actualization.

persuasion A deliberate attempt to influence the attitudes and/or behavior of another person.

PET scan (positron-emission tomography) A brain-imaging technique that reveals activity in various parts of the brain, based on patterns of blood flow, oxygen use, and glucose consumption.

phobia (FO-bee-ah) A persistent, irrational fear of some specific object, situation, or activity that poses little or no real danger.

phonemes The smallest units of sound in a spoken language.

physical drug dependence A compulsive pattern of drug use in which the user develops a drug tolerance coupled with unpleasant withdrawal symptoms when the drug use is discontinued.

pineal gland The endocrine gland that secretes the hormone that controls the sleep/wakefulness cycle.

pituitary gland The endocrine gland located in the brain that releases hormones that activate other endocrine glands as well as growth hormone; often called the "master gland."

place theory The theory of hearing that holds that each individual pitch a person hears is determined by the particular location along the basilar membrane of the cochlea that vibrates the most.

placebo (pluh-SEE-bo) An inert or harmless substance given to the control group in an experiment as a control for the placebo effect.

placebo effect The phenomenon that occurs in an experiment when a participant's response to a treatment is due to his or her expectations about the treatment rather than to the treatment itself.

plasticity The capacity of the brain to adapt to changes such as brain damage.

population The entire group of interest to researchers, to which they wish to generalize their findings; the group from which a sample is selected.

positive reinforcement Any pleasant or desirable consequence that follows a response and increases the probability that the response will be repeated.

postconventional level Kohlberg's highest level of moral development, in which moral reasoning involves weighing moral alternatives; "right" is whatever furthers basic human rights.

posttraumatic stress disorder (PTSD) A prolonged and severe stress reaction to a catastrophic event or to severe, chronic stress.

pragmatics The patterns of intonation and social roles associated with a language.

preconscious The thoughts, feelings, and memories that a person is not consciously aware of at the moment but that may be easily brought to consciousness.

preconventional level Kohlberg's lowest level of moral development, in which moral reasoning is based on the physical consequences of an act; "right" is whatever avoids punishment or gains a reward.

prejudice Attitudes (usually negative) toward others based on their gender, religion, race, or membership in a particular group.

prenatal development Development from conception to birth.

presbyopia (prez-bee-O-pee-uh) A condition, occurring in the mid- to late 40s, in which the lenses of the eyes no longer accommodate adequately for near vision, and reading glasses or bifocals are required for reading.

preterm infant An infant born before the 37th week and weighing less than 5.5 pounds; a premature infant.

primacy effect The tendency for an overall impression of another to be influenced more by the first information that is received about that person than by information that comes later. The tendency to recall the first items in a sequence more readily than the middle items.

primary appraisal A cognitive evaluation of a potentially stressful event to determine whether its effect is positive, irrelevant, or negative.

primary auditory cortex The part of each temporal lobe where hearing registers in the cerebral cortex.

primary drives A state of tension or arousal that arises from a biological need and is unlearned.

primary mental abilities According to Thurstone, seven relatively distinct capabilities that singly or in combination are involved in all intellectual activities.

primary reinforcer A reinforcer that fulfills a basic physical need for survival and does not depend on learning.

primary visual cortex The area at the rear of the occipital lobes where vision registers in the cerebral cortex. The part of the brain in which visual information is processed.

problem solving Thoughts and actions required to achieve a desired goal that is not readily attainable.

problem-focused coping A direct response aimed at reducing, modifying, or eliminating a source of stress.

projective test A personality test in which people respond to inkblots, drawings of ambiguous human situations, or incomplete sentences by projecting their inner thoughts, feelings, fears, or conflicts onto the test materials.

prosocial behavior Behavior that benefits others, such as helping, cooperation, and sympathy.

prospective forgetting Not remembering to carry out some intended action.

prototype An example that embodies the most common and typical features of a concept.

proximity Physical or geographic closeness; a major influence on attraction.

pruning The process through which the developing brain eliminates unnecessary or redundant synapses.

psychiatrist A mental health professional who is a medical doctor.

psychoactive drug Any substance that alters mood, perception, or thought; called a controlled substance if approved for medical use.

psychoanalysis (SY-ko-ah-NAL-ih-sis) The term Freud used for both his theory of personality and his therapy for the treatment of psychological disorders; the unconscious is the primary focus of psychoanalytic theory. The first psychodynamic therapy, which was developed by Freud and uses free association, dream analysis, and transference.

psychodynamic therapies Psychotherapies that attempt to uncover repressed childhood experiences that are thought to explain a patient's current difficulties.

psycholinguistics The study of how language is acquired, produced, and used and how the sounds and symbols of language are translated into meaning.

psychological disorders Mental processes and/or behavior patterns that cause emotional distress and/or substantial impairment in functioning.

psychological drug dependence A craving or irresistible urge for a drug's pleasurable effects.

psychological perspectives General points of view used for explaining people's behavior and thinking, whether normal or abnormal.

psychologist A mental health professional who possesses a doctoral degree in psychology.

psychology The scientific study of behavior and mental processes.

psychoneuroimmunology (sye-ko-NEW-ro-IM-you-NOLL-oh-gee) A field in which psychologists, biologists, and medical researchers combine their expertise to study the effects of psychological factors on the immune system.

psychosexual stages A series of stages through which the sexual instinct develops; each stage is defined by an erogenous zone around which conflict arises.

psychosis (sy-CO-sis) A condition characterized by loss of contact with reality.

psychosocial stages Erikson's eight developmental stages for the entire lifespan; each is defined by a conflict that must be resolved satisfactorily for healthy personality development to occur.

psychosurgery Brain surgery performed to alleviate serious psychological disorders or unbearable chronic pain.

psychotherapy Any type of approach that uses psychological rather than biological means to treat psychological disorders.

puberty A period of rapid physical growth and change that culminates in sexual maturity.

punishment The removal of a pleasant stimulus or the application of an unpleasant stimulus, thereby lowering the probability of a response.

random assignment The process of selecting participants for experimental and control groups by using a chance procedure to guarantee that each participant has an equal probability of being assigned to any of the groups; a control for selection bias.

rational-emotive therapy A directive form of psychotherapy, developed by Albert Ellis and designed to challenge clients' irrational beliefs about themselves and others.

realistic conflict theory The view that as competition increases among social groups for scarce resources, so do prejudice, discrimination, and hatred.

recall A memory task in which a person must produce required information by searching memory.

recency effect The tendency to recall the last items in a sequence more readily than those in the middle.

receptors Protein molecules on the surfaces of dendrites and cell bodies that have distinctive shapes and will interact only with specific neurotransmitters.

reciprocal determinism Bandura's concept of a mutual influential relationship among behavior, cognitive factors, and environment.

recognition A memory task in which a person must simply identify material as familiar or as having been encountered before.

recognition heuristic A strategy in which decision making stops as soon as a factor that moves one toward a decision has been recognized.

reconstruction An account of an event that has been pieced together from a few highlights, using information that may or may not be accurate.

reflexes Built-in responses to certain stimuli that neonates need to ensure survival in their new world.

rehearsal The act of purposely repeating information to maintain it in short-term memory.

reinforcement Any event that follows a response and strengthens or increases the probability that the response will be repeated.

reinforcer Anything that follows a response and strengthens it or increases the probability that it will occur.

relationship therapies Therapies that attempt to improve patients' interpersonal relationships or create new relationships to support patients' efforts to address psychological problems.

relearning method A measure of memory in which retention is expressed as the percentage of time saved when material is relearned compared with the time required to learn the material originally.

reliability The ability of a test to yield nearly the same score when the same people are tested and then retested on the same test or an alternative form of the test.

REM dream A type of dream occurring almost continuously during each REM period and having a storylike quality; typically more vivid, visual, and emotional than NREM dreams.

REM rebound The increased amount of REM sleep that occurs after REM deprivation; often associated with unpleasant dreams or nightmares.

REM sleep A type of sleep characterized by rapid eye movements, paralysis of large muscles, fast and irregular heart and respiration rates, increased brain-wave activity, and vivid dreams.

replication The process of repeating a study to verify research findings.

representative sample A sample that mirrors the population of interest; it includes important subgroups in the same proportions as they are found in that population.

representative heuristic A thinking strategy based on how closely a new object or situation is judged to resemble or match an existing prototype of that object or situation.

repression Completely removing unpleasant memories from one's consciousness, so that one is no longer aware that a painful event occurred.

resistance stage The second stage of the general adaptation syndrome, when there are intense physiological efforts to either resist or adapt to the stressor.

resting potential The slight negative electrical potential of the axon membrane of a neuron at rest, about –70 millivolts.

restorative theory of sleep The theory that the function of sleep is to restore body and mind.

reticular formation A structure in the brainstem that plays a crucial role in arousal and attention and that screens sensory messages entering the brain.

retina The layer of tissue that is located on the inner surface of the eyeball and contains the sensory receptors for vision.

retrieval The process of bringing to mind information that has been stored in memory.

retrieval cue Any stimulus or bit of information that aids in retrieving particular information from long-term memory.

retrieval failure Not remembering something one is certain of knowing.

retrograde amnesia (RET-ro-grade) A loss of memory for experiences that occurred shortly before a loss of consciousness.

reuptake The process by which neurotransmitters are taken from the synaptic cleft back into the axon terminal for later use, thus terminating their excitatory or inhibitory effect on the receiving neuron.

reversibility The realization that any change in the shape, position, or order of matter can be reversed mentally.

right hemisphere The hemisphere that controls the left side of the body and, in most people, is specialized for visual-spatial perception.

rods The light-sensitive receptor cells in the retina that look like slender cylinders and allow the eye to respond to as few as five photons of light.

Rorschach Inkblot Method (ROR-shok) A projective test composed of 10 inkblots that the test taker is asked to describe; used to assess personality, make differential diagnoses, plan and evaluate treatment, and predict behavior.

sample A part of a population that is studied to reach conclusions about the entire population.

saturation The purity of a color, or the degree to which the light waves producing it are of the same wavelength.

scaffolding A type of instruction in which an adult adjusts the amount of guidance provided to match a child's present level of ability.

scapegoating Displacing aggression onto members of minority groups or other innocent targets not responsible for the frustrating situation.

Schachter-Singer theory A two-factor theory stating that for an emotion to occur, there must be (1) physiological arousal and (2) a cognitive interpretation or explanation of the arousal, allowing it to be labeled as a specific emotion.

schedule of reinforcement A systematic process for administering reinforcement.

schemas The integrated frameworks of knowledge and assumptions a person has about people, objects, and events, which affect how the person encodes and recalls information.

scheme Piaget's term for a cognitive structure or concept used to identify and interpret information.

schizophrenia (SKIT-soh-FREE-nee-ah) A severe psychological disorder characterized by loss of contact with reality, hallucinations, delusions, inappropriate or flat affect, some disturbance in thinking, social withdrawal, and/or other bizarre behavior.

scientific method The orderly, systematic procedures that researchers follow as they identify a research problem, design a study to investigate the problem, collect and analyze data, draw conclusions, and communicate their findings.

secondary appraisal A cognitive evaluation of available resources and options prior to deciding how to deal with a stressor.

secondary reinforcer A reinforcer that is acquired or learned through association with other reinforcers.

secondary sex characteristics Those physical characteristics that are not directly involved in reproduction but distinguish the mature male from the mature female.

selection bias The assignment of participants to experimental or control groups in such a way that systematic differences among the groups are present at the beginning of the experiment.

self-actualization Developing to one's fullest potential.

self-efficacy The perception a person has of his or her ability to perform competently whatever is attempted.

self-serving bias The tendency to attribute one's successes to dispositional causes and one's failures to situational causes.

semantic memory The type of declarative memory that stores general knowledge, or objective facts and information.

semantics The meaning or the study of meaning derived from morphemes, words, and sentences.

semicircular canals Three fluid-filled tubular canals in the inner ear that sense the rotation of the head.

sensation The process through which the senses pick up visual, auditory, and other sensory stimuli and transmit them to the brain.

sensory adaptation The process in which sensory receptors grow accustomed to constant, unchanging levels of stimuli over time.

sensory memory The memory system that holds information from the senses for a period of time ranging from only a fraction of a second to about 2 seconds.

sensory receptors Highly specialized cells in the sense organs that detect and respond to one type of sensory stimuli—light, sound, or odor, for example—and transduce (convert) the stimuli into neural impulses.

separation anxiety The fear and distress shown by a toddler when the parent leaves, occurring from 8 to 24 months and reaching a peak between 12 and 18 months.

serial position effect The finding that, for information learned in a sequence, recall is better for the beginning and ending items than for the middle items in the sequence.

serotonin (ser-oh-TOE-nin) A neurotransmitter that plays an important role in regulating mood, sleep, impulsivity, aggression, and appetite.

set point The weight the body normally maintains when one is trying neither to gain nor to lose weight.

sexual disorders Disorders with a sexual basis that are destructive, guilt- or anxiety-producing, compulsive, or a cause of discomfort or harm to one or both parties involved.

sexual orientation The direction of one's sexual preference—toward members of the opposite sex (heterosexuality), toward one's own sex (homosexuality), or toward both sexes (bisexuality)

sexual response cycle The four phases—excitement, plateau, orgasm, and resolution—that make up the human sexual response in both males and females, according to Masters and Johnson.

sexually transmitted diseases Infections that are spread primarily through intimate sexual contact.

shaping An operant conditioning technique that consists of gradually molding a desired behavior (response) by reinforcing any movement in the direction of the desired response, thereby gradually guiding the responses toward the ultimate goal.

short-term memory (STM) The memory system that codes information according to sound and holds about seven (from five to nine) items for less than 30 seconds without rehearsal; also called working memory.

situational attribution Attributing a behavior to some external cause or factor operating within the situation; an external attribution.

Skinner box A soundproof chamber with a device for delivering food to an animal subject; used in operant conditioning experiments.

sleep apnea A sleep disorder characterized by periods during sleep when breathing stops and the individual must awaken briefly to breathe.

sleep cycle A period of sleep lasting about 90 minutes and including one or more stages of NREM sleep, followed by REM sleep.

sleep spindles Sleep Stage 2 brain waves that feature short periods of calm interrupted by brief flashes of intense activity.

slow-wave sleep Deep sleep; associated with Stage 3 and Stage 4 sleep.

social cognition The mental processes that people use to notice, interpret, and remember information about the social world.

social facilitation Any positive or negative effect on performance that can be attributed to the presence of others, either as an audience or as co-actors.

social loafing The tendency to put forth less effort when working with others on a common task than when working alone.

social norms The attitudes and standards of behavior expected of members of a particular group.

social phobia An irrational fear and avoidance of any social or performance situation in which one might embarrass or humiliate oneself in front of others by appearing clumsy, foolish, or incompetent.

social psychology The subfield that attempts to explain how the actual, imagined, or implied presence of others influences the thoughts, feelings, and behavior of individuals.

Social Readjustment Rating Scale (SRRS) Holmes and Rahe's measure of stress, which ranks 43 life events from most to least stressful and assigns a point value to each.

social roles Socially defined behaviors considered appropriate for individuals occupying certain positions within a given group.

social support Tangible and/or emotional support provided in time of need by family members, friends, and others; the feeling of being loved, valued, and cared for by those toward whom we feel a similar obligation.

socialization The process of learning socially acceptable behaviors, attitudes, and values.

sociocognitive theory of hypnosis A theory suggesting that the behavior of a hypnotized person is a function of that person's expectations about how subjects behave under hypnosis.

sociocultural approach The view that social and cultural factors may be just as powerful as evolutionary and physiological factors in affecting behavior and mental processing and that these factors must be understood when interpreting the behavior of others.

somatoform disorders (so-MAT-uh-form) Disorders in which physical symptoms are present that are due to psychological causes rather than any known medical condition.

somatosensory cortex (so-MAT-oh-SENS-or-ee) The strip of tissue at the front of the parietal lobes where touch, pressure, temperature, and pain register in the cerebral cortex.

spaced practice Learning in short practice sessions with rest periods in between.

specific phobia A marked fear of a specific object or situation; a general label for any phobia other than agoraphobia and social phobia.

spinal cord An extension of the brain, from the base of the brain through the neck and spinal column, that transmits messages between the brain and the peripheral nervous system.

split-brain operation A surgical procedure, performed to treat severe cases of epilepsy, in which the corpus callosum is cut, separating the cerebral hemispheres.

spontaneous recovery The reappearance of an extinguished response (in a weaker form) when an organism is exposed to the original conditioned stimulus following a rest period.

SQ3R method A study method involving the following five steps: (1) survey, (2) question, (3) read, (4) recite, and (5) review.

Stage 4 sleep The deepest stage of NREM sleep, characterized by an EEG pattern of more than 50% delta waves.

standardization Establishing norms for comparing the scores of people who will take a test in the future; administering tests using a prescribed procedure.

state-dependent memory effect The tendency to recall information better if one is in the same pharmacological or psychological state as when the information was encoded.

stereotypes Widely shared beliefs about the characteristic traits, attitudes, and behaviors of members of various social groups (racial, ethnic, or religious), including the assumption that the members of such groups are usually all alike.

stimulants A category of drugs that speed up activity in the central nervous system, suppress appetite, and can cause a person to feel more awake, alert, and energetic; also called "uppers."

stimulus (STIM-yu-lus) Any event or object in the environment to which an organism responds; plural is *stimuli*.

stimulus motives Motives that cause humans and other animals to increase stimulation when the level of arousal is too low (examples are curiosity and the motive to explore).

storage The process of keeping or maintaining information in memory.

stranger anxiety A fear of strangers common in infants at about 6 months and increasing in intensity until about 12 months, and then declining in the second year.

stress The physiological and psychological response to a condition that threatens or challenges a person and requires some form of adaptation or adjustment.

stressor Any stimulus or event capable of producing physical or emotional stress.

stroke The most common cause of damage to adult brains, arising when blockage of an artery cuts off the blood supply to a particular area of the brain or when a blood vessel bursts.

structuralism The first formal school of thought in psychology, aimed at analyzing the basic elements, or structure, of conscious mental experience.

subjective night The time during a 24-hour period when the biological clock is telling a person to go to sleep.

subliminal perception The capacity to perceive and respond to stimuli that are presented below the threshold of awareness.

substance abuse Continued use of a substance after several episodes in which use of the substance has negatively affected an individual's work, education, and social relationships.

substantia nigra (sub-STAN-sha NI-gra) The structure in the midbrain that controls unconscious motor movements.

successful aging Maintaining one's physical health, mental abilities, social competence, and overall satisfaction with life as one gets older.

successive approximations A series of gradual steps, each of which is more similar to the final desired response.

superego (sue-per-EE-go) The moral system of the personality, which consists of the conscience and the ego ideal.

suprachiasmatic nucleus (SCN) A pair of tiny structures in the brain's hypothalamus that control the timing of circadian rhythms; the biological clock.

survey A descriptive research method in which researchers use interviews and/or questionnaires to gather information about the attitudes, beliefs, experiences, or behaviors of a group of people.

symbolic function The understanding that one thing—an object, a word, a drawing—can stand for another.

sympathetic nervous system   The division of the autonomic nervous system that mobilizes the body's resources during stress and emergencies, preparing the body for action.

synapse   (SIN-aps) The junction where the axon terminal of a sending neuron communicates with a receiving neuron across the synaptic cleft.

synesthesia   The capacity for responding to stimuli simultaneously with normal and unusual perceptions.

syntax   The aspect of grammar that specifies the rules for arranging and combining words to form phrases and sentences.

systematic desensitization   A behavior therapy that is based on classical conditioning and used to treat fears by training clients in deep muscle relaxation and then having them confront a graduated series of anxiety-producing situations (real or imagined) until they can remain relaxed while confronting even the most feared situation.

tactile   Pertaining to the sense of touch.

taste aversion   The intense dislike and/or avoidance of a particular food that has been associated with nausea or discomfort.

taste buds   Structures in many of the tongue's papillae that are composed of 60 to 100 receptor cells for taste.

telegraphic speech   Short sentences that follow a strict word order and contain only essential content words.

temperament   A person's behavioral style or characteristic way of responding to the environment.

temporal lobes   The lobes that are involved in the reception and interpretation of auditory information; they contain the primary auditory cortex, Wernicke's area, and the temporal association areas.

teratogens   Harmful agents in the prenatal environment, which can have a negative impact on prenatal development or even cause birth defects.

thalamus   (THAL-uh-mus) The structure, located above the brainstem, that acts as a relay station for information flowing into or out of the forebrain.

Thematic Apperception Test (TAT)   A projective test consisting of drawings of ambiguous human situations, which the test taker describes; thought to reveal inner feelings, conflicts, and motives, which are projected onto the test materials.

theory   A general principle or set of principles proposed to explain how a number of separate facts are related.

theory of dissociated control   The theory that hypnosis is an authentic altered state of consciousness in which the control the executive function exerts over other subsystems of consciousness is weakened.

thymus gland   The endocrine gland that produces hormones that are essential to immune system functioning.

timbre   (TAM-burr) The distinctive quality of a sound that distinguishes it from other sounds of the same pitch and loudness.

time out   A behavior modification technique used to eliminate undesirable behavior, especially in children and adolescents, by withdrawing all reinforcers for a period of time.

token economy   A behavior modification technique that motivates and rewards appropriate behavior with tokens that can be exchanged later for desired goods or privileges.

top-down processing   Information processing in which previous experience and conceptual knowledge are applied to recognize the whole of a perception and thus easily identify the simpler elements of that whole.

trait   A personal characteristic that is stable across situations and is used to describe or explain personality.

transduction   The process through which sensory receptors convert the sensory stimulation into neural impulses.

transference   An emotional reaction that occurs during psychoanalysis, in which the patient displays feelings and attitudes toward the analyst that were present in another significant relationship.

triarchic theory of intelligence   Sternberg's theory that there are three types of intelligence: componential (analytical), experiential (creative), and contextual (practical).

trichromatic theory   The theory of color vision suggesting that three types of cones in the retina each make a maximal chemical response to one of three colors—blue, green, or red.

Type A behavior pattern   A behavior pattern marked by a sense of time urgency, impatience, excessive competitiveness, hostility, and anger; considered a risk factor in coronary heart disease.

Type B behavior pattern   A behavior pattern marked by a relaxed, easygoing approach to life, without the time urgency, impatience, and hostility of the Type A pattern.

unconditional positive regard   Unqualified caring and nonjudgmental acceptance of another.

unconditioned response (UR)   A response that is elicited by an unconditioned stimulus without prior learning.

unconditioned stimulus (US)   A stimulus that elicits a specific unconditioned response without prior learning.

unconscious   (un-KON-shus) For Freud, the primary motivating force of human behavior, containing repressed memories as well as instincts, wishes, and desires that have never been conscious.

underextension   Restricting the use of a word to only a few, rather than to all, members of a class of objects.

undifferentiated schizophrenia   A catchall term used when schizophrenic symptoms either do not conform to the criteria of any one type of schizophrenia or conform to more than one type.

uplifts   The positive experiences in life, which may neutralize the effects of many hassles.

validity   The ability of a test to measure what it is intended to measure.

variable   Any condition or factor that can be manipulated, controlled, or measured.

variable-interval schedule   A schedule in which a reinforcer is given after the first correct response that follows a varying time of nonreinforcement, based on an average time.

variable-ratio schedule   A schedule in which a reinforcer is given after a varying number of nonreinforced responses, based on an average ratio.

ventromedial hypothalamus (VMH) The part of the hypothalamus that acts as a satiety (fullness) center to inhibit eating.

vestibular sense (ves-TIB-yu-ler) The sense that detects movement and provides information about the body's orientation in space.

viral STDs Sexually transmitted diseases that are caused by viruses and are considered to be incurable.

visible spectrum The narrow band of electromagnetic waves that are visible to the human eye.

visual cliff An apparatus used to test depth perception in infants and young animals.

wavelength A measure of the distance from the peak of a light wave to the peak of the next.

Weber's law The law stating that the just noticeable difference (JND) for all the senses depends on a proportion or percentage of change in a stimulus rather than on a fixed amount of change.

Wernicke's aphasia (VUR-nih-keys) Aphasia that results from damage to Wernicke's area and in which the person's speech is fluent and clearly articulated but does not make sense to listeners.

Wernicke's area The language area in the left temporal lobe involved in comprehending the spoken word and in formulating coherent speech and written language.

withdrawal symptoms The physical and psychological symptoms (usually the exact opposite of the effects produced by the drug) that occur when a regularly used drug is discontinued and that terminate when the drug is taken again.

working backward A heuristic strategy in which a person discovers the steps needed to solve a problem by defining the desired goal and working backward to the current condition; also called *backward search*.

Yerkes-Dodson law The principle that performance on tasks is best when the arousal level is appropriate to the difficulty of the task: higher arousal for simple tasks, moderate arousal for tasks of moderate difficulty, and lower arousal for complex tasks.

zone of proximal development A range of cognitive tasks that a child cannot yet do but can learn to do through the guidance of an older child or adult.

zygote Cell that results from the union of a sperm and an ovum.

Name Index

Abeles, N., 264
Abell, S., 348
Abraham, H., 127
Abrams, D., 431
Acklin, M. W., 359
Adam, M., 205
Adams, J. H., 45
Adams, M. J., 186
Adams, R. J., 249
Addi-Raccah, Q., 261
Addis, M., 407, 415, 416
Ader, D. N., 19
Adesman, A., 63
Adler, A., 9, 253, 345
Adler, R., 261, 322
Agras, W. S., 407
Ainsworth, M. D. S., 253, 417
Åkerstedt, T., 110
Akse, J., 344
Al'absi, M., 184
Albrecht, K., 312, 313
Alexander, G. E., 264
Alleman, J., 417
Allen, B. P., 358
Allen, G., 44
Allen, K. W., 404
Allport, G., 349, 446
Alpert, G. W., 330
Alsaker, F. D., 258
Altarriba, J., 415
Altermatt, E., 223
Aluja, A., 350
Amato, S., 248
American Cancer Society, 370
American Medical Association, 179
American Psychiatric Association, 117, 179, 264, 326, 377, 379
American Psychological Association, 179, 415
Amirkhan, J. H., 427
Amundsen, A., 327
Andersen, B. L., 297
Anderson, C. A., 159, 442, 444
Anderson, J., 437
Anderson, K. B., 442
Anderson, L. P., 157
Anderson, R., 380
Andreasen, N. C., 46, 127, 408
Andrews, G., 417
Anglin, J., 254
Anokhin, A., 327
Anstey, K., 263
Apgar, V., 249
Apkarian, A. V., 49

Aram, D., 255
Archer, J., 22, 442
Arehart-Treichel, J., 387–388
Aristotle, 5
Armstrong, M., 125
Aronson, E., 436, 448
Aronson, J., 222
Arushanyan, E., 124
Asch, Solomon, 430–431
Assefi, S., 126
Atkins, R., 252
Atkinson, John, 282
Atkinson, R. C., 170
Au, J. G., 123
Augoustinos, M., 448
Austenfeld, J., 317
Axel, R., 83
Axelsson, A., 98
Ayalon, H., 261
Ayers, M., 260
Ayllon, T., 154, 402
Azar, B., 13
Azerinsky, Eugene, 111–112
Azrin, N. H., 152, 154, 402

Babor, T., 406
Bach, P., 407
Baddeley, A. D., 172, 175, 181
Baer, J., 404
Baer, L., 411
Bagby, R. M., 357
Bagley, C., 298
Bahrick, Harry, 186
Bailey, J. M., 299
Baker, B., 261
Baker, E., 120
Baldwin, J. D., 294
Baldwin, J. I., 294
Ball, S. G., 376
Ballenger, J. C., 410
Balon, R., 411
Baltes, M., 267
Baltes, P. B., 236, 267
Bandura, A., 157, 159, 255, 257, 347, 405, 443
Barch, D., 382, 383
Bargh, J., 97
Bargmann, C., 83
Baringa, M., 110
Barlett, Frederick, 174
Barlow, D. H., 407
Barnhardt, P. L., 120
Bartlett, A., 344
Bartlett, F. C., 175, 180
Bartoshuk, L. M., 249
Bartzokis, G., 263

Basic Behavioral Science Task Force, 159
Bass, Ellen, 177
Bassi, M., 377
Bassili, J. N., 436
Bates, M., 124
Bateson, G., 180
Batson, C. D., 438
Baumgardner, A. H., 427
Baumrind, D., 256, 259
Bavelier, D., 74
Baynes, K., 51
Bazan, S., 431
Beach, F. A., 298
Bean, P., 415
Bear, R., 154
Beauchamp, G. K., 249
Beck, A. T., 379, 407
Beck, J., 249
Beckham, Albert Sidney, 7
Beeder, A. B., 127
Beets, M., 324
Begleiter, Henri, 327
Behrens, 94, 316
Beirut, L., 327
Békésy, G. von, 82
Bekker, M. H. J., 374
Belcourt-Dittloff, A., 315
Bell, A. P., 299
Bell, M. A., 57, 252
Bellis, M., 330
Belloch, A., 406
Belsky, J., 253
Bem, D., 97
Bem, S. L., 257
Benes, F. M., 382
Benjafield, J. G., 5
Benjamin, L. T., 7, 26
Benjet, C., 402
Bennett, S. K., 354
Bennett, W. I., 98
Benotsch, E., 332
Ben-Porath, Y. S., 356
Beran, M., 210
Berckmoes, C., 52
Berenbaum, S. A., 225, 257, 298
Berger, Hans, 55
Berkowitz, L., 442
Bernal, M. E., 414
Bernardi, L., 119
Bernat, E., 97
Berndt, T. J., 260, 378
Bernstein, D., 176, 179
Bernstein, I. L., 144
Berscheid, E., 429
Besharat, M., 386

Beyrer, C., 328
Bialystok, E., 211
Billiard, M., 118
Bilmes, M., 344
Binet, Alfred, 215
Biondi, M., 374
Birch, H. G., 251
Bird, T., 63
Bishop, J., 253
Bishop, R., 170
Bisiach, E., 52
Bjork, R. A., 120
Bjorklund, D. F., 181
Black, D. W., 127
Blaiser, M. J., 192
Blanch, A., 350
Blasco, M., 265
Blascovich, J., 445
Blatt, S. J., 415
Bliese, P. D., 324
Blinn-Pike, L., 259
Bliss, T. V., 184
Bloom, B. S., 227
Bloomer, C. M., 95
Blumer, D., 378
Blyth, D. A., 258
Boerger, E., 116
Bogen, Joseph, 52
Bogenschultz, M., 130
Bohannon, H. N., III, 179
Boivin, D. B., 110
Bolino, M., 360
Bonanno, G. A., 267
Bonke, B., 184
Bonson, K., 124
Borbely, A. A., 114
Borbely, Alexander, 114
Boring, E. G., 95
Bornstein, R. F., 438
Bosse, R., 265
Botez, M. I., 44
Bouchard, T. J., Jr., 63, 219–220, 220, 352, 353
Boul, L., 260
Bourassa, M., 127
Bowden, C., 410
Bowen-Reid, T., 315
Bower, G. H., 187, 191
Bowers, K. S., 120, 121, 177
Boyle, Robert, 81
Bracken, P., 378
Braun, A., 116, 249
Brawman-Mintzer, O., 373
Breckler, S. J., 435
Brennan, P. A., 440
Brent, D., 380

Subject Index

Note: Boldface type indicates key terms and the page numbers where they are defined.

Color vision, 78–80
  theories of, 78–80
Commitment, 323
Compazine, 408
Compliance, 432
Componential intelligence, 214
Compulsion, 376
Computed tomography (CT) scan, 55
Concept, 201–202
Conception, 247
Concrete operations stage, 237
Conditioned fear response, 142
Conditioned response, 139
  changing, 140–142
  extinction of classically, 141
  generalization of, 141
Conditioned stimulus, 139
Conditions of worth, **348**–349
Condoms, 327
Condon, Richard, 109
Conduction deafness, 98
Cones, 76, 79
Confederate, 426
Conformity, 430–431
Confounding variables, 15
Confucianism, 354
Conscientiousness, 351
Conscious, 341
Consciousness, 110
Consequences Test, 227
Conservation, 237
Consolidation, 170, 187
Consolidation failure, 187
Constancy, perceptual, 92
Contact comfort, 252
Context, memory and, 181–182
Context-dependent memory, 181
Contextual intelligence, 214
Continuity, 91
Continuous reinforcement, 148
Control, 323
  lack of, and unpredictability, 312
Control group, 15
Conventional level, 242
Convergence, 92
Convergent thinking, 226
Conversion disorder, 385
Convolutions, 46
Cooing, 254
Coping, 317–318
  avoidant strategies, 321
  emotion-focused, 317–318
  problem-focused, 317
Cornea, 76, 79
Coronary heart disease, 319–320
Corpus callosum, 46, 51
Correlational method, 17–18
  strengths and weaknesses of, 17–18
Correlation coefficient, 17, AP.*5*–7
Corticoids, 61
Cortisol, 292–293
Costa, Paul, 350, 351
Counseling psychologists, 26, 413
Couples therapy, 400, 412
Crack, 126
Craik, Fergus, 172
Creativity, 225
  intelligence and, 225–227

Crick, Francis, 62
Critical periods, 248
Critical thinking, 21–22
Cross-dressing, 299
Cross-modal perception, 90
Crowding, 443
Crystallized intelligence, 263
Culturally sensitive psychotherapy, 414
Culture, 277
  altered states of consciousness and, 121
  memory and, 180–181
  mood disorders and, 377–378
  personality and, 354–355
Culture-fair intelligence tests, 217
Cumulative recorder, 150
Curvilinear relationship, AP.*6*–7

Dahmer, Jeffrey, 369
Dalmane, 126
Dark adaptation, 76–77
Darrow, Clarence, 340
Darwin, Charles, 6
Data, describing, with tables and graphs, AP.*1*–5
Date, getting a, 300
Death and dying, 266–267
Decay theory, 186
Decibels (dB), 81
Decision making, 202–205
Declarative memory, 173
Defense mechanism, 342, 344
Dehydroepiandrosterone (DHEA), 386
Delta waves, 55, 113
Delusions, 381
Delusions of grandeur, 381
Delusions of persecution, 381
Dement, William, 118
Dementia, 264
Dendrites, 38
Denial, 321
  death and, 266
Deoxyribonucleic acid (DNA), 62
Depakote, 410
Dependent variables, 15
Depressants, 122, 126
Depression
  alcohol abuse and, 326
  death and, 266
  life stresses and, 379
  mood disorders and, 377–378
  psychotic, 377
  in sexual dysfunction, 386–387
Depth perception, 92
Derailment in schizophrenia, 381
Description as goal of psychology, 4
Descriptive research methods, 11–13
Descriptive statistics, AP.*1*–7
  correlation coefficient, AP.*5*–7
  describing data with tables and graphs, AP.*1*–5
  measures of central tendency, AP.*1*
  measures of variability, AP.*3*
  normal curve, AP.*3*–5
Designer drugs, 127
Developing brain, 56–57
Developmental psychology, 26, 236

Developmental theories
  Erickson's theory of psychosocial develop-
    ment, 245–247
  Kolhberg's theory of moral development, 241
  Piaget's theory of cognitive development, 236–240
  Vygotsky's sociocultural approach, 241
*Diagnostic and Statistical Manual of Mental
  Disorders, Fourth Edition, Text
  Revised* (**DSM-IV-TR**), 372, 387
*Diagnostic and Statistical Manual of Mental Dis-
  orders, Fourth Edition* (DSM-IV), 372
  major categories of mental disorders, 372
Difference threshold, 74
Diffusion of responsibility, 439
Diffusion tensor imaging (DTI), 56
Directive therapy, 399
Discrimination, 141, 150, **444**
  open discussions of, 448
  roots of, 444–446
Discriminative stimulus, **150**–151
Disinhibitory effect, 158
Disorganized/disoriented attachment, 253
Disorganized schizophrenia, 383, 384
Displacement, 171
Display rules, 290
Dispositional attribution, 427
Dissociated control, theory of, 121
Dissociation, 385
Dissociative amnesia, 385–386
Dissociative disorders, 372, 385–386
Dissociative fugue, 386
Dissociative identity disorder (DID), 386
Divalproex, 410
  for bipolar disorder, 379
Divergent thinking, 226–227
Diversity education, 448
Dizygotic twins, 63
Domestic violence, 441
Dominant-recessive pattern, 62
Door-in-the-face technique, 432
Dopamine, 41, 42, 122, 125, 379
Double-blind technique, 16
Dreams, 115–118
  activation-synthesis hypothesis of, 117
  analysis of, 398
  interpreting, 116–117
  lucid, 116
  non-rapid eye movement (NREM) sleep, 115
  rapid eye movement (REM) sleep, 115
Drive, 279
Drive-reduction theory, 279
Drug dependence, 123–124
  physical, 123
  psychological, 124
Drugs. *See also specific*
  anticonvulsant, 410
  antidepressant, 373, 376, 409
  antipsychotic, 408
  designer, 127
  effect of, on brain, 122
  over-the-counter, 122
  psychoactive, 121–128
Drug therapy, 408–410
Drug tolerance, 123

Pavlov, Ivan
  classical conditioning and, 138–140, 141, 143, 145
Pavlovian conditioning, 138
Peak experiences, 281, 348
Peer groups, 256, 258
Pegwood system in improving memory, 192
Pelvic inflammatory disease, 327
Penfield, Wilder, 47, 48, 174
Penis envy, 342, 346
Perception, 73, **74**
  cross-modal, 90
  extrasensory, 97
  influences on, 88–90
  of motion, 93–95
  principles of, 91–96
  puzzling, 95–96
  subliminal, 97, 98
Perceptual constancy, 92
Perceptual development, 249–250
Perceptual organization and constancy, 91–92
Perceptual set, 90
Performance, relationship between arousal and, 280
Performance anxiety, 375
Performance-approach orientation, 283
Performance-avoidance orientation, 282–283
Peripheral nervous system (PNS), 58–59
Perls, Fritz, 399
Perls, Thomas, 235
Permeability, 38
Permissive parents, 256
Personal fable, 238
Personality, 340
  culture and, 354–355
  learning theories and, 346–347
  neurotic, 346
Personality assessment, 355–359
  inventories, 355–358
  observation, interviews, and rating scales, 355
  projective tests, 358–359
Personality disorders, 372, **387**–388
Personality inventories, 355–358
Personality types, 268
  heart disease and, 319–320
Personal space, **442**–443
Personal unconscious, 344
Person-centered therapy, 399, 412
Persuasion, 437
  repetition and, 438
  subliminal, 97
Pessimism, 323
Petry, Nancy, 405
Pheromones, 295
Phi phenomenon, 10, 95
Phobias, 374–375
  animal, 375
  situational, 375
  social, 375
  specific, 375
Phonemes, 208, 254
Phonological awareness, 255
Physical attractiveness, 428–429
Physical challenge, workplace stress and, 313
Physical changes
  in early and middle adulthood, 260
  in later adulthood, 262–263

Physical drug dependence, 123
Physical variables, workplace stress and, 313
Physiological psychology, 23, 26
Piaget, Jean, 236–240, 242
Pineal gland, **60**, 110
Pinna, 82
Pitch, 81
Pituitary gland, **60**
Placebo, **16**
Placebo effect, **16**
Place theory, **83**
Plasticity, 46, **48**–49, 57
Plateau phase in sexual response cycle, 297
Plato, 5
Pleasure principle, 341
Polygenic inheritance, 62
Polysomnograms, 111
Pons, 44
Ponzo illusion, 95
Population, 12, AP.7
Positive bias, 175
Positive correlation, AP.5
Positive reinforcement, 147
Positron emission tomography (PET) scan, 55
Postconventional level, 242–243
Posttraumatic stress disorder (PTSD), 314–315
Poverty, health and, 324
Power tools, hearing loss and, 99
Pragmatics, 208
Precognition, 97
Preconscious, 341
Preconventional level, 242
Prediction as goal of psychology, 4
Pregnancy, teenage, 259
Prejudice, 444
  level of, 446–447
  open discussions of, 448
  roots of, 444–446
  unlearning, 448
Premack, David, 208–209
Prenatal androgens, 257
Prenatal development, 247
Presbyopia, 76, **260**
Pretend play, 237
Preterm infants, 249
Primacy effect, 181
Primary appraisal, 316–317
Primary auditory cortex, **50**
Primary drives, 283
Primary effect, **181**, 426
Primary mental abilities, 213
Primary Mental Abilities Tests, 213
Primary reinforcer, 147
Primary visual cortex, **50**, 77
Prior judgments, willingness to modify or abandon, 21
Prior knowledge, influence on perception, 90
Private speech, 241
Proactive interference, 187
Problem-focused coping, 317
Problem solving, 205–206
Procrastination, winning battle against, 160–161
Progesterone, 62, 297
Projective tests, 358–359

Prosocial behavior, **438**–439
  bystander effect, 439
  reasons for helping, 438
Prospective forgetting, **188**–189
Prototype, **202**
Proximity, 91, **428**
Prozac, 409
Pruning, 56
Psychedelics, 127
Psychiatric social workers, 413
Psychiatrists, **413**, 414
Psychoactive drugs, 121–128, **122**
  behavioral effects of, 124–128
Psychoanalysis, 9, 25, **340**–344, 346, **398**, 412, 413
  conscious, preconscious, and unconscious in, 341
  defense mechanisms, 342
  evaluating Freud's contribution, 344
  id, ego, and superego in, 341–342
  psychosexual stages of development, 342–343
Psychodynamic therapies, 371, **398**
Psycholinguistics, **208**
Psychological disorders, 369
  explaining, 371–372
  prevalence of, 370
Psychological drug dependence, 124
Psychological perspectives, 24–25
Psychological research, participants in, 19–20
Psychologists, 414
Psychology
  biological, 23–24
  cognitive, 9–11, 10–11
  defined, **3**
  evolutionary, 22–23
  feminine, 346
  founding of, 5–6
  Gestalt, 10
  goals of, 4–5
  humanistic, 9
  individual, 345
  industrial, 6
  majoring in, 26–27
  minorities in, 7
  schools of thought in, 8–11
  specialties in, 26
  women in, 7
Psychoneuroimmunology, 322
Psychosexual stages of development, 342–343
Psychosis, 381
Psychosocial development, 245–247
Psychosocial stages, 245–247
Psychosurgery, 411
Psychotherapy, 397
  for bipolar disorder, 379
  culturally sensitive, 415
  for major depressive disorders, 377
  for panic disorders, 374
  Psychotic depression, 377
Puberty, sexual behavior and, **258**–259
Public speaking, overcoming fear of, 389
Punisher, 146
Punishment, 151
  operant conditioning and, 151–153
  Pupils, 76, 79
Puzzle box, 146

Credits

PHOTOS

CHAPTER 1: p. 1: © Brian Bailey/Getty Images; **6:** © David Young-Wolff/PhotoEdit; **8:** Archives of the History of American Psychology—The Robert V. Guthrie Papers; **10:** © Lon C. Deihl/PhotoEdit; **11:** © Carlos Lopez-Barillas/Getty Images; **12:** AP/ Wide World Photos; **13:** © Howard Huang/ Getty Images/The Image Bank; **18:** © Steve Skjold/PhotoEdit; **24 left:** © James Strachan/Getty Images/Stone; **24 right:** © Leland Bobbe/Getty Images/Stone.

CHAPTER 2: p. 36: © Gandee Vasan/Getty Images/The Image Bank; **37:** Reprinted with permission from Damasio H, Grabowski T, Frank R, Galaburda AM, Damasio AR: The return of Phineas Gage: Clues about the brain from a famous patient. *Science*, 264:1102–1105, © 1994. American Association for the Advancement of Science. Photo courtesy of H. Damasio, Human Neuroanatomy and Neuroimaging Laboratory, Department of Neurology, University of Iowa.; **39 top:** © BioPhoto/Photo Researchers, Inc.; **39 bottom:** © BioPhoto Photo Researchers, Inc.; **41:** © Bill Aron/PhotoEdit; **48:** Photo James Prince; **49:** © Bernardo Bucci/CORBIS; **50:** © Anthony Edgeworth; **56:** © Alexander Tsiaras/Photo Researchers, Inc.

CHAPTER 3: p. 72: © Marin Barraud/Getty Images/Stone; **75:** © Philip Condit II/Getty Images/Stone; **77:** © Carolina Biological Supply Company/Phototake; **80 left:** © Robert Harbison; **80 right:** © Robert Harbison; **85:** © Omikron/Photo Researchers, Inc.; **87:** © Gerard Vandeystadt/Photo Researchers, Inc.; **89:** Courtesy of Daniel J Simons; **93:** Courtesy of Geotyme Enterprises; **94 top left:** © Kent Meireis/The Image Works; **94 top middle left:** © James Randklev/Getty Images/The Image Bank; **94 top middle right:** © Bernd Euler/plus 49/The Image Works; **94 top right:** © Mike Yamashita/Woodfin Camp & Associates; **94 bottom left:** © Craig Tuttle/CORBIS; **94 bottom middle:** © Randi Anglin/Syracuse Newspaper/The Image Works; **94 bottom right:** © Pete Turner/Getty Images/The Image Bank; **96:** © Richard Lord Ente/The Image Works; **98:** © Martin Rogers/Stock Boston, LLC.

CHAPTER 4: p. 108: © Chip Simons/Getty Images/The Image Bank; **111:** © David Frazier/Getty Images/Stone; **113 top:** © Russell D. Curtis/Photo Researchers, Inc.; **113 bottom:** © Kent Meireis/The Image Works; **115:** Courtesy of Sean Drummand; **117:** MATRIX RELOADED, Keanu Reeves, Lung Yun Chao, 2003, © Warner Brothers/courtesy Everett Collection; **118:** psihoyos.com; **120:** © Michael Newman/PhotoEdit; **121:** © Robert Frerck/Getty Images/Stone; **125:** © Tony Freeman/PhotoEdit; **128:** © Michael Richards/PhotoEdit.

CHAPTER 5: p. 136: © Jeffrey L. Rotman/CORBIS; **140:** © Bettmann/CORBIS; **144 top:** Courtesy of the National Fluid Milk Processor Promotion Board; **144 bottom:** © Yellow Dog Productions/Getty Images/The Image Bank; **145:** © Kevin Laubacher/Getty Images/Taxi; **147:** © Arthur Tilley/Getty Images/Taxi; **148:** © Christoph Wilhelm/Getty Images/Taxi; **150:** © Nina Leen/Time & Life Pictures/Getty Images; **154:** © Will & Demi McIntyre/Photo Researchers, Inc.; **157:** Stanford University News Service; **158:** Courtesy of Dr. Albert Bandura, Stanford University; **159:** © 2003 Laura Dwight.

CHAPTER 6: p. 168: ©Bill Bachmann/The Image Works; **169 left:** Susan Schwartzenberg, © Exploratorium, www.exploratorium.edu; **169 right:** © Franco Magnani; **172 top:** © Kent Wood/Photo Researchers, Inc.; **172 bottom:** © Chris Trotman/CORBIS; **175 top:** © Royalty Free/CORBIS; **175 bottom:** © Grantpix/Photo Researchers, Inc.; **178:** © SINER JEFF/CORBIS SYGMA; **179:** © Greg Whitesell/Getty Images; **180:** © M & E Bernheim/Woodfin Camp & Associates; **183:** adapted from Maguire et al., 2000; **183:** adapted from Maguire et al., 2000; **185:** © Michael Newman/PhotoEdit.

CHAPTER 7: p. 199: © Ethan Miller/Las Vegas Sun/Reuters/CORBIS; **201:** AP/Wide World Photos; **202 left:** © Jim Simncen/Getty Images/Stone; **202 right:** ©Art Wolfe/Getty Images/Stone; **204:** © Tony Freeman/PhotoEdit; **206:** © Topham Picture Point/The Image Work; **207:** AP/Wide World Photos; **210:** © FRANS LANTING/Minden Pictures; **211:** © Bob Daemmrich/The Image Works; **214 left:** © Bernard Wolf; **214 middle:** © Rafael Macia/Photo Researchers, Inc.; **214 right:** © B&C Alexander/Photo Researchers, Inc.; **216:** Archives of the History of American Psychology—University of Akron; **220:** © Portfield/Chickering/Photo Researchers, Inc.; **223:** Stanford University News Service.

CHAPTER 8: p. 234: © David Young-Wolff/PhotoEdit; **235:** Amy Snyder, ©Exploratorium, www.exploratorium.edu; **241:** © Frank Siteman/PhotoEdit; **244:** Photo Dan Lapsley; **248 left:** © Francis Leroy/Science Photo Library/Photo Researchers, Inc.; **248 middle:** Lennart Nilsson/Bonniers; **248 right:** Lennart Nilsson/Bonniers; **250:** © Mark Richards/PhotoEdit; **252:** © Martin Rogers/Stock Boston, LLC.; **253:** © Laura Dwight/PhotoEdit; **255:** © Bob Daemmrich Photography; **261:** © Will and Demi McIntyre/Photo Researchers, Inc.; **264:** © Jim Craigmyle/CORBIS.

CHAPTER 9: p. 276: © Lucy Nicholson/Reuters/CORBIS; **279:** © Anthony Neste; **280:** © Don Mason/CORBIS; **282:** © REUTERS/Robert Galbraith/CORBIS; **286:** AP/Wide World Photos; **290:** Reprinted by permission of the Human Interaction Laboratory/© Paul Ekman 1975; **291:** © David Young-Wolff/PhotoEdit; **292:** © PhotoDisc/Getty Images; **295:** Courtesy of David M. Buss; **297:** © Tom & DeAnn McCarthy/CORBIS; **299:** © Barbara Peacock/Getty Images/Taxi; **300:** © Lori Adamski Peek/Getty Images/Stone.

CHAPTER 10: p. 307: © Ryan McVay/Getty Images/Photodisc Green; **308:** MARTIN BUREAU/AFP/Getty Images; **309:** © Michael Greenlar/The Image Works; **313 top:** © Spencer Grant/PhotoEdit; **313 bottom:** © M. Granitsas/The Image Works; **315:** © Ariel Skelley/CORBIS; **320:** © Jose Luis Pelaez, Inc./CORBIS; **321:** © Thomas S. England/Time & Life Pictures/Getty Images; **323:** © Ronnie Kaufman/CORBIS; **325:** Courtesy of Edith Chen; **329:** AP/Wide World Photos; **330:** © Sonda Dawes/The Image Works.

CHAPTER 11: p. 339: © FujiPhotos/The Image Works; **340:** © Bettmann/CORBIS; **341:** © Hulton-Deutsch Collection/CORBIS; **344:** © Michael Newman/PhotoEdit;

345: © Bettmann/CORBIS; 346: Louis Fabian Bachrach; 347: ©Zefa Visual Media—Germany/Index Stock Imagery; 349: © Bettmann/CORBIS; 352: © Ariel Skelley/CORBIS; 354: © Chris Arend/Getty Images/Stone.

CHAPTER 12: p. 367: © Zave Smith/CORBIS; **369 left:** © Robert Harbison; **369 right:** © Dean Conger/CORBIS; **376:** © Spencer Grant/PhotoEdit; **380:** AP/Wide World Photos; **383:** Courtesy of Deanna M. Barch, Ph.D.; **384 top:** © Will Hart; **384 bottom:** © Arthur Tilley/Getty Images/Taxi.

CHAPTER 13: p. 396: © Michael Newman/PhotoEdit; **398:** AP/Wide World Photos; **399:** © Michael Rougier/ Time Life Pictures/Getty Images; **401 top:** © Royalty-Free/ CORBIS; **401 bottom:** © Bruce Ayers/Getty Images/Stone; **402:** © David Young-Wolff/PhotoEdit; **404:** © Geri Engberg/The Image Works; **405:** Courtesy of Nancy Petry; **411:** © W & D McIntyre/Photo Researchers, Inc.; **415:** © Michael Newman/PhotoEdit; **417:** © Jose Pelaez/ CORBIS.

CHAPTER 14: p. 424: © Jim West/Alamy; **425:** From the film *Obedience* copyright 1965 by Stanley Milgram and distributed by Penn State Media Sales.; **426:** © Larry Dale Gordon/Getty Images/The Image Bank; **428:** © J. Christopher Briscoe/Photo Researchers, Inc.; **429:** © Zen Sekizawa/Getty Images/Taxi; **430:** William Vandevert/Scientific American; **434 top:** © Mark Richards/PhotoEdit; **434 bottom:** Philip G. Zimbardo, Inc.; **437:** AP/Wide World Photos; **438:** © AFP/Getty Images; **439:** © Robert Brenner/PhotoEdit; **441:** Courtesy of Miki Paul; **446:** © Gary A. Conner/PhotoEdit.

TEXT AND ART

Figure 1.3, p. 23: Reprinted from *Psychological Science*, 7, B. P. Buunk, A. Angleitner, V. Oubaid, and D. M. Buss, "Sex differences in jealousy in evolutionary and cultural perspective: Tests from the Netherlands, Germany, and the United States," pp. 359–363, copyright © 1996, with permission from Blackwell.

Try It 6.1, p. 187: Reprinted from *Cognitive Psychology*, 11, R. S. Nickerson and M. J. Adams, "Long-term memory for a common object," pp. 287–307, exercise on p. 297, copyright © 1979, with permission from Elsevier.

Try It 7.1, p. 206: From *Solve It!: A Perplexing Profusion of Puzzles* by James F. Fixx, copyright © 1978 by James F. Fixx. Used by permission of Doubleday, a division of Random House, Inc.

Figure 7.1, p. 209: Adapted with permission from *Science*, 172, David Premack, "Language in chimpanzee?," pp. 808–822, Figure 1, p. 809. Copyright © 1971 AAAS.

Figure 7.2, p. 212: Reprinted from *Psychological Science*, 14, Kenji Hakuta, Ellen Bialystock, and Edward Wiley, "Critical evidence: A test of the critical-period hypothesis for second-language acquisition," pp. 31–38, copyright © 2003, with permission from Blackwell.

Figure 7.8, p. 221: Reprinted with permission of the Society for Research in Child Development.

Figure 7.9, p. 224: Reprinted from *Scientific American*, 267, Doreen Kimura, "Sex differences in the brain," pp. 118–125, Figure from pp. 120, 121, copyright © 1992, with permission from Jared Schneidman.

Figure 7.10, p. 226: Adapted from *Neuropsychologia*, 38, I. Carlsson, P. E. Wendt, and J. Risberg, "On the neurobiology of creativity: Differences in frontal activity between high and low creative subjects," pp. 873–885, copyright © 2000, with permission from Elsevier.

Figure 8.1, p. 239: From Laura E. Berk, *Child Development*, 3/e, © 1994. Published by Allyn and Bacon, Boston, MA. Copyright © 1994 by Pearson Education. Reprinted by permission of the publisher.

Figure 10.5, p. 319: From *Dynamics of Health and Wellness*, 1st edition by Green, J./Shellenberger, R., © 1991. Reprinted with permission of Brooks/Cole, a division of Thomson Learning: www.thomsonrights.com. Fax 800 730-2215.

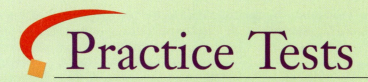# Practice Tests

Answers can be found in the *Student Solutions Manual*.

Chapter 1: Introduction to Psychology

Multiple Choice

1. Psychology is defined as
   a. the scientific study of the mind.
   b. the formal study of human behavior and learning processes.
   c. the scientific study of behavior and mental processes.
   d. the science of behavior and mental illness.

2. A counseling psychologist is working with a married couple to promote better communication in their relationship. Which goal of psychology is the psychologist trying to accomplish?
   a. description
   b. explanation
   c. prediction
   d. influence

3. Unlike basic research, applied research is intended to
   a. solve practical problems.
   b. advance scientific understanding.
   c. seek new information.
   d. describe, but not influence, the quality of life.

4. The first psychological laboratory was established by
   a. Ernst Weber.
   b. Gustav Fechner.
   c. Wilhelm Wundt.
   d. Sigmund Freud.

5. The early school of psychology devoted to studying the basic elements of conscious mental experiences was
   a. functionalism.
   b. structuralism.
   c. behaviorism.
   d. humanism.

6. What problem was commonly encountered by early female researchers in the field of psychology?
   a. They could not get men to allow them to do research.
   b. The better schools refused to allow women to study with men.
   c. The schools they attended refused to confer advanced degrees.
   d. They were denied access to laboratories.

7. What person is most closely associated with the school of behaviorism, which studies only observable, measurable behavior?
   a. John B. Watson
   b. Sigmund Freud
   c. Abraham Maslow
   d. Max Wertheimer

8. Dr. Smith believes that depression is a consequence of faulty thinking. With which theoretical perspective would Dr. Smith most agree?
   a. biological
   b. humanistic
   c. psychoanalytic
   d. cognitive

9. A researcher is studying patterns of social play in 8-year-olds by watching children on a playground and documenting their behaviors. Which research method is she using?
   a. survey
   b. laboratory observation
   c. case study
   d. naturalistic observation

10. A survey-taker makes sure that the people surveyed closely mirror the population of interest. He is ensuring that he has a
    a. representative sample.
    b. representative population.
    c. biased sample.
    d. random population.

11. A professor asks her class to record how often they study. Her students may tend to report studying more than they really do, thereby giving a
    a. candid response.
    b. social desirability response.
    c. representative response.
    d. random response.

12. The variable that is presumed to vary as a result of the manipulation of another variable is called a(n)
    a. confounding variable.
    b. dependent variable.
    c. independent variable.
    d. mitigating factor.

13. Dr. Needles is testing the effects of a new drug. One group receives the drug, while a comparison group receives an injection of a harmless solution. The group that receives the drug is called the
    a. experimental group.
    b. control group.
    c. prediction group.
    d. placebo group.

14. In Dr. Needles's experiment, neither he nor the participants know who gets the drug and who gets the harmless solution. This method is called
    a. the single-blind method.
    b. the double-blind method.
    c. the hidden-purpose method.
    d. deception.

15. Which of the following correlation coefficients indicates the strongest relationship between two variables?
    a. .67
    b. −.43
    c. −.85
    d. 1.25

16. Research participants must be told the purpose of the study in which they are participating and its potential for harming them. This is the ethical consideration known as
    a. prior approval.
    b. applicable disclosure.
    c. appropriate disclosure.
    d. informed consent.

17. Which of the following is *not* a characteristic exhibited when one engages in critical thinking?
    a. independent thinking
    b. suspension of judgment
    c. open-minded acceptance
    d. willingness to modify prior judgments

18. Dr. Jarrod, a psychologist, is part of an interdisciplinary team that includes biologists, biochemists, and medical researchers, who study the nervous system. To which field does Dr. Jarrod likely belong?
    a. evolutionary psychology
    b. biopsychosociology
    c. chemical psychology
    d. neuroscience

19. Dr. Benson studies the factors that promote productivity in an office environment for a large company. Which type of psychologist is Dr. Benson likely to be?
    a. social psychologist
    b. industrial-organizational psychologist
    c. educational psychologist
    d. counseling psychologist

20. Which type of psychologist is most likely to study how human behavior is affected by the presence of other people?
    a. social psychologist
    b. developmental psychologist
    c. educational psychologist
    d. clinical psychologist

True or False

21. Replication is used to verify that a study's findings are accurate with a different group of participants.

22. Wilhelm Wundt and William James belonged to the same early school of psychology.

23. Humanistic psychology focuses on the uniqueness of human beings and their capacity for growth.

24. Descriptive research methods accomplish all three goals of psychology equally well.

25. Experiments allow for the greatest experimenter control as well as permitting cause-effect conclusions to be drawn.

26. A perfect positive correlation is indicated by the coefficient 1.00.

27. If stress and illness are positively correlated, it means that stress causes illness.

28. The APA permits the use of animals in research.

29. Information-processing theory compares the human brain's workings to those of a computer.

30. The view that human behavior is shaped by physiological factors is called the sociocultural approach.

Essay

31. Explain what separates the science of psychology from common sense. Include in your response why a theory cannot rely on anecdotal evidence.

32. Name and describe four major psychological perspectives. According to each perspective selected, what is the primary reason for your behavior?

33. Suppose you wanted to test whether a new drug helped improve scores on a memory test for college students. Design an experiment to do so. Include how you would select your sample, and label the independent and dependent variables, as well as the experimental and control groups. Also, describe one confounding variable you would avoid.

Multiple Choice

1. What separates psychology from simple common sense?
   a. use of folk wisdom
   b. reliance on logical inference
   c. reliance on the scientific method
   d. use of cultural stories and anecdotes

2. Which term refers to a set of principles proposed to explain how a number of separate facts are related?
   a. theory
   b. hypothesis
   c. concept
   d. idea

3. Dr. Carson conducts an experiment and achieves results that support her theory. She conducts another study, hoping to achieve the same results as in the first experiment. What process is Dr. Carson conducting?
   a. validation
   b. replication
   c. redundant experimentation
   d. observation

4. Laura wants to find out why her boyfriend has been so grumpy lately. Which goal of psychology is Laura trying to accomplish?
   a. description
   b. explanation
   c. prediction
   d. influence

5. Wilhelm Wundt studied the perception of various sensory stimuli using the method of
   a. functionalism.
   b. sensory adaptation.
   c. introspection.
   d. sensory deprivation.

6. The leading advocate of the early school of psychology devoted to the study of how humans use mental processes to adapt to their environment was
   a. Wilhelm Wundt.
   b. Edward Titchener.
   c. Sigmund Freud.
   d. William James.

7. Which school of psychology posits that individuals perceive objects and patterns as whole units?
   a. cognitive psychology
   b. Gestalt psychology
   c. psychoanalysis
   d. information-processing theory

8. The school of psychology led by Rogers and Maslow that emphasizes individual uniqueness and the capacity for growth is called
   a. behaviorism.
   b. psychoanalysis.
   c. cognitive psychology.
   d. humanism.

9. When a television network predicts the winner of an election, it is relying on which research method?
   a. survey
   b. naturalistic observation
   c. experiment
   d. correlational study

10. The factor that is manipulated by the researcher in an effort to determine its effects on something else is called a(n)
   a. confounding variable.
   b. dependent variable.
   c. independent variable.
   d. mitigating factor.

11. The group that does *not* receive exposure to the independent variable in an experiment is the
   a. experimental group.   c. prediction group.
   b. control group.   d. variable group.

12. Dr. Janus teaches two sections of Introductory Psychology, one at 8 a.m. and one at 1 p.m. He decides to conduct an experiment on the effect of using PowerPoint slides to lecture on the grades of each class. Students in the 1 p.m. section see PowerPoint slides for a lecture, whereas students in the 8 a.m. class see notes on a chalkboard. Dr. Janus plans to compare the two groups' performance on the exams, but a colleague points out that his study has a confounding variable. What is that confounding variable?
   a. the intellectual levels of the students in each section
   b. the motivation of the students in each section
   c. the difficulty of the course material
   d. the times of the two sections

13. Which is an advantage of the experimental method?
   a. the artificiality of the lab situation
   b. the lack of experimenter control
   c. the ability to draw cause-effect conclusions
   d. none of the above

14. "There is a positive correlation between ice cream sales and domestic violence reports." This statement suggests that
   a. ice cream consumption causes domestic violence.
   b. domestic violence makes people want to eat ice cream.
   c. domestic violence calls increase and ice cream sales increase at the same time.
   d. domestic violence calls increase and ice cream sales decrease at the same time.

15. Which of the following is a primary cause of participant-related bias?
    a. lack of representativeness in the sample
    b. unethical researchers
    c. confounding variables
    d. use of the case study method

16. Which of the following is *not* a provision of the APA's ethics code?
    a. Research must receive approval from all institutions involved in a study.
    b. Deception of subjects is always unethical.
    c. Subjects may be paid for participation in research.
    d. Researchers must report findings and make data available to others.

17. A theory has heuristic value when
    a. it stimulates debate and motivates individuals to pursue research.
    b. it leads to the development of solutions to real-world problems.
    c. it generates testable hypotheses.
    d. it replaces a previously believed theory.

18. A therapist utilizes techniques from a variety of theoretical approaches. Her approach is said to be
    a. psychoanalytic.
    b. eclectic.
    c. transcendental.
    d. radical.

19. Adaptation and survival are central themes in the _____ school of psychology.
    a. biological
    b. cognitive
    c. evolutionary
    d. behavioral

20. Dr. Runge diagnoses and treats individuals with severe mental disorders such as schizophrenia. Dr. Runge is most likely which type of psychologist?
    a. physiological psychologist
    b. developmental psychologist
    c. clinical psychologist
    d. counseling psychologist

True or False

21. The scientific method involves a systematic investigation that always leads to a solution of a real-world problem.

22. Minority psychologists have grown in their representation in the field of psychology over the past several decades.

23. The conscious mind is the primary focus of psychoanalysis.

24. An experiment accomplishes the goal of description and the goal of explanation.

25. A research result is considered valid if the experiment contains confounding variables.

26. A positive correlation between two variables means that the first variable causes the second variable; a negative correlation means the opposite.

27. Debriefing is required as soon as possible after a study if deception has been used.

28. One reason for using animals in research is that more medical procedures can be done on animals than on humans.

29. The different perspectives in psychology differ only in how they explain abnormal behavior.

30. Developmental psychologists specialize in doing therapy with children.

Essay

31. Describe the four basic goals of psychology and give a real-world example of each.

32. Describe the differences between an experiment and descriptive research methods. What are the advantages and disadvantages of each?

33. Name and describe four types of psychologists, including what they do and where they typically work.

Chapter 2: Biology and Behavior

Multiple Choice

1. The neurons that relay messages from the sense organs to the central nervous system are
    a. afferent (sensory) neurons.
    b. efferent (motor) neurons.
    c. interneurons.
    d. operant neurons.

2. Which part of the neuron receives messages from other cells?
    a. dendrite
    b. cell body
    c. axon
    d. synapse

3. When a neuron's axon carries a positive electrical potential of about 50 millivolts, it is said to be firing. This state is called the
   a. resting potential.
   b. synaptic charge.
   c. action potential.
   d. ionic storm.

4. Sarah seems to be depressed, isn't sleeping well, and has little appetite. Which neurotransmitter is most likely to be involved in the problem?
   a. serotonin
   b. dopamine
   c. epinephrine
   d. acetylcholine

5. Jesse is wiring together his home theater system, and he accidentally touches a live wire. He gets a painful shock and quickly jerks his hand away. The reflex of pulling his hand back is dictated by the
   a. brain.
   b. spinal cord.
   c. arm.
   d. heart.

6. A severe injury to the medulla would likely result in
   a. coma.
   b. paralysis.
   c. memory loss.
   d. death.

7. Which area of the brain regulates several body functions, including hunger, thirst, sexual behavior, and internal body temperature?
   a. thalamus
   b. hypothalamus
   c. amygdala
   d. substantia nigra

8. Danielle is left-handed. When she is taking notes in class, which part of her brain is directing the movements of her hand?
   a. left frontal lobe
   b. right frontal lobe
   c. left temporal lobe
   d. right temporal lobe

9. The visual cortex is located in the
   a. frontal lobe.
   b. parietal lobe.
   c. temporal lobe.
   d. occipital lobe.

10. Coral suffers from epilepsy. Her doctor wants to perform an operation that he believes will improve the quality of Coral's life. What is the most likely change that Coral's doctor wants to make in her brain?
    a. He plans to perform a prefrontal lobotomy.
    b. He plans to remove her amygdala.
    c. He plans to sever her corpus callosum.
    d. He plans to scrape the Broca's area.

11. Which part of the nervous system is primarily responsible for regulating the body's internal environment?
    a. autonomic nervous system
    b. somatic nervous system
    c. central nervous system
    d. synaptic nervous system

12. During an exam, which brain-wave pattern are you most likely to exhibit?
    a. alpha wave
    b. beta wave
    c. delta wave
    d. slow wave

13. Kelvin is undergoing some tests to look for signs of physical damage to his brain. He also needs to be sure that certain parts of his brain are working properly. Which type of diagnostic technique would reveal both structures and activity?
    a. fMRI
    b. MRI
    c. CT scan
    d. PET scan

14. Which individual is most likely to recover a lost brain function following a head injury?
    a. 60-year-old woman
    b. 25-year-old man
    c. 45-year-old man
    d. 15-year-old girl

15. Which of the following statements about gender differences in the adult brain is *true*?
    a. Men are better able to find their way out of a maze than are women due to the higher activity of men's right frontal cortex.
    b. Men have less white matter in the brain than do women.
    c. Women have more white matter in the left brain than do men.
    d. Women have more gray matter in the area of the brain that controls emotions than do men.

16. Marisa is riding a roller coaster. As it surges over the high point to plunge downward, her heart races, her breathing quickens, and blood flow to her skeletal muscles increases. Which division of the peripheral nervous system is most active?
    a. somatic
    b. central
    c. sympathetic
    d. parasympathetic

17. Chemical substances that are released in one part of the body but affect other parts of the body are called
    a. neurons.
    b. electrons.
    c. hormones.
    d. neurotransmitters.

18. Which organ is responsible for regulating blood sugar by releasing insulin and glucagon into the bloodstream?
    a. pancreas
    b. pituitary
    c. spleen
    d. thyroid

19. In a dominant-recessive pattern set of inheritance rules, which pair of genes would result in the expression of a recessive trait?
    a. two dominant genes
    b. one dominant gene and one recessive gene
    c. two recessive genes
    d. none of the above

20. Which type of study is *not* likely to be used in the field of behavioral genetics?
    a. an experiment
    b. a twin study
    c. an adoption study
    d. all of the above would be used in the field of behavioral genetics

True or False

21. The myelin sheath allows neural impulses to travel faster.

22. Any neurotransmitter can fit into any receptor.

23. The limbic system is a series of brain structures involved in emotion.

24. Wernicke's aphasia involves difficulty with comprehension of speech.

25. The right hemisphere of the brain is responsible for most language functions.

26. Pain perception occurs in the somatosensory area of the cerebrum.

27. The somatic nervous system can be divided into the sympathetic and parasympathetic nervous systems.

28. An MRI is a more powerful way to view the brain than an EEG.

29. The gonads are responsible for the production of sex hormones.

30. There are 22 pairs of chromosomes in the human body.

Essay

31. Describe the process of neural conduction across the synapse.

32. Name and describe the effects of five neurotransmitters.

33. Review the specialized functions of the right and left hemispheres of the cerebral cortex.

PRACTICE TEST 2

Multiple Choice

1. The neurons that carry signals from the central nervous system to organs, glands, and skeletal muscles are
    a. afferent (sensory) neurons.
    b. efferent (motor) neurons.
    c. interneurons.
    d. operant neurons.

2. The gap between the axon terminal of one neuron and the dendrite of another neuron is the
    a. dendrite.
    b. cell body.
    c. axon.
    d. synapse.

3. The period of time (1–2 seconds) during which it is impossible for a neuron to fire is called the
    a. resting potential.
    b. refractory period.
    c. action potential.
    d. synaptic remission.

4. Individuals with Alzheimer's disease often have difficulty learning new information and retaining it in memory. Which neurotransmitter is likely involved in this difficulty?
    a. serotonin
    b. dopamine
    c. epinephrine
    d. acetylcholine

5. The central nervous system is made up of
    a. the brain only.
    b. the brain and spinal cord.
    c. the brain, spinal cord, and pituitary gland.
    d. all the neurons except those in the brain.

6. Which area of the brain is most crucial in your efforts to store information in long-term memory?
    a. cerebellum
    b. corpus callosum
    c. amygdala
    d. hippocampus

7. Before traveling to higher brain centers, most sensory information must pass through the:
   a. cerebral cortex.
   b. thalamus.
   c. hypothalamus.
   d. substantia nigra.

8. The auditory cortex is located in the
   a. frontal lobe.
   b. parietal lobe.
   c. temporal lobe.
   d. occipital lobe.

9. Which part of the brain controls the pituitary gland?
   a. frontal lobe
   b. cerebellum
   c. thalamus
   d. hypothalamus

10. John suffers a traumatic brain injury that makes it difficult for him to comprehend speech. The likely site of his injury is the
    a. left frontal lobe.
    b. right frontal lobe.
    c. left temporal lobe.
    d. right temporal lobe.

11. If the frontal lobe controls voluntary movements, then which division of the peripheral nervous system does the frontal lobe control?
    a. somatic
    b. autonomic
    c. sympathetic
    d. parasympathetic

12. Slice-by-slice cross-sectional images of the brain are produced by
    a. fMRI.   c. CT scan.
    b. MRI.   d. PET scan.

13. Which of the following is a specialized function of the left hemisphere of the brain in most people?
    a. control of the production of written language
    b. control of the left side of the body
    c. visual-spatial skills
    d. interpretation of nonverbal behavior

14. While in a deep sleep, which brain-wave pattern are you most likely to exhibit?
    a. alpha wave   c. delta wave
    b. beta wave   d. gamma wave

15. Lenora is driving in heavy traffic and is suddenly "cut off" by a darting sedan. She is startled, but soon recovers her composure. Her heart rate and breathing slow to normal rates. Which division of the nervous system took over as she calmed down?
    a. sympathetic
    b. parasympathetic
    c. somatic
    d. central

16. Jennifer was in an accident that caused some damage to her motor cortex. If she is able to walk again, it will be because of the _____ of parts of the brain.
    a. plasticity
    b. recoverability
    c. efficiency
    d. lateralization

17. Which of the following is the most common cause of damage to adult brains?
    a. drug use
    b. traumatic brain injuries due to accidents
    c. Alzheimer's disease
    d. strokes

18. Melatonin, the hormone that regulates sleep and wakefulness, is produced and regulated by the
    a. adrenal glands.
    b. pineal gland.
    c. thymus gland.
    d. pituitary gland.

19. In which of the following patterns of inheritance is a trait influenced by both genes and environmental factors?
    a. polygenic inheritance
    b. sex-linked inheritance
    c. multifactorial inheritance
    d. dominant-recessive inheritance

20. Which of the following studies allows researchers to disentangle the effects of heredity and the environment?
    a. an experiment
    b. a twin study
    c. an adoption study
    d. a family study

True or False

21. The resting potential for a neuron is 50 millivolts.

22. Dopamine is a neurotransmitter that has relevance in both schizophrenia and Parkinson's disease.

23. Simple sobriety tests are designed to test the functioning of the cerebellum.

24. The spinal cord is responsible for reflexes that help us avoid injury.

25. The limbic system includes the hippocampus, the reticular formation, and the amygdala.

26. The two cerebral hemispheres are connected by a band of nerves called the corpus callosum.

27. As we age, the ability of the brain to reorganize itself and recover from damage is reduced.

28. If a split-brain patient is blindfolded and given a pen to hold in her left hand, she will not be able to name the object being held.

29. An EEG can reveal what is happening in individual neurons.

30. Fraternal twins result when two sperm cells fertilize a single egg.

Essay

31. Describe the functions of the thalamus and the hypothalamus.

32. Name and describe the function of each of the four lobes of the brain.

33. Describe four glands and the hormones they produce, including the function of those hormones.

Chapter 3: Sensation and Perception

Multiple Choice

1. Jenna accidentally steps on a pin. The stimulation of her skin and transmission of the information regarding this touch to the central nervous system is the process of
   a. penetration.
   b. sensation.
   c. perception.
   d. registration.

2. To sense a change in weights being carried, the additional weight added must be 2% higher than what you carried before. This difference threshold is calculated using
   a. Weber's law.
   b. an absolute threshold.
   c. Planck's law.
   d. Gestalt laws.

3. The process of converting sensory stimulation into neural impulses is called
   a. sensory conduction.
   b. transformation.
   c. sensory adaptation.
   d. transduction.

4. The outer part of the eye that serves to protect the eye, and on which you would place your contact lenses, is called the
   a. lens.
   b. cornea.
   c. pupil.
   d. papillary opening.

5. On a rainy day, Jake sees that his flashy new red car doesn't look as bright and shiny; the color seems duller. This is because
   a. Jake's rods are more relied upon, and rods don't allow color perception.
   b. Jake's cones are more relied upon, and cones don't allow color perception.
   c. Jake's rods and cones are both used, and neither allows color perception.
   d. Jake suffers from red-green color blindness.

6. Connie squints to better see the board in class. She is trying to get the light waves to strike which part of her retina?
   a. rods
   b. optic nerve
   c. fovea
   d. iris

7. Which theory best explains visual phenomena such as color vision and afterimages?
   a. trichromatic theory
   b. opponent-process theory
   c. Weber's law
   d. signal detection theory

8. The loudness of a sound corresponds to which physical characteristic of a sound wave?
   a. amplitude
   b. frequency
   c. wavelength
   d. timbre

9. Which of the following is the sensory receptor for hearing?
   a. eardrum
   b. pinna
   c. cochlea
   d. hair cells

10. Which theory best explains how sensory receptors in our ear encode sound wave frequencies over 1,000 Hz?
    a. frequency theory
    b. place theory
    c. both frequency theory and place theory
    d. neither frequency theory nor place theory

11. Glenda purchases some new perfume to attract her boyfriend's attention. The perfume is meant to stimulate which sensory system?
    a. olfactory
    b. gustatory
    c. tactile
    d. auditory

12. Linda's friends all drink coffee, but Linda finds the taste of coffee very bitter, more so than do her friends. Which is one explanation for Linda's dislike of coffee?
    a. She is not addicted to caffeine.
    b. She is a "nontaster."
    c. She is a "supertaster."
    d. She has damaged taste buds.

13. Monique experiences a leg cramp in her calf. She massages the muscle while gritting her teeth and finds she feels less pain. Which theory explains this decrease in pain?
    a. place theory
    b. frequency theory
    c. opponent-process theory
    d. gate-control theory

14. A toddler plays with blocks by sorting them into piles by color, so that the red blocks make up one pile, the blue blocks make up a second pile, and the green blocks make up a third pile. She is using which Gestalt principle of perceptual organization?
    a. proximity
    b. similarity
    c. continuity
    d. closure

15. Gary sees a friend standing near a fence. The fence partially blocks his view of his friend, so Gary realizes the fence is closer to him than is his friend. Which monocular depth cue is Gary using?
    a. linear perspective
    b. relative size
    c. interposition
    d. texture gradient

16. The "old woman/young woman" image is an example of
    a. the phi phenomenon.
    b. an impossible figure.
    c. an ambiguous figure.
    d. an autokinetic illusion.

17. Which of the following involves an illusion utilizing two equal lines with diagonals extending outward from one line, making it appear longer than the line with diagonals extending inward?
    a. Müller-Lyer illusion
    b. moon illusion
    c. Ponzo illusion
    d. linear perspective illusion

18. Brandi is learning to read by sounding out a word one letter at a time. Which type of processing is she using?
    a. bottom-up processing
    b. top-down processing
    c. perceptual set
    d. Gestalt principle of closure

19. Leroy is studying and trying to ignore his roommate's phone conversation in the other room. He is engrossed in his psychology textbook until he hears his name mentioned, when he suddenly becomes aware of what his roommate is saying on the phone. Which perceptual concept does this example demonstrate?
    a. phi phenomenon
    b. cross-modal perception
    c. just noticeable difference
    d. cocktail party phenomenon

20. Which type of extra-sensory perception might be claimed by individuals who try to predict the outcome of a football game?
    a. clairvoyance
    b. synesthesia
    c. precognition
    d. telepathy

True or False

21. We perceive different colors based on the wavelength of light striking our retina.

22. A blind spot exists in our vision because an area on the retina lacks visual receptors.

23. Someone with color blindness cannot perceive any colors at all.

24. The same note played on different instruments sounds different because of a change in timbre.

25. The sensory receptors for the olfactory system are located in the olfactory bulbs.

26. Different areas of the tongue specialize in processing different taste sensations.

27. The body produces natural painkillers called endorphins.

28. You are able to perceive a quarter as round even when viewing it from an angle due to perceptual constancy.

29. Illusions fool our perceptual system only when our attention decreases.

30. Subliminal perception can influence behavior to some degree.

Essay

31. Explain the progression of a sound wave from its arrival at the eardrum to its arrival in the brain.

32. Describe how gate-control theory explains both our perception of pain and how psychological factors affect this perception.

33. Name and describe five Gestalt principles of perceptual organization.

Multiple Choice

1. Chris switches on his stereo. Sound waves stimulate receptors in his ear. It is only when the signals are processed in his brain that he recognizes the sounds as the music of Metallica. This recognition by the brain is called
   a. sonic stimulation.
   b. sensation.
   c. perception.
   d. registration.

2. Carrie purchases a new clock that chimes every hour. At first she finds the new chime distracting, but eventually she stops noticing the hourly noise. What process has taken place?
   a. sensory adaptation
   b. phi phenomenon
   c. the noise has fallen below the absolute threshold
   d. transduction

3. When you are complimented on the color of your eyes, which part of the eye is being noticed?
   a. cornea
   b. iris
   c. pupil
   d. lens

4. Which is the opening to the eye?
   a. cornea   c. pupil
   b. iris   d. lens

5. With age, the lens loses its ability to accommodate for near vision. What is this condition called?
   a. myopia
   b. hyperopia
   c. malopia
   d. presbyopia

6. Which of the following is *not* a type of cell according to the opponent-process theory of color vision?
   a. yellow/blue
   b. white/black
   c. blue/red
   d. red/green

7. The degree to which light waves producing a color are of the same wavelength is called
   a. brightness.
   b. maxima chroma.
   c. saturation.
   d. hue.

8. Which of the following animals can respond to sounds with the highest pitch?
   a. humans
   b. dogs
   c. bats
   d. dolphins

9. Which of the following statements best explains how we detect the location from which a sound is coming?
   a. Different hair cells fire to encode location.
   b. The difference in the intensity of sound reaching each ear helps us determine location.
   c. Hair cells fire in different frequencies depending on the location of the sound.
   d. The eardrum is struck harder when a sound is nearer than when it is farther away.

10. Which taste sensation is triggered by the substance glutamate?
    a. sweet
    b. bitter
    c. salty
    d. umami

11. Hal hurts his back while moving furniture. He realizes he has to complete the job and, while doing so, notices a reduction in pain. This is due to the activity of
    a. endorphins.
    b. serotonin.
    c. the spinal cord.
    d. norepinephrine.

12. Viewing either a white vase or two black faces in profile in a single image is an example of
    a. an ambiguous figure.
    b. an impossible figure.
    c. figure proximity.
    d. figure-ground.

13. Which of the following is *not* a monocular depth cue?
    a. linear perspective
    b. convergence
    c. interposition
    d. motion parallax

14. If you stare at a single unmoving light in a dark room, it will appear to move. What is this phenomenon called?
    a. autokinetic illusion
    b. phi phenomenon
    c. Ponzo illusion
    d. moon illusion

15. Which of the following explains how we know that a stop sign says "stop" even if some of the letters are hidden?
    a. bottom-up processing
    b. top-down processing
    c. perceptual set
    d. Gestalt principle of closure

16. Carla is driving across the state. She begins to focus only on the road in front of her, and she is taken by surprise when a car appears "out of nowhere" to cut her off. Which phenomenon is occurring here?
    a. phi phenomenon
    b. cocktail party phenomenon
    c. unfocused misperception
    d. inattentional blindness

17. We tend to perceive objects that are close together as belonging to the same group. This illustrates the Gestalt principle of
    a. similarity.
    b. continuity.
    c. proximity.
    d. closure.

18. Many complex perceptual tasks require the brain to integrate information from more than one sense, a process called
    a. cross-modal perception.
    b. extra-sensory perception.
    c. cross-sensory perception.
    d. multifactorial perception.

19. The capacity for responding to stimuli with unusual perceptions along with typical ones is called
    a. psychasthenia.
    b. extra-sensory perception.
    c. cross-modal perception.
    d. synesthesia.

20. Subliminal messages are presented
    a. above the threshold of awareness.
    b. below the threshold of awareness.
    c. only when the target is distracted.
    d. only when the subject is expecting them.

True or False

21. The absolute threshold is the minimum amount of sensory information that can be detected 100% of the time.

22. Sensory receptors may grow accustomed to constant, unchanging levels of stimuli over time.

23. Rods and cones fire in sequence to encode the wavelength of light.

24. There are more cones than rods in the human retina.

25. The ossicles in the middle ear are the three smallest bones in the human body.

26. The prevalence of chronic pain varies widely across different cultures.

27. The kinesthetic sense provides information about the positions of body parts relative to one another.

28. A pirate wearing an eye patch over one eye would have no depth perception.

29. Illusions occur due in part to learning.

30. Our expectations of what we will perceive can affect our actual perceptions.

Essay

31. Explain the two theories of color vision. Why is more than one theory needed to explain the perception of color?

32. Describe how we sense odors, including how neurons encode specific odors and their intensity.

33. Describe how you use both top-down processing and bottom-up processing when you read.

Chapter 4: States of Consciousness

PRACTICE TEST 1

Multiple Choice

1. A mental state other than wakefulness, such as sleep or meditation, is called
    a. consciousness.
    b. meta-consciousness.
    c. altered state of consciousness.
    d. conscientiousness.

2. Circadian rhythms exist for
    a. appetite.
    b. learning efficiency.
    c. energy level.
    d. all of the above.

3. Which hormone is most related to the sleep/wake cycle?
    a. adrenaline
    b. serotonin
    c. melatonin
    d. glucagon

4. _____ occurs in four stages.
    a. Biorhythm
    b. Consciousness
    c. REM sleep
    d. NREM sleep

5. Which EEG pattern is typical of someone who is re-laxed and drowsy, but not yet asleep?
   a. alpha waves
   b. beta waves
   c. delta waves
   d. sleep spindles

6. Jonas stayed up all night at a party. The next night when he slept, he had nightmares. This was probably because of
   a. sleep privation.
   b. REM rebound effect.
   c. NREM sleep disturbance.
   d. more time spent in stage 3 sleep.

7. Which theory best explains the function of sleep in humans?
   a. restorative theory of sleep
   b. circadian theory of sleep
   c. a combination of both the restorative and circa-dian theories of sleep
   d. neither the restorative nor the circadian theory of sleep

8. Laura describes a dream she had to her friend, Jessica. Jessica explains her view of what the dream means. Jessica is offering her opinion of which aspect of Laura's dream?
   a. manifest content
   b. latent content
   c. lucid content
   d. symbiotic content

9. Which of the following best describes the activation-synthesis hypothesis of dreaming?
   a. Dreams are symbolic of unconscious conflicts.
   b. Dreams offer a symbolic opportunity to rehearse solutions to real-world problems.
   c. Dreams are the brain's way of consolidating memories.
   d. Dreams are the brain's attempt to make sense of the random firing of brain cells during REM sleep.

10. The technical term for talking in one's sleep is
    a. somniloquy.
    b. somnambulism.
    c. parasomnia.
    d. hypersomnia.

11. Which of the following major sleep disorders may be treated through surgery?
    a. insomnia
    b. sleep apnea
    c. narcolepsy
    d. somniloquy

12. Nightmares and sleep terrors
    a. occur during different stages of sleep.
    b. are both seen during REM sleep.
    c. are the same thing.
    d. predict mental illness.

13. Terrell spends time every morning sitting alone, qui-etly concentrating on the sound of his own breath-ing. He says that the 20 minutes of quiet time clear his mind and cause him to feel rested and alert. Ter-rell is experiencing the benefits of
    a. hypnosis.
    b. medication.
    c. breathing control.
    d. meditation.

14. Which of the following statements about hypnosis is true?
    a. Memory is more accurate under hypnosis.
    b. People can perform superhuman acts while un-der hypnosis.
    c. People are more suggestible while hypnotized.
    d. Hypnosis can be used to regress adults back to their childhood.

15. Which theory of hypnosis posits that the behavior of a hypnotized person is a function of his or her own expectations about how people behave while hypno-tized?
    a. sociocognitive theory of hypnosis
    b. theory of dissociated control
    c. cognitive dissonance theory
    d. neodissociated theory of hypnosis

16. Which of the following is *not* a psychoactive drug?
    a. marijuana
    b. nicotine
    c. caffeine
    d. all of the above are psychoactive drugs

17. Alcohol is classified as a
    a. stimulant.
    b. depressant.
    c. hallucinogen.
    d. narcotic.

18. Blake uses cocaine. He finds he needs more cocaine now to receive the same effect he once received from smaller amounts of the drug. This symptom of co-caine dependence is called
    a. withdrawal.
    b. drug escalation.
    c. drug tolerance.
    d. psychological drug dependence.

19. At what point does casual use of a psychoactive drug become abuse?
    a. when the use of the substance occurs regularly
    b. when the individual feels a craving for the drug
    c. when use of the drug has begun to negatively af-fect important aspects of the person's life and functioning
    d. when the individual realizes that he or she wants to stop using the substance

20. The neurotransmitter associated with the feelings of reward or pleasure produced by many psychoactive substances is
    a. serotonin.
    b. dopamine.
    c. acetylcholine.
    d. diazepam.

True or False

21. Chronic jet lag can result in permanent memory deficits.

22. Exposure to bright sunlight during early morning hours and avoidance of bright light in the evening may help restore circadian rhythms.

23. Sleep deprivation may negatively affect mood, but has little effect on cognitive performance.

24. Dreams occur only during REM sleep.

25. Chronic insomnia can last for years and affects about 10% of all adults.

26. Meditation can help some people with depression.

27. Hypnosis has been effective in helping patients control pain.

28. Substance abuse is a more severe problem than substance dependence.

29. An individual who is addicted to cocaine and tries to quit using will often feel nervous and "hyper."

30. Marijuana has been associated with apathy and a decline in school performance.

Essay

31. Describe the progression through the various stages of the sleep cycle, including the EEG pattern typical of each stage.

32. Distinguish between the dream theories espoused by Freud and Hobson.

33. Distinguish between the general effects of stimulants, depressants, and hallucinogens, including the typical pattern of withdrawal symptoms for each.

PRACTICE TEST 2

Multiple Choice

1. An awareness of one's own thoughts, feelings, perceptions, sensations, and external environment is called
    a. objective reality.
    b. meta-awareness.
    c. consciousness.
    d. circadian reality.

2. Which of the following is *not* considered an altered state of consciousness?
    a. wakefulness
    b. sleep
    c. hypnosis
    d. drug intoxication

3. The biological clock that controls circadian rhythms is the
    a. suprachiasmatic nucleus.
    b. reticular formation.
    c. hypothalamus.
    d. substantia nigra.

4. Manny has worked the night shift at his job for some time. He sometimes has to run errands for his family during the day, and he finds himself being less attentive and having a slower reaction time when he does so. This period during which he has reduced attention and efficiency is called
    a. low biorhythm period.
    b. narcolepsy.
    c. hypersomnia.
    d. subjective night.

5. During which stage of sleep are you likely to find an EEG pattern of sleep spindles?
    a. stage 1
    b. stage 2
    c. stage 3
    d. REM sleep

6. The typical sleep cycle lasts approximately
    a. 60 minutes.
    b. 90 minutes.
    c. 4 hours.
    d. 8½ hours.

7. Which of the following is *not* a characteristic of REM sleep?
    a. vivid dreams
    b. eye movements
    c. increased brain-wave activity
    d. movement of the limbs

8. About half of a full night's sleep is spent in which stage?
    a. REM
    b. stage 2
    c. stage 3
    d. stage 4

9. Which theory of sleep is consistent with evolutionary theory?
    a. restorative theory of sleep
    b. circadian theory of sleep
    c. memory consolidation theory of sleep
    d. none of the above are consistent with evolutionary theory

10. Who suggested that dreams are symbolic representations of unconscious urges and desires?
   a. Wood, Wood, and Boyd
   b. evolutionary theorists
   c. J. Allan Hobson
   d. Sigmund Freud

11. Somnambulism, or sleepwalking, occurs during a partial arousal from which stage of sleep?
   a. REM
   b. stage 2
   c. stage 3
   d. stage 4

12. Narcolepsy
   a. is caused by prenatal exposure to toxins.
   b. can be treated with depressants.
   c. can be treated with stimulants.
   d. is rarely seen in adults.

13. Which of the following is *not* a potential health benefit of meditation?
   a. lowering blood pressure
   b. burning fat cells
   c. reducing heart attack risk
   d. lowering cholesterol levels

14. Which theory suggests that hypnosis induces a split between two aspects of the control of consciousness?
   a. dissociated control
   b. sociocognitive
   c. neodissociation
   d. neocognitive control

15. What percentage of people can reach the deepest levels of the hypnotized state?
   a. 5%
   b. 25%
   c. 50%
   d. 80%

16. Ways of inducing altered states of consciousness are found in _____ cultures.
   a. Western
   b. Asian
   c. African
   d. all

17. Depressants have a calming, sedating effect because they work on receptors for which neurotransmitter?
   a. GABA
   b. serotonin
   c. epinephrine
   d. dopamine

18. Physical dependence is characterized by _____ and _____.
   a. tolerance; withdrawal
   b. intoxication; pleasure
   c. intoxication; withdrawal
   d. pleasure; dosing increases

19. A class of depressants that are derived from the opium poppy and offer pain-relieving effects are the
   a. hallucinogens.
   b. psychedelics.
   c. cannabinoids.
   d. narcotics

20. Psychoactive substances produce a pleasurable effect by acting on which part of the limbic system of the brain?
   a. suprachiasmatic nucleus
   b. reticular formation
   c. hippocampus
   d. nucleus accumbens

True or False

21. An altered state of consciousness involves a change in awareness.

22. NREM dreams are less frequent and less memorable than REM dreams.

23. REM sleep is the stage in which we reach our deepest level of sleep.

24. During lucid dreams, the individual is aware that he or she is dreaming and able to influence the dream.

25. Sleep terrors are more vivid than nightmares and are more likely to keep the dreamer awake afterward.

26. Even staying up a bit later on Friday and Saturday nights can negatively affect one's mood on Monday morning.

27. A hypnotized person is under the complete control of the hypnotist.

28. Opiates mimic the body's own endorphins and thus are useful in pain management.

29. Alcohol serves to make men more aggressive, sexually aroused, and able to perform sexually.

30. Marijuana can be best classified as a hallucinogen.

Essay

31. Name and describe four parasomnias.

32. Review the three theories of hypnosis.

33. Distinguish between physical and psychological drug dependence.

Chapter 5: Learning

Multiple Choice

1. The individual most directly responsible for the process of classical conditioning is
   a. B. F. Skinner.
   b. Ivan Pavlov.
   c. John B. Watson.
   d. Edward Thorndike.

2. Billy's father always yells at him to "come here now" before administering a spanking. Billy begins to cry when his father yells that phrase at him. In this example of classical conditioning, which is the *conditioned stimulus*?
   a. the spanking
   b. Billy's crying
   c. Billy's father's yell of "come here now"
   d. Billy's father

3. The weakening and eventual disappearance of a conditioned response that is caused by repeated presentation of the conditioned stimulus without the presence of the unconditioned stimulus is called
   a. discrimination.
   b. generalization.
   c. spontaneous recovery.
   d. extinction.

4. The type of classical conditioning that accounts for learning when conditioned stimuli are linked together to form a series of signals is called
   a. chaining.
   b. second-stage conditioning.
   c. higher-order conditioning.
   d. latent learning.

5. Jerry bought a dog specifically to serve as a watch dog. He teaches his dog to bark whenever the doorbell rings. However, the dog also barks at the telephone or a doorbell rung on television. Which process explains these additional responses?
   a. spontaneous recovery
   b. higher-order conditioning
   c. generalization
   d. discrimination

6. John B. Watson's work with Little Albert was significant because it demonstrated
   a. a conditioned fear response.
   b. the limitations of classical conditioning.
   c. discrimination procedures.
   d. conditioning the behavior of a rat.

7. Janie once ate fish at a restaurant and later felt ill. Now the very smell of cooked fish makes her nauseous. What has Janie experienced?
   a. conditioned fear response
   b. taste aversion
   c. taste generalization
   d. conditioned fussiness response

8. Bill completes his drug rehabilitation program. His counselor strongly urges him to avoid going to places where he used to use drugs. His counselor, knowledgeable about classical conditioning, says this so that
   a. Bill doesn't experience peer pressure to use drugs.
   b. Bill can start fresh in more areas of his life.
   c. Bill doesn't get rewarded for drug use.
   d. Bill doesn't come into contact with stimuli previously associated with drug use.

9. Thorndike's experiments using the cat who had to learn to escape the puzzle box for food illustrated which behavioral law?
   a. law of rewards
   b. law of consequence
   c. law of effect
   d. law of gravity

10. Which of the following is the clearest example of operant conditioning?
    a. A firefighter races to the fire truck when the fire alarm rings.
    b. A driver begins to press the gas pedal when a traffic signal turns green.
    c. A rat runs through a maze successfully after being placed in it a second time.
    d. A dog sits because it has previously been given a treat for sitting.

11. The process of shaping a response involves reinforcing each of a series of steps which become increasingly more similar to the desired response. This process thus relies on
    a. successive approximations.
    b. gradual discovery.
    c. the "eureka" phenomenon.
    d. planning with foresight.

12. What causes extinction in operant conditioning?
    a. withholding punishment
    b. withholding reinforcement
    c. shaping
    d. reinforcing successive approximations

13. Cindy cries for candy when in the store with her mother. Her mother, wanting Cindy to be quiet, gives in and gets her some candy, at which point Cindy becomes silent. The next time they go to the store, the process repeats itself. Which of the following best describes what has happened?
    a. Cindy's behavior is positively reinforced, and her mother's behavior is positively reinforced.
    b. Cindy's behavior is positively reinforced, and her mother's behavior is negatively reinforced.
    c. Cindy's behavior is negatively reinforced, and her mother's behavior is positively reinforced.
    d. Cindy's behavior is negatively reinforced, and her mother's behavior is negatively reinforced.

14. A traffic signal uses different colors to trigger different behaviors: green for go, red for stop. This is most similar to which concept in operant conditioning?
    a. negative reinforcement
    b. shaping
    c. discriminative stimulus
    d. generalization

15. Which of the following is the best example of a primary reinforcer?
    a. money
    b. a diploma
    c. water
    d. a greeting card

16. A professor gives his class a quiz each Monday. Consequently, students do not study much during the week, but "cram" throughout the weekend to earn a good grade. Their behavior best corresponds to which schedule of reinforcement?
    a. fixed ratio
    b. variable ratio
    c. fixed interval
    d. variable interval

17. When Billy misbehaves, his parents make sure to apply punishment immediately and consistently, and to use the harshest possible punishment so that Billy will "get the message." Which of the following is a recommendation you might make to help their use of punishment be more effective?
    a. make punishment less severe
    b. make punishment more severe
    c. punish him less consistently
    d. wait a bit after his misbehavior before punishing him

18. Seligman's experiments with dogs that did not escape the shock administered, even when they could have, demonstrates which principle?
    a. avoidance learning
    b. learned helplessness
    c. escape learning
    d. positive reinforcement

19. Carrie is trying to complete a jigsaw puzzle. She has struggled with it for some time until she suddenly sees how the pieces fit together. Which type of learning is Carrie exhibiting?
    a. insight learning
    b. latent learning
    c. shaping
    d. observational learning

20. Carl learns how to change a flat tire by watching his mother do so. She would change a tire, and then have him show her each step as well. Which type of learning does this demonstrate?
    a. insight learning
    b. latent learning
    c. shaping
    d. modeling effect

True or False

21. Memorizing a phone number long enough to dial it, and then forgetting it, fits the text definition of learning.

22. Classical conditioning takes place most readily when the unconditioned stimulus occurs just before the conditioned stimulus.

23. John B. Watson coined the term "behaviorism" for the school that proposed limiting psychology to the study of overtly observable behavior.

24. The cognitive view of the classical conditioning suggests that the repeated pairing of the conditioned stimulus and the unconditioned stimulus is the critical element for conditioning to occur.

25. The "operant" in operant conditioning refers to a voluntary behavior.

26. The partial reinforcement effect occurs when reinforcement is intermittent and learning proceeds more quickly.

27. Punishment can suppress behavior, but not extinguish it.

28. Biofeedback can be used to train individuals to control internal responses such as heart rate and brainwave pattern.

29. Behavior modification programs require a therapist to administer them.

30. The process of latent learning depends on reinforcement taking place.

12. Vern has too much to drink at a party. The next day he gets a phone call from a woman he met at the party, but he does not remember her name. According to the state-dependent memory effect, under which condition is Vern most likely to remember her name?
    a. when he is sober
    b. when he hears her voice
    c. when he sees her face
    d. when he is drunk

13. The physiological process responsible for the formation of memories is called
    a. hippocampal potentiation.
    b. long-term potentiation.
    c. LLP.
    d. action potential.

14. Which of the following hormones has *not* been related to memory processes, according to your text?
    a. cortisol
    b. estrogen
    c. testosterone
    d. epinephrine

15. Jacquez believes that as you get older, memories that haven't been used will just fade away and disappear. His position is most consistent with which cause of forgetting?
    a. decay theory
    b. encoding failure
    c. consolidation failure
    d. proactive interference

16. David studied French in high school, but switched to learning Italian in college. Whenever he tries to speak French, he catches himself instead translating his English phrases into Italian. Why is David forgetting his French?
    a. encoding failure
    b. proactive interference
    c. retroactive interference
    d. decay theory

17. Which of the following is *not* a form of motivated forgetting?
    a. repression
    b. progressive forgetting
    c. suppression
    d. retrograde amnesia

18. Cassie is playing Trivial Pursuit with friends. Whenever she is asked a question, she gets frustrated because insists she knows the answer but can't seem to remember it. What is Cassie experiencing?
    a. state-dependent memory
    b. tip-of-the-tongue phenomenon
    c. retrograde amnesia
    d. repression

19. Another name for "cramming"—generally considered less effective than other methods of studying—is
    a. memorizing.
    b. studying.
    c. massed practice.
    d. motivated learning.

20. Roy G. Biv, an acronym representing the colors of the visual spectrum, is a type of
    a. chunking exercise.
    b. elaborative rehearsal.
    c. pegging.
    d. mnemonic device.

True or False

21. Elaborative rehearsal is the best method for remembering complex information like material for this class.

22. Recall tasks are typically considered to be easier than recognition tasks.

23. A reconstruction of an event may be based on inaccurate information.

24. Eyewitness testimony is reliable evidence in criminal court cases.

25. Human memory abilities can be significantly enhanced in certain cultures.

26. Your strongest, most long-lasting memories are usually those fueled by your emotions.

27. Hermann Ebbinghaus conducted the first experimental studies on learning and memory.

28. Studying similar subjects decreases the amount of interference experienced.

29. Overlearning involves studying so hard you can't remember what you studied.

30. Engaging in spaced practice will help you remember more in less study time.

Essay

31. Describe the "reconstructive" nature of memory, including the impact of schemas and cognitive bias.

32. What is long-term potentiation, and how is it related to learning?

33. Describe a plan for studying that incorporates four recommendations from your text to improve your memory.

Essay

31. Describe how the cognitive view of classical conditioning differs from Pavlov's view of classical conditioning.

32. Design a program of punishment to prevent a child from engaging in a dangerous behavior, such as playing with electrical cords. Discuss how the punishment program meets the recommendations in the text for making punishment more effective.

33. Describe how you might use the process of shaping to teach a rat to press a lever in a Skinner box.

Chapter 6: Memory

Multiple Choice

1. Any steps you take to try to commit something to memory are part of the _____ process.
   a. consolidation
   b. encoding
   c. retrieval
   d. placement

2. When you call information for a phone number, but you don't have a pen to write down the number, which part of your memory must attempt to maintain the number while you run around looking for a pen?
   a. sensory memory
   b. long-term memory
   c. short-term memory
   d. encoded memory

3. The strategy of grouping bits of information into larger units that are easier to remember is called
   a. displacement.
   b. rehearsal.
   c. assimilation.
   d. chunking.

4. For information in long-term memory to be used, it must be
   a. encoded.
   b. moved into sensory memory.
   c. retrieved.
   d. chunked.

5. Memories of a vacation spent with your family would be considered
   a. semantic memories.
   b. episodic memories.
   c. procedural memories.
   d. nondeclarative memories.

6. Which of the following is *not* one of the three types of nondeclarative memories?
   a. information learned in class
   b. motor skills
   c. simple classically conditioned responses
   d. habits

7. A memory researcher asks subjects to memorize a list of words, and finds it takes them 30 minutes to do so. Two weeks later, he asks the same subjects to memorize the list of words again, and they do so in 15 minutes. The percentage of time saved, 50%, is known as the
   a. savings score.
   b. relearning score.
   c. rote score.
   d. recognition score.

8. An integrated framework about people, objects, and events that is stored in long-term memory is called a
   a. memory.
   b. schema.
   c. reconstruction.
   d. retrieval cue.

9. Henry is in college, and he has difficulty remembering events from the first few years of his life. This is due to
   a. repression of early traumas.
   b. infantile amnesia, and indicative of a problem.
   c. infantile amnesia, and quite normal.
   d. the fact that he has yet to experience recovered memories.

10. There is a good chance that you remember exactly where you were and what you were doing when you first heard about the attacks on September 11, 2001. Such a vivid memory is called a(n) _____ memory.
    a. flashbulb
    b. snapshot
    c. autobiographical
    d. first-order

11. According to the serial position effect, which items on a list are *least* likely to be recalled?
    a. the first few
    b. the middle few
    c. the last few
    d. all items are equally likely to be remembered or forgotten

Multiple Choice

1. The act of maintaining information in the memory is called
   a. placement.   c. coding.
   b. storage.   d. filing.

2. Your instructor suggests that when you study, you should relate psychological concepts to events you have encountered in your day-to-day life. She is encouraging you to engage in
   a. maintenance rehearsal.
   b. elaborative rehearsal.
   c. rote memorization.
   d. the method of loci.

3. Which of the following memory systems holds information for as little as a fraction of a second?
   a. sensory memory
   b. long-term memory
   c. episodic memory
   d. short-term memory

4. As you read these questions, you most likely use the _____ part of your memory to answer correctly.
   a. semantic
   b. episodic
   c. consolidated
   d. nondeclarative

5. What type of memory task is involved in answering fill-in-the-blank questions?
   a. recognition   c. encoding
   b. episodic retrieval d. recall

6. Trying to remember a phone number by repeating it over and over again is called
   a. maintenance rehearsal.
   b. relearning.
   c. overlearning.
   d. elaborative rehearsal.

7. Sometimes erroneous information is supplied to an eyewitness after an event is over. This can affect the accuracy of eyewitnesses' recollections—a phenomenon called the
   a. disinformation effect.
   b. faulty memory syndrome.
   c. misinformation effect.
   d. misleading memory.

8. Which of the following events is *least* likely to be considered a "flashbulb" memory?
   a. attending your high school graduation
   b. participating in your wedding
   c. eating your breakfast this morning
   d. watching your favorite sports team win a championship game

9. Research on childhood memories has demonstrated that
   a. hypnosis is an effective technique for bringing early memories of trauma into consciousness.
   b. simply imagining experiences can lead to false memories.
   c. we have no memory for events that occurred before age 7.
   d. fictitious childhood memories can be experimentally induced.

10. Why does your text suggest people of various cultures can perform unique and amazing memory tasks?
    a. Some cultures value memories more than others.
    b. Some ethnic groups seem to have a biological predisposition to memory tasks.
    c. People of all cultures are better able to remember that which matters to them.
    d. Some cultures place greater emphasis on teaching memory skills.

11. You may find that you perform better on exams if you study in the same room in which you will later take the test because of
    a. autobiographical memories.
    b. flashbulb memories.
    c. the context-dependent memory effect.
    d. the state-dependent memory effect.

12. Which region of the brain is responsible for many of the functions necessary for episodic and semantic memory?
    a. hypothalamic
    b. Wernicke's area
    c. medulla
    d. hippocampal

13. The inability to form long-term memories following a brain injury is called
    a. retrograde amnesia.
    b. proactive amnesia.
    c. retroactive amnesia.
    a. anterograde amnesia.

14. Which of the following statements regarding hormones and memory is *false*
    a. Estrogen and progesterone decrease the risk of dementia in postmenopausal women.
    b. Epinephrine and norepinephrine are involved in the imprinting of emotionally laden memories.
    c. Excessive levels of cortisol are related to poor performance on memory tasks.
    d. Several hormones have been shown to be significantly related to memory functioning.

15. You know how to play the flute but decide to learn to play the clarinet. Unfortunately, you have trouble because you keep trying the same finger positions on the clarinet that you would use for the flute! Your previous experience is interfering with your attempt to learn something new. Your text calls this:
    a. retroactive amnesia.
    b. anterograde amnesia.
    c. retrograde interference.
    d. proactive interference.

16. Which researcher studied memory using lists of nonsense syllables?
    a. Freud
    b. Ebbinghaus
    c. Tulving
    d. Loftus

17. Lonnie is struggling in school. He meets with his professor and tells her about his study habits, which seem to be ineffective. The professor suggests that Lonnie try studying differently, and that his difficulty remembering material on the exams is due to
    a. encoding failure.
    b. proactive interference.
    c. consolidation failure.
    d. prospective forgetting.

18. Jessica hates going to the dentist, and she completely forgot about her last appointment. This is an example of
    a. repression.
    b. proactive interference.
    c. prospective forgetting.
    d. anterograde amnesia.

19. Studying by reading material and then closing your eyes to see how much you can recall is called
    a. recitation.
    b. spaced practice.
    c. overlearning.
    d. organization.

20. Which of the following is *not* a type of mnemonic device?
    a. method of loci
    b. repetition method
    c. pegword system
    d. first-letter technique

True or False

21. Chunking is a strategy that increases the capacity of sensory memory.

22. Research indicates that the two types of declarative memory function independently.

23. Remembering how to drive your car is a nondeclarative memory.

24. Long-term potentiation is a temporary decrease in the strength of neuronal firing.

25. Because of the primary and recency effects, you are least likely to recall items in the middle of a sequence.

26. Memories with significant emotional impact activate the amygdala.

27. The process of consolidation is most closely related to the process of memory retrieval.

28. Schemas may both aid and distort memory.

29. The more certain a witness is of his or her testimony, the more likely it is to be accurate.

30. Mnemonic devices help you remember things for only a short period of time.

Essay

31. Define elaborative rehearsal and explain how it facilitates learning.

32. Describe the controversy surrounding recovered repressed memories.

33. Describe the forms of motivated forgetting.

Chapter 7: Cognition, Language, and Intelligence

PRACTICE TEST 1

Multiple Choice

1. Acquiring, storing, retrieving, and using information, based on sensation, perception, problem solving, and conceptualizing, is called
    a. thinking.
    b. memorizing.
    c. cognition.
    d. recognition.

2. Which of the following would *not* be considered a concept?
    a. animals
    b. your dog Spike
    c. mammals
    d. dogs

3. Individual instances of a concept that are stored in memory from personal experience are called
   a. prototypes.
   b. specifics.
   c. formal concepts.
   d. exemplars.

4. Which of the following is the most likely prototype of a bird?
   a. sparrow
   b. penguin
   c. ostrich
   d. turkey

5. You are trying to decide what kind of breakfast cereal to buy. You notice a new cereal that you recall seeing advertised on television and choose to buy it. This kind of decision making fits best with the concept of the
   a. elimination by aspects strategy
   b. recognition heuristic
   c. algorithm
   d. representativeness heuristic

6. A cognitive rule of thumb, known as a(n) _____, says that the probability of an event or the importance it is given is based on its existence in prior memory.
   a. probability heuristic
   b. representative heuristic
   c. recognition heuristic
   d. availability heuristic

7. Kayla is playing blackjack and has a hand totaling 17. She knows that she will likely lose if she gets another card but she does so anyway because she has a "gut feeling" she will get a lucky card. On what is Kayla's decision making based?
   a. probability heuristic
   b. elimination by aspects
   c. intuition
   d. analogy heuristic

8. When you learn a specific procedure for solving a math problem that will always lead you to the correct answer, you are learning a(n)
   a. analogy.
   b. availability heuristic.
   c. algorithm.
   d. means-end analysis.

9. Juanita visits her adviser at college and afterward figures out when she will graduate by counting how many classes she has left and determining how many terms it will take to complete them. She is using
   a. working backward.
   b. means-end analysis.
   c. a mental set.
   d. an algorithm.

10. _____ leads to the tendency to apply a familiar strategy to the solution of a problem without carefully considering the special requirements of the problem.
    a. Trial-and-error thinking
    b. An analogy
    c. Functional fixedness
    d. Your mental set

11. How many phonemes are in the word *psychology*?
    a. 4   c. 8
    b. 6   d. 10

12. Intonation and social rules are part of which component of language?
    a. phonics
    b. pragmatics
    c. syntax
    d. semantics

13. The language in which you think largely determines the nature of your thoughts. This is called the
    a. bilingual theory.
    b. relative cognition model.
    c. meta-cognitive strategy.
    d. linguistic relativity hypothesis.

14. Thurston believed that seven distinct capabilities are involved in all intellectual activities, which he referred to as
    a. primary mental abilities.
    b. the *g* factor.
    c. IQ.
    d. the triarchic theory.

15. Wes is a con artist who flunked out of school. He is unemployed but runs "scams" to earn his living. He has played a bum, a cop, a priest, and a businessman as part of his efforts to cheat people, and he has never been caught. Wes likely would score best on a test of which of Sternberg's types of intelligence?
    a. experiential intelligence
    b. contextual intelligence
    c. componential intelligence
    d. none of the above

16. Phillip is an 8-year-old with a mental age of 6. According to Stern's formula, what is his IQ?
    a. 60
    b. 75
    c. 100
    d. 133

17. When you take a test and afterward believe it did not accurately measure your knowledge of the material covered, you are questioning the test's
    a. validity.
    b. cultural fairness.
    c. reliability.
    d. standardization.

18. Dynamic assessment
    a. is the latest trend in aptitude testing.
    b. is the only way to assess for mental retardation.
    c. provides a means to minimize cultural bias.
    d. is a technique used to differentiate gifted individuals from those who excel in only one domain.

19. Early interventions designed to enrich the environment of poor children
    a. rarely have an effect.
    b. have demonstrated that such efforts can have lasting effects.
    c. support the heritability of intelligence.
    d. demonstrate that nature cannot be altered by nurturing.

20. When you figure out a solution to your problem and you put it into action, you are engaging in the process of
    a. preparation.
    b. incubation.
    c. illumination.
    d. translation.

True or False

21. You are more likely to learn a formal concept from a textbook as opposed to a natural concept.

22. Framing, or presenting information a certain way to emphasize an outcome or gain, has a limited effect on decision making.

23. Anything the human brain can do, an artificial intelligence program can do just as well or better.

24. Morphemes, the smallest units of meaning in the English language, are always words.

25. Bilingualism during childhood is associated with an improved ability to think about language.

26. The SAT is an aptitude test designed to predict college performance.

27. Mental retardation is based solely on one's IQ score.

28. Lewis Terman's study found that mentally gifted individuals had more mental health problems than the general population.

29. Research shows that racial differences in IQ are due to genetic factors.

30. Women tend to do better than men on mathematical calculation tests.

Essay

31. Discuss the advantages and disadvantages of relying on heuristics in making decisions.

32. What have attempts to teach language to nonhuman primates demonstrated?

33. Distinguish between Spearman's *g*-factor approach to intelligence and Gardner's theory of multiple intelligences.

PRACTICE TEST 2

Multiple Choice

1. Which of the following is *not* typically considered an act of cognition?
    a. remembering information
    b. solving a math problem
    c. perceiving a stimulus
    d. moving toward an object

2. Although you may think of a tomato as a vegetable, it is actually a fruit. When you categorize a tomato as a fruit, you are using
    a. a formal concept.
    b. a natural concept.
    c. a prototype.
    d. an exemplar.

3. Which pairing best demonstrates a concept and a prototype of that concept?
    a. transportation—rickshaw
    b. mammal—platypus
    c. bird—penguin
    d. furniture—sofa

4. You take multiple-choice tests by reading each possible answer and crossing out each one that does not fit, before choosing the remaining answer. Which strategy are you using?
    a. anology
    b. elimination by aspects
    c. heuristic
    d. random guesswork

5. You see a news story about a plane crash and decide to cancel your trip to Hawaii because you decide that plane crashes have a high likelihood of occurrence. You are relying on the
    a. recognition heuristic.
    b. representativeness heuristic.
    c. availability heuristic.
    d. law of averages.

6. A thinking strategy based on how closely a new object or situation is judged to resemble an existing prototype is a(n)
   a. probability heuristic
   b. representative heuristic.
   c. recognition heuristic.
   d. availability heuristic.

7. Corinne's computer sometimes "freezes" when she is surfing the web. Once, she smacked the monitor and the problem was corrected. Since then, the first thing she tries when it freezes is to smack the monitor. She is using a(n)
   a. recognition heuristic.
   b. representativeness heuristic.
   c. availability heuristic.
   d. analogy heuristic.

8. "The glass can be half empty or half full." This sentence best illustrates
   a. framing.   c. qualifying.
   b. explaining.   d. replacing.

9. Will solves mazes in his leisure time. When he is doing a maze and reaches a difficult decision on a path to take, he will often look at the end of the maze and try to follow the path until he reaches his position. Will is using the strategy of
   a. means-end analysis.
   b. working backward.
   c. an algorithm.
   d. mental set.

10. Using a screwdriver to hammer in a nail demonstrates the ability to rise above
    a. restrictive range.
    b. the availability heuristic.
    c. functional fixedness.
    d. framing.

11. Which of the following is *not* a morpheme?
    a. re-   c. -ive
    b. -ed   d. -s

12. The meaning or study of meaning of words is called
    a. morphology.
    b. semantics.
    c. syntax.
    d. psycholinguistics.

13. According to the linguistic relativity hypothesis
    a. Eskimos have many words for snow because they think about snow more than other peoples.
    b. thinking influences perceptions and, as a consequence, language.
    c. because most cultures have just one word for snow, they think about snow in a more limited way than do the Eskimos.
    d. if snow were more common throughout the world, there would be more words for it.

14. Who is most closely associated with the idea that there is one general factor (*g* factor) underlying our mental abilities?
    a. Sternberg
    b. Gardner
    c. Thurstone
    d. Spearman

15. According to the triarchic theory of intelligence, if someone does very well in school, he or she would be considered high in which type of intelligence?
    a. componential intelligence
    b. experiential intelligence
    c. contextual intelligence
    d. standardized intelligence

16. Carol takes the same intelligence test 2 years in a row, and her scores both times are the same. Based on this information, this test would be considered to have good
    a. standardization.
    b. reliability.
    c. norms.
    d. validity.

17. On the Wechsler scale, the average range of IQ is considered to be between
    a. 80 and 100.
    b. 90 and 100.
    c. 90 and 110.
    d. 80 and 120

18. Which of the following best defines the nature versus nurture argument in intelligence research?
    a. How much of intelligence is inherited and how much is due to environmental factors?
    b. How much impact does socialization have on reaching potential?
    c. Is intelligence is a learned skill?
    d. Does the kindness of others have an effect on the development of intelligence?

19. Which of the following is the *best* definition of creativity?
    a. the ability to create original art using imagination and simple skills
    b. the ability to produce original, valuable ideas or solutions to problems
    c. the natural inclination to create something from nothing
    d. the ability to use intelligence in unconventional ways

20. What some people call insight, that sudden awareness of a solution to a problem, is
    a. preparation.
    b. incubation.
    c. illumination.
    d. translation

True or False

21. Formal concepts are also known as fuzzy concepts.

22. When an object is visualized, the areas of the brain involved with processing visual information show increased activity.

23. People rely on intuition only to make less important decisions.

24. Heuristics in general can lead to quick decisions but also leave us open to making errors.

25. The language learning of both humans and chimps depends on operant conditioning.

26. Learning a second language early in life actually leads to a change in the activity level in Broca's area.

27. Stern's formula for the calculation of IQ is no longer used today.

28. Women tend to outperform men on measures of perceptual speed.

29. Tasks requiring creativity and tasks on intelligence tests rely on different methods of problem solving.

30. There are no established tests of creativity.

Essay

31. Describe the limitations of artificial intelligence.

32. What did Lewis Terman find in his study of the mentally gifted?

33. You are debating Arthur Jensen, Richard Herrnstein, and Charles Murray. How would you counter their arguments regarding race and intelligence?

Chapter 8: Human Development

Multiple Choice

1. The idea that development occurs in distinctive phases that are easily distinguishable from each other is the central premise of
   a. continuous development.
   b. stage theories.
   c. environmental theory.
   d. nature versus nurture.

2. Wendy is 18 months old and just learning to speak. She meows whenever she sees a cat. One day, while she is watching television, a rabbit appears, and Wendy points and meows. What process has Wendy attempted regarding her existing scheme of cats?
   a. assimilation
   b. conservation
   c. accommodation
   d. hypothetico-deductive thinking

3. Sanford enjoys playing hide-and-seek with his mother. Sanford can play this game only because he has achieved what Piaget would call
   a. conservation.
   b. reversibility.
   c. hypothetico-deductive thinking.
   d. object permanence.

4. Piaget's cognitive stages in chronological order are
   a. sensorimotor, concrete operations, preoperations, formal operations.
   b. preoperations, concrete operations, formal operations, sensorimotor.
   c. preoperations, formal operations, concrete operations, sensorimotor.
   d. sensorimotor, preoperations, concrete operations, formal operations.

5. During which of Piaget's stages are children able to understand abstract concepts such as "freedom"?
   a. formal operations
   b. preoperations
   c. concrete operations
   d. sensorimotor

6. Luis behaves well at school because he wants to please his teacher. Which of Kohlberg's levels of moral development best fits Luis?
   a. sensorimotor
   b. preconventional
   c. conventional
   d. postconventional

7. According the Erikson, adolescence is known as the period of
   a. industry versus inferiority.
   b. autonomy versus shame and doubt.
   c. identity versus role confusion.
   d. trust versus mistrust.

8. Ginny is 82 years old. She often looks back on her life with satisfaction, believing that she accomplished a lot, had a loving family, and contributed to the world. Which of Erikson's stages best fits Ginny?
   a. industry versus inferiority
   b. ego integrity versus despair
   c. generativity versus stagnation
   d. autonomy versus shame and doubt

9. The developing human organism as it develops from the ninth week until birth is called a(n)
   a. embryo.
   b. zygote.
   c. gamete.
   d. fetus.

10. Because of the risk of fetal alcohol syndrome, pregnant women are advised to
    a. drink no more than one glass of wine per day.
    b. limit their drinking during the first trimester of pregnancy.
    c. completely abstain from alcohol during pregnancy.
    d. abstain from all hard liquor and limit consumption of other alcoholic beverages.

11. Harmful agents in the environment that can have a negative effect on prenatal development are called
    a. critical periods.
    b. teratogens.
    c. prenatal poisons.
    d. antagonists.

12. Brandi is 2 months old. She is generally happy most of the time, enjoys meeting new people, and has a regular routine to her day. Which temperament best describes her?
    a. slow-to-warm-up
    b. inconsistent
    c. easy
    d. difficult

13. Shawn is 18 months old. Lately, whenever his mother leaves him with his grandmother, he cries as if he is afraid. Their pediatrician said not to worry because _____ is common among children his age.
    a. stranger anxiety
    b. separation anxiety
    c. attachment disorder
    d. avoidance anxiety

14. "Mama give cookie me" could be an example of
    a. babbling.
    b. underextension.
    c. overextension.
    d. telegraphic speech.

15. Barry tells his father that he and his mother "goed to the store." This error is an example of
    a. overextension.
    b. overregularization.
    c. underextension.
    d. underregularization.

16. Which parenting style appears to produce the best results in the United States?
    a. authoritative
    b. authoritarian
    c. permissive
    d. absent

17. Cassandra is a teenager who hates school. She has developed a plan to have a perfect life that involves quitting school with her boyfriend and getting rich and famous by being on *American Idol*. Cassandra's plan would best be described by which term?
    a. a personal fable
    b. naive idealism
    c. imaginary audience
    d. hypothetico-deductive thinking

18. The most common symptom of menopause is
    a. menarche.
    b. hot flashes.
    c. dizziness.
    d. high blood pressure.

19. The only intellectual ability to show a continuous decline from age 30 to 80 is
    a. spatial ability.
    b. perceptual speed.
    c. creativity.
    d. mathematic ability.

20. The three leading causes of death in both men and women older than age 65 are heart disease, cancer, and
    a. Alzheimer's disease.
    b. stroke.
    c. COPD.
    d. meningitis.

True or False

21. Developmental psychology as it is studied today focuses on childhood and adolescence as times of change, and adulthood as a time of stagnation.

22. According to Piaget, a 3-year-old child would assume that you can see what she sees.

23. Vygotsky's sociocultural approach to cognitive development puts more emphasis on the impact of language development than does Piaget's theory.

24. Newborns can recognize stimuli to which they were exposed prior to birth.

25. One conclusion drawn from the visual cliff experiment was that babies have no perception of depth until they learn to walk.

26. Securely attached infants tend to develop more advanced social skills when they are preschoolers than their peers who were not securely attached.

27. The nativist position suggests that language development occurs primarily through operant conditioning.

28. Gender roles occur through the sole influence of biological factors.

29. Fluid intelligence peaks in one's twenties, but crystallized intelligence increases throughout the lifespan.

30. White males older than age 75 have the highest suicide rate of any group in the United States.

Essay

31. Name and describe four types of conservation tasks used by Piaget.

32. Distinguish between how learning theorists and nativists explain language development.

33. Describe how social learning, cognitive developmental, and gender-schema theorists explain gender role development.

Multiple Choice

1. Which of the following did *not* propose a stage theory of development?
   a. Ainsworth
   b. Erikson
   c. Piaget
   d. Kohlberg

2. An infant can be said to possess a scheme for nursing at his or her mother's breast. When the infant has to modify this scheme to nurse from a bottle, which process can be said to occur?
   a. accommodation
   b. assimilation
   c. maturation
   d. symbolic function

3. Shayna wants two cookies, but her mother wants her to have only one. Her mother breaks one cookie in half, and Shayna happily believes she has two. Shayna has not yet developed the concept of
   a. egocentrism.
   b. object permanence.
   c. symbolic function.
   d. conservation.

4. Chris pretends that playing cards are actually people interacting with one another. Piaget would say that Chris is using
   a. hypothetico-deductive thinking.
   b. object permanence.
   c. symbolic function.
   d. conservation.

5. Kohlberg believed that moral development is closely related to
   a. parental relationships.
   b. religious training.
   c. cognitive development.
   d. language development.

6. Quentin behaves well so that he can avoid getting spanked by his parents. Kohlberg would say that he is at which level of moral development?
   a. preconventional
   b. conventional
   c. postconventional
   d. none of the above

7. Erikson's first stage, the outcome of which depends on how responsive a child's caregiver is to that child's needs, is called
   a. industry versus inferiority.
   b. autonomy versus shame and doubt.
   c. basic trust versus mistrust.
   d. initiative versus guilt.

8. The cell that results from the union of a sperm and egg, corresponding to the first 2 weeks of pregnancy, is called the
   a. embryo.
   b. zygote.
   c. fetus.
   d. neonate.

9. During which prenatal period do the major organs of the body develop?
   a. period of the embryo
   b. fetal period
   c. teratogenic period
   d. period of the zygote

10. Which of the following statements about neonates is *false*?
   a. Newborns can turn their heads in the direction of a sound.
   b. Newborns show preferences for certain tastes and odors.
   c. Newborns are blind at birth, and develop sight starting around 5 weeks of age.
   d. Newborns possess certain built-in responses right from birth.

11. Temperament
    a. is genetically determined and unaffected by the environment.
    b. appears to be correlated with personality later in life.
    c. can rarely be detected within the first few weeks of life.
    d. can be reliably categorized in only 35% of infants.

12. Karen clings tightly to her mother in virtually all situations. She will not explore new environments. If her mother leaves the room for a few minutes, Karen will be angry at her mother and not allow her mother to hold her. Which type of attachment is Karen demonstrating?
    a. secure
    b. avoidant
    c. resistant
    d. disorganized/disoriented

13. The phoneme vocalization that occurs usually between 4 and 6 months after birth is called
    a. cooing.
    b. babbling.
    c. utterances.
    d. telegraphic speech.

14. Seeing her father in a kilt, Sally exclaimed, "Daddy is a girl! He's wearing a skirt!" With this statement, Sally is exhibiting that she has not yet acquired the concept of
    a. gender identity.
    b. gender stability.
    c. gender roles.
    d. gender constancy.

15. Which approach suggests that children learn gender roles primarily by being rewarded for behaviors that are considered gender-appropriate?
    a. biological view
    b. gender-schema theory
    c. social learning theory
    d. cognitive developmental theory

16. Sixteen-year-old Carlos loves action movies. Whenever he sees a new action film, he tries to copy the kinds of stunts he sees on the screen. He is convinced he can never be seriously hurt doing so, because of
    a. the personal fable.
    b. the imaginary audience.
    c. naive idealism.
    d. adolescent angst.

17. Presbyopia is considered an unavoidable change that occurs
    a. before age 40.
    b. around the mid- to late forties.
    c. around retirement age.
    d. just prior to the onset of menopause.

18. Relationship satisfaction tends to decline in adults following the birth of a child. Research has shown this decline to be primarily due to conflicts over
    a. the financial burdens of having a child.
    b. the decline in intimacy following the birth of a child.
    c. the increase in work-related stress following the birth of a child.
    d. the division of labor in raising a child.

19. Which type of intelligence peaks in the early twenties and slowly declines thereafter?
    a. emotional   c. crystallized
    b. fluid   d. vestibular

20. Which of the following is *not* a physical change typically associated with aging?
    a. becoming more nearsighted
    b. hearing loss
    c. a breakdown of myelin
    d. impaired night vision

True or False

21. It is generally agreed that cognitive development occurs in discrete stages.

22. Vygotsky's "zone of proximal development" refers to those tasks a child has mastered.

23. Erikson's stage theory is unique in its emphasis on development throughout the lifespan.

24. Characteristics of children with fetal alcohol syndrome include mental retardation and hyperactivity.

25. If a child does not meet a developmental milestone for a motor skill within 2 months later than the average child, then that child is considered unhealthy.

26. On average, girls experience their adolescent growth spurt earlier than boys.

27. Adolescents tend to choose friends who have similar backgrounds and values.

28. Approximately 80% of women with school-aged children work outside the home.

29. Physical exercise has little impact on the health of older adults.

30. More than 75% of all cases of senility are the result of Alzheimer's disease.

Essay

31. Describe each of Piaget's stages of cognitive development, being sure to describe the abilities and limitations at each stage.

32. Describe the three parenting styles. Which produces the best results?

33. What effects does the timing of puberty have on males and females?

Chapter 9: Motivation, Emotion, and Human Sexuality

Multiple Choice

1. Keisha wants to make good grades because her parents promised her a new car if she makes the honor roll. Keisha's motivation is
   a. intrinsic.
   b. extrinsic.
   c. social.
   d. homeostatic.

2. Human behavior is motivated by certain innate tendencies shared by all individuals, according to
   a. instinct theory.
   b. drive-reduction theory.
   c. homeostatic theory.
   d. arousal theory.

3. Which of the following statements is *true* according to the Yerkes-Dodson law?
   a. Performance on simple tasks is best when the arousal level is low.
   b. Performance on both simple and difficult tasks is best when the arousal level is high.
   c. Performance on moderately difficult tasks is best when the arousal level is low.
   d. Performance on difficult tasks is better when arousal is low.

4. Which needs did Maslow believe must be satisfied first?
   a. physiological
   b. safety
   c. belonging and love
   d. esteem

5. Which of the following factors *inhibits* eating?
   a. low blood levels of glucose
   b. stomach contractions
   c. increased levels of cholecystokinin (CCK)
   d. increased levels of insulin

6. Which of the following is a primary drive?
   a. curiosity
   b. emotional insecurity
   c. thirst
   d. loneliness

7. You conduct a hunger experiment with rats. In one rat, you damage the ventromedial hypothalamus. In the second rat, you stimulate the lateral hypothalamus. Then you offer food to each of the rats. What will happen?
   a. The first rat will eat; the second rat will not eat.
   b. The first rat will not eat; the second rat will eat.
   c. Both rats will eat.
   d. Neither rat will eat.

8. Cherelle has weighed approximately 120 pounds for most of her adult life. She doesn't work hard to lose weight, nor does she try to gain weight. You conclude that 120 pounds represents Cherelle's
   a. set point.
   b. metabolic rate.
   c. body mass index.
   d. homeostatic score.

9. The hormone that directly affects the hypothalamus and plays a primary role in weight regulation is
   a. adrenalin.
   b. leptin.
   c. serotonin.
   d. insulin.

10. Which factor seems most highly correlated with male bulimics?
    a. age
    b. education
    c. sexual orientation
    d. intelligence

11. What is the shortest of the four phases in the sexual response cycle?
    a. plateau
    b. resolution
    c. excitement
    d. orgasm

12. The area of the hypothalamus that governs sexual behavior is twice as large in heterosexual men than it is in homosexual men, according to research done by LeVay. What is the main criticism of LeVay's research?
    a. He did not use universal precautions.
    b. He did not account for AIDS as a variable.
    c. LeVay used only a small sample.
    d. His research was never replicated.

13. Inez devotes all of her energy to school. She sets high standards of performance for herself in an effort to accomplish all she can. Inez could be said to have a high
    a. need for success.
    b. need for recognition.
    c. need for achievement.
    d. need for glory.

14. Yvonne insists she must get the highest grade on every test so that she can exceed her peers and enhance her own self-worth. According to goal orientation theory, which goal orientation best fits Yvonne?
    a. mastery-approach orientation
    b. mastery-avoidance orientation
    c. performance-approach orientation
    d. performance-avoidance orientation

15. On realizing that the shadow behind you is a man with a gun, your heart begins to race and at the same time you feel afraid. With which of the following theories of emotion is this scenario most consistent?
    a. Cannon-Bard theory
    b. Lazarus theory
    c. James-Lange theory
    d. Schachter-Singer theory

16. Which theory of emotion says that emotion-provoking stimuli trigger a cognitive appraisal, followed by emotional and physiological arousal?
    a. James-Lange theory
    b. Cannon-Bard theory
    c. Schachter-Singer theory
    d. Lazarus theory

17. Which of the following would *not* be considered a basic emotion?
    a. embarrassment   c. anger
    b. fear   d. joy/happiness

18. Many members of traditional British culture consider Americans to be vulgar because of Americans' tendency to spontaneously demonstrate whatever emotion they feel. The conflict between cultures is caused by differing
    a. impressions.   c. emotional ranges.
    b. display rules.   d. basic emotions.

19. The facial feedback hypothesis states that
    a. we recognize the emotions of others in their facial expression, and change our own emotions to match.
    b. our emotions directly affect our facial muscles so that we produce an expression to match the emotion.
    c. muscular movements involved in certain facial expressions produce the corresponding emotion.
    d. facial expressions change the intensity of the emotion one is feeling.

20. Which of the following has been suggested as providing a biological explanation for some of the emotional differences between the genders?
    a. Women process emotions in both cerebral hemispheres, while men tend to use predominantly the left hemisphere to process emotions.
    b. The amygdala is significantly larger and shows more activity in women than in men.
    c. Men's brains route emotional responses through the frontal lobe, thereby tempering their emotional responses with rational planning.
    d. There are no real emotional differences between the genders.

True or False

21. A motive can be biological or social in nature, but no behavior serves both types of motives at once.

22. Extrinsic motivation is consistent with Skinner's concept of reinforcement.

23. The phenomenon of sensation seeking is best explained by drive-reduction theory.

24. Individuals with bulimia nervosa are often of normal weight.

25. Women appear to have the strongest desire for sex around the time of ovulation when they are most likely to conceive a child, as evolutionary theory would predict.

26. Androgens are present only in men; estrogen and progesterone are present only in women.

27. Younger siblings show a higher need for achievement than older siblings.

28. The amygdala is activated by fear before any direct involvement of the cerebral cortex occurs.

29. Blind babies develop facial expressions of emotions in the same sequence and at the same time as infants who can see.

30. Women report more intense emotional experiences than men, but men generate more extreme physiological reactions indicating emotional response.

Essay

31. Describe environmental cues for hunger.

32. Define anorexia nervosa and bulimia nervosa, and describe the negative effects of each disorder.

33. Discuss the role of cognition in each of the four theories of emotion discussed in this chapter.

PRACTICE TEST 2

Multiple Choice

1. Gerrard just got a promotion at work. He told his family that he didn't really care about the extra money—he was thrilled because he liked his work and took pride in doing a good job. Gerrard's motivation is
   a. intrinsic.
   b. extrinsic.
   c. social.
   d. homeostatic.

2. According to drive-reduction theory, a drive is created when the body's balanced internal state is disturbed. This balanced state is called
   a. hypothalamic equity.
   b. internal consistency.
   c. homeostasis.
   d. symmetry.

3. Which of the following is *not* consistent with Maslow's hierarchy of needs?
   a. Before looking for his friends, a man first finds an umbrella to keep himself dry.
   b. A woman deprives herself of food to lose weight and gain approval from her friends.
   c. A woman first starts a career to support herself before starting to date.
   d. An individual first meets biological and psychological needs before achieving self-actualization.

4. Removal of which brain area will lead to an animal's overeating enough to cause obesity?
   a. amygdala
   b. lateral hypothalamus
   c. ventromedial hypothalamus
   d. thalamus

5. Which of the following environmental factors inhibits eating?
   a. foods high in fat and sugar
   b. boredom
   c. being around others who are eating
   d. none of the above inhibits eating

6. As you get older, you find you cannot eat the same quantity and types of foods you ate when you were younger without putting on extra weight. This is due to a change in your
   a. metabolic rate.
   b. body mass index.
   c. homeostasis.
   d. leptin secretion rate.

7. Grace is obsessed with her body. She thinks she is fat when she is actually alarmingly thin. She counts every calorie and, no matter what the scale says, she is convinced that she is grossly overweight. Grace probably suffers from
   a. bulimia nervosa.
   b. anorexia nervosa.
   c. CDD.
   d. depressive bulimia.

8. Gender differences are seen in all of the following *except*
   a. the incidence of homosexuality.
   b. the role of hormones in sexual interest.
   c. the likelihood of engaging in premarital sex.
   d. the incidence of bulimia nervosa.

9. Which of the following is *true* according to the evolutionary principle of parental investment?
   a. Men seek long-term relationships with women thought to be good at child rearing.
   b. Women seek younger men who are strong and healthy.
   c. Both men and women seek short-term relationships with individuals thought to provide "good breeding."
   d. Women seek older men who are stable and emotionally attached.

10. What do men experience during the resolution phase?
    a. multiple orgasms
    b. plateau
    c. refractory period
    d. ejaculation

11. In Laumann's survey, what percentage of men reported having felt some same-sex desires?
    a. 1%
    b. 5%
    c. 10%
    d. 25%

12. Which of the following has *not* been suggested as a way to encourage the development of high need for achievement in children?
    a. giving children fewer responsibilities so they can concentrate on schoolwork
    b. teaching children to think independently from the time they are very young
    c. offering sincere praise for a child's accomplishments
    d. stressing the achievement of excellence and persistence

13. What is the name of the test used to reveal a person's needs and the strength of them?
    a. Thematic Apperception Test
    b. Rorschach test
    c. house-tree-person
    d. MMPI

14. Adam studies enough in school to ensure that he scores at least as high as the class average on every exam. Which goal orientation best describes Adam?
    a. mastery-approach orientation
    b. mastery-avoidance orientation
    c. performance-approach orientation
    d. performance-avoidance orientation

15. After falling, a child often looks toward the mother before reacting. Depending on how the mother responds, the child will respond to the fall by either laughing or crying. Which of the following would best explain this phenomenon?
    a. James-Lange theory
    b. Cannon-Bard theory
    c. Schacter-Singer theory
    d. Lazarus theory

16. Which theory suggests that emotion-provoking stimuli are transmitted to the brain and nervous system simultaneously, causing both physiological and emotional responses?
    a. James-Lange theory
    b. Cannon-Bard theory
    c. Schachter-Singer theory
    d. Lazarus theory

17. Which of the following are both universal and un-learned?
    a. impressions
    b. display rules
    c. emotional ranges
    d. basic emotions

18. Which of the following statements is *true* concerning brain lateralization and emotions?
    a. Sad feelings are associated with greater activity in the left side of the brain.
    b. Angry feelings produce more pronounced stimulation on the right side of the brain.
    c. Women show less lateralization than men when it comes to perceiving the emotions of others.
    d. Perception of others' emotions appears to be lateralized to the left side of the brain.

19. Which of the following is an example of a display rule?
    a. Americans express pleasure with a smile.
    b. Japanese people grimace when disgusted.
    c. Laughter first appears at about 4 months of age.
    d. Girls will smile when presented with a gift, even if they do not like it.

20. Your psychology professor suggested that you hold a pencil between your teeth. As your mouth curved into a smile, you began to feel happy. Your professor was demonstrating
    a. the James-Lange theory.
    b. the facial feedback hypothesis.
    c. social referencing.
    d. the Cannon-Bard theory.

True or False

21. Intrinsically motivated behaviors are typically considered more enjoyable than extrinsically motivated behaviors.

22. Humans have several instincts that serve to motivate behavior.

23. Low-carbohydrate diets may reduce a person's metabolic rate, which in turn drains the dieter's energy so that he or she is less able to exercise.

24. No matter which treatment program is used, most individuals with anorexia nervosa experience relapses.

25. There is ample evidence for some kind of genetic predisposition that increases the likelihood of homosexuality in men, but not in women.

26. Men are more likely to have sexual fantasies of doing something sexual to someone else, whereas women are more likely to have sexual fantasies of having something sexual done to them.

27. Individuals with a high need for achievement choose easier tasks on which they are more certain to have success.

28. College and high school students who adopt one of the mastery orientations are more likely to procrastinate and get poorer grades.

29. Research has indicated that it is always healthy to express one's emotions.

30. Women appear to be more physiologically sensitive to negative emotions than men are.

Essay

31. Compare and contrast the drive-reduction theory and the arousal theory of motivation.

32. Describe the phases of the human sexual response cycle, highlighting the main differences between men and women throughout the cycle.

33. Describe gender differences in the experience and expression of emotions.

Chapter 10: Health and Stress

Multiple Choice

1. Which of the following is *not* part of the text's definition of stress?
   a. a physiological response
   b. an emotional response
   c. a psychological response
   d. a situation that requires adaptation

2. Which type of stressors seem to cause more stress?
   a. hassles
   b. uplifts
   c. annoyances
   d. catastrophes

3. Hank has a stressful job, but he always looks forward to coming home to his wife, who never fails to bring a smile to his face and relieve some of his stress. According to Richard Lazarus, Hank's time with his wife would be described as
   a. a hassle.
   b. an approach-approach situation.
   c. a counter-stressor.
   d. an uplift.

4. Would you rather have a terrible toothache or the undesirable experience of having the tooth drilled and the cavity filled? This choice represents which type of conflict?
   a. approach-avoidance
   b. approach-approach
   c. avoidance-avoidance
   d. double approach-avoidance

5. According to Albrecht, which of the following factors is *not* related to job satisfaction and effective functioning at work?
   a. the clarity of the job description and evaluation criteria
   b. having a variety of tasks to accomplish
   c. being one's own boss
   d. having some amount of accountability on the job

6. A prolonged stress reaction following a catastrophic experience is called
   a. postdramatic stress disorder.
   b. posttraumatic stress disorder.
   c. general adaptation syndrome.
   d. exhaustion.

7. Which of the following has been found to moderate levels of racial stress in African Americans?
   a. a strong sense of ethnic identity
   b. a high degree of hostility
   c. historical racism
   d. being one of only a few African Americans in a given setting, such as a classroom or workplace

8. According to Seyle's GAS concept, when an organism fails in its efforts to resist a stressor, what happens?
   a. resistance failure
   b. exhaustion
   c. fight-or-flight syndrome
   d. alarm

9. According to Richard Lazarus, an event appraised as stressful could involve
   a. harm or loss.
   b. threat.
   c. challenge.
   d. all of the above.

10. Which of the following is the best example of a secondary appraisal?
    a. Carol does not believe her exam performance is related to anything she does.
    b. Marsha thinks that majoring in chemistry will be a challenge.
    c. Jan decides that she isn't smart enough to do well in school.
    d. Cindy tries to choose easier classes that won't be a threat to her grade point average.

11. Mrs. Genova has been told that she has terminal cancer and only a few months left to live. After a brief time, she set out to tie up the loose ends of her life, updating her will, giving away special possessions, and saying her goodbyes. Mrs. Genova is employing which approach to coping with her illness?
    a. variate-focused
    b. problem-focused
    c. emotion-focused
    d. solution-focused

12. The biomedical model focuses on _____, giving explanations based on biological factors without taking social or psychological matters into account.
    a. stress
    b. health
    c. wellness
    d. illness

13. Which element of the Type A behavior pattern is most strongly related to coronary heart disease?
    a. time urgency
    b. hostility
    c. competitiveness
    d. impatience

14. Which of the following is *not* a risk factor for cancer, according to health psychologists?
    a. smoking
    b. promiscuous sexual behavior
    c. excessive alcohol consumption
    d. all of the above are risk factors for cancer

15. The key components of the immune system are the white blood cells known as
    a. antigens.
    b. antibodies.
    c. lymphocytes.
    d. leukocytes.

16. Which of the following infectious diseases has *not* been correlated with periods of high stress?
    a. rubella
    b. mononucleosis
    c. flu
    d. genital herpes

17. Which of the following qualities is *not* considered part of the trait of hardiness?
    a. control
    b. commitment
    c. caring
    d. challenge

18. What percentage of the adult population in the United States still smokes, according to your text?
    a. more than 40%
    b. less than 25%
    c. about 10%
    d. less than 10%

19. Shrinkage of which part of the brain has been shown in MRI studies done on alcoholics?
    a. medulla
    b. temporal lobes
    c. cerebral cortex
    d. pons

20. A diagnosis of AIDS is made when
    a. the presence of HIV reaches a critical level in the body.
    b. HIV is detected in the blood.
    c. there is evidence of HIV-related damage to the immune system.
    d. the damage to the immune system due to HIV leads to opportunistic infections.

True or False

21. The parasympathetic nervous system initiates the fight-or-flight response.

22. The hassle most commonly cited by college students is not getting enough sleep.

23. Survivor guilt is a common symptom of individuals who live through a catastrophic event.

24. Prolonged stress can lead to permanent increases in blood pressure, suppression of the immune system, and weakening of muscles.

25. Research has indicated that problem-focused coping is the best stress management strategy.

26. A sedentary lifestyle is the primary modifiable risk factor contributing to death from coronary heart disease.

27. Once a stressful experience has passed, stress no longer actively suppresses the immune system.

28. Women are more likely than men to seek medical care.

29. Being exposed to second-hand smoke doubles one's risk of having a heart attack.

30. The most common infectious disease in the United States is AIDS.

Essay

31. Describe the biopsychosocial model of health and illness.

32. Describe the Type A and Type B behavior patterns.

33. Describe four personal factors that reduce the impact of stress and illness.

PRACTICE TEST 2

Multiple Choice

1. You are about to ask your boss for a much-needed raise. The physiological response involving the release of hormones that cause you to feel anxious is called the
    a. stress adaptation response.
    b. ready-or-not response.
    c. fight-or-flight response.
    d. get-it-over-with response.

2. What is the SRRS?
    a. Stress Response Rating Scale
    b. Stress Rate Response Scale
    c. Social Readjustment Rating Scale
    d. Serial Response-Rated Stressors

3. If you like all kinds of sweets, do you want cake or ice cream? This choice represents which type of conflict?
    a. approach-avoidance
    b. approach-approach
    c. avoidance-avoidance
    d. double approach-avoidance

4. What does your book report as the number one hassle for college students?
    a. worry about the future
    b. lack of sleep
    c. physical appearance
    d. not enough hours in the day

5. Which of the following is *not* typically considered a result of job stress?
    a. family conflict
    b. reduced job effectiveness
    c. tardiness and absenteeism
    d. substance abuse

6. Posttraumatic stress disorder (PTSD)
   a. affects approximately 20% of the population.
   b. is usually seen only in men who have been involved in combat.
   c. may be experienced only by those who are directly affected by some trauma.
   d. is often associated with the development of other psychological problems.

7. Historical racism has been associated with
   a. PTSD.
   b. increased substance abuse.
   c. cardiovascular reactivity.
   d. depression.

8. Cara works two jobs while trying to support her two children and take care of her elderly father. She initially struggled with this arrangement, but more recently she feels as though she is handling the stress better. Which stage of the general adaptation syndrome seems to best fit Cara?
   a. resistance stage
   b. alarm stage
   c. assessment stage
   d. avoidance stage

9. Mr. Stanley has cancer. He spends all of his spare time reading and doing research into alternative medicine and experimental treatments for his disease. He is determined to beat it. Mr. Stanley is using which approach to cope with his illness?
   a. variate-focused
   b. problem-focused
   c. emotion-focused
   d. solution-focused

10. Dr. Laslow is conducting a biopsychosocial evaluation of a patient. He has evaluated the patient's mood, stress management skills, level of exercise, diet, and personality. What has Dr. Laslow forgotten?
    a. He has not assessed biological factors.
    b. He has not assessed psychological factors.
    c. He has not assessed social factors.
    d. He has not forgotten anything.

11. Which of the following statements about the Type B behavior pattern is *false*?
    a. Type B individuals are generally relaxed and easygoing.
    b. Type B individuals experience low levels of time urgency.
    c. Type B individuals are at least as successful as Type A individuals.
    d. Type B individuals are less ambitious than Type A individuals.

12. The field that includes psychologists, biologists, and medical researchers who study the effects of psychological factors on the immune system is called
    a. psychoneuroimmunology.
    b. immunopsychology.
    c. neurology.
    d. psychobiology.

13. Which of the following has *not* been linked to lowered immune response?
    a. academic pressures
    b. poor marital relationships
    c. job responsibilities
    d. sleep deprivation

14. Religious faith
    a. has been shown to have a direct effect on health.
    b. has been shown to be correlated with better health habits.
    c. is a form of problem-focused coping.
    d. is frequently accompanied by denial, and together they have a negative effect on health status.

15. Which of the following is *not* a potential benefit of social support?
    a. reduced likelihood of developing cancer
    b. increased probability of surviving a heart attack
    c. encouragement of health-promoting behaviors
    d. reduced depression and enhanced self-esteem

16. Which statement concerning ethnic differences in health conditions is *false*?
    a. The rate of AIDS among African Americans is three times higher than among White Americans.
    b. Among all U.S. ethnic groups, the infant mortality rate is lowest for Chinese Americans.
    c. Hispanic Americans suffer more heart problems than non-Hispanic White Americans.
    d. Rates of diabetes are higher for Native Americans than for all other ethnic groups.

17. Which of the following is *not* considered a negative consequence of smoking?
    a. higher incidence of chronic bronchitis and breathing problems
    b. increased risk of heart disease
    c. higher incidence of anxiety disorders and depression
    d. increased risk of respiratory tract infections and tumors

18. The most frequently abused substance is likely
    a. alcohol.
    b. caffeine.
    c. cocaine.
    d. marijuana.

19. The incidence of many sexually transmitted diseases (STDs) has increased over the last 30 years because of all of the following *except*
    a. more permissive attitudes about sex.
    b. increased use of the birth control pill.
    c. increased use of vaginal spermicides.
    d. increased sexual activity among younger people.

20. AIDS progresses more quickly in all of the following *except*
    a. men.
    b. smokers.
    c. the very young.
    d. people older than age 50.

True or False

21. While people vary in what they view as a hassle, those events seen as catastrophes are universal.

22. Unpredictable stressors are more difficult to cope with than predictable stressors.

23. PTSD is a common response to typical life stressors.

24. Racial stress can be experienced only in an environment where racism occurs.

25. Ignoring a stressor can be an effective way of managing stress.

26. Research indicates that the most effective elements of a strategy of coping with cancer are social support, focusing on the positive, and distraction.

27. Having a rich social life may reduce a person's risk of catching a cold virus.

28. Men are more likely to die following open-heart surgery than women are.

29. Ninety percent of ex-smokers report that they quit on their own.

30. Viral STDs are more amenable to treatment than bacterial STDs are.

Essay

31. Review the variables that must be within a person's comfort zone to experience job satisfaction, according to Albrecht.

32. Describe Lazarus and Folkman's psychological model of stress.

33. Discuss the lifestyle factors that put one at risk for developing coronary heart disease.

Chapter 11: Personality Theory and Assessment

Multiple Choice

1. You don't usually think about your phone number, but if someone asked you for it, you could easily recall it and make yourself aware of it. Your phone number is likely stored in your
    a. unconscious.
    b. conscious.
    c. preconscious.
    d. subconscious.

2. George wants a new stereo badly. He decides he will buy a new one by putting it on his credit card, without worrying too much about the debt he is accruing. George is acting based on the wishes of his
    a. id.
    b. ego.
    c. superego.
    d. unconscious mind.

3. Alice feels good about how neat and organized she keeps her room. This pride represents her
    a. ego.
    b. conscience.
    c. id
    d. ego ideal.

4. Lysette cannot believe it when her friends tell her that her boyfriend is cheating on her. She insists they must be mistaken. Which Freudian defense mechanism might Lysette be exhibiting?
    a. repression
    b. projection
    c. displacement
    d. denial

5. Tabitha has always been a flirtatious and promiscuous woman. She is very vain, and she tends to seek attention from anyone around her. Freud might suggest that she had problems at which psychosexual stage of development?
    a. anal
    b. phallic
    c. oral
    d. latency

6. Which theorist suggested that we share the universal experiences of humankind throughout evolution?
    a. Carl Jung
    b. Sigmund Freud
    c. Karen Horney
    d. Alfred Adler

7. Which theorist suggested that behavior, cognitive factors, and the environment have a mutually influential relationship?
   a. Abraham Maslow
   b. Julian Rotter
   c. Albert Bandura
   d. Karen Horney

8. Which of the following statements about the differences between people with high self-efficacy and low self-efficacy is *false*?
   a. People with high self-efficacy show greater persistence than those with low self-efficacy.
   b. People with high self-efficacy set lower goals that are more realistic than those with low self-efficacy.
   c. People with high self-efficacy have more confidence than those with low self-efficacy.
   d. All of the above statements are true.

9. Someone with an internal locus of control is most likely to explain a high test grade as due to
   a. luck.
   b. an easy exam.
   c. hard work.
   d. prayer.

10. Which group of theories is most likely to suggest that individuals can reach their full potential for growth?
    a. psychoanalytic
    b. trait
    c. learning
    d. humanistic

11. Ben goes along with what his friends want to do even though he would prefer to do something else. He does so because he wants to be accepted. Carl Rogers would explain Ben's behavior by saying that he has been exposed to
    a. conditions of worth.
    b. conditions of self-actualization.
    c. conditions of unconditional positive regard.
    d. conditions of friendship.

12. You are trying to set up two of your friends for a date. One asks you to describe the other's personality, which you do using five to eight characteristics. According to Allport, what kind of traits have you listed?
    a. cardinal traits
    b. surface traits
    c. central traits
    d. source traits

13. Zach is an emotional, nervous, and moody person, but he is always good-natured, warm, and cooperative. On which two Big Five traits would Zach likely be rated highly?
    a. Extroversion and Neuroticism
    b. Openness to Experience and Agreeableness
    c. Conscientiousness and Extroversion
    d. Agreeableness and Neuroticism

14. According to the Minnesota twin study, which of the following statements concerning twins and personality is *true*?
    a. Identical twins are similar on several personality factors, whether reared together or apart.
    b. Identical twins are similar on several personality factors, but only if they were reared together.
    c. Identical twins are similar on several personality factors, but only if they were reared apart.
    d. Identical twins are not similar on any personality factors.

15. Genes exert more influence on which Big Five traits?
    a. Extroversion and Neuroticism
    b. Openness to Experience and Agreeableness
    c. Conscientiousness and Extroversion
    d. Agreeableness and Neuroticism

16. Nicole responds to some questionnaires that ask her questions about her behaviors and personality characteristics. What kind of personality assessment has she undergone?
    a. behavioral assessment
    b. personality inventory
    c. projective test
    d. structured interview

17. Which of the following provides a standardized format for the data from observations or interviews?
    a. personality inventory
    b. rating scale
    c. projective test
    d. behavioral checklist

18. Which of the following is often used by career counselors?
    a. Minnesota Multiphasic Personality Inventory (MMPI)
    b. Myers-Briggs Type Indicator (MBTI)
    c. Thematic Apperception Test (TAT)
    d. California Personality Inventory (CPI)

19. Which of the following is a projective test?
    a. Minnesota Multiphasic Personality Inventory (MMPI)
    b. Myers-Briggs Type Indicator (MBTI)
    c. Thematic Apperception Test (TAT)
    d. California Personality Inventory (CPI)

20. Which of the following is considered by the examiner in evaluating responses to the Rorschach Inkblot method?
    a. the content of the response
    b. whether shape or color influenced the response
    c. whether the whole blot or only part of it is used in the response
    d. all of the above are considered

True or False

21. The ego operates according to a principle that demands immediate gratification.

22. Freud's theories have been criticized as defying scientific testing.

23. Low self-efficacy is correlated with an increased risk for depression.

24. People with an internal locus of control are more likely to procrastinate than people with an external locus of control.

25. According to Maslow, self-actualized individuals are autonomous and thus do not pursue personal relationships.

26. Observable qualities of personality are referred to as source traits.

27. The Big Five traits have been found in cross-cultural studies in Canada, Poland, Germany, Hong Kong, and Portugal.

28. The trait of aggressiveness is more influenced by parental upbringing than by genetics.

29. The MMPI contains validity scales to detect faking or lying.

30. The Rorschach Inkblot method continues to have poor interrater agreement due to the lack of a scoring system.

Essay

31. What are the primary distinctions between the theories of the neo-Freudians and Freud's theory?

32. Describe the situation versus trait debate.

33. How does personality differ based on the individualism/collectivism dimension of a culture?

Multiple Choice

1. Which of the following is *not* an element of one's personality, according to the text definition?
    a. behaviors
    b. feelings
    c. thoughts
    d. biological mechanisms

2. You stare at the clock during class, very aware of how slowly the time seems to pass. This awareness is contained in your
    a. unconscious.
    b. conscious.
    c. preconscious.
    d. subconscious.

3. Kia feels guilty for lying to a friend. This guilt is part of her
    a. ego.
    b. conscience.
    c. id
    d. ego ideal.

4. The ego operates according to the reality principle, which means that the ego
    a. considers the constraints of the environment while trying to satisfy id impulses.
    b. demands immediate gratification.
    c. has to utilize defense mechanisms to reduce anxiety.
    d. counters any fantasy wishes of the id.

5. Which is the correct order of Freud's stages?
    a. anal, phallic, oral, latency, genital
    b. anal, oral, genital, latency, phallic
    c. oral, anal, genital, latency, phallic
    d. oral, anal, phallic, latency, genital

6. According to Freud, what process leads to superego development?
    a. fixation
    b. sublimation
    c. identification
    d. reaction formation

7. Which theorist suggested that inferiority feelings could prevent personal development?
    a. Carl Jung
    b. Sigmund Freud
    c. Karen Horney
    d. Alfred Adler

8. Horney disagreed with Freud on
    a. his division of personality into id, ego, and superego.
    b. his concept of penis envy.
    c. his disregard of cultural and environmental influences on personality.
    d. all of the above.

9. Which group of theories is most likely to suggest that personality is shaped most by childhood experiences?
   a. psychoanalytic
   b. humanistic
   c. learning
   d. trait

10. Which of the following is *not* part of Bandura's concept of reciprocal determinism?
   a. environment
   b. behavior
   c. unconscious conflicts
   d. cognitive factors

11. Someone with an external locus of control is most likely to explain a high test grade as due to
   a. attending class each day.
   b. an easy exam.
   c. studying hard.
   d. intelligence.

12. Which aspect of Rogers' person-centered therapy contributes to the development of a fully functioning person?
   a. conditions of worth
   b. self-actualization
   c. unconditional positive regard
   d. self-esteem

13. Lee is a careful person. In fact, if you asked him to describe his entire personality in one word, he'd say the word would be "careful." According to Allport, *careful* is Lee's
   a. cardinal trait.
   b. surface trait.
   c. central trait.
   d. source trait.

14. Which personality test did Raymond Cattell develop?
   a. Minnesota Multiphasic Personality Inventory (MMPI)
   b. Sixteen Personality Factors Questionnaire (16PF)
   c. Thematic Apperception Test (TAT)
   d. California Personality Inventory (CPI)

15. Trait theories
   a. state that situational factors override personal characteristics.
   b. focus on the role of the unconscious.
   c. take a more optimistic view of human nature than humanists do.
   d. look at personal characteristics that are stable across situations.

16. What do adoption studies say about hereditary influences on personality?
   a. Adopted children are most similar in personality to other children in the adopted family.
   b. Adopted children are most similar in personality to their biological parents.
   c. Adopted children are most similar in personality to their adopted parents.
   d. Adopted children's personalities are not like anyone in their biological or adopted families.

17. People in individualistic cultures
   a. emphasize the importance of group success.
   b. define themselves in terms of their group membership.
   c. are accorded honor and prestige for personal achievement.
   d. have personalities no different than people in collectivistic cultures.

18. Which of the following does *not* increase the accuracy of behavioral assessment?
   a. using projective tests
   b. using rating scales
   c. using multiple raters or observers
   d. using structured interviews

19. The Minnesota Multiphasic Personality Inventory (MMPI)
   a. is a personality inventory.
   b. was developed to diagnose psychiatric disorders.
   c. contains ten clinical scales as well as several validity scales.
   d. all of the above.

20. Why are projective tests "projective"?
   a. They involve the use of a projector to display the images.
   b. They make projections about the future behavior of the subject.
   c. The subjects project their unconscious thoughts and feelings onto the test.
   d. The subjects project the meaning of the test to the examiners.

True or False

21. Several studies have shown that people try to repress unpleasant thoughts.

22. While Freud's theory was popular a long time ago, no one today believes it offers anything of value to our understanding of personality.

23. The tendency for people to believe in a god is an archetype.

24. Self-efficacy is based on objective standards of performance.

25. Self-esteem is based in part on comparisons of actual to desired traits.

26. Scores on the Big Five traits have been related to the characteristics of someone's home.

27. Consistent with the stereotype of "grumpy old men," agreeableness declines as we age.

28. Genes serve to constrain the ways in which environments affect personality traits.

29. The United States is ranked as the most individualistic culture, such that minority groups within the United States also become individualistic.

30. The halo effect happens when an interviewer focuses on positive traits of an interviewee that are irrelevant to the purpose of the interview.

Essay

31. Name and describe five Freudian defense mechanisms.

32. Name and describe the traits that constitute the five-factor theory of personality.

33. Distinguish between projective and objective methods for personality assessment, providing examples of each.

Chapter 12: Psychological Disorders

PRACTICE TEST 1

Multiple Choice

1. Gretchen likes to keep everything. She has things stacked in corners and every closet is filled to the top. Lots of people save things, but Gretchen's "saving" has reached the point that every surface in her home is covered. She is embarrassed to have company—yet she continues to "save" things. What is it about Gretchen's behavior that makes it considered "abnormal?"
   a. It is illegal.
   b. It is maladaptive.
   c. It is dangerous.
   d. It is unexplained.

2. Which perspective contends that early childhood experiences are behind the manifestation of psychological disorders?
   a. psychosocial
   b. psychodynamic
   c. cognitive
   d. biopsychosocial

3. Which type of disorder has the highest lifetime prevalence in the United States?
   a. anxiety disorders
   b. mood disorders
   c. substance abuse/dependence
   d. schizophrenia

4. Eric does not like to be in public places—especially where there are a lot of people and getting away would be difficult. He fears he will have a panic attack and will not be able to get away or obtain help. Eric could probably be diagnosed with
   a. agoraphobia.
   b. panic disorder.
   c. bipolar disorder.
   d. generalized anxiety disorder.

5. Which of the following would be considered a social phobia?
   a. fear of enclosed places
   b. fear of injections
   c. fear of public speaking
   d. fear of flying

6. Mark is a "clean freak." He spends hours upon hours mopping, dusting, and in general sanitizing his house. Mark's cleaning behaviors might be described as a(n)
   a. phobia.
   b. obsession.
   c. delusion.
   d. compulsion.

7. Which patient is most at risk for a recurrent episode of depression?
   a. John, who first became depressed at age 24
   b. Mary, who first became depressed at age 50
   c. Carol, who first became depressed at age 14
   d. Henry, who first became depressed at age 40

8. The rate of depression among women is generally _____ that of men.
   a. about half
   b. twice
   c. about four times
   d. one-fourth

9. Which factors play a major role in bipolar and major depressive episodes?
   a. biological and cognitive
   b. social and biological
   c. personal and social
   d. cognitive and personal

10. The word "psychotic" refers to
    a. dangerousness.
    b. nervousness.
    c. loss of contact with reality.
    d. social isolation.

11. Marianne believes that she is a world-famous movie star. Her neighbors see her occasionally in her front yard, waving to them as if they were her adoring crowd. Marianne suffers from
    a. delusions of grandeur.
    b. delusions of persecution.
    c. an anxiety disorder.
    d. bipolar disorder.

12. Schizophrenia has been associated with abnormal activity of the neurotransmitter
    a. serotonin.
    b. norepinephrine.
    c. acetylcholine.
    d. dopamine.

13. Individuals with which type of schizophrenia have periods where they display little or no body movement, often remaining in bizarre positions for hours?
    a. undifferentiated
    b. disorganized
    c. paranoid
    d. catatonic

14. Which of the following disorders is diagnosed more often in men than in women?
    a. major depression
    b. generalized anxiety disorder
    c. schizophrenia
    d. phobia

15. Following an accident, Michael became blind. Doctors can find no medical cause for his blindness. They should consider a diagnosis of
    a. conversion disorder.
    b. dissociative disorder.
    c. reaction formation.
    d. hypochondriasis.

16. The disorder that involves an individual having several different personalities, one host and at least one alter, is called
    a. dissociative identity disorder.
    b. dissociative fugue.
    c. dissociative amnesia.
    d. conversion disorder.

17. Sarah is a female but she believes she should be a male. Sarah's problem might be considered an example of
    a. gender identity disorder.
    b. conversion disorder.
    c. sexual dysfunction.
    d. personality disorder.

18. James finds it arousing when his girlfriend wears a sexy negligee. James would be diagnosed with
    a. a paraphilia.
    b. gender identity disorder.
    c. a sexual dysfunction.
    d. no disorder at all.

19. Which cluster of personality disorders includes disorders that are most likely to be confused with schizophrenia, especially paranoid schizophrenia?
    a. cluster A
    b. cluster B
    c. cluster C
    d. cluster D

20. Tina is one of those people you can never predict. One minute she's your best friend; the next, she hates you and considers you to be her worst enemy. She has fits of inappropriate anger, recklessness and occasional suicidal gestures. Tina may be an example of a(n)
    a. histrionic personality.
    b. dependent personality.
    c. borderline personality.
    d. antisocial personality.

True or False

21. *Insanity* is a term used by mental health professionals to describe those suffering from psychological disorders.

22. Mental illness is diagnosed in 20 times more Americans than is cancer.

23. Antidepressant drugs are effectively used in the treatment of obsessive-compulsive disorder (OCD).

24. Research indicates that 1 year after their initial diagnosis of major depressive disorder, more than 90% of patients still show symptoms.

25. About 90% of individuals who commit suicide leave clues.

26. Schizophrenia involves the possession of multiple personalities within the same body.

27. Smelling something that is not there is an example of a hallucination.

28. A hypochondriac is someone who fakes an illness to get attention.

29. Dissociative amnesia may be caused by a traumatic head injury that impairs the functioning of the hippocampus.

30. Genes strongly influence the development of gender identity disorder.

Essay

31. Review the questions that may be asked to determine whether someone's behavior is abnormal.

32. Describe the risk factors for suicide, including gender, age, and ethnic differences in suicide rates.

33. Distinguish between the positive and the negative symptoms of schizophrenia.

PRACTICE TEST 2

Multiple Choice

1. Velma is deathly afraid of elevators. She works on the fifth floor of an office building, so she climbs the stairs to and from work each day. She makes sure she is never late and, in general, her avoidance of elevators doesn't cause her any problems, other than her own secret embarrassment over what she considers a "silly fear." By which criterion would Velma's behavior be considered abnormal?
  a. It is illegal.
  b. It is maladaptive.
  c. It is dangerous.
  d. It causes personal distress.

2. Which perspective is based on the belief that abnormal behavior is caused by problems such as chemical imbalances or genetics?
  a. psychosocial
  b. biological
  c. biochemical
  d. sociobiological

3. Which psychological disorder has the highest annual prevalence rate in the United States?
  a. major depressive disorder
  b. schizophrenia
  c. specific phobia
  d. obsessive-compulsive disorder

4. Chronic, excessive worry for 6 months or longer is called
  a. generalized anxiety disorder.
  b. localized anxiety disorder.
  c. adjustment disorder.
  d. panic disorder.

5. The most common type of specific phobia involves
  a. fears of blood, injuries, or injections.
  b. fears involving animals.
  c. fears of situations like elevators or heights.
  d. fears involving the natural environment, such as storms.

6. Persistent, recurrent, involuntary thoughts or images that invade the consciousness and cause personal distress are called
  a. obsessions.
  b. compulsions.
  c. ruminations.
  d. delusions.

7. Jerry feels sad and guilty. He says that his life is meaningless and he feels helpless. Based only on this information, you suspect that Jerry is suffering from a mood disorder called
  a. a manic episode.
  b. a suicidal episode.
  c. major depression.
  d. minor depression.

8. Abnormal levels of which neurotransmitter are most strongly linked to depression and suicidal thoughts?
  a. dopamine
  b. norepinephrine
  c. acetylcholine
  d. serotonin

9. Which ethnic group in the United States is most likely to commit suicide?
  a. African Americans
  b. White Americans
  c. Asian Americans
  d. Hispanic Americans

10. Hallucinations are an example of a
  a. delusion.
  b. negative symptom.
  c. positive symptom.
  d. neutral symptom.

11. Clay has been diagnosed with schizophrenia. He is difficult to understand when he speaks, because he shifts from one subject to another without any real warning or connection. This symptom is called
  a. derailment.
  b. a delusion.
  c. inappropriate affect.
  d. grossly disorganized behavior.

12. Marcus shows almost no emotional expression. He speaks in a monotonic voice and seems more like a robot than a person. Marcus is exhibiting
  a. a personality disorder.
  b. bipolar disorder.
  c. inappropriate affect.
  d. flat affect.

13. Which of the following is *not* a brain abnormality found in people with schizophrenia?
    a. slow communication between the left and right hemispheres
    b. reduced volume in the hippocampus, amygdala, and thalamus
    c. higher levels of neural activity in the frontal lobes
    d. defects in the neural circuitry of the limbic system

14. Which of the following statements about gender differences in schizophrenia is *false*?
    a. Men are more likely to develop schizophrenia than women are.
    b. Men develop schizophrenia at an earlier age than women do.
    c. Men respond better to treatment of schizophrenia than women do.
    d. Men are more likely to suffer a relapse of schizophrenic symptoms than women are.

15. Aaron is preoccupied with his physical health. If he gets a cold, he is sure it is pneumonia. Every headache leads him to the doctor, convinced he has a brain tumor. Aaron most likely has a disorder called
    a. conversion disorder.
    b. dissociative disorder.
    c. reaction formation.
    d. hypochondriasis.

16. Carrie suffers a complete loss of memory, including personal identity. She travels far away from home and assumes a new identity. Which diagnosis best fits Carrie?
    a. dissociative identity disorder
    b. dissociative fugue
    c. dissociative amnesia
    d. conversion disorder

17. What percentage of patients with dissociative identity disorder are women?
    a. 33%   c. 75%
    b. 50%   d. 90%

18. For which type of disorder is someone most likely to be treated with Viagra?
    a. sexual dysfunction.
    b. gender identity disorder
    c. paraphilia
    d. personality disorder

19. Which of the following would *not* be considered a paraphilia?
    a. the desire to have sex with children
    b. sexual arousal based on nonhuman objects such as clothing
    c. the desire to change sexes
    d. the desire to be humiliated by one's sexual partner

20. Ted Bundy was charming and likeable, at first. But Bundy was a serial killer—completely devoid of a conscience. He killed with no remorse; he had a complete disregard for the rights of others. Bundy was considered to have a(n)
    a. histrionic personality.
    b. dependent personality.
    c. paranoid personality.
    d. antisocial personality.

True or False

21. The term "intern syndrome" has been used to describe the tendency for individuals learning about disorders to notice that they or someone they know have some of the symptoms described.

22. To be committed to a mental hospital, the only criterion is whether an individual has a psychological disorder.

23. The lifetime prevalence for depression is higher in the United States than in any other country.

24. Phobias are most often treated using medications such as Valium.

25. Severely depressed people may suffer from delusions or hallucinations.

26. Individuals with bipolar disorder typically cycle between depressed and manic states with no periods of normalcy as long as they go untreated.

27. Women are more likely than men to attempt suicide, but men are more likely than women to be successful in committing suicide.

28. Cocaine abuse can alter dopamine activity in the brain and increase a person's risk for developing schizophrenia.

29. Approximately 95% of patients with dissociative identity disorder report early histories of severe trauma or abuse.

30. Individuals with a personality disorder tend to respond well to medications, but not to other types of therapy.

Essay

31. Review how the biological, biopsychosocial, psychodynamic, learning, and cognitive perspectives explain psychological disorders.

32. Review the subtypes of schizophrenia.

33. Describe the behaviors that are associated with the three clusters of personality disorders.

Chapter 13: Therapies

Multiple Choice

1. Which group of therapy approaches are based on the notion that psychological well-being depends on self-understanding?
   a. behavior therapies
   b. relationship therapies
   c. insight therapies
   d. all forms of psychotherapy are based on that notion

2. Which approach attempts to uncover childhood experiences in an effort to explain a person's current difficulties?
   a. psychodynamic therapy
   b. interpersonal therapy
   c. person-centered therapy
   d. cognitive therapy

3. Valora became angry with her therapist and shouted at him, "You are just like my father!" Freud would consider her outburst to be an example of
   a. dissociation.
   b. free association.
   c. transference.
   d. genuineness.

4. What is the goal of person-centered therapy?
   a. to uncover unconscious conflicts and resolve them
   b. to assist clients' growth toward self-actualization
   c. to replace maladaptive behaviors with more adaptive responses
   d. to challenge clients' irrational beliefs about themselves and others

5. The individual most closely associated with Gestalt therapy is
   a. Fritz Perls.
   b. Sigmund Freud.
   c. Carl Rogers.
   d. Aaron Beck.

6. Interpersonal therapy (IPT) is especially helpful in treating
   a. alcoholism.
   b. narcissism.
   c. specific phobias.
   d. depression.

7. Which type of problem is interpersonal therapy (IPT) *not* specifically designed to address?
   a. severe problems in coping with the death of a loved one
   b. deficits in interpersonal skills
   c. behavioral problems exhibited in school
   d. difficulties in adjusting to life after a divorce

8. One factor that is associated with relapse rates among patients with schizophrenia is family members with
   a. high RR.
   b. high EE.
   c. low EE.
   d. low RR.

9. Juan's school uses a reward system to encourage students to do their homework and have good behavior. Children earn gold stars for completing assignments and paying attention to the teacher, and later can exchange stars for snacks or even a day without homework. Which behavior modification technique is Juan's school using?
   a. time out
   b. systematic desensitization
   c. flooding
   d. token economy

10. Which technique is designed to treat phobias by exposing the client to extended periods of contact with the feared object or event until the anxiety decreases?
    a. aversion therapy
    b. flooding
    c. systematic desensitization
    d. exposure-desensitization

11. Exposure and response prevention is an approach that has proved successful in treating
    a. personality disorders.
    b. narcissism.
    c. depression.
    d. obsessive-compulsive disorder.

12. In Ellis's ABC model, the *A* represents
    a. the action taken.
    b. the actual problem.
    c. the activity of the client.
    d. the activating event.

13. Joan's therapist encourages her to subject her beliefs to real-world "tests." Which approach is her therapist taking?
    a. cognitive therapy
    b. person-centered therapy
    c. rational-emotive therapy
    d. interpersonal therapy

14. Neuroleptics is another term for
    a. antipsychotics.
    b. sedatives.
    c. anti-Parkinsonian drugs.
    d. antiseizure medications.

15. Which drug is someone most likely to take for bipolar disorder?
    a. Xanax
    b. Clozapine
    c. Lithium
    d. Prozac (fluoxetine)

16. Cynthia wants to be a psychiatrist. What degree will she need after college?
    a. Ph.D.
    b. M.D.
    c. Psy.D.
    d. Ed.D.

17. The bond between therapist and client that is thought to be a factor in the effectiveness of psychotherapy is called
    a. attachment.
    b. counselor–client bonding.
    c. the psychosocial relationship.
    d. the therapeutic alliance.

18. What does research suggest about the success of psychotherapy?
    a. It is most successful with single adults.
    b. The longer someone is in therapy, the more improvement he or she seems to make.
    c. Brief therapy is generally most effective with married couples.
    d. Patients in therapy do better with psychologists than with psychiatrists.

19. Which of the following behaviors would be considered unethical for a therapist?
    a. informing clients about the cost and expected duration of a therapy
    b. alerting the authorities if a client threatens to harm someone
    c. treating an ex-girlfriend in therapy
    d. explaining the purpose of tests given to clients as part of therapy

20. Culturally sensitive therapy is important because
    a. it ensures that proper medication will be prescribed.
    b. cultural factors need to be considered when choosing a therapeutic intervention.
    c. the development of a therapeutic alliance is not possible if the client and therapist have different backgrounds.
    d. cultural insensitivity is the underlying cause of most mood disorders.

True or False

21. A psychodynamic therapist would interpret a client's being late to a session as a form of resistance.

22. Person-centered therapy is an example of a directive therapy.

23. A Gestalt therapist might help a client with unfinished business using the empty chair technique.

24. Family therapy tends to be ineffective as a treatment option for adolescent drug abusers.

25. Alcoholics Anonymous (AA) is a form of self-help group.

26. Aversion therapy is no longer utilized due to ethical concerns about it.

27. Tardive dyskinesia is a movement disorder brought on by long-term use of antidepressants.

28. Maintenance doses of antidepressants may be needed following a major depressive episode to reduce the probability of a relapse.

29. Rapid transcranial magnetic stimulation (rTMS) appears to have the same benefits as electroconvulsive therapy (ECT) but carries significantly fewer risks.

30. Therapists can actually be too sensitive to gender issues and assume an incorrect cause for problems as a result.

Essay

31. Compare and contrast Ellis's rational-emotive therapy and Beck's cognitive therapy.

32. What are the three types of drugs used to treat depression, and how do they work?

33. Describe five types of mental health professionals, including their training and services provided. Which of these careers best matches your interests?

Multiple Choice

1. Which group of therapies assumes that people have the freedom and ability to make their own decisions and lead rational lives?
   a. psychoanalytic
   b. humanistic
   c. behavioral
   d. directive

2. Frank's therapist asks him to say whatever comes to mind. His therapist is employing
   a. free association.
   b. unconditional positive regard.
   c. transference.
   d. the empty chair technique.

3. The individual most closely associated with person-centered therapy is
   a. Fritz Perls.
   b. Sigmund Freud.
   c. Carl Rogers.
   d. Aaron Beck.

4. Lorraine's therapist encourages her to resolve her issues with her father by speaking to an empty chair as if he were sitting there. The therapist then has Lorraine occupy the chair and respond as her father would. Lorraine is undergoing
   a. person-centered therapy.
   b. psychoanalysis.
   c. Gestalt therapy.
   d. rational-emotive therapy.

5. For which of the following has family or couples therapy *not* been shown to be effective?
   a. adolescent drug use
   b. communication problems
   c. sexual dysfunctions
   d. phobias

6. Which of the following is *not* a benefit of group therapy?
   a. Group therapy works more quickly than individual therapy does.
   b. Group therapy is less expensive than individual therapy is.
   c. Group therapy allows for feedback from other group members as well as the therapist.
   d. Group therapy teaches each individual that others share their problems.

7. A study by Morgan and Flora (2002) demonstrated that those prisoners who participated in group therapy progressed more quickly than those who did not participate for all of the following problems *except*
   a. anxiety.
   b. alcoholism.
   c. low self-esteem.
   d. depression.

8. Which term refers to the systematic application of learning principles to help a person eliminate undesirable behaviors and replace them with adaptive ones?
   a. cognitive management
   b. behavior modification
   c. learning application
   d. systematic desensitization

9. Loretta has a fear of spiders. Her therapist trains her to relax, and helps her make a list of situations involving spiders that escalate in terms of how much anxiety they provoke. What technique is Loretta's therapist using?
   a. aversion therapy
   b. flooding
   c. systematic desensitization
   d. exposure and response prevention

10. Which of the following, when used to rid a client of an undesirable habit or harmful behavior such as smoking or drinking, often involves unpleasant associations with electric shock or drugs that induce nausea and vomiting?
    a. aversion therapy
    b. flooding
    c. systematic desensitization
    d. exposure and response prevention

11. According to Ellis
    a. emotional reactions are direct consequences of events.
    b. a person's beliefs determine how he or she reacts to an event.
    c. the consequences of an action are more important than the action itself.
    d. adaptive behaviors must be learned.

12. Which of the following approaches would be considered a nondirective therapy?
    a. rational-emotive therapy
    b. Gestalt therapy
    c. cognitive therapy
    d. person-centered therapy

13. Jessica puts a lot of pressure on herself in school. She believes that she must make an A on every exam or else she is stupid. What would Beck call this unreasonable but unquestioned idea that rules Jessica's life?
    a. a condition of worth
    b. an unconscious conflict
    c. an automatic thought
    d. an irrational belief

14. For which of the following disorders has cognitive therapy been shown to be effective?
    a. depression
    b. insomnia
    c. generalized anxiety disorder
    d. all of the above

15. Fluoxetine (Prozac) is which kind of drug?
    a. tricyclic
    b. selective serotonin reuptake inhibitor (SSRI)
    c. neuroleptic
    d. monoamine oxidase (MAO) inhibitor

16. What does your text suggest about the effectiveness of medications such as Xanax and Prozac?
    a. They are effective only with long-term use.
    b. Psychotherapy is usually much more effective in conjunction with medication.
    c. Psychotherapy alone seems to work as well as psychotherapy and drugs together.
    d. Prozac, in particular, is highly addictive.

17. Which of the following professionals do *not* conduct psychological tests?
    a. psychiatrists
    b. clinical psychologists
    c. school psychologists
    d. licensed professional counselors

18. Which of the following professionals do *not* need a doctoral-level degree?
    a. psychiatrists
    b. clinical psychologists
    c. counseling psychologists
    d. licensed professional counselors

19. Which of the following is *not* an ethical requirement of professionals doing psychological testing?
    a. The test should be completed in a single session so as not to inconvenience the client.
    b. The test must be reliable and valid.
    c. The professionals must explain the purpose of testing to clients.
    d. Test results must be provided to clients in a confidential manner.

20. When working with immigrants, which of these factors do researchers consider to be most important to successful treatment?
    a. The therapist should be very familiar with the client's culture.
    b. The therapist must be able to separate psychopathology from anxiety and sadness over the immigration experience.
    c. The client must be willing to assimilate into the culture in which he or she is living.
    d. The therapist must educate the client about the value system of his or her new country.

True or False

21. Because psychodynamic therapies require such a commitment of time and expense, they are not utilized today except in rare circumstances.

22. Gestalt therapy helps people become more self-accepting by realizing that their behavior is due to societal influences.

23. Relationship therapies work with an individual's internal struggles as well as with his or her interpersonal relationships.

24. When accompanied by medication, family therapy can reduce relapse rates for individuals with schizophrenia.

25. Time out has been shown to be effective in reducing undesirable behaviors in children and adolescents.

26. Participant modeling, which is based on observational learning, has been effective in treating depression but not phobias.

27. Rational-emotive therapy and cognitive therapy have similar goals; they simply involve different methods of accomplishing them.

28. The mental hospital population has increased in the United States due to the recent breakthroughs in drug therapy.

29. Selective serotonin reuptake inhibitors (SSRIs) cause irreversible sexual dysfunction.

30. Gender-sensitive therapy takes into account the effects of gender on both the client's *and* the therapist's behavior.

Essay

31. Describe how interpersonal therapy (IPT) addresses interpersonal problems associated with major depression.

32. Describe the use of electroconvulsive therapy (ECT), including the arguments for and against its use.

33. Review the research on the effectiveness of psychotherapy.

Chapter 14: Social Psychology

Multiple Choice

1. In Stanley Milgram's obedience study, the "learner" was a(n)
   a. confederate.
   b. naive subject.
   c. unwilling participant.
   d. victim.

2. Your grandmother always told you that first impressions create lasting impressions. She is essentially describing
   a. the actor-observer effect.
   b. the recency effect.
   c. the primacy effect.
   d. a situational attribution.

3. Creighton's boss is particularly grumpy today. He knows that she's been under a lot of stress at home, and figures that is the reason for her grumpiness. Creighton is making a
   a. self-serving bias.
   b. random attribution.
   c. dispositional attribution.
   d. situational attribution.

4. Shea failed her law school entrance exams. She said it was because there was too much noise in the room and the questions were ridiculous. Shea's excuses are an example of
   a. false attribution.
   b. the primacy effect.
   c. dispositional attribution.
   d. self-serving bias.

5. Heather never gave Bobby much thought until she found out that he likes her. Lately she's been thinking that she likes him, too. Her attraction is largely based on
   a. the mere exposure effect.
   b. proximity.
   c. reciprocity.
   d. a situational attribution.

6. Which of the following is a major factor in attractiveness?
   a. exaggerated features
   b. wide-set eyes
   c. skin tone
   d. symmetry

7. The matching hypothesis is similar to the idea that
   a. birds of a feather flock together.
   b. a penny saved is a penny earned.
   c. a bird in the hand is worth two in the bush.
   d. familiarity breeds contempt.

8. Changing or adopting an attitude or behavior to be consistent with the social norms of a group or their expectation is called
   a. obedience.
   b. conformity.
   c. familiarity.
   d. triangulation.

9. Which of the following is a similarity in Milgram's and Asch's results?
   a. In both studies, all participants conformed or obeyed to the maximum level possible.
   b. In both studies, the deception used on the participants was considered ethically unacceptable by critics.
   c. In both studies, if at least one other person refused to conform or obey, the participant was less likely to conform or obey as well.
   d. In both studies, the majority of participants refused to conform or obey.

10. Phillip was offered a job that provided weekends off. Once he said yes and gave notice at his old job, the new employer told him he would have to work every Saturday until noon. Phillip's new boss used the
    a. mere-exposure effect.
    b. door-in-the-face technique.
    c. foot-in-the-door technique.
    d. low-ball technique.

11. Two teams were playing a game of tug-of-war. Gerald was tired, so he just pretended to be pulling, knowing that no one could tell the difference. Gerald's approach to the game is an example of
    a. socialization.
    b. social facilitation.
    c. social loafing.
    d. the triangular effect.

12. If you work better in front of other people, the effect of those other people is called a(n)
    a. audience effect in social facilitation.
    b. co-action effect in social facilitation.
    c. audience effect in social loafing.
    d. co-action effect in social loafing.

13. Investigations following the latest NASA shuttle disaster suggested that many of the engineers and other workers saw problems but failed to speak up because no one else did. They all work well together and were accustomed to everything going right. In their zeal to launch the shuttle and continue to work effectively and cohesively, they failed to investigate problems that were quite evident. Some suggested that the NASA scientists were victims of:
    a. groupthink.
    b. social facilitation.
    c. obedience.
    d. compliance.

14. Zimbardo's prison study showed that
    a. social roles influence behavior.
    b. behavior is beyond the influence of social bias.
    c. prisons are inherently corrupt.
    d. social loafing is culturally bound.

15. Which of the following is a deliberate attempt to change the attitude or behavior of another person?
    a. stereotyping
    b. persuasion
    c. extortion
    d. cognitive dissonance

16. Frank is overweight and seems unable to stick to any diet. Although his diet efforts suggest that he wants to lose weight, he denies it and says that he is happy with his body the way it is. Frank is trying to reduce his feelings of
    a. cognitive dissonance.
    b. negative persuasion.
    c. self-esteem.
    d. attributional asymmetry.

17. Which of the following is *not* one of the identified elements of persuasion?
    a. the source of the communication
    b. the message
    c. the decision-making process
    d. the audience

18. When Kitty Genovese was stabbed to death near her apartment, later investigations found that nearly 40 people witnessed the attack—yet no one called for help. Some would say that this case is an example of
    a. altruism.
    b. prejudice.
    c. the bystander effect.
    d. antisocial behavior.

19. What did Cloninger find with regard to crime, aggression, and biology?
    a. Twins are twice as likely to be violent if they are raised together by their biological parents.
    b. Adopted children are more likely to be criminals if their adoptive parents are criminals.
    c. Adopted children are no more likely to be criminals than others, even if their adoptive parents are criminals.
    d. Biology and genetic factors have no effect on aggressive behavior.

20. Kathy's sorority has a rule against dating boys from certain fraternities. Kathy may date only boys who belong to two specific fraternities. Her sorority considers any other boys to be "undesirables." According to the definitions in your chapter, Kathy's sorority is an example of
    a. an in-group.   c. a crowd.
    b. an out-group.   d. social pressure.

True or False

21. Research has indicated that Americans are more likely to make situational attributions than Koreans for both desirable and undesirable behaviors.

22. There are significant cultural differences in attractiveness ratings of the opposite sex.

23. In Asch's conformity experiments, 75% of the participants conformed to the incorrect response of the majority at least once.

24. Research indicates that in the presence of others, an individual has lower performance on easier tasks but excels at more difficult tasks.

25. Social loafing is more common in collectivistic cultures such as China than in the United States.

26. Zimbardo's Stanford prison experiment had to be ended in 6 days because the behavior of the participants began to get out of hand.

27. Generally speaking, people with low IQs are easier to persuade than people with high IQs.

28. Being altruistic carries no benefits for the altruistic person.

29. Individuals who were abused as children are more likely to be aggressive than adults who were not abused in childhood.

30. People perceive more diversity among members of their own ethnic group, and more similarity among members of other groups.

Essay

31. What do men and women rate as the most important qualities in a mate? Review both the similarities and the differences in what men and women seek.

32. Describe Stanley Milgram's obedience study. What conclusions could be drawn from it? Could the same study be conducted today?

33. Describe the social learning theory of aggression. What does the research say about a relationship between TV violence and viewer aggression?

Multiple Choice

1. Naomi blames her own poor performance on an exam on her instructor's poor teaching skills. In the next moment, she makes fun of another student who did poorly on the test, saying she knows he is not very smart. Naomi is exhibiting
   a. the self-serving bias.
   b. situational attribution.
   c. the actor-observer effect.
   d. the halo effect.

2. Beverly's husband is always leaving her little love notes and giving her gifts for no reason. She believes his behaviors reflect the fact that he's a sweet guy. She is making a
   a. self-serving bias.
   b. random attribution.
   c. dispositional attribution.
   d. situational attribution.

3. Which two factors are most likely to contribute to why a man might be attracted to the "girl next door"?
   a. proximity and mere exposure
   b. mere exposure and reciprocity
   c. reciprocity and proximity
   d. proximity and the halo effect

4. Which of the following is most likely to be correct based on social psychology research on attraction?
   a. Opposites attract.
   b. Love is a many-splendored thing.
   c. Absence makes the heart grow fonder.
   d. Birds of a feather flock together.

5. The mere-exposure effect is contrary to the idea that
   a. familiarity breeds contempt.
   b. out of sight, out of mind.
   c. positive feelings arise from repeated exposure to a stimuli.
   d. that which we see often, we like.

6. You are a participant in a conformity study conducted by Solomon Asch. You are most likely to avoid conforming to an incorrect response given by the rest of the group if
   a. there are 10 other participants conforming as opposed to 3.
   b. at least one of the other participants breaks with conformity.
   c. there are 3 other participants conforming as opposed to 10.
   d. none of the other participants breaks with conformity.

7. In Milgram's original study of obedience, what percentage of participants administered the "maximum" voltage?
   a. 20%
   b. 40%
   c. 60%
   d. 80%

8. A technique used to gain a favorable response from someone by first asking for small favors is the
   a. mere-exposure effect.
   b. door-in-the-face technique.
   c. foot-in-the-door technique.
   d. bait-and-switch technique.

9. Which of the following is a good way to avoid the effects of social loafing on a group project for class?
   a. Have the whole group get the same grade for the project.
   b. Instruct each group member to take responsibility for the group's performance.
   c. Allow group members to have their individual contributions to the project remain anonymous.
   d. Have the members of the group get individual grades, each based on their own contribution.

10. Zimbardo's prison experiment was directed at studying
    a. social facilitation.
    b. social loafing.
    c. social roles.
    d. social deficits.

11. A supporter of a politician tries to persuade you to vote for his candidate by appealing to your fears about what might happen if the opposing candidate wins. This supporter is *most* demonstrating which component of your attitude?
    a. emotional component
    b. cognitive component
    c. behavioral component
    d. none of the above

12. The more people must sacrifice or suffer to become a member of an organization, the more _____ they are likely to become toward the group.
    a. positive
    b. negative
    c. oppositional
    d. prejudiced

13. Under which conditions does an attempt at persuasion work best if it presents both sides of an issue as opposed to just one side?
    a. when the audience is not well informed
    b. when the audience cares about the issue
    c. when the audience already agrees with the point of view
    d. when the audience is somewhat intelligent

14. A celebrity is a spokesperson for a product. He is attractive and likable, and he plays a humorous, if somewhat dumb, character on television. Sales of the product actually decrease once his commercial airs. Why might this be so?
    a. Persuasion does not depend on attractiveness.
    b. Persuasion depends only on the quality of the product.
    c. Persuasion also depends on credibility.
    d. Persuasion does not depend on attractiveness.

15. Mr. Arnold donated $5 million to the college for a new student center. He accepted the college's invitation to name the building after him. Mr. Arnold's behavior demonstrates
    a. altruism.
    b. prosocial behavior.
    c. social support.
    d. diffusion of responsibility.

16. The bystander effect is greatly reduced by:
    a. counseling.
    b. anonymity.
    c. catastrophe.
    d. public appeal.

17. Which of the following suggests that aggression results when we make attributions about the motives of people involved when an aversive event occurs?
    a. frustration-aggression hypothesis
    b. theory of personal space
    c. social learning theory of aggression
    d. cognitive neoassociationistic model

18. The general tendency to look at people and situations from the perspective of one's own racial or cultural group is called
    a. stereotyping.
    b. discrimination.
    c. ethnocentrism.
    d. cultural racism.

19. David is failing algebra. He told his parents not to worry, though. He had decided to ask the Vietnamese student in his class to tutor him, in exchange for his help with English. "Those Asians are always good at math," he said. David's statements are demonstrating a(n)
    a. stereotype.
    b. prejudice.
    c. faulty logic.
    d. out-group bias.

20. Which of the following statements is *true*, according to your text?
    a. Prejudice has all but been eradicated.
    b. Most people agree that conditions for minorities are better than they were 50 years ago.
    c. African Americans believe that prejudice has worsened and is more institutionalized.
    d. Attitudes are a strong predictor of behavior.

True or False

21. Deception is no longer used in social psychology research.

22. Job interviewers are more likely to recommend physically attractive people in part because of the halo effect.

23. Infants show preferences for attractive faces over unattractive faces.

24. Research indicates that women are more likely to conform than men are.

25. The presence of others affects our performance due to heightened arousal.

26. Attitudes predict behavior the majority of the time.

27. Diffusion of responsibility is even more likely to occur during catastrophes because so many more people are involved.

28. The size of personal space varies for individuals and across situations.

29. Playing violent video games is correlated with aggression.

30. People often say that they don't engage in more social contact with others of different races due to fear of rejection.

Essay

31. Describe the Stanford prison experiment conducted by Philip Zimbardo. What conclusion could be drawn from the study?

32. How can cognitive dissonance be applied to a person's smoking behavior?

33. Review the possible biological causes of aggression.